To Alexandra, who supports me,
cheers me on, and carries me through . . .

To Gabrielle and Suzanne, who already
possess a passion for cooking.

FRANÇOIS-RÉGIS GAUDRY
AND FRIENDS
present

ARTISAN | NEW YORK

WHY DID CUCINA ITALIANA CONQUER THE WORLD?

The great historian of Italian cuisine Alberto Capatti, first president of the University of Gastronomic Sciences in Pollenzo and member of the scientific committee of Casa Artusi and the European Institute of Food History and Cultures (IEHCA), was kind enough to share with us his thoughts on the success of Italian cuisine today.

REGIONAL, NATIONAL . . . AND GLOBAL CUISINE

During the 1920s, Italy was hampered by its regional and cultural divisions. These circumstances would take time to resolve themselves, and as a consequence caused a fragmented and dispersed national cuisine. Even today, people from Calabria do not see their gastronomic culture as part of a cohesive whole. At the same time, beginning at the end of the nineteenth century, Italian emigration, particularly to America, occurred on a remarkable scale and offered simple foods perfectly suited to the New World. The muffuletta, a sandwich of Sicilian origin that has been a tradition in New Orleans since 1906, is a good example; it quickly became the symbol of New Orleans. Regional, national, and global cuisine has been a reality for Italy for a little over a century now, offering an extraordinarily diverse array to those who take time to explore it. Today, one can find grocery stores filled with quality Italian products, and menus of Michelin-starred chefs now offer a seductive image of gourmet Italy. And books such as *La scienza in cucina e l'arte di mangiar bene* (*Science in the Kitchen and the Art of Eating Well*), published by Actes Sud, have been monumental in bringing Italian food and culture into kitchens around the world.

ACCESS TO QUALITY

As for quality? Italian food products are guaranteed by European certification labels, which protect very famous food products including Italian cheeses such as Parmesan. But the cuisine itself plays a role in this story, including the popularity of mozzarella, loved for its freshness and lightness, and even most recently *burrata* from Apulia, which was once unknown. Imitations, however, are still produced, which can originate in Italy and be sought after. This is the case with balsamic vinegar from Modena, which has the distinction of having both PDO (Protected Designation of Origin) and PGI (Protected Geographical Indication) designations: you can, therefore, at a high price, buy the authentic product from private sellers who operate an *acetaia* (an artisanal balsamic vinegar producer) and produce it on-site. Access to the ingredients of this regional and global cuisine can sometimes be difficult, dictated by the circumstances. But a well-connected commercial network, and especially a competent consumer who can opt to go beyond traditional supermarkets to obtain ingredients directly from farmers via specialty grocers with strict standards, are key to sourcing the highest-quality ingredients that will produce the most authentic cuisine.

THE POWERHOUSE OF WHEAT

The power of Italian cuisine is its large-scale use of wheat flour, the basic ingredient for many popular Italian foods such as pasta, focaccia, pizza, etc. Italian cuisine can thus travel anywhere around the globe and be reproduced. Pizza, a word that needs no translation, is the perfect example: in California in the 1950s, Pizza Hut became America's first pizza restaurant chain. It is remarkable to note that this "flat pie" spread all over the world at the same time it was conquering the last regions in Italy where it was still unknown: the Alps. Even considering the fact that its primary ingredients easily cross borders—tomatoes export well, and mozzarella can be made anywhere—what has determined the success of pizza is that it can be topped with any local ingredient, from pineapple to *würstel* (Vienna sausage), and even cassoulet. Wheat flour, which Italy has always struggled to produce in quantity to meet its own needs, has become the keystone of a global system where recipes for spaghetti, ravioli, and stuffed focaccias take center stage.

WHY LET'S EAT ITALY?

One day in 2017, while I was tasting all the specialties of Piedmont in a trattoria in Alba, my traveling companion (a producer of organic hazelnuts from the Langhe) witnessed that I was as happy as a clam and asked me: *"Saresti stato Italiano nella vita precedente?"* ("Would you have been Italian in a previous life?") I replied: "I have two loves: my country [France] and Italy."

If I had to dig for the roots of my passion for Italy, I would uncover a magical spectacle I experienced in my childhood: my mother standing at the end of her old stainless steel pasta roller rolling out large sheets of pasta, which she then dried on the white-cloth-covered dining-room table. The lasagnas she made were small masterpieces that made our family and friends salivate. Her *aubergines alla parmiggiana* and *saltimbocca* had no equal. My mother cooks as naturally as she breathes, and Italy has always been part of her. She grew up in a Corsican family that, like many other families on the île de Beauté, was diverse. I remember those large tables of people where we spoke loudly in French, Corsican, and Italian, and where I heard my uncles and aunts from Genoa and Tuscany utter this sentence, which made people laugh a little grudgingly: "The Corsicans are Italians who have gone astray. . . ." My parents are very French, but they raised me with the idea that Italy, like France, has a sense of beauty and goodness.

Another member of my family was also an influence in my gustatory exploration of Italy: my first cousin, Stéphane Solier, whom I recruited to assist with this ambitious book. A Latin scholar and specialist in classical literary works, he has lived for nine years in Rome, working as a teaching assistant at the university and as a cultural attaché at the French embassy. He welcomed me many times to the Eternal City. Together, we tasted dishes that became instant favorites and eternal obsessions for us: Roman pastas (including the famous carbonara that I have become a champion of in France), *puntarelle* salad, and *carciofi alla giudia* (a traditional Jewish dish with artichokes). From Rome and throughout the rest of the Italian peninsula, Italian cuisine has become, for me, a holy grail, a reason for living, and a professional conquest!

During my journey as a food journalist, I met Alessandra Pierini, who has become a kind of spiritual guide. I remember our meeting in her first grocery store, located on rue Rodier (Paris, 9th). It was 2010. It was an immediate professional and friendly kinship between the two of us. Ale (that's her nickname) took me everywhere in Italy, from her native Liguria to Sicily, via Piedmont, Milan, Sardinia, the Dolomites, Tuscany, and Naples . . . and all these regions have become a part of the menu of our *Let's Eat* radio programs that air in France; so many of the programs have been blessed by Alessandra's soothing voice, her encyclopedic knowledge, and her precise recipes!

Obviously, after the publication of *Let's Eat France!*, Italy seemed the obvious choice to continue the *Let's Eat* program, but an obvious choice I approached with care, not only immersing myself in Italian cuisine but also insisting I surround myself with a large network of experts, researchers, chefs, artisans, lovers of Italian culture and cuisine, and Italian illustrators, involving around a dozen trips to Italy. For three years, we have explored every corner of one of the most exciting culinary heritages in the world. The result lives up to our expectations: a Franco-Italian declaration of love for *la cucina italiana* resulting in an ambitious and comprehensive book everyone can savor.

Buon viaggio in Italia!

François-Régis Gaudry

ITALIAN CUISINE
A USER'S GUIDE

Italian Cuisine in 20 Dates

MASSIMO MONTANARI*

1154

Arab geographer al-Idrisi is the first to mention the existence of a **dry pasta factory**. In his writings, the factory, located in Trabia (Palermo), controlled the entire production chain and exported pasta throughout the Mediterranean basin.

AROUND 1300

Around this date, the **first Italian cookbook** (*Liber de coquina*) was published. Written at the Angevin court of the Kingdom of Naples and believed to have been modeled after an example from the Swabian period, the book was published in Palermo at the court of Frederick II of Sicily. Tastes were different then, but some now-iconic dishes of Italian cuisine were already included, such as lasagna and other varieties of pasta.

AROUND 1450

Maestro Martino, Italy's most famous cookbook author of the Middle Ages, wrote ***De arte coquinaria***, which gained wide circulation in Europe thanks to the support of his humanist friend Platina (Bartolomeo Sacchi).

AROUND 1475

Platina publishes ***De Honesta voluptate et valetudine*** (*Honest Pleasure and Good Health*). In terms of gastronomy, the work is inspired by the cookbook of Maestro Martino, his friend and collaborator, but the recipes are presented in a more literary way as a text focused on nutrition.

1477

Piedmontese doctor Pantaleone da Confienza publishes *Summa lacticiniorum*, **the oldest treatise on dairy products in Europe**.

1548

Milanese scholar Ortensio Lando publishes *Commentario delle più notabili e mostruose cose d'Italia* (*Commentary on the Most Notable and Tremendous Things in Italy*), **a travel guide to Italy noting the main regional culinary specialties**. This is the first Italian gastronomic guide.

1570

Bartolomeo Scappi publishes *Opera dell'arte del cucinare* (commonly referred to as *L'Opéra*), a monument of Italian Renaissance cuisine.

CIRCA 1630

As Naples goes through a period of famine, **pasta becomes an essential part of people's diets for the first time**. Neapolitans begin to be referred to as *mangiamaccheroni* (macaroni eaters), an epithet that will eventually be applied to all Italians.

1690

First mention of the so-called *espagnole* tomato sauce in Antonio Latini's cookbook *Lo scalco alla moderna*, published posthumously as *The Modern Steward*.

1716

Cosimo III de' Medici defines the territories where the **Chianti appellation** can be used. This is the first example of a PDO (Protected Designation of Origin).

1775

The first Italian book entirely devoted to the making of ice cream appears: *De' sorbetti* by Filippo Baldini.

1839

First mention of *spaghetti al pomodoro* ("with tomatoes") in the *Cucina teorico-pratica* (*Theoretical and Practical Cuisine*) by Ippolito Cavalcanti, the second edition of which includes an appendix on popular Neapolitan cuisine. The book discusses, for the first time, this new seasoning with a promising future, complementing the more traditional combination of pasta and cheese.

1891

Pellegrino Artusi publishes the first edition of *La scienza in cucina e l'arte di mangiar bene* (*Science in the Kitchen and the Art of Eating Well*). In his work, he seeks to create a common culture in a country very recently unified (1861). The work promotes the culinary traditions of a large number of cities and regions and is the founding text of modern Italian cuisine. Artusi will produce fifteen editions, enriched by the contributions of readers, up to 1911.

1929

Birth of the monthly magazine *La Cucina Italiana* (*Italian Cuisine*), which remains an important reference in the gastronomic culture of the country.

1931

The *Guida gastronomica d'Italia* by the Touring Club Italiano is born. It's the first organized collection of the gastronomic traditions of Italian regions and provinces.

1957

Mario Soldati films *Viaggio nella valle del Po* (*Journey along the Po Valley*) for Italian television. He talks about the agricultural and food realities of the country, as well as the emerging food industry. This report marks the official appearance of the topic of gastronomy on public television.

1959

After years of research in southern Italy, particularly in Cilento in Campania, the American doctor Ancel Keys publishes *Eat Well and Stay Well*, which paves the way for the international promotion of what will be referred to as the **"Mediterranean diet."**

1977

Gualtiero Marchesi opens his first restaurant in Milan. By combining nouvelle cuisine and Italian traditions, he rejuvenates Italian cuisine.

1986

Carlo Petrini founds the Slow Food Association in Bra (Cuneo, Piedmont). In just a few decades, it will spread throughout Italy and the world. The association promotes gastronomic knowledge by integrating haute cuisine with popular traditions.

2016

For the first time, the restaurant of an Italian chef, **La Francescana de Massimo Bottura (Modena), is voted best restaurant in the world** by the World's 50 Best Restaurants.

** Professor at the University of Bologna, specialist in the Middle Ages and food.*

Cucina Povera

Lovers of Italian cuisine keep the expression *cucina povera* on the tips of their tongues. What does this expression mean?

Although there are many nutritionally and sociologically "rich" specialties in Italy, Italian cuisine is often referred to as "poor" (*povera*). Inspired by *arte povera*, the expression *cucina povera* appeared in the 1970s to denote simple, frugal, and inexpensive recipes inherited from rural traditions. We tend to associate cucina povera with southern Italy even though it is found throughout all of Italy's provinces.

THE MAIN INGREDIENTS

—BREAD

Italy has created treasured, inventive dishes, both sweet and savory, that reuse this everyday food.

—OFFAL

This is the *quinto quarto* (fifth quarter), which includes all the pieces (viscera, glands, internal organs, head, feet, etc.) of farm animals considered to be of lower rank. These are included in the makeup of many dishes.

—*BACCALÀ* (SALTED COD), *STOCCAFISSO* (DRIED COD), ANCHOVIES IN SALT OR OIL

These marine resources were the fish of the poor because they are inexpensive and nonperishable.

—PIG FAT

Lard or bacon is the quintessential peasant's fat: flavorful and providing needed calories. Pork fat was replaced by duck fat in the Jewish community.

—CHEESE

Invented as a way to preserve milk, cheese is an important source of animal protein but is also considered a condiment (on pasta).

—VEGETABLE PROTEINS

Legumes, cereals, polenta, and chestnuts, to name a few, are all restorative raw ingredients that are easy to grow and harvest.

—VEGETABLES

Cabbage, squash, and potatoes were grown in vegetable gardens because of their yield and size, providing a generous resource.

—WILD PLANTS

A manna available in nature, delivering flavor and many nutrients.

THE TECHNIQUES

—PRESERVING

Preserving food using salt, vinegar, or oil; dried or smoked products . . . these methods were created out of the need in precarious rural economies to guarantee a regular year-round resource.

—COOKING IN A KETTLE

A large pot was present in all countryside households in which everything was cooked or reheated (soups, pasta, stews, etc.).

—PASTA

Prepared at home, without eggs, with wheat flour or less noble cereals (like *grano arso*, "burnt wheat", collected after the burning of grain fields such as buckwheat).

—FRYING

A cooking method that made ingredients golden, crispy, and high in calories, with a fat that could be reused several times (usually lard).

Flours

Bread, pizza, pasta . . . flour is absolutely everywhere! Each recipe has its own particular flour, flour type, and strength. For recipes that call for type 00 flour, you can use all-purpose flour for the same results.

FLOUR TYPES

Italy categorizes flour with criteria that are a bit vague for the average consumer. Here is an equivalence table based on extraction rate, which indicates the portion of the wheat kernel remaining after milling.

ITALIAN FLOURS BY "TIPO" (TYPE)	EXTRACTION RATE	USES
00	70%	Neapolitan pizza
0	73%	Cakes
1	80%	White bread
2	90%	Semi-whole bread
Whole wheat (integral)	95%	Whole wheat bread

A MATTER OF STRENGTH

Each flour has a different strength—which affects the "elastoplastic" qualities of a dough—directly related to its protein (gluten) level. Measured with the *W* index, the strength makes it possible for flour to absorb more or less water (for more or less hydrated loaves) and to obtain dough rise times of varying lengths. It is important to know the strength of a flour when fermentation will take place.

Italian Manitoba flour, for example, can be type 00 or 0, and is rich in proteins (13 to 15 percent), especially those that are gluten forming. Its *W* index varies from 350 to 400. Given its high level of resistance, it is used for long or very long rising times (bread, pizza, brioches, panettone, etc.).

	W90–170	W180–250	W260–350	W>350
TIPO ("TYPE") 00	Cookies, pâte brisée, pâte sucrée (short-crust pastry doughs)	Loaf cakes, sponge cake (genoise), choux dough, pastry cream, everyday breads with short fermentation	Medium-fermentation pizza dough, baguette, small loaves, bread for toast	Viennoiseries (brioches, baba), baked items with long fermentation, including pizza dough
TIPO ("TYPE") 0	Cookies, pâte brisée, pâte sucrée (short-crust pastry doughs)	Loaf cakes, sponge cake (genoise), choux dough, pastry cream, everyday breads with short fermentation	Choux dough, puff pastry, ciabatta, small loaves, medium-fermentation baguettes	Viennoiseries, breads with long fermentation (panettone), *rosette soffiate*, ciabatta
TIPO ("TYPE") 1		Ordinary breads		
TIPO ("TYPE") 2		Ordinary breads		
WHOLE WHEAT (INTEGRAL) FLOUR		Bread and pizza		

Equipment

COMMON EQUIPMENT

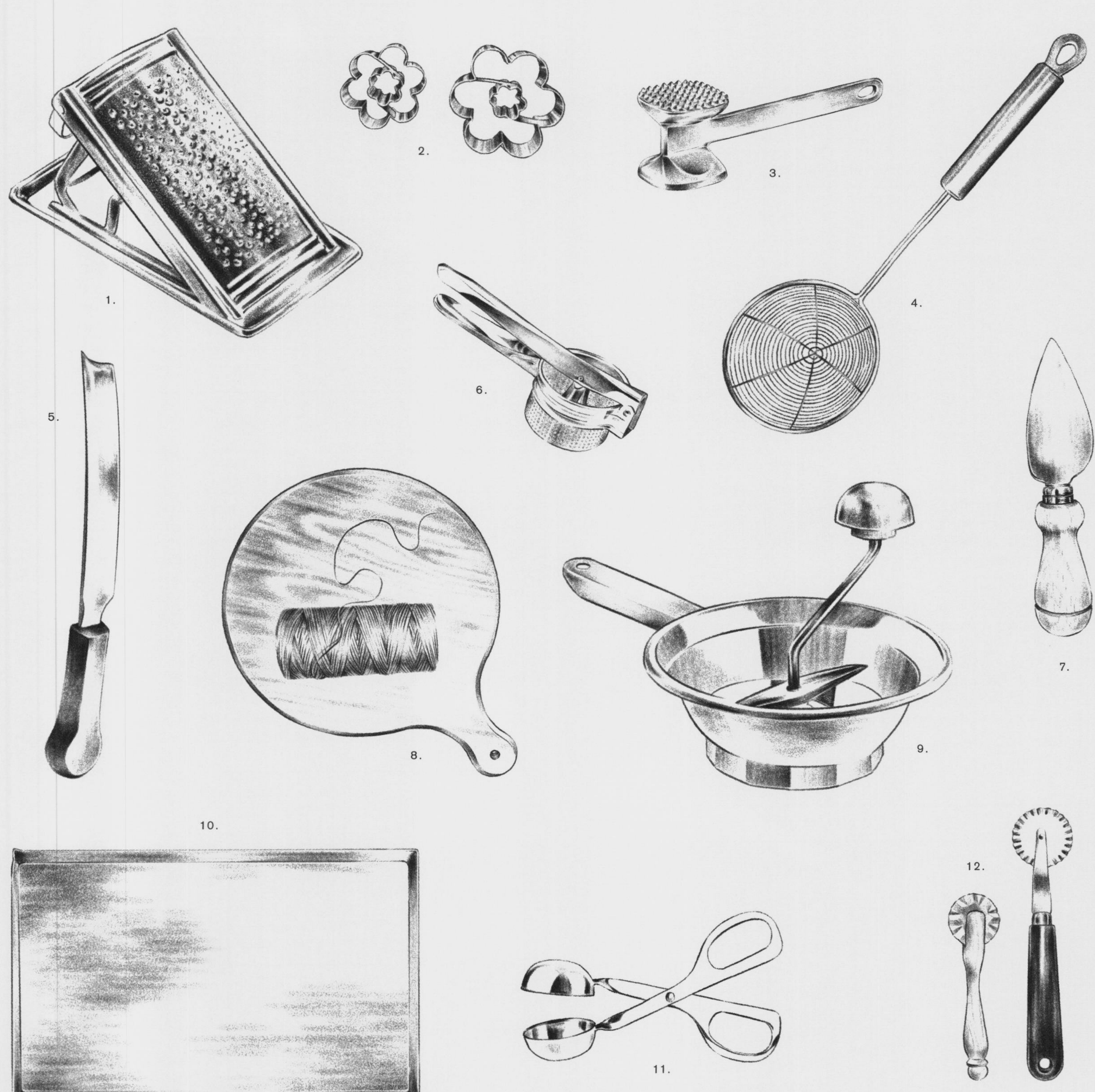

1. PARMESAN GRATER—*GRATTUGIA PER PARMIGIANO*

2. CANESTRELLI COOKIE CUTTERS—*STAMPINI PER CANESTRELLI*

3. MEAT TENDERIZER—*BATTICARNE*

4. OPEN SPIDER (STRAINER)—*RAGNO*

5. HAM BONING KNIFE—*COLTELLO PER DISOSSARE IL PROSCIUTTO*

6. FOOD PRESS—*SCHIACCIAPATATE/PASSATELLI*

7. PARMESAN KNIFE—*COLTELLO PER PARMIGIANO*

8. BOARD + STRING, FOR POLENTA—*TAGLIERE E FILO PER POLENTA*

9. VEGETABLE/TOMATO MILL—*PASSAVERDURA/POMODORO*

10. FOCACCIA TRAY—*TEGLIA PER FOCACCIA*

11. MEATBALL TONGS—*PINZA PER POLPETTE*

12. PIZZA WHEEL, left—*ROTELLA TAGLIAPIZZA*, **PASTA WHEEL**, right—*ROTELLE PER PASTA*

PASTA SPECIFIC

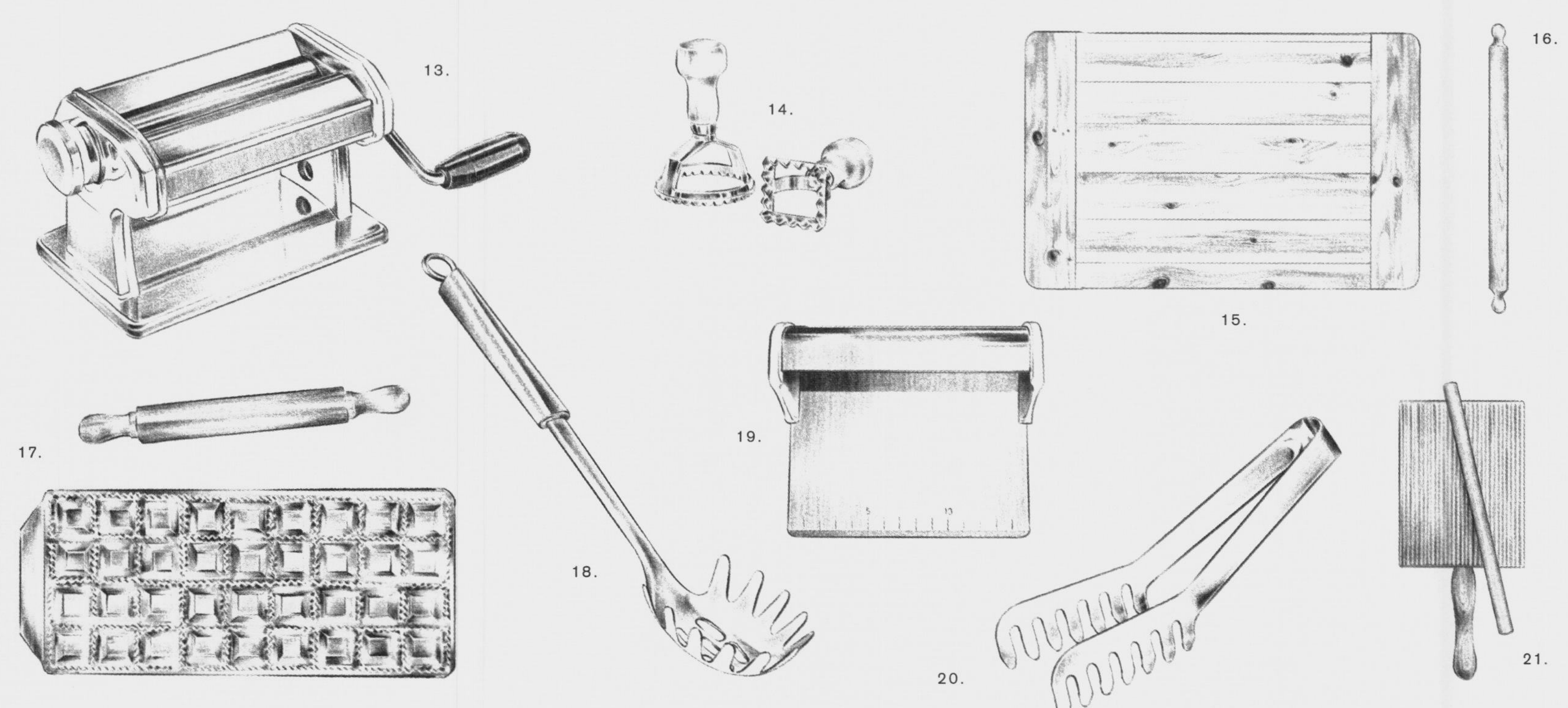

13. PASTA ROLLER—*MACCHINA PER LA PASTA*

14. RAVIOLI CUTTERS—*STAMPINI PER RAVIOLI*

15. WOODEN KNEADING BOARD—*SPIANATOIA PER PASTA*

16. 31½-INCH (80 CM) ROLLING PIN—*MATTARELLO PER PASTA*

17. RAVIOLI MOLD + ROLLER—*STAMPO PER RAVIOLI ROLL + MATTARELLO*

18. SPAGHETTI SPOON—*CUCCHIAIO PER SPAGHETTI*

19. PASTA CUTTER—*RASCHIETTO*

20. SPAGHETTI TONGS—*PINZA PER SPAGHETTI*

21. GNOCCHI BOARD + ROD, FOR GARGANELLI—*RIGAGNOCCHI + BASTONCINO PER GARGANELLI*

REGIONAL EQUIPMENT

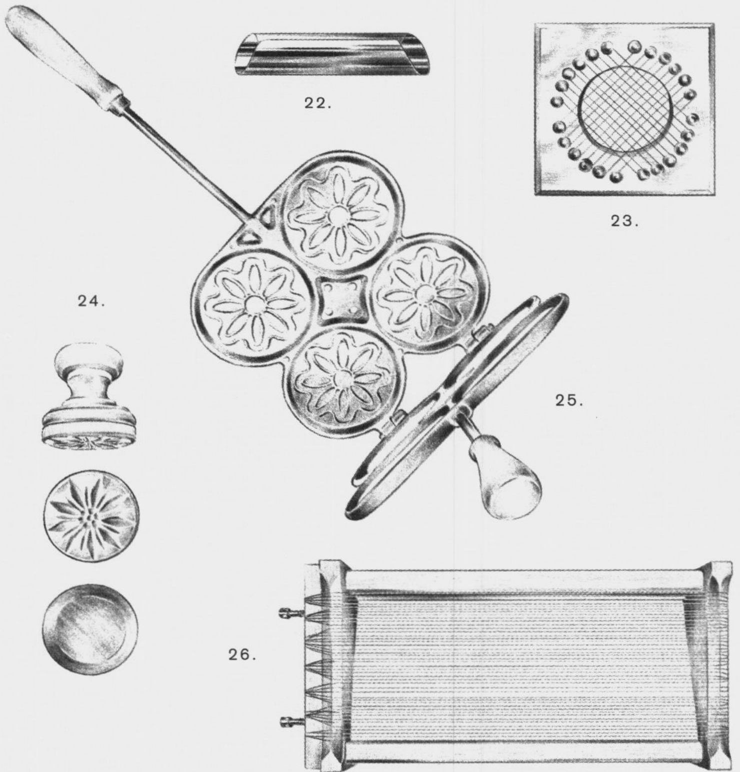

22. CANNOLI TUBES (SICILY)—*ROTOLO PER CANNOLI*

23. PUNTARELLE CUTTER (LAZIO)—*TAGLIAPUNTARELLE*

24. COOKIE CUTTERS FOR CROXETTI (LIGURIA)—*STAMPO PER CROXETTI*

25. TIGELLE MOLD (EMILIA-ROMAGNA)—*PIASTRA PER TIGELLE*

26. PASTA CUTTER (ABRUZZO)—*CHITARRA PER SPAGHETTI*

SPECIALTY EQUIPMENT

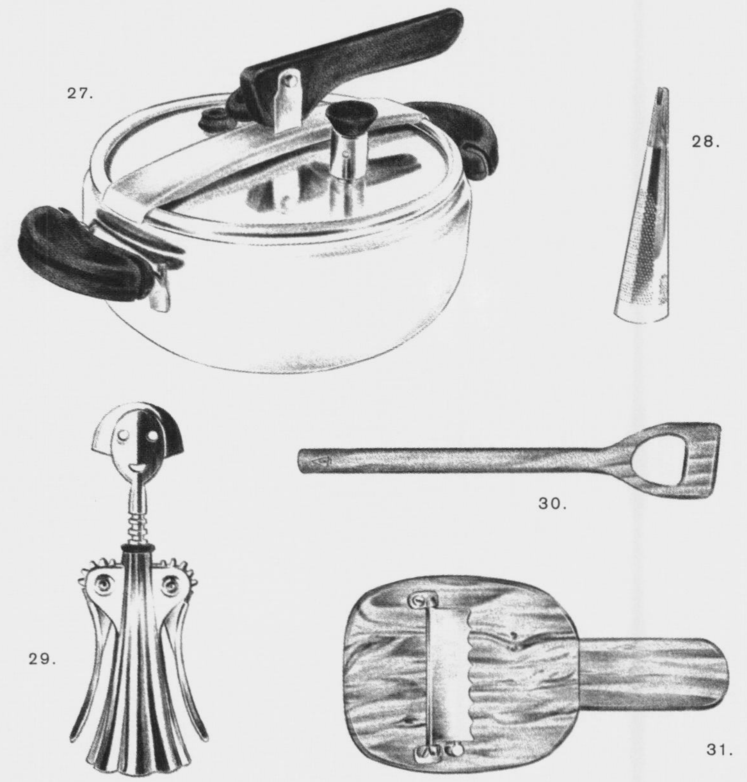

27. PRESSURE COOKER, LAGOSTINA—*PENTOLA A PRESSIONE*

28. "TODO" PARMESAN GRATER, ALESSI—*GRATTUGIA PER PARMIGIANO*

29. ANNA G. CORKSCREW, ALESSI—*CAVATAPPI*

30. ALBERTO GOZZI RISOTTO SPOON—*CUCCHIAIO PER RISOTTO*

31. ETTORE SOTTSASS TRUFFLE GRATER, ALESSI—*TAGLIATARTUFO*

The Meal

THE DAY IN DINING

IN MOST REGIONS

COLAZIONE
The first meal of the day (breakfast). Various hours.

PRANZO
The midday meal (lunch). In the north, between 12:30 and 1 p.m.; central, between 1 and 1:30 p.m.; south, around 2 p.m.

CENA
The evening meal (dinner). In the north, between 7:30 and 8 p.m.; central, between 8 and 8:30 p.m.; south, starting from 9 p.m.

IN CERTAIN NORTHERN UPPER CLASSES

PRIMA COLAZIONE
The first meal of the day (breakfast).

COLAZIONE
The midday meal (lunch).

PRANZO
The evening meal (dinner).

CENA
An evening meal (dinner), between 10 and 11 p.m., and sometimes until late; more formal with more guests.

BUT ALSO . . .

LO SPUNTINO
A snack that holds off hunger while waiting for lunch or dinner.

LA MERENDA
A snack for children or a light meal for adults. It can be sweet (*pane con la marmellata*, Nutella, biscotti), or salty (*pane con il prosciutto, salame* [salami], *formaggio* [cheese], pizza, or focaccia).

A TAVOLA!—DINNER'S READY

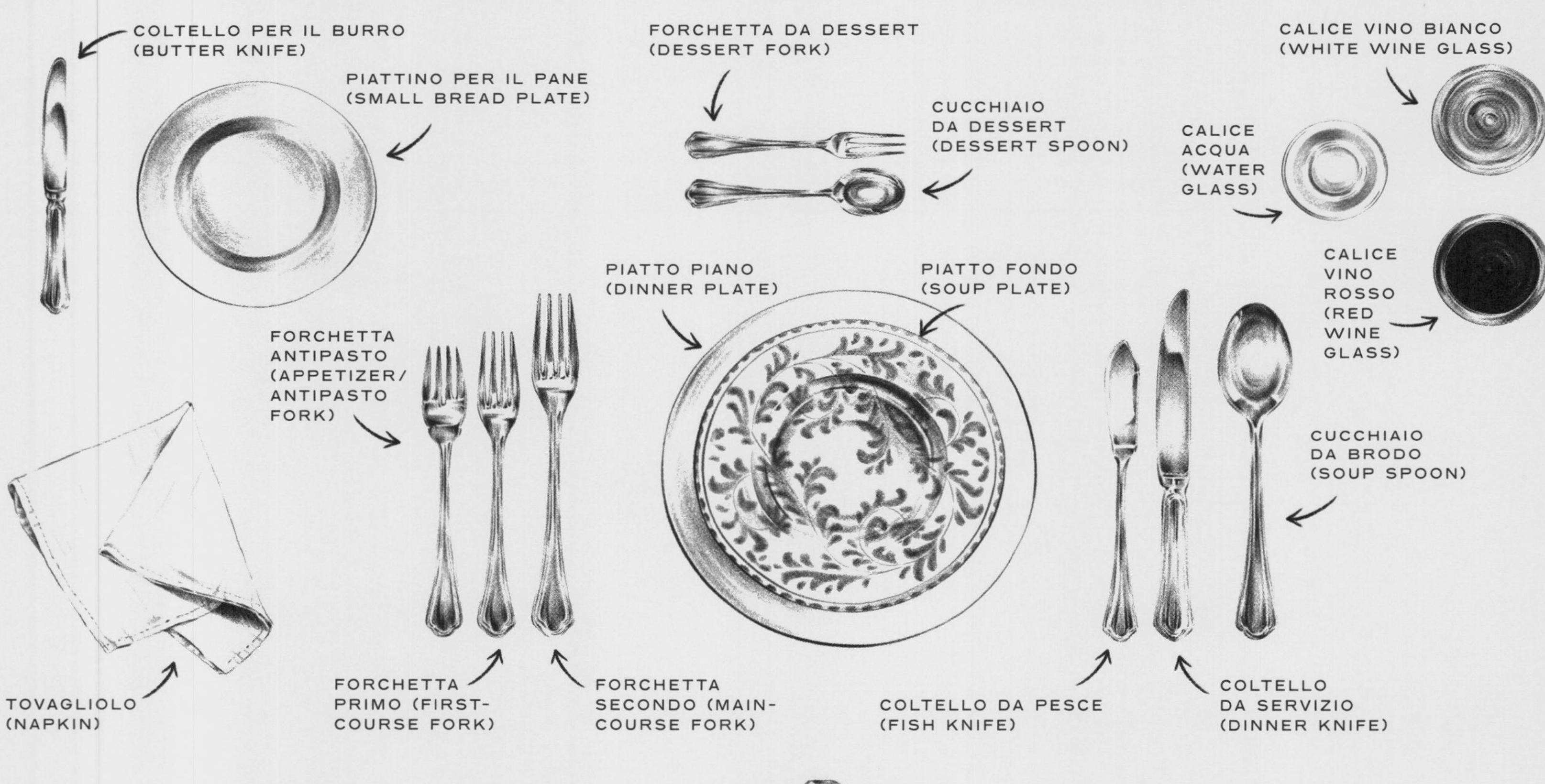

BROCCA D'ACQUA (WATER PITCHER)

ACQUA NATURALE O GASSATA (FLAT OR SPARKLING WATER)

BOTTIGLIA DI VINO (WINE BOTTLE)

VINO DELLA CASA (TABLE/ HOUSE WINE)

BIRRE/BIBITE (BEER/COOL BEVERAGE)

ORDINE DEI PIATTI—THE ORDER OF DISHES

1.

ANTIPASTI
APPETIZER/STARTER

- **_FREDDI_** — COLD
- **_CALDI_** — HOT

2.

PRIMI PIATTI
FIRST COURSES

- **_IN BRODO (ZUPPA, MINESTRA . . .)_** — IN BROTH (SOUPS, STEWS . . .)
- **_ASCIUTTI_** — DRY
  - **_RISI & RISOTTI_** — RICE & RISOTTOS
  - **_PASTA_** — PASTA

3.

SECONDI PIATTI
MAIN COURSES

- **_UOVA, PESCI, CROSTACEI, FORMAGGI COTTI . . ._** — EGGS, FISH, SHELLFISH, COOKED CHEESES . . .
- **_CARNI (BIANCHE, ROSSE, SELVAGGINA . . .)_** — MEAT (WHITE, RED, GAME . . .)

\+ **_CONTORNI_** — ACCOMPANIMENTS/SIDE DISHES (GRILLED VEGETABLES . . .)

4.

DESSERT
DESSERTS

- **_FORMAGGIO_** — CHEESE
- **_DOLCI_** — SWEETS
  - **_CALDI (ZABAIONE . . .)_** — HOT (SABAYON . . .)
  - **_FREDDI (GELATI, TORTE . . .)_** — COLD (ICE CREAM, TARTS)
- **_FRUTTA_** — FRUITS

5.

CAFFÈ
COFFEE

→ **_AMMAZZACAFFÈ_** ("COFFEE KILLER"), **_DIGESTIVO_** (DIGESTIF)

The Art of Talking about the Stomach with the Hands

How do you stop an Italian from talking? Tie his hands together! Inherited from ancient Greek gesticulator rhetoric, speaking with the hands is one of the most identifiable features of someone who is Italian. Here is a small glossary to help you understand when speaking with an Italian at the table or while chatting about cooking.

I'M HUNGRY!

Place the edge of the open hand at stomach level and pat the side rhythmically.

Or rub the stomach with a wide-open hand in a repeated circular motion.

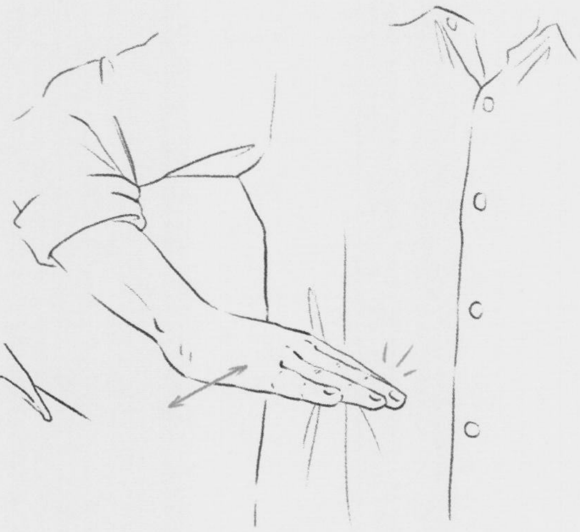

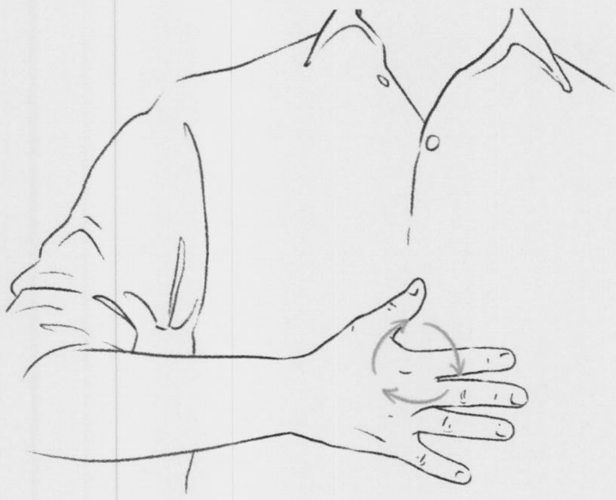

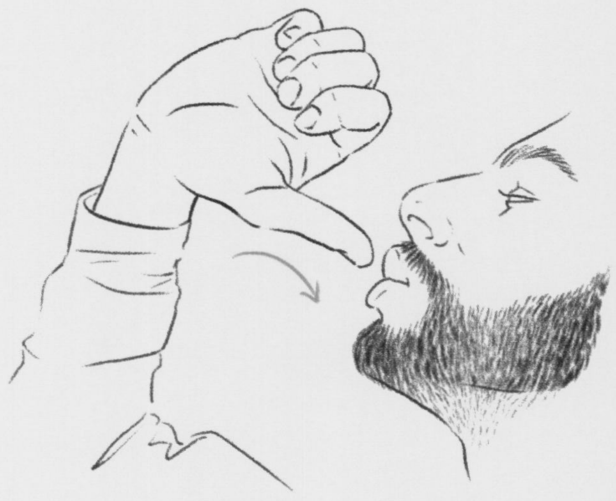

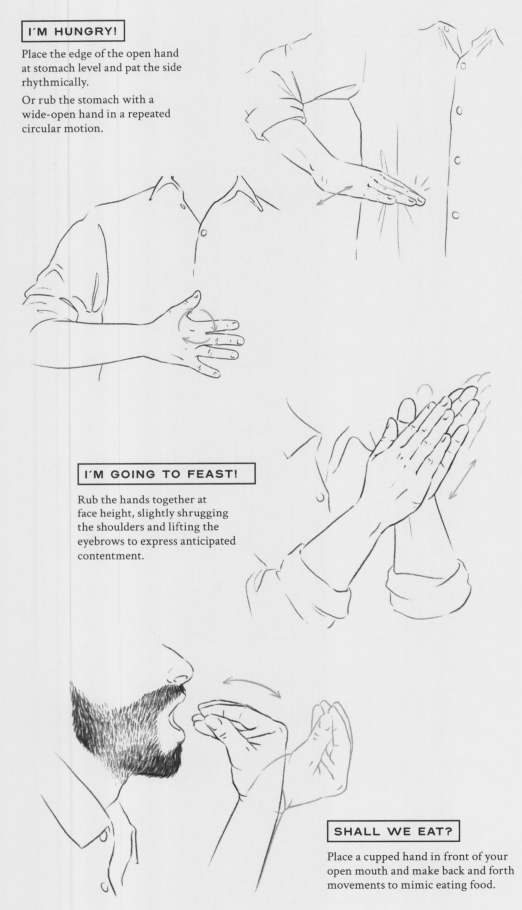

I'M THIRSTY

Bend the index finger, middle finger, ring finger, and little finger down and point the thumb toward the mouth to mimic drinking.

I'M GOING TO FEAST!

Rub the hands together at face height, slightly shrugging the shoulders and lifting the eyebrows to express anticipated contentment.

SHALL WE ENJOY A PLATE OF SPAGHETTI?

With a closed fist, use the index and middle fingers pointing as two chopsticks and imitate the movement of the fork turning several times to roll up spaghetti.

SHALL WE EAT?

Place a cupped hand in front of your open mouth and make back and forth movements to mimic eating food.

SHALL WE HAVE A COFFEE?

Pretend to hold a cup of coffee with the thumb, index, and middle fingers gathered near the mouth, and rotate your hand toward the mouth as if to take a sip.

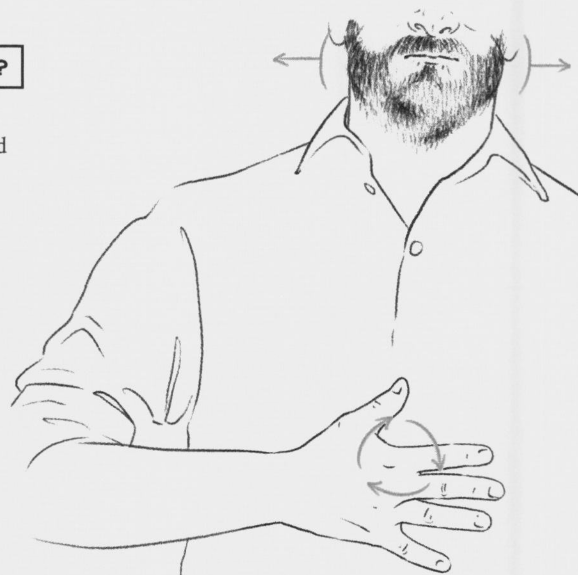

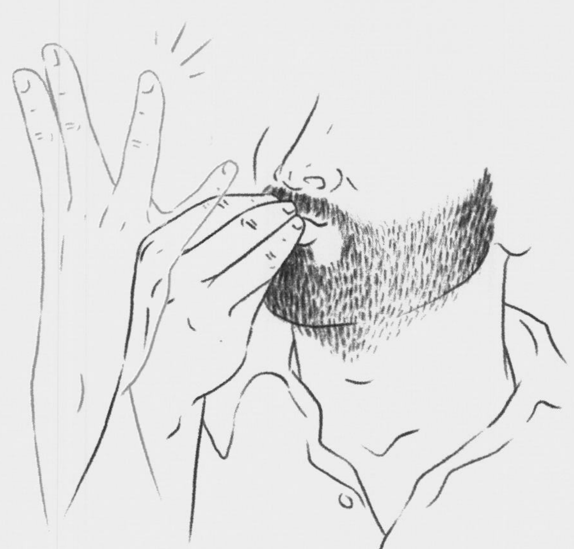

IT'S EXQUISITE!

Place a cupped hand in front of your closed mouth. Place all five fingertips on the lips and act out a kiss (*il bacio*) while opening the hand in front of the face, with the eyes closed for more emphasis.

I AM FULL!

Pat the stomach with the wide-open hand in a repeating circular motion, puffing the cheeks to mimic being overfilled.

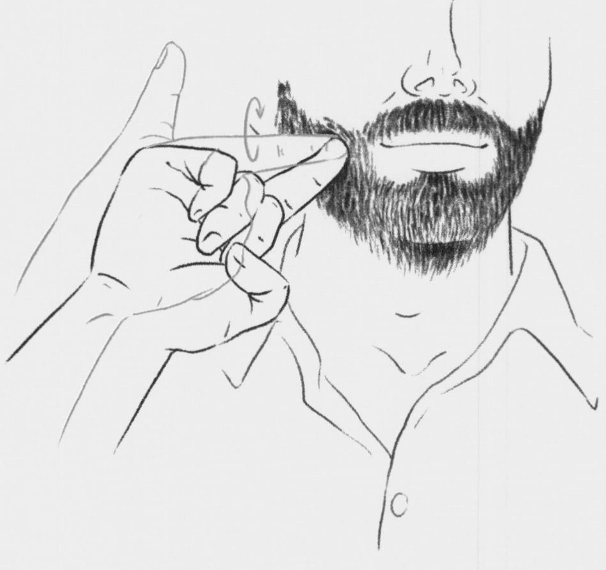

I LOVE IT!

Point the index finger against the cheek, thumb up, and rotate the hand three or four times with your finger as a pivot point (like a screwdriver) with the eyes wide open.

BLECK! IT'S DISGUSTING!

Slowly raise both hands (as if signaling "hands off") and tilt your head to the left with an expression of disgust (eyes closed, mouth tightened).

I'M LICKING MY FINGERS!

Place the open hand fanned out in front of the mouth and, with the tongue slightly sticking out, pass the fingers one by one in front of the mouth as if licking them.

Cooking Pasta

When it comes to pasta, non-Italians make many faux pas! *Basta* the mistakes with pasta.

LA COTTURA—COOKING

Choose artisanal pasta. Look for "*trafilata al bronzo*" on the packaging, which indicates that the pasta has been extruded through a bronze die, which gives it a rough texture to ensure sauce sticks to it well. But this designation is now also used by commercial pasta manufacturers. It is difficult to know the origin of the cereals listed on the package, but the indication IGP (*Indicazione Geografica Protetta*, Protected Geographical Indication) "Pasta di Gragnano" is proof of its authenticity. A quality pasta can also be recognized by the flavorsome aroma of cereals when you open the package.

THE RIGHT PROPORTION

In Italy, pasta is a *primo piatto* (first course) and not a main course. Three to 3½ ounces (80 to 100 g) of pasta per person is sufficient for a primo piatto, or up to 4¼ ounces (120 g) for a *piatto unico* (single course).

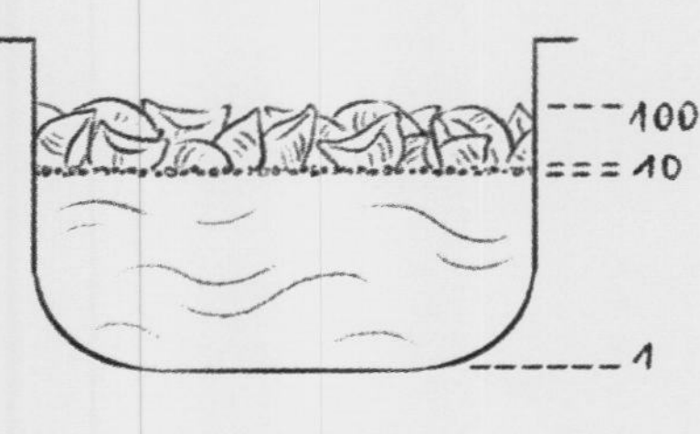

4 CUPS (1 L) WATER
2 TEASPOONS (10 G) COARSE SALT
3½ OUNCES (100 G) PASTA

LOTS OF WATER AND SALT IN THE POT

Pasta should float around comfortably in a large pot of water, and never covered. This is to ensure the pasta noodles do not stick to each other and therefore cause them to have a starchy taste. The water should be abundantly salted when it reaches a boil and not before, and not after the pasta is added. Here the 1/10/100 rule applies: prevention is less costly than correction!

DO NOT BREAK SPAGHETTI IN HALF

Doing so would be sacrilege! There's a reason spaghetti is long. Besides, spaghetti rarely breaks into two equal halves but often into pieces of different lengths, which compromises its ability to cook evenly. Only *candele*, ziti, or smooth penne pastas, which are considered a spaghetti as the Italians like to define them, are acceptable in the south for breaking to use in recipes.

RESPECT COOKING AL DENTE

Al dente means that the pasta should have a bit of resistance when chewed. And contrary to popular belief, al dente pasta is much more digestible than cooked pasta because it encourages chewing. But this is a subjective idea: northern Italians, who cook pasta just a little, do not always agree with those from the south, who cook it even less! To achieve the right texture, your best bet is to rely on the lower range of the cooking time indicated on the package. If the pasta is to be panfried, drain it two minutes beforehand. The very trendy pasta-doneness test of tossing it against the wall ("If it sticks, it's done," they say) is as far-fetched as it is messy! The best way to test is to taste it: the pasta should display a firm elasticity. When you bite into a strand of spaghetti, you should see a small white dot in the middle of the strand. This indicates that the core is still a little underdone, which is what you want.

DRAIN THE PASTA

Do not cool pasta under cold running water then finish cooking it later! Pasta should be drained in a large colander and immediately cooked in the sauce. In Italy, they say that pasta breathes: when it's hot, its pores open up to accommodate the sauce.

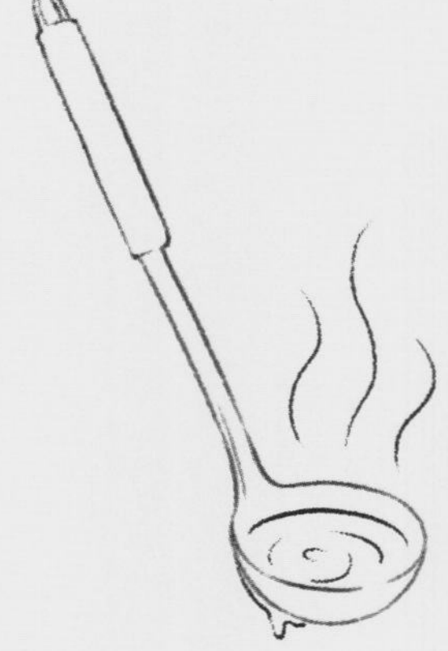

COOK WITH THE PASTA WATER

The water in which the pasta was cooked is an essential recipe ingredient. Always ladle out a large quantity of pasta water during cooking to set aside in a bowl. Make no mistake, in Italy, pasta is always added to the sauce and not the other way around! When you pour your pasta into the pan of sauce, add a little of the pasta water to help bind the sauce and smooth it out, thanks to the starch in the pasta water. Then season your pasta directly in the pan.

THREE HABITS THAT SHOULD BE BANNED . . .

PUTTING CREAM IN CARBONARA

Should you bind a sauce made with egg yolk and lardons with a little cream? This is an affront to Rome's culinary heritage! Egg yolk, the Parmesan and Pecorino-Romano duo, and the pasta cooking water are all you need to make a thick, smooth sauce . . . as long as you exercise care when making it. And, made in this way, it's more easily digestible.

SERVING PASTA AS A SIDE DISH

Like rice, mashed potatoes, and vegetables, pasta is often served, outside of Italy, as a complement to a meat or fish dish. For example, in France, *escalope à la Milanaise* is served with tagliatelle or spaghetti. This would be heresy in Italy, where *costoletta alla milanese* is perfect with just a salad or a few sautéed potatoes. In Italy, pasta is too important to be reduced to the rank of a *contorno* (side dish).

PLACING CHEESE ON SEAFOOD PASTA

In the spring of 2019, a diplomatic incident occurred in London: Massimo Donati, the chef of Maximo trattoria, forbade a customer from sprinkling his plate of crab ravioli with Parmesan. The customer took revenge by posting a negative review on Tripadvisor. The Parmigiano Reggiano Consortium stepped in, reminding everyone, perhaps just for advertising purposes, of the "versatility" of this famous cheese from Emilia-Romagna. After all, there are many recipes in southern Italy that combine *cozze e pecorino* (mussels and pecorino)! This combination is the exception, however. Cheese over seafood remains a firmly established taboo.

—A GEOGRAPHICAL REASON: Fish was consumed in coastal areas, while cheese was mostly produced inland, so these two ingredients had little opportunity to come together.

—A HEALTH REASON: In theories by Hippocrates and Galen, reference was made to digestive complications associated with the chemical transformation of fish once in contact with cheese. The belief in separating them continued throughout the Middle Ages and the Renaissance, reaching modern Italian cookbooks.

—A RELIGIOUS REASON: In Israel, during the time of Christ, there was a cultural barrier between shepherds and fishermen. They could trade cheese and fish, but in a limited way, and in cooking they never mixed them in the same dish or in the same recipe . . .

PASTA IN NUMBERS*

Italians are the world leaders in pasta production—**3.2 MILLION TONS**—and consumption—**53 POUNDS (24 KG) PER PERSON PER YEAR**. They eat it **FOUR OR FIVE TIMES A WEEK** for lunch.

ITALIANS' FAVORITE PASTA DISHES**

- *CARBONARA*
- *PASTA AL RAGÙ*
- *PASTA POMODORO E BASILICO*

***According to a 2019 BVA Doxa poll for The Fork*

Over the past decade or so, central Italy has become the area of greatest pasta consumption, where 45 percent of residents eat pasta every day, compared to 32 percent in the south and 24 percent in the north.

Over the period of a year, nearly four out of ten packages of dry pasta are sold south of Rome, while the northwest is the leader in fresh pasta.

**According to a 2017 BVA Doxa poll*

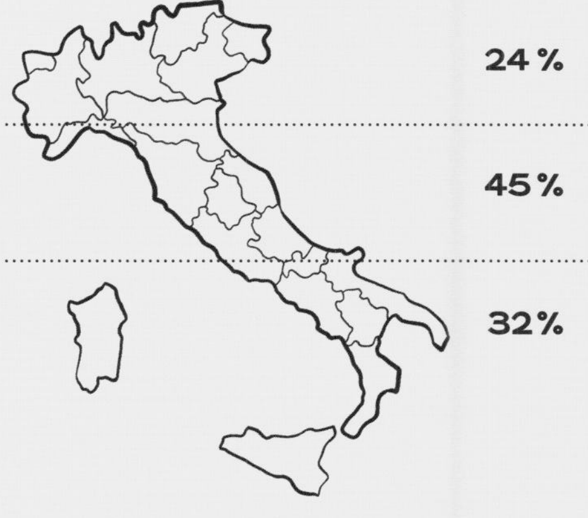

AL DENTE, A NEW CUSTOM

ITALIANS HAVE NOT ALWAYS CONSUMED PASTA COOKED FIRM (AKA "AL DENTE")

→ In the first recipes for pasta from the Middle Ages, the cooking time was long: one hour for vermicelli and up to two hours for Sicilian macaronis . . . Poaching in broth, water, or milk was often followed by parboiling. At the time, there was a taste for soft, tender cheeses, and the dietary precepts recommended prolonged cooking of pasta in order to avoid body blockages and kidney stones.

→ From the seventeenth century, the Florentine cook Giovanni del Turco, desiring to simplify medieval recipes, recommended cooking pasta less and strengthening it by moistening it with fresh water, in particular to preserve the integrity of certain fragile pasta shapes, such as fresh tagliatelle.

→ It is probable that the idea of short cooking times for pastas began in the streets of Naples, thanks to the figure of the *maccaronaro*, who would quickly prepare steamed macaronis any time of the day for a modest sum of money. The Neapolitan duke Ippolito Cavalcanti mentioned for the first time the notion of al dente in his 1837 guide *Cucina teorico-pratica*. He uses as an example the Neapolitan spaghetti as still "green" (in the sense of "not ripe") and elastic to the bite.

→ The idea of al dente pasta would be adopted by the bourgeoisie class and throughout the Italian peninsula thanks to Italian unification.

Tasting Spaghetti

The Italians criticize the rest of the world for lack of elegance and efficiency when it comes to eating the star of the pasta world: spaghetti. Here's a little lesson in how to do it correctly.

WHAT TO DO

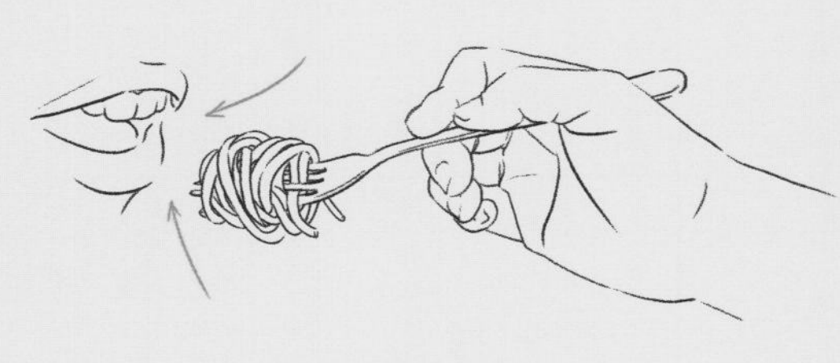

1

Pick up some spaghetti with your fork. Lift the fork and focus on maneuvering the spaghetti strands through the tines.

2

Place the tines of the fork against the curved edge of the plate and turn the fork to make a ball of spaghetti. The strands of the pasta will wrap around the tines to form a compact bite.

3

Lift the fork fully to your mouth. Taking bites that are too big risks getting stained with sauce or letting the spaghetti hang out of your mouth.

WHAT NOT TO DO

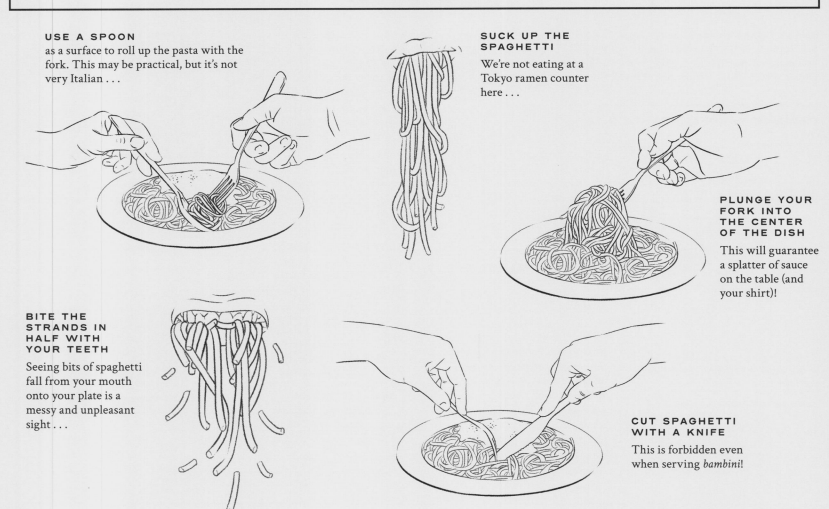

USE A SPOON
as a surface to roll up the pasta with the fork. This may be practical, but it's not very Italian . . .

SUCK UP THE SPAGHETTI
We're not eating at a Tokyo ramen counter here . . .

PLUNGE YOUR FORK INTO THE CENTER OF THE DISH
This will guarantee a splatter of sauce on the table (and your shirt)!

BITE THE STRANDS IN HALF WITH YOUR TEETH
Seeing bits of spaghetti fall from your mouth onto your plate is a messy and unpleasant sight . . .

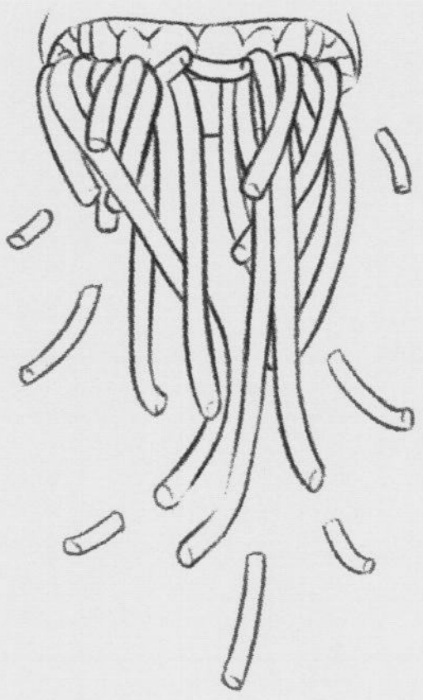

CUT SPAGHETTI WITH A KNIFE
This is forbidden even when serving *bambini*!

Glossary

Here is a little primer on techniques and terms specific to Italian cuisine.

ABBRACCIARE (IL CONDIMENTO): meaning "to kiss." Used to describe pasta that "blends" well with its seasonings.

ACQUACOTTA (lit. "cooked water"): an aromatic soup made from vegetables, wild herbs, and water and enhanced with aromatics (lesser calamint, wild carrot, wild fennel . . .) common to central Italy. You can enrich it with stale bread, scrambled eggs, or porcini mushrooms. See *zuppa*.

ACQUA PAZZA (ALL') (lit. "in crazy water"): a recipe for poached white fish or lightly flavored broth used for poaching (olive oil, tomatoes, water—or seawater in former times).

AFFOGARE: to drown. 1. Cooking eggs or fish by submerging them halfway in water at a maximum temperature of 200°F (90°C). 2. In pastry, to soak a dessert in a liquid (liqueur, chocolate, coffee, etc.).

AMMAZZACAFFÈ (lit. "coffee killer"): an alcoholic drink served at the end of the meal, after coffee, to "kill" the aftertaste.

AMMOLLICARE: to sprinkle with fresh or dried bread crumbs. A step in the preparation of fish, meats, and vegetables very common in southern Italy, applied just before placing the dish in the oven to create a thin crust on top.

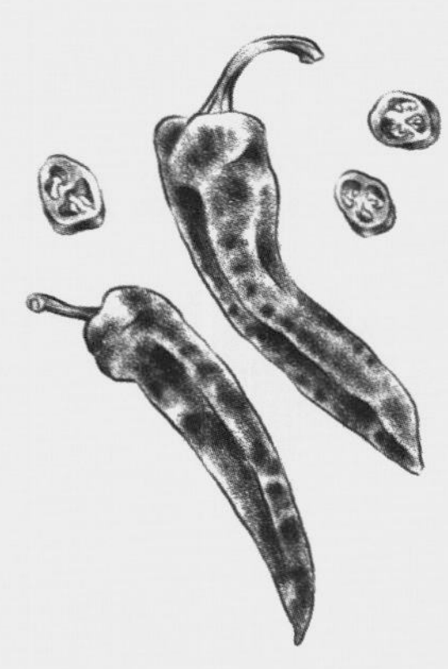

ALL'ARRABBIATA (lit. "enraged"): a dish cooked with a large amount of chile.

ARROSTO MORTO (lit. "dead roast"): method of cooking meats that consists of browning the meat in a fat without other liquids, as is done for roasts, then cooking it slowly by adding broth, wine, or water. See *umido* and *morto*.

ASTRATTO: see *elioconcentrato*.

BAFFA: a whole fillet. 1. Each of the two halves of a fish (often smoked salmon or stockfish) stripped of the head, tail, backbones, and spine. *Baffa*, which often comes in the shape of a large rectangular piece, can be split into *filetti* (thin fillets). 2. Also a whole lobe (roe) of bottarga or a piece of speck.

BATTUTA: to make into tartare using a knife. A preparation that mainly applies to the Fassona breed of calves (Piedmont).

BATTUTO: minced bacon and herbs. A condiment prepared by "beating" and chopping bacon or pork fat, celery, onion, garlic, carrot, and parsley with a large kitchen knife.

BIANCO (IN) (lit. "in white"): 1. Seasoning (of pasta, meat, fish, vegetables) that does not include the use of tomato sauce. 2. To eat *in bianco* in Italian culture means to eat without sauce: it is a way of serving dishes (rice, pasta) with "light" seasonings, in particular using butter (or oil) and Parmesan, whether by choice or because of a restricted diet. 3. Related to escalopes (thin cutlets): brown them only lightly.

BIANCA/ROSSA: a pizza topping with a base of mozzarella (*bianca*) or a base of tomato sauce (*rossa*).

BIGA: a pre-ferment. A technique for pre-fermentation of pizza dough, consisting of a mixture of water, flour, and yeast left to stand between sixteen and forty-eight hours. The pre-ferment acts as a leavening agent when incorporated into the final dough. Called a *poolish* when it is liquid.

BISTECCA: a deformation of the word *beefsteak* (a recent addition to the Italian language, introduced at the end of the nineteenth century from the Anglo-American community in Florence). The original Italian word was *braciola* (coal). Today, *bistecca* refers to both pork chops (*bistecca di maiale*) and steak.

BRACE (ALLA) (lit. "over the embers"): grilled, cooked on a grill (*gratella*) over the almost-extinguished embers (indirect, slow cooking). See *ferri, griglia,* and *spiedo*.

BRASATO (lit. "braise"): 1. Food (meat, fish, vegetables) stewed over low heat to maintain its internal juices. 2. Applied to beef, the term refers to a specific dish of Lombard or Piedmont cuisine in which a tender piece, such as rump steak (most often marinated ahead of time in a full-bodied wine such as Barolo or Barbaresco and aromatics) is browned in a fat, then cooked over low heat and covered (*umido*) in the wine used in the marinade. See *stracotto*.

BRILLARE (lit. "to pearlize"): related to the preparation of risottos by toasting the rice in a base of butter and onion before fully cooking it.

BRODETTO (lit. "small broth"): 1. Sauce made from eggs beaten in a broth with lemon juice. 2. Fish soup common near the Adriatic coast, made of various types of fish cooked over low heat in a chopped mixture (*soffritto*) of onions, parsley, garlic, pepper, salt, spices, and wine, to which pieces of fresh or canned tomatoes are added.

BRODO (DI PESCE): fish broth. The bones and heads are boiled with a bouquet garni, then strained. Different from *fumetto*.

CACCIATORA (ALLA) (lit. "by hunting"): a method of cooking chicken, rabbit, or game by sautéing it in oil with garlic and wine or wine vinegar with a sprig of rosemary.

CAPULIATO (lit. "minced"): a traditional Sicilian seasoning made from sun-dried tomatoes, sliced then marinated in olive oil, with basil and other herbs (oregano, garlic, chile, etc.). Used to season pasta, bruschetta, or focaccia.

CARPIONE: a marinade from northwestern Italy. A sort of escabeche made from an onion *soffritto*, sage (or bay leaf), sometimes celery and carrot, salt, water, and vinegar, which is usually used to cook freshwater fish (tench, eel, carp, etc.) but also ocean fish and vegetables (squash, zucchini).

CHANTILLY: not Chantilly cream in the sense of lightly sweetened whipped cream but instead a diplomat cream or crème madame. A mixture of pastry cream and whipped cream, with or without gelatin (without gelatin is *crème madame*).

CORNICIONE (lit. "cornice," "molding"): the edge of a pizza (the crust).

CROGIOLARE: to simmer; to cook over low heat with little liquid.

DENTE (AL): a cooking method reserved for pasta, rice, cereals, and certain vegetables that consists of stopping the cooking when the food still has a firm consistency, sometimes by rinsing it briefly under cold water to reduce the heat stored in the food.

ELIOCONCENTRATO (CONCENTRATED IN THE SUN) OR ESTRATTO DI POMODORO (IN SICILIAN, ASTRATTO OR STRATTU): a tomato concentrate made by sun drying.

FARINA/SEMOLA: flour/semolina. The difference between the two products is based on the coarseness: a finer grain size for *farina* (flour) or a coarser grain size for semolina. But beware: this also refers to *farina granita* (cornmeal). In this case, corn is broken down into *farina bramata* (medium- or large-grain cornmeal), *farina fioretto* (fine-grain cornmeal) and *farina fumetto* (very fine-grain cornmeal). The terms *grits* or *gritz* ("sand" in Old English) generally refer to coarsely ground durum wheat semolina or cornmeal.

FERRI (AI) (lit. "on irons"): grilled, cooked on a flat cooking pan or a cast-iron griddle often with grill marks; to sear and mark foods that are not in direct contact with the flame. See *brace, griglia,* and *spiedo.*

FIORENTINA: a piece of beef and a method of cooking. 1. Sirloin steak with the tenderloin attached. Recommended thickness: 2 inches (5 cm) or, as measured in Tuscany, "three fingers." Traditional accompaniment: white bean salad. 2. To grill this meat over hard charcoal. The meat is seared and grilled just on the surface to prevent the juices from running out. The steak is turned only once to allow time just to heat the interior so that it remains red and bloody (rare). Salt is not added until after cooking to retain the juices. Finally, a few drops of olive oil with a little freshly ground black pepper are added.

FIORETTO: see *farina.*

FUMETTO: 1. Stock (fish) very similar to *brodo,* but all the ingredients have first been panfried over high heat in very hot oil, then covered with water, and finally strained. The consistency is thicker than brodo. 2. See *farina.*

FUNGHETTO (A) (lit. "like a small mushroom"): a way of preparing eggplant, common in Campania, by cutting the eggplant into small cubes and sautéing them like mushrooms.

GRIGLIA (ALLA) (lit. "on the grill"): grilled, cooked quickly over a direct heat source through a grill (*gratella*). See *brace, ferri,* and *spiedo.*

GUAZZETTO: a seasoning usually obtained by combining tomatoes, garlic, wine, or stock in a pan, intended for cooking fish (cod, gurnard, or red mullet, for example).

IMPANATURA: see *panatura.*

IMPAZZIRE (lit. "go crazy"): inadvertently breaking a mayonnaise or emulsion, causing the ingredients to separate.

INTINGOLO: a sauce or juice obtained by cooking meat, fish, or vegetables.

INZUPPARE: to soak, to moisten baked foods (bread, toasted breads, cookies) in liquid to soften and flavor them. For example, to make *zuppa inglese* or the dessert tiramisu.

LIEVITO MADRE (lit. "mother starter"): a pre-ferment or starter.

MANTECARE: shake vigorously. An operation that involves the rather long and vigorous working of two ingredients—raw or cooked—to soften them and make them homogeneous and creamy. 1. For risotto, at the end of cooking, *mantecatura* (to work) occurs after adding butter and/or Parmesan. For the Venetian *baccalà mantecato* (a kind of cod brandade), this is done in olive oil. 2. This method also gives its name to a particular type of ice cream, called *mantecato.* 3. It also applies to pâtés (duck liver, fish) and pasta.

MENARE OR MISSIARE (lit. "to hit"): to vigorously mix polenta with the elbow raised.

MINESTRA: a soup. Very widespread in Italy, especially in the north. It involves cooking vegetables and/or meat in a broth, like *zuppa,* but it has a more liquid consistency (the broth is not absorbed, *inzuppato*) and especially involves adding pasta or rice. Its lighter version is consommé, a soup generally with a white stock made from poultry, veal, or beef that is then clarified and served in a cup. The term *minestra asciutta* ("dry soup") is used for pasta in sauce (*spaghetti al pomodoro, tagliatelle al ragù, penne all'arrabiata*) or risottos.

MINESTRONE: a thick soup, somewhere between *minestra* and *zuppa.* Prepared with more or less broth, hence its thicker consistency than *minestra,* composed of many ingredients: a mixture of roughly chopped fresh seasonal vegetables, thickening vegetables (potatoes, squash, legumes), fat (oil, bacon, etc.), and cereals. Le Virtù from Abruzzo is included in this category.

MORTO (lit. "death"): in Tuscany, this describes pork tenderloin cooked in a dish as opposed to traditional cooking on a spit.

ONDA (ALL') (lit. "on the wave"): a degree of cooking and the density of risotto when it reaches a creamy consistency. The name derives from the rippling movement of the rice during the phase of *mantecatura* when it folds up on itself and, when serving, delicately follows the shape of the dish.

PANATURA: to bread. The method that consists of covering a dish, meat, or fish with dried bread crumbs (dry bread or dried out) or fresh, finely crumbled bread crumbs before cooking. Not to be confused with *impanatura* (breading), which consists of flouring a food, dredging it in beaten eggs, then coating it in dried or fresh bread crumbs.

PASSATA (lit. "ground," "passed through"): a tomato preparation that is more liquid than *polpa* because the tomatoes are crushed and mixed with their juices. It is subdivided into:

- **VELLUTATA**: sauce. A finer consistency due to the removal of seeds and skin.
- **RUSTICA**: coarser and grainier.

The *passata* is raw or pasteurized at 149°F (65°C) during its manufacture. To keep its character intact, it is barely heated. It is often used with eggs, white meats, or meatballs in sauce.

PASTA SECCA (lit. "dry pasta"): pasta made by drawing or by rolling out and drying, made from semolina flour and water.

PASTASCIUTTA (lit. "drained/dried pasta"): traditional Italian pasta dish (the pasta is cooked in water, drained, then seasoned). Not to be confused with *pasta secca.*

PASTICCIO: pasta gratin. A preparation from central and southern Italy based on pasta seasoned or stuffed with sauces, meats, and/or vegetables, then baked in the oven. The word *pasticcio* tends to more and more frequently replace *timballo.*

PELATI: whole peeled tomatoes, briefly blanched, and preserved in their juices. They cook very quickly, which is why they are preferred for "flash" fish preparations or as a seasoning for pasta or pizzas.

PEZZETTONI (lit. "large pieces"): a classic canned tomato format, easier to use than *pelati.* Used when the pulp is not blended, but stripped of its skin and seeds, ready to use.

PEZZI (lit. "pieces"): canned tomatoes, diced, raw, or pasteurized at 149°F (65°C).

PICCATA (LOMBARDY) OR FRITTURA PICCATA (LATIUM): 1. A method of cooking very thin escalopes (cutlets) of cushion (*noix*) of veal in a small sauce usually made of butter and lemon juice or Marsala sprinkled with chopped parsley (sometimes with mushrooms or tomatoes). 2. In the Italian national lexicon, a very thin escalope (cutlet).

PINZIMONIO (OR, IN ROMAN DIALECT, CAZZIMPERIO): a preparation based on a custom of serving very fresh raw vegetables (fennel, celery, carrots, radish) to dip in an a mixture of oil, lemon juice, salt, and pepper.

PISTO (CAMPANIA): a mixture of ground spices (cloves, cinnamon, nutmeg, cardamom, pepper, etc.) mainly used in baking.

POLPA (lit. "pulp"): a preparation of slightly acidic tomato, made solely of seeded tomatoes, cut into pieces and enhanced with their juices. Used especially for long cooking times or high temperatures, particularly suitable for soups, stews, daubes (*brasati*), or even raw to season a *bruschetta rustica.*

POMODORO: tomato. In a sauce: see *passata, pelati, pezzettoni, pezzi, polpa, purea, salsa, sugo.*

PUREA DI POMODORO: tomato purée. A preparation of tomato that is denser than *salsa,* obtained through the process of filtration.

Q.B. (QUANTO BASTA) (lit. "just enough," "what is needed"): sufficient, judged by one's discretion. This term is noted in a recipe next to foods whose quantity is not specified but left to the discretion of the cook.

QUINTO QUARTO ("fifth quarter"): the offal, or what is left after the carcass of a slaughtered animal is cut into four quarters: red offal (liver, heart, etc.), white offal (testes), edible tissue (intestines, stomach). Considered a treasure of *cucina povera*.

RAGÙ: meat in sauce. A seasoning for pasta or other *primi piatti* (first courses such as polenta, pasta gratins such as *timballo* or *pasticcio*) made with simmered meat, herbs, with or without tomato sauce. There are two main types of ragù: 1. Made with finely minced meat (*ragù alla bolognese*, sauce Bolognese). 2. Based on whole pieces of meat cooked for a very long time (southern recipes: *ragù napoletano, ragù alla potentina*).

RIPASSARE (IN PADELLA): to sauté in a pan with oil, garlic, and chile for a few minutes over high heat. Mainly refers to vegetables previously boiled.

SALMORIGLIO: a condiment from southern Italy made with lemon juice, olive oil, garlic, salt, and herbs. Common to Sicily and Calabria, it accompanies meats, seafood, or fish, in particular swordfish.

SALSA DI POMODORO (OR SUGO DI): a tomato sauce. Not to be confused with *passata. Salsa di pomodoro* is prepared from a *soffritto* in northern Italy, or made with unpeeled garlic in the south, to which fresh or canned tomatoes are added (*passata, polpa . . .*). It's perfect when used on its own as is or as a starting point for more elaborate sauces.

SALTARE: to jump, to make jump. 1. For meats: to brown or panfry in a pan with fat. 2. For pasta: to place the pasta in a pan with the accompanying sauce and briefly stir it or shake the pan so the juice adheres well to the pasta (see *abbracciare*). 3. For vegetables: sauté vegetables in butter or another fat.

SAOR (from **SAPORE**) (lit. "flavor"): a sweet-and-sour condiment common in Veneto made with onions, raisins, and pickled pine nuts. Applies to fish (the dish *sarde in saor*, which uses sardines), meats, or vegetables (*zucca*: winter squash, eggplants, radicchio).

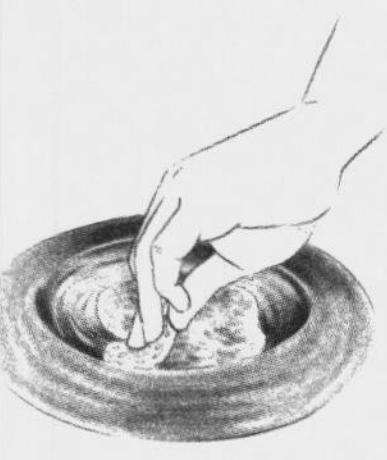

SCARPETTA (FARE LA) (lit. "make a little shoe"): to soak. An expression of southern French origin, which could relate to the comparison of bread as a shoe that "skates" on the sauce, or by a derivative of the word *scarsetta* (poverty).

SCIUÉ SCIUÉ: in a hurry. A Neapolitan adverb applied to quick, easy cooking. For example, spaghetti or a *sugo* (sauce) *sciué sciué* (a tomato sauce briefly cooked in oil).

SFOGLIA (DI PASTA ALL'UOVO): rolled out (as in pasta made from eggs).

SOFFRITTO: minced celery, carrots, and onion (sometimes with aromatic herbs) browned over low heat in olive oil to prepare as the base for a sauce, soup, risotto, stew (*stufato*), etc. Sometimes bacon or pancetta is added.

SPADELLARE: to brown in a pan, to fry. A process of seasoning and thoroughly mixing the pasta with an accompanying sauce directly over high heat.

SPEZZATINO (lit. "small piece"): a stew. The preparation of small, lower-rank pieces of meat (veal, beef, lamb, pork, etc.) simmered for a long time in a liquid (see *umido*) after being browned in butter, onions, herbs, and possibly fresh or canned tomatoes. During cooking, vegetables are often added (peas, potatoes).

SPIEDO (ALLO): on the spit.

STRACCETTI (lit. "rags," "cloths"): meaning strips, very fine ribbons of beef or veal, usually floured and fried in a pan, then served with vegetables or, in Rome, with arugula.

STRACOTTO (lit. "very cooked"): method of cooking in a liquid (see *umido*) that applies to beef, veal, pork, donkey, or horse. A term used primarily in northern and central Italy. Equivalent to *brasato* and *stufato* by its long cooking time. It differs from stufato because theoretically it does not involve marinating the meat but instead larding and browning it before cooking it in wine, or in broth and milk. *Stracotto* can be used as a stuffing for pasta like the *anolini* from Piacenza.

STUFATO (lit. "steamed," "cooked on a wood-burning stove"): a stew. Cooking in a liquid (see *umido*), over low heat, covered (in a steamer) with beef, veal, lamb, or pork. This term used in central and southern Italy, due to slow cooking, and is compared to the terms *brasato* and *stracotto* used in north-central Italy, but in stufato a marinade is used, the meat can be cut into small pieces that do not necessarily brown, and tomato and vegetables (potatoes) can be added.

SUCCO: juice (from fruit).

SUGO: juice, sauce. 1. A smooth sauce prepared with different ingredients to add to pasta or rice: *spaghetti con sugo di pomodoro* (a sauce made from tomato flesh, olive oil, and basil); *riso con sugo di funghi* (rice with mushroom sauce). 2. Juice obtained by browning meat in oil or butter with salt, herbs, and other ingredients (*sugo dello stufato*, meat stew). 3. The liquid obtained from pressing oranges or tomatoes; in this case, *sugo* is more common than the synonym *succo*.

TAGLIATA: beef sirloin about ¼ inch (5 mm) thick, very tender, grilled or panfried and served with the cooking juices (olive oil, salt, black pepper, aromatic herbs).

TIMBALLO (lit. "timpani," "flared mold"): a gratin; a dish made with pasta or rice. The composition is based on pasta or rice seasoned with layers of meat in sauce (*ragù*) or juice. Everything can be cooked inside short crust or pie dough, wrapped in slices of eggplant or ham, and placed in a mold. Similar to *pasticcio, bomba di riso, lasagna napoletana*, or *sartù*.

TRAFILATURA (IN BRONZO) (lit. "bronze-extruded"): a method that allows the desired shape of pasta to be obtained. This method using bronze dies gives the texture of the pasta a rougher, almost artisanal character, which allows its sauce to adhere to it perfectly.

TRIFOLARE/TRIPOLARE: to panfry, to sauté. To brown food in a pan with a little oil, garlic, and parsley. Used mainly to describe cooking mushrooms, eggplants, and kidneys.

TRUSARE (dialect, from Latin *trusare*, "to push vigorously"): to vigorously mix risotto.

UCCELLETTO (ALL') (lit. "like the little bird"): a method of cooking vegetables specific to Tuscany in which they are browned in oil (or bacon fat) and sage, just like game birds, then seasoned with salt, black pepper, and fresh tomatoes.

UMIDO (IN) (lit. "moisture"): a cooking method for meats, fish, and vegetables that involves a long preparation time. The food is cooked, often covered, over low heat in a sufficient amount of liquid (tomato sauce, wine, or broth). This technique may involve a preliminary step where the primary ingredient is browned. See *arrosto morto, brasato, ragù, spezzatino, stracotto, stufato*.

ZIMINO (OR INZIMINO, ZEMIN): a liquid preparation similar to court-bouillon, but distinguished by the use of chard and/or spinach, tomatoes, garlic, chopped parsley, and other herbs. It is used to cook and season fish and mollusks (cuttlefish, salted cod), legumes (chickpeas, beans), and meats, most often offal (*lampredotto, caillette Florentine*) in Tuscany and Liguria.

ZUPPA: soup. A "poor man's" dish, filling and rather rich, very common in Italy: *zuppa* involves cooking food (vegetables, fish) without adding pasta or rice, unlike *minestra* and minestrone, but often with the addition of bread (sliced—according to the etymology of the term—or as croutons) when serving. See *acquacotta*. Belonging to this family are *sauersuppe* from Haut-Adige (bread, tripe, onions), the Florentine *carabaccia* (onions), the Lucca *garmugia* (spring vegetables, meat), *zuppa di pane* to prepare the Tuscan *ribollita, crapiata de Matera* (legumes), the Sardinian *mazzamurru* (bread, tomatoes, pecorino), and *seupe* from Valle d'Aosta.

GOURMAND GEOGRAPHIES

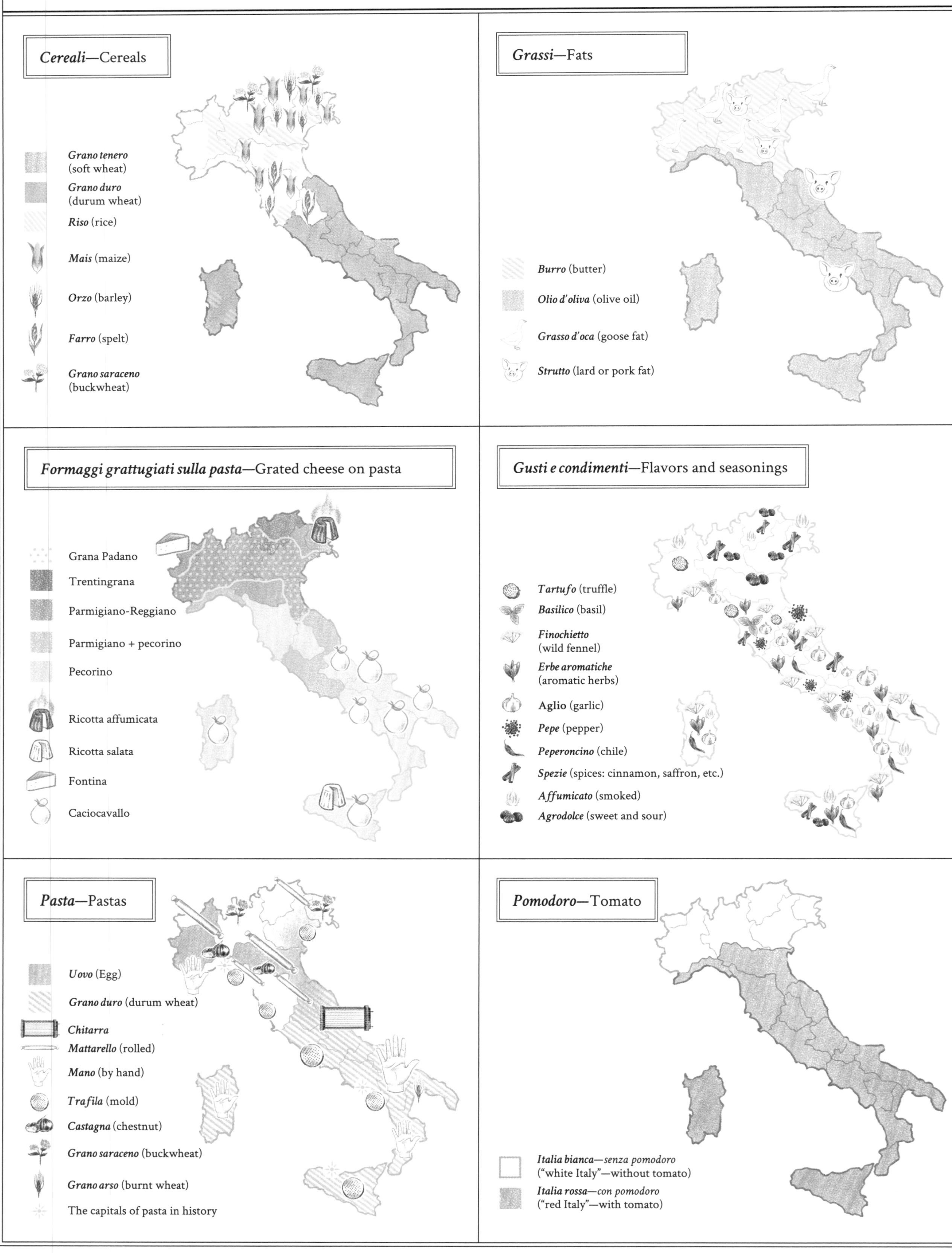

Cereali—Cereals
Grano tenero (soft wheat)
Grano duro (durum wheat)
Riso (rice)
Mais (maize)
Orzo (barley)
Farro (spelt)
Grano saraceno (buckwheat)
Grassi—Fats
Burro (butter)
Olio d'oliva (olive oil)
Grasso d'oca (goose fat)
Strutto (lard or pork fat)
Formaggi grattugiati sulla pasta—Grated cheese on pasta
Grana Padano
Trentingrana
Parmigiano-Reggiano
Parmigiano + pecorino
Pecorino
Ricotta affumicata
Ricotta salata
Fontina
Caciocavallo
Gusti e condimenti—Flavors and seasonings
Tartufo (truffle)
Basilico (basil)
Finochietto (wild fennel)
Erbe aromatiche (aromatic herbs)
Aglio (garlic)
Pepe (pepper)
Peperoncino (chile)
Spezie (spices: cinnamon, saffron, etc.)
Affumicato (smoked)
Agrodolce (sweet and sour)
Pasta—Pastas
Uovo (Egg)
Grano duro (durum wheat)
Chitarra
Mattarello (rolled)
Mano (by hand)
Trafila (mold)
Castagna (chestnut)
Grano saraceno (buckwheat)
Grano arso (burnt wheat)
The capitals of pasta in history
Pomodoro—Tomato
Italia bianca—senza pomodoro ("white Italy"—without tomato)
Italia rossa—con pomodoro ("red Italy"—with tomato)

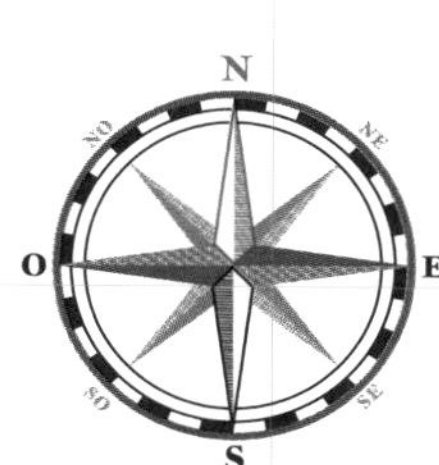

THE WINE MAP *of* ITALY

SCALE
0 — 60 mi (100 km) — 100 mi (200 km) — 190 mi (300 km)

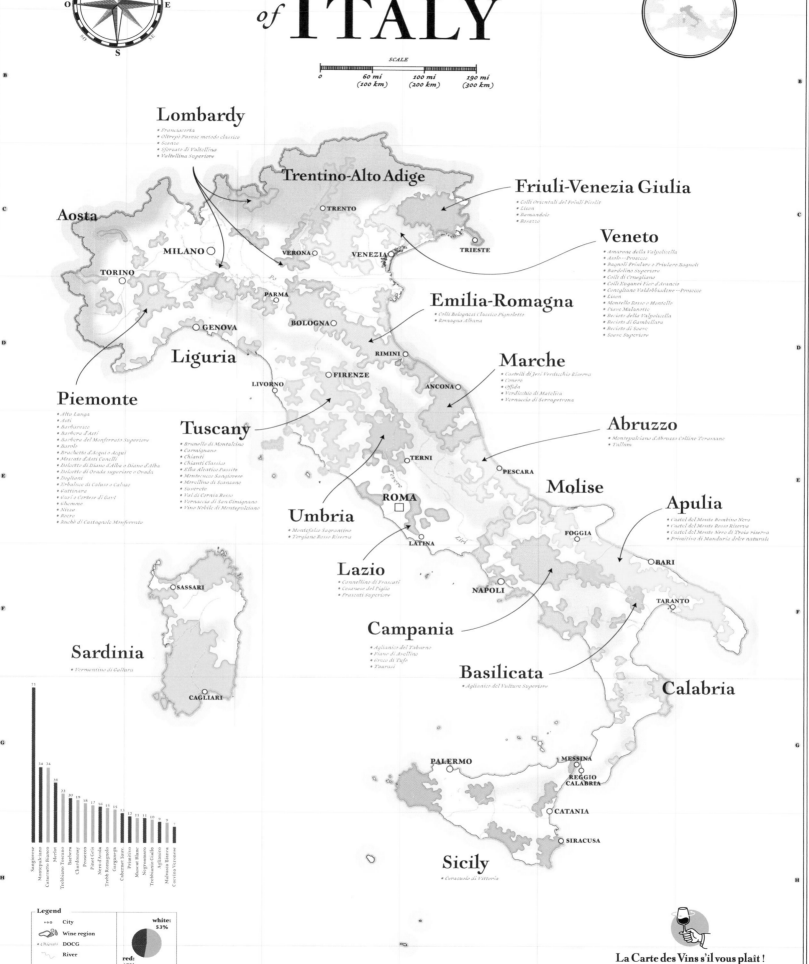

Lombardy
- *Franciacorta*
- *Oltrepò Pavese metodo classico*
- *Scanzo*
- *Sforzato di Valtellina*
- *Valtellina Superiore*

Trentino-Alto Adige

Friuli-Venezia Giulia
- *Colli Orientali del Friuli Picolit*
- *Lison*
- *Ramandolo*
- *Rosazzo*

Aosta

Veneto
- *Amarone della Valpolicella*
- *Asolo --Prosecco*
- *Bagnoli Friularo o Friularo Bagnoli*
- *Bardolino Superiore*
- *Colli di Conegliano*
- *Colli Euganei Fior d'Arancio*
- *Conegliano Valdobbiadene --Prosecco*
- *Lison*
- *Montello Rosso o Montello*
- *Piave Malanotte*
- *Recioto della Valpolicella*
- *Recioto di Gambellara*
- *Recioto di Soave*
- *Soave Superiore*

Emilia-Romagna
- *Colli Bolognesi Classico Pignoletto*
- *Romagna Albana*

Liguria

Marche
- *Castelli di Jesi Verdicchio Riserva*
- *Conero*
- *Offida*
- *Verdicchio di Matelica*
- *Vernaccia di Serrapetrona*

Piemonte
- *Alto Langa*
- *Asti*
- *Barbaresco*
- *Barbera d'Asti*
- *Barbera del Monferrato Superiore*
- *Barolo*
- *Brachetto d'Acqui o Acqui*
- *Moscato d'Asti Canelli*
- *Dolcetto di Diano d'Alba o Diano d'Alba*
- *Dolcetto di Ovada superiore o Ovada*
- *Dogliani*
- *Erbaluce di Caluso o Caluso*
- *Gattinara*
- *Gavi o Cortese di Gavi*
- *Ghemme*
- *Nizza*
- *Roero*
- *Ruchè di Castagnole Monferrato*

Tuscany
- *Brunello di Montalcino*
- *Carmignano*
- *Chianti*
- *Chianti Classico*
- *Elba Aleatico Passito*
- *Montecucco Sangiovese*
- *Morellino di Scansano*
- *Suvereto*
- *Val di Cornia Rosso*
- *Vernaccia di San Gimignano*
- *Vino Nobile di Montepulciano*

Abruzzo
- *Montepulciano d'Abruzzo Colline Teramane*
- *Tullum*

Molise

Umbria
- *Montefalco Sagrantino*
- *Torgiano Rosso Riserva*

Apulia
- *Castel del Monte Bombino Nero*
- *Castel del Monte Rosso Riserva*
- *Castel del Monte Nero di Troia riserva*
- *Primitivo di Manduria dolce naturale*

Lazio
- *Cannellino di Frascati*
- *Cesanese del Piglio*
- *Frascati Superiore*

Campania
- *Aglianico del Taburno*
- *Fiano di Avellino*
- *Greco di Tufo*
- *Taurasi*

Sardinia
- *Vermentino di Gallura*

Basilicata
- *Aglianico del Vulture Superiore*

Calabria

Sicily
- *Cerasuolo di Vittoria*

TRENTO
MILANO
VERONA
VENEZIA
TRIESTE
TORINO
Po
PARMA
GENOVA
BOLOGNA
RIMINI
FIRENZE
LIVORNO
ANCONA
TERNI
Tevere
PESCARA
ROMA
LATINA
Liri
FOGGIA
BARI
SASSARI
NAPOLI
TARANTO
CAGLIARI
PALERMO
MESSINA
REGGIO CALABRIA
CATANIA
SIRACUSA

Sangiovese	Montepulciano	Catarratto Bianco	Merlot	Trebbiano Toscano	Barbera	Chardonnay	Prosecco	Pinot Gris	Nero d'Avola	Trebb Romagnolo	Garganega	Cabernet Sauv.	Primitivo	Muscat Blanc	Negroamaro	Trebbianio Giallo	Aglianico	Malvasia Bianca	Corvina Veronese
71	34	34	28	22	20	19	18	17	16	15	15	13	12	11	11	10	9	9	7

Legend
- City
- Wine region
- *• Chianti* DOCG
- River

white: 53%
red: 47%

La Carte des Vins s'il vous plait !
www.lacartedesvins-svp.com

SEASON

PRIMAVERA/ESTATE (SPRING/SUMMER)

CATEGORY

PRIMO PIATTO (FIRST COURSE)

LEVEL

FACILE (EASY)

GENOESE PESTO

In this famous sauce originating in Genoa in Liguria, the basil expresses itself with power and delicacy. Here are the secrets . . .

ALESSANDRA PIERINI

A LITTLE HISTORY

The first codification of pesto can be attributed to Giovanni Battista Ratto in *La cuciniera genovese*, published in 1863. Its most illustrious ancestor is certainly the Roman *moretum*, a kind of cheese enriched with aromatic herbs and ground in a mortar with oil, vinegar, walnuts, or pine nuts—so many of the ingredients in which the Italian Riviera overflows. Pesto is also a descendant of *agliata*, a medieval specialty made from crushed garlic, enlivened with fish in Sardinia, almonds and ricotta in Sicily, and basil in Liguria.
In the Genoese dialect, pesto is pronounced *péstu* (past participle of the Genoese verb *pestâ*, "to pound"), from which *pistou* in Provence (garlic, basil, olive oil) originates.

THE RECIPE

In Genoa and Liguria, each family has its version. You will never find two identical pestos! But the basic ingredients are always included.

MAKES 14 OUNCES (400 G) OF PASTA

4 bunches (2⅛ to 2½ oz/60 to 70 g leaves) Genoese DOP basil

1 clove Vessalico garlic

1 ounce (30 g) pine nuts

⅔ teaspoon (3 g) coarse sea salt

1½ to 2⅛ ounces (45 to 60 g) grated 24-month-old Parmesan cheese

¾ to 1½ ounces (20 to 40 g) Pecorino Fiore Sardo DOP cheese

1⅔ to 2½ cups (400 to 600 mL) Riviera Ligure DOP olive oil

Wash the basil leaves in cold water and let them dry on a clean kitchen towel without crumpling them.

In a mortar, crush the garlic with the pine nuts.

Once these two ingredients have been reduced to a creamy consistency, add a few grains of salt and the basil leaves, without packing them, to completely fill the mortar.

Crush the basil against the sides of the mortar using a slight twisting motion of the pestle.

When the basil releases its clear green liquid, add the cheeses.

Drizzle in the olive oil, while stirring, to make the paste creamier. This step must be completed as quickly as possible to avoid oxidation of the basil.

ADVICE FROM A GENOESE

For a creamier sauce, thin it just before serving with a little pasta cooking water, which is rich in starch.

Never heat pesto! It is a sauce that is prepared and used strictly when cold.

Pounded or blended?

Purists swear by a mortar, as long as it's made of smooth white Carrara marble, cool enough to preserve the color of the chlorophyll in the basil leaves. It's even more ideal if it is equipped with the four characteristic "ears," which make it easy to grip and rotate on the work surface. It is a perfect match along with a pestle made of soft fruitwood (from a pear tree, for example), which avoids overheating the ingredients. But a pesto made in a blender can be very good, too! To avoid stressing the leaves, cool the glass blender jar well before using it and blend the pesto in short bursts.

THE MORTAR-MADE PESTO WORLD CHAMPIONSHIP

This was a brilliant idea conceived by the Palatifini Association, chaired by Roberto Panizza, the king of pesto. Every two years since 2007, one hundred competitors challenge each other in the Palazzo Ducale in Genoa to prepare the best pesto in the world made using a mortar!

WHICH PASTAS?

In Genova, *trofie, trenette, croxetti,* gnocchi, and lasagna are the pastas of choice. Elsewhere, it's spaghetti or linguine . . . and *basta!*

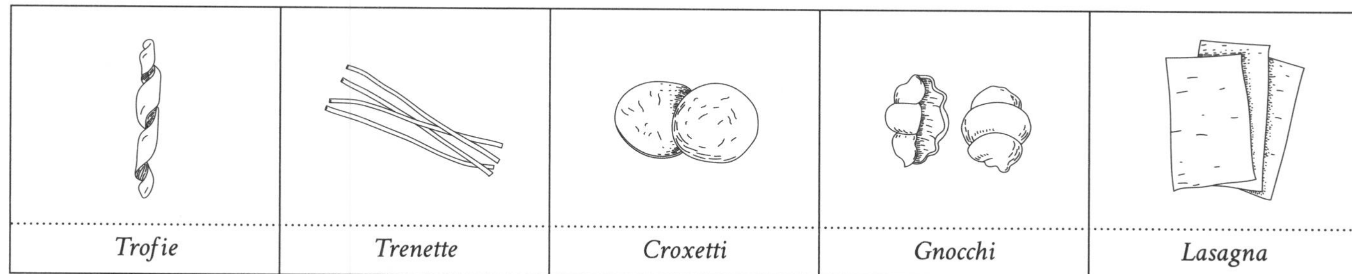

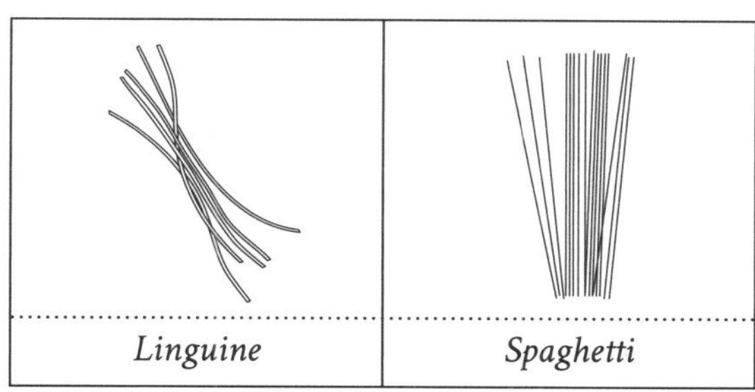

BASIC INGREDIENTS

THE CHEESES

Some only use Parmesan, but tradition recommends a mixture of two-thirds **PARMIGIANO-REGGIANO DOP** aged twenty-four months to one-third **PECORINO FIORE SARDO DOP** (an aged cheese round made from Sardinian sheep's milk) for more character.

THE BASIL

Since 2005, the **GENOESE DOP** benefits from a **PDO** (Protected Designation of Origin). It is grown mainly in the west of the city of Genoa and guarantees the pesto maintains its characteristic flavor. For a much more intense aromatic version, look for stems that do not exceed 4 to 4¾ inches (10 to 12 cm) in length and that have small leaves. This basil is distinguished by its absence of minty scent, and it is always sold with the roots attached, still inside a clump of soil, a sign of extreme freshness.

THE SALT

In the traditional mortar preparation, coarse salt is very important because it absorbs the essential oils produced by the crushed basil leaves and prevents them from darkening. It also helps crush the leaves more easily.

THE PINE NUTS

The Italian varietal **PINUS PINEA** has a very subtle taste, which contrasts nicely with that of garlic. Avoid non-European pine nuts, which have a different flavor.

THE OLIVE OIL

The olive oil **RIVIERA LIGURE DOP**, with its delicate and fresh fruitiness, goes well with the other ingredients without dominating them.

THE GARLIC

VESSALICO garlic offers an intense fragrance and a delicate taste that does not dominate the other ingredients, while still being very digestible.

SKIP TO
GARLIC, P. 192;
HIS MAJESTY THE BASIL, P. 121;
OLIVE OIL, P. 140.

— NAPLES — THE TOP 10 PIZZERIAS

For generations, families of *pizzaioli* have tied their names to the art of hand-tossed dough. Let's meet the Neapolitan dynasties of the wood-fired oven.

ALBA PEZONE

In Campania, people don't say ***"Andiamo a mangiare una pizza?"*** ("Are we going to eat a pizza?"), but instead ***"Andiamo da Vincenzo?"*** ("Are we going to Vincenzo?").

DA ATTILIO · Attilio Bachetti

VIA PIGNASECCA, 17, NAPOLI

Opened in 1938 by his grandfather, whose name, Attilio, the business bears. This pizzeria, located in one of the most popular areas of Naples, La Pignasecca, is a safe bet.

THE PIZZA: authentic. Long fermentation of the dough, which is light and aromatic. Local toppings, cooked using *pampuglie* (wood chips).

TO TRY: *Appennini*. Star-shaped, stuffed with ricotta, filled in the center with *fior di latte*, panfried zucchini or porcini mushrooms, and pancetta.

VINCENZO CAPUANO

PIAZZA VITTORIA, 8, NAPOLI

Vincenzo, who still works with his grandfather, was one of the pioneers of modern pizza.

THE PIZZA: fine dough, tender and supple, exuberant crust, classic or more gourmet fillings.

TO TRY: Parmigiana, with an eggplant mille-feuille.

LA NOTIZIA · Enzo Coccia

VIA MICHELANGELO DA CARAVAGGIO, 53/55 AND 94/A, NAPOLI

Enzo revived pizza *bianca* (without tomato) and instituted gourmet pizza in the 1990s.

THE PIZZA: selected toppings (PDO, PGI, products protected by Slow Food, sourced olive oils).

TO TRY: *Capodimonte*—San Marzano tomato, buffalo sausage from Paestum, fior di latte from Agerola, pecorino, black pepper.

DA MICHELE · Fabrizio Condurro

VIA CESARE SERSALE, 1/3, NAPOLI

Since 1870, five generations of this family of *maestri pizzaioli* have succeeded each other running this temple of Neapolitan pizza.

THE PIZZA: the menu only offers two: marinara and Margherita.

TO TRY: both!

I MASANIELLI

Francesco Martucci

VIALE GIULIO DOUHET, 11, CASERTA

Named after Masaniello, a seventeenth-century Neapolitan revolutionary, because Francesco is a rebel at heart.

THE PIZZA: the ingredients par excellence are sourced from a short distance from the pizzeria. Cooking sometimes combines three techniques for the same pizza: steaming, frying, and wood-fired oven.

TO TRY: *Futuro di marinara*—cream of roasted Datterino tomato, Ischia oregano, Salina capers, wild garlic pesto, Trapani anchovies.

CONCETTINA AI TRE SANTI

Ciro Oliva

VIA ARENA ALLA SANITÀ, 7 BIS, NAPOLI

This representative of the new wave in pizza has existed since 1951 in the very diverse district of Rione Sanità. He is the creator of pizza *sospesa* ("prepaid" pizza, purchased for those who cannot afford it).

THE PIZZA: surprising "zero-salt" pizza dough, seasoned with herbs and spices; bizarre and sometimes eccentric toppings.

TO TRY: 'O Raù—calzone stuffed with buffalo ricotta, seven-hour meat stew, forty-eight-month-old Parmigiano, basil.

PEPE IN GRANI · Franco Pepe

VICOLO S. GIOVANNI BATTISTA, 3, CAIAZZO

Twenty-five miles (40 km) from Naples, housed in a former eighteenth-century palace, this pizzeria has become a destination thanks to the visionary work of Franco.

THE PIZZA: balanced toppings, not excessive, from a network of local producers. À la carte—up to six variations of the Margherita!

TO TRY: Margherita *sbagliata* ("failed" Margherita—that is to say, with inverted toppings: mozzarella and olive oil are added, then tomatoes and basil cream are added once the pie is out of the oven).

PIZZERIA TRATTORIA PRIGIOBBO

Fratelli Prigiobbo

VIA PORTACARRESE A MONTECALVARIO, 96, NAPOLI

A discreet neighborhood pizzeria-trattoria, opened in the 1940s and operated by the same family ever since. An invaluable establishment whose legacy can pass down only through the family's care.

THE PIZZA: always prepared with the same consistent standards by brothers Ciro and Gennaro.

TO TRY: Margherita *all'ombra*, with just a hint of tomato.

ANTICA FRIGGITORIA LA MASARDONA

VIA GIULIO CESARE CAPACCIO 27, NAPOLI

Mecca of the Neapolitan pizza *fritta*, located in the train station district since 1945. Starting at 10 a.m., Enzo Piccirillo (grandson of Masardona) treats hungry gourmets. Cristiano, his son, is located in Rome. A pilgrimage to this establishment is essential . . .

THE PIZZA: golden, crisp, light, puffed, not greasy, topped well, very tasty.

TO TRY: *Senza Pomodoro* ("white," without tomato)—sheep's-milk ricotta, fresh smoked provola, *ciccolil* (Italian pork cracklings), black pepper, basil.

PIZZERIA TOTÒ E GINO SORBILLO

Gino Sorbillo

VIA DEI TRIBUNALI, 32, NAPOLI

Its story begins in 1935 with Gino's grandparents, who had twenty-one children—all pizzaioli! A veritable celebrity of the Neapolitan landscape.

THE PIZZA: huge but light, very thin and elastic dough, with toppings protected by Slow Food.

TO TRY: the classic Margherita.

SKIP TO
PIZZE NAPOLETANE, P. 54;
HOMEMADE PIZZA, P. 52.

SEASON

TUTTO L'ANNO (YEAR-ROUND)

CATEGORY

PRIMO PIATTO/ PIATTO UNICO (FIRST OR SINGLE COURSE)

LEVEL

FACILE (EASY)

Present everywhere in Italy and a dish made by all families, minestrone is as universal as it is comforting.

ILARIA BRUNETTI

WHAT AM I?

Minestrone is a thick soup made from vegetables, legumes, and starches (pasta, rice, and/or other cereals). Its ingredients are dictated by the season and the vegetables available. It can be enhanced with a touch of meat (bacon, pancetta, etc.). It also varies in how it's cooked: the vegetables can be boiled in water or browned first with a base of *soffritto* (minced celery, carrots, and onions).

THROUGHOUT THE SEASONS: SOME ESSENTIALS

IN WINTER
Savoy cabbage, black cabbage, broccoli, fennel, leeks.

IN SPRING
Green peas, beans.

IN SUMMER
Zucchini, thin green beans (haricots verts), eggplant, tomatoes, borlotti beans.

IN AUTUMN
Squash, mushrooms.

YEAR-ROUND
Onions, carrots, celery, potatoes, chard, chicory.

REGIONAL VARIATIONS

ALLA MILANESE: in Lombardy rice and, when in season, savoy cabbage are always included; it is enriched with pancetta and/or pork rind, added to a soffritto or just before serving. It is often sprinkled with Grana Padano.

ALLA GENOVESE: rich in vegetables, ranging from eggplants to haricots verts, and seasoned with Genoese pesto; it is served hot in winter, warm or cold in summer. It's a close cousin of the Provençal *soupe au pistou*.

TOSCANO: rich in vegetables and made with spelt or pasta. In Tuscany, minestrone often includes local *pancetta tesa* or *lardo di Colonnata*.

PIEMONTESE: very thick, cooked with fresh egg-based pasta. You can enrich it using a ham bone or poultry carcass, added during cooking.

In everyday language, *minestrone* means a "confused collection," a "mess."

THE RECIPE

Ilaria Conti, a Ligurian chef based in Paris, takes this recipe from her grandmother Iole.

SERVES 4

- 1 bunch chard
- 3 small zucchini
- 3½ ounces (100 g) thin green beans (haricots verts)
- 1 eggplant
- 3½ ounces (100 g) spinach
- 3½ ounces (100 g) peas
- 2 stalks celery
- 1¾ ounces (50 g) squash
- 3 small potatoes
- 4 or 5 leaves cabbage or black cabbage from Tuscany
- 2 small carrots
- 1 white onion
- 5¼ ounces (150 g) fresh shelled borlotti beans (or coco white beans from Paimpol)
- Extra-virgin olive oil
- 5¼ ounces (150 g) *ditalini* pasta (or another small size, such as orzo . . .)
- 2⅛ ounces (60 g) Genoese pesto
- 2⅛ ounces (60 g) Parmesan cheese

Small dice all the vegetables and place them, along with the shelled beans, in a saucepan with 8½ cups (2 L) salted boiling water and 1 tablespoon olive oil. Cook for 30 to 40 minutes. Take a third of the soup, blend it, and transfer it back to the saucepan. Bring back to a boil and cook the pasta. Top each serving with a drizzle of oil, 1 tablespoon of the pesto, and some grated Parmesan.

Il Tocco Della Chef (Chef's Tip)

To preserve the color and texture of her minestrone, Ilaria cooks the vegetables once the water has started boiling, while her grandmother starts cooking them in cold water (the traditional approach). For added flavor, Ilaria slices all the vegetables the night before and leaves them in the pot with the basil, covering them with water. The next day, she drains them, saves the soaking water, and boils it to cook the vegetables.

FROM THE RIGHT OR LEFT?

In his famous song "Destra-Sinistra" (1994), the great singer-songwriter Giorgio Gaber, singing in his legendary irony, illustrated through examples the ideological difference between left and right: the bathtub is on the right, the shower is on the left; the jeans are on the left, but with a jacket are on the right. And of course his examples had to include food: a "pretty *minestrina*" (a consommé including small pastas) is on the right, the minestrone is "always on the left." What's more, the *culatello* (a charcuterie from Parma) is on the right, the mortadella is on the left.

SKIP TO
THE SOUPS OF ITALY, P. 146; GENOESE PESTO, P. 20; LEGUMES, P. 150.

THE MOKA POT

La moka is the Italian coffeemaker that allows you to prepare your espresso at home on the stovetop. Here is a brief history of an iconic *macchinetta* and its artistic variations.

MARIELLE GAUDRY

MOKA EXPRESS

Why the word *moka*? This term comes from a varietal of high-quality coffee originating in Arabia and, since the end of the eighteenth century, has become a generic term to mean "coffee." The moka pot is the work of Alfonso Bialetti, an engineer who got his start in aluminum in France before returning to his native Piedmont in 1919, where he began working with what he found to be a promising material in his home workshop.

Inspired by the washing machine design of the times, in which water was pressurized by boiling, he created the Moka Express in 1933, an art deco–style coffeemaker made from an alloy of aluminum and stainless steel. This little machine grew out of his small workshop to a thriving business eventually listed on the stock exchange (Bialetti Industrie). The company started offering a range of other machines in the 2000s (including induction pots and frothers).

LA MOKA CONSISTS OF 3 PARTS

And the *caffettiera* Napoletana?

Despite its name meaning "Neapolitan coffeemaker," it is an older French invention by Morize, a Parisian tinsmith, dating from 1819.

It didn't take long for the use of this coffee pot to spread throughout Italy, and it was used for decades for home coffee brewing.

The *cuccumella*, as the Neapolitans call it (the diminutive of the word *cuccuma*, a Latin term for a copper or terra-cotta container), falls into the category of drip coffeemakers.

Unlike the moka pot, which requires no handling until the coffee is poured into the cup, the *cuccumella* is first placed over heat, then flipped over, off the heat, so that the water pours by gravity through the coffee grounds.

LA MOKA GALLERY

A TOUR OF SOME ICONIC DESIGNS OF *LA MOKA*.

BIALETTI

Moka Express
DESIGNER: Alfonso Bialetti
INVENTED: 1933

LAVAZZA

Carmencita
DESIGNER: Marco Zanuso
INVENTED: 1979

AN INVALUABLE ACCESSORY

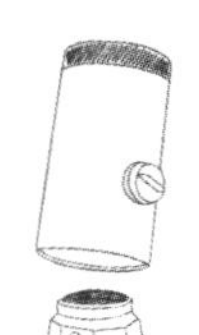

Le Dosacaffè
This coffee-making accessory delivers the perfect dose of coffee through the simple turn of a knob. It was invented for those who are a bit clumsy after they wake up and need a little assistance to measure out their coffee grounds!

ALESSI

9090
DESIGNER: Richard Sapper
INVENTED: 1979

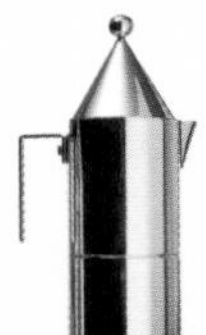

La Cocina
DESIGNER: Aldo Rossi
INVENTED: 1980

La Cupola
DESIGNER: Aldo Rossi
INVENTED: 1988

Pulcina
DESIGNER: Michele De Lucchi
INVENTED: 2015

Ossidiana
DESIGNER: Mario Trimarchi
INVENTED: 2016

Moka
DESIGNER: David Chipperfield
INVENTED: 2019

A FEW RULES TO RESPECT

→ Use clean, cold mineral water.

→ Do not tamp down the coffee grounds in the filter.

→ Maintain low heat under the coffeemaker to allow a slow extraction, and never boil the coffee.

→ Stir the coffee well with a spoon in the upper chamber before serving it.

→ Do not clean the machine with dish soap. Simply rinse it with water, as the tannins in the coffee will season the inside of the coffeemaker over time and ensure the unique taste of your homemade java.

SKIP TO
EQUIPMENT, P. 6; TIRAMISU, P. 188.

SEASON

TUTTO L'ANNO (YEAR-ROUND)

CATEGORY

SEGUNDO PIATTO (MAIN COURSE)

LEVEL

FACILE (EASY)

POLPETTE

MEATBALLS

Whether small and firm for eating elegantly with the fingers, or plump with a moist center and submerged in tomato sauce, *polpette* are a treasure of at-home cooking.

ILARIA BRUNETTI

"This is a dish that everyone knows how to make, beginning with the jackass, which was perhaps the first to provide the model for the meatball for the human race."

—*La scienza in cucina e l'arte di mangiar bene* (*Science in the Kitchen and the Art of Eating Well*, 1891), Pellegrino Artusi

THE METAMORPHOSIS OF *POLPETTE*

The word most likely comes from *polpa*, meaning "flesh," due to the boneless meat used in its preparation.

In Italy, you can find meatballs used in ancient cooking (*globi*, made from cheese and honey, and *offulae*, made from meat or grains). The first recipe appeared in 1400 CE in the *Libro de arte coquinaria* by Maestro Martino, a Renaissance cook, but it was actually veal cutlets wrapped in bacon and cooked on a spit. The filling has become ennobled over time, with the addition of spices, raisins, and vinegar. In 1648, in the treatise *L'economia del cittadino in villa* (*The Economy of the Citizen in the Country*) by the Bolognese agronomist and gastronome Vincenzo Tanara, we find the first ground-meat *polpette*, filled with ricotta, Parmesan, garlic, raisins, eggs, bread soaked in broth, spices, and currants.

THE SOUL OF THE POLPETTA

THE BASE: ground meat or, sometimes, leftovers from a stew pot, bread soaked in milk, eggs, and Parmesan.

THE METHOD: fried in oil, panfried, or in a sauce.

Variations

IN NAPLES, raw beef is mixed with pork, pine nuts, and raisins. After frying, they are cooked in tomato sauce.

THE LIGURIANS add mushrooms to it.

IN SICILY, they opt for onions, pecorino, and mint.

IN TUSCANY, boiled veal and potatoes are mixed in.

IN BOLOGNA, it's all pork, with ground pork loin, ham, and mortadella.

IN VENICE, mortadella is combined with beef for dumplings served as *cicchetti*.

IN MOLISE, lamb is king.

IN APULIA, it can be found made with a base of horse meat.

IN MILAN, *mondeghili* are ground beef–stew meatballs, breaded as in the Milanese style.

Il Polpettone

The *polpettone* is a large cylindrical meatball about 9¾ inches (25 cm) long. It's made essentially from the same ingredients as that of its little round cousins with, preferably, a mixture of ground meats (pork, beef, and/or veal) and often enriched with a runny center of mozzarella or whole hard-boiled egg, or even wrapped in charcuterie. It can be cooked in a pan or in the oven.

THE RECIPE

It's my mother Irene's recipe, simple and foolproof, resulting in irresistible meatballs.

SERVES 4 TO 6

- 3½ cups (150 g) fresh bread crumbs
- Scant ½ cup (100 mL) milk
- 1⅓ pounds (600 g) ground beef
- 3½ ounces (100 g) grated Parmigiano-Reggiano cheese
- 2 small eggs
- A small bunch fresh parsley, chopped
- Salt and freshly ground black pepper
- Flour, for rolling
- Oil, for frying

Soak the bread crumbs in the milk to soften them; drain, then add the beef, Parmesan, eggs, and parsley and season with salt and pepper. Mix by hand or with a fork.

Using your hands, form balls the size of Ping-Pong balls and roll them in flour to coat. Fry them in hot oil, in either a deep fryer or in a high-sided pan, until browned, turning them frequently for even cooking. Remove and let drain briefly on a paper towel–lined plate, then transfer to a clean plate and serve.

SOME SUGGESTIONS . . .

→ You can cook the polpette in a skillet in olive oil for several minutes over high heat, adding a drizzle of white wine. Cover the pan to finish cooking them over medium heat.

→ They can be made very small to serve as an aperitif along with a homemade mayonnaise.

→ To make them as they do in Naples, add a handful of raisins and pine nuts to the filling. In a saucepan, brown a small chopped onion and a clove of garlic in olive oil, add 4 cups (1 L) tomato sauce, season with salt, bring to a boil, and add the previously fried polpette. Simmer for 30 minutes over low heat.

Sulla Punta Della Lingua (On the Tip of the Tongue)

Polpetta avvelenata ("poisoned meatball"): a term in political jargon, meaning an insult hidden behind a compliment.

Fare/ridurre qualcuno in polpette ("reduce someone to meatballs"): crushing someone, usually with a joke.

Polpettone: a dud movie or book.

Polpetta con elastico ("meatball with a rubber band," in Calabria): a promise made by politicians before elections . . . and not kept.

Un fari purpetti ("do not make meatballs," in Sicily): a suggestion to change your attitude to avoid a retaliation.

SKIP TO

PELLEGRINO ARTUSI, P. 32; CICCHETTI VENEZIANI, P. 228.

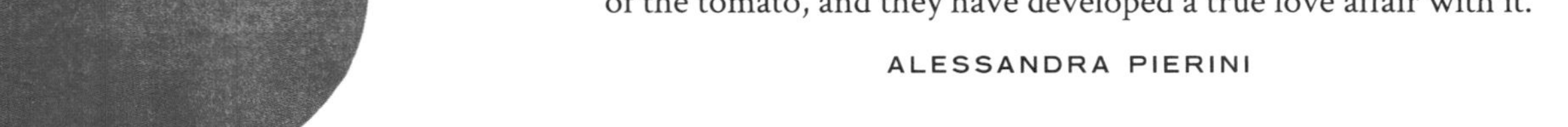

A LOVE FOR TOMATOES

The Italians were the first in the world to discover the gastronomic potential of the tomato, and they have developed a true love affair with it.

ALESSANDRA PIERINI

The long saga of the tomato

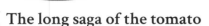

SEVENTH CENTURY The tomato (*Solanum lycopersicum*), originally a wild edible plant, is transported by the Aztecs to Mexico where it is domesticated.

1519 The tomato (from the Incan *tomalt*, meaning "pulpy fruit with seeds") is introduced in Europe by the Spaniards. The kingdom of Sardinia (ruler of Spain) may be one of the first lands to have known it and exported it to Liguria.

SIXTEENTH–SEVENTEENTH CENTURIES
Tomatoes are considered poisonous and used mainly as an ornamental plant.

1544 The Latin term *mala aurea*, in Italian *pomo d'oro* (golden apple), appears in a treatise by the botanist physician Andrea Mattioli to define the fruits—at the time yellow—of the tomato. He notices that in some parts of Italy, peasants have been frying them in oil.

OCTOBER 31, 1548
Arrival of the tomato in Tuscany when Cosimo de' Medici receives a basket of these fruits on his property near Pisa, a gift from his wife, Eleanor of Toledo.

1554 Arrival of the red tomato in Italy, the result of different genetic selections. For its alleged aphrodisiac virtues, the French call it the *pomme d'amour* (apple of love). In Sicilian dialect, it is still called *puma d'amuri*.

1570 The tomato officially becomes part of the Solanaceae family of flowering plants.

1694 Chef Antonio Latini publishes two first tomato-based recipes in Naples in his book *Scalco alla moderna*, including *salsa di pomodoro alla spagnola* (Spanish tomato sauce). Already consumed by the rural classes in the south, the fruit then conquers the bourgeoisie class.

1705 The Jesuit Francesco Gaudenzio, in *Il pan unto toscano* (*Tuscan Oil Bread*), celebrates the happy marriage of tomato and olive oil.

1770 Ferdinand of Bourbon sows the first seeds of the San Marzano variety between Naples and Salerno, given to him by the viceroy of Spain, Manuel de Amat.

1790 The Roman cook Francesco Leonardi writes the recipe for *all'amatriciana*, the red version of traditional white *pasta alla gricia*, served with tomatoes.

1837 The Genoese violinist Niccolò Paganini, passionate about cooking, composes the recipe for ravioli with tomato sauce.

1839 The first written recipe for tomato pasta, *vermicelli ca'pummarola*, appears in Ippolito Cavalcanti's Neapolitan-dialect cookbook.

1857 Carlo Dalbono presents ragù for the first time in his work *Usi e costumi di Napoli* (*Traditions and Customs of Naples*), used mainly as a tomato sauce with simmered meat that covers the cheese on pasta, making a red version of *cacio e pepe* (cheese and pepper).

1860 With the Expedition of the Thousand campaign under the leadership of Garibaldi, and the unification of the country, the tomato arrives in all regions of northern Italy.

1875 The Piedmontese Francesco Cirio opens the first factory for canned peeled tomatoes in Campania.

1888 Brandino Vignali starts the production of tomato extract in Parma, by drying concentrated tomato juice in the sun.

1889 Official birth of the legendary Margherita pizza with tomato, mozzarella, and basil—the three great symbols of Italianism.

1891 Pellegrino Artusi makes a distinction between *sugo* and *salsa di pomodoro* and provides the recipes.

1912 In the Parma region, there are more than sixty manufacturers of canned tomatoes.

1951 Ugo Mutti produces the first tomato paste sold in tubes.

SPECIALTIES THAT TURNED RED

BEFORE THE ARRIVAL OF THE TOMATO	AFTER THE ARRIVAL OF THE TOMATO
Pizza mastunicola, Campania. Pork fat, cheese, black pepper, basil.	***Pizza marinara.*** Tomato, garlic, oregano, olive oil, and all pizza *rosse* (red).
Pan cotto (baked bread), Tuscany. A soup of dry bread in a broth of spices and vegetables.	***Pappa al pomodoro.*** Bread, tomato, garlic, basil, and olive oil.
Princisgrass, Marche. Lasagna made with ham, truffles, butter, cream, and Parmesan.	***Vincisgrassi.*** Lasagna made with beef, pork fat, chicken offal, tomato, béchamel, Parmesan.
Cipollata, Emilia-Romagna, Tuscany. Stewed pork, sausage, pancetta, and lots of onions.	***Friggione.*** Sauce made with onions and tomatoes simmered in lard. To accompany meat, sausage, cotechino, and polenta.
Sburrita, Tuscany. Cod soup with garlic, olive oil, wine, aromatic herbs, and chile. Served with toast rubbed with garlic.	***Cacciucco.*** Soup of fish, shellfish, and mollusks cooked in wine, tomato, and pepper, served with toast rubbed with garlic. Also available in a version without tomato.
Gricia, Lazio. Seasoning of Pecorino-Romano, *guanciale* (cured pork cheek), and pepper for rigatoni or spaghetti.	***Amatriciana.*** Tomato, *guanciale* (cured pork cheek), Pecorino-Romano, and black pepper served on spaghetti.
Aglio, olio, peperoncino, Campania, Lazio. Garlic, oil, and chile to season spaghetti.	***Arrabbiata.*** Garlic, oil, chile, and tomato served on penne pasta.
Crostino, Tuscany. A slice of toasted bread, salted, then rubbed with garlic and olive oil.	***Bruschetta.*** Slice of toasted bread, salted, rubbed with garlic, tomato, and olive oil.
Pan lavato, Toscane. Salad of bread, onions, cucumbers.	***Panzanella.*** Salad of bread, onions, tomato, and basil.

DID YOU SAY TOMATO?

ABRUZZO: *pammador, pummadore, tumat.*

APULIA: *pemedore, pummitoru.*

BASILICATA: *pummidore.*

CALABRIA: *pimmadoru, pumadora-piru, pumadora, pumadoreja, pumadoru, pumaroru, pummadoru.*

CAMPANIA: *prommarola, pummarola.*

EMILIA-ROMAGNA: *pandor* (Modena), *pomdor, pomdor, tomaca, tumaca.*

FRIULI-VENEZIA GIULIA: *tomat.*

LAZIO: *pemmadore, pummidora, pummidoro.*

LIGURIA: *pumata* (Ventimiglia), *tomata, tumata.*

LOMBARDY: *pomates, pomatis, pumañs, pumudamuri, tumat, tumates* (Como), *tumatis.*

MARCHE: *pundor.*

PIEDMONT: *tomatisa, tumati, tumatica.*

SARDINIA: *tomata, tramata, tremata, tumata, tammata.*

SICILY: *puma d'amuri.*

UMBRIA: *pummidori.*

SKIP TO
PIZZA AS POP ICON, P. 246;
PIZZA FRITTA, P. 218.

HOMEMADE TOMATO SAUCE

Simple but excellent-quality ingredients are the universal ingredients to an everyday Italian *salsa*.

ALESSANDRA PIERINI

Salsa or *sugo di pomodoro*?

There is a lot of confusion between these two terms, and they are often used interchangeably.

Salsa (sauce) from Latin ***salsus*** (salty), and ***sugo*** (sauce) from the Latin ***sucus*** (juice)

are terms that indicate a tomato-based condiment, not to be confused with *passata* (the basic purée, which can be used as a base for salsa or sugo).

Pellegrino Artusi explains the difference:

→ *Salsa* corresponds to cooking tomato preserves (*passata*) with other ingredients, as a tradition within families and in peak season for later use in the kitchen.

→ *Sugo* corresponds to a cooked sauce. It consists of sautéing onion, garlic, and celery (*soffritto*) in olive oil with tomatoes (fresh or canned) cut into pieces with a few leaves of parsley and basil.

At the end of cooking, everything is strained to smooth it out. It is used in stews, on pasta, or in risotto, as is or as a starting point for the creation of more elaborate sauces (*sugo di pomodoro con pesce, sugo di pomodoro con funghi,* for example).

TWO SCHOOLS

In Italian cooking, there are two great schools of thought for cooking the legendary *salsa di pomodoro*, a master recipe to use on its own or as a base for other recipes.

NORTH OF ROME

In a saucepan, start with a soffritto (chop 1 stalk celery, 1 carrot, and 1 onion and brown them in oil and/or butter), add 1⅛ pounds (500 g) of tomatoes (fresh, or homemade or canned purée), salt, and pepper, and simmer over low heat for 30 to 45 minutes. The sauce can be processed through a vegetable mill to make it smoother. The result will be orangey in color, silky, and light. It can accompany pasta for four people, served as a condiment for *polpette* (meatballs), fish fillets, au gratin vegetables, and *involtini* (stuffed meat rolls), as a few examples.

SOUTH OF ROME

In a skillet, crush and brown 2 cloves of garlic (often whole and in their skins) in olive oil before adding 1⅛ pounds (500 g) of tomatoes (fresh, or homemade or canned purée) for quick cooking over medium heat (often while cooking the pasta). If the tomato is whole, it should not be crushed until the end of cooking. The result is bright red and tangy, and the tomato is highlighted more this way. From this base, for four people, you can use it for pasta (especially spaghetti, linguine, or penne), to cook an *arrabbiata* (spicy sauce), a *sugo alla Norma* (eggplant sauce), a *sugo di pesce* (a sauce based on fish), or a *parmigiana* (eggplant gratinée), or to serve with cuttlefish, as a few examples.

RECIPE

PASSATA DI POMODORO

The *passata*, or *conserva di pomodoro*, is the queen of tomato preserves, especially in the south, where tomatoes are abundant all summer long. This would be the time to make a homemade purée.

MAKES 4 CUPS (1 L) OF PASSATA

4½ pounds (2 kg) tomatoes (San Marzano, Roma, or on the vine . . .), very ripe but firm

6 basil leaves, washed and dried

2 teaspoons (12 g) fine salt

Equipment

Four 1-cup (250 mL) jars, sterilized in boiling water

Wash, dry, and quarter the tomatoes. Remove and discard the seeds, stems, and cores. Place the quarters in a heavy-bottomed saucepan and cook for 15 minutes over low heat, stirring occasionally. Process the flesh through a vegetable mill to remove the skin and create a velvety consistency. If it is still too runny, cook for another 5 minutes. Add the basil and salt. Use immediately or transfer the hot purée to clean jars. The purée will keep in the refrigerator for up to 3 weeks. *Note:* If you have a tomato press that separates the seeds and skin from the pulp, you can use it to mash the tomatoes before cooking and skip the vegetable mill.

Sulla Punta Della Lingua (On the Tip of the Tongue)

"Amore, tesoro, saosiccia e pommatoro" (Lazio): Literally "Love, treasure, sausage, and tomato," a tongue-in-cheek rhyme that combines pleasant names to make fun of lovers.

"Stongo cu 'o culo dint' 'e ppummarole" (Campania): "My butt is in tomatoes," which means to be broke (in ruins).

SKIP TO
A LOVE FOR TOMATOES, P. 26;
PENNE ALL'ARRABBIATTA, P. 252;
SPAGHETTI AL POMODORO, P. 289.

TOMATOES

In the "land of the tomato," each varietal represents iconic recipes, symbols of Italian identity around the globe.

ALESSANDRA PIERINI

① CILIEGINO GIALLO

Yellow cherry tomato

Throughout Italy

TASTE—soft, sweet, and crisp.

IN COOKING—raw, salad, cold pasta, sauce, with fish and seafood, focaccia, *contorno* (side dish).

② MINI CILIEGINO

Mini cherry tomato

Throughout Italy

TASTE—sweet, slightly acidic.

IN COOKING—raw, in salad.

③ CUORE DI BUE OTELLO

Otello Beef Heart

South-Central Italy

TASTE—intense, smooth flavor, thick skin.

IN COOKING—salad, *pinzimonio* (an assortment of fresh vegetables with sauce).

④ ⑤ ⑥ DATTERINO ROSSO, GIALLO, ARANCIO

Red, yellow, orange plum tomato

Southern Italy

TASTE—very sweet.

IN COOKING—raw, salad, confit, for pizza, quick sauces for pasta, jam.

⑦ GRAPPOLO

Tomato on the vine

Lazio, Campania, Sicily, Sardinia

TASTE—tasty and luscious, with notes of fresh grass and cut hay.

IN COOKING—salad, sauce, stewed, stuffed, au gratin.

⑧ MARINDA OR MERINDA

Sicily

TASTE—intense, vegetal, fragrant, juicy.

IN COOKING—salad, baked, *panzanella* (bread salad).

⑨ CIRANO

Campania

TASTE—delicate and rather smooth, firm, not very fibrous.

IN COOKING—cooked, canned.

⑩ PIZZUTELLO DI PACECO

Pointue de Paceco

Sicily

TASTE—fragrant, fine, delicate.

IN COOKING—raw, for pizza, canned, *pesto alla trapanese* (Trapani pesto), dried.

⑪ POMODORO CORBARINO

Campania

TASTE—flavorful, sweet and sour.

IN COOKING—sauce, for pizza, canned.

⑫ POMODORINO DI PACHINO IGP

Small Pachino tomato

Sicily

TASTE—sweet, floral, firm, slightly spicy.

IN COOKING—salad, pasta sauce, confit, fish contorno, dried, *capuliatu* (a condiment made from sun-dried tomatoes).

⑬ TORPEDINO

Lazio

TASTE—balanced, fairly sweet, aromatic.

IN COOKING—green: in salad, bruschetta; ripe: sauce, canned, baked with fish, dried.

⑭ ZEBRINO

Striated

Southern Italy

TASTE—good sweet-acid balance, crunchy.

IN COOKING—salad, fish carpaccio, tartare.

⑮ SAN MARZANO

Campania

TASTE—sweet and sour, compact, fragrant. Picked green or red.

IN COOKING—salad, *freselle* (bread salad), baked dishes, sauce, ragù, pizza, *passata* (purée), canned, concentrate, jam.

⑯ GIGANTE NERO

Black Giant

Lazio, Sardinia, Sicily

TASTE—smooth, sweet, fleshy.

IN COOKING—salad, eaten with salt.

⑰ CUORE DI BUE PIEMONTESE

Piedmontese Beef Heart

Piedmont

TASTE—sweet, juicy, dense.

IN COOKING—salad, stuffed, sauce, soup, caprese.

⑱ COSTOLUTO FIORENTINO

Ribbed Florentine

Tuscany

TASTE—delicate, smooth, vegetal taste of forest floor, firm.

IN COOKING—gratin, sauce, bruschetta, panzanella, *pappa al pomodoro* (soup).

⑲ CUPIDO

Cupid

Sardinia

TASTE—very sweet, fruity.

IN COOKING—raw, cold contorno, sauce, pizza.

⑳ POMODORO FIASCONE OR RE UMBERTO

Campania

TASTE—fresh, vegetal, firm, and melting in the center.

IN COOKING—canned food, pizza, stewed, ragù.

㉑ ㉒ PIENNOLO DEL VESUVIO GIALLO E ROSSO

Small vine tomato from Vesuvius
DOP/Slow Food

Campania

TASTE—sweet and sour, very intense, almost smoky, bitter, and mineral-like aftertaste.

IN COOKING—sauce, contorno, preserve.

㉓ CAMONE

Sicily, Apulia, Piedmont

TASTE—tasty, fleshy, crunchy

IN COOKING—salad, stuffed raw, with burrata.

㉔ CUORE DI BUE ALBENGA

Albenga Beef Heart

Liguria

TASTE—sweet, heavy, compact, very balanced.

IN COOKING—gratinée with eggplant, stuffed, *condijun* (close relative of the Niçoise salad).

㉕ NASONE DEL CAVALLINO O CIRIONE

Veneto

TASTE—slightly tart, compact, and firm.

IN COOKING—raw, salad.

㉖ CUORE DI BUE GIALLO

Yellow Beef Heart

Southern Italy

TASTE—delicate, little acidity.

IN COOKING—salad, sauce.

㉗ REGINELLA OR CAMONE SARDO

Sardinian Camone

Sardinia

TASTE—intense, crunchy with balsamic notes.

IN COOKING—rice or pasta salad, *pane frattau* (a kind of lasagna with Sardinian bread and pecorino).

㉘ CILIEGINO PENNUTO ZEBRATO

Cherry tomato with a striped pattern

Sardinia

TASTE—rich, firm, persistent.

IN COOKING—raw, canned, with pasta and fish.

㉙ POMODORO ROSA DI SORRENTO

Sorrento pink tomato

Campania

TASTE—fruity, delicate, fleshy.

IN COOKING—salad, sauce, gratin, savory tarts, caprese, with *colatura* (anchovy juice).

㉚ NERINA

Sardinia, Sicily

TASTE—sweet, fragrant, crunchy.

IN COOKING—salad, canned, focaccia.

SKIP TO
HOMEMADE TOMATO SAUCE, P. 27;
SPAGHETTI AL POMODORO, P. 289;
INSALATA CAPRESE, P. 95.

The States of the Tomato

Canned, in a jar, or freshly prepared, the *pomodoro* is found in recipes in all regions throughout Italy in its many forms.

ALESSANDRA PIERINI

All-Purpose Preparations

Passata (lit. "passed through")

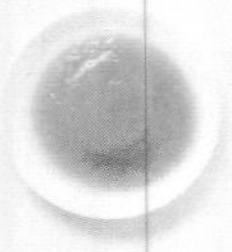

A preparation obtained from fresh and well-ripened tomatoes, crushed, with their juices, to create a very thick juice. It can be *vellutata* (velvety) with the skin and seeds removed to make it thinner, or *rustica* (rustic), thicker and lumpier.

TASTE: intense, creamy sweetness.

USES: in cooking for *primi piatti* (first courses), sauce, creamy soups, gratin, fish soups, long cooking and high temperatures.

Polpa (lit. "pulp," "flesh")

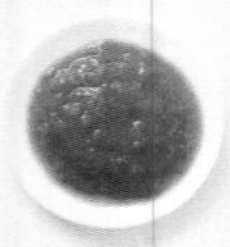

The tomatoes are peeled, cut into pieces (1½ to 4 in/4 to 10 cm), and mixed with their thick juice (*passata*) for a more consistent appearance. The *polpa* is made up of about 70 percent chunks and 30 percent passata.

TASTE: very close to fresh tomato, slightly tangy.

USES: raw on bruschetta, cooked for sauce, ragù, lasagna, *guazzetto*, *secondi piatti* (main courses) of meat or fish, and a long cooking time. Used for pizza when finely processed.

Cubetti (lit. "small cubes")

or *dadini* (small dice), *pezzi* (pieces) or *pezzettoni* (large pieces)

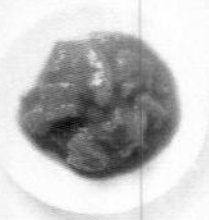

Tomatoes cut into cubes (½ to ⅔ inch/14 to 16 mm), less thick than for polpa, with their juice, without skin or seeds.

TASTE: grassy, fresh, good texture, less thick juice.

USES: for cooking in chunky sauces, in cold dishes.

Pelati (whole peeled tomatoes)

This is the closest product to the raw produce. Tomatoes, often with an elongated shape, are blanched to be peeled and stored in their juice or in water. Their seeds are maintained, and they contain a great deal more water.

TASTE: perfect sweet-acidic balance, firm and consistent tomatoes.

USES: these must be crushed before use or during cooking. For quick preparations, such as pizza, *spaghetti al pomodoro*.

Concentrato (concentrate)

or *estratto* (extract)

The tomatoes are crushed, cooked, strained, and cooked again to reduce them and obtain a very thick tomato paste. Depending on the degree of concentration, it can be *doppio* (double) or *triplo* (triple). In Sicily, they practice *elioconcentrato* or *strattu*, a technique of naturally concentrating tomatoes by long exposure to the sun.

TASTE: soft, very intense taste of cooked tomato, very intense red color.

USES: as a condiment and flavor enhancer in soups and minestrone, to add color to dishes, a sauce base for meat-based stews (ragù, *spezzatino* . . .) or legumes.

Filetti (lit. "fillets")

or *pacchetelle* (or *spaccatelle* in the southern dialect)

The method used by artisanal canneries in particular. The tomato is cut into quarters with its juice more or less thick, often with the skin and seeds. Uses either the elongated, firmer tomato, or the *pomodorini del Piennolo*.

TASTE: sweet-and-sour flavor, melting consistency close to ripe, fresh tomato.

USES: for quick cooking, as an accompaniment to fish, for pasta, on focaccia.

Pomodorini (cherry tomatoes)

Whole tomatoes, peeled or not, in their juice.

TASTE: sweet, crunchy, and juicy.

USES: lightly heated and seasoned for use a side dish with fish, quick pasta sauces.

Specific Preparations

Pomodorini secchi

(dried tomatoes)

Fresh tomatoes cut in half, salted, and traditionally sun dried. A method for preserving tomatoes. Elongated tomatoes (San Marzano type), cherry, or Datterino are generally used. Similar to semidried tomatoes, which are semidried in the oven at a low temperature to keep them moist and soft, and marinated in oil.

Confettura di pomodoro

(tomato jam)

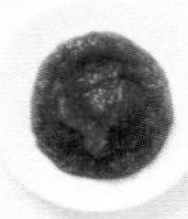

Peeled tomatoes cooked with sugar and, sometimes, lemon juice, until thickened. Used on bread, with cheese, or with roasts.

Acqua di pomodoro

(tomato water)

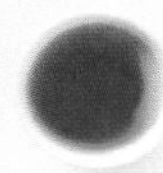

Essence or liquid extract of tomato. For jellies, risottos, pasta.

Polvere di pomodoro

(tomato powder)

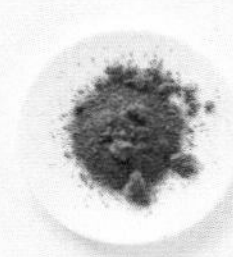

Cherry tomatoes, seeded, lightly salted, sun dried, then crushed. Used as a spice.

Insalata di pomodori cuore di bue

(beef heart tomato salad)

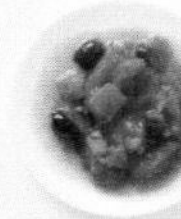

Tomatoes picked when ripe; cut; seasoned with shallot, basil, oregano, salt, black pepper, olive oil; and placed in a jar a few hours after picking.

Ketchup

Sweet and tangy condiment made from tomato, vinegar, and sugar. For meats, *bollito misto* (a stew) . . .

EACH TOMATO HAS ITS OWN CHARACTER

Tomato varietals are numerous and come in different shapes, sizes, colors, consistencies, and degrees of ripeness. They can be divided into categories, depending on their use.

***DA INSALATA* (FOR SALAD) OR *DA TAVOLA* (FOR THE TABLE)**

APPEARANCE: rounded, more or less crushed, smooth or ribbed surface, few seeds, thin skin, consistent pulp. Consumed from green to yellow, or red when ripe.

VARIETALS: Cuore di Bue, Camone, Marinda, Costoluto, Reginella, Ciliegino, di Sorrento . . .

***DA SALSA* (FOR SAUCE), *DA CONSERVA* (FOR CANNING), OR *DA SUCCO* (FOR JUICE)**

APPEARANCE: elongated or pear-shaped, fleshy, thick skin, compact flesh and not watery, uniform intense red.

VARIETALS: San Marzano, Corbarino, Nasone, Datterino, Cirano, Pachino, Pizzutello, Tondino . . .

***DA SERBO* (LONG STORAGE)**

In the past, this was the only way to ensure fresh produce out of season: choose from low-dehydration varieties.

APPEARANCE: round or ovoid, firm skin, thick, small and often in clusters, red or yellow. Common in southern Italy. Not irrigated, very concentrated aromas.

VARIETALS: Siccagno, Piennolo del Vesuvio, Principe Borghese Siciliano . . .

SKIP TO
RAGÙ BOLOGNESE, P. 330;
HOMEMADE PIZZA, P. 52;
SPEZZATINO, P. 85.

Passata
(lit. "passed through")

Polpa
(lit. "pulp," "flesh")

Concentrato
(concentrate)

Cubetti
(lit. "small cubes")

Pelati
(whole peeled tomatoes)

Filetti
(strips or slices)

Pomodorini
(cherry tomatoes)

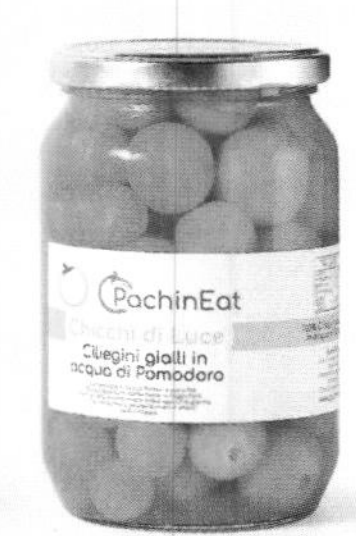

Pomodori secchi
(dried tomatoes)

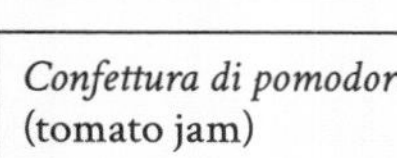

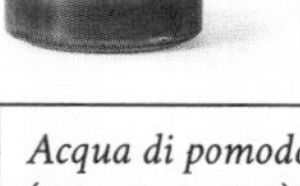

Confettura di pomodoro
(tomato jam)

Polvere di pomodoro
(tomato powder)

Acqua di pomodoro
(tomato water)

Ketchup

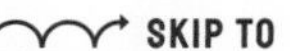
SKIP TO
PENNE ALL'ARRABBIATA, P. 252;
AMATRICIANA, P. 177;
PACCHERI ALLO SCORFANO, P. 206;
HOMEMADE PIZZA, P. 52.

Pellegrino Artusi

PROFILE

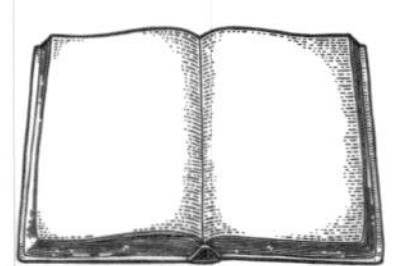

A MULTIFACETED BOOK

La scienza in cucina e l'arte di mangiar bene (*Science in the Kitchen and the Art of Eating Well*), commonly referred to as "The Artusi," was self-published in fifteen editions (in the first edition, Artusi dedicated the book to his two cats!). It is still a benchmark today for any traditional recipe.

→ The book overflows with historical anecdotes delivered in a friendly tone and with a subtle wit.

→ It is not aimed at professionals but instead at middle-class families, bringing together everyday recipes from all over Italy and sparingly incorporating regional or French terms (which were in vogue at the time).

→ It was testimony to a recently reunified Italy in search of a new national identity.

He penned the Italian gastronomic bible, which is considered a pillar of home cooking, a historical document, and a work of art to be savored for its finesse.

ILARIA BRUNETTI

IN DEFENSE OF THE ITALIAN LANGUAGE . . .

"Henceforth in Italy, if you don't speak like a barbarian, specifically when it comes to fashion and cuisine, no one understands you; to be understood, therefore, I will have to call this side dish not *passato di* . . . but *purée di* . . . , or more barbarously 'chewed potatoes.'"

(*Passato di patate*, No. 443)

. . . AND THE "CHARACTER OF THE NATION"

"'Short additions and long tagliatelle,' say the Bolognese. . . . I do not approve of this fashion consisting, in order to conform to foreigners' tastes, of finely breaking up *cappellini*, *tagliarini*, and other similar pasta before putting them in broth because, being characteristic of Italy, they must on the contrary, preserve the character of the nation."

(*Tagliatelle à la mode de Romagne*, No. 71)

RECIPE

98. RAVIOLI ALL'USO DI ROMAGNA

Below is the recipe for Romagna-style ravioli, numbered 98 in Artusi's famous book. In the past, ravioli were quenelles (dumplings) of stuffing not enclosed inside pasta, like the *gnudi* of Tuscany.

The people of Romagna, because of the climate that requires hearty sustenance, and perhaps also because they are used to heavy foods, generally have only contempt for boiled vegetables: so I have often heard it said in the trattoria: "Waiter, a portion of stew, but without spinach!" Or "With that [spinach] you can use it as a Band-Aid on your backside."

Here is the recipe for *Ravioli all'uso di Romagna* without chard or spinach.

5¼ ounces (150 g) ricotta, ¼ cup plus 2 tablespoons (50 g) flour, ⅓ cup (40 g) grated Parmesan cheese, 1 whole egg, 1 yolk, salt.

Make a smooth dough combining all the ingredients and place the dough on a lightly floured work surface. Shape it into a log, then divide it into 14 or 15 small identical pieces (shape them according to use). Boil for 2 to 3 minutes in unsalted water and season with cheese and the juices of cooked meats; they can be served as a side for braised beef or a *fricandeau*.

DECLARATIONS OF PRINCIPLE

"If one doesn't have the tendency to be a successful cook, I don't think one needs to be born holding a saucepan to be successful; passion is all that's required."

(*Author's preface*)

MARIETTA AND THE PANETTONE

Marietta Sabatini was Artusi's housekeeper to whom he dedicated the recipe for Panettone Marietta (No. 604): "She is such a good cook and so kind and honest that she deserves that I dedicate this cake to her, that which she taught me." Along with the cook Francesco Ruffilli, she contributed to the success of Artusi's book by cooking all the recipes, so much so that on his deathbed, he left them all his property and copyrights.

HERITAGE

→ Since 1996, the Festa Artusiana has celebrated Artusi's birthday in Forlimpopoli.

→ In 2007, a former convent was opened as a cooking school for amateurs, named Casa Artusi, with a library, restaurant, and shop.

KEY DATES

AUGUST 4, 1820
Born in Forlimpopoli (Emilia-Romagna).

1851
After a violent robbery and assault on Pellegrino's sister, the Artusi family moves to Florence.

1865
He retires from his successful career as a businessman and devotes himself entirely to his passions: cooking and literature.

1891
The first edition of *La scienza in cucina e l'arte di mangiar bene* (*Science in the Kitchen and the Art of Eating Well*).

MARCH 30, 1911
Dies in Florence.

SKIP TO
FRESH PASTA, P. 294.

SEASON

TUTTO L'ANNO (YEAR-ROUND)

CATEGORY

SECONDO PIATTO (MAIN COURSE)

LEVEL

FACILE (EASY)

SALTIMBOCCA ALLA ROMANA

VEAL WITH PROSCIUTTO AND SAGE

This is another iconic Italian recipe that has spread throughout the world! In just two steps and with only three ingredients, it reveals the flavors of Rome.

FRANÇOIS-RÉGIS GAUDRY

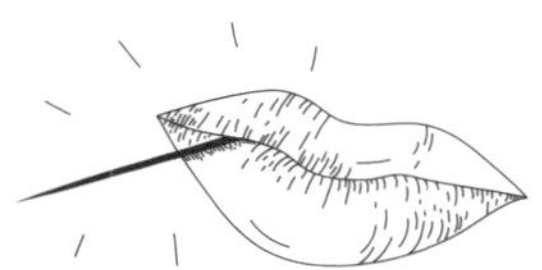

ITS ORIGINS

Saltare in bocca means "to jump in the mouth." This gourmet dish is composed of veal cutlets skewered (with a toothpick) with sage leaves and prosciutto, then sautéed in butter.

Ada Boni, Italian chef and author of the famous *Talismano della felicità* (1929), traces its origins to the area near Brescia, probably due to the presence of *saltimbocca alla bresciana* in some cookbooks. The dish appeared on the menu of the trattoria Le Venete in Rome.

It was after tasting the dish in this former splendor of Roman cuisine, during the nineteenth century, that Pellegrino Artusi reproduced the recipe in his treatise *La scienza in cucina e l'arte di mangiar bene* (*Science in the Kitchen and the Art of Eating Well*, 1891).

THE RECIPE

Denise Solier-Gaudry has always made this recipe for her family, having learned it from a book on Roman cooking. It eventually became a "madeleine de Proust" to her son, reminding him of his childhood.

SERVES 4

- 8 very thin veal cutlets (about 70 g)
- 8 slices prosciutto, such as di Parma
- 8 sage leaves
- 3 tablespoons (40 g) butter
- Scant ½ cup (100 mL) white wine
- Salt and freshly ground black pepper

If the cutlets are a little thick, flatten and tenderize them with a weight or a rolling pin. Wrap the cutlets with the prosciutto (covering them almost completely). Place a sage leaf in the center of each cutlet on top of the prosciutto and secure it with a toothpick.

In a large skillet, melt half the butter until foaming. Cook the cutlets over high heat, 1 minute on the prosciutto side and 2 minutes on the opposite side. Add the wine and season with salt and pepper. Remove the cutlets and set them aside to stay warm. With the pan still over high heat, reduce the sauce a little, add the remaining butter, then pour the sauce over the cutlets and serve.

Il Tocco Della Nonna (Grandmother's Tip)

To make the sauce creamy, Roman grandmothers like to lightly flour the cutlets, but only on the side without the prosciutto. When prepared this way, don't forget to serve bread at the table . . . to soak up the sauce!

VARIATIONS

CHANGE THE FORMAT: to make this dish into an appetizer instead, cut small 2⅓- to 2¾-inch (6 to 7 cm) cutlets from large slices of veal, cover them with prosciutto of the same size, arrange a small sage leaf on top, and secure it with a toothpick. Serve as an aperitif.

CHANGE THE MEAT: replace veal with beef or chicken. Some chefs use speck instead of prosciutto to add a smoky note.

MAKE *INVOLTINI*: these are saltimbocche rolled up and held in place by a toothpick, with the prosciutto and sage rolled up inside.

TO SERVE WITH THEM: some cooks place mozzarella or provolone slices between the veal and the prosciutto; you can add capers, chopped artichokes, or chopped red onions to the pan.

Tips from Artusi

→ "Place half a sage leaf on each (a whole leaf may be too much)." But if you like the fresh, resinous taste of sage, don't hesitate to use a large leaf!

→ "Don't leave them for long over the heat on the prosciutto side, to prevent the ham from hardening."

→ Artusi does not mention white wine. But this doesn't prevent the Romans from using a little of the wine to make their saltimbocche a little extra special!

SKIP TO
THE WAR OF THE HAMS, P. 311;
SAGE, P. 257.

SEASON
TUTTO L'ANNO (YEAR ROUND)

CATEGORY
DOLCE (DESSERT)

LEVEL
DIFFICOLTÀ MEDIA (MEDIUM DIFFICULTY)

PANNA COTTA

Originally from Piedmont, this "cooked cream" has become a popular dessert throughout Italy and is one of its best sweet ambassadors abroad.

FRANÇOIS-RÉGIS GAUDRY

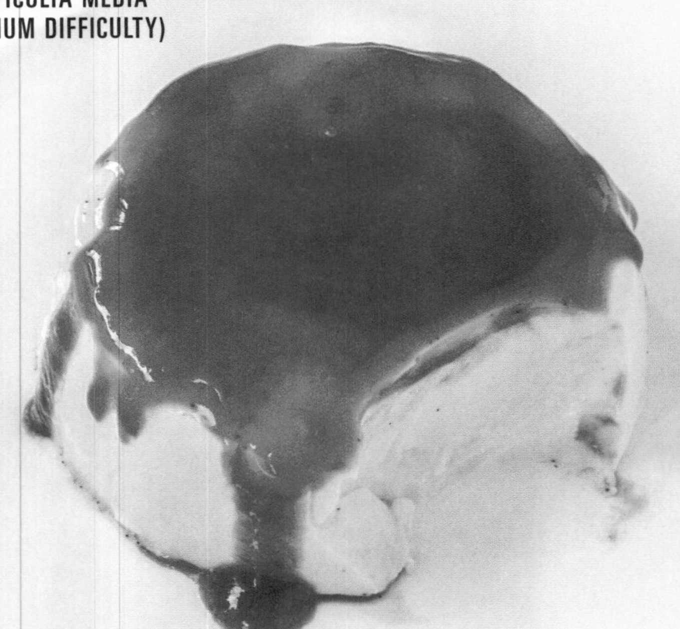

A MODERN NAME

Panna cotta literally means "cooked cream."

But the Italian word *panna* does not exist in the Piedmontese dialect, which prefers *fior dël làit* (flower of milk) to denote cream. The term *panna cotta* probably didn't appear until the 1900s.

ITS ORIGINS

→ Is Ettore Songia, starred chef of I Tre Citroni in Cuneo (Piedmont), the one who created this dessert in the mid-1960s, as his family attests? He was undoubtedly the first to codify the recipe and to put its name on the menu of a gourmet restaurant. However, its origins seem further back than this. Legend has it that a Hungarian woman from the Langhe region made this dessert to use up excess milk from her day's milking.

→ The panna cotta could be a descendant close to *latte e mella*. Traces of a recipe strangely resembling today's panna cotta can be found in a letter that poet Giacomo Leopardi wrote to his father in 1827 about his stay in Bologna:

"The recipe for *latte e melle* is very simple because it consists of *fior di latte* and cream, unsalted gelée, and sugar."

The panna cotta debates

WHICH CREAM?

Definitely cream with 31 to 35 percent fat.

A GELLING AGENT?

The risk when using a gelling agent is that the dessert becomes overly "set" and has a rubbery texture! Instead, it must remain smooth and creamy. While the modern Piedmontese recipe uses a small amount of gelatin (derived from pork or fish), today some Italian chefs make the original panna cotta with no gelling agent at all.

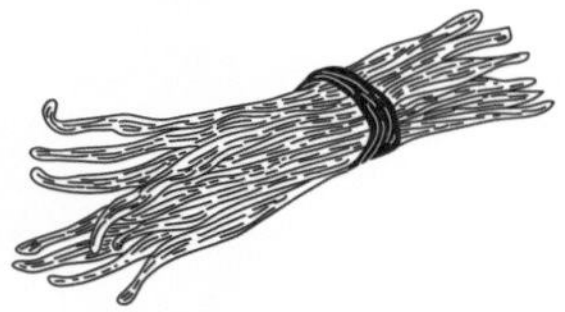

WITH VANILLA?

This spice is perfectly suited for flavoring panna cotta and was used probably beginning the 1970s.

WHAT ACCOMPANIMENT?

Caramel sauce, red-fruit sauces, exotic fruits (mango, passion fruit . . .), crème de café, or chocolate sauce!

THE RECIPE

The Piedmontese version is creamy, such as the one by Daniele Rota, chef at the pub Antiche Sere in Turin.

SERVES 4 OR 5

- ⅓ ounce (10 g) organic sheet gelatin
- Scant ½ cup (100 mL) whole milk
- 2 cups (500 mL) cream with 35% fat
- ½ cup (100 g) superfine sugar
- ½ vanilla bean

Soften the gelatin in a bowl of cold water. In a saucepan, heat the milk without boiling it. Drain the gelatin well and combine it with the milk until melted. In a separate saucepan, place the cream, sugar, and vanilla bean. Bring to a boil, stirring constantly. Turn off the heat, add the milk mixture, and stir to thoroughly combine.

Once the cream is infused, remove the vanilla pod. Pour everything into a mold or individual ramekins. Let rest in the refrigerator for 24 hours before serving with the accompaniment of your choice.

VARIATIONS

Organic gelatin can be replaced by:
2½ teaspoons (3 g) agar-agar: add to the milk at the same time.
4 large (120 g) egg whites: beat them lightly with a fork without stiffening them and pour the boiled cream with the sugar and vanilla over them, mixing well. Milk is not necessary when the recipe is made in this way.

THE GELATIN-FREE RECIPE

Andrea Maggi, the Roman chef of restaurant Aglio e Olio (Paris 11th), has the accomplishment of making panna cotta without a gelling agent. Its creamy texture, paired with orange marmalade, is irresistible!

SERVES 6

- 3 cups (700 g) cream (35% fat)
- ⅓ cup plus 1 teaspoon (60 g) sugar
- Citrus, such as lime or bergamot, for zesting

Cook 2 cups (500 g) of the cream over low heat for 45 minutes. Chill the remaining cream. At the end of 45 minutes, the cream should have reduced by half (check by weighing it). Place it back over the heat and add the sugar. Bring to a boil. Off the heat, add the scant cup (200 g) of very cold cream. Whisk to combine.

Into each bowl or ramekin, pour the cooked cream, then chill it for 3 hours.

When ready to serve, grate citrus zest on top.

A good idea

Place a generous tablespoon of orange marmalade at the bottom of each bowl before pouring in the cooked cream.

SKIP TO
CROSTATA ALLA CONFETTURA, P. 66; GIANDUJA, P. 180.

THE BRONTE PISTACHIO

Why is the pistachio from the Bronte region considered the best in the world?
The secrets of this Sicilian green gold are revealed here.

FRANÇOIS-RÉGIS GAUDRY

WHAT AM I?

Pistachio is the fruit of the true pistachio tree (*Pistacia vera*), a Mediterranean tree that looks similar to the fig tree, in the Anacardiaceae family. Growing in clusters, pistachio is a drupe composed of a pericarp (a soft yellow-red membrane), an endocarp (a woody shell that opens into two halves), and a pale-green elongated nut with fuchsia tones.

Il pistacchio verde di Bronte

(*Pistacia vera* cv. Napoletana, grafted on *P. terebinthus*) is a cultivar grown in the regions of Bronte, Adrano, and Biancavilla (province of Catania), with a PDO (Protected Designation of Origin) since 2009 and Slow Food protection. The sector currently has around 3,000 producers spread over 6,900 acres (2,800 ha). Harvesting is done every other year due to a physiological characteristic of pistachio trees, which alternate fertile and nonfertile years. In the Bronte region, it is therefore common to remove the buds during so-called nonfertile years to prevent them from being attacked by insects. The volcanic soil gives this nut powerful aromas and a unique flavor and sweetness.

Laura Lupo and Alberto Caudillo grow organic Bronte pistachios and transform them into natural products of exceptional quality: oils, pure pastes, flours . . . and a crema di pistacchio, a delicious spread containing 38 percent of this precious green gem! www.aricchigia.com

THE PISTACHIO IN ALL ITS BRILLIANCE!

1. Pistacchio fresco (fresh)
USES: creative cuisine.

2. Pistacchio essiccato con guscio (dried with the shell)
USES: aperitif.

3. Pistacchio essiccato et sgusciato (dried and shelled)
USES: cooking.

4. Pistacchio pelato (blanched)
USES: mortadella and charcuterie.

5. Olio di pistacchio (pistachio oil)
USES: pastries and savory dishes.

6. Pasta pura di pistacchio (pure pistachio paste)
USES: gelati, granita, and pastries.

7. Farina di pistacchio (pistachio flour)
USES: biscotti and desserts.

8. Granella di pistacchio (crushed)
USES: Sicilian pesto for pasta, pastries, and desserts.

RECIPE

BUSIATE AL PESTO SICILIANO

In Bronte, Alfredo Proto, the chef of Protosteria, excels in this revisited Sicilian tradition.

9 ounces (250 g) *busiate* (a short twisted Sicilian pasta that is coated well in sauce, or use *caserecce*)

½ onion

2 tablespoons (30 mL) olive oil

1¾ ounces (50 g) medium-sliced pancetta, cut into small strips

2 tablespoons Pistachio Pesto (see recipe above)

Freshly ground black pepper

1 ounce (25 g) aged *caciocavallo* (Sicilian cow's-milk cheese) or grated ricotta salata or pecorino cheese

¼ cup (20 g) crushed Bronte pistachios

- Cook the pasta in a large pot of salted boiling water.
- Meanwhile, finely chop the onion and brown it in a pan with the olive oil. Add the pancetta and cook for 3 to 4 minutes over medium heat, adding 2 tablespoons of the pasta cooking water to bind it.
- Stir in the pistachio pesto; season with pepper. Drain the pasta and pour it into the sauce.
- Serve immediately with the grated cheese and crushed pistachios.

Pesto siciliano al mortaio (Sicilian mortar pesto)

Pistachio producer Laura Lupo makes her pistachio pesto in a brass mortar dating from 1870, passed down through her family from generation to generation.

In a mortar (or a blender), place 9 ounces (250 g) blanched pistachios and add a pinch of fleur de sel and a few turns of the pepper mill. Start by crushing (*pestare*, or "mashing with a pestle") the ingredients while dry. When the pistachios are coarsely crushed, drizzle in olive oil while continuing to mash. You want to achieve a fluid paste with nuts that are not too finely ground. This pesto accompanies pasta, fresh cheeses, and roasted vegetables.

An Arabic Heritage

The Arabs introduced their culture to Sicily between the eighth and ninth centuries. The Sicilian dialect has maintained this connection: derived from the Arabic *fristach* and *frastuch*, the terms *frastuca* and *frastucara* indicate the fruit and the tree, respectively. In the Brontese dialect, the term *frastucata* designates a dessert made from pistachio, and *frastuchino* designates the green color of this fruit.

SKIP TO
SWEETS FROM THE CONVENT, P. 204;
FRESH PASTA, P. 294;
IN THE LAND OF GELATI, P. 50.

GRISSINI & CO.

Popular far beyond its original borders, this mini dry baguette made from wheat flour, water, yeast, and oil has conquered Italy and the world. But *grissini* are far from the only Italian crackers one can enjoy today.

JACQUES BRUNEL

EVERTHING ORIGINATES FROM THE GRISSINI!

Some people trace the origins of grissini to Turin in the fourteenth century. At that time, to deal with inflation, bakers produced a thin version of the local baguette (*grissia*), thus giving rise to the *grissino*.

But there is another story, a bit more glorious, concerning the Duke of Savoy Victor Amadeus II. During the first half of the seventeenth century, this young prince of fragile health had difficulty digesting ordinary bread, which was baked too quickly and spoiled by bacteria. His baker developed a more hygienic and digestible biscuit, made with a little water, two-thirds wheat flour, and one-third rye flour, sometimes with a bit of cornmeal. Having become the delicacy of aristocrats, these "little sticks of Turin" (according to Napoléon I, who had them transported with him to relieve his ulcers) were wider and longer than those we know today, and even twisted.

GRISSINI · *Piedmont*

Today, grissini form a large family of varieties, of which stand out the *stirato* ① and the handmade *rubatà* (less straight) and with turned ends, available in three lengths: 4¾ inches (12 cm) ②, 12 inches (30 cm) ③, and 19 inches (48 cm) ④. A practical means to stir your soup or to enjoy wrapped in thin ham, grissini are available in mini ⑤, very fine *torinesi* ⑥, with cornmeal ⑦, or as puff pastry, in olive oil, with rosemary, walnuts . . . and are today enjoyed most commonly as an aperitif.

SCHIACCIATINA ⑧ · *Northern Italy*

Liguria, Tuscany, and Piedmont are the strongholds of these dry but tasty breads, flattened in the shape of tongues (hence their other name, *lingue*) ⑨, which all of Italy adores. Naturally a little salty and very low in fat, they are enjoyed in versions with rosemary, olives, or chile . . . and spread with tapenade or anchovy cream.

GHIOTTINA ⑩ · *Tuscany*

The sister to the *schiacciatina*, this flat bread is distinguished by its thickness and a larger (square) format. With or without rosemary, its almost soft crunch is an invitation to enjoy it with ham.

LINGUA DI SUOCERA ⑪ · *Piedmont*

This "mother-in-law's tongue" is not biting, as the name suggests; it is just very long (19 inches/ 48 cm) and a little swollen. Similar to *schiacciatina*, it is a crunchy flat bread enriched with oil and herbs (rosemary, oregano, etc.) and is the ideal support for a host of toppings.

TARALLI ⑫ · *Southern Italy*

Popular throughout the south, this crisp bread in the shape of a small ring is made from various flours depending on the region, moistened with oil and water (or white wine), and often flavored with onion, garlic, chile, sesame, or fennel seeds. There are tiny ones (*tarallini*) ⑬ and also sweet versions.

TARALLI GRANDI ⑭ · *Apulia*

This extra-large oblong version of *taralli* also belongs to the famous family of scalded doughs that are twice cooked: first poached in water, then baked in the oven, as is done when making pretzels.

TARALLI NAPOLETANI ⑮ · *Campania*

These large crumbly taralli, twisted into rings, are enjoyed in Naples with a glass of cold beer in their *nzogna e pepe* (lard and pepper) version, enriched with almonds.

TARALLI FROLLI ⑯ · *Campania*

Created near Naples, these large, crumbly taralli are preferred as a sweet version, but there are excellent savory ones, too, topped with fennel seeds.

TARALLI DI GRANO ARSO ⑰ *Apulia*

Browned by the sun, the wheat kernels from late harvests left on the ground take on toasted aromas with notes of hazelnut. They thus produce taralli of distinct character. Some farmers even develop this flavor by roasting, or even smoking, their crops.

SCALDATELLE · *Campania*

These long, thin taralli also belong to the family of scalded doughs. Their uniqueness lies in their dough, which is enriched with fennel seeds and sometimes eggs.

BIBANESI® ⑱ · *Veneto*

Invented in Bibano di Godega near Vittorio Veneto, these globule-shaped grissini, named after their brand name, are addictive when eaten with cheese and are the pride of Treviso today.

ITALIAN CRACKERS · *Across Italy*

Across Italy, the popular variations are too numerous to count. Among them are Quadri ⑲, whose name was created by a brand to designate these traditional small squares of dry bread with an airy texture, ideal for toast. Another new product with a traditional feel is Figuli ⑳, a diamond-shaped bite popular for aperitifs.

SKIP TO FLOURS, P. 5

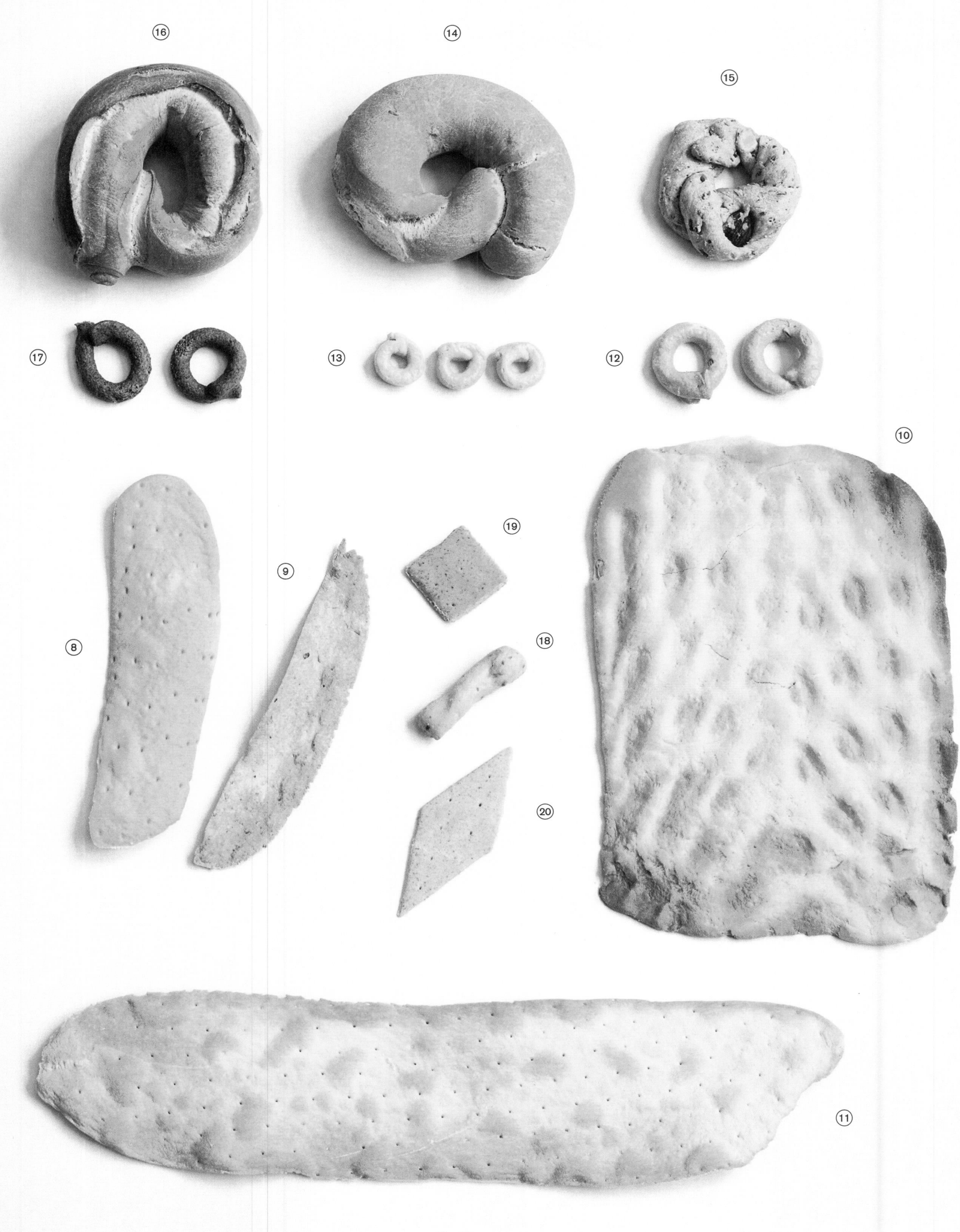
⑯
⑭
⑮
⑰
⑬
⑫
⑩
⑲
⑨
⑱
⑧
⑳
⑪

BREADS FOR SURVIVAL

Is dry bread a loss? No, it's a lifesaver! Created from the need to preserve breads, these baked specialties occupy a prominent place in Italian cuisine.

JACQUES BRUNEL

SCHÜTTELBROT ①

Trentino-Alto Adige

This "shake bread" (the meaning of *schüttelbrot*) is a fairly crisp flatbread made from rye flour seasoned with spices (cumin, anise, or fennel), dried after baking, and enjoyed with speck or cheese.

PANE CARASAU ②, GUTTIAU ③, PISTOCCU ④...

Sardinia

Adopted by the Sardinian shepherds, this rustic flatbread, round and as thin as paper (hence its nickname *carta da musica*, or "sheet music"), would fit nicely into their saddlebags. Made from fine semolina flour (or barley in poorer families, and now also rice or corn), this leavened bread rises during baking and is split before being baked again. Crumbly and crisp, it can be kept for a year.

There is a very tasty variety called *biscottadu integrale* ⑤ and made with whole flours of ancient Sardinian wheats (*trigu murru, trigu rubiu, arista niedda,* and *trigu moru*) enriched with lard, proofed, then cooked over a wood fire.

Rectangular and thicker, the *carasau* when made from cornmeal is called *pistoccu* and, once moistened, becomes an edible container for various fillings. Its salty, oil-enriched version is called *pane guttiau* (drizzled with oil).

Alternated with layers of tomato sauce topped with a poached egg, the slices of *pane carasau*, when moistened, form the *pane frattau*, a Sardinian alternative to lasagna.

PANE IN PANNOS ⑥

Sardinia

Literally "bread in a towel," this round bread, 9¾ to 12 inches (25 to 30 cm) in diameter, was made in the past to celebrate saints in mid-September as well as for weddings and Easter. It's very rare today. Prepared with hard-wheat flour, water, natural yeast (*madrighe* in Sardinian), and salt, the dough is placed in an oven on low heat to help it rise. It is then removed from the oven, covered with a linen cloth, and placed in a basket to finish rising. The bread is completed by baking, then peeling it into two halves that are stacked on top of each other. *Pane in pannos* is used in soups or sheep broth, with pecorino or baked vegetables. Maria Antonietta Mazzone, who provided these explanations, protects and continues this tradition in Sardinia.

PAN BISCOTTO ⑦

Throughout Italy

Successor to the *buccellatum* of Roman soldiers (a munitions bread that was, when there was time, "baked twice," or *bis-coctus*, for longer keeping), this dry flat bread adopted by shepherds and peasants is common throughout Italy. It is also found in a white version (called *pane tostato*) ⑧, one made of whole grain ⑨, or as *caponatina* ⑩.

FRESELLE OR FRISELLE ⑪

Southern Italy

These small round breads from Apulia and Campania are hard because they are baked twice. A large hole through the center allowed a rope to be passed through so the bread could be immersed for a few seconds in ocean water. Once moistened, *freselle* was eaten with anchovy (or tomato and olive oil by peasants). In Brindes or Otranto, it is nicknamed the "bread of the crusaders" because it's from these ports that one set sail for the Levant, equipped with a garland of *friselle*. A smaller, close cousin is Calabrian *frese* ⑫, often eaten with tomatoes, whose juice softens the bread.

BISCOTTI DEL MARINAIO ⑬

Throughout Italy

The first Italians to eat dry bread were Roman sailors. Due to the lack of an oven to bake fresh breads, fishermen carried with them on boats flatbreads made with little water, then dried. The bread was therefore not eaten until it was moistened (or, better, crumbled into soup). This sea cracker, called *panis nauticus* by Pliny the Elder, became the common food of sailors from the maritime republics (Venice, Pisa, Genoa, and its territories, such as Sardinia), where this tradition generated an entire range of products. In Liguria, the Genoan *pandolce*, enriched with pine nuts and dried fruits, is a sweet version of this.

SKIP TO
ARTICHOKES, P. 100;
FLOURS, P. 5.

③
②
④
⑨
⑧
①
⑤
⑥

THE FIG

Sweet, fleshy, and succulent, the fig is one of the symbols of Italian summers and invites you to enjoy all the pleasures it offers.

SACHA LOMNITZ

Varietals

There are the *bianchi*, with green or yellow skin, and the *neri*, which are red, brown, or purple in color.

Some bear fruit only once at the end of summer:

→ *Verdino*, the most widespread, pear-shaped and quite small, with green skin and pink-red flesh;

→ *Brogiotto nero*, slightly flattened, with purple-black skin and red flesh;

→ *Dattero*, in the shape of a spinning top, with brown skin and red flesh;

→ *Gentile*, heart-shaped, with green skin and pink flesh.

Others fruit twice per year:

→ *Dottato*, a very light green with yellow flesh, most often dried; it ripens at the end of June and in August. It produces two PDO products (dried figs of Cosenza, Calabria; and *bianchi del Cilento*, Campania) and two Slow Food–protected products (*fico secco di Carmignano*, Tuscany; and *fico monnato di Prignano Cilento*, Campania);

→ *Callara*, pear-shaped, with red skin and pink flesh; ripens at the end of June and in September.

A QUESTION OF GENDER

In Italian, the tree is often a masculine noun but its fruit is a feminine noun.

THE EXCEPTION: the *fico* is both the tree and the fruit.

The *fica* (or *figa* in the north) commonly refers to the female sex. The fig is also a very common sex symbol in history and the arts.

ANATOMY

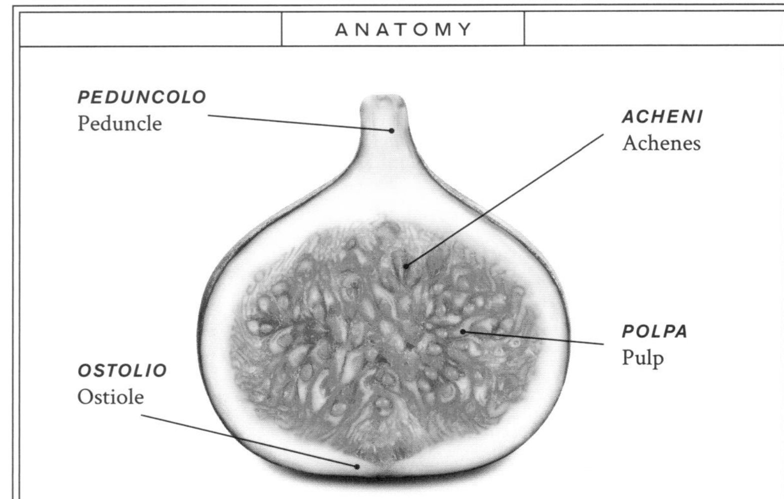

Presence in Italy

Native to the Caucasus and the shores of the Black Sea, the fig spread throughout the Mediterranean basin during antiquity and was highly appreciated.

Italian production is concentrated in the south (Apulia, Calabria, Sicily, and Campania).

In all its versions

→ Fresh, it joyfully accompanies charcuterie or traditional pasta dishes and risottos.

→ It flavors ice creams and *semifreddi* (frozen desserts).

→ As a jam, it fills the famous *crostata* (jam tart) and accompanies cheeses.

→ The *lonzino di fico* (Ancona, Marche), protected by Slow Food, is a roll of dried figs and nuts wrapped in fig leaves tied by a thread like the *lonza*, a type of salumi. Enjoyed with dessert or afternoon tea.

THE ART OF THREADING FIGS

Calabria is famous for its cottage industry in dried figs:

· ***Treccia* or *jetta***, a braid of figs strung on a *canna* (reed) and baked in the oven.

· **The *corolle***, necklaces of figs on a branch of myrtle, then baked.

· ***Fichi imbotttiti* or *crocette***, stuffed with almonds or walnuts (sometimes citrus peel), covered in chocolate or baked in the oven.

· ***Palloni di Fichi***, small baked fig balls, covered with fig-tree honey and preserved in a fig leaf.

SURPRISE!

The fig is not a fruit, but a floral receptacle closed on itself in which the fertilized female flowers become small seeds.

Composed of more than 80 percent water, fresh figs are a concentrate of mineral salts . . . and calories (280 calories per 3½ ounces/100 g!).

To pollinate the tree, fig-tree wasps deposit their larvae, which will safely grow in the fruit.

In the past, the milk from figs was used to curdle milk and make cheese.

FICHI MANDORLATI

Luigi Chezzi, from Aradeo (Salento), gives us his recipe for dried figs with grilled almonds, a snack and a traditional Apulian dessert.

INGREDIENTS

2¼ pounds (1 kg) ripe but firm fresh figs

5¼ ounces (150 g) almonds

2 lemons

Cloves (as many as there are figs)

Several bay leaves

· Halve the figs lengthwise, leaving both halves attached to the stalk. Dry them in the sun for 5 to 10 days, flesh side up. Cover them with a cotton cheesecloth, turn them often, and bring them in each day at sunset.

· Once dehydrated and rough, immerse them in boiling water, drain them, and pat dry with a cloth.

· Toast the almonds for 10 minutes at 350°F (180°C). Stuff each fig with 1 or 2 almonds, grated lemon zest, and a clove. Close them up and place them in a baking dish. Bake for 20 minutes at 300°F (150°C).

· Once the figs have cooled, place them in a jar, alternating each layer with bay leaves. Close the jar tightly and let stand for 1 month in a cool place. They can be stored for up to 1 year in an airtight container.

SKIP TO
CROSTATA ALLA CONFETTURA, P. 66; ALMONDS, P. 173.

SEASON
TUTTO L'ANNO (YEAR ROUND)

CATEGORY
SECONDO PIATTO (MAIN COURSE)

LEVEL
DIFFICOLTÀ MEDIA (MEDIUM DIFFICULTY)

CO(S)TOLETTA ALLA MILANESE

VEAL MILANESE

In Italy's fashion capital, veal cutlets are dressed in a delicate golden coating. It's quite an art!

FRANÇOIS-RÉGIS GAUDRY

ITS ORIGINS

The first mention of *cotoletta* dates from the Middle Ages: *lombolos cum panitio* (ribs coated with bread crumbs) appeared on the lunch menu of the monks of Sant'Ambrogio during solemn festivities in 1134 according to a description reported by Pietro Verri, the eighteenth-century Lombard historian. It is on the basis of these writings that the municipality of Milan granted the *denominazione comunale* (De.Co.) to the *costoletta alla Milanese* in 2008.

ON FRYING AMONG ITALY, AUSTRIA, AND FRANCE

→ According to the Italians, the Austrian marshal Joseph Radetzky brought this recipe to Austria after it was discovered in the kingdom of Lombardy-Veneto for which he served as governor from 1848 to 1857.

→ According to the Austrians, the Milanese are the successors to the dish wiener schnitzel, a specialty from Vienna of which there are versions prior to the one from Milan, although they are floured but not breaded.

→ What if France held the paternity? In *La Science du maître d'hôtel cuisinier* (*The Science of the Master Hotel Cook*, 1749), Menon mentions breaded and fried chops, marinated in melted butter, cloves, and various herbs. This recipe would have arrived in Milan during the Napoleonic campaigns with the name *cotolette Rivoluzione francese* (French Revolution cutlets).

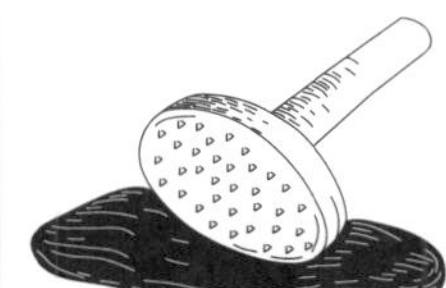

THE GOLDEN RULES

WHICH CUT OF VEAL?

Veal chops come from the first five ribs in the rack of veal. You should ask the butcher to keep the bones in for a weight of about 12 ounces (350 g) each.

HOW DO YOU FLATTEN IT?

The gentle method: flatten it with your hands to obtain a thickness of about 1 inch (2–3 cm).

The forceful method: beat the chops with a *batticarne* (tenderizer) to widen them, which takes the form of *orecchia d'elefante* (elephant's ear).

WHICH FAT?

Use clarified butter, because it does not burn when cooked! Directions for clarifying: Melt the butter over very low heat, skimming off the milk proteins that form as a foam on the surface. Continue to heat to evaporate the whey, then strain.

WHAT ACCOMPANIMENT?

A lemon wedge to add brightness to the flavor is common but not very traditional. As a *contorno* (side dish), serve vegetables or green salad.

What do you call it?

CUTÙLETA	**COTOLETTA**	**COSTOLETTA**	**ESCALOPE (MILANESE)**
in Western Lombard dialect	*in everyday language*	*for purists*	*boneless cutlets*

Its cousins

COTOLETTA ALLA BOLOGNESE —*Emilia-Romagna*
After frying, grated Parmesan and prosciutto are added and browned in a skillet with broth.

COTOLETTA ALLA PALERMITANA —*Sicily*
The chop is brushed with olive oil, covered with egg-free bread crumbs, garnished with grated pecorino and chopped parsley, then baked or broiled.

SKIP TO
MIGRANT CUISINE, P. 194.

THE RECIPE

Cesare Battisti makes one of the best veal cutlets in Milan in his upscale trattoria and sanctuary of traditions, Ratanà.

MAKES 1 COTOLETTA

One 12-ounce (350 g) bone-in veal chop
Salt
Bread crumbs
2 large (100 g) eggs
2/3 cup (130 g) clarified butter
10 sage leaves (optional)
Butter

Using a sharp knife, clean and loosen the bone from the chop. Remove the membrane that surrounds the chop to prevent it from curling during cooking. Mash the chop carefully with your hands. Season with salt on both sides.

Pour the bread crumbs into a shallow dish. Beat the eggs in a second shallow dish. Dredge the chop in the eggs then in the bread crumbs, coating evenly.

Melt 1 spoonful of clarified butter in the pan. Add the sage.

Cook the chop over low heat on one side for 6 minutes. Baste frequently with melted butter. Add fresh butter. Flip the chop and cook for another 6 minutes.

Transfer the chops to a paper towel–lined plate. The meat must rest for 4 minutes so the juices distribute into the flesh rather than seeping out when cut. Season with salt and serve with a few fried sage leaves.

Pulcinella

Arlecchino

Gianduia

La Commedia dell'Arte

Arlecchino, Pulcinella, Pierrot . . . who knew these characters from the *Commedia dell'arte* were such mischievous gourmands?

STÉPHANE SOLIER

ON THE ART OF FARCE

In the sixteenth century, the success of the *Commedia dell'arte* (Italian comedy) was due to the improvisational talent (*arte*) of its acrobatic actors and to fairly simple plots filled with witticisms. These often played on the irrepressible appetites of its masked figures (*maschere*), both serving as symbols of Italy's specific regional traits and of humanity's faults. They spent their time searching for food, thus embodying the eternal quest for sustenance of the Italian people.

Harlequin, from stage to stovetops

Dressed in a colorful costume, Arlecchino (Arlequin in French) is also, in culinary jargon:

—the name of preparations put together to remain distinct and recognizable by their nature or color (an accompaniment *à l'arlequine*).

—the names of the leftovers from restaurant tables that kitchen assistants sold at a discount to the *gargotiers* (seedy restaurants) of Paris's Les Halles, under the July Monarchy.

—the name proposed by the Mussolinian "lists of substitutions" (*elenchi di sostituzioni*) from 1941 to 1943 to replace and translate the "too-English" word *cocktail* . . . but without success!

THREE GOURMET INTRIGUES

Harlequin, the fly eater

When his stomach growls out of hunger, Arlecchino is capable of anything! In *Lazzo della mosca* (the fly pantomime), after dreaming of a delicious banquet worthy of Lucullus, he catches a "very fat" fly, plays with it in a series of funny antics and somersaults, before swallowing it under the hilarious gaze of the audience.

Pulcinella, His Majesty of Maccheroni

The Neapolitan people found in Pulcinella, the insatiable devourer of *maccheroni*, a worthy representative: it was during the seventeenth century that inhabitants of the city abandoned their vegetarian diet (which was based on cabbage, earning them the nickname *mangiafoglie* [leaf-eaters]) to become authentic *mangiamaccheroni* (pasta eaters).

During one of his many adventures, Pulcinella became king and was no longer served his favorite dish, as it was considered unworthy of his rank. Rather than giving up his coveted pasta, he replied, upset: *"E mò, mò me sprincepo!"* ("And now, now I dethrone myself!").

Gianduja . . . a melting heart

This man with heart embodies the good humor and joviality of his homeland region, Piedmont. The name of this lover of good wine and good food, *Gioan d'la douja*, means "John of the mug" in local dialect.

During the carnival of 1865, a confection was distributed in the streets of Turin. This delicacy, invented by Turin pastry chefs during the continental blockade imposed by Napoléon, was made from cocoa combined with hazelnuts from the Langhe. The treat took the name of . . . *gianduja* (*gianduia*), and the little chocolates were called *gianduiotto*, named after their "patron saint"!

SKIP TO
GIANDUJA, P. 180.

GENEALOGY OF A GOURMANDISE

GOURMET MASKS FROM THE ATELLAN FARCE . . . *Masked buffoon farce from the Latin theater of the fourth century BCE.*			. . . THE FREELOADERS OF THE GRECO-ROMAN COMEDY *Fifth to first century BCE.*		
MACCUS	DOSSENNUS/MANDUCUS	BUCCO	PARASITUS	LIGURITOR	COQUUS

THE CLOWN Stupid peasant, party animal, gluttonous.	**THE SCHOLAR** Cunning and pretentious hunchback, greedy, libidinous.	**THE SIMPLETON** Hungry, talkative, liar, cunning parasite.	Hungry slave or guest, sycophant, cunning.	Slave "licker of dishes," subjected to deprivation.	Master of the kitchens, boastful and arrogant, thief in his spare time.

PULCINELLA	BALANZONE	ARLECCHINO ARLEQUIN	GIOPPINO	STENTERELLO	MEO PATACCA	BEPPE NAPPA	BRIGHELLA BRIGUELLE
NAPLES, CAMPANIA	BOLOGNA, EMILIA-ROMAGNA	BERGAMO, LOMBARDY	BERGAMO, LOMBARDY	FLORENCE, TOSCANY	ROME, LAZIO	MESSINA-SCIACCA, SICILY	BERGAMO, LOMBARDY
A peasant greedy for maccheroni, fool, and coward who charms with his witticisms.	Talkative and pretentious doctor, fat as Bologna "The Fat" and lover of good food.	Naive but skillful servant, with an easy way and a permanent appetite.	Peasant with three goiters, sympathetic and lazy, cunning and frequent cravings.	Penniless, fearful but cunning, skinny and starving.	Quarrelsome soldier with a big heart, inseparable from his flask of wine.	Foolish servant, lazy, an inveterate guzzler.	Cunning and manipulative servant, sometimes a cook or innkeeper.

SEASON

TUTTO L'ANNO (YEAR-ROUND)

CATEGORY

STREET FOOD

LEVEL

FACILE (EASY)

FOCACCIA

Focaccia is the legendary bread of Liguria. In Umbria, it's a dessert. In Sicily, it is filled with anchovies, escarole, and cheese. This is a spotlight on a specialty as delicious as it is multifaceted.

ALESSANDRA PIERINI

FOCACCIA ALLA GENOVESE

A recipe from Maurizio Pinto, chef of the restaurant Voltalacarta, Genoa, Liguria.

SERVES 6

4 cups (500 g) all-purpose flour, plus 1 tablespoon (10 g), as needed

⅓ ounce (10 g) fresh baker's yeast

1½ cups (350 mL) water

⅓ cup (80 mL) extra-virgin olive oil, plus a drizzle for the plate

1 teaspoon (4 g) sugar

2 teaspoons (12 g) fine salt plus 1 pinch

1 pinch coarse salt

Place the flour on a work surface and make a well in the center. Dilute the yeast in 1¼ cups (300 mL) of the water and pour the mixture into the well with 2 tablespoons (30 mL) of the olive oil and the sugar. Knead by hand for 1 minute, add the 2 teaspoons (12 g) salt, and continue kneading for a few minutes until a smooth and supple dough is achieved. If the dough is sticking too much to your hands, add a little more flour. Shape it into a ball and let rest for 20 minutes on a floured work surface, covered with a clean cloth. Place the dough, still in a ball shape, on an oiled baking sheet, cover again with the cloth, and let stand for 30 minutes.

Preheat the oven to 425°F (220°C). Prepare the oil wash in a bowl by mixing the remaining scant ¼ cup (50 mL) water, remaining scant ¼ cup (50 mL) oil, and the pinch of fine salt. Mix well.

Spread out the dough with your hands so that it covers the entire surface of a 12 by 15¾-inch (30 by 40 cm) baking sheet. Let stand for 20 minutes. Spread the dough again on the baking sheet and use your fingertips to form the typical focaccia dimples. Pour the oil wash over the entire surface. Let rise for another 2 hours.

Sprinkle the focaccia with the coarse salt. Bake for 15 minutes, or until light golden.

VARIATIONS

→ *Con le cipolle*—with onions: slice a white onion very finely, season it with salt, and brush on some olive oil. Add the onion just after applying the oil.

→ *Con la salvia, con il rosmarino*—with sage, with rosemary: finely chop 10 fresh sage leaves or a few sprigs of rosemary, mix them into the flour, and knead with the other ingredients.

→ *Con pomodorini e olive*—with cherry tomatoes and olives: place halved cherry tomatoes and pitted olives in the dimples before baking.

Who am I?

Its name comes from the Latin *focus* (fire, hearth), to designate a food cooked in an oven or on embers. Common to all ancient peoples—Egyptians, Phoenicians, Carthaginians, Greeks, and of course Romans—this very popular food made from flour, water, and yeast can be seasoned with olive oil, herbs, or honey, and stuffed with cheese or other foods.

HOW DO YOU RECOGNIZE IT?

IT IS RICHER IN FAT (oil or lard) than bread, but less seasoned than a pizza.

IT IS OFTEN SPREAD BY HAND onto rectangular trays and is mostly found in bakeries or *focacceria.*

IT CAN BE EATEN AT ANY TIME OF DAY, alone or with charcuterie and cheese or, as in Genoa, with a cappuccino for breakfast.

THE OTHER FOCACCIA

Generally, it is made in the north with toppings, and in the south it is stuffed.

THE MOST WELL-KNOWN

Liguria: *con formaggio di Recco,* a thin bread stuffed with fresh cheese and eaten very hot.

Apulia: The *barese,* thick and very soft thanks to potato, which replaces part of the flour; often topped with olives and/or cherry tomatoes.

Calabria: two layers of dough filled with elderberry seeds, anchovies, and onions.

Basilicata: stuffed with tomatoes, mozzarella, artichokes, olives, mushrooms, grated pecorino, and chile.

Tuscany: also called *ciaccia* or *schiacciata,* a bread dough made with olive oil.

SWEET VERSIONS

Veneto: *veneta,* a large sweet bread flavored with orange or lemon.

Liguria: *di Lerici,* with almonds, candied fruits, raisins, and Marsala.

Piedmont: *di Chieri,* a complex preparation made from flour, milk, butter, and sugar.

SKIP TO

BREAKFAST, P. 65;
HOMEMADE PIZZA, P. 52;
FLOURS, P. 5.

BEER

Long considered a simple summer refreshment, *birra Italiana* has recently found a new lease on life with the wave of craft breweries.

EUGENIO SIGNORONI

A BRIEF HISTORY

BEGINNING OF THE TWENTIETH CENTURY: Despite the creation and establishment of a network of breweries for brands such as Peroni, Poretti, Moretti, and Wührer, annual per capita consumption stagnates at 5⅛ cups (1.2 L), compared to 34 gallons (127.6 L) for wine. This production is often managed by brewers from Germany or Switzerland who mainly produce light German beers, such as Pilsner and Vienna.

AFTER 1945: Almost all of these brands are acquired by large multinationals, and until the mid-1980s the presence of beer in Italy remains marginal. Competing with water and soda, beer is relegated to a drink to have with pizza.

1980s–1990s: The first Italian microbreweries open, although many close a few years later, most likely from being too far ahead of their time.

SINCE 1996: The real birth and spread of Italian craft beer.

ITALIAN ARTISANAL BEER

In 1996, occurring almost simultaneously in Lombardy, Piedmont, Veneto, and Lazio, several new producers (five of which are still active) were established, venturing for the first time to produce beer inspired by international canonical styles yet with a local interpretation. From there, circulation intensified, growth became relentless, and, by the end of 2018, the number of Italian craft beer brands surpassed nine hundred. In 2016, Italy was the first country in the world to pass a law to set the criteria for craft beer.

ARTISANAL OR AGRICULTURAL BREWERY

According to Italian law, an *artisanal brewery* is defined as independent from any other beer producer, produces less than 5.3 million gallons (200,000 hL) per year, and offers products that are neither pasteurized nor microfiltered. When at least 51 percent of the raw materials (barley and hops) are self-produced, the brewery is then defined as *agricultural*.

THE STARS OF THE FOUNDING BREWERIES

XYAUYÙ—BALADIN · *Piozzo (Piedmont)*

An intense and dark amber beer, with oxidized notes, reminiscent of straw wines. It is Teo Musso's masterpiece and the product that best represents Italian beer's ability to be creative.

MOTOR OIL—BEBA · *Villar Perosa (Piedmont)*

Dark but graceful. Simple but not trivial. Easygoing, to share with friends. This stout sums up the brewery of the brothers Sandro and Enrico Borio in a single beer.

TIPOPILS—BIRRIFICIO ITALIANO · *Lurago Marinone (Lombardy)*

An emblematic beer of the artisan movement, Agostino Arioli's Pilsner has become an international model. Arioli adds the technique of raw hopping—adding hops after the first fermentation—creating an intense and unusual aromatic profile for this blond.

MONTESTELLA—LAMBRATE · *Milano (Lombardy)*

A pub Pilsner that is a brilliant expression of how this brewery approaches beer, which made pubs its preferred place and showed Milan to appreciate this drink in its historic Via Adelchi location, where many of its enthusiasts come together.

QUINN—TURBACCI · *Mentana (Lazio)*

Opened at the end of 1995. It is the oldest brewery still in operation. The Quinn is its historic Pilsner: simple, pleasant, and full of character.

ITALIAN GRAPE ALE (IGA)

From the beginning, the goal of Italian producers was to seek a solid connection to their territories. And if, in the early years, chestnuts and fruits attested to this relationship, it was the grape that became the real distinctive ingredient in many of offerings. In recent years, a new category has been emerging in Italy, one that is internationally recognized, called the Italian Grape Ale (IGA). Its individual characteristic is that it uses grapes in all its forms in fermentation: whole fruits, juice, must, *sapa* or *vincotto* (cooked and reduced grape must).

① **BB10—BARLEY** · *Maracalagonis (Sardinia)*

The first grape beer to be marketed was created by Nicola Perra using Grenache sapa added after boiling on a dark base, with intense notes of dark chocolate and licorice.

② **NEBIULIN-A—LOVERBEER** · *Marentino (Piedmont)*

It is the must of the Nebbiolo grape variety that enriches the sour beer that Valter Loverier ferments and long ages in wooden barrels. The result: a beer of rare elegance to which the grapes add flavor and depth.

③ **FUNKY ROSE—SIÈMAN** · *Villaga (Veneto)*

High-fermentation beer with the addition of Tai Rosso must, a local grape variety from Colli Berici. Siemàn (meaning "six hands" in the local dialect) is a unique company in the Italian landscape. Producers of both wine and beer, they use the grapes for their two productions, especially for the fermentation phase.

④ **Û BACCAROSSA—CA' DEL BRADO** · *Pianoro (Emilia-Romagna)*

For now, the boys at Ca' del Brado have decided to only manage the fermentation and wood aging of their beers. This beer with Centesimino grapes from a local biodynamic company is a splendid example of an IGA in an acidic version.

THE ESSENTIAL BEERS

⑤ **QUARTA RUNA—MONTEGIOCO** · *Montegioco (Piedmont)*

Volpedo's very fragrant peaches match Riccardo Franzosi's lager, which has become a benchmark for many brewers who have chosen to use fruit in their production.

⑥ **SAISON—CANTINA ERRANTE** · *Barberino Tavernelle (Tuscany)*

Cantina Errante is one of the most recent projects in the artisanal landscape. These beers are matured in fine wood barrels that previously held wine and as a result have incredible character and depth. They have become classics of Italian production in a very short time.

⑦ **DOPPELBOCK—ELVO** · *Graglia (Piedmont)*

Josif Vezzoli's Doppelbock is a salute to low fermentation. Produced with local water (the softest in Europe), it achieves the feat of being fluid even with a full body and high alcohol content.

⑧ **SYRENTUM—SORRENTO** · *Massa Lubrense (Campania)*

The blond beer from Giuseppe Schisano and Francesco Galano is a celebration of Sorrento lemons whose zest is one of its ingredients. It has the scent of a sunny day from the Amalfi Coast mixed with that of a Neapolitan pastry.

⑨ **MARGOSE—BIRRANOVA** · *Triggianello (Apulia)*

It's the sea and its salty water that make their appearance in this Apulian interpretation of a very old style of German beer. Donato Di Palma presents his version of Gose—a beer with spontaneous top fermentation—in an inspiration that unites the north and the south of the Old World.

⑩ **O.G.111—CARROBIOLO** · *Monza (Lombardy)*

Creativity, precision, and elegance are the stylistic elements of all the production of Pietro Fontana and this "barley wine" with peated malt; it's an extraordinary expression of it.

⑪ **PINK IPA—ALMOND '22**—*Spoltore (Abruzzo)*

Jurij Ferri is a wizard of spices, and this IPA (India Pale Ale, a style of high-fermentation beer of English origin) with pink peppercorn is a fine example with its spicy, balsamic, and floral notes combined with the intense sensations of American hops.

SKIP TO
CACIO E PEPE, P. 175; PIZZE NAPOLETANE, P. 54.

EVENTS NOT TO BE MISSED

EurHop! (October, Rome)

Arrogant Sour Festival (May, Reggio Emilia)

Birraio dell'Anno (January, Florence)

PIZZA E BIRRA

Is there a more emblematic association of Italy than beer and pizza? Yet this link that seems so strong today (36 percent of Italians say they prefer to drink beer with pizza) emerged in the 1950s for reasons beyond what is gastronomic. Pizzerias at the time were not allowed to sell alcoholic drinks over 8 percent ABV (alcohol by volume) and therefore offered beer instead, which was simple, cheap, thirst quenching, and low in alcohol.

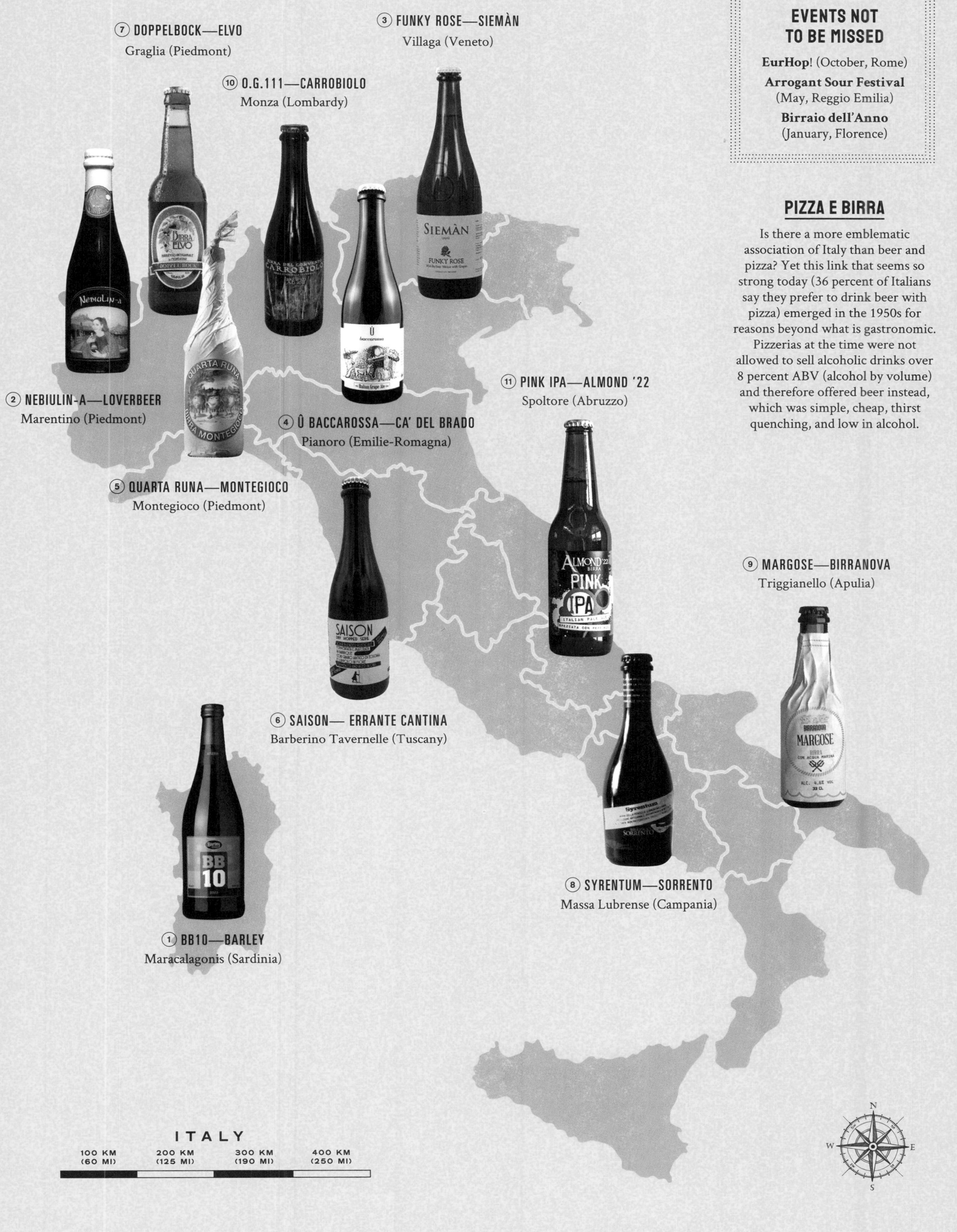

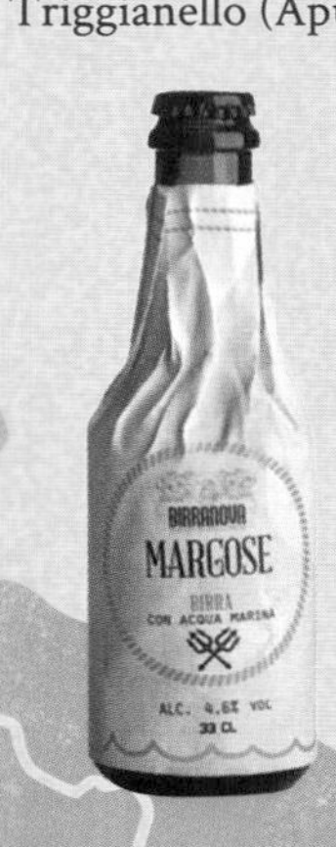

⑦ DOPPELBOCK—ELVO
Graglia (Piedmont)
③ FUNKY ROSE—SIEMÀN
Villaga (Veneto)
⑩ O.G.111—CARROBIOLO
Monza (Lombardy)
② NEBIULIN-A—LOVERBEER
Marentino (Piedmont)
⑪ PINK IPA—ALMOND '22
Spoltore (Abruzzo)
④ Û BACCAROSSA—CA' DEL BRADO
Pianoro (Emilie-Romagna)
⑤ QUARTA RUNA—MONTEGIOCO
Montegioco (Piedmont)
⑨ MARGOSE—BIRRANOVA
Triggianello (Apulia)
⑥ SAISON— ERRANTE CANTINA
Barberino Tavernelle (Tuscany)
⑧ SYRENTUM—SORRENTO
Massa Lubrense (Campania)
① BB10—BARLEY
Maracalagonis (Sardinia)
SIEMÀN
FUNKY ROSE
CARROBIOLO
BIRRA ELVO
QUARTA RUNA
BIRRA MONTEGIOCO
SAISON
ALMOND '22
PINK IPA
MARGOSE
BB 10
ITALY
100 KM (60 MI)
200 KM (125 MI)
300 KM (190 MI)
400 KM (250 MI)
N
W
E
S

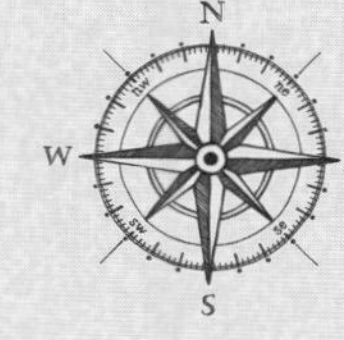

BOTTARGA

Whether from mullet or tuna, these dried fish eggs are the caviar of the Mediterranean!

ALESSANDRA PIERINI

WHO AM I?

Bottarga is a double pouch of eggs (roe) primarily from female mullet (*Mugil cephalus*), bluefin tuna (*Thunnus thynnus*), or yellowfin tuna (*Thunnus albacares*), pressed, salted, and dried.

History

Its name derives from the Arabic *batàrikh* (dried fish eggs), which comes from the Greek *oatarichia* (fish eggs preserved in salt). The Egyptians—experts in the art of salting and mummification—then the Phoenicians and their Sardinian colonies Tharros and Othoca produced it more than 3,000 years ago to feed fishermen. The Arabs spread it throughout the Mediterranean, Spain, Italy, and southern France.

A CERTAIN EXPERTISE

The double pouch of mature eggs is carefully and meticulously removed by hand to keep it intact. It is then rinsed and placed under salt for about a week before being pressed between two wooden planks, then dried. You can recognize bottarga (*butàriga* in Sardinian) of artisanal mullet by the piece of flesh attached to the base of the double pouch, *unghia* (nail), *su biddiu* in Sardinian, maintained to prevent it from emptying out and to suspend it while handing for drying.

MULLET OR TUNA?

MULLET

FISHING SEASON—September.

FISHING REGIONS—Sardinia (Cabras), Tuscany (the Orbetello lagoon, a Slow Food partner).

APPEARANCE—flattened sausage shape. *Chiara* (light) ① is softer and less refined, a golden hazelnut color, amber. *Scura* (dark) ② is drier and more refined, dark orange-brown; from 3½ to 14 ounces (100 to 400 g), sous vide, whole (*baffa*), or grated.

AGING—from 30 to 60 days.

TASTE—delicate but frank, aromatic, with a bitter almond aftertaste.

TUNA

FISHING SEASON—May.

FISHING REGIONS—Sicily, Sardinia (Carloforte), Campania, Calabria.

APPEARANCE—parallelepipedal shape, pink to dark brown; 1¾ to 2⅔ pounds (800 g to 1.2 kg) whole (*baffa*), 7 to 14 ounces (200 to 400 g); piece ③; sous vide or grated ④.

AGING—from 30 to 90 days.

TASTE—intense, salty, and pronounced.

OTHER BOTTARGA FISH

Spigola or *branzino* (sea bass), *pesces pada* (swordfish), *ricciola* (amberjack/yellowtail), *palamita* (bonito), lake fish (trout, shad . . .).

RECIPE

SPAGHETTI ALLA BOTTARGA

SERVES 4

3 ounces (80 g) mullet bottarga (or tuna bottarga in Sicily)

¼ cup plus 2 tablespoons (90 mL) olive oil, plus more for drizzling

2 cloves garlic, peeled, halved, and the germ removed

14 ounces (400 g) spaghetti

Zest of 1 lemon

- Cut three-fourths of the bottarga into very thin strips and set aside. Bring a pot of salted water to a boil. Meanwhile, gently heat the oil in a large pan with the garlic. As soon as the garlic begins to brown, turn off the heat.
- Cook the spaghetti al dente, drain, setting aside 3 tablespoons (45 mL) of the pasta cooking water. Remove the garlic, pour the pasta into the pan, and place back over the heat. Sauté, add the strips of bottarga, the lemon zest, and the reserved cooking water. Stir well to combine.
- Serve hot, with a drizzle of olive oil and the bottarga cut into strips directly on the plates. Grate the remaining bottarga on the plates when ready to serve. Salt is typically not needed because the bottarga is salted.

Varitions

→ The recipe is often accompanied with parsley, but artichokes, asparagus, and ricotta are also used . . .

→ Roman chef Sergio Risdonne of restaurant Chez Marie en Corse in Linguizzetta cooks minced garlic and anchovies in butter in a skillet, then deglazes the pan with white wine. He then incorporates the grated and sliced bottarga into the spaghetti.

How Do You Enjoy It?

→ On bread, with olive oil or butter and lemon zest.

→ With artichokes, asparagus, celery, potatoes, eggs.

→ In pasta or risotto.

→ With ricotta, mozzarella, burrata.

→ On oysters.

WARNING!

Today, 95 percent of the raw material used to make mullet bottarga comes from Africa, Israel, the Philippines, or Australia. Production in the western Mediterranean remains the privilege of a few passionate fishermen or small family businesses, but it fails to meet the ever-growing demand.

SKIP TO

A LEADING COUNTRY FOR CAVIAR, P. 360; SPAGHETTI AI RICCI DI MARE, P. 283.

SEASON

TUTTO L'ANNO (YEAR-ROUND)

CATEGORY

PRIMO PIATTO (FIRST COURSE)

LEVEL

DIFFICILE (DIFFICULT)

LASAGNE VERDI ALLA BOLOGNESE

SPINACH PASTA LASAGNA BOLOGNESE

Colorful layers of spinach pasta interspersed with *ragù bolognese* and béchamel sauce: this is the legend of Bologna—real heartiness on a plate.

FRANCESCA GAMBERINI

LASAGNA AND BOLOGNA

The recipe for lasagna is not commonly found in culinary texts because it is influenced by at-home traditions. Even today in Bologna, it is customary to prepare this dish for family on Sundays or on public holidays. Here is its story:

FIRST CENTURY—Apicius presents a recipe for *lagana*, the predecessor of lasagna.

1282—a first version of lasagna from Bologna (boiled and flavored with cheese) is mentioned in *Memoriale bolognese*.

DURING THE RENAISSANCE—the mention of alternating layers of an egg-based pasta and cheese appears.

MID-NINETEENTH CENTURY—spinach, traditionally sandwiched between the layers, is boiled and integrated into the pasta itself, accompanied by meat juices.

1935—the recipe is described as *lasagne verdi* (green lasagna) by Paolo Monelli in *Il Ghiottone errante*.

2003—the International Academy of Italian Cuisine submits the recipe for *lasagna verdi alla bolognese* to the chamber of commerce.

ITALY'S OTHER LASAGNAS

NEAPOLITAN LASAGNA—Campania. Semolina pasta prepared with Neapolitan ragù, ricotta, mozzarella, and other cheeses.

VINCISGRASSI—Marche. With beef and chicken offal and mushrooms. The pasta contains oil, eggs, and white wine.

LASAGNA WITH VITERBO LENTILS—Lazio.

LASAGNA BENEVENTO STYLE—Campania. Similar to the Neapolitan version, but moistened with chicken broth before cooking.

SAGNE CHINA—Calabria. Similar to the Neapolitan version, but enriched with hard-boiled eggs, Scamorza cheese, vegetables, pork, etc.

SKIP TO
FRESH PASTA, P. 294;
PELLEGRINO ARTUSI, P. 32;
RAGÙ BOLOGNESE, P. 330.

THE RECIPE

SERVES 6

For the pasta noodles

- 4¾ cups (600 g) all-purpose flour (or type 00 pastry flour or T45)
- 6 large (300 g) eggs
- 10½ ounces (300 g) spinach or wild nettle leaves
- Freshly grated nutmeg

For the béchamel

- 14 tablespoons (200 g) unsalted butter
- ¾ cup (100 g) all-purpose flour, sifted
- 4 cups (1 L) whole milk
- Fine salt
- Freshly grated nutmeg

To assemble

- 1¾ pounds (800 g) Ragù Bolognese
- 4 cups (400 g) grated Parmesan cheese
- Butter

Equipment

Baking dish, approximately 9¾ by 14 by 2⅓ inches (25 by 35 by 6 cm)

Make the pasta noodles

· Knead together the flour, eggs, boiled spinach (wrung out and pressed through a strainer), and a little nutmeg. Roll out finely with a rolling pin or pasta roller and cut into 6 by 4-inch (15 by 10 cm) rectangles. Boil a few pasta sheets at a time in salted boiling water for a few minutes (when they float to the surface, they are ready). Remove them from the water, let cool for a few minutes in a bowl of cold water, then dry them on a clean kitchen towel.

Make the béchamel

· Melt the butter in a saucepan over low heat, then incorporate the flour and whisk to combine. Cook this mixture, called a roux, until golden brown. Add the milk, salt, and nutmeg and finish cooking to the desired thickness. Let cool in a container, covered with plastic wrap.

Assemble the dish

· Preheat the oven to 350°F (180°C). Butter the baking dish and place a layer of the noodles on the bottom, then cover with an even layer of the ragù, then one layer of béchamel, followed by a sprinkle of the Parmesan. Continue in this way until all the ingredients are used; there should be at least six layers. Cover the last layer of noodles with béchamel mixed with a little ragù, a few pieces of butter, and the remaining Parmesan.

· Bake for about 30 minutes. When the surface is golden, remove the lasagna from the oven, let stand for 5 minutes, and serve.

WHERE TO ENJOY LASAGNA IN BOLOGNA?

TRATTORIA DA ME (Via San Felice, 50), opened in 1937 by Danio and Ada,] grandparents of Elisa, the current owner and chef. They offer lasagna verdi only on Sundays at noon, just as they have done for the last eighty years.

RISTORANTE DIANA (Via Volturno, 5), guardian of the Bolognese tradition since 1909.

Did you know?

GARFIELD,
the famous cat from the comic strips, is a lasagna fanatic.

FERDINAND II,
King of the Two Sicilies, whose kingdom was annexed in 1861 for the benefit of a unified Italy, was nicknamed *Re lasagna* (the Lasagna King) because of his passion for the dish.

SQUASH

This vegetable is the queen of the autumn season. An easy and low-calorie vegetable, *zucca* (*sùca* in the north and *cocuzza* in the south) forms the base of many traditional Italian dishes. Here are the six most common Italian varietals.

ALESSANDRA PIERINI

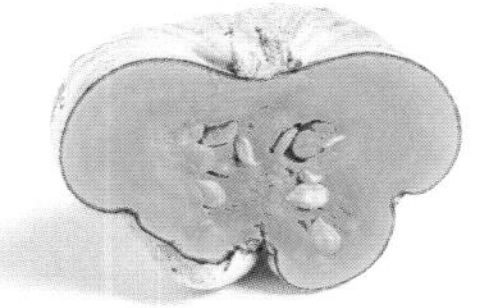

① ZUCCA BERRETTINA DI LUNGAVILLA

SCIENTIFIC NAME—*Cucurbita maxima.*

VERNACULAR NAMES—berretta or cappello del prete (beret or priest's hat), bertagnina, piacentina.

REGION OF ORIGIN—Lombardy and Emilia-Romagna.

APPEARANCE—round, turban-shaped, with a less developed lower section, light gray-green color.

FLESH—yellow, sweet, fruity with a slight nutty taste, firm, with little fiber and a floury texture.

IN COOKING—ideal for *nüsat,* a savory tart common to the Pavia region (see recipe at right). You can mix the flesh with ricotta, bread crumbs, and nutmeg and fry in olive oil for vegetarian meatballs. When baked, it is sliced and cooked with olive oil and crushed hazelnuts.

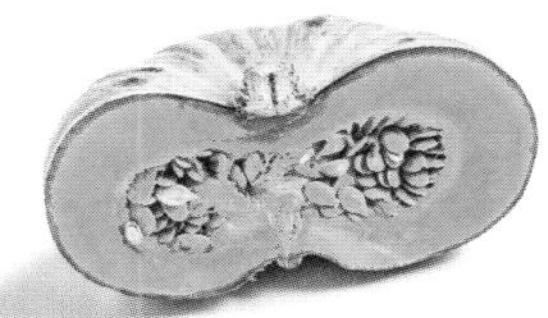

② ZUCCA MANTOVANA

SCIENTIFIC NAME—*Cucurbita maxima.*

VERNACULAR NAME—zucca mantovana.

REGION OF ORIGIN—Lombardy.

APPEARANCE—round, slightly flat, gray-green skin. There is an elongated variety (*violina*).

FLESH—sweet and delicate, orange-yellow, tender, pasty, and compact.

IN COOKING—it can be made into gnocchi or used in risotto. Used to fill *tortelli* and *cappellacci ferraresi.* Using the violina variety, slices are cooked in milk; dredged in flour, egg, bread crumbs; and fried in butter.

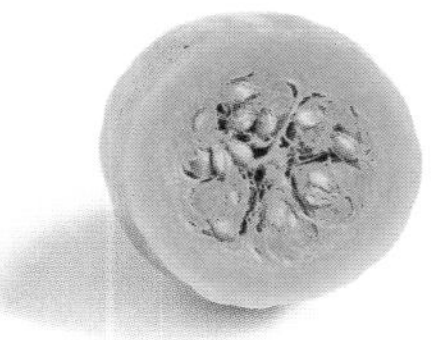

③ ZUCCA DI ALBENGA

SCIENTIFIC NAME—*Cucurbita moschata.*

VERNACULAR NAMES—zucca torta, tromboncino, trombetta (trumpet), or creeping.

REGION OF ORIGIN—Liguria.

APPEARANCE—elongated, cylindrical, twisted with a more bulbous end. Orange-beige skin. It can reach over 3 feet (1 m) long.

FLESH—light orange, sweet, melting, with a light taste of fresh almond and chestnut; it is also eaten very young and green, like zucchini.

IN COOKING—in Calabria, it is used *ripiena* (stuffed with meat, eggs, bread crumbs, pecorino, garlic, and parsley). In Liguria, one makes *farinata di zucca,* a savory tart stuffed with grated squash, Parmesan, and oregano, or the *torta dolce di Pietra Ligure,* a cake with squash, pine nuts, and raisins. It is also made into jams.

④ ZUCCA MARINA DI CHIOGGIA

SCIENTIFIC NAME—*Cucurbita maxima.*

VERNACULAR NAMES—santa, barucca, baruffa, marina de ciosa.

REGION OF ORIGIN—Veneto.

APPEARANCE—voluminous, round and squat in the middle, with rough, irregular, green skin.

FLESH—dark yellow to orange, thick, breaks up well, juicy, sweet with a hint of chestnut.

IN COOKING—marinated *saor*-style (sweet-and-sour with olive oil, vinegar, sugar, onions, raisins, and pine nuts); raw, grated into a salad; Sicilian *agrodolce* (see recipe at right); in risottos and soups with rice; in *pan zal,* a sweet yellow bread from Friuli-Venezia Giuli, with boiled squash, cornmeal, rye flour, dried figs, and grappa.

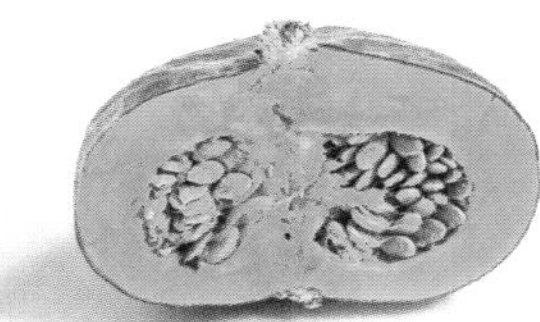

⑤ ZUCCA DELICA

SCIENTIFIC NAME—*Cucurbita maxima.*

VERNACULAR NAME—zucca delica.

REGION OF ORIGIN—Lombardy, Veneto, Emilia-Romagna, Sicily.

APPEARANCE—small, round, dark green with slight grooves that, when ripe, turn brownish.

FLESH—intense yellow, firm but tender, dry, very sweet and fragrant, with a nutty taste.

IN COOKING—suitable for all uses. Baked au gratin and in gnocchi, purées, ravioli, risottos, breads and cakes, confit.

⑥ ZUCCA LUNGA DI NAPOLI

SCIENTIFIC NAME—*Cucurbita moschata.*

VERNACULAR NAMES—piena di Napoli, cocozza zuccarina.

REGION OF ORIGIN—Campania.

APPEARANCE—elongated cylindrical shape, thin green skin with small light brown furrows. It can weigh up to 44 pounds (20 kg)!

FLESH—almost red-orange, quite firm, sweet and musky.

IN COOKING—raw in salad; cooked into soups, jams, gratins. In *pasta e cocozza* (Naples), with *ditali, tubetti,* or *pasta mista* cooked directly in creamed squash with Parmesan, garlic, parsley, and chile.

 **SKIP TO**

TORTELLI DI ZUCCA, P. 371; MARINADES, P. 322.

ZUCCA IN AGRODOLCE (SWEET-AND-SOUR SQUASH)

This very popular recipe in Sicily was born in the Vucciria market in Palermo. It was called *ficatu ri setti cannola* (liver of the seven spouts) because it was prepared for those who could not afford to buy the beloved Italian *agrodolce* liver, which was reserved for nobles. This dish was sold by street vendors near the Fountain of the Seven Spouts.

$1\frac{2}{3}$ cups (400 mL) olive oil

$1\frac{1}{3}$ pounds (600 g) peeled squash (marina di Chioggia) or pumpkin

3 cloves garlic, peeled

$1\frac{1}{2}$ teaspoons (20 g) sugar, or more to taste

$\frac{1}{4}$ cup (60 mL) white wine vinegar

Salt and freshly ground black pepper

30 mint leaves, chopped

- Heat the olive oil in a skillet or deep fryer until it reaches 340°F (170°C). Cut the squash into $\frac{1}{3}$-inch-thick (1 cm) rounds, then fry them for 2 minutes on each side. Drain on paper towels.
- Thinly slice the garlic and heat it for 5 minutes in the same oil used to fry the squash, adding the sugar and vinegar.
- Arrange the squash slices in a dish, season with salt and pepper, and sprinkle with the mint. Let cool and enjoy.

NÜSAT (SQUASH TART)

This is a savory squash tart from Lombardy traditionally cooked on the day before Christmas.

SERVES 4

$1\frac{3}{4}$ pounds (800 g) squash (berrettina or pumpkin), peeled and sliced

1 white onion, minced

$\frac{1}{4}$ cup (60 mL) olive oil

2 tablespoons (30 g) unsalted butter, plus more for the dish

1 large (50 g) egg

$\frac{2}{3}$ cup (60 g) grated Parmesan cheese

$\frac{2}{3}$ cup (60 g) dried bread crumbs, plus more for the dish

1 pinch freshly grated nutmeg

1 pinch salt

A few crushed walnuts, for serving

- Bake the squash for 40 minutes at 350°F (180°C).
- Sauté the onion in a pan with the olive oil and butter for 5 minutes over medium heat.
- Mash the squash flesh with a fork. Combine it in a bowl with the egg, Parmesan, bread crumbs, nutmeg, and salt. Add the cooked onion and stir.
- Pour the mixture into a buttered baking dish sprinkled with bread crumbs (the preparation should not exceed $1\frac{1}{8}$ inches/3 cm in height).
- Bake at 300°F (150°C) for 30 to 35 minutes. Serve warm, with crushed walnuts sprinkled over the top.

In the Land of Gelati

Of all sweet delights, ice cream is without a doubt the Italians' favorite.

ALBA PEZONE, LOÏC BIENASSIS, VALENTINE OUDARD

ICE CREAM'S DISTANT ANCESTORS

→ According to Pliny the Elder, the Emperor Nero liked to "boil water, put it in glass flasks, and cool it in the snow" (*The Natural History*, p. 77).

→ In Tang China (618–907 CE), ice cream preparations were made from milk.

→ From the Middle Ages in Persia and the Middle East, sherbets and frozen fruit-based drinks were consumed.

→ In Italy, Giambattista della Porta in *De magia naturali* (1589) explains how to freeze wine in a container by immersing it in a mixture of saltpeter and snow. This technique, which had been used for centuries, was mentioned in the mid-thirteenth century by the Arab physician Ibn Abi Usaybi'a.

First recipes

→ In the *Codex Atlanticus*, Leonardo da Vinci (1452–1519) provides the recipe for "Turks' water": sugar, rose water, and ice water make up what could be the first written version of sorbet.

→ In 1682, the *Nouveau Confiturier* by French chef François de La Varenne spoke of ice cream, "orange blossom snow," and "coriander snow": actually a sorbet, since it contains neither milk nor cream.

→ The second volume of *Lo scalco alla moderna* (1694) by Antonio Latini is the first mention presented in an Italian-language book of *sorbetti* and other *acqueaggiacciate*.

THERE IS NO "RIGHT TIME" FOR GELATO

It can be enjoyed any time of day—and all year round!

Gelato terms

CONO
A crunchy cone made from a rolled wafer.

COPPETTA
A small disposable jar.

COPPA GELATO
A glass cup, generally holding several flavors, served at the table.

GELATAIO
A master ice cream maker.

GELATERIA
The name for a gelato vendor.

SORBETTO
Ice cream made from the flesh and juice of fruits, without fat, eggs, or milk; with a *grana fine* (refined texture, smooth, homogeneous) and powerful aromas.

GRANITA
A type of sorbet with a granular and fine texture (but not crystallized), made from fruit or coffee.

GREMOLATA
A granita containing pieces of fruit.

NOT HERE!

Do not go looking for Italian soft-serve ice cream! Soft-serve is an industrial ice cream and does not come from Italy but from the United States, where it was invented in the 1930s.

A small tour of frozen specialties

Tartufo

SEMIFREDDO: a kind of rich ice cream made with eggs and whipped cream, comparable to the parfait of Antonin Carême. In the large family of *semifreddi* are *zuccotto* (a hemisphere-shaped dome covered with sponge cake) and *spumone* (a frozen mousse composed of three flavors) . . .

TARTUFO: created in Pizzo (Calabria) in 1953, this little dome (a hazelnut ice cream on a layer of chocolate ice cream filled with melted bittersweet chocolate, covered with cocoa powder) looks like a black truffle, from which its name is derived. There is also a *bianco* version (plain or *zabaione* ice cream, with a coffee center, covered with meringues).

AFFOGATO: to those who have a hard time choosing between dessert and coffee at the end of the meal, the Italians have provided a solution with *affogato* ("drowned"), which is a hot espresso poured on top of a scoop of vanilla ice cream.

AND ALSO . . .

CASSATA GELATA: a sponge cake filled with ricotta and candied fruit; the frozen version of Sicilian *cassata*.

TORTE GELATO: ice cream cake, made with or without a cake layer.

GELATO AL BISCOTTO: rum and amaretti ice cream between two cookies, from Naples.

PROFITEROLES: small choux-dough puffs topped with ice cream or pastry, covered with chocolate.

TRONCHETTI: frozen logs . . .

Granita, the original ice cream?

This mixture has a base of water, sugar, and fruit and is traditionally enjoyed in Sicily for breakfast, accompanied by a brioche *col tuppo* (a brioche topped with a small bun). It dates back to the Muslim rule of the island ininth to tenth centuries). Snow from Mount Etna and surrounding areas was collected, stored in *nivieri* (converted caves), then scraped and drizzled with syrups made from fruits or flowers.

Sicilian flavors

(1) **LIMONE** (lemon): all of Sicily.

MANDORLE (almonds): raw and chopped in Syracuse, grilled in Modica.

GELSOMINO OR SCURSUNERA (jasmine or oyster plant [*scorsonere*]): Trapani.

(2) **GELSO NERO** (blackberry from the mulberry tree): Trapani.

PISTACCHIO (pistachio): Bronte.

(3) **FICO E FICO D'INDIA** (fig and prickly pear): Sicily and Calabria.

CAFFÈ (coffee): often topped with whipped cream, throughout Sicily.

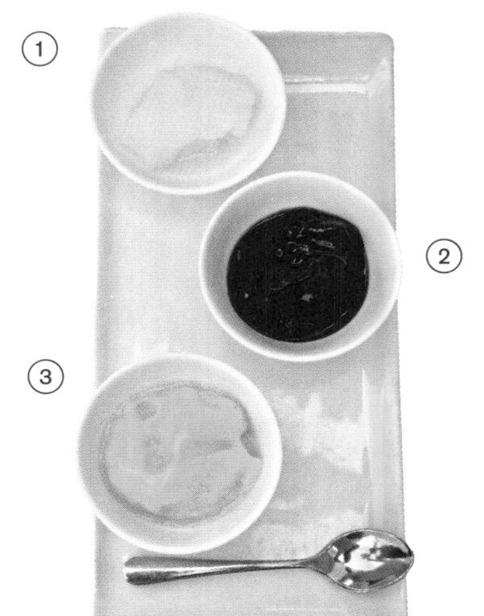

THE KING OF GRANITA

In Noto, a superb Baroque village in the province of Syracuse, stands Caffè Sicilia, the laboratory–tea room of pastry genius Corrado Assenza. He defines granita as "the pure, natural, and fresh expression of the land."

FLAVORS OF THE REGIONS

Ice cream makers rely on local products.
Here is a little tour of Italy's flavors of gelati.

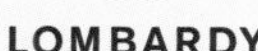

LOMBARDY

Cremaoro (coffee), *castagne/cachi* (chestnut/persimmon).

♥ **A NOTABLE ADRESS:** Gnomo Gelato (Milan).

PIEDMONT

Langhe hazelnuts, *zabaione*, *farina bona* (roasted corn), *ramassin* (small plum).

♥ **A NOTABLE ADRESS:** Casa Marchetti (Turin).

TUSCANY

Parmigiano alle pere (Parmesan with pear), *castagne del Mugello IGP* (chestnut).

♥ **A NOTABLE ADRESS:** Carapina (Florence).

SICILY

Limone di Santa Flavia (lemon), *cachi di Misilmeri* (persimmon), *fior di latte*, *bacio di dama* (with the flavors of the chocolate-hazelnut cookie), and the *granita alla pesca gialla di Leonforte* (granita with yellow peach).

♥ **A NOTABLE ADRESS:** Cappadonia Gelati (Palermo).

EMILIA-ROMAGNA

Crema bolognese (a very yellow cream, vanilla, very rich in eggs), *morbido all'amarena* (hazelnuts, almonds, cocoa, sour cherries), *granlatte* (milk and cream), *crema italiana* (eggs and lemon zest).

♥ **A NOTABLE ADRESSES:** Stefino (Bologna), Gelateria Leoni (Cesena).

LAZIO

Total *croccante* (crunchy nuts, toasted separately then dredged in bramble honey, then in *fior di latte* ice cream), *liquirizia* (Amarelli licorice), *cachi* (persimmon).

♥ **A NOTABLE ADRESS:** Fiordiluna (Rome).

CAMPANIA

Caffè (coffee), *amalfi* (Amalfi lemon and limoncello), *nocciola* (hazelnut).

♥ **A NOTABLE ADRESS:** Cerasella (Naples).

SKIP TO
ALMONDS, P. 173;
THE BRONTE PISTACHIO, P. 35;
LAND OF LEMONS, P. 352.

HOMEMADE PIZZA

TECNICA *Iconica*

It is possible to make a delicious pizza at home.
Here are the secrets to success.

ALESSANDRA PIERINI

THE RECIPE

This is a perfect pizza crust dough, soft and chewy at the same time. Alba Pezone, cook, founder of a cooking school, and creator of the original Neapolitan, shares her recipe with us. We have tested it and enthusiastically approve it! Allow a proofing time of 8 to 10 hours.

MAKES APPROXIMATELY 3 PIZZAS TO SHARE

4 cups (500 g) flour, type 00 (W260; or use a soft-wheat all-purpose flour) or T45 flour (or pastry flour)

¾ teaspoon (5 g) fresh baker's yeast

¾ to 1⅓ cups (300 to 320 g) water, at room temperature

⅔ to 2 teaspoons (10 to 12 g) fine salt

The Dough

❶ Place the flour and crumbled yeast on a work surface.

❷ ❸ Slowly trickle in three-fourths of the water.

❹ Knead quickly until a rough dough is obtained. Incorporate the salt in pinches, then drizzle in the remaining water.

❺ ❻ Knead for about 15 minutes (in a bowl or on the work surface), until you obtain a smooth, homogeneous, and elastic dough that detaches easily from the work surface or sides of the bowl.

❼ ❽ Shape into a ball and set aside in a bowl that can hold three times its volume.

❾ Cover with plastic wrap and proof for 4 hours at a temperature of around 64°F (18°C), protected from drafts.

☞ *Tip*

You can knead the dough in a stand mixer fitted with a dough hook. Start on setting 1 (the lowest speed), and as soon as you add all the water, increase the speed to setting 2.

1

2

3

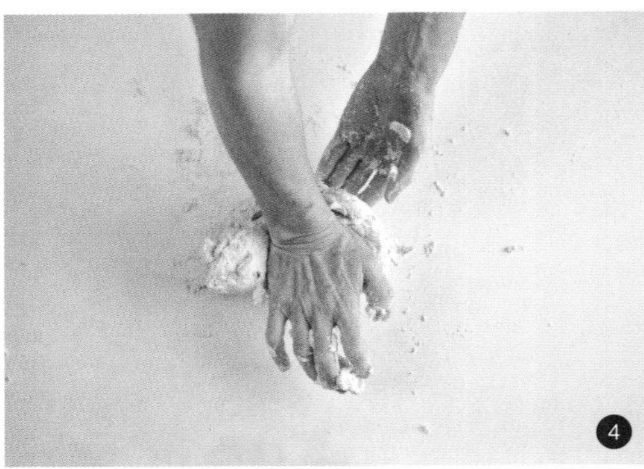
4

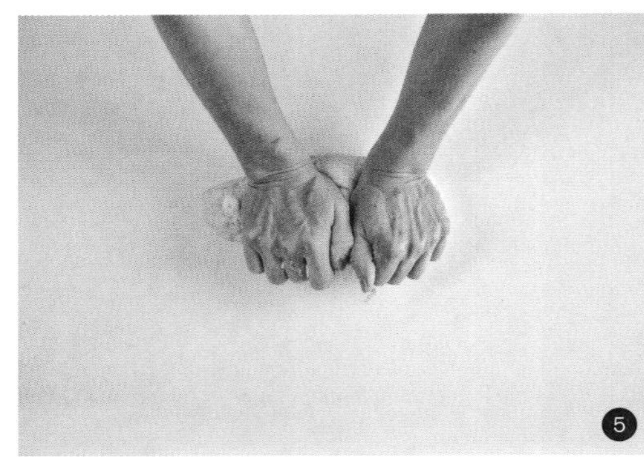
5

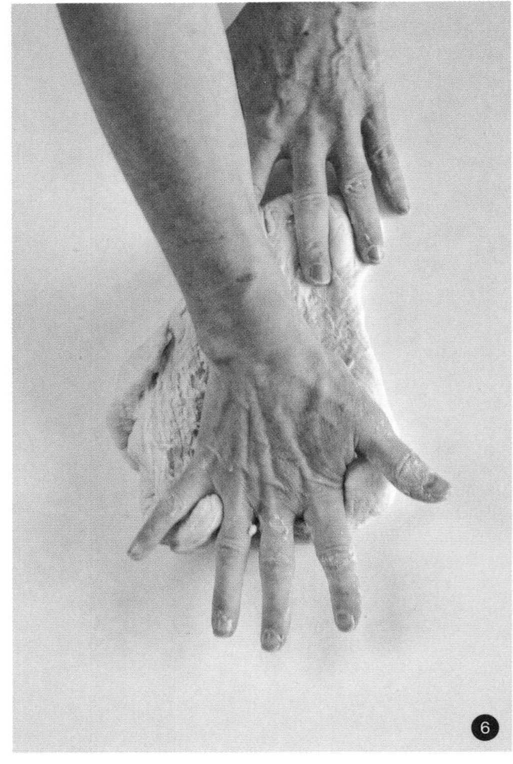
6

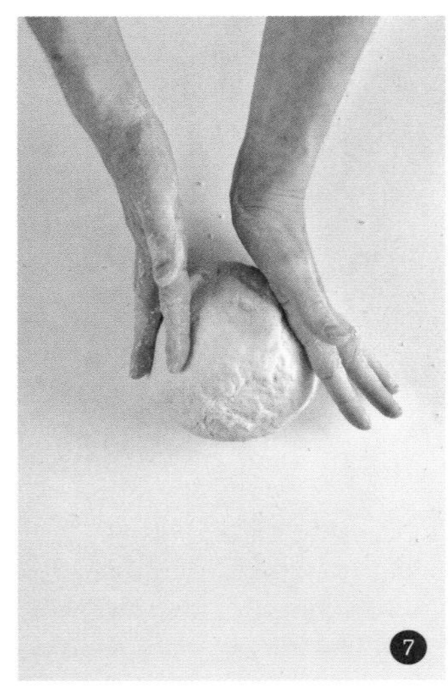
7

8

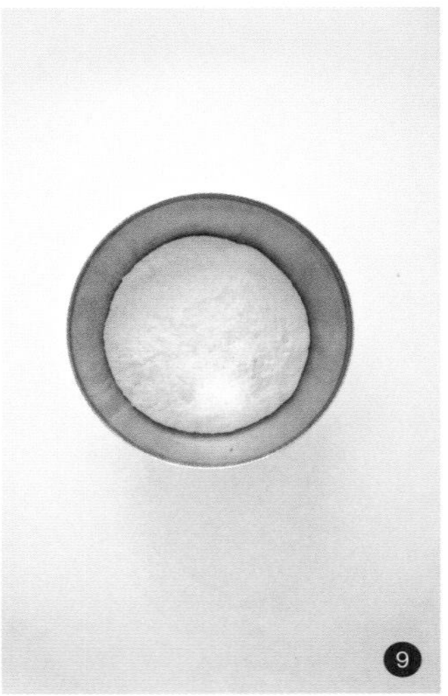
9

After 4 hours of proofing, the dough is ready.

⑩ Divide the dough into balls weighing 10 ounces (280 g) each. Place them on a rimmed baking sheet, spacing them out to make room for spreading. Cover the baking sheet with plastic wrap (without crushing the dough balls), and let rise for another 4 hours at a temperature of around 64°F (18°C), away from drafts.

⑪ ⑫ ⑬ Spread the dough out thinly by hand, then place it on an oiled metal baking sheet and spread on the toppings.

BAKING: Preheat the oven to 475°F (250°C) or the highest temperature your oven can reach. Bake the pizza for 12 to 15 minutes.

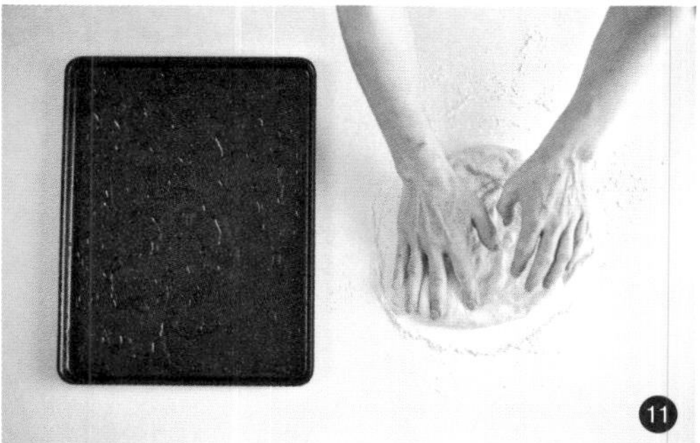

Three Classic Toppings

Now that you know all the secrets to a great pizza dough, you can start composing your pizzas. Here are three classic versions!

POMODORO E MOZZARELLA

— Tomato and mozzarella —

¼ cup (60 mL) tomato *passata*,
6 slices *fior di latte* mozzarella,
A good drizzle of olive oil,
A few basil leaves arranged on top, once baked.

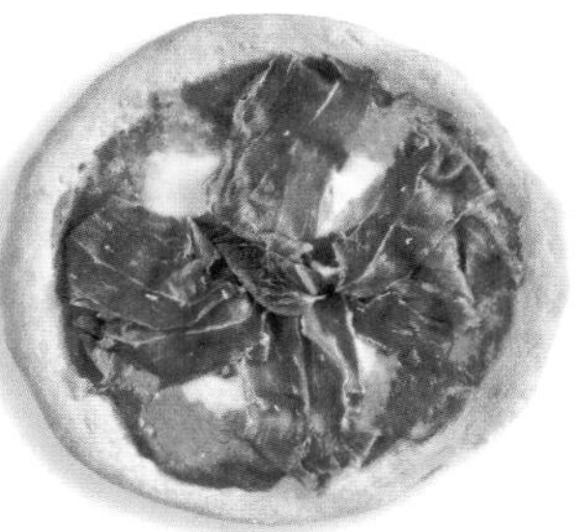

PROSCIUTTO CRUDO

— Prosciutto —

¼ cup (60 mL) tomato *passata*,
6 slices *mozzarella di bufala*,
4 thin slices prosciutto,
A good drizzle of olive oil,
A few basil leaves arranged on top, once baked.

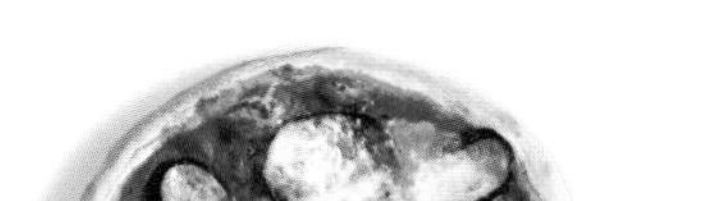

VEGETARIANA

— Vegetarian —

¼ cup (60 mL) tomato *passata*,
6 slices *fior di latte* mozzarella,
1 small zucchini, thinly sliced,
4 slices eggplant,
½ red bell pepper, sliced,
A good drizzle of olive oil,
A few basil leaves arranged on top, once baked.

SKIP TO
PIZZA AS POP ICON, P. 246;
THE MOZZARELLA FAMILY, P. 182;
HOMEMADE TOMATO SAUCE, P. 27.

PIZZE NAPO

THE CLASSICS

THE PIZZAIOLO

◆◆◆

Guillaume Grasso

◆◆◆

This French *pizzaiolo* from Naples who lives in Paris* has produced the five most authentic recipes in Naples and five more recent versions, according to the book published by the Associazione Verace Pizza Napoletana (True Neapolitan Pizza Association), whose certification colors he displays in his restaurant. His pizzas, once topped and seasoned, are placed in a wood-fired oven at 850°F (450°C)!

*GUILLAUME GRASSO, LA VERA PIZZA NAPOLETANA PARIS 15TH

MARGHERITA

Homage to Queen Margherita di Savoia (1851–1926) in the official colors of her country.

→ Peeled San Marzano tomatoes
→ Mozzarella
→ Grana Padano, Parmigiano-Reggiano, pecorino (optional)
→ Basil leaves (added once baked)
→ Extra-virgin olive oil

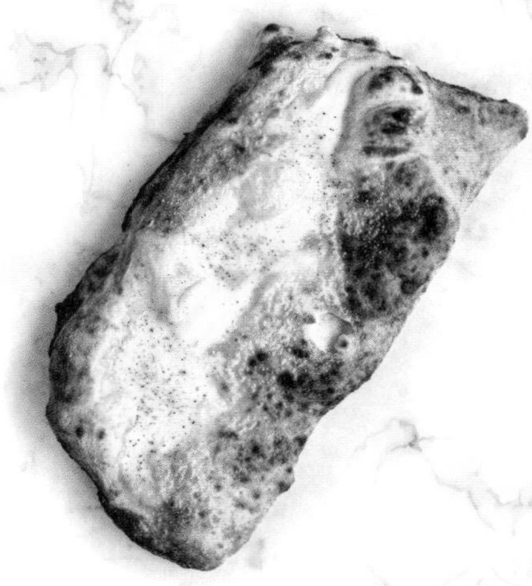

RIPIENO BIANCO

The "white filling" calzone, as one hears it called in Naples.

→ Pork cracklings
→ Neapolitan sausage
→ Ricotta

CAPRICCIOSA

According to mood: its ingredients vary depending on what's available.

→ Peeled San Marzano tomatoes
→ Garlic (optional)
→ *Fior di latte*
→ Slices of cooked ham
→ Mushrooms
→ Artichokes
→ Parmigiano-Reggiano
→ Extra-virgin olive oil
→ Basil leaves (added once baked)

MARINARA

This was comfort food for fishermen after a long day's work.

→ Peeled San Marzano tomatoes
→ Garlic
→ Oregano
→ Extra-virgin olive oil

MASTUNICOLA

The oldest of the *vasunicola* pizzas (from the colloquial term for basil, *vasunicola*).

→ Lard
→ Pecorino
→ Black pepper
→ Basil leaves (added once baked)

LETANE

From the original Margherita to the *quattro formaggi*, here is a display of ten traditional Neapolitan pizzas.

ANNA MARÉCHAL

THE MODERN TAKES

VEGETARIANA

A celebration of the vegetable garden.

→ Peeled San Marzano tomatoes
→ *Fior di latte*
→ Mushrooms
→ Artichokes
→ Grana Padano, pecorino, Parmigiano-Reggiano
→ Eggplant (added once baked)
→ Zucchini (added once baked)
→ Basil leaves (added once baked)

ACCIUGHE

Also called *Romana* because of the Roman passion for anchovies.

→ Peeled San Marzano tomatoes
→ Piennolo tomatoes from Vesuvius
→ Anchovies (added once baked)
→ Oregano
→ Garlic
→ Black olives (optional)

DIAVOLA

The "devil" is hiding in the sausage . . .

→ Peeled San Marzano tomatoes
→ Spicy sausage (Neapolitan salami or Calabrian *spianata*)
→ *Fior di latte*
→ Chile (optional)
→ Grana Padano, Parmigiano-Reggiano, pecorino
→ Basil leaves (added once baked)
→ Extra-virgin olive oil

QUATTRO FORMAGGI

Four variable main ingredients; the key is balance.

→ Ricotta
→ Gorgonzola
→ Smoked provola
→ Parmigiano-Reggiano, pecorino, Grana Padano
→ Extra-virgin olive oil

RUCOLA

Arugula takes center stage.

→ *Fior di latte*
→ *Mozzarella di bufala* (added once baked; optional)
→ Cherry tomatoes (added once baked)
→ Arugula (added once baked)
→ Parmigiano-Reggiano shavings (added once baked)

SKIP TO
HIS MAJESTY THE BASIL, P. 121;
TOMATOES, P. 28;
HOMEMADE PIZZA, P. 52.

. . . AND THE OTHERS

Some are large and thin and crisp, while others have plump *cornicioni* (crusts) . . . Let's explore the various regional styles of pizza.

ANTONIO PUZZI

The First Emigrant *Pizzaioli*

Tramonti is a small village of 4,000 inhabitants located between the mountains of the Amalfi Coast. This is where entrepreneur Luigi Giordano, nicknamed Gigino 'a casettara, set out to conquer Novara and Piedmont, where he created cheese dairies and pizzerias.

GENOA

According to legend, in the fifteenth century Admiral Andrea Doria was particularly fond of a "flat bread" topped with anchovies and onions: the *pissalandrea* or "Andrea's pizza." The Genoese called it *pissaladiera* then exported it to Nice under the name of *pissaladière*. But the name is more likely derived from *pissalat* ("salted fish," such as anchovies used as a topping).

THE PIZZA: thick, but it should not exceed ¾ inch (2 cm). Its edge is slightly crisp and its dough is soft. It is topped with desalted anchovies, tomato sauce, garlic, and sometimes black Taggiasca olives.

THE INSTITUTION: Zena Zuena, Via Cesarea, 78 (pizzaiolo Denis Pirrello).

TURIN

The first capital of Italy, it was the base for pizzaioli of the "Tramonti school," who invented the *pizza al padellino* (panfried pizza) there.

THE PIZZA: after it has risen and matured, the dough (sometimes with the addition of oil) is placed in an oiled pan about 8 inches (20 cm) in diameter. Once covered with peeled tomatoes then chilled, the pizza is topped with the other ingredients just before it's slid into the oven. It has a crunchy edge and a thick, soft bottom crust.

THE INSTITUTION: Cit Ma Bon, Corso Casale, 34 (pizzaiolo Savino Tavano).

ROME

At the end of the twentieth century, thanks to the work of many bakeries, pizza became diversified in Rome: it can be thin and crisp, thick and cooked in an ovenproof dish, round or square—in other words, multifaceted, just like Rome itself!

THE PIZZA: for the most locally authentic version, the dough proofs directly on the baking pan on which it bakes; the crust is open and crisp, seasoned only with olive oil and salt, and topped with charcuterie or a richer selection of toppings.

THE INSTITUTION: Pizzarium, Via della Meloria, 43 (pizzaiolo Gabriele Bonci).

PALERMO AND SYRACUSE

There are two iconic Sicilian pizzas.

THE PIZZAS: the *sfincione* from Palermo is thick, soft, and baked with a topping of tomato sauce, onions, cheese (usually *caciocavallo*), anchovies, and bread crumbs. In the neighboring town of Bagheria, it is served up *bianco*, without tomato. The Syracuse *pizzolo* is split and stuffed halfway through baking with a few slices of cheese so that the halves adhere. Then it is topped with oil, grated cheese, and thyme before being placed in the oven again.

THE INSTITUTION: Antico Forno Valenti, Via Francesco Aguglia, Bagheria (pizzaiolo Maurizio Valenti).

VENETO

Pizza culture did not spread to this "land of rice" until the beginning of the nineteenth century, when certain millers (thanks to the intuition of Giuseppe Vignato) prompted pizzaioli to conceive pizzas as delicacies.

THE PIZZA: the dough must rise for a long time, but its hydration level can vary, and the toppings are gourmet and innovative.

THE INSTITUTION: Saporè, Piazza del Popolo, 46, San Martino Buonalbergo (pizzaiolo Renato Bosco).

And Women?

The world of pizza making seems to be predominantly male. However, in Naples, following World Wars I and II, many widows placed large pots over the fire outside the *bassi* (typical ground-floor dwellings of the city) and made *pizza fritta*. We are indebted to them for returning women to pizza making.

Although now few in number, they still excel in the art of pizza making. Maria Cacialli in Naples (Campania), Petra Antolini in Verona (Veneto), Rosa Casulli in Putignano (Apulia), Roberta Esposito in Aversa (Campania), Francesca Gerbasio in Sala Consilina (Campania), and Federica Mignacca (who tours Italy with her "Montanarina Story" project) are among the most in-demand "ladies of pizza" in Italy.

Pizza al taglio

Pizza "by weight" can be round and thin, sold in *spicchi* (in quarters); thick and cooked in *teglia* (on a baking sheet), sold in squares or rectangles, crisp with an open honeycomb-like crust, as in Rome, or denser and soft such as in the north.

SKIP TO
PIZZA AS POP ICON, P. 246;
PIZZA FRITTA, P. 218;
PIZZA JOURNEYS, P. 196.

SEASON
TUTTO L'ANNO (YEAR-ROUND)

CATEGORY
SECONDO PIATTO (MAIN COURSE)

LEVEL
FACILE (EASY)

CONIGLIO ALLA LIGURE

LIGURIAN RABBIT

Facing the sea, Liguria offers a rich rural repertoire, like this delicious rabbit with wild herbs, Vermentino white wine, and Taggiasca olives common throughout the region.

ALESSANDRA PIERINI

THE RECIPE*

SERVES 4

- 1 sprig rosemary
- 6 sage leaves
- 4 bay leaves
- 2 sprigs marjoram
- 2 sprigs thyme
- ¼ cup plus 2 tablespoons (90 mL) olive oil
- 3 cloves garlic, crushed and peeled
- 1 rabbit, cut into pieces
- Scant ½ cup (100 mL) dry white wine
- Fine salt and freshly ground black pepper
- 25 Taggiasca olives in olive oil (or olives from Nice), pitted
- ¼ cup (30 g) pine nuts

Finely chop the herbs except the bay leaves.

Place the herbs in a casserole dish with the olive oil, garlic, and rabbit pieces. Cook over medium heat and stir.

Deglaze the dish with the white wine, season with salt and pepper, cover, and cook over low heat for 30 to 40 minutes, turning the pieces of rabbit from time to time for even cooking. Stir in a little water, if necessary, to prevent the meat from drying out.

Add the olives and pine nuts, and cook for another 10 minutes.

ALESSANDRA'S TIP

Add toasted and crushed pistachios to give the recipe some punch and crunch!

**Recipe taken from the book* La Pasta allegra, *by Sonia Ezgulian and Alessandra Pierini, Éditions de l'Epure, 2019.*

And with pasta?

This recipe can also include pasta, for example tagliatelle, pappardelle, *mafaldine*, etc., which would be served directly in the dish with the rabbit. Once the cooking is complete, just remove the bones, place the shredded meat back in the dish, cook the pasta al dente in a separate pan, and pour it straight into the sauce with the meat. Add a drizzle of olive oil and serve immediately.

FROM HATS TO CASSEROLE

Ligurian rabbit is a recipe of rural traditions originating in the Savona inlands where rabbits were farmed. Their fur was used to make hats, and the consumption of rabbit meat quickly spread throughout Liguria, according to this recipe, which has very few variations.

It has experienced a resurgence in popularity since 2013 thanks to the film *La grande bellezza*, by Paolo Sorrentino. In the scene where a dinner is given in honor of a nun, Cardinal Bellucci, questioned by his guests about spirituality, responds in a totally offbeat way, with recipe suggestions, one of which he details as follows:

"Twelve well-cooked [rabbit] pieces, thyme, bay leaf, rosemary, red wine, Taggiasche olives: this is Ligurian rabbit."

SKIP TO
OLIVES, P. 214; OREGANO, P. 340; SAGE, P. 257.

CARNIVAL & DELICACIES

Sugar and fat: this is what it's all about when celebrating Carnival in Italy. Here is a tour of Italy and its fried sweets.

MARTINA TUSCANO

An air of celebration . . .

Carnevale, or rather *Carne Levare* (to free oneself from meat), is the etymology of the word referring to the moment when one consumes rich fatty foods for the last time before Lent. This period is marked by excess with parties, galas, and costumes, permitting one to shed the burdens of socially acceptable behavior and established order.

AN ARRAY OF SWEETS!

Whether soft or crisp, soaked in honey, or dusted with confectioners' sugar, Carnival treats should be fried. It's about celebrating fat and abundance!

CHIACCHIERES ⑧ (lit. "gossips")
Thin and crispy beignets (a fritter) also called *bugie* ⑥ (Piedmont, Liguria), *crostoli* ③ (Friuli), *galani* ① (Veneto), *lattughe* (Mantua), *cenci* ④ (Tuscany), *cunchielli* (Molise), *guanti* (Naples) or *girelle* ⑤ if they are rolled into a snail shape, and *maraviglias* (Sardinia). Legend has it that Queen Margherita di Savoia (1851–1926), a great talker, asked her pastry chef for cakes to enjoy between bouts of gossiping, hence their name. Their French cousins are called *bugnes* (Lyon), *merveilles* (Bordeaux), and *oreillettes* (Provence) . . .

FRITTELLES
Small, round, chewy beignets (fritters), also called *brighelle* (Umbria), *fritole* (Venice), *caragnoli* (Molise), *castagnole* ⑨ (in many regions), *scroccafusi* (Marche), *tortelli* (Lombardy).

CIAMBELLES OR BASTONCINI
Beignets with holes in the center or elongated. They also go by *graffe* (Naples), *berlingozzi* (Tuscany), *zeppole* (Sardinia and Campania), *crispelle di riso* (Sicily). For *Carnival arancini* (Marche), the dough is rolled into a snail shape.

BEIGNETS are sometimes covered in honey, such as the *cicerchiata* (Abruzzo, Umbria, Calabria), *scorpelles* (Molise), *brignolus* (Sardinia), *struffoli* ② (Campania), or *pignolata* (Sicily and Calabria).

THE KINGDOM OF THE CARNIVAL

In Cocagne, the imaginary land of plenty, idleness, and self-serving pleasure, Renaissance literature depicts the King of Carnival. As Pieter Bruegel depicted in his painting in 1559, the king gladly fought his rival, Lent, a symbol of famine.

SKIP TO
NEAPOLITAN PASTRIES, P. 123; SWEET TREATS OF CHRISTMAS, P. 314.

THE EXCEPTIONS

Nonfried cakes are found, but more rarely:

~

In Campania

The *migliaccio*, made with ricotta and semolina, and the *sanguinaccio*, with chocolate and pig's blood.

In Apulia

Dita degli apostoli ("Apostles' fingers"), crêpes stuffed with ricotta and chocolate.

In Sardinia

Caschettas di Belvi ⑦, small delicacies made from hazelnuts, chestnut honey, and spices, once offered by husbands to their wives on wedding days.

RECIPE

CASTAGNOLES ⑨

MAKES APPROXIMATELY 50 CASTAGNOLES

2 cups (250 g) all-purpose flour, plus more to form the balls
1 teaspoon (4 g) baking powder
2 large (100 g) eggs
⅓ cup (60 g) granulated sugar
Zest of 1 unwaxed lemon
1 pinch salt
1 or 2 teaspoons Marsala or anise liqueur
3½ tablespoons (50 g) unsalted butter, cut into small cubes
Peanut oil, for frying
Confectioners' or superfine sugar, for coating

- Sift the flour and baking powder together on a work surface and form a wide well with high sides. Add the eggs, granulated sugar, lemon zest, and salt to the well.
- Combine the ingredients by hand, then add the Marsala and butter.
- Continue to mix until you have a very firm and homogeneous dough. Let rest for 30 minutes.
- Take pieces of dough of about ⅓ ounce (10 g) each and roll them in the palm of your hand, using a little flour, to obtain smooth balls.
- In a large, high-sided skillet, fry the *castagnoles* in hot peanut oil, until they turn a uniform golden color.
- Set aside to drain on paper towels, then roll them in confectioners' sugar until completely coated.
- Serve hot or cold.

Tips for good frying

The correct temperature for the frying oil is 350°F (175°C). To check the temperature, you have to drop a small piece of dough into the oil and watch how it reacts:

→ ***If it remains at the bottom:*** the correct temperature has not yet been reached.

→ ***If it barely rises to the surface:*** the oil has reached 350°F (175°C).

→ ***If it immediately turns brown:*** the oil has exceeded 375°F (190°C) and must therefore be allowed to cool a little.

APERITIVO

France has the *aperitif*, in Spain it's *tapas*, and in Italy it's the . . . *aperitivo*! It's for those long-awaited hours at the end of the day when you can finally lean against the bar or sit on the terrace while sipping a refreshing drink to enjoy with gourmet bites.

ILARIA BRUNETTI ET ANNA MARÉCHAL

APERITIVO

A bicchiere e via . . .

("One drink and I'm off . . .")

WHERE? At the local bar.

WHAT TO DRINK? A simple spritz, a draft beer, an unpretentious prosecco, or an alcohol-free aperitif.

WHAT SNACKS? Chips or olives.

WHAT'S THE ETIQUETTE? Lean on *al bancone* (at the bar) or sit at the table, but don't linger too long.

APERITIVO

Stappiamoci una buona bottiglia

("Let's uncork a good bottle")

WHERE? In a popular wine bar.

WHAT TO DRINK? From any beautiful bottle.

WHAT SNACKS? Charcuterie and cheese platters.

WHAT'S THE ETIQUETTE? Sit calmly composed in the company of friends who love good food.

APERITIVO

Glamour

WHERE? In a trendy lounge bar.

WHAT TO DRINK? A trendy cocktail.

WHAT SNACKS? Finger food, of course!

WHAT'S THE ETIQUETTE? Smartly dressed, of course!

APERITIVO

A generous abbuffata

(spread)

WHERE? In a popular bar in college towns.

WHAT TO DRINK? Plenty of spritz, Americano, Negroni, or wine.

WHAT SNACKS? A self-serve buffet.

WHAT'S THE ETIQUETTE? Try to look dignified while piling as much food as possible onto very small plates. It's an ideal approach for when money is a little tight.

INSTRUCTIONS

Today, the aperitivo is an important ritual in bars and cafés with friends or colleagues . . . and even at home! It usually takes place between 6:30 and 9 p.m. (even later in the south) and before dinner.

TO DRINK AND TO EAT

→ From the Latin *apertare* (to open), *aperitivo* is a warm, convivial, and popular time that is supposed to whet the appetite. Hippocrates, the fifth-century Greek physician, relieved his patients' hunger with bitter-tasting drinks. This technique, adopted by herbalists in modern times, is reflected in the tradition of bitters included in Italian cocktails.

→ In 1786 in Turin, Antonio Benedetto Carpano perfected vermouth, a bitter and invigorating recipe made from white wine, absinthe, and herbs. King Victor Emmanuel II crowned it the official aperitif of the court.

→ During the nineteenth century, the aperitivo culture from the north spread. Piedmontese wine producers Martini and Rossi created Martini Bianco (a vermouth made from moscato and aromatic herbs). Lombard Gaspare Campari made his own bitter liqueur from herbs and macerated fruits.

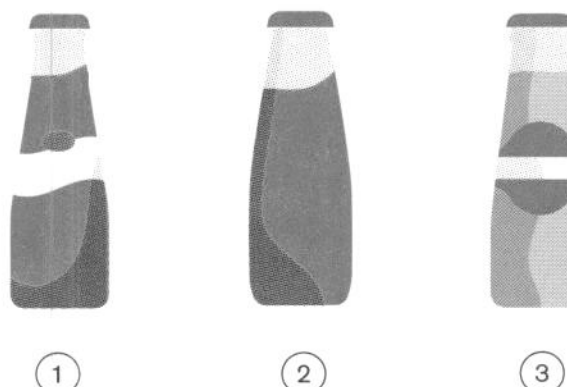

ALCOHOL-FREE BUT WITH FLAVOR!

These drinks, made slightly bitter to stimulate the appetite and served in single-dose bottles, make an alcohol-free aperitivo sparkling and cheerful.

① **GINGERINO (RECOARO)**
Orange-red, typical of the northeast, made with citrus extract, herbs, and spices.

② **SANBITTER (SANPELLEGRINO)**
Made with spices and herbs. *Rosso*, the original, is an intense red color, while *bianco* is clear, with a more delicate flavor.

③ **CRODINO (CAMPARI)**
Nicknamed the *analcolico biondo* (alcohol-free blond), amber yellow, made with lots of spices and matured in oak barrels.

AN APERITIVO FOR EVERY APPETITE

SIMPLE: with each drink, you are provided free snacks (*taralli*, olives, small canapés, focaccia, house-made fried foods, etc.).

ELABORATE: an all-you-can-eat buffet! Born in Milan and especially popular throughout the north, this version provides prepared dishes (salads, bruschetta, pasta, meatballs, etc.) to replace dinner. There are foods to suit all tastes and all budgets (access to the buffet is included in the price or sometimes with a small additional charge), from broke students to trendy Milanese. It is called *apericena* (the dinner aperitif) in Milan.

SKIP TO
AMARO, P. 210; SPRITZ, P. 94; COCKTAILS, P. 190.

THE CULTIVATION OF RICE

Wheat and rice are Italy's two staples. Pasta and risotto have already conquered the world, but many other gourmand variations using the little grains of rice wait to be discovered.

ANNA PRANDONI

THE CHRONICLE OF A CONQUEST

Rice is a plant native to parts of Southeast Asia, the earliest traces of which date back 5,000 to 6,000 years. Even today, around 92 percent of the world's production of rice is in Asia.

FIRST CENTURY BCE
Arrival of rice in the West; used as medicine.

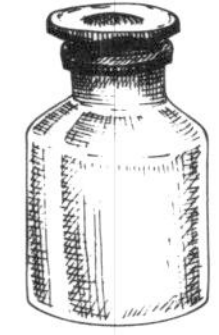

MIDDLE AGES
Rice makes its appearance in cooking, probably introduced by the Arabs in Sicily or by the Aragonese rulers in Naples.

1340
In an edict, Milan tax collectors are ordered to impose high taxes on "spices that come from Asia, via Greece" (including rice, then considered a spice).

1475
Gian Galeazzo Sforza, duke of Milan and a great supporter of rice being grown on his lands, sends a bag of rice to the dukes d'Este of Ferrara to spread its cultivation.

SIXTEENTH CENTURY
In some regions of Italy, rice fields that occupy 12,300 acres (5,000 ha) during the fifteenth century expand to 123,500 acres (50,000 ha) in the sixteenth century.

SEVENTEENTH CENTURY
In Lombardy, rice becomes an essential ingredient. From the Po plain, rice cultivation has spread to Emilia-Romagna and Tuscany although its yield is not the same due to lack of water.

Growth Cycles

FALL—PRESEEDING
The soils are prepared for spring with "false" seeding so weeds can grow and be destroyed.

SPRING—SEEDING
Between March and April, seeding and fertilization begin.

SUMMER—IRRIGATION AND FERTILIZATION
In mid-June, the rice is 6 to 8 inches (15 to 20 cm) high; irrigation and fertilization begin, in rotation. Before August 10, a preventive fungicidal treatment is applied.

FROM HARVEST TO STORAGE

The harvest (September and October), performed with machines, is followed by sifting and drying. Starting from 21 percent moisture, the rice reduces to 12 percent, ferments, and increases back to 14 percent for commercial sale.

THE STAGES OF PRODUCTION

At this point, the rice is ready to be processed. To do this, it undergoes several steps:

THRESHING: the rice is subjected to a first cleaning to go from a raw state to a semiprocessed state.

HUSKING: this step consists of removing the husk from the rice grains. This results also in brown rice.

BLEACHING: this is the last step necessary to obtain white rice.

PACKAGING

RICE IN COOKING

FRYING

Arancini (Sicily): round or elongated rice balls filled, breaded, and fried.

Supplì (Lazio): rice croquettes stuffed with mozzarella, fried, and topped with ragù.

SOUPS AND MAIN DISHES

Minestra di riso e rape (Aosta Valley): soup made with rice, turnips, and milk.

Risi e bisi (Veneto): thick soup of rice and peas flavored with parsley and Grana Padano.

Tiella di riso cozze e patate (Apulia): rice, mussels, and potatoes layered in a gratin dish and baked.

Paella algherese (Sardinia): a dish of Spanish origin, rich in chicken, spicy salami, vegetables, and seafood.

Riso e prezzemolo (Lombardy): a very basic soup, made from rice in broth flavored with parsley.

Riso e latte salato (Lombardy): rice cooked in milk and enriched with grated Grana Padano.

Riso in cagnone (Lombardy): rice boiled and seasoned with butter, sage, garlic, and Grana Padano.

Bomba di riso (Emilia-Romagna): rice timbale stuffed with pigeon.

Sartù (Campania): rice timbale seasoned with meat sauce, chicken livers, and enriched with meatballs, hard-boiled eggs, peas, and mozzarella.

Paniscia (Piedmont): rice with beans, cabbage, sausage, and pork.

RISOTTOS

All'isolana (Veneto): with a mixture of various meats, flavored with cinnamon.

Col tastasal (Veneto): with sausage meat.

Con i bruscandoli (Veneto): with hints of hops.

Alla padovana (Veneto): with sausages, poultry offal, chicken meat, pork, turkey, marrow, and peas.

Alla milanese (Lombardy): with saffron and marrow.

Alla certosina (Lombardy): "*à la chartreuse,*" with crayfish, perch, peas, and mushrooms.

Alla monzese (Lombardy): with red wine and sausages

Alla pilota (Lombardy): with *salamelle*, fresh sausages typical of Mantua.

Al Barolo (Piedmont): moistened with Barolo, a red wine.

DESSERTS

Bostrengo (Marche): a thick tart made with cereals, dried fruits, nuts, and raisins.

Torta di riso or torta degli addobbi (Emilia-Romagna): a rice cake enriched with almonds and candied fruit.

Riso in prigione ("imprisoned" rice) or ***riso e latte dolce*** (sweet rice pudding) (Emilia-Romagna, Piedmont, Lombardy . . .): a very simple dessert made from rice cooked in milk, to be eaten with a spoon.

①

③

⑤

②

④

⑥

RECIPE

TORTA DI RISO DOZE

Daniela Vettori, passionate about the history of Ligurian cuisine, shares the secrets of this rice cake typical of villages near La Spezia, traditionally baked in a copper dish in a wood-fired oven.

SERVES 8 TO 10

½ cup (120 g) round or originario rice

5¼ cups (1.25 L) whole milk

2 medium unwaxed lemons

7 large (350 g) fresh eggs

1 cup plus 2 tablespoons packed (250 g) brown sugar

2 tablespoons (30 mL) liqueur (orange, anise, limoncello . . .)

Cook the rice al dente in 1 cup (250 mL) of the milk with the entire zest of 1 lemon (this will be strained out later). Preheat the oven to 300°F (150°C). In a bowl, beat the eggs with the brown sugar. Add the remaining 4¼ cups (1 L) milk and combine with the cooked rice, the grated zest of the second lemon, and the liqueur. This mixture will be very liquid. Pour everything into a ovenproof dish and spread out the rice on the bottom using a wooden spoon. Bake for about 1 hour. You can sprinkle the cake with brown sugar and caramelize the top under the broiler for a few minutes at the end of the cooking time.

COMUNE—Standard ①

MOST COMMON—*originario.*

SHAPE—small round grains.

COOKING TIME—12 to 13 minutes.

USES—unblended soups with dried beans (during cooking, it tends to release starch), desserts.

OTHER TYPES—Balilla, Pierot, Razza 253, Cripto, and Americano 1600.

SUPERFINO—Superfine

MOST COMMON—*arborio* ② and *carnaroli* ③.

SHAPE—large grains, long or very long.

COOKING TIME—16 to 18 minutes.

USES—risottos: it releases very little starch during cooking, which is why it is recommended for preparations in which the grains must remain well separated.

OTHER TYPES—Roma, Argo, and Baldo.

SEMIFINO—Semifine ④

THE MOST COMMON—*Vialone nano.*

SHAPE—long, narrow grains.

COOKING TIME—14 to 16 minutes.

USES—risottos and minestrone.

OTHER TYPES—Rosa Marchetti, Maratelli, Italico Padano, and Lido.

FINO—Fine ⑤

THE MOST COMMON—*S. Andrea.*

SHAPE—round grains of medium length, or semilong.

COOKING TIME—13 to 15 minutes.

USES—hors d'oeuvre, white rice, timbale, pilaf.

OTHER TYPES—Rinaldo Bersani (Ribe), Razza 77, Europa, and Ringo.

RISO VENERE ⑥

This black rice originates in the region of Vercelli (Piedmont), but its ancestors were from China. It was created in 1997 by the research center of the Sapise Seed Cooperative (Sardo Piemontese Sementi), which crossed two varietals: a very hardy local white rice and an Asian black rice. This rice, which bears the Italian name of Venus, the goddess of love (it was considered a powerful aphrodisiac in China), has a round purplish black grain and is very aromatic. Its pronounced scent is reminiscent of fresh bread with a delicately nutty taste. Eaten cooked in water or in a pilaf, this rice has a very good firmness and remains firm and chewy, making it ideal in salads and a perfect accompaniment to fish, shellfish, white meats, or vegetables. Allow 40 to 50 minutes of cooking time.

SKIP TO

RISOTTO, P. 78; SUPPLÌ VS. ARANCINI, P. 362; RISI E BISI, P. 207; RISOTTO ALLA MILANESE, P. 290.

Carlo Petrini

PROFILE

HIS PHILOSOPHY

A great thinker and unifier, Carlo Petrini defended the dignity and legitimacy of food science. According to him, gastronomy is culture, and the pleasure associated with it is freedom. Thanks to the rediscovery of taste and in praise of slowness—symbolized by the snail—Carlo Petrini and Slow Food have redefined relationships between food and agriculture and gastronomy and agronomy, while taking definitive and local actions anchored in the modern day. In other words, to support both natural biodiversity and the cultural diversity of mankind.

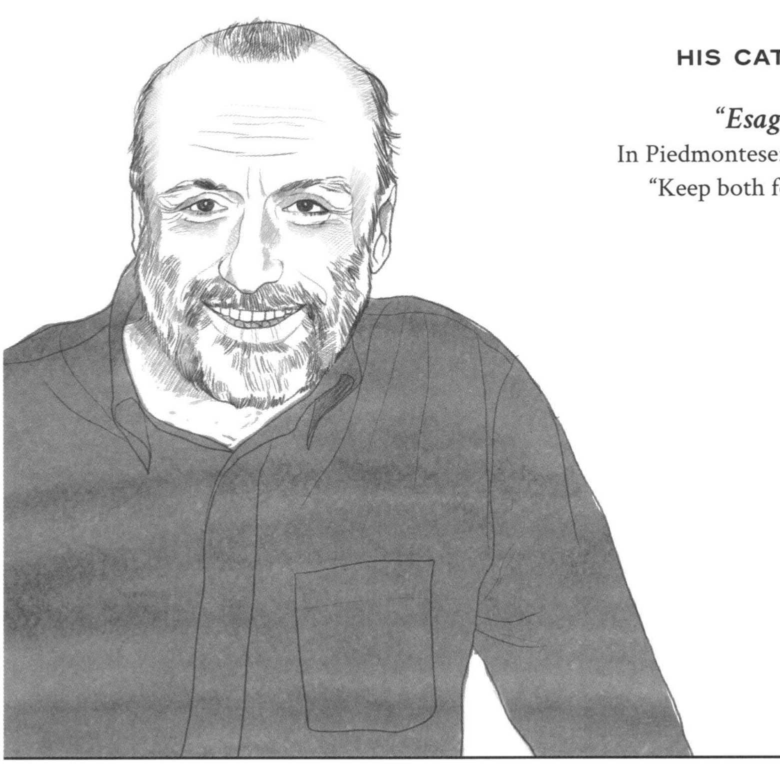

A native of Piedmont and a journalist by training, the founder of Slow Food is an endless defender of biodiversity and the concept of eating well.

ANNA MARÉCHAL

HIS CATCH PHRASE

"Esageròma nen"
In Piedmontese: "Don't exaggerate" or "Keep both feet on the ground."

HIS FAVORITE DISHES

BAGNA CAUDA
(garlic and anchovy dip)
A Piedmontese dish made with garlic, olive oil, vegetables, and anchovies.

THE CLASSIC *PASTA AL POMODORO*
Pasta in tomato sauce.

ONION SOUP,
which he enjoys on each trip to Paris at Au Pied de Cochon, a restaurant in Les Halles, open 24 hours.

HIS MISSIONS

→ Make food an anthropological, philosophical, and political concern, international in scope.

→ Protect, save, and promote local products and varietals that are rare or lost, thanks to the Slow Food safeguards and the Ark of Taste. "An eloquent concept: The ark is the boat on which Noah saved the animal species. We want do the same for foods: protect agriculture from extinction." —*Gazzetta d'Alba*, 2007

IN THE FOOTSTEPS OF BRILLAT-SAVARIN

The creation of Slow Food was inspired by Jean-Anthelme Brillat-Savarin. Petrini's favorite quote by Brillat-Savarin is: "*The pleasures of the table belong to all ages, to all conditions, to all countries, and to every day; they can be associated with all the other pleasures and remain the last to console us for the loss of the rest.*"

The Slow Food Manifesto was signed in Paris by a group of *oenogastronomes* near the theater from the Opéra-Comique, 160 yards (150 m) from the building where Brillat-Savarin, the author of the *Physiology of Taste*, lived.

HIS BIOGRAPHY IN 5 DATES

1949
Born in Bra (Piedmont).

1986
McDonald's is set to open a location at the Spanish Steps in Rome. This becomes a scandal and the birth of the Slow Food movement.

1987
Participates in the creation of *Gambero Rosso*, a supplement of the newspaper *Il Manifesto*. He acts as wine critic and writes the first guide *Vini d'Italia*.

1989
Signing of the Slow Food Manifesto promoting food that is good, clean, and fair.

2004
Creation of the International University of Gastronomic Sciences in Pollenzo and the Terra Madre association, a global community of members committed to better nutrition.

INTERNATIONAL RECOGNITION

→ The British newspaper the *Guardian* classifies him in 2008 among the "50 personalities who can save the planet."

→ In 2013, he receives the highest environmental award by the United Nations, the Champions of the Earth program, in the "inspiration and action" category.

→ He publishes, in 2014 in Italy, *Deux idées de bonheur* (*Two Ideas of Happiness*) with the Chilean writer Luis Sepúlveda, discourse and digressions concerning gastronomy in which they discuss current affairs, literature, and politics as well their idea of happiness.

Carlo Petrini (second from left) at the First International Slow Food Congress in Venice, from November 29 to December 2, 1990.

SKIP TO
BAGNA CAUDA, P. 119;
SPAGHETTI AL POMODORO, P. 289.

Slow Food®

This Italian movement, which has spread globally, is committed to defending biodiversity at the local level as well as virtuous agricultural practices and, above all, good food for everyone.

CARLO DE PASCALE

THE SLOW FOOD ECOSYSTEM

HEADQUARTERS: Bra (Piedmont), birthplace of Carlo Petrini.

A UNIVERSITY: UNISG (Università di Scienze Gastronomiche), opened in 2004 in Pollenzo (Piedmont). A second campus is located in Colorno (Emilia-Romagna).

A PUBLISHING HOUSE: Slow Food Editore, which publishes the magazines of the association as well as gastronomic and tourism books.

TRADE FAIRS: Salone del Gusto, Slow Fish, Slow Meat, Slow Cheese, Slow Wine, Slow Beer . . . the year is punctuated by demonstrations and gatherings for the promotion of good food.

A WORLDWIDE MOVEMENT BORN IN ITALY

Slow Food is an NGO (nongovernmental organization) created in 1986 by Carlo Petrini, Italian sociologist and journalist, in reaction to the planned opening of a McDonald's at the Spanish Steps in Rome. Emanating from a left-wing cultural and gourmand perspective, Slow Food became international in 1989 with the ambition of constituting "a movement for the rights for all to enjoy the pleasures of the table" in reaction to the frenetic fast-paced lifestyle. The first manifesto was signed at the Opéra-Comique in Paris. From its beginning, Slow Food has aimed to bring about a new gastronomy where social and environmental sustainability are essential. "Slow," represented by a snail logo, represents a positive and constructive attitude aimed at taking the time to save, produce, savor, and, above all, to live.

A LITTLE SLOW-FOODIAN DICTIONARY

BUONO, PULITO E GIUSTO
"GOOD, CLEAN, AND FAIR"
This has been the Slow Food slogan from the beginning:
→ *Buono,* "good," because everything begins with taste.
→ *Pulito,* "clean," because Slow Food cannot conceive that what is good is not sustainable.
→ *Giusto,* "fair," because respect of the environment is nothing without social justice.

—

FONDAZIONE SLOW FOOD PER LA BIODIVERSITÀ ONLUS
SLOW FOOD FOUNDATION FOR BIODIVERSITY
Born in Florence in 2003, the foundation is the organization that coordinates other projects and institutions of the NGO Slow Food such as the Ark of Taste, Sentinels, and the Alliance of Chefs.

TERRA MADRE
Created in 2004, this foundation is a network of producers, chefs, and academics aiming to make possible "Good, clean, and fair" food at the local level. This network is also the origin of a worldwide meeting that takes place every two years, the Salone del Gusto, which attracts hundreds of thousands of visitors to Turin.

—

ALLEANZA SLOW FOOD DEI CUOCHI
THE ALLIANCE OF CHEFS
More than 1,100 chefs across the world who support small local producers and who use in their kitchens the products of the *presidi* and the Ark of Taste.

PRESIDI
THE SENTINELS OF TASTE
The *presidi* designate structures that support small traditional productions and promote the terroirs, the trades, and the know-how. They also support safeguarding indigenous races and varietals of foods. It is a key and standout element of Slow Food.

—

ARCA DEL GUSTO
THE ARK OF TASTE
The Ark of Taste is a participatory global catalog of forgotten agricultural products to draw attention to them and help protect them. Both a record of biodiversity and gustatory richness, the Ark serves as a base of reference to the *presidi.*

—

CONVIVIUM
Slow Food chapters, the Convivium is a group of members who act at the local level as local chapters. The Convivium contributes to different actions and organizes activities around eating well.

SLOW FOOD IN NUMBERS (2020)

· 100,000 ·	· 585 ·	· 5,175 ·	· 220,000 ·	· 1,147 ·	· 160 ·
MEMBERS	SENTINELS	PRODUCTS IN THE ARK OF TASTE	VISITORS TO SALONE DEL GUSTO IN 2018	CHEF MEMBERS OF THE ALLIANCE	COUNTRIES IN THE MOVEMENT

4 OUTSTANDING *PRESIDI*

Asiago Stravecchio DOP
VENETO
Semicooked hard cheese benefiting from a PDO since 1978. A group of producers wanted go further by saving alpine Asiago, which allows a long, even very long ripening and makes it one of the world's exceptional cheeses.

Pesca nel sacchetto
SICILY
"Peaches in the bag!" Every year in June in Leonforte, peach farmers wrap peaches still on trees in tissue paper. The fruits ripen slowly, sheltered from wind and parasites, sometimes through November, and develop intense aromas.

Fagiolo rosso di Lucca
TUSCANY
The red bean from Lucca, which is found in *primi* soups, *pasta e fagioli,* and an accompaniment for a *secondo piatto.* This bean, similar to *borlotto,* is tastier and more tender. It nearly disappeared before the pleasure of eating traditional legume-based dishes was rediscovered in the *osteries* (pubs).

Mortadella classica
EMILIA-ROMAGNA
This is a great example of the value added by Slow Food. *Mortadella classica* has a specification much more demanding than PGI. Less pink, to the point of being almost gray, less conspicuously scented, its difference stands out when tasted, revealing a rare and exceptional food. It is an artisanal product, even for Bologna; it is the last of such products.

SKIP TO
MORTADELLA, P. 160; FISHING HUTS, P. 303; LEGUMES, P. 150.

·CAFFÈ·AL·BAR·

MARIELLE GAUDRY

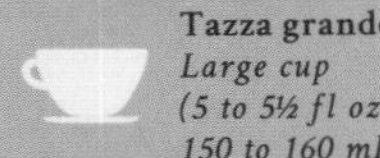

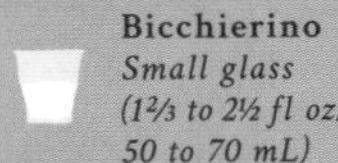
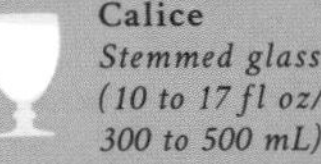

Tazzina	Tazza grande	Bicchiere alto	Bicchierino	Piccolo bicchiere	Bicchiere da martini	Calice
Small cup	*Large cup*	*Tall glass*	*Small glass*	*Small round glass*	*Martini glass*	*Stemmed glass*
(1⅔ to 2½ fl oz/ 50 to 70 mL)	*(5 to 5½ fl oz/ 150 to 160 mL)*	*(5 to 5½ fl oz/ 150 to 160 mL)*	*(1⅔ to 2½ fl oz/ 50 to 70 mL)*	*(6¾ fl oz/ 200 mL)*	*(8½ fl oz/ 250 mL)*	*(10 to 17 fl oz/ 300 to 500 mL)*

· NATIONAL ·

CAFFÈ
5 teaspoons (25 mL) of espresso coffee
The standard Italian coffee

CORTO/RISTRETTO
A short espresso (<5 teaspoons/25 mL)

LUNGO
A long espresso (>5 teaspoons/25 mL)

DOPPIO
Double espresso (2 × 5 teaspoons/25 mL)

MACCHIATO
1 espresso + 1 dash of *caldo* (with hot milk) or *freddo* (with cold milk) milk foam

CAPPUCCINO
1 espresso + roughly ½ cup (125 to 135 mL) of whipped milk and milk foam + optional cocoa powder

CAFFELLATTE
1 espresso + roughly ½ cup (125 to 135 mL) of milk

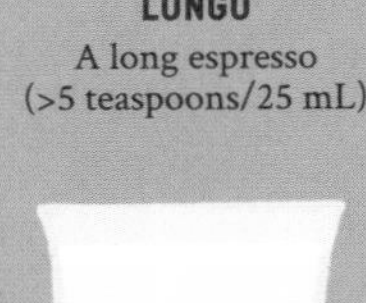

LATTE MACCHIATO
1 espresso + 9 tablespoons (130 mL) hot milk with milk foam

MOCACCINO
3½ ounces (100 g) dark chocolate + 1 espresso + just over ¾ cup (200 mL) of milk + cocoa powder

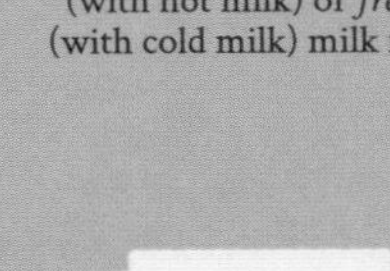

SCHIUMATO
1 espresso + scant ¼ cup (50 mL) of milk foam applied with a spoon

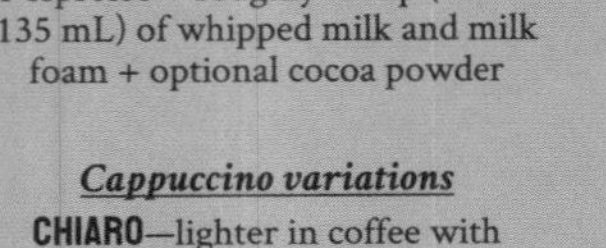

Cappuccino variations

CHIARO—lighter in coffee with a little more milk
SCURO—stronger in coffee and less milk
AL VETRO—served in a glass
DECAFFEINATO—made with decaffeinated coffee
SECCO—without milk, only milk foam
SENZA SCHIUMA—without foam

MAROCCHINO
1 espresso + 5 teaspoons (25 mL) of milk foam + cocoa powder

SHAKERATO
Double espresso + 3 ice cubes + 1 teaspoon (4 g) sugar, shaken

CORRETTO
1 espresso + ½ teaspoon (3 mL) of liqueur (grappa, anise . . .)

CAFFÈ CON PANNA
1 espresso + 2 tablespoons (30 mL) fresh whipped cream

COFFEE FREDDO
1 espresso prepared in advance and stored in the refrigerator

CAFFÈ AL GINSENG
1 espresso + 1 teaspoon (5 g) ginseng extract + ⅔ teaspoon (4 g) sugar + 1 teaspoon (5 mL) vegetable-based drink

ESPRESSO AMERICANO
Double espresso + 2 tablespoons (30 mL) hot water

ESPRESSINO
1 espresso + scant ¼ cup (50 mL) whipped milk + cocoa powder

CAFFÈ D'ORZO
2 tablespoons (30 mL) soluble barley (an alternative to caffeine)

· REGIONAL ·

Turin
BICERIN
Just over ¾ cup (200 mL) coffee + scant ¼ cup (50 mL) heavy cream + 2 tablespoons (30 mL) milk + 7 ounces (200 g) chocolate + 2 teaspoons (4 g) sugar

Rome
CAFFÈ COMPLETO
1 espresso + 1½ ounces (40 g) chocolate + ¼ cup (60 mL) sweetened whipped cream (¼ cup/50 g sugar) + cocoa powder

Salento, Apulia
CAFFÈ IN GHIACCIO
1 espresso + 2 ice cubes
Variation:
CON LATTE DI MANDORLE
+ 2 teaspoons (10 mL) almond milk

Campania
CAFFÈ ALLA NOCCIOLA NAPOLETANA
1 espresso + 3½ ounces (100 g) hazelnut cream (1½ ounces/40 g roasted hazelnuts + 4 teaspoons/20 mL cream) + 6 tablespoons (40 g) confectioners' sugar

Calabria
CAFFÈ CALABRESE
1 espresso + 1 teaspoon (5 mL) cognac + 1 piece licorice + 1 teaspoon (4 g) cane sugar

Marche
MORETTA DI FANO
1 espresso + 2 teaspoons (10 mL) brandy + 4 teaspoons (20 mL) anise liqueur + 2 teaspoons (10 mL) rum + 2 teaspoons (8 g) cane sugar + lemon zest

Veneto
CAFFÈ PADOVANO OU CAFFÈ PEDROCCHI
(named after this historic café in Padua)
1 espresso + scant ¼ cup (50 mL) mint whipped cream (¼ cup plus 2 teaspoons/70 mL cream, 4 teaspoons/20 mL whole milk, 4 teaspoons/20 mL mint syrup) + cocoa powder

Tuscany
PONCE ALLA LIVORNESE
1 ristretto + 4 teaspoons (20 mL) rum + 2 teaspoons sugar (8 g) + lemon zest

***Decaffeinato:** this is an espresso without caffeine, but all coffees can be ordered decaffeinated, according to taste.*

BREAKFAST

More than any other meal, *prima colazione* embodies Italian identity.

MARTINA LIVERANI

It's called *colazione*

Colazione comes from *collatio*, which meant "meeting" in late Latin and originally referred to the meal monks ate after the last evening service. Today, the colazione is a private time. Whether enjoyed at home or in a café, standing or sitting, Italians enjoy this meal as a moment of solitude. *Prima* (first) refers to the first meal of the day. This term can also (rarely) be used to refer to lunch.

Italiano vero?

The colazione is, in general, a sweet, quick meal that often includes a coffee or cappuccino and a croissant. Ironically, none are of Italian origin. But what about coffee? This is Italy's most famous immigrant! The croissant? It was invented in Vienna after an after-dark attack by the Ottomans: the town bakers, the only people awake at the time of the attack, were able to sound the alarm, which helped drive back the invaders. To celebrate this achievement, the *kipferl*, ancestor of all croissants, including the Italian *cornetto*, was created.

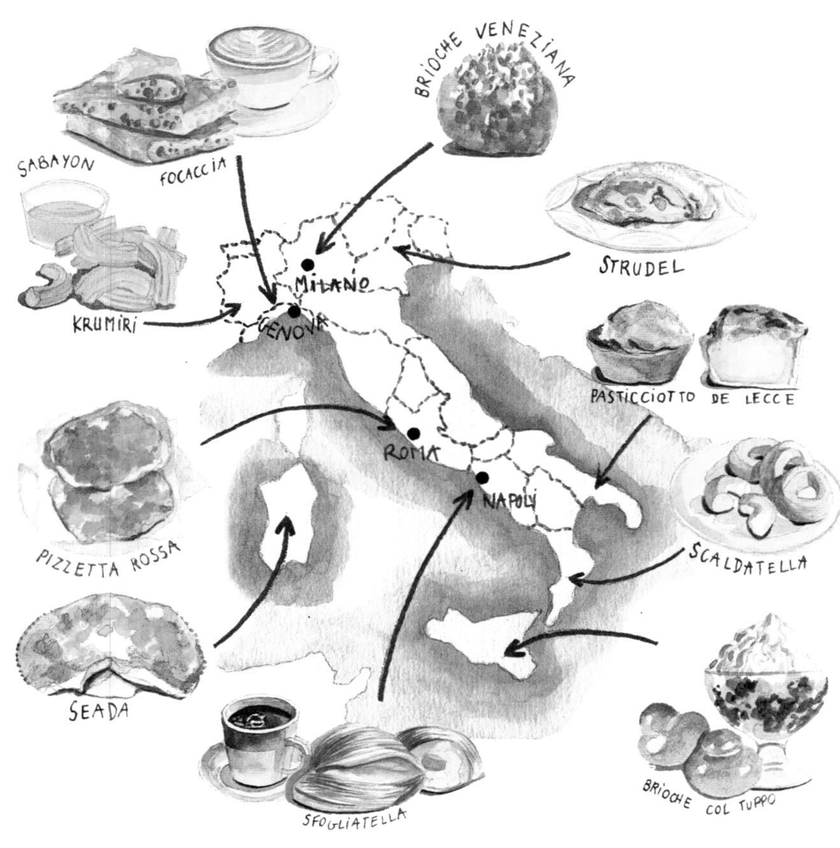

A TOUR OF ITALY BY BREAKFAST

Certain regional breakfast specialties still exist, however. They can seem almost exotic (albeit tasty) in the face of the undisputed domination of coffee and croissants.

IN GENOA
Focaccia dipped in a latte.

IN NAPLES
Coffee with *sfogliatelle*, a kind of puff pastry shell filled with cream or ricotta.

IN SICILY
A breakfast with brioches, say *col tuppo* (with a bun) and a granita.

IN THE DOLOMITES
The day begins with strudel.

IN PIEDMONT
Enjoy a *zabaione* and *krumiri* cookies.

IN SARDINIA
One eats *seadas*, fried ravioli with pecorino and honey.

IN MILAN
Coffee is served with a brioche referred to as *veneziana* (covered with coarse sugar and/or almond glaze).

IN ROME
The morning starts with a coffee and a *maritozzo* (a small pastry filled with whipped cream) or, for those who prefer a savory flavor, a tomato *pizzetta*.

IN HOMES IN CALABRIA
Scaldatelle (or *scaddateddi*), salted and flavored with cumin, which evoke pretzels, are enjoyed.

IN SALENTO
The *pasticciotto de Lecce*, a flaky pastry filled with pastry cream, is the popular choice.

• A RECENT RITUAL •

As Alessandro Marzo Magno recounts in his book *Il genio del gusto* (2014), breakfast is a modern practice:

"Cappuccino, which serves as the centerpiece of many Italian breakfasts, was born from the bar coffee machine using espresso. . . . Before these machines came into existence at the start of the twentieth century, an Italian cappuccino with a foamy top wasn't possible; at best one had to enjoy a latte."

SUGAR COMES TO THE TABLE

During the Great War, Italians unwittingly adopted a sweet breakfast for the first time, as soldiers were given morning rations that included chocolate, cookies, coffee, and milk. But until the 1950s, breakfast was a rather salty and savory meal, made up of leftovers from the day before (bread, cheese, eggs, and various other items). Sweet foods were a luxury reserved for special occasions until the 1960s, when the boom in the economy brought cookies, spreads (Nutella was created in 1964), commercially produced yogurts and jams, and instant cereals and cocoa into homes.

AN INDUSTRIAL COLAZIONE?

The pastry industry has also contributed to the standardization of breakfast. The company Tre Marie in Milan invented the first line of frozen croissants in the 1980s, which became the standard products in Italian bars all over the country. From there emerged the idea, then the custom, of accompanying one's espresso or cappuccino with a hot and fragrant croissant. At home, the dominance of Mulino Bianco (the Barilla Group's breakfast and snacks brand) has taken hold with a series of unforgettable ads depicting an ideal family gathered for breakfast around commercially produced cookies and pastries (hence the expression *famiglia del Mulino Bianco*, "a Mulino Bianco family," to describe domestic, yet artificial, bliss.

SKIP TO
CORNETTO, P. 350; STRUDEL, P. 379; ZABAIONE, P. 203; COOKIES, P. 154.

SEASON
TUTTO L'ANNO (YEAR-ROUND)

CATEGORY
DOLCE (DESSERT)

LEVEL
DIFFICOLTÀ MEDIA (MEDIUM DIFFICULTY)

CROSTATA ALLA CONFETTURA

FRUIT TART

A rustic dessert popular among the oldest Italian pastry shops, this lattice tart is a family classic, enjoyed for breakfast or afternoon tea.

MARIELLE GAUDRY

A LATTICED TART

→ Modern culinary encyclopedias and dictionaries define it as a traditional round dessert baked in the oven with a crust made most often with shortbread; covered with jam, pastry cream, or fresh fruit; and decorated with strips of dough across the top arranged in a crisscross (lattice) pattern.

→ Its name comes from the Latin *crusta* (crust). Martino da Como's *Libro de arte coquinaria* mentions it in the fifteenth century, and it caused a sensation at the papal court banquets in Bartolomeo Scappi's opera (1570).

→ The distinguishing characteristic of the *crostata alla confettura* is its lattice top, to which it owes its name *all'alsaziana* (Alsatian-style) but which, according to legend, was invented by a nun from the convent of San Gregorio Armeno (Naples), a nod to the gate through which the cloistered sisters would walk to attend services.

THE RECIPE

This is the recipe of Irene Stefanelli, a Friulian mother, who learned it from her mother, Ameriga.

SERVES 6

2½ cups (300 g) pastry flour or all-purpose flour
¾ cup (150 g) superfine sugar
10½ tablespoons (150 g) unsalted butter, softened
1 pinch salt
Zest of 1 lemon
2 large (38 g) egg yolks
1 large (50 g) egg
1⅓ cups (250 g) apricot jam (or strawberry, blueberry, orange . . .)

Equipment
11-inch-diameter (28 cm) tart pan, preferably ceramic, with fluted or smooth edges

On a floured work surface or in a large bowl, place the flour, sugar, butter, salt, and lemon zest. Add the egg yolks and the whole egg. Mix by hand until a smooth dough is obtained. Shape into a ball, cover with plastic wrap, and refrigerate for at least 2 hours.

Roll out the dough to form a circle 1 inch (3 cm) larger in diameter than the pan and 2.5 mm thick. Transfer the dough to the pan, then prick the bottom all over with a fork. Scrape in the jam and spread it out evenly. Carefully cut away the excess dough with a knife. Refrigerate for 1 hour.

Preheat the oven to 325°F (170°C). Using the remaining dough, form a ball and roll it out to a rough rectangle 2 mm thick. Using a crimped pasta cutter, cut even strips of dough and place them in a crisscross pattern on top of the tart to the edge of the pan. Bake for 30 to 45 minutes.

PASTA FROLLA (SWEET PASTRY DOUGH)

ALL-PURPOSE FLOUR = TIPO 0 FLOUR
The equivalent of all-purpose flour is Italian "0," ideal for obtaining a fine-textured dough.

BUTTER
Butter alone makes up 30 to 50 percent of the total ingredients. It determines the texture of the dough. The fattier the ingredients in the dough, the more crumbly it will be.

GRANULATED VS. CONFECTIONERS' SUGAR
While coarse-grained granulated sugar provides a crunchier (but more brittle) dough, the fine texture of confectioners' sugar makes it smoother (but more moist). You choose!

EGGS
The yolks make the dough crumblier, but the whites make it more elastic.

SALT
The ideal amount of salt should not exceed 0.45 percent of the total weight of the dough.

To these basic ingredients can be added, according to taste: **LEMON ZEST, THE SEEDS OF HALF A VANILLA BEAN,** and also **A LITTLE BAKING POWDER,** although this use is less common.

VARIATIONS

CROSTATA DI RICOTTA
A great classic that replaces the jam with ricotta, filled with dried fruits and candied citrus.

CROSTATA DI RICOTTA E CIOCCOLATO
The height of indulgence with chocolate chips added to the ricotta.

CROSTATA DI VISCIOLE
This version with sour cherries is widely enjoyed in Lazio, Marche, and Trentino. A Jewish recipe: with a layer of almond paste or ricotta.

CROSTATA DI FRUTTA
Filled with fresh fruit and pastry cream.

CROSTATA AL CIOCCOLATO OR ALLA NUTELLA
For chocolate fans.

SKIP TO
THE FIG, P. 40;
CHOCOLATE SPREADS, P. 248.

OCTOPUS

A majestic sea creature, *polpo* is a standout ingredient among foods offered by the sea.

NADIA POSTIGLIONE

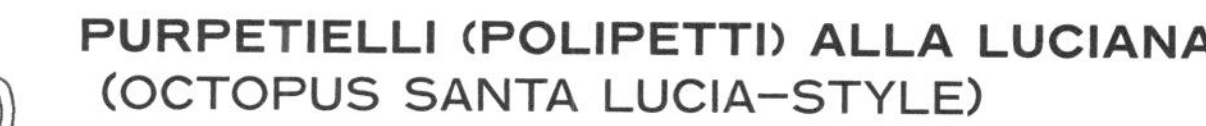

RECIPE

PURPETIELLI (POLIPETTI) ALLA LUCIANA (OCTOPUS SANTA LUCIA–STYLE)

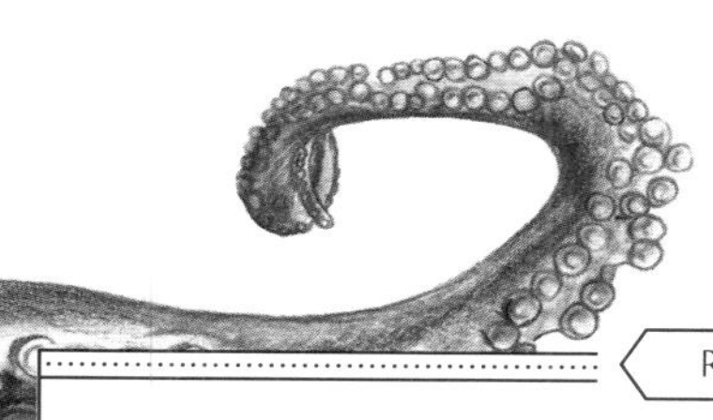

This recipe takes its name from the village of Santa Lucia, the seaside district in the historic center of Naples. It is said that the fishermen of the village, the Luciani, employed a special method for octopus fishing using terra-cotta amphorae, then cooked them fresh on the shore.

SERVES 6

2¼ pounds (1 kg) cleaned baby octopus
Scant ¼ cup (50 mL) white wine
Scant ½ cup (100 mL) olive oil
2 cloves garlic, peeled
5 tomatoes (preferably ones used for making sauce), chopped
1 bunch parsley, chopped
Freshly ground black pepper

- In a casserole dish, preferably made of terra-cotta, set the octopus over medium heat, cover, and cook for several minutes.
- Add the wine and cover again. After 5 minutes, add the oil, garlic, tomatoes, and half of the parsley.
- Cover and cook over low heat for at least 1 hour. The octopus should be tender but not breaking apart. Season with pepper and add the remaining parsley.
- Serve with croutons. Alternatively, use the sauce to coat spaghetti with the octopus added.

IL POLPO O POLIPO (OCTOPUS VULGARIS)

From the Greek *polypous* ("several feet"), *polpo* is a cephalopod referred to by the Latin name of *octopus* ("eight feet"). It can be identified by the double row of symmetrical suction cups located on its tentacles. It is also referred to, especially if it is large in size, by the name *piovra* ("many tentacled").

IL MOSCARDINO (ELEDONE MOSCHATA)

The musky octopus is smaller, with one row of suction cups per tentacle. It is widespread in Veneto by the name of *folpo*, where it is prepared with oil, garlic, and parsley in a dish by the name *folpetti lessi*. It is common in *bacari* (popular taverns).

A TOUR OF ITALY

In stew

POLPO IN PIGNATA—*Apulia*: prepared without adding liquid, with tomato, onion, and pepper.

PURPICEDDI MURATI—*Sicily*: small octopus cooked with tomato paste and chile.

POLPO ALL'INFERNO—"Infernal," *Liguria*: with garlic, onion, chile, and potatoes.

POLPO UBRIACO—"drunk," *Tuscany*: cooked in red wine, with onion and bay leaf.

AGLIATA DI POLPO—Sardinia: with boiled garlic, in a sauce made with tomato, garlic, and vinegar.

POLPO IN PURGATORIO—"In purgatory," *Molise*: small octopuses cooked with their ink sacks, red onions, wine, and pepper.

In salad

A STRICASALE—*Sicily*: with parsley, garlic, olive oil, and lemon.

ALL'EOLIANA—"Aeolic style," *Sicily*: with tomatoes, parsley, and capers.

TRAPANESE—*Sicily*: with olives, radish, celery, and garlic.

DI POLIGNANO—*Apulia*: with potatoes, tomatoes, parsley, and onion.

POLPO ALLA TELLARESE—*Liguria*: with potatoes and olives, seasoned with garlic, oil, lemon, and parsley. According to legend, the village Tellaro was saved in 1660 from a pirate attack by a giant octopus that climbed a bell tower and rang the bells to wake up the entire town.

TIELLA DI POLIPO DI GAETA—*Lazio*: a double-crust pie with tomato, parsley, and local olives.

BRODO DI POLPO—*Campania*: today this is prepared only at home but was a classic street food sold by women in Naples. Baked in pots full of octopuses, the broth was served in a glass with a piece of tentacle.

With pasta

MACCARONES DE BUSA CON RAGÙ DI POLPO—*Sardinia*: fresh pasta, typical of the region, shaped using a wire rod (the busa) and served with a ragout of red octopus.

SPAGHETTI ALLA LUCIANA: spaghetti seasoned with a sauce of small octopus in tomato sauce (see recipe above).

Two Schools of Cooking

IMMERSING IN BOILING WATER
Quickly immerse the tentacles three times to make them curl before fully submerging the octopus.

STARTING IN COLD WATER
Immerse the octopus in cold water and bring to a boil. Cook for 30 to 40 minutes per 2¼ pounds (1 kg); halve the time if using a pressure cooker. Let cool in its water.

The practice of the "curly octopus"

In Bari, the practice of *polpo arricciato* consists of beating the mollusk for a long time on a hard surface to soften its flesh and make its tentacles curl.

SKIP TO
GARLIC, P. 192; CALAMARI, P. 242.

GOURMET CINEMA

— SCOLA, MATTOLI, MONICELLI, FERRERI —

THESE ITALIAN FILMMAKERS KNOWN FOR THEIR VERY DIFFERENT STYLES MAKE UP AN ON-SCREEN ANTHOLOGY OF FIVE MEMORABLE CULINARY SCENES. LAURENT DELMAS

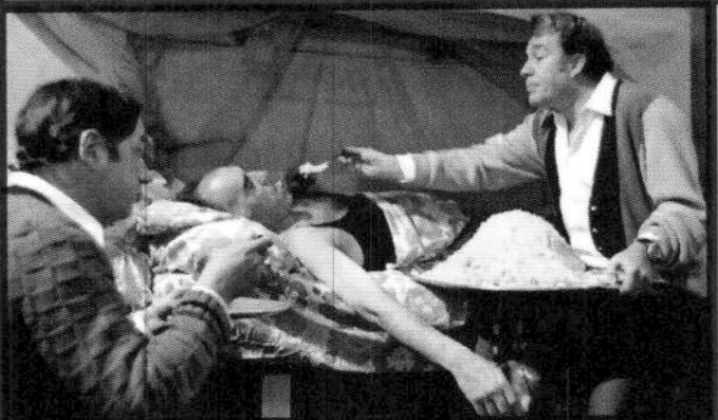

THE BIG FEAST

La grande abbuffata

MARCO FERRERI, 1973

THE FILM

Ugo the chef (Ugo Tognazzi), Philippe the judge (Philippe Noiret), Marcello the airplane pilot (Marcello Mastroianni), and Michel the producer and television presenter (Michel Piccoli) come together for a gastronomic weekend in a beautiful Parisian residence. They are joined by Andréa the teacher (Andréa Ferréol). Together, they will attempt to feast to the point of their demise . . .

THE SCENE

The last dish Ugo devoured before he died is symbolic. First, because among the four protagonists, Ugo has the most at stake (he is a great chef, owner of the restaurant Le Biscuit à Soupe), and second, because he dies while eating his "masterpiece" dish. "This is my last meal of *la grande bouffe*. I die swallowing the last spoonful of this pâté. In reality, I tried to kill myself three times for not knowing how to make it," proclaims Ugo.

THE DISH

A reproduction of the dome of Saint Peter's Basilica in Rome, a monumental duck pâté en croute.

WE ALL LOVED EACH OTHER SO MUCH

C'eravamo tanto amati

ETTORE SCOLA, 1974

THE FILM

This film is a true reflection of Italian society in the late 1960s, including all its enthusiasm and disenchantment.

THE SCENE

Antonio (Nino Manfredi), Gianni (Vittorio Gassman), and Nicola (Stefano Satta Flores), three former resistance fighters, meet in a small restaurant in Rome. They almost forget for a time over a lively meal the mediocrity of their existence and their lost dreams. As pathetic musketeers, they cross their forks, exclaiming: "One for all! All for one!"

THE DISH

In the trattoria so aptly named *Il re della mezza* (the king of the half portion), the penniless heroes feast on "poor" dishes of Roman tradition, in a triumph of macaroni, *bucatini all'amatriciana*, *porchetta*, pasta e ceci, and *picchiapò* (beef stew with tomato and onions). It's a celebration of good things with friends . . . along with a heaping portion of nostalgia!

BIG DEAL ON MADONNA STREET

I soliti ignoti

MARIO MONICELLI, 1958

THE FILM

Tiberio (Marcello Mastroianni), Dante Cruciani (Totò), Peppe (Vittorio Gassman), and Mario Angelletti (Renato Salvatori), four small inconsequential thieves, decide one day to rob the safe of a pawn shop by burrowing through the wall of the adjoining apartment to which they have the key.

THE SCENE

The thieves do break through the wall, but it's actually the partition that separates the room they start in from . . . their kitchen in the same apartment! Their only booty is therefore the contents of the refrigerator and a saucepan. It's an occasion for the four guests to compliment the cook: "*Femmina piccante pigghiala per amante; femmina cuciniera pigghiala per mugliera.*" ("A spicy woman, to take as a mistress; a Cordon-bleu woman, to take as a wife.")

THE DISH

Pasta e ceci (pasta and chickpeas) eaten from the pan.

VIVA ITALIA!

I nuovi mostri

ETTORE SCOLA, 1977

THE FILM

In the sketch "Hostaria!" Scola blatantly scoffs at the culinary snobbery of some of his contemporaries, able to consume anything if the address is fashionable enough.

THE SCENE

A waiter (Vittorio Gassman) and a cook (Ugo Tognazzi), who are lovers, fight in the kitchens of their restaurant, throwing food and other objects at each other. The cook then goes back to the stove . . .

THE DISH

"Gross soup" (*zuppone alla porcara*), a mixture in which all the ingredients are combined, including a shoe, a cigar . . . all the thrown objects from one of their quarrels. In the dining room, diners find this dish delicious and proclaim: "a fairly sophisticated soup of great finesse, *à la française*!"

POVERTY AND NOBILITY

Miseria e nobiltà

MARIO MATTOLI, 1954

THE FILM

Naples in the nineteenth century: two poor families share the same unsanitary apartment.

THE SCENE

It's been three days since the residents of the apartment have eaten when Eugenio, a young aristocrat in love, offers them a deal: a Pantagruelian meal for their participation in a huge scam.

THE DISH

A dish of steaming spaghetti served in a soup tureen, greedily and mischievously devoured by Totò with both hands.

SKIP TO
AMATRICIANA, P. 177;
MAFIA DISHES, P. 139.

SEASON

TUTTO L'ANNO (YEAR-ROUND)

CATEGORY

PRIMO PIATTO/ SECONDO PIATTO (FIRST OR MAIN COURSE)

LEVEL

DIFFICOLTÀ MEDIA (MEDIUM DIFFICULTY)

LA GENOVESE

GENOVESE SAUCE

Its name is perhaps misleading, because it's known as a Neapolitan specialty! Here are the stories and recipe of this delicious white sauce made with onions and meat that goes perfectly with pasta.

ALBA PEZONE

"IN THE GENOA STYLE"

→ In the fourteenth century, *Liber de coquina*, a cookbook focusing on southern French cuisine and used in the Angevin court, attests to the existence of *tria ianuensis* (pasta from Genoa), which is pasta cooked in water and seasoned with fried onions, spices, cheese, and boiled meat.

→ The recipe's modern version could be found during the fifteenth century in a pub in the port of Naples run by a former Genoese sailor.

→ Another more lyrical possibility behind its name: it was invented by a very famous chef nicknamed o'Genovese who was a cook in the city around the same time.

A CLASSIC

In 1839, Genovese sauce officially entered the repertoire of Neapolitan cuisine thanks to Ippolito Cavalcanti, Duke of Buonvicino, who provided the recipe in his treatise *Cucina Teorica–Practica* (*Theoretical–Practical Cuisine*), under the name *raguetto alla genovese* (little ragù *à la Genovese*).

INGREDIENTS

ONION, either Ramato di Montoro (copper in color) or Rosso di Tropea (red), with exceptional sweetness.

MEAT (BEEF) has the supporting role here. Less-noble cuts of beef requiring longer cooking times are used: chuck, shoulder, neck, breast, top rib, skirt, shank, shin . . .

NO BAY LEAF, which is too strong, but yes to *piperna* (wild thyme, an aromatic herb from Ischia Island, spicy and tasty).

DO NOT GIVE IN TO THE TEMPTATATION OF TOMATO! La Genovese is a "white" sauce. However, in one variation, the small cherry tomatoes from Vesuvius can bring a brilliant and coppery-colored nuance to the dish (add only one tomato for two servings, maximum).

DURING MORE SPARCE TIMES, Neapolitans practice *la finta* (false) Genovese sauce: a very appetizing stew of caramelized onions but without meat!

WHICH PASTA?

Use *ziti spezzati a mano*, a very long, smooth, hollow-tube pasta, broken up before cooking, used in the past for wedding feasts (*ziti* means "fiancés"). Otherwise, *paccheri* and *rigatoni* (short and thick pasta) are permitted.

THE COOKING

In the casserole dish, Genovese sauce must *pippiare*, a Neapolitan verb for braised, very long cooking over a low heat (four to five hours, covered) so that it concentrates flavors and takes on the amber color. In Naples, Genovese sauce is a Sunday dish. The cooking begins on Friday; the dish matures on Saturday and is served on Sunday.

Service

It's a two-in-one dish, *primo* (first) and *secondo* (second): The first will be the *pasta alla genovese* (the pasta topped with caramelized onions), and the second the *stracotto* (stewed meat), served after the pasta.

THE RECIPE

Courtesy of Alfonso Mattozzi, chef at Ristorante Europeo Mattozzi in Naples.

SERVES 6 TO 8

- 5½ to 6½ pounds (2.5 to 3 kg) red onions
- 2 carrots
- 2 stalks celery
- 3⅓ pounds (1.5 kg) beef for braising (you can mix the pieces)
- Flour
- Thyme
- Olive oil
- 3 or 4 small tomatoes from Vesuvius (otherwise, olive or cherry tomatoes)
- Wine (white or red)
- Meat broth (beef or chicken)
- Salt
- 1½ pounds (700 g) ziti, broken by hand
- Freshly grated 24-month-old Parmesan cheese
- A few basil leaves, chopped
- Freshly ground black pepper

Peel and cut the onions into thin rings. Peel and cut the carrots and celery into small dice. Cut the meat into large cubes (2 inches/5 cm) and lightly flour them.

In a cast-iron pot, brown the carrots, celery, a few rings of the onion, and the thyme in olive oil over high heat. Add the meat and brown on all sides.

Remove the meat and reduce the heat. Add the remaining onions, drizzle with olive oil, and cook, covered, for 15 minutes, stirring frequently to avoid scorching.

Return the meat to the pot, then add the tomatoes and crush them. Add a little wine and cook until evaporated.

Add enough broth just to cover the meat and season lightly with salt. Bring to a boil, then cover and cook for 4 hours over low heat. If necessary, add a little water (or broth) from time to time to prevent the meat from drying out and the sauce from sticking to the pan.

After cooking, the sauce should be amber in color, the onions caramelized, and the meat well glazed. If the dish contains too much liquid, remove the lid and let reduce until the liquid is concentrated and syrupy in consistency.

Let the meat rest, covered. Reheat before serving.

Cook the ziti in a large pot of salted boiling water. Use broken pieces, as they will help bind (*mantecare*) the pasta with the sauce. Drain the ziti when still very al dente, keeping aside a ladle of the pasta cooking water. Pour the cooked pasta into another large skillet along with the Genovese sauce and the reserved pasta water. Sauté over high heat for 1 to 2 minutes, along with some Parmesan and chopped basil.

Transfer the ziti to a large bowl, sprinkle with more Parmesan and basil, and season with pepper.

Serve the meat separately, as a *secondo piatto*, after the pasta.

SKIP TO
ONIONS, P. 292.

THE ART OF PORK FAT

From bacon to lard, *il maiale* (pork) is a source of fat that Italians love to use. Here is an overview of this indulgent ingredient.

FRANÇOIS-RÉGIS GAUDRY

① LARDO D'ARNAD DOP

Aosta Valley

Lard from the back and shoulder of pork, at least 1⅛ inches (3 cm) thick, cured in wooden boxes (chestnut, oak, or larch) sprinkled with brine with a mixture of aromatic herbs, spices, and black pepper.

TASTING NOTES—white to light pink color, sometimes with thin veins. Melting texture. Smooth flavor, persistent, with spicy and herbaceous notes.

USES—traditionally eaten with *pan dür* (black bread from the Aosta Valley) spread with honey. Also with boiled chestnuts, honey, and *motzetta* (dried meat of beef, chamois, deer, or wild boar).

② LARDO DI COLONNATA IGP

Tuscany

Lard from the back of pork, at least 1⅛ inches (3 cm) thick, cured in marble bowls in a mixture of sea salt, ground black pepper, fresh rosemary, fresh garlic, and other spices. Curing lasts a minimum of six months in a naturally ventilated and humidified environment.

TASTING NOTES—white color, with rosy or slightly brown tinges; may show some veins of lean meat. Silky texture. Delicate and fresh flavor, sapid and long on the palate, it has a certain smoothness and notes of spices and aromatic herbs.

USES—thinly sliced on toast; in Tuscan minestrone. Now appears in creations of top chefs.

③ GUANCIALE

Cured pork cheek, composed of fat and crossed with veins of muscle. It is a traditional product from Lazio and Abruzzo, abundantly seasoned with pepper, sometimes with rosemary, sage, and garlic. The *guanciale dei monti Lepini di maiale nero* and *guanciale amatriciano* are renowned products. It can be smoked (Friuli) and is also found in Veneto, Tuscany, Umbria, Molise, Calabria, and Sardinia.

TASTING NOTES—firmer than pancetta, its flavor is more full-bodied, even spicy, sometimes with slight notes of rancidity.

USES—indispensable ingredient in many Roman pasta dishes (*gricia*, *amatriciana*, carbonara).

④ PANCETTA

This is cured pork belly common to many regions of Italy. This can be *arrotolata* (rolled up like a big salami), *steccata* (folded tight on itself), or *tesa* (in the shape of a flat parallelepiped). In some regions (Trentino-Alto Adige, Friuli, Veneto, etc.), it is *affumicata* (smoked). Two pancetta specialties benefit from a DOP (*Denominazione di origin protetta*), aka PDO (Protected Designation of Origin):

PANCETTA PIACENTINA DOP · *Emilia-Romagna*

Cylindrical in shape and weighing 8¾ to 17½ pounds (4 to 8 kg), it is made at an altitude of over 2,900 feet (900 m) in the province of Plaisance (Emilia-Romagna) from pigs born, raised, and slaughtered in Lombardy and Emilia-Romagna. It is dry salted, rolled, encased in a natural pork casing, and dried for a minimum of four months.

TASTING NOTES—bright red meat, white fat. Melting texture and sweet flavor.

USES—it is enjoyed as an aperitif, to fill PGI (Protected Geographical Indication) *piadina romagnola,* and in many recipes, from pasta sauces to roasted meats.

PANCETTA DI CALABRIA DOP · *Calabria*

This breast meat, with its rind, is between 1⅛ and 2 inches (3 and 5 cm) thick and comes from pigs raised and slaughtered in Calabria. It is salted, washed with water, marinated in wine vinegar, covered with *impepatura* (chile powder), and cured for at least thirty days.

TASTING NOTES—rosy red color, tangy flavor, slightly spicy.

USES—traditionally consumed with pasta, legumes, fresh beans, etc.

---

⑤ PANCETTA COPPATA

The fusion of two pieces from the pig: a breast (*pancetta*) wrapped around a boneless spine (*coppa* or *capocollo*). The coppa is a leaner piece, although marbled with visible intramuscular fat. This technique is widespread among three primary regions: Emilia-Romagna, Lombardy, and Veneto. It is often found under the name *pancetta magra* (lean) and is mainly commercially manufactured.

TASTING NOTES—two flavors in one: the melting fat of the sweet-flavored pancetta, and the creamy texture of the coppa.

USES—enjoyed as an aperitif; only used in a few traditional recipes.

⑥ FILETTO LARDELLATO

Literally "larded fillet," it is a salted and dried pork tenderloin surrounded in fat. It's a first cousin of the Corsican *lonzu.* It is sometimes found under the name *filone,* mainly in Friuli, where it is lightly smoked.

TASTING NOTES—a contrast between the lean meat, with a dense texture and delicate flavor, and the melting fat, which is flavorful and smooth.

USES—mainly present on charcuterie boards.

⑦ STRUTTO

The lard is obtained by melting pork fat (without meat). Cold, it is white, shiny, smooth, and odorless. When hot, it is oily and transparent, with a faint but characteristic odor. Its use in Italy probably dates back to the Etruscans. It was supplanted by olive oil, the production of which spread between the seventh and sixth centuries BCE. It regained importance in the Middle Ages under the influence of barbarian invasions. It is a fat still very present in the cuisines of Lombardy, Emilia-Romagna, Marche, and Campania.

TASTING NOTES—it gives the dishes in which it is integrated an umami character, serving as a flavor enhancer.

USES—it is an essential ingredient in many dishes:

→ In the dough of certain breads and breadsticks (pizza, brioches, *piadine* from Marche and Emilia-Romagna, *schiacciatina* from Mantua, *crescentina* and *gnocco fritto* from Modena, *coppia ferrarese* IGP from Ferrara, *taralli* from Apulia, etc.).

→ In *torte* and fritters (*erbazzone* from Emilia-Romagna, *casatiello* from Naples, *seadas* and *pardulas* from Sardinia, etc.).

→ In pastry, where it provides a crumbly texture (*cannolo* from Sicily, *sfogliatella* from Naples, etc.).

→ Deep-fried, thanks to its high smoke point of 480°F (250°C): *carnival chiacchiere,* Lombardy *patacia,* etc.

THE ANATOMY OF PORK FAT

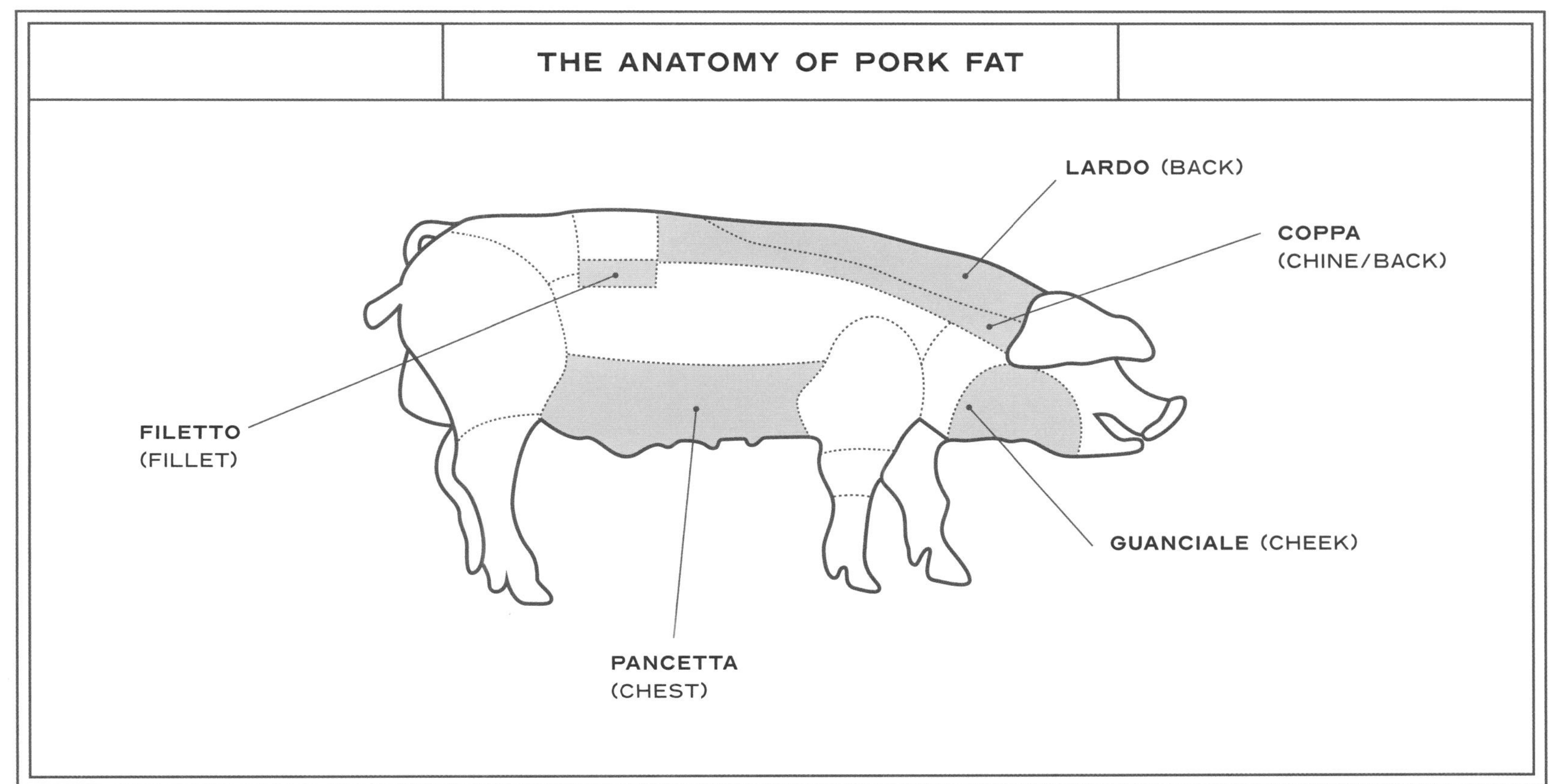

SKIP TO
SAUSAGE, P. 332; THE WAR OF THE HAMS, P. 311.

IMAGINARY MUSEUM

This art gallery of five themes invites you to sit down at the table with some of the artists who have left their mark on Italian art.

CHRISTOPHE BROUARD

SELFISH GOURMETS

***The Beaneater*, Annibale Carracci, 1583–1585, oil on canvas (22 by 27 inches/57 by 68 cm), Galleria Colonna, Rome.**

This iconic work is part of the comic tradition and celebrates the riches of the Bolognese *terroir* as much as it enjoys the ill-mannered mores of the peasant—busy, open mouthed, eagerly plunging his wooden spoon into his bowl of beans. Placed in the foreground, among onions, bread, and a jug with its glass of wine, is *torta d'erbe*, a Bolognese dish par excellence and the true star of the table!

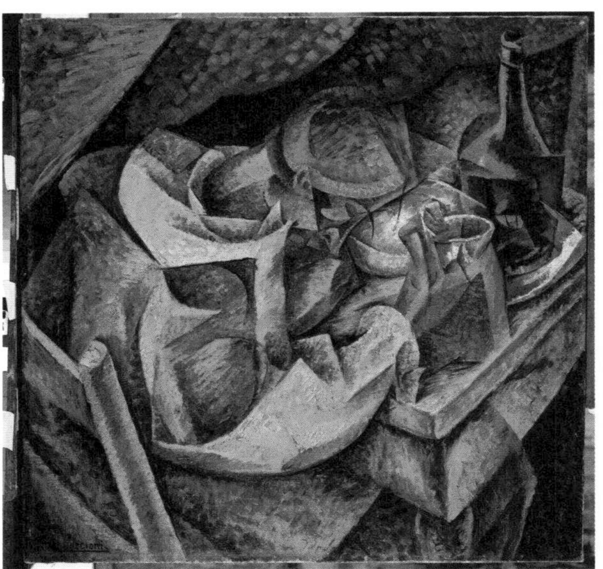

***The Drinker*, Umberto Boccioni, 1914, oil on canvas (33 by 34 inches/86 by 87 cm), collection of Riccardo and Magda Jucker, Milan.**

Aware of the legacy left by Carracci (an artist who also portrayed a drinking character in his painting *Boy Drinking*, Oxford, Christchurch College), futurist Umberto Boccioni established a more tormented image of the dining companion, almost at odds with the codes established by the futurist theorist Marinetti fifteen years later. With the help of alcohol, the man, seen from above, collapses in the noisy confusion of a tavern.

STILL LIFES

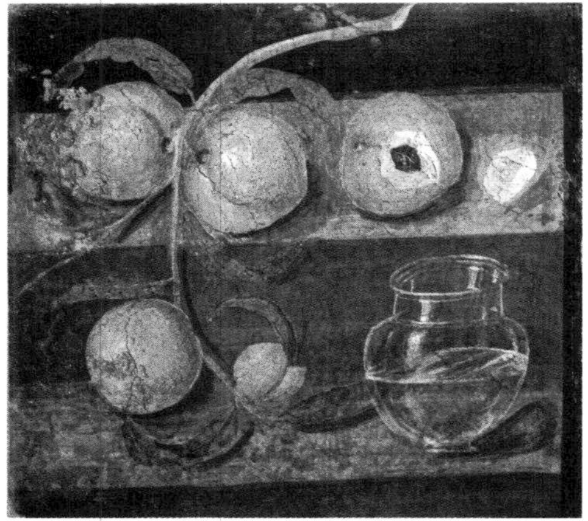

***Still Life with Peaches and a Water Jar*, Pompeii, second style, 80–20 BCE, fresco (14 by 13 inches/35 by 34 cm), National Archaeological Museum of Naples.**

On a Pompeian red background are a branch with four peaches and a pitcher of water. On the top shelf, a peach has been cut open, but is not ripe enough to eat. This work represents how, between realism and illusionism, to evoke a xenium (a gift of food that a host must offer to his guests), nourish through mimicry the pleasure of the guest-spectator, and, at the same time, encourage him to seize the day (*carpe diem*).

***Still-Life with Birds*, the Master of Hartford, first quarter of the seventeenth century, oil on canvas (41 by 68 inches/104 by 173 cm), Galleria Borghese, Rome.**

Posed or exposed? Covering the surface of a long, narrow table, abundant game birds—some still hunted today, including partridge, pheasant, mallard, woodcock, and others that are more surprising: an owl, jay, and woodpecker—are arranged in such a way as to almost be objects of study. What could the artist's intention be? And why confront us with an owl with an intimidating expression? The work offers much to think about regarding the opulence of these hunted prizes . . .

***Basket of Fruit*, Caravaggio, between 1594 and 1602, oil on canvas (18 by 25 inches/46 by 64.5 cm), Pinacoteca Ambrosiana, Milan.**

Nature finds in Michelangelo Merisi, known as Caravaggio, one of its best interpreters. Like the bounty of Bacchus, the basket is abundantly filled with autumnal fruits—a cluster of black grapes, shiny apples, spoiled quince, and a fig peeking through large leaves—composing an allegory of the riches of the Italian land. Through its detailed imperfections it suggests vanity and the cycle of life, from withering until death.

SACRED MEAL

The Last Supper, **Jacopo Bassano (aka Jacopo da Ponte), 1546–1547, painting on canvas (12 by 20 inches/30 by 51 cm), Galleria Borghese, Rome.**

During the fifteenth century, the use of an oblong composition made it possible to represent each of the protagonists of this biblical scene and to introduce pittances, such as suckling pig (by Duccio), shellfish, or eel (by Leonardo da Vinci). Bassano's *The Last Supper* is part of this tradition: in a very profane representation, Christ extends, in the middle of a richly furnished table (with bread, pomegranate, apples, wine), a dish containing the head of a paschal lamb, an explicit metaphor of his own sacrifice, to Judas.

In 2003, the Genoese artist Vanessa Beecroft depicted in a filmed performance (*VB52*) a Eucharistic meal during which women create, at their discretion, arrangements of colors, often monochromatic: jellies, plants, and juices, echoing outfits and hairstyles. Dinner companions thus embody the artist herself in her intimate and conflicting relationship with food.

AT THE HEART OF PRODUCTS

La Vucciria, **Renato Guttuso, 1974, oil on canvas (118 by 118 inches/300 by 300 cm), Palazzo Chiaramonte Steri, Palermo.**

A striking masterpiece by the Sicilian artist, this view of the Vucciria market in Palermo is an invitation to explore the belly of the port city. By favoring a tight framing and shedding the principles of linear perspective inherited from the Renaissance, the artist shows us a world built on startling oxymorons: an abundance of foods around which people are intermingling, and the organization of the market superimposed with bustling activity . . . This work is as much a tribute to the rich Sicilian *terroir* as it is to the Italian avant-garde of the turn of the century, embodied by the futurists.

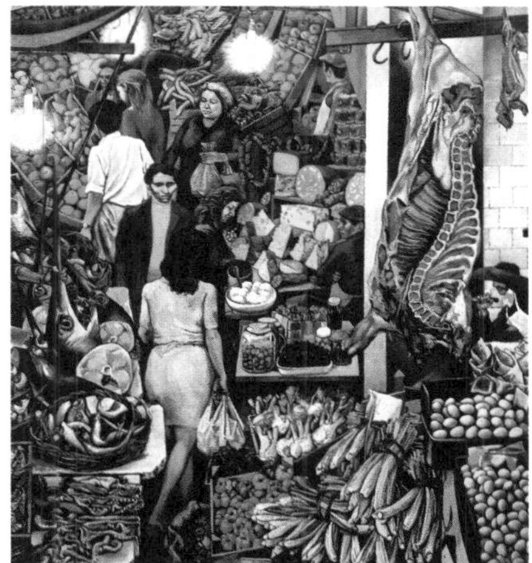

The Ricotta Eaters, **Vincenzo Campi, circa 1580, oil on canvas (30 by 35 inches/77 by 89 cm), Musée des Beaux-Arts, Lyon.**

Called *Buffonaria* in Campi's widow's will, this painting consecrates the preparation of cheese in a strange way. While we witness the devouring of ricotta by four jester-looking characters (inspired by the *Commedia dell'arte*), the painter has represented on the front part of the cheese a series of hollowed-out cavities that could suggest a sort of human skull: an ambivalent symbol, in contradiction with the lightness of the scene and equated with idleness or death. A possible echo can be seen in Pasolini's film *La Ricotta* (1963).

The Butcher's Shop, **Bartolomeo Passarotti, 1575–1580, oil on canvas (44 by 60 inches/112 by 152 cm), Gallerie Nazionali di Arte Antica (Palazzo Barberini), Rome.**

In the butcher's lair, business and death reign supreme. It is difficult today to grasp the symbolic dimension of this iconography in the Italy of religious reform. The physical rapprochement of man with animal hybridizes the kingdoms of the living: by exhibiting the boar's head, the young butcher seems to claim the sexual power of the creature, known as one of the most luxurious animals since Aristotle.

RECONSTRUCTED NATURE, FRENZIED DISHES

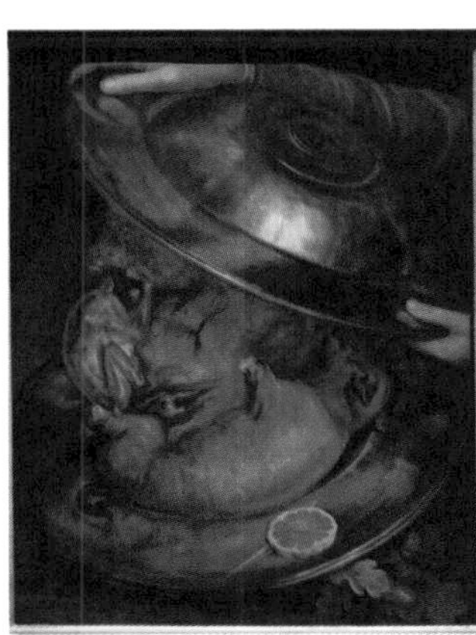

The Cook, **Giuseppe Arcimboldo, c. 1570, oil painting on wood (21 by 16 inches/52.5 by 41 cm), National Museum, Stockholm.**

If there is one trend that strives to revive food in a different form, it is the one embodied by Arcimboldo! The Lombard painter inspires several compatriots in the rewriting of the natural order. His upside-down paintings are the incarnation of this, such as *The Cook*, made up of beautiful roasted meats that, once the painting is turned over, reveal a human profile. A tasty irony: so becomes cooked one who believes himself to be a cook!

Autumn, **Giovanni Paolo Castelli (aka Lo Spadino), 1690–1700, oil on canvas (52 by 37 inches/131 by 94 cm), Dorotheum, Vienna.**

Heir to the genre and master of still life at the end of the seventeenth century, the Roman Spadino excelled in the representation of allegories of the seasons. Here he offers a true baroque parody of Arcimboldesque art, associating pomegranates, apples, and quinces with the arabesque motif of a deity who greedily swallows a bunch of grapes through a mouth made of figs.

GNOCCHI DI PATATE

POTATO GNOCCHI

Half pasta, half potato, these little bumps of pasta are rolled all over "the boot." They can be served up in a large variety of sauces, and it's a snap to make them yourself. Let's get rolling!

ILARIA BRUNETTI

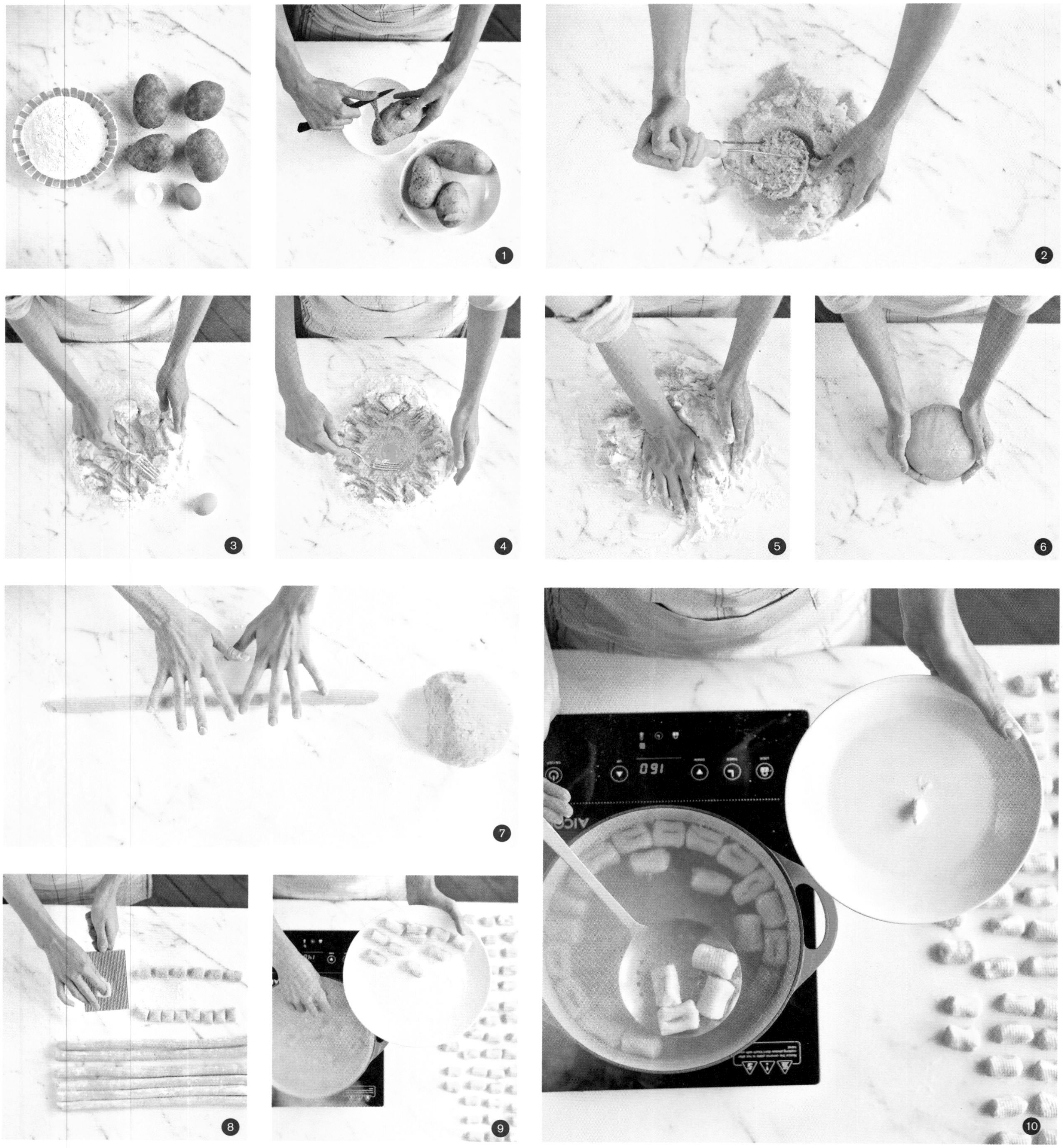

THE TECHNIQUE

SERVES 4 TO 6

2¼ pounds (1 kg) starchy potatoes (Roseval, Bintje . . .)

About 2 cups (250 g) all-purpose flour, plus more for the work surface

1 large (50 g) egg

Salt

❶ ❷ ❸ Cook the potatoes with their skins on in boiling water (starting them in cold salted water) or by steaming (if steamed, they will absorb less water). Peel the cooked potatoes, then mash them while still hot on a lightly floured work surface. Let cool. Pour the flour onto the work surface near the mashed potatoes.

❹ Using a fork, form a well in the center of the potatoes. Add the egg to the well and fold it in.

❺ Gradually incorporate the flour. The drier the flesh of the potatoes, the less flour will be required. Season with salt and gently work the dough with the palms of your hands until it is smooth.

❻ Form a ball.

❼ Cut pieces of dough and form them into sausage shapes ¾ inch (2 cm) in diameter. Cut them into ⅓-inch-long (1 cm) sections.

❽ Roll the gnocchi using a *rigagnocchi* or the tines of a fork.

❾ Place the gnocchi in a pot of salted boiling water.

❿ As soon as they rise to the surface, remove them with a skimmer or slotted spoon and serve immediately with a pat of butter or your chosen sauce.

The Sauces

BURRO E SALVIA (butter and sage)

Over very low heat, melt 7 tablespoons (100 g) butter with a dozen sage leaves; pour over the gnocchi and top with grated Parmesan.

AL POMODORO (tomato sauce)

Serve the gnocchi with a very red *al pomodoro* sauce.

ALLA SORRENTINA

Take 2¼ pounds (1 kg) peeled tomatoes, fresh or canned. Core and dice them. Cook in a pan in olive oil and garlic for half an hour. Season with fresh basil. Transfer to a serving dish and pour the sauce over the gnocchi. Top with 10½ ounces (300 g) of well-drained diced mozzarella and some grated Parmesan, then brown in the oven.

RAGÙ DI CARNE (meat sauce)

A classic made with chopped meat and a dash of tomato sauce!

AND ALSO . . .

A Genoese pesto, sauces with flavors of the sea (including fish and shellfish . . .), meat, or vegetable sauces . . . Just like pasta, gnocchi lend themselves to a wide variety of flavorings and sauces.

What are they?

In the land of Bengodi described in Boccaccio's *Decameron* (circa 1350–1353), gnocchi—called *maccheroni ammaccare* (knead)—roll down from the top of a mountain of grated Parmesan . . .

Present on Italian tables long before the arrival of potatoes, gnocchi were made with flour or bread crumbs, eggs, and cheese. It was after the famine of the eighteenth century, which forced peasants to feed on strange tubers from the Americas, that potatoes were added as part of the gnocchi recipe, eventually becoming the main ingredient.

THE GOLDEN RULES

1

The choice of potatoes is essential: the flesh must be firm and starchy, like that of Bintje or Roseval.

2

The dough should not be overworked, otherwise it will become sticky. As soon as it is smooth, it is ready.

3

To accompany liquid sauces, you can make smaller gnocchi, without marking them.

4

Once prepared, the gnocchi should be cooked immediately. To store them, simply shape them with a little more flour, blanch them, and season them with a drizzle of olive oil. You can then keep them chilled or arrange them well spaced on a tray and place them in the freezer. Once frozen and firm, transfer them to freezer bags.

THE RIGAGNOCCHI

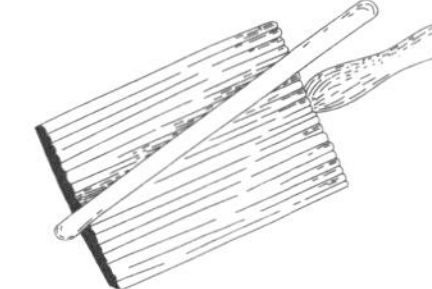

Literally "scratch-gnocchi," this small wooden tool is used to make the ridges characteristic of gnocchi that help them absorb sauce. The tool is also used to make *garganelli*, tube-shaped pasta shells from Emilia-Romagna.

SKIP TO
THE GNOCCHI UNIVERSE, P. 76;
GNOCCHI DOLCI, P. 187.

Sulla Punta Della Lingua (On the Tip of the Tongue)

Ridi, ridi, che la mamma ha fatto gli gnocchi!
"Laugh, laugh, Momma made some gnocchi!"

This expression is used when a child bursts out laughing for no reason, as if the only thing that can justify such happiness is Momma's gnocchi.

Giovedì gnocchi!
"Gnocchi Thursday!"

The expression dates back to the time when the religious calendar was strictly followed: Friday being *magro* (lean) day, a day without meat, so you needed to eat a hearty dish like gnocchi the day before.

Los ñoquis del 29
"The gnocchi of the 29th"

In Argentina, a country that experienced heavy Italian immigration, tradition has it that gnocchi is eaten on the twenty-ninth of the month with pesos placed on one's plate, a tribute to Saint Pantaleon, who thanked peasants for sharing their meager meal with him, ensuring them good harvests and prosperity. But it also represents that at the end of the month, there is often only enough money left in one's pocket for simple dishes, such as *ñoquis*!

Papà del Gnoco, a character of the Carnival of Verona, with a giant *gnocco* resting on his big golden fork.

THE GNOCCHI UNIVERSE

While potato gnocchi have conquered the whole of Italy, every region—especially the north—has specialties that enrich the world of gnocchi with myriad flavors and shapes.

ILARIA BRUNETTI

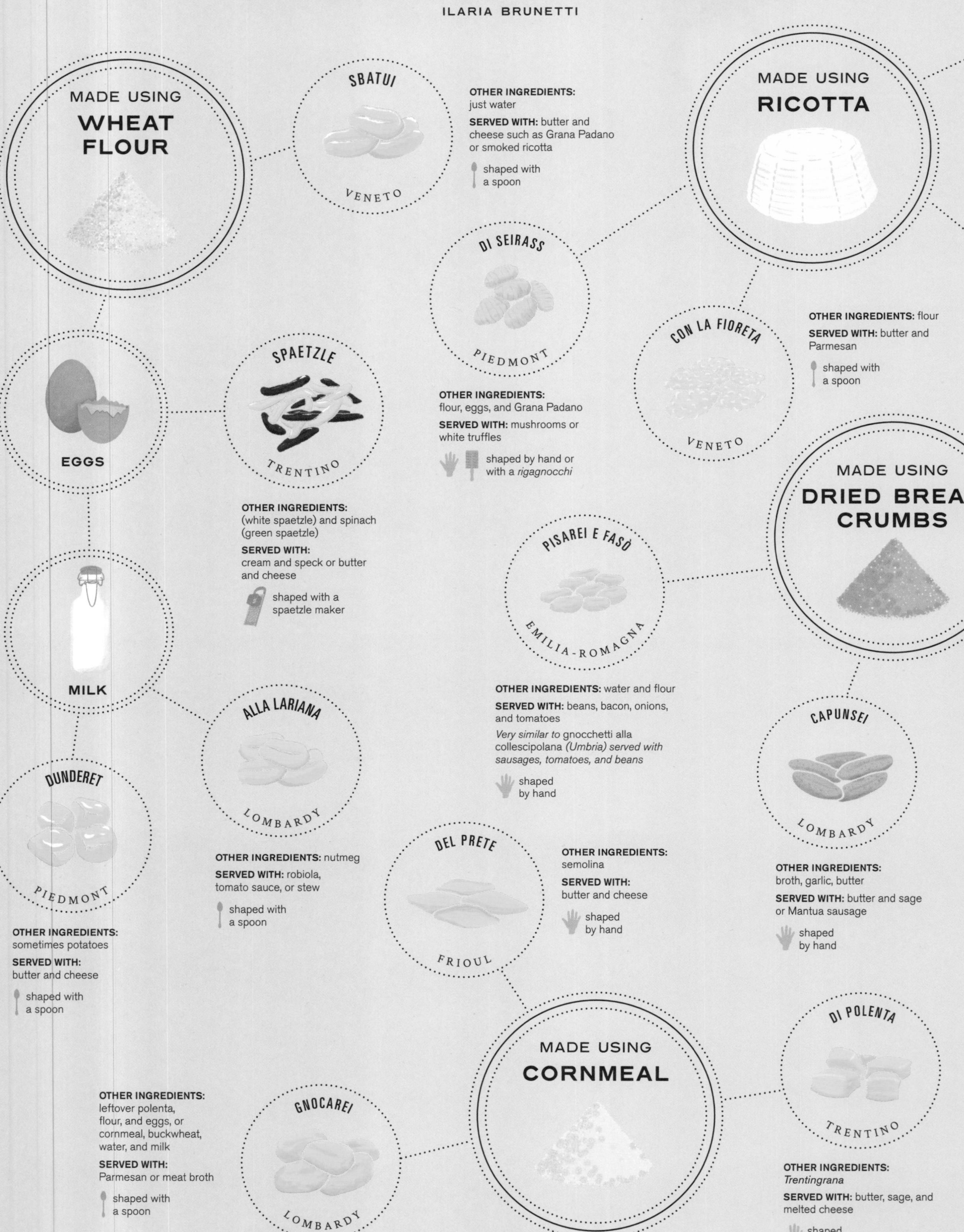

In Tuscany, they are called gnudi

OTHER INGREDIENTS: eggs, flour, sometimes chard, Parmesan

SERVED WITH: butter and sage or butter and Parmesan

 shaped by hand or a spoon

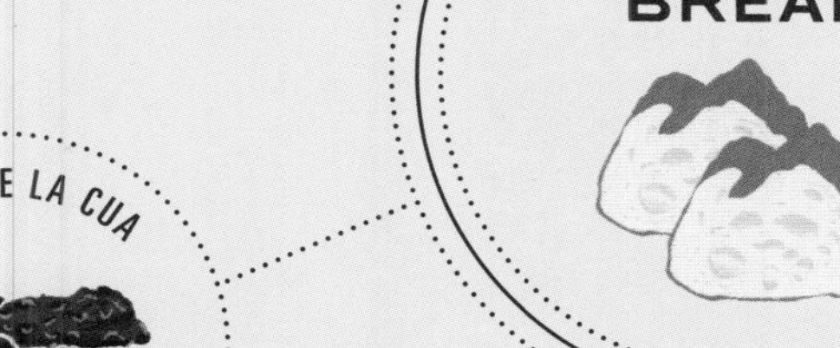

MADE WITH

STALE BREAD

MARICONDE

LOMBARDY

OTHER INGREDIENTS: milk, Grana Padano, eggs, butter

SERVED: in a broth

shaped with a spoon

OTHER INGREDIENTS: spinach or chard, milk, sometimes potatoes

SERVED WITH: Silter cheese

shaped with a spoon

Full name: pizzoccheri della Valchiavenna

OTHER INGREDIENTS: eggs and milk

SERVED WITH: a sauce made from butter, sage, bitto, scimut or Casera cheese

shaped with a spoon

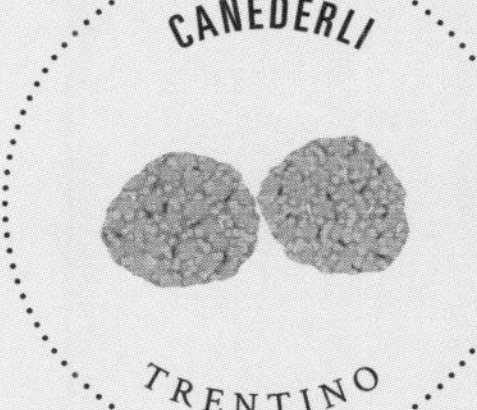

OTHER INGREDIENTS: eggs, milk, onions, chives, parsley, cheese, speck, sometimes liver or spinach

SERVED: in the cooking broth or with butter and cheese

shaped by hand

OTHER INGREDIENTS: eggs, with or without potatoes, flour

SERVED WITH: butter and sage or smoked ricotta

 shaped with a spoon or a *rigagnocchi*

OTHER INGREDIENTS: eggs, Grana Padano, and chard or wild herbs

SERVED WITH: butter and sage

shaped with a spoon

OTHER INGREDIENTS: eggs, flour, and Tumin dal Mel fresh cheese

SERVED WITH: butter and Parmesan

 shaped by hand

RAVIOLES DELLA VAL VARAITA

PIEDMONT

OTHER INGREDIENTS: wheat flour

SERVED WITH: butter and pancetta

shaped with a spoon

OSSOLANI

PIEDMONT

OTHER INGREDIENTS: squash, potatoes, and chestnut flour

SERVED WITH: butter and cheese

 shaped with a spoon or a *rigagnocchi*

OTHER INGREDIENTS: wheat flour, sometimes buckwheat flour

SERVED WITH: a sauce made from Fontina and tome cheese

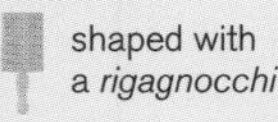 shaped with a *rigagnocchi*

MADE USING

POTATOES

OTHER INGREDIENTS: milk, butter, and Parmesan

SERVED: baked in the oven, with butter and Parmesan

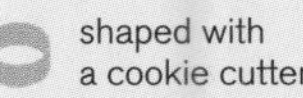 shaped with a cookie cutter

OTHER INGREDIENTS: stuffed with a whole pitted plum

SERVED WITH: butter, sugar, and cinnamon

shaped by hand

OTHER INGREDIENTS: chestnut flour, wheat flour, sometimes eggs

SERVED WITH: butter and sage

shaped with a *rigagnocchi*

OTHER INGREDIENTS: butter, eggs, Parmesan

SERVED: in broth

shaped with a spoon

MADE USING

SEMOLINA

RISOTTO

An emblematic dish of Italian culinary heritage, typical to northern Italy, risotto comes in endless variations. Here are all the secrets for a perfect result.

ANNA PRANDONI

COOKING RICE IS AN ART . . .

Legend has it that the creation of risotto is due to a somewhat clumsy Sicilian cook. Stemming from a failed attempt to properly form *arancini*, the famous fried rice balls, he served a risotto as we know it today.

In reality, the technique of cooking risotto emerged at the beginning of the sixteenth century and arose from the care needed to prepare a rice soup with just the right amount of liquid. Instead of immediately pouring the rice into the water or broth, the liquid was gradually added to the rice during cooking to allow the cook to adjust the amount of liquid as closely as possible to what was needed.

A DISH TO MAKE WITH LOVE

Care, attention, dedication . . . risotto requires love and experience because only practice can achieve a perfect result. It's an impatient dish: it doesn't wait and demands to be enjoyed while still hot. However, it can adapt to changes. If there is any left over, it can be sautéed with a pat of butter in a saucepan to form a delicious golden crust on the bottom. By adding a few eggs to leftovers, it can be made into croquettes, coated in bread crumbs, and fried.

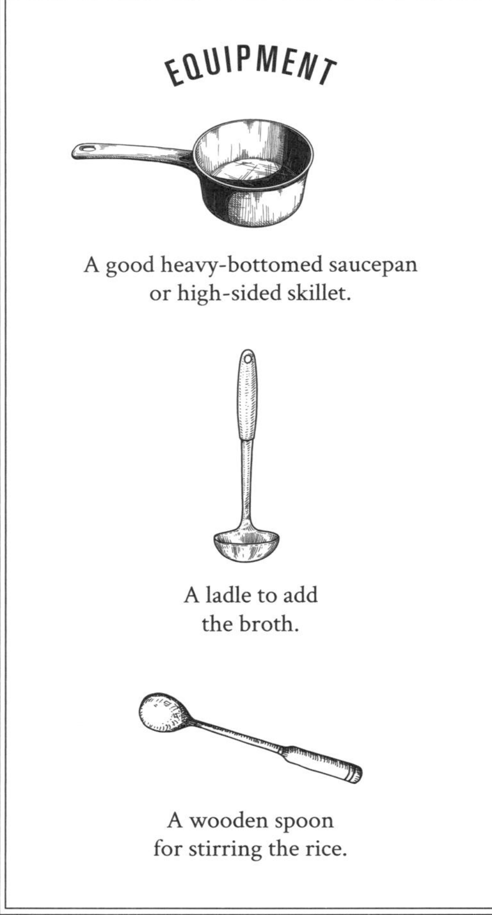

EQUIPMENT

A good heavy-bottomed saucepan or high-sided skillet.

A ladle to add the broth.

A wooden spoon for stirring the rice.

Ingredients

Broth

It must match the ingredients that characterize the risotto: fish, meat, or vegetables.

Wine and onion

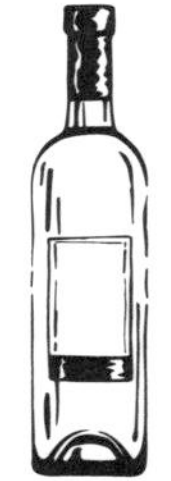

You should use a quality wine, preferably a dry white wine. Red wine is reserved for certain specific recipes, such as *barolo risotto.* Many modern chefs use shallot instead of onion for a more delicate-tasting *soffritto.* Another technique involves cooking the onion separately over low heat and adding it to the rice after the *tostatura* (toasting of the rice) phase, which prevents it from overbrowning or burning during this step.

Oil or butter for the tostatura?

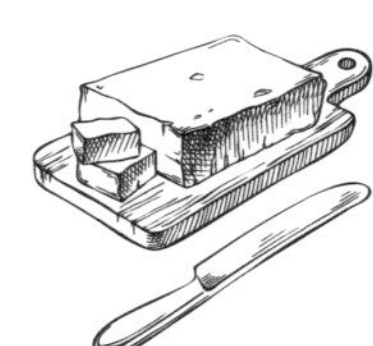

Disagreement continues. Since risotto is basically a traditional recipe from northern Italy, we prefer butter and opt for oil only in *risotti* that contain fish.

THE CHOICE OF RICE

• ARBORIO •

COOKING CHARACTERISTICS
Releases more starch than other types of rice and results in a creamier risotto.

PERFECT FOR . . .
A rustic risotto, such as with sausage or mushrooms.

• CARNAROLI •

COOKING CHARACTERISTICS
With its long grains, it offers excellent resistance to cooking and results in a nicely loose risotto.

PERFECT FOR . . .
A *risotto alla milanese* or one with seafood.

• VIALONE NANO •

COOKING CHARACTERISTICS
Smaller grains. It remains more compact and swells in volume.

PERFECT FOR . . .
A risotto with fish or spring vegetables.

ADAPTATIONS

ALLO ZAFFERANO
SAFFRON

This is the distinction of *risotto alla milanese.* Saffron is infused into the broth used for cooking, giving it its characteristic golden-yellow color.

AL TARTUFO
TRUFFLE

Whether white or black, truffle enhances a simple Parmesan risotto.

AGLI AGRUMI
CITRUS

Very fragrant, like lemon or bergamot risotto.

CON IL PESCE
FISH

In seafood risotto, also called fisherman's risotto, fish and other seafood are added, either filleted or diced. It is prepared *bianco* (white) or by adding tomato. Cheese is not allowed!

CON LE VERDURE
VEGETABLES

You can make a risotto with any vegetable, from the classic pumpkin to artichoke, mushroom, and asparagus risotto. The primavera variant is a creation of the genius of Cipriani, the founder of Harry's Bar in Venice, who added diced spring vegetables from the garden.

AL FORMAGGIO
CHEESE

Parmesan risotto is the simplest. It is prepared by following the main recipe but adding a double quantity of grated Parmesan. You can also use Taleggio, Gorgonzola, or Valtellina Casera, among other cheeses.

CON LA CARNE
MEAT

Among the classics are *risotto alla monzese,* with *luganiga,* a rustic pork sausage, and risotto with chicken livers, but you can prepare risotto with any type of meat.

• VARIATIONS •

In "enriched" risotti, certain ingredients—notably fish and shellfish, but also mushrooms—must be added after the *soffritto* is made, and are sautéed in the soffritto if necessary. Others, like sausages or vegetables, are part of the soffritto itself, without the onion. The rice is then added, but in both cases there is no real *tostatura.*

Cremoso o all'onda?

Risotto all'onda ("in waves," meaning fluid) is often contrasted with *risotti cremosi* (creamy, more compact risotto). In reality, there is no real difference between them: an *all'onda* risotto is a *cremoso* risotto that has reached a point of equilibrium, neither too thick nor too liquid. The best result is achieved when, while stirring briskly, a wave—*un'onda*—forms in the risotto.

In Veneto, risotto looks more like soup. The ingredients are cooked in water and the rice is added to the resulting broth that is completely absorbed during cooking. The key, therefore, lies in the exact proportions between the liquid, including the liquid contained in the vegetables, and the rice.

SKIP TO
THE CULTIVATION OF RICE, P. 60; SAFFRON, P. 291; SUPPLÌ VS. ARANCINI, P. 362; RISOTTO ALLA MILANESE, P. 290.

HOW TO MAKE RISOTTO

THE TECHNIQUE

SERVES 4

1 small onion, chopped

7 tablespoons (100 g) unsalted butter

2 cups (400 g) Vialone Nano rice (or carnaroli or arborio)

Scant 1/4 cup (50 mL) white wine

4 to 6 cups (1 to 1.5 L) broth (depending on the rice used)

3/4 cup (75 g) grated Grana Padano or Parmesan cheese

The five traditional steps:

1 *Il soffritto* (the aromatic additions). Soften the onion in half the butter for 15 minutes.

2 *La tostatura* (toasting). Add the rice to fry and lightly toast, about 3 minutes, until it turns shiny. Be careful because the rice will not absorb the liquid if it is overtoasted.

3 *Il vino* (wine). Pour in the wine and stir until evaporated.

4 *Il brodo* (the broth). Gradually add the hot broth with a ladle. Allow the rice to absorb the liquid before adding more. Allow between 16 and 19 minutes of cooking time.

5 6 *La mantecatura* (creaming). Off the heat, finish by adding the remaining butter and the Grana Padano and stirring to combine. Let stand for at least 1 minute.

7 8 9 Spread the risotto onto each plate, tapping the edge of the plate with one hand while turning it with the other.

THE OTHER HOME OF COUSCOUS

Sicily is the land of *cuscus*, first cousin of the famous dish of the Maghreb.

MORGANE MIZZON

FROM TURKEY TO ITALY

→ In its carnivorous version, couscous originates from the Maghreb (the region encompassing northwestern Mediterranean Africa). Between the ninth and eleventh centuries, Sicily, under Arab domination, inherited this family-style dish. In particular, the city of Trapani, located in the far west of Sicily facing the Tunisian coast, adopted the recipe to the point that it become one of its specialties.

→ In Italy, one speaks of *cuscus trapanese*, or *cùscusu* in the Sicilian dialect. These terms come from the Arabic *kuskus*, derived from the Berber *seksu*, meaning "well rounded."

PATRIMONY

Now well established in the culinary landscape of the island, this dish is recognized as a "traditional agri-food product of Sicily," a distinction granted by the Ministry of Agricultural Policy.

Every year since 1998, a world couscous championship has been held in the small town of San Vito lo Capo, located about 19 miles (30 km) from Trapani.

Cousins

→ In Carloforte and Calasetta in Sardinia, *cuscus tabarchino* or *cascà*, a vegetarian couscous flavored with herbs and spices, is served.

→ In Sardinia, *fregula con le arselle* is prepared, a kind of soup made with large grains of semolina pasta and clams.

WHAT DOES THE DISH LOOK LIKE?

COUSCOUS

It must be worked by hand with a very specific action referred to as the *incocciatura*. This involves hydrating the grains little by little, swirling them gently in a bit of water. This step is traditionally performed in a *mafaradda* (in Sicilian dialect), a large terra-cotta dish over which water is poured. The couscous is then drained, dried in the open air, and cooked in the upper part of a *couscoussier*.

BROTH

On the lower level of the couscoussier is cooked the *ghiotta di pesce*, a rich soup made from Mediterranean fish and scorpion fish cooked together in a flavored broth, then drained. Bream, redfish, and gurnard are among the most commonly used species of fish.

COOKING

The couscous is steamed in the couscoussier, with either water flavored with bay leaves, parsley, and onions, or with fish broth taken from the ghiotta di pesce.

SERVING

Once cooked, the couscous should soak in the broth for half an hour. It's traditionally served in a wide, shallow dish, ideally the mafaradda, with a few cooked mussels, clams, and shrimp. The fish soup is then poured over it.

SKIP TO
FREGULA CON LE ARSELLE (SARDINIAN PASTA WITH CLAMS), P. 152;
COOKING WITH SEAWATER, P. 317.

MODICA CHOCOLATE

It's the black gold of Sicily! This chocolate is made according to the Aztec tradition in a small baroque-style city located in the southeast of the island.

STÉPHANE SOLIER

ONE OF A KIND IN THE WORLD

With the exception of not using the *metate*, a preheated concave stone used to grind cocoa beans that was replaced at the end of the nineteenth century by machines, the artisan chocolatiers of Modica make chocolate according to the pre-Columbian tradition:

The cocoa is worked without conching—that is to say, "cold"—in a bain-marie, at a temperature not exceeding 113°F (45°C) to retain its aromas.

The cocoa is mixed with sugar, the crystals of which remain whole.

The result

The chocolate has a gritty and sandy texture and is less "buttery," with a more pronounced cocoa flavor. There is a gradual release of aromatic elements (cocoa, sugar, then spices, including the traditional vanilla and cinnamon).

THE SABAINI REVOLUTION

Craftsman Simone Sabaini has perfected the traditional recipe and has won the distinction of making the best chocolate from Modica for nine years.

Her secrets

→ Working with chocolate at even lower temperatures and for longer times to stabilize the molecules and maintain its shiny appearance for longer.

→ Selecting exceptional raw ingredients.

→ Rigorous personal recipes.

→ A nonstop pursuit of innovation: creating chocolate with aromatic additions (herbs, spices, tobacco, etc.).

The history of a tradition

SEVENTEENTH CENTURY
The Jesuits, masters of cocoa plantations in Latin America, settle in Sicily. They teach Sicilians and unemployed persecuted Jews the Aztec art of grinding cacao.

1746
The Spanish possession of the commune of Modica protects the *cicolateri* who work with the bitter cacao, which arrives by land from Palermo or by sea from Livorno and Malta, on behalf of the house of Grimaldi.

SECOND HALF OF THE EIGHTEENTH CENTURY
Local elites consume hot chocolate, sweetened with cane sugar, introduced to Sicily by the Arabs and served for morning snacks and at social gatherings.

LATE NINETEENTH CENTURY
With the appearance of the first coffees, the dark nectar reaches other social classes. The traditional methods of chocolate making are gradually abandoned, but are safeguarded by a few craftsmen.

2018
The Modican tradition is protected by a PGI.

2020
Project to include Modica chocolate in the Intangible Cultural Heritage of UNESCO.

SKIP TO
GIANDUJA, P. 180;
CHOCOLATE SPREADS, P. 248.

SEASON

TUTTO L'ANNO (YEAR-ROUND)

CATEGORY

ANTIPASTO STREET FOOD

LEVEL

FACILE (EASY)

MOZZARELLA IN CARROZZA

FRIED MOZZARELLA

Sandwiched between bread, dredged in egg, breaded, then fried: in this recipe, mozzarella gets the heat. This antiwaste recipe guarantees you'll become addicted.

ALESSANDRA PIERINI

Travel sickness

Born in the Neapolitan countryside during the eighteenth century, *mozzarella in carrozza* ("mozzarella in a carriage") was initially enclosed between two slices of round sourdough bread (*cafone*), which resembled the wheels of a carriage.

At the time, the milk, transported by carts, curdled quickly during its journey and arrived in a fairly advanced state. Mozzarella, which was practically made inside the carriage due to this long journey, was no longer fresh enough to eat raw, but was perfect for cooking.

ITS EVOLUTION

ORIGINALLY, the recipe used *mozzarella di bufala* (buffalo mozzarella), which is more watery and needs to sit longer before using. Today, *fior di latte* is often recommended.

WHEN FIRST CREATED, mozzarella in carrozza was round, but today its shape is more triangular, rectangular, or square. It is very often prepared with white bread or stale bread.

VARIATIONS

MILK is used instead of flour, or 2 to 3 tablespoons of milk are added to the beaten eggs for a smoother result. This is very useful for softening stale bread.

THE ROMAN VERSION uses fior di latte instead of mozzarella di bufala and adds anchovy fillets or cooked ham to the mozzarella slices before the sandwich is closed. Gourmands will be sure to add capers, sun-dried tomatoes, or basil.

IN VENICE, in *bacari* (wine bars), mozzarella in carrozza is plump and golden, and encloses anchovies in white sandwich bread dredged in fritter batter.

THE RECIPE

SERVES 4

- 9 ounces (250 g) mozzarella di bufala or fior di latte
- 8 slices sandwich bread, measuring 4¾ by 4¾ inches (12 by 12 cm), crusts removed
- Salt
- ¾ cup (100 g) all-purpose flour
- 1½ cups (150 g) dried bread crumbs
- 2 large (100 g) eggs
- Freshly ground black pepper
- Oil, for frying

Cut the mozzarella into thin slices. Let dry on paper towels to remove excess liquid. Divide the mozzarella over 4 slices of the bread, being careful not to let it extend over the edges of the bread. Season with salt and close with the remaining bread slices, pressing down lightly with your hand, especially on the edges, to compress the sandwiches.

Place the flour and bread crumbs in two separate shallow bowls. Lightly beat the eggs in a shallow plate and season with salt and pepper. Cut the sandwiches on the diagonal and dredge them carefully in the flour, then in the beaten eggs, making sure to soak the surface and edges. Let the excess egg drain. Evenly coat all sides with the bread crumbs. Refrigerate for 30 minutes.

Heat the oil to 340°F (170°C) in a deep fryer or saucepan high enough to be able to completely submerge the breaded triangles in the oil. Fry only a few pieces at a time, until golden brown, turning them halfway through the cooking time (allow 2 to 3 minutes). Drain on paper towels and serve hot.

Il Tocco di Alessandra (Alessandra's Tips)

Prepare your homemade bread crumbs using leftover bread, biscotti, or very dry *grissini*—this will change everything!

AND IF THERE IS NO BREAD . . .
You can make this recipe without bread. When this is the case, it takes on another name: *mozzarella fritta.* Dip the drained mozzarella slices in the beaten egg and then into the bread crumbs. Fry the breaded mozzarella in the hot oil, 1 minute per side.

A DOUBLE DREDGE in bread crumbs (eggs plus bread crumbs) before frying in oil guarantees an extraordinarily crispy result.

FOR A LIGHTER VERSION, bake the sandwiches in a preheated 350°F (180°C) oven on a baking sheet lined with oiled parchment paper for 20 minutes (turning them halfway through cooking).

SKIP TO
THE MOZZARELLA FAMILY, P. 182; CICCHETTI VENEZIANI, P. 228.

Nadia Santini

PROFILE

This self-taught cook is the first Italian chef to be awarded three Michelin stars.

ANNA MARÉCHAL

KEY DATES

1953
Nadia Cavaliere is born in San Pietro Mussolino (Veneto).

1974
She and her husband, Antonio Santini, take over the restaurant Dal Pescatore, opened in 1926 by his grandfather.

1982
First Michelin star.

1996
Third Michelin star.

2013
Awarded "best chef in the world" by the Prix Veuve Clicquot.

A FAMILY MATTER

→ **FIRST GENERATION**: the pub Vino e Pesce was founded in 1926 by Antonio and Teresa Santini, the grandparents of Antonio Santini, in Canneto sull'Oglio (Lombardy).

→ **SECOND GENERATION**: their son Giovanni continues the business, specializing in fried fish and Lambrusco produced by his father. Vino e Pesce becomes Dal Pescatore (meaning "at the fisherman's house"), in homage to Antonio's first profession.

→ **THIRD GENERATION**: Nadia Santini, with no training other than political science and food science, learns the profession in the kitchen alongside Teresa Santini and Bruna, her stepmother. With her husband, Antonio, they transform the family pub into a worldwide model of gastronomy.

→ **FOURTH GENERATION**: Nadia and Antonio's children join the adventure: Giovanni works in the kitchen with his mother. Alberto, a sommelier by training, follows in his father's footsteps in the dining room, accompanied by his wife, Valentina.

RECIPE

CIALDE DI PARMIGIANO (PARMESAN TUILES)

SERVES 4

1½ tablespoons (20 g) unsalted butter

1½ cups (150 g) grated Parmigiano-Reggiano cheese

• Melt a small pat of butter in a nonstick skillet over medium heat. When the butter is melted, soak up the excess fat with a paper towel.

• Spoon small piles of the Parmesan into the pan and cook for a few seconds until the edges start to brown.

• Use tongs to remove the hot tuiles and place them on a rolling pin to bend them. Let rest for a few minutes and serve hot.

A PRIVILEGED TERROIR

Equidistant from Parma, Cremona, and Mantua, located in the Oglio Sud natural park in the heart of the Po plain, the restaurant, with around thirty seats, benefits from the resources of its environment, including Vialone Nano rice and fish from fresh headwaters. The kitchen garden's produce and fresh fish caught by the family round out the local provisions.

Nadia Santini composes dishes also inspired by her experiences at tables in France (such as restaurants Troisgros and Bocuse), in the tradition of Gualtiero Marchesi and "new Italian cuisine."

HER SPECIALTIES

STUFFED PASTA

Tortelli di zucca (squash tortellini with butter and Parmesan), a dish emblematic of the neighboring city of Mantua, the recipe for which has been passed down in the family for three generations. Also deserving mention is the *agnolini in brodo all'anguilla alle braci* (in a braised eel broth), which connects Nadia's love for stuffed pasta with the lake resources of the Oglio.

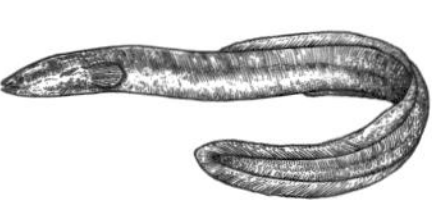

FISH

In the spirit of the restaurant's name, the Santinis cook freshwater fish with finesse. One of the house's flagship dishes is also part of an ancestral Italian culinary tradition: *anguilla in carpione al profumo di arancia* (eel in escabeche with flavors of orange).

WINE

The wine list is among the best in the world and represents all the major wine regions. In keeping with the original brand, led by Lambrusco, the fourth-generation Santinis consider the gastronomic experience to be a complete journey between the *cantina* (cellar) and the plate.

PARMIGIANO-REGGIANO

Nadia Santini, who grew up in a rural environment, knows and uses this king of Italian cheeses like no one else. Parmesan is a component of many of her signature recipes, and she originated the now cult preparation whose popularity took off in the 1980s: *cialde de parmigiano*, or Parmesan tuiles.

SKIP TO
GUALTIERO MARCHESI, P. 163;
MARINADES, P. 322;
FRESH PASTA, P. 294;
TORTELLI DI ZUCCA, P. 371.

ALIMENTARI

Located all over Italy and in particular in isolated villages, these general food markets are buzzing with life as much as they are showcases for delectable products.

MARTINA LIVERANI

Martina Liverani, journalist and writer, created the weekly publication *Dispensa, Generi Alimentari e Generi Umani* in 2013, where she recounts, and displays in images, many stories.

LOCAL FOOD NETWORKS

In past days, in small villages or in neighborhoods, the *alimentari* were the only places where you could buy food and essentials from bread and shoelaces to soap and canned tuna. They had colloquial names: *Sali e Tabacchi* (Salts and Tobacco), *Generi alimentari* (General Foods), *Salumi e Affini* (Salumi and Similar Products) that bear witness to a world where gastronomy and human relationships were closely linked.

Today, they have returned to the towns and villages! These food markets have become nerve centers for finding excellent-quality products in short supply. Grocers always call their customers by their first names, offer home delivery, and prepare sandwiches for lunch, children's snacks, or even picnics for those spending a day at sea or hiking through the mountains. These "retro-modern" businesses have become symbols of resistance to large shopping centers.

Isabella—*Generi alimentari a Castana* (Pavia)

Gioacchino—*Generi alimentari a Veniano* (Como)

Giovanna and Michele—*Generi alimentari a Castelvetrano* (Trapani)

Vincenzo—*Generi alimentari a Salemi* (Trapani)

Antonio and Anna—*Generi alimentari a Cerchiara di Calabria* (Cosenza)

SKIP TO
PANINO, P. 166; LET'S GO OUT TO EAT, P. 92.

SEASON
TUTTO L'ANNO (YEAR-ROUND)

CATEGORY
SECONDO PIATTO (MAIN COURSE)

LEVEL
DIFFICOLTÀ MEDIA (MEDIUM DIFFICULTY)

SPEZZATINO

ITALIAN BEEF STEW

This cousin of the perhaps better-known French boeuf Bourguignon is served up as a big and hearty family stew.

CÉLINE MAGUET

A stew with two secret weapons.

Behind every successful *spezzatino* are two key steps all good *cuoco* (cooks) must master.

(1) **THE *SOFFRITTO***
It's the browned onion-carrot-celery trio that gives flavor to the sauce, which serves as the base.

(2) **THE WELL-EXECUTED MAILLARD REACTION**
The Maillard reaction creates the crust and the perfect color of a steak, and the caramelized browned bits that are deglazed in the pan . . . By adhering to the hot pan, the meat is browned and gains a golden crust, and it leaves behind juices that will caramelize and provide flavor to the stew!

A HISTORY OF BUTCHERING

De spezzato ("cut into pieces") in a spezzatino is the one step that should be performed by the butcher, so that the beef shoulder, which is the first choice for this dish, or the upper shoulder or skirt steak can be cut properly! The tissues of these cuts melt and their collagen is released, creating all the magic in texture that occurs in these slow-cooked dishes.

SPEZZATINO FOR ALL TASTES

Beef is not the only meat that makes a good spezzatino. Each region has its preferences . . .

DI VITELLO (veal) *spezzatino alla cacciatora*—Lazio.

DI PECORA (sheep) *pezzata*—Umbria, Marche.

DI CINGHIALE (wild boar)—Umbria, Tuscany, Sardinia.

DI CAPRIOLO (venison)—Umbria, Trentino-Alto Adige, Friuli.

DI MAIALE (pork) *toc' de purcit*—Friuli; *cif* and *ciaf*—Abruzzo; *sfrionza*—Campania.

DI CAVALLO (horse) *pezzetti*—Apulia; *pastisada*—Veneto.

DI ASINO (donkey) *pastizzà de musso*—Veneto.

THE RECIPE

Here is the Tuscan *spezzatino di manzo* (beef), adapted by Mattia Carfagna, a gourmet from a large family of winegrowers and originally from the island of Giglio, in Tuscany.

SERVES 4

- 1 carrot
- 2 stalks celery
- 1 large onion
- Olive oil
- 3 sage leaves
- 1 sprig thyme
- 1 sprig rosemary
- 2 quarts (2 L) vegetable or beef stock
- 3/4 cup (180 mL) white or red wine
- 3 1/3 pounds (1.5 kg) beef shank, cut into 1 1/2- to 2-inch (4 to 5 cm) cubes

To make the soffritto, peel and finely chop the carrot, celery, and onion. In a large lidded ovenproof pot, cook the vegetables over low heat in a drizzle of olive oil. When the vegetables have started to soften, add the herbs and stock, then cover. When the liquid has evaporated, add half the wine and cook for another 20 to 40 minutes, or until the vegetables have cooked down and are lightly browned. Remove the vegetables from the pot and set aside.

Over high heat, heat a drizzle of oil in the same pot, then sear the meat cubes on all sides to brown them. Cook until the bits adhered to the bottom of the pan have browned, then add the remaining wine to deglaze the pan, using a wooden spoon to scrape up the caramelized browned bits from the bottom. Return the soffritto to the pot, then reduce the heat to low. Once the wine has been absorbed, cook the stew as if making a risotto: add a little stock at a time after the previous addition has evaporated.

After 30 minutes, add just enough stock to almost cover the meat: the meat must emerge from the top by about 1 inch (2.5 cm). Cover and simmer for at least 2 hours over very low heat, until the liquid has evaporated. The sauce must be smooth and thick and the meat tender. If the meat is still tough, continue adding more stock. Serve with mashed potatoes or polenta.

Il Tocco Della Chef (Chef's Tip)

At the end of the cooking time, add 1 tablespoon (15 mL) honey and 1 3/4 ounces (50 g) chocolate or cocoa nibs and a pinch of salt. Cook for an additional 15 minutes, then serve.

SKIP TO
POLENTA, P. 114;
RUSTIC COW BREEDS, P. 258;
RAGÙ BOLOGNESE, P. 330.

PARMIGIANO-REGGIANO

A gritty cow's-milk cheese distinguished by a PDO, Parmesan—despite its popularity—still possesses many secrets.

ANGELA BARUSI

ITS ORIGINS

It was during the twelfth century that the first dairies appeared in the Cistercian and Benedictine monasteries of Parma and Reggio Emilia where monks began processing milk in large boilers to produce a hard cheese that could be matured very slowly. The Parmesan produced at that time already resembled what we know today.

Its *Terroir*

The original production area is small but unique in its composition. It includes the provinces of Parma, Reggio Emilia, Modena, Bologna (Emilia-Romagna), and Mantua (Lombardy). Surrounded by the chain of the Apennine Mountains and the Po and Reno Rivers, it is blanketed with wide plains and gentle hills. Everything happens in this region, from growing the feed on which the cows graze to final packaging of the cheese.

Storage tips

When vacuum-packed, Parmesan can be stored for several months in its original unbroken packaging. Once opened, it becomes a fresh product again and should be handled as such.

Freshly cut, it should be wrapped in plastic wrap or placed in a closed glass or plastic container and stored in the refrigerator at 38° to 46°F (4° to 8°C). A young cheese (aged sixteen to eighteen months) can be kept for fifteen days; store a more mature cheese (more than twenty-four months) for about one month.

Freezing is not recommended.

CATTLE BREEDS

Four cattle breeds contribute to Parmesan's richness:

FRISONA ITALIANA
the most common and most productive breed.

BIANCA MODENESE
protected by Slow Food, its milk has an optimal ratio of fat and protein content.

BRUNA ITALIANA
its milk is specially adapted for making cheese thanks to its high casein and fat content.

ROSSA REGGIANA
its milk is particularly rich in proteins, calcium, and phosphorus.

CHOOSING THE BEST AGED PARMESAN

DISHES	AGING	USES	WHY?
Minestrone, vegetable soups, creamy and puréed soups	24 months or more	Grated	Excellent solubility. The aromas combine perfectly with the liquid. Shorter-matured ones will be less soluble and less tasty, leaving a lumpy deposit on the spoon and at the bottom of the dish.
Fresh pasta; with ragù or for cream-based sauces	30 months	Grated	Does not lump, and releases intense aromas and fragrances.
Dried pasta; with tomato oil or butter	15–18 months	Grated	Its sweetness goes perfectly with the acidity of tomatoes.
STUFFED PASTAS			
Vegetables	24 months	Grated	Provides consistency and flavor.
Fish	14–16 months	Grated	Provides sweetness and character, enhancing the delicate flavor of fish.
Meats	24 months	Grated	Enhances the taste without dominating other flavors.
Cheese	30 months	Grated	The palatability and spicy notes of a long ripening give flavor and character to single-ingredient fillings.
MAINS			
Stuffed meats	24 months	Grated	Improves flavor and binds ingredients.
Roulades	14–16 months	Shavings	Gives a buttery, milky flavor.
Main courses of fish/shellfish	24 months	Grated	Balances the sweet and fatty taste characteristic of shellfish.
Green salads and fruit salads (not recommended for citrus fruits)	18–24 months	Shavings	Added at the last minute, it brings flavor and slightly spicy milky notes.
Dessert: cream, cookies, and ice cream	18–20 months	Grated	Provides sweetness and light flavor, but also consistency and fat.

PARMESAN RINDS

After being carefully scraped and cleaned, Parmesan's rind can be used to flavor different dishes, thanks to its particular taste.

→ In purées and vegetable soups, the rinds can be placed in the liquid to cook, then cut into small cubes.

→ Rinds can be grilled or browned in a saucepan with a drizzle of oil after being boiled in water or broth.

→ They are very good cut into cubes, then warmed in the microwave and served as an aperitif.

THE LITTLE WHITE DOTS

The characteristic small white bits that are visible when eating Parmesan are crystals of the amino acid tyrosine: they are an indication of ripening time because they increase in number and size over time.

FEED

In its area of origin, Parmesan's unique characteristics are due in part to the biodiversity of the alfalfa and grass fields and natural meadows where the cattle forage. Some of these fields have not been plowed for centuries and support more than sixty varieties of local grasses. These transmit flavors and aromas to the milk as well as specific lactic acid bacteria that, combined with the uniqueness of the local cattle herd, give Parmesan its characteristic sensory profile and its ability to undergo very long aging.

SKIP TO
ITALY'S BEAUTIFUL CHEESES, P. 222;
RISOTTO, P. 78.

12 months
24 months
36 months
48 months
60 months
72 months
101 months
140 months

A Good Interior

Parmesan is made up of only 30 percent water along with 70 percent nutrients, which is why it is particularly rich in protein, calcium, vitamins, and minerals. It is naturally lactose-free and very rich in free amino acids that are easily absorbed, and its long aging makes it highly digestible. Additives and preservatives are not allowed in its production.

THE WHEELS

Selection and marketing

To become Parmesan, wheels that have reached twelve months of aging are subjected to rigorous examination by experts from the consortium responsible for protecting the appellation. This test, called the *battitura*, involves tapping the wheel in several places with a special hammer. The sounds produced should be homogeneous, indicating the absence of defects in the structure of the cheese. Only wheels that pass this examination are marked using a hot iron with the oval symbol that certifies them as Parmigiano-Reggiano PDO.

To age, or not to age

Once branded, the cheese can be sold, but generally the aging continues, and each dairy decides what degree of maturity it wishes to give its wheels: 18, 24, 36, 40 months, or, rarely, longer.

PARMESAN IN NUMBERS

50,000 people involved in the production chain.

1,111,900 acres (**450,000** ha) of agricultural land in 174 municipalities.

1,450,000 tons of local feed.

2,820 dairy farms.

265,000 cows over 24 months old to produce the milk.

1,920,000 tons of milk processed into Parmesan.

400,000 tons of milk produced by **64,000** cows in the mountains.

330 dairies.

137 gallons (**520** L) of milk to produce a single wheel.

13½ gallons (**13.5** L) of milk to produce 2¼ pounds (1 kg) of cheese.

About **3,700,000** wheels produced in 2019.

A SMALL SENSORY GUIDE			
AGING	ODORS AND AROMAS	TEXTURE	FLAVORS
14-16 MONTHS	Fresh milk and yogurt; blanched grass and vegetables; fresh fruits.	Elastic, poorly soluble.	Harmonious and delicate taste; sweet and tasty.
24-28 MONTHS	Butter; walnuts and hazelnuts; citrus; meat broth.	Soluble, crumbly, and grainy.	Balance between sweetness and acidity; sometimes a little spicy.
30-36 MONTHS	Cheese crust; walnuts and hazelnuts; nutmeg and pepper; banana and pineapple; meat broth and leather.	Very crumbly, grainy, and soluble.	Sweet and salty; very tasty, with a slight acidity; moderately spicy.

THE RELIGION OF COFFEE

Although they are not the biggest European consumers, Italians hold *caffè* sacred.

MARIELLE GAUDRY

WHO AM I?

ORIGINS—wild coffee is a shrub of the species *arabica* (from the tropical forests of Ethiopia) or *canephora* (from West Africa).

BOTANICAL IDENTITY
Coffea arabica (arabica) and *C. canephora* (robusta) both belong to the Rubiaceae family.

ARRIVAL IN EUROPE—Italy is the European gateway to coffee. From the 1600s, shipments of bags of yellow-green coffee beans left the Yemeni port of Moka for Venice, then for other ports in Italy served by sea routes. From there it spread across the continent at lightning speed.

Caffè Sospeso

This Neapolitan tradition of solidarity, literally meaning "suspended coffee," was born at the end of World War II. It consists of paying in advance at the bar for an additional coffee for a person in need. The custom quickly spread throughout the country, then crossed its borders. With the changeover to the euro, it has run out of steam a bit, but its resurgence is occurring in Naples, mainly thanks to the initiative of various associations. A national day (*giornata del caffè sospeso*) was established in 2011 to recognize this practice. It occurs on December 10, also celebrated as World Human Rights Day.

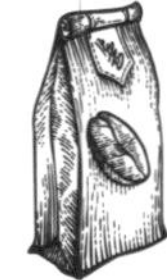

STORING YOUR COFFEE AT HOME

Opt for storing whole coffee beans, which are less expensive and keep better, and grind them in a suitable grinder as needed.

Before opening the beans, keep the original coffee package in a cool spot and avoid storing it in a closed cabinet where temperatures tend to rise.

Once the package has been opened, transfer its contents to an airtight container.

ROASTING

Italy is the second-largest producer of roasted coffee in Europe (over 400,000 tons in 2019), after Germany.

THE OVEN TEST

A crucial and final stage in coffee processing, roasting is the cooking of the beans. It occurs as closely as possible to the moment when the coffee will be consumed, which should be within the next thirty days after roasting. Roasting causes the bean to change its color (it's green when it is picked), increase its volume, and lighten its weight due to the loss of water. It takes place in a drum oven whose temperature and cooking time can be adjusted according to the varietals used and the results desired.

Unlike large industrial roasters with accelerated roasting methods ("flash" roasting), traditional roasting takes great care of the beans to enhance all their aromas and organoleptic characteristics. Italy is known for its so-called dark roasting (*torrefazione scura*): the beans are roasted longer and therefore darker. And the farther south you go in Italy, the deeper the roasting.

The Holy Trinity of *Caffè*

The quality of an espresso is measured by its crema, body, and aroma.

THE CREMA
makes a beautifully homogeneous hazelnut color, created by the perfect chemical reaction between water, temperature, pressure, and coffee.

BODY
is distinguished by its substance, fat, and viscosity, which ideally should be dense and velvety.

AROMA
is intense and elegant, with varied notes ranging from toast, chocolate, caramel, and nuts to a floral or fruity bouquet.

THE MAIN ROASTERS

There are no fewer than eight hundred roasters in Italy. Only about sixty are considered excellent for the quality of the beans processed and their artisanal and respectful know-how: they know the plantations from which they source their beans, and they favor slow roasting. Here is a selection.

Laboratorio di Torrefazione Giamaica Caffè—Verona, Veneto
ROASTER: Gianni Frasi, taken over by Simone Fumagalli
FOUNDED: 1947

Torrefazione Caffè Lelli—Bologna, Emilia-Romagna
ROASTER: Leonardo Lelli
FOUNDED: 1996

Torrefazione Lady Cafè—San Secondo, Emilia-Romagna
ROASTER: Massimo Bonini
FOUNDED: 2005

Caffè San Domenico—Sant'Antonino di Susa, Piedmont
ROASTER: Roberto Messineo
FOUNDED: 1998

Torrefazione Trinci—Cascine di Buti, Tuscany
ROASTER: Andrea Trinci
FOUNDED: 1939

"Il caffè buono si beve al bar"

Although elsewhere the term *café* can mean both the drink and the place where it is consumed, in Italy, *café* more commonly refers to the establishment rather than the drink. You can drink your *caffè* there in the morning, after lunch, or during an afternoon break, standing directly at the counter (*al bar*). A brief, friendly, and sacred moment around a coffee that is appreciated for its special qualities.

SKIP TO
THE MOKA POT, P. 24; BREAKFAST, P. 65.

ESPRESSO MACHINES

Here are the important dates in Italian technology that gave birth to espresso, a beverage enjoyed all over the globe.

HIPPOLYTE COURTY

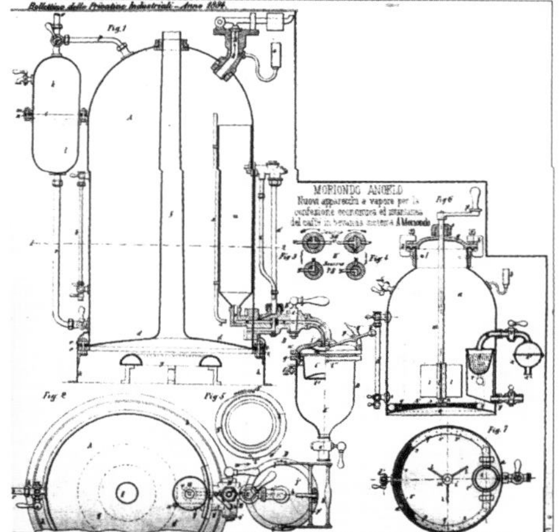

1884

Angelo Moriondo invents the first coffee machine in Turin to work with steam pressure. All that remains of it are sketches and souvenirs from the world's fair . . .

1901

Luigi Bezzera takes over Moriondo's work and creates the Tipo Gigante. However, it remains in the prototype stage.

1903

Desiderio La Pavoni develops the Ideale, the first espresso machine produced and marketed. Its shell-like silhouette still sits at center stage in some of the most beautiful bars in the world today.

1938

Barista Achille Gaggia designs an espresso machine that uses not steam pressure but instead hot water, thanks to a faucet-connected machine (**Torcio** or **Lampo**).

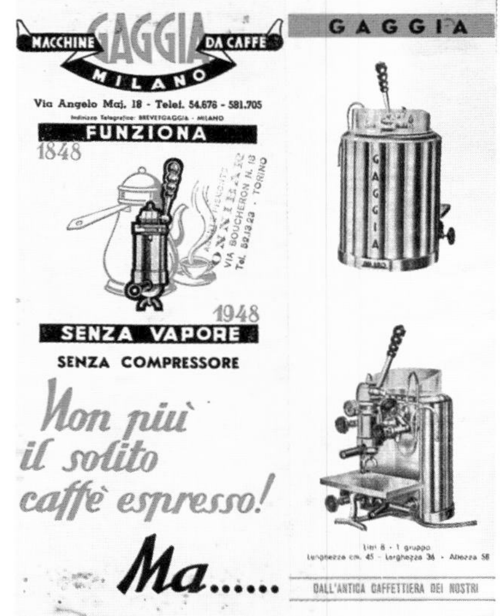

1948

Achille Gaggia creates a revolutionary machine: the lever-operated espresso machine! The pressure goes from 1.5 bars to 8 or 9. Made using hot water instead of steam, espresso now tastes like coffee rather than something burnt. As a result, Italy discovers the crema, smoothness, and flavor of coffee. Espresso becomes popular, the **Tipo Classica** machine invades bars throughout Italy, and Gaggia schmoozes with movie stars.

1961

Ernesto Valente takes the coffee machine to another dimension and eclipses Gaggia's machine. He replaces the lever with an electric pump and the boiler with a heat exchanger, and invents preinfusion. Espresso has never been easier to make, and the result is so consistent. The **Faema E61** becomes the icon of bars and *la dolce vita*. The modern espresso machine is born.

1970

La Marzocco, in Florence, develops a dual-boiler machine called the **GS** to produce steam for milk and hot water for espresso.

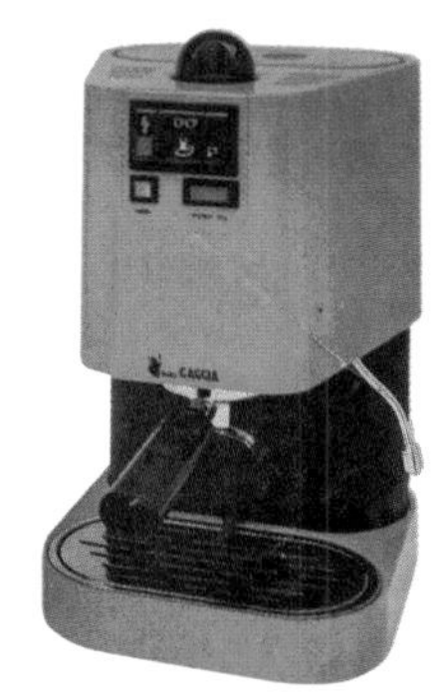

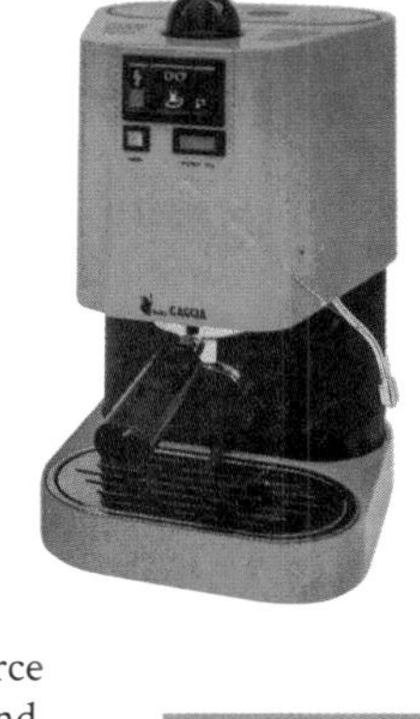

1977

The **Baby Gaggia**, an all-plastic household espresso machine, comes to kitchens and becomes popular in households. (This is not the first such machine. Gaggia began marketing the Gilda in 1952.) *Il caffè espresso* is no longer just a social and public experience, but also an individual experience.

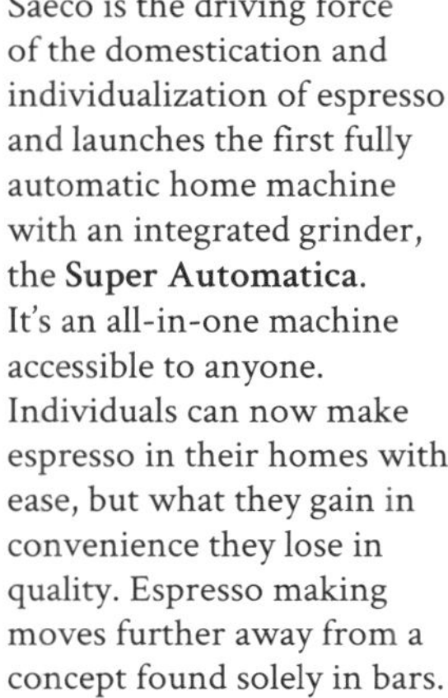

1985

Saeco is the driving force of the domestication and individualization of espresso and launches the first fully automatic home machine with an integrated grinder, the **Super Automatica**. It's an all-in-one machine accessible to anyone. Individuals can now make espresso in their homes with ease, but what they gain in convenience they lose in quality. Espresso making moves further away from a concept found solely in bars.

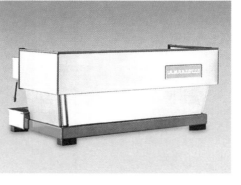

1993

La Marzocco, in Florence, markets the **Linea Classic**, an espresso machine for specialty coffee. From this true merger of technology, espresso changes from being simply an icon of Italian bars to a beverage served in coffee shops around the world. Espresso is no longer solely Italian, although the equipment is.

SKIP TO
HISTORIC CAFÉS, P. 265.

EASTER CAKES

The Easter holiday, which celebrates spring and the resurrection of Christ, marks the end of the fast of Lent with myriad sweets that carry strong symbolism.

SERENA CIRANNA

· BOILED EGG COOKIES ·

In southern Italy, the tradition during Easter is to bake dry cakes imbedded with whole hard-boiled eggs, which serve as both pagan and Christian symbols of rebirth.

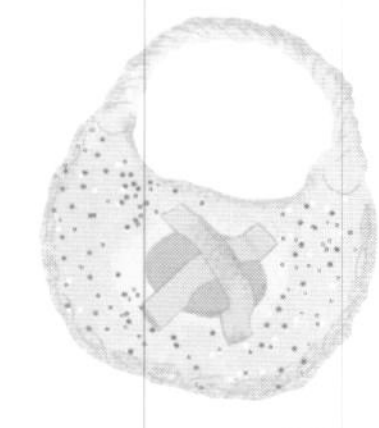

Panarelle*—Basilicata*

These shortbread cookies, originally made using olive oil, come in several shapes, the most traditional of which is a basket, or *panaredd* in local dialect. It encases a hard-boiled egg.

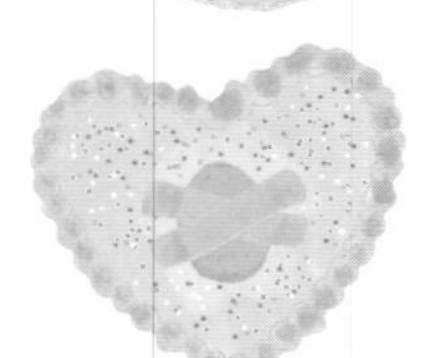

Scarcelle*—Apulia*

These shortbread cookies take many shapes (doves, hearts . . .). They typically encase an odd number of eggs, which is believed to bring good luck.

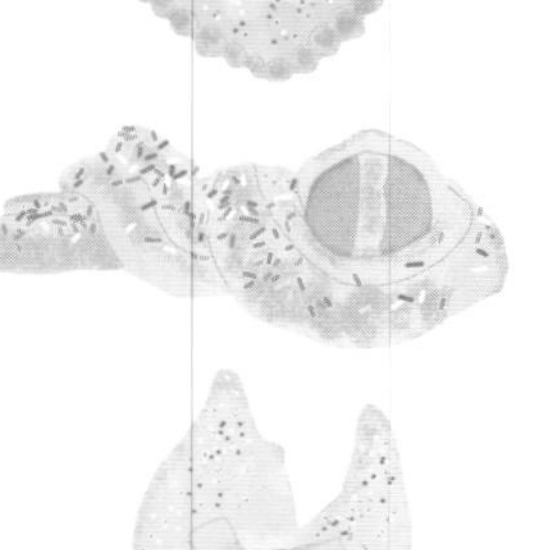

Cuzzuppa*—Calabria*

This cake is made with lard or olive oil, flavored with lemon, and sometimes topped with *annaspero* (a glaze made with sugar, egg white, and lemon juice). One is offered to each member of the family, and their size varies depending on the importance of the person. The number of eggs also has a meaning (seven announces a marriage, for example).

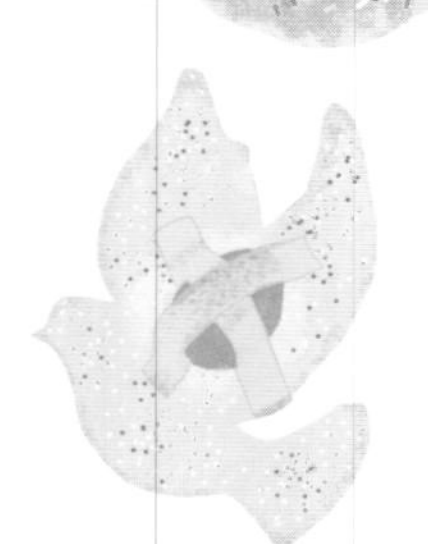

Aceddu cull'ovu*—Sicily*

Meaning literally "a bird with its egg," these tender cookies symbolize peace and rebirth. Also called *cuddura* and originally representing a dove, they are now available in different shapes, depending on the city.

· MODERN CLASSICS ·

Created by innovators of Italian confectionery, these recent creations have become classics on tables at Easter.

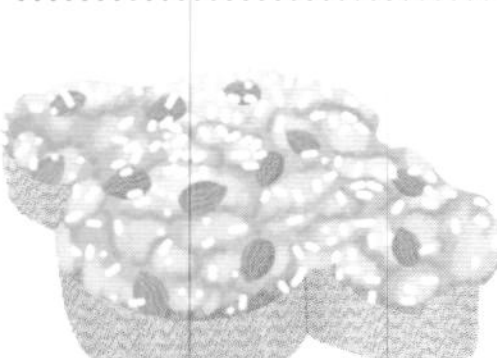
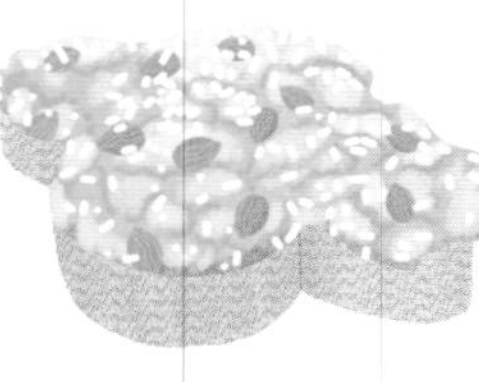

Colomba pasquale*—Lombardy*

The Motta company, which produces panettone, had the idea at the beginning of the twentieth century to use the same manufacturing process and the same ingredients to produce their frozen almond dessert in the shape of an "Easter dove," today popularized by artisan pastry chefs.

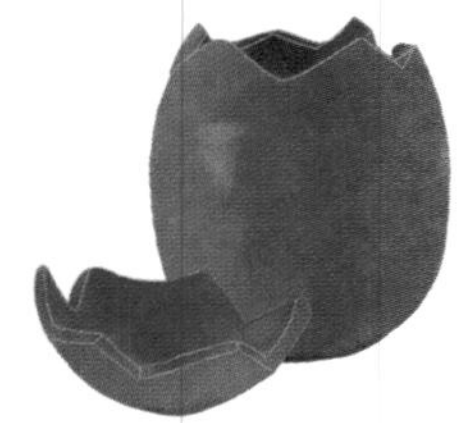

Uovo di Pasqua*—throughout Italy*

The exchange of eggs is a long tradition in the Christian world, inspired by ancient pagan practices or linked to the ban on egg consumption during Lent. Starting in the twentieth century, chocolate eggs have been very successful, especially in Piedmont.

· THE SICILIAN MARZIPAN LAMB ·

A veritable sculpture to admire rather than to eat, this little lamb made of almond paste decorates tabletops and shop windows. Among its most famous versions are the Favara marzipan lamb (Agrigento), with a pistachio center.

· SWEET BREADS AND CAKES ·

After fasting comes all the pleasures! The egg, forbidden during Lent, makes a comeback in an array of pastries.

Ciambelle pasquali*—Piedmont*

These lemon-, anise-, or pine nut–flavored "Easter fritters" are submerged in boiling water, then baked and decorated with cherries. They are often accompanied by a glass of sweet Asti sparkling wine.

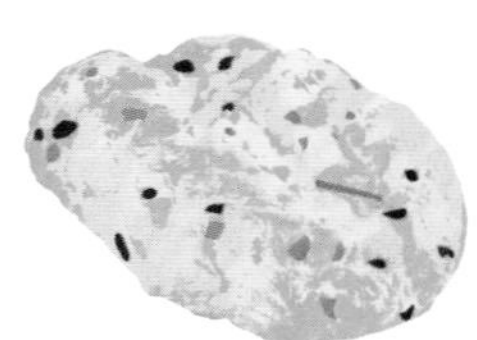

Resta*—Lombardy*

Common to Como, this yellow bread made from raisins, citron, and other candied citrus fruits was originally eaten on Palm Sunday (before Easter). Its name refers to its crust decorated with a fish bone (sometimes a stalk of wheat), a symbol of rebirth. Inside, an olive or cherry branch is a reminder of the arrival of spring.

Ciaramicola*—Umbria*

Common to Perugia, this cake is a tribute to the city's coat of arms whose colors it bears. The reddish interior, made from flour, sugar, butter, Alchermes liqueur, and orange peel, creates a nice contrast with the white glaze and the dragées that decorate its top.

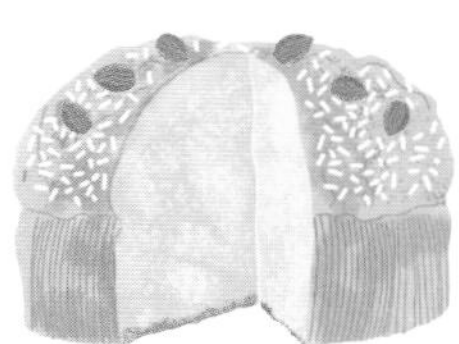

Fugassa*—Veneto*

This is a "poor man's" dessert made with flour, baker's yeast, sugar, vanilla, and almonds. With a shape reminiscent of a panettone, this cake is baked in the oven after a very long proofing time. Its name is the equivalent of *focaccia* in the Venetian dialect.

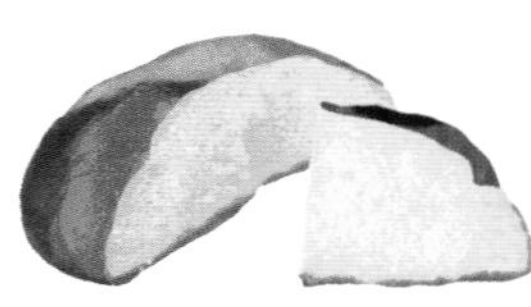
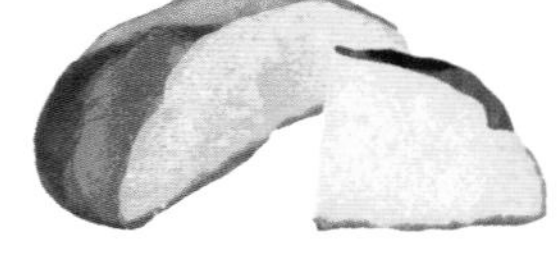

Pinza triestina*—Friuli-Venezia Giulia*

Emblematic of the city of Trieste, this bread, enriched with butter, honey, and eggs, can be enjoyed with salty or sweet foods. The three slashes on its surface evoke the Holy Trinity but also facilitate its rising in the oven.

· RICOTTA-BASED CAKES ·

This fresh cheese is widely used in Easter cakes in Italy. It offers a spring freshness and lightness to baked products.

Pardulas*—Sardinia*

These small sun-shaped cakes, also called *formaggelle* (small cheeses), made from sheep's-milk ricotta and flavored with saffron and orange zest, pay homage to pastoral traditions.

Pastiera napoletana*—Campania*

This classic of Neapolitan tradition is one of the most famous ricotta-based cakes. It is said that this cake would have elicited a smile in public from the austere Maria Theresa of Austria, wife of King Ferdinand II of Bourbon.

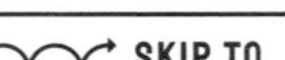

SKIP TO

RICOTTA, P. 219; PASTIERA, P. 91.

SEASON
TUTTO L'ANNO (YEAR-ROUND)

CATEGORY
DOLCE (DESSERT)

LEVEL
DIFFICOLTÀ MEDIA (MEDIUM DIFFICULTY)

PASTIERA

RICOTTA AND ORANGE BLOSSOM CAKE

This Easter cake can be baked starting on Holy Thursday so that its sweet pastry, ricotta and wheat filling, and aroma of orange blossom develop into delicious harmony.

ALESSANDRA PIERINI

A fairy-tale pastry

Its first written recipe is found in the fable "La Gatta Cenerentola" (1634) by Giambattista Basile, the origin of the famous story of Cinderella. The recipe is said to be an enhanced version of a cake that accompanied pagan festivals in ancient Rome to celebrate the return of spring, during which the priestesses of Ceres in procession carried pastries made from eggs, a symbol of renewal.

FROM MYTHOLOGY . . .

It is said that the inhabitants of the Gulf of Naples offered it to the mermaid Parthenope, who rose from the water each spring to lull them with her melodious songs:

→ The flour, a symbol of the strength and wealth of the earth.

→ The ricotta, an offering of pastoral culture.

→ The eggs, attributes of new life.

→ The wheat boiled in milk, a link between agriculture and livestock.

→ The orange blossom water, a divine libation glorifying the golden fruits of the region.

→ A sweet element to commemorate the sweetness of the siren's song, which envelops the entire universe.

The *pastiera* was born from the union of all these ingredients.

Another legend explains that Neapolitan sailors' wives brought baskets at night containing wheat, ricotta, eggs, and candied fruits to the beaches as offerings to the god Neptune to protect their husbands at sea. In the morning, all these foods miraculously metamorphosed into pastiera.

. . . TO RELIGION

It is thanks to the nuns of the former monastery of San Gregorio Armeno in Naples, experts in the art of pastiera, that this recipe has become firmly established as a symbolic dessert of Easter.

THE RECIPE

This version was provided by Gerardo Scognamillo, a Neapolitan pastry chef who immigrated to Marseille.

SERVES 8 TO 10

For the shortbread pastry

4 cups (500 g) all-purpose flour, plus more for rolling

1 cup (200 g) granulated sugar

Zest of 1 unwaxed lemon

14 tablespoons (200 g) unsalted butter, at room temperature

2 large (38 g) egg yolks

1 pinch salt

For the filling

10½ ounces (300 g) raw wheat, or 1⅓ pounds (600 g) cooked wheat

Scant ½ cup (100 mL) milk

2 tablespoons (30 g) unsalted butter, plus 1 tablespoon (20 g) for greasing the pan

Zest of 1 unwaxed lemon

7 large (133 g) egg yolks, plus 1 large (19 g) egg yolk for finishing (or use a little milk)

2 cups (400 g) granulated sugar

1⅓ pounds (600 g) ricotta cheese

2 tablespoons (30 mL) orange blossom water

1½ ounces (40 g) candied citron

1½ ounces (40 g) candied orange

5 large (180 g) egg whites

3 tablespoons (20 g) confectioners' sugar

For the pastry, combine the flour, granulated sugar, and lemon zest. Add the butter and work the ingredients together using a wooden spoon. Stir in the egg yolks. Add the salt and combine just until you achieve a smooth dough. Press the dough into a disk and chill for 1 hour.

For the filling, wash the raw wheat and place it in a saucepan with three times its volume of unsalted water. Gently bring to a boil, cook for 1 hour over low heat, then drain.

Transfer the cooked wheat to a pot and add the milk, butter, and lemon zest. Cook for 15 minutes, or until the milk is absorbed into the wheat and a creamy consistency is achieved.

Combine the egg yolks with the granulated sugar, then stir in the ricotta, orange blossom water, cooked wheat, and candied fruits. Beat the egg whites to stiff peaks. Incorporate them delicately into the ricotta mixture; the consistency should be quite liquid.

Preheat the oven to 350°F (180°C). On a floured work surface, roll out the dough using a rolling pin to a thickness of just slightly less than ¼ inch (5 mm). Butter an 11-inch (28 cm) round cake pan or springform pan, at least 3 inches (8 cm) high, and line it with the round of dough. Trim off excess dough from the edges and cut the scraps into ⅓-inch-wide (1 cm) strips long enough to extend across the top of the cake. Scrape the filling into the mold and spread it out. Arrange the dough strips on top in a crisscross pattern. Brush the strips with egg yolk or milk. Bake for 1 hour 15 minutes, or until the surface is golden. Turn off the oven and let the cake cool in the oven. Dust with the confectioners' sugar just before serving.

VARIATIONS

This can be made with lard instead of butter, with or without pastry cream, mixed wheat or not, with or without candied fruits. In the region of Caserta, some people replace the wheat with rice.

Italy, land of bitter oranges,

is the home of the unique Slow Food sentinel orange blossom water. It is produced in Vallebona (Imperia, Liguria) by Pietro Guglielmi.

SKIP TO
SWEETS FROM THE CONVENT, P. 204; CITRUS, P. 106; RICOTTA, P. 219.

LET'S GO OUT TO EAT

Eating establishments of all sorts abound in Italy. Here is a tour of "the boot" to help discover all the choices for a bite out.

STÉPHANE SOLIER

NATIONAL EATERIES

RISTORANTE

From French *restaurant* (to restore), introduced in Italian in 1877.
An establishment with rather elaborate cuisine, either national or international. It has a fixed menu with bottled wines. For special occasions.

$$$+ —VARIABLE PRICES

OSTERIA (OR HOSTARIA)

From Old French *oste* (innkeeper).
Referring to the innkeeper of popular inns where a bed, breakfast, wine, and snacks were available. Today, it's a modest establishment similar to a trattoria (simple homemade dishes, inexpensive, daily menu, table wine) or a trendy bistro spotlighted by Slow Food (serving ethical and local cuisine, quality wines).

$$$-$$ —VARIABLE PRICES

AGRITURISMO

Compound word (*agri* + *tourism*).
An agricultural structure emphasizing green and sustainable Italian tourism and whose activities include those devoted to providing accommodations and food that promote farm-raised products. The menu is limited to local products.

$$$-$$ —VARIABLE PRICES

TRATTORIA

From French *traiteur* (seller of prepared foods).
A rather modest establishment with traditional local and regional cuisine. The menu is limited to a few dishes, and it most often serves everyday wines.

$$ —USUALLY INEXPENSIVE

LOCANDA

From Latin *locare* (to rent).
A tavern or inn with sleeping rooms and traditional cuisine similar to a trattoria. Serves foods that are typical of the region.

$$ —USUALLY INEXPENSIVE

TAVOLA CALDA

Meaning "hot table" (serving hot dishes at any time).
A snack bar or cafeteria with prepared simple foods (roasted items, fried foods, vegetables, etc.). For on-site dining or takeout.

$ —MODEST PRICES

PIZZERIA

From Italian *pizza*.
An establishment where they prepare, bake (usually in a wood oven), and serve pizzas, fried foods, and other easy-to-eat dishes in an informal atmosphere and setting. For on-site dining or takeout.

$ —USUALLY LOW PRICES

TAVERNA

From Latin *taberna* (stall, cabaret, or inn).
Originally these were often modest establishments dedicated to serving wine, with a refined rustic atmosphere.

$ —SIMPLE FOOD SERVICE, EVERYDAY WINES, MODEST PRICES

REGIONAL EATERIES

LATTERIA

An old dairy or milk shop (*latte*).
A Milanese canteen for laborers.

TRANI

A typical wine bar in Milan, originally run by locals from Trani (Apulia). Offering meals without fuss, card games, and singers.

PIOLA

From French *piaule*/*piôle* (tavern), from Old French *pier* (to drink).
A Piedmontese cabaret, especially in Turin. Offering Piedmontese wines and specialties (charcuterie, cheeses, anchovies, hard-boiled eggs, omelets).

FRIGGITORIA

Establishment of fried foods (*friggere*) for takeout.
Found throughout Italy but very common in Genoa (offering paper cones of fried fish, or *cartoccio di pesce*), Naples (risen pizzas [*cresciuta*], *pizza fritta* . . .), and Palermo (chickpea fritters [*pani e panelle*], potato croquettes [*crocchè*] . . .).

FRASCA/OSMIZA

From *frasca* (branches) and Slovenian *osmiza* (eight, for the number of opening days originally permitted).
A country inn from Friuli open to the public for the sale of local products and traditional dishes (mostly cold), cheeses, and charcuterie.

BANCARELLA

Literally "little bench."
Has stands and mobile stalls everywhere in the markets. Sells *cibo di strada* (street food): *arancini* (rice croquettes), *cartocciata* (filled turnovers), *arrusti e mancia* (horsemeat sandwich), *pani ca meusa* (sandwich of veal spleen and lungs) . . .

CHIOSCO (OR CIOSCO)

From medieval Turkish *kieuchk* or *kiösk* (palace, salon).
A kiosk selling traditional thirst-quenching drinks (seltzer water, lemon and salt, syrups . . .) in Catania and throughout Sicily.

BACARO

Perhaps from the Venetian expression *far bàcara* (to party).
A Venetian establishment serving wine by the glass (an *ombra*), spritz, and snacks (*cicchetti*).

PUTIA/PUTICA

From the Greek *apotheke* (shop).
Popular restaurants present throughout Sicily, especially in Catania and Messina. Often offering large tables where one enjoys grilled meats.

FRASCHETTA

New wine establishments in the Castelli Romani (Ariccia), with salty-snack service. Castelli wine, *porchetta* (roast suckling pig), charcuterie and cheeses, and pasta from the Roman tradition (carbonara, *amatriciana* . . .).

FIASCHETTERIA

Typical Tuscan wine retail shop, with wine sold in flasks, originally accompanied by cold plates and pastas in broth. Offering local wines, homey dishes, and local charcuterie (*soppressata*, *finocchiona* . . .).

SEASON
TUTTO L'ANNO (YEAR-ROUND)

CATEGORY
BEVANDA (BEVERAGE)

LEVEL
FACILE (EASY)

SPRITZ

The popularity of this orange-red aperitif has moved beyond the borders of Venice, where it originated.

MARIELLE GAUDRY

CAMPARI OR APEROL?

Originally from Milan (1860, Lombardy), Campari (spritz bitter) has a bright red color, is rather bitter, and has won the hearts of many.

Originally created in Canale (1919, Piedmont), Aperol (spritz *dolce*) has an orange color and is sweeter than Campari.

AN ALTERNATIVE?

Cynar, a bitter created in 1952, is produced from artichoke leaves and plants. It is amber in color and more bitter than Aperol. Its alcohol level reaches 16.5 percent. The quantity added to a spritz is the same as other bitters.

STILL OR SPARKLING WINE?

While some recipes stick to dry white wine, especially in Trieste, sparkling wine is another choice, such as a Prosecco from Veneto.

SPARKLING WATER OR STILL?

Acqua frizzante (carbonated water) is the preference, though others disregard it.

ORANGE OR LEMON?

A slice of orange in the Aperol version, lemon in the Campari version.

AN OLIVE OR NOT?

For a final touch, opt for a large green olive (Bella di Cerignola from Apulia or Nocellara del Belice from Sicily), not pitted, at the end of a toothpick.

WHY A GERMANIC NAME?

While under Austrian occupation in the nineteenth century, Venice witnessed soldiers, merchants, officials, and diplomats arriving from Vienna. Accustomed to beer, the diplomats found the local wines too alcoholic and got into the habit of asking the waiter to literally "squirt" (*spritzen* in German) water into their wine. Starting in 1900, this first version of the spritz took on a sparkling twist with the use of seltzer water. It then became available in different forms depending on the region, with the creation of amaro, a bitter liqueur made from oranges and an infusion of plants.

The most common is the Venetian version. It's nicknamed *sprisseto* and served in *bacari* (wine bars) with Campari or Aperol.

SPRITZ *Veneziano*

The ultimate Venetian spritz is made with Select. Created in Venice in 1920, Select is a dazzling ruby-red bitter with a bitterness between that of Aperol and Campari. It offers an astonishing aromatic complexity on the nose, with notes of citrus and flowers. It is served according to artistic guidelines and with great fanfare in Piazza San Marco (Gran Caffè Quadri, €20) or at the Rialto market standing at the counter (Al Merca, €2.50). It's up to you to choose your version of *la dolce vita*.

A SPLASH OF FREEDOM

Although the Veneziano spritz recipe was codified in 2011 by the IBA (International Bartenders Association) in precise proportions (¼ cup/ 60 mL Prosecco, 3 tablespoons/40 mL Aperol, 1 splash sparkling water), in Venice it varies frequently from one bartender to another, in both method and quantities.

OSCAR QUAGLIARINI'S RECIPE

Italian bartender

MAKES 1 LARGE WINEGLASS

- ½ cup (120 mL) Prosecco
- Ice cubes
- 3 tablespoons plus 1 teaspoon (50 mL) Aperol
- 1 splash sparkling water
- 1 orange wheel
- 1 green olive

SEASON

ESTATE (SUMMER)

CATEGORY

ANTIPASTO/ SECONDO PIATTO (APPETIZER OR MAIN COURSE)

LEVEL

FACILE (EASY)

INSALATA CAPRESE

TOMATO, MOZZARELLA, AND BASIL SALAD

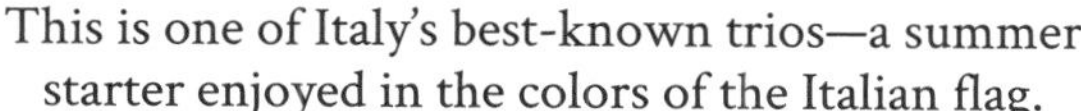

This is one of Italy's best-known trios—a summer starter enjoyed in the colors of the Italian flag.

ANNA MARÉCHAL

Its origins

One thing is certain: the caprese salad was, as its name suggests, born on the island of Capri in the Gulf of Naples. There are several conflicting theories, however, regarding how it came to be:

→ It was invented at the Quisisana hotel in the 1920s following Filippo Tommaso Marinetti's work *The Manifesto of Futurist Cooking*. As a vegetarian recipe, it denigrated common pasta dishes.

→ A story of more humble origins, however, says it was created around 1920 by a patriotic shipyard worker who combined the three ingredients in homage to his homeland and the colors of its flag.

→ It is also said that this salad was popular with King Farouk, who was exiled to Capri in 1952 after a military coup in Egypt. The story further claims it was created in his honor by the chef of the Hotel Gatto Bianco, where Farouk was staying. This highly publicized version of the story popularized the dish beyond Italy's borders.

IF THE CAPRESE WERE . . .

A PIZZA:
It would be the Margherita.

GNOCCHI:
They would be prepared *alla sorrentina*.

A PRODUCT:
It would be the Marrone di Caprese Michelangelo DOP. This PDO chestnut is produced in the municipality of Caprese Michelangelo, north of Anghiari in the province of Arezzo (Tuscany). It is particularly starchy.

A DESSERT:
It would be the *torta caprese*, an addicting flourless chocolate and almond cake!

SKIP TO
TOMATOES, P. 28; OLIVE OIL, P. 140.

The flavor of this salad, in the three colors of the Italian flag, shines when composed of three farm-raised products from Campania.

TOMATOES

They should be ripe but have a fairly firm consistency. The Sorrento or Cuore di Bue (beef heart) varietals, dense and tasty, lend themselves well to this salad. Their large and irregular dimensions go well with the slices of mozzarella.

MOZZARELLA

Mozzarella di bufala Campana DOP, with its enticing and delicate flavors, or *fior di latte* (a cow's-milk cheese), which is lighter. The latter cheese is used often in the salad's *treccia* (braided) version.

BASIL

The Neapolitan variety—the most widespread—with its large, intense green leaves, is ideal.

SEASONING

A powerful, aromatic, and fruity olive oil along with salt and pepper. Forget pesto, Parmesan, balsamic vinegar, and other additions that tend to overembellish. Simplicity is the way to go here.

THE RECIPE

This salad is built around just three ingredients and a balance of seasonings. Good olive oil, salt, pepper, and *basta*!

SERVES 4

1⅓ pounds (600 g) Sorrento tomatoes

10½ ounces (300 g) fior di latte, at room temperature

Fleur de sel and freshly ground black pepper

Extra-virgin olive oil

10 basil leaves

Cut the tomatoes lengthwise into thin slices (¼ inch/5 mm). Discard any excess juice that accumulates. Drain the fior di latte, then cut it into slices of the same thickness.

On a serving dish, preferably a white one, alternate the slices of tomato and the slices of cheese, overlapping them slightly along one entire row. Repeat this step. Season the tomatoes with a pinch of fleur de sel and a few turns of the pepper mill. Drizzle the olive oil over the salad. Arrange the basil leaves on top, then serve.

VARIATIONS

→ The ingredients can be diced, seasoned, and served in a bowl.

→ Oregano is often used as a seasoning. You can infuse it in the olive oil before drizzling it on top.

→ Some people insert anchovies, capers, or olives between the slices of tomato and cheese.

PANETTONE

A soft and fragrant brioche-style cake offering an abundant filling, artisanal panettone is an unparalleled delight for Christmas. Here are ten truly gourmand versions representing both tradition and creativity.

ALESSANDRA PIERINI

PANETTONE TRADIZIONALE MILANO

Traditional Milanese

Traditional versions

PANETTONE TRADIZIONALE MILANO

Traditional Milanese · 2¼ POUNDS (1 KG)

PRODUCER—Pasticceria Il Chiosco (Lonigo, Veneto). After getting his start working with the best pastry chefs in Italy, Francesco Ballico set out on his own in 1996 by purchasing a former town bar, now transformed into an elegant pastry shop.

INGREDIENTS—raisins, candied orange, Mieli Thun orange blossom honey, Bourbon-Madagascar vanilla.

PANETTONE TRADIZIONALE BASSO

Traditional short · 2 POUNDS (900 G)

PRODUCER—Olivieri 1882 (Arzignano, Veneto), a family of pastry chefs, chocolatiers, and ice cream makers established in 1882. Today, Nicola Olivieri runs the business, and his artisanal panettone is ranked among the best in the country.

INGREDIENTS—raisins, candied orange, orange paste, honey, Tahitian vanilla.

PANETTONE TRADIZIONALE GLASSATO

Traditional, with glaze · 2¼ POUNDS (1 KG)

PRODUCER—Luigi Biasetto (Padua, Veneto), crowned world pastry champion in 1997 and winner of the 2018 prize for best panettone in Italy at the prestigious I Maestri del Panettone competition in Milan.

INGREDIENTS—raisins, candied orange, acacia honey, vanilla, orange, lemon.
Glaze: almonds, cocoa.

PANETTONE TRADIZIONALE MILANO

Traditional Milanese · 1⅞ POUNDS (850 G)

PRODUCER—Opera Waiting (Poggibonsi, Tuscany). Aided by his brother Gianluca and his wife, Elisa Polvani, Gabriele Ciacci has selected ancient wheats and the best raw ingredients (mainly organic).

INGREDIENTS—candied orange, raisins, candied citron, sainfoin honey, vanilla.

PANETTONE TRADIZIONALE MANDORLATO

Traditional, with almond glaze · 2¼ POUNDS (1 KG)

PRODUCER—Malafronte (Gragnano, Campania). Founded in the nineteenth century by Giuseppe Malafronte, this family bakery also became a pastry shop in the 1980s thanks to the efforts of third-generation Ciro Malafronte; the shop is now operated by his three children.

INGREDIENTS—raisins, candied orange, candied citron, honey, salt, natural flavors.
Glaze: apricot kernels, almonds.

Creative versions

PANETTONE AI MARRONS GLACÉS

With candied chestnuts · 2¼ POUNDS (1 KG)

PRODUCER—Mauro Morandin (Saint-Vincent, Aosta Valley). Mauro took over the pastry shop founded by his father, Rolando, where he works with the highest-quality ingredients. His internationally renowned panettone has won numerous competitions.

INGREDIENTS—candied chestnuts.
Filling: hazelnuts, chestnuts, cocoa butter, alcohol, natural Bourbon vanilla flavor.

PANETTONE ALLE AMARENE

With morello cherries · 2¼ POUNDS (1 KG)

PRODUCER—Malafronte (Gragnano, Campania). *See* Panettone Tradizionale Mandorlato.

INGREDIENTS—morello cherries, honey, salt, natural flavors.

PANETTONE AL GIANDUJA

With gianduja · 1⅔ POUNDS (750 G)

PRODUCER—Olivieri 1882 (Arzignano, Veneto). *See* Panettone Tradizionale Basso.

INGREDIENTS—Valrhona 55% dark chocolate, Piedmont hazelnut paste IGP, candied orange paste, cocoa, honey, Tahitian vanilla.
Glaze: almonds, hazelnuts, cocoa, pine nuts.

ALBIMOKKA

With candied apricots and coffee · 1⅔ POUNDS (750 G)

PRODUCER—Massimo Ferrante (Campomorone, Liguria). Running his pastry shop since 1991 (an annexed café was bult in 2012), Massimo is assisted by his wife and son. He was awarded the Best Traditional Panettone prize in 2019 at the Panettone World Cup in Lugano, Switzerland.

INGREDIENTS—candied apricot, salt, vanilla, coffee.
Glaze: chocolate, coffee liqueur.

PANETTONE AL PISTACCHIO

With pistachio · 2¼ POUNDS (1 KG)

PRODUCER—Aricchigia (Bronte, Sicily). An artisanal producer founded by Laura Lupo on the slopes of Mount Etna, using local raw ingredients such as Bronte pistachios DOP and Sicilian almonds from the family farm.

INGREDIENTS—30 percent pistachio flavors.
Glaze: 20 percent pistachio flavors.

SKIP TO
SWEET TREATS OF CHRISTMAS, P. 314; "MIELICROMIA," P. 338.

BEHIND THE SCENES OF THE PANETTONE

As a symbol of Italian Christmas, this festive cake delights the palate, satisfies the appetite, and warms the heart.

ANNA PRANDONI

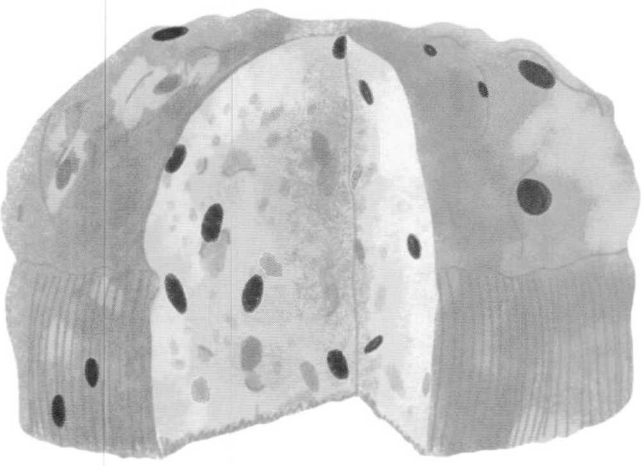

WHAT AM I?

It's a slow-fermentation, dome-shaped, typically Milanese cake (not brioche!), baked in the oven and filled with raisins and candied fruits. Panettone is produced and consumed only during the Christmas season. It makes an appearance for only a short time, but it's the sweetest time of year.

ITS ORIGINS

→ Starting at the beginning of the nineteenth century, artisanal panettone became a permanent resident of Milan. However, its story begins much earlier and has become an object of imagination, if not legend.

→ There are many who place its beginnings at the court of Ludovico Maria Sforza during the second half of the fifteenth century, where a boy named Toni allegedly rescued dessert, which had been burned by the chef of the court, by offering an improvised version based on candied fruits and raisins, called *pan del Toni*, from which the current name is derived.

→ Documents from the thirteenth century describe the custom of enjoying a slice of *pandolce* (a kind of raisin-filled sponge cake) on the day of San Biagio (Saint Blaise, February 3) in the rural communities around Milan.

→ In the nineteenth century and at least until World War I, Milanese production of panettone grew, maintaining a handcrafted style intended for the social elite.

→ With the economic boom of the postwar period, panettone production became industrialized while trying to maintain a certain quality. Angelo Motta and Gino Alemagna created a more accessible panettone, which spread throughout the country while remaining faithful to original craftsmanship.

The tradition of San Biagio

In Milan, it's tradition to set aside aside a piece of panettone shared during the Christmas meal to eat stale with the family on February 3 as a way to ward off sore throats and colds. On this day, in order to sell the unsold loaves, merchants offer the *panettoni di San Biagio* at reduced prices as the last vestige of the holiday season.

THE PROFESSIONAL TECHNIQUE

Artisanal panettone is extremely complex to make: you need two different types of dough with very long proofing times. Here are the steps to its preparation.

STEP 1

To make a classic Milanese panettone, start by mixing the flour, some of the sugar, the malt, and the yeast, and let the dough proof for about twelve hours.

STEP 2

The second step consists of incorporating the eggs, butter, sugar, vanilla, and candied fruits (raisins and orange peel) into the dough. At the end of this step, the panettone dough is soft, smooth, and shiny.

STEP 3

After a first *puntatura* (rest) and once the desired weight is determined, shaping begins. You *pirlare* (roll) the panettone: the dough is turned by hand to give it its shape.

STEP 4

The panettone is then placed in a round *pirottino*, the classic paper mold for baking panettone, and left undisturbed to rise one last time for six to eight hours.

STEP 5

Before baking, the top is slashed in a cross, originally as a religious symbol, and a piece of butter is placed in the *scarpatura* (slash mark).

STEP 6

Baking takes one hour and requires a temperature of around 199°F (93°C) at the center of the cake.

STEP 7

Once baked, the *panettoni* are turned upside down to hang to retain their shape and to rest for fourteen hours before packing.

SKIP TO
SWEET TREATS OF CHRISTMAS, P. 314;
SACROSANCT CUISINE, P. 346.

How do you choose a good panettone?

A perfect combination of what you see, feel, touch, and taste is an unfailing indicator of a quality product that keeps its promises!

SEE

→ A uniform and well-developed honeycomb structure.

→ A crust that is well adhered to the dough, about 2.5 mm thick, golden brown in color, and without scorch marks.

→ The quantity, size, and density of candied fruits: they must be visible, well distributed throughout the interior, and in reasonable quantity.

→ Expiration date: the shorter it is, the more likely the panettone has been prepared without preservatives.

SMELL

The freshness perceived by the nose corresponds to that of the raw ingredients used. A sweet and pleasant smell is a good sign.

TOUCH

The panettone must "string." That is to say, when a piece is pulled from the center, it should pull apart in large strips, as if it were cotton.

TASTE

The balance among tastes is fundamental. Sweet, salty, sour, and bitter must be in perfect harmony. The soft structure should melt on the tongue, and the bite should not feel rubbery.

The variations

In addition to traditional panettoni, which follow specific guidelines (chocolate, glazing, creams), other fillings, both sweet and savory, are now added. Here are some of the most surprising:

RADICCHIO DI TREVISO

CAPOCOLLO DI MARTINAFRANCA
(a charcuterie from the Murge)

'NDUJA CALABRAISE
(spicy pork sausage)

GORGONZOLA, OLIVES,
or even **MARINE PLANKTON.**

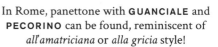

In Rome, panettone with **GUANCIALE** and **PECORINO** can be found, reminiscent of *all'amatriciana* or *alla gricia* style!

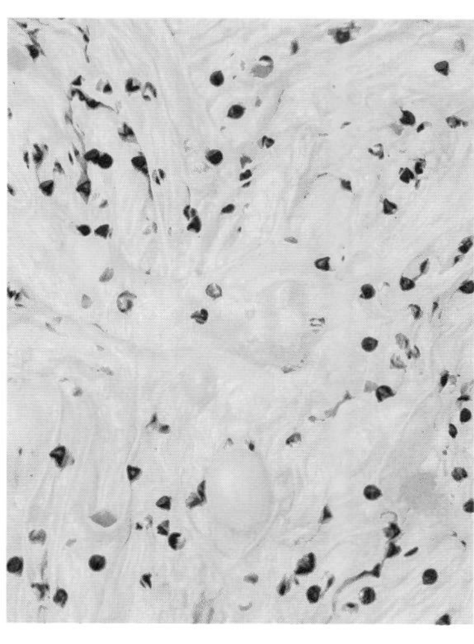

Behind the scenes at the Olivieri 1882 bake shop in Arzignano, Veneto (see page 97).

ARTICHOKES

The tender-hearted *carciofo* (artichoke) has conquered all of Italy, the world's largest producer and consumer of this edible thistle.

STÉPHANE SOLIER

ITALY'S EXCELLENT ARTICHOKES

By selecting plants with the most beautiful and least thorny flower buds, Italy's artichoke cultivators have achieved fleshy and tender plants in a variety of shapes. And above all, they are a tasty balance between slight bitterness and sweetness.

The elongated (or cylindrical)

CARCIOFO VIOLETTO ① ("purple)

HARVEST—December to March.

ORIGIN—Sicily, Apulia, Liguria (Violetto di Provenza [Violet of Provence] or di Perinaldo, Slow Food), Tuscany, Romagna.

IN COOKING—raw or as a *primo* (in pasta or risotto) or *secondo* (in stew), *piatto* (first or main course).

The thorny and elongated

VIOLETTO DI SANT'ERASMO - CASTRAURA ② (Slow Food)

HARVEST—beginning of April for the *castraure* (central bloom of the first flowering, in the shape of a tulip), then from the end of April to the end of June for the others.

ORIGIN—this varietal, which grows in the Venetian Lagoon, is distinguished by its slight salty aftertaste. Sweetness takes precedence over bitterness.

IN COOKING—raw, with a drizzle of olive oil and lemon, fried in a very light batter or served with *schie* (small prawns from the lagoon).

SPINOSO DI ALBENGA ③

HARVEST—December to April.

ORIGIN—plain of Albenga and coast of Savona and Imperia (Liguria).

IN COOKING—raw, in *pinzimonio* (an olive oil dip); perfect in fricassee (*alla ligure*) or in *torta pasqualina* (a rustic chard tart with prescinsêua cheese or ricotta, eggs, borage, and aromatic herbs; Liguria).

SPINOSO DI SARDEGNA DOP ④

HARVEST—beginning of September to the end of May.

ORIGIN—Sardinia.

IN COOKING—raw, in pinzimonio; in fritters with mint and Sardinian ricotta or in savory pies; associated with lamb or bottarga; canned in oil.

CARCIOFO TEMA DEL SULCIS DOP ⑤

HARVEST—October to April.

ORIGIN—South of Sardinia.

IN COOKING—raw or grilled (*arrustu*).

SPINOSO DI SICILIA ⑥

(Di Menfi, Slow Food; di Palermo)

HARVEST—late November to late April.

ORIGIN—Sicily.

IN COOKING—raw, braised, fricasseed, fried, boiled, stuffed with ricotta, canned in oil.

SKIP TO
CORATELLA DI ABBACCHIO CON I CARCIOFI, P. 341; CLASH OF THE ARTICHOKES, P. 102.

The rounded

CARCIOFO ROMANESCO DEL LAZIO IGP

Also called Mammolo, Mamma, or Cimarolo ⑦ and its version Romanesco Rosso ⑧ or Apollo ⑨

HARVEST—February to May (the Apollo is fatter and ready earlier: late December to May).

ORIGIN—Lazio.

IN COOKING—ideal for *romanissimes carciofi alla giudia* (fried), *alla romana* (stewed), *alla matticella* (stuffed with herbs and braised), *vignarola* (spring salad of vegetables), *coratella* (*fressure d'agneau*, a dish with lamb's pluck), or *mamme ripiene* (stuffed with meat and pecorino) from Tuscany.

Other sizes

The medium artichoke

CARCIOFETTA ⑩

The small artichoke

CARCIOFINO ⑪

Close cousins

CARDO OR CARDO DA COSTE ⑫

Cardoon (with its ribs)

Most Popular varietals

Gobbo del Monferrato (Piedmont, Slow Food; ideal for *bagna cauda*), di Chieri (Piedmont), di Bologna, *alato, triste.*

TASTE—slightly bitter, with hints of celery.

IN COOKING—boiled, prepared as a gratin, fried; in soup, flan, tarts . . .

CARDO SELVATICO ⑬

Wild cardoon

ORIGIN—found throughout southern Italy and on the islands.

IN COOKING—especially using the flower bud (*gemma*, also called *carciofino* or *gureu* in Sardinia), with more pronounced bitterness, fried, baked, or canned in oil.

And also . . .

Elongated varietal

CARCIOFO BRINDISINO IGP

Round varietals

CARCIOFO OR TONDO DI PAESTUM IGP

(Campania)

CARCIOFO VIOLETTO DI CASTELLAMMARE

(Campania, Slow Food)

CARCIOFO BIANCO DI PERTOSA

(Campania, Slow Food)

RECIPE

LASAGNE DE PANE CARASAU CON I CARCIOFI (SARDINIAN LASAGNA WITH ARTICHOKES)

This Sardinian artichoke lasagna recipe pays homage to the flavors of one of the artichoke's favorite lands.

SERVES 8

15 to 20 Sardinian spiny artichokes or *poivrades* (Violetto di Provenza)
Juice of ½ lemon
6 tablespoons (90 mL) olive oil
8 cloves garlic, halved and peeled
Scant ½ cup (100 mL) dry white wine
5 or 6 sprigs mint, chopped
2⅔ pounds (1.2 kg) fine tomato pulp (*polpa*)
Salt and freshly ground black pepper
14 ounces (400 g) fresh sheep's-milk ricotta
7 to 9 ounces (200 to 250 g) *pane carasau* (traditional Sardinian flatbread)
7 ounces (200 g) grated dry Sardinian pecorino

- Clean the artichokes and remove their outer leaves. Keep part of the stem and peel it. Trim the ends ¾ to 1⅛ inches (2 to 3 cm) from the tip. Cut the artichokes into eight sections and set them aside in cold water with the lemon juice added.
- In a skillet over medium heat, brown the artichoke sections for 10 minutes in 3 tablespoons (45 mL) of the olive oil with 5 garlic cloves. Deglaze the pan with the wine, cover, and cook for 5 minutes. Add a little water if necessary; the artichokes should be tender but still slightly firm. At the end of the cooking time, sprinkle with the mint and combine.
- In the same pan used to sauté the artichokes, brown the remaining 3 garlic cloves in the remaining 3 tablespoons oil, add the tomato pulp, and reduce over medium heat for 20 to 25 minutes. Lightly season with salt and pepper. Remove the garlic, let cool, and add 10½ ounces (300 g) of the ricotta.
- Preheat the oven to 350°F (180°C). In an ovenproof dish, spread two ladles of the tomato sauce. Place the pane carasau overlapping on top of each other, breaking them up if necessary, to cover the bottom of the dish. Add two ladles of tomato sauce on top, then arrange some artichokes (16 pieces per layer), a few portions of the remaining ricotta, and a good handful of the pecorino. Cover with more pane carasau and continue layering until all the ingredients are used, finishing with two ladles of tomato sauce, 9 pieces of artichoke, three or four portions of ricotta, and a good handful of pecorino. Bake for 20 to 25 minutes. Let stand for 10 minutes before serving.

SEASON

PRIMAVERA (SPRING)

CATEGORY

ANTIPASTO (APPETIZER)

LEVEL

FACILE (EASY)

CLASH OF THE ARTICHOKES

Rome is one of the best places in Italy for enjoying artichokes. Two legendary recipes make an appearance in spring: one stewed, the other fried in olive oil!

FRANÇOIS-RÉGIS GAUDRY

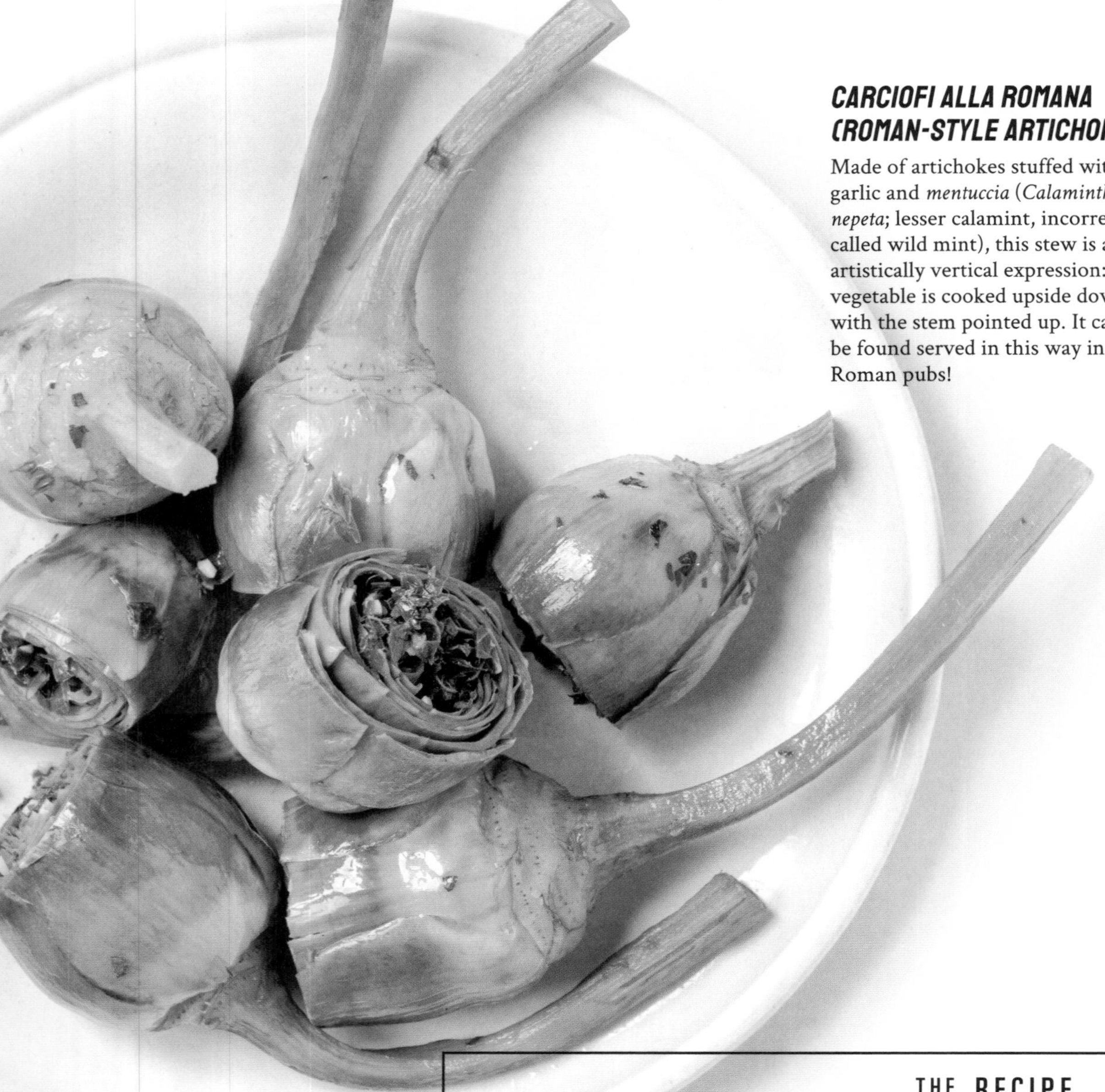

CARCIOFI ALLA ROMANA (ROMAN-STYLE ARTICHOKES)

Made of artichokes stuffed with garlic and *mentuccia* (*Calamintha nepeta*; lesser calamint, incorrectly called wild mint), this stew is an artistically vertical expression: the vegetable is cooked upside down with the stem pointed up. It can be found served in this way in Roman pubs!

ORIGIN

The ancestor of this dish is a recipe by Roman cook Apicius (first century CE) made using cardoons, fried or boiled, with lots of spices (including mint). But there is also a relation to *carciofi alla matticella*, an ancestral recipe originating in Velletri in the region of the Castelli Romani (Roman Castles). The artichokes are stuffed with mentuccia, garlic, and salt, then brushed with olive oil and cooked in hot embers of vine shoots. It was a typical winegrower's snack, accompanied by fresh beans, bruschetta, and pecorino.

METHOD

Wrap the artichokes with parchment paper, wrapping tightly around the stems to ensure the stems also steam. This old method continues to this day among pub families and kitchens. A paper bag brought from the bakery or the grocery store (a natural paper bag is best) also works.

WHERE IN ROME TO ENJOY THEM

Lo Scopettaro, Lungotevere Testaccio, 7, Rome: a Roman trattoria that has been open since 1930 in the popular and charming district of Testaccio.

THE RECIPE

SERVES 4

- 8 Romaneschi artichokes
- Juice of 1 lemon
- 1 bunch mentuccia (lesser calamint), or use cultivated mint
- 3 cloves garlic
- Salt and freshly ground black pepper
- Just over ¾ cup (200 mL) olive oil

Cut the stems of the artichokes, leaving a few inches attached to the base. Peel the remaining cut stems. Remove the outer leaves in two or three layers, until you reach the tender leaves. Using a paring knife, cut off the tips of the leaves, using an upward spiral movement from the stem to the flower. Immerse them, along with the peeled stems, in a bowl of cold water with the lemon juice added to prevent blackening. Spread out the middle leaves to form a cavity and, using a melon baller, remove the fuzzy choke if there is any.

Pluck the leaves from the mentuccia. Peel the garlic and remove the germ. Finely chop the mentuccia leaves and garlic, then season with salt and pepper. Stuff the artichoke centers with this mixture.

In a high-sided sauté pan, place the artichokes upside down (with the stems pointing up) along with the trimmed stems. Season with salt, then add the olive oil with 1 cup (250 mL) water, up to the base of the stems. Cover with a lid or parchment paper and cook over medium heat for 20 minutes, or until the vegetables feel tender when pierced with the tip of a knife.

Serve the artichokes warm, upside down, with their cooking juices.

VARIATIONS

Some recipes include white wine, which replaces half the cooking water. Others add a touch of parsley. Chef Claudio Gargioli (Armando al Pantheon, in Rome) cooks artichokes lying on their side and refrains from adding herbs.

Which artichoke?

Il Carciofo Romanesco del Lazio IGP, harvested between mid-February and May in the coastal region located northwest of Rome between Ladispoli and Civitavecchia. In the food stalls in the capital, it can also be found under the names of *cimaroli* and *mammole*. Almost every part is eaten: the leaves, the heart, even the stem! Other varietals, such as the Violetto di Provenza, lend themselves to these recipes, as long as they are fresh and firm, with tight leaves.

CARCIOFI ALLA GIUDIA (JEWISH-STYLE ARTICHOKES)

Well-bloomed artichoke flowers with a tender heart and crispy copper-colored petals sculpted from frying in olive oil. This is one of the not-to-be-missed specialties of Rome's Jewish community.

ORIGIN

This emblematic dish of Judeo-Roman cuisine was born in Rome's Jewish community, probably in the sixteenth century. Some claim the dish was prepared by women to break the fast on Yom Kippur (the Day of Atonement). But it's probably a specialty of Passover, when spring vegetables embody renewal. The artichoke undoubtedly played the role of the bitter food represented on the seder table to symbolize the bitterness of life in Egypt.

METHOD

Deep-frying in oil twice is the essential cooking method here. The first frying is long enough to cook the artichoke to the heart; the second frying is faster and is used to crisp the petals!

THE RECIPE

SERVES 4

8 Romaneschi artichokes
Juice of 1 lemon
Salt
4 cups (1 L) olive oil

Cut the stems of the artichokes, leaving a few inches attached to the base. Remove the outermost fibrous leaves, but no more than this. Using a paring knife, cut the tips of the leaves only if they are too fibrous. Immerse the artichokes in a bowl of cold water with the lemon juice added until ready to cook. Peel back the two or three layers of softer leaves, spreading them apart with the thumbs of both hands. Use a melon baller to remove the fuzzy choke, if necessary. "Beat" two artichokes together head-to-head so that the leaves open, and place them on the counter with the stems up. Season with salt, including between the leaves.

Heat the olive oil over medium heat in a sauté pan or casserole dish. Immerse as many artichokes upside down as the pot can hold, without overlapping each other. Fry them for 20 to 25 minutes, holding them with tongs or a skimmer. While they are cooking, fill a bowl with water. Using your fingers, sprinkle drops of water over the frying oil to help crisp the leaves. Watch out for splashing! Repeat this step several times. The artichokes are cooked when their sides are golden brown and their hearts are tender. Drain them on paper towels, upside down, and let cool completely.

Just before serving, immerse the artichokes again for a few minutes in the hot frying oil and press them firmly with a skimmer against the bottom of the pan so they open up like sunflowers. The artichokes will come out golden and crisp. Serve hot.

VARIATIONS

Some recipes call for cooking the artichokes in a pot of salted boiling water for 20 minutes before deep-frying them only once for 10 minutes.

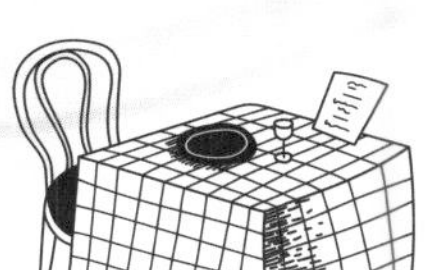

WHERE IN ROME TO ENJOY THEM

Al Pompiere, Via di S. Maria de 'Calderari, 38, Rome: a historic pub opened since 1928 where you can enjoy Judeo-Roman specialties.

SKIP TO
THE OTHER PROMISED LAND, P. 278; ARTICHOKES, P. 100; MINT, P. 202.

STOCKFISH AND SALT COD

Stoccafisso (stockfish) and *baccalà* (salt cod), both codfish, are the cornerstones of cooking on lean days in Italy.

NADIA POSTIGLIONE

· TWO INGREDIENTS, ONE DNA ·

They are both prepared from cod of the species *Gadus morhua*.

STOCCAFISSO

FROM THE DUTCH *STOCVISCH*, "STICK FISH"

Stockfish is arctic cod that has been dried by outdoor winds when the temperature is above 32°F (0°C). Suspended from special wooden supports called stocks and sheltered from the rain, the cod dries slowly. It's a specialty of the Lofoten Islands (Norway).

HOW DO YOU REHYDRATE IT?

Rehydration time: two days
Stockfish, sold whole, must first be cut open to remove the black vesicle inside. Place the stockfish in a large bowl, cover it with plenty of cold water, and refrigerate, changing the water every two hours. Then return the bowl to the refrigerator and change the water four times a day for two days.

BACCALÀ

FROM LATIN *BACULUS*, "STICK"

Refers to salt cod. Near the end of the fifteenth century, fishing boats sailed from all over Europe to the Grand Banks of Newfoundland to fish for the cod that were in abundance there. The cod, gutted and salted on board for storage, eventually reached Italian tables.

HOW DO YOU REHYDRATE IT?

Soaking time: three days
Rince the cod under running water to remove all the salt. Cut the fillet into slices and place them in a large (preferably glass) bowl. Cover with cold water. After a few hours, change the water. Refrigerate. Change the water three times a day, rinsing the slices with each change.

The *baccalajuolo*, a legendary figure in Neapolitan gastronomy, is a specialist in the art of soaking and rehydrating salt cod.

THE SUCCESS OF COD

Cod consumption spread through Italy starting from the mid-sixteenth century, when the Catholic Church advocated stricter fasting practices. The coinciding discovery of abundant schools of cod in the Labrador Sea (located between Greenland and Canada) allowed cod's large-scale commercialization. Inexpensive and not highly perishable, stockfish and salt cod gradually spread inland, transforming popular Italian cuisine.

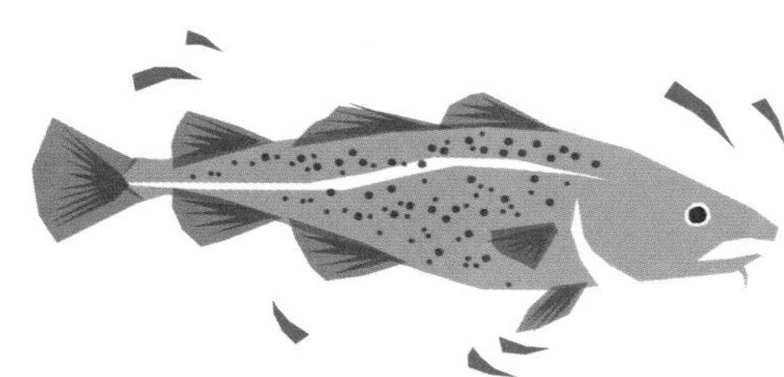

3 ways to cook them

"RED" RECIPES, WITH TOMATO

***Stoccafisso alla livornese* (Tuscany):** white wine, tomato sauce, chile.

***Baccalà all'anconetana* (Marche):** potatoes, cherry tomatoes, anchovies, black olives.

***Stocco messinese alla ghiotta* (Sicily):** potatoes, pine nuts, capers, and raisins.

***Pesce stocco di Mammola* (Calabria):** potatoes, dried chiles, and olives.

***Stoccafisso accomodato Liguria* (Liguria):** potatoes, Taggiasca olives, anchovies.

"WHITE" RECIPES, WITHOUT TOMATO

***Stoccafisso alla badalucchese* (Liguria):** chopped hazelnuts, pine nuts, mushrooms, and crumbled amaretti cookies.

***Brandacujun* (Liguria):** mixture of stockfish, potatoes, parsley, garlic, and oil.

***Baccalà arrosto alla ceraiola* (Umbria):** roasted salt cod with rosemary, white wine, and dried bread crumbs.

***Baccalà mantecato* (Veneto):** with a reduction of cream, extra-virgin olive oil, and garlic.

FRIED SALT COD

***Filetti di baccalà alla romana* (Lazio):** battered fillets

***Baccalà fritto napoletano* (Campania):** pieces dredged in flour and fried.

***Frittelle di baccalà alla ligure* (Liguria):** fritters.

***Zeppoline alla calabrese* (Calabria):** fritters, with raisins.

MAMMOLA'S STOCKFISH

In the town of Mammola on the slopes of the Calabrian Apennine Mountains, an excellent stockfish is produced, unique in the way it's rehydrated in marble basins using water from local sources.

★ THE BATTLE OF BACCALÀ ★

IN NAPLES

...

Naples has for centuries been the importation and distribution center of salt cod in southern Italy. Its inhabitants are extremely devoted to the product. The biggest importers and experts in salt cod soaking are now concentrated in the province of Vesuvius, a historic salt cod enclave, notably in the town of Somma.

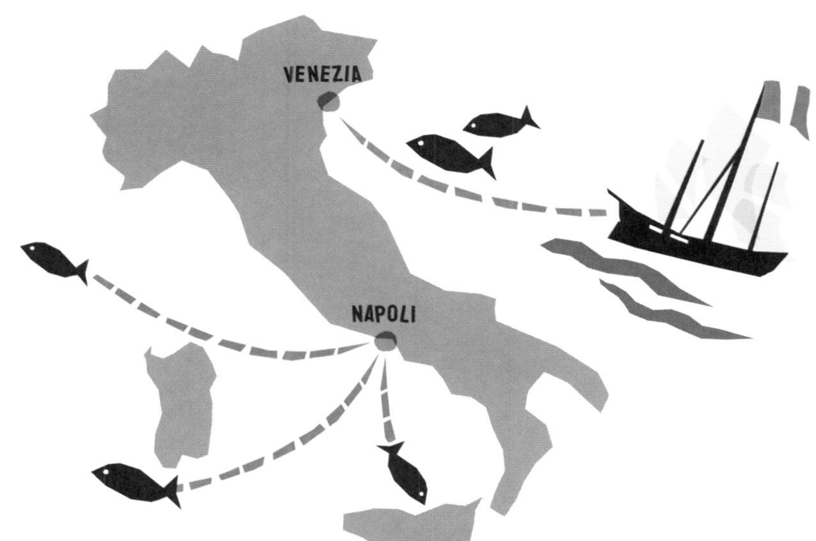

IN VENICE

...

What would Venetian cuisine look like today if in 1431 the noble merchant Pietro Querini had not been shipwrecked in the Lofoten archipelago? After landing on the islands, Querini was impressed by the rows of cod hanging and drying in the north wind. He returned loaded with this precious exotic cargo, changing the culinary history of his region.

RECIPE

ZEPPULELLE DI BACCALÀ (SALT COD FRITTERS)

SERVES 6

2 cups (250 g) all-purpose flour
Salt and freshly ground black pepper
1 large (19 g) egg yolk
1⅔ teaspoons (7 g) baking powder
10½ ounces (300 g) desalted cod (see opposite)
1 gallon (4 L) frying oil

- Place the flour on a work surface and make a well in the center. Add 1 cup (250 mL) lukewarm water, a pinch of salt, a pinch of pepper, the egg yolk, and the baking powder. Thoroughly combine until you obtain a fluid mixture (but not too fluid).
- Cover with plastic wrap and let stand for 30 minutes.
- Rinse and dry the cod. Remove the skin. Break the flesh with your hands into shredded pieces and incorporate it into the dough.
- Heat the oil in a deep fryer or high-sided saucepan.
- Add a spoonful of the batter and fry for a few minutes, turning often, until golden brown. Continue until all the batter is used.
- Season with a pinch of pepper and salt, and enjoy hot. You can vary the ingredients and use, for example, fried zucchini blossoms to create an assortment of *zeppulelle*.

RECIPE

BACCALÀ ALLA VICENTINA (VENETO-STYLE STOCKFISH)

An absolute icon of Venetian cuisine for lean days, this dish of Vicenza (Veneto) is, in fact, prepared with stockfish (interestingly called *baccalà* in Veneto). Here is the authentic recipe of the Confraternita del Baccalà alla Vicentina.

SERVES 6

1¾ pounds (800 g) stockfish
1 sweet onion, finely chopped
1 clove garlic, finely chopped
3 sardines, in salt
1½ cups (360 mL) extra-virgin olive oil
1 bunch parsley, chopped
All-purpose flour
1⅔ cups (400 mL) fresh whole milk
Salt and freshly ground black pepper
¼ cup (30 g) grated Grana Padano cheese

- Rehydrate the stockfish (see opposite).
- Remove the bones and cut the flesh into slices about 2⅓ inches (6 cm) thick.
- In a small saucepan, brown the onion, garlic, and sardines over low heat in the olive oil.
- After 8 to 10 minutes, when the onion is softened, add the parsley and turn off the heat.
- Lightly flour the stockfish slices. In (preferably) an earthenware casserole dish, carefully arrange the stockfish slices.
- Cover with the cooked onion mixture, pour the milk carefully over the top, season with salt and pepper, and sprinkle with the Grana Padano.
- Simmer over low heat for at least 3 hours, without stirring, but gently shaking the pot to mix the liquids. This dish is traditionally served with grilled polenta.

SKIP TO
CICCHETTI VENEZIANI (VENETIAN SNACKS), P. 228; POLENTA, P. 114.

CITRUS

Cultivated in Liguria and in all regions of southern Italy, citrus fruits add a fragrant note to Italy's landscape.

ALESSANDRA PIERINI

Origins

Citrus fruits are the fruits of trees belonging to the Rutaceae family and mainly of the genus *Citrus*. The term in Italian, *agrume*, comes from the late Latin *acrumen* ("with a sour flavor"), itself borrowed from the classical Latin *acer* (sour).

Originally from Asia, citrus fruits came to Italy during the Middle Ages, even though the citron was already known to the Romans as the *citreum*.

CHINOTTO DI SAVONA ①

Myrtle-leaf orange • Slow Food (*Citrus myrtifolia*)

ORIGIN: Liguria

TASTE: sharp, intense, notes close to bitter orange.

IN COOKING: not eaten raw but used in pastry, candied, in syrup, in maraschino liqueur, in *mostarda* (preserved fruits), and in jelly for cheeses. The dried leaves are used in relaxing and digestive herbal teas.

ARANCIA AMARA OR MELANGOLO ② ③

Bitter orange, sour orange (*Citrus aurantium*)

ORIGIN: Liguria, Sardinia

TASTE: bitter, sour, intense, and floral.

IN COOKING: not eaten raw but used instead in marmalade, liqueur, amaro (a bitter liqueur), orange wine, *labritti co' li facioli* (tendons and beef cartilage cooked with beans and seasoned in oil), and *melangolo* (bitter orange—Umbria).

ARANCE ROSSE

Blood orange (*Citrus sinensis*)

Moro (PGI) ④, Sanguinello (PGI) ⑤, Tarocco (PGI) ⑥, Fragolino ⑧

ORIGIN: Calabria, Sicily

TASTE: sweet, intense, slight acidity of red fruits; juicy purplish red pulp.

IN COOKING: juiced; raw, in fruit salad; candied.

ARANCE BIONDE

Sweet orange (*Citrus sinensis*)

Belladonna ⑦, Navelina ⑨

ORIGIN: southern Italy

TASTE: very sweet, fragrant.

IN COOKING: juiced; raw; *aranzada* (candied zest, honey, almonds—Sardinia); *diavolina* (dragée); in panettone, *pandolce*, marmalade; in salads, often with fennel; in marinades.

MANDARANCIO OR TANGERINO ⑩

Tangerine (*Citrus* × *tangerina*)

ORIGIN: Sicily

TASTE: sweet, delicate, close to orange but less tangy.

IN COOKING: raw; as a salad with radicchio (Treviso) or fennel; in a cocktail; in tarts.

MANDARINO ⑪

Mandarin (*Citrus deliciosa* or *reticolata*)

ORIGIN: Sicily, Calabria

TASTE: juicy, sweet-and-sour, fragrant, aromatic with a hint of bitterness.

IN COOKING: raw; with red mullet, in tartare with shrimp; with duck; in semifreddo (ideal); in pastry. The Tardivo di Ciaculli (Sicily) Slow Food variety with Modica chocolate.

CLEMENTINE

Clementines (*Citrus clementina*)

Clementina ⑫, Clementina tardiva ⑬

ORIGIN: Sicily, Calabria

TASTE: sweet, very balanced in acidity, juicy, and very fruity.

IN COOKING: raw; in mostarda; with shellfish; with squash; with ricotta and dill; with endive and walnuts; in pastry.

CEDRO ⑭

Citron (*Citrus medica*)

ORIGIN: Campania, Calabria

TASTE: refreshing, sharp and bitter, close to lemon.

IN COOKING: juiced; candied; with fish, mollusks, shellfish; to season pasta with ricotta and almonds; raw, in pieces or in carpaccio with olive oil, oregano, chives, olives; marinades; in preserves with olives; in granita, syrup, sweets, digestifs.

BERGAMOTTO ⑮

Bergamot (*Citrus bergamia*)

ORIGIN: Calabria

TASTE: powerful, zesty, bitter, tangy, very aromatic, between lime and bitter orange.

IN COOKING: in vinaigrette; with fish; in risotto; in desserts, cocktails, liqueur, and herbal teas.

KUMQUAT ⑯

Kumquat (*Fortunella margarita*)

ORIGIN: Sicily

TASTE: sweet and harsh at the same time, between orange and lemon.

IN COOKING: in pasta sauces; with pork, duck, or chicken; as a sauce for panna cotta or chocolate tart; whole raw.

LIMONI

Lemons (*Citrus limon*)

Foglia di Sorrento (Campania) ⑰, Di Rocca Imperiale (Calabria) ⑱, Primofiore di Siracusa (Sicily) ⑲, Verdello di Siracusa (Sicily) ⑳, Pane di Paestum (Campania) ㉑, Costa d'Amalfi (Campania) ㉒

TASTE: lively, sour, tangy, fragrant. Depending on the variety, it can also be sweeter.

IN COOKING: in pasta, risottos, ravioli; with fish, shellfish; in limoncello; in marinades; with bottarga; *delizia al limone* (a Neapolitan cake); in gelato, *sorbetto*, granita; *canarino* (herbal tea).

POMPELMO ROSA ㉓

Grapefruit (*Citrus paradisi*)

ORIGIN: Sicily

TASTE: fairly sweet, fruity, between an orange and white grapefruit.

IN COOKING: sweet-and-sour recipes; risottos; shellfish; in salad with *friggitelli* (small green bell peppers); in fruit salads; caramelized with black pepper.

POMPIA ㉔

Pompia • Slow Food (*Citrus monstruosa*)

ORIGIN: Sardinia

TASTE: bitter, assertive, vegetal, slightly acidic, between citron and grapefruit.

IN COOKING: not eaten raw; *pompia intrea* (whole candied), *pompia prena* (with almonds); *saranzada* (cut into thin strips with honey and almonds served on orange or lemon leaves); in jams, liqueur.

TACLE ㉕

Sweet orange (*Citrus sinensis* 'Tarocco' × *clementina*)

ORIGIN: Sicily

TASTE: sweet, between clementine and blood orange, discreetly tangy.

IN COOKING: juiced; desserts and pastry.

VINTAGE DRINKS

Chinotto is also a soda made from the extract of a citrus fruit of the same name. It has a caramel brown color and bittersweet taste. During the postwar years, it was a popular national drink and served as a local and natural alternative to American drinks.

Cedrata is a cool, thirst-quenching, sparkling yellow-green drink made from citron, created in 1886 by the Lombard company Tassoni.

These two beverages have recently regained some popularity.

SKIP TO
LAND OF LEMONS, P. 352;
IN THE LAND OF GELATI, P. 50;
EASTER CAKES, P. 90; MOSTARDA, P. 377.

7
15
2
20
22
11
8
6
25
3
1
18
17
9
21
4
24
23
12
19
14
13
10
16
5

Massimo Bottura

PROFILE

HIS MENTORS

GEORGES COGNY: it was from this Franco-Italian chef at Locanda Cantoniera in Piacenza (Emilia-Romagna) that Bottura learned French culinary techniques, starting in 1986.

ALAIN DUCASSE: this chef from the Landes welcomed Bottura for an internship in 1993 at the Hôtel de Paris, his Michelin three-star restaurant in Monaco.

FERRAN ADRIÀ: the Catalan father of molecular gastronomy invited Bottura in 2000 to work with him at El Bulli, in Rosas (Catalonia).

HIS NETWORK

FRANCESCHETTA 58: his modern pub from Modena, the little sister of his three-star restaurant.

CASA MARIA LUIGIA: his twelve-bedroom guesthouse in the Emilian countryside.

HIS RESTAURANTS FOR A CAUSE: in 2015, on the occasion of the Universal Exhibition in Milan, Massimo Bottura set up, with the Catholic organization Caritas le Refettorio, a refectory that collects unsold food and redistributes it to people living in poverty through meals prepared by volunteer chefs. Building on this successful experience, this chef from Modena and his American wife, Lara Gilmore, created the Food for Soul foundation to promote this charitable project around the world, from Italy to Rio and from London to Paris . . .

This Michelin three-star chef is the most influential man in Italian gastronomy.

FRANÇOIS-RÉGIS GAUDRY

"My muscles are made with Parmesan cheese, and balsamic vinegar runs through my veins!"
On Va Déguster, France Inter, 2019.

HIS BIOGRAPHY IN 5 DATES

SEPTEMBER 30, 1962
Born in Modena (Emilia-Romagna).

1995
Takes over Osteria Francescana, a traditional Modena trattoria, which he transforms into a gourmet restaurant.

2011
Earns three stars in the Michelin Guide.

2014
Publication by Phaidon of his monograph, *Vieni in Italia con me* (*Never Trust a Skinny Italian Chef*).

2016 AND 2018
Osteria Francescana is named "World's Best Restaurant" by the UK's World's 50 Best Restaurants ranking.

SKIP TO
BALSAMIC VINEGAR, P. 280

HIS SIGNATURE DISHES

OOPS! MI È CADUTA LA CROSTATINA AL LIMONE
(*"Oops! I dropped the lemon tart"*)

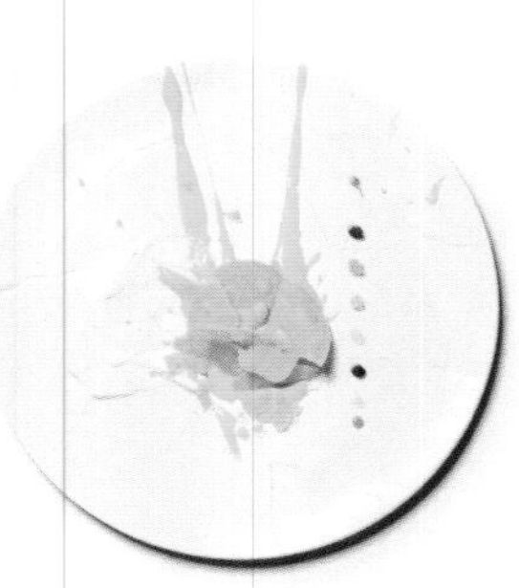

One evening while working in the kitchen, Japanese pastry chef Takahiko Kondo dropped a lemon and oregano tart on the floor. Its exploded design inspired a new plating technique.

UNA PATATA IN ATTESA DI DIVENTARE UN TARTUFO
(*"A potato waiting to become a truffle"*)

From the humble potato to the precious white Alba truffle, it's all in one dish! In appearance, this dessert is just a potato, but the first stroke of the spoon through its skin reveals a soufflé made with the potato flesh filled with crème anglaise and truffle. A visually stunning and flavorful illusion.

TUTTE LE LINGUE DEL MONDO
(*"All the languages of the world"*)

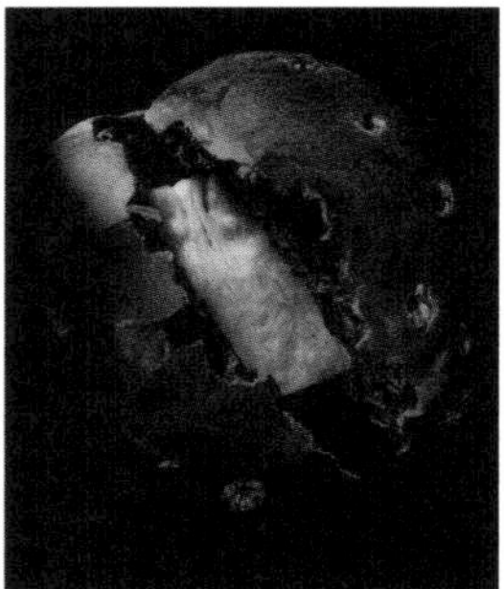

A veal tongue cooked at low temperature in a black "cocoon" made of flour, salt, ground coffee, and activated charcoal, then served with an eclectic range of condiments from several geographical origins (Indian dahl, spicy salsa . . .), all on the same plate.

CAMOUFLAGE: UNA LEPRE NEL BOSCO
(*"Camouflage: a hare in the woods"*)

Is it a bit of undergrowth? A piece of fabric? No, it's hare stew in its purest form. Blood, bones, red wine, spices, and cocoa compose a powdery and vaporous landscape that reproduces the gamey flavors of this traditional dish.

WHITE TRUFFLE, THE GEM OF PIEDMONT

According to Italian composer Gioachino Rossini, this lumpy fungus is the "Mozart of mushrooms." The *tartufo bianco* is the crown on any dish.

CHARLES PATIN O'COOHOON

THE WHITE LADY

LATIN NAME: *Tuber magnatum pico.*

COMMON NAMES: *tartufo bianco, oro bianco* (white gold).

APPEARANCE: smooth yellow skin, white to brown-red flesh.

HARVEST ZONE: its birthplace is Piedmont (the Alba white truffle), but it is also found in Lazio, Calabria, Marche (Acqualagna white truffle), Tuscany (San Miniato white truffle), and Umbria.

SEASON: September to January.

PRICE: between €375 and €500 for 3½ ounces (100 g).

An incredible mushroom

The first records of the truffle appear in 79 CE in Pliny the Elder's *Natural History*. This Roman naturalist considered it a botanical miracle because it grows with no roots. The Greeks and Romans attributed aphrodisiac virtues to it. Plutarch believed that it arose from the combined action of water, heat, and lightning. According to the Roman poet Juvenal, the truffle was born from lightning thrown by Jupiter at the base of an oak tree.

ODOR OF SANCTITY

Money itself may have no odor, but the value of a truffle lies in its aroma. Composed of 120 volatile molecules, the truffle has very little flavor. It is retronasal olfaction (the perception of odors from the oral cavity while eating and drinking) that allows it to develop its notes of honey, hay, lime blossom, and garlic. Tasting a truffle with a stuffy nose would be a shame!

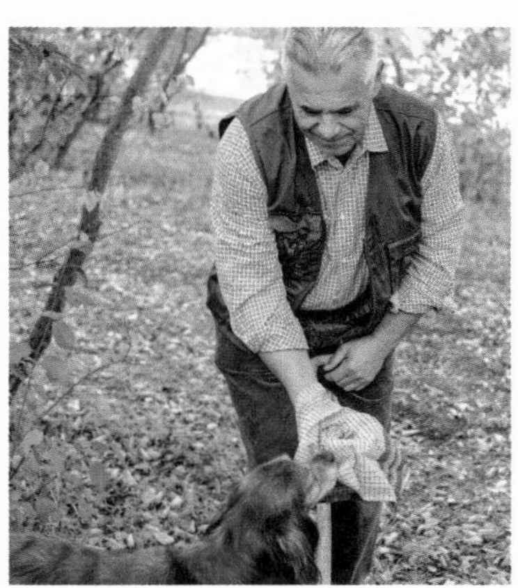

ANATOMY

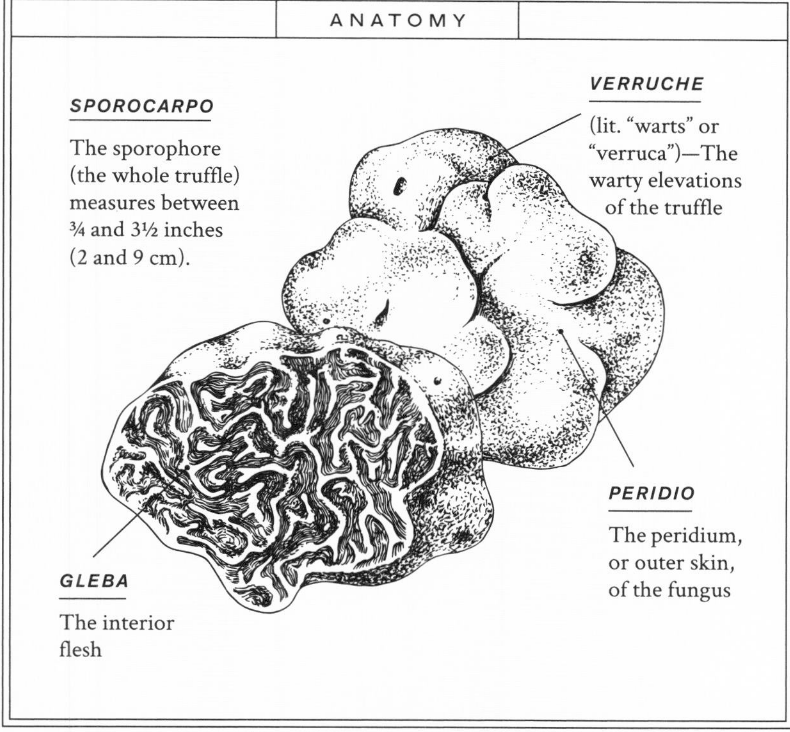

DESTINED FOR STARDOM

In 1929, Giacomo Morra, a hotel-restaurant owner from Alba, came up with the idea of launching the Fiera del Tartufo Bianco, the Alba International White Truffle Fair. The following year he created Tartufi Morra, the first company to market the white truffle. In 1933, *Time* magazine called him the "king of the truffle."

This great ambassador was also a great promoter. As early as 1949, he gifted the glamorous actress Rita Hayworth the finest truffle of the year; Marilyn Monroe, Alfred Hitchcock, and Winston Churchill would follow . . . The truffle thus became a highly coveted object.

ALWAYS RAW

→ On scrambled or fried eggs
→ On fresh egg pasta or risotto
→ On carpaccio or tartare
→ With a fondue

SKIP TO
MUSHROOMS, P. 240.

RECIPE

TAJARIN AL TARTUFO (TRUFFLE PASTA)

SERVES 4

1⅛ pounds (500 g) *tajarin* (long fresh egg pasta from Piedmont) or *tagliolini*

7 tablespoons (100 g) butter

White pepper

1 ounce (25 g) white truffle

- Bring a large pot of salted water to a boil. Add the pasta and cook for 1 to 2 minutes. In a skillet set over medium heat, melt the butter.
- Drain the pasta, reserve the cooking water, and add the pasta to the skillet.
- Add half a ladle of the cooking water to bind the mixture. Stir well to combine.
- Season with white pepper, grate the truffle on top, and serve immediately.

Oak

Poplar

Willow

THE TREE THAT SHELTERS A RARITY

Dogs and pigs hunt for it under the clay soils at the base of deciduous trees. These particular trees have roots that promote the development of the mycelium of the truffle. Oak has the most affinity with truffles, followed by poplar, willow, lime, hornbeam, and hazel.

COMMON OAK · *Quercus robur*

AUSTRIAN OAK · *Quercus cerris*

SESSILE OAK · *Quercus petraea*

DOWNY OAK · *Quercus pubescens*

BLACK POPLAR · *Populus nigra*

WHITE POPLAR · *Populus alba*

EASTERN COTTONWOOD · *Populus deltoides*

ASPEN · *Populus tremula*

PUSSY WILLOW · *Salix caprea*

WHITE WILLOW · *Salix alba*

BROAD-LEAVED LINDEN · *Tilia platyphyllos*

EUROPEAN HOP HORNBEAM · *Ostrya carpinifolia*

EUROPEAN FILBERT · *Corylus avellana*

And the black truffle?

Italy is the other country for *Tuber melanosporum*. In fact, it was the Milanese doctor and botanist Carlo Vittadini who named it in 1831 in his publication *Monographia tuberacearum*. The black truffle reigns supreme in Umbria, where it is called *tartufo nero di Norcia* or *di Spolato*.

THE TRUFFLE: reddish to brownish lumpy skin, purple-black flesh, with white veining.

THE HUNTING: collected between November and March at the base of deciduous trees such as the downy oak, live oak, hornbeam, and hazel tree.

THE DISH: *pappardelle alla Norcia*. Cook 14 ounces (400 g) pappardelle al dente. Heat a pan with 2 tablespoons (30 mL) olive oil and 1 finely chopped garlic clove. Add 4 crumbled fresh sausages (without the casing), then ⅔ cup (150 g) ricotta and a half ladle of pasta cooking water. Stir over the heat. Add the drained pasta to the pan. Grate a few truffle shavings on top and serve.

SPOTLIGHT ON CAPERS

With its green and briney notes, *Capparis spinosa* is an essential seasoning in Italian cuisine. Here we peel away its layers to reveal the caper . . . from stem to bud!

CHARLES PATIN O'COOHOON

IT COMES FROM FAR AWAY

Originally from the Mediterranean region, the caper was traded by the ancient Greeks. The Romans later used it to spice up sauces, especially fish dishes.

A CAPER OR NOT?

The caper	*The caper berry*

It's important to not confuse the caper and the caper berry . . . The caper is the bud of the caper plant flower, while the caper berry is the fruit of the caper plant.

THE LIFE CYCLE OF THE CAPER

If the caper is not picked, it will grow larger and eventually flower. The purple-and-white flower blooms for twenty-four hours before fading away. In the center of this flower, the gynophore (the stem that supports the pistil) continues to grow until it produces the fruit of the plant, called the caper berry, which contains the seeds.

THE SIZES

Historically, there were eight sizes of capers:

LILLIPUT—from ⅛ to ¼ inch (4 to 7 mm)
OCCHIO DI PERNICE—barely ⅓ inch (8 mm)
OCCHIELLO—⅓ inch (9 mm)
LACRIMELLA—from ⅓ to ½ inch (9 to 12 mm)
PUNTINA—½ inch (12 mm)
MEZZANELLA—above ½ inch (13 to 14 mm)
CAPPERONE—⅔ inch (15 mm)

Today, Pantelleria capers are grouped into three categories:

PICCOLO—up to ⅓ inch (8 mm)
MEDIO—from ⅓ to ½ inch (9 to 12 mm)
GRANDE—above ½ inch (13 mm)

In Salina, these three categories have different names:

PUNTINA—up to ⅓ inch (8 mm)
CAPPERO—from ⅓ to ½ inch (9 to 12 mm)
CAPPERONE—above ½ inch (13 mm)

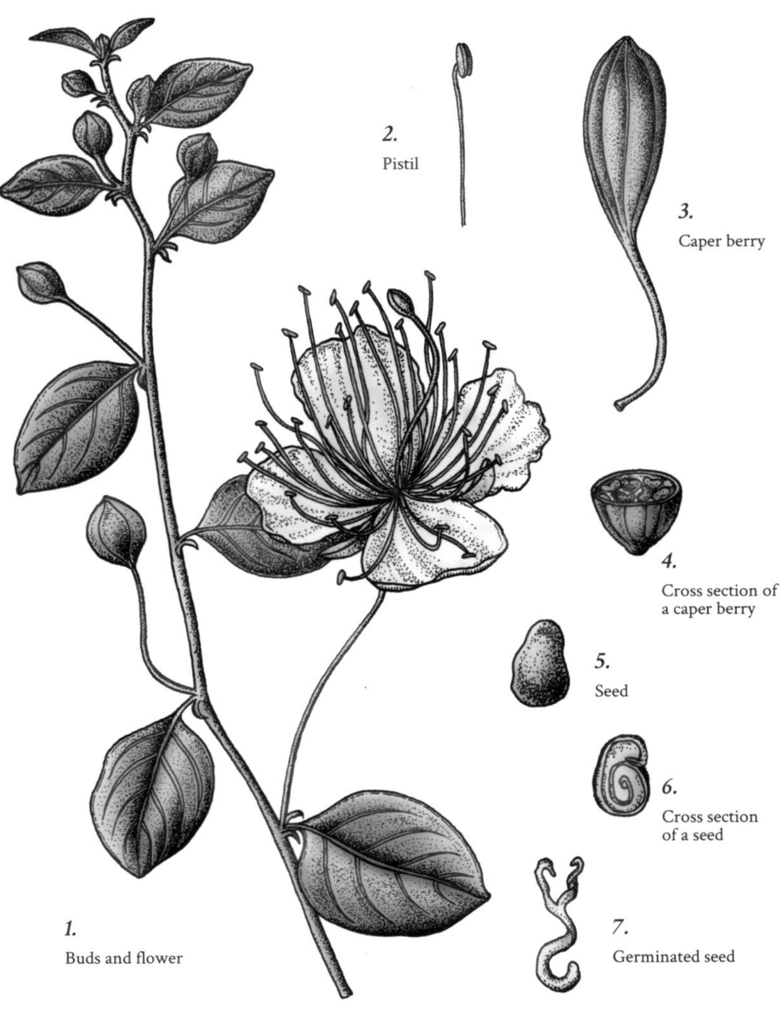

1. Buds and flower
2. Pistil
3. Caper berry
4. Cross section of a caper berry
5. Seed
6. Cross section of a seed
7. Germinated seed

How do you store capers?

Caper growers don't like soaking them in vinegar, as this overly aggressive storage method can spoil their flavor. They prefer to preserve them in salt, a simple process but one that takes twenty days.

METHOD

- Place the picked capers (without washing them) in a container, then add 40 percent of their weight in medium-grain gray salt (if the salt grains are too fine, the salt will be quickly absorbed into the capers; if the grains are too large, they will damage the buds).
- Stir every day for ten days.
- At the end of this time, weigh the capers, add 20 percent of the weight in salt, then stir again every day for ten days.
- Finally, add 25 percent of their weight in salt and transfer everything to jars.
- At this point, the capers are edible.
- Before serving, rinse them in cold water, and let them soak for two hours.

FOOD FOR THOUGHT

According to archbishop and writer François Fénelon, in his *Abrégé des vies des ancien philosophes* (1740; published posthumously), Plato "lived . . . only on capers in Sicily."

THE BUD WAR

Almost all of the production of capers comes from island cultures: the Aeolian Islands (Sicily), Aegadian Islands (Sicily), Ustica (Sicily), Tremiti Islands (Apulia), Sardinia . . . The most famous are Pantelleria and Salina.

PANTELLERIA: this volcanic island has become the caper capital of the world, where the world's only PGI caper grows. It is picked by hand between June and mid-August, before being preserved in sea salt from the Trapani salt mines. Each plant yields between 2¼ and 4½ pounds (1 and 2 kg) of capers, for an annual production of 16,000 tons.

SALINA: between May and August on this Aeolian island located in northern of Sicily, a special varietal of the cultivar Nocellara is harvested, which produces a rounder and firmer bud than its cousin from Pantelleria. It is protected by Slow Food.

THE MOST FAMOUS OF THE "CAPRI-GROWERS"

Giorgio Armani, Madonna, Sting . . . the island of Pantelleria has welcomed many famous personalities. But its most invested resident is Carole Bouquet. Living since 2005 at an altitude of 1,300 feet (400 m) in Rekhale (in the south), this French actress grows a vineyard of Passito di Pantelleria (a local Muscat grape) and harvests nearly 1,500 pounds (700 kg) of capers each year.

Sulla Punta Della Lingua (On the Tip of the Tongue)

In Tuscan, the expression "*Cappero!*" is not quite as nice as the caper itself. It translates to "What a fool!" In contrast, the plural form and expression "*Capperi!*" is an exclamation of surprise, close to *mamma mia!*, a euphemism to replace a more vulgar word.

SKIP TO
CAPONATA (SICILIAN EGGPLANT SALAD), P. 220.

1. *Cucunci* (caper berries) in vinegar

2. Caper berries with salt

3. Caper berries in olive oil

4. Caper plant leaves in olive oil

5. Capers in salt (large size)

6. Capers in olive oil (medium size)

9. Capers in oil (small size)

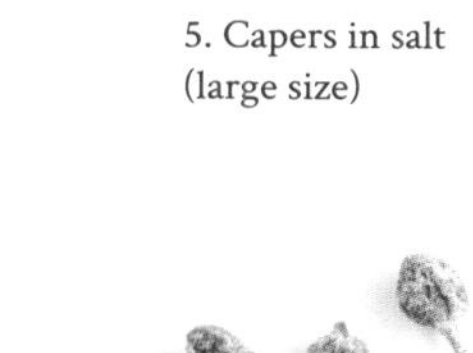

7. Cream of capers with olive oil

8. Capers in salt (medium size)

10. Selargino capers in salt (small size)

11. Crunchy capers

12. Crushed caper berries

13. Caper powder

1. *Cucunci* (caper berries) in vinegar

ORIGIN—Pantelleria (Sicily)
PRODUCER—Azienda Agricola Gianflora

2. Caper berries with salt • Slow Flood

ORIGIN—Aeolian Islands (Sicily)
PRODUCER—Azienda Agrobiologica Salvatore D'Amico

3. Caper berries in olive oil

ORIGIN—Pantelleria (Sicily)
PRODUCER—La Nicchia

4. Caper plant leaves in olive oil

ORIGIN—Pantelleria (Sicily)
PRODUCER—Bonomo e Giglio for Incuso

5. Capers in salt (large size)

ORIGIN—Racale (Apulia)
PRODUCER—I Contadini

6. Capers in olive oil (medium size)

ORIGIN—Pantelleria (Sicily)
PRODUCER—Azienda Agricola Konza Kiffi

7. Cream of capers with olive oil

ORIGIN—Pantelleria (Sicily)
PRODUCER—Azienda Agricola Konza Kiffi

8. Capers in salt (medium size)

ORIGIN—Pantelleria (Sicily)
PRODUCER—Serragghia di Giotto Bini

9. Capers in oil (small size)

ORIGIN—Calabria
PRODUCER—Torre Saracena

10. Selargino capers in salt (small size)

ORIGIN—Selargius (Sardinia)
PRODUCER—Marco Maxia

11. Crunchy capers

ORIGIN—Pantelleria (Sicily)
PRODUCER—Bonomo e Giglio for Incuso

12. Crushed caper berries

ORIGIN—Pantelleria (Sicily)
PRODUCER—Bonomo e Giglio for Incuso

13. Caper powder

ORIGIN—Pantelleria (Sicily)
PRODUCER—La Nicchia

SEASON

TUTTO L'ANNO (YEAR-ROUND)

CATEGORY

PRIMO PIATTO (FIRST COURSE)

LEVEL

FACILE (EASY)

SPAGHETTI ALLE VONGOLE

SPAGHETTI WITH CLAMS

The simplicity of Italian cuisine is expressed in this seafood dish whose fame goes far beyond the borders of its native Campania.

ILARIA BRUNETTI

YOU CHOOSE!

WINE OR NO WINE?

Wine delivers slightly acidic notes, an essential component for some yet one to avoid for others, who feel it alters the delicate taste of the mollusks.

SHELLS OR NO SHELLS?

Traditionally, the clams are not shelled. But removing them in advance prevents the spaghetti from cooling down while the diner is shelling them.

TOMATO OR NO TOMATO?

While the clams are cooking, a few (seasonal!) cherry tomatoes are allowed.

SPAGHETTI ALLE VONGOLE FUJUTE ("FLYING" CLAMS)

Spaghetti with clams . . . without clams? The idea came from actor Eduardo De Filippo, who, one evening when too tired to eat his *spaghetti alle vongole* at a restaurant, prepared pasta at home with what he had on hand: parsley, garlic, chile, olive oil, tomatoes from Piennolo. He said he could still smell the taste of the sea!

THE RIGHT CLAMS*

VONGOLA VERACE

Venerupis decussata, aka European gray palourde

APPEARANCE—oval, 1⅓ to 2¾ inches (35 to 70 mm) wide. Tight and concentric stripes, color ranging from light gray to dark brown-gray.

TASTE—delicate, because it likes the somewhat salty waters of the lagoons.

VONGOLA COMUNE

Chamelea gallina, aka small prairie clam

APPEARANCE—rounded triangular shape, 1 to 1¾ inches (25 to 45 mm). The exterior is gray or light yellow, with continuous brownish stripes, in polka dots or zigzags.

TASTE—although smaller, they are tastier.

TELLINE

Donax trunculus, aka wedge clam

APPEARANCE—triangular wedge-shaped, ⅓ to 1⅛ inches (10 to 30 mm). Smooth, yellowish shell.

TASTE—as tasty as it is small!

**According to Serena Lanza, Italian biologist*

THE RECIPE

The quality of this pasta dish relies, more than anything else, on the freshness of the palourde clams. These can be replaced by cockles or wedge clams.

SERVES 4

- 2¼ pounds (1 kg) palourde clams
- Salt
- ½ cup (125 mL) olive oil, plus more for serving
- 2 cloves garlic
- 1 red chile (fresh or dried), seeded and cut into thin strips
- 1 small bunch flat-leaf parsley
- ¼ cup (60 mL) dry white wine
- 14 ounces (400 g) spaghetti (or linguine)

To soak and rinse the clams, dispose of any broken or open shells and those filled with sand. Immerse the rest in a large volume of salted water (1¼ ounces/35 g salt per 4 cups/1 L) for 2 to 3 hours, changing the water two or three times during soaking to remove all the sand.

In a large skillet, heat ¼ cup (60 mL) of the olive oil and brown 1 of the garlic cloves, peeled or unpeeled, one-quarter of the chile, and a few sprigs of parsley. Add the clams, sauté over high heat for 1 minute, then add the wine and cook until the liquid has evaporated. Reduce the heat, cover, and cook until the shells have opened. Be careful not to overcook the clams or they will become rubbery.

Strain the clams from their juice, and strain the juice through a clean thin kitchen towel or a fine-mesh strainer to remove any grit.

Shell three-quarters of the clams. Discard the parsley stems. Chop the remaining parsley and set aside.

Place the spaghetti in a pot of salted boiling water. Heat the remaining ¼ cup (60 mL) olive oil in the skillet with the remaining garlic clove and the strained clam juice. Add more of the chile according to taste.

Three to 4 minutes before the end of the pasta cooking time, drain the spaghetti, reserving a few ladles of the cooking water. Add the pasta to the skillet. Finish cooking over high heat, adding a ladle of the cooking water if the pasta is too dry. Off the heat, stir in the clams, chopped parsley, and a drizzle of olive oil. Stir briefly and serve immediately.

ORANGE WINE

White in nature but red in style, it stirs up passions and has experienced a rebirth in Italy. Let's take a clear look into this sometimes-cloudy wine.

JÉRÔME GAGNEZ

A little history

Could orange wine be a primitive form of wine? This good question deserves attention: it could be that the taste for this style of wine is far from being a new fad and is instead a return to basics. The first traces of winemaking (eight thousand years ago) were discovered in Georgia in the Caucasus, where winemakers placed white grapes in amphora (ancient Greek jars, aka *kvevri*), macerating the skins in the juice.

This method is still used in Georgia today, and it spread over the centuries to Slovenia and Friuli.

BUT WHAT IS IT?

As the name suggests, this is a wine with an orange color—nothing surprising in this case. However, it's unique in how it is made: by macerating the skins, and sometimes the grape stems, in the juice. In other words, orange wine is a white wine vinified in the manner of red wine.

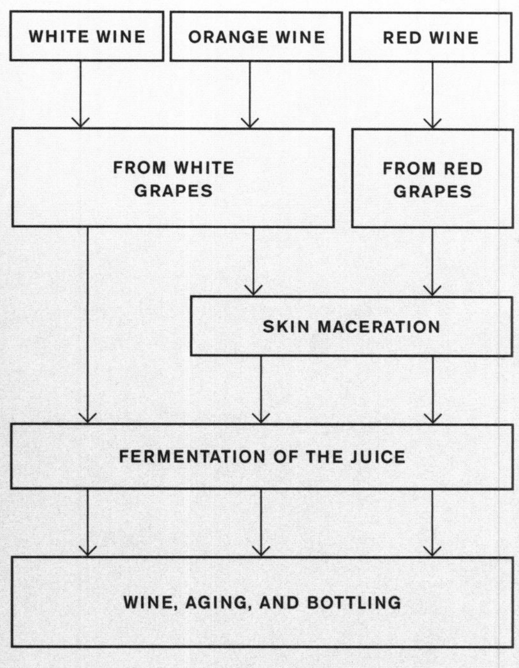

FROM FRIULA TO SICILY

It was in Friuli where this winemaking method reappeared in the 1990s, thanks to two winegrowers:

Stanko Radikon and Josko Gravner.

Many have followed suit throughout Italy, including in Sicily, where Frank Cornelissen is one of its pioneers.

Tasting...

The nose

offers a fairly wide palate that goes from more or less ripe citrus fruits to notes of root plants such as cinchona and gentian (especially when the stem is macerated), including floral notes.

•

The palate

presents a more or less tannic substance depending on the length of maceration and the grape varietal used. Contrary to popular belief, it is not the longest macerations that produce the most tannic wines. The fundamental taste difference between a white wine and an orange wine is the dimension of tannins.

HOW ABOUT FLAVOR?

IT DEPENDS ON SEVERAL FACTORS

1—THE TYPE OF GRAPE

You can use any white grape to produce an orange wine. Each winemaker chooses the grape varietal according to the desired end result. What is tasted on the palate is obviously very different whether using Muscat, Vitovska, or Ribolla Gialla grapes.

2—THE MACERATION TIME

This can vary from one day to several months. It is believed that Georgians macerated for a very long time, probably up to six or seven months. Since the extraction of tannins from the skin in the wine is a way to avoid its oxidation, this approach was likely favored for this reason. The longer the maceration time, the more it promotes two complementary phenomena: a better extraction of tannins and a better absorption of the tannins in the wine (for a less tannic impact on the palate).

3—THE CONTAINER USED FOR MACERATION AND MATURATION

A barrique; a wooden, stainless steel, or concrete vat; an amphora . . . each winegrower has preferences and, consequently, achieves a different result.

Three choice wines

From left to right:

VITOVSKA PAOLO VODOPIVEC
Friuli-Venezia Giulia

RIBOLLA GIALLA, JOSKO GRAVNER
Friuli-Venezia Giulia

VEJ BIANCO ANTICO, PODERE PRADAROLO
Emilia-Romagna

SKIP TO
FRANCESCO "JOSKO" GRAVNER, P. 199;
GATHERING GRAPES, P. 158.

POLENTA

This poor man's dish, which gleams golden, is a delight on winter evenings . . . and a delight of Italian cuisine.

STÉPHANE SOLIER

FROM GRAIN TO MASH

ANTIQUITY: *puls* (a spelt mash) was the national dish of the Roman people. It was called *polenta* when made from barley.

MIDDLE AGES: polenta made from chestnuts, spelt, or mixed cereals (*polenta mugna*, *nera*, or *taragna* . . .) are widely (and still today) consumed, from the north to the south in Italy.

SIXTEENTH CENTURY: maize, which arrived from Mexico, was planted by the Venetians in their more barren inlands, Friuli, where it became a good source of income and staved off famine.

SEVENTEENTH CENTURY: acclimated to cooking according to local customs—as a porridge!—the yellow grain infiltrated the country.

Turkish or American?

Maize is American. Why, then, is it still called *granturco* ("Turkish wheat") in Italian? In the sixteenth century, most of the products imported from abroad came from the East, and Venice readily traded with Turkish ports. Consequently, the grain would be so named to distinguish it from the native soft wheat.

ITALIAN NUGGETS

Here are some remarkable varietals of maize *di Storo*: Sponcio (Ark of Taste Slow Food), Veneto; *mais di Storo*, Trentino; *pignulet ottofile*, Piedmont; *mais marano*, Veneto; Biancoperla (Slow Food), Veneto.

Paese che vai, polenta che trovi

"Wherever you go you will find a different polenta . . ."

Contrary to popular belief, polenta is found everywhere in Italy! Yes, it is most known for being a dish of the mountains and valleys of the north; so much so that *polentoni*, the "polenta eaters," is a word the southerners use to refer to their northern rivals. But this nickname is misleading. Polenta has also won the hearts—and stomachs—of the *terroni* (southerners).

Polenta in Italy has its own style based on geography. In the north, it can be creamy, though it can also be found served in a firm form. In central and southern Italy, it is served creamier.

VARIABLE TEXTURES:

→ The ratio between water and/or milk and flour.
→ The cooking time.
→ The variety of maize.
→ The grain size.

LIFESAVING OR HARMFUL?

A bowl of polenta fed the mountain peasants but also weakened them: when consuming maize as their primary food source, they were deprived of essential vitamins and amino acids, which led to pellagra, a disease characterized by generalized weakness. How can this dangerous problem be avoided? By combining polenta with other ingredients from the local *terroirs*!

GRIND VARIATIONS

While the colors may differ from the classic golden yellow to black, including the rarest *rossa* (red), it is the grain size that creates the distinction.

TARAGNA (maize and buckwheat)
Grind thickness: +++
Uses and appearance: rustic, dark polenta

INTEGRALE (raw, not sifted)
Grind thickness: +++
Uses and appearance: granular polenta

GROSSA (coarse semolina)
Grind thickness: +++
Uses and appearance: firm polenta (for frying or broiling)

BRAMATA (just shelled and ground maize)
Grind thickness: ++
Uses and appearance: classic polenta, long cooking

FINE (fine)
Grind thickness: +
Uses and appearance: soft polenta

FIORETTO (very fine)
Grind thickness: –
Uses and appearance: polenta for baking, soft polenta, pastry, bread baking, bread crumbs

FUMETTO (flour)
Grind thickness: – –
Uses and appearance: pastry, bread baking, breading

The art of enhancing polenta

SIMPLY COOK IT BY INCORPORATING . . .

→ **Cheese and butter** (northern Italy): local cheeses (Fontina, Montasio, Asiago, etc.).

→ **Meat:** sausages (Trentino, Lombardy), *grasei*, pork cracklings (Emilia-Romagna).

→ **Vegetables:** squash (Friuli); string beans or broad (fava) beans (*polenta infasolà* or *infavà*, Veneto); potatoes (Trentino); string beans, potatoes, and black cabbage (*polenta incatenata*, Liguria); chicory and other wild vegetables (*pizza e minestra*, Molise; *macafana*, Trentino; *frascatula*, Calabria); with the herb costmary (Lombardy).

SERVE IT WITH . . .

→ **Stewed meat** (northern and central Italy): from beef to game.

→ **Sausages or pork chops** (throughout Italy).

→ **Seafood:** from salt cod (Veneto, Piedmont) to cuttlefish and *moscardini* (small octopus) to eels (Friuli, Veneto).

ONCE FIRM, CUT IT INTO PIECES (SLICED/DICED) AND . . .

→ **Fry it:** eat it simply or with local products, such as bacon, sage, or porcini mushrooms (throughout Italy).

→ **Grill it:** serve it as an accompaniment to a dish or as a base for applying spreads (Veneto, Friuli).

→ **Bake it and brown it:** in layers with cheese, meat sauce, and/or vegetables, or as small gnocchi (especially in northern Italy, but also in south central Italy).

A GOLDEN MUSE

As a symbol of the subsistence diet of the Italian people throughout the ages, polenta's praises have been sung all through literature, from Manzoni to Pasolini, including by the Romagnan Giovanni Pascoli and the Sardinian Nobel Prize winner Grazia Deledda.

It also animates the imagination of Italians in painting and cinema, where it symbolizes festive sharing:

La Polenta (1740) by the Venetian master of genre painting, Pietro Longhi.

Polenta e bisati (eels) in *Païsa* (1946) by Roberto Rossellini.

The steaming *Polenta* of the Dalco family of Emilian sharecroppers in *Novecento (1900)* (1976) by Bernardo Bertolucci, on an aptly named *Polenta* soundtrack by Ennio Morricone.

PREPARE POLENTA

Traditionally, polenta is prepared by stirring cornmeal in hot water constantly and for a long time—referred to as *menare* (beating)—for up to an hour! Some cooks add butter and cheese.

—

You can *mantecare* (work it) to make it creamy after it is seasoned.

—

1 teaspoon (6 g) coarse salt

1 part cornmeal to 4 parts liquid

For a creamier polenta, add just over ¾ cup (200 mL) of cream or whole milk to the water

Butter

Parmesan cheese

In a saucepan of salted boiling water, gradually sprinkle in the cornmeal while stirring with a large wooden spoon to prevent lumps from forming. Stir frequently over low heat until the polenta thickens, then cook, stirring often, for 40 to 50 minutes.

The polenta is ready to accompany fish or meat in sauce, or simply enhance it with cheese: 5 minutes before the end of the cooking time, add a little butter and Parmesan, then stir until thoroughly combined.

LA POLENTA À LA SAUCE CARNAVALESQUE

Following the advice of Rosaura to Arlecchino in *La Dame de Qualité* (scene 9, act I) by the Venetian dramatist Carlo Goldoni (1744):

"We'll fill a nice pot with water and put it on the stove. When the water begins to murmur, I will take this powder as beautiful as gold, called yellow flour, and, little by little, will let it melt in the saucepan in which you, Arlecchino, with the help of a learned rod [a large wooden spoon], you will draw circles and lines [to avoid the formation of lumps]. When the material is condensed, we will remove it from the heat and both together, one with the help of a large spoon, we will let it run onto a dish. We will spread over it, with small strokes of the hand, an abundant piece of fresh, yellow, and delicate butter, then as much well-scraped yellow cheese [Parmesan], then? Then, Arlecchino and Rosaura, one on one side, the other on the other, each armed with a fork, we will take two or three bites at a time of this polenta, so well prepared, and we will partake of a meal of an emperor."

SKIP TO
THE GNOCCHI UNIVERSE, P. 76.

RECIPE

GNOCCHI DI POLENTA (POLENTA GNOCCHI)

From Paolo Dolzan, chef of Ristorante PerBacco, Mezzolombardo (Trentino-Alto Adige).

SERVES 8

Salt

7¾ to 9 ounces (220 to 250 g) cornmeal

1¾ ounces (50 g) Trentingrana cheese (or Parmesan or Grana Padano), grated

10½ ounces (300 g) Casolet (a Trentin cheese), a tome of fresh cow's-milk cheese, or a young Morbier

5 tablespoons (80 g) unsalted butter, plus 1 teaspoon (5 g) for greasing the dish

6 to 8 sage leaves

- Preheat the oven to 350°F (180°C).
- Bring 4 cups (1 L) salted water to a boil in a large saucepan. Add the cornmeal and cook over low heat for 40 to 45 minutes while stirring. Remove from the heat and let cool until a thick consistency is achieved.
- Add a handful of the Trentingrana, stir, and let cool until the polenta can be handled with the hands. Transfer it to a work surface and, using your hands, form a log measuring ½ inch (1.5 cm) in diameter. Shape into gnocchi by cutting small pieces ¾ inch (2 cm) long.
- Butter a baking dish. Place the gnocchi in the dish. Cut the Casolet into ⅓-inch (1 cm) cubes and place them on top of the gnocchi. In a separate pan, cook the butter (do not let it burn) with the sage leaves, and pour it over the gnocchi. Bake for 10 to 15 minutes. When browned and bubbling, remove it from the oven and serve hot.

CANNOLO

This dessert, made of tube-shaped fried dough filled with a ricotta cream, is king in Sicily. It is also a strong symbol of Italianism.

MARIELLE GAUDRY

ITS ORIGINS

The creation of cannoli can be traced back to the Muslim presence in Sicily (897–1091). They were, in fact, created by the women of the province of Caltanissetta (*kalt el nissa*, Arabic for "castle of women"). But the question remains: were they created by nuns to celebrate Carnival or created by the concubines of Saracen emirs gathered in harems who experimented with cooking, creating a similar pastry? In his book *Siciliani a tavola*, the duke and gastronome Alberto Denti Di Pirajno argues that the rich flavor of the *cannolo* would betray its Muslim origins.

It was the pastry chefs of Palermo who perfected and popularized this dessert before it then spread throughout the island, and eventually around the world.

IL CARNEVALE

The cannolo was first made for Carnival. It can now be found all year round, although it is recommended to be eaten during the time when ricotta is at its best, December through May.

• SACRED CANNOLI •

"Leave the gun, take the cannoli!"

This line from the movie *The Godfather* (Francis Ford Coppola, 1972) has become a classic.

Coppola admitted that actor Richard Castellano, who played Peter Clemenza, completely improvised the second part of this line. It echoes the scene earlier in the film where his wife reminds him not to forget to buy cannoli at the bakery. A promise is a promise, but cannoli are sacred!

CANNOLO & CO.

The name *cannolo* comes from the Latin *canna*, which means "stick." It refers to the reeds of the rivers of southern Europe. Cut into sections, the reeds were the perfect tool for rolling the cannoli dough. Some pastry shops and traditional Italian mothers still employ bamboo tubes, although aluminum tubes are used more frequently today. In Sicilian, the crisp tube of fried dough obtained when making cannoli is referred to as *scorcia* (crust, bark).

In Sicilian, *cannolo* also means "faucet," which led to another legend explaining its creation: the sisters of the convent of Santa Maria di Monte Oliveto in Palermo in the middle of Carnival jokingly filled a bathtub with ricotta cream and replaced the faucets with faucet-shaped pastries . . .

Naughty Cannolo

For Giuseppe Coria,* the Sicilian author of regional cookbooks, its tube shape is a phallus, a symbol of fertility and strength, which has the power to ward off the evil eye.

**Profumi di Sicilia: Il libro della cucina siciliana* (Vito Cavalotto, 2006).

THE GREAT FIEFS OF CANNOLO IN SICILY

PALERMO
Miniature version (*cannolicchi*).

PIANA DEGLI ALBANESI
Province of Palermo: giant cannoli with excellent ricotta made from the milk of sheep raised on a plateau at an elevation of 2,600 feet (800 m).

DATTILO
Province of Trapani: cannoli with a ricotta that is more natural, less processed, and less sweet.

AVERAGE SIZE

SICILIAN CANNOLO: 2¾ TO 4 INCHES (7 TO 10 CM)

CANNOLICCHI—PALERMO: 2 INCHES (5 CM)

***CANNOLO GIGANTI*—PIANA DEGLI ALBANESI:** 8 INCHES (20 CM)

Which ricotta?

Trying to select the best cannolo in Sicily is a waste of time, as the island's recipes differ simply because the ricotta used in the filling is so different. It is not made in the same way from one province to another on the island. To make the ricotta cream filling, cow's-milk ricotta (*ricotta iblea*) is preferred in the Ragusane region, while sheep's-milk ricotta (*ricotta di pecora*) or goat's-milk ricotta (*ricotta di capra*) is used in Catania. Before being combined with sugar, it is typically strained to make it creamier and smoother.

Which alcohol?

The alcohol added to the dough also varies. In the east, it is traditionally white wine; in the west, it's Marsala. The color of the dough, as well as its texture, changes in these cases. In Messina, they say the dough is crumbly and white, while in Palermo, it is thicker and darker.

What decoration?

In Catania or Messina, they like to dip the two ends of the cannoli in crushed Bronte pistachios. Elsewhere, it can be almonds or hazelnuts. In Palermo, they prefer to add a piece of candied fruit (an orange or cherry on top). You can also find chocolate chips used all over the island.

With or without chocolate?

Cocoa powder is an integral part of cannoli dough, in small quantities of course, but it is almost always present. Chocolate, beyond the chips used for decoration, is sometimes used in the ricotta cream. For more interest, the cannolo can be filled entirely with chocolate cream or with two creams (one without chocolate, the other with chocolate), or the shell can be coated on the inside with melted chocolate before the cream is added.

THE TECHNIQUE

By Giacomo Timpanaro, chef of the Vuciata Kitchen Market restaurant in Catania.

MAKES 60 TO 70 CANNOLI

For the dough

2¼ pounds (1 kg) all-purpose flour, plus more for dusting
1 cup (100 g) confectioners' sugar
⅓ cup (30 g) unsweetened cocoa powder
1 tablespoon (20 g) salt
7 tablespoons (100 g) unsalted butter, at room temperature
2 large (100 g) eggs
Scant ½ cup (100 mL) dry white wine
6 cups (1.5 L) neutral oil, such as sunflower or rapeseed, for frying
Superfine sugar, for rolling the shells

For the filling

2¼ pounds (1 kg) sheep's-milk ricotta
¾ cup (150 g) superfine sugar
Crushed pistachios, for garnish

Equipment

Stand mixer
Pasta roller
One 4¾ by 4¾-inch (12 by 12 cm) square cookie cutter
Metal tubes measuring ¾ inch (2 cm) in diameter
Deep fryer

Steps

1 For the dough, combine the flour, confectioners' sugar, cocoa, and salt in the bowl of a stand mixer fitted with the dough hook and mix at low speed. Add the butter, eggs, and half the white wine and continue to mix.

2 Add the remaining white wine and mix until you obtain a light brown, sandy, firm, compact paste.

3 Finish kneading the dough by hand until smooth, then form a ball. Place it in an airtight container and refrigerate for 24 hours. Remove it 15 minutes before using.

4 Flour a work surface. Cut one-fourth of the dough and press it out by hand, then roll it out with a rolling pin or with a pasta roller to 2 to 3 mm thick.

5 Using the cookie cutter, cut the dough into even squares.

6 Place a metal tube down the diagonal of a dough square and fold the two corners over onto the tube.

7 Immerse the wrapped tubes in a deep fryer for 2 minutes, until browned.

8 Transfer them to paper towels to drain. When cooled, remove the metal tubes, then gently roll the fried dough shells in superfine sugar. Set aside.

9 For the filling, mix together the ricotta and superfine sugar and scrape the mixture into a pastry bag. Fill the cannoli with this mixture.

10 Finish by dipping the ends in crushed pistachios.

11 Enjoy within 15 minutes for the best freshness and crispness.

1

2

3

4

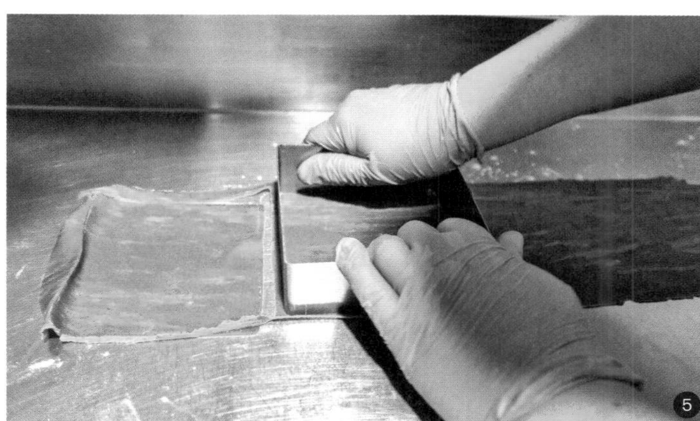
5

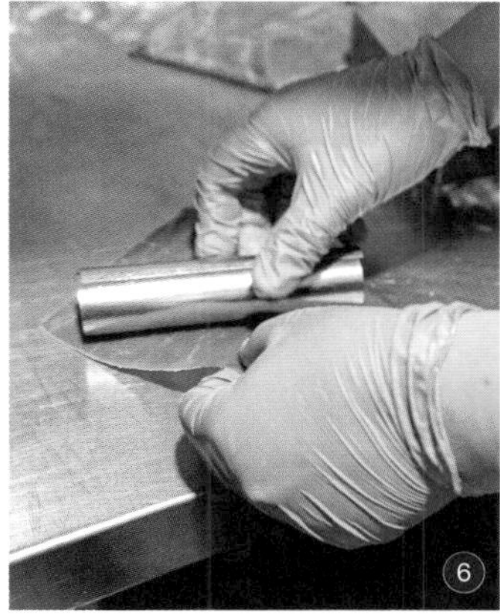
6

7

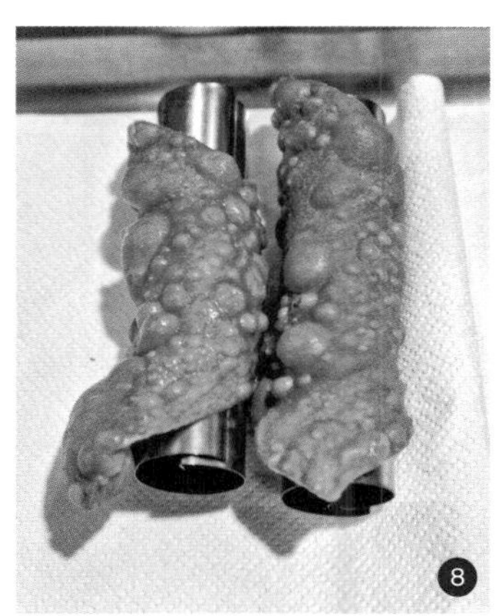
8

9

10

11

SKIP TO
RICOTTA, P. 219;
THE BRONTE PISTACHIO, P. 35;
SWEETS FROM THE CONVENT, P. 204.

SAGRA, A SACRED FESTIVAL

Throughout Italy, many local products are celebrated through sacred festivals. Here is a short list of these festive feasts over the seasons.

MARTINA TUSCANO

SAGRA

The word *sagra* comes from the Latin *sacrum* (sacred object). The term designated ceremonies celebrating new places of worship at fairs and markets. The current use of the word, in the sense of a collective gathering, can be attributed to the Florentine writer Boccaccio (1313–1375) and confirmed by poet Gabriele d'Annunzio in his 1915 speech "La Sagra dei mille." Since the 1970s, the granting of heritage status has turned these religious commemorations into gastronomic festivals, which frequently revolve around a local product or dish. Sagras express a popular gastronomic culture rooted in a land that helps promote traditional practices and products. But their proliferation can sometimes combine folkloric revival, territorial marketing, wine, and gastronomic tourism . . . A tour of the most authentic sagras is a must!

SAGRAS: HOW THEY WORK

The exact dates vary, but sagras usually take place over several days, outdoors, in the heart of the city. Visitors move from booth to booth to eat or sit at tables set up for the occasion. Entrance is free, and each booth sets the prices for its dishes.

THE FOUR SEASONS OF THE SAGRA

January

SAGRA DEL BROCCOLO FIOLARO

FIOLARO BROCCOLI

Creazzo, Veneto

The sandy limestone terrain and the regional climate provide an ideal growing environment for this vegetable with long leaves. Its tasty young shoots, known as *fioi* (meaning "children" in the Venetian dialect), which emerge after the first frost, are served panfried at this fair, which combines music with gastronomy.

February

SAGRA DEL CHIODO DI MAIALE

PORK "NAIL"

Aulla, Tuscany

Once a pig has been slaughtered, part of the meat is chopped for inclusion in sausage casings cooked in *testi*, traditional terra-cotta molds. It is then eaten as a snack as if to "drive a nail"—that is to say, to fill one's stomach. Other pork specialties can be tasted at the booths, depending on the market.

March

SAGRA DEL CARCIOFO

ARTICHOKE

Siamaggiore, Sardinia

With long stems, purple veins, and long yellow thorns, this artichoke varietal, native to the island, is known for its delicate taste and its tender, crisp heart. Whether served fried, in risotto, or in salad among shows and concerts, it's the king of the party!

April

SAGRA DEL CINGHIALE

BOAR

Certaldo, Tuscany

The hills of the Tuscan Maremma are a boar's paradise, duly and hungrily celebrated in local stews. Charcuterie, salami, or pappardelle are cooked for lunch and dinner in the main room of the town hall.

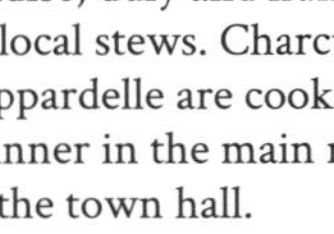

May

SAGRA DEL PESCE

FISH

Camogli, Liguria

Each year, this event attracts thousands of visitors, who arrive to taste fresh fish offered by the Camogli fishermen's cooperative and fried in a spectacular twenty-eight-quintal pan. The festival is dedicated to Saint Fortunato, patron saint of fishermen. Fireworks can be viewed on the beach in the evening.

June

SAGRA DELLE CILIEGIE

CHERRIES

Raiano, Abruzzo

Raiano's cherry sagra is a tribute to Saint Venance, patron saint of the city and of gourmets, whom the cherry symbolizes. This festival adorns the streets of the village in red, while parades and music take place.

July

SAGRA DELLA CIPOLLA ROSSA DI TROPEA

TROPEA RED ONION

Tropea, Calabria

For a single day, Tropea celebrates the sweetness of the onion that made it famous, with dances, parades, and many local dishes. The "red gold of Calabria" can be tasted in sweet-and-sour dishes, as an accompaniment to salt cod, with tuna fillets, or in savory *torte.*

August

SAGRA DEL CHISCIOI

BUCKWHEAT FRITTERS WITH CHEESE AND CHICORY

Valtellina, Lombardy

This little-known dish sums up the area: it consists of buckwheat-flour fritters and Casara fresh cheese served on a bed of finely chopped chicory. The party takes place in the Olmi Park and also offers local cheeses, charcuterie, and wines.

September

SAGRA DELLA PORCHETTA

PORCHETTA

Ariccia, Lazio

The famous porchetta, a suckling pig prepared with herbs and cooked on a spit, can be eaten as a main course or in a sandwich against a backdrop of concerts and fireworks.

October

SAGRA DELL'UVA E DEL BARDOLINO

GRAPE AND WINE OF THE BARDOLINO

Bardolino, Veneto

The mild climate, whether in summer or winter, leaves its mark on the grapes that make this light red wine. In the historic center of the city, there is a large market with music and many dishes to be tasted.

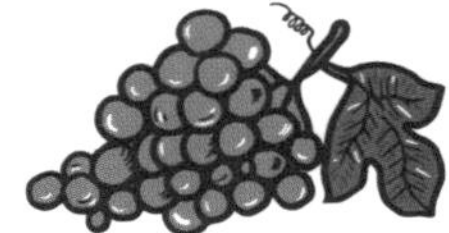

November

SAGRA DELLA ZUCCA E DEL SUO CAPPELLACCIO

SQUASH AND THE LITTLE HAT

San Carlo, Emilia-Romagna

The firm and sweet flesh of the Violina squash, common throughout the region, is the perfect filling of these *tortelli*, so named because their shape recalls the hats (*cappelli*) formerly worn by peasants. This party takes place indoors, in the town hall.

December

SAGRA DELLA PETTOLA

FRITTERS

Rutigliano, Apulia

In the spotlight at this festival are savory fritters (with anchovies, tomato, salt cod, *cime di rapa* [broccoli rabe]), but also sweet ones (with pine nuts, raisins, or honey) whose name derives from the Greek *pettele* (pillow) and which accompany the meals of Christmas celebrations in Apulia, Campania, Calabria, and Basilicata. The party takes place in the historic town center, with lots of musical entertainment.

SEASON

TUTTO L'ANNO (YEAR-ROUND)

CATEGORY

ANTIPASTO/ PIATTO UNICO (APPETIZER OR SINGLE COURSE)

LEVEL

FACILE (EASY)

BAGNA CAUDA

GARLIC AND ANCHOVY DIP

Less heavy than cheese fondues, milder than the Provençal-style anchovy dip with raw garlic, *bagna cauda*, as it's called in Piedmont, remains a rustic dish meant for sharing and for dipping!

MARIE-AMAL BIZALION

A PIEMONTESE-STYLE GARLIC SAUCE

Bagna cauda is a hot dish made with anchovies and garlic into which vegetables, cooked or raw, are dipped. Legend has it that this dish celebrated the end of the fall harvest.

MYSTERIOUS ROOTS

Was bagna cauda inspired by the recipe for *anchoïade*, the Provençal-stye raw garlic and anchovy paste used for spreading on bread? The first mention of this version dates from the fourteenth century: Antonio Guaineri, a doctor, noticed the passion the Piedmontese peasants had for a cooked garlic cream.

The addition of anchovies, although they were imported from the Provençal coast as early as the twelfth century, was not documented until 1766, in *Il cuoco piemontese perfezionato a Parigi* (anonymous). At the time, garlic was grown in Piedmont but not olives. Garlic was therefore used in local products along with walnut or hazelnut oils instead of olive oil.

THE IDEAL *STAGIONE* (SEASON)

Opt to make this recipe when vegetables (used for dipping) are at their peak and, with a little luck, you'll also find the famous Piedmontese giant Cardo gobbo di Nizza Monferrato, the only cardoon that can be eaten raw. For centuries, Piedmontese winemakers and their harvest workers have celebrated the end of the harvest sitting around this dish.

BAGNA CAUDA HAS ITS DAY

Since 2013, the Astigiani Association ("Inhabitants of Asti") has organized "Bagna Cauda Day" at the end of November. For three days, the town of Asti and the surrounding area celebrate the love of this dish through artistic, fun, and gourmet events.

"Con la cauda bagna ogni verdura as cumpagna."
("With bagna cauda, all vegetables taste good.")

PIEMONTESE EXPRESSION

THE RECIPE

SERVES 6

10½ ounces (300 g) desalted anchovies

Cooked or raw vegetables, according to the season (potatoes, cardoons, bell peppers, onions, Jerusalem artichokes, carrots, celery, cauliflower, artichokes . . .)

5 heads garlic

1¼ cups (300 mL) fresh whole milk (more or less may be need)

¼ cup (60 mL) olive oil

Remove the backbones from the anchovies and rinse the fish. Immerse them in a bowl of cold water for 10 minutes. Peel the vegetables. Cut the vegetables to be eaten raw into sticks, rounds, or quarters, whatever shape makes sense for dipping them in the sauce.

Boil the other vegetables (potatoes, Jerusalem artichokes; beware, as cardoons require a long cooking time) and roast the peppers (optional) and onions under the broiler.

Peel the garlic and place the cloves in a fondue pot, preferably one made of terra-cotta. Add just enough milk to cover them. Simmer over very low heat for about 1 hour, or until the garlic becomes tender; it will have absorbed the milk and started to brown a little.

Crush the cooked garlic with a fork. Drain the anchovies and pat dry. Add the anchovies and olive oil to the garlic. Cook over low heat, stirring, until the mixture becomes creamy, 5 to 10 minutes.

Place the pot in the center of the table over the appropriate propane burner supplied with the pot or use a tea-light candle. Place the vegetables in one or more serving dishes surrounding the pot. Guests dip their vegetables into the sauce, using their fingers or a fork, in the same way as with a cheese fondue.

THE OFFICIAL RECIPE

Cooking garlic in milk is an indulgent option but not one accepted by the Accademia Italiana della Cucina, founded in 1953. In the purist's version of the recipe, the garlic is cooked down in olive oil with a drizzle of walnut oil added, and the anchovy is soaked in red wine before being dried. Adding a little fresh butter at the end of the cooking time is recommended to further enrich everything.

Fujot, fojot... Lacking a pot?

Bagna cauda is cooked over very low heat in a terra-cotta dish or, if that is not available, in an enameled cast-iron pan before being transferred to what's called a *fujot* or *fójot* (stove) in local dialects. This is an earthenware dish with a tall, hollowed-out base, under which embers were placed (today a candle is used) to keep the sauce warm during the meal. Of course, the fujot can be replaced by a fondue pot with a heating base.

SKIP TO
THE AMAZING ANCHOVY, P. 236; VITELLO TONNATO, P. 305; MIGRANT CUISINE, P. 194.

DANTE AND *THE DIVINE COMEDY*

The sin of gluttony, as is well known, leads straight to hell! Who are these contemporaries of Dante (1265–1321)? And what happens to them when they succumb to temptation?

STÉPHANE SOLIER

WHO AM I?

Considered the father of the modern Italian language, Florentine Dante Alighieri (1265–1321) illuminates the entire Renaissance with his aura, thanks to his work *The Divine Comedy* (1303–1321), subdivided into three canticles: *Hell*, *Purgatory*, and *Paradise*.

PURGATORY

Coming out of Hell, Dante and Virgil see the souls of the repentant lying dead atop Mount Purgatory. In the sixth circle, they meet the former gourmands, tormented by eternal hunger and thirst:

All souls had dark, cavernous eyes, pale faces, and so emaciated that the skin stuck to the bones. . . . This spark rekindled in me the memory of that changed face, and I recognized that of Forese. . . . And he me: "All these people who weep while singing, for having given over to their mouths, in hunger and thirst here, make themselves holy. . . . This one (and he pointed to it) is Buonagiunta, Buonagiunta of Lucca; and, beyond him, this other, whose face is the most emaciated, had in his arms the Holy Church. He was from Tours, and by fasting he atones for the Bolsene eels prepared Vernaccia style." . . . I saw Messer Marchese who, with a throat less dry, had time to drink in Forlì, and yet never felt his thirst quenched. . . .

Translation of extracts from Dante by F. R. de Lamennais, Flammarion, 1910

WHO ARE THESE REPENTANT ONES?

Poets, nobles, high-ranking religious personalities, but above all three characters possessing legendary gourmandism:

→ Forese Donati, a relative of Dante by marriage. In insulting sonnets with buttoned foils, Dante reproached him for being a glutton and a thief.

→ French Pope Martin IV (1281–1285), originally from Tours, whose favorite dish was eels that he killed in a white wine called Vernaccia and whose epitaph mentions this guilty passion.

→ Marchese (or Marchesino) degli Argugliosi, chief magistrate of Faenza in 1296, with a reputation as a heavy drinker.

HELL

Guided by the soul of Virgil, the poet arrives, in song VI, at the third circle of Hell, occupied by the souls of gourmands, including a certain Ciacco:

Showers of heavy hail, black water, and snow swept through the dark air; foul is the earth that receives them. Cerberus, cruel beast and monstrous form, with three mouths, barks at those who are submerged there. . . . He tears their spirits, flays them, and cuts them up. The rain makes them howl like dogs. . . . A shadow, heaving, sat down when it saw us walk past it. . . . "Your name was Ciacco: because of the serious sin of gluttony, I am, as you can see, broken in the rain. And I, sad soul, am not alone. . . ."

Who is Ciacco? A certain Giacomo (Jacques), of which Ciacco is the diminutive form, who is a parasite who gorges on banquets of the time? The Florentine poet Ciacco dell'Anguillara, from whom we were presented two popular compositions? More likely, and simply, a *pig* in the Florentine language, an allegory of all the gourmands of the world!

AND DANTE HIMSELF?

Lost "in a dark forest," an allegory of sin, perhaps in which, of the three circles of Hell, the poet himself can take his place? Or in the second one, that of the lustful, as he thinks himself? Or in the third, that of the gourmands?

A short story from the beginning of the fifteenth century by Giovanni Sercambi could provide a clue: an invitation to lunch to Dante by Robert of Anjou, son of the King of Naples Charles II, in 1309, shows a poet who is both gourmand and spiritual (Giovanni Sercambi, *Novelle* LXXI, *in* Massimo Montanari, *Les Contes de la table*, Seuil, 2016).

THE LAW OF *CONTRAPPASSO*

Gourmands couldn't be missing in the Hell and Purgatory of *The Divine Comedy*. These sinners from the poet's circle, who served as models of pleasure seekers, are judged by the law of nature wherein punishment befits a crime, as in "an eye for an eye." In this case, the punishments are exactly opposite to the sin committed: either devouring or eternal hunger.

SKIP TO
SACROSANCT CUISINE, P. 346.

HIS MAJESTY THE BASIL

Italy has turned this "royal herb" with distant origins into one of the most revered aromatic emblems of its cuisine.

ILARIA BRUNETTI

Neapolitan basil

It is the best known and most widespread varietal of the *Ocimum basilicum* family.

· LEAF ·

Large, bullous, with wavy edges, intense green.

· AROMA ·

Menthol, due to linalool and methyl chavicol.

· ICONIC DISH ·

Pummarola (Neapolitan tomato sauce).

WHAT AM I?

SCIENTIFIC NAME: *Ocimum basilicum.*

FAMILY: Lamiaceae, which includes lavender, mint, rosemary, sage, thyme, and savory.

ORIGIN OF THE NAME: from the Greek *βασιλικόν* (*basilikon*), a term meaning "royal herb," possibly due to its use in mummification techniques at the court of the pharaohs of ancient Egypt.

GEOGRAPHICAL ORIGIN: India. Because it was forbidden in cooking, it was used in sacred rituals and in Ayurvedic medicine. It gradually crossed the Middle East, finally reaching Italy.

FLAVORS: intense, minty, with lemony or anise notes.

SEASON: from June to September.

THE VARIETALS: the genus *Ocimum* has a large number of varietals native to Asia (such as Indian holy basil), Latin America (such as Mexican cinnamon basil), and Africa (such as lemon basil). It is in Africa where the greatest diversity of species is found.

BEYOND THE TABLE . . .
Basil essential oil is highly prized and renowned for its antispasmodic, anti-inflammatory, and analgesic properties.

Basilico Genovese DOP

Genovese basil is the only basil to have obtained, in 2005, the PDO label. The specifications define its geographical area as on the Tyrrhenian side of Liguria for its ideal microclimate, and it must be grown on natural soil.

· LEAF ·

Medium, oval-elliptical, convex, light green, with smooth edges.

· AROMA ·

Delicate and persistent, due to the prevalence of eugenol and methyl eugenol in its essential oil composition, far from the minty character of its Neapolitan cousin.

· ICONIC DISH ·

Genovese pesto, in which it is the only basil varietal allowed.

A tavola!

Basil is usually added at the end of a dish's cooking time so that the heat does not alter its aroma. An essential addition to several iconic dishes, from rich *caponata* (eggplant salad) to the simpler caprese salad, its flavor matches well with many vegetables but also with fish, poultry, and even certain fruits, such as strawberries and lemon.

It does not like to be dried: to preserve it, freeze it or infuse it in extra-virgin olive oil. But the best approach is to always have a pot growing on the windowsill!

A ROMANTIC PLANT

Lisabetta of Messina, protagonist of Boccaccio's *Decameron* (1350–1353), kept the head of her lover Lorenzo, beheaded by her brothers opposed to their love, in a vase filled with basil leaves, which she watered with her tears.

Tuscan giant basil

Cultivated in Valdarno, this "lettuce leaf" varietal is from the same family as the Neapolitan variety but is much less well-known.

· LEAF ·

Very large, bright green, light emerald.

· AROMA ·

Intense and slightly minty, close to Neapolitan.

· ICONIC DISH ·

Panzanella, a salad made with bread and tomatoes.

RECIPE

ZUCCHINI FRITTERS WITH BASIL

This Apulian delight involves cooked basil, with great results!

Grate a large washed zucchini and drain it in a colander for 1 hour. Mix with 2 teaspoons flour, 2 teaspoons Pecorino Romano, an egg, and 10 chopped basil leaves. Let stand for 5 minutes and, if too runny, add more flour and cheese. Submerge spoonfuls of this mixture in very hot frying oil and cook until golden brown.

Recommended basil: Neapolitan or Tuscan, for their minty note, which goes well with zucchini.

SKIP TO
CAPONATA (SICILIAN EGGPLANT SALAD), P. 220;
INSALATA CAPRESE, P. 95;
PANZANELLA (BREAD SALAD), P. 168;
GENOESE PESTO, P. 20.

SEASON

TUTTO L'ANNO (YEAR-ROUND)

CATEGORY

STREET FOOD

LEVEL

FACILE (EASY)

PIADINA ROMAGNOLA

FLATBREAD SANDWICH

Originally a snack enjoyed by laborers, this stuffed flatbread, commonly prepared in areas along the Adriatic, has become a renowned specialty street food with a protected know-how.

MARTINA LIVERANI

A SIMPLE PLEASURE

The *piadina* has ancient rural origins. The Etruscans in the region consumed a circular-shaped substitute for unleavened bread. This tradition then spread during the Middle Ages when the Romagnols (inhabitants of Romagna) prepared alternatives to bread, since bread was taxed at that time. At the end of the twentieth century, the "bread of the Romagnols" conquered the countryside and the towns. Families and workers alike have made this snack their own.

Piadina Romagnola has been protected by a PGI since 2014.

Traditional fillings

→ *Squacquerone*, a regional cheese (a creamy delight that is both sweet and slightly tangy), and prosciutto.

→ Sardines and shallots, around coastal areas.

→ Salami or mortadella, very simple and delicious.

→ Almost any type of cheese and vegetables, raw or cooked.

→ Chocolate, honey, or caramelized figs, as dessert.

There is only one requirement: the piadina must be prepared and cooked just before eating, enjoyed while still hot, and held in the hands.

THE RECIPE

MAKES 6 PIADINES

4 cups (500 g) high-protein all-purpose flour or T65 flour

1⅔ teaspoons (10 g) salt

1 pinch baking soda

Just over ¾ to 1 cup (200 to 250 mL) slightly lukewarm water

1¾ ounces (50 g) lard

Combine the flour, salt, and baking soda on a work surface. Make a well in the center, add the lukewarm water and lard, and knead until you get a smooth dough. Let rest for 30 minutes.

Form six balls, then roll them into thin disks about 3 inches (8 cm) in diameter using a rolling pin.

Cook them on a hot *testo* (alternatively, in a nonstick skillet or crêpe maker), pricking them with the tines of a fork. Flip the piadina until cooked on both sides, just when it begins to smell like hot bread. Set aside until ready to fill. Enjoy hot, eating them with your hands!

For a vegetarian version, replace the lard with the same amount of olive oil.

SKIP TO
ITALY'S BEAUTIFUL CHEESES, P. 222; SALUMI, P. 308.

OFFICIAL VERSIONS

Bordered by the Adriatic and protected by the Apennine Mountains, Romagna is a small region, but there are many versions of the piadina. The consortium that protects it with the PGI label distinguishes two versions:

PIADINA ROMAGNOLA

THICKNESS—min. ⅛ inch (4 mm), max. ⅓ inch (8 mm).

DIAMETER—min. 6 inches (15 cm), max. 10 inches (25 cm).

TEXTURE—compact, stiff, and crumbly.

DIRECTIONS FOR USE—cut into quarters to use as bread.

PIADINA ROMAGNOLA DI RIMINI

THICKNESS—max. ⅛ inch (3 mm).

DIAMETER—min. 9 inches (23 cm), max. 12 inches (30 cm).

TEXTURE—soft and flexible.

DIRECTIONS FOR USE—fill, then roll up or fold in half.

And also...

IL CRESCIONE

Also called calzone or *cassone* (in Rimini), it is a typical preparation based on the piadina. The ⅛-inch-thick (4 mm) flatbread is filled, folded, and closed before baking. It is often stuffed with greens and/or herbs (spinach, chard leaves, or wild herbs), with or without cheese, but there are several versions.

LA CRESCIA SFOGLIATA

In the Marche region is found a cousin of the piadina, whose dough is made with eggs and black pepper. Once rolled out, it is laminated with lard.

THE *TESTO*

The piadina is characterized by its fast and vigorous cooking approach and its "leopardlike" appearance (due to the patches of browning) when cooked on a *testo romagnolo*, a small round pan with a nonstick base and a very low rim, made of either cast iron or aluminum.

These two materials are excellent for conducting heat, which allows fast and even baking of unleavened bread.

NEAPOLITAN PASTRIES

"See Naples and die" is the popular expression. Vesuvius, the bay, the *sfogliatelle* and many other sugary delicacies make this Campanian city a capital of sweets.

ALBA PEZONE

Graffa

A crown-shaped fritter with an ancient history, whose yeast-raised dough is made from a mixture of flour, potatoes, and lard. Today, the recipe has been lightened, but the cooking method remains unchanged; it is the frying that makes it delicious. It is found everywhere (bread shops, pastry shops, bars).

Struffoli

The origin of this small mounded pastry, composed of fried balls of dough coated in honey and decorated with candied fruits, almonds, and colorful sprinkles, is very old (it dates back to ancient Greece). *Struffoli* are on all Neapolitan tables during the Christmas holidays.

Sfogliatella

This icon of Neapolitan pastry began in the convent of Santa Rosa (Salerno) in the eighteenth century but owes its fortune to pastry chef Pasquale Pintauro at the beginning of the nineteenth century on the ancient and popular shopping thoroughfare of Via Toledo. The *sfogliatella riccia*, in the shape of a shell, contains a rich, soft filling (ricotta, semolina, candied zest, vanilla, and cinnamon) in a flaky and crisp pastry. The *sfogliatella frolla*, round and plump, wraps the same filling in a case of crumbly sweet pastry dough. The Santa Rosa, an ancestor or variant of sfogliatella riccia, topped with pastry cream and an Amarena cherry, is typical of the Amalfi Coast.

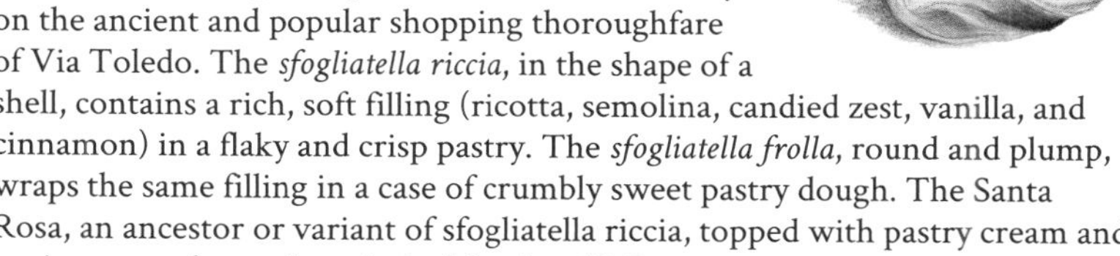

Biscotto all'amarena

Formerly a dessert whose filling made it possible to recycle tart bases and other cakes that had become too dry or soft, today it is a cookie made in pastry shops: a crumbly sweet pastry dough surrounds a very rich filling made from genoise sponge cake, chocolate, and Amarena cherry preserves, with a thin and crackly icing.

Zuppetta dolce

Also called *torta diplomatica*, this crispy and melting mille-feuille alternates puff pastry (the first and last layers) with genoise sponge cake (two layers soaked in liqueur in the center), each layer being covered with diplomat cream (pastry cream lightened with whipped cream) and Amarena cherry preserves, dusted with confectioners' sugar. It's a great classic pastry for Sundays.

Zeppola di San Giuseppe

Prepared for Saint Joseph's Day celebrations on March 19, this is an airy cream puff pastry, shaped like a crown, baked or fried, topped with pastry cream and an Amarena cherry.

Delizia al limone

Created in the 1980s, this pastry showcases Amalfi lemon: a dome of genoise sponge cake topped with tangy lemon cream, soaked in limoncello, covered with a melting lemon glaze.

Testa di moro

Always present on the *guantiera* (pastry tray) on Sundays, this is a dome of genoise sponge cake soaked in rum, topped with a chocolate cream, and covered with chocolate sprinkles.

The Latest One: Fiocco di neve

Created less than ten years ago from the imagination of Ciro Poppella, a young Neapolitan pastry chef, *fiocco di neve* (snowflake) is a candid and evanescent little brioche filled with a light ricotta cream. This innovation is a star in Naples today and will undoubtedly become a tradition.

Babà

A Neapolitan pastry par excellence. Despite its French origins, this yeast-raised cake is available in *classico* (classic, soaked in rum syrup) or *guarnito* (topped with whipped cream and wild strawberries, or pastry cream and Amarena cherries). In the past, it was always served on its golden cake board and enjoyed when seated at a table or standing at a counter; today, it is also available in a dish or glass for eating on the go. Its name has even become everyday language: "*Tu si 'nu babà!*" ("You are so cute!")

Caprese

This cake, which was created in Capri long before the modern-day craze for flourless chocolate cake began, gets its texture from the omission of flour based on the recipe for almond tart filling. Delicious, and often served with a small glass of chilled limoncello.

RECIPE

Cream together ¼ cup plus 2 tablespoons (80 g) granulated sugar with 10 tablespoons (140 g) unsalted butter until creamy. Add 4 large (200 g) eggs, beat everything together, then add 1¾ cups (200 g) almond flour and 1 teaspoon (4 g) baking powder. Incorporate 5 ounces (140 g) melted dark chocolate into the batter. Bake in a greased mold at 350°F (180°C) for 35 minutes. Once cooled, turn the cake out of the mold and dust with confectioners' sugar.

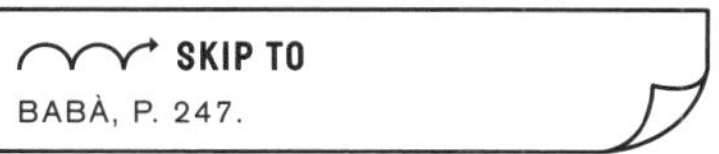

SKIP TO
BABÀ, P. 247.

PASTA INVENTORY

PASTA CORTA (SHORT PASTAS)

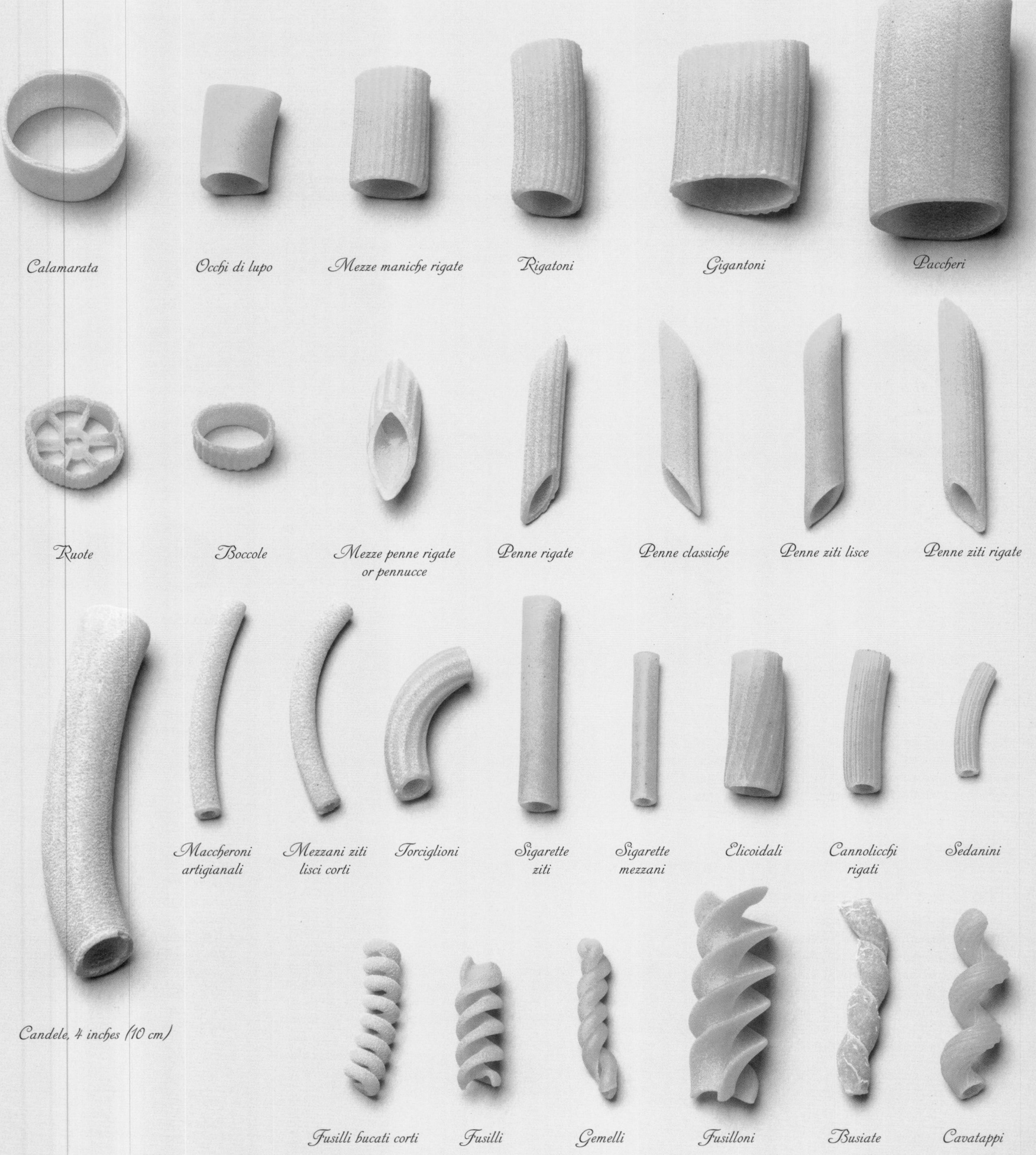

Calamarata

Occhi di lupo

Mezze maniche rigate

Rigatoni

Gigantoni

Paccheri

Ruote

Boccole

Mezze penne rigate or pennucce

Penne rigate

Penne classiche

Penne ziti lisce

Penne ziti rigate

Candele, 4 inches (10 cm)

Maccheroni artigianali

Mezzani ziti lisci corti

Torciglioni

Sigarette ziti

Sigarette mezzani

Elicoidali

Cannolicchi rigati

Sedanini

Fusilli bucati corti

Fusilli

Gemelli

Fusilloni

Busiate

Cavatappi

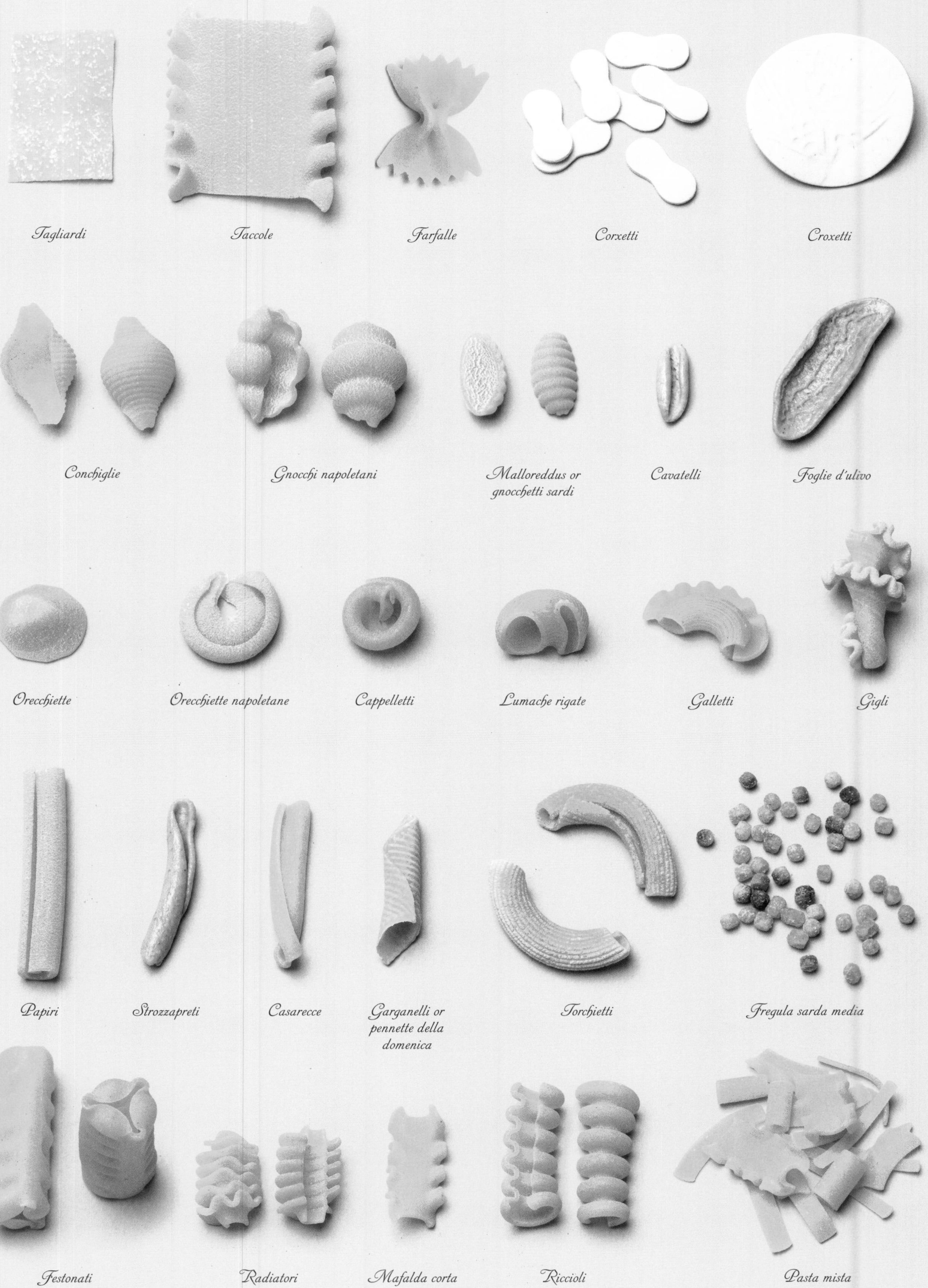

Tagliardi · Taccole · Farfalle · Corxetti · Croxetti

Conchiglie · Gnocchi napoletani · Malloreddus or gnocchetti sardi · Cavatelli · Foglie d'ulivo

Orecchiette · Orecchiette napoletane · Cappelletti · Lumache rigate · Galletti · Gigli

Papiri · Strozzapreti · Casarecce · Garganelli or pennette della domenica · Torchietti · Fregula sarda media

Festonati · Radiatori · Mafalda corta · Riccioli · Pasta mista

Bucatini
Spaghetti
Spaghettoni garganesi XXL
Vermicelli
Spaghetti alla chitarra
Fedelini
Spaghettini
Capelli d'angelo
Capellini
Chitarroni
Tagliolini
Maccheroncini di Campofilone
Pici
Strangozzi
Tagliatelle a nido
Pizzoccheri

Sagnette abruzzesi *Scialatielli* *Lasagna riccia ondulata*

Ravioli · *Agnolotti* · *Cappelletti* · *Tortellini*

Agnolotti del plin · *Mezzelune* · *Cappellacci* · *Pansoti*

Casonsei · *Marubini* · *Fagottini* · *Caramelle*

Ravioloni · *Tortelli* · *Anolini* · *Cjalson*

Tortelloni · *Fazzoletti* · *Tortelli con la coda* · *Culurgiones*

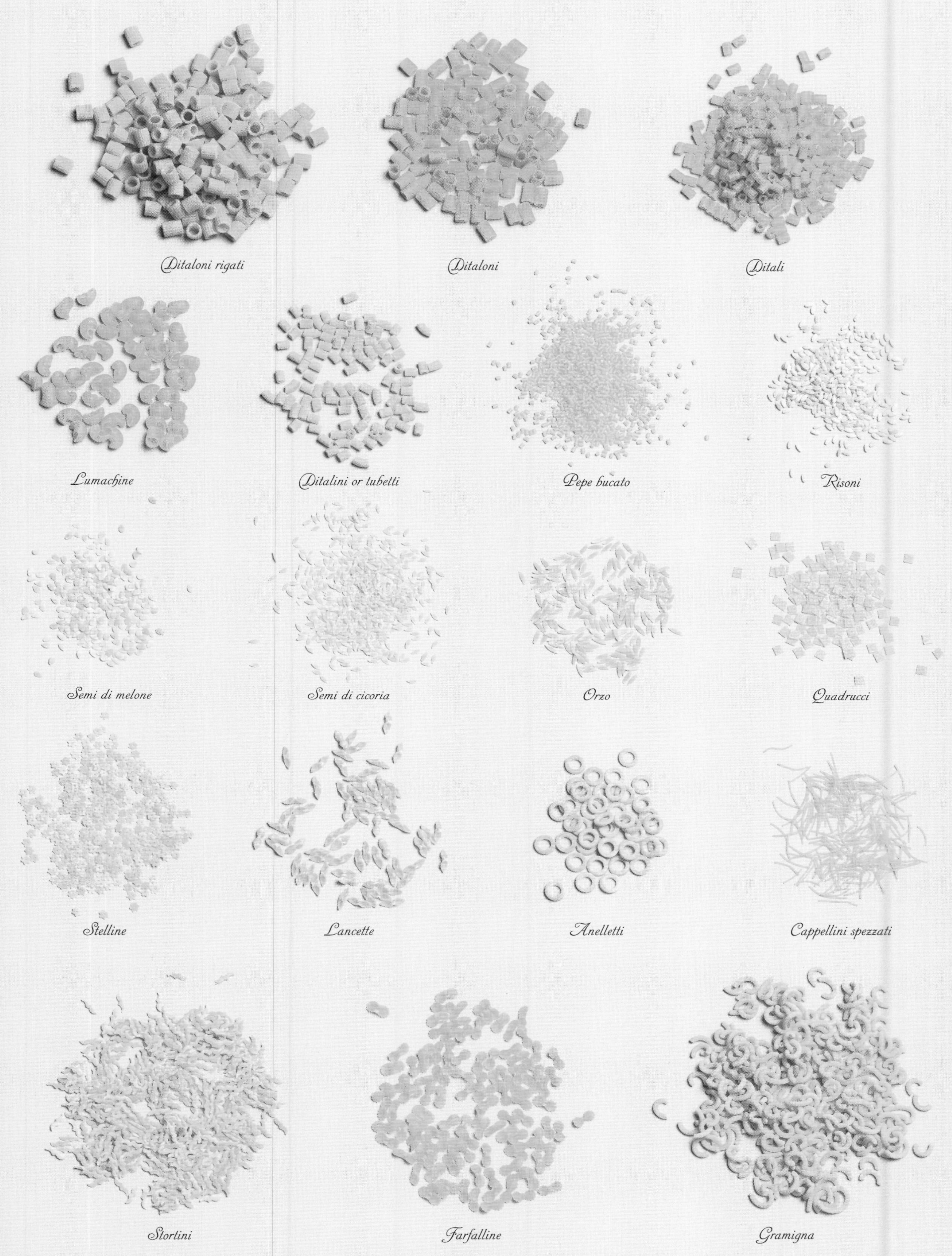

Ditaloni rigati

Ditaloni

Ditali

Lumachine

Ditalini or tubetti

Pepe bucato

Risoni

Semi di melone

Semi di cicoria

Orzo

Quadrucci

Stelline

Lancette

Anelletti

Cappellini spezzati

Stortini

Farfalline

Gramigna

Tiramisù
Candele
Lasagna
Lumaconi
Conchiglioni
Pennoni rigati
Cannelloni
Caccavella

Pasta reale

(Emilia-Romagna, Campania)

An invigorating dough made from flour, eggs, and butter. All the ingredients are mixed together in boiling water to form a dough. The dough is transferred to a pastry bag, piped into small balls ¾ inch (2 cm) in diameter, then baked in the oven. The result: mini puffs, which are immersed in a meat broth just before serving.

Loriggbitas

(Sardinia—Slow Food)

Of Sardinian origin, the name derives from their shape, *sa loriga*, the braided iron ring attached to animals. This dough, made from semolina flour and salted water, is still prepared by hand by women following artisanal methods. Formerly cooked for All Saints' Day with a sauce made from farm-raised rooster, it is also served with generous sauces made from pork, game, shellfish, asparagus, or mushrooms.

Dromsa

(Calabria)

An ancient recipe from the Arbëreshë (Albanian) community living in the Calabrian mountains, prepared with flour spritzed with water with a bunch of dried oregano that, after being combined quickly with the hands, then sifted, forms irregular and fragrant lumps. It is cooked in a richly spiced simmering tomato sauce, served with pecorino.

Filindeu

(Sardinia—Slow Food)

The name means *fili di Dio* (son of God). The recipe is passed down from mother to daughter and has roots in the region of Barbagia. Made from semolina flour and salted water, using meticulous and dexterous hand movements, long threads of dough are woven by hand and placed on a large board to dry. They are broken up and cooked in mutton broth, then sprinkled with very fresh and tangy pecorino (Casu Axedu).

Testarolo

(Liguria, Tuscany—Slow Food)

Originally from Lunigiana, a region in the Apennine Mountains between Liguria and Tuscany, this is one of the oldest forms of pasta still in existence, a large flat circle 15¾ to 19½ inches (40 to 50 cm) in diameter made from wheat flour (sometimes buckwheat or chestnut flour) and water, cooked first over embers in a *testo*, a vessel covered with clay or cast iron, then cut into diamond shapes and immersed in boiling water. It is served with Genoese pesto.

BISTECCA ALLA FIORENTINA

FLORENTINE STEAK

This is one of Tuscany's gastronomic jewels, found at many restaurants throughout the region. Let's light a fire under this satisfying piece of grilled beef!

FRANÇOIS-RÉGIS GAUDRY

ITS ORIGINS

Bistecca alla fiorentina's history is attached, as its name suggests, to the capital of Tuscany. This tradition dates back to the Medici era. Legend has it that on August 10, 1565, on San Lorenzo Day (he was tortured on a grill!), the city was illuminated by bonfires on which were roasted large pieces of beef that were distributed to the population. English knights who enjoyed partaking of the meat cried, "Beefsteak! Beefsteak!" The word was later Italianized. However, the consumption of grilled beef did not become widespread in Italy until the nineteenth century.

THE BREED

There is no *bistecca* (steak) without the Chianina, a cattle breed that owes its name to the Val di Chiana, a valley located between Tuscany and Umbria. This large cow, with its porcelain-white coat, has been known since antiquity for its excellent tenacity for work. It has gradually been converted into a meat breed. The Maremmana, Marchigiana, and Romagnola breeds are also suitable for bistecca. The meat is usually taken from *vitellone* (young male calf [veal]) or the *scottona* (heifer).

THE CUT

Bistecca is the sirloin steak, a piece of meat crossed by a T-shaped bone also referred to as the T-bone. It comes from the *lombata* (loin), the lower part of the back that corresponds to the lumbar vertebrae. On one side of the bone is the filet mignon, and on the other, the strip steak.

Its thickness and weight vary depending on the animal. Its ideal cut size is 1½ to 2⅓ inches (4 to 6 cm) thick for a weight of 1¾ to 3⅓ pounds (800 g to 1.5 kg). Traditionally, it is aged for at least fifteen days.

THE GOLDEN RULES FOR COOKING

OVER A WOOD FIRE—over a wood fire is obligatory! The coals, preferably of oak or olive wood, should be glowing but flameless and just covered with a thin layer of ash.

NO FAT—this is a warning from Pellegrino Artusi in *La scienza in cucina e l'arte di mangiar bene* (*Science in the Kitchen and the Art of Eating Well*, 1891): "If you season it first with oil or something else, like many people do, it will taste like smoke and be cloying."

NO SALT—it may dry out the meat. The steak is not salted until it is eaten.

THE MEAT MUST BE HANDLED WITHOUT BEING PIERCED—to prevent the juices from escaping.

THE TECHNIQUE

1. The bistecca is seared on a grill close to the coals (at around 660°F/350°C) for 1 minute on each side so that a crust forms on the meat.
2. The grill is then raised over a lower heat, and the meat is cooked for 3 to 5 minutes on each side, depending on the weight, and turned only once.
3. At the end, the steak should be cooked "upright," resting on the side of the bone, for several minutes.

Serving

Bistecca can be enjoyed rare, as Pellegrino Artusi attests: ***"It should not be overcooked, as it should provide abundant juice to the dish on which it is cut."***

This steak is traditionally served with a green salad, cannellini beans, or grilled vegetables.

THE STAR BUTCHER

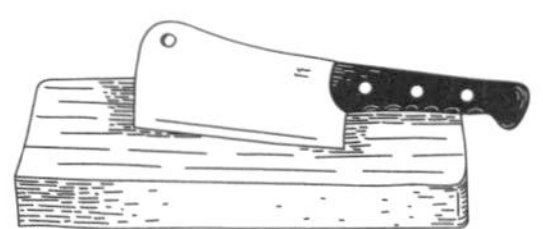

Next to his wood-fired oven, Tuscan **DARIO CECCHINI** has carved out a worldwide reputation for himself. His secrets: Chianina meat of excellent origin, strict accordance to the rules of the art of preparation, and a particular taste for spectacle!

Antica Macelleria Cecchini, Panzano, Chianti (Tuscany).

Photos taken at the restaurant Regina Bistecca, 14, Via Ricasoli.

SKIP TO
PELLEGRINO ARTUSI, P. 32;
RUSTIC COW BREEDS, P. 258.

SEASON

TUTTO L'ANNO (YEAR-ROUND)

CATEGORY

ANTIPASTO STREET FOOD

LEVEL

DIFFICOLTÀ MEDIA (MEDIUM DIFFICULTY)

TORTA FRITTA

FRIED DOUGH

Fried diamond-shaped crisps, puffed and airy . . . these are a great snack, especially when accompanied by local specialties.

ALESSANDRA PIERINI

"Fried tart"

In Emilia-Romagna, this beignet made from flour, yeast, and lard was originally served as a dessert, dusted with confectioners' sugar. Later, salt replaced sugar and fried dough became a substitute for bread to accompany local charcuterie and cheeses as a snack or aperitif. Today, *torta fritta*—so called in Parma—has also become a staple *cibo di strada* (street food). It is called *gnocco fritto* in Reggio Emilia and Modena, *pinzin* in Ferrara, *chisulén* in Piacenza, and *crescentine**—often in the plural—in Bologna.

*Beware! In Modena, *crescentina* means a small bread baked in *tigelles*, two terra-cotta disks used for baking in a wood-fired oven (Bologna).

ACCOMPANIMENTS

· LARD ·

Cut into very thin slices or reduced to a cream with garlic and rosemary (*lardo pesto*).

· CHARCUTERIE ·

Coppa, pancetta, prosciutto di Parma, mortadella, sausage.

· CHEESE ·

Parmigiano-Reggiano, Gorgonzola, Taleggio, Squacquerone, or Stracchino (fresh cow's-milk cheeses without the rinds, very creamy and soft).

· WINE ·

Especially Lambrusco, but also the other sparkling wines of the region (Pignoletto, Malvasia, Fortana).

Torta fritta can also be eaten on its own, piping hot and lightly salted on the outside.

SKIP TO
ITALY'S BEAUTIFUL CHEESES, P. 222;
SALUMI, P. 308;
PARMIGIANO-REGGIANO, P. 86.

THE RECIPE

This recipe comes from my mother, Rosetta, who prepares mountains of these for family reunions. You need a patient person in charge of frying the torta fritta, because they must be served as you go so that they stay warm.

MAKES APPROXIMATELY 40 PIECES

4 cups (500 g) pastry flour, plus more for dusting

2⅓ teaspoons (9 g) fresh baker's yeast

½ teaspoon (2 g) sugar

1 cup plus 1 tablespoon (250 g) water, at room temperature

1 ounce (30 g) lard or unsalted butter

2 teaspoons (12 g) fine salt, plus more as needed

4 cups (1 L) frying oil or lard

· Sprinkle the flour on a work surface. Dissolve the yeast and sugar in a bowl with 3 tablespoons (50 g) of the water and incorporate it into the flour with the lard. Combine well. Add the remaining water and the salt and knead until you get a smooth, supple dough. Shape it into a ball, then let it proof for 2 to 3 hours on a floured work surface covered with a clean cloth in a warm room and away from drafts. It should double in size.

· Roll out the dough using a rolling pin or a dough sheeter to a thickness of 2 to 3 mm, then, using a knife or a fluted pastry cutter, cut out diamond shapes measuring 2 to 2¾ inches (5 to 7 cm). Let rise for 1 hour, covered, on the floured work surface.

· Heat the oil in a deep fryer or deep saucepan. Fry only 2 or 3 pieces at a time so they are fully immersed in the oil. When puffed, turn them over, usually after 1 minute. When lightly browned, remove them with a skimmer and place them on paper towels to drain. Season with salt and serve immediately.

VARIATIONS

→ The dough can be cut into rectangles or circles.

→ Sparkling water can replace yeast to puff up the dough.

→ Lard (ideal for a crunchy texture) or butter can be replaced with olive oil, and the water with lukewarm milk.

→ In Tuscany, these are called *ficattola, coccolo,* or *donzella.* These are bite-size pieces of unrolled fried dough.

A CLOUDLIKE DOUGH

Torta fritta dates back to the Lombards (sixth century), as evidenced by the presence of lard in the batter and as used for the frying fat. This fat was very popular among barbarians and dominated through the Middle Ages. The first written testimony of the torta fritta dates back to Carlo Nascia, court cook for the Duke of Parma. In his book *La quattro banchetti destinati per le quattro stagioni dell'anno* (*Four Banquets for the Four Seasons of the Year*, 1659), he speaks of *pasta al vento* ("dough in the wind"), describing it as a cloud of finesse and lightness. Since then, the recipe has been part of the Emilia-Romagna tradition, especially among families living in the countryside, thanks to the accessibility and simplicity of the ingredients.

THE LAGOON IS A TERROIR

It has over a thousand years of history and receives ten million tourists a year, but who would imagine that Venice and its lagoon conceal an authentic gastronomic and winemaking region?

SAMUEL COGLIATI

WATER-BASED MARKET GARDENS

The islands of the lagoon are made up of fertile river silts. The tradition of market gardening still exists, thanks to vegetable gardens of small, mainly local, production. The delicate and salty characteristic of the land gives the vegetables extra flavor.

The hot spot of market gardening is the island of Sant'Erasmo, with its delicious vegetables:

Purple artichokes—*castraure*

Thin green asparagus—*sparasei*

Small summer beans—*baéte*

Zucchini and bitter chicories—*radiceti* . . .

The voice of the sea

Looking at its dark green waters, an observer wouldn't suspect that Venice's lagoon is full of fish. "And yet," assures Cesare Benelli, local restaurateur and expert on the area, "we can trace almost everything we find there from the sea." Going even further, the lagoon is a breeding ground: fish lay their eggs there, which are used as food by predators. "This is why," Benelli explains, "the fish and shellfish have an incomparable flavor." Almost everything is wild, caught in nets that remain suspended, thus respecting the bottom of the shallow lagoon. Cuttlefish, *go* (goby), *bisati* (eels), *scorbola* (mantis shrimp), *schie* (gray shrimp), *scampi* (langoustines) . . .

The moeches

Twice a year (April to May and October to November), the green crabs (*Carcinus aestuarii*) molt by leaving their shells. During this time, they have an exquisite tenderness. The Venetians gather them for frying like fritters and eating whole. While the crabs are crisp on the outside, their flesh remains soft on the inside and exudes fine and powerful sea flavors. This treat, known as *moeche* (pronounced "mo-ay-kay"), is available to savor only in Venice . . .

WILD HERBS, HIDDEN TREASURES

Along the shores of the coast of Cavallino-Treporti, there are tasty plants and wild herbs, ideal to use in condiments and salads, served as raw vegetables, or cooked in the traditions of the lagoon.

Salicornia—sea beans (samphire)

Enula marina—golden samphire

Fiori di carota—wild carrot flowers

Porcellana di mare—sea purslane

Minutina—buck's-horn plantain

Critmo marittimo—sea fennel

CAN A WINE BE BRINY?

In Venice, people worship wine. For a long time, ships imported barrels from the eastern Mediterranean where the republic had its trading posts. But the Venetians did not neglect local production, which was sometimes carried out in the heart of the city. Some vestiges have withstood the test of time. Volunteers from the association Laguna nel Bicchiere ("Lagoon in the Glass") maintain a few rows of vines scattered throughout the city. The most substantial small vineyard is probably that of the island of San Michele, with its white grape varietals (Glera, Malvasia, Dorona): these wines have the unique characteristic of a slightly briny flavor! New winemakers have been inspired by it, including Gianluca Bisol in Mazzorbo (cuvée Venissa) or Michel Thoulouze in Sant'Erasmo (cuvée Orto).

EL SELVÀDEGO, "THE WILD"

Venice and water are one, but the old aristocracy did not live on fish alone. The notables of the Venetian Republic have always had a fondness for game, for which the lagoon offers many choices. Even today during the autumn season, in the surroundings of Burano, Torcello, and farther inland, people hunt:

Ducks (*ànare*), which a few rare restaurants sometimes offer.

Mallards (*masolini*), sometimes also offered at restaurants.

Whistling ducks (*ciossi*), which cannot be sold, so are prepared as home-cooked dishes.

Winter teals (*salsegne*), for domestic consumption only.

A few gourmet addresses

In 1992, the association I Ristoranti della Buona Accoglienza was founded. It brings together thirteen restaurants in Venice that are committed to "protecting and showcasing the extraordinary productions of the lagoon terroir."

SEASON
INVERNO (WINTER)

CATEGORY
VERDURE (VEGETABLE)

LEVEL
FACILE (EASY)

PUNTARELLE ALLA ROMANA

CHICORY SALAD WITH GARLIC AND ANCHOVY

RICETTA Iconica RICETTA

LAZIO

Tender green shoots intermingled and coated with an anchovy vinaigrette—it's a marriage of bitterness and flavor. From chopping to seasoning, here are the secrets to this iconic Roman winter salad.

FRANÇOIS-RÉGIS GAUDRY

LA PUNTARELLE, A SALAD AT THE CUTTING EDGE

Literally meaning "small spikes," the term *puntarelle* refers to the flower stalks of a very popular chicory varietal cultivated in Lazio and southern Italy.

ITS LATIN NAME

Cichorium intybus var. *foliosum.*

ITS COMMON NAMES

Cicoria di Catalogna (Catalonian chicory) and *cicoria asparago* (asparagus chicory), because the large buds that grow in its center resemble asparagus. In the region of Rome, it is the cultivar *Cicoria di Catalogna frastagliata di Gaeta* that is cultivated primarily today.

THE SEASON

The winter months (harvested ideally in January and February).

ITS ORIGINS

A descendant of wild chicory, which was consumed in ancient Egypt. The tradition of seasoning it with a "pesto" made from anchovies is thought to trace back to ancient Rome.

ITS FLAVOR

Slightly bitter and crunchy, with a subtle taste of almond.

Tournicoti

Why do puntarelle curl in contact with cold water? As can be seen, puntarelle shoots have two colors, each of which has a different composition: internal white fibers, which are rather elastic, and external green fibers, which are more rigid. In contact with water, the white part tends to absorb more water and therefore warps. Since it gives at the pressure difference between the green part and the white part, the shoots then bend, and always in the same direction: concave. The green fibers wrap in toward the center. Visually, it has a frizzy look!

THE RECIPE

This Roman salad is rustic and easy to prepare, but it takes a bit of preparation to be at its best. The day before, or at least two hours before preparation, immerse the puntarelle in a bowl of cold water and place everything in the refrigerator.

SERVES 4

1 head puntarelle (1¾ to 2¼ pounds/ 800 g to 1 kg)

1 clove garlic

8 to 10 anchovy fillets in olive oil

2 tablespoons (30 mL) white wine vinegar

5 to 6 tablespoons (75 to 90 mL) olive oil

Salt and freshly ground black pepper

Prepare the puntarelle as indicated in the paragraph "Trimming the Puntarelle, the Method" (above).

Prepare the seasoning: peel the garlic clove, remove the germ from the center, and crush the garlic in the bottom of a mortar.

Add the anchovy fillets and mash again.

Pour in the vinegar and olive oil, and pound the mixture to obtain a slightly thick dressing.

If using a food processor, take care to pulse easily so as not to heat the ingredients.

Season with salt (be careful, the anchovies are already salted).

Drain the puntarelle carefully, place it in a bowl, pour the dressing over the top, and toss well. Add a few turns of the pepper mill over the top, and serve.

TRIMMING THE PUNTRELLE, THE METHOD

In the markets of Rome, puntarelle can be found already sliced, soaking in cool water.

When the entire head is purchased, the long leaves must be removed, maintaining the large light green heart as well as some tender ribs and tips. Using a large, sharp knife, cut the heart lengthwise in about ¼-inch-thick (5 mm) slices, then in strips a few millimeters wide. Wash them. There is also a "puntarelle cutter," a kind of grid of crossed wires allowing the puntarelle to be sliced into uniform strips.

Place water and ice cubes in a mixing bowl and immerse the strips for at least thirty minutes. The ice water will help rid them of some of their bitterness and cause them to curl up on themselves, taking on a coiled look.

AND COOKED PUNTARELLE?

→ To make a tasty side dish: finely chop the stems and leaves, drop them in a heated pan with a drizzle of olive oil, a touch of garlic, a few anchovy fillets (and maybe a few capers). Cook for five to ten minutes over medium heat.

→ To accompany spaghetti, moisten lightly cooked puntarelle with a little pasta cooking water to create a liaison and add al dente spaghetti.

→ For a risotto: add cooked puntarelle to risotto before serving it.

→ For an omelet: beat six eggs with a fork. Add cooked puntarelle. Cook the omelet until slightly colored.

SKIP TO
THE AMAZING ANCHOVY, P. 236;
GARLIC, P. 192;
BITTER LETTUCES, P. 170.

ARTE BIANCA

Ever since the word *flour* entered the Latin language and the Romans mastered *arte bianca* ("white art," referring the trade of the baker), bread has occupied a fundamental place in the Italian diet.

ADRIANO FARANO*

PANEM ET CIRCENSES

"Bread and circuses." Such was the tactic, according to the poet Juvénal, of the authorities of the Roman Empire to buy social peace, proof that the inhabitants of the Italian peninsula were crazy about bread as early as two thousand years ago! The Pompeian baker Modestus certainly paid the price of this adoration when Mount Vesuvius erupted in 79 CE: he could not escape in time because he was waiting for his last eighty-one loaves to finish baking, as discovered by archaeologists.

There are numerous Pompeian frescoes illustrating the importance of the bakery in the ancient Campanian city.

ITALIAN BREAD: A BRIEF HISTORY

32,000 YEARS AGO
The first loaf. It is made from oat flour in the Paglicci cave in Apulia.

SEVENTH TO FIRST CENTURY BCE
The *confarreatio* (marriage in ancient Rome). Spouses of the aristocracy exchange bread, probably unleavened, made from starch flour (*far* in Latin, from which the word *flour* is derived).

FROM THE THIRD CENTURY BCE
A *terroir* of wheat. Demeter, goddess of the harvest, offers wheat to the Sicilians to thank them for having comforted her following the abduction of her daughter Persephone. Sicily thus becomes "the breadbasket of the Roman people," according to an expression attributed to Cato by Cicero.

FROM THE MIDDLE AGES TO THE MID-TWENTIETH CENTURY
Communal ovens. Breads are prepared in each household, placed on the nuptial bed to proof, then wrapped in sheets and marked with the initials of the father's name . . . even if it was the women who did all the work! They were then cooked in communal wood-fired ovens for a fee.

IN 1915
A senator of wheat. Agronomist Nazareno Strampelli creates the Senatore Cappelli varietal of wheat to thank the parliamentarian who lent him fields. The old varietals were quickly replaced by modern wheat species with higher yields and less digestible gluten.

IN 1925
The battle of wheat. Benito Mussolini launches Battaglia del Grano, a program to boost wheat production with the aim of reducing imports from abroad. In six years, production increases from 25 million to 81 million quintals.

THE PRAYER OF THE BREAD

Because it is the only food that the Christian rite of the Eucharist transforms into divine flesh, bread has been the subject of beliefs often linked to religion. In Calabria, after placing the bread in the oven, the following prayer is recited:

"Santa Rosalia bianco e rosso como a tía Santu Nicola u criscidinta ca nuje u criscimmu fora."

("Saint Rosalie, white and red like you, Saint Nicholas, make it grow inside, and we will make it grow on the outside.")

Sulla Punta Della Lingua (On the Tip of the Tongue)

Chi ha i denti non ha il pane, chi ha il pane non ha i denti.
"Whoever has teeth has no bread, whoever has bread has no teeth." (Possessions often end up in the hands of those who do not know how to manage them.)

Non è pane per i tuoi denti.
"This is no bread for your teeth." (You can't afford it.)

Rendere pan per focaccia.
"Give bread for focaccia." (Take revenge, give someone a taste of his own medicine.)

Portare a casa la pagnotta.
"Bring home a loaf of bread." (Earn your keep.)

Non si vive di solo pane.
"We don't just live on bread." (Man cannot live on bread alone.)

PANE SCIOCCO

Why in Florence do people still eat *pane sciocco* ("foolish bread") without salt? Some might say it's because salt attracts moisture and therefore hastens mold forming on the bread, but the real answer lies with the longtime rivals in Pisa, who, by controlling access to the sea, increased taxes on salt in the twelfth century. The response of the embittered Florentines? "We call your bluff, and will just do without!"

BREAD AT THE CENTER OF THE MEAL

At the table of Michelin three-star chef Niko Romito (Reale, Abruzzo), bread made from ancient solina wheat is now a full-fledged dish on his tasting menu. The movement to rediscover ancient grains is in full swing.

The best bakers

__Brisa (Bologna, Emilia-Romagna):__
A student in Bologna, Abruzzese Pasquale Polito founded a bakery specializing in sourdough bread and "local" flours that showcase the grain traditions throughout Italy.

__Bonci (Rome, Lazio):__
The king of *lievitati* (leavened doughs) is a tall man with tattooed arms. For Gabriele Bonci, bread, panettone, and *pizza al taglio* (by the slice) are all to be conquered! Beware of his yeasts! His specialty is *pasta madre* (sourdough starter).

__Vulaiga (Fobello, Piedmont):__
Nestled in a mountain village, this *panificio* is the work of Eugenio Pol, a true guru of sourdough bread and ancient wheats, who doesn't hesitate to combine unusual ingredients such as in his *farro monococco* bread (made with einkorn wheat), marjoram, and *guanciale* (cured pork cheek).

__Perino Vesco (Turin, Piedmont):__
Andrea's bakery offers sourdough breads made from *farro monococco* flour, as well as the famous *grissini stirati a mano* (hand-pulled grissini).

LA *PASTA MADRE*

Italian arte bianca uses the term *pasta madre* to describe this pre-ferment for bread. This great miracle of life can be re-created at any time. The older it is, the more the pasta madre has a variety of lactic acid bacteria and yeasts capable of giving bread a wide range of aromas and making it more digestible.

*Adriano Farano is a bread specialist. He founded the Pane Vivo bakery (Paris, 20th arr.).

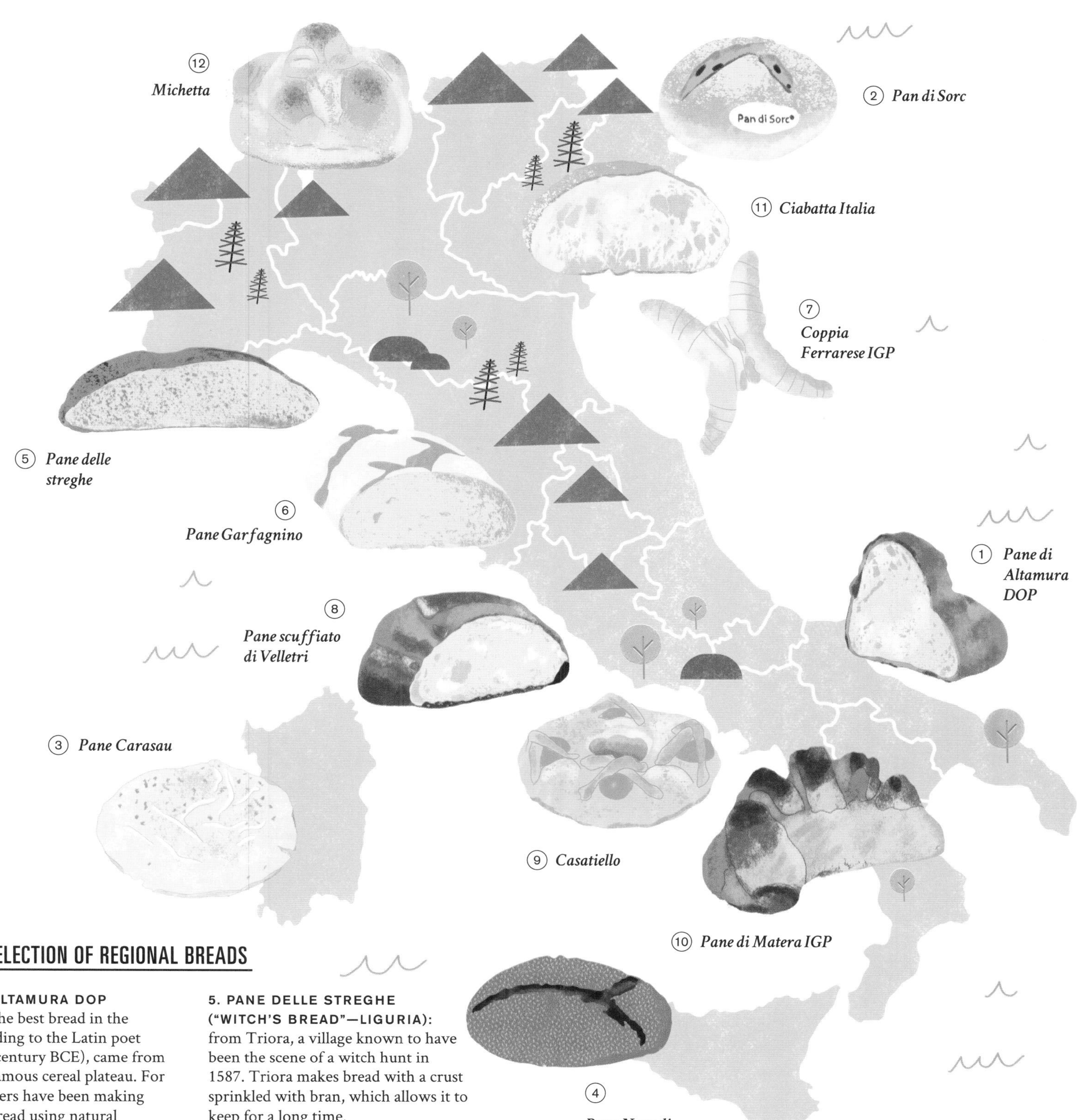

A SMALL SELECTION OF REGIONAL BREADS

1. PANE DI ALTAMURA DOP (APULIA): "The best bread in the world," according to the Latin poet Horace (first century BCE), came from Murgia, the famous cereal plateau. For centuries, bakers have been making hard-wheat bread using natural sourdough starter.
Weight: 1⅛ to 11 pounds (500 g to 5 kg).

2. PAN DI SORC (FRIULI): filled with figs, raisins, and fennel seeds, it is made from rye flour, wheat flour, and cornmeal of the old varietal known as Cinquantino, because it grows in "fifty days."
Weight: about 9½ ounces (270 g).

3. PANE CARASAU (SARDINIA): literally "toasted bread" in Sardinian, it is as thin as sheet music.
Weight: 10½ ounces (300 g).

4. PANE NERO DI CASTELVETRANO (SICILY): so called because of its dark color, characteristic of ancient varietals of hard-wheat flours, native to the region of Trapani.
Weight: 1⅛ to 2¼ pounds (500 g to 1 kg).

5. PANE DELLE STREGHE ("WITCH'S BREAD"—LIGURIA): from Triora, a village known to have been the scene of a witch hunt in 1587. Triora makes bread with a crust sprinkled with bran, which allows it to keep for a long time.
Weight: 1¾ to 2 pounds (800 to 900 g).

6. PANE GARFAGNINO (TUSCANY): this very light bread is made of one-third crushed potatoes, which was a practical ingredient when the wheat crops were poor.
Weight: 2¼ pounds/1 kg (round) or 4½ pounds/2 kg (oval).

7. COPPIA FERRARESE IGP (EMILIA-ROMAGNA): a twisted bread in the shape of a cross, now protected by labels, and made from soft-wheat flour and lard.
Weight: 3 to 9 ounces (80 to 250 g).

8. PANE SCUFFIATO DI VELLETRI (LAZIO): cooked over a wood fire, this bread is created from a double fermentation, which allows it to be very honeycombed (*scuffiato* in the local dialect).
Weight: 1⅛ pounds (500 g).

9. CASATIELLO (CAMPANIA): featuring a whole egg covered with dough in the form of a cross, this Neapolitan Easter bread is made with soft-wheat flour, lard, and black pepper. It is baked in a ring-shaped mold.
Weight: 1⅛ to 4½ pounds (500 g to 2 kg).

10. PANE DI MATERA IGP (BASILICATA): this large loaf with a unique taste and beautiful yellow crumb from Cappelli hard-wheat flour is created using ancient know-how. It keeps for a long period of time.
Weight: 2¼ or 4½ pounds (1 or 2 kg).

11. CIABATTA ITALIA (VENETO): this small, world-famous bread has a recent history. It was registered in 1982 as a commercial product under the name *ciabatta* by its creator, a visionary miller who found a flour capable of absorbing high levels of hydration.
Weight: about 7 ounces (200 g).

12. MICHETTA (LOMBARDY): this small bread made from T00 flour is a staple of Milanese panini.
Weight: 1¾ to 3⅛ ounces (50 to 90 g).

THE DELIGHTS OF LICORICE

Black and seductive, *liquirizia* is not just a confection.

GIANNA MAZZEI

WHAT AM I?

SCIENTIFIC NAME: *Glycyrrhiza glabra.*

FAMILY: Fabaceae (same as legumes).

HABITAT: a Mediterranean plant cultivated in central, southern, and island regions of Italy.

HARVEST: in the fall, from plants at least three years old. The roots and runners (stemlike growths of the plant for propagation) are harvested, then dried in the sun.

TASTE: sweet and balsamic.

ACTIVE INGREDIENT: glycyrrhizin, known for its sweet flavor; it is often used as a sweetener.

COLOR: straw yellow when fresh; ocher when dried. To obtain the shiny black that characterizes it, the roots are dried, crushed, pressed, and moistened with boiling water.

CALABRAIS COFFEE

This unusual match, common to Calabria, offers a tasty and energizing break! Just put a pinch of licorice powder (obtained by grinding a candy or a pure licorice lozenge) in a saucepan, add 1 teaspoon brown sugar and a drop of eau-de-vie or cognac, flambé, and drizzle with a hot espresso.

PRODUCTION

In Italy, licorice is widespread in Calabria, the region that produces the most, but it's also made in Abruzzo, Molise, Apulia, and Sardinia.

The Cordara varietal, produced in Calabria and granted a PDO, is considered the best in the world. It is so named because its appearance is reminiscent of a disordered interweaving of strings.

Pura Liquirizia Saila ABRUZZO | Tabu' Perfett LOMBARDY | Girella or Rotella (roll) | Polvere (powder)

Radice (root for herbal teas) | Sukai (soft) | Passaro Pura Liquirizia CALABRIA | Leone pastilles PIEDMONT | More (blackberries)

Grezza (natural) | Pesci (soft fish) | Gommose Leone (soft) PIEDMONT | More (soft blackberry) | Golia Perfetti (candies) LOMBARDY

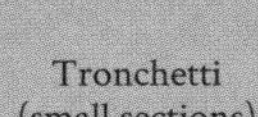

Fralementi (tiny bits) | Spezzata (in chips) | Licorice mint Leone | Licorice anise Leone | Pure licorice Leone | Tronchetti (small sections)

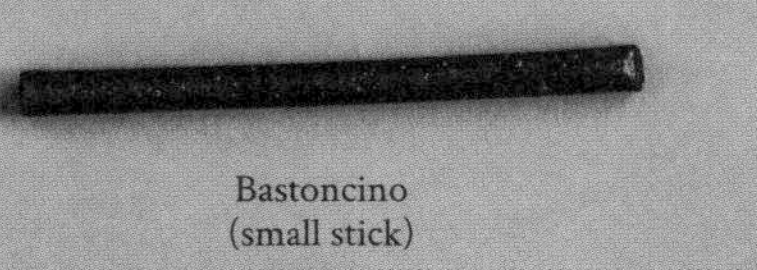

Bastoncino (small stick) | Radice (root) | Frantumata (block in pieces)

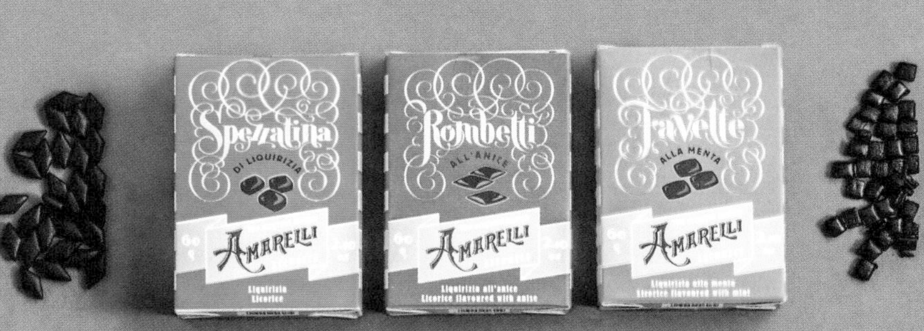

Rombi (diamonds) | Spezzatina Amarelli CALABRIA | Rombetti Amarelli CALABRIA | Amarelli favor CALABRIA | Spezzatina (little bits)

A PLANT THAT WANTS TO DO US GOOD

→ Licorice's digestive, purifying, and anti-inflammatory properties have been known since antiquity. It is mentioned in traditional Chinese medicine and has been used in Asia for more than five thousand years; the Shiites used it to quench their thirst on long walks in the desert. It arrived in Europe in the fifteenth century, brought by Dominican friars who used it as a dye or as an herbal tea infusion.

→ It produces a satiating effect.

→ It is useful in cases of arterial hypotension but is contraindicated in cases of hypertension.

→ In cosmetics, in the form of an ointment, it is known for its soothing nature and as a treatment against skin spots.

Licorice in all its forms

ROOT—the raw root is harvested, peeled, and dried. It is chewed for pleasure or as a tobacco substitute when quitting smoking. In slices, it can be used in infusions or macerations.

POWDERED—for the preparation of ice cream or liqueur or to flavor apple or pear jams, or even honey. Also excellent in lemon and licorice risotto; the saffron and licorice risotto of Michelin three-star chef Massimiliano Alajmo is famous.

IN CONFECTIONERY—sweet, bitter, salty, tastes like candy, it is also used in the preparation of liqueurs, to flavor vodka or beer, or in spiced milk.

SKIP TO
CANDIES, P. 286;
THE RELIGION OF COFFEE, P. 88; LIQUORI, P. 366.

MAFIA DISHES

The Mafia is a popular subject in cinema, inspiring many stories. Even in jail, nostalgia for the mother country and its dear cuisine is revered. Here are three cult scenes cooked up by Scorsese, Leone, and Coppola.

LAURENT DELMAS

GOODFELLAS

Martin Scorsese

1990

THE SCENE OF THE CRIME—in prison, members of the Lucchese clan, including Henry (Ray Liotta) and Jimmy (Robert De Niro), watch Scorsese's own father in the role of Vinnie prepare meat-based tomato sauce according to a recipe from Catherine Scorsese, the mother of the Italian American filmmaker. With a particularly artful way of very finely chopping garlic: using a razor blade, as being imprisoned would demand!

WHAT'S THE DISH?—this is, of course, ragù (see recipe opposite)! A debate ensues between the onion camp and the garlic camp, who seem to prevail, as shown in the close-up of the cutting of a garlic clove. The main secret, however, is the use of three kinds of meat, when typically only one is used.

THE KILLER LINE—"In prison, dinner was always a big thing."

RECIPE

MAMMA SCORSESE'S RAGÙ

SERVES A LARGE TABLE OF INMATES

- 1 large sweet onion, chopped
- 2 tablespoons (30 mL) olive oil
- Scant ½ cup (100 mL) tomato paste
- 3 cloves garlic
- 2 carrots, sliced into thick rounds
- 1 potato, peeled and sliced into thick rounds
- 5 tablespoons (13 g) finely chopped fresh basil
- 5 tablespoons (13 g) finely chopped fresh flat-leaf parsley
- 1 pinch ground cayenne
- Salt
- 4½ pounds (2 kg) chopped fresh tomatoes
- 32 ounces (900 g) tomato sauce
- 1 ounce (25 g) fresh bread
- ¼ cup (60 mL) milk
- 6 ounces (170 g) pork sausage
- 6 ounces (170 g) ground veal
- 6 ounces (170 g) ground beef
- 1 large (50 g) egg
- ⅓ cup (40 g) grated Parmesan cheese

· In a large pot, brown the onion in the oil. Add 2 cups (500 mL) water, the tomato paste, very finely chopped garlic (if possible, chopped with a razor), carrots, potato, half the basil and parsley, and the cayenne; season with salt. Bring to a boil, partially covered, and simmer gently for 1 hour, stirring from time to time.

· In a separate pan, combine the chopped tomatoes and tomato sauce.

· In a bowl, soak the bread in the milk. Add this mixture to the pot along with the meats, egg, Parmesan, remaining basil and parsley, and one-fourth of the tomato sauce mixture. Season with salt. Add the remaining sauce mixture, then cook for 1 hour, stirring frequently.

· Remove the carrots and potato. The sauce is ready. Serve it with pasta.

THE GODFATHER

Francis Ford Coppola

1972

THE SCENE OF THE CRIME—in a kitchen, Peter Clemenza (Richard S. Castellano), one of the thugs of the Corleone family, tells Michael Corleone (Al Pacino) how to cook spaghetti and meatballs, according to the recipe of this Italian American filmmaker's mother.

WHAT'S THE DISH?—Coppola reportedly said regarding this scene, "I detailed the recipe because if the movie had been a flop, at least the viewers would have had a good spaghetti sauce recipe."

THE KILLER LINE—Clemenza: "Come over here, kid, learn something. You never know, you might have to cook for twenty guys someday. You see, you start out with a little oil. Then you fry some garlic. Then you throw in some tomatoes, tomato paste, you fry it. Ya make sure it doesn't stick. You get it to a boil, you shove in all your sausage and your meatballs . . . and a little bit o' wine, and a little bit o' sugar . . . That's my thing."

ONCE UPON A TIME IN AMERICA

Sergio Leone

1984

THE SCENE OF THE CRIME—we owe to this sentimental Italian director the introduction of a little sweetness into this world of thugs and spicy sauces. In a scene that has become legendary, one of the hero's young friends, Patsy (Brian Bloom), intends to obtain the favors of shy Peggy (Julie Cohen). When he goes to her house, she makes him wait a long time while she finishes her bath . . .

WHAT'S THE DISH?—the boy wanted to seduce Peggy with a superb Russian charlotte full of cream and candied fruit, delicately wrapped. But once alone, he can't resist the torment of greedy temptation for long: he first runs his fingers over the cake, then devours it hungrily. Instead of Peggy's favors, the cherry on the cake for Patsy will be . . . the maraschino that tops the pastry!

THE KILLER LINE—"Wait."

AND ALSO . . .

The Sopranos: Carmela's chicken Parmesan cutlets and Tony Soprano's barbecued lamb; *Godfather 2*'s bread and red onion soup . . .

SKIP TO

LIQUORI, P. 366; POLPETTE (MEATBALLS), P. 25; RAGÙ BOLOGNESE, P. 320.

OLIVE OIL

Inseparable from Italian cuisine, *olio di oliva* has its *terroir*, its varietals, and its know-how.

ALESSANDRA PIERINI

4000 BCE: the *ulivo* or *olivo* (olive tree, *Olea europaea* var. *sativa*) thrives in Asia Minor and Syria. The oil obtained by pressing its fruits, the olives, is used as a medicine and lamp oil.

2500 BCE: the Code of Hammurabi (a Babylonian legal text) regulates the production and trade of olive oil and attests to its presence in Mesopotamia. The olive tree quickly takes root throughout the Mediterranean basin, where the climate is ideal for its development.

EIGHTH CENTURY BCE: the Greeks cultivate the olive tree for consumption, and they take it into Sicily and among the Etruscans (who occupy central Italy).

FOURTH CENTURY BCE: the Romans spread its use in all their conquered territories as far as northern Europe and impose the payment of taxes in the form of olive oil. They improve its cultivation and

(CE) production and begin to classify the oil according to different types of pressing. It is an expensive commodity, reserved especially for the richest; commoners use bacon or lard.

SIXTH CENTURY CE: after the fall of the Roman Empire, olive tree cultivation is abandoned almost everywhere.

ELEVENTH CENTURY: the best land is reclaimed for the production of cereals and the cultivation of olive trees, which is very profitable.

TWELFTH–FIFTEENTH CENTURIES: Italy becomes one of the largest producers of olive oil, especially due to the know-how of Cistercian and Benedictine monks. In some regions, however, the use of animal fats is preferred to oil, replaced during Lent by cheaper walnut oil.

SIXTEENTH–SEVENTEENTH CENTURIES: there is a great boom in the production of olive oil with the invention of the hydraulic press.

EIGHTEENTH–TWENTIETH CENTURIES: the olive tree and its fruits begin to be classified according to their geographical origin. Olive oil is gaining in popularity and, in the second half of the twentieth century, due to the economic boom, becomes an everyday ingredient, while butter is associated with the codes of French haute cuisine.

TWENTY-FIRST CENTURY: recent decades are declared an absolute success for olive oil, in part thanks to the promotion of the healthy Mediterranean diet, also called the Cretan diet.

LAND OF OLIVE

Italy has the largest olive heritage in the world with more than five hundred varietals, including forty-three PDO and four PGI oils. Olive oil is produced in all regions, except in the Val d'Aosta, where the first productions should soon start to emerge thanks to the hard work of a small group of producers who have recently begun experimental crops in the middle of the region's mountains.

1

2

3

THE OLIVE TREE, AN INTEGRAL PART OF THE LANDSCAPE

To date, four olive landscapes are recognized by the Italian Ministry of Agriculture as part of historic rural landscapes:

→ The *terrazzamenti* (terraced olive groves) of Vallecorsa (Lazio).

→ The historical park of Venafro (Molise).

→ The Pedemontana Olivetata chain in Assisi-Spoleto (Umbria).

→ The polycultural landscape of Trequanda (Tuscany).

But also: (1) the terrazzamenti of Liguria, overlooking the sea; (2) the gentle Tuscan hills crisscrossed with vineyards and olive trees; (3) the olive groves at the foot of nourishing Mount Etna; and (4) the enormous thousand-year-old olive trees of Apulia.

4

Olio extravergine di oliva

Extra-virgin olive oil (in Italian, *olio EVO*) is a pure fruit juice obtained naturally by cold mechanical extraction (less than 81°F/27°C). The quality is defined by legislation based on physicochemical criteria (the acidity level is less than 0.8 percent per 3½ ounces/100 g) and an organoleptic evaluation. As a result of pressing, we can obtain:

→ A monocultivar (monovarietal) oil, made from a single varietal of olive. It has a strong taste linked to the terroir and the cultivar itself.

→ A blended oil, made from different varietals of olives. It has a more balanced taste that expresses what is desired from its producer more than the region's character.

The degree of ripeness of the fruit, the production process, the *frangitura* (extraction), and storage methods also determine the flavor of the oil.

AN AROMATIC PALETTE

In Italy, olive oils are grouped into two main families of fruitiness:

FRUTTATO VERDE (harvested green): more intense aromas, obtained from olives harvested green (unripened) or *invaiate* (when purple-green in color) and before full maturity (October to early November). From a nutritional standpoint, these oils are considered to be more qualitative because they are richer in polyphenols. It is the most common type of oil in Italy.

FRUTTATO MATURO (harvested ripe): oil obtained from black olives harvested at full maturity (November and December).

FRUITY: all the taste and olfactory sensations, perceived directly on the tongue and through the nose, that characterize the oil and change according to the varietal of the olive, provided it is fresh, healthy, and picked at the correct degree of ripeness.

THE MOST EMBLEMATIC OLIVE VARIETALS

	LIGHT	MEDIUM	INTENSE
The main olive varietals have been classified into three aromatic families according to their level of intensity (light, medium, intense). Each of these families can be produced in green or ripe stages, thus offering a rich palette of tastes and uses.	*varietals:* GRIGNANO (Veneto), TAGGIASCA (Liguria), LECCINO E OLIVASTRA DI SEGGIANO (Tuscany), OTTOBRATICA (Calabria) . . .	*varietals:* CASALIVA (Lombardy), FRANTOIO E MORAIOLO (central Italy), OGLIAROLA SALENTINA (Apulia), CARBONCELLA (south central), ITRANA (Lazio), NOCELLARA DEL BELICE E BIANCOLILLA (Sicily) . . .	*varietals:* SAN FELICE (Umbria), CORATINA (Apulia), TONDINA (Calabria), TONDA IBLEA (Sicily), BOSANA (Sardinia) . . .
	→ Simple dishes with a delicate taste, more typical of northern cuisine.	*→ More structured and consistent dishes; multipurpose.*	*→ Rich, complex, juicy, more suitable for southern cuisine.*
HARVESTED GREEN → Lively, fiery, vegetal taste with a hint of fresh grass. Bitter and/or pungent (or fiery) and/or astringent, positive attributes that testify to the olives being very fresh when crushed. Fluid texture.	TASTE—delicate, balanced spice and bittersweet note. Scents of fresh almond, pine nuts, apple.	TASTE—rounder, fresh aroma, clean, balsamic; spice and bitter more pronounced but balanced. Notes of grass, raw artichoke, green tomato, bell pepper, aromatic herbs. Slightly pungent and bitter. Multipurpose.	TASTE—powerful and persistent, with quite marked and fiery bitterness and very spiced peppery finish. Notes of green leaves, raw artichoke, cardoon, arugula.
	USES—risotto; shellfish; light frying; seafood; steamed fish; pesto; tender lettuces; squash blossoms; *fagioli al fiasco*; squash; *scaloppina al limone* (lemon cutlets); *coniglio alla ligure* (Ligurian rabbit); pastry.	USES—white meat; carpaccio; grilled fish; *guazzetto* (stewed in broth), tuna; grain soups; hard-boiled egg; pizza; pasta in sauce, *con le sarde* (with sardines), *alla Norma*; stuffed vegetables; asparagus; fresh cheeses; mozzarella; *salsa verde*.	USES—red meat, game; *bresaola*; radicchio, bitter lettuces, radish, arugula; bruschette with garlic, *pinzimonio*; soup and pasta with legumes; artichokes, bell peppers; minestrone; *orecchiette alle cime di rapa*; *ribollita*; *cavolo nero* (black cabbage); recipes with capers and oregano.
HARVESTED RIPE → Softer, subtle, and round on the palate. Creamy and buttery texture; little or no bitterness and/or fieriness.	TASTE—delicate, fresh, slightly bitter. Notes of dried fruits, sourdough bread, flowers, linden, pear.	TASTE—balanced. Notes of wood, red or yellow fruits, apple, preserved tomato, and ripe olives.	TASTE—expressive. Notes of toasted almond, banana, toast, cut hay, cooked endive, plum.
	USES—risotto; shellfish, freshwater fish; white meat; frying; mayonnaise; gnocchi; *agrodolce*; pastry, fruit salad; vanilla ice cream.	USES—*carpione* (marinade); salad of oranges or lemons; poultry; fish; cooked vegetables; *bigoli in salsa* (pasta with anchovies); mushrooms; lentils; cakes.	USES—guinea fowl, duck, rabbit; octopus; vegetable soups; melon; dark chocolate; chocolate sorbet; desserts.

Note: Recipes *in bianco* (undressed or unseasoned) such as rice, pasta, potatoes, but also focaccia and breads, with a fairly neutral taste, can accommodate all fruity nuances of olive oils.

SKIP TO
OLIVES, P. 214;
GENOESE PESTO, P. 20.

BOTTLES OF GREEN GOLD

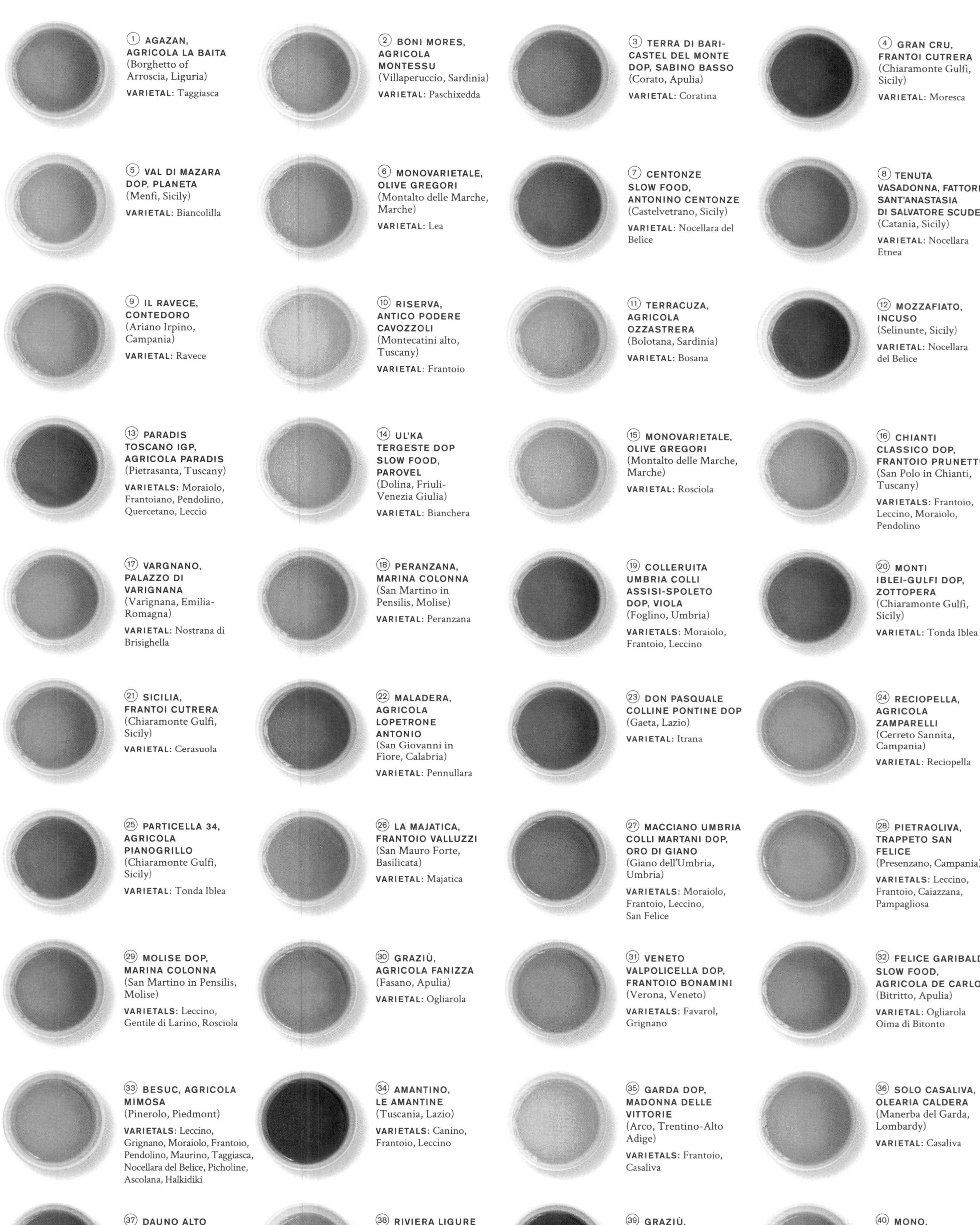

(1) **AGAZAN, AGRICOLA LA BAITA** (Borghetto of Arroscia, Liguria)
VARIETAL: Taggiasca

(2) **BONI MORES, AGRICOLA MONTESSU** (Villaperuccio, Sardinia)
VARIETAL: Paschixedda

(3) **TERRA DI BARI-CASTEL DEL MONTE DOP, SABINO BASSO** (Corato, Apulia)
VARIETAL: Coratina

(4) **GRAN CRU, FRANTOI CUTRERA** (Chiaramonte Gulfi, Sicily)
VARIETAL: Moresca

(5) **VAL DI MAZARA DOP, PLANETA** (Menfi, Sicily)
VARIETAL: Biancolilla

(6) **MONOVARIETALE, OLIVE GREGORI** (Montalto delle Marche, Marche)
VARIETAL: Lea

(7) **CENTONZE SLOW FOOD, ANTONINO CENTONZE** (Castelvetrano, Sicily)
VARIETAL: Nocellara del Belice

(8) **TENUTA VASADONNA, FATTORIA SANT'ANASTASIA DI SALVATORE SCUDERI** (Catania, Sicily)
VARIETAL: Nocellara Etnea

(9) **IL RAVECE, CONTEDORO** (Ariano Irpino, Campania)
VARIETAL: Ravece

(10) **RISERVA, ANTICO PODERE CAVOZZOLI** (Montecatini alto, Tuscany)
VARIETAL: Frantoio

(11) **TERRACUZA, AGRICOLA OZZASTRERA** (Bolotana, Sardinia)
VARIETAL: Bosana

(12) **MOZZAFIATO, INCUSO** (Selinunte, Sicily)
VARIETAL: Nocellara del Belice

(13) **PARADIS TOSCANO IGP, AGRICOLA PARADIS** (Pietrasanta, Tuscany)
VARIETALS: Moraiolo, Frantoiano, Pendolino, Quercetano, Leccio

(14) **UL'KA TERGESTE DOP SLOW FOOD, PAROVEL** (Dolina, Friuli-Venezia Giulia)
VARIETAL: Bianchera

(15) **MONOVARIETALE, OLIVE GREGORI** (Montalto delle Marche, Marche)
VARIETAL: Rosciola

(16) **CHIANTI CLASSICO DOP, FRANTOIO PRUNETTI** (San Polo in Chianti, Tuscany)
VARIETALS: Frantoio, Leccino, Moraiolo, Pendolino

(17) **VARGNANO, PALAZZO DI VARIGNANA** (Varignana, Emilia-Romagna)
VARIETAL: Nostrana di Brisighella

(18) **PERANZANA, MARINA COLONNA** (San Martino in Pensilis, Molise)
VARIETAL: Peranzana

(19) **COLLERUITA UMBRIA COLLI ASSISI-SPOLETO DOP, VIOLA** (Foglino, Umbria)
VARIETALS: Moraiolo, Frantoio, Leccino

(20) **MONTI IBLEI-GULFI DOP, ZOTTOPERA** (Chiaramonte Gulfi, Sicily)
VARIETAL: Tonda Iblea

(21) **SICILIA, FRANTOI CUTRERA** (Chiaramonte Gulfi, Sicily)
VARIETAL: Cerasuola

(22) **MALADERA, AGRICOLA LOPETRONE ANTONIO** (San Giovanni in Fiore, Calabria)
VARIETAL: Pennullara

(23) **DON PASQUALE COLLINE PONTINE DOP** (Gaeta, Lazio)
VARIETAL: Itrana

(24) **RECIOPELLA, AGRICOLA ZAMPARELLI** (Cerreto Sannita, Campania)
VARIETAL: Reciopella

(25) **PARTICELLA 34, AGRICOLA PIANOGRILLO** (Chiaramonte Gulfi, Sicily)
VARIETAL: Tonda Iblea

(26) **LA MAJATICA, FRANTOIO VALLUZZI** (San Mauro Forte, Basilicata)
VARIETAL: Majatica

(27) **MACCIANO UMBRIA COLLI MARTANI DOP, ORO DI GIANO** (Giano dell'Umbria, Umbria)
VARIETALS: Moraiolo, Frantoio, Leccino, San Felice

(28) **PIETRAOLIVA, TRAPPETO SAN FELICE** (Presenzano, Campania)
VARIETALS: Leccino, Frantoio, Caiazzana, Pampagliosa

(29) **MOLISE DOP, MARINA COLONNA** (San Martino in Pensilis, Molise)
VARIETALS: Leccino, Gentile di Larino, Rosciola

(30) **GRAZIÙ, AGRICOLA FANIZZA** (Fasano, Apulia)
VARIETAL: Ogliarola

(31) **VENETO VALPOLICELLA DOP, FRANTOIO BONAMINI** (Verona, Veneto)
VARIETALS: Favarol, Grignano

(32) **FELICE GARIBALDI SLOW FOOD, AGRICOLA DE CARLO** (Bitritto, Apulia)
VARIETAL: Ogliarola Oima di Bitonto

(33) **BESUC, AGRICOLA MIMOSA** (Pinerolo, Piedmont)
VARIETALS: Leccino, Grignano, Moraiolo, Frantoio, Pendolino, Maurino, Taggiasca, Nocellara del Belice, Picholine, Ascolana, Halkidiki

(34) **AMANTINO, LE AMANTINE** (Tuscania, Lazio)
VARIETALS: Canino, Frantoio, Leccino

(35) **GARDA DOP, MADONNA DELLE VITTORIE** (Arco, Trentino-Alto Adige)
VARIETALS: Frantoio, Casaliva

(36) **SOLO CASALIVA, OLEARIA CALDERA** (Manerba del Garda, Lombardy)
VARIETAL: Casaliva

(37) **DAUNO ALTO TAVOLIERE DOP, OLIO DI SERRA** (Sarracapriola, Apulia)
VARIETALS: Provenzana, Risciola

(38) **RIVIERA LIGURE RIVIERA DEI FIORI DOP, DELICATEZZE DELLA RIVIERA** (Borgo d'Oneglia, Liguria)
VARIETAL: Taggiasca

(39) **GRAZIÙ, AGRICOLA FANIZZA** (Fasano, Apulia)
VARIETAL: Coratina

(40) **MONO, OLEIFICIO ANGELINI** (Ascoli Piceno, Marche)
VARIETAL: Ascolana Tenera

THE HAZELNUT

From Mesopotamia to today's modern confections, the uses for the *nocciola* (hazelnut) seem endless, and it has become perfectly acclimated to Italy.

GIANNA MAZZEI

WHAT AM I?

SCIENTIFIC NAME: *Corylus avellana.*

FAMILY: Betulaceae.

ORIGINS: either in Mesopotamia or Asia Minor. It was quickly adopted by the Greeks and Romans. It began its proliferation in Italy starting in the second century BCE.

BEST FRIEND: the truffle, through a symbiotic relationship. The hazelnut tree is an excellent symbiote for the truffle fungus. Hazelnut trees, grown in suitable environments, develop mycorrhizae that produce truffles.

In cooking

Savory: grilled, in salads, in pesto, with baked sea bream, with poultry, in breads.

As dessert: hazelnut meringues, *brutti ma buoni* ("ugly but good," a dry cookie from Tuscany), *baci di dama* ("lady's kisses," a confection from Piedmont, made of two rounded cookies sandwiching chocolate), nougat, ice creams, brittles, and *addormenta suocere* ("sleep mother-in-law," caramelized hazelnuts made into pralines).

RECIPE

TORTA DI NOCCIOLE SENZA FARINA (FLOURLESS HAZELNUT CAKE)

This flourless hazelnut cake is a traditional Piedmontese delight.

4 large (200 g) eggs
¾ cup (150 g) granulated sugar
2¼ cups (250 g) hazelnut flour
1 teaspoon (4 g) baking powder
Confectioners' sugar, for dusting (optional)
Crushed hazelnuts, for garnish (optional)

- Preheat the oven to 350°F (180°C).
- Separate the egg whites from the yolks. Whisk the yolks with the granulated sugar until light and fluffy. Beat the egg whites to stiff peaks without overbeating them.
- Mix the hazelnut flour with the yolk-sugar mixture, then add the baking powder and combine. Gently fold in the beaten egg whites using a spatula by lifting and turning the spatula from the bottom to the top of the batter. Pour the batter into a mold 8 or 9½ inches (20 or 24 cm) in diameter and bake for 35 minutes. Let cool, then dust with confectioners' sugar and crushed hazelnuts, if desired.

LOVELY MARRIAGES

CHEESE

Pecorino scoiattolino ("little squirrel"), produced in Tuscany by De' Magi, is a cheese matured in "straw" made from the Piedmontese hazelnut Tonda Gentile delle Langhe PDO. "Straw," in this case, refers to the waste (pieces, perisperm, and essential oils) resulting from the production of hazelnut paste. The rind of this cheese is edible.

SAUSAGE

Salame alla Nocciola Piemonte IGP, a pork sausage with a sweet and savory contrast, is one of the essential products of this region.

CHOCOLATE

Gianduja, a soft paste made of chocolate and hazelnuts, is a union so successful that it became a flagship delicacy in Italy and eventually throughout the world. The combination of hazelnut and chocolate is the result of two factors: the historical period when cocoa exports into Piedmont were restricted and cocoa was therefore expensive to use; and the peculiar character of the hazelnut Tonda Gentile delle Langhe PDO that, when roasted, is reminiscent of the flavor of cocoa.

ESPRESSO ALLA NOCCIOLA

For a hazelnut espresso, place 1 to 2 teaspoons of hazelnut paste (obtained by processing the hazelnuts for several minutes) at the bottom of a cup, pour hot coffee over the top, sweeten if necessary, and top with whipped cream and chopped hazelnuts.

THE MOST APPRECIATED ITALIAN VARIETALS

① NOCCIOLA DI GIFFONI IGP

Campania

Round, white and aromatic flesh. Ideal for desserts and for being ground.

② NOCCIOLA LIGURE—MISTO CHIAVARI

Liguria

Slow Food Ark of Taste: cultivated by hand in terraces according to an ancient tradition with combinations of variable cultivars, but generally composed of Tapparona, *dall'orto*, Sraeghetta, Bianchetta, and Del rosso, with, in smaller quantities, Menoia, Longhera, and Trietta. Ideal for natural hazelnut oil, baci di dama, chocolates (confectionery), spreads, and nougats. As a flour, it can be used in desserts and doughs.

③ NOCCIOLA ROMANA DOP

Lazio

Almost spherical, crunchy, and compact in texture, it has a fine and persistent flavor. Its production has an ancient history, occurring between Viterbo and Rome. Ideal for desserts, ice creams, creams, liqueurs, and savory dishes.

④ NOCCIOLA TONDA DEI NEBRODI

Sicily

Incomparable aroma, delicate flavor, and intense aftertaste. Ideal for almond paste, brittles, nougat, ice cream, and *rametti* (typical Sicilian cookies), or simply topped with chocolate.

⑤ TONDA GENTILE DELLE LANGHE OR NOCCIOLA TRILOBATA PIEMONTE

Piedmont

Large, with a subtle aroma and delicate flavor, it is protected by a thin but very hard shell. It is the most popular type. Grown in the lower region of Piedmont, the best example of this varietal is the Piemonte Nocciola IGP, universally considered the best in the world. Ideal for any type of preparation, sweet or savory; perfect with chocolate.

SKIP TO
GIANDUJA, P. 180; NOUGATS, P. 326; CAFFÈ AL BAR, P. 64.

SEASON

TUTTO L'ANNO (YEAR-ROUND)

CATEGORY

DOLCE (DESSERT)

LEVEL

FACILE (EASY)

CASTAGNACCIO

CHESTNUT FLOUR CAKE

As soft as it is tasty, this rustic cake made with chestnut flour is one of the sweet symbols of Tuscany.

FRANÇOIS-RÉGIS GAUDRY

An arboreal metaphor

This cake combines the fruits of three emblematic Tuscan trees: the chestnut (*castagno*), which grows in the mountains; the olive tree, present everywhere; and the pine tree from the seaside and plains. When you add raisins and rosemary to the cake, all the landscapes of the region come together in just one dish! As a nod to its tree-sourced ingredients, as well as to its dense texture, *castagnaccio* has been dubbed *pane di legno* (wooden bread).

ITS ORIGINS

→ Although Tuscany has made this chestnut flour–based cake one of its flagship desserts, it is also common, in different forms, in other regions with a strong tradition of chestnut-tree farming: Umbria, Piedmont, Lazio, Liguria, Emilia-Romagna, Calabria . . . In these mountainous regions, the chestnut was the bread of the poor, and castagnaccio constituted a meal (as was the case for the traveling actors Mimmo and Dea in the movie *Polvere di stelle* by Alberto Sordi, 1973).

→ In his *Commentario delle più notabili e mostruose cose d'Italia* (*Commentary on the Most Notable and Tremendous Things in Italy*, 1553), the Augustinian humanist Ortensio Lando seems to attest to the Tuscan origin of castagnaccio: he even attributes it to a certain man named Pilade da Lucca.

→ In 1891, in *La scienza in cucina e l'arte di mangiar bene* (*Science in the Kitchen and the Art of Eating Well*), Pellegrino Artusi codified the modern version of this cake which he mentions "*migliaccio,* commonly called *castagnaccio.*" The term *migliaccio* at the time referred to any preparation baked in the oven from a mixture of millet flour, water, and oil.

THE RECIPE

The cake is only ¾ inch (2 cm) thick, which gives it a texture that is both soft and dense. This version is by Paolo Gori, chef of Da Burde in Florence. It can be served with ricotta cheese or whipped cream.

SERVES 6

3⅔ cups (400 g) chestnut flour
5 tablespoons (30 g) confectioners' sugar (optional)
1 pinch salt
3⅓ cups (800 mL) water
Tuscan olive oil
⅓ cup (50 g) pine nuts
A few rosemary needles

Equipment

1 rectangular mold, 10¼ by 14½ inches (26 by 37 cm)

Preheat the oven to 425°F (220°C). Sift the flour into a bowl. If your flour is not sweet enough, stir in the confectioners' sugar.

Add the salt and gradually stir in the water, stirring with a whisk to avoid lumps. You should achieve the consistency of crêpe batter.

Grease the mold using olive oil and scrape in the batter; it should be about ¾ inch (2 cm) deep. Add the pine nuts on top, then finely chop the rosemary and sprinkle it over the top.

Lightly drizzle the top with oil and bake for 30 to 35 minutes. Let cool before serving.

VARIATIONS

According to other regional versions of castagnaccio, you can also add raisins, crushed walnuts, orange zest, and fennel seeds to the batter before baking it.

"In some provinces of Italy there is absolutely no knowledge of chestnut flour, and I don't think anyone has tried to introduce the use of it; and yet, for most people, and for those who do not fear gassy foods, this is inexpensive, healthy, and nutritious."
PELLEGRINO ARTUSI

EVERY NAME UNDER THE SUN

Castagnaccio has different names in Tuscany, depending on the region and the thickness of the cake.

WHEN THE CAKE IS THIN

→ *Patona* in Lunigiana (the historic region between Liguria and Tuscany).
→ *Castigna* in Fosdinovo, a commune of the province of Massa-Carrara.
→ *Migliaccio* in Florence.
→ *Ghirighio* in the region of Florence.

WHEN IT IS THICKER

→ *Torta di neccio* in Lucca.

WHEN IT IS VERY THICK (1⅛ INCHES/3 CM OR MORE)

→ *Toppone* in Livorno.
→ *Baldino* in Arezzo.

SKIP TO
CHESTNUTS, P. 364;
PELLEGRINO ARTUSI, P. 32.

THE SOUPS OF ITALY

Soups are emblematic of *cucina povera*. Let's take a dive into these hearty dishes.

ILARIA BRUNETTI

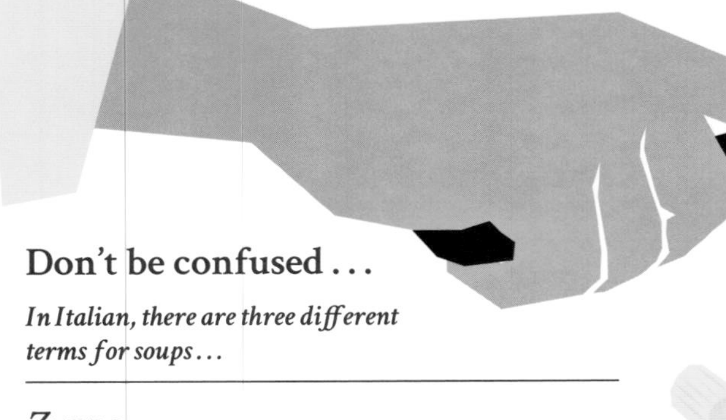

Don't be confused . . .

In Italian, there are three different terms for soups . . .

Zuppa

A soup that generally includes bread, either in soaked or grilled slices or as croutons. The term derives from the Gothic word *suppa* (a soaked slice), which referred to stale bread steeped in broth, a dish that served as the base diet for commoners. Just like with any rule, there are many exceptions . . . some with no bread at all!

Minestra

Often based on vegetables, sometimes with meat, cooked in water or broth. Instead of bread, pasta or grains are added. A famous exception is the *minestra maritata*, which does not include any grains. The term derives from the Latin *menestrare* (to administer) because it was served by the head of the family. One warning: *minestre asciutte* (dry soups) refers to *primi piatti* (first courses, such as pasta, risotto, and rice) prepared as nonliquid dishes!

Minestrone

Unlike minestra, which can be made with just one vegetable, minestrone is characterized by its wide variety of vegetables, including potatoes as well as legumes; sometimes grains or pasta are added. When puréed, it's referred to as *passato*.

ZUPPE WHERE BREAD IS KING

PANCOTTO (throughout Italy): bread cooked in broth and butter, with Grana Padano in the north (also called *panada*) and with oil and pecorino in south central Italy, where you can also add vegetables.

ACQUACOTTA ("cooked water"—central Italy): made with vegetables and wild herbs, sometimes with beaten egg and stale bread that has been soaked or toasted on the side.

PAPPA AL POMODORO (Tuscany): a famous marriage of bread and tomatoes flavored with basil.

SEUPA ALLA VALPELLINZESE (Aosta Valley): rye bread, savoy cabbage, Fontina cheese, and meat broth, layered and baked in the oven. If leeks replace the cabbage, it is referred to as *puarò*.

ZUPPA ALLA PAVESE (Lombardy): in a skillet, toast eight slices of bread with butter; divide the slices among four deep plates, break an egg over each slice, and grate some Parmesan on top; pour 1 cup (250 mL) broth onto each plate (but not over the yolk).

LEGUMES, A SOURCE OF PROTEIN IN CUCINA POVERA

ZUPPA DI LENTICCHIE E CASTAGNE (Abruzzo)—with lentils (or sometimes chickpeas) and roasted chestnuts: cook 1 cup (200 g) lentils with a bay leaf in water; chop 1¾ ounces (50 g) bacon and 9 ounces (250 g) roasted chestnuts and panfry with thyme and marjoram; add a few spoonfuls of tomato sauce and the lentils along with some of the cooking water; cook for 10 minutes, and serve with toast.

JOTA (Friuli): beans, fermented cabbage, potatoes, smoked pancetta, and, sometimes, pork chops.

ZUPPA DI CICERCHIE (Umbria)—vetches (leguminous plants) with tomatoes, onions, and potatoes, flavored with sage and rosemary.

MINESTRA CRAPIATA (Basilicata): spelt and hard wheat with beans, chickpeas, lentils, and vetches.

MINESTRA MESC-CIÚA (Liguria): chickpeas, white beans, and spelt seasoned with good-quality local oil.

MINESTRA DI ORZO E FAGIOLI (Friuli)—barley and beans, with pancetta or bacon, onions, carrots, and potatoes, served with aged Montasio cheese.

THE COMFORT OF MINESTRONE

With a base made up of a wide variety of seasonal vegetables, legumes, sometimes pancetta or bacon, and often grains, minestrone is a family dish par excellence, which does not really have officially documented recipes. Nevertheless, certain cities have their preferences for preparation:

→ In Genoa: served hot or cold, often with *bricchetti* (matchstick-shaped pasta made from hard wheat).

→ In Milan: preferably with rice, often with pancetta or pork rind.

→ North of Lake Garda (Veneto): boiled chestnuts are added.

GRAINS HONORED IN THESE *MINESTRE*

MINESTRA DI ORZO E PATATE (Trentino-Alto Adige, Aosta Valley)—barley and potatoes: in a large saucepan, brown 1 carrot, 1 onion, 1 stalk celery, 3 potatoes, and 3½ ounces (100 g) speck, all finely diced. Add 9 ounces (250 g) rinsed pearled barley, cover with 6 cups (1.5 L) hot water or broth, and cook for 1 hour.

MINESTRA DI FARRO (Tuscany, Umbria): spelt with onions, carrots, and celery, served with pancetta and pecorino. It can be enriched with other vegetables or roasted chestnuts.

PASTA E PATATE (Campania)—pasta and potatoes: a very thick soup; cauliflower or peas can be substituted for potatoes.

RISO E ERBORIN (Lombardy): rice and parsley cooked in water or broth with butter and Grana Padano added; in Veneto, potatoes are added and the dish is referred to as *riso, patate e parsemolo*.

PASTA E FAGIOLI (throughout Italy)—pasta and beans: a happy marriage with several variations.

A PLACE FOR VEGETABLES

ZUPPA DI CICORIA, CACIO E UOVA (Abruzzo)—chicory, cheese, and egg: meat broth poured over beaten eggs, completed with panfried wild chicory and pecorino. In Campania, zucchini is added.

ZUPPA DI ORTICHE (Molise)—nettles: this soup won't sting your tongue! Clean the nettles (wear gloves) to obtain 1⅓ pounds (600 g) of stems. Sauté a small onion with olive oil and 1¾ ounces (50 g) pancetta, add 2 diced ripe tomatoes and, after 10 minutes of cooking, add the nettle stems; season with salt, cover with water, and simmer. Serve with toast.

RIBOLLITA (Tuscany): the famous soup containing bread, Tuscan black cabbage, beans, and vegetables.

MINESTRA DI RISO E VERZA (Lombardy, Campania): rice and savoy cabbage, *di magro* (without meat) in the south, with pancetta in the north.

MINESTRA DI TENERUMI (Sicily): a rare treat outside the island, with potatoes, tomatoes, and *cucuzze* zucchini and *tenerumi* (their leaves). With or without pasta.

ZUF DI ZUCCA (Friuli): cornmeal and squash cooked in water and milk, with butter and cold milk added at the end of the cooking time.

THE DELICACY OF *BRODO* (BROTH)

ZUPPA IMPERIALE (Emilia-Romagna): beef broth with dice-shaped pasta made from semolina flour, eggs, and Parmesan, then baked. It is found with pecorino in Abruzzo.

SCRIPPELLE 'NFUSS (Abruzzo): thin savory crêpes (*scrippelle*) cooked with bacon, sprinkled with pecorino, rolled, and served in chicken broth.

BRODETTO PASQUALE (Lazio)—a broth for Easter: made with capon or lamb and beef, with beaten eggs, marjoram, lemon, and pecorino.

MINESTRA DI PASTA REALE (Emilia-Romagna)—royal pasta: of French origin, these are small choux puffs served in beef broth. Prepare choux pastry with ½ cup (65 g) all-purpose flour, 3½ tablespoons (50 g) unsalted butter, scant ½ cup (100 mL) water, and 2 large (100 g) eggs; cook; and serve in the hot broth.

TRIDDI IN BRODO (Apulia): a pasta made from hard-wheat flour, pecorino, and parsley, broken up with three (*tridd* in the local dialect) fingers and cooked in chicken broth.

ANOLINI IN BRODO (Emilia-Romagna): pasta filled with stewed beef or cheese, similar to tortellini, served in a capon or beef broth.

WHEN MEAT JOINS

ZUPPA SCOTTIGLIA (Tuscany): also called *cacciucco*, it is made with mixed meats of chicken, veal, and beef—or with lamb, pork, and wild boar—and cooked with tomatoes, black pepper, lemon zest, and herbs.

SAURE-SUPPE (Trentino-Alto Adige)—sour soup: with tripe, onions, vinegar, and lemon zest, served on slices of stale rye bread.

CISRÀ (Piedmont): tripe with chickpeas (*cisi* in the local dialect), pancetta, and pork chops. Typically served for the Day of the Dead.

MINESTRA MARITATA (Campania)—"married": the marriage is between meats (pork sausage, chicken, and beef) and vegetables (chicory, broccoli, escarole . . .), without grains added.

MINESTRA DUMEGA (Lombardy): for celebrations, the soup is traditionally enriched with *dumega*, a variety of local barley, pork rind, and pork feet.

MINESTRA DI RISO E FEGATINI (Lombardy)—rice and chicken livers: cook 10½ ounces (300 g) Vialone Nano rice in 6 cups (1.5 L) meat broth; brown 6 chicken livers in butter, add them to the rice, and serve with parsley and Parmesan.

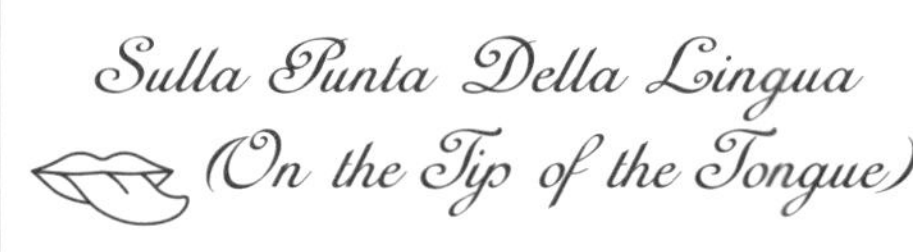

Se non è zuppa è pan bagnato.
"If it's not soup, it's wet bread."
Said when two things appear different but are in fact the same.

Minestra riscaldata.
"Rewarmed soup."
Refers to a romantic relationship that resumes after a breakup.

Gallina vecchia fa buon brodo.
"An old hen makes good broth."
With age comes wisdom.

La solita minestra.
"Always the same soup."
Always the same thing.

SKIP TO
PASTA AND BEANS, P. 276; FROM THE SEA, P. 244; TORTELLINI IN BRODO (TORTELLINI IN BROTH), P. 328; MINESTRONE, P. 23; PAPPA AL POMODORO, P. 367; CHICKPEA, THE KING OF THE POOR, P. 293.

SEASON

TUTTO L'ANNO (YEAR-ROUND)

CATÉGORIE

PIATTO UNICO (SINGLE COURSE)

NIVEAU

FACILE (EASY)

MACCO DI FAVE

FAVA BEAN PURÉE

APULIA, SICILY, BASILICATA, CALABRIA

With roots in Italy's southern rural culture, this frugal but nourishing dish is an expression of three simple ingredients—fava beans, olive oil, and wild fennel—mashed into a rustic puree with a unique consistency.

NADIA POSTIGLIONE

THE GENEALOGY OF MACCO

From the Latin *maccare* (crush), mashed fava beans (broad beans) were served on the tables of the ancient Romans. Apicius, in his cooking treatise (first century CE), offers various recipes for fava beans and mashed peas, with black pepper and ginger or with honey and vinegar. At the beginning of the Middle Ages, *macco* was a purée of different legumes, widely consumed by commoners in Italy.

THE RECIPE

Inspired by the Accademia Italiana della Cucina (Italian Academy of Cooking).

SERVES 4

- 1⅛ pounds (500 g) dried fava (broad) beans (preferably Cottoia), shelled
- 3 tablespoons (45 mL) extra-virgin olive oil, preferably an intense oil with fruity and spicy notes
- 1 yellow onion, chopped
- 1 clove garlic, unpeeled
- Salt and freshly ground black pepper
- 6 or 7 small wild fennel fronds, chopped

Rinse the beans, place them in a large bowl, cover with hot water, and soak for about 8 hours.

In a casserole dish (preferably one made of terra-cotta), heat 2 tablespoons (30 mL) of the olive oil over medium heat and brown the onion and garlic. Drain and rinse the beans, then add them to the dish. Cook for several minutes, until browned.

Add about 2 cups (500 mL) hot water (just enough to cover the ingredients), and season with salt.

Cover and cook over low heat for about 1 hour. Gradually skim off any surface impurities as they rise and stir regularly to help the beans soften; add more hot water if the mixture thickens too much. When the macco is cooked, coarsely mash the beans.

Just before serving, season with pepper and the fennel. Stir the macco for several minutes and serve with the remaining 1 tablespoon (15 mL) olive oil drizzled on top.

THE SOUL OF SOUTHERN CUISINE

Sicily is the land of fava beans and macco. This ancient mashed dish has been an essential source of protein in the diet of the peasant classes for centuries. In *Liber de coquina*, an anonymous fourteenth-century medieval cookbook probably written in Sicily, there are two recipes for puréed fava beans, or *fabas fractas*.

A FEW SICILIAN VARIATIONS

→ Raffadali (Agrigento) is the village whose preference is *macco di fave*. This version is an extremely stripped-down form, including only fava beans, wild fennel, and olive oil.

→ In Ramacca (Catania), on the eve of Saint Joseph's Day (March 19), townspeople gather in the village square to eat *pasta col macco*, a macco of beans and lentils with tubettini or broken spaghetti.

→ In season, with fresh fava beans flavored with fennel seeds, chile, or rosemary.

→ With squash (Palermo).

→ With carrots (Trapani).

→ With chard, spinach, or even tomato (Sicily).

→ With a mixture of vegetables and pork rind (Syracuse).

→ The next day, leftover macco is rolled in flour and fried.

BEYOND SICILY

CALABRIA—with pasta and chile.

APULIA, BASILICATA—accompanied by wild chicory.

VENETO, LOMBARDY—*fava menata* (crushed fava beans), a kind of mashed bean soup.

LIGURIA—*marò*, a pesto made from fresh fava beans used to top meats.

A philosophical hostility . . .

The Greek mathematician and philosopher Pythagoras considered the bean to be a forbidden food because the hollow stem of the plant was in direct contact with hell, and, being by nature "flatulent," it could welcome the souls of the dead. He is said to have died while fleeing from men paid to assassinate him because he refused to walk through a bean field in the Calabrian countryside.

SKIP TO
LEGUMES, P. 150;
PASTA AND BEANS, P. 276.

COOKING WITH BREAD

Why throw extra bread away when you can transform, reuse, or enhance it? From bread crumbs to large chunks, there is no limit to creativity when it comes to cooking with either dried or stale bread.

JACQUES BRUNEL

PANE INTERO *whole loaf*

CAPPON MAGRO · *Liguria*
An ancient Genoese salad (a pyramid of cooked vegetables, fish, and seafood) made up of hardtack (*pane del marinaio*), soaked stale bread, or fresh bread crumbs. Its name evokes a luxury dish (capon, although it contains none) made from rustic ingredients. It was eaten at Christmas.

CAPONATA ESTIVA · *Campania*
In the same spirit as *cappon magro*, this Neapolitan snack combines *friselle* (small round buns), rehydrated and rubbed in oil and garlic, with fresh tomatoes and tuna, or marinated fish or boiled beef.

PIZZA DI PANE · *Campania*
Once softened in a little hot water and oil, stale bread arranged on the bottom of a glass baking dish can be the base of a crispy pizza if you have tomatoes, mozzarella, or anchovy fillets. Just bake for 25 minutes.

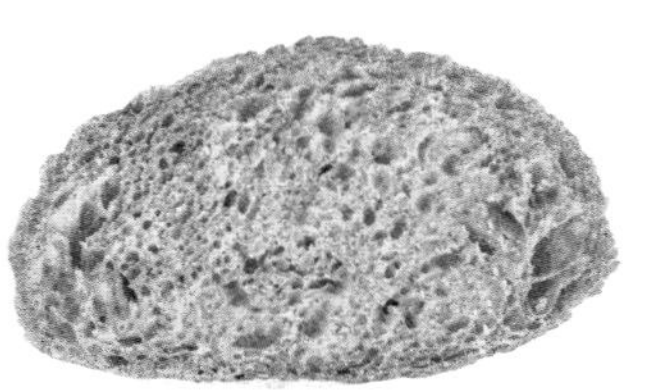

FETTA *slices*

BRUSCHETTA · *throughout Italy*
Once grilled, then rubbed with garlic and oil, a slice of rustic country bread can be topped with various condiments (sun-dried tomatoes, tapenade, anchovies, etc.). This is one of the most popular antipasti.

PANCOTTO · *Apulia*
Several soups are grouped together under the name *pancotto* (cooked bread), the most famous being a vegetable version with tomatoes, celery, potatoes, garlic, and chile, enriched with pecorino.

CAPONATA LUNGA · *Sicily*
Slices of bread are grilled once baked and offer the ideal support for a tomato sauce.

MINESTRA CON IL PANE SOTTO · *throughout Italy*
In water, alternate a layer of sliced stale bread and a layer of cooked vegetables (carrots, onions, lentils, white beans, etc.), then sprinkle with grated pecorino, until you obtain a thick and tasty soup.

SCHIACCIATA TOSCANA, FOCACCIA CROCCANTE · *Tuscany*
Crispy on the outside but tender inside, these two semidried breads are best served with charcuterie or tomatoes.

FETTUNTA · *Tuscany*
Rubbed with garlic, this slice of toasted bread is a wonderful when moistened with a grand cru olive oil.

MOLLICA *crumbs*

POLPETTE · *throughout Italy*
These crisp meatballs are made with stale bread (or not) soaked in milk and seasoned with parsley, sometimes including cheese. They are usually served with tomato sauce once panfried.

CUBETTI DI PANE O CROSTINI *croutons or toast*

PAPPA AL POMODORO · *Tuscany*
As good served cold as it is hot, this derivative of pancotto combines fresh tomatoes, garlic, and basil in a thick, creamy soup that was once intended for children.

TORTA MIASCIA · *Lake Como, Lombardy*
Simple and quick to prepare, this sweet tart repurposes stale pieces of bread with an apple, raisins, and lemon zest.

BUDINO DI PANE · *Italy*
A little dried bread torn in pieces and soaked in milk, eggs, and raisins . . . After baking for 1 hour in a bain-marie, the result is a delicious and inexpensive bread pudding.

PANZANELLA · *Tuscany*
This rustic masterpiece is a salad with simple ingredients (local stale bread made without salt, rehydrated with vinegar, tomatoes, red onions, cucumber, olive oil, and basil).

CROSTINI · *Veneto*
Toasts with elaborate toppings (chicken livers, *baccalà mantecato*, creamed vegetables, etc.).

CANEDERLI · *Trentino-Alto Adige*
Common in Germanic and Slavic Europe, *Knödels* (bread meatballs) are the original version of dumplings and *canederli*. In the former South Tyrol and Friuli, they are made with stale bread, eggs, milk, pieces of speck, and fresh herbs.

BRICIOLE *fresh bread crumbs*

PICI ALLE BRICIOLE · *Tuscany*
Hand-rolled, these large spaghetti from Siena achieve a delicious crunch when grilled stale bread is coarsely grated into a filling of garlic and local pecorino.

SPAGHETTI CA'MUDDICA · *Sicily*
Pieces of dried white bread crumbs replace Parmesan and accompany raisins, oil, garlic, and anchovy fillets in this poor man's dish, giving it heft. It's also good on *pasta con le sarde* (Sicilian pasta with sardines).

PANE GRATTUGIATO *dried bread crumbs*

PEPERONI MBUTTUNATI · *Campania*
Bell peppers stuffed with black olives, anchovies, and capers, then rolled in bread crumbs and baked.

PASSATELLI · *Emilia-Romagna*
Dried bread crumbs are one of the ingredients in these large pasta, along with eggs, grated Parmesan, and sometimes lemon.

CROCCHÈ · *throughout Italy*
Made with mashed potatoes, with either mozzarella and sometimes pig's feet, this croquette is coated with bread crumbs before being fried.

ARANCINI · *Sicily*
Designed to use leftover risotto, these croquettes incorporating cheese, meat, and peas are breaded with dried bread crumbs and then fried.

MOZZARELLA IN CARROZZA · *southern Italy*
This mozzarella sandwich is coated with bread crumbs before being immersed in hot oil and fried.

STRUDEL DI MELE · *Trentino-Alto Adige*
Before closing up these strudel turnovers, those living in the mountains always grate a little dry *spaccatina* (a local lard bread) inside to absorb the juice from the apples, which gives the cake a wonderful crunch.

SKIP TO
PANZANELLA (BREAD SALAD), P. 168;
POLPETTE (MEATBALLS), P. 25;
SUPPLÌ VS. ARANCINI, P. 362.

LEGUMES

Leguminous plants (Fabaceae family) are the most protein-rich plants. In cooking, the fresh or dried seeds can be used, and sometimes the pods. Here is an exploration of this large family of nutritious plants.

ALESSANDRA PIERINI

FAVA (BROAD) BEANS *Vicia faba*

Fava larga di Leonforte
Sicily · Slow Food

TASTE—subtle, vegetal, slightly bitter.

COOKING—salads, chunky soups, purées, stews, slow-cooked dishes.

Favetta di Sicilia
Sicilian small fava (broad) bean

TASTE—tender, vegetal.

COOKING—preserves, salads, risottos, purées.

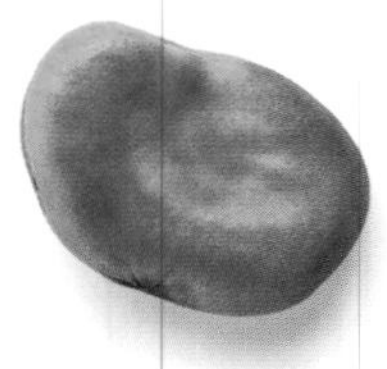

Fava cottoia di Modica
Sicily · Slow Food

TASTE—starchy, sweet.

COOKING—purées, pastas, soups.

SKIP TO
PASTA AND BEANS, P. 276; THE ART OF RIBOLLITA, P. 368; THE SOUPS OF ITALY, P. 146; CHICKPEA, THE KING OF THE POOR, P. 293.

LENTILS *Lens culinaris*

Lenticchia della Val d'Erice
Sicily

TASTE—delicate, almost sweet.

COOKING—creamy soups, creams, slow-cooked dishes.

Lenticchia di Castelluccio di Norcia IGP
Umbria · IGP

TASTE—rich, reminiscent of hazelnuts.

COOKING—stews, purées, chunky soups.

Lenticchia nera delle Colline Ennesi
Sicily · Slow Food

TASTE—vegetal, of fresh hazelnut; delicate.

COOKING—chunky soups, with fish, shellfish.

Lenticchia etrusca variegata
Lazio

TASTE—pronounced, slightly earthy.

COOKING—pork-based stews, salads.

Lenticchia di Ustica
Sicily · Slow Food

TASTE—fine, herbaceous.

COOKING—chunky soups, vegetable soups, creamy soups.

Lenticchia dell'Altopiano di Colfiorito
Umbria

TASTE—delicate, close to chestnuts.

COOKING—salads, with game, fish.

Lenticchia dei Monti Sicani
Sicily

TASTE—fine, sweet, vegetal.

COOKING—salads, chunky soups, with fish.

CHICKPEAS *Cicer arietinum*

Cece dei Monti Sicani
Sicily

TASTE—subtle, smooth.

COOKING—pork-based stews, stews, creams.

Cece nero dei Monti Sicani
Sicily

TASTE—herbaceous, delicate.

COOKING—chunky soups, salads.

Cece del solco dritto di Valentano
Lazio · Slow Food

TASTE—flavorful, slightly sweet.

COOKING—chunky soups, salads.

Cece rugoso
Marche

TASTE—pronounced, slightly starchy.

COOKING—chunky soups, slow-cooked dishes.

SMALL WILD PEAS *Pisum arvense*

Roveja di Civita di Cascia
Umbria · Slow Food

TASTE—assertive, quite complex.

COOKING—salads, chunky soups, vegetable soups, creamy soups.

INDIAN OR GRASS PEA *Lathyrus sativus*

Cicerchia
Central Itay

TASTE—delicate, melting.

COOKING—salads, chunky soups, creams, purées.

Fagiolo Corona
Throughout Italy
TASTE—fleshy, tender, delicate.
COOKING—sauces, in salads, with meat.

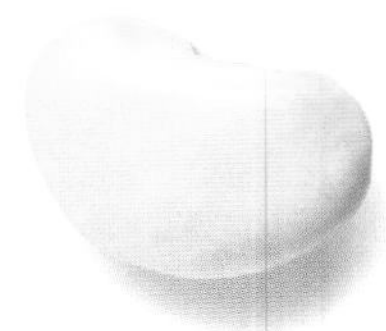

Fagiolo Ciavattone di Sorano
Tuscany
TASTE—very melting, rich, fragrant.
COOKING—slow-cooked dishes, salads.

Fagiolo Diavolo di Cascia
Umbria
TASTE—flavorful, tender, melting.
COOKING—salads, chunky soups, slow-cooked dishes with tomato.

Fagiolo Badda di Polizzi Generosa
Sicily · Slow Food
TASTE—flavorful, with notes of chestnut, almond; herbaceous and even briny; slightly astringent.
COOKING—chunky soups, with pastas.

Fagiolo rosso classico (classic red bean)
Throughout Italy
TASTE—starchy, fairly sweet and melting.
COOKING—slow-cooked dishes, stews, purées, salads.

Fagiolo Bala rossa della Val Belluna
Veneto · Slow Food
TASTE—pronounced, reminiscent of chestnuts.
COOKING—creams, chunky soups, vegetable soups.

Fagiolo giallo della stoppia di San Lorenzo
Lazio
TASTE—tender, sweet.
COOKING—chunky soups, vegetable soups, slow-cooked dishes.

Fagiolo di Lamon IGP
Friuli-Venezia Giulia · IGP
TASTE—delicate and melting.
COOKING—chunky soups, pastas, salads.

Fagiolo rosso di Lucca
Tuscany · Slow Food
TASTE—pronounced, melting.
COOKING—salads, chunky soups, with pastas.

Fagiolo Verdolino aquesiano
Lazio
TASTE—creamy, sweet.
COOKING—chunky soups, braised dishes.

Fagiolo Borlotto (coco white bean)
Throughout Italy
TASTE—intense.
COOKING—chunky soups, salads, pork-based stews, with sausages.

Fagiolina del Trasimeno
Umbria · Slow Food
TASTE—tender, flavorful, juicy.
COOKING—creams, chunky soups, salads.

Fagiolo rosso di Viterbo
Lazio
TASTE—unctuous, pronounced.
COOKING—with meats, charcuterie, pork-based stews.

Fagiolo Gialet bellunese
Friuli-Venezia Giulia · Slow Food
TASTE—subtle, tender.
COOKING—creamy soups, with fish, in soups with barley.

Fagiolo di Controne
Campania · Slow Food
TASTE—fine, firm.
COOKING—salads, with pastas, shellfish.

Fagiolo Occhio nero di Oliveto Citra (black-eyed pea)
Campania
TASTE—slightly pronounced, quite firm.
COOKING—chunky soups, with pastas, rice.

Fagiolo del Purgatorio di Gradoli
Lazio · Slow Food
TASTE—slightly sweet and delicate.
COOKING—slow-cooked stews, vegetable soups, creams.

Fagiolo Cannellino di Atina DOP
Lazio · DOP
TASTE—soft and delicate, evokes hazelnut.
COOKING—chunky soups, vegetable soups; with white meats, mollusks, shellfish.

Fagiolo Cosaruciaru di Scicli
Sicily · Slow Food
TASTE—soft, light, tender.
COOKING—creamy soups, salads, chunky soups.

Fagiolo nero (black bean)
Throughout Italy
TASTE—intense, spicy.
COOKING—sauces, creams, chunky soups.

Fagiolo Perlina or Tondino dei Sibillini
Marche
TASTE—delicate, tender.
COOKING—chunky soups, creamy soups, braised.

Fagiolo Risina or di Spello
Umbria
TASTE—marked, creamy.
COOKING—chunky soups, with fish, in butter.

Fagiolo di Sorana IGP
Tuscany · IGP
TASTE—refined, delicate.
COOKING—salads, with butter.

Fagiolo Giallorino del Compitese · *Tuscany*
TASTE—very fragrant, delicate.
COOKING—chunky soups, vegetable soups, with fish, charcuterie.

Fagiolo Zolfino di Reggello
Tuscany · Slow Food
TASTE—fleshy, subtle.
COOKING—chunky soups (*ribollita*), slow-cooked dishes, purées.

SEASON

AUTUNNO, PRIMAVERA (AUTUMN, SPRING)

CATEGORY

PRIMO PIATTO (FIRST COURSE)

LEVEL

FACILE (EASY)

FREGULA CON LE ARSELLE

SARDINIAN PASTA WITH CLAMS

This very thick seafood soup is one of the most popular variations of these small Sardinian pasta balls that are similar to couscous.

ILARIA BRUNETTI

LA FREGULA

These are large grains of semolina pasta most often—yet incorrectly—called *fregola*. The term comes from the Latin *ferculum*, which means "plateau" or "plate" or "dish."

THE ARSELLE CLAM

In Italy, it's known as the *tellina* or *arsella* clam. In Sardinia, *arselle*—*cocciule* in the local dialect—are either gray European palourde clams or cockles. Here are distinctions:

COCCIULA PINTADA (colored) or ARSELLA BIANCO-NERA: a clam recognizable by its white-and-black striated shell.

COCCIULA NIEDDA or ARSELLA NERA (black): a palourde clam with a very dark shell. Its flesh is the tastiest.

COCCIULA BIANCA or RIGÀRA or ARSELLA BIANCA (white): a common clam, with a white ribbed shell, considered to be of little interest.

COCCIUA LADA (or *scrobicularia plana*): larger and even tastier, this rare variety is on the verge of extinction.

THE RECIPE

Chef Simone Tondo (Racines, Paris 20th) shares the recipe of his grandmother Marise, who was his first and most important "master of the stove" and who taught him how to be free in the kitchen . . . and elsewhere.

SERVES 4

- 1 clove garlic, peeled
- Extra-virgin olive oil
- 1⅛ pounds (500 g) palourde clams or cockles, soaked
- Scant ¼ cup (50 mL) white wine
- 4 to 6 cups (1 to 1.5 L) vegetable stock
- 8½ ounces (240 g) fregula pasta
- 1 small bunch parsley

In a saucepan, brown the whole garlic clove over medium heat with 2 to 3 tablespoons (30 to 45 mL) olive oil. Add the clams, then the wine. Cook until the liquid evaporates, then cover and cook just long enough for the shells to open, no more than 5 minutes. Turn off the heat; strain the liquid from the pan and set it aside. Remove some of the clams from their shells and set aside at room temperature. Bring the stock to a boil and cook the fregula until tender. Add the clams and their strained cooking liquid 2 minutes before the end of the pasta cooking time. The mixture should be souplike. Add a drizzle of olive oil and a few chopped parsley leaves.

Il Tocco Dello Chef (Chef's Tip)

Simone likes to complete the dish with fresh basil leaves and oven-baked Datterino tomatoes with olive oil, thyme, and salt.

CLASSIC VARIATIONS

In rosso: with peeled tomatoes or just a touch of tomato paste.

Arselle e bottarga: enhanced with mullet bottarga or, more rarely, tuna, another island specialty, grated or cut into very thin slices.

Arselle e carciofi: a delight, with the addition of purple Sardinian artichokes.

Fregula in 6 steps

It can be found quite easily in markets, but making fregula at home is much easier than you might think.

1. Dissolve 1 pinch salt and 1 pinch saffron (optional) in a scant ½ cup (100 mL) lukewarm water.

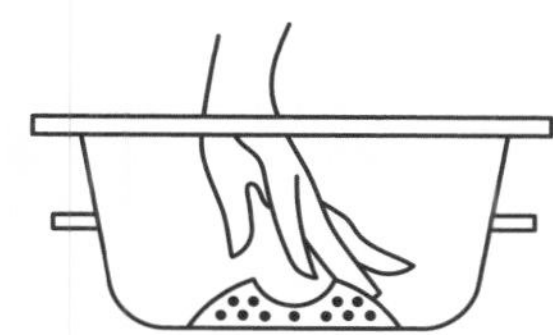

2. Sprinkle 1⅓ cups (250 g) durum wheat semolina flour in a large deep dish and pour a little salted water in the center. Mix with one hand, stirring clockwise, then counterclockwise.

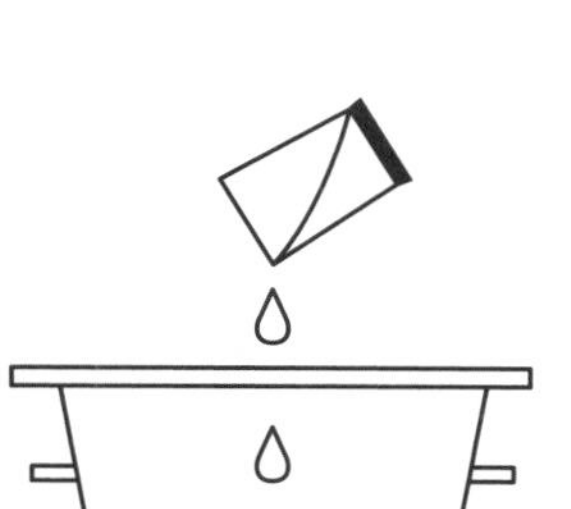

3. As the flour absorbs the liquid, add more water as needed.

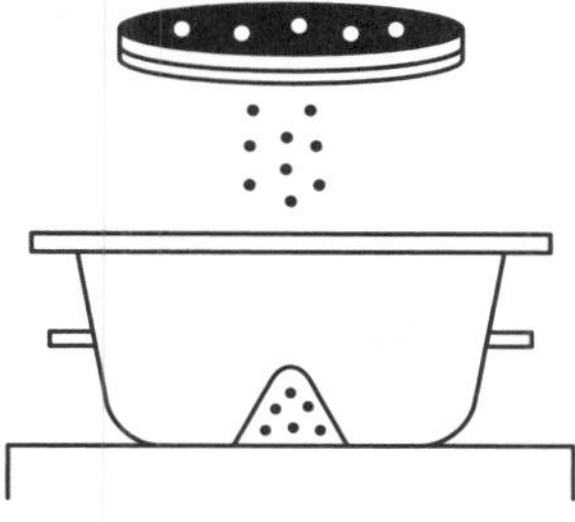

4. When large round grains begin to form, sift them to remove excess particles.

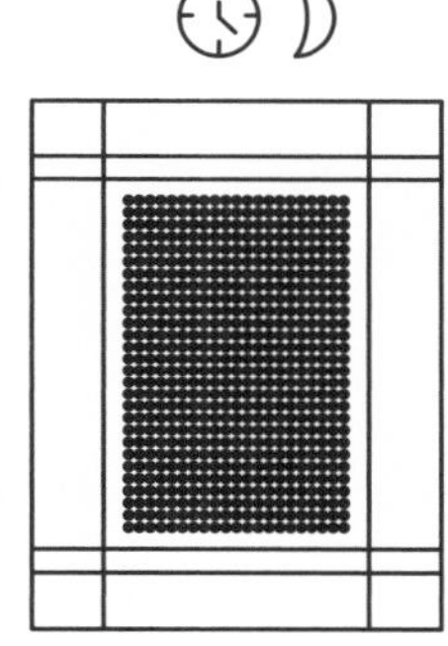

5. Arrange the grains on a clean cloth to dry for several hours or up to overnight.

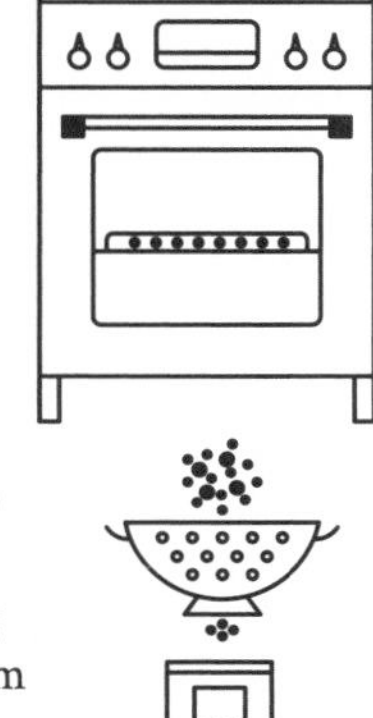

6. Roast in the oven at 300°F (150°C) for 15 minutes: the degree of roasting can be adjusted according to taste. Separate larger grains from smaller ones using a colander; this allows for even cooking. Let cool.

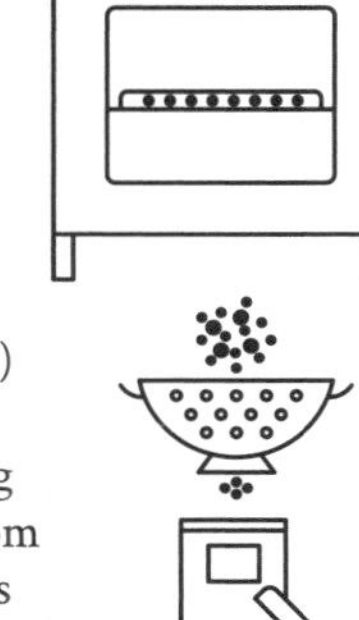

SKIP TO
SPAGHETTI ALLE VONGOLE (SPAGHETTI WITH CLAMS), P. 112;
THE OTHER HOME OF COUSCOUS, P. 81;
FLOURS, P. 5.

PERSIMMON

A little-known fruit with a big personality, *il caco* has found its place in Italian culinary heritage.

GIANNA MAZZEI

WHAT AM I?

SCIENTIFIC NAME: *Diospyros kaki.*

NICKNAME: food of the gods; from the Greek *dios* (god) and *pyros* (fruit, grain).

COUNTRY OF ORIGIN: China.

SEASON: fall and winter.

CHARACTER: variable.

ANECDOTE: the only living thing that survived the atomic bombing of Nagasaki was a persimmon tree. Since then, it has been considered a symbol of peace.

A perfect fruit when ripe

Persimmon is a fruit with a strong personality. It is unpleasant on the palate when it is not ripe, due to large amounts of tannins it contains. The sensation produced is reminiscent of 100 percent cacao dark chocolate. Someone who has tasted the astringency of an unripe persimmon may be discouraged from ever tasting the ripe fruit! The fact that persimmon is harvested and often sold before maturity is one of the reasons misunderstandings about its character can arise.

The flesh should be eaten only when fully ripe. When the fruit is soft and its orange skin looks like it's about to split open, it is ready to be enjoyed. As it matures, sugars increase and tannins decrease, inviting in more sweetness.

STORIES AND LEGENDS

In Campania, it is called *legnasanta* (holy wood) because, once opened, a shape recalling Christ on the cross can be seen in its flesh.

The persimmon contains a seed that, when cut open vertically, reveals a white germ. The interpretation of its form takes on different meanings depending on the tradition to which it refers.

In Sicily, this germ is seen as a diaphanous hand reminiscent of that of the Madonna and is called the *manuzza di Maria* (the little hand of Mary).

HOW DO YOU RIPEN IT?

To speed up the ripening process, place the persimmon in a paper bag with a few apples or in a container with a lid. The ethylene produced naturally by the apples accelerates the fruit's ripening.

SKIP TO
GIUSEPPE VERDI, P. 216.

POPULAR TYPES

SOFT-FLESH PERSIMMON: a soft variety whose more compact parts, in the shape of thin small tongues, are its treasures.

KAKI POMME: arriving in Europe in the early 1900s, this variety is not a cross between apple and persimmon. It's crispy but contains fewer tannins and can be cut into slices or diced.

IN COOKING

→ Baked in olive oil, salt and pepper, and dried bread crumbs, it goes well with roasts.

→ It is excellent dredged in oil and rosemary, floured, and fried.

→ The soft-flesh variety—which has the consistency close to a jam—should not be peeled but cut in half and eaten with a spoon. One gourmet's option: first dip the spoon in a glass of Marsala wine.

→ The flesh, cooked in butter and sugar, is excellent as a crêpe filling.

→ Italian opera composer Giuseppe Verdi, a gourmand of the persimmon, would cut it in half, sprinkle it with sugar, then drizzle it with champagne.

COOKIES

Italy is the homeland of the biscotti, hard cookies created from the need to transport nonperishable foods. There are a multitude of forms and recipes. Here is an overview of these crunchy Italian delights.

ALESSANDRA PIERINI

• DIP YOUR COOKIE •

As a ritual at the end of the harvest, workers liked to dip very dry cookies in a glass of wine. In fact, the end-of-meal ritual of dipping a dry cookie in a glass of *passito* (a wine made from grapes dried on the vine) is still very much alive today, such as with the *cantuccini* cookies dipped in the vin santo dessert wine of Tuscany.

WITH SPICES

(1) ***Susamielli*** **· Lazio, Apulia, Campania**
TEXTURE: from crumbly to hard.
Also known under the names *sapienze* or *sesamielli*. Shortbread, citrus zest, cinnamon, nutmeg, honey, and Neapolitan *pisto* (a mixture of cloves, vanillin, cinnamon, nutmeg, confectioners' sugar, and black pepper).

(2) ***Mustacciuoli*** **or** ***mostaccioli*** **or** ***mustazzola*** **· Molise, Umbria, Apulia, Campania, Calabria, Sicily**
TEXTURE: from crumbly to hard.
Flour, honey, spices, and, depending on the region, dried fruits, cocoa, coffee, liqueurs, or wine.

(3) ***Brigidini*** **· Tuscany**
TEXTURE: crumbly.
Very fine and brittle tuiles made from flour, eggs, anise, and sugar. Similar to *berlingozzi* and *berlingacci*, but sweeter.

(4) ***Pevarini*** **· Veneto**
TEXTURE: crumbly and crunchy.
Dense shortbread made of flour, baking powder, molasses, honey, black pepper, cinnamon, nutmeg, ginger, and cloves.

(5) ***Bicciolani di Vercelli*** **· Piedmont**
TEXTURE: crumbly.
Flour, butter, sugar, eggs, honey, cinnamon, mace, coriander, white pepper, vanilla, cocoa, and lemon zest.

(6) ***Roccoco*** **· Campania, Apulia**
TEXTURE: from crumbly to hard.
Shortbread enriched with almonds, honey, orange peel, and Neapolitan pisto.

WITH ALMONDS

(7) ***Crunchy amaretti*** **· Piedmont, Liguria, Lombardy, Emilia-Romagne**
TEXTURE: crunchy.
Sweet and bitter ground almonds (13 percent minimum), sugar, and egg white.

(8) ***Soft amaretti*** **· those of Monbaruzzo and Voltaggio in Piedmont, Sassello in Liguria, and Oristano in Sardinia are the most famous**
TEXTURE: from soft to very soft.
Sweet and bitter ground almonds (35 percent minimum), sugar, and egg white. See recipe on the following page.

(9) ***Paste di mandorle*** **· Sicily, Sardinia—also called** ***sospiri*****—Calabria, Apulia**
TEXTURE: soft.
Ground sweet almonds, sugar, egg white, and lemon zest.

(10) ***Ricciarelli*** **· Tuscany**
TEXTURE: from soft to very soft.
Ground sweet almonds, honey, orange zest, eggs, sugar, vanilla; oval-shaped and dusted with confectioners' sugar.

WITH DRIED AND/OR CANDIED FRUIT

(11) ***Cavallucci*** **· Tuscany, Marche, called** ***morselletti*** **in Lazio**
TEXTURE: crumbly and crunchy.
Flour, sugar, honey, anise, nuts, almonds, candied orange, and candied citron.

(12) ***Tegole*** **· Aosta Valley**
TEXTURE: crumbly.
Tuiles made from hazelnut and almond flours, wheat flour, sugar, and egg white.

(13) ***Brutti e buoni*** **· Piedmont, Tuscany**
TEXTURE: crunchy and crisp.
Meringue of egg whites with sugar and/or ground hazelnuts and/or almonds.

(14) ***Papassini*** **· Sardinia**
TEXTURE: crunchy.
Flour, raisins, walnuts, almonds, orange zest, anise, nutmeg, and cooked grape must; dense and of various shapes.

BREAD DOUGH DERIVATIVES

(15) ***Torcetti*** **or** ***torchietti*** **· Aosta Valley, Piedmont, central Italy**
TEXTURE: crumbly and crunchy.
Butter, sugar, and flour; similar to flaky pastry. The preparation and cooking method are very similar to those of savory grissini.

(16) ***Taralli glassati*** **· Campania, Calabria, Basilicata, Lazio**
TEXTURE: crumbly and crunchy.
A sweet version of the savory *taralli* with flour, sugar, lard, eggs, and anise, rum, or grappa.

FROM SHORTBREAD—FROLLINI

(17) ***Paste di meliga*** **· Piedmont, those from Monregalese are Slow Food sentinels**
TEXTURE: crumbly and soft.
Finely ground cornmeal, sugar, eggs, and vanilla.

(18) ***Offelle di Parona*** **· Lombardy**
TEXTURE: crumbly and soft.
Flour, eggs, butter, sugar, and olive oil.

(19) ***Krumiri*** **· Piedmont**
TEXTURE: crumbly and soft.
Wheat flour and cornmeal, sugar, butter, eggs, and vanilla.

(20) ***Canestrelli liguri*** **· Liguria, Piedmont**
TEXTURE: crumbly and soft.
Flour, lots of butter, sugar, and eggs; dusted with confectioners' sugar.

(21) ***Zaleti, zaeti,*** **or** ***xaeti*** **· Veneto, Trentino, Friuli**
TEXTURE: crumbly and soft.
Cornmeal and wheat flour, butter, sugar, eggs, raisins, pine nuts, and lemon zest.

THE MOST UNUSUAL

(22) ***'Mpanatigghi*** **· Sicily, from Modica**
TEXTURE: crumbly and soft.
Shortbread; filled with veal (formerly game), Modica chocolate, dried fruits, and spices. Introduced to the island by the Spaniards in the sixteenth century, this recipe made it possible to eat meat in secret during Lent.

THE TRUE BISCUITS (TWICE-COOKED)

(23) ***Cantuccini*** **· Tuscany, also known as** ***biscotti di Prato, piparelli*** **in Sicily, and** ***morselletti cilentani*** **in Campania**
TEXTURE: from crunchy to hard.
There are several variations, but the most traditional are made with almonds. See recipe on the following page.

(24) ***Biscotti della salute*** **or** ***del Lagaccio*** **· Piedmont, Liguria**
TEXTURE: crumbly and crunchy.
Biscotti made from flour, sugar, butter, anise or fennel, and salt.

(25) ***Baicoli*** **· Veneto, also known as** ***pan biscotto***
TEXTURE: crumbly and crunchy.
Flour, sugar, butter, egg white, and salt.

(26) ***Anicini*** **· Liguria, Sardinia, Piedmont**
TEXTURE: crumbly and hard.
Various sweet slices made from eggs, flour, sugar, and anise.

FILLED

(27) ***Nucatuli*** **or** ***nucatula*** **· Sicily**
TEXTURE: crunchy and hard.
Dough is made from semolina flour, sugar, and lard filled with dried figs, walnuts, almonds, orange zest, cinnamon, and honey.

(28) ***Baci di dama*****, "lady's kisses" · Piedmont especially, but also Liguria, Aosta Valley**
TEXTURE: crumbly.
Two round cookies made with hazelnut and almond flours, sandwiching a chocolate filling. See recipe on the following page.

(29) ***Pasticciotti*** **· Sicily, Apulia, Campania**
TEXTURE: crumbly and soft.
Shortbread filled with jams or creams, depending on the region.

(30) ***Tozzetti*** **· south central Italy**
TEXTURE: from crunchy to hard.
Dough made with flour, butter, vanilla, and lemon zest; filled with nuts, honey, and spices.

FOR SOAKING

(31) ***Savoiardi*** **· Piedmont, Sicily, Sardinia where they are called** ***biscotti di Fonni*** **or** ***pistoccus.***
TEXTURE: crumbly and soft.
See recipe on the following page.

(32) ***Biscottini di Novara*** **· Piedmont**
TEXTURE: crunchy and crumbly.
Flour, sugar, and eggs, without fat; shaped like savoiardi but flatter.

OF A RELIGIOUS NATURE

(33) ***Quaresimali*** **· mainly Liguria, but also Tuscany, Campania, Apulia, Sicily**
TEXTURE: from hard to crunchy and crumbly.
Often made from almonds but also hazelnuts or pine nuts; quite firm, surrounded by shortbread; prepared during Lent.

(34) ***Ossa dei morti*** **or** ***biscotti/fave dei morti*****, "biscotti/beans of the dead" · Throughout Italy, with variations**
TEXTURE: hard.
Made with flour, sugar, eggs, almonds, and, depending on the region, enriched with dried or candied fruits, spices, and sweet wines; made to celebrate the deceased at the beginning of November.

(35) ***Nacatole*** **· Calabria**
TEXTURE: crumbly.
Shortbread with anise; they used to be offered along with wedding invitations but are now prepared for Christmas.

(36) ***Mostaccioli*** **or** ***spaccadenti*****, "tooth breaker" · Calabria**
TEXTURE: hard.
Very hard dough made from flour, honey, and grape must; they take allegorical forms of human figures, animals, or symbolic objects and are found during all religious festivities.

LESS COMMON BUT ALSO GOOD

Ferratelle (Abruzzo), **bicciolani** and **tirulen** (Piedmont), **bigi** (Lombardy), **susumelle** (Calabria), **essi** and **buranesi** (Veneto), **biscotti di Panicaglia** (Tuscany), **biscotti di Castellammare** (Campania) . . .

ONCE UPON A TIME . . . A TWICE BAKING

From the late Latin *biscoctus*, meaning "twice-cooked" (*bis-cuit*), this twice-baked, very hard, and long-lasting bread existed as far back as Roman times. Until the Middle Ages, the only sweeteners used in cooking were honey and cooked grape must. It was not until 996 CE that sugar arrived in Venice and the eleventh to twelfth centuries that the trade in spices (pepper, cinnamon, anise, etc.), creams, jams, and exotic ingredients increased. Today, the definition of *biscuit* applies to any small, dry, crumbly, or crunchy cake made with flour, sugar, eggs, and fat.

Fare il biscotto
"To make a biscotto": to cheat, to break a rule for one's own gain.

Mettersi in mare senza biscotti
"Go ahead [out to sea] without biscotti": be careless, face a situation without preparation or adequate means.

FROM SURVIVAL COOKIES TO HOLIDAY TREATS

The first purpose of the hard cookie was purely utilitarian: to provide a food reserve for soldiers and sailors during long voyages. Since medieval times, cookies have been enriched with honey, raisins, and juices and nectars from plants, to be enjoyed during religious ceremonies (Christmas, baptisms, Lent, Carnival, etc.). Eventually, these hard cookies (aka biscuits/biscotti) began to appear in the salons of the upper middle classes of the nineteenth century and became more sophisticated, to be enjoyed with tea, hot chocolate, and liqueurs.

RECIPES

SAVOIARDI (LADYFINGERS)

MAKES APPROXIMATELY 25 COOKIES

½ cup (50 g) confectioners' sugar, plus more for dusting

¾ cup (150 g) superfine sugar, plus 2 tablespoons (25 g)

6 large (300 g) eggs

1¼ cups (150 g) all-purpose flour or T55 flour

⅓ cup (50 g) potato starch, sifted

1 teaspoon (5 g) cornstarch, sifted

1 pinch salt

- Preheat the oven to 475°F (250°C). Line a baking sheet with parchment paper.
- In a bowl, combine the confectioners' sugar and the 2 tablespoons (25 g) superfine sugar. Set aside.
- Separate the egg whites from the yolks. In a bowl, beat the egg yolks and the remaining ¾ cup (150 g) superfine sugar until a thick mixture is obtained.
- Gradually add the flour, potato starch, cornstarch, and salt; mix well.
- In a separate bowl, beat the egg whites to stiff peaks, then fold them into the mixture.
- Fit a piping bag with a plain piping tip and fill the bag with the dough. Pipe cookies of equal length into a "tongue" shape onto the prepared baking sheet.
- Dust the surface with the mixture of confectioners' and superfine sugars, then bake for 15 to 20 minutes, until the cookies are golden brown.
- Once cooled, dust them again with confectioners' sugar.

SOFT AMARETTI

MAKES APPROXIMATELY 15 COOKIES

1¾ cups (200 g) finely ground sweet almonds

3½ tablespoons (25 g) bitter almond flour (or a few drops of bitter almond extract, or bitter apricot kernel flour)

1¾ cups (180 g) confectioners' sugar, plus more for dusting

2 large (60 g) egg whites

- Preheat the oven to 350°F (180°C). Line a baking sheet with parchment paper.
- In a bowl, combine the ground sweet almonds and bitter almond flour with the confectioners' sugar.
- Beat the egg whites to stiff peaks, then incorporate them into the nut mixture until you get a fairly moist and sticky dough.
- Using your hands, form 1⅛-inch (3 cm) balls, place them on the prepared baking sheet, and press them to flatten them slightly.
- Dust with confectioners' sugar, and bake for 10 to 15 minutes. They should form a crust but remain light in color.
- Remove from the oven and let cool on the baking sheet. They will stay moist for several days in an airtight container.

CANTUCCINI

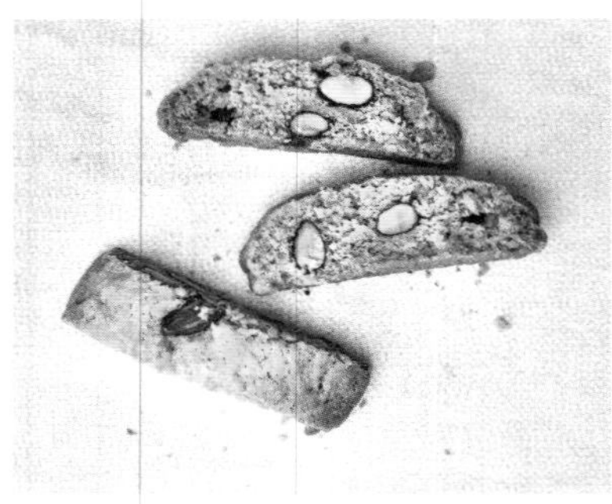

MAKES APPROXIMATELY 20 COOKIES

3 large (150 g) eggs

¾ cup plus 2 tablespoons (180 g) sugar

2 cups (250 g) all-purpose flour or T55 flour, plus more for dusting

1 teaspoon (4 g) baking powder

½ vanilla bean, split lengthwise and seeds scraped out

Zest of 1 organic orange

1 pinch salt

½ cup (80 g) whole roasted almonds

- Preheat the oven to 350°F (180°C). Line a baking sheet with parchment paper.
- Separate the egg whites from the yolks of two of the eggs; set the remaining egg aside to use as an egg wash. In a bowl, beat the egg whites to stiff peaks; set aside. In a separate bowl, whisk the yolks with the sugar until lightened.
- Add the flour, baking powder, vanilla seeds, orange zest, and salt to the yolk-sugar mixture. Stir everything together until you get a smooth but sticky dough. Add the almonds and combine.
- Gently fold in the beaten egg whites.
- Shape two loaves measuring 8 inches (20 cm) long and 2 to 2⅓ inches (5 to 6 cm) in diameter using a little flour on the work surface and the dough, then place the loaves on the prepared baking sheet.
- Lightly beat the remaining egg with a fork and brush the loaves with the egg.
- Bake the loaves for 20 minutes. As soon as they start to brown, remove them, let cool, then cut crosswise into ¾-inch-thick (2 cm) slices. Return them to the oven, lowering the temperature to 320°F (160°C).
- After 10 minutes, turn them over and continue baking for another 10 minutes, until golden and firm to the touch.

BACI DI DAMA

MAKES APPROXIMATELY 20 COOKIES

½ cup (100 g) sugar

1 cup (100 g) hazelnut flour or almond flour

1 cup (100 g) all-purpose flour or T55 flour

1 large (19 g) egg yolk

5 tablespoons (70 g) unsalted butter, at room temperature

1 pinch salt

3 ounces (80 g) gianduja or praline chocolate, chopped

- In a bowl, combine the sugar and hazelnut flour. Add the all-purpose flour, egg yolk, butter, and salt, and stir to thoroughly combine.
- Shape the dough into a loaf, cover with plastic wrap, and let rest in the refrigerator for 30 minutes.
- Cut off pieces of the dough, shape the pieces into 1-inch (2.5 cm) balls, and place them on a baking sheet lined with parchment paper. Refrigerate for 30 minutes.
- Preheat the oven to 350°F (180°C). Remove the cookies from the refrigerator and bake for 15 to 20 minutes, until golden. Remove from the oven and let cool on the baking sheet.
- While the cookies are baking, melt the chocolate in a bain-marie. Once melted, continue to stir as it cools until it is a fairly thick consistency.
- Spread a little chocolate on the flat side of a cookie and sandwich it with another cookie. Repeat with the remaining cookies. Set aside until the chocolate has set, and enjoy.

Alessandra's tip:
These cookies can also be filled with any store-bought chocolate spread!

SKIP TO
LIQUORI, P. 366;
CHOCOLATE SPREADS, P. 248.

SEASON

TUTTO L'ANNO (YEAR-ROUND)

CATEGORY

DOLCE (DESSERT)

LEVEL

DIFFICILE (EASY)

SEADAS

FRIED CHEESE POCKETS

Two deep-fried disks of dough joined together by a center of melted cheese flavored with lemon zest and served topped with warm honey . . . golden, like the Sardinian sun.

GIANNA MAZZEI

ITS ORIGINS

→ It's called *seada* (plural *seadas*), but also *sebada, sevada, casgiulata*. The name derives from the Latin *sebum* (tallow, animal fat), due to its oily appearance once fried.

→ Although common to areas traditionally linked to sheep farming, it has spread throughout the island.

→ Originally created *manna cantu su prattu*, that is to say, "as big as a plate," seadas have since been resized to their current smaller size, between 4 and 6 inches (10 and 15 cm) in diameter.

INGREDIENTS

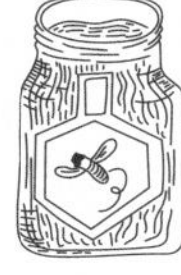

· THE DOUGH ·

When made of semolina flour and lard, it takes the name *pasta violada*. In Sardinian, *violare sa pasta* means to prepare the dough with lard.

· THE CHEESE ·

The original recipe uses *casu friscu*, a fresh, unsalted sheep's-milk cheese that is both sweet and tangy and should not be matured for more than four to five days. The Sardinian trick to bringing out the acidity of the cheese is to wrap it in a damp cloth and let it sit for a few days at room temperature. There are two ways to prepare it: traditionally, by melting it; or *a sa mandrona* (the lazy way), by simply grating this same cheese.

· THE HONEY ·

Orange blossom (floral and fruity), arbutus (bitter), chestnut (not very sweet).

THE RECIPE

Here is an adapted version I learned from my Sardinian aunt Francesca (she measures nothing!).

MAKES 12 SEADAS

2¾ cups (500 g) semolina flour, plus more as needed
Salt
1¾ to 2⅛ ounces (50 to 60 g) lard
1⅛ pounds (500 g) fresh sheep's-milk cheese, soured
Scant ½ cup (100 mL) milk (optional)
1 tablespoon (13 g) sugar (optional)
Zest of 1 large unwaxed lemon
Frying oil
Honey

Place the semolina on a work surface and make a well in the center. Dissolve a pinch of salt in 1 cup (250 mL) lukewarm water and gradually pour it into the well, kneading with your fingers to obtain a firm, smooth, and elastic dough. Do not add the water all at once, as you may need a little less than you expect. Add the lard, then knead the mixture for about 10 minutes, until smooth and homogeneous. Wrap the dough in plastic wrap and place it in the refrigerator.

In a saucepan over very low heat, melt the cheese, stirring with a wooden spoon. If it is too dry, add some milk; if it is too runny, add a little semolina. When it becomes stringy, add the sugar (if using) and the lemon zest. Mix well and remove from the heat. Prepare a bowl of cold water to wet your fingers and handle the hot cheese, then form the cheese into disks approximately 4 inches (10 cm) in diameter on parchment paper or a cutting board. Let cool.

Roll out the dough and shape it into disks measuring ¾ inch (2 cm) larger in diameter than the cheese. Place a disk of cheese in the center of one disk of dough and set another disk of dough on top. Seal the edges while trying to press out any air, then cut around the circumference with a scalloped pasta roller (to mimic the rays of the sun). Fry the seadas in plenty of oil and arrange them in a dish. If the honey has crystallized, heat it in a saucepan or double boiler. Pour the honey over the seadas, and serve piping hot.

THE VARIATIONS

→ You can replace the semolina flour with T00 flour (or all-purpose flour), or make a mixture of the two, and use orange zest instead of lemon, or add it to the honey drizzled on the seadas (in this case, do not add it to the filling).

→ Today, olive oil or frying oil is preferred over lard.

→ There is a savory version that includes parsley and cheese. Some people mistakenly believe that this is the ancestor of the sweet version, when in fact it arose out of necessity at a time when there was no honey.

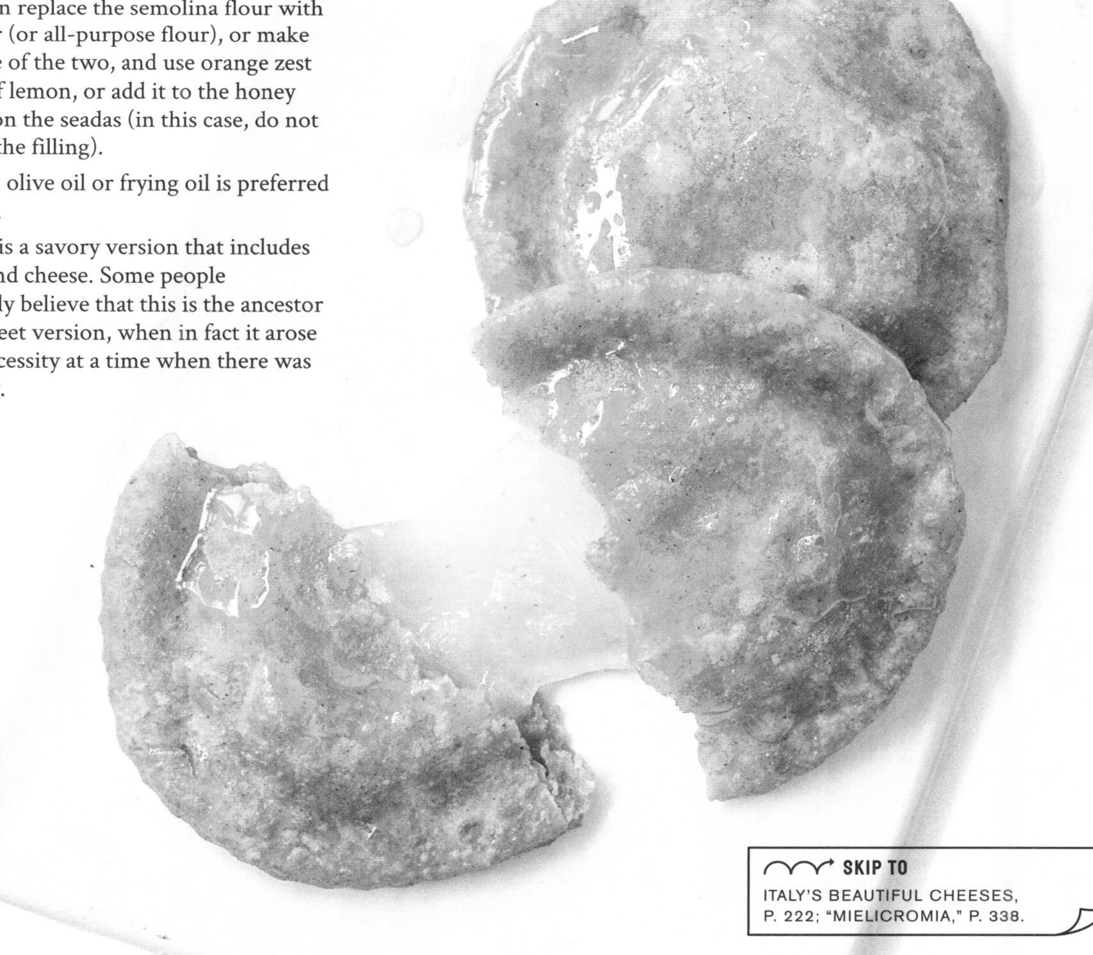

SKIP TO
ITALY'S BEAUTIFUL CHEESES, P. 222; "MIELICROMIA," P. 338.

GATHERING GRAPES

The Greeks called it *Oenotria*, "the land of wine." With more than 350 grape varietals identified, Italy has managed to preserve its extraordinary winegrowing richness. Each vine offers its own character and distinct terroir to the wines produced from its fruit.

SAMUEL COGLIATI

THE AROMATIC FAMILY

Some fruits are naturally more fragrant than others. What a fragrance there can be in certain grape varietals!

ALEATICO

Slow to ripen, it no longer enjoys its former popularity. Fruity, fresh and delicate, muscatlike, it nevertheless produces smooth wines with an attractive ruby color, lightly effervescent, and sweet.

A DOC: Aleatico di Gradoli
A DOMAIN: Le Coste (Gradoli, Latium)

—

MALVASIA BIANCA DI CANDIA

One of the most widely used aromatic grape varietals in Italy. It is especially along the northern and central Apennine mountain range that it produces golden, captivating, dry or sweet whites, often sparkling and festive.

A PGI: Emilia
A DOMAIN: Crocizia (Langhirano, Emilia-Romagna)

—

RUCHÉ (PRONOUNCED "ROU-KAY")

In central Piedmont, the bouquet of the vinous, penetrating, colorful, and generous red wines impart this grape's aromas of Asian spices and flowers.

A DOC AND DOCG: Ruché di Castagnole Monferrato
A DOMAIN: Cascina Tavijn (Scurzolengo, Piedmont)

—

ZIBIBBO OU MOSCATO D'ALESSANDRIA

This may be the king of muscats. It is used for drying on the vine, especially in western Sicily and on the island of Pantelleria. This is where naturally sweet nectars with an amazing aromatic radiance are born.

A DOC: Passito di Pantelleria
A DOMAIN: Salvatore Murana (Pantelleria, Sicily)

THE POWERFUL FAMILY

In a Mediterranean climate, it isn't difficult to find a grape that provides fleshiness and character to its juice.

AGLIANICO

In the lands of Campania or on the volcanic slopes of Vulture (Basilicata), this grape brings tannins, alcohol, and a great deal of structure to its red wines.

A DOC: Aglianico del Vulture
A DOMAIN: Paternoster (Barile, Basilicata)

—

UVA LONGANESI

On the plains near the Adriatic coast of Romagna, this varietal produces a black wine called *bursôn*, concentrated and original, yet a little rustic.

A PGI: Ravenna
A DOMAIN: Zini (Boncellino, Emilia-Romagna)

—

PECORINO

Muscular without being "body built." Between Marche and Abruzzo, its white wines are fat, flavorful, and with firm fruitiness along with chewiness.

A DOCG: Offida
A DOMAIN: Aurora (Offida, Marche)

—

PRIMITIVO

Close to the Californian Zinfandel, of which Primitivo is its real name. Settled in the south of Apulia, this varietal creates fleshy and full-bodied reds and rosés, enveloped in a softness that is sometimes almost sweet.

A DOC: Primitivo di Manduria
A DOMAIN: Candido (San Donaci, Apulia)

THE ELEGANT FAMILY

Of course, elegance doesn't come solely from the vines: terroir has a lot to do with it. Yet there can be no great wine without a great vine!

GROPPELLO GENTILE

Found in the Lombard area of Lake Garda, this varietal is no longer as successful as it used to be. Yet this thin-skinned varietal produces light, airy reds, scented with red fruits and spices.

A DOC: Garda Classico
A DOMAIN: Le Sincette (Polpenazze del Garda, Lombardy)

—

NERELLO MASCALESE

The undisputed queen of Etna, it is one of the most famous grape varietals in the south. Its tannic and distinguished reds improve with long aging in the cellar.

A DOC: Etna
A DOMAIN: Calabretta (Randazzo, Sicily)

—

ROSSESE

Grows in Dolceacqua, a town in Liguria on the French border. It produces garnet-colored wines with much character and strong but plump flavor.

A DOC: Rossese di Dolceacqua
A DOMAIN: Antonio Perrino Testalonga (Dolceacqua, Liguria)

—

VITOVSKA

On the limestone plateaus of Carso, on the Italian-Slovenian border, this grape gives rise to straightforward, flavorful, focused whites, with easy-drinking character and aging potential.

A DOC: Carso
A DOMAIN: Kante (Duino Aurisina, Friuli-Venezia Giulia)

THE TENSE FAMILY

These grapes don't have to offer a dreadfully acidic quality. If well managed, the quality can offer pleasing drinkability.

THE LIGHT FAMILY

Watch out for the equation that suggests concentration of flavor equals quality! Light wines can change this notion . . .

ASPRINIO

In the town of Aversa, in Campania, these high-growing grapes are harvested by climbing a ladder to a height of several meters . . . As its name says, it produces dry and lemony whites, sometimes sparkling.

A DOC: Aversa
A DOMAIN: I Borboni (Lusciano, Caserta)

–

GRIGNOLINO

Both a noble and popular grape varietal, it produces lightly colored, fresh reds, with a very dry flavor thanks in particular to firm and subtle tannins. Its homeland is Monferrat (Piedmont).

A DOC: Monferrato Casalese
A DOMAIN: Cantine Valpane (Ozzano, Emilia-Romagna)

–

PRIÉ BLANC

On the edge of Mont Blanc, in Morgex and La Salle, a few vines grow at an elevation of up to 4,100 feet (1,250 m)! The local white is tangy and light. It is also known to have potential for champagnization.

A DOC: Morgex and La Salle
A DOMAIN: Vintage (Saint Christophe, Aosta Valley)

–

TERRANO

In Carso, it has an acidic tension that is rare among red grape varietals. Its wines are sharp, sometimes harsh in their youth, but so original!

A DOC: Carso
A DOMAIN: Zidarich (Duino Aurisina, Friuli-Venezia Giulia)

FAVORITA

A relative of Vermentino (southern Piedmont), it is the source of fresh and smooth whites that stand out for their frank fruitiness. Dry or sweet (sometimes lightly effervescent).

A DOC: Langhe
A DOMAIN: Fratelli Alessandria (Verduno, Piedmont)

–

PIGNOLETTO

The white grape varietal from Bologna and its surroundings. Unfortunately, it is not often highlighted. The suave and very dry wines that it produces can nevertheless be pleasant and thirst-quenching.

A DOC: Colli Bolognesi
A DOMAIN: Maria Bortolotti (Zola Predosa, Emilia-Romagna)

–

MAGLIOCCO

This Calabrian vine, widespread especially in the north of the region, produces bright, warm reds with a fine and delicate texture. To drink as fruit forward.

A PGI: Calabria
A DOMAIN: L'Acino (San Marco Argentano, Calabria)

–

SCHIAVA

From southern Tyrol, it barely tints its wines, the color of which is an ethereal garnet. However, the presence of taste and the fine touch of the tannins make it a grape that should not be neglected!

A DOC: Alto Adige
A DOMAIN: Girlan (Cornaiano, Trentino-Alto Adige)

WHAT ABOUT OTHER POPULAR VARIETALS?

Pinot Gris is the fourth most cultivated grape in Italy; Merlot comes in fifth, Chardonnay ninth, Cabernet Sauvignon thirteenth* . . . Yet Merlot and Chardonnay fear hot weather: they therefore do not often find a place in Italy. Bordeaux plants, on the other hand, do well in Trentino or on the Tuscan coast (Bolgheri). Pinot Gris has taken root in Friuli, where some winegrowers highlight its fleshy and powerful side, for example by macerating it with skins on.

**Sources: OIV 2017; Kym Anderson/ The University of Adelaide, 2013.*

WHAT IS A NATIVE VARIETAL?

Native varietals are often compared to international varietals. But any grape varietal can be both local and cultivated elsewhere. Over the millennia, plants have moved with humans, mutated, and been hybridized and selected.

SKIP TO
INDIGENOUS GRAPE VARIETALS, P. 307;
WINE FROM FIRE, P. 165;
HIGH-ELEVATION WINES, P. 381.

MORTADELLA

Often mistreated by commercial production, this bologna, nicknamed as a tribute to its origins in Bologna, has a rich history and an artisanal tradition that should lend it prestige.

ALESSANDRA PIERINI

WHAT AM I?

Mortadella is a kind of large pink sausage, compact and cylindrical, made principally with lean finely chopped pork and fat, seasoned with salt, black pepper, spices, and often pistachios. It is encased in a synthetic or natural casing and cooked slowly (up to twenty-four hours), suspended from a string, in a dry-air oven at around 167°F (75°C).

For a long time, it was a snack enjoyed by the rural classes, placed between two slices of rustic bread and accompanied by a glass of Lambrusco or Barbera wine. Incorrectly considered to be a very fatty charcuterie meat (it is around 20 percent fat), when it is of excellent quality it is only lightly salted. It should be a uniform bright pink color with pearly white bits of fat throughout.

Mortadella di Bologna (Emilia-Romagna) has been a PGI designation since 1998 but can also be made in other regions of northern and central Italy.

WITH OR WITHOUT PISTACHIOS?

The PGI designation allows both versions. In Bologna, the one without pistachio is preferred, as in the ancient recipe, while in the central and southern parts of Italy, this green and crunchy note is a must.

ITS ORIGINS

~

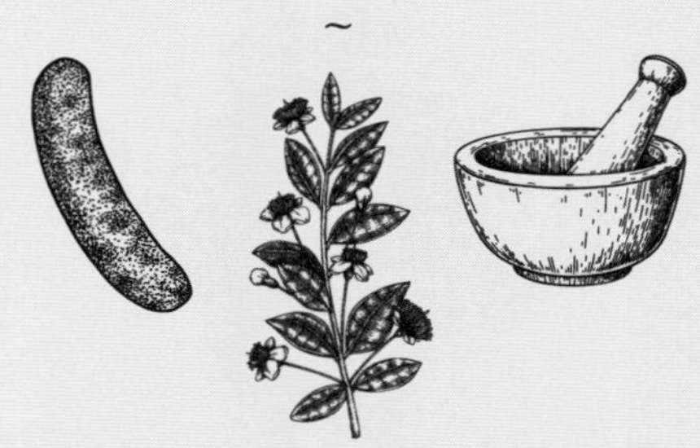

Is its name from the Latin *farcimen murtatum* or *myrtatum*, designating a sausage stuffed with myrtle, or is it from *mortarium*, for the mortar in which the Romans ground the pieces of meat and pig fat with spices? The latter theory is supported by a stone tablet dating from the Roman imperial period showing seven young pigs in a pasture and a mortar with a pestle.

•

In the thirteenth century, the former corporation of Bologna pork butchers called the Salaroli codified the official recipe, thus establishing the first specifications for the product, adopted in 1661 by Cardinal Girolamo Farnese.

•

In 1557, Cristoforo da Messisbugo detailed in his cookbook the ingredients and the production stages of mortadella.

HOW SHOULD YOU EAT IT?

IN *SOTTILISSIME* (VERY VERY THIN) SLICES

Cut with an *affettatrice* (slicer) or a sharp knife by an experienced butcher: on *pizze*, *bruschette*, crostini, or focaccia; as a starter wrapped around *grissini*; on a fried egg; stuffed with fresh cheeses (ricotta, goat's-milk cheese, *stracchino* . . .), with pistachios, walnuts, or pine nuts; with figs.

CUBED

In salads; as an aperitif; on its own or on a skewer with cheese and vegetables.

CHOPPED

In sauces, ravioli fillings (always found in the famous tortellini), *torte*, meatballs, fish, *involtini* (meat roulades).

A DELICATE STEP

The cooking phase is crucial. If performed incorrectly, it can give the mortadella an irregular shape, melt the diced fat (*lardelli*), or alter its pink color due to excess heat. Mortadella often has a diameter of 8 to 12 inches (20 to 30 cm) and weighs 22 to 66 pounds (10 to 30 kg), but some made for competitions can weigh up to 220 pounds (100 kg), and should be handled with great care.

MORTADELLA IN THE MOVIES

OFTEN ASSOCIATED WITH CURVY AND JOVIAL FEMALE PERSONALITIES, IT HAS BEEN A STAR OF THE BIG SCREEN.

LA MORTADELLA (AKA LADY LIBERTY)

MARIO MONICELLI
1971

Neapolitan Sophia Loren, attempting to travel to New York with a mortadella in her luggage, is stopped at customs, where she decides to eat the mortadella on-site.

UNA GIORNATA PARTICOLARE (AKA A SPECIAL DAY)

ETTORE SCOLA
1977

In this film, Sophia Loren, playing a hostess, brings a large slice of mortadella to the table following the soup course.

BAMBOLA

JUAN JOSÉ BIGAS LUNA
1996

The sensual Valeria Marini poses sitting on a huge mortadella for a photo to be sent to her fiancé, who is in prison.

Taste

Its intoxicating and incomparable scent is delicate, slightly spiced; the fat melts in the mouth with a roundness, softening the peppery notes in a smooth balance. Its aroma is a call to the taste buds, encouraging another bite with its pleasant flavor.

SKIP TO
TORTELLINI IN BRODO (TORTELLINI IN BROTH), P. 328; SOPHIA LOREN, P. 336.

① MORTADELLA DI PRATO

Marini · *Agliana-Prato, Tuscany—PGI Slow Food*

Produced since 1900, it is presented as a small cooked sausage. The meat and fat, which are chopped with a knife, are mixed with spices, garlic, and Alkermes red liqueur, resulting in a deep pink color; it's then cooked in water or steamed. Intense and very spiced flavor.

② MORTADELLA CLASSICA DI BOLOGNA

Bonfatti Renazzo di Cento · *Bologna—Slow Food*

A classic, produced according to the ancient recipe of Bologna and now very rare. Meat from Italian pork is cooked in stone skillets between 167° and 171°F (75° and 77°C) with salt, black peppercorns, ground white pepper, mace, coriander, and garlic, encased in pork bladder.

③ MORTADELLA AL PISTACCHIO

Levoni · *Castellucchio Mantua, Lombardy*

Very rich in taste and fragrant, with intense green pistachios and pleasant notes of nutmeg and black pepper.

④ SALAME ROSA

Artisanal quality · *Bologna*

Produced in Bologna since the Middle Ages during the same time as the classic mortadella, which has always been the leader, this *salame* (sausage) presents large lean and drier pieces of meat with a rich taste close to roasted ham, aromatic and persistent.

⑤ MORTADELLA DI MORA ROMAGNOLA

Artisanal quality · *Bologna—Slow Food*

Produced with the ancient local Mora Romagnola breed of pigs. It has a more pronounced meaty taste due to the inclusion of fewer spices, but it is very elegant.

⑥ MORTADELLA DI GRIGIO DEL CASENTINO

Le Selve di Vallolmo, Poppi · *Arezzo, Tuscany*

Only the best cuts of the belly and shoulder of this ancient Tuscan breed are used to produce a very lean, fine-textured, but more rustic mortadella; the fat is chopped with a knife. It has a gentle garlicky flavor and includes pistachios.

Mortadella in all its forms

Once a product that only nobles could afford, it has now become, thanks to commercial production, a more accessible food, but this is often at the expense of quality.

The difference lies in the choice of the ingredients (such as free-range pigs or local breeds fed on noble grains or acorns or chestnuts), the use of a slow cooking process, the casing and the natural flavors, and the absence of polyphosphates and flavor enhancers, which only artisanal production can guarantee.

pasta pazza

It's not just foreigners who create all kinds of crazy pasta dishes! After the economic and political crisis that rocked Italy in the 1970s, an appetite for renewal resonated in the kitchen. Using spectacular or kitschy sauces, cream, and alcohol galore, here are four "crazy pastas" that Italians might prefer to forget but that you can prepare at home if you're looking for extra entertainment with your meals.

FRÉDÉRICK
E. GRASSER HERMÉ

SPAGHETTI WITH STRAWBERRIES

THE CRAZY DISH—strawberries in a pasta dish or in risotto? This was a curious idea that Italians may have borrowed from the French. In France during the 1980s, nouvelle cuisine was in full swing, with the tomato-strawberry gazpacho by Michel Guérard as one example of its many forms.

MAKE IT HOW? Serves 4. Sauté 14 ounces (400 g) cooked spaghetti in a pan in a mixture of butter and cream. Add 4½ ounces (125 g) sautéed strawberries. Stir well to combine, then serve with freshly grated pecorino or Parmesan. Season with salt and pepper.

KITSCHY INDEX:

❶❷❸④⑤

→ Visually it's similar to tomato sauce . . .

VODKA PENNE PASTA

THE CRAZY DISH—this dish was first mentioned in the cookbook *L'Abbuffone* (1974) by actor Ugo Tognazzi, which mentions pasta *all'infuriata*, a vodka-soaked variation of *arrabbiata*. Both sides of the Atlantic claim the origins of this now cult dish: a Bologna restaurant owner and a Roman cook at the behest of a vodka maker on one side of the ocean, and a New York student and the Neapolitan chef of a Manhattan restaurant on the other. This culinary curiosity continued and even evolved in the 1980s: it gave birth to *penne alla moscovita* (salmon, cream, caviar, and vodka).

MAKE IT HOW? Cook al dente 9 ounces (250 g) penne pasta, add it to a creamy, spicy, garlicky tomato sauce. Once the pasta is well coated with the sauce, add (at least!) ⅓ cup (80 mL) vodka, and cook until the vodka evaporates or flambé it for a moment. Serves 2.

KITSCHY INDEX:

❶❷❸❹⑤

→ Eat or have a drink? . . . There's no need to choose!

CHOCOLATE TAGLIATELLE

THE CRAZY DISH—tagliatelle witnessed every color in the 1980s: made with tomato, spinach, beet juice . . . and even chocolate! The use of cocoa in savory recipes existed in regional traditions (game stews, sweet gnocchi in Umbria, *coda alla vaccinara* in Rome . . .), and nouvelle cuisine undoubtedly fanned the flames.

MAKE IT HOW? When making fresh pasta, combine the flour with unsweetened cocoa powder (⅓ cup/30 g cocoa per ¾ cup/100 g of flour). When cooked, this pasta is delicious combined with Gorgonzola and walnuts.

KITSCHY INDEX:

❶❷③④⑤

→ Sweet and savory is in fashion!

PASTA SERVED IN THE PARMESAN WHEEL

THE CRAZY DISH—how do you go from adding Parmesan to pasta to the other way around? This is undoubtedly a clever way of using this king of cheeses all the way down to its rind. Sophia Loren attributes this fad of the 1960s to her friend Guido Furiassi, a Milanese restaurateur. The 1970s contributed a psychedelic flambéed version of this dish using vodka.

MAKE IT HOW? Hollow out a half round of Parmesan and spoon the pasta directly into the wheel, adding melted Parmesan to the cream sauce. For the fiery version, flambé the cheese wheel with a half glass of vodka. Serve directly in the cheese wheel.

KITSCHY INDEX:

❶❷❸❹❺

→ A daring and exuberant gesture . . . but perhaps a bit excessive?

SKIP TO
PENNE ALL'ARRABBIATA, P. 252;
POP PASTA, P. 221;
SOPHIA LOREN, P. 336.

Gualtiero Marchesi

PROFILE

FOR A NEW ITALIAN CUISINE

France and its nouvelle cuisine influences were fundamental to Marchesi, but his goal was to renew the identity of Italian cuisine without mimicking that of neighboring countries. He reduced cooking times, lightened seasonings, and respected ingredients.

"I consider my cuisine both Italian and nouvelle. Italian, because it does not deny anything regarding the great regional gastronomic traditions of our country, but at the same time it is nouvelle because it keeps its eyes open to the evolution—past, present, and future—of life's conditions."

(La mia nuova grande cucina italiana, 1980)

CUCINA TOTALE

Marchesi was the first to design a "total cuisine": from dishes to tablecloths, his vision embraces the entire dining experience. His cooking delivers what is essential, but he maintains the theatrical aspect of the room.

KEY DATES

MARCH 19, 1930
Born in San Zenone al Po (Lombardy).

1968–1976
His period abroad in France (Ledoyen, Chapeau Rouge, Maison Troisgros).

1977
The opening of his eponymous restaurant in Milan and his first star in the Michelin Guide.

1981
Creation of *riso e oro* (rice and gold), his legendary risotto.

1985
Achieves three Michelin stars, a first in Italy.

1986
Designated Knight of the Italian Republic.

2014
Founding of his *accademia* in Milan, a cooking school for professionals and amateurs.

DECEMBER 26, 2017
Dies in Milan.

Known as "Maestro," Marchesi revolutionized Italian cuisine and changed the world's view of Italian (haute) gastronomy.

ANNA PRANDONI

AN AESTHETE

He was an accomplished musician and passionate about art. Even though his focus was cuisine, he was always inspired by the works of great painters, because, as he stated, "We are what we have seen." For example:

QUATTRO PASTE
("Four pastas")

Four different sizes of pasta *in bianco* (without sauce) on the plate, as a nod to the four portraits of Andy Warhol's *Shot Marilyns* painting.

UOVO ALLA BURRI
("Burri-style egg")

An egg scorched with a blowtorch, a nod to materialist artist Alberto Burri, famous for his combustions on paper.

L'ACROME DI BRANZINO
("Achromatic branzino")

In reference to the achromatic (colorless) paintings by Piero Manzoni.

FRANCE: I LOVE YOU . . .

In 1990, France's minister of culture, Jack Lang, appointed Gualtiero Marchesi Knight of the Order of Arts and Letters.

. . . BUT NO THANKS

In 1993, Marchesi moved his restaurant to L'Albereta in Franciacorta, where he retained his three Michelin stars until 2008, when the Michelin Guide took one away. He then refused the distinction of the star rating system and disappeared forever from the guide.

HIS LINEAGE

In addition to influencing all the great Italian chefs of today, Marchesi trained several at his side: Enrico Crippa, Carlo Cracco, Ernst Knam, Andrea Berton, Pietro Leemann, Davide Oldani, and Paolo Lopriore, to name a few.

SKIP TO
A LEADING COUNTRY FOR CAVIAR, P. 360; ENRICO CRIPPA, P. 254.

SIGNATURE DISHES

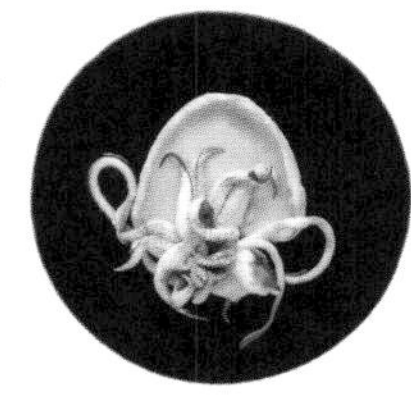

SEPPIA AL NERO
("Cuttlefish in black," 1983)

An immaculate cuttlefish resting on a reflective pool of its ink: a gastronomic manifesto that sublimates the ingredient.
"I glorified the nature of the cuttlefish, taking to extreme consequences the idea that form, each form, is substance. When this concept transforms itself into a rule, cooking becomes simpler, and seriously engages in capturing the essence of the discourse: in other words, how does one transform nature into food without betraying it."

DRIPPING DI PESCE
("Dripping fish," 2004)

This dish was inspired by Jackson Pollock's technique of dripping colors onto canvas. Resting on a lightened mayonnaise with calamari and clams are splashes of tomato, squid ink, and parsley sauces. When eaten, by gathering together the pieces of seafood on the spoon, a canvas of the artist is created.

ROSSO E NERO
("Red and black," 2006)

Two pieces of monkfish, dipped in squid ink and fried, rest atop a spicy tomato sauce.

"I arranged the pieces of monkfish, like enigmatic marks of artist Alberto Burri, as archetypal shapes and volumes, solid and fluctuating at the same time. One sees red and black, with white appearing impetuously and unexpectedly when the guest's knife reveals—with such presence—the immaculate centers."

GNOCCHI DI PATATE CRUDE

RAW POTATO GNOCCHI

Can you make gnocchi from raw potatoes? This is a typical recipe from the Dolomites, a mountainous region of Trentino-Alto Adige, which is best made with local charcuterie.

ILARIA BRUNETTI

THE TECHNIQUE

By Silvana Segna, chef at Locanda Alpina in Brez (Trento).

SERVES 2

2 raw potatoes, either white fleshed (such as Kennebec or Lenape) or yellow fleshed (such as Bintje)

1 large (19 g) egg yolk

3 tablespoons (25 g) all-purpose flour, plus more as needed

Salt

1 tablespoon (14 g) unsalted butter

5¼ ounces (150 g) thinly sliced pancetta (or speck)

Steps

1. Peel the potatoes.
2. Grate the potatoes with a coarse grater. Squeeze the grated flesh by hand to drain away the excess liquid.
3. Add the egg yolk to the grated potato flesh, and combine with a spoon.
4. Add the flour while stirring.
5. Season with a pinch of salt. Stir until the mixture is slightly tacky but not too wet. Add more flour, if necessary.
6. Bring a large pot of salted water to a boil. Using a spoon, form gnocchi approximately ¾ inch (2 cm) long.
7. Immerse the gnocchi in the boiling water.
8. While the gnocchi cook, melt the butter in a saucepan over medium heat and add pieces of the pancetta to the pan.
9. Cook until browned.
10. When the gnocchi rise to the surface, they are done.
11. Remove the gnocchi from the pot using a skimmer.
12. Cook the gnocchi in the pan with the butter and pancetta until they have taken on the color of the sauce.
13. Serve hot.

SKIP TO
THE GNOCCHI UNIVERSE, P. 76;
THE ART OF PORK FAT, P. 70.

1

2

3

4

5

6

7

8

9

10

11

12

13

WINE FROM FIRE

Thanks to its sometimes lively mountains such as Vesuvius and Etna, Italy is an emblematic country of volcanic wines. Let's take a walk through these red-hot *terroirs*.

JÉRÔME GAGNEZ

THE VINEYARD OF VESUVIUS

LOCATION: overlooking the Bay of Naples, halfway between Pompeii and Naples.

VINES: all around the foot of the volcano.

HIGH POINT: 4,200 feet (1,281 m).

GEOLOGICAL PROFILE: a limestone base covered by volcanic rocks containing limestone inclusions.

THE WINE TO DRINK: look for the wine named Lacryma Christi, because Christ, as it's told, would have shed tears on the side of Vesuvius either in reaction to the corruption created by Lucifer in Naples or in the face of the beauty of this bay. The wine is produced between 328 and 1,300 feet (100 and 400 m) in elevation and benefits from a Mediterranean climate refreshed by this altitude. Only the native grape varietals are used here: Piedirosso (locally Palummina), Sciascinoso, and Aglianico for the reds and rosés; Coda di Volpe Bianca, Verdeca (majority), Falanghina, Catalanesca, and Greco for the whites.

THE VINEYARD OF PANTELLERIA

LOCATION: almost halfway between Sicily and Tunisia.

VINES: they are placed in a hollow (*vite ad alberello*), then the branches are pressed to the ground in a radial arrangement to allow the plant to protect itself from the wind that blows here almost three hundred days a year. Rare dry wines and sweet wines are produced on Pantelleria. Equally incredible is the wine produced from these vines. Superlative in intensity, with captivating aromas.

HIGH POINT: Montagna Grande, 2,700 feet (836 m).

GEOLOGICAL PROFILE: 100 percent volcanic rocks, especially ignimbrite.

THE WINES TO DRINK: Moscato di Pantelleria and Passito di Pantelleria. They are both produced from the Muscat of Alexandria grape, locally known as Zibibbo. The Passito is the representative of a very old Italian tradition, known as *passito*, which consists of allowing the grapes to dry on the vine. The juice obtained is very concentrated in sugar, acidity, and aromas, which products extraordinary sweet wines.

VOLCANIC GEOGRAPHY

Volcanoes, some more or less active than others, are found in the southern part of Italy. Several vineyards have developed around them. There are four primary ones.

Terroirs of high elevation and warm soils

The vines planted on volcanoes grow several hundred meters above sea level. Their elevation induces an essential climatic factor for developing the character of the wines. An undeniable natural freshness is the result. The composition of soils is different from one volcano to another, but all have a high concentration of minerals and are highly fertile. These minerals have a distinct influence on the character of the wine, in particular on its tactile dimension—that is to say, the texture on the palate and the balance between the different flavors. The result is complex wines with marked salinity, sometimes minerally, always thin-bodied and with a sleek structure. With their flavor and balance, these unique wines sometimes have surprising aging capability.

THE ETNA VINEYARD

LOCATION: in Sicily, on the eastern coast of the island, north of Catania.

VINES: spread over the southern, eastern, and northern slopes of the mountain.

HIGH POINT: 10,900 feet (3,330 m).

GEOLOGICAL PROFILE: volcanic rocks with rare inclusions such as gabbro or sandstone.

THE WINES TO DRINK: the DOCs Etna Rosso, Etna Rosso Riserva, Etna Rosato, Etna Spumante, Etna Bianco, and Etna Bianco Superiore make up all the wines produced on the volcano. The grape varietals used are Nerello Mascalese and Nerello Cappuccio for the reds and rosés. The whites are produced from the Carricante and Catarratto grape varietals. A few vines of Trebbiano and Minella Bianca complete them.

THE AEOLIAN ISLANDS VINEYARD

LOCATION: a few nautical miles north of Sicily, the Aeolian archipelago consists of seventeen volcanic islands, seven of which are inhabited.

VINES: only four islands produce wine over a total area of 222 acres (90 ha). Salina and Lipari represent 90 percent of the volume produced; Stromboli and Panarea share the remaining 10 percent.

HIGH POINT: Salina, Monte Fossa delle Felci, 3,100 feet (962 m).

GEOLOGICAL PROFILE: volcanic rocks with numerous inclusions of sedimentary and metamorphic rocks.

THE WINES TO DRINK: Malvasia delle Lipari. These very rare wines, mostly sweet, are almost exclusively made from the Malvasia grape varietal. The local tradition is to harvest the grapes when fully ripe and then dry them in the sun for ten to fifteen days. This results in a natural drying that concentrates the sugars, acids, and aromas.

SKIP TO
GATHERING GRAPES, P. 158;
ORANGE WINE, P. 113;
HIGH-ELEVATION WINES, P. 381.

An emblem of *cibo di strada* (street food), this Italian sandwich takes forms from simple everyday homemade versions to gastronomic creations.

ANNA PRANDONI

PANINO

IN SEARCH OF THE LOST INVENTORS

JOHN MONTAGU → FALSE!
The Earl of Sandwich: in 1762, he was served slices of meat held between two slices of bread so he could continue playing cards. He may have contributed his name to it, but popular English theater of the sixteenth century and Shakespeare had already mentioned the idea.

THE CHINESE → MAYBE!
The *rou jia mo*, a small round loaf in the middle of which is placed meat, is found mentioned during the seventh to tenth centuries.

THE JEWISH POPULATION → MAYBE!
In the first century, Rabbi Hillel the Elder inaugurated the tradition of eating a mixture of fruits and spices between two slices of unleavened bread with bitter herbs in remembrance of the suffering of the Jews in Egypt.

THE ANCIENT GREEKS AND ROMANS → TRUE!
The idea of combining bread with an accompaniment, which could be cheese, lard, onions, or figs, was part of the eating habits of the ancient peoples. This habit continued over time without being given a name or codified.

ITS HISTORY

NINETEENTH CENTURY: Italy's first contact with the Anglo-Saxon tradition of the sandwich is as part of the Grand Tour of young English nobility in Europe. At the end of the century, it is eaten as a meal by the poor.

1910: the first distinction in Italian between the *panini gravidi* (literally "pregnant sandwiches") and the other sandwiches in *L'arte cucinaria in Italia* by Alberto Cougnet.

1930S: in search of quick modern meals, futurists Marinetti and Fillìa (authors of *The Manifesto of Futurist Cooking*) recognize in the *panino* a perfect icon. *Tra i due* ("between the two") replaces the English name and becomes the counterpart of the *tramezzino* (snack sandwiches), a term coined by poet Gabriele D'Annunzio.

1968: under American influence, the *panino* becomes a true meal everyone can enjoy, and even a festive dish (Sophia Loren, *In cucina con amore*, 1971).

1980S: panino, linked to the imagination of the American consumer, becomes the symbol of fast food in Milan, while evolving toward opulent shapes with gourmet ingredients.

SOME FAMOUS PANINI

ROUND LEAVENED BREADS

Michetta .... A small loaf with charcuterie (Lombardy).

Rosetta .... A rounded rose-shaped bread, perfect with speck (South Tyrol) or with mortadella (Emilia-Romagna).

Pani ca mèusa (or *vastedda* or *mafaldina*) .... A soft bread from Palermo filled with finely chopped veal spleen (*milza*) and cooked in lard *(Sicily)*.

5 e 5 .... A traditional flatbread from Livorno into which a *farinata*, a flat cake made of chickpea flour, is inserted (Tuscany).

Sole .... Topped with *lampredotto*, the veal caillette, typical of Florentine *cucina povera* (Tuscany).

Panino con la porchetta .... Slices of porchetta (boneless pork roast filled with herbs) in a *ciriola* oval-shaped bread, or *casereccio di Lariano* or *di Genzano*, thick loaves with a golden rind (Lazio).

Panino con il polpo grigliato .... With grilled octopus (Apulia).

BASED ON BIANCA OR FOCACCIA PIZZA

Schiacciata .... A sort of focaccia, but crispier, filled with local prosciutto and olive oil (Tuscany).

Pizza bianca .... Pizza dough with mortadella (Rome).

Panuozz .... A sandwich of pizza dough, filled with various ingredients—*scamorza*, *friarielli* (broccoli rabe shoots), or sausage (Naples).

Puccia pugliese .... Bread made from semolina flour with various fillings—tuna and tomatoes, green vegetables, and ricotta . . . (Apulia).

Ciabatta farcita .... Ciabatta bread, filled with mozzarella and tomatoes, charcuterie, vegetables . . . (throughout Italy).

RUSTIC COUNTRY BREAD

Tramezzino .... Two triangular slices of sandwich bread, filled (northern Italy).

Toast prosciutto cotto e fontina .... Toasted sandwich bread filled with cooked ham and cheese from the Aosta Valley (throughout Italy).

HOMEMADE BREAD

Panonta .... Filled with several layers of omelet, sausage, and bell peppers . . . (Molise).

Pane cunzato .... Semolina bread topped with *primosale* (a sheep's-milk cheese), anchovies, fresh tomatoes, oregano, and olive oil (Sicily).

Panino con la frittata .... Omelet sandwich (throughout Italy).

"PANINI"—THE OTHER MEANING

What are often referred to in other countries as paninis have little similarity to the Italian *panini*. Elsewhere, these are a commercially produced soft thin bread, toasted in a sandwich press, topped with cheese and other ingredients.

Founded in 2015, the Accademia del Panino Italiano carries out research and projects concerning panino, including PaninoMap, an app that lists the worldwide addresses where panini (and more generally, sandwiches) are made on-site to order.

SKIP TO
TRAMEZZINO, P. 319; FRITTATA, P. 356; PIADINA ROMAGNOLA (FLATBREAD SANDWICH), P. 122; TRIPPA ALLA ROMANA, P. 380.

SEASON
TUTTO L'ANNO (YEAR-ROUND)

CATEGORY
PRIMO PIATTO (FIRST COURSE)

LEVEL
FACILE (EASY)

MALLOREDDUS ALLA CAMPIDANESE

RICETTA *Iconica* RICETTA

SARDINIA

PASTA WITH SAUSAGE, TOMATO, AND SAFFRON

Although we often associate the islands with flavors from the sea, this rustic pasta dish is a testament to Sardinians' love for products from the land.

ILARIA BRUNETTI

A story related to wheat

In Roman times, around 250 BCE, Sardinia, along with Sicily, was considered the breadbasket of Rome. In 1706, in his book *Voyage du père Labat en Espagne et en Italie* (*Voyage of Father Labat in Spain and Italy*), clergyman Jean-Baptiste Labat praised the delicacy of Sardinian wheat, which provides "excellent *maccheroni* suitable for noble tables."

MALLOREDDUS

Malloreddus or *gnocchetti sardi* are short pastas made with durum wheat semolina flour, water, salt, and sometimes saffron, which is popular throughout the island. The pasta's name comes from the diminutive of *malloru* ("bull" in Sardinian), because they bulge like the belly of a small calf.

HOW DO YOU PREPARE THEM?

Once the dough is shaped into a ball (use just over ¾ cup/200 mL of water and ⅓ teaspoon/2 g salt for 2¼ cups/400 g durum wheat semolina flour), let it rest for 30 minutes, covered with a thin kitchen towel or placed in a plastic bag. Form long sausage-shaped logs about ¼ inch (5 mm) in diameter, cut them into small pieces, ⅓ to ⅔ inch (1 to 1.5 cm) long, and roll them with your index finger against a rough surface (traditionally these were then placed in a wicker basket, *su ciuliri* in the local language, where they were dried).

THE SAUCE

Malloreddus lend themselves to different sauces—from meat, vegetables, cheese, wild herbs, fish, and shellfish—or to soups. But their best-known use, even beyond Sardinia, is undoubtedly *alla campidanese*, from a region from southern Sardinia, prepared in a sauce made of tomato, pork sausage (traditionally flavored with wild fennel seeds), and grated Pecorino Sardo.

A TOUR OF THE ISLAND OF *GNOCCHETTI SARDI*

The same pasta—sometimes with small variations in size—have different names and seasonings depending on the area of Sardinia.

CIGGIONI
Province of Sassari—sheep ragù.

CHIUSONI
Gallura region—tomato sauce and pork.

CASSULI
Carloforte—Genoese pesto, tomatoes, and sometimes tuna.

ZIZZONES OR MACCARONES FURRIADOS
Province of Goceano—melted fresh cheese.

MACCARONES CRAVOS
Province of Nuoro—tomato sauce and pecorino cheese.

THE RECIPE

It was this recipe from her grandmother Marisa that made chef Simone Tondo (Racines, Paris 2nd) fall in love with cooking.

SERVES 4

- 1 onion
- 2 tablespoons (30 mL) olive oil
- 14 ounces (400 g) fresh sausage with wild fennel seeds (or use plain fresh sausage and add fennel seeds to the tomato sauce)
- ¼ cup (60 mL) white wine
- 14 ounces (400 g) tomato sauce
- 1 pinch ground saffron
- Salt
- 14 ounces (400 g) malloreddus pasta
- 3 to 3½ ounces (80 to 100 g) Pecorino Sardo, aged ideally 6 months

Finely chop the onion and brown it in the olive oil in a pan over low heat. Add the sausage, crumbling it into small pieces with your hands, and brown it with the onion for 5 minutes. Deglaze the pan with the wine. Cook for another 5 minutes, then add the tomato sauce and saffron. Season with salt. Cover and cook over low heat for at least 1 hour.

Cook the malloreddus in salted boiling water, drain, then add the noodles to the sauce. Divide the pasta among serving plates. Sprinkle with the grated pecorino.

SKIP TO
FENNEL, P. 233; SAFFRON, P. 291; PASTA INVENTORY, P. 124; SAUSAGE, P. 332.

SEASON

PRIMAVERA, ESTATE (SPRING, SUMMER)

CATEGORY

ANTIPASTO/ PRIMO PIATTO (APPETIZER OR FIRST COURSE)

LEVEL

FACILE (EASY)

PANZANELLA

BREAD SALAD

When properly prepared, bread moistened in a salad with tomatoes and onions can deliver a most refreshing experience.

SACHA LOMNITZ

THE STORY OF A MIRACLE

The tradition of *panmolle* (soaked bread) accompanied with vegetables appeared long before the arrival of tomatoes in Italy. But did this idea arise from peasants who used dry bread in their dishes or from sailors who would soak their bread in seawater and eat it with legumes? According to a legend from the fourteenth century, this idea is a gift from the blessed Sienese merchant Giovanni Colombini. By wetting a crust of bread and a dry olive tree with his tears, he fed the destitute who followed him with salted bread in olive oil.

TO QUOTE IN PASSING . . .

A simple poor man's dish par excellence, *panzanella* has inspired great authors and renowned artists.

→ *Pan lavato* (washed bread), as mentioned in Boccaccio's *Decameron* (1349–1353), helps restore hope to a woman afflicted with a thousand ailments.

→ Bronzino, a mannerist painter in the Medici court during the sixteenth century, declared his complete love for panzanella in a poem in praise of the onion.

THE RECIPE

Michele Farnesi, chef of Dilia restaurant (Paris 20th), offers a traditional version inherited from his family from Lucca.

SERVES 4

1⅛ pounds (500 g) ripe tomatoes (such as Costoluto Fiorentino or beef heart)

Salt

3 tablespoons (45 mL) red wine vinegar

6 tablespoons (90 mL) olive oil (preferably Tuscan extra-virgin)

1⅛ pounds (500 g) stale bread

1 red onion

Small bunch basil

Ideally, prepare this salad the day before or a few hours in advance of serving. If doing so, do not season it too much to avoid breaking down the vegetables. Cut the tomatoes into cubes or quarters, season with salt, drizzle with the vinegar and olive oil, and let them drain. Dice or tear the bread into pieces and mix it with the tomatoes in a bowl. Let rest in the refrigerator while the bread softens. Slice the onion into thin strips and add it to the bowl. Finely chop the basil and add it to the bowl. Adjust the seasoning (salt, vinegar, and oil), if necessary.

THE CHEF'S VERSION

Cut the stale bread into large cubes, toast them in the oven, then immerse them two-thirds of the way in the juice from the tomatoes to soften them, keeping the top third of the bread cubes crisp. Arrange the other ingredients on the crisp side of the bread. You can use anchovies in a green sauce, or perhaps very simply ricotta and fresh onion.

ELSEWHERE IN ITALY

Panzanella can be found throughout central Italy.

UMBRIA—with *cipollotto nocerino* (a small sweet onion), thin slices of *sedano nero* (black celery) from Trevi, and thinly sliced carrots.

MARCHE—with minced garlic and *mentuccia* (*Calamintha nepeta*, lesser calamint) in place of basil, lettuce leaves, or parsley.

LAZIO—with *casareccio di Genzano* IGP bread with a dark crust, a soft, airy crumb, and the scent of grains. Arrange the large slices soaked in water at the bottom of serving plates, then cover them with tomato, cucumber, onion, and, as an option, capers.

The variations

Purists will tell you that true Tuscan panzanella contains only soaked bread, tomato, onion, basil, and cucumber. However, it can be creatively embellished to liven up the family table:

***Nonna* Rossella,**
Mina and Neri's grandmother, adds hard-boiled eggs.

***Mamma* Fede,**
Tito's mom, enriches it with anchovy fillets in oil.

***Zio* Checco,**
Tito's uncle, likes it with crumbled tuna; *cugini* (cousins) Camilla, Irene, and Samuele add pressed ham.

***Nonno* Paolo,**
Tito's best friend's grandfather, toasts the bread.

Kudos to all the families who create their own! Add what inspires you: arugula, fennel, sheep's-milk cheese . . .

SKIP TO
PAPPA AL POMODORO, P. 367;
BREADS FOR SURVIVAL, P. 38;
THE ART OF RIBOLLITA, P. 368.

THE (RE)NAISSANCE OF VEGETABLES

During the *Rinascimento* (Renaissance), the Italians exceled with their accomplishments not only in painters' workshops but also in the fields. What delights did their harvest baskets contain?

XAVIER MATHIAS

Great Agronomists

Italians during the fifteenth century not only shined in the fields of painting and sculpture but also in agriculture! Italian agriculture exercised a near dominance over the discovery and rediscovery of vegetables. Over the centuries, all kitchens benefited from the richness of the Italian harvest.

Through hybridization to obtain new species or subspecies, and with the ability to cultivate crops to produce even more appetizing products, the Italians spread the beauty of the Renaissance through their fields. They stood out not only for their ability to properly cook vegetables but also for their agricultural expertise in cultivating them. In 1544, the Italian Mattioli published *Commentarii in libros sex Pedacii Dioscoridis*, a work on botany that all European courts used as reference.

Rabelaisian Heritage

During a stay in Rome, François Rabelais maintained correspondence with a French clergyman and sent him a number of seeds "which the Holy Father can sow in his secret garden at Belvedere." He is said to have introduced three principal vegetables into France: the artichoke, romaine lettuce, and the melon.

VEGETABLES FROM ITALY

ARTICHOKE · *CARCIOFO*
→ In 1575, chronicler L'Estoile reported that Catherine de' Medici, who was crazy about the artichoke, ate so much of it that she *cuida crever* (almost died). Considered at the time to be a fruit, it was through the Italian court that this humble thistle became so respected!

EGGPLANT · *MELANZANA*
→ Although its Italian name probably comes from the Latin *mela insane* (unhealthy apple), the Italians enjoyed it as early as the thirteenth century after its introduction to Sicily by Arab merchants.

CELERY · *SEDANO*
→ Its etymological root comes from Italy (*seleri* in Lombard), where it was known to the Romans as a medicinal plant. It was introduced into cooking during the great plague that affected Sicily during the seventeenth century. Ribbed varietals spread throughout at a later time.

CAULIFLOWER AND BROCCOLI · *CAVOLOFIORE E BROCCOLO*
→ A creation of the Romans, broccoli was developed from the finest specimens of wild cabbage. It was very quickly enjoyed by the elites, to the detriment of the other cabbages, which were left to the tables of the commoners. It was a delight of Catherine de' Medici, who was responsible for its use spreading throughout France.

Cauliflower, likely indigenous to the Near East, was known to the Romans but fell into oblivion. It was rediscovered in Europe during the sixteenth century when Genoese sailors brought it back from the Levant. In the mid-nineteenth century, romanesco cabbage (*broccolo romanesco*) was developed from Roman varietals of cauliflower.

ZUCCHINI · *ZUCCHINA*
→ It's actually a small summer squash consumed when not fully matured, a strange and delicious habit that emerged in Italy during the nineteenth century. During the eighteenth century, gardeners and farmers in Italy had selected a group of varietals that lent themselves perfectly to this use thanks to their small size and ability to continually provide new growth—provided they were picked regularly. This is the cultigroup of zucchini.

FENNEL · *FINOCCHIO*
→ *"Finocchio e pane mi bastua!"* ("All I need is bread and fennel!") This is a popular Venetian saying that gives us an idea of the importance of this sweet, bulbous vegetable.

TOMATO · *POMODORO*
→ Almost all of Europe was long suspicious of this nightshade plant. It was not until 1778 that *Solanum lycopersicum*, its scientific name, migrated to the category of vegetable plant in the catalog of ornamental plants by the Vilmorin-Andrieux House, the famous French seed producer. In contrast, as early as the sixteenth century, the Italians had adopted what they nicknamed the *pomodoro* (golden apple, or "apple of love"). Provence, under the dual influence of Spain in the west and Italy in the east, successfully developed the first tomato crops at the beginning of the seventeenth century.

SKIP TO
ARTICHOKES, P. 100;
FENNEL, P. 233; ZUCCHINI, P. 234;
CABBAGE & CO., P. 334;
EGGPLANT, P. 266.

BITTER LETTUCES

Cultivated in Italy since the fifteenth century, these chicories from the Asteraceae family enhance Italy's winter dishes and are renowned for their digestive properties. This is all the more reason to enjoy them.

ALESSANDRA PIERINI

(1)

CICORIA BIANCA OR PAN DI ZUCCHERO

Common chicory

(Cichorium intybus)

ORIGIN—Lombardy and northern Italy.

PROFILE—long, crisp light green to white leaves, very compact; bitter, with an almond note (the heart is sweeter). Harvested from September to November.

IN COOKING—raw in salads, but most often steamed or cooked au gratin.

(2)

SCAROLA

Escarole

(Cichorium endivia var. *latifolium)*

ORIGIN—southern Italy.

PROFILE—moderately bitter; crunchy heart surrounded by jagged leaves. Harvested from October to March.

IN COOKING—raw in salads; panfried; baked/roasted; steamed; as a stuffing; in savory pies, risottos, soups.

(3) (4)

RADICCHIO ROSA DEL VENETO AND ROSA DI SIMONE

Radicchio

(Cichorium intybus)

ORIGIN—Veneto.

PROFILE—delicate, with a slight note of bitterness balanced by a somewhat sweet finish; color ranging from soft pink to pastel purple. Harvested from November to March.

IN COOKING—as a salad; in risottos; braised.

(5)

RADICCHIO ROSSO DI TREVISO TARDIVO IGP OR SPADONE

Treviso red chicory

(Cichorium intybus)

ORIGIN—Veneto.

PROFILE—intense red-purplish color with white streaks; the most elegant and refined version has lanceolate leaves; delicately bitter. Harvested between October and February.

IN COOKING—in risottos, soups, pastas, focaccia, stuffings; fried, braised, marinated, baked/roasted, in salads, in sweet-and-sour dishes, in jam. It goes well with creamy cheeses (Gorgonzola, Taleggio), walnuts, and hazelnuts.

(6)

ROSA DI GORIZIA

Gorizia Rose

(Cichorium intybus sativum)

ORIGIN—Friuli-Venezia Giulia.

PROFILE—intense and slightly bitter; glossy leaves from deep pink to garnet red. Harvested between late November and January. Very rare. Protected by Slow Food.

IN COOKING—raw or cooked; for an aperitif with hard-boiled egg, as served in the *frasche* risottos; *orzotto* (barley-based risotto); in *frico*; in potato and bean soup; in pastry. The extract is used in the composition of amari or grappa.

(7) (8)

RADICCHIO ROSSO DI CHIOGGIA IGP AND DI VERONA IGP

Round and semilong chicory

(Cichorium intybus var. *silvestre)*

ORIGIN—Veneto.

PROFILE—from sweet to moderately bitter; very compact intense red leaves with white veins and leaves. The one from Chioggia is round, in a ball; the one from Verona is more oval and pointed. There is an early varietal (April to July) and a late varietal (September to March).

IN COOKING—raw in salad; braised; baked; in savory pies, risottos, pasta. After infusion and distillation, an amaro is made.

(9) (10)

RADICCHIO VARIEGATO DI LUSIA AND DI CASTELFRANCO IGP

Classico/variegated chicory

(Cichorium intybus)

ORIGIN—Veneto.

PROFILE—delicate, fairly sweet, bitter aftertaste; compact central ball and relaxed outer leaves, marbled with purple-red on a white-yellow background, thin and crisp. Harvested from October to January.

IN COOKING—raw in salads, especially with walnuts and Gorgonzola, rarely cooked; whole leaves are usually rolled and stuffed.

(3) (8) (7)

(9)

(15) (13)

(11)

RADICCHIO ROSSO DI TREVISO PRECOCE IGP

Early Treviso radicchio

(Cichorium intybus)

ORIGIN—Veneto.

PROFILE—bitter; less dense than the late variety, larger and more flexible leaves, intense red; the head is compact and elongated. Harvested from September to October.

IN COOKING—raw in *pinzimonio* (a preparation of olive oil, vinegar, salt, and black pepper as a dip for raw vegetables), but preferably cooked, braised, or grilled; in pasta, risottos; in creams, jellies.

(12)

PUNTARELLA

Catalonian chicory

(Cichorium intybus)

ORIGIN—Veneto (Cicoria Catalogna di Chioggia), Lazio (Cicoria Catalogna Frastagliata di Gaeta).

PROFILE—pleasantly bitter, tender and crunchy texture; large bulb surrounded by leaves similar to a dandelion, with a heart of stems in the shape of asparagus. Harvested from mid-October to mid-February.

IN COOKING—the raw heart in salad with garlic and anchovies; leaves sautéed in pasta or as an accompaniment.

(13) (14) (15)

CICORIA A GRUMOLO ROSSA, VERDE E MISCUGLIO DI CAMPO OR PAESANA

Red-heart chicory, mixed green, or field chicory

(Cichorium intybus)

ORIGIN—northern Italy (Zuccherina di Trieste, Friuli-Venezia Giulia; Radicio Verdon da Cortel, Veneto; Ceriolo, Capolino, Sciroeu, Lombardy; Gorgnalini, Emilia-Romagna).

PROFILE—bitter, fresh, crunchy, herbaceous; thick, rose-shaped leaves. Harvested in winter and spring.

IN COOKING—as a salad with hard-boiled egg, shellfish, charcuterie, or cheeses; sautéed; in stuffings.

SKIP TO
GORGONZOLA, P. 318; AMARO, P. 210; PUNTARELLE ALLA ROMANA, P. 135.

(1) (4) (2) (6) (12) (10) (5) (11) (14)

RECIPE

SCAROLA 'MBUTTUNATA (STUFFED ESCAROLE)

- Wash and drain a head of escarole, split it in half, and stuff it with 4 anchovy fillets (ideally those canned in oil from Cetara), about a dozen pine nuts and raisins, and 3 or 4 pitted black olives (from Gaeta, if possible). Season lightly with pepper.
- Close up the head of escarole gently, tie with kitchen twine to secure, and brown it over low heat in a sauté pan with plenty of olive oil, garlic, and a handful of capers, covered, for about 20 minutes.
- Turn it over to evenly brown on all sides. When done, it should be golden brown, tender, and moist.

SEASON

TUTTO L'ANNO (YEAR-ROUND)

CATEGORY

DOLCI (DESSERT)

LEVEL

FACILE (EASY)

SALAME DI L'ITALIA CIOCCOLATO

ITALIAN CHOCOLATE SALAMI

RICETTA Iconica RICETTA

THROUGHO[UT] ITALY

A great classic as simple as it is addictive, this chocolate dessert is a delight for both young and old.

ILARIA BRUNETTI

This is not a salami...

. . . but instead a dessert, well known and appreciated throughout Italy. Made with cocoa powder or chocolate, biscuits (hard cookies), butter, eggs, and a hint of rum, it's formed into a large log shape. The cookies represent the fat found in a typical salami. The log is sometimes coated in confectioners' sugar and wrapped with a string for more realism.

WHERE DOES IT COME FROM?

→ Some say it originates from Portugal, where it can still be found.

→ Others believe it is originally from Sicily, where it is called *salame turco* (Turkish sausage). In this version, almonds from Aversa or pistachios from Bronte are added, and Marsala replaces the rum.

→ In Piedmont, where it is also common, the region's famous hazelnut is part of the recipe.

→ It can now be found throughout Italy, each region with its own version!

THE RECIPE

This recipe comes from my mother, Irene. It dates back to my great-grandmother Paolina, so it has been handed down through the generations. I've yet to find anyone who can resist it.

SERVES 6

¾ cup (100 g) whole almonds

7 ounces (200 g) dark chocolate

14 tablespoons (200 g) unsalted butter

2 large (38 g) very fresh egg yolks

¼ cup (50 g) sugar

1 tiny glass (about 2 tablespoons/30 mL) rum

9 ounces (250 g) hard cookies, such as Petit Beurre or Thé Lu (in Italy, these are called Oro Saiwa: dry, crisp, and without butter), crushed

---

Preheat the oven to 285°F (140°C). Boil the almonds for 2 minutes. Drain them, then run them under cold water to remove the skins by squeezing the nuts lightly between your thumb and forefinger. Spread them over a baking sheet and place in the oven for 10 minutes to dry. Coarsely chop them once cooled.

Finely chop the chocolate and place it in a bowl. Melt the butter in a saucepan over low heat, then let cool. In a separate bowl, beat together the egg yolks and sugar. Add the melted butter, chocolate, rum, almonds, and cookies.

With this quantity, you can prepare a large "salami" 12 inches (30 cm) long and 2⅓ inches (6 cm) in diameter, or make two small ones, which will be easier to cut and eat with your fingers. Arrange the mixture lengthwise on a piece of parchment paper and form it into a salami shape.

Wrap up the salami in the parchment, closing the ends securely. Roll it on top of the work surface to create a log shape, then place it in the freezer. Remove it about 10 minutes before enjoying it, cut into slices.

SKIP TO

THE BRONTE PISTACHIO, P. 35;
THE HAZELNUT, P. 144;
ALMONDS, P. 173.

ALMONDS

Pampered by the hot and dry climate of Apulia and Sicily, the *mandorla* is one of the flagship ingredients of Italian pastry, but it also shines in savory recipes.

ALESSANDRA PIERINI

WHAT AM I?

The fruit of the almond tree (*Prunus dulcis*), native to Asia. It arrived in Sicily in 2500 BCE thanks to Phoenician trade, then spread throughout the Mediterranean basin.

But it's also the kernel of some stone fruits (*armellina*). Those of apricot or peach, with their bitter aftertaste, are used in baking to intensify the taste of sweet almond.

SWEET OR BITTER?

The main subspecies are:

LA SATIVA, the most widespread, sweet, and edible.

AMARA, smaller and drier, bitter, to be consumed in minute quantities because it contains the toxic chemical hydrocyanic acid.

The most famous varietals

Mandorla della val di Noto

(Sicily, Slow Food), which includes three varietals:

→ ***Pizzuta d'Avola***: elliptical, wide, flat, and regular with a small tip (*pizzu* in Sicilian), the most sought after especially for making *confetti* (dragées), including the famous Sulmona (Abruzzo); crunchy and rich in essential oils; intense, sweet, and milky taste.

→ ***Romana*** **or** ***corrente d'Avola***: triangular, irregular; intense, vanilla flavor with a bitter honey aftertaste.

→ ***Fascionello***: round, irregular; the least aromatic of the three but very mild, fattier, with a supple texture.

Mandorla di Torritto

(Apulia, Slow Food): small and plump; balanced taste, intense and sweet at the same time, with buttery, slightly acidic, melt-in-the-mouth and oily notes.

BUT ALSO:

Mandorla di Navelli (Abruzzo), *piacentina* (Emilia-Romagna), *sarda* (Sardinia).

HARVESTING

Harvesting takes place in two stages: fresh almonds are picked from May to June before reaching full maturity (they remain tender and subtly sweet for a month); the remaining almonds are harvested dry from August to September.

RECIPE

PESTO ALLA TRAPANESE (SICILIAN TOMATO AND ALMOND PESTO)

SERVES 4

14 ounces (400 g) fresh ripe but firm tomatoes (Roma, beef heart, etc.) or canned peeled tomatoes

⅓ cup (50 g) blanched almonds

2 cloves garlic (preferably red garlic from Nubia), peeled

20 basil leaves

⅓ cup (30 g) grated aged pecorino cheese

1 drizzle olive oil

Salt and freshly ground black pepper

- Place the tomatoes in a pot of boiling water for 2 to 3 minutes, drain, then let cool and remove the skins. Working in batches, combine the almonds, garlic, tomatoes, and basil in a blender and blend until you get a homogeneous and fairly liquid mixture. (Alternatively, you can use a mortar.) Transfer the pesto to a deep dish, add the pecorino and olive oil, stir well to combine, and season with salt and pepper.
- Stir in freshly drained pasta until combined, then serve. Ideal with *busiate* (a twisted and rough-textured pasta, typical of Sicily), *bucatini*, or *spaghettoni*.

Tip: Before serving, sprinkle with toasted dried bread crumbs or grated tuna bottarga.

THE ALMOND IN ALL ITS FORMS!

① IN THE SHELL

Long-lasting flavor and aroma.

② SKIN ON

For *torrone*, *croccante*, granita, dragées, liqueurs; with goat's-milk or blue-veined cheeses.

③ BLANCHED

For *pesto alla trapanese*; velvety; added at the end of cooking with vegetables (cauliflower, broccoli, asparagus, zucchini, eggplant); creams; *cuscus dolce*; *torta caprese*; dragées; *amaretti*; *ricciarelli* (cookies); *mandorlato* (nougat).

④ CRUSHED

As a final sprinkling for salads, soups, pasta, risotto; fillings; fruit salads.

⑤ GROUND/FLOUR

As a coating for white meats and fish; pastry; almond paste (*marzapane* or *pasta reale*; *frutta martorana*).

⑥ OIL

Fish; pastry.

⑦ AS A SPREAD

A pure paste with added sugar, oil, and cocoa butter.

⑧ AS PURE PASTE

Mixed with water, to replace milk; gelato; chocolate confections; pastry.

And also . . .

Sliced, grilled, as a milk, in marzipan . . .

SKIP TO

COOKIES, P. 154; SWEETS FROM THE CONVENT, P. 204; NOUGATS, P. 326.

THE GENEALOGY OF ROMAN PASTA

The Italian capital isn't just about the Colosseum, Saint Peter's Basilica, and the Trevi Fountain. It also boasts some of Italy's most famous pasta dishes, each with a fascinating family tree.

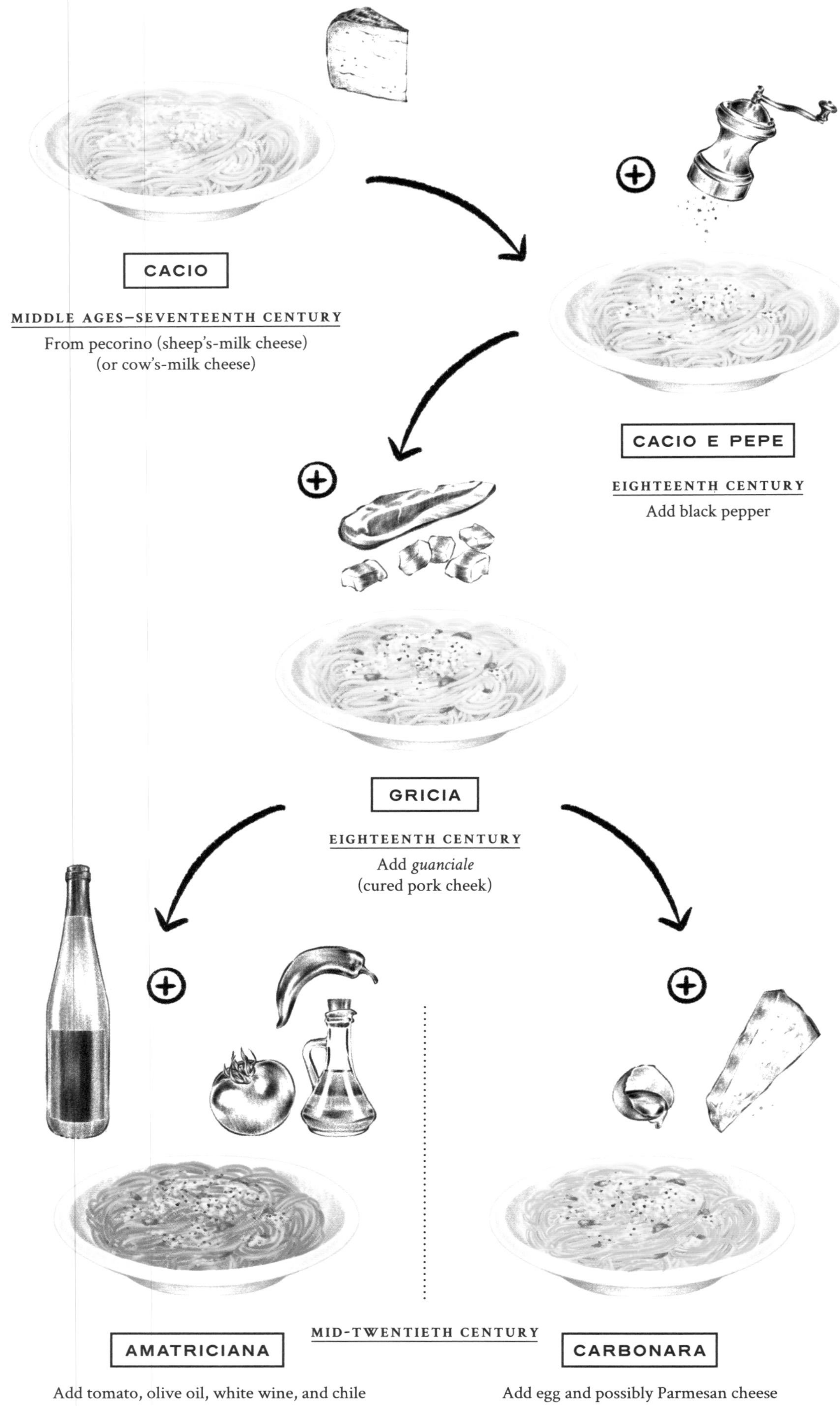

CACIO

MIDDLE AGES–SEVENTEENTH CENTURY

From pecorino (sheep's-milk cheese) (or cow's-milk cheese)

CACIO E PEPE

EIGHTEENTH CENTURY

Add black pepper

GRICIA

EIGHTEENTH CENTURY

Add *guanciale* (cured pork cheek)

MID-TWENTIETH CENTURY

AMATRICIANA

Add tomato, olive oil, white wine, and chile

CARBONARA

Add egg and possibly Parmesan cheese

ADDRESS BOOK

CACIO E PEPE

DA CESARE
(Cesare al Casaletto)
→ *Via del Casaletto, 45*
TRATTORIADACESARE.IT

GRICIA

ARMANDO AL PANTHEON
→ *Salita dei Crescenzi*
ARMANDOALPANTHEON.IT

AMATRICIANA

OSTERIA PALMIRA
→ *Via Abate Ugone 29*
OSTERIAPALMIRA.IT

CARBONARA

SALUMERIA ROSCIOLI
→ *Via dei Giubbonari, 21, 00186*
SALUMERIAROSCIOLI.COM

ALSO TRY THESE ROMAN PASTA DISHES BY . . .

Luciano Monosilio
LUCIANO CUCINA ITALIANA
Piazza del Teatro di Pompeo, 18

Adriano Baldassarre
L'AVVOLGIBILE
Circonvallazione Appia, 56

Tommaso Pennestri
TRATTORIA PENNESTRI
Via Giovanni da Empoli, 5

Sarah Cicolini
SANTO PALATO
Piazza Tarquinia, 4a/b

SEASON

TUTTO L'ANNO (YEAR-ROUND)

CATEGORY

PRIMO PIATTO (FIRST COURSE)

LEVEL

DIFFICOLTÀ MEDIA (MEDIUM DIFFICULTY)

CACIO E PEPE

PASTA WITH CHEESE AND BLACK PEPPER

Pecorino Romano, black pepper, and *basta*! Although seemingly simple, this emblematic Roman dish requires a bit of skill.

FRANÇOIS-RÉGIS GAUDRY

A SHEPHERD'S DISH

Dry pasta, black pepper, and Pecorino Romano cheese: these nonperishable ingredients once filled the bags of Lazio shepherds during the seasonal movement of their flocks.

The invigorating marriage of *maccheroni* with cheese is documented as early as the fourteenth century in *Liber de coquina* (anonymous), the oldest treatise on cooking from the Christian West. Black pepper was included in the eighteenth century. This spice would "warm you up" during cold weather.

Cacio e pepe became a classic dish at Roman *locande* (inns) during the nineteenth century. Innkeepers had the reputation of overusing cheese and also adding salt to *intorzare* (trick) the customers into drinking more wine.

BLACK PEPPER, FROM ARISTOCRACY TO *CUCINA POVERA*

→ A precious spice reserved for the aristocratic classes during antiquity, black pepper made a fortune for the Republic of Venice in the Middle Ages.

→ It became more widespread during the eighteenth and nineteenth centuries, thanks to the growing trade with the Portuguese, then the English and Dutch.

→ Starting from the nineteenth century, it became a part of peasant cuisine and an ingredient in cucina povera.

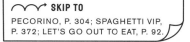

SKIP TO
PECORINO, P. 304; SPAGHETTI VIP, P. 372; LET'S GO OUT TO EAT, P. 92.

THE GOLDEN RULES

Despite its minimal number of ingredients, cacio e pepe is one of the most difficult pasta recipes to make. It cannot be simplified to precise proportions; instead, it must be practiced.

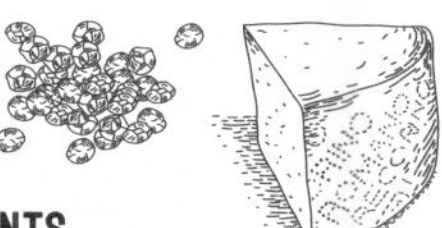

INGREDIENTS

No olive oil, no butter, no cream—just the pasta cooking water, cheese, and black pepper!

THE CHEESE

Use Pecorino Romano, ideally aged for twelve months. In order to create a good emulsion, it should not be grated too finely or too coarsely. It also serves to salt the dish.

THE BLACK PEPPER

Use a good-quality black pepper and grind it fresh, but not too finely.

THE PASTA

SPAGHETTI—this is the most popular type of pasta and the best compromise.

RIGATONI—traditional, but seen less often, as it's more difficult to emulsify with the cheese.

TONNARELLI—a long pasta, the Roman variant of *maccheroni alla chitarra* from Abruzzo: there are many fans of this style, but the pasta is porous and tends to absorb too much of the sauce.

THE CHEESE CREAM

The "original" version is simple and without embellishment, but the success of this recipe relies on an emulsion made with the cheese and the pasta cooking water, added in approximately equal parts. The sauce must be sufficiently creamy while also remaining quite "dry" and not too rich. If the temperature of the water is too hot, the cheese may become stringy and compact into a ball; if the temperature of the water is too cool, the emulsion will be grainy.

THE NUMBER OF SERVINGS

It's best to prepare cacio e pepe for two people, with four as the maximum. Beyond that, success in making the dish will be more or less random.

THE RECIPE

Roman cook Giovanni Passerini (Restaurant Passerini, Paris 12th) makes a classic cacio e pepe.

SERVES 4

14 ounces (400 g) spaghetti
Coarse salt
Freshly ground black pepper
2 cups (200 g) grated Pecorino Romano cheese

Cook the spaghetti in 1 gallon (4 L) boiling water with 1 tablespoon (20 g) salt (the cheese is very salty).

Meanwhile, in a large hot—but not too hot—skillet, add a good 7 or 8 turns of the pepper mill, pour in about 6 tablespoons (90 g) tap water, and let the pepper cook for a few minutes. Increase the heat and bring to a boil, then turn off the heat and let the pepper infuse; the water should turn a light brown color and stay warm.

When the spaghetti is cooked al dente, set aside a ladleful of the pasta cooking water, then drain the pasta and add it to the skillet (with the heat still off), distributing it evenly over the bottom of the pan. Add enough of the reserved pasta cooking water to partially cover the pasta, about half of what would fully submerge the pasta. Wait several seconds for the pasta to cool a little. Keep the warm pasta water and a cup of cold tap water nearby.

Sprinkle ¾ cup (70 g) of the pecorino over the pasta, distributing it well. Using a spatula or tongs, mix the pasta in a circular fashion with one hand while pushing and pulling the pan by its handle with your other hand. The mixture should become creamy. If the cheese is thin, add a drizzle of cold water. If the cheese remains grainy, add a little of the warm cooking water.

Divide the spaghetti among four plates, sprinkle with the remaining pecorino, and top with a few turns of pepper. Serve.

Il Tocco Dello Chef (Chef's Tip)

When black truffle is in season, grate it over the top . . . and the cacio e pepe takes on another dimension!

SESASON

TUTTO L'ANNO (YEAR-ROUND)

CATEGORY

PRIMO PIATTO (FIRST COURSE)

LEVEL

DIFFICOLTÀ MEDIA (MEDIUM DIFFICULTY)

GRICIA

PASTA WITH CHEESE, BLACK PEPPER, AND PORK

It doesn't have quite the same popularity as *cacio e pepe*, but this pecorino, black pepper, and *guanciale* combination is often considered the most authentically Roman dish.

FRANÇOIS-RÉGIS GAUDRY

ITS ORIGINS

→ A peasant dish originating in the region of Amatrice, a town in Lazio on the border with Abruzzo, *gricia* is said to be the ancestral dish of *amatriciana* before the arrival of the tomato in the region during the eighteenth century. In other words, it's an *amatriciana bianca* (white amatriciana).

→ It shares the flavor of Pecorino Romano and black pepper with cacio e pepe, but it is distinguished by the addition of guanciale and lard (the latter is less frequently used today), two sources of animal protein that could be preserved for long periods. Acccording to some historians, before this mixture became a sauce used for pasta, it was intended to accompany bread.

WHERE DOES ITS NAME COME FROM?

TWO THEORIES

From the town of Grisciano (in the province of Rieti), 9 miles (15 km) from Amatrice. This would explain why the old spelling *griscia* is sometimes used.

From the word *gricio*, which, during the nineteenth century in Rome and its surrounding area, designated a seller of bread and other foodstuffs originating in the canton of Grisons (Graubünden), Switzerland.

THE RECIPE

This is Giovanni Passerini's favorite Roman pasta (Restaurant Passerini, Paris 12th). Why? "It is less rich than a carbonara and less 'camouflaged' than an amatriciana!" He usually cooks it with short *mezze maniche* pasta.

SERVES 4

Coarse salt
10½ ounces (300 g) guanciale (cured pork cheek)
14 ounces (400 g) mezze maniche pasta
Freshly ground black pepper
¾ cup (80 g) grated Pecorino Romano cheese

Bring 1 gallon (4 L) water to a boil with 1 tablespoon (20 g) salt (the guanciale and pecorino are salted). Remove the rind from the guanciale. Slice the meat ¼ inch (5 mm) thick, then into sticks about 1⅛ inches (3 cm) long and ⅔ inch (1.5 cm) wide. Brown the guanciale in a large pan over low heat to melt the fat, then increase the heat and fry until golden brown.

Cook the pasta al dente. Set aside about 1 cup (250 mL) of the cooking water, then drain the pasta and add it to the pan with the guanciale. Stir, add a little of the cooking water, and cook for 2 minutes to bind everything together, adding more of the cooking water if necessary. The starch in the pasta and the fat will bind with the water. Remove from the heat and let stand for 1 minute. Season with a few turns of the pepper mill.

Sprinkle half the pecorino over the pasta in three parts, stirring vigorously to avoid lumps. The pecorino should not become stringy! Divide among four plates, then sprinkle evenly with the remaining pecorino. Season again with a few turns of the pepper mill.

☞ *Il Tocco Dello Chef (Chef's Tip)*

Add a few fresh mint leaves to each dish. It's delicious!

PASTA CHOICES

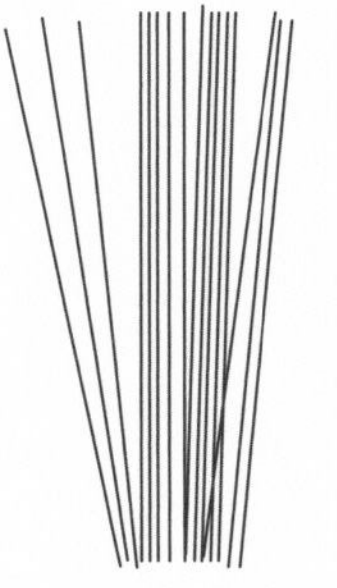

Spaghetti

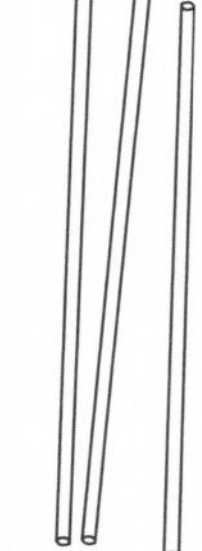

Bucatini

Rigatoni

Mezze maniche

SKIP TO
THE ART OF PORK FAT, P. 70; THE TASTE OF SHAPE, P. 317; PECORINO, P. 304.

SEASON
TUTTO L'ANNO (YEAR-ROUND)

CATEGORY
PRIMO PIATTO (FIRST COURSE)

LEVEL
FACILE (EASY)

AMATRICIANA

PASTA WITH GUANCIALE AND TOMATO

From Rome to rest of the world via Abruzzo, this pasta dish of rural origins is a living legend!

FRANÇOIS-RÉGIS GAUDRY

UNA GRICIA ROSSA

→ Born between the regions of Lazio and Abruzzo, *amatriciana* (or *matriciana* in Roman dialect) takes its name from the city of Amatrice. This recipe is the *rossa* (tomato) descendant of the dish *gricia*. Cultivated from the 1750s in the region of Naples, the tomato quickly spread to the kingdom of the Bourbons, on which Amatrice depended.

→ It was only from the middle of the nineteenth century that this rural recipe became known in Rome. Impacted by the pastoral crisis of the time, the shepherds of the Amatrice region went to the city to sell their products. Some even opened *locande* (inns), where the recipe was discovered. (These inns at the time were nicknamed *matricio.*)

The official sauce

Since 2019, *amatriciana tradizionale* has benefited from the STG (*specialità tradizionale garantita*) label: made of *guanciale amatriciano* (cured pork cheek produced in the region), dry white wine, tomato, Pecorino di Amatrice or Pecorino Romano DOP, extra-virgin olive oil, chile, salt, and black pepper.

PASTA CHOICES

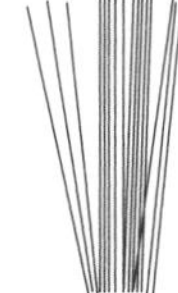

Spaghetti—this is the mandatory format of the official recipe of the city of Amatrice.

Bucatini—this is the format preferred by the Romans.

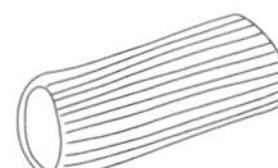

Rigatoni et tonnarelli—this is becoming more and more in vogue.

GARLIC AND/OR ONION?

This is forbidden in the official recipe but used in some versions, before adding the bacon.

FAT?

The use of olive oil seems to be more recent. In the old recipe, the fat of the guanciale and possibly lard were the only known fats.

AMATRICIANA, A MOVIE STAR

This recipe is celebrated by many directors: Ettore Scola in *C'eravamo Tanto Amati* (*We All Loved Each Other So Much*), 1974; the "Exemplary Citizen" sketch in *Viva Italia* (*I Nuovi Mostri*), 1977; Alberto Sordi in *Un Tassinaro a New York* (*A Taxi Driver in New York*), 1987; Giorgio Pàstina in *Cameriera bella presenza offersi* (*Housemaid*), 1951 . . .

A KOSHER VERSION

The Jewish community in Rome has adapted amatriciana to the rules of kashruth: dried beef replaces guanciale and pecorino is omitted in this version of the recipe.

THE RECIPE

A native Roman, Luana Belmondo shares her family secrets with us: "My mother prepared amatriciana on Mondays with ingredients from the pantry and the guanciale that my father would cure in our cellar. At home, the eldest were served first; I was the last served, but I got the best part because the sauce was at the bottom of the dish!"

SERVES 4

- 4¼ ounces (120 g) guanciale (cured pork cheek; from Amatrice, if possible)
- 1 tablespoon (15 mL) olive oil
- 2½ tablespoons (40 g) white wine
- 6 fresh San Marzano tomatoes (out of season, use 12 ounces/350 g canned whole peeled tomatoes instead)
- Salt
- 1 small piece chile
- 14 ounces (400 g) bucatini or spaghetti
- 3 to 3½ ounces (80 to 100 g) grated Pecorino Romano cheese

Cut the guanciale into strips. Brown them in a skillet over medium heat in the olive oil until the fat becomes transparent and lightly browned. Add the wine and let it evaporate. Transfer the guanciale to a plate.

Break up the tomatoes by hand and add them to the hot pan. Season lightly with salt, then add the chile. Cook to reduce the sauce, about 10 minutes, crushing the tomato pieces with a wooden spoon. Add the guanciale and stir to combine.

Cook the pasta al dente in plenty of salted boiling water. Drain, setting aside about a cup (250 mL) of the pasta cooking water, and add the pasta to the sauce. Stir well to combine, and add a little cooking water to the sauce if it appears too dry. Add two-thirds of the pecorino. Serve immediately, topped with the remaining pecorino.

Il Tocco Di Luana (Luana's Tip)

"I always add a sage leaf to the tomato sauce."

A RECIPE WITH ITS OWN STAMP

In 2008, an Italian stamp was dedicated to Amatrice and all the ingredients of its famous pasta dish.

SKIP TO
GOURMET CINEMA, P. 68; THE OTHER PROMISED LAND, P. 278;
A LOVE FOR TOMATOES, P. 26.

SEASON

TUTTO L'ANNO (YEAR-ROUND)

CATEGORY

PRIMO PIATTO (FIRST COURSE)

LEVEL

DIFFICOLTÀ MEDIA (MEDIUM DIFFICULTY)

CARBONARA

PASTA WITH EGG YOLK, GUANCIALE, AND CHEESE

This could be the most famous Italian pasta dish in the world. But strangely, few are familiar with its origins, and its execution is often less than successful. Here are all its secrets.

ELEONORA COZZELLA*

A RECIPE OF THE RECONSTRUCTION

Carbonara is the hallmark dish of Rome's postwar years, when food restrictions and money shortages gradually faded and a new optimism emerged. Until 1950, this dish did not appear in any cookbook, literary work, newspaper article, or movie.

ITS ANCESTORS

Some food historians have tried to trace the past of carbonara to ancient recipes in which pasta-egg-cheese or pasta–pork fat–cheese combinations appeared.

→ The most famous historical dish in which pasta and egg come together dates to 1778. The recipe, in *Il cuoco galante* by Vincenzo Corrado, a cook and writer from Naples, indicates how "thin pasta noodles can be cooked in a white capon broth, or even in brown beef broth, or in milk, and [how when] cooked, it can be served bound with or without egg yolks."

→ In 1839, in *Cucina teoricopratica* by Ippolito Cavalcanti (duke of Buonvicino, also a cook and writer), the first combination of pasta, egg, and cheese appeared in the recipe *maccarune co caso e ova sbattute* (*maccheroni* with cheese and beaten egg).

→ In 1881, in *Il principle dei cuochi* by Francesco Palma, a recipe even closer to carbonara can be found: maccheroni with cheese and eggs and including pork fat.

→ In *Memorie di Amélie*, an anonymous collection of recipes from the end of the nineteenth century, the author, married to a Neapolitan, mentions "maccheroni with egg" seasoned with lard, beaten eggs, grated cheese, and black pepper, but the dish is a soup intended to be eaten with a spoon, and includes a lot of chopped parsley and basil.

→ In Rome, *gricia*, the pasta dish with *guanciale*, has been well-known since the sixteenth century, and the trio of pork fat, cheese, and egg in pasta has since been common in kitchens throughout the country.

The mystery of the name

Although there were many recipes based on pork fat, cheese, and egg, they were not called *carbonara*, so it's perhaps the name that could help unravel the mystery of its origins.

ALTHOUGH MANY SUPPORT the idea of it being a dish consumed during meetings of the members of the Carbonari (a secret society during the first half of the nineteenth century with strong political convictions), this idea should be ruled out.

THE THEORY that a chef in Carbonia (a town in Sardinia) who worked in Rome invented it seems doubtful and without merit.

THE IDEA that this was a dish eaten by the coal workers of the Apennine Mountains is plausible but not verifiable.

THE POETIC NOTION that the name comes from the black pepper sprinkled on the dish that evokes a shower of tiny fragments of coal is appealing, but has no real evidence.

REALISTICALLY, the name could have originated from the fact that its ingredients were found on the black market, which in Roman parlance was called the *mercato carbonaro.* This black market was abundantly supplied with food from the US army. The Italian American connection begins to make sense . . .

THE AMERICAN CONNECTION HYPOTHESIS

On July 26, 1950, an article in the newspaper *La Stampa* recounted a traditional festival in the Trastevere district. Speaking with one of the capital's restaurateurs, Cesaretto alla Cisterna, the journalist writes that he was the first to welcome "the American officers—who had landed in Italy in 1943 against the fascist and Nazi forces—came to Trastevere in the past in search of *spaghetti alla carbonara.*" This is the first mention in the Italian press of the dish destined to become one of the symbols of Roman cuisine.

HISTORY AND SOCIOLOGY OF A "TRADITION"		
ACT I ON THE ROAD TO ROMANIZATION (1950–1960)	BACON ⟶ PANCETTA	
ACT II INTERPRETATIONS 1980s	**THE *BORGHESE* (BOURGEOISE) VERSION** **VEHICLE:** *cookbooks by ladies from rich, worldly families* **CREAM:** *cookbooks by Carnacina, Veronelli, Gualtiero Marchesi, Alain Senderens* **BLACK PEPPER:** *a spice that was still very expensive a few years earlier* **PARMESAN CHEESE**	**POPULAR VERSION** **VEHICLE:** popular trattorias **WITHOUT CREAM** **WITHOUT BLACK PEPPER** **PECORINO**
ACT III THE INVENTION OF TRADITION** Since the early 1990s	EGG YOLK, GUANCIALE, PECORINO	

***Phenomenon analyzed by sociologists Eric J. Hobsbawm and Terence Ranger. A tradition invented in the name of shared values and a fantasized past is integrated by a group of a given region once everyone is persuaded that it is the "original," "old," "traditional" version . . .*

PASTA CHOICES

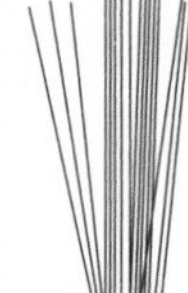

Spaghetti

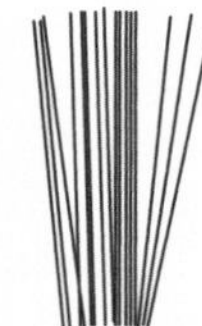

Spaghettoni

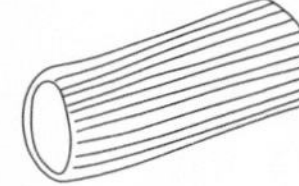

Rigatoni or *mezze maniche*

THE ANSWER TO THE MYSTERY

This preparation's history is intimately linked to the presence of the American army in Rome between 1943 and 1945. American soldiers circulated among the local youth, distributing cigarettes and the music of Glenn Miller and Cole Porter and popularizing the boogie-woogie, chocolate bars, and chewing gum. Most important, the soldiers traded their K rations (the standardized individual provisions provided to troops) containing bacon and powdered eggs . . . which often ended up on the black market.

In statements, bar owners of the time say they prepared the first carbonara using bacon and powdered eggs at the request of soldiers who asked for spaghetti for breakfast—that is to say, spaghetti accompanied with eggs and bacon. It was in this context that carbonara was born, an expression of Italian creativity and genius with American influences.

It became so trendy that Herbert L. Matthews, Rome correspondent for the *New York Times*, paid tribute to the food of trattorias and celebrated the trend of carbonara in an article dated July 12, 1954.

THE RECIPE

One of the best carbonara in the world is that of chef Nabil Hadj Hassen, who left his native Tunisia to devote his talents to the kitchen of Salumeria Roscioli in Rome.

SERVES 4

9 ounces (250 g) guanciale (cured pork cheek)

14 ounces (400 g) spaghettoni noodles

Salt

1 large (50 g) egg

3 large (57 g) egg yolks

7½ ounces (210 g) Pecorino Romano cheese

1½ ounces (40 g) Parmesan cheese (aged 24 months)

2½ tablespoons (20 g) freshly ground black pepper

Remove the black pepper and rind from the guanciale. Cut the meat into ⅓-inch-thick (1 cm) slices, then into ⅓-inch (1 cm) cubes, starting from the edge. In a pan, brown the cubes over high heat. When some of the fat has melted and one side is crisp, begin stirring until all the fat is melted, then reduce the heat to low and let the guanciale "confit" in its fat for about 20 minutes. When the cubes are crispy, remove the pan from the heat but keep them warm; reserve the melted fat.

Add the spaghettoni to a pot of salted boiling water. Lightly beat the egg and egg yolks together in a bowl. Grate the cheeses and combine them, then add about 2 cups (190 g) of the cheeses and 2 tablespoons (15 g) of the pepper to the eggs and stir to combine. (You can crush the pepper in a mortar rather than using a pepper mill to obtain larger pieces.) There is no need to season with salt, as the cheese and guanciale are salty.

When the pasta is almost cooked, set aside a few ladles of the pasta cooking water, then drain the pasta and transfer it to a saucepan with the eggs, cheese, and pepper, and mix well over low heat. Let stand for about 1 minute, then add the crispy guanciale and a spoonful of its melted fat.

Making circular movements and moving top to bottom in the pan to create an emulsion, coat the pasta with the beaten eggs, cheese, guanciale, and its fat. Work quickly, adding a little pasta water to help form the emulsion. The success of the carbonara depends entirely on this step, which lasts barely a minute.

Serve immediately, sprinkling each plate with the remaining cheese and some pepper.

	SALT	CHEESE	BINDER	SPICE
FOLLOWING THE ARTISTIC WAY	✓ *Guanciale*	✓ *Pecorino*	✓ *Egg yolk*	✓ *Black pepper*
TOLERATED	*Pancetta*	*Pecorino and Parmesan*	*Egg yolk and a little egg white*	*White pepper*
NO, THAT'S NOT HOW IT'S DONE	✗ *Bacon*	✗ *Just Parmesan*	✗ *Oil*	
DON'T EVEN THINK ABOUT IT!!!!	✗ *Lardons*	✗ *Cream*		✗ *Garlic, onion*

*Author of *La carbonara perfetta: Origini ed evoluzione di un piatto culto*, Cinquesensi Editore, 2019.

SKIP TO

THE ART OF PORK FAT, P. 70; PARMIGIANO-REGGIANO, P. 86; PECORINO, P. 304.

GIANDUJA

This comforting combination of finely ground hazelnuts with chocolate, which inspired the world's best-selling brand of chocolate spread, originates from Piedmont.

MARIE-AMAL BIZALION AND ALESSANDRA PIERINI

Not Everything Can Be the Real Gianduja!

Gianduja, also spelled *gianduia*, is a creamy chocolate with origins in Turin, made from cacao and hazelnut paste. The most common version is milk chocolate with a minimum of 15 percent hazelnuts, but the original recipe is based on dark chocolate with a high percentage of hazelnuts. It is found commercially in the form of:

classic bars or with whole hazelnuts

small trapezoidal chocolates wrapped in gold foil (*gianduiotti*)

chocolate spread

At the request of Piedmontese artisan chocolate makers, gianduja is in the running to be granted the PGI label in order to protect its historical origins and to require the exclusive use of the Nocciola del Piemonte IGP hazelnut.

BORN FROM A BLOCKADE

In 1806, Napoleon closed the borders of his empire, to which Piedmont belonged, to imports from Great Britain and its colonies. Cacao became a rare commodity, so Turin's pastry chefs added a high proportion (up to 70 percent) of chopped roasted local hazelnuts instead.

In 1865, these small chocolates were initially called *givu* ("cigar butt" in Piedmontese), but their name quickly became *gianduiotto*, the diminutive form of Gianduia, a character from the *Commedia dell'Arte* who had represented the symbol of the struggle for independence since the end of the eighteenth century. The same year, during Carnival, the Caffarel-Prochet company had the idea of having the Gianduia character distribute the first candies made in this way and wrapped in paper, a wrapping that has remained unchanged.

① GIANDUJA CENTO GRAMMI

A chocolate bar of gianduja
3½ OUNCES (100 G)

INGREDIENTS—Piedmont IGP hazelnuts, milk, cocoa butter, cocoa beans.

MAKER—Guido Castagna (Giaveno, Turin). This chocolatier has mastered the entire production process from bean to bar using a natural and artisanal method. He also roasts his Piedmontese hazelnuts.

TASTE—soft and delicate, it leaves a pleasant sensation of smoothness when tasted.

② NOCCIOLONE

A long block (ingot) of gianduja, filled with whole roasted hazelnuts — 9 OUNCES (260 G)

INGREDIENTS—Piedmont IGP hazelnuts (51 percent), sugar, cacao, cocoa butter, milk.

MAKER—D. Barbero (Asti). A chocolate maker since 1883, he specializes in the production of nougat and gianduja. This chocolate house is respected throughout Italy for the quality of its artisanal production.

TASTE—an explosion of flavors and textures with the suppleness of chocolate and the crunch of hazelnuts; irresistible.

③ BLOCCO DI GIANDUJA CON NOCCIOLE

A large block of gianduja with hazelnuts — 4½ POUNDS (2 KG)

INGREDIENTS—Piedmont IGP crème de noisette (28 percent), sugar, Piedmont hazelnuts (15 percent), cocoa butter, milk, cocoa mass.

MAKER—Venchi (Coni). In 1800, Silvano Venchi began producing chocolates in his shop, but it wasn't until 1878 that his heirs launched a *giandujotto* with 32 percent hazelnuts. Their expertise is recognized around the world.

TASTE—as smooth as you can imagine and very generous in hazelnuts. It is nevertheless quite sweet.

④ CIOCCOLATO GIANDUJA CON NOCCIOLE INTERE

Gianduja with whole hazelnuts
2¼ POUNDS (1 KG)

INGREDIENTS—Piedmont IGP hazelnuts (55 percent), sugar, cocoa mass, cocoa butter, powdered milk.

MAKER—D. Barbero (Asti).

TASTE—this large appetizing tablet seduces with its crunch and aroma once sliced; it is striking with its assertive nutty taste.

⑤ GIANDUIOTTO CLASSICO

Classic

INGREDIENTS—sugar, Piedmont hazelnuts IGP (25 percent), cocoa butter, whole milk powder, cocoa mass.

MAKER—D. Barbero (Asti).

TASTE—soft and creamy, quite pronounced taste of nuts and a slight bitterness at the end that counterbalances the sugar.

⑥ GIANDUIOTTO ANTICA RICETTA

Old recipe

INGREDIENTS—Piedmont hazelnut paste IGP (33 percent), sugar, whole milk powder, cocoa mass, cocoa butter, anhydrous milk fat.

MAKER—Venchi (Coni).

TASTE—quite a seductive attack of roasted and chocolaty notes; a slightly fatty finish.

⑦ GIANDUIOTTO CLASSICO

Classic

INGREDIENTS—sugar, Piedmont hazelnuts (28 percent), cocoa mass, milk powder, cocoa butter, almonds, vanilla powder.

MAKER—Caffarel (Turin). This is the chocolate factory, founded in 1826, to whom we owe the creation of the first gianduiotto. Its products are known in more than forty countries.

TASTE—creamy and smooth, with a vanilla aftertaste. Very sweet finish.

⑧ GIANDUJOTTO CLASSICO

Classic
⅓ OUNCE (10 G)

INGREDIENTS—sugar, Piedmont hazelnuts, cocoa mass, whole milk powder, cocoa butter, vanilla.

MAKER—Guido Gobino (Turin). After working in his father's chocolate factory, he founded his brand in 1996. He is considered one of the greatest artisan chocolatiers in the world, both nationally and internationally.

TASTE—soft and silky texture and notes of roasted caramel; quite dense and compact.

⑨ GIUINOTT

Meaning "young man" in the Piedmontese dialect
⅛ OUNCE (5 G)

INGREDIENTS—Piedmont IGP hazelnuts (40 percent), cane sugar, Chuao Venezuelan cocoa beans, cocoa butter.

MAKER—Guido Castagna (Giaveno, Turin). This master chocolatier has reinterpreted the traditional recipe by changing the shape and weight. His gianduiotto has received a gold medal six times at the International Chocolate Awards of London.

TASTE—smaller than the usual size, soft, melting in a perfect harmony of flavors, elegant, and ultra-addicting.

THE *TORTA GIANDUIA*

Common in Piedmont, this rich cake is the triumph of two common products of the region: hazelnuts and chocolate. A chocolate and hazelnut cake soaked with Abricotine liqueur, filled with chocolate cream, then glazed with dark chocolate.

SKIP TO
LA COMMEDIA DELL'ARTE, P. 42;
THE HAZELNUT, P. 144.

RECIPE

GIANDUJA CREAM

This recipe, easy to make at home, is shared by Confetteria Avvignano (Turin, Piedmont), founded in 1883. A favorite Turin confection that brings pleasure to the eyes as well as the palate.

MAKES APPROXIMATELY 6⅓ OUNCES (180 G)

½ cup (50 g) chopped hazelnuts

¾ ounce (20 g) dark chocolate or unsweetened cocoa powder

¼ cup plus 2½ tablespoons (40 g) confectioners' sugar

¼ cup plus 2 teaspoons (70 mL) milk

- Process the hazelnuts until a homogeneous, dense, and oily paste is obtained.
- Gently melt the chocolate in a saucepan.
- Pour all the ingredients into a bowl and stir gently to remove any lumps.
- Pour the mixture (which at this stage should be slightly liquid) into glass jars. Seal and store in the refrigerator.

CHOOSE GREAT HAZELNUTS

The original recipe calls for Nocciola del Piemonte IGP hazelnuts, considered the best hazelnut in the world. For this recipe, it can be replaced by the Corsican hazelnut from Cervione, the only PGI hazelnut from France, with a slightly woodsier flavor.

THE MOZZARELLA FAMILY

In the family of pulled-curd cheeses, we think first of mozzarella.
But there are many other cousins of this famous white ball of cheese . . .

ALESSANDRA PIERINI

MOZZARELLA

Whether from cow's or buffalo's milk, mozzarella comes in different sizes, but it's at the size of 9 ounces (250 g) that it's considered the best. The cheese can also be smoked naturally with hay, as is traditional, or immersed in a liquid smoke extract.

Fior di latte (cow's milk)

① PERLINA (SMALL PEARL) ½ OUNCE/15 G

② CILIEGINA (SMALL CHERRY) 1 OUNCE/25 G

③ NODINO (KNOT) 1¾ OUNCES/50 G

④ FIOR DI LATTE ("FLOWER OF MILK") 9 OUNCES/250 G

⑤ SFOGLIA (SHEET)

Bufala (buffalo's milk)

⑥ OVOLINO (SMALL EGG) ⅔ OUNCE/18 G

⑦ CILIEGINE (SMALL CHERRY) 1¾ OUNCES/50 G

⑧ BOCCONCINO AFFUMICATO (SMALL CORK, SMOKED) 1¾ OUNCES/50 G

⑨ MOZZARELLA 9 OUNCES/250 G

⑩ SMOKED MOZZARELLA 9 OUNCES/250 G

⑪ MOZZARELLA 1⅛ POUNDS/500 G

⑫ TRECCIA (BRAID) 9 OUNCES/250 G

⑬ TRECCIA (BRAID) 1⅛ POUNDS/500 G

⑭ TRECCIA (BRAID) 4½ POUNDS (2 KG)

⑮ ZIZZONA (BREAST) 2¼ POUNDS (1 KG)

OTHER PULLED-CURD CHEESES

⑰ BURRATA

Typical of Apulia, native to Andria, made from cow's milk (rarely from buffalo's milk), stuffed, most of the time closed with a string. The round, elastic outer shell, similar to mozzarella, contains a creamy and soft filling, *stracciatella* ⑲, made from shredded mozzarella mixed with fresh cream. A recent invention, it was created in 1956 from the need to recycle excess mozzarella. From 4½ ounces (125 g) (*burratina* ⑯), it can also be smoked ⑱.

→ It is eaten in salads or with pasta.

㉒ CACIOCAVALLO

Produced in southern Italy, made from cow's milk (rarely buffalo's milk), it looks like a large pear weighing 2¼ to 4½ pounds (1 to 2 kg). Its name, which means "straddling cheese," comes from the fact that it is matured as two pieces, tied together with a string and straddling a wooden beam. Soft when fresh (up to two months), it becomes pungent and dry when older (like the Silano DOP ㉓).

→ When fresh, *caciocavallo* is used in baked dishes, savory pies, and lasagna; aged, it can be eaten in fillings or grated over pasta or risottos. It can also be smoked ㉔. In Sicily is found *caciocavallo ragusano*, the only one to have a large parallelepiped shape, with a pronounced pungent taste, used to grate on top of pasta. *Provola*, of which the Sicilian Nebrodi and Madonie are Slow Food sentinels, is very close to caciocavallo.

⑳ SCAMORZA

Also called *mozzarella passita* (dried), this 7-ounce to 1⅛-pound (200 to 500 g) pear-shaped cheese made from cow's milk (rarely buffalo's milk) originated in southern Italy; a string is passed under the head to hang the cheeses in pairs to drain. It is consumed from the first day of production (when it is slightly tart, supple, and delicate) and up to two months later (with a firmer texture and stronger flavor). In Apulia, there is one made from sheep's milk that is eaten fresh or dry (grated).

→ As an accompaniment to charcuterie, in gratins, savory pies, focaccia, pizza. It can also be smoked ㉑.

㉕ PROVOLONE

Produced mainly in the south of Italy but also in the Po plain, it comes in a multitude of shapes and sizes: cylinder, pear, melon, and with a weight that can vary from 6½ to 220 pounds (3 to 100 kg)! It is produced either mild (softer, with a delicate fragrance and a milky flavor with herbaceous nuances) or pungent (drier, with a very pronounced taste with animal notes ㉖). The *provolone del Monaco di razza agerolese* (Campania) is a Slow Food sentinel.

→ As a table cheese; in fondues; grilled on the barbecue; grated over pasta; or in gratins.

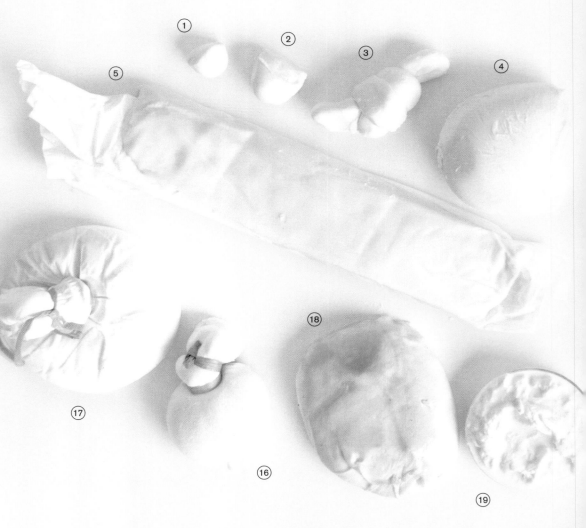

23
21
24
25
20
22
11
15
9
26
12
7
6
13
14
10
8

ITS ORIGIN

Pliny the Elder testifies in his *Natural History* (first century CE) of the production of cow's-milk cheese, which was widespread in ancient Campania. It was probably a pulled-curd cheese, *provatura* or *provola*, still made today.

The water buffalo (*Bubalus bubalis*) is the origin of this cheese. Buffaloes from India are said to have been introduced to Sicily by the Saracens in the tenth century and then migrated in Norman times to the Neapolitan region, where the humid, hot, and marshy lands were well suited to their breeding.

From the thirteenth century, the Benedictine monks of the Santa Maria convent in Capua (Campania) developed its production to offer it to pilgrims passing through. *Mozzarella Aversana*, which continues to be produced in this region, is considered the best.

ARTISANAL METHOD

Whole milk is heated, and a natural lactic acid starter (*siero innesto*) and rennet are added. This produces a curd that must rest to acidify. It is then broken up using a *spino* (a sort of large balloon whisk on a long wooden handle) and placed in a bath of whey. After a few hours, boiling water is added and the curd softens. Using a stick, it is kneaded, shaped, and stretched, still by hand, so that it begins to pull or string. This elastic *filatura* of curd is then folded back on itself and *mozzata* (pinched off) by the *casaro* (cheesemaker).

The resulting balls are dropped into cold water and salted using one of two methods:

→ In the Caserta region, mozzarella is first soaked in brine, then shaped. The skin will be more present and resistant, the taste saltier, and the appearance more matte and opaque.

→ In the Salerno region, salt is added directly to the preserving liquid in the packaging, for a milder, delicate, and more melting taste and a brighter appearance.

INDUSTRIAL MANUFACTURING

Outside of the certified process, this process can be automated, and fresh milk can even be replaced by chilled or frozen powdered milk or curd. The aim is to lower costs and speed up production.

GOOD TO KNOW

To produce 2¼ pounds (1 kg) of cow's-milk mozzarella (or *fior di latte*), you need between 1¾ and 2⅛ gallons (7 and 8 L) of milk.

For 2¼ pounds (1 kg) of buffalo's-milk mozzarella, you need between 1 and 1⅓ gallons (4 and 5 L) of milk. This better yield is due to the fact that buffalo's milk is richer in fat.

RAW OR PASTEURIZED MILK?

Originally, mozzarella was produced only with raw milk, but since the 1950s, pasteurization has often been employed. This change has had two consequences: greater food safety, and the inevitable standardization of the cheese's flavor. Today, each *caseificio* (creamery) can choose to use raw or pasteurized milk.

CITRIC ACID OR LACTIC ACID STARTER CULTURE?

To develop all of its aromas and to be more digestible, mozzarella must have a certain degree of acidity, which is obtained naturally thanks to lactic acid cultures from a fermentation lasting several hours. This is the main advantage of artisanal *caseifici* (creameries). Nonnatural acidification is achieved by adding citric acid, which makes mozzarella immediately ready for the market but also makes it an industrial product. In some cases, lactic acid bacteria and citric acid can be used at the same time to speed up production but without compromising the mozzarella's flavor too much.

PRESERVATION

In the region in which it's produced, mozzarella is eaten raw, at room temperature, on the day it is made, without ever being refrigerated, since the preserving liquid that covers it ensures its preservation. Starting from the second day, it is used for cooking. For consumers located far from where the mozzarella is produced, and for whom refrigeration is therefore essential, it is best to consume it quickly after letting it come to room temperature (or briefly soaking it in its packaging in hot water), because cold temperatures damage its consistency and aromas.

CURIOSITIES

LA BUFALA AS A DIGESTIF

Buffalo's milk in Campania is also consumed in the form of alcohol, called *guappa.* This drink is homage to the *bufalari* (buffalo breeders), as is its name, attributed to the prettiest and most productive buffalo in the herd. This alcohol perpetuates the custom of warming up on winter mornings with a glass of fresh buffalo's milk washed down with alcohol.

THE SIKHS, GUARDIANS OF TRADITION

The Sikhs have been present in Italy, organized as small groups, for the past fifteen years. Their cultural sensitivity to buffalo ranching makes their presence indispensable on today's dairy farms. Most come from the Punjab region, on the border between India and Pakistan, the heart of the Sikh community.

From *mozza* to *mozzarella*

It's called *mozza*, from the word *mozzare*, which is the gesture made by the cheesemaker consisting of pinching off the ball of stretched curd by hand while the curd is still hot (obtained from curdled milk) before shaping it.

In 1563, the doctor and botanist Pietro Andrea Mattioli wrote: "This buffalo milk, with which one fashions balls tied with sedges, called *mozze* . . ."

It was not until 1570 that the word *mozzarella* appeared in Bartolomeo Scappi's cookbook: "fresh butter, fancy *ricotte*, fresh *mozzarelle*, and a drop of milk."

IT GOES BY MANY NAMES!

Mozzarella

The generic name; it can be made from cow's or buffalo's milk.

Mozzarella di latte di bufala

Made with buffalo's milk that does not have the PDO label. The expression *mozzarella di bufala* is prohibited in this case.

Mozzarella di bufala campana DOP

Made from fresh whole Italian buffalo's milk, which obtained its PDO in 1996. Before that date, it was the only one that could bear the name *mozzarella.* It is produced in Campania (the provinces of Naples, Caserta, and Salerno), south of Rome (Lazio), north of Apulia, and part of Molise. It goes informally by *bufala.*

Fior di latte ou fiodilatte ("flower of milk")

Made with fresh whole cow's milk. Since 1996, fior di latte has been recognized as *specialità tradizionale garantita* (STG) in the regions of Campania, Basilicata, Calabria, Apulia, Molise, Sicily, and Lazio.

Mozzarella con latte di bufala

Made with both cow's and buffalo's milk.

Mozzarella di Gioia del Colle DOP

Made with cow's milk; obtained its PDO in 2019. It comes from a particularly high-quality production from two provinces of Apulia and one province of Basilicata.

BUFALA OR FIOR DI LATTE?

To fully enjoy the taste of these pulled-curd cheeses, they must be eaten very fresh. Once sliced, they should release drops of milk, and their consistency should be firm and elastic and somewhat resistant to the bite.

MOZZARELLA DI BUFALA	FIOR DI LATTE (OR MOZZARELLA)
APPEARANCE AND CONSISTENCY Porcelain white, pronounced but thin shell, smooth surface, not viscous. When sliced, it releases a milky liquid. Meticulously made, elastic and tenacious, good resistance to the bite. It becomes supple and melting on subsequent days after it's made, or if it has been chilled for a long time, which can cause its fibers to break.	**APPEARANCE AND CONSISTENCY** Shiny, even outer skin, thin and off-white, with yellowish tinges due to the presence of beta-carotene in the cow's milk. The flesh is more fibrous, composed of several sheets of pulled curd that overlap.
TASTE A musky scent slightly reminiscent of moss, undergrowth, animal-like, with aromas of fresh milk. On the palate, it is smoother, with aromatic notes of yogurt and fresh grass and a pleasant acidity. It has a creamy aftertaste; the palate is enveloped in a comforting, creamy sensation.	**TASTE** It has an aroma of cooked milk with a taste very similar to fresh milk and subtly tangy, lighter, and smoother. One can perceive fibers of the moderately elastic pulled curd on the palate.
IN CUCINA **Raw**, at room temperature, and unseasoned to appreciate all the complexity of the milk. **In salad**, without slicing it too far in advance, with a fruity olive oil, with ripe and firm tomatoes, with fresh basil or oregano (fresh or dry). **Not recommended for cooking because it produces a lot of liquid**; it is better to drain it well and add it only at the end of the cooking time (on pizza, for example).	***IN CUCINA*** **Raw**, in salad, with olive oil; perfect with oregano, basil, wild fennel, marjoram; used in caprese salad. **Cooked**: *mozzarella in carrozza*, fried mozzarella, eggplant Parmesan, pizza, pasta, *panzerotti*, gratins, *supplì*, *gnocchi alla sorrentina*, panini . . .

A precious liquid

In artisanal production, the solution, or liquid, in which the mozzarella is preserved guarantees optimal preservation of the cheese and its organoleptic characteristics: it is the *liquido di governo*. It is customized by the cheesemaker according to the acidity of the cheese and from the fermentation of the water that remains after production. In nonartisanal production, this liquid is often replaced by salted water with the addition of citric acid.

Sulla Punta Della Lingua (On the Tip of the Tongue)

Una bufala

"to tell a *bufala*": to provide false information.

SKIP TO
ITALY'S BEAUTIFUL CHEESES, P. 222; MOZZARELLA IN CARROZZA, P. 82.

THE THREE VOICES OF STRACCIATELLA

As if to justify the etymology of its name (*stracciare* means "to tear"), *stracciatella* is "torn" between three very distinct and perfectly delicious identities.

ELVIRA MASSON

A CHEESEMAKER'S SPECIALTY

Stracciatella is the creamy, stringy center of *burrata*. This means it's decadent! Native to Apulia, it can also be found sold on its own, packaged in white containers. There is a smoked version, *stracciatella affumicata*.

A LITTLE HISTORY: this recent specialty more than likely originated with burrata at the beginning of the twentieth century. Lorenzo Bianchino, a farmer from Apulia, could not make the delivery to his customers due to bad weather, so he decided to use the leftovers of his unsold mozzarella. After shredding them, he combined them with fresh cream, then stuffed the resulting mixture into a ball of stretched curd. Burrata was thus born, and its melting heart was immediately greeted with great success.

METHOD: it is eaten like burrata, rather plain, simply prepared, with tomatoes, roasted zucchini, a nice olive oil, and a lot of black pepper to counterbalance the cream. It has recently begun to appear on pizzas, added as soon as they emerge from the oven, or as a topping for pasta.

A festive soup

In Rome, *stracciatella* refers to a broth made with eggs and Parmesan cheese, traditionally served during the Christmas holidays. It has regional variations: *stracciatella alla pesarese* in the Marche, *minestra del paradiso* in Emilia-Romagna, and more specifically *brodo con la tevdura* in the region of Reggio Emilia.

A LITTLE HISTORY: a fine example of *cucina povera*, this popular dish, whose peasant origin is difficult to trace, makes a delicious and colorful broth.

METHOD: use one egg and one handful of grated Parmesan cheese per person. In a salad bowl, break the eggs and beat them with a fork along with the Parmesan. Incorporate this mixture into hot vegetable or meat broth. The cheese coagulates and forms small strings, the *straccetti*.

An ice cream

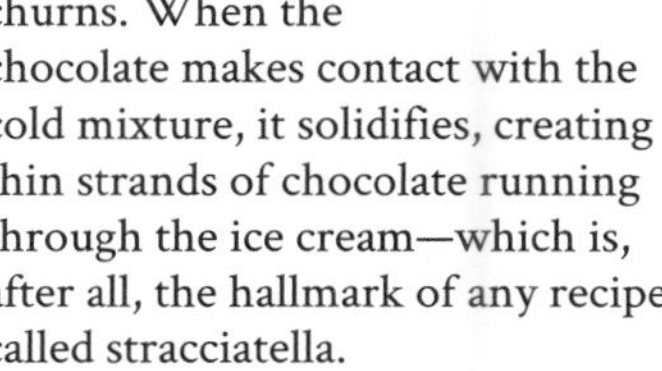

Stracciatella is also a dessert! Take the famous *fior di latte* ice cream (made from whole milk, cream, and sugar), flavor it with vanilla, and add melted dark chocolate directly into the ice cream maker as it churns. When the chocolate makes contact with the cold mixture, it solidifies, creating thin strands of chocolate running through the ice cream—which is, after all, the hallmark of any recipe called stracciatella.

A LITTLE HISTORY: this dessert was invented in 1961 by Enrico Panattoni, owner of the La Marianna café in Bergamo, Lombardy. He gave it the same name as the popular Roman soup because it had the same jagged appearance.

METHOD: a scoop of stracciatella can be enjoyed plain, or as a variation of *affogato*, with hot coffee poured over the top.

SKIP TO
IN THE LAND OF GELATI, P. 50.

SEASON

TUTTO L'ANNO (YEAR-ROUND)

CATEGORY

ANTIPASTO/ SECONDO PIATTO (APPETIZER/ MAIN COURSE)

LEVEL

DIFFICOLTÀ MEDIA (MEDIUM DIFFICULTY)

SARDE A BECCAFICO

SICILIAN STUFFED SARDINES

This Sicilian interpretation of sardines was born as a dish of the poor, but its popularity and fame have far exceeded that of the noble dish it was intended to imitate.

ILARIA BRUNETTI

THE ORIGIN

Beccafico (*becfigue*, or in English, ortolan) comes from the name of the small bird that is particularly fond of the sweet fruit from which its name is derived. Appreciated by the Romans, these birds were hunted by Sicilian aristocrats under the reign of the Bourbons in the nineteenth century, and were cooked, stuffed with their offal, by the *monsù*, their French cooks. The less well-off Palermitans, just as much gourmands, reproduced this dish, which was considered a luxurious delight, using what they had in abundance around them: sardines, whose tails resemble that of a bird, with bread crumbs used for stuffing. According to an ancient belief, the pine nuts added were reputed to prevent food poisoning that a not-so-fresh fish might cause . . .

THE RECIPE

Here is the version by Francesco Di Natale, a chef from Syracuse who brought his region's cooking to Bologna: he adds pecorino to the stuffing, as in Catania, but he bakes the sardines in the oven, as in Palermo.

SERVES 4
(ENOUGH FOR A MAIN COURSE)

2 tablespoons (20 g) very small Sicilian Passolina raisins or dried currants

¼ cup (60 mL) sweet white wine

1⅓ cups (160 g) dried bread crumbs

Extra-virgin olive oil

1 onion, peeled and finely diced

1 ounce (30 g) anchovies in oil

2 tablespoons (20 g) pine nuts

1 ounce (30 g) peppered Sicilian pecorino (otherwise a well-aged Sardinian pecorino)

2¼ pounds (1 kg) fresh sardines

Bay leaves (as many as there are sardines)

Juice of ½ lemon

Juice of ½ orange

- Soak the raisins for 10 minutes in the wine with a little water added. Lightly toast the bread crumbs on a pan with a small drizzle of olive oil, being careful not to burn them. In a separate pan, cook the onion with a drizzle of olive oil until very tender; combine it with the bread crumbs. Chop the anchovies very finely, then add them to the onions and bread crumbs along with the raisins (drained first), pine nuts, pecorino, and a drizzle of oil. The texture of the mixture should be sandy.
- Carefully rinse and peel the sardines. Cut off the heads but leave the tails. Open each belly and clean out the inside. Cut off the dorsal fin, being careful not to separate the two fillets.
- Preheat the oven to 400°F (200°C). Spread the sardines open with the flesh side up. Place a small spoonful of the stuffing mixture on top, roll up the sardine, and secure it with a toothpick, leaving the tail pointing up. Arrange them in a dish, and place a bay leaf between each one. If the sardines are too small, place the stuffing on an open sardine and cover it with a second sardine (like a sandwich), then place this on a bay leaf. Drizzle with oil and the citrus juices, then bake for 5 minutes.

Variations

IN PALERMO

The sardines are wrapped around a stuffing made with dried bread crumbs, pine nuts, and raisins and baked in the oven.

IN CATANIA

The stuffing is enriched with *caciocavallo* cheese and arranged between two open sardines, which are then breaded and fried in oil.

IN MESSINA

This version is less well-known but is similar to the Palermo version, often including capers in the stuffing; once fried, the sardines are placed in tomato sauce.

THE CONTEMPORARY VERSION

In 2013, Michelin two-star Sicilian chef Ciccio Sultano (Duomo restaurant, in Ragusa) reinterpreted this dish in an unprecedented way. On a small slice of sesame bread, he placed an oyster stuffed with bread crumbs and, on top, a sardine fillet that had previously been cooked sous vide; the arrangement is accompanied by a cold lemon soup. Not for traditionalists!

SKIP TO
FISH, P. 300.

GNOCCHI DOLCI
SWEET GNOCCHI

Before becoming the name for the dish we know today, *gnocco* referred to a knot tied in a piece of fabric, as well as to an anise-flavored bread. This highly adaptable food can even be made into . . . a dessert!

ILARIA BRUNETTI

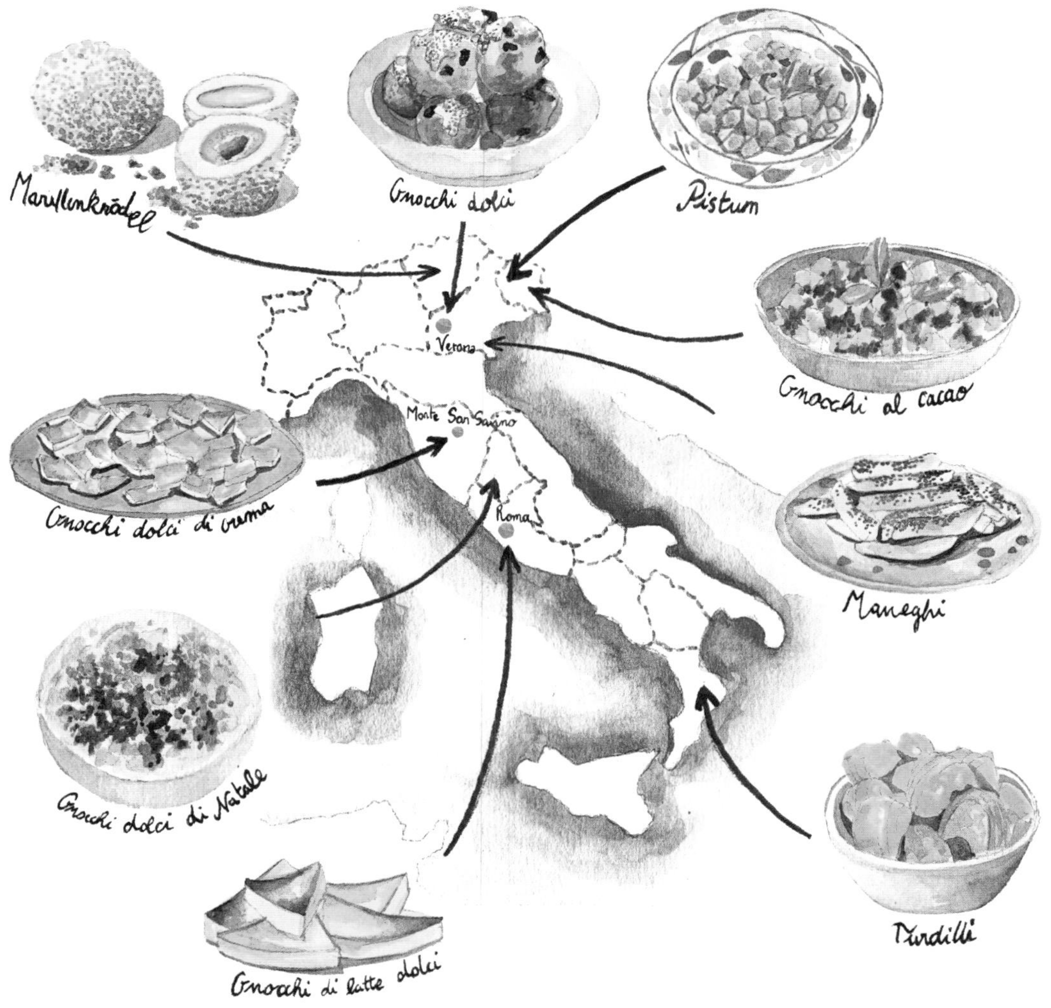

RECIPE

GNOCCHI DI LATTE (MILK GNOCCHI) AS PREPARED IN ROME BY ADA BONI*

SERVES 4

6 large (114 g) egg yolks
3 tablespoons (25 g) all-purpose flour
1 tablespoon (8 g) cornstarch
1 teaspoon (3 g) potato starch
1 tablespoon (13 g) sugar
1 pinch salt
1 pinch freshly grated nutmeg
2 cups (½ L) milk
3½ tablespoons (50 g) unsalted butter
Melted butter, for brushing
Grated Parmesan cheese
Ground cinnamon

- Combine the egg yolks, flour, cornstarch, potato starch, sugar, salt, and nutmeg in a bowl. Add the milk, then stir to combine using a whisk. Transfer this mixture to a heavy-bottomed saucepan. Add the butter and cook over low heat, stirring with a wooden spoon, for 10 minutes. From time to time, remove the pan from the heat and mix vigorously, making sure that the mixture thickens but does not stick to the pan. The mixture should develop a smooth, elastic consistency.
- Preheat the oven to 350°F (180°C). Brush a baking dish with melted butter. Wet a work surface (ideally marble) with a little water. Scrape the mixture onto the surface and spread it out to about ⅓ inch (1 cm) thick. Let cool completely so that it firms up. Cut the dough into diamond shapes and arrange them over the bottom of the greased baking dish. Sprinkle with Parmesan and cinnamon. Continue alternating the layers in this way. Brush the top with a little butter and bake for 20 minutes. Serve the gnocchi piping hot.

**Great ambassador of early-twentieth-century Roman cuisine and author. Recipe from the cult book* Il Talismano della Felicità, *1953.*

A quick tour through "the Boot"...

• IN FRIULI-VENEZIA GIULIA •

Cocoa gnocchi can be found! These are classic potato gnocchi served with a blend of cocoa, candied fruit, sugar, cinnamon, and smoked ricotta. Formerly served as a main course and today served as a dessert, this specialty has become a rarity. The same applies to ***pistùm***, which is gnocchi made with dried bread crumbs, raisins, candied citron, sugar, spices, and herbs.

• IN VENETO •

On the border of Emilia-Romagna, warm up in winter with ***maneghi***, elongated gnocchi made from sweet potatoes, served with butter, sugar, grated Grana Padano, and cinnamon. In the city of Verona, sweet gnocchi are called beignets, made with potatoes, raisins, pine nuts, vanilla, milk, flour, and yeast and found during Carnival.

• IN TRENTINO-ALTO ADIGE •

After a beautiful day of skiing, you can comfort yourself with sweet ***knöedels***, large potato gnocchi stuffed with whole pitted fruit (apricot for the *marillenknödel*, plum for the *zwetschgenknödel*), rolled in dried bread crumbs flavored with cinnamon, and served with a good amount of melted butter.

• IN TUSCANY •

In the village of Monte San Savino, they make ***gnocchi dolci di crema***, diamonds of thick pastry cream, baked in the oven and sprinkled with confectioners' sugar.

• IN UMBRIA •

Sweet Christmas gnocchi are thick, water-and-flour-based pastas seasoned with a mixture of nuts, cocoa, Alkermes (a liqueur), dried bread crumbs or crushed amaretti cookies, lemon, and cinnamon.

• IN ROME •

In addition to the famous ***gnocchi di semolino***, called gnocchi *à la romaine* (Roman-style), we also find **sweetened *gnocchi di latte***: a batter made from milk, eggs, sugar, starch, butter, and nutmeg, spread and cut into diamond shapes, which are then sprinkled with Parmesan and cinnamon and baked in the oven.

• IN CALABRIA •

Tradition dictates that Christmas dinner ends with fun and festive ***turdilli***, flour-based striped cakes rolled into a spiral.

SKIP TO
SWEET TREATS OF CHRISTMAS, P. 314.

SEASON

TUTTO L'ANNO (YEAR-ROUND)

CATEGORY

DOLCI (DESSERT)

LEVEL

FACILE (EASY)

TIRAMISU

This creamy dessert is known around the world. Its acceptable variations are sometimes a source of disagreement among those who love it. Perhaps some clarity to the argument is needed.

MARIELLE GAUDRY

Fighting for tiramisu

Friuli-Venezia Giulia—in the 1950s, Norma Pielli, owner of the hotel-restaurant Albergo Roma (Tolmezzo), liked to serve an invigorating dessert to visiting hikers and those living in the mountains. It was called *tireme su* (pick me up) in the local language.

Veneto—the restaurant Le Beccherie in Treviso lays claim to the invention of tiramisu in the 1960s. Owner Alba Campeol is said to have asked her cook Roberto Linguanotto to create a dessert that would appeal to both young and old. The recipe, perfected over the years, didn't appear on the menu until 1972.

If the STG (*specialità tradizionale garantita*) label, which was requested in 2013 from Brussels by the president of the province of Treviso, is not granted, a declaration of war on his Friulian neighbors may result! In 2017, a decree from the Italian Ministry of Agriculture ruled in favor of the Friuli-Venezia Giulia region. Tiramisu was added to the list of PAT (*prodotti agroalimentari tradizionali*), traditional agrifood products of the region.

THE GOLDEN RULES

WHICH COOKIES SHOULD BE USED?

The traditional recipe is made from *savoiardi*, a crisp ladyfinger cookie. The thinner and crispier *pavesini* can be used as an alternative. Sponge cake–based ladyfingers (sometimes known as boudoir biscuits), which are dry and narrow, are to be avoided because they soak up too much liquid too quickly.

AN ARTISANAL MASCARPONE OR NOTHING!

It's all about a (good) creamy taste and texture. When the mascarpone is fresh, it makes all the difference.

ADD CREAM OR NOT?

You choose! Its addition to the filling is controversial, as the texture of the mascarpone itself should be sufficiently creamy if mixed properly with the egg.

ADD ALCOHOL OR NOT?

The recipes of Treviso and Tolmezzo, which have been declared official recipes, do not contain it, but it is quite common to add one spoonful of Marsala (a Sicilian fortified wine) or amaretto (a liqueur from Lombardy made of bitter almonds) to the strong coffee.

BEAT THE EGG WHITES OR NOT?

Beating the egg whites to a meringue offers lightness to the cream filling.

WHICH COFFEE?

It should be full-bodied and made just before use, such as a strong espresso.

A ROUND OR RECTANGULAR DISH?

It was originally made in a round dish, but a rectangular dish has become more common because it is more practical for cutting and serving.

THE RECIPE

By Norma Pielli, in Tolmezzo. This is the first version of tiramisu, said to have been written in the 1950s. It's a tried-and-true recipe in both proportion and method.

SERVES 6 TO 8

12½ cups (3 L) coffee or espresso coffee

4 large (200 g) eggs

¾ cup (150 g) sugar (the original recipe calls for 1½ cups/300 g because the Italians consumed very sweet desserts from 1950 to 1960)

1⅛ pounds (500 g) artisanal mascarpone cheese

1⅛ pounds/500 g (or 26 to 30) *savoiardi* (ladyfinger cookies)

½ cup (50 g) unsweetened cocoa powder

Equipment

A rectangular baking dish, 9¾ inches (25 cm) long

Transfer the coffee to a deep dish to cool. Separate 3 of the eggs. Beat the egg whites to stiff peaks using an electric mixer. In a separate bowl, combine the remaining whole egg, the egg yolks, and the sugar. Beat well with a whisk to lighten the mixture.

Gradually add the mascarpone, stirring gently from the bottom to the top of the mixture to obtain a smooth and creamy texture. Gently fold in the beaten egg whites, stirring gently until just incorporated.

Dip the ladyfingers one by one in the coffee to soak them lightly, then arrange them in the bottom of the baking dish, one next to the other, to cover the entire bottom of the dish. Pour half the cream filling over the top of the cookies. Place the dish in the refrigerator for 45 minutes to set this first layer.

Repeat these same steps, starting with the cookies soaked in coffee to create the next layer, then spreading the remaining cream over the top. Place the tiramisu in the refrigerator for at least 6 hours.

When ready to serve, dust the top completely with a thin layer of the cocoa powder.

THE TIRAMISU WORLD CUP

An annual competition organized in Treviso since 2017.

TWO CATEGORIES IN THE COMPETITION:
The classic recipe and the creative recipe.

SKIP TO
MASCARPONE, P. 239; THE OTHER PROMISED LAND, P. 278; COOKIES, P. 154.

Tiramisu Day

MARCH 21

THE OFFICIAL DAY ESTABLISHED IN 2017

GOOD FOR MIND AND BODY

It is said that *tiramisu* is the second-most-pronounced Italian word in the world! In folklore, it is credited for aphrodisiac virtues stemming from its use of strong coffee and the expression *tireme su* (in current Italian, *tirami su*), literally meaning "pick me up"—in both mind and body.

GRAPPA

Winemaking countries traditionally distill their grape pomace to make brandies or eaux-de-vie. In Italy, it's *grappa* that ends every good meal!

CÉLINE MAGUET

"La grappa purifica, disinfetta e santifica."
"Grappa purifies, disinfects, and sanctifies." —PROVERB

ITS HISTORY

During the Renaissance, grappa was a simple homemade alcohol produced under the thatch-roofed cottages of northern Italy, near the Alps, often secretly in order to avoid the taxes on alcohol. After the country was unified in the nineteenth century, domestic distillation gradually disappeared in favor of artisanal distilleries, which perfected the stills used to make it. During World War I, soldiers from the south, who shared Veneto trenches with soldiers from the north, discovered grappa. After returning home, they spread the news of grappa throughout their region. From regional production to consumption, grappa has become a national spirit.

GRAPPA AND COFFEE, TWO INSEPARABLE BEVERAGES

A quick lesson for speaking the language of the barista at the café counter!

"Un caffè corretto per favore!" This is one way to improve your coffee: by adding a splash of grappa.

"Posso avere un rasentin?" When requested in northern Italy, a *rasentin*, which is a splash of grappa in the cup, helps clean the cup from which you just drank your coffee.

"Un caffè e un ammazzacaffè!" Literally "coffee killer," this means following your coffee with a shot of grappa to clean your palate.

GRAPPA IN COOKING

PAIR WITH A CHEESE:
Enjoy a young grappa with a blue-veined cheese; enjoy an aromatic grappa (distilled from Moscato or Gewürztraminer) with a semiaged cheese; enjoy an aged grappa with a smoked cheese.

SAVOR WITH A SQUARE OF BITTER DARK CHOCOLATE.

ENJOY IN DESSERTS:
With fritters and fruit preserves (cherries, peaches, grapes) during Carnival.

SEASON FIRST COURSES:
Incorporated into a risotto (*grappa di moscato*) or gnocchi.

How is grappa made?

Derived from *grappolo* or *graspo*, meaning "cluster," grappa earns its name! After the grape harvest, the grapes are fermented, then pressed (or vice versa). The juice will become wine, and the pomace—the material left after the grapes are pressed—goes off to distilleries to be processed through one of two methods:

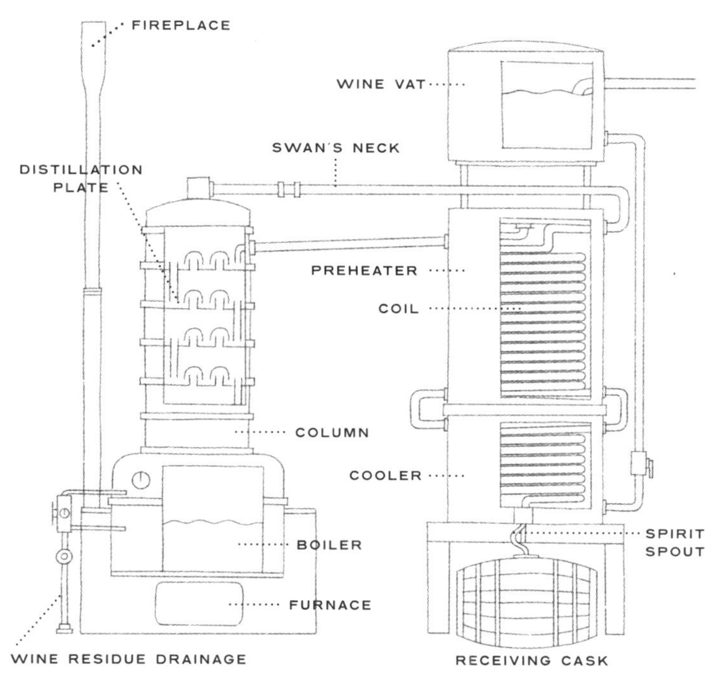

CONTINUOUS DISTILLATION

Coming from the United States and borrowed from the petroleum industry, this method shortens working time and handling, but often at the expense of the quality of the distilled product.

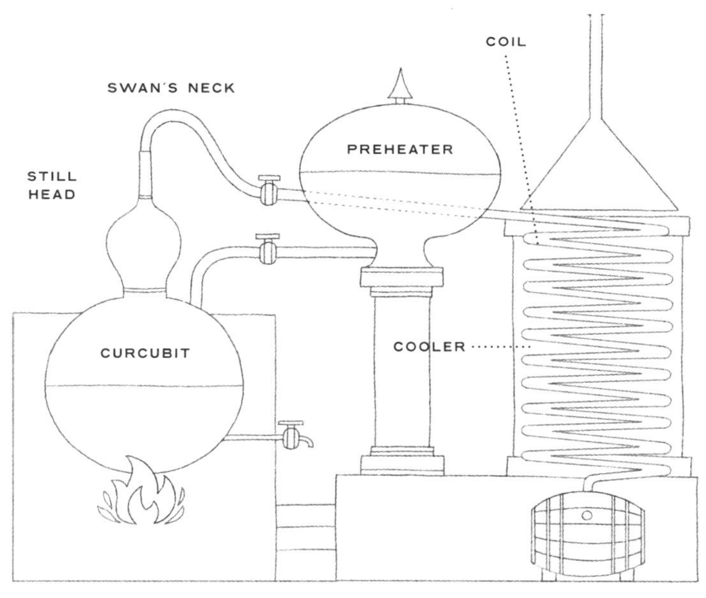

THE ALEMBIC (POT STILL)

Commonly used in the Charentes for Cognac, this method is slower and more exacting. The brandy is distilled several times in order to remove bad alcohols at the top and bottom and to keep only the heart, which contains the fine and expressive aromas of the fruit.

The grappe family

All aspects of the process, from maturing to the varietals of grapes used, are good criteria for classifying grappa. Here are some selected bottles.

GRAPPA GIOVANE **(YOUNG)**

Bottled after distillation or left for a few months in vats.

Grappa bianca, Nardini
An eau-de-vie in its youth, full of passion; fruity and floral.

GRAPPA INVECCHIATA **(AGED)**

After distillation, the grappa is aged twelve to eighteen months (*riserva invecchiata*) in barrels.

Grappa eighteen years, Gino Barile
This distillery extends its aging in oak barrels to a very high level (up to thirty-five years), giving its grappa hints of toasted walnuts, sandalwood, and captivating flowers.

GRAPPA DI MONOVITIGNO **(SINGLE VARIETAL)**

Produced from the pomace of a single grape varietal.

Grappa Barbaresco, Romano Levi distillery
Romano Levi was an artisanal grappa purist. This grappa from Barbaresco (using the Nebbiolo grape), balanced between fruit and spices, pays him a fine tribute.

GRAPPA AROMATICA **(AROMATIC)**

Produced from very aromatic grape varietals such as Brachetto, Malvasia, Moscato, and Traminer.

Grappa di Traminer, Capovilla distillery
Vittorio Gianni Capovilla, one of the maestros of grappa, is obsessed with the quality of his grape pomace. Here he went for Gewürztraminers for their citrusy notes.

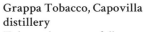

GRAPPA AROMATIZZATA **(FLAVORED)**

A grappa to which natural flavors have been added (herbs, roots, fruits . . .).

Grappa Tobacco, Capovilla distillery
Tobacco leaves are fully expressed, and with them, warm notes of cocoa and exotic fruits.

SKIP TO
GATHERING GRAPES, P. 158; CAFFÈ AL BAR, P. 64; LIQUORI, P. 366.

COCKTAILS

Spritz, Negroni, Americano . . . these classic cocktails fill glasses around the world! Here ten cultured cocktails* highlight a bit of Italian gastronomy in liquid form.

JORDAN MOILIM

> **Very often constructed around bitterness, Italian cocktails are characterized by minimal ingredients and the use of traditional spirits.**

***These cocktails were prepared by bartender Oscar Quagliarini in the restaurant Grazie, Paris 3rd.*

What are the essentials?

Vermouth, an infused fortified wine, or the famous **Campari**, a bitter maceration of herbs and fruits. They give the cocktails their dominant red color.

Negroni 1

Invented in 1919 at Café Casoni in Florence, it owes its name to Count Camillo Negroni who, weary of always drinking the same Americano, suggested the barman replace sparkling water with gin. This is a favorite cocktail among bartenders.

IN AN OLD-FASHIONED GLASS WITH ICE CUBES

- 2 TABLESPOONS PLUS 2 TEASPOONS (40 ML) GIN
- 2 TABLESPOONS PLUS 2 TEASPOONS (40 ML) RED VERMOUTH
- 2 TABLESPOONS PLUS 2 TEASPOONS (40 ML) CAMPARI
- GARNISH: ORANGE SLICE

Negroni Sbagliato 3

Like many inventions, this one was the result of an error. It was in 1972 that Mirko Stocchetto, bartender of bar Basso in Milan, created this variation of the Negroni by accidentally replacing gin with sparkling wine. Just as nice as the original version, this Negroni *sbagliato* (literally "failure") has established itself as a classic.

IN A HIGHBALL GLASS WITH ICE

- 2 TABLESPOONS PLUS 2 TEASPOONS (40 ML) RED VERMOUTH
- 2 TABLESPOONS PLUS 2 TEASPOONS (40 ML) CAMPARI
- 2 TABLESPOONS PLUS 2 TEASPOONS (40 ML) PROSECCO
- GARNISH: ORANGE SLICE

2

This is one of the oldest Italian cocktails. Invented in 1861 by Gaspare Campari (Lombard founder of the eponymous liqueur), this drink was named in tribute to its great success with Americans who came to the Italian coasts in the early 1920s.

IN AN OLD-FASHIONED GLASS WITH ICE CUBES

- 2 TABLESPOONS PLUS 2 TEASPOONS (40 ML) RED VERMOUTH
- 2 TABLESPOONS PLUS 2 TEASPOONS (40 ML) CAMPARI
- ¼ CUP (60 ML) SODA
- GARNISH: LEMON ZEST

4

Invented at the end of the nineteenth century, it was the first name given to the Americano before the version was topped off with soda. This cocktail, one of the favorites of the Italians, brings together two great Italian cities with its blend of Campari from Milan and vermouth from Turin.

IN AN OLD-FASHIONED GLASS WITH ICE CUBES

- 2 TABLESPOONS PLUS 2 TEASPOONS (40 ML) CAMPARI
- 2 TABLESPOONS PLUS 2 TEASPOONS (40 ML) VERMOUTH CARPANO PUNT E MES
- GARNISH: LEMON ZEST

Bellini 5

Now a staple brunch cocktail in the United States, the Bellini was first concocted in Venice in 1948. Giuseppe Cipriani, founder of Harry's Bar in Venice, wanted to create a fruity and refreshing tall drink by associating white peach nectar with Prosecco. There is a variation of the cocktail (the Rossini) based on strawberry purée and another based on orange juice (the Mimosa).

IN A CHAMPAGNE COUPE

- 2 TABLESPOONS PLUS 2 TEASPOONS (40 ML) PEACH PURÉE
- TOP OFF WITH CHAMPAGNE

Spritz 6

In the mid-nineteenth century, when Veneto was occupied by the Austrian Empire, German soldiers would ask the bartender for *spritzen,* that is, to "squirt" Italian wine with water to help lighten it. The first spritz were then composed of white wine and sparkling water, before various liqueurs were added in the twentieth century, including Aperol, the bitter aperitif that's now an essential ingredient in this Venetian cocktail.

IN A ROUND WINE GLASS

- ¼ CUP (60 ML) APEROL
- ADD ICE
- ⅓ CUP PLUS 2 TEASPOONS (90 ML) PROSECCO
- 1 TABLESPOON PLUS 1 TEASPOON (20 ML) SPARKLING WATER
- GARNISH: ORANGE SLICE

Campari shakerato 7

It's difficult to trace the exact origin of this "shaken" version of the Campari, the only clue being that the famous red liqueur and the cocktail shaker both appeared around 1860. They were destined to meet!

IN A CHAMPAGNE COUPE

- ⅓ CUP PLUS 2 TEASPOONS (90 ML) CAMPARI
- 2 TEASPOONS (10 ML) GIN
- SHAKE, STRAIN, AND SERVE IN THE CHAMPAGNE COUPE

Zucca shakerato 8

Little known beyond Italy's borders, this cocktail is made from rhubarb and enriched with bitter orange and cardamom. It's also called Rabarbaro Zucca (the name has nothing to do with the *zucca* [zucchini], it's the name of a rhubarb liqueur created in 1845 by Ettore Zucca). This spirit is usually enjoyed with sparkling water or shaken with a few ice cubes.

IN A HIGHBALL GLASS WITH ICE

- ⅓ CUP PLUS 2 TEASPOONS (90 ML) RABARBARO ZUCCA
- SHAKE, STRAIN, AND SERVE IN THE HIGHBALL GLASS
- GARNISH: ORANGE SLICE

Garibaldi 9

Little is known about the origins of this revolutionary cocktail . . . its name coming from the red shirt of Giuseppe Garibaldi, a real political hero who notably worked for the construction of a unified Italy in the middle of the nineteenth century.

IN A HIGHBALL GLASS

- 3 TABLESPOONS PLUS 1 TEASPOON (50 ML) CAMPARI
- TOP OFF WITH ORANGE JUICE
- ADD ICE
- GARNISH: ORANGE SLICE

Cardinale 10

An icon of *la dolce vita,* this cocktail was created in 1950 at the legendary Excelsior Hotel in Rome. The cocktail culture being so omnipresent at the time thanks to the strong American influence, even some cardinals were tempted by this seductive trend. An improbable meeting between Cardinal Schumann and Giovanni Raimondo, a star mixologist at the time, gave birth to this cocktail, still sipped today between strolls on the Via Veneto.

IN AN OLD-FASHIONED GLASS WITH ICE CUBES

- 2 TABLESPOONS PLUS 2 TEASPOONS (40 ML) CAMPARI
- 2 TABLESPOONS PLUS 2 TEASPOONS (40 ML) GIN
- 2 TABLESPOONS PLUS 2 TEASPOONS (40 ML) DRY VERMOUTH
- GARNISH: ORANGE SLICE

SKIP TO
CARPACCIO, P. 198; SPRITZ, P. 94; PROSECCO & CO., P. 250.

6 7 8 9 10

GARLIC

Praised by Hippocrates for its medicinal virtues, nicknamed *rosa fetida* (foul rose) by the ancient Greeks, since the dawn of time *aglio* has conquered vampires while also flavoring Italian dishes.

GIANNA MAZZEI

WHAT AM I?

SCIENTIFIC NAME: *Allium sativum*.

FAMILY: Liliaceae.

HARVEST: June, July, and August.

ORIGIN: central Asia.

PROPERTIES: antibacterial, prebiotic, antioxidant, and protective of the cardiovascular system.

FLAVOR: its characteristic odor is due to various organic sulfur compounds, including alliin and its derivatives (such as allicin and diallyl disulfide).

Its history

Garlic has been used since antiquity:

In cooking, as a staple in the diet of the Greek and Roman peoples.

For its almost miraculous healing properties, so much so that Hermes offered it to Ulysses as an antidote to the sorceress Circe's spells (*Odyssey*, X, 302–307).

The Middle Ages also attributed protective virtues against contagious diseases to it, as well as the power to drive out evil spirits and ward off the evil eye.

IN COOKING

Garlic is essential in many dishes such as bruschetta, Genoese pesto, and Ligurian *aggiada* (made with garlic sauce, bread crumbs, vinegar, olive oil, and salt). It is also the heart of *spaghetti aglio, olio e peperoncino* (garlic, oil, and chile). It is excellent preserved in oil or marinated.

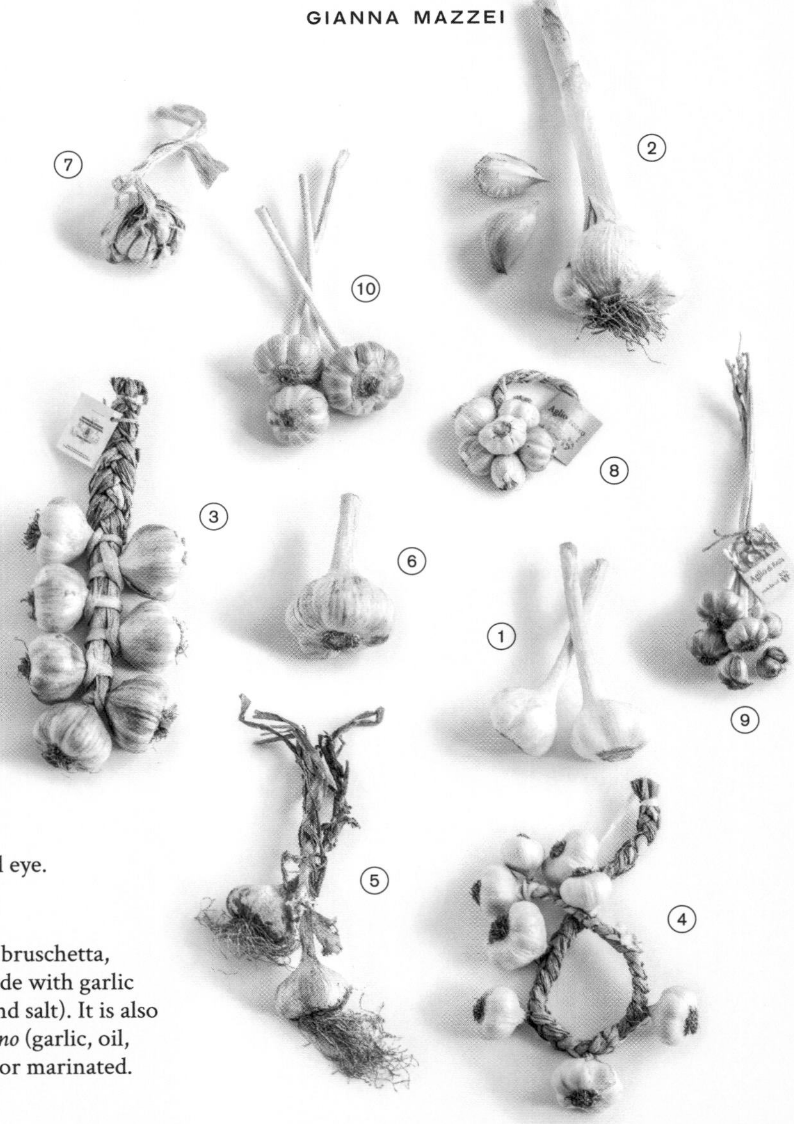

A TOUR OF ITALY

WHITE: THE STRONGEST

(1) ***Aglio bianco Polesano DOP***—Veneto
Silver-white color, very persistent fragrance.

(2) ***Aglione della Valdichiana***—Tuscany · Ark of Taste Slow Food
A rare garlic and very large (up to 1¾ pounds/800 g), very fragrant, mild, sweet, and digestible. It is used in *pici all'aglione* where it is used to generously flavor tomato sauce.

PINK: DELICATE AND AROMATIC

(3) ***Agli di Vessalico***—Liguria · Slow Food Sentinel
Very digestible, delicately pungent flavor (thanks to the soil and the mild climate of the valley, located between the Alps and the Ligurian coast).

(4) ***Aglio di Voghiera DOP***—Emilia-Romagna
Sometimes streaked with pink, sweet, and refined (much appreciated even by those who do not typically like garlic).

(5) ***Aglio di Ufita***—Campania · Slow Food Sentinel
Endangered; very intense aroma; main ingredient in the typical fresh garlic omelet from the region.

(6) ***Aglio rosa di Nicastro***—Calabria
Only around ten producers market it during the three days of the Saints Peter and Paul fair.

(7) ***Aglio rosa di Papaglionti***—Calabria
Smaller than the others, very pungent.

RED: SLIGHTLY PUNGENT

(8) ***Aglio rosso di Nubia DOP***—Sicily · Slow Food Sentinel
Traditionally presented in braids of around a hundred bulbs, very intense flavor; essential in the preparation of pesto *alla trapanese*.

(9) ***Aglio di Resia***—Friuli-Venezia Giulia · Slow Food Sentinel
Also called *strok*, reddish, slightly grassy, and assertively balsamic; each phase of its production follows the lunar cycle.

(10) ***Aglio rosso di Sulmona***—Abruzzo
Vinous color, strong flavor, pungent aroma; cultivated for centuries, only in the Sulmona basin and in the Peligna Valley.

AND ALSO:

Aglio rosso Maremmano (Tuscany); ***Aglio di Caraglio*** (Piedmont · Slow Food Sentinel); ***Aglio bianco Piacentino IGP*** (Emilie-Romagna), called *re dell'aglio* (the king of garlic).

RECIPE

AGLIATA DI POLPO IN AGRODOLCE (SWEET-AND-SOUR OCTOPUS WITH GARLIC)

This typical Sardinian recipe was passed on to me by my father, Virgilio Mazzei, sommelier and culinary explorer.

SERVES 4

4½ pounds (2 kg) octopus
¾ to 1 cup (100 to 150 g) all-purpose flour
2 cups (½ L) frying oil
2 large heads garlic, peeled
¼ cup (60 mL) olive oil
5 or 6 sun-dried tomatoes, chopped (optional)
6 quarts (1.5 L) tomato purée
6 to 8 tablespoons (100 to 130 g) tomato paste
¼ cup (60 mL) red vinegar
2 to 3 tablespoons (25 to 35 g) superfine sugar

- Clean the octopus and boil it whole. Once cooked, rinse it to remove the skin. Cut it into large pieces, coat it lightly with flour, and fry it in a pan in hot frying oil for 2 to 3 minutes. Set aside.
- Chop the garlic and brown it lightly in a high-sided pan in the olive oil. Add the sun-dried tomatoes and cook for several minutes. Add the tomato purée, a little water, and the tomato paste, then cook over low heat.
- Stir together the vinegar and sugar and add the mixture to the sauce. Cook over low heat for 30 minutes. Add additional water, if necessary, to keep the mixture liquid.
- Place the pieces of octopus in a dish, cover with the sauce, and stir to coat well. Let cool to room temperature.
- Make ahead, ideally 8 to 10 hours before serving, so that the flavors have time to blend.

SKIP TO
GENOESE PESTO, P. 20; OCTOPUS, P. 67; BAGNA CAUDA (GARLIC AND ANCHOVY DIP), P. 119; ALMONDS, P. 173.

SEASON

TUTTO L'ANNO (YEAR-ROUND)

CATEGORY

PRIMO PIATTO (FIRST COURSE)

LEVEL

FACILE (EASY)

SPAGHETTI AGLIO, OLIO E PEPERONCINO

SPAGHETTI WITH GARLIC, OLIVE OIL, AND CHILE

RICETTA Iconica RICETTA

This surprisingly simple spaghetti dish from Naples can spice up any impromptu dinner.

ILARIA BRUNETTI

FEW INGREDIENTS, BUT ALWAYS EXCELLENT!

SPAGHETTI
Preferably artisanal.

OLIVE OIL
Select one with an intense fruity taste, such as the oil of the Frantoio varietal—Tuscany, Umbria, or Nocellara del Belice from Sicily. You can use only a portion of it for cooking, then use the remainder (two or three tablespoons) to drizzle over the spaghetti just before serving.

GARLIC
A delicate garlic will allow you to enjoy the dish without regret, such as red garlic from Nubia (Sicily), or Vessalico (Liguria), or pink garlic from Lautrec (Tarn). If you prefer an even more delicate taste, leave the cloves whole, just to flavor the oil, and remove them before adding the spaghetti to the pan.

CHILES
There is nothing better than a red chile from Calabria!

LA SPAGHETTATA DI MEZZANOTTE (MIDNIGHT SPAGHETTI)

This "midnight spaghetti" embodies Italian conviviality: after a night out with friends or at the end of the evening with family, there is nothing like a quick and simple improvised meal to satisfy hunger pangs, for kids or adults. It's one last moment enjoyed together before the day's end.

THE RECIPE

SERVES 4

14 ounces (400 g) spaghetti or vermicelli, spaghettoni, or linguine

Salt

2 to 3 cloves garlic

6 tablespoons (90 mL) extra-virgin olive oil

1 or 2 fresh red chiles (in season) or dried

1 small bunch parsley, chopped

- Place the spaghetti in a pot of salted boiling water. Peel the garlic cloves, halve them, remove the germ in the center, and cut the garlic into small cubes or slice it into very thin strips.
- Heat the olive oil over medium heat in a pan large enough to accommodate the spaghetti, add the garlic, and cook until lightly browned. Core and seed the chiles, cut them into thin strips, and add them to the pan; turn off the heat.
- Ladle out about a cup (250 mL) of the pasta cooking water and set it aside. Once the spaghetti is al dente, drain it. Add the spaghetti to the pan set back over high heat, stir in the reserved cooking water, and add the parsley. Sauté the spaghetti to coat them well in the sauce. Serve immediately. Olives, anchovies, and/or toasted bread crumbs are also often added.

MISTAKES TO AVOID

BURN THE GARLIC OR PARSLEY
. . . and your spaghetti will have a bitter taste.

TOO MUCH CHILE
. . . and you'll set your guests' taste buds on fire.

SERVING THE PASTA TOO DRY OR TOO OILY
Follow the recipe but, above all, practice makes perfect.

SKIP TO
THE SPAGHETTI FAMILY, P. 201; CHILE PEPPERS, P. 359

MIGRANT CUISINE

Many Italians settled throughout Europe and the Americas with their suitcases full of recipes, which they adapted to their host countries. The result is clever culinary crossbreeding.

FRANÇOIS-RÉGIS GAUDRY

EXPATRIATE SPECIALTIES

Although these were invented by Italians, the Italian homeland shuns them.

CAESAR SALAD

The famous salad made with romaine lettuce, croutons, and grated Parmesan, and seasoned with a spicy garlic and anchovy dressing.

The inventor: Caesar Cardini, originally from the Lake Maggiore region of Italy and chef at a restaurant in Tijuana, Mexico. On July 4, 1924, he was inspired by a family recipe to hastily feed the many customers who had come into his restaurant that day.

CARUSO SAUCE

A sauce made with cream, mushrooms, chopped ham, crushed nuts, and grated cheese to accompany tortellini, spaghetti, cappelletti, and other pastas. It's a big hit throughout South America, but not in Italy!

The inventor: Raimondo Monti, owner of the Mario e Alberto restaurant in Montevideo, Uruguay. He created this recipe in the 1950s to pay tribute to the famous Neapolitan singer Enrico Caruso.

FETTUCINE ALFREDO

Long pasta noodles similar to tagliatelle are served with a rich and creamy sauce made from butter and grated Parmesan cheese. Cream, broccoli, peas, or chicken versions parade out of the kitchens of Italian restaurants in the United States.

The inventor: Alfredo Di Lelio, chef of a trattoria in Rome. He was probably inspired in 1908 (or 1914) by a recipe of the great fifteenth-century cook Maestro Martino. In the United States, this immigrant seized on the opportunity for this simple recipe in the 1920s, as a symbol of Italianism.

MUFFULETTA

A Louisiana sandwich generously filled with salami, ham, mortadella, cheese, and an olive salad with capers and pickled vegetables.

The inventor: Salvatore Lupo, a Sicilian immigrant who operated his store Central Grocery in New Orleans, hijacked muffuletta, the traditional round Sicilian bread, in 1904. It was an immediate success.

PASTA PRIMAVERA

Tagliatelle noodles with spring vegetables dressed in cream, butter, and grated cheese.

The inventor: Sirio Maccioni, chef at Le Cirque restaurant in New York. He is said to have created this recipe in 1975 at the Canadian summer residence of Italian baron Carlo Amato on Roberts Island, Nova Scotia. He brought it back to his Manhattan restaurant, and a 1977 *New York Times* article made it famous throughout the United States.

ITALIAN AMERICAN COMBOS

When authentic Italian recipes become acclimatized in the Americas . . . they are at risk of becoming a little distorted.

BAGNA CAUDA

Immigrants from Piedmont who settled in Argentina established the tradition of this anchovy dip for vegetables. Garlic is used in abundance, as in the original version, but the olive oil is replaced with cream. Every July 20, descendants of the immigrants celebrate this dish in the town of Humberto Primo, in the province of Santa Fe.

CHICKEN PARM

An abbreviation of chicken Parmigiana, these breaded chicken cutlets baked au gratin with tomato sauce and mozzarella cheese are the carnivore's version of *parmigiana di melanzane* (eggplant Parmesan).

CHICKEN SCARPARIELLO

Literally "shoemaker's chicken." Chicken pieces are sautéed with sausage, onions, garlic, bell peppers, potatoes, and sometimes chile. This version is a far distance from *pasta alla scarpariello*, the Neapolitan pasta with cherry tomatoes, basil, and grated cheese . . .

CIOPPINO

This tomato fish soup is bursting with shrimp, mussels, and crabs. It was invented by Genoese immigrants at the end of the nineteenth century at Fisherman's Wharf in San Francisco. It's a (very) distant cousin of *ciuppin*, a Ligurian fish soup.

CLAMS CASINO

In nearly every Italian restaurant in America, you can find this dish, which consists of clams stuffed with bacon, garlic, and parsley then baked au gratin. They were said to have been invented in the 1900s at the Little Casino, an Italian restaurant in Rhode Island.

ITALIAN BEEF SANDWICH

It's a hoagie roll filled with slices of roast beef and sautéed vegetables. This iconic street food was invented in the 1930s at Al's Beef in Chicago, still known for this specialty.

LOBSTER FRA DIAVOLO

Literally "Brother Devil," Fra Diavolo, aka Michele Pezza (his real name), was an Italian soldier and rascal. But it's also the nickname for lobster prepared with a very spicy tomato sauce served over spaghetti, a specialty invented in the 1920s on Long Island.

SPAGHETTI AND MEATBALLS

This is what happens when *polpette* (traditional Italian meatballs) meet spaghetti under a slathering of tomato sauce . . . What would be considered heresy in Italy (where polpette are rarely served with pasta) has now become an iconic dish of Italian cuisine. The dish was probably popularized by New York immigrants in the early twentieth century, when meat was very accessible and spaghetti was still one of the only pasta formats available.

MILANESA

The South American version of *co(s)toletta alla milanese*, developed by Italian immigrants at the end of the nineteenth century. In Argentina and Uruguay, *milanesa a la napolitana* is a version with tomato, mozzarella, and sometimes ham.

PEPPERONI

It's a fusion of the English word *pepper* with the Italian *peperoni*, both referring to bell peppers. *Pepperoni* is a salami born from Italian inspiration, seasoned with paprika and/or hot pepper (*peperoncino* in Italian). This American cousin of *piccante salsiccia* sits proudly as a topping on New York–style pizza.

SHRIMP SCAMPI

Scampi is the Italian word for langoustine, a type of large prawn. Italian immigrants undoubtedly adapted their recipe to include shrimp. In their native country, they made this dish with langoustines poached in white wine and sautéed with olive oil (or butter) and garlic.

SKIP TO
INSALATA CAPRESE, P. 95; POLPETTE (MEATBALLS), P. 25; PARMIGIANA DI MELANZANE (EGGPLANT PARMIGIANA), P. 274

MIGRANT CUISINE

PIZZA JOURNEYS

Is pizza the world's most customizable dish? Since the nineteenth century, this globally recognized dish has adapted to wherever Italian immigrants have settled and has given rise to curiously creative versions.

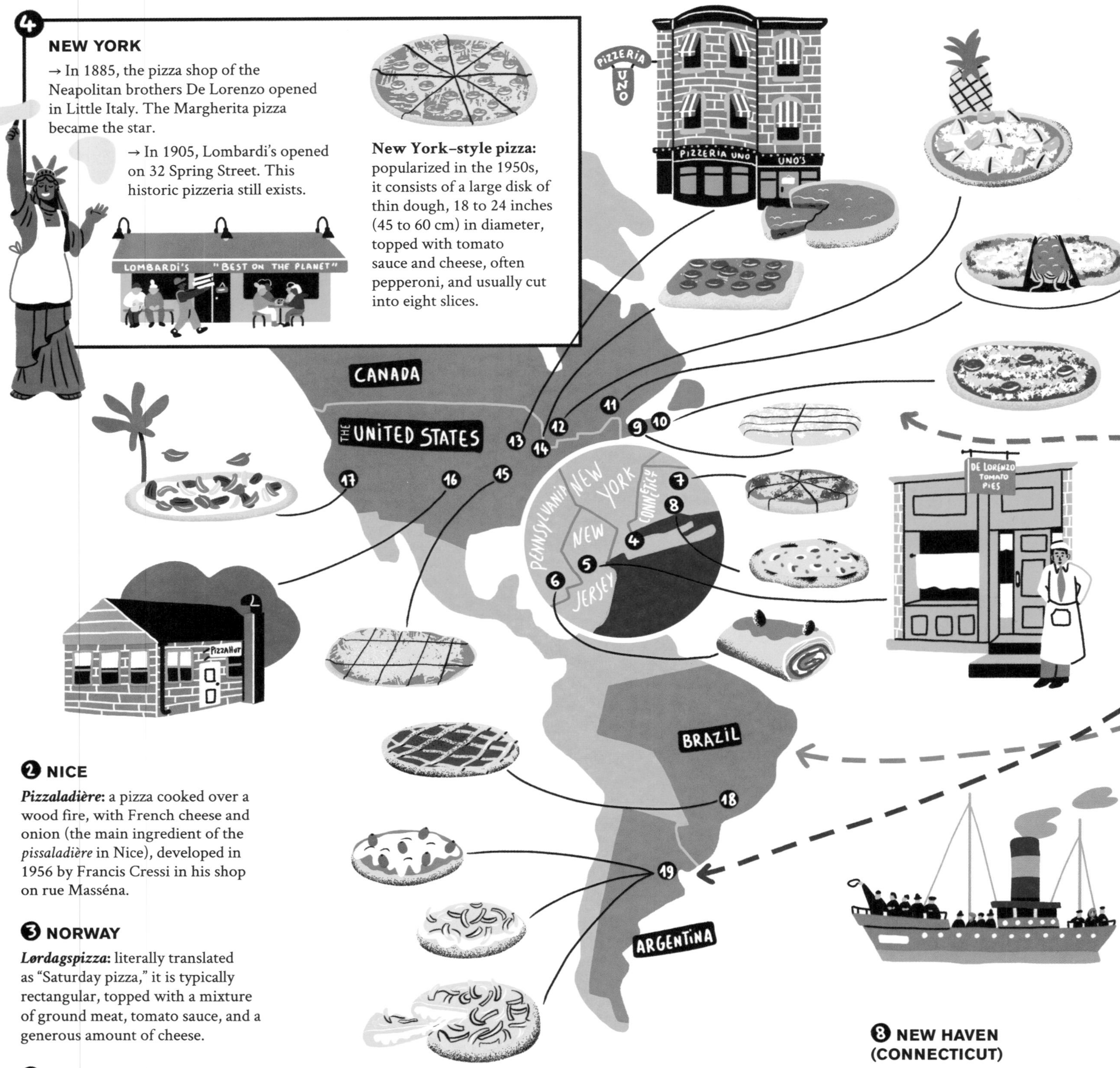

❹ NEW YORK

→ In 1885, the pizza shop of the Neapolitan brothers De Lorenzo opened in Little Italy. The Margherita pizza became the star.

→ In 1905, Lombardi's opened on 32 Spring Street. This historic pizzeria still exists.

New York–style pizza: popularized in the 1950s, it consists of a large disk of thin dough, 18 to 24 inches (45 to 60 cm) in diameter, topped with tomato sauce and cheese, often pepperoni, and usually cut into eight slices.

❷ NICE

***Pizzaladière*:** a pizza cooked over a wood fire, with French cheese and onion (the main ingredient of the *pissaladière* in Nice), developed in 1956 by Francis Cressi in his shop on rue Masséna.

❸ NORWAY

***Lørdagspizza*:** literally translated as "Saturday pizza," it is typically rectangular, topped with a mixture of ground meat, tomato sauce, and a generous amount of cheese.

❺ TRENTON (NEW JERSEY)

Tomato pie: in 1936, the De Lorenzo brothers invented this American-style pie baked on a baking sheet on which mounds of cheese are place before adding tomato. Today, there are still two De Lorenzo's addresses: Robbinsville, New Jersey, and Yardley, Pennsylvania.

❻ PHILADELPHIA (PENNSYLVANIA)

***Pizza arrotolata* or pizza Stromboli:** rolled pizza with mozzarella and deli meats, invented in 1950 at Romano's Italian Restaurant & Pizzeria, near Philadelphia.

❼ CONNECTICUT

Greek pizza: made with a soft and oily dough similar to focaccia, abundantly topped, and baked in a pan. It was invented by a Greek from Albania in Connecticut in 1954. It is widespread in New England and eastern New York State.

❽ NEW HAVEN (CONNECTICUT)

New Haven–style pizza: a pizza with a thin and soft crust blackened by cooking over a wood fire, invented at Frank Pepe, a pizzeria founded in 1925. A plain pizza is topped with tomato sauce, oregano, and grated Pecorino Romano cheese. The white clam pie is a white pizza with clams, olive oil, oregano, garlic, and grated cheese.

THE PATH OF IMMIGRANTS

Mid-nineteenth century to 1920s: from Naples to Marseille, New York, and North America.

From 1876 to 1920: from all over Italy to Brazil.

End of the nineteenth century: from Naples and Genoa to Argentina

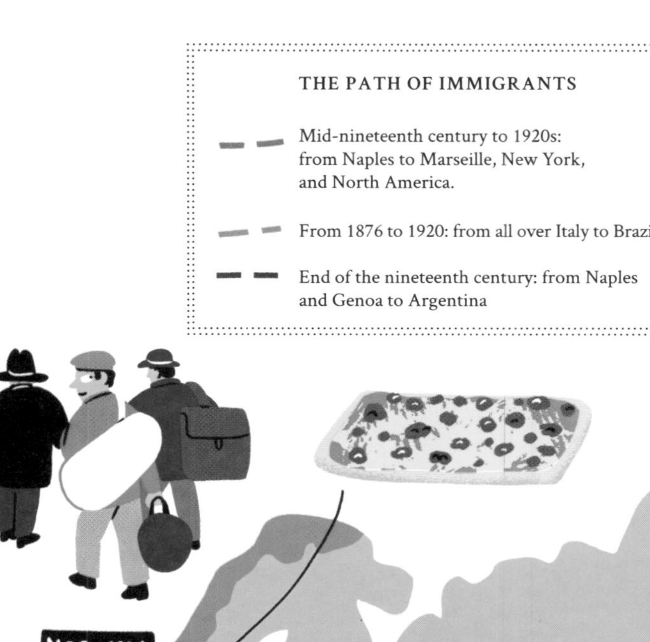

NORWAY

FRANCE

Genoa

ITALY

Naples

1 MARSEILLE

→ In 1903, the cantina of an Italian from Sorrento (Campania) located on rue de la Guirlande served *pizza bianca*, "white" pizza (with "Roman cheese," lard, and basil).

→ In the 1930s, Sauveur di Paola, a pizza maker from Formia (Lazio), promoted the *pizza rossa* ("red" pizza) with tomatoes. His restaurant, opened on rue d'Aubagne in 1943, still exists today.

→ In 1962, Jean Méritan, a steward from Marseille, invented the pizza truck, a revolutionary vehicle equipped with a wood-fired oven mounted on a trailer towed by a van. Little by little, pizza makers took to vans. This Marseilles invention spread throughout France.

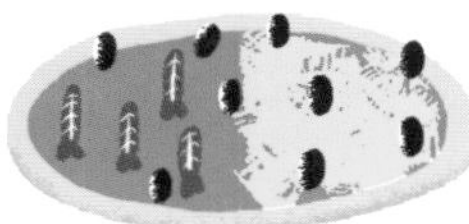

Half-and-half pizza (*pizza moitié-moitié*): half anchovy, half Emmental, invented by the Provençaux of France.

***Pizza figatellu-brocciu*:** a result of pizza meeting the Corsican community; it is very popular in Marseille.

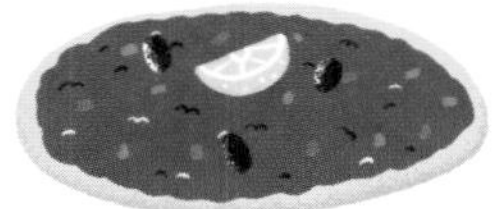

Meat pizza (*pizza à la viande*): a version derived from *lahmacun*, a typical Armenian dish, probably invented in the Armenian community.

NAPOLI

9 CANADA (ATLANTIC COAST)

Garlic fingers: a pizza topped with garlic butter, parsley, and cheese and cut into rectangular slices in the shape of fingers.

10 NOVA SCOTIA

Pictou County pizza: topped with "brown sauce" and a Halifax-made pepperoni called Brothers, named after the company that produces it, Chris Brothers Meats & Deli.

11 QUEBEC

Pizza-ghetti: an iconic junk food consisting of half a pizza and a portion of spaghetti topped with a tomato-based sauce.

12 CHATHAM (ONTARIO)

Hawaiian pizza: Sam Panopoulos, a Canadian businessman of Greek descent, along with his brothers staked claim on this invention in 1962 of this pizza made with tomato, cheese, ham, and pineapple in their restaurant the Satellite. This recipe has become very popular in Colombia.

13 CHICAGO (ILLINOIS)

Chicago-style pizza: also called "deep-dish pizza," it was developed in 1943 by Texan Ike Sewill and Italian Rik Riccardo at Pizzeria Uno. It's a layered pizza covered with runny cheese and tomato sauce, on a crust rolled out with a rolling pin and baked in a pan in an electric oven.

14 DETROIT (MICHIGAN)

Detroit-style pizza: a rectangular pizza with a thick, crispy, and chewy crust. It's traditionally topped with Wisconsin brick cheese, then tomato sauce spread on top of other toppings (rather than directly on the crust). It was created in 1946 at Buddy's, now a pizza chain.

15 SAINT LOUIS (MISSOURI)

Saint Louis–style pizza: a crunchy unleavened crust, cracker-style, topped with commercially produced Provel cheese and always cut into squares.

16 WICHITA (KANSAS)

The first Pizza Hut opened its doors on June 15, 1958. In 2019, this chain had 18,703 outlets around the world.

17 CALIFORNIA

California-style pizza (or gourmet pizza): combines a thin and crunchy crust, typical of New York, with ingredients from Californian cuisine (duck, hoisin sauce, barbecue chicken, peppers, smoked salmon, and goat cheese, etc.). It was invented in the late 1970s by Alice Waters (Chez Panisse, in Berkeley) and popularized by American chefs Ed LaDou and Wolfgang Puck (Spago, Los Angeles).

18 SÃO PAULO (BRAZIL)

Pizza Catupiry: named after a cream cheese created in 1911 by Mario and Isaira Silvestrini, an Italian immigrant couple in the state of Minas Gerais. Local ingredients are added: crayfish, chicken, corn, hearts of palm . . .

19 BUENOS AIRES (ARGENTINA)

***Muzzarella*:** thick crust (called *media mesa*) topped with lots of cheese, tomato sauce, and olives. Other recipes include jam, tomato slices, red bell pepper, and *longaniza* (a spiced dry sausage from Spain).

***Fugazza con queso*:** pizza topped with cheese and onions.

***Fugazzeta*:** cheese sandwiched between two pizza crusts, topped with onions.

SKIP TO
THE HISTORY OF PIZZA, P. 270;
PIZZE NAPOLETANE, P. 54.

SEASON

TUTTO L'ANNO (YEAR-ROUND)

CATEGORY

SECONDO PIATTO (MAIN COURSE)

LEVEL

FACILE (EASY)

CARPACCIO

Before referencing a preparation made of thin slices of raw meat or fish, this red-colored dish was an emblem of Venice and a tribute to one of its most famous painters.

FRANÇOIS-RÉGIS GAUDRY

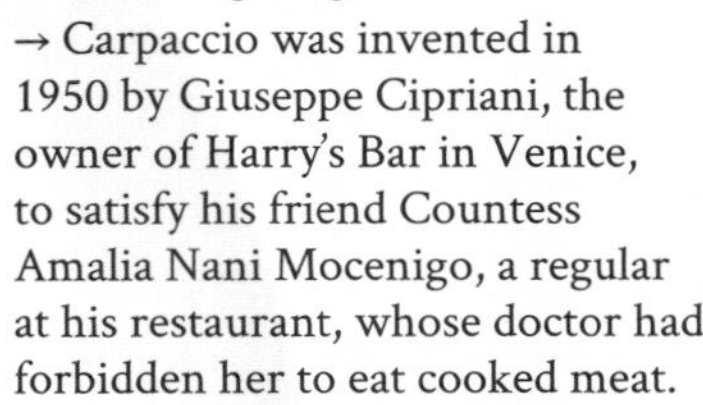

A family legend

→ Carpaccio was invented in 1950 by Giuseppe Cipriani, the owner of Harry's Bar in Venice, to satisfy his friend Countess Amalia Nani Mocenigo, a regular at his restaurant, whose doctor had forbidden her to eat cooked meat.

→ According to a myth supported by Cipriani's family, Giuseppe settled on the name *carpaccio* for his creation by visiting a retrospective organized that same year in the Republic of Venice featuring Vittore Carpaccio. The deep reds of this famous Venetian painter of the Renaissance reminded him of the color of raw beef.

→ But according to documents in the archives of the Doge's Palace, the Carpaccio exhibit did not take place in 1950 but instead in 1963. It is most likely that Giuseppe Cipriani had been making his recipe for many years but did not decide to name it *carpaccio* until the 1960s.

A PIEDMONT INFLUENCE?

Could carpaccio be a recipe inspired by the Alba-style raw meat dish *carne cruda all'albese*? This traditional antipasto from the Langhe region, which spread throughout Piedmont, is made from thin slices of raw Fassona veal, cut with a knife, seasoned with lemon juice, olive oil, salt, and pepper. In season, you can add a few slices of white Alba truffle.

Arugula and Parmesan Carpaccio

This "tufted" version of carpaccio has been very popular in Italy and around the world since the 1980s.

To make it, buy precut meat or a piece of knuckle or sirloin (allow 3½ ounces/100 g per person). Place the meat in the freezer, then cut it into very thin slices once it hardens. Arrange the slices over the entire surface of a plate, then let come to room temperature. When ready to serve, whisk lemon juice with salt and olive oil, drizzle the plate with a spoonful of this mixture, then season it with a few turns of the pepper mill.

Season the arugula with the remaining sauce and arrange it in the center of the meat. Place Parmesan shavings on top. You can also add, depending on your preferences, lightly toasted pine nuts, capers, or Taggiasca olives. Serve immediately.

THE CARPACCIO OF HARRY'S BAR

This famous preparation is served as a *secondo piatto* (main course) to distinguish it from the recipe from Alba. Never freeze the meat before slicing it; this is one of the golden rule's at Harry's Bar in Venice. Properly trimming a piece of beef and slicing it thinly takes practice and dexterity. You can also ask your butcher to do it with a slicer, as long as you use the meat within two hours to prevent it from turning black.

SERVES 6

About 2¼ pounds (1 kg) beef sirloin (about 1⅓ pounds/600 g after cleaning)

Salt

1 cup (250 g) mayonnaise

1 to 2 teaspoons (5 to 10 mL) Worcestershire sauce

1 teaspoon (5 mL) fresh lemon juice

2 to 3 tablespoons (30 to 45 mL) milk

Freshly ground black pepper

Clean the piece of meat by removing all traces of fat, nerves, or cartilage until you get a small cylinder of tender meat. Place the meat in the refrigerator until it is very cold. Using a sharp knife or, better still, a household meat slicer, cut very thin slices from the meat. Arrange the slices on six large plates to completely cover their surface, salt the top of the meat lightly, and refrigerate for at least 5 minutes.

Combine the mayonnaise with the Worcestershire and lemon juice. Add the milk to obtain a homogeneous but thick sauce. Adjust the seasoning, adding more salt, pepper, Worcestershire, or lemon juice to the sauce as needed.

Immediately before serving, dip a spoon in the carpaccio sauce several times and drizzle it over the plates, decorating the slices à la Kandinsky. Serve immediately.

SKIP TO
RUSTIC COW BREEDS, P. 258.

Francesco "Josko" Gravner

PROFILE

"For great wine you have to have clean water, obtained at the source, not at the mouth."

A RETURN TO BASICS

1952
Born in Goritz (Friuli-Venezia Giulia).

MID-1970S
A graduate in agronomy, he takes over his family business, founded in 1901. He begins practicing traditional viticulture.

1996
He loses 95 percent of his vineyard harvests due to hail damage. He then changes his way of thinking about wine and, with the small quantity of Ribolla he has harvested, experiments with his first macerations.

1997
He abandons the use of chemicals and macerates all his wines for four days in large wooden vats without temperature control.

2001
He undertakes a complete vinification in terra-cotta amphorae (ancient winemaking vessels) with indigenous yeasts. All his wines are clarified and unfiltered. The industry's press is highly critical of them.

2006
He begins aging all his wines in amphorae.

2013
His daughter Matja joins the company and takes care of the commercial end of the business.

SINCE 2019
His nephew Gregor works in the vineyard and the cellar.

AMPHORAE

In 1987, a friend gave him a Georgian amphora (*kvevri*). Fascinated, Josko traveled to Georgia three years later to learn about its local winemaking tradition and to bring back more of these vessels. He found eleven with a capacity to hold 528 gallons (2,000 L), nine of which broke during transport. Determined not to give up, he proceeded with the first fermentations in amphorae, which he buried, according to traditional methods used in the Caucasus.

A key figure in the history of winemaking in Italy and a pioneer in the return to fermenting in ancient vessels, this winegrower from Friuli has revolutionized winemaking.

PAOLO TEGONI

"I drink to your health, Josko! Remember this man is the best winegrower in the world! And he knows it!"

(LUIGI VERONELLI, JOURNALIST AND GASTRONOME)

THE MOON

Josko works according to the precepts of biodynamics. The lunar calendar plays a fundamental role, indicating the best days for work in the vineyards and in the cellar.

NEW MOON: a good time to sow, but not for winemaking in the cellar.

WAXING MOON: ideal period for doing a lot of work in the vineyard, but also for casking and bottling.

FULL MOON: a good time for grafting, pruning, or working the soil; in the cellar, it's a good time for casking and bottling.

WANING MOON: excellent for harvesting, pruning, and cellar operations.

HIS WINES

Since 2013, his production consists entirely of white wine obtained from Ribolla grapes and red wine made from Pignolo grapes.

THOSE OF YESTERDAY, TODAY, AND TOMORROW . . .

RIBOLLA: made from the Ribolla grape varietal cultivated in the region for more than a thousand years. Starting in 2001, the grapes were fermented for extended periods with indigenous yeasts and without temperature control in buried Georgian amphorae. After removal from the vat and pressed, the wine was transferred back to the amphora, where it remained for five months, after which it was aged in large oak barrels for six years.

ROSSO BREG: obtained from Pignolo grapes, it was fermented in contact with the skins in wooden vats until 2005. Starting in 2006, it was transferred into a buried amphora with indigenous yeasts and without temperature control. Aged for five years in oak barrels, it was then aged for at least five years in the bottle.

8.9.10: made with a selection of Ribolla grapes entirely botrytised (affected by noble rot). It was obtained using the best grapes from three successive harvests (2008, 2009, and 2010), hence its name. After fermentation in amphorae and a long maceration, it was aged in small oak barrels and bottled when the moon was waning in July 2015.

RARE (IN DANGER OF DISAPPEARING)

BIANCO BREG: made from a blend of several grape varietals (Chardonnay, Sauvignon, Pinot Gris, and Riesling Italico). The fermentation of the grapes was performed separately, but they were aged together. The rest of the vinification follows that of Ribolla. The 2012 vintage was the last to be sold. The international grape varietals were subsequently uprooted.

ROSSO GRAVNER: made from Merlot and Cabernet Sauvignon from the Hum and Runk vineyards (until 2004), it fermented in open oak vats for twenty-one days, without temperature control. After four years in oak barrels, it was aged for at least six months in the bottle.

RUJNO: Rosso Gravner cuvée was produced only in the best years. Fermentation took place with indigenous yeasts and in contact with grape pomace in open oak vats for five weeks, without temperature control. The wine was aged four years in oak barrels and six years in the bottle.

SKIP TO
NATURAL WINE, P. 320;
ORANGE WINE, P. 113.

la Molisana
SOLO GRANO ITALIANO
DECORTICATO A PIETRA
Mugnai da quattro generazioni
Aria pura di montagna
Acqua cristallina di sorgente
SPAGHETTI N°15
COTTURA 11 MINUTI
TRAFILATA AL BRONZO
Garofalo
SPAGHETTI
RUMMO
MAESTRI PASTAI IN BENEVENTO DAL 1846
METODO Lenta Lavorazione
ECCEZIONALE TENUTA ALLA COTTURA
SPAGHETTI Nº 3
500g ℮
dal 1886
Spaghetti n°12
Lenta Essiccazione
PER UNA PASTA DI QUALITÀ SUPERIORE
Semola a grana grossa
Acqua fredda di montagna
Trafila ruvida al bronzo
MADE IN ITALY
500 g ℮
Spaghetti
SPIGABRUNA
PASTA DI SEMOLA DI GRANO DURO BIOLOGICA CAPPELLI
SPAGHETTI BIO
MANCINI PASTIFICIO AGRICOLO
SPAGHETTI
PASTA DI SEMOLA DI GRANO DURO
500 g ℮
NET WT. 17,6 oz
FEUDO MONDELLO
SICILIA
PASTA DI SEMOLA INTEGRALE DI GRANO DURO
DAI NOSTRI CAMPI LA NOSTRA PASTA
MACINAZIONE A PIETRA
SPAGHETTI
i Grani di Luchino
gli Spaghetti dei Martelli
famiglia di pastai
1000 g ℮ 35.2oz (2.2 lb)
PRODUCT OF ITALY
SPAGHETTI di GRAGNANO
PASTA di GRAGNANO I.G.P.
Pastificio dei Campi
FABBRI
SPAGHETTI
minardo
Spaghetti
PASTA ARTIGIANALE
DURANTE
SPAGHETTI
Pastificio
FAELLA
dal 1907
PASTA DI GRAGNANO I.G.P.
Trafilata in bronzo
AFELTRA
100% Grano Italiano
PASTA DI GRAGNANO I.G.P.
Pasta Artigianale
BENEDETTO CAVALIERI
1918
100° ANNIVERSARIO
Spaghettoni di Benedetto Cavalieri
500g℮
MONOGRANO
FELICETTI
spaghetti
Setaro
Pasta
Torre Annunziata
(Napoli)
PASTA DI SEMOLA DI GRANO DURO
Lavorazione artigianale
Trafila in bronzo
GENTILE
GRAGNANO
NAPOLI
Pasta di Gragnano I.G.P.
TRAFILATA AL BRONZO

THE SPAGHETTI FAMILY

This is the pasta format par excellence! Its name derives from the word *spago* (string), for its thin, elongated shape. Spaghetti factories abound and prosper. Here is a roundup of the most respected *pastifici* (pasta factories) in Italy.

ALESSANDRA PIERINI

1	2	3	4	5	6	7	8

9	14
10	15
11	16
12	17
13	18
	19

ARTISANALLY PRODUCED

Selected wheat, bronze dies, slow drying: these are all the elements of artisanally produced spaghetti. Tasting: chewiness, thickness, flavor, and the ability to perfectly absorb their sauce.

(19) GENTILE · *Gragnano, Campania*

Founded in 1876 on the property of the same name, this historic *pastificio* has helped make Gragnano IGP pasta known around the world. It is located in the ancient Valle dei Mulini (Valley of Mills), the cradle of flour production. The Zampino family, owners since the 1980s, select wheat exclusively from Apulia. **COOK TIME:** 12 minutes.

(10) MINARDO · *Modica, Sicily*

In 2007, Giorgio Minardo founded this company, which became certified organic in 2008. He uses only ancient Sicilian wheats of the timilia and russello varietals, milled on-site using mineral water from the Nebrodi mountains, while maintaining the wheat germ, the part richer in nutrients. **COOK TIME:** 10 minutes.

(12) BENEDETTO CAVALLIERI

Maglie, Apulia

This is a one-hundred-year-old family-operated pasta factory selects hard wheat from Apulia and Basilicata. Spaghetti represents almost 30 percent of their total production. Their *spaghettoni* deserves special mention. **COOK TIME:** 16 to 17 minutes.

(16) DURANTE · *Cagli, Marche*

This pastificio, founded in 2008 on the banks of the Metauro River, uses spring water and local organic wheat of the Senatore Cappelli, Tirex, and Marco Aurelio varietals. The two founders are Ugo Guerra, a descendant of pasta makers, and Stefano Leoni, heir to grain producers. **COOK TIME:** 13 minutes.

(15) FABBRI · *Strada in Chianti, Tuscany*

Founded in 1893 in the village square, this family business works with the best ancient Italian wheat thanks to the fourth generation, embodied by Giovanni, and the fifth generation, with Marco and Lisa. Their spaghetti (dried for three to six days at less than 100°F/38°C) is considered among the best in Italy. **COOK TIME:** 12 minutes.

(18) MONOGRANO FELICETTI

Predazzo, Trentino-Alto Adige

This pasta has been produced in the heart of the Dolomites since 1908 by the Felicetti family. Riccardo, the grandson, has developed a production line that combines clean air and water drawn from over 3,200 feet (1,000 m) with the best varietals of organic Kamut wheat from Umbria, Apulia, Basilicata, and Canada. **COOK TIME:** 10 minutes.

(11) FAELLA · *Gragnano, Campania*

Gaetano Faella began this factory in 1907. This family of craftspeople has always worked only with Italian wheat and has contributed to the world renown of Gragnano, the capital of PGI pasta. **COOK TIME:** 10 to 12 minutes.

(14) PASTIFICIO DEI CAMPI

Gragnano, Campania

Giuseppe and Giovanna Di Martino, third-generation manufacturers, carry on a tradition of over five hundred years in the birthplace of PGI pasta. Their hard wheat is Italian, mainly from Apulia. Among the varietals: Saragolla, Simeto, and Grecale. **COOK TIME:** 8 minutes.

(9) MARTELLI · *Lari, Tuscany*

This family business has focused since 1926 on five pasta formats produced from Italian hard wheat ground by the Florentine Borgioli mill in Calenzano. The drying time of their spaghetti is at least fifty hours. **COOK TIME:** 9 to 10 minutes.

(13) SETARO · *Torre Annunziata, Campania*

Their story began in 1939 with grandfather Nunziato and continues with Vincenzo, Nunziato, and Giovanni. This factory produces nearly one hundred formats from Apulian wheat. **COOK TIME:** not indicated because it depends on the drying conditions.

(17) AFELTRA · *Gragnano, Campania*

Established in 1848 and crowned with the PGI label, this factory has created the Slow Food sentinel *fusilli a mano di Gragnano* (long, spiraled pasta made by hand). The durum wheat semolina is 100 percent Italian and mixed with spring water from the Lattari Mountains. **COOK TIME:** 8 to 10 minutes.

COMMERCIALLY PRODUCED

Tons of semolina is being transported each day to provide the world with the best pasta-making flour. Tasting: good consistency and good cooking performance; these pastas offer very good support for sauces.

(1) LA MOLISANA · *Campobasso, Molise*

Created by the Carlone family in 1912, the brand was acquired in 2011 by the Farro family of flour millers, who exclusively use Italian wheat from Apulia, Molise, Marche, Lazio, and Abruzzo. Today, this pasta is among the most consumed in Italy. **COOK TIME:** 10 minutes.

(2) GAROFALO · *Gragnano, Campania*

Founded in 1789 by Michele Garofalo with an exclusive concession for the production of pasta thanks to his expertise, the company is still an eminent spokesperson for the PGI label today. **COOK TIME:** 10 minutes.

(3) RUMMO · *Benevento, Campania*

In 1846, Antonio Rummo founded a flour mill and a fresh pasta factory before refocusing efforts on dry pasta. Since 2000, Rummo has strived to reduce the environmental footprint of its production. The wheat used comes from Italy, Australia, and Arizona. **COOK TIME:** 9 minutes.

(4) DE CECCO · *Fara San Martino and Caldari, Abruzzo*

Filippo De Cecco, son of one of the two founding brothers, designed a system of hot-air fans to replace sun drying. His invention enabled production to increase and international exports to begin in 1889. The wheat used by this multinational company, founded in 1886, comes from Italy, California, and Arizona. **COOK TIME:** 12 minutes.

FARM PRODUCED

Farmers are now getting their hands dirty by producing flour from their own organic cereals and making pasta using spring water and traditional methods. Tasting: excellent hold and body, producing fragrant, porous, and slightly floury pastas, which add smoothness to a sauce.

(7) FEUDO MONDELLO

Monreale, Sicily

Since the mid-nineteenth century, the Agosta family has cultivated the lands of the former Mondello stronghold in the Belice Valley in northwest Sicily. They produce locally distributed pasta with ancient and local varietals of wheat grown and ground on-site. **COOK TIME:** 10 minutes.

(5) SPIGABRUNA · *Pietrelcina, Campania*

This farm cultivates various organic cereals, including Senatore Cappelli hard wheat. Rosa Viola, who started the business about fifteen years ago, produces and processes cereals on-site with her team. **COOK TIME:** 7 minutes.

(6) MANCINI · *Fermo, Marche*

In 1938, Mariano Mancini founded this family farm dedicated to the cultivation of vegetables and cereals. Massimo, the grandson, started the pasta factory in 2010. He selects the best cereals, including the rare organic Khorasan wheat. **COOK TIME:** 9 to 11 minutes.

(8) MULINO VAL D'ORCIA

Pienza, Toscany

The Grappi Luchino agricultural company has been in existence since 1992 in the heart of the Val d'Orcia, a UNESCO World Heritage Site. The business, run by the same family for generations, covers more than 250 acres (100 ha), 85 percent of which is organically grown (especially hard wheat). **COOK TIME:** 8 to 10 minutes.

SKIP TO
PASTA INVENTORY, P. 124;
THE TASTE OF SHAPE, P. 317.

MINT

The herb that shoots up spontaneously all over Italy is an essential herb in the kitchen, especially in Rome, where it lends its delicate scent to many typical dishes.

JILL COUSIN

Mint in Italian Cooking

ZUCCHINE A SCAPECE, *Campania*: zucchini (or eggplant) fried then marinated in vinegar and spearmint.

CULURGIONES, *Sardinia*: ravioli stuffed with potatoes, pecorino, and mint.

COTOLETTE ALLA PALERMITANA, *Sicily*: breaded veal cutlets with fresh mint added after cooking.

ALICI AL FORNO ALLA MENTA, AGLIO E LIMONE, *Sicily*: anchovies baked on a bed of garlic and mint.

AGNELLO CON PISELLI, *Apulia*: lamb simmered with peas and mint, served at Easter.

ZUCCHINE MARINATE CON MENTA OR CONCIA DI ZUCCHINE, *Lazio*: carpaccio of sliced raw zucchini marinated in lemon and spearmint.

GELATO MENTA E CIOCCOLATO, *Lombardy*: Pennyroyal mint and chocolate ice cream.

SKIP TO
CLASH OF THE ARTICHOKES, P. 102; MARINADES, P. 322.

A small mint garden

From the Labiaceae family, several varietals of mint grow wild or are cultivated in Italy. Among them are *Mentha menta* and its close cousin *Lamium mentuccia*. Here are the most common varietals.

· MENTUCCIA ROMANA ·

Lesser calamint (*Calamintha nepeta*), so called in Rome and Tuscany but known as *nepitella* or *nepetella* elsewhere in Italy, is a wild variety. A creeping perennial shrub, it has small rounded slightly fuzzy leaves, with a subtle scent moving between mint and oregano, and pink flowers in season. It is also cultivated and sold at fresh produce markets.

· MENTA POLLEGIO ·

Pennyroyal mint (*Mentha pulegium*), with freshly scented and slightly oval leaves, is used in candies.

· MENTA VERDE ·

Spearmint (*Mentha spicata*), with oval, jagged leaves, often grows spontaneously in gardens. Very fragrant, it is also cultivated and sold in bunches. It is the most used varietal.

A ROMAN IDYLL

Mentuccia romana is inseparable from the cuisine of the Italian capital. Here are three representative dishes:

CARCIOFI ALLA ROMANA (Roman artichokes): artichokes cooked in a casserole dish with garlic and chopped fresh mentuccia.

TRIPPA ALLA ROMANA (Roman tripe): tripe stew with tomato, garnished after cooking with fresh mentuccia and pecorino.

VIGNAROLA: a casserole of artichokes, peas, fava (broad) beans, romaine lettuce, and asparagus, served with fresh mentuccia and parsley.

RECIPE

SPAGHETTI MARITATI

This pasta recipe with chopped walnuts and mint is typical of the village of Casalbordino (Abruzzo), where chef Riccardo Ferrante (restaurant Solina, Paris 12th) grew up. *Maritati* means "married," for its happy combination of walnuts and spearmint.

SERVES 4

- 1 bunch spearmint
- 2⅔ cups (250 g) walnut halves
- 2 cloves garlic
- ¼ cup (60 mL) olive oil
- ¼ cup (30 g) ground sweet pepper
- 1 handful coarse salt
- 1⅛ pounds (500 g) fresh *spaghetti alla chitarra**

· Remove the leaves from the mint and finely chop the leaves. Chop the walnuts with a knife, then combine them with the chopped mint; set aside. Peel and thinly slice the garlic cloves and lightly brown them in the olive oil in a saucepan over medium heat. Add the sweet pepper, then deglaze the pan with a ladleful of water.

· Boil a large pot of salted water and cook the spaghetti. When the spaghetti is al dente, ladle out about a cup (250 mL) of the cooking water and set aside; drain the spaghetti.

· Pour the spaghetti into the saucepan with the garlic mixture, then stir vigorously clockwise, adding a little of the pasta cooking water. A natural cream, formed by the starch from the pasta and the olive oil, will coat the pasta. Continue stirring, adjusting the sauce with cooking water or olive oil as necessary. Serve the spaghetti mounded slightly on the plate, and sprinkle with the walnut-mint mixture.

****The art and method:*** *spaghetti alla chitarra* is a pasta format typical of Abruzzo. Preparing these long square ribbons requires a utensil called a *chitarra* ("guitar"), fashioned from a frame of beechwood over which thin steel wires are stretched.

SEASON
TUTTO L'ANNO (YEAR-ROUND)

CATEGORY
DOLCE (DESSERT)

LEVEL
DIFFICOLTÀ MEDIA (MEDIUM DIFFICULTY)

ZABAIONE

CUSTARD WITH FORTIFIED WINE

With its characteristic yellow color, reputation as an aphrodisiac, and zing of alcohol, *zabaione* (sabayon) has been delighting all of Italy for generations.

GIANNA MAZZEI

What am I?

Spelled *zabaione*, but also *zabajone* or *zabaglione*, it is a dessert made with eggs, sugar, and fortified wine. Campania, Lombardy, Tuscany, Piedmont, Veneto, and Emilia-Romagna claim its origins, which yet remain a mystery.

→ The first known recipe can be found in the *Cuoco napolitano*, an anonymous Neapolitan manuscript dating from the end of the fifteenth century.

→ In *Le Libro de arte coquinaria* (1456–1467), Maestro Martino recommends eating it before going to sleep. He also suggests it as a stimulant for the mind.

→ Bartolomeo Scappi, in his *Opera dell'arte del cucinare* (1570), in addition to specifying the wines to use—Malvasia or Trebbiano di Pistoia—gives instructions so detailed that they can still be followed exactly as written today. He indicates that zabaione is suitable for the sick and infirm. These three versions of the recipe include cinnamon.

→ It is said that it was popular at the French court of Catherine de' Medici, where she introduced it; she liked to eat it frozen.

→ Famous for its nourishing, toning, strengthening, and energizing properties, zabaione is also renowned for its aphrodisiac qualities.

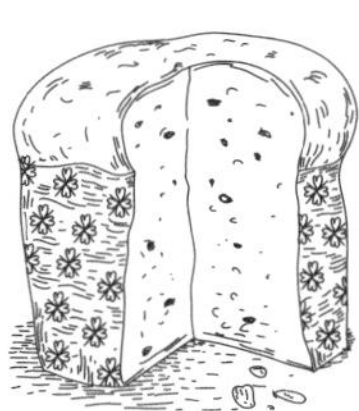

HOW DO YOU ENJOY IT?

It can be enjoyed on its own or with *amaretti*, *savoiardi* (ladyfinger cookies), *langues de chat* ("cat's tongues"), or *paste di meliga* (small cookies made with butter and cornmeal). It is excellent with a slice of panettone or *pandoro*. It is used to fill *torta Ostiglia* and *torta Elvetia*, two rich tarts from northern Italy. It can be eaten hot, warm, or cold.

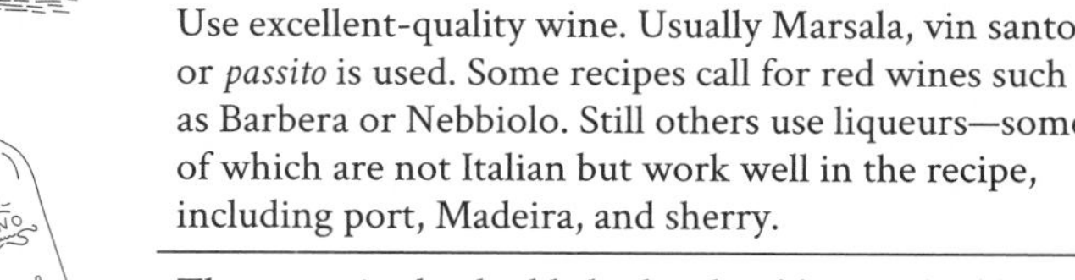

THE GOLDEN RULES

Use very fresh eggs.

Use excellent-quality wine. Usually Marsala, vin santo, or *passito* is used. Some recipes call for red wines such as Barbera or Nebbiolo. Still others use liqueurs—some of which are not Italian but work well in the recipe, including port, Madeira, and sherry.

The water in the double boiler should never boil but always remain slightly simmering.

Traditionally, the unit of measurement for measuring the wine is half an eggshell.

THE MAGIC BREAKFAST

In the Italian tradition, there is also the "grandmother" version, commonly known as *uovo sbattuto*, which is a cousin of eggnog. In a cup, using a teaspoon, vigorously combine the yolk of a fresh egg with sugar—the more sugar is added, the creamier the texture will be—until you obtain a light and frothy cream. It can be consumed as is or with the addition of a few drops of milk, coffee, or Marsala.

THE RECIPE

Here is the traditional version from Mantua.

SERVES 4

4 extra-fresh (76 g) egg yolks
¼ cup plus 2 tablespoons (80 g) sugar
8 eggshell halves (about ⅓ cup/80 g) Marsala or other fortified wine

Place the egg yolks in a saucepan set in a bain-marie and add the sugar. Whisk by hand or using an electric mixer until you obtain a clear and frothy cream. Add the Marsala in a thin stream while constantly whisking. When the mixture is well combined, set the saucepan over another saucepan of slightly simmering water (or transfer the mixture to a bowl and set it over the pan) to make a double boiler. Maintain medium heat, or even low heat, to avoid lumps and to prevent the cream from sticking to the side of the pan. Continue whisking until a thick, velvety consistency is achieved, 10 to 15 minutes.

THE LAZY VERSION

Instead of using the traditional bain-marie, it is possible to prepare the zabaione directly over the heat source. The method for the ingredients is the same, but you have to be careful when the foam begins to deflate because this is the moment when it thickens. It's also at this moment that the zabaione must be removed from the heat before it sticks to the side of the pan.

SKIP TO
COOKIES, P. 154.

Sweets from the Convent

Let's open the doors into this sweet Eden that is reviving the traditions of Sicilian pastry.

ALESSANDRA PIERINI

A SACRED PLACE

Next to the Church of Santa Caterina d'Alessandria, a baroque jewel in Palermo, is a Dominican convent of the same name that was home to cloistered nuns from the seventeenth to the twentieth centuries. It has recently reopened to the public to offer contemporary cakes and pastries produced in the former pastry shop where the nuns operated in complete secrecy.

This place is now aptly named I Segreti del Chiostro (the Secrets of the Cloister) and owes its existence to Maria Oliveri, an art historian. She revived the specialties produced by twenty-one Palermo monasteries that ceased their activities more than forty years ago. None of the secret recipes were documented; they were merely passed down by spoken word from the oldest to the youngest. Maria interviewed the last few custodians of these sweet treasures.

Paradise behind closed doors . . .

Until the nineteenth century, the sisters were the only real pastry chefs in the city, and this represented an important source of income for the survival of their convents. They sold gourmand selections on Sunday mornings through a turnstile that allowed them to communicate with the outside world without being seen.

Cannolo (Cannoli)

INGREDIENTS: hard-wheat flour, lard, sugar, eggs, Marsala wine, ricotta, dark chocolate, pistachios, candied fruit.

ORIGIN: Badia Nuova Monastery, also called S. Maria di Monte Oliveto. Built in 1512 in the historic center, it hosted the community of the Clare sisters.

Genovesi (Genoese)

INGREDIENTS: flour, eggs, sugar, lard or butter, ricotta, milk, chocolate or pistachio.

ORIGIN: Monastery of Santa Caterina.

Nucatoli

INGREDIENTS: flour, lard, eggs, sugar, Marsala wine, almonds.

ORIGIN: Monastery of Santa Elisabetta. Founded in 1551 by Franciscan nuns, it was transformed into a cloistered convent in 1607.

Biscotti papali

(cookies of the pope)

INGREDIENTS: flour, eggs, butter, sugar, Marsala wine, *cedrata* (candied citron zest with honey).

ORIGIN: Monastery of Santa Caterina.

Biscotti ricci

(curly cookies)

INGREDIENTS: almonds and/or pistachios, sugar, egg white, milk.

ORIGIN: Monastery of the Reepentite (literally "redeemed sinners"). The convent, built in 1524, quickly became a welcome place of redemption for women considered of little virtue, who found spirituality in the Franciscan order. In 1866, following a law suppressing certain religious orders, the monastery was expropriated.

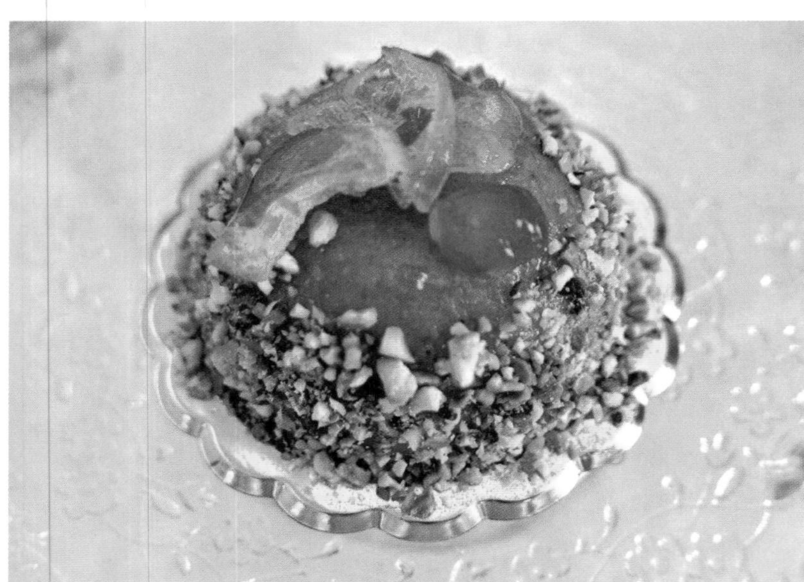

Trionfo di gola

(triumph of gluttony)

INGREDIENTS: flour, eggs, sugar, milk, cornstarch, almonds, pistachios, apricot jam, candied fruit.

ORIGIN: Monastery of Sant'Andrea delle Vergini. Built in 1300 for the Benedictine order, it was partially destroyed by bombings in 1943 during World War II and rebuilt, but is now abandoned.

Sospiri di Monaca

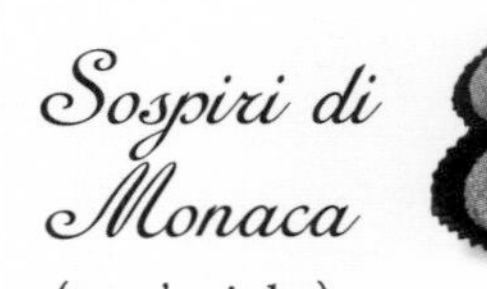

(nun's sighs)

INGREDIENTS: almonds, sugar, liqueur, candied fruits.

ORIGIN: Monastery of La Martorana.

Maria Stuarda (Mary Stuart)

INGREDIENTS: flour, lard, eggs, sugar, *zuccata* (pumpkin candied with sugar and cinnamon).

ORIGIN: Monastery of Santa Caterina. This convent, one of the largest and most important in Palermo, built in 1311, welcomed daughters from the most prominent families. The last three nuns of the Dominican order were transferred out in 2014. Now open to the public, it can be visited like a museum where visitors have access to the I Segreti del Chiostro pastry shop.

Minne di vierge

(virgins' nipples)

INGREDIENTS: flour, lard, sugar, eggs, Marsala wine, ricotta, dark chocolate, candied fruits, *cedrata* (candied citron zest with honey).

ORIGIN: Monastery of Sant'Andrea delle Vergini.

Pasticciotti del paradiso

(pastries from heaven)

INGREDIENTS: flour, eggs, lard, sugar, Marsala wine, candied orange, zuccata.

ORIGIN: Monastery of Santissimo Salvatore, the first monastery built in Palermo along with the adjacent church in 1072 during Norman times. It housed the congregation of sisters of the Order of Saint Basil the Great. The fact that Queen Costanza of Altavilla and the patron saint of Palermo Rosalie donned the Basilian convent habit has crowned it with prestige.

Panino di Santa Caterina

(Saint Catherine's little bread)

INGREDIENTS: almonds, eggs, zuccata, sugar.

ORIGIN: Monastery of Santa Caterina.

Frutta martorana

(Fruits of Martorana)

INGREDIENTS: almonds, sugar.

ORIGIN: Monastery of La Martorana. It was the third to be built by Eloisa and Goffredo Martorana, in 1194, under Benedictine rule. The name of the founders has remained with it, to indicate the famous marzipan fruits (*frutta martorana*) invented by the nuns here.

Cassata fridda

(cold casssata)

INGREDIENTS: flour, eggs, sugar, dark chocolate, ricotta, candied fruit.

ORIGIN: Monastery of Santa Teresa. The Discalced Carmelites occupied this place from 1653 to 1866, when they were transferred to the Assunta convent.

Fedde del Cancelliere

(chancellor's buttocks)

INGREDIENTS: almonds, pistachios, milk, sugar, apricot jam, cornstarch.

ORIGIN: Monastery of the Cancelliere. Founded in 1171 as the Monastero di Santa Maria dei Latini, this second Palermo convent of the time was inhabited by the Benedictines. In the thirteenth century, it changed its name in honor of the founding chancellor (*cancelliere*). It was destroyed by bombings in 1943 during World War II and never rebuilt.

Cassatelle

(small cassatas)

INGREDIENTS: soft- and hard-wheat flours, lard, sugar, Marsala wine, white wine vinegar, ricotta, dark chocolate.

ORIGIN: Badia Nuova Monastery.

A little less than saintly, perhaps?...

There are many convent-produced pastries that have names suggesting a bit of naughtiness!

→ The recipe for cannoli is said to have been invented by the women of the harem of a Saracen emir established in Sicily, to pay homage to his manly attributes. The recipe was passed on to the nuns at the end of Arab rule.

→ The rather indecent looking *minne di vergine*, originally created to echo the hills of the Sambuca region, are alluring in their resemblance to the *cassatelle di Sant'Agata* (a traditional Sicilian pastry) dedicated to Saint Agatha, the patron saint of Catania, who was martyred after having her breasts cut off.

→ The naughty *fedde del Cancelliere* could resemble, according to historian Mary Taylor Simeti, the female sex organ rather than buttocks.

→ The curious *sospiri di monaca*, a kind of almond paste fingers, merrily suggest other earthly pleasures!

AND ALSO:

Biscotti papali, couscous dolce, cassata antica, buccellatini di Suor Aurora, pantofole, gelo di mellone, agnello pasquale, amaretti, *sussameli, cosi duci,* granita . . .

SKIP TO
CANNOLO, P. 116; DISHES FROM THE VATICAN, P. 382; NEAPOLITAN PASTRIES, P. 123.

SEASON
TUTTO L'ANNO (YEAR-ROUND)

CATEGORY
PRIMO PIATTO (FIRST COURSE)

LEVEL
DIFFICOLTÀ MEDIA (MEDIUM DIFFICULTY)

PACCHERI ALLO SCORFANO

PASTA WITH SCORPION FISH

Emblematic of Campania, this pasta dish with scorpion fish is a tasty derivative of *acqua pazza*, a broth made from poached fish, and an ancestral cooking technique.

NADIA POSTIGLIONE

THE SEA ON THE PLATE

→ Acqua pazza (literally "crazy water") is said to be the descendant of a sailor's technique of cooking fish in seawater. Another story says it was born in the nineteenth century in taverns in Naples, where inhabitants cooked with seawater to get around the taxes placed on salt . . .

→ Although absent from historical cookbooks, it is defined in Tommaseo's 1865 dictionary of the Italian language as "a clear and tasteless broth."

→ Today, it is illegal to use seawater directly in cooking. The current version of acqua pazza involves cooking fish in court-bouillon with tomato, oil, white wine, and herbs.

Pairing with pasta

When reduced by cooking, acqua pazza becomes a denser sauce intended to accompany pasta. In Campania, *paccheri allo scorfano* is one of the most typical expressions of this, in which the oil and the tomato produce an aromatic emulsion, creating an ideal sauce.

THE RECIPE

It is recommended to use a whole fish, as much of the flavor is concentrated in the head. The cooking time of the fish varies according to its weight: plan on 15 minutes for 10½ ounces (300 g), 20 minutes for 1⅛ pounds (500 g).

SERVES 4

7 ounces (200 g) Piennolo del Vesuvio tomatoes (canned when out of season) or Datterini tomatoes
Salt
2 cloves garlic, peeled
⅓ cup plus 2 tablespoons (110 mL) olive oil
1 Mediterranean scorpion fish (*rascasse* or *chapon*; scales and backbone removed), preferably at least 1⅛ pounds (500 g), or 2 small
Scant ½ cup (100 mL) white wine
½ bunch parsley, chopped
12 ounces (350 g) paccheri de Gragnano IGP pasta
A few basil leaves, chopped
Freshly ground black pepper

Cut the tomatoes in half, remove the seeds, strain the juice, and set the juice aside. Bring a pot of salted water to a boil for the pasta.

Cook the whole garlic cloves in a pan with the olive oil. Remove them once golden. Gently place the fish in the pan, cook for a few minutes, then add the wine. Add the juice from the tomatoes, lower the heat, sprinkle with half the parsley, and cover. Cook for 10 minutes to brown. Add the tomato halves, cook for 5 minutes, then turn off the heat.

Lift out the fish and place it on a work surface. Crumble the flesh, removing any bones and any thorns from the skin, and add it to the sauce. Season with salt, if necessary. You can also keep the whole fish warm and eat it after the pasta.

Cook the pasta. A few minutes before the end of the recommended cooking time, set aside a cup (250 mL) of the cooking water and drain the pasta. Place the pasta in the saucepan with the reserved cooking water, the remaining parsley, and the basil. Season with salt and pepper, then cook over high heat for a few minutes before serving.

THE THREE USES OF ACQUA PAZZA

① This fish is eaten by itself as a *secondo piatto* (main course).

② The pasta with just the sauce is consumed as a *primo piatto* (first course). The flesh of the fish is eaten afterward (as the secondo piatto).

③ The pasta is eaten with the sauce and the shredded fish flesh as a primo piatto.

INGREDIENTS

THE PASTA

In this dish, the *pacchero* (meaning "slap" in the Neapolitan dialect) is a large short pasta in the shape of a smooth (*lisco*) or grooved (*rigato*) tube, which absorbs the sauce; the sauce, in turn, is enhanced by the consistency of the pasta. You can also use *maniche mezze* (a large tubular grooved pasta), linguine, or *spaghettoni* (large spaghetti).

POMODORINI DEL PIENNOLO DEL VESUVIO

Oval and pointed in shape, these small tomatoes grow on the slopes of Mount Vesuvius. Their flavor is unique, not very sweet, with very strong vegetal and mineral notes.

FISH

Scorpion fish (*rascasse*) are a culinary passion of the Neapolitans. In 1773, in *Il cuoco galante*, the cook Vincenzo Corrado mentions its firm white flesh and recommends it with a tomato sauce. *Chapon* (a close cousin to the rascasse), gurnard, monkfish or, as a more refined option, sea bream can also work for this recipe.

SKIP TO
COOKING WITH SEAWATER, P. 317; FISH, P. 300; TOMATOES, P. 28.

SEASON
PRIMAVERA (SPRING)

CATEGORY
PRIMO PIATTO (FIRST COURSE)

LEVEL
DIFFICOLTÀ MEDIA (MEDIUM DIFFICULTY)

RISI E BISI

ITALIAN RICE AND PEAS

Halfway between a risotto and a soup, this Venetian-style marriage of rice and peas is a celebration of spring!

FRANÇOIS-RÉGIS GAUDRY

What am I?

→ Derived from the Venetian dialect *rixi e bixi*, *risi e bisi* translates to "rice and peas," although peas are called *piselli* in Italian.

→ Rice cooked with vegetables? This is probably a heritage from Byzantium, with whom Venice had intense trade relations during the eleventh century.

→ Common in Venice, Vicenza, and Verona, this specialty lies somewhere between a fluid risotto (the rice grain is not toasted in the fat, but it must maintain its texture) and a thick *minestra* (it is traditionally eaten with a spoon). It was offered to the doge in the banquet hall of the Palazzo Ducale on April 25, Saint Mark's Day.

TWO ICONIC INGREDIENTS

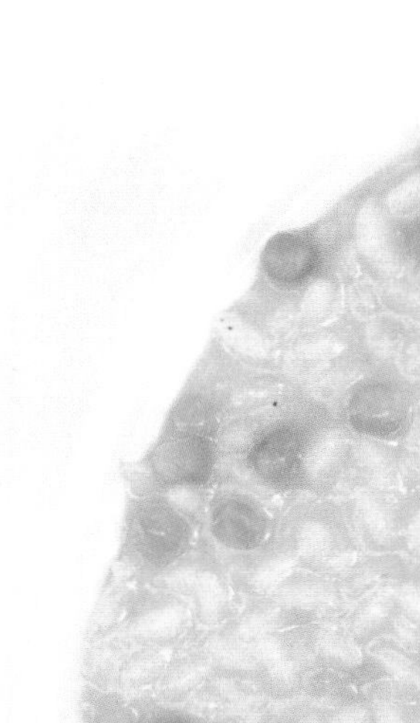

Riso di Grumolo delle Abbadesse (a product protected by Slow Food), a rice of the varietal Vialone Nano, cultivated in the provinces of Vicenza and Padua.

Bisi di Lumigagno, named after a small village in the province of Vicenza. The historic varietal cultivated on the hills of Berici is *verdoni*: it is resistant to the cold and develops early (it is harvested in April and May). This pea is also used in the preparation of another traditional dish: *tajadele coi bisi*, which is fresh pasta served with peas sautéed with spring onion and white wine.

THE RECIPE

This classic version requires simultaneous cooking of the rice and peas. Eleonora Zuliani, chef at Il Bacaro restaurant (Paris 11th), offers a modernized risotto-style version. She adds white wine, a cream of peas, and a touch of chives instead of the traditional parsley!

SERVES 4

1 stalk celery
1 carrot
1 yellow onion
2¼ cups (320 g) shelled fresh peas
Salt
2 small fresh white onions
7 tablespoons (105 mL) olive oil
1⅔ cups (320 g) Vialone Nano rice
Scant ½ cup (100 mL) dry white wine
4 tablespoons (60 g) unsalted butter, chilled and diced
⅓ cup (30 g) grated Parmesan cheese
Freshly ground black pepper
A few chives, chopped

The day before (preferably)

In a large pot, combine the celery, carrot, and yellow onion. Cover these vegetables with cold water (you need at least 1½ quarts/1.5 L water) and bring to a boil. Lower the heat and simmer for 30 minutes. Let cool, strain, and keep the broth cool.

The next day

Bring the vegetable broth to a boil, lower the heat, and let simmer.

Cook 1¾ cups (250 g) of the peas with a scant ½ cup (100 mL) of the broth and a pinch of salt for about 5 minutes. Using a blender, blend off the heat, then let cool.

Roughly chop the white onions, then cook with 3 tablespoons (50 mL) of the broth and a pinch of salt. After about 10 minutes, they should be soft. Blend and keep warm.

In a saucepan, heat 3 tablespoons (45 mL) of the olive oil. Add the rice and stir to give the rice a pearly sheen. When the temperature of the rice is too hot to touch (it will be too hot to keep the back of your hand on top), add the wine, cook until it evaporates, and pour in a good ladleful of the broth. Continue cooking in this way, gradually adding broth, stirring between additions.

After 10 minutes, add the remaining ½ cup (70 g) peas and cook for 10 minutes, then add the blended peas and onions. Season lightly with salt.

After 14 minutes, remove the pan from the heat and make the *mantecatura* (the creaming): add the butter, Parmesan, and remaining 4 tablespoons (60 mL) olive oil and stir to thoroughly combine. Season with salt and pepper. Arrange on serving dishes, and sprinkle with the chopped chives.

VARIATIONS

→ Pea pods can be added to the vegetable broth to enhance the pea flavor.

→ A few sprigs of wild fennel fronds are often added.

→ This dish is commonly served with pancetta: replace part of the cooking butter with pancetta, cut into strips.

→ Probably of Jewish origin, *risi, bisi e oca* includes the addition of pieces of goose breast confit (*oca*).

Did you know?

Add strawberries to risi e bisi and you have a dish in the colors of the Italian flag. In the midst of Risorgimento (Italian unification) in the nineteenth century, "*risi, bisi e fragole*" became a slogan, a cry of protest against Austrian occupation.

SKIP TO
THE OTHER PROMISED LAND, P. 278; RISOTTO, P. 78; THE SOUPS OF ITALY, P. 146.

ASPARAGUS

Appearing as white, green, or purple, asparagus is a direct expression of the climate in which it grows. Here is an overview of the various regions of production around the Italian peninsula.

NADIA POSTIGLIONE

WHAT AM I?

SCIENTIFIC NAME

Asparagus officinalis.

COMMON NAME

Asparago.

ETYMOLOGY

From Latin *asparagus,* possibly from Persian *speregha* (bud).

HISTORY

Cultivated by the Egyptians along the Nile, known to the Greeks, and loved by the ancient Romans, asparagus spread to northern Europe during the Roman expansion. In the nineteenth century, its cultivation intensified in northern Italy with the arrival of a new white varietal from France: *asperge d'Argenteuil* (Argenteuil asparagus).

CONSERVATION

Also esteemed for its healing properties, asparagus was so popular in cooking among the Romans that it was dried and stored in brine or vinegar for consumption all year round.

TOUR OF ITALY

PURPLE ASPARAGUS ①

Very rare, with a fleshy consistency, it has a delicate and fruity flavor, with a slight bitter note.

Liguria

Known since the fifteenth century for its intense purple color linked to its genetic makeup, Violetto di Albenga (Slow Food) is a unique varietal. These late-developing asparagus were once covered with untreated cotton bales to protect them from the heat.

WHITE ASPARAGUS ②

Grown without exposure to sunlight by being covered with a heap of soil (called a *baulatura*), it is soft, fragrant, tender, and not very fibrous; almost the entire stalk can therefore be consumed.

Veneto

Since the sixteenth century, Veneto has remained the land of choice for white asparagus, with the varietals *bianco di Cimaldomo* IGP, *bianco di Bibione, bianco di Mambrotta, bianco di Padova, bianco del Sile, bianco di Rivoli Veronese,* and, in particular, *bianco di Badoere* IGP (very aromatic) and *bianco di Bassano del Grappa* DOP, among the most appreciated in Italy, with a strong note of fresh-cut grass.

Friuli-Venezia Giulia

Introduced as a local crop in the vineyards to contain moisture in the soil, *asparagus bianco del Friuli* was already famous in the nineteenth century. In Tavagnacco, it is particularly buttery and fragrant.

Lombardy

This region is suitable for growing white asparagus with pinkish heads. The pink hue is achieved by measured exposure to sunlight and sometimes due to the particular composition of the soil. Among the most popular varietals are *bianco di Cilavegna, di Cantello* IGP, *bianco di San Benedetto Po,* and the famous *rosa di Mezzago,* not very fibrous and with an intense taste.

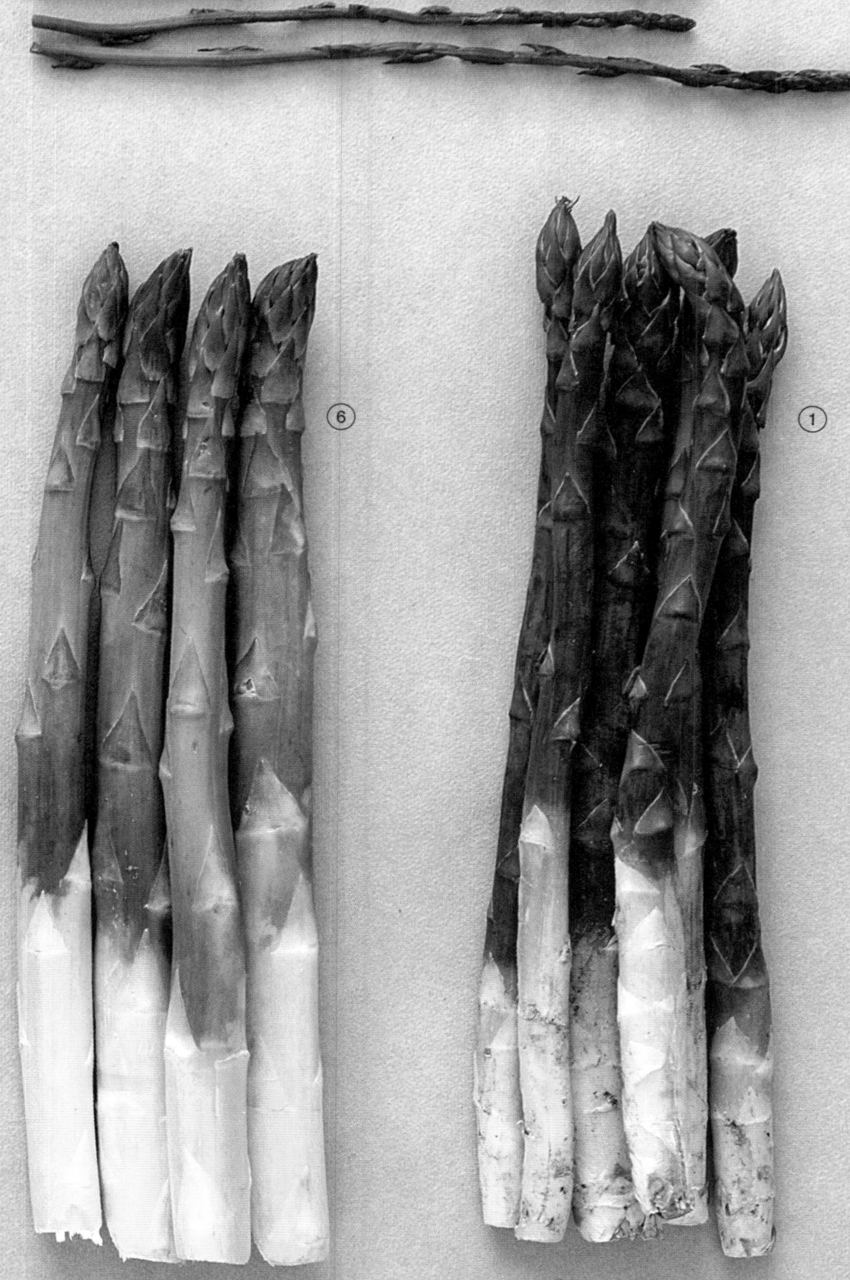

IN COOKING

ASPARAGI E CIAIRIGHÌ

Lombardy

The asparagus are boiled, sautéed in butter, and served with a fried egg. A classic.

TACCONELLE CON ASPARAGI SELVATICI E VENTRICINA

Molise

Diamonds of egg pasta with tomato sauce, seared wild asparagus, and *ventricina*, a pork sausage with spices and wild fennel seeds, typical of Abruzzo and Molise.

AL PROSCIUTTO

Emilia-Romagna

Green asparagus blanched al dente, wrapped in a slice of prosciutto, and baked au gratin with butter and Parmesan.

IN CARTOCCIO

Sardinia

Previously prepared on the grill, today wild asparagus are seasoned with garlic, olive oil, and sun-dried tomatoes, then wrapped in foil (*in cartoccio*) before being baked.

RISOTTO

Northern Italy

Asparagus, especially white, find their full expression prepared in this way. The broth for the risotto is made from the peels. Precooked, cut asparagus are added to the rice at the very end of the cooking time.

GREEN ASPARAGUS

It grows in sunlight, which allows photosynthesis of chlorophyll. It can be thin (3), medium (4) or thick (5) and has a strong flavor, with a smoother finish reminiscent of artichoke.

Apulia

This region is currently the largest producer, with the *capitanata* varietal in particular.

Piedmont

There are different niche productions, such as the varietals *valmacca*, *di Vinchio*, and *poirino*. *Asparago di Santena* 6, appreciated by Camillo Cavour (politician and father of the unification of Italy), is soft and not very fibrous.

Emilia-Romagna

The varietal *verde di Altedo* IGP, not very fibrous, expresses a marked herbaceous note.

Veneto

The varietal *amaro di Montine* (of the species *Asparagus maritimus*) grows along the coast and has a marked bitter note.

There is also *Argenteuil* (Tuscany), *asparago di Canino* (Lazio), and *asparago di Campidano* (Sardinia).

WILD ASPARAGUS (7)

Asparagus acutifolius, with its thin, fibrous stem, grows wild in the Mediterranean scrub brush, at the edge of woods and along drystone walls. It is widespread throughout the central region, the south, and the islands. Appreciated for its marked bitter note, it is used in cooking for *frittates* (omelets), risottos, sauces, soups, and preserves in oil.

Among the best known varietals are asparagus Pineta (Emilia-Romagna), Calabria IGP (Calabria), Murgia (Apulia), and Tissi (Sardinia), with an intense aroma.

SKIP TO
THE WAR OF THE HAMS, P. 311; RISOTTO, P. 78.

AMARO

Italian tradition dictates that each meal end with a bitter beverage to facilitate digestion, prompt a nap, or encourage chitchat with friends.

MARTINA LIVERANI

WHAT AM I?

An amaro (Italian for "bitter") is an alcoholic drink whose name expresses its dominant taste. Amaros are obtained from distilled spirits from a base of grains or fruit and generally flavored through infusion with herbs and other edible substances such as bark, berries, and roots. The minimum alcohol content must be 15 percent and the amount of sugar per 4 cups (1 L) must be less than 10 percent; otherwise, it is considered a liqueur.

From region to region, the taste of these *elisir spiritoso* changes depending on the plants used and the duration of the infusion. Of all the countries, Italy produces the greatest variety of amaros, with more than 870 types.

THE ORIGINS

→ The history of amaro (from Latin *amarus*) is linked to that of the medieval Arab alchemy school al-Kimiya, which spread the first alcoholic infusions of herbs cultivated for healing purposes.

→ Knowledge of distillations arrived from Jerusalem in 1099, notably at the medical college of Salerno.

→ These first experiments for medical purposes were reproduced in the form of infusions in monasteries and abbeys, especially by the Franciscans.

→ During the first years of the Renaissance, the medicinal objectives of these preparations were gradually abandoned, and unsweetened bitter decoctions began to resemble modern liqueurs, appreciated in their own right.

→ Thanks to the discovery of Indian and South American spices, which arrived in Europe via the Dutch and English East India Companies and the flourishing companies of the cities of Venice and Florence, the production of these distillates reached a decisive turning point.

→ The consumption of liqueurs and amaros for purposes of pleasure officially began at the court of Catherine de' Medici (late sixteenth century) with the first known evidence of delicious preparations served for receiving her guests.

The great classics

Here is a selection of iconic labels that have made Italy the great land of amaros. Bitterness levels range from 1 to 5.

AMARO MONTENEGRO (2/5)

ORIGIN: created in Zola Pedrosa, Bologna (Emilia-Romagna), in 1885 out of the passion of alchemist Stanislao Cobianchi and then called Elisir Lungavita (Elixir of Long Life), it was just ten years later sold under its current name.

RECIPE: forty herbs and plants, including oregano, cilantro, orange, nutmeg; 23% ABV.

TASTE: delicately bitter, citrus, balanced.

AMARO AVERNA (3/5)

ORIGIN: the Benedictine monks of Santo Spirito Abbey in Caltanissetta (Sicily) donated the recipe to Salvatore Averna, who has been marketing it since 1868. The brand now belongs to the Campari Group.

RECIPE: lemon, orange, and pomegranate essential oils mixed with roots, spices, and other secret herbs; 29% ABV.

TASTE: aromatic, herbaceous, Mediterranean aromas, harmonious, intense.

FERNET BRANCA (5/5)

ORIGIN: developed by Bernardino Branca, this quintessential Italian digestif has been produced since 1845 by the Fratelli Branca distillery in Milan (Lombardy).

RECIPE: twenty-seven plants, including rhubarb, saffron, cinnamon, chamomile, gentian; 39% ABV. Since the 1970s, the company has sold a mint version made with peppermint oil.

TASTE: herbaceous, balsamic, full-bodied, persistent, very bitter.

CYNAR (4/5)

ORIGIN: icon of the 1960s, created in 1948 by Venetian Angelo Dalle Molle, it is consumed as an aperitif as much as a digestif and has belonged to the Campari Group since 1995.

RECIPE: extract of artichoke leaves (*cynara* in Greek and Latin) and thirteen herbs; 16.5% ABV. It can be used in a spritz instead of Aperol, which is sweeter, or Campari, which is more bitter.

TASTE: vegetal, tannic, robust but balanced, persistent bitter note.

AMARO LUCANO (3/5)

ORIGIN: developed in 1894 by Pasquale Vena, pastry chef at Pisticci Scalo, Matera (Basilicata), still owned by the family today.

RECIPE: thirty herbs, including wormwood, gentian, sage, orange, elderflower, angelica; 28% ABV.

TASTE: citrus, floral, balsamic, bitter with a strong character.

RAMAZZOTTI (4/5)

ORIGIN: created in Milan (Lombardy) in 1815 by Bolognese Ausano Ramazzotti. Now owned by Pernod Ricard.

RECIPE: thirty-three herbs and spices, including cardamom, myrrh (with flavor of anise), orange, artichoke stem, cloves; 30% ABV.

TASTE: full-bodied, balanced, long finish, spiced, citrus.

BRAULIO (5/5)

ORIGIN: made in 1826 by pharmacist Francesco Peloni from Bormio (Lombardy) and sold since 1875, the recipe today belongs to the Campari Group. It is the most common Italian alpine amaro.

RECIPE: juniper, absinthe, gentian, muscat, yarrow, and other secret ingredients aged in oak barrels. 21% ABV.

TASTE: aromatic, balsamic, persistent, woodsy, very bitter.

VECCHIO AMARO DEL CAPO (3/5)

ORIGIN: created in 1965 from an idea of Giuseppe Caffo, from the Caffo distillery in Limbadi (Calabria) near the picturesque Capo Vaticano, from which it gets its name.

RECIPE: twenty-nine ingredients, including tangerine, orange, licorice, juniper, chamomile, anise; 35% ABV.

TASTE: herbaceous, citrus, delicately bitter with hints of vanilla.

The new wave

Today, harvesting herbs, roots, and wild berries is again valued, accompanying the return to traditional production of amaros. Rare natural treasures have thus been rediscovered—such as helichrysum in Sardinia, rock samphire (aka sea fennel) in Apulia, and *mentuccia* (*Calamintha nepeta*, lesser calamint)—and more creative compositions have been tested using radicchio, olive tree leaves, truffles, or even muscari (aka grape hyacinth, cultivated as an ornamental plant).

AMARO DENTE DI LEONE

La Valdôtaine (Saint Marcel, Aosta Valley)

An infusion of dandelion and other alpine herbs. Balsamic, soft, and velvety; 32.6% ABV.

CARAMARO

Tosti (Canelli, Piedmont)

An infusion made from wine and selected herbs, including thistle and artichoke leaves. Spiced, balanced, and harmonious; 17% ABV.

JUITH

Attimi Perfetti (Castelrotto, Trentino-Alto Adige)

With jujube (date), chamomile, mint leaves, and orange blossom. Sweet, fragrant, with a tangy finish; 33% ABV.

AMARO DEL CICLISTA

Casoni (Final Emilia, Emilia-Romagna)

The name recalls the exhaustive rides great-grandfather Casoni would take on his bicycle to see the woman who would become his fiancée, an effort rewarded with a glass of amaro. It's a mixture of about fifteen herbs, including rhubarb, gentian, licorice, juniper. Sweet, flavorful, with a spicy finish; 23.5% ABV.

AMARO FORMIDABILE

Formidabile Liquori & Affini (Roma, Lazio)

A maceration of aromatic and medicinal plants, including red quinquina, palmate rhubarb, wormwood, gentian, and star anise. Citrus, aromatic, with a long finish; 33.5% ABV.

AMARA

Rossa Sicily (Misterbianco, Sicily)

An infusion of blood orange zest and herbs. Citrusy, very fragrant, pleasant, and balanced; 30% ABV.

AMARISCHIA

Amarischia (Caviano, Campania)

Herbs selected according to the ancient recipe of the monks of Ischia with aloe, gentian, arugula, common rush, and wild thyme. Pleasant, balanced, vegetal, and slightly bitter; 30% ABV.

SKIP TO
LIQUORI, P. 366.

SEASON

TUTTO L'ANNO (YEAR-ROUND)

CATEGORY

SECONDO PIATTO (MAIN COURSE)

LEVEL

FACILE (EASY)

POLLO ALLA DIAVOLA

DEVIL'S-STYLE CHICKEN

RICETTA Iconica RICETTA

LAZIO, TUSCANY

Split, splayed, and seasoned galore with cayenne pepper, this dish will spice up any Sunday dinner.

CÉLINE MAGUET

A FOWL SQUABBLE

Tuscany and Rome fight over who can claim the origins of this recipe. In cookbooks from their two bordering regions, this fiery chicken figures prominently. From its carving to its cooking, the methods are the same in both regions. For now, there is no indication of who will succeed in staking their claim as the inventors of this dish between these two cities whose meat cultures are quite considerable.

DID YOU SAY "DIABOLICAL"?

So where does its evocative name "devil's chicken" come from? Does it originate from the flames shooting up around the skillet, reminiscent of the flames of hell, or is it from the generous dose of cayenne pepper? Pellegrino Artusi, father of modern Italian cuisine, lays it out for us in *La scienza in cucina e l'arte di mangiar bene* (*Science in the Kitchen and the Art of Eating Well*, 1891): "It is called *pollo alla diavola*, because it must be seasoned with strong cayenne pepper and served with a very spicy sauce, and thus whoever eats it, feeling his mouth catch fire, may be tempted to send to the devil [*mandare al diavolo*] both the chicken and the one who cooked it." Tempting, don't you agree?

A cinematic chicken

→ Director Vittorio De Sica mentions, in his letters, Marcello Mastroianni's passion for *pollo alla diavola*: He enjoyed it on the set of *Sunflower* (1970).

→ Chiara Rapaccini, Mario Monicelli's companion, recounts in her memoirs (*La bambina buona*, Sonzogno, 2011) that for her first meal with the director, she cooked pollo alla diavola, which she had flattened, for lack of a more suitable utensil, with his Golden Lion statue, won at the Venice Film Festival!

THE RECIPE

SERVES 4

- 1 whole chicken
- Olive oil
- 1 clove garlic, finely chopped
- 1 tablespoon (8 g) cayenne pepper (or to taste)
- 1 handful coarse salt
- 3 sprigs rosemary
- 6 sage leaves

Slit the chicken along the backbone (you can use a pair of kitchen shears) to open it up. To ensure even cooking, firmly flatten the chicken, breast side down, using a meat mallet.

In a bowl, combine a few tablespoons of olive oil with the garlic, cayenne, salt, rosemary, and sage. Massage the whole chicken thoroughly with this mixture. Let rest for 15 minutes.

Heat 2 to 3 tablespoons (15 to 45 mL) of olive oil in a pan or casserole dish over high heat, and place the chicken breast side down against the bottom of the pan. Place a heavy object on the chicken (such as heatproof weight or chef's press) and cover the pan. After about 5 minutes, lower the heat to medium. Cook for 15 minutes. Flip the chicken over and cook for another 20 minutes. For a small chicken, allow 40 to 45 minutes; increase the cooking time to 50 to 60 minutes for a chicken weighing about 2¼ pounds (1 kg). Serve with potatoes or a salad.

NOT TO BE CONFUSED WITH . . .

POLLO ALLA CACCIATORA
Lazio and Tuscany

This is another clash of claims between Lazio and Tuscany! The recipe varies depending on the region. *Pollo alla cacciatora* (hunter's chicken) is made with chicken cooked in herbs and white wine in Rome, but in Tuscany, the bird is stewed in tomato sauce and red wine. The saying goes in Tuscany that if the chicken is fresh, it is prepared alla cacciatora, and if it is a little older, it's prepared alla diavola.

POLLO CON I PEPERONI
Lazio

A simple name for an equally simple recipe to prepare: chicken cooked in a tomato sauce with bell peppers and white wine. This is a cousin to Basque-style chicken.

POLLO AL MATTONE
Tuscany

Similar to pollo alla diavola, it is the cooking technique that makes it unique. The chicken, split and splayed and weighed down with a brick (*mattoni*), is simply pan or oven roasted.

SKIP TO
PELLEGRINO ARTUSI, P. 32;
CHILE PEPPERS, P. 359.

FARRO, ANCIENT GRAINS

These ancient cereals cultivated in central Italy are not only delicious but have excellent nutritional qualities . . . two reasons to get to know them!

ELVIRA MASSON

SCIENTIFIC NAME
Triticum monococcum

COMMON NAME
Farro piccolo (einkorn; only one grain per shell)

SCIENTIFIC NAME
Triticum dicoccum

COMMON NAME
Farro medio (emmer)

SCIENTIFIC NAME
Triticum spelta

COMMON NAME
Farro grande (spelt)

COMPLEX CEREALS

FAMILY: Poaceae (grasses).

ORIGIN OF THE NAME: Italian *farro* derives from Latin *far* (common wheat).

GEOGRAPHICAL ORIGIN: the earliest cultures of farro date back to 5000 BCE in central Europe and Asia. Italy is one of its historic cradles.

APPEARANCE: similar to wheat, these grains have the shape of a grain of rice with an orange color. The special attribute is that the grains are enveloped in their protective husks and rich in fiber.

FLAVOR: subtle, between hazelnut and cashew. Dense texture, resistant to the bite. A concentrate of fiber, protein, iron, zinc, and antioxidants. Low in gluten, it's a nutrition bomb!

AN ANCIENT GRAIN

In Tuscany, farro has been cultivated since the Etruscans. Even today, along the roads of the small region called Garfagnana located at the foot of the Apuan Alps, near Lucca, farro fields stretch as far as the eye can see.

The husk provides protection from pests, disease, and chemicals, making it a highly desirable grain. But its yield is quite low, which is why wheat is often preferred.

FARRO FAMOSO

• Farro di Monteleone di Spoleto (*Triticum dicoccum*), native to Umbria, has a PDO. This varietal dates from the sixteenth century.

• Farro della Garfagnana (*Triticum dicoccum*), which carries a PGI in Tuscany, is cultivated at an elevation of 980 to 3,200 feet (300 to 1,000 m) using organic farming methods.

Label legend

Integrale: whole grains, with husks.

Semiperlato: semipearl; the grain has been lightly sanded and freed from its interior.

Perlato: pearl, or totally refined.

Spezzato: crushed. It is also called *farricello*. This is the main ingredient in *minestra di farro spezzato* in Umbria, a rustic soup with leeks, potatoes, onions, tomato *passata*, and pecorino.

Soffiato: puffed. It is used as a breakfast cereal, in biscuits and cookies, or to make granola.

In cooking

PREPARATION—to facilitate cooking, washing and soaking the grains for about twelve hours beforehand is recommended.

COOKING—from fifteen (for pearl) to forty-five minutes (for whole), depending on the varietal.

USES—low in gluten, it does not lend itself well to breadmaking and performs best in cooking where it will be served whole, in soup, cooled in a salad, or sweetened.

RECIPE

FARROTTO (FARRO MADE RISOTTO-STYLE)

This cooking technique is very popular in the central regions of Italy, where farro is widely cultivated and cooked (Umbria, Tuscany, Abruzzo . . .). Farrotto is made with cheeses typical of each region and seasonal vegetables.

· Heat 4 cups (1 L) stock in a saucepan.
· In another saucepan, brown 1 chopped onion in olive oil.
· Add the farro (use 3½ ounces/100 g per person), then add a few ladles of hot stock to cover the farro with liquid. Allow at least 50 minutes of cooking time.
· Mix regularly, adding additional stock as it evaporates. Incorporate the onion, then slowly add a selected cheese.
· Enjoy with a drizzle of olive oil.

SKIP TO
RISOTTO, P. 78.

OLIVES

In brine, in oil, dried, added to a martini, or to top a pizza, there is an *oliva* for every occasion.

ALESSANDRA PIERINI

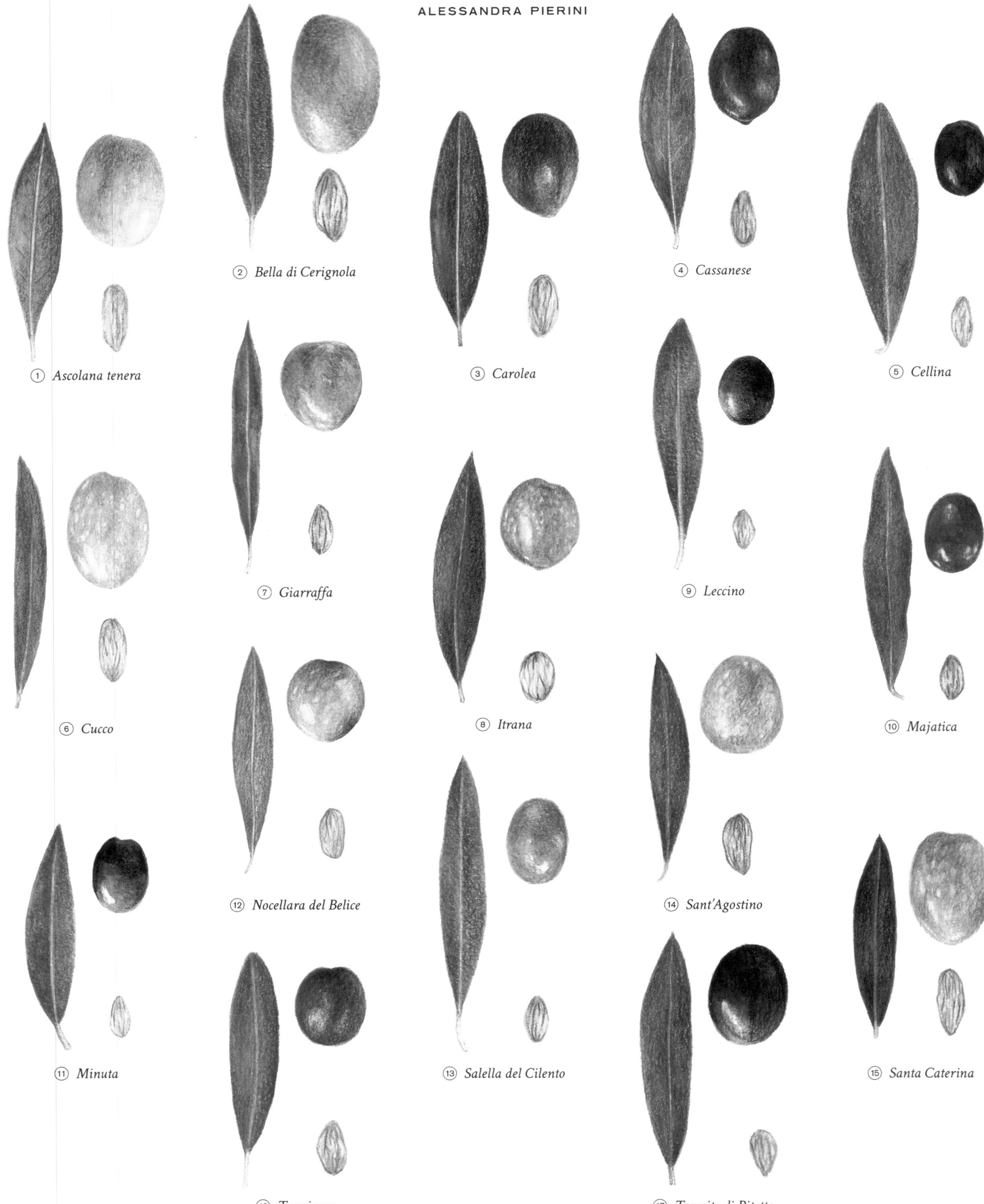

① *Ascolana tenera*
② *Bella di Cerignola*
③ *Carolea*
④ *Cassanese*
⑤ *Cellina*
⑥ *Cucco*
⑦ *Giarraffa*
⑧ *Itrana*
⑨ *Leccino*
⑩ *Majatica*
⑪ *Minuta*
⑫ *Nocellara del Belice*
⑬ *Salella del Cilento*
⑭ *Sant'Agostino*
⑮ *Santa Caterina*
⑯ *Taggiasca*
⑰ *Termite di Bitetto*

① ASCOLANA TENERA

Marche and Abruzzo

COMMON NAMES—*liva da Concia, liva ascolana, liva di San Francesco.*

APPEARANCE—ellipsoidal shape, green, large and heavy (up to ⅓ ounce/9 g, ⅞ inche/21 mm).

IN COOKING—mild, with a crunch; famous in the olive recipe *all'ascolana* (a stuffing of meat, garlic, and parsley, breaded and fried) or in brine.

INTERESTING FACT—it was granted PDO in 2005 under the name *ascolana del Piceno.*

② BELLA DI CERIGNOLA

Apulia

COMMON NAMES—*cerignolese, oliva a ciuccio.*

APPEARANCE—usually green (crunchy flesh), sometimes black (soft flesh), ellipsoidal in shape, very large (⅓ to ⅔ ounce/11 to 18 g, ⅞ to 1 inch/22 to 25 mm), compact.

IN COOKING—fruity and herbaceous; prepared in brine, soft, delicate; alone as an aperitif or in pasta, fish, or white-meat recipes; in cocktails.

INTERESTING FACT—it was granted PDO in 2000 under the name *bella della Daunia.*

③ CAROLEA · *Basilicata, Calabria, Apulia, Sicily*

COMMON NAMES—*olivona, calabrese, cumugnana, nicastrese, catanzarese.*

APPEARANCE—green or black, large (about ¼ ounce/6 to 8 g, about ¾ inch/18 to 19 mm), fleshy, firm, and ellipsoidal in shape.

IN COOKING—in brine with chile, garlic, and oregano; baked with *baccalà* and broccoli; in oil with eggplant and zucchini slices.

INTERESTING FACT—very ancient, already present before the arrival of the Greeks in the seventh century BCE; it is cultivated up to 2,600 feet (800 m) in elevation.

④ CASSANESE · *Calabria*

COMMON NAME—*grossa di Cassano.*

APPEARANCE—black, medium size (⅛ ounce/4 g, ⅔ inch/17 mm), irregular elliptical shape.

IN COOKING—dried in the sun to keep its typical bitter taste or in salt, then canned with olive oil, chile, lemon, orange zest, or mint leaves.

INTERESTING FACT—used for *bagnarola*, a preparation made with fish, olives, capers, dried bread crumbs, Parmesan, parsley, lemon, and pepper.

⑤ CELLINA · *Apulia*

COMMON NAMES—*morella, oliva barese, oliva di Nardò.*

APPEARANCE—black, small (¹⁄₁₆ to ⅛ ounce/2 to 3 g, ½ inch/12 mm), firm.

IN COOKING—taste reminiscent of blackberries; in brine in a terra-cotta container (*capasa*) with bay leaves, fennel fronds, and lemon slices; in *pucce* (breads with olives); in *mpille* (breads with vegetables, tomatoes, capers, olives); in the recipe *lepre alla cacciatora* (hunter's hare).

INTERESTING FACT—in a document dating from 1095, it is listed under the name *hocellina*, from late Latin *aucèllus* (bird), an animal very fond of this fruit.

⑥ CUCCO · *Abruzzo*

COMMON NAMES—*chietina, coglioni di gallo, lancianese, olivoce.*

APPEARANCE—black but mostly green, round, large (about ¼ ounce/6 to 8 g, ¾ inch/19 mm).

IN COOKING—delicate, with a bitter aftertaste that fades if kept in brine; for tomato bruschette or to season pasta.

INTERESTING FACT—in the local language, it is called *oliva da cuccare* (to swallow) for its spherical cherrylike shape.

⑦ GIARRAFFA · *Sicily*

COMMON NAMES—*becco di corvo, cacata di chioggia, cefalutana, ciocca, giardara, giarrafara, giarraffella, giarraffu mammona, pizzu di corvu, raffa, raffu.*

APPEARANCE—green (crunchy and vegetal flesh) or black (milder), elongated, heart-shaped, large (⅓ ounce/10 g, about ¾ inch/18 to 20 mm).

IN COOKING—slightly salty with a slightly bitter aftertaste; in *agghiotta* (fish with tomatoes, celery, onion, capers, and olives).

INTERESTING FACT—it is harvested in September and October and from November to January.

⑧ ITRANA · *Lazio*

COMMON NAMES—*oliva di Gaeta* (often harvested ripe, so black in color), *aitana, aitanella, cicerone, gaetana, di Esperia, tanella, trana.*

APPEARANCE—green or purplish black, medium to large in size (⅛ to ¼ ounce/4 to 6 g, ½ inch/12 mm), firm.

IN COOKING—very tasty, fruity, almost vinous; on pizza, fish, salads; in *pizzaiola*; with *spaghetti alla puttanesca* or *baccalà*.

INTERESTING FACT—when green, it is used for extracting oil; traditionally, it is also eaten crushed, *schiacciata*, or *appassita* (dried in the sun); DOP since 2016.

⑨ LECCINO · *Tuscany, Apulia*

COMMON NAME—*colombina.*

APPEARANCE—from black to purplish pink, small to medium (¹⁄₁₆ to ⅛ ounce/2 to 4 g, ⅓ inch/10 mm), fleshy, elongated ovoid shape.

IN COOKING—pronounced and intense taste, pungent and aromatic; for tapenades, salads, focaccia.

INTERESTING FACT—this is the most cultivated varietal, used for oil or as a table olive.

⑩ MAJATICA · *Basilicata*

COMMON NAMES—*maggiatica, gentile di Matera, oliva di Ferrandina, pasola, paesana.*

APPEARANCE—black, plump, small (¹⁄₁₆ to ⅛ ounce/2 to 4 g, ½ inch/12 mm).

IN COOKING—to accompany charcuterie, aged pecorino, orange salad, or baccalà in a casserole; the green olive is used for extracting oil.

INTERESTING FACT—20 percent of the production is reserved for the traditional oven-drying method, which gives it the name *oliva infornata di Ferrandina* (protected by Slow Food); the olives, left to wilt after harvest, are immersed in boiling water and dried in the oven with oregano and wild fennel.

⑪ MINUTA · *Sicily*

COMMON NAME—*mezza oliva.*

APPEARANCE—black with green undertones, small (⅛ ounce/3 g, about ⅓ inch/9 to 10 mm).

IN COOKING—*alivi 'a puddastredda* (pitted and fried in oil and garlic); *alivi cunzati* (crushed and boiled, seasoned with garlic, mint, oregano); in brine (*tinello*) with a mixture of water, sea salt, and aromatic herbs from the Nebrodi Mountains (wild fennel, garlic, bay leaf, and rosemary) or pressed in layers (*a suppresso*) in wooden or ceramic containers with salt and aromatics.

INTERESTING FACT—defined by agronomists as a "living fossil plant," its tree is very similar to the wild olive tree of ancient origin, and is particularly resistant to cold and disease; protected by Slow Food.

⑫ NOCELLARA DEL BELICE

Sicily

COMMON NAMES—*aliva di Castelvetrano, aliva tonda, bianculidda, tunna, nuciddara, mazara, nebba, trapanese.*

APPEARANCE—intense green, round, large (⅛ to ¼ ounce/5 to 7 g, about ¾ inch/18 to 20 mm), fleshy, crunchy, and dense, less often black.

IN COOKING—fruity, delicate, slight bitterness on the finish; ideal for *caponata* (Sicilian eggplant salad), with fish, *pane cunzato* (bread soaked in oil and topped), and in cocktails.

INTERESTING FACT—granted a PDO in 1998, it is included in three PDO oils: Valle del Belìce, Valli Trapanesi, and Val di Mazara.

⑬ SALELLA DEL CILENTO

Campania

COMMON NAMES—*lioi, licinella, monticedda, salentina.*

APPEARANCE—green, fleshy, small (⅛ ounce/3 g, ⅓ inch/10 mm).

IN COOKING—the *pane del pescatore* (fisherman's bread) topped with salted anchovies and olives; as an aperitif with cheese and charcuterie.

INTERESTING FACT—the traditional canned preparation of *oliva salella ammaccata* ("broken") *del Cilento* with olive oil, garlic, oregano, and thyme is protected by Slow Food.

⑭ SANT'AGOSTINO · *Apulia*

COMMON NAMES—*cazzarola, grossa di Andria, oliva pane.*

APPEARANCE—green, ovoid, large and heavy (¼ ounce/7 g, about ¾ inch/18 to 20 mm).

IN COOKING—in brine with wild fennel for an aperitif, a must with focaccia *pugliese*.

INTERESTING FACT—it is one of the largest table olives with *bella di Cerignola* and *ascolana*.

⑮ SANTA CATERINA · *Tuscany*

COMMON NAMES—*lucchese, di San Biangio, di San Giacomo.*

APPEARANCE—green, large (¼ to ⅓ ounce/7 to 9 g, ⅔ inch/16 mm), plump.

IN COOKING—in *cinghiale in umido* (wild boar casserole), in variations of *panzanella*, on bruschette.

INTERESTING FACT—it is the most cultivated varietal of table olive in Tuscany.

⑯ TAGGIASCA · *Liguria*

COMMON NAMES—*lavagnina, Oneglia pignola, di Taggia.*

APPEARANCE—in *véraison* (the onset of ripening) from purple to black, small (¹⁄₁₀ ounce/2.5 g, ⅔ inch/15 mm), ovoid, fleshy.

IN COOKING—fruity, aromatic, and sweet with an almond aftertaste; it is the standout in *coniglio alla ligure* and in *stoccafisso*; used with pasta, eggplant, fish, and on Genoese focaccia; canned, often pitted in olive oil.

INTERESTING FACT—it owes its name to the Benedictine Convent of Taggia (Imperia), where its cultivation began over a thousand years ago.

⑰ TERMITE DI BITETTO · *Apulia*

COMMON NAMES—*cima di Bitetto, mele di Bitetto, oliva mela, baresana.*

APPEARANCE—green, purplish, or black, round, medium (⅛ ounce/4.5 g, about ½ inch/12 to 14 mm).

IN COOKING—soft and crunchy; for focaccia, *panzerotti*, with baked fish or in *guazzetto*.

INTERESTING FACT—the black ones are eaten fresh after harvest; sweet, they are fried with garlic and cherry tomatoes in olive oil and eaten hot as an aperitif after being salted (*olive nere fritte*).

SKIP TO
CAPONATA (SICILIAN EGGPLANT SALAD), P. 220; CONIGLIO ALLA LIGURE (LIGURIAN RABBIT), P. 57.

Giuseppe Verdi

PROFILE

A MISANTHROPE . . . BUT SOPHISTICATED!

Considered misanthropic, Verdi retired in 1847 at barely thirty-four years of age with his wife, the soprano Giuseppina Strepponi, whom he tenderly called his *pasticcio* (little pâté), to his villa in Sant'Agata in the heart of the austere Po plain. He would leave his villa only to supervise his works. Although he followed an ascetic diet while working (during which he subsisted only on coffee), he was otherwise a lover of good food:

→ A maestro in the art of haggling over calves, cows, and poultry in regional markets.

→ An ingenious manager of the construction of a dairy, a fruit and vegetable market, and an icehouse in which ice from his lake was used, in particular to keep his *culatello di Zibello*, a delicious charcuterie from the region.

→ Self-sufficient with a well-stocked food pantry: fish from his lake, poultry and eggs from his barnyard, waterfowl from the banks of the river Po, vegetables from his kitchen garden.

→ Demanding when it came to his kitchen and table equipment: cast-iron stove bought in Paris in 1864, silverware, Sèvres porcelain, engraved Christofle cutlery.

KEY DATES

1813
Born in Roncole (Emilia-Romagna).

1851
Presentation of the opera *Rigoletto*, inspired by the play *Le roi s'amuse* by Victor Hugo, at the Fenice theater in Venice.

1853
Composes his opera *La Traviata*, after the novel *La Dame aux camélias* by Alexandre Dumas, fils, at the Fenice opera house in Venice.

1861
Election to the first national parliament of a unified Italy.

1901
Dies in Milan (Lombardy).

Considered the greatest maestro of Italian opera in the nineteenth century, he was also a gastronome. Let's make a toast to this stylish composer!

STÉPHANE SOLIER

THE WAR OF THE COMPOSERS

The two *maestri* Rossini and Verdi not only crossed swords over bel canto, they also faced each other as tournedos . . .

TOURNEDOS À LA ROSSINI
A sauce made with truffles, foie gras, and Madeira.

TOURNEDOS À LA VERDI
A sauce made with semolina, tomatoes, Parmesan, and onions.

"The kitchen at Sant'Agata deserves mention of its picturesque grandeur of collection of prints and art objects and all its implements of Pantagruelic alchemy. . . . More than anything, Verdi likes to see shining around him, among his guests, the spiritual and sincere gaiety which follows good meals; he is a disciplined man and as such he rightly considers the meal to be a work of art."
Giuseppe Giacosa, poet and librettist, 1889.

THE KITCHEN, FROM GRANDFATHER TO SON

→ From ancestors who were farmers, bakers, and innkeepers since the sixteenth century in Emilia-Romagna.

→ From parents who were proprietors of Osteria Vecchia, a farm/inn and food market in Roncole (Parma).

WHEN THE OPERA BECOMES A MEAL . . .

Verdi's career as a composer is a nod to gastronomy.

NABUCCO

After the premiere of this opera in 1842, Milan was in an uproar over the young Verdi. The city's pastry shops offered Verdi *feuilletés* (puff pastries), and cooks invented *salsa alla Verdi* (a sauce with Parma ham) . . .

OTELLO

During the long dry patch while he was writing *Otello* (1879–1887), every Christmas the publishers Tito and Giulio Ricordi would send the master a panettone to encourage him to complete his opera. A miniature chocolate Othello, "the Moor of Venice," once topped the cake and was gradually completed in its form, first without legs and sexless, then with half a body . . .

RIGOLETTO

It was by performing the role of Gilda in Verdi's *Rigoletto*, performed in 1887 in Brussels, that soprano Helen Porter Mitchell, better known by her stage name, Nelly Melba, came to prominence. Shortly after, Auguste Escoffier created the famous dessert peach Melba. Thanks, Verdi!

ESCOFFIER'S MUSE

In his *Guide culinaire* (1902), Auguste Escoffier pays homage to the sophistication of the Italian composer by dedicating a large number of recipes to him, often based on Parmesan and truffles: *consommé Verdi*, *oeufs Verdi* (eggs), *filets de sole Verdi* (sole fillets on a bed of seasoned *maccheroni*), *poulet sauté Verdi* (sautéed chicken on a bed of Piedmontese risotto, slices of foie gras and truffles), or *salade Aïda* . . .

HIS FAVORITE DISHES

COSTOLETTA ALLA MILANESE, with lots of butter.

POLENTA, of which he dreamt when he was away from Italy.

RAVIOLI ALLA GENOVESE

RISOTTO ALLA MILANESE, the art of which he perfectly mastered: "If they knew how he composes *risotto alla milanese*, God knows what applause would rain down on him" (letter from his wife, February 19, 1861).

SPALLA DI SAN SECONDO (charcuterie made from pork shoulder), of which it is claimed he invented the dish (followed with a long cooking once dredged) and how to enjoy it, at room temperature.

PANNA COTTA

PERE COTTE, pears cooked in wine.

AMARETTI, "The eighth wonder of the world" (letter from April 5, 1865).

THE MASTER'S CELLAR

BORDEAUX WINES AND MOËT & CHANDON CHAMPAGNE

CHIANTI

ASTI SPUMANTE, for after dessert.

SKIP TO
CO(S)TOLETTA ALLA MILANESE (VEAL MILANESE), P. 41; POLENTA, P. 114; RISOTTO ALLA MILANESE, P. 290.

SEASON

TUTTO L'ANNO (YEAR-ROUND)

CATEGORY

PRIMO PIATTO (FIRST COURSE)

LEVEL

FACILE (EASY)

SPAGHETTI ALLA PUTTANESCA

SPAGHETTI WITH MARINARA AND OLIVES

This recipe, dating to the beginning of the twentieth century, plays the role of prima donna in the Neapolitan gastronomic repertoire—and the wildest rumors circulate about its origins.

SONIA EZGULIAN

The scandalous pasta of Naples

Why is the name of this recipe associated with prostitutes (*puttane*)?

→ Some say its garish colors (the green from the parsley, the red from the tomatoes, the purple from the olives) recall the colorful outfits worn by prostitutes.

→ Others tell of the dish's creation by a French streetwalker who, while walking the cobblestones of the Quartieri Spagnoli in Naples, brought her native Provence with her through these ingredients.

→ Most, however, tell the story of such a dish that the Neapolitan prostitutes (or their pimps) would keep simmering on the stove to attract customers with its tantalizing aroma or to offer as a way to restore energy after a night of frolicking.

THE ESSENTIALS

Its ancestor is said to be marinara sauce (olive oil, olives, and capers). It was not until the 1950s that *puttanesca* as we know it today appeared.

If possible, choose Gaeta olives (or Niçoise), Pomodorini del Piennolo tomatoes, and very finely chopped garlic and anchovies.

Use long pastas: spaghetti, vermicelli, linguine, or penne.

THE RECIPE

Two versions of this dish have been in head-to-head competition since the beginning of the twentieth century. The Neapolitan version, which uses long pasta exclusively, is made without anchovies. The version from Lazio, which goes well with penne or spaghetti, includes anchovies. Today in Naples, it can sometimes be found with anchovies or even with tuna.

SERVES 4

14 ounces (400 g) spaghetti

Salt

6 tablespoons (90 mL) olive oil

8 anchovy fillets in salt, rinsed and dried

2 cloves garlic, peeled

14 ounces (400 g) fresh in-season Piennolo tomatoes (preferably), peeled (or use canned peeled tomatoes)

1 tablespoon (9 g) salted capers

1 pinch chopped red pepper

16 to 20 black olives (preferably Gaeta or Niçoise), pitted

Freshly ground black pepper

4 sprigs flat-leaf parsley, chopped

Cook the spaghetti in a large pot of salted boiling water until al dente.

Heat 4 tablespoons (60 mL) of the olive oil in a large skillet. Finely chop the anchovy fillets, then the garlic. Add the anchovies and garlic to the pan and cook for several minutes. Coarsely crush the tomatoes and add them to the pan, then add the capers and red pepper. Roughly chop the olives and add them to the pan. Season to taste with salt and black pepper. Simmer over high heat for 6 to 7 minutes, stirring occasionally.

Set aside some of the pasta cooking water, then drain the pasta and add it to the pan with 2 tablespoons (30 mL) of the cooking water and the remaining 2 tablespoons olive oil. Stir for 1 or 2 minutes over high heat, sprinkle with the parsley, and serve immediately.

SONIA'S CREATIVE VARIATION

I admit that I make this recipe often because I love its straightforward flavors and its quick preparation. I like to replace the first 4 tablespoons (60 mL) of olive oil with 2 tablespoons (30 g) of butter for extra creaminess, as is allowed in some Italian variations. I carried my tribute of this recipe to the point of creating a veal and pork sausage seasoned with the ingredients of puttanesca: tomato (paste), anchovies, capers, olives, and parsley.

SKIP TO

TOMATOES, P. 28; OLIVES, P. 214; THE AMAZING ANCHOVY, P. 236; SPOTLIGHT ON CAPERS, P. 110.

SEASON

TUTTO L'ANNO (YEAR-ROUND)

CATEGORY

STREET FOOD

LEVEL

DIFFICOLTÀ MEDIA (MEDIUM DIFFICULTY)

PIZZA FRITTA

FRIED PIZZA

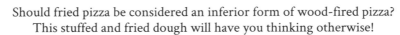

Should fried pizza be considered an inferior form of wood-fired pizza? This stuffed and fried dough will have you thinking otherwise!

ALBA PEZONE

ITS ORIGINS

With its own popular identity, *pizza fritta* has a history related to women. During World War II, Neapolitan housewives left their homes to make ends meet. The most daring among them from the working-class neighborhoods decided to set up a *focone* (a wide and deep skillet) on sidewalks to sell pizzas to go, filled like a turnover and fried. To avoid competing with each other, they each chose separate days to sell their product. Customers, whose names were jotted in notebooks, could pay eight days later, hence the Neapolitan phrase *a ogge a otto* ("eat it today, pay in eight days").

Pizze Fritte, da Assunta
Via Giuseppe Simonelli, 58 80134 Napoli
tel. +39 334 369 5502

A PIZZA FRITTA WORD GUIDE

RIPIENA	Stuffed, with the filling on the inside.
GRANDE	For those with big appetites (up to 16 inches/40 cm in diameter).
PISCITIELLO	Meaning *little fish*, but in the city's historic center, it means a half-moon-shaped pizza fritta (or half of a large one). Called *battilocchio* in the station district (literally "eye flap," designating a woman's hat covering the eyes, or it could mean a lost person in the figurative sense).
TRADIZIONALE	Without tomato, which attests to its ancient origin dating from before the arrival of the tomato in Naples.
COMPLETA	Stuffed with ricotta, provola, *ciccioli*—a kind of Neapolitan pork crackling—tomato, black pepper. Starting from a *completa*, the variations are then made by omitting certain ingredients (without *ciccioli*, without pepper . . .) or by adding ingredients (a lot of ricotta, a lot of *provola* . . .). And then there are the seasonal versions: with panfried escarole, olives, and capers (typical around Christmas) or with sautéed bell peppers or eggplant (for summer).
MONTANARA	A variation topped with tomato and mozzarella (see recipe below). It is said to be the meal of the native workers who went to work on the coast. It is first mentioned in 1600 in a text by Antonio Valeriani as a "typical Sunday recipe." It is also represented in the anthology film *L'oro di Napoli* (*The Gold of Naples*) by Vittorio De Sica (1954).

THE RECIPE (A MONTANARA)

Pizza fritta is difficult to prepare at home because properly frying it can be a delicate operation. Here is a recipe for the *montanara* version, a traditional homemade pizza fritta with the toppings instead of a stuffed dough, therefore easier to make.

FOR 12 TO 15 FRIED *PIZZETTE* (LITTLE PIZZAS)

For the dough

4 cups (500 g) all-purpose flour, plus more for dusting
¾ teaspoon (5 g) fresh baker's yeast
1¼ to 1⅓ cups (300 to 320 g) water, at room temperature
1⅔ to 2 teaspoons (10 to 12 g) fine sea salt
Peanut oil, for frying

For the toppings

1 clove garlic
2 tablespoons (30 mL) olive oil
14 ounces (400 g) peeled tomatoes
2 pinches dried oregano
Salt and freshly ground black pepper
2 mozzarella di bufala cheese
1 cup (100 g) grated pecorino or Parmesan cheese
12 to 15 basil leaves

To make the dough, place the flour in a large stainless steel bowl and crumble the yeast over the top. Drizzle in three-quarters of the water. Knead quickly, until you get a rough dough. Work in the salt, then drizzle in the remaining water. Knead for about 15 minutes (in the mixing bowl or on the work surface), until you obtain a smooth, homogeneous, and elastic dough that detaches from the side of the bowl. Shape the dough into a ball and transfer it to a large bowl capable of holding three times its volume. Cover the bowl with plastic wrap, then let rise for 4 hours at a temperature close to 64°F (18°C), away from drafts.

Divide the dough into balls weighing 1¾ to 2⅛ ounces (50 to 60 g) each. Space them out on a baking sheet. Cover with plastic wrap and let rise for another 4 hours at around 64°F (18°C), away from drafts.

Transfer the dough to a lightly floured work surface. Using your fingertips, press each dough ball into a disk. Fry the pizzettes on both sides in oil heated to 338° to 356°F (170° to 180°C). Set aside on paper towels to drain.

To prepare the toppings, peel and finely chop the garlic. In a saucepan, heat the olive oil. Brown the garlic in the oil, then add the tomatoes and oregano. Season with salt and pepper. Simmer over medium heat for 15 minutes. Shred the mozzarella into pieces and let drain.

Top each pizzette with a spoonful of sauce, a piece of mozzarella, a pinch of the pecorino, and a basil leaf. Serve immediately.

TIPS

→ You can knead the dough in a stand mixer fitted with the dough hook. Start on speed 1, then increase to speed 2.

→ If you prepare the montanara in advance, place them in the oven at 475°F (250°C) for 10 seconds before serving so that they crisp up again.

RICOTTA

Here's a little tour of a creamy Italian cheese made using whey, the by-product of other cheeses.

ALESSANDRO DE CONTO

ITS ORIGINS

It is known that the Greeks made ricotta—the Cyclops Polyphemus prepares it in his cave in the *Odyssey* (IX, 184)—and, following the Greeks, the Etruscans and the Romans also produced it, as the agronomists Cato and Columella demonstrated (second to first centuries BCE). Made from whey, a by-product of the cheesemaking process that was also used as pig feed, ricotta served as poor folks' food.

FRESH RICOTTA

① **COW** · *northern Italy*

Delicate and soft, it can be coarse and gritty when it is artisanal or smooth and velvety when it is industrially made. It is available in varying quantities, from 3½ ounces to 4½ pounds (100 g to 2 kg). Industrial varieties are homogenized for preservation.

USES—plain; in sauces or with pasta; to fill savory tarts or fresh pasta; in pastry.

② **GOAT** · *northern Italy and parts of the south*

Delicate and sour, it has a slight goaty taste. It is found in varying quantities, from 3½ ounces to 4½ pounds (100 g to 2 kg). The one sold in smaller quantities is better.

USES—plain; a rather recent product that has not found its place in traditional dishes.

③ **SHEEP** · *south central Italy*

With a strong taste, it is mild and grainy. Born in Lazio, as is Pecorino Romano, the famous ricotta Romana DOP is the first ricotta to benefit from this PDO label.

USES—plain; used to fill fresh pasta and savory tarts and to make many traditional desserts from the south (*pastiera, cassata, cannolo, pardulas*. . .).

④ **BUFFALO** · *southern Italy*

Creamy and slightly sticky, it is distinguished by its aroma of coconut and almond. *Ricotta di bufala Campana* DOP (buffalo's-milk ricotta from Campania), which is derived from *mozzarella di bufala* DOP, is a recent product.

USES—plain, with a drizzle of oil and some black pepper or lemon zest; for topping pizza; as a sauce for pasta; for making meatballs or to stuff vegetables for baking.

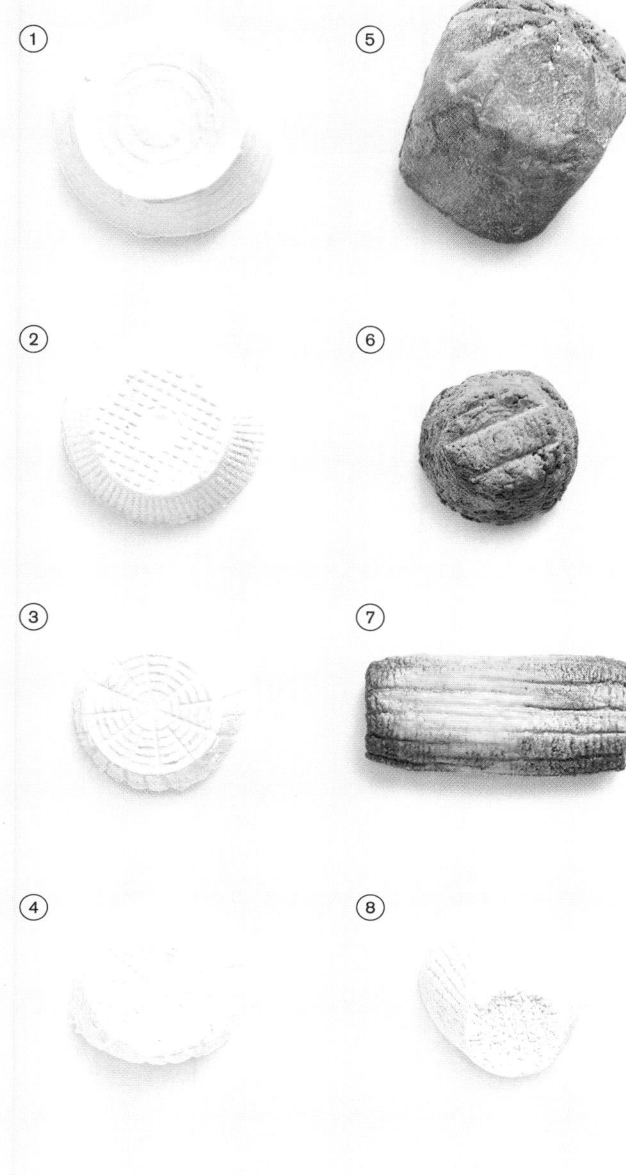

HOW TO MAKE IT?

Ricotta (from the Latin *recoctus*, meaning "cooked twice") is obtained by cooking the whey left over from cheesemaking. A fatty cheese will give off a weak whey and make a dry ricotta; a semifat cheese will give off a richer whey and make an unctuous ricotta. It's also possible to add up to 20 percent milk and/or fresh cream to give the product a creamy consistency.

1 → The whey is heated to approximately 185°F (85°C).

2 → After a few minutes, the first pieces of curdled milk rise to the surface (this is called flocculation). This results in the coagulation of whey proteins.

3 → The curds are removed with a skimmer, then placed in containers to drain.

4 → Once cooled, the ricotta can be packaged. You can also eat it while still hot by buying it directly from the producer!

SMOKED RICOTTA

Ricotta can be preserved by smoking, salting, baking, or all of these techniques combined. It is then perfect to be grated on *primi piatti* (pasta, rice, soups . . .).

⑤ ***Ricotta affumicata al forno o al camino*** (cow's-milk ricotta smoked in the oven or over a fire, Friuli-Venezia Giulia): grated onto *cjarsons*, sweet or savory ravioli from Friuli generously topped with melted butter.

⑥ ***Ricotta affumicata di capra*** (smoked goat's-milk ricotta, Veneto and Friuli-Venezia Giulia): grated over gnocchi in tomato sauce.

⑦ ***Salata e affumicata,*** ⑧ ***ricotta salata*** (salted and smoked ricotta, and salted ricotta, Sicily, Sardinia, Calabria) and the different local variations of *marzotica e infornata* (baked, Apulia); *mustia* (Sardinia): grated over Sicilian *pasta alla Norma*.

TWO RARITIES

SEIRASS DEL FEN · *Piedmont*

Slow Food Sentinel

A ricotta obtained from cow's milk or a mixture of milks (cow's-sheep's-goat's) and wrapped in hay. *Seirass* means "serum" in the Piedmontese language. In the past, this round-shaped ricotta, weighing around 4½ pounds (2 kg), was prepared only in the mountains and then covered with hay (*fen* is dried umbrella pine fescue) for protection during transport. It is eaten fresh or after being matured for three to four months, with Piedmontese *grissini* (breadsticks), jam, and honey. It is also used in making a *crostata* (a free-form rustic pie), or it can be grated.

RICOTTA SALATA DELLA VALNERINA · *Umbria*

This rare cone-shaped sheep's-milk ricotta is covered with bran or herbs, which help preserve it. It is excellent with vegetable soups or with a strong-flavored local extra-virgin olive oil.

SKIP TO
NEAPOLITAN PASTRIES, P. 123;
SWEETS FROM THE CONVENT, P. 204;
FRESH PASTA, P. 294.

SEASON

ESTATE (SUMMER)

CATEGORY

ANTIPASTO/ CONTORNO (APPETIZER OR SIDE DISH)

LEVEL

FACILE (EASY)

CAPONATA

SICILIAN EGGPLANT SALAD

This cold eggplant ragout is one of the emblems of Sicilian cuisine. The secret to its success is its wonderful sweet-and-sour taste.

ILARIA BRUNETTI

WHEN THE *CAPONE* IS AWAY, THE EGGPLANT WILL PLAY

It is said that in the eighteenth century, *caponata* was an aristocratic dish made from *capone*, a Sicilian term for mahi-mahi. Since the wider population did not have access to this expensive and rare fish, they replaced it with pieces of eggplant. Others argue that the word *caponata* comes from the Latin term *caupona*, which means a tavern where sailors were served simple and tasty dishes, while still others relate it to the Greek *capto*, which means "to cut."

It's in a can!

Caponatina is an industrially made canned caponata manufactured in Palermo since 1916 and exported mainly to the United States. By extension, the term *caponatina* now refers to a simplified caponata made with baked vegetables, without sweet-and-sour sauce.

WITH OR WITHOUT BELL PEPPERS: THAT IS THE QUESTION

Each microregion of Sicily has its own version: there are more than thirty traditional recipes! The main difference is the presence of bell peppers, which are absent from the Palermo version—the most well-known—but used frequently elsewhere.

· IN PALERMO ·
Eggplant, celery, onions, tomato sauce, green olives, capers, vinegar, sugar, basil, pine nuts, almonds.

· IN MESSINA ·
Same as the Palermo version, plus fresh tomatoes, peeled and in pieces.

· IN CATANIA ·
Yellow and red bell peppers, eggplant, celery, onions, tomatoes, white olives, capers, vinegar, sugar.

· IN AGRIGENTO ·
Friggitelli bell peppers (*arramascati* in Sicilian), eggplant, celery, white onions, tomatoes, green and black olives, capers, vinegar, sugar, honey, garlic, chile, raisins, basil, pine nuts or almonds.

· IN CIANCIANA ·
Artichokes, celery, onions, peeled tomatoes, green olives, sugar, vinegar, lemon juice.

· IN BIVONA ·
In this village known for its fragrant fruits, peaches and pears are used!

THE RECIPE

A never-fail caponata by Fabrizio Ferrara, the Sicilian chef and owner of Osteria Ferrara (Paris 11th).

SERVES 4

1 large purple eggplant
Salt
1 tablespoon plus 1¾ teaspoons (20 g) sugar
1 stalk celery
½ white onion
5¼ ounces (150 g) peeled tomatoes
7 tablespoons (80 g) extra-virgin olive oil
2 tablespoons (30 g) red wine vinegar or sherry
¼ cup (30 g) capers
¼ cup (30 g) raisins
⅓ cup (50 g) green olives
A few fresh basil leaves
¼ cup (30 g) pine nuts

Cut the eggplant into ¾-inch (2 cm) cubes and put them in a bowl. Sprinkle with 1⅔ teaspoons (10 g) salt, then with the sugar. Let marinate for 30 minutes. Cut the celery into ⅓-inch (1 cm) slices (save a few leaves for garnish, if you'd like). Chop the onion. Purée the tomatoes.

Heat the olive oil in a pan, add the cubed eggplant, and cook over high heat until lightly browned. Deglaze the pan by adding the vinegar. Reduce the heat, add the celery and onion, cook for 1 to 2 minutes, then stir in the tomatoes. Season with salt, if necessary; let cook until thickened and somewhat reduced. Add the capers, raisins, and olives 5 minutes before the end of the cooking time. Chill for at least 5 hours. Taste and adjust the seasoning, if needed, to achieve the right level of sweet and sour, then serve cold, with basil or celery leaves and pine nuts on top.

CHEF'S ADVICE

Not blanching the celery before panfrying it, as tradition would have it, allows it to retain its crunchy texture.

This recipe is even better when prepared the day before serving it!

A TAVOLA! HOW SHOULD YOU EAT YOUR CAPONATA?

→ Simply, with just some mozzarella and a big slice of thick rustic bread.

→ With a tuna steak, briefly seared in the pan.

→ With good mackerel fillets in olive oil.

→ To accompany rabbit, either roasted in the oven or cooked in a casserole dish.

→ With a soft-boiled egg on top.

→ As it is enjoyed in Syracuse, in a sandwich with pecorino or, for big appetites, with a grilled sausage.

SKIP TO
EGGPLANT, P. 266; OLIVES, P. 214; SPOTLIGHT ON CAPERS, P. 110.

Pop Pasta

Pasta hasn't conquered just our stomachs! It has also infiltrated music, cinema, and comics around the world.

PIERRE-BRICE LEBRUN

THE MACARONIC LANGUAGE

This writing style was invented in the fifteenth century, probably by writer Tifi Odassi, who penned *Carmen macaronicum*, a burlesque piece of seven hundred pages whose hero was a *maccheroni* maker. This piece was written in Paduan Italian mixed with Latin, combining common words with Latin endings—thus the birth of the macaronic style. Rabelais used the macaronic style on numerous occasions in his work *Pantagruel*, and it was used more recently by Raymond Queneau in *Exercices de style* (*Exercises in Style*, 1947).

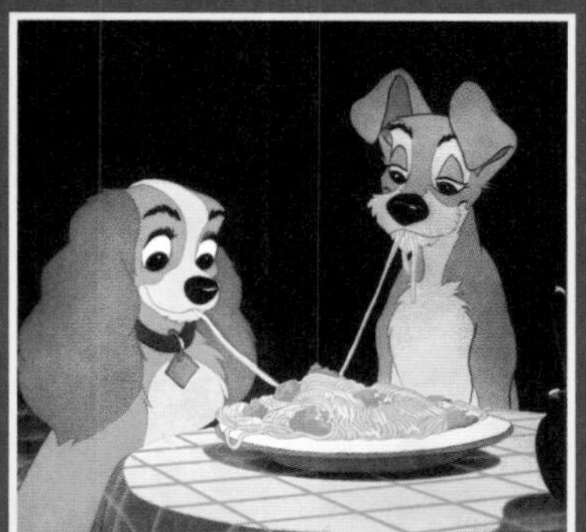

***Lady and the Tramp*, Walt Disney**

In this Walt Disney cartoon, released in 1955, Tramp, in order to woo Lady, takes her to Tony's to share a plate of spaghetti and meatballs (on a checkered tablecloth under the light of a candle stuck into a bottle of Chianti) in a passionate romanticism set to the music of an accordion. *Ah!* Such emotion!

MIRÁCOLI SAUCE

From an appetizing and sunny yellow cardboard box decorated with the Italian flag, Belgian brand Mirácoli—which has never set foot on the Italian peninsula—offers a complete, easy-to-prep meal: a bag of pasta to cook, a bag of sauce to reheat, a bag of grated cheese, and the "famous secret spice mix," all of which propelled Mirácoli into the collective Belgian culinary unconscious. *Miracoli* means "miracles": the real miracle is that someone eats it!

***Il Signor Spaghetti*, Goscinny and Attanasio**

Il Signor Spaghetti is the hero of a series of humorous comics created by cartoonist Dino Attanasio in 1952 and scripted by René Goscinny. In the album *Spaghetti et la peintoure à l'houile* (1961), he is joined by his cousin Prosciutto, a pest who is a goof up! Spaghetti is a likeable caricature of an Italian who is always well dressed, resourceful, fatalistic, and in good spirits.

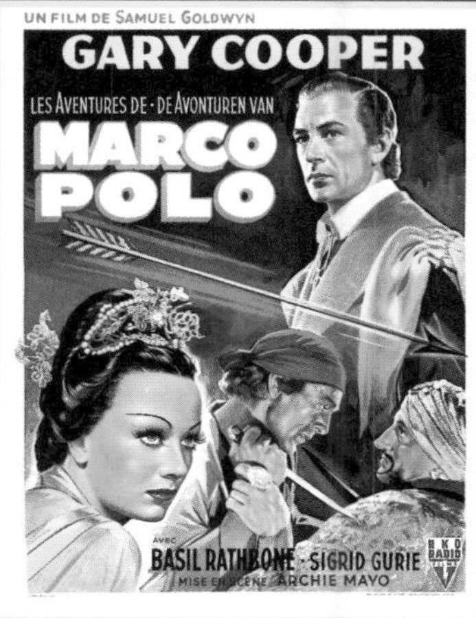

***The Adventures of Marco Polo* (1938), with Gary Cooper**

In this Hollywood blockbuster directed by Archie Mayo (with the help, in two scenes, of John Ford, who says he was never paid for the work), a sailor named Spaghetti observes—as he goes ashore to fetch water—Chinese people cooking pasta. He brings the pasta back to an astonished Marco Polo . . .

Pastafarianism

This religion, born in 2005 in Oregon, is a parody aimed at denouncing the absurdity of religious dogmas, whatever they may be. It professes that a Flying Spaghetti Monster, invisible and undetectable, created the universe. Pastafarianism has achieved the feat of being officially recognized as a religion in New Zealand (with permission to perform marriages), Utah, the Netherlands, and Taiwan (China). Its followers, whose numbers are increasing, wear a colander on their heads during ceremonies. They follow the principles set forth in the Gospel of the Flying Spaghetti Monster (available online).

The over-the-top BBC prank

On April 1, 1957, the very serious British news program *Panorama* aired a three-minute clip on the spaghetti harvest in Castiglione, on the shores of Lake Lugano in Ticino. The harvest, they reported, had been particularly good that year, thanks to an exceptionally mild winter and the virtual disappearance of the spaghetti weevil. The report was presented by the very respectable—and very austere—Richard Dimbleby. It featured a Swiss farming family delicately picking spaghetti off branches and placing them in wicker baskets. When the BBC received hundreds of calls from viewers asking where to get a spaghetti tree, the station diplomatically replied, "Put a strand of spaghetti in a can of tomato sauce and pray."

"BUT LORD, IT'S ONLY A LITTLE PASTA . . ."

From 1975 to 2000, the character Don Patillo sang the praises of Panzani pasta on French television, in advertisements for the brand created in Niort in 1950 by Jean Panzani, whose parents were from Florence (he made his first noodles in 1940 in his in-laws' attic). French actor, singer, and impersonator André Aubert (1923–2010) portrayed Don Patillo in TV commercials by imitating the fictional protagonist Don Camillo, made famous by French actor and singer Fernandel, imploring the Lord's forgiveness when God reproaches him for his sin of gluttony: "But Lord, it's only a little pasta . . ."

SKIP TO
PIZZA AS POP ICON, P. 246;
GOURMET CINEMA, P. 68;
SPAGHETTI VIP, P. 372.

ITALY'S BEAUTIFUL CHEESES

FROM THE ALPS TO THE PO PLAIN, FROM THE APENNINE MOUNTAINS TO THE ISLANDS, ITALY OFFERS RICH AND DIVERSE TERROIR. HERE IS AN INVENTORY OF THE COUNTRY'S SPLENDID CHEESES —ALESSANDRO DE CONTO

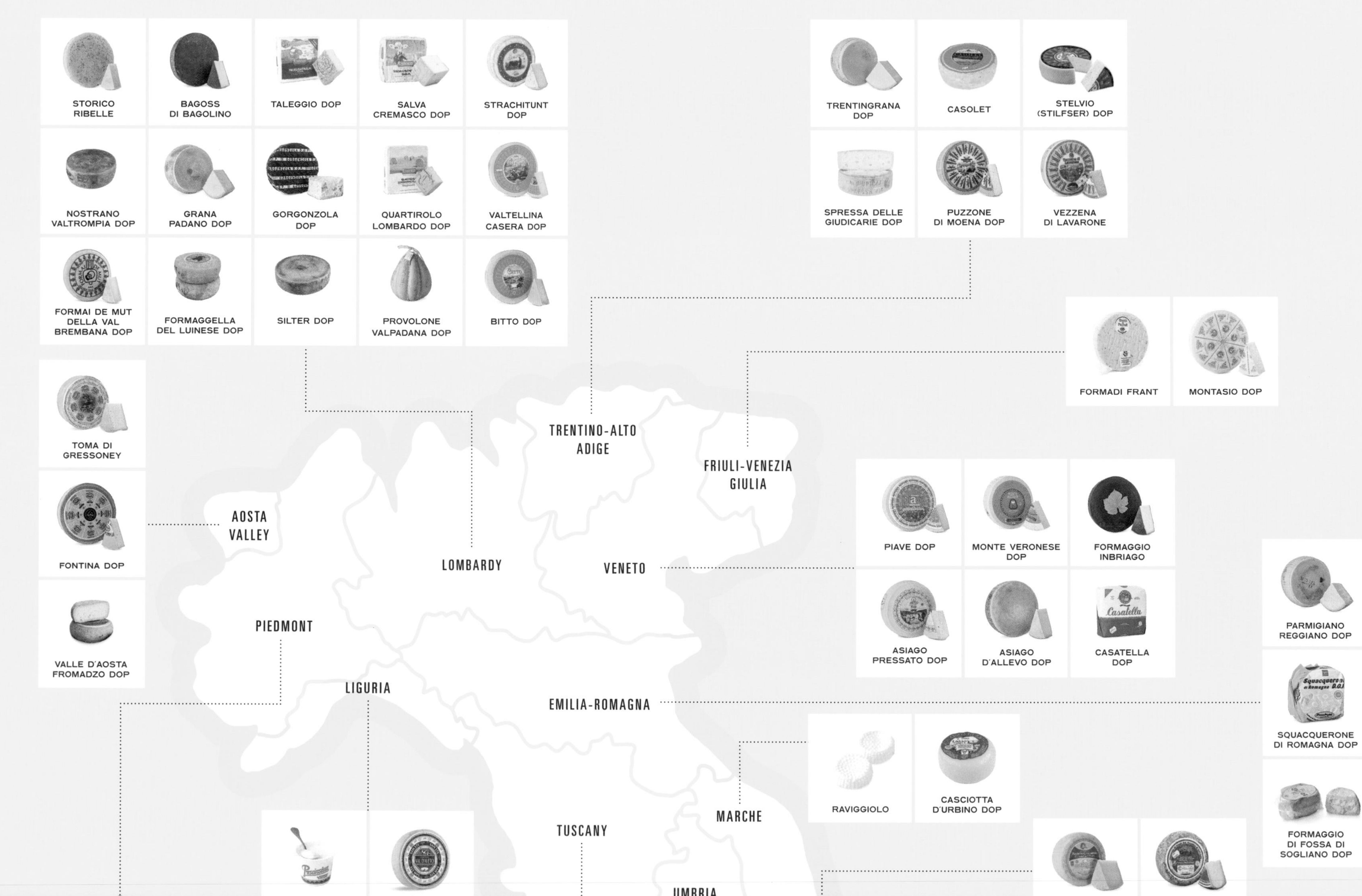

PECORINO DI PIENZA
PECORINO TOSCANO DOP
PECORINO DELLE BALZE VOLTERRANE DOP
MARZOLINO
LAZIO
MOLISE
MANTECA
MURAZZANO DOP
BETTELMATT
TOMA PIEMONTESE DOP
CASTELMAGNO DOP
BRA DOP
OSSOLANO DOP
RASCHERA DOP
MONTEBORE
ROBIOLA DI ROCCAVERANO DOP
SARDINIA
PECORINO DI NORCIA
CAMPANIA
APULIA
BASILICATA
MARZOLINA
CACIOFIORE DELLA CAMPAGNA ROMANA
PECORINO DI PICINISCO DOP
CONCIATO ROMANO
FIORDILATTE DEI MONTI LATTARI
PROVOLONE DEL MONACO DOP
MOZZARELLA DI BUFALA CAMPANA DOP
CALABRIA
CANESTRATO DI MOLITERNO IGP
CANESTRATO PUGLIESE
PECORINO DI FILIANO DOP
CACIORICOTTA
CACIOCAVALLO SILANO DOP
BURRATA DI ANDRIA IGP
CACIOCAVALLO PODOLICO DEL GARGANO
PECORINO CROTONESE DOP
PECORINO DEL MONTE PORO
SICILY
CASIZOLU
PECORINO ROMANO DOP
PECORINO SARDO DOP
PECORINO DI OSILO
FIORE SARDO DOP
VASTEDDA DEL BELICE DOP
RAGUSANO DOP
PIACENTINU ENNESE DOP
PECORINO SICILIANO DOP
PROVOLA DEI NEBRODI DOP
PROVOLA DELLE MADONIE AFFUMICATA
PECORINO PEPATO
TUMA PERSA DI PASCOLO

LEGEND
TYPES OF MILK

COW'S MILK | SHEEP'S MILK | GOAT'S MILK | BUFFALO'S MILK | PEPPER | BUTTER | SAFFRON

FRIULI-VENEZIA GIULIA

MONTASIO DOP

FAMILY—semicooked.

AFFINAGE—from 2 to more than 18 months.

FLAVOR—sweet, milky, fresh grass when young; mild, flavorful, with hints of umami as it ages.

FORMADI FRANT

FAMILY—made based on a collection of different cheeses.

AFFINAGE—from 30 to 180 days.

FLAVOR—intense, with aromas of spices and cream.

VENETO

ASIAGO PRESSATO DOP

FAMILY—uncooked pressed.

AFFINAGE—a minimum of 20 days.

FLAVOR—mild, with hints of yogurt and fermented milk.

ASIAGO D'ALLEVO DOP

FAMILY—semicooked pressed.

AFFINAGE—a minimum of 90 days and up to 18 months in the very ripened version.

FLAVOR—mild with notes of hay, scents of pasture, exotic fruits, and slightly pungent in the very ripened version.

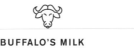

CASATELLA DOP

FAMILY—soft cheese.

AFFINAGE—several days.

FLAVOR—mild, milky, yogurt and fresh cheese.

PIAVE DOP

FAMILY—cooked pressed.

AFFINAGE—from 20 days to 18 months.

FLAVOR—milky and simple; mild, with hints of caramel and vanilla when ripened.

MONTE VERONESE DOP

FAMILY—semicooked (whole-milk version) or cooked (half-fat version).

AFFINAGE—a minimum of 25 days for the whole-milk version, up to 24 months for the half-fat version.

FLAVOR—milky and buttery when young; it becomes powerful, with notes of grilled fruit and wildflower meadow when ripened.

FORMAGGIO INBRIAGO

FAMILY—semicooked pressed.

AFFINAGE—a minimum of 40 days followed by at least 15 days of ripening in wine and/or must.

FLAVOR—assertive, with hints of Merlot or Cabernet in the classic version.

TRENTINO-ALTO ADIGE

TRENTINGRANA DOP

FAMILY—cooked pressed.

AFFINAGE—at least 18 months.

FLAVOR—mild, with hints of pasture and umami.

CASOLET

FAMILY—raw unpressed.

AFFINAGE—around 20 days.

FLAVOR—buttery and milky.

SPRESSA DELLE GIUDICARIE DOP

FAMILY—semicooked pressed.

AFFINAGE—a minimum of 90 days.

FLAVOR—mild, with scents of hay and fresh grass.

STELVIO (STILFSER) DOP

FAMILY—pressed, washed rind.

AFFINAGE—a minimum of 60 days.

FLAVOR—mild, buttery, with hints of fermented fruit.

PUZZONE DI MOENA DOP

FAMILY—pressed, washed rind.

AFFINAGE—a minimum of 60 days.

FLAVOR—intense and aromatic, with notes of humid cellar and undergrowth.

VEZZENA DI LAVARONE

FAMILY—cooked pressed.

AFFINAGE—a minimum of 4 months.

FLAVOR—mild and rich with notes related to pastures; as the ripening progresses, exotic notes are accentuated, in particular pineapple.

LOMBARDY

BITTO DOP

FAMILY—cooked pressed.

AFFINAGE—a minimum of 60 days.

FLAVOR—mild, with notes of cooked butter and grilled fruit.

PROVOLONE VALPADANA DOP

FAMILY—pulled curd.

AFFINAGE—a minimum of 60 days.

FLAVOR—mild and milky in the milder version; slightly biting, with hints of lactic ferments in the pungent version.

SILTER DOP

FAMILY—cooked pressed.

AFFINAGE—a minimum of 100 days.

FLAVOR—mild, with hints of dried fruits and pasture grasses.

FORMAGGELLA DEL LUINESE DOP

FAMILY—semicooked pressed.

AFFINAGE—20 days.

FLAVOR—delicate, with light goaty scents.

FORMAI DE MUT DELLA VAL BREMBANA DOP

FAMILY—cooked pressed.

AFFINAGE—45 to 120 days.

FLAVOR—mild, with notes of cooked butter, wildflower meadow, and toasted hazelnuts.

VALTELLINA CASERA DOP

FAMILY—cooked pressed.

AFFINAGE—a minimum of 60 days.

FLAVOR—mild, with aromas of cellar and dried fruits.

QUARTIROLO LOMBARDO DOP

FAMILY—raw unpressed (washed rind in the ripened version).

AFFINAGE—a few days for the fresh version, at least 40 days for the ripened version.

FLAVOR—milky, with hints of yogurt in the fresh version; with cellar notes and yeast in the ripened version.

GORGONZOLA DOP

FAMILY—unpressed blue-veined.

AFFINAGE—a minimum of 50 days (mild); at least 80 days (pungent).

FLAVOR—melting, with notes of apple and ripe pear in the mild version; intense, slightly flavorful and pungent, with intense marbling in the pungent version.

GRANA PADANO DOP

FAMILY—cooked pressed.

AFFINAGE—9 months.

FLAVOR—mild, slightly savory with a scent of cooked milk, hints of hay and broth.

NOSTRANO VALTROMPIA DOP +

FAMILY—cooked pressed

AFFINAGE—a minimum of 12 months

FLAVOR—intense and aromatic, with notes of spice and exotic fruits

STRACHITUNT DOP

FAMILY—raw unpressed blue-veined.

AFFINAGE—a minimum of 75 days.

FLAVOR—intense, with notes of banana, yeast, and ripe fruit.

SALVA CREMASCO DOP

FAMILY—raw unpressed, washed rind.

AFFINAGE—a minimum of 75 days.

FLAVOR—mild, good acidity, with hints of yogurt and cellar.

TALEGGIO DOP

FAMILY—raw unpressed, washed rind.

AFFINAGE—a minimum of 35 days.

FLAVOR—milky and buttery, with notes of forest and wet wood.

BAGOSS DI BAGOLINO +

FAMILY—cooked pressed.

AFFINAGE—a minimum of 12 months.

FLAVOR—intense, with notes of grass, hay, and saffron.

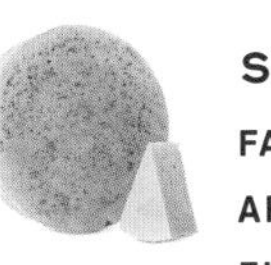

STORICO RIBELLE

FAMILY—cooked pressed.

AFFINAGE—a minimum of 120 days.

FLAVOR—soft, complex, with hints of toasted hazelnuts and exotic fruits.

PIEDMONT

MURAZZANO DOP

+ 40%

FAMILY—raw unpressed.

AFFINAGE—a few days.

FLAVOR—mild, with hints of cream and raw butter.

BETTELMATT

FAMILY—cooked pressed.

AFFINAGE—from 60 to 300 days.

FLAVOR—intense, slightly bitter, with notes of alpine herbs and flowers.

TOMA PIEMONTESE DOP

FAMILY—semicooked pressed.

AFFINAGE—aminimum of 30 days.

FLAVOR—mild and melting, with notes of butter and milk.

CASTELMAGNO DOP

+ OU 10%

FAMILY—raw pressed.

AFFINAGE—a minimum of 60 days.

FLAVOR—unique, with slightly acidic notes of lemon and yogurt.

BRA DOP

+ OU 10%

FAMILY—semicooked pressed.

AFFINAGE—minimum 45 days in the soft version and a minimum of 180 days in the hard version.

FLAVOR—mild, with hints of yogurt, tender; lightly flavorful, with sensations of toasted fruit.

OSSOLANO DOP

FAMILY—semicooked pressed.

AFFINAGE—a minimum of 60 days.

FLAVOR—mild and fragrant, with hints of soft caramel and pasture.

RASCHERA DOP

FAMILY—semicooked pressed.

AFFINAGE—a minimum of 30 days.

FLAVOR—mild, with notes of raw butter and milk.

ROBIOLA DI ROCCAVERANO DOP

+ 20%

FAMILY—raw unpressed.

AFFINAGE—a few days.

FLAVOR—mild and fresh, with light floral scents.

MONTEBORE

FAMILY—raw unpressed.

AFFINAGE—from 30 to 300 days.

FLAVOR—mild, with hints of cooked butter and mushroom.

AOSTA VALLEY

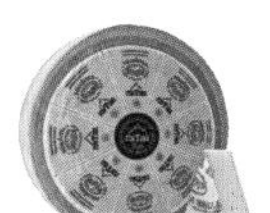

FONTINA DOP

FAMILY—semicooked pressed.

AFFINAGE—a minimum of 60 days.

FLAVOR—mild, melting, with scents of cellar and undergrowth.

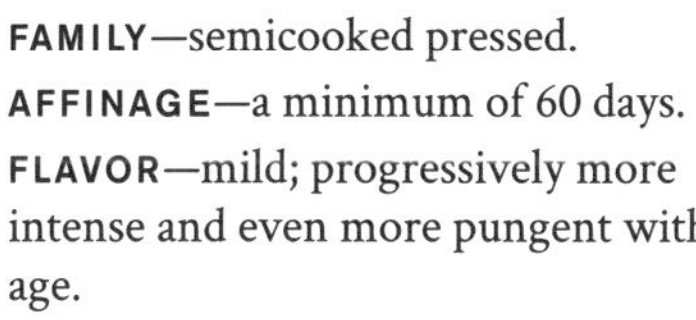

VALLE D'AOSTA FROMADZO DOP

+ UN PEU

FAMILY—semicooked pressed.

AFFINAGE—a minimum of 60 days.

FLAVOR—mild; progressively more intense and even more pungent with age.

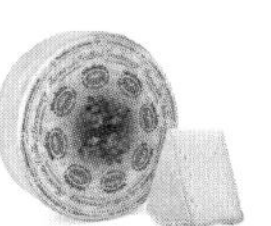

TOMA DI GRESSONEY

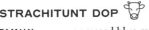

FAMILY—semicooked pressed.

AFFINAGE—from 60 to 180 days.

FLAVOR—mild, with intense notes of mountain grasses.

LIGURIA

PRESCINSEUA

FAMILY—fresh and sour curd.

AFFINAGE—a few days.

FLAVOR—slightly acidic and fermented.

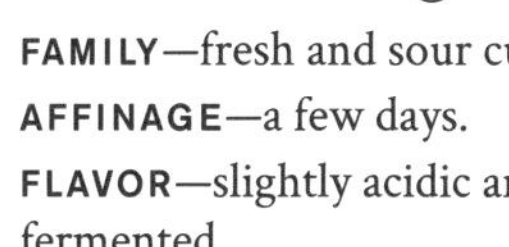

SAN STE'

FAMILY—semicooked pressed.

AFFINAGE—from 60 to 300 days.

FLAVOR—from mild and milky to slightly pungent and bitter.

EMILIA-ROMAGNA

PARMIGIANO REGGIANO DOP

FAMILY—cooked pressed.
AFFINAGE—a minimum of 13 months.
FLAVOR—mild, fruity, with hints of umami and dried fruits.

SQUACQUERONE DI ROMAGNA DOP

FAMILY—raw unpressed.
AFFINAGE—several days.
FLAVOR—mild and milky.

FORMAGGIO DI FOSSA DI SOGLIANO DOP

AND/OR

FAMILY—semicooked pressed cheese, ripened buried in a hole.
AFFINAGE—a minimum of 160 days.
FLAVOR: intense, light in flavor, with mineral and mushroom notes.

TUSCANY

PECORINO DELLE BALZE VOLTERRANE DOP

FAMILY—semicooked pressed.
AFFINAGE—a minimum of 45 days.
FLAVOR—mild, with slight acidity and a fragrance of thistle.

PECORINO TOSCANO DOP

FAMILY—semicooked pressed.
AFFINAGE—a minimum of 20 days.
FLAVOR—mild, with hints of cooked butter and cream; notes of grilled fruits emerge during ripening.

PECORINO DI PIENZA

FAMILY—semicooked pressed.
AFFINAGE—from a few days to 6 months.
FLAVOR—mild and melting when young; with hints of hazelnut and cellar as it ages.

MARZOLINO

FAMILY—semicooked pressed.
AFFINAGE—a minimum of 15 days.
FLAVOR—mild, fresh and buttery.

APULIA

CANESTRATO PUGLIESE DOP

FAMILY—semicooked pressed.
AFFINAGE—a minimum of 60 days.
FLAVOR—aromatic, intense, slightly pungent.

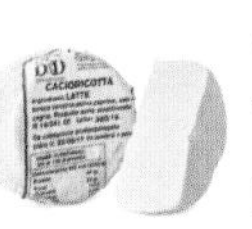

CACIORICOTTA

/ OR BOTH

FAMILY—pressed cheese.
AFFINAGE—a minimum of 30 days.
FLAVOR—flavorful, aromatic, sometimes pungent.

BURRATA DI ANDRIA IGP

FAMILY—pulled curd filled with cream.
AFFINAGE—a few days.
FLAVOR—mild, fresh, milky.

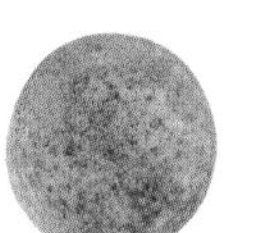

CACIOCAVALLO PODOLICO DEL GARGANO

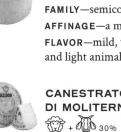

FAMILY—pulled curd.
AFFINAGE—a minimum of 180 days.
FLAVOR—intense, fruity, with a slight flavor; pungent when very ripe.

BASILICATA

CACIOCAVALLO SILANO DOP

FAMILY—pulled curd.
AFFINAGE—a minimum of 30 days.
FLAVOR—mild, milky, with notes of cooked butter.

PECORINO DI FILIANO DOP

FAMILY—semicooked pressed.
AFFINAGE—a minimum of 180 days.
FLAVOR—mild, with notes of cellar and light animallike fragrance.

CANESTRATO DI MOLITERNO IGP

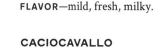

+ 30%

FAMILY—semicooked pressed.
AFFINAGE—a minimum of 90 days.
FLAVOR—complex and slightly flavorful, with vegetal and cellar notes.

CALABRIA

PECORINO CROTONESE DOP

FAMILY—semicooked pressed.
AFFINAGE—a minimum of 60 days.
FLAVOR—mild and flowery when young; intense and pungent when very ripened.

PECORINO DEL MONTE PORO

+ POSSIBLY

FAMILY—semicooked pressed.
AFFINAGE—a minimum of 90 days.
FLAVOR—aromatic, with hints of wildflower meadow.

SICILY

PECORINO SICILIANO DOP

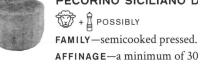

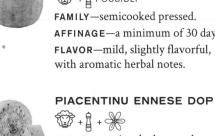

+ POSSIBLY

FAMILY—semicooked pressed.
AFFINAGE—a minimum of 30 days.
FLAVOR—mild, slightly flavorful, with aromatic herbal notes.

PIACENTINU ENNESE DOP

+ +

FAMILY—semicooked pressed.
AFFINAGE—a minimum of 60 days.
FLAVOR—mild, aromatic, with strong notes of saffron and Mediterranean herbs.

RAGUSANO DOP

FAMILY—pulled curd.
AFFINAGE—a minimum of 90 days.
FLAVOR—mild, with hints of honey and sweet fruit; it becomes pungent with prolonged ripening.

VASTEDDA DEL BELICE DOP

FAMILY—pulled curd.
AFFINAGE—a few days.
FLAVOR—mild, milky, with hints of ferments and slight acidity.

PROVOLA DEI NEBRODI DOP

FAMILY—pulled curd.
AFFINAGE—a minimum of 10 to 15 days.
FLAVOR—mild, with notes of pasture, cooked butter, and Mediterranean herbs.

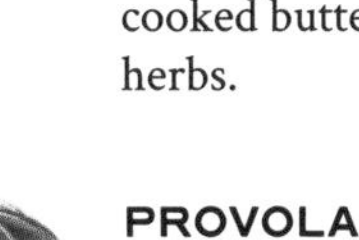

PROVOLA DELLE MADONIE AFFUMICATA

FAMILY—pulled curd.
AFFINAGE—a minimum of 10 to 15 days.
FLAVOR—mild, delicate and smoky.

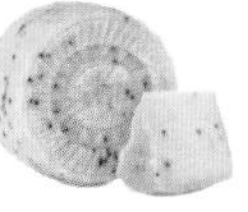

PECORINO PEPATO +

FAMILY—semicooked pressed.

AFFINAGE—a minimum of 20 days.

FLAVOR—mild, slightly savory, and quite pungent.

TUMA PERSA DI PASCOLO

FAMILY—semicooked pressed.

AFFINAGE—a minimum of 120 days.

FLAVOR—intense and slightly pungent, with scents of grass and hay.

SARDINIA

FIORE SARDO DOP

FAMILY—semicooked pressed.

AFFINAGE—minimum 105 days.

FLAVOR—intense, flavorful, with strong smoky notes.

PECORINO ROMANO DOP

FAMILY—cooked pressed.

AFFINAGE—a minimum of 150 days.

FLAVOR—flavorful, with notes of Mediterranean herbs.

CASIZOLU

FAMILY—pulled curd.

AFFINAGE—a minimum of 30 days.

FLAVOR—mild, with hints of fermented milk and Mediterranean herbs.

PECORINO SARDO DOP

FAMILY—semicooked pressed.

AFFINAGE—a minimum of 20 days (mild version), at least 60 days (ripened version).

FLAVOR—mild and aromatic.

PECORINO DI OSILO

FAMILY—semicooked pressed.

AFFINAGE—a minimum of 60 days.

FLAVOR—mild and very fragrant.

MARCHE

CASCIOTTA D'URBINO DOP + 20%

FAMILY—semicooked pressed.

AFFINAGE—a minimum of 20 days.

FLAVOR—mild, melting, and milky.

RAVIGGIOLO

FAMILY—fresh cheese.

AFFINAGE—a few hours.

FLAVOR—fresh, with notes of milk and yogurt.

CAMPANIA

MOZZARELLA DI BUFALA CAMPANA DOP

FAMILY—pulled curd.

AFFINAGE—a few days.

FLAVOR—mild, fragrant, with aroma of coconut and almond; in some versions there is a presence of animallike notes.

PROVOLONE DEL MONACO DOP

FAMILY—pulled curd.

AFFINAGE—a minimum of 120 days.

FLAVOR—mild, sometimes intense and aromatic; it offers pungent sensations with prolonged ripening.

FIORDILATTE DEI MONTI LATTARI

FAMILY—pulled curd.

AFFINAGE—a few days.

FLAVOR—mild, fresh, with notes of milk and pasture.

CONCIATO ROMANO

+ +

FAMILY—cheese ripened in amphorae.

AFFINAGE—from a few months to over a year.

FLAVOR—intense, with fermented notes and ripe fruit.

LAZIO

PECORINO DI PICINISCO DOP + 25%

FAMILY—raw pressed dough.

AFFINAGE—a minimum of 30 days.

FLAVOR—mild, with strong scents of mountain grasses.

CACIOFIORE DELLA CAMPAGNA ROMANA

FAMILY—raw unpressed.

AFFINAGE—around 20 days.

FLAVOR—mild, buttery, with strong notes of wild artichoke.

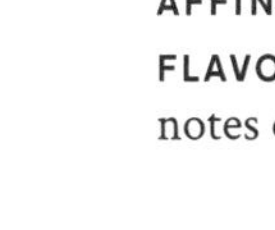

MARZOLINA

+ OR

FAMILY—raw pressed dough.

AFFINAGE—from a few days to a year or more.

FLAVOR—soft and creamy when young, with notes of the olive oil in which it is ripened; pungent when aged.

ABRUZZO

PECORINO DI FARINDOLA

FAMILY—semicooked pressed.

AFFINAGE—a minimum of 120 days.

FLAVOR—intense, with notes of green vegetables, mushroom, and moss.

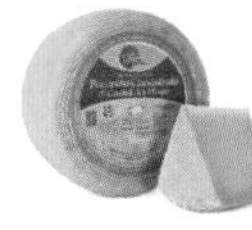

CANESTRATO DI CASTELDELMONTE

FAMILY—semicooked pressed.

AFFINAGE—a minimum of 90 days.

FLAVOR—intense and slightly pungent, with notes of pasture and sheep's fleece.

OMBRIE

PECORINO DI NORCIA

FAMILY—semicooked pressed.

AFFINAGE—from 120 to 180 days.

FLAVOR—mild, slightly pungent, with slightly animallike notes of hay and pasture.

MOLISE

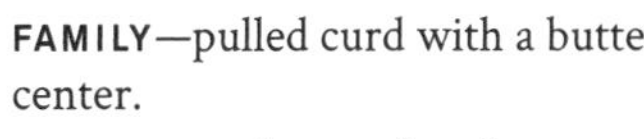

MANTECA +

FAMILY—pulled curd with a butter center.

AFFINAGE—from a few days to a year.

FLAVOR—mild, seductive with hints of cooked milk when young; becomes intense and pungent during ripening.

SEASON

TUTTO L'ANNO (YEAR-ROUND)

CATEGORY

ANTIPASTO (APPETIZER)

LEVEL

FACILE (EASY)

CICCHETTI VENEZIANI

VENETIAN SNACKS

If you're looking for a perfect snack for aperitif time, here is a tasty small-plate option, Venetian-style.

ILARIA BRUNETTI

I CICCHETTI

Cicchetti, or *cicheti* in Venetian, are small bites—often in the form of spreads for toast—served to accompany a glass of wine in the *bacari* (wine bars). They include fish-based specialties such as marinated anchovies or sweet-and-sour eel, or assorted fried and other meat-based foods, from simple charcuterie to offal. The name derives from the Latin *ciccum*, meaning "thing of little value" or, according to some, from *chiquet*, a dated French term for a small glass of wine.

HOW TO DO IT

The Venetians generally limit themselves to one or two cicchetti per person, sold by the piece, to accompany a drink before a meal. Tourists often order more in quantity to make a unique meal for a low price. You eat them with your fingers.

Sarde in saor

LEXICON

BACARO

A small and modest Venetian *osteria* where you go for a drink, usually a simple glass of house wine (*vino della casa*) and a few cicchetti; larger dishes are sometimes consumed, but rarely. The first official *bacaro* was Bacaro Grande, opened in the Rialto district in 1866, but this type of place existed long before under the name *malvasia*, due to the wine it served there. There are many theories about the origin of the term: it could come from Bacchus due to its wine origins; from the local expression *far bacàra*, meaning to party, because of the convivial atmosphere; or from *bacaresi*, the winemakers and growers who sold their wine in Piazza San Marco in the seventeenth century.

OMBRA

A glass of wine one drinks in a bacaro. So called because the bacaresi followed the shadow of the famous square's bell tower during the day to keep their wine cool.

BIANCHETO

A glass of unpretentious white wine.

ANDAR PER OMBRE

Go from bacari to bacari for a drink . . . or more!

CICCHETTO

Be aware that this term outside of Venice can have a different meaning. If you offer a *cicchetto* outside of Venice, it means a shot of alcohol.

SARDE IN SAOR (SWEET-AND-SOUR SARDINES)

Here is the traditional recipe. But in Eleonora Zuliani's restaurant (Il Bacaro, Paris 11th), she offers her own version that replaces frying with more delicate cooking: with the oil at 194°F (90°C) poured over the sardines, then set aside to cool. The flesh of the fish thus becomes tender and delicate. These sardines can be served as an antipasto.

SERVES 4

- 14 ounces (400 g) white onions
- Scant ½ cup (100 mL) olive oil
- Salt
- 1¼ cups (300 mL) red wine vinegar
- 1 tablespoon (10 g) raisins (optional)
- 20 sardines, preferably from the Mediterranean (about 1¾ pounds/ 800 g)
- 1¼ cups (150 g) all-purpose flour
- 4 cups (1 L) frying oil
- 1 tablespoon (3 g) chopped parsley
- 1 tablespoon (8 g) toasted pine nuts (optional)
- Freshly ground black pepper

Thinly slice the onions. Heat the olive oil in a skillet over low heat. Add the onions and cook, without letting them take on any color, until they are tender, adding water if necessary, about 30 minutes. Season with salt, add the vinegar and the raisins (if using) and turn off the heat.

Remove the head and entrails from the sardines, rinse the fish quickly, and dry them carefully. Lightly flour the fish and fry them in hot frying oil (in small batches); place them on paper towels to drain, then season with salt. Be careful not to overcook the sardines, as the maceration in the onion and vinegar will finish cooking them.

In a high-sided dish, arrange the sardines and onions in layers. Cover with plastic wrap and place in the refrigerator for 24 hours.

To serve, arrange the sardines, covered with onions, on plates. Sprinkle with the parsley, top with a few toasted pine nuts, if desired, and lightly season with pepper.

Ovetto e acciuga

Musetto

Tartina con cotto e kren

A TOP 10 LIST

of cicchetti

*

BACCALÀ MANTECATO
Cream of salt cod on grilled white polenta (see recipe at right).

*

TARTINA CON COTTO E KREN
Toast with ham and horseradish.

*

TARTINA CON SOPPRESSA VENETA
Toast with local sausage.

*

MUSETTO
Cooked sausage made from pork head on a slice of bread.

*

OVETTO E ACCIUGA
Hard-boiled egg with anchovies.

*

POLPETTA
Beef meatball.

*

NERVETTI
Veal tendrons and beans.

*

SARDE IN SAOR
Sweet-and-sour sardines (see recipe opposite).

*

FRITTATA ALLE ERBE
A sort of omelet with herbs.

*

FOLPETTI
Small octopi, with oil and parsley.

But also

Sardines or marinated anchovies, all types of fried items (vegetables, breaded mozzarella or *in carrozza*, fish . . .), toast with butter and anchovies, spleen boiled and seasoned with oil, small sandwiches (*paninetti*) and *tramezzini* . . .

Tartina con soppressa veneta

Baccalà mantecato

Nervetti con fagioli

BACCALÀ MANTECATO (CREAM OF SALT COD ON GRILLED WHITE POLENTA)

The traditional recipe calls for *stoccafisso*, dried cod (strangely called *baccalà* in Veneto, or salt cod in the rest of Italy), but Eleonora Zuliani prefers baccalà; as it will be easier to find and work with. With a larger portion, this *cicchetto* is also served as an antipasto.

SERVES 4

14 ounces (400 g) salt cod, sliced
1 stalk celery
4 cloves garlic
1 bay leaf
1 1/4 cups (300 mL) peanut oil
2 cups (500 mL) olive oil
1 anchovy
Salt and freshly ground black pepper
A few sprigs parsley

Soak the cod for 3 days, changing the water twice a day.

Place the pieces in a pot of cold water with the celery, garlic, and bay leaf. Bring to a boil, lower the heat, and cook in simmering water until the flesh comes off the central ridge (about 1 hour).

Gently collect the fish with a skimmer and reserve the cooking water. Remove all the bones from the fish but keep the skin, which is rich in collagen and will make the dish creamy.

Immediately work the still-hot flesh using the flat beater of a stand mixer (or use a wooden spoon), adding the peanut oil in a thin stream, alternating with a little cooking water, to obtain a mousselike consistency. Add the olive oil. Add the anchovy. Season with salt, if needed.

Serve, seasoned with pepper and sprinkled with chopped parsley on slices of toasted white polenta.

Frittata

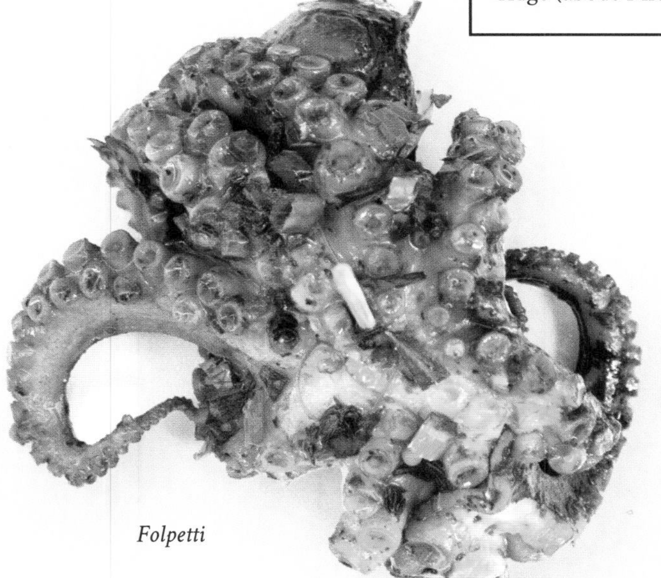

Folpetti

Polpetta

SKIP TO
STOCKFISH AND SALT COD, P. 104;
FRITTATA, P. 356;
MARINADES, P. 322.

GOURMAND

Fashion and gastronomy have always formed beautiful alliances on the table, canvas, or fabric. Let's browse this panorama of collector's items.

JACQUES BRUNEL

Gattinoni, 2015

THE CASE OF ARMANI

This *imperatore* was one of the first to offer a complete fashion experience to its customers through furniture, fine meals, and hotel stays. There are ten Armani restaurants and cafés in the world today. The first opened in 1998 in Paris. Massimo Mori, its director, explains: "Focused on simple and beautiful products, gastronomy and fashion go hand in hand in Italy. The *bella figura* presupposes a healthy body. Clientele do not come here for the white truffle, but instead for simple, carefully sourced products."

A QUICK FOOD-CLOTHING CHRONOLOGY

ANTIQUITY

Bacchus, god of sacred drunkenness, wears grapes. Ceres, the embodiment of the fertile earth, holds a sheaf of wheat in her hand. Mars, the warrior, extends an olive branch.

The leaves of the bay laurel were worn as a crown for victors (a victorious general, an athlete, or the king of poets).

FROM THE MIDDLE AGES

Exported throughout Europe, brocades from Venice, inspired by the East, incorporate gourmand motifs including pomegranates and capers.

The red *cornicello* (echoing a red chile pepper) is worn as a pendant throughout southern Italy. It is a very old phallic symbol and serves as protection against the evil eye.

IN THE TWENTIETH CENTURY

Salvador Dalí for Elsa Schiaparelli, 1937

1930s: Salvador Dalí designs a lobster for Elsa Schiaparelli as a print on a dress. He dreams of adding mayonnaise . . . An animal lover, she adorns her creations with *farfalle* (butterflies), perhaps inspired by pasta.

1930s–1960s: the duke and jeweler Fulco di Verdura transforms pomegranate, grapes, and scallops into jewelry.

1950s: Silks printed in Como shimmer with candy and caramels . . . Designer Emilio Pucci launches prints of fish, fruits, and vegetables.

1960s: Mariuccia Mandelli (Krizia) designs a dress with a pineapple pattern.

1970s: Ken Scott, an American adopted by Italy, blends pop art and indulgence with a "collard" trench coat and asparagus print dresses.

1997: Fendi launches the "baguette" bag, the shape of which is inspired by the French bread.

Fashion dresses the table

In 2003, Sandro Veronesi (Italian fashion brand Calzedonia) launched Signorvino, a wine shop chain that also serves food.

—

Is Milan the capital of fashionable tables? Besides being a leather goods maker, Trussardi joins La Scala, Bulgari, and Dolce & Gabbana at the table with restaurants opened in Milan. Prada bought the historic Marchesi pastry shop and is gradually expanding it.

—

Not content with having opened Gucci Garden in Florence, Gucci, entrusted to the great Massimo Bottura, has opened Italian cafés of various sizes from Dubai to Shanghai.

—

Known for his leopard prints, Roberto Cavalli has opened a club-restaurant in the Ibiza marina, built next to 21,520 square feet (2,000 sq m) of garden, the latest in a host of tables carrying the brand from Beirut to Saint-Tropez.

Dolce & Gabbana, 2018

ADORNMENTS

Fashion labels food

Head of Diesel, Marni, Maison Margiela, etc., Renzo Rosso also produces wine and olive oil because, he says, "organic will be the next luxury."

At the head of Geox (the brand of famous breathable shoes), Mario Moretti Polegato handed to his brother the management of the family vineyard, which today is at the forefront of Prosecco production.

The Ferragamo shoemaker stepped into winemaking with the brands Il Borro and Castiglion del Bosco.

In 1994, the Marzotto group (Valentino, Hugo Boss . . .) bought Ca' del Bosco, a wine estate focused on Franciacorta (sparkling wine).

FIVE FEASTS ON A HANGER

5 LOOKS

FUTURO REMOTO

Provocative jeweler Gianni De Benedittis dumps a plate of pasta on your neck with his spaghetti-and-fork gold and silver necklace.

•

ALESSANDRO CONSIGLIO

In 2002, her rather rigid evening dresses consisted of foods prepared sous vide: *bresaola*, ham, and apple segments . . .

•

MOSCHINO

In the footsteps of Franco Moschino, American Jeremy Scott dedicated the label's 2014 summer collection to junk food: red-and-gold McDonald's-style suits and Budweiser sets . . .

•

GATTINONI COUTURE

In 2015, the Roman fashion house designed an ode to bread into its fabrics: a tulle dress embroidered with Kaiser panini, a large focaccia hat, a bustier as a sheaf of wheat, and pants embroidered all over with crackers.

•

DOLCE & GABBANA

Under the slogan "Italians do it better," the duo filled their 2017 summer collection with nods to national foods: dresses with fish prints, tomato sauce, ice cream cones, lobster, pasta . . .

Moschino, 2014–2015

Dolce & Gabbana, 2017

Dolce & Gabbana, 2017

Dolce & Gabbana, 2018

THE MISSONI FAMILY BUDINO

This chocolate pudding (*budino*) is a staple of this Lombard family, renowned for its knits with colorful prints as much as for its passion for gastronomy. This recipe is taken from *The Missoni Family Cookbook*, written by Francesco Missoni and published by Assouline in 2018.

SERVES 5

1¼ cups (250 g) superfine sugar

1 cup (120 g) all-purpose flour

4 cups (1 L) milk, at room temperature

1 pound (450 g) 70% cacao dark chocolate, finely chopped

14 tablespoons (200 g) unsalted butter

Whipped cream, for serving

Equipmant

One 10¼-inch (26 cm) Bundt pan

· Combine the sugar and flour in a bowl. Put the milk in a separate bowl, then add the sugar-flour mixture, whisking just until incorporated.

· Strain the mixture through a fine-mesh strainer into a saucepan set over low heat. Increase the heat to medium and stir in the chocolate and butter until melted. Reduce the heat slightly and cook, stirring constantly, for 3 minutes, until the pudding reaches a thick consistency (the temperature will reach 212°F/100°C). Reduce the heat again to low and cook, stirring constantly, for 7 minutes, then remove from the heat.

· Pour cold water into the Bundt pan and let stand for a few minutes to cool the pan. Pour out the water, then wipe the mold completely dry. Scrape the hot pudding into the pan and set it aside to cool.

· When the pudding reaches room temperature, cover the mold with plastic wrap and refrigerate for about 2 hours, or until chilled.

· To unmold, hold a plate firmly over the top of the mold. Carefully invert the mold and the plate together to release the pudding. The budino should release completely, falling out onto the plate. If not, dip the bottom of the Bundt pan in hot water for 5 to 10 seconds, then try again.

· Serve chilled, with whipped cream.

FENNEL

In Italy, fennel is used as both a vegetable and a spice. From the seed to the bulb, *il finocchio* lends anise flavor to many preparations.

GIANNA MAZZEI

Male

Female

Seeds

Wild

WHAT AM I?

An herbaceous plant (*Foeniculum vulgare*) of the Apiaceae family, *finocchio* (fennel) is native to the Mediterranean, and its wild form was already being used in ancient Rome, in particular to mask the taste and smell of spoiling foods, a practice that lasted until the Middle Ages. It was cultivated starting from about the sixteenth century.

There are two main varietals:

→ **COMMON GARDEN FENNEL** (*finocchio dolce*), of which mostly the base (the heart, erroneously referred to as the bulb) is eaten, but also the stalks and fronds.

→ **WILD FENNEL** (*finocchio selvatico* or *amaro*, also called *finocchietto*), of which the leaves, stems, flowers, roots, and fruits (erroneously called seeds) are eaten. But beware of overconsumption: the fruits, consumed in excessive amounts, can have hallucinogenic effects.

FINOCCHIO SELVATICO

It thrives in the Mediterranean climate and grows wild throughout Italy. It prefers the sun but can tolerate partial shade.

APPEARANCE: green leaves resembling hay (hence its Latin name, *foeniculum*) and umbel-type small yellow flowers.

ENVIRONMENT: uncultivated fields, meadows, vegetable gardens, along pathways, and along sunny walls; it also adapts to limestone and rocky soils and slopes. It prefers seaside areas and low hills but can be found growing at elevations up to 3,200 feet (1,000 m).

HARVESTING: the flower from mid-August to the end of September; fruits in early fall; buds and feathery leaves from spring to fall.

PROPERTIES: carminative, galactophorous, emmenagogic, diuretic, antiemetic, aromatic, antispasmodic, anti-inflammatory. It protects the liver.

TASTE: herbaceous and balsamic aroma, reminiscent of licorice.

RECIPE

SORBETTO AL FINOCCHIETTO (FENNEL SORBET)

This wild fennel sorbet acts as a palate cleanser between courses of hearty meals.

MAKES APPROXIMATELY 1 PINT

¾ ounce (20 g) fennel fronds
½ cup (100 g) sugar
3 quarts (3 L) water
2 large (60 g) egg whites
2 tablespoons (30 mL) fresh lemon juice

- Wash the fennel ronds, crush them, and combine them with the sugar.
- Place the water, fennel, and sugar in a saucepan and boil for 2 minutes. Cover and let cool. Beat the egg whites to stiff peaks. Remove the fennel from the pan, then add the lemon juice and beaten egg whites to the cooking liquid. Stir gently. Transfer to an ice cream maker and churn.
- **If you do not have an ice cream maker:** Freeze the mixture in a large glass dish with low sides. After 1 hour, break up the ice crystals with a whisk, and return the dish to the freezer. Repeat this step every 30 minutes for about 4 hours.

Cooking finocchio dolce

The white bulb, which is both crunchy and juicy, imparts its sweet taste of aniseed into salads. It can also be boiled, grilled, and cooked au gratin.

The best-known varietals are *bianco perfezione, dolce di Firenze, finocchio di Parma, finocchio di Fracchia, gigante di Napoli, grosso di Sicilia, wanderomen,* and *romanesco.*

There is a distinction between female fennel and male fennel, although this is not scientific and relies only on the fennel's shape. The female is elongated and excellent baked; the male is rounded and perfect for enjoying raw.

IN COOKING

THE SEEDS—dragées, breads, *taralli* (kinds of grissini baked as rings), fresh and dried sausages, pancetta, warm wine, in *finocchini* (traditional Piedmontese cookies), and in *finocchiona* and *sbriciolona*, two irresistible Tuscan sausages.

THE FLOWERS—in porchetta from upper Lazio, Umbria, and Tuscany; marinated olives, mushrooms, and eggplant.

FRESH FRONDS—Sicilian sardine pasta, Sardinian bread soup, Sicilian pesto, *bombetti in porchetta* from Marche (whelk or periwinkle shellfish); in liqueur; in soups, fish dishes, salads, meatballs, sausage ragouts; with beans, cheese, eggs.

Sulla Punta Della Lingua (On the Tip of the Tongue)

Infinocchiare: to confuse, to deceive.

Since fennel served to mask the taste and smell of certain spoiling foods, innkeepers would offer sweet fennel to chew when serving questionable wine to their customers. In addition, the locally produced fennel seed was much cheaper than the precious spices imported from the East and created an "illusion" of certain flavors when added to particular dishes.

SKIP TO

PASTA CON LE SARDE (SICILIAN PASTA WITH SARDINES), P. 306; MACCO DI FAVE (FAVA BEAN PURÉE), P. 148; FULVIO PIERANGELINI, P. 323.

ZUCCHINI

Once considered a second-rate squash in other parts of the world, the *zucchina* flourishes under the Italian sun.

JILL COUSIN

The "Italian Squash"

After sixteenth-century colonists of the New World discovered *askutasquash* from Native Americans, Italians in the eighteenth century had the idea of consuming a variety of shiny and watery squash before it had fully ripened. Various hybridizations resulted in the zucchini we know today.

ZUCCHINI IN COOKING

Here are several Italian specialties using cooked zucchini:

→ ***Minestrone alla milanese*** (Lombardy)
A soup made with long, green zucchini.

→ ***Zucchine trifolate*** (throughout Italy)
Zucchini simply sliced and sautéed with garlic and parsley.

→ ***Scarpaccia*** (literally "old shoe," Tuscany)
A flat zucchini cake made with flour, milk, and egg and embellished with Parmesan cheese that is a favorite at all summer tables. There is also a sweet version, *scarpaccia viareggina*, native to the town of Viareggio.

→ ***Zucchine marinate con menta*** (Lazio)
Zucchini marinated in lemon and spearmint, plated as a carpaccio.

→ ***Zucchine a scapece*** (Campania)
Zucchini fried then marinated in vinegar and mint.

→ ***Fritelle di zucchine*** (throughout Italy)
Zucchini fritters. Sometimes the flesh is used and sometimes the flowers, as in southern Italy, which are often stuffed with ricotta.

→ ***Zucchine 'mbuttunate*** (Calabria)
Zucchini stuffed with sausage, dried bread crumbs, and cheese; cooked in a pan; and served with tomato sauce, basil, and grated *caciocavallo* cheese.

ZUCCHINI AS A MODEL

In the sixteenth century, the cultivation of zucchini was in full swing on Italian soil, as can be seen in the painting *La Fruttivendola* by Italian painter Vincenzo Campi, housed at the Pinacoteca art gallery in Milan. In the image, a vegetable seller offers zucchini for sale on her small stand.

RECIPE

FIORI DI ZUCCHINE FRITTE, MOZZARELLA, ACCIUGHE, BASILICO
(FRIED ZUCCHINI BLOSSOMS, MOZZARELLA, ANCHOVIES, BASIL)

The Sicilian-born chef Fabrizio Ferrara (Osteria Ferrara, Paris 11th) opts not for zucchini blossoms stuffed with ricotta and mint, which is very common in southern Italy, but for the equally classic recipe using mozzarella and anchovy.

SERVES 4

1⅔ cups (200 g) T55 flour or all-purpose flour
Fleur de sel
1⅔ cups (400 mL) very cold sparkling water
A few ice cubes
4½ ounces (125 g) mozzarella cheese
8 zucchini blossoms
8 anchovy fillets in oil
8 basil leaves
2 quarts (2 L) frying oil (peanut or sunflower oil)
4 teaspoons (20 mL) extra-virgin olive oil
Freshly ground black pepper

· Place the flour in a bowl and add some salt. Gradually add the sparkling water. Using a spoon or your hand, combine the mixture until you obtain a smooth batter. Add the ice cubes, then place the bowl in the refrigerator.

· Cut the mozzarella into strips the length of the blossoms. Place the strips on paper towels or a plate to drain.

· Place an anchovy fillet and a basil leaf on each strip of mozzarella.

· Remove the pistil from the zucchini blossoms, being careful not to tear the flowers. Slide a strip of the mozzarella, anchovy, and basil inside each blossom. Close the flowers by carefully twisting the tip a little. Place in the refrigerator.

· In a high-sided saucepan, heat the oil. When the temperature reaches 350°F (180°C), dredge the zucchini blossoms in the batter and place them in the oil. Cook for a few minutes, until the flowers are crispy, then serve.

☞ *Il Tocco Dello Chef (Chef's Tip)*

Accompany these with a carpaccio of citron fruit, which brings freshness and a delicate citrus bitterness to the fried blossoms.

A ZUCCHINI INVENTORY

① ZUCCHINA TROMBETTA D'ALBENGA

Liguria—**crookneck**

(*Cucurbita moschata*) A variety producing a long green fruit that can reach 3 feet (1 m) in length and ends in a ball shape where the seeds are clustered. The green flesh, very firm and sweet, is eaten raw.

② ZUCCHINO TONDA VERDE

Emilia-Romagna—**round green zucchini (summer squash)**

(*Cucurbita pepo*) A small round and spherical zucchini with sweet and fragrant flesh. It is delicious stuffed.

③ ZUCCHINA GIALLA

Throughout Italy—**yellow squash**

(*Cucurbita pepo*) Its yellow fruits, which taste like pumpkin, are mainly used for making risottos.

④ TENERUMI

In Sicily, the name given to the long greens of the cucuzza squash used to prepare *pasta con i tenerumi*, a soup made from spaghetti, tomato, cucuzza squash, and tenerumi.

⑤ ZUCCA LUNGA SERPENTE DI SICILIA

Southern Italy—**cucuzza squash**

(*Lagenaria longissima*) Very long and cylindrical in shape, reminiscent of the elongated body of a snake, this zucchini offers a soft and firm flesh. It is eaten in soup or in pasta. It is a climbing plant. Also called *cucuzza longa, cucozza, cucuzzella, zucca lagenaria, zucca verde, zucchetta da pergola.*

⑥ ZUCCHINO STRIATO PUGLIESE

Apulia—**striped zucchini**

(*Cucurbita pepo*) The fruits, dark green streaked with light green, have a very sweet flesh.

Let's take a look at zucchini . . .

In late spring, zucchini blossoms adorn Italian tables. Beautiful and delicate, the blossoms are often stuffed after harvest and eaten as a fritter, the *frittelle di fiori di zucchina*. Only the male flowers ⑦ are harvested to allow the zucchini to develop on the female flowers ⑧. It is very easy to differentiate them: the male flower is supported on a thin stem while the female is supported by a slightly swollen stem that will produce the fruit.

SKIP TO

SQUASH, P. 48; MARINADES, P. 322; THE (RE)NAISSANCE OF VEGETABLES, P. 169.

THE AMAZING ANCHOVY

From Liguria to Sicily, this small fish is one of the most appreciated in Italy for its assertive and slightly pungent flavor. Here is an exploration of this amazing fish from the waters to the kitchen.

CHARLES PATIN O'COOHOON

LATIN NAME—*Engraulis encrasicolus.*

COMMON NAME—common anchovy. Two words define it in Italian: *acciuga* and *alice.* These terms are synonyms, although traditionally *alice* refers to fillets of small anchovies canned in oil, and *acciuga* refers to the whole anchovy preserved in salt.

APPEARANCE—it has bluish highlights and a silver back.

TASTE—the pronounced flavor of its flesh with its salty notes is as comfortable accompanied by meat as it is by vegetables.

HOW IS IT FISHED?

BY LAMPARO

This is a technique that dates back to the fourteenth century. The anchovies are caught at night using nets and a *lamparo,* a powerful lamp that attracts them.

BY CIÀNCIOLO

This is a very old method of catching fish from the water's surface, encircling them with a twisting and sliding net called a *ciànciolo.*

RECIPE

BAGNUN DI ACCIUGHE* (TOMATO ANCHOVY SOUP)

This soup has been simmering in pots in the town of Sestri Levante, near Genoa, since the nineteenth century.

SERVES 4

- 2¼ pounds (1 kg) whole fresh anchovies
- 6 cloves garlic (set aside 1 clove for the toasts), peeled
- 2 bunches parsley
- ¼ cup (60 mL) olive oil
- 6 fresh tomatoes, peeled and chopped
- 1 teaspoon (3 g) capers
- Several olives
- Salt and freshly ground black pepper
- ¼ cup (60 mL) dry white wine
- Several small slices baguette, toasted
- Oregano (optional)
- Basil (optional)

· Wash, clean, and dry the anchovies. In a large saucepan, brown 5 of the garlic cloves and the parsley in the olive oil. Add the tomatoes, capers, and olives. Season with salt and pepper. Add the wine and simmer for 10 minutes over medium heat. Add the anchovies and cook for another 10 minutes.

· Rub the toasts with the remaining garlic clove. Arrange them on serving plates and arrange the anchovies on top. You can also add a little oregano to the soup and season with a few basil leaves, if desired.

*Based on *Vera cuciniera genovese,* by Renzo Bagnasco.

How to Choose Your Anchovy

It should have a bright eye and a stiff, shiny body. The paler the anchovy, the less fresh it is.

IN OIL OR IN SALT: A DELICIOUS DILEMMA!

Here are the two most common ways to preserve anchovies for several months so you can keep enjoying them even outside of fishing season (March to July).

· WITH OIL ·

Allow for about 10½ ounces (300 g) of fresh anchovies per jar. Cover the anchovies in coarse salt for 72 hours in a bowl. Rinse and dry them. Remove the central bone before removing the fillets. In a small lidded glass jar, place the anchovy fillets in successive layers, then cover them with a fruity olive oil. Pack them well while expelling as much air as possible. Close the lid tightly. Keep refrigerated.

· SALT ·

Remove the heads and entrails of 2¼ pounds (1 kg) fresh anchovies. Gently wipe off the bodies. In a small lidded glass jar, place a layer of gray salt, then set some anchovies on the salt, belly side down. Cover with more salt, then continue layering in this way, alternating fish and salt (plan on about 9 ounces/ 250 g of fish per jar), ending with a layer of salt on top. Place a small weighted object on top to pack them down, then close the lid tightly (with the weight still in place). Keep refrigerated. After 5 days, remove the weight and any impurities that have collected on top. Add another layer of salt. Close the jar and refrigerate.

Great classic dishes starring anchovy

***SPAGHETTI ALLA PUTTANESCA* (SPAGHETTI WITH PUTTANESCA SAUCE)**

Neapolitan prostitutes are credited with the origin of this pasta dish made with capers, olives, tomatoes, and anchovies. There are two possibile explanations for this: the very strong aroma this delicious dish emits (which may attract customers) or the practicality for preparing it between appointments.

***SCAPECE DI ACCIUGHE* (ANCHOVY ESCABECHE)**

This recipe for fried anchovies marinated in vinegar and tomatoes is typical of southern Italy.

***BAGNA CAUDA* (GARLIC AND ANCHOVY DIP)**

This Piedmontese cousin of the Provençal-style dish called *anchoïade* is a dip made from anchovies, garlic, and olive oil, traditionally served with vegetables.

SALSA VERDE

This is a cold uncooked sauce made with parsley, anchovies, and vinegar, typical of Piedmont. It often accompanies *bollito misto* (a stew).

The anchovy festival

Along the Cinque Terre, in Monterosso al Mare, the Sagra dell'Acciuga, a festival dedicated to the *Engraulis encrasicolus* is celebrated in August.

ACCIUGHE SOTTO SALE DEL MAR LIGURE

This is the only anchovy to have a PGI (protected geographical indication). After fishing, the fish are placed in a fan shape in wood barrels, then covered with sea salt. Historically, the Republic of Genoa controlled its commerce. The sale of anchovies was subject to a tax, the *gabella piscium.* The vendors were called *chiapparoli,* in reference to Chiappa, a district of Genoa where they traded.

COLATURA DI ALICI
ANCHOVY FISH SAUCE

This amber-colored sauce is derived from fermented anchovies. Just a few drops of this "liquid anchovy" are enough to enhance the flavor of a dish.

Fishing

Fishing for anchovies takes place from March to July. During this period, the anchovy is lower in fat content and is therefore more suitable for salting.

Preparing

The head and entrails of the anchovies are removed. There is an old Italian word, *scapare*, which means "to tear off the heads" of anchovies and sardines before salting them.

Packing

The anchovies are packed in layers in a chestnut barrel called a *terzigno*. They are placed back to stomach, not stomach to stomach (which would speed up fermentation), alternating with sea salt.

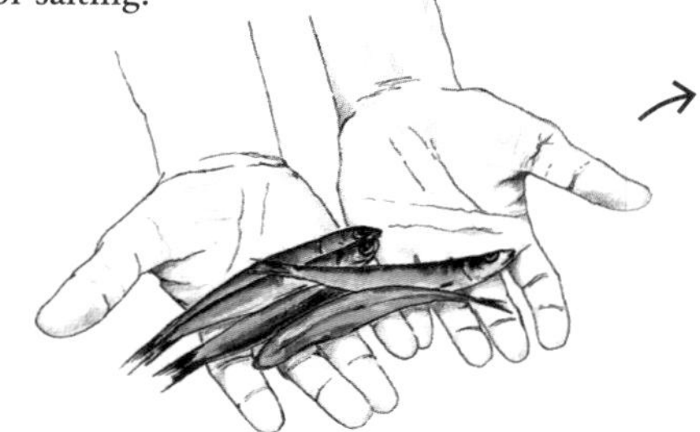

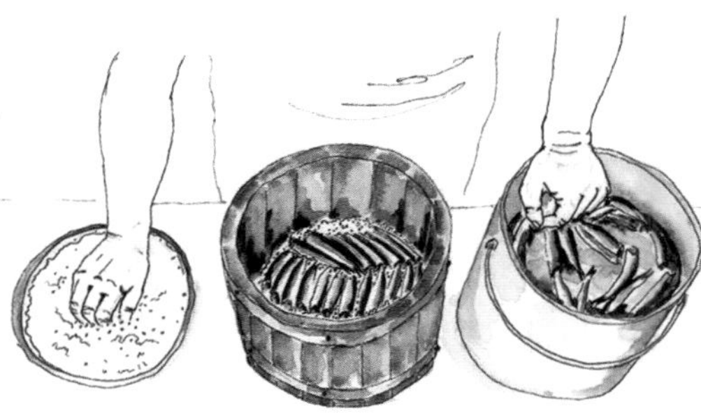

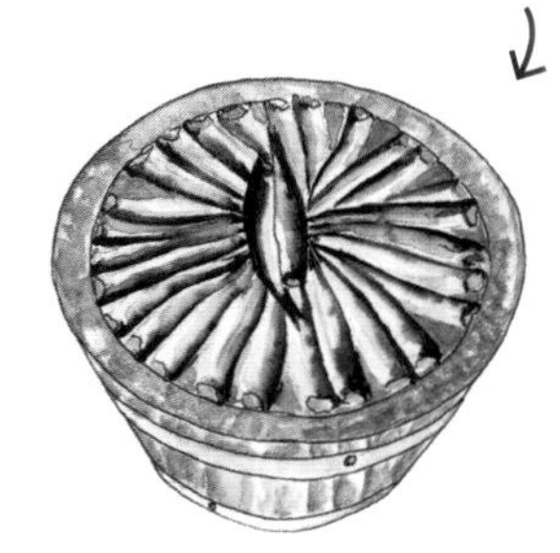

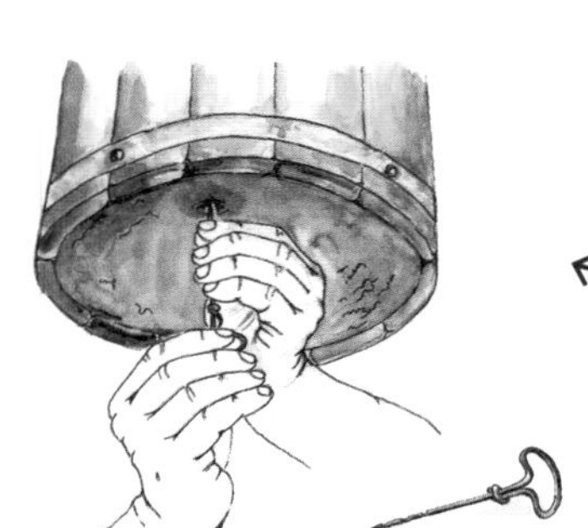

Pressing and aging

When the layers are finished, the barrel is covered with a wooden lid, the *tompagno*, on which stones are placed to exert downward pressure.

Aging lasts between four and six months, to be completed by the holidays. Some producers extend the aging up to twenty-four months to obtain a concentrated but more balanced liquid, rounder and softer in flavor. The anchovies exude a liquid that flows between the layers of fish and collects all the organoleptic properties of the fish. This liquid, which is both salty and very fragrant, acts as a natural flavor enhancer.

Collecting

With just a twist, the underside of the barrel is pierced to collect the precious liquid: the juice *cola* (flows), which gives *colatura* its name. A distillate with brown-mahogany tinges is the result.

The aroma of antiquity!

Colatura descends from garum, a fermented fish sauce the Romans used during antiquity. To make it, fish were matured with their entrails, then left to macerate in a large jar with salt, spices, and aromatics.

Colatura appeared in the thirteenth century in the rectory of San Pietro in Tuczolo, near Amalfi (Campania). The Cistercian monks arranged cleaned anchovies in wine barrels in salt before collecting and cooking the liquid produced.

Pairing with colatura

Mix a little pasta cooking water with 1 teaspoon (5 mL) colatura per person. Use it to season tomato-based spaghetti.

•

Deglaze a fish with a few drops of colatura.

•

Like *nuoc nam* (fish sauce), its Asian equivalent, colatura goes perfectly into a wok of vegetables.

COLATURA AT THE TABLE!

In Cetara, Gennaro Castiello and Gennaro Marciante opened **Acquapazza**, considered a gold-standard destination, which combines artisanal anchovy production and restaurants dedicated to colatura.

ACQUAPAZZA,
CORSO GARIBALDI, 36, CETARA

CETARA, A CITY OF CHOICE!

In this small port on the Amalfi Coast, anchovy is king. The fish spawns in the Gulf of Salerno, a particularly saline sea that gives flavor to the flesh of the anchovy. The fish are also smaller there, with a more concentrated flavor. The city celebrates colatura the first week of December during the *festa della colatura di alici*.

SKIP TO
BAGNA CAUDA (GARLIC AND ANCHOVY DIP), P. 119; SAGRA, A SACRED FESTIVAL, P. 118; SPAGHETTI ALLA PUTTANESCA, P. 217.

SEASON
ESTATE (SUMMER)

CATEGORY
PRIMO PIATTO (FIRST COURSE)

LEVEL
DIFFICOLTÀ MEDIA (MEDIUM DIFFICULTY)

PASTA ALLA NORMA

SICILIAN PASTA AND EGGPLANT

Originating in Catania, *pasta alla Norma* brings together on one plate all the symbols of a Sicilian summer: pasta, tomatoes, eggplant, ricotta salata, and basil. But be aware, this dish has its standards.

ILARIA BRUNETTI

THE NORMA, A STORY . . .

How was the Norma invented? Two opposing theories exist.

→ The playwright Nino Martoglio is said to have named this dish in the 1920s. Invited to the table of a certain Saridda D'Urso in Catania, he is said to have exclaimed:

"Donna Saridda, chista è na vera Norma!"

("Madame Saridda, this is a veritable Norma!"), comparing the harmonious perfection of the *maccheroni cu li milinciani* (with eggplant) to that of the opera *Norma* by the great composer Vincenzo Bellini.

→ A less-credited theory is the legend claiming this dish made its debut in society on the same day, and in the same city, as the premiere of *Norma*, presented on December 26, 1831, at the Catania theater.

THE RECIPE

By Fabrizio Ferrara, chef and proprietor of Osteria Ferrara (Paris 11th).

SERVES 4

1 medium oblong eggplant
Salt
Extra-virgin olive oil
½ white onion, finely chopped
1 clove garlic
14 ounces (400 g) tomatoes, peeled and diced
14 ounces (400 g) maccheroni
¼ cup (60 g) ricotta salata
Leaves from ½ bunch basil

Cut three-quarters of the unpeeled eggplant into ⅔-inch (1.5 cm) cubes. Using a mandoline, cut the remaining eggplant into very thin slices. Place the cubes and slices in a colander, add a handful of salt, and let rest for 30 minutes to soften.

Cook the cubes in a pan over high heat with ¼ cup (60 mL) olive oil until browned. Add the onion, garlic, and tomatoes. Let simmer for 5 minutes.

Fry the eggplant slices in oil heated to 300°F (150°C). Remove and set aside on paper towels to drain.

Cook the maccheroni al dente in salted boiling water. Set aside a little of the cooking water, then drain the pasta and sauté in the pan with the sauce. If necessary, add a spoonful of the pasta cooking water. Divide the pasta among serving plates, grate the ricotta over the top, add the fried eggplant slices, and finish with the basil.

Cooking the eggplant two ways brings a richness to the dish as well as a play of textures.

SKIP TO
EGGPLANT, P. 266; HIS MAJESTY THE BASIL, P. 121; RICOTTA, P. 219.

FOR A PASTA ALLA NORMA BY THE RULES . . .

THE PASTA

Use short pasta, preferably *maccheroni*, but rigatoni, penne, *mezze maniche*, or *mezzi paccheri* can be used. In Trapani, *busiate* is also used.

THE TOMATOES

Use fresh or canned, but they must always be of high quality, because the balance between acidity and sweetness, which is only found in fine tomatoes, is fundamental to the success of the dish. The San Marzano and Perino varietals work very well.

THE EGGPLANT

Preferably purple and oblong. The traditional recipe of Catania calls for eggplant in very thin slices, while in Messina the preference is small dice. In both cases, frying is the only method allowed for cooking them.

THE RICOTTA

In Messina, ricotta salata from Catania is replaced by *ricotta infornata* (baked ricotta), with a flavor that is more delicate and slightly toasted.

GOURMAND HERESY

As a Friulian, I sometimes use smoked ricotta from my region, the taste of which goes well with eggplant.

MASCARPONE

Often imagined as limited to the dessert tiramisu, this smooth, fatty, and lightly buttery cream is a recurring ingredient in northern Italian cuisine in both sweet and savory recipes.

CÉLINE MAGUET

ORIGIN

Before becoming famous for various industries, the Po plain was known for its extensive cattle-breeding grounds. Starting from the end of the sixteenth century, mascarpone has been produced there from cow's milk, as indicated from the first traces of production found south of Milan in the province of Lodi. Mascarpone was produced from November to March during mild temperatures to ensure its conservation.

A mysterious name

The origin of its name is still a mystery. It most likely comes from the Lombard dialect *maschpa* (cream of milk) or from *mascherpa,* a Lombard expression meaning "released," a description that fits the attributes of mascarpone, which tends to ooze when it's not stored in a container.

In Milan, people often say in the local language *"È rimasto come quel della mascherpa!"* ("He stayed put like mascarpone!"), a reference to a young boy from Lodi who went to the Milan market to sell his mascarpone. Once there, he found his basket was completely empty, the cream having melted from the heat. The expression stuck as a way to refer to someone who has experienced great disappointment.

RECIPES

HOMEMADE MASCARPONE

Don't have mascarpone in the fridge? Make some yourself!

MAKES 10½ OUNCES (300 G)

2 cups (500 mL) raw cream

1¾ teaspoons (8 mL) fresh lemon juice

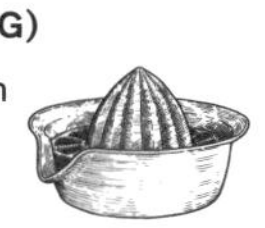

· In a saucepan, heat the cream over low heat while stirring with a whisk but without thinning it out too much. When the temperature reaches 185°F (85°C, a low simmer), add the lemon juice while continuing to stir. Cook for 8 to 10 minutes, until the cream thickens. Remove from the heat and let cool at room temperature for 30 minutes.

· Strain the cream through a fine-mesh strainer lined with a thin cloth (or cheesecloth), then place it in the refrigerator to drain for 7 to 8 hours. The longer you leave the mascarpone in the fridge, the thicker it will become. When the desired consistency is reached, transfer the mascarpone to an airtight container. It will keep in the refrigerator for 3 to 4 days.

MASCARPONE CREAM

This livens up any party and is also fabulous on *pandoro* and panettone, two great rival cakes.

FOUR INGREDIENTS AND A LITTLE KNOW-HOW:

· Whisk 2 large (38 g) egg yolks (do not discard the egg whites) with ¼ cup plus 1 tablespoon (60 g) sugar until the mixture is lightened in color.

· Combine 1 cup (200 g) mascarpone with 3 tablespoons (45 mL) rum. Stir this delicious mixture into the egg yolk mixture.

· Beat the 2 egg whites (60 g) to stiff peaks, then gently fold them into the mascarpone mixture.

· Serve with panettone or pandoro, or use the cream to fill a brioche.

IT'S NOT HOW YOU MAKE CHEESE!

Mascarpone is (legally) a cheese in name but not (technically) in fact.

Its recipe is simple

Lemon juice or citric acid is added to cream. The mixture is then heated in a bain-marie to form a kind of curd without using a ferment, animal rennet, or anything else—*niente.* The difference between this and cheese is based on this addition of "nothing else." Cheese, by definition, is milk or cream to which a ferment has been added to create a curd. For mascarpone, the so-called curdling does not take place, but it is this approach that gives it its creamy consistency.

IMPORTANT RULES

In risotto, don't even think about it!

It's like adding cream to carbonara . . . heresy.

In desserts, yes!

It perfectly replaces other thick creams.

SKIP TO

ITALY'S BEAUTIFUL CHEESES, P. 222; TIRAMISU, P. 188; PANETTONE, P. 96.

MUSHROOMS

Here is an overview of the most beautiful fungi growing in Italy, from spring to winter . . .

PATRIZIO MENCHI

SPRING

Dormiente (dormant)

March mushroom
(*Hygrophorus marzuolus*)

CAP: between 2 and 6 inches (5 and 15 cm), fleshy, gray, with pearl undertones; its gills are pale, grayish.

STEM: white, cylindrical, dense.

FLESH: white, with a very subtle aroma of withered rose and a pleasant flavor.

HARVEST: after the spring thaw, in the woods with varied vegetation and where white fir predominate. It's difficult to see because it is mostly buried in the ground: it likes to "sleep" under the snow. It is uncommon and is the first mushroom of the year.

COOKING: in *risotto ai dormienti*. Prepare a risotto according to a traditional recipe and stir in the cleaned and chopped mushrooms after the white wine is absorbed.

Prugnolo / Fungo di San Giorgio

St. George's mushroom
(*Calocybe gambosa*)

CAP: between 1½ and 3 inches (4 and 8 cm) in diameter, fleshy; its color varies from white to ocher; its gills are off-white.

STEM: ivory color, dense.

FLESH: thick, white, with a pronounced floury scent; very sought after.

HARVEST: it often grows near members of the rose family (Rosaceae) and near blackthorn trees. Its characteristic flourlike smell helps locate it.

COOKING: it can complement egg pastas and soups, or just be sautéed.

Morchella spugnola / Morchella conica

Morel (*Morchella esculenta*)

CAP: up to 8 inches (20 cm) high and about 2 inches (5 cm) in diameter. Very distinct miter shape, gray-brown color.

STEM: whitish and hollow.

FLESH: very elastic; its scent is subtle, sometimes imperceptible.

HARVEST: on damp ground and in coniferous woods.

COOKING: consume it only after cooking it, because raw morels contain toxins. Very tasty, it can be cut into small pieces and sautéed; used in stuffings (made with egg and bread crumbs), risotto, omelets . . .

SUMMER

Galletto / Finferlo

Girolle/golden chanterelle
(*Cantharellus cibarius*)

CAP: up to 4¾ inches (12 cm) in diameter, not particularly distinguishable from the stem; yellow color, more or less intense.

STEM: cylindrical and slightly flared.

FLESH: clear, yellowish, fibrous; its aroma is reminiscent of the skin of the white peach; it is not attacked by worms, making it easy to store.

HARVEST: in hilly deciduous forests and in mountainous coniferous woods; from early summer through late fall.

COOKING: the most cooked wild mushroom in Europe; used both in sauces and as an accompaniment; excellent canned in oil.

Prataiolo

Meadow mushroom
(*Agaricus campestris*)

CAP: white, its diameter varies between 2 and 4¾ inches (5 and 12 cm); very fleshy, with pink gills (when young) or darker (when older).

STEM: short, slightly cylindrical.

FLESH: white, with a pleasant smell and a sweetish taste.

HARVEST: very common in meadows in early summer through fall. Do not confuse it with the yellow-staining mushroom (*Agaricus xantodermus*), which is very similar but distinguishable by its unpleasant odor and its foot that turns yellowish when touched.

COOKING: raw, sautéed in a pan, as a topping.

DISTINCTIVE ATTRIBUTE

Very close relative of the button or common mushroom (*Agaricus bisporus*), a cultivated variety on sale in all supermarkets.

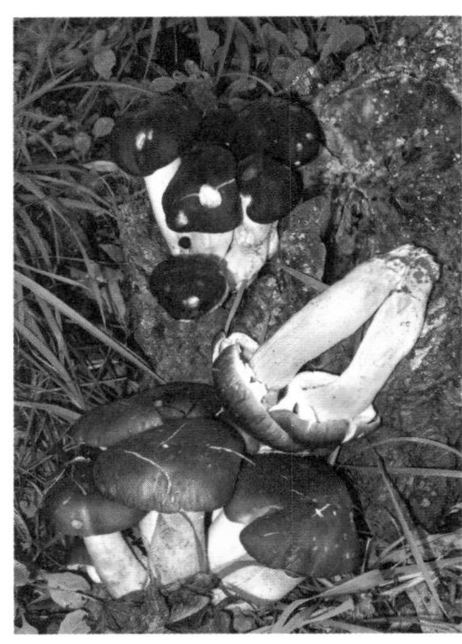

Pioppino

Poplar mushroom (*Cyclocybe aegerita*)

CAP: can reach 6 inches (15 cm) in diameter and be hemispherical or convex; off-white to buff brown.

STEM: firm, fibrous, and plump.

FLESH: white, slightly brownish at the base of the foot, and tender.

HARVEST: from branches of poplars, elms, and dead or living maple trees.

COOKING: it can be made into sauces or preserved in oil, but remove the lower part of the foot.

DISTINCTIVE ATTRIBUTE

It's the first mushroom to have been cultivated.

Photographs by Gianfronco and Silvio Di Cocco (Gruppo Micologico Fiorentino—P.A. Micheli).

AUTUMN

Fungo porcino ("pig mushroom," Liguria), *Cappellet* (Lombardy), *Moccione* (Tuscany), *Brisa* (Veneto)

Porcini (*Boletus edulis*)

CAP: between 2 and 9¾ inches (5 and 25 cm) in diameter, convex in shape, thick and fleshy; the cuticle (or cap skin, removed when peeling mushrooms) turns greenish yellow when ripe; the pores are white and turn yellow and olive green with age.

STEM: white to light beige, widened at the base.

FLESH: thick and firm, notes of undergrowth with a nutty taste.

HARVEST: August to October in deciduous (oak, beech) and coniferous (fir, spruce) forests.

COOKING: raw or cooked. To dry porcini mushrooms: clean the porcini and pat dry. Cut them lengthwise into ⅛-inch-thick (3 mm) strips. Dry them for 2 hours at 122°F (50°C). Let stand for 15 minutes in the open air. Repeat this step until the texture becomes brittle. Once dry and cool, store in jars, protected from light.

DISTINCTIVE ATTRIBUTE

Il fungo di Borgotaro grows in Emilia-Romagna on 81,500 acres (33,000 ha); it is the only porcini to have a PGI.

Pennenciola / Fungo sanguinello

Saffron milk cap (*Lactarius deliciosus*)

CAP: orange in color, between 2 and 6 inches (5 and 15 cm), funnel-shaped.

STEM: short, hollow, orange.

FLESH: firm, brittle, and grainy, it oozes an orange latex that becomes greenish when exposed to air and that distinguishes it from other edible orange milk caps, which exude whitish latex.

HARVEST: associated mainly with umbrella pine, it grows in coniferous woods from early fall to late winter.

COOKING: excellent braised or in sauces with a tangy taste or canned in oil.

Cimballo ("cymbal")/*Fungo di San Martino* ("St. Martin's mushroom")

Trooping funnel, monk's head (*Clitocybe geotropa*)

CAP: between 2⅓ and 8 inches (6 and 20 cm), funnel-shaped, with a leather-colored central depression.

STEM: cylindrical, large, stocky.

FLESH: white or off-white, very aromatic.

HARVEST: until early winter, in deciduous and coniferous woods and in glades. Often grows in circular groups, always in the same place if conditions are favorable.

COOKING: very tasty, it can be enjoyed in sauces, as an accompaniment, or on crostini (spread on toast); dried; its taste and flavors are reminiscent of truffle, so much so that it can sometimes be prepared the same way.

DISTINCTIVE ATTRIBUTE

Like the oyster mushroom, it is more prized than the porcini in certain regions of Italy (Maremma).

Ovolo ("small egg")/*Fungo reale* ("royal mushroom")

Caesar's mushroom (*Amanita caesaria*)

CAP: bright orange in color, it measures up to 7 inches (18 cm). The gills are tight and golden yellow.

STEM: cylindrical, thicker, and ovoid at the base, with an ample volva.

FLESH: thick cap, a more granular foot; faint odor and pleasant taste.

HARVEST: uncommon, it grows in deciduous forests and regions with a temperate climate; avoid picking those covered with mold, which change their odor.

COOKING: ideal raw, prepared as carpaccio; if it is cooked, it should be eaten separately, without any other ingredient, to preserve its delicate flavor.

Mazza di tamburo ("drumstick")/ *Bubbola* ("bagatelle")

Parasol mushroom (*Macrolepiota procera*)

CAP: between 4 and 9¾ inches (10 and 25 cm), slightly brownish, initially spherical and then widely spread out in the shape of a parasol with numerous hazel-colored scales.

STEM: can reach 15¾ inches (40 cm), hollow in its upper part, with brown stripes and a moveable ring.

FLESH: soft and fragile, pleasant smell and nutty taste.

HARVEST: in the clearings of deciduous forests, in meadows, until late autumn.

COOKING: only the cap is eaten; breaded and fried, or thinly sliced and arranged in alternating layers with potato slices then baked in the oven.

Cardoncello / Ferlengo

King oyster mushroom (*Pleurotus eryngii*)

CAP: diameter from 1⅛ to 4 inches (3 to 10 cm); its foot may be off-center and its color varies from off-white to dark buff.

STEM: whitish color, tapered, and plump.

FLESH: white, firm, compact, and elastic; slight odor of flour.

HARVEST: common on the roots of eryngos (flowering plants of the Apiaceae family); it can be collected in large quantities in summer and until late autumn.

COOKING: excellent canned in oil, but also sautéed, au gratin, grilled . . .

DISTINCTIVE ATTRIBUTE

In some regions of Italy (the south and the islands), the oyster mushroom, which can even be cultivated, is more popular than the porcini mushroom.

WINTER

Finferla / Fiammiferino

Yellow foot (*Craterellus lutescens*)

CAP: diameter between ⅓ and 2 inches (1 and 5 cm), with a central depression; orange-brown in color, it has a fibrous appearance.

STEM: irregular, tapered, orange.

FLESH: fibrous, elastic. Emits a persistent fragrance of fruit; sweet flavor.

HARVEST: in moist coniferous woods in late fall and winter; very common, it lines the forest.

COOKING: used in flavorful side dishes (beef cheek; pastas, such as pappardelle . . .). When it is dried, it can be simply rehydrated to its original texture.

Trombette dei morti / Corno dell'abbondanza

Trumpet of death, black trumpet, horn of plenty (*Craterellus cornucopioides*)

CAP: between 1⅛ and 3 inches (3 and 8 cm) in diameter, does not stand out well from the stem because the fungus is shaped like a narrow funnel; the inside is black, the outside a whitish gray.

STEM: blackish, 1½ to 2⅓ inches (4 to 6 cm) high, hollow like any mushroom.

FLESH: fine and grayish, elastic, with a slightly fruity scent.

HARVEST: grows in clumps in deciduous woods and covers very large areas; one of the last mushrooms of the season.

COOKING: dried and chopped, it is used as a seasoning; very good fresh, but must cook for a long time because of its fibrous consistency (in soups).

SKIP TO

RISOTTO, P. 78; WHITE TRUFFLE, THE GEM OF PIEDMONT, P. 109; THE SOUPS OF ITALY, P. 146.

CALAMARI

Abundant in the waters that surround the entire Italian peninsula, the *calamaro* (squid) is an Italian love story, and a must on tables along the seaside.

STÉPHANE SOLIER

WHAT AM I?

NAME: European squid (*Loligo vulgaris*), also called *calamari* when used as food.

SEASON: September to February.

APPEARANCE: pinkish purple with red undertones; diamond-shaped wings on the upper half of the body.

TASTE: firm and tender flesh, very sought after, delicately briny, almost sweet.

A STORY OF LOVE: the Romans enjoyed it in quenelles (*isicia*), in ragout (*patina*), or stuffed (*lolligo farsilis*).

CLEANING SQUID

→ Rinse with cool water. Gently remove the head, without rupturing the ink sac, to extract part of the entrails.

→ Cut off the tentacles and the arms above the eyes. Remove the beak and eyes from the head.

→ Cut the head and wings into sections and peel them with the back of a knife.

→ Empty the inside of the body tube by first removing the cuttlebone (the strip of cartilage).

→ Place two fingers in the body and remove the remaining entrails. Peel the outside with the back of a knife. Rinse everything with clean water.

→ Storing larger squid in the freezer overnight softens them.

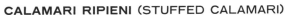

RECIPES

CALAMARI RIPIENI (STUFFED CALAMARI)

Mirjam Montefusco, an outstanding cook and the Corso-Italian aunt of François-Régis Gaudry, regularly digs into the recipes of her two countries to the delight of family and friends.

SERVES 3

6 small squids (5¼ to 7 ounces/150 to 200 g each) or 3 large

2 cloves garlic, peeled

3 tablespoons (45 mL) extra-virgin olive oil

Salt

½ cup (50 g) stale bread crumbs

4 or 5 sprigs parsley

1 egg

4 teaspoons (20 mL) dry white wine

14 ounces (400 g) canned finely chopped tomatoes (*polpa*), or 2¼ pounds (1 kg) ripe tomatoes (make into a *passata* in advance)

1 cayenne pepper (optional)

- Clean the squids and reserve the entire body tubes. Finely chop the bodies and tentacles. In a skillet, brown 1 garlic clove over medium heat in 1 tablespoon (15 mL) of the olive oil. Add the chopped squid and sauté for 10 minutes. Season lightly with salt. Chop the bread crumbs and add them to the pan, stirring to moisten them. Stir well for 5 minutes over low heat. Remove the garlic, then transfer the contents of the pan to a large bowl. Finely chop the parsley and add it to the bowl. Add the egg. Mix well by hand or with a fork.
- Gently fill the squid bodies three-quarters full with the stuffing. Close them using a toothpick. In a lidded pot, heat 2 tablespoons (30 mL) of the olive oil. Halve the remaining garlic clove and cook until browned. When the garlic is a golden brown, add the stuffed squid bodies to the pan and brown them over medium heat, turning them regularly and carefully. Add the wine and let cook until the liquid has evaporated. Add the tomato *polpa* or *passata* and the cayenne pepper, if using. Season with salt. Cook, covered, for 30 minutes (40 minutes for larger squid), then uncover and let the sauce reduce for several minutes. Remove the garlic before serving.

Variation: Heat 1 tablespoon (15 mL) olive oil in a pan and brown the cayenne pepper (cut into thirds) and 1 clove garlic, halved. Add 2¼ pounds (1 kg) green chard (preferably wild), season with salt, and sauté for 10 minutes. Add the sautéed chard to the pot with the squid, and stir gently for 5 minutes over low heat. Serve.

CALAMARI FRITTI (FRIED CALAMARI)

Christian Menchi, Corso-Tuscan owner of the restaurant U Capezzu (Santa Severa, Haute-Corse, France), inherited his taste and methods for cooking local seafood from his Corsican grandmother Lucile and his mother, Mirjam Montefusco.

- Clean 1¾ pounds (800 g) squid (4 small or 2 to 3 large).
- Cut the head and mantle into ¼-inch-wide (5 mm) rings and the wings, arms, and tentacles into two or three pieces each. Rinse them with clean water and dry well with paper towels.
- In a bowl, combine ⅓ cup plus 1 tablespoon (50 g) flour and ¼ cup (30 g) cornmeal. Dredge the squid pieces in the flour mixture, and remove any excess flour by tossing them briefly in a strainer.
- Fry the squid rings in vegetable oil (such as sunflower oil) heated to 338°F (170°C) for 2 to 3 minutes, or until golden brown. Season with salt, and serve with an aioli.

SKIP TO
THE STATES OF THE TOMATO, P. 30; LINGUINE AL NERO DI SEPPIA (CUTTLEFISH INK LINGUINE), P. 361; OCTOPUS, P. 67.

SEASON

TUTTO L'ANNO (YEAR-ROUND)

CATEGORY

SECONDO PIATTO (MAIN COURSE)

LEVEL

FACILE (EASY)

FEGATO ALLA VENEZIANA

CALF'S LIVER AND ONIONS

Once upon a time in the city of Venice, a liver was simmered with small onions . . . and became an emblematic dish of the Venetian Republic.

FRANÇOIS-RÉGIS GAUDRY

ITS ORIGIN

→ Referred to as *figà àea Venessiana* by the Venetians, *il fegato alla veneziana* is a dish of contrasts: the strength of the liver (pork or veal) combined with the sweetness of the onion. Don't forget the *agrodolce* (sweet-and-sour) touch brought by the vinegar or white wine that makes this *piatto* a decidedly serene specialty!

→ Tempering the potency of organ meats has been a method since antiquity. It was customary to fatten pigs and geese with figs and to calm the heat of the meat with fruit sugar or honey. The word *fegato* comes from the Latin *ficatum*—itself derived from *ficus* (fig), because *iecur ficatum*, liver fattened with figs, was widely practiced. The Venetians, to temper the strength of the liver, promptly combined it with onions, which were abundant in the lagoon, and whose antibacterial properties made it possible to preserve fish.

→ This recipe first appeared in 1790 under the mention of *fegato di mongana alla veneziana* (*mongana* meant milk-fed veal) in *L'Apicio moderno*, a collection of recipes by Roman cook Francesco Leonardi.

THE INGREDIENTS

LIVER

Among organ meats, the liver is a favorite piece, considered the seat of feelings and strength. This dish had aristocratic status.

Originally, pork liver was used, which had a stronger flavor. Today, this specialty is commonly prepared with calf's liver, but rabbit liver, which is tasty and delicate, is also enjoyed.

THE ONION

One of the flagship vegetables in Venetian cuisine. The traditional varietal of onion used in this recipe is the *cipolla bianca di Chioggia*: a sweet white onion cultivated in the province of Chioggia in Veneto.

THE VINEGAR

It contributes to the sweet-and-sour taste of the recipe, but it was once used for its antibacterial properties. Some domestic versions use lemon instead of vinegar.

THE RECIPE

It is often on the menu of Il Bacaro (Paris 11th), the Venetian trattoria of chef Eleonora Zuliani.

SERVES 4

- 1⅛ pounds (500 g) white or yellow onions
- 1⅛ pounds (500 g) calf's liver, as a single slice
- 3 tablespoons (45 mL) olive oil
- Salt
- 2 tablespoons (30 mL) red wine vinegar
- 1 tablespoon (15 mL) Marsala wine (optional)
- 1 tablespoon (20 g) unsalted butter
- Freshly ground black pepper
- 2 sprigs flat-leaf parsley, chopped

Cut the onions into thin rings about ⅛ inch (4 mm) thick. Trim the veins and skin from the liver, cut it into ¼-inch-thick (5 mm) strips, then into pieces about 1½ inches (4 cm) wide.

Pour 2 tablespoons (30 mL) of the olive oil into a nonstick pan and cook the onions over low heat, without browning them, for about 30 minutes; add water regularly. Season with salt, and transfer them to a plate; keep warm.

Wipe out the pan and add the remaining 1 tablespoon olive oil. Sear the liver pieces over high heat for about 30 seconds, stirring with a wooden spoon. Add the cooked onions, mix well, then add the vinegar and Marsala, if using. Continue cooking for 1 minute. Season with salt.

Remove from the heat, add the butter in small pieces, season generously with pepper, and sprinkle with the parsley.

Il Tocco Della Chef (Chef's Tip)

Add a sage leaf to the oil just before browning the liver pieces. Sage goes perfectly with liver! Ideally this recipe is accompanied, as is done in Venice, with polenta.

Close relatives

FEGATO ALLA SBRODEGA

The liver is cooked longer in broth, with half the onions, and most often with garlic and parsley.

FEGATO 'MBRIAGON (UBRIACONE, "DRUNKEN")

For this "drunk" liver, the liver is cut into strips, floured, and simmered in red wine.

FEGATO ALLA VICENTINA

This dish uses white wine instead of wine vinegar.

SKIP TO

THE LAGOON IS A TERROIR, P. 134; POLENTA, P. 114; ONIONS, P. 292.

FROM THE SEA

Here are some recipes with humble origins that have now become refined dishes. Let's take a walk along the coast and dive into some delicious seafood soups.

ILARIA BRUNETTI

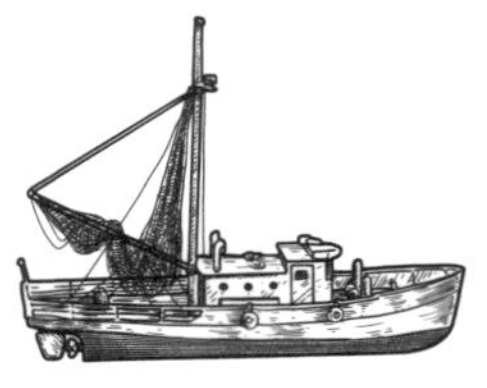

THE ORIGINS

Today considered a delicacy, fish soups were once modest dishes: fishermen prepared these aboard their boats using seawater and fish too small or damaged to sell. In the seventeenth century, when the consumption of fish increased to respect the religious calendar, soups containing prized fish and precious spices appeared on noble tables.

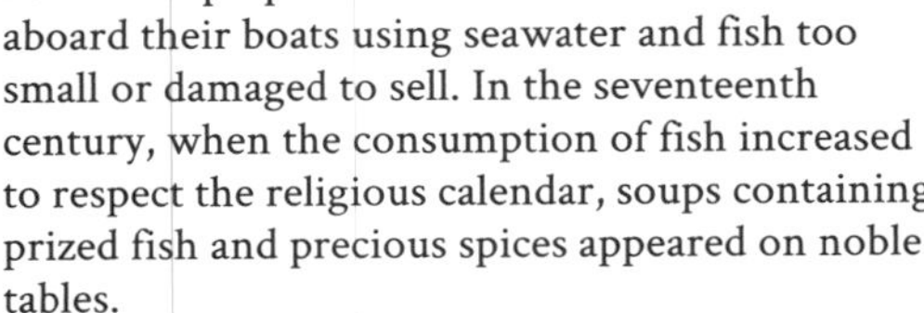

THE COASTAL ANATOMY OF *BRODETTO*

FROM FRIULI TO VENETO
It's made with fish from the Venetian lagoon, often using a single type of fish sliced and usually without tomatoes and with vinegar; it is typically served with grilled white polenta.

IN EMILIA-ROMAGNA
The flavor is assertive, with onions, vinegar, tomatoes, and pepper. Toward the mouth of the river Po, eel reigns supreme; traveling down the coast, gurnard, scorpion fish, small fish, sharks, mussels, and palourde clams are used.

FROM MARCHE TO MOLISE
The richest versions are found here, with many varieties of fish (often John Dory and scorpion fish), mollusks, and some crustaceans; the fish are cooked whole, placed in terra-cotta molds, adding them from the largest to the smallest according to their cooking times. They are often made with tomatoes or chile pepper added and sometimes enhanced with green bell peppers, all served with grilled bread.

RECIPE

BRODETTO ALLA VASTESE (TRADITIONAL VASTO SEAFOOD SOUP)

By Riccardo Ferrante,* chef of Solina Pasta Fresca (Paris 12th).

SERVES 4

- 5¼ ounces (150 g) clams (cockles, wedge clams, or palourde)
- 5¼ ounces (150 g) mussels
- 4 mantis shrimp or langoustines, or 2 spider crabs
- 4 red mullets
- 4 small whiting fish
- 4 small cuttlefish or calamari
- 4 *ghiozzi testoni* (giant gobies, or use small scorpion fish, sole, or wedge sole)
- Just over ¾ cup (200 mL) olive oil
- 6 cloves garlic, peeled
- 1 bell pepper, cored, seeded, and sliced lengthwise
- 1⅛ pounds (500 g) fresh and juicy tomatoes, chopped
- 1 bunch parsley, coarsely chopped
- 1 bunch basil, coarsely chopped
- 1 red chile

Equipment
Terra-cotta cooking pot or a large low-sided pot

- Clean the clams and mussels and rinse them of any salt. Clean the fish, or ask the fishmonger to clean them. Rinse them.
- In the cooking pot, heat the olive oil and add the whole garlic cloves, the bell pepper, tomatoes, parsley, basil, and whole chile. Cook over high heat.
- Once the tomatoes start to release their liquid, add the shrimp, then the fish, starting from the largest to the smallest size (red mullet, whiting fish, cuttlefish, testoni). Spread them out well and place them little by little on the sauce, then on top of each other. The brodetto is never stirred together, hence the importance of placing the fish according to their size and cooking times. Cover and cook for 7 minutes.
- Add the clams and mussels. As they cook, the shellfish will add water and salinity to the mixture. Cover and cook again for 7 minutes.
- Check the fish to determine if they are cooked through. If not, cook for a few minutes longer until done. Serve immediately.
- After serving, there will be some sauce left in the dish. There are two opposing traditions for using this sauce:
  → The first is to *fare la scarpetta* (meaning mop up with bread).
  → The second is to cook spaghetti al dente and coat it with the remaining sauce.
  You choose!

**His family recipe was documented by Céline Maguet.*

DECRYPTION OF AN "ITALIAN" FISH SOUP

THE BASE: an assortment of fresh fish, according to the catch of the day; often mollusks, sometimes crustaceans. If the fish are cooked in pieces, a broth is prepared with their heads and spines as the base of the soup.

THE ACIDIC NOTE: this is essential and is provided by vinegar, white wine, or tomatoes.

THE VEGETABLES AND CONDIMENTS: always garlic, often onion and chile (in the south); sometimes capers and black olives (Sicily, Liguria), celery, bell peppers; more rarely other vegetables.

THE HERBS: very often parsley; sometimes basil; more rarely oregano (Sicily) or saffron (Sardinia, Marche, Liguria).

THE SIDE DISH: very often grilled bread; sometimes polenta (Friuli and Veneto).

Do not confuse . . .

ZUPPA—A SOUP
This is usually a more rustic soup prepared with an assortment of fish *da taglio* (for cutting) such as gummy shark, or *da sugo* (pieces for simmering) such as red mullet. It's rarely mixed.

BRODETTO—A TYPE OF FISH STEW
It is available all along the Adriatic coast, mostly with fish *da brodo* (in broth) such as gurnard and fish prepared da sugo.

GUAZZETTO—A RAGOUT
A preparation made with noble fish, such as sea bream, panfried with fresh tomatoes, garlic, wine, or broth. It is also sometimes prepared with cod, frog, and even meats.

SKIP TO
COOKING WITH SEAWATER, P. 317;
FISHING HUTS, P. 303.

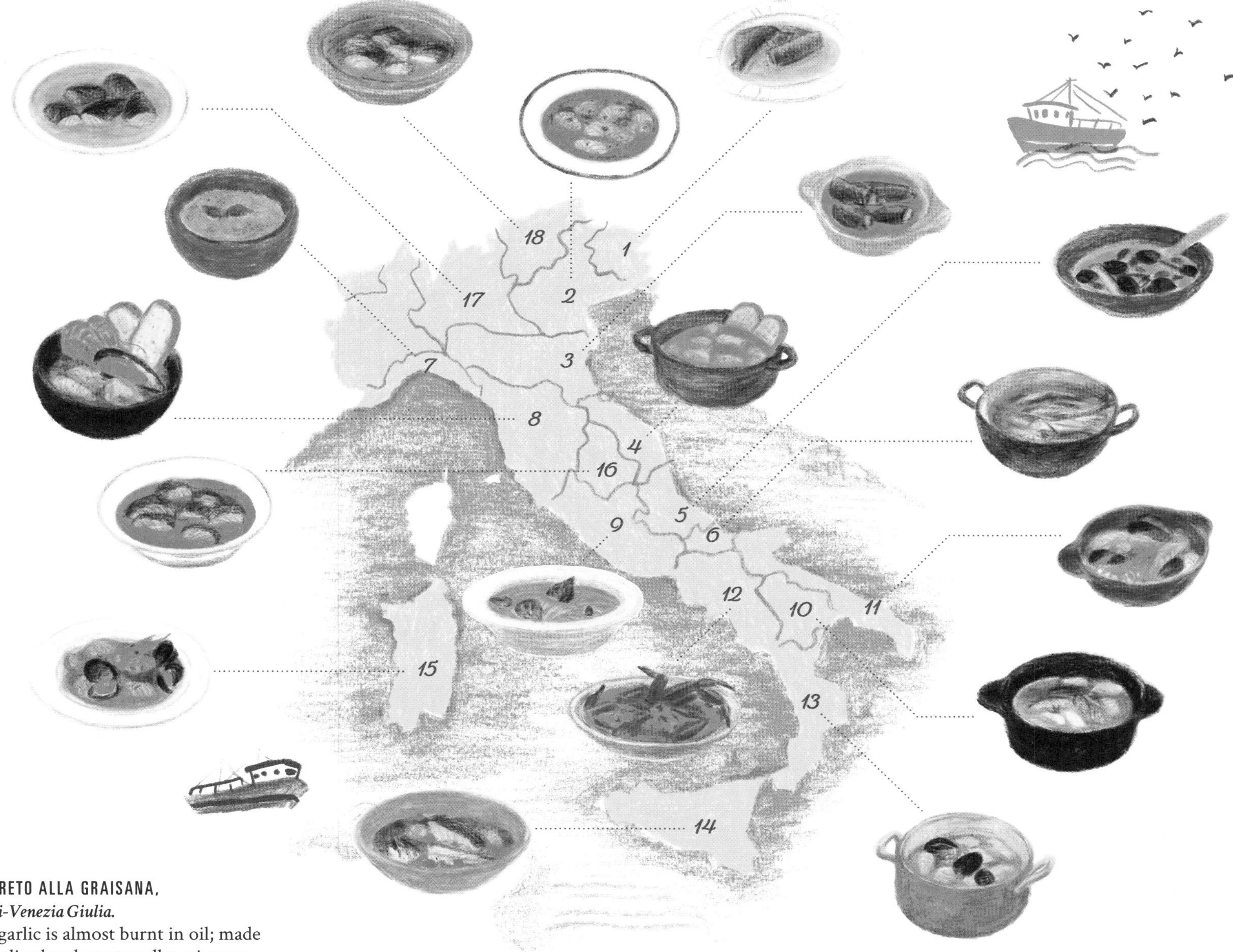

1. BORETO ALLA GRAISANA, *Friuli-Venezia Giulia.*
The garlic is almost burnt in oil; made with sliced turbot or mullet, vinegar, and black pepper. A traditional dish for fishermen who lived in *casoni* (fishing huts), it is found today also including an assortment of fish or shellfish.

2. BRODETTO CIOSOTO, *Veneto.*
Made with gobies, which are cooked sliced, often with other fish from the Venetian lagoon in their broth, with onion, garlic, white wine, vinegar, and sometimes tomatoes.

3. BRODETTO A BECCO D'ASINO (literally "donkey's kiss," an expression that means "done quickly"), *Emilia-Romagna.*
Typical of Comacchio, with eels, onions, tomato paste, and vinegar.

4. BRODETTO ALL'ANCONETANA, *Marche.*
Tradition calls for thirteen varieties of fish (as a remembrance of the Last Supper), along with garlic, onion, vinegar, tomatoes, chile or black pepper, and parsley.

5. BRODETTO ALLA VASTESE, *Abruzzo.*
(see recipe opposite) An assortment of fish, calamari, mussels, clams, with tomatoes, bell peppers, chile, parsley, and basil.

6. BRODETTO ALLA TERMOLESE, *Molise.*
Very close to *alla Vastese*, its neighbor from Vasto, but more liquidy.

7. CIUPPIN, *Liguria.*
A less thick soup, with rockfish, garlic, anchovies, white wine, parsley, sometimes onions and celery. Some add saffron to it.

8. CACCIUCCO, *Tuscany.*
There are two famous versions: one from Livorno, which is more rustic with a pronounced taste of garlic and chile, and another from Viareggio, in which the flavors are more mellow.

9. MINESTRA DI BROCCOLI E ARZILLA, *Lazio.*
Broken spaghetti cooked in a soup made of skate broth with its flesh, romanesco cabbage, tomatoes, and anchovies seared in oil, garlic, and parsley.

10. ZUPPA DI PESCE LUCANA, *Basilicata.*
Very simple, with different sliced fish, garlic, and chile.

11. ZUPPA DI PESCE ALLA GALLIPOLINA, *Apulia.*
It includes up to twenty-one varieties of fish, with mussels, clams, sometimes langoustines, onions, and tomatoes. Some still use seawater to make it.

12. GUAZZETTO DI GRANCHIO, *Campania.*
In this typical soup from the coast at the foot of Vesuvius, the *fellone* (spider) crab is cooked with garlic, parsley, and a few tomatoes; a very tasty sauce to which vermicelli or *paccheri* can be added.

13. QUADARU O QUADARO, *Calabria.*
The name refers to the copper pot in which an assortment of fish is cooked with garlic, sea lettuce, tomatoes, and—according to tradition—seawater, all spicy hot.

14. ZUPPA DI PESCE ALLA SIRACUSANA, *Sicily.*
An assortment of fish (including mahi-mahi) filleted and cooked over low heat with celery, tomatoes, capers, bay leaf or parsley, chile, garlic, and bone broth.

15. SA CASSOLA, *Sardinia.*
A soup that tradition begs at least seven marine ingredients (fish, shellfish, and crustaceans) with tomatoes, onion, garlic, chile, and basil. The name comes from the pan in which it is cooked.

When it's all about fresh water . . .

16. TEGAMACCIO, *Umbria.*
Eel and perch cooked with tomatoes, wine, and chile in an earthenware pot that lends the soup its name.

17. ZUPPA DI PESCE ALLA LARIANA, *Lombardy.*
Trout, pike, and other freshwater fish are filleted, fried, and served in a broth prepared with their bones and flavored with saffron.

18. ZUPPA DI PESCE DI LAGO, *Trentino-Alto Adige.*
Close to the Lombard version, but bay leaf replaces saffron.

PIZZA AS POP ICON

Whether in old movie reels or television programs, pizza has frequently been in the limelight. Here is a world tour of various productions in which this guest star has taken center stage.

STÉPHANE SOLIER

IN FILM

In Hollywood just as in *cinecittà*, as deep dish or rolled, pizza has made audiences salivate since the 1940s.

SAINT JOHN THE BEHEADED (SAN GIOVANNI DECOLLATO)

D'AMLETO PALERMI, 1940

Featured pizza—its first on-screen appearance at a popular Naples tavern. The large Totò shares a steaming pizza just out of the oven. Iconic!

THE PIZZA TRIANGLE/ DRAMA OF JEALOUSY (DRAMMA DELLA GELOSIA TUTTI I PARTICOLARI IN CRONACA)

Pizza from the heart—A florist (Monica Vitti) shares the love of bricklayer Oreste (Marcello Mastroianni) and *pizzaiolo* Nello (Giancarlo Giannini) between a mortadella sandwich and a *pizza Margherita* in the shape of a heart.

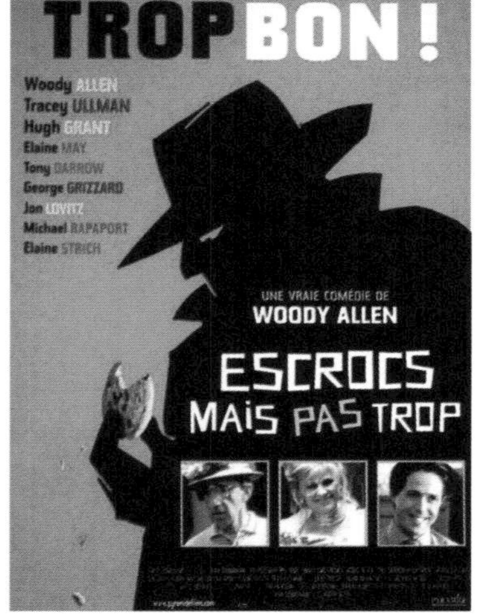

SMALL TIME CROOKS

BY WOODY ALLEN, 2000

Criminal pizza: an ex-mobster decides to rent an old pizzeria to rob a bank. Will the disappointments overcome his desire for pizza?

EAT, PRAY, LOVE

BY RYAN MURPHY, 2010

Sabbatical pizza—In search of meaning, Liz Gilbert (Julia Roberts) decides to take charge of her life and go where things are more authentic. For food, it's Italy . . . and the double mozzarella pizza from L'Antica Pizzeria Da Michele in Naples, where the scene was filmed on location.

IN TELEVISION

Enjoyed alone or with friends, in the street or at home, pizza plays the supporting role in many classics of the small screen.

FRIENDS

BY MARTA KAUFFMAN AND DAVID CRANE, 1994–2004

Friendly pizza—This famous sitcom celebrates pizza. And Joey Tribbiani (Matt LeBlanc) is its most dedicated fan.

BREAKING BAD (S03-E02)

BY VINCE GILLIGAN, 2008–2013

Flying pizza—The famous scene where Walter White (Bryan Cranston), in a rage, hurls his pizza onto the roof of his garage . . . In tribute, the most die-hard fans made a pilgrimage to the shooting location to imitate the gesture, much to the chagrin of the garage's real owner.

SKIP TO
POP PASTA, P. 221;
SPAGHETTI VIP, P. 372;
PIZZE NAPOLETANE, P. 54.

SEASON

TUTTO L'ANNO (YEAR-ROUND)

CATEGORY

DOLCE (DESSERT)

LEVEL

DIFFICOLTÀ MEDIA (MEDIUM DIFFICULTY)

BABÀ

RUM-SOAKED CAKES

Ricetta Iconica Ricetta

CAMPANIA

This sweet treat turns the heads of Neapolitans, who stake claim to its origins . . . but wrongly so?

ALBA PEZONE

ITALIANO VERO?

→ Let's be clear: baba didn't originate at the foot of Mount Vesuvius but instead much farther north, in the Franco-German Grand Est of the eighteenth century, thanks to the genius of Stanisław Leszczynski, a dethroned Polish king who was also a gourmand.

→ In the eighteenth century, Nicolas Stohrer, descendant of Stanisław's Polish pastry chef and himself a pastry chef to Stanisław's daughter Maria Leszczynska (wife of King Louis XV), popularized a rum-soaked version, the *baba au rhum,* in his pastry shop on rue Montorgueil in Paris.

→ Its name comes from a traditional Polish recipe (*baba* or *babka*) or from the king's favorite story collection, *The Thousand and One Nights.*

FROM PARIS TO NAPLES . . .

These two capitals compete, scrutinize each other, and copy each other. It was Maria Carolina, queen of the Two Sicilies and sister of Marie Antoinette, who partly introduced French cuisine and fashion to Naples. Naples adopted baba to the point that its French origins were forgotten: in 1836, in an Italian cooking manual written by Chef Angeletti for Marie-Louise of Austria, baba appeared as a dessert . . . in the Neapolitan tradition.

Baba in all its forms

ITS DIAMETER MAY VARY FROM 1⅛ TO 15¾ INCHES (3 TO 40 CM), in the shape of a mushroom or a charlotte.

IT'S SOLD IN A JAR (in rum syrup or other alcohol),

DRY (to soak at home), or

FRESH (topped with whipped cream, cream, and fruit).

SKIP TO
NEAPOLITAN PASTRIES, P. 123.

WHY DO THE NEAPOLITANS LOVE IT SO MUCH?

Because its attributes are a metaphor for their city:

GOLDEN AND POROUS, like tuff, the soft volcanic rock on which Naples is built.

FLEXIBLE, like the tolerance the city practices.

POPULAR AND ARISTOCRATIC, like its inhabitants.

OPULENT, like its churches and palaces.

EXCESSIVE and almost volcanic, like Vesuvius.

Sulla Punta Della Lingua (On the Tip of the Tongue)

If a Neapolitan says to you ***"Si proprio 'nu babbà"*** ("You're a real baba"), he is giving you a most wonderful compliment!

THE RECIPE

This is my *babà napoletano* recipe, a real treat!

MAKES 6 BABÀ

For the dough

- 1 teaspoon (8 g) fresh baker's yeast
- ⅓ cup (90 g) low-fat milk, lukewarm
- 1¾ cups (225 g) high-protein flour
- 1 tablespoon plus 1¾ teaspoons (20 g) sugar
- 1 teaspoon (6 g) salt
- 2 large (100 g) eggs
- 3 tablespoons (45 g) unsalted butter, cut into pieces, at room temperature, plus more for the molds

For the syrup

- 4 cups (1 L) water
- 1¼ cups (300 mL) dark rum (or other fruit-based alcohol, such as limoncello or Cointreau), plus more for drizzling
- 2 cups (400 g) sugar
- 1 vanilla bean
- 1 stalk lemongrass
- ½ lemon, sliced
- 1 lime, sliced

Equipment

- Stand mixer fitted with a dough hook or handheld mixer
- Baba or muffin molds

To make the dough, crumble the yeast into the milk in the bowl of the stand mixer fitted with the dough hook or in a mixing bowl. Add the flour, sugar, and salt and knead on speed 1. Incorporate the eggs, one at a time, then knead on medium speed for 5 minutes, until the dough comes away from the side of the bowl. Add the butter and knead again for 5 minutes, until the dough again comes away from the side of the bowl; it should be smooth and very elastic.

Butter the baba molds and line a baking sheet with parchment paper. Scrape the dough into a piping bag fitted with a plain piping tip and fill the prepared molds two-thirds full. Cut the dough with scissors to release it from the piping bag. Place the molds on the baking sheet. Let rise at room temperature for 2½ hours; the dough should double in volume.

Preheat the oven to 325°F (170°C). Bake the babas for 30 minutes, then unmold them onto the baking sheet. Place them back in the oven for 30 minutes at 325°F (160°C) to dry them. Let cool to room temperature.

To make the syrup, combine the syrup ingredients in a saucepan. Bring just to a boil (the syrup must be very hot but not kept at a boil), then cover, remove from the heat, and let stand for 5 minutes.

Immerse the babas in the syrup headfirst; when they begin to swell, turn them over using a skimmer or a slotted spoon. Soak them well in the syrup; they should double in volume. Place them on a rack set over a baking sheet to drain.

Serve the baba in cups, drizzled with the syrup and rum.

CHOCOLATE SPREADS

Whether enjoyed slathered on bread, cakes, or cookies or just eaten with a spoon, these twelve artisanal chocolate spreads are sure to satisfy.

ALESSANDRA PIERINI

① NOCCIOLATA
18.5%

② GIACOMETTA
32%

③ CREMA NOVI
45%

④ CREMA GIANDUJA
45%

⑤ CREMA ALLA NOCCIOLA TEO & BIA
47%

⑥ CREMA SPALMABILE ALLA NOCCIOLA
50%

⑦ CREMA SPALMABILE DI CACAO E NOCCIOLE
50%

⑧ CREMA GIANDUJA
52%

⑨ CREMA ALLA NOCCIOLA LIGURE
52%

⑩ CREMA DI NOCCIOLA
60%

⑪ CREMA DI LANGA
65%

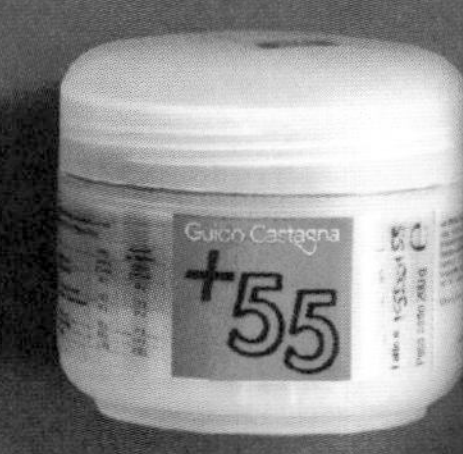

⑫ +55 CREMA DI NOCCIOLE
68%

① NOCCIOLATA

Creamy texture, quite dark in color. Beautiful chocolate and vanilla notes; the hazelnut is subtle.

PRODUCER—Rigoni di Asiago (Asiago, Veneto). A family business founded in 1923, it originally produced honey but expanded in the 1970s to add jams to its product line. Certified organic since 1992, it secured its success in 2008 with this spread.

INGREDIENTS—hazelnut paste (18.5 percent), cane sugar, sunflower oil, skim milk powder, low-fat cocoa powder (6.5 percent), cocoa butter, soy lecithin, vanilla extract.

Risk of addiction:

② GIACOMETTA

A creamy and smooth texture with a pleasant cocoa flavor, slightly astringent, rather dark in color.

PRODUCER—Giraudi (Castellazzo Bormida, Piedmont). Giovanni Battista Giraudi founded this family of chocolate makers, ongoing since 1907 and today headed by Giacomo Boldi, his nephew.

INGREDIENTS—roasted Piedmont hazelnuts IGP (32 percent), brown sugar, sunflower oil, low-fat cocoa powder (40 percent), whole milk powder, soy lecithin.

Risk of addiction:

③ CREMA NOVI

Creamy, oozy; slightly grainy and rustic texture. Nice praline sensation; hazelnut is more present than cocoa.

PRODUCER—Elah-Dufour Novi (Novi Ligure, Piedmont). Novi is a former cooperative of confectioners and chocolate makers founded in 1903, and today belongs to the Genoese industrial group Elah-Dufour.

INGREDIENTS—hazelnuts (45 percent), sugar, low-fat cocoa powder (9 percent), skim milk powder, cocoa butter, soy lecithin, pure vanilla extract.

Risk of addiction:

④ CREMA GIANDUJA

Much more fluid than average in texture; light, delicate. Vegetal flavor of fresh hazelnut. A delight!

PRODUCER—Guido Gobino (Turin, Piedmont). The father, Giuseppe, started working for the company in 1964 and became the owner in 1980. His son Guido succeeded him in 1985. He is considered one of the best chocolate makers in Italy.

INGREDIENTS—Piedmont hazelnuts IGP (45 percent), sugar, bitter cocoa powder, skim milk powder, soy lecithin, vanilla bean.

Risk of addiction:

SKIP TO
THE HAZELNUT, P. 144;
GIANDUJA, P. 180.

⑤ CREMA ALLA NOCCIOLA TEO & BIA

Very sweet profile, with a texture close to Nutella. Very tasty, even if it's relatively short on the palate.

PRODUCER—MB Alimentari (Alessandria, Piedmont). Pastry chocolatiers since 2004, Monica Baldo and Giuseppe Magné focus on organic, gluten-free, and lactose-free products.

INGREDIENTS—Piedmont hazelnuts (47 percent), cane sugar, low-fat cocoa powder.

Risk of addiction:

⑥ CREMA SPALMABILE ALLA NOCCIOLA

Surprising texture, crunchy at times. There is an emphasis on the vegetal flavors of hazelnut.

PRODUCER—D. Barbero (Asti, Piedmont). The production house of this chocolatier and *nougatier*, founded in 1863, is known for its traditional hazelnut-based chocolates.

INGREDIENTS—Piedmont hazelnut paste (50 percent), cane sugar, low-fat Ecuadorian cocoa powder (12 percent), cocoa butter, soy lecithin.

Risk of addiction:

⑦ CREMA SPALMABILE DI CACAO E NOCCIOLE

A beautiful color and consistency. Dominant toasted hazelnut flavor. A tad too sweet.

PRODUCER—Marco Colzani (Carate Brianza, Lombardy). A demanding agronomist and oenologist, he created his company in 2016. He mainly produces jams, fruit juices, and chocolates.

INGREDIENTS—Piedmont hazelnuts IGP (50 percent), cane sugar, cocoa powder.

Risk of addiction:

⑧ CREMA GIANDUJA

A creamy appearance and texture. The first bite meets a certain acidity from cocoa, followed by gourmand flavors.

PRODUCER—Maison della Nocciola (Settimo Vittone, Piedmont). The Caffa family has specialized for 150 years in the transformation of hazelnuts, especially in cookies, dragées, and chocolates.

INGREDIENTS—Piedmont hazelnuts IGP 52 percent, cane sugar, low-fat cocoa 8 percent, skim milk powder, cocoa butter, soy lecithin, vanilla.

Risk of addiction:

⑨ CREMA ALLA NOCCIOLA LIGURE

Liquid texture, satisfying nutty flavor and aroma. For enthusiast palates.

PRODUCER—Il Parodi (Campomorone, Liguria). Since 2016, Andrea Parodi has been involved in increasing production of the 4,500-year-old Misto-Chiavari hazelnut, which is very important for local biodiversity.

INGREDIENTS—toasted Ligurian hazelnuts (Slow Food Ark of Taste, 52 percent), cane sugar, low-fat cocoa powder, cocoa butter, soy lecithin.

Risk of addiction:

⑩ CREMA DI NOCCIOLA

Comforting, old-style, voluptuous, and dangerously addictive!

PRODUCER—Papa dei Boschi (Lequio Berria, Piedmont). José Noé is at the helm of a 120-acre (50 ha) hazelnut farm in the Langhe region dating back three generations. He sells hazelnuts and derivative products.

INGREDIENTS—Piedmont hazelnuts IGP (60 percent), sugar, skim milk powder, low-fat cocoa powder, Bourbon vanilla.

Risk of addiction:

⑪ CREMA DI LANGA

Very liquid texture; rather bitter taste likely due to the absence of sugar (sucrose). Nice effort.

PRODUCER—Altalanga Azienda Agricola (Alba, Piedmont). Gian Franco Cavallotto, who founded his company in 2013, organically grows the famous hazelnut *tonda e gentile* on a preserved site.

INGREDIENTS—Piedmont hazelnuts IGP (65 percent), low-fat cocoa powder, chicory root, agave syrup powder (9 percent), maltodextrin, sunflower lecithin, pure vanilla extract.

Risk of addiction:

⑫ +55 CREMA DI NOCCIOLE

It has the appearance of a butter balm and the highest percentage of hazelnuts represented, yet remains subtle and balanced.

PRODUCER—Guido Castagna (Giaveno, Piedmont). Master chocolatier since 2001, he chooses the best raw materials for his products, which have won several awards in international competitions.

INGREDIENTS—Piedmont hazelnuts IGP (68 percent), cane sugar, cocoa butter.

Risk of addiction:

AND NUTELLA AMONG ALL THIS?

This is the best-known chocolate hazelnut spread of all! Entire shelves of Nutella products populate shops, and its sugar level is so high (2 ounces/57 g per 3½ ounces/100 g), it can trigger severe addictions . . . The brand, created in 1964 by the Piedmontese chocolate giant Ferrero, has established itself throughout the world thanks to storytelling that is as powerful as its hazelnut percentage is low (13 percent, originating mainly from Turkey).

Nutella has turned into gold for the Ferrero family: At the time of this book's publication, Giovanni Ferrero (son of Michele, inventor of Nutella) is the richest man in Italy.

PROSECCO & CO.

Since 2016, Italy has been the world's leading producer of sparkling wines. But take note: it's not all Prosecco!

SAMUEL COGLIATI

PROSECCO

A sparkling Italian white wine made from the Glera grape varietal, Prosecco is produced in five provinces of Veneto (Belluno, Venice, Padua, Treviso, and Vicenza) and, more recently, four provinces of Friuli-Venezia Giulia (Gorizia, Pordenone, Trieste, and Udine).

APPELLATIONS: a vast Prosecco DOP, three DOCG wines (Conegliano-Valdobbiadene, Asolo, Colli di Conegliano), as well as other lesser known DOPs and IGTs.

DOP → *Denominazione di origine protetta*

DOCG → *Denominazione di origine controllata e garantita*

IGT → *Indicazione geografica tipica*

METHOD: In addition to the sparkling wines produced in closed vats, which are easy to drink yet not strong, some winemakers preserve the true tradition of producing natural sparkling wines. Always fresh and thirst-quenching, the best Prosecco has a smooth softness.

TO TASTE: Casa Coste Piane, Marchiori, Silvano Follador.

A LITTLE HISTORY

→ Viticulture has been practiced in Conegliano, north of Treviso (Veneto), since Roman times.

→ In 1754, Arcadian poet Aureliano Acanti made the first specific mention of Prosecco in *Il roccolo*, an ode to the wines of the Vicenza region.

→ In the eighteenth and nineteenth centuries, viticulture developed first under the leadership of the Republic of Venice, then Austria.

→ 1969: birth of the DOC Prosecco dei Colli di Conegliano Valdobbiadene.

→ Since this time, the vibrancy of the Veneto region, commercial promotion, and the more advantageous price of production using closed vats (as compared to the Champagne method) have contributed to the success of Prosecco.

THE TRADITIONAL METHOD: THE GREAT CLASSICS

In Italy, the making of Prosecco is modeled on the Champagne method and the wine is similar in terms of taste. Some territories have stepped to the forefront over time. Enjoyed young, the wines are lively, fresh and delicate, exuberant, and dominated by acidity; after a few years of aging, they acquire more complexity (spices, brioche and buttery notes, etc.).

DOCG FRANCIACORTA, LOMBARDY

Grapes: Chardonnay mostly; Pinot Noir, Pinot Blanc, and, very rarely, Erbamat. **To taste:** Faccoli, Clarabella, or Villa Crespia.

DOC TRENTO, TRENTINO

Grapes: Very predominantly Chardonnay; Pinot Noir, Pinot Blanc, or Pinot Meunier. **To taste:** Ferrari (see box opposite), Bellaveder, or Castel Noarna.

OLTREPÒ PAVESE, LOMBARDY

Grapes: Very predominantly Pinot Noir, sometimes supplemented with Pinot Blanc or Pinot Gris. **To taste:** Castello di Stefanago and Casa Zuffada.

ALTO ADIGE, SOUTH-TYROL

Grapes: Very predominantly Chardonnay, sometimes with Pinot Noir or Pinot Blanc. **To taste:** Haderburg, Arunda Vivaldi.

THE ASTOUNDING SUCCESS OF PROSECCO

66 PERCENT OF ITALIAN SPARKLING WINE PRODUCTION

486 MILLION BOTTLES PER YEAR

MORE THAN 11,000 WINEGROWERS

The Renewal of an Ancestral Method

Wines made by the *méthode ancestrale* are also called pét-nat wines (short for *pétillant naturel*, "natural sparkling"). Although they are the trendiest bubbles, this method is ancient: it was used to make Champagne before the eponymous "Champagne method" (*méthode traditionelle*) came into being. In pét-nat wines, fermentation takes place spontaneously in the bottle, without any added sugar or yeasts (which are used to trigger secondary fermentation in the traditional method). Often, these wines are not disgorged—that is to say, the sediment within the bottle is not removed as it is in other sparkling wines; instead, it remains in the bottle, giving the wine a slight cloudiness.

In Italy, you can find Prosecco *col fondo* (on its lees), which is refreshing and delicious; some artisanal Lambruschi, a little rustic but expressive; Garganega whites in Veneto; and even some Trebbiani in Emilia-Romagna.

An Italian Dom Pérignon?

It's not a sports car, but the comparison is hardly off base. Founded in 1902, the Ferrari house (Trento) doesn't produce just in large volume. Mauro Lunelli had the intuition to vinify the Chardonnay from the Pianizza vintage separately, making it a prestigious cuvée. With the 1972 vintage, the "Giulio Ferrari—Riserva del Fondatore" cuvée was born. It became a sort of Italian Dom Pérignon cuvée, but with more finesse, thanks to the expertise of cellar master Ruben Larentis. The 2008 vintage embodies the classicism of a round and brilliant blanc de blancs. The 2008 rosé (70 percent Pinot Noir) is sumptuous, mature, and bold. As for the extremely rare "Collezione" version, recently disgorged, it is the pinnacle of Ferrari elegance.

OFF THE BEATEN TRACK

Away from established appellations, here are some exceptional bottles to taste:

MALVIRÀ CUVÉE "RIVE GAUCHE" EXTRA-BRUT ROSÉ, PIEDMONT: a *metodo Charmat* (tank method) rosé made from Nebbiolo; balanced and delicious.

LA DISTESA "GIULIETTA" CUVÉE, MARCHE: a Verdicchio with complexity and power, thanks to a very long aging *sur latte* (with the bottles stacked on their sides).

CUVÉE "ARIONE" MUNI—DANIELE PORTINARI, VENETO: a naturally dry Durella, brilliant with tension, with a fine and strong texture.

BRUT NATURE "DUE DEI," SICILY: a rare example of a traditional method wine using the Grillo wine grape on Marsala *terroir*; sophisticated.

SKIP TO
WHEN RED WINE SPARKLES, P. 313;
GATHERING GRAPES, P. 158.

SEASON

TUTTO L'ANNO (YEAR-ROUND)

CATEGORY

PRIMO PIATTO (FIRST COURSE)

LEVEL

FACILE (EASY)

PENNE ALL'ARRABBIATA

SPICY TOMATO AND CHILI PASTA

RICETTA Iconica RICETTA

LAZIO

This spicy Roman pasta is one of the best known in the world, but it is also the subject of heated debate.

JORDAN MOILIM

AN ENRANGED SAUCE

Arrabbiata, the past participle of the verb *arrabbiare*, means "enraged" or "furious." This is because of the chile pepper that perks up this sauce along with its devilishly red color. *All'arrabbiata* means a tomato and chile–based preparation accompanying meats: *bistecca di manzo all'arrabbiata* is a spicy variation of the dish *pizzaiola*.

WAS IT THE INVENTION OF AN INNKEEPER?

Legend has it that *penne all'arrabbiata* originated in the early twentieth century in a Roman trattoria, the idea of an innkeeper who wanted to offer his customers an alternative to *amatriciana*. He kept the tomato but added garlic, eliminated the *guanciale* (cured pork cheek), replaced the bucatini with penne, and, most important, increased the amount of *peperoncino*.

A STAR OF CINEMA

Penne all'arrabbiata appears in Federico Fellini's *Roma* (1972), alongside other Roman specialties such as *rigatoni con la pajata*, *carbonara*, and *lumache con mentuccia e peperoncino* (snails with mint and chile pepper). They are also on the menu of the film *La Grande Bouffe* (*Blow-Out*) by Marco Ferreri (1973).

THE ARRABBIATA DEBATES

SHORT OR LONG PASTA?

This sauce mainly accompanies penne pasta, but it is sometimes found coating bucatini.

FRESH OR DRIED CHILE?

Fresh chile brings more fruity flavors to the sauce, while ground chile lends smokier notes. In Italy, ground chile is often used. All chile varietals are acceptable, although the one from Calabria is the most popular.

PARSLEY OR BASIL?

This debate is heated: parsley often wins, but for purists, neither is added.

PECORINO OR PARMESAN?

If you could only choose one, it would be Pecorino Romano, for its saltiness and its connection to Rome. However, purists prefer to go without cheese and adding a drizzle of olive oil right at the end to season it.

THE RECIPE

Here's a delicious but rigorous version of this fiery pasta. There is no pecorino or fresh herbs to temper its fury.

SERVES 2

Olive oil

2 teaspoons (6 g) cayenne pepper or red chile flakes, to taste

1 clove garlic, peeled

6⅓ ounces (180 g) Pomodorini tomatoes (or tomato *passata*)

Salt and freshly ground black pepper

7 ounces (200 g) penne pasta

In a high-sided pan, heat 2 tablespoons (30 mL) olive oil over medium heat.

Add the cayenne and let it gently fry for several minutes to impart flavor into the oil. Meanwhile, finely chop the garlic. Add it to the pan.

Before the garlic browns, add the tomatoes. Gently crush them with a spoon to release their juices.

Season with salt and black pepper. Add more cayenne if you want a very hot sauce. Cover and let the sauce reduce and thicken slightly over low heat for several minutes.

While the sauce simmers, cook the pasta in salted boiling water. A good minute before the time indicated on the package, set aside a ladleful of the cooking water and drain the penne. (Do not overcook the penne, as it will continue to cook in the sauce.)

Add the pasta directly to the sauce. Increase the heat. If the sauce has reduced a little too much, add a bit of the reserved pasta cooking water to thin it slightly.

Stir or flip the pasta in the pan until fully coated with sauce. Add a drizzle of olive oil and serve immediately.

Jamie Oliver's tip

This British star chef is not afraid of anything . . . not even of infuriating Roman chefs!

Not content to add just one twist to this recipe by including a few anchovies, Jamie also recommends adding a hint of vodka to support the power of the chile and to lend complexity to the sauce.

SKIP TO

TOMATOES, P. 28; PIZZAIOLA, P. 268; CHILE PEPPERS, P. 359.

AMARENA

Gently tart, this sour cherry is a treasure trove of ancient flavors.

GIANNA MAZZEI

WHAT AM I?

SCIENTIFIC NAME: *Prunus cerasus.*

FAMILY: Rosaceae.

SEASON: summer (June and July).

TASTE: sweet, slightly acidic.

ORIGIN: legend has it that the Roman general Lucullus (first century BCE), famous for his sumptuous and refined banquets, brought the first sour cherry trees from Turkey to Italy.

FAMOUS RELATIONS

Prunus avium: wild cherry, or bird cherry. Its domesticated form produces sweet cherries.

Prunus cerasus var.*marasca*: so-called acidic or sour cherries, used in cocktails.

Prunus cerasus var. *austera*: called Visciola and known under the name morello cherry, it is the champion of cherries, and the variety dropped into the glass of Champagne preferred by James Bond.

In cooking

Plain, with a little sugar, and lightly crushed on a slice of bread: it's an old-style snack.

IN SYRUP

—with blue cheeses or ricotta.
—to garnish ice creams, creams, yogurt, or panna cotta.
—to fill tarts, cakes, and cookies: such as *crostata di ricotta e visciole ebraico-romanesca*, Neapolitan amarena cookies, and *pasticciotti* of Apulia.
—on *zeppole di San Giuseppe* (a fried dough topped with pastry cream).

CANDIED

—in pastry in *zelten trentino* (a type of honey loaf with candied fruit).
—with almond paste and in some cannoli.

MACERATED: CHERRY WINES

The pits are used to produce maraschino, a colorless liqueur.

DRIED IN PRESERVES

Wild boar sauce from Maremma Laziale (Lazio).

RECIPE

AMARENA IN SYRUP AL SOLE (MADE IN THE SUN)

This ancient recipe, which uses the heat from the sun to create a syrup from sugar and cherry juices, comes from Annamaria Troiano, a great cook from Pescara and guardian of the Abruzzo tradition.

MAKES 4 CUPS (1 L) SYRUP

2¼ pounds (1 kg) amarena sour cherries

2¼ pounds (1 kg) sugar

- Sterilize glass jars and their lids. Remove the stems and wash the cherries. Dry them completely by spacing them out on a clean cloth.
- Pit the cherries and place them in a bowl, retaining any juices. Add the sugar and stir well to combine. Divide the cherries among the jars, close the lids, and place them outside, exposed to the sun, from morning to dusk. For the next 30 to 40 days, leave the jars outside in the sunlight during the day; the heat will turn the sugars into syrup and preserve the cherries. Remember to gently shake the jars to obtain a homogeneous syrup.
- After 30 to 40 days, check for mold. If mold is present, throw away all the cherries and syrup and start again. Store in the refrigerator or in a cool, dark place.

If the sun is not out . . .

- Gently combine the pitted cherries and their juices with 3¾ cups (750 g) sugar. Cover the bowl with a cloth and let macerate at room temperature for 24 hours.
- Strain the liquid into a saucepan. Bring to a boil and cook the syrup for 15 minutes. Skim off any impurities, if present. Add the cherries and boil for 8 to 10 minutes more. Using a slotted spoon, transfer the cherries to the jars and set aside; continue to boil the syrup for 15 to 20 minutes more. Let cool.
- Cover the cherries with the syrup. Tap the base of each jar on the counter to remove any air bubbles. If necessary, add more syrup. Close the jars tightly.
- Wrap the jars in kitchen towels, place in a saucepan, and cover with cold water. Bring to a boil, then simmer for 30 minutes over low heat. Let the jars cool in the pan.
- Store in a cool, dark place.

FABBRI 1905

The brand known today by this name was founded under the name "Premiata Distilleria Liquori G. Fabbri" by Gennaro Fabbri. The syrup *Marena con frutto*, inspired by a recipe by his wife Rachele Buriani, was created in the 1920s.

The special attribute of this amarena cherry is that it is semicandied in syrup and therefore maintains some of its firmness along with its sweetness.

To market this specialty product, the Fabbri family, passionate about art, entrusted the creation of the special jar to famous Faenza ceramist Riccardo Gatti. On the occasion of its one-hundreth anniversary, the company created the Fabbri Prize for Art, a triennial event that places Amarena Fabbri at the center of artistic exhibitions.

The best varietals of amarena

TESIO DI SERLE
Lombardy

BRUSCHE DI MODENA, IGP/ PDO FOR THE PRESERVES
Emilia-Romagna

METEOR
Throughout Italy

MONTMORENCY
Throughout Italy

DI CASTELVETRO
Emilia-Romagna

DI CANTIANO
Marche, considered the best amarena in Italy

DI PESCARA
Abruzzo

DI TROFARELLO
Piedmont

DI VERONA
Veneto

DI VIGNOLA
Emilia-Romagna

SKIP TO
CROSTATA ALLA CONFETTURA, P. 66; LIQUORI, P. 366.

Enrico Crippa

PROFILE

An avant-garde chef but one who isn't oblivious to tradition, this Lombard living in Piedmont is causing a stir in the land of the white truffle!

FRANÇOIS-RÉGIS GAUDRY

KEY DATES

1971
Born in Carate Brianza (Lombardy).

1987
Apprentices in Gualtiero Marchesi's restaurant in Milan.

1996
Creation of the Gualtiero Marchesi restaurant in Kobe, then chef of the Rihga Royal Hotel in Osaka until 1999.

2005
Opening of Piazza Duomo in Alba with the Ceretto family of winegrowers.

2012
Receives three Michelin stars.

TRAINING IN FRANCE

Christian Willer at the Palme d'Or in Cannes, Ghislaine Arabian at Ledoyen in Paris, Antoine Westermann at Le Buerehiesel in Strasbourg, Michel Bras in Laguiole . . . Enrico Crippa has built on his experiences in great French gastronomic institutions and his culinary connection with Italy's neighboring country.

ORTO

A few kilometers from Alba, in Monsordo Bernardina on the Ceretto family estate, Enrico Crippa tends to the restaurant's vegetable garden following the principles of biodynamics: 43,000 square feet (4,000 sq m) of land and 4,300 square feet (400 sq m) of greenhouses. Every day, he arrives to pick vegetables, herbs, and flowers.

SIGNATURE DISHES

Piazza Duomo

Through all its windows, the dining room of Piazza Duomo overlooks Piazza del Duomo. But there is also quite a view on the inside. The walls and vaulted ceilings are adorned with a fresco signed by artist Francesco Clemente: on a pink background, a giant grapevine leaf branches out into a succession of magical images inspired by the landscapes of the Langhe.

CARPACCIO DI RICCI DI MARE

A pecorino sauce caressing a sea urchin carpaccio, a nod to a traditional accord practiced in Apulia.

INSALATA 21... 31... 41... 51...

This salad is a Piedmontese cousin of the famous vegetable metaphor of the dish *gargouillou* from Aubrac created by Crippa's mentor, French chef Michel Bras. Insalata 21... 31... 41... 51... is a lush arrangement of leaves, shoots, and petals. The numbers 21, 31, 41, or 51 stand for the varieties of lettuces and flowers included, according to the seasons, either wild or grown in the restaurant's vegetable garden, and to be enjoyed with the help of tweezers. The final gesture is to sip the dressing at the bottom, a delicious dashi broth (kombu seaweed and dried bonito) accented with a touch of orange, which partially seasons the last few leaves.

SHOT CAMPARI TRAMEZZINO

A Campari-tomato-orange shot to electrify the captivating *tramezzino*, the tiny sandwiches invented in Turin at the beginning of the twentieth century, seen here made from a soft bread made with chickpea flour filled with a *crème de fromage*, shavings of Parmesan, anchovies, egg yolk, and crisp chicory.

RISOTTO CACAO

A pinch of cocoa powder elevates this excellent Piedmontese risotto.

CREMA DI PATATE

A hint of lapsang souchong tea is added to echo the floral and earthy notes of the white truffles flavoring creamed potatoes.

SKIP TO
CARPACCIO, P. 198;
GUALTIERO MARCHESI, P. 163.

SEASON

TUTTO L'ANNO (YEAR-ROUND)

CATEGORY

ANTIPASTO, PRIMO PIATTO (APPETIZER/ FIRST COURSE)

LEVEL

FACILE (EASY)

FARINATA

CHICKPEA FLATBREAD

It's the queen of Ligurian street foods—a flatbread made of chickpea flour, which can be eaten at any time of the day. It's even easy enough to make at home!

ALESSANDRA PIERINI

THE RECIPE

SERVES 4 (MAKES 2 *FARINATA*)

2¾ cups (250 g) chickpea flour

4 cups (1 L) water

1⅔ teaspoons (10 g) salt

½ cup (100 g) olive oil, plus more for greasing the pan

Freshly ground black pepper

Equipment

One 12-inch (30 cm) round nonstick pie pan

In a large bowl, combine the flour and water, ensuring there are no lumps. Whisk in the salt. Let stand for 3 to 4 hours at room temperature .

Skim off any foam that has formed on the surface, then add the olive oil. Stir gently to combine. Preheat the oven to the maximum temperature, ideally 475°F (250°C) or higher. Grease the bottom and sides of the pan with a little olive oil. Place the empty pan in the oven to heat it for about 2 minutes (this will create a crust on the flatbread). If your pan looks dry, grease the bottom of the dish again. It should be heavily greased. Pour in the batter to a depth of about ¼ inch (5 mm). Bake for about 15 minutes, or until the crust is golden brown. Enjoy hot, seasoned with pepper.

A DISTINCT CHARACTER

Farinata is a very thin unleavened flatbread (or crêpe) made from chickpea flour, olive oil, water, and salt, cooked in a very hot oven, preferably a wood-burning oven; and served piping hot. In Savona, the preference is for a version made from wheat flour.

It can be seasoned with rosemary, onions, black pepper, sausage, fresh cheese, artichokes, and, especially, *bianchetti* (anchovy and sardine whitebait). It should be golden and crisp. Its thickness should not exceed ⅛ to ¼ inch (4 to 5 mm), and it should have the flavor of olive oil but not be too greasy. The surface should be cracked and a little rough, but without large spots or burns. It's a street food par excellence, to be eaten straight from the oven, rolled up in greased paper (*la peppià*), and seasoned with black pepper.

COUSINS, MORE AND LESS DISTANT

THE FIRST COUSINS

CALDA-CALDA
in Massa-Carrara

BELLA CALDA
in Piedmont

CECINA
in Pisa

TORTA DI CECI
in Livorno

FAINÈ
in Sardinia

SCIOCCA
on the west coast of Genoa
(with yeast added)

SOCCA
in neighboring Nice, France

CADE
in Toulon

SECOND COUSINS . . . OR OTHER

KARANTIKA OR CALENTICA
in Algeria

CALENTITA
in Uruguay and Argentina

Between history . . .

Farinata has existed in Genoa since the fifteenth century. Then called *scriblita* (*tarte* or *focaccia* in Latin, then as part of the Genoese dialect) and often eaten between two slices of bread, it was for years considered a food for lean Fridays and was also often prepared by dockworkers. It was prepared in *sciamadde* (from *fiammata*, meaning flambéed), small stalls in which a hot fire was always burning, a small number of which still exist today. Traveling female vendors roamed the streets with large round cast-iron dishes (*testo*) on their heads, offering farinata, shouting: **GÔ A FAÏNÂ CÄDA** ("I have hot farinata").

. . . and legend

Farinata is said to have been invented in 233 BCE during a battle between the Romans and the Ligurians in present-day Tuscany. The Ligurians got the idea from their Roman adversaries to use their metal shields as a dish in which to cook a mixture of water and flour over fire. Another version of the story claims that this dish was created in 1284 during a battle between the Genoese and Pisans at Meloria. The Genoese ships survived a storm, but the "Pisa gold" (chickpea flour) stored in the holds accidentally mixed with seawater that came aboard. The result, once dried in the sun, was delicious farinata.

SKIP TO
CHICKPEA, THE KING OF THE POOR, P. 293; LEGUMES, P. 150.

SEASON

TUTTO L'ANNO (YEAR-ROUND)

CATEGORY

STREET FOOD, SECONDO PIATTO (MAIN COURSE)

LEVEL

DIFFICOLTÀ MEDIA (MEDIUM DIFFICULTY)

PORCHETTA

An emblem of village festivals, this stuffed and roasted pork dish can be eaten sliced, hot, cold, alone, or accompanied with other foods . . . It's a true Italian meaty classic!

MINA SOUNDIRAM

THE ORIGINS

Several regions contend for the origins of this boned, seasoned, and roasted whole pig.

ARICCIA—Lazio
In pre-Roman times (fifth century BCE), priests from this city prepared and offered sacrificial pigs at the temple of Jupiter on Mount Cavo.

RIETI—upper Lazio
This recipe has been made here since the Etruscan period (sixth century BCE). An inhabitant of Poggio Bustone is said to have come up with the idea when he witnessed a fire of aromatic plants in which pigs perished.

CAMPLI—Abruzzo
This dish has been enjoyed here since the Middle Ages, served on the tables of princes but also in markets. A fair has been held each year in its honor since 1964.

NORCIA—Umbria
This city has been known since Roman times for pig breeding (hence the term *norcino*, "he who works with pork meat") and for the practice of stuffing pork.

→ The creation of porchetta is also claimed by Emilia-Romagna, and during the twentieth century it spread to more northern regions such as Veneto, where it is now popular.

GLOSSARY

PORCHETTARO
A person who makes porchetta by profession. How should you use this word in a sentence? "He traded in his suit for a *porchettaro*'s apron," for example.

PORCHETTATO
"Prepared in the style of porchetta." A cooking method inspired by porchetta, applied to other meats such as lamb and rabbit but also lake fish such as carp or pike.

The different schools

There are two great traditions for seasoning porchetta, depending on the region:

Rosmarino (rosemary) or ***ramerino*** in Tuscan, in southern Tuscany, lower Lazio, and Abruzzo.

Finocchio selvatico or ***finocchietto*** (wild fennel) in upper Lazio, Umbria, Marche, and Romagna.

REGIONAL SPECIALTIES

PORCHETTA DI ARICCIA—IGP (*Lazio*)
The most well-known, with a PGI since 2011. Scented with rosemary, garlic, and black pepper, it is recognizable by its crisp and delicious crust! Made only from female pigs.

PORCHETTA DI SELCI—PAT (*Lazio*)
This small town won the Traditional Italian Regional Food Product (*prodotto agroalimentare tradizionale*, or PAT) designation in 2019, which protects its rosemary, garlic, and black pepper porchetta.

PORCHETTA DI POGGIO BUSTONE—PAT (*Lazio*)
Since 1930, a food fair has been held in the village center on the first Sunday in October. Cooked in a wood-burning oven, the porchetta is seasoned with black pepper, rosemary, fresh garlic, and sometimes chile.

PORCHETTA DI VITERBO—PAT (*Lazio*)
Completely empty except for liver, cylindrical in shape, flavored with black pepper, garlic, and wild fennel.

PORCEDDU (*Sardinia*)
This suckling pig, which is marinated and seasoned with garlic and herbs (rosemary, wild fennel, and especially myrtle) then roasted over a wood fire, is a cousin of porchetta, except that it is not stuffed or rolled but instead cooked whole and placed vertically on a spit.

HOW TO

THE MEAT
Use a well-sourced meat with good provenance, preferably from a young female pig (hence the feminine form of the word *porchetta*), whose meat is said to be leaner and tastier.

THE PREPARATION
Boning, blanching, salting, seasoning—the offal can also be stuffed—rolling, binding, and cooking: a process passed down within families and in the butcher shops of *porchettari* (see Glossary, left).

THE COOKING
On a spit in a wood-burning oven for three to eight hours, depending on the size of the animal. (Steel ovens are more common today.)

THE SERVING
Often served in slices, porchetta is also available in sandwiches! Associated with street vendors, it is served everywhere during fairs, markets, or harvest meals. It is also eaten in the *fraschette* (casual restaurants around Rome) of the Castelli Romani (Roman Castles).

44.93

The length, in meters (147.4 feet), of the longest porchetta in the world, listed in the Guinness World Records—a spectacle created in Monte San Savino (Tuscany) in 2010 by Aldo Iacomoni, Walter Iacomoni, Giuliano Di Goro, and Gino Mencuccini.

THE RECIPE

"The porchetta was brought to my childhood village in Calabria by a successful family from Tuscany. I make it according to the Tuscan school of thought, but with Roman influences, too, because my aunt lived in Ariccia! And the wild fennel reminds me of Calabria."
—Alessandro Candido, chef at restaurant Candide (Paris 10th)

SERVES 6 TO 8

4½ pounds (2 kg) pork belly
16 cloves pink garlic, peeled
Leaves from 5 sprigs rosemary
¼ ounce (8 g) wild fennel flowers
3 tablespoons (40 g) sea salt
1 tablespoon (8 g) freshly ground black pepper (preferably from Madagascar)
Olive oil

Equipment
Kitchen string

Bone the pork belly and lay it out flat with the inside up; leave the rind intact. Preheat the oven to 425°F (220°C).

Chop the garlic, rosemary, and fennel flowers together. Season with salt and pepper. Add a good drizzle of olive oil to create a paste. Spread the paste over the pork, then roll up the pork.

Using the kitchen string, tie the pork to bind it. Pierce it with the tip of a knife in several places (this will ensure it does not burst open during cooking).

Wrap the porchetta in aluminum foil and place it on a wire rack set over a roasting pan to ensure even cooking of the crust, to prevent the porchetta from burning, and to catch the excess fat drippings.

Roast for 1 hour. Remove the aluminum foil, lower the oven temperature to 350°F (180°C), and continue roasting. Allow 1 hour of roasting time per 2¼ pounds (1 kg). Remove the porchetta and let it rest for 12 hours at room temperature. Enjoy hot or cold. When enjoyed warm, the flavors of the meat and herbs are more expressive.

SKIP TO
LET'S GO OUT TO EAT, P. 92; SAGRA, A SACRED FESTIVAL, P. 118; FENNEL, P. 233.

SAGE

Present in many Italian dishes, *salvia* is an excellent herb for health.

GIANNA MAZZI

WHAT AM I?

SCIENTIFIC NAME: *Salvia officinalis.* From the Latin *salvus* (safe, healthy) because of its healing properties.

FAMILY: Lamiaceae.

ORIGIN: Mediterranean basin and Asia. It is cultivated throughout Italy.

USE: fresh, dried, or frozen.

RECIPE

FAGIOLI ALL'UCCELLETTO (TUSCANY)

Also called, ironically, *fagioli all'uccelletto escapato* (*all'uccelletto escapato* meaning "escaped bird"), this poor man's dish has the flavor of game but does not contain any meat. This recipe is inspired by No. 384 of *La scienza in cucina e l'arte di mangiar bene* (*Science in the Kitchen and the Art of Eating Well*, 1891) by Pellegrino Artusi.

SERVES 4

10½ ounces (300 g) dried cannellini beans or navy beans, rehydrated by soaking
2 cloves garlic, peeled
6 tablespoons (90 mL) olive oil
1 sprig sage
Salt and freshly ground black pepper
10½ ounces (300 g) peeled tomatoes

- Boil the beans in a saucepan over low heat, then let cool. Crush the garlic cloves and lightly brown them in a pan in the olive oil along with the sage. Drain the beans and add them to the pan. Season with salt and pepper and cook for several minutes. Add the tomatoes. Cook over low heat, stirring, for about 30 minutes.
- Enjoy on its own or with sausages, boiled meats, or a tripe ragout.

SACRED SAGE!

The ancient Greeks preserved food by covering it with sage leaves. The Romans did the same, but they considered the herb sacred. It was picked during grand ceremonies, then used to treat all ailments as a powerful healing agent.

IN COOKING

→ Sage is part of the sacred trio for roasts: chopped with rosemary and garlic, it flavors roasted meats, fish, or potatoes.

→ Its leaves browned in butter are used to season gnocchi and ravioli but are also used to stuff fresh pasta.

→ Battered and fried sage is perfect as an aperitif. Dip the leaves one by one in fritter batter made with ¾ cup (100 g) flour, just over ¾ cup (200 mL) cold beer, and a pinch of salt and pepper, then fry them in hot oil.

→ Indispensable in *saltimbocca alla romana* (veal cutlets cooked with prosciutto and sage), in crostini with chicken livers, and with pork.

→ It enhances legume- and grain-based soups.

→ It flavors one of the variations of Genoese focaccia.

SKIP TO
SALTIMBOCCA ALLA ROMANA (VEAL WITH PROSCIUTTO AND SAGE), P. 33; PELLEGRINO ARTUSI, P. 32.

A CHART OF RUSTIC BREEDS

Italy is rich with an immense diversity of livestock. Here is an inventory of the peninsula's native breeds.

CHARLES PATIN O'COOHOON

MEAT BREED 🥩 DAIRY BREED 🍼 MEAT & DAIRY BREED 🥩 🍼

COWS

Although in ancient Rome pork provided most of the fresh or preserved meat, cattle breeding gradually came to the fore in Italy, and with it *manzo* (beef) and *formaggi vaccini* (cow's-milk cheese).

AGEROLESE
🥩 🍼

ORIGIN: Agerola, Campania, since the eighteenth century.

APPEARANCE: medium height, dark coat, short horns directed forward.

MEAT: fat.

MILK: rich, used for Provolone del Monaco.

BRUNA ALPINA
🍼

ORIGIN: Alps in the sixteenth century.

APPEARANCE: large in size, color ranging from fawn gray to chestnut, small horns pointing forward.

MILK: rich, used for certain cheeses such as Bagoss di Bagolino (a Lombard large-format cheese).

CABANNINA
🥩 🍼 *Slow Food*

ORIGIN: Rezzoaglio, Liguria, since the nineteenth century.

APPEARANCE: small size, brown color with a light stripe.

MEAT: flavorful, used in *tuccu*, a Genoese sauce.

MILK: used to make *sarazzu*, a sort of aged ricotta.

CALVANA
🥩

ORIGIN: Calvana and Mugello mountains in the Tuscan Apennine mountains since the eighteenth century.

APPEARANCE: large, with a pearly white color, light horns with dark tips.

MILK: a very flavorful veal.

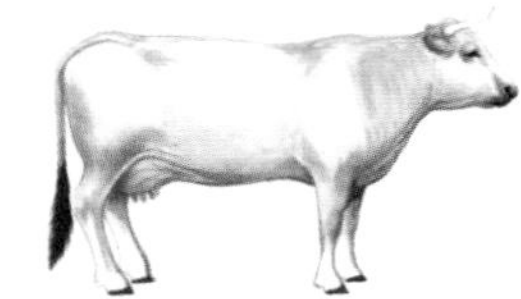

CHIANINA
🥩

ORIGIN: Val di Chiana, Tuscany, since antiquity.

APPEARANCE: largest domesticated bovine in the world, a uniform white coat, short horns with black tips.

MILK: lean and flavorful, light red in color with a little bit of fat. Used for the famous *bistecca alla fiorentina*.

GRIGIO ALPINA
🥩 🍼 *Slow Food*

ORIGIN: Trentino-Alto Adige, since the Middle Ages.

APPEARANCE: medium height, silvery gray coat and light crescent-shaped horns, dark at the ends.

MEAT: delicious in cured meats (*kaminwurzen*, small smoked sausages).

MILK: used to make Vezzena di Lavarone, Slow Food.

GARFAGNINA
🥩 🍼

ORIGIN: Garfagnana, Tuscany.

APPEARANCE: medium size, light gray color with bluish tinges, raised horns.

MEAT: rustic with a lot of flavor and good texture.

MILK: used to make Romecchio.

MARCHIGIANA
🥩

ORIGIN: Marche, since the nineteenth century.

APPEARANCE: large size, pale gray coat, powerful head, short neck with a hump for males.

MEAT: tender and rosy, fine grain.

MAREMMANA
🥩 *Slow Food*

ORIGIN: the marshes of Maremma, Tuscany, and Lazio, since the time of the Etruscans.

APPEARANCE: tall, silvery gray color, lyre-shaped horns.

MEAT: rustic and low in fat, strong flavor, dark red color, delicious for roasting.

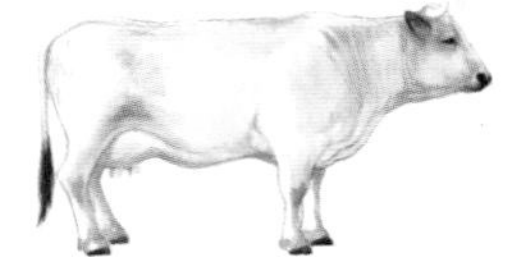

MODENESE
🥩 🍼 *Slow Food*

ORIGIN: Modena, Emilia-Romagna.

APPEARANCE: tall, white color, pedicle between the horns.

MEAT: tender and rosy veal.

MILK: used for Parmigiano-Reggiano cheese.

MODICANA
🥩 🍼 *Slow Food*

ORIGIN: province of Modica, Sicily, since the sixteenth century.

APPEARANCE: medium height, dark coat, yellowish horns at the ends.

MEAT: rustic and with a great deal of carotene.

MILK: used for ragusano cheeses from the Hyblaean mountains or Caciocavallo from the Sicani mountains.

PASTURINA
🥩

ORIGIN: Arezzo, Tuscany.

APPEARANCE: robust, grayish white color, lyre-shaped horns.

MILK: tasty and juicy, delicious for grilling.

PISANA
🥩 🍼

ORIGIN: province of Pisa, since the eighteenth century.

APPEARANCE: medium height, plain dark chestnut color, short horns curving forward.

MILK: rustic and tender, delicious in ragù.

PIEMONTESE
🥩 🍼 *Slow Food*

ORIGIN: Piedmont, since the nineteenth century.

APPEARANCE: heavy, white coat, short horns.

MEAT: a beautiful red, very low in fat, and very tender.

MILK: used for Castelmagno or Raschera cheeses.

PODOLICA
🥩 🍼 *Slow Food*

ORIGIN: Middle East, arrived in the fifth century.

APPEARANCE: medium height, gray color, lyre-shaped horns.

MEAT: lean, rich in carotene and essential fatty acids.

MILK: used for *caciocavallo* cheese.

PONTREMOLESE

ORIGIN: provinces of La Spezia, Liguria, and Massa Carrara, Tuscany.

APPEARANCE: rustic, wheat yellow color, lyre-shaped horns.

MEAT: a very tender veal.

MILK: used for *fior di cacio*.

PUSTERTALER

ORIGIN: Val Pusteria, Trentino-Alto Adige, since the nineteenth century.

APPEARANCE: medium height, red or blue-gray spotted coat, short horns.

MEAT: fat with good tenderness.

MILK: production of mountain cheeses (*saras del fen, pustertaler bergkase di montagna della Val Pusteria*).

REGGIANA

ORIGIN: province of Reggio Emilia since the twelfth century.

APPEARANCE: tall, red wheat color.

MEAT: flavorful.

MILK: historic breed for Parmigiano-Reggiano cheese.

RENDENA

Slow Food

ORIGIN: Val Rendena, Trentino-Alto Adige, since the eighteenth century.

APPEARANCE: medium height, plain brown-black color, short horns.

MEAT: eaten fresh or dried in thin slices (*carne salada*).

MILK: used for making *razza rendena*.

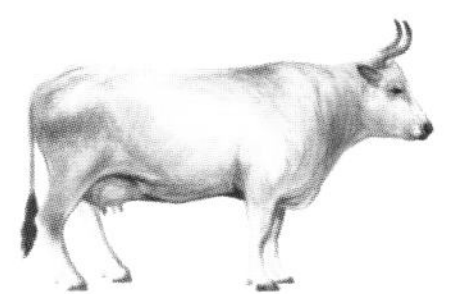

ROMAGNOLA

Slow Food

ORIGIN: Emilia-Romagna.

APPEARANCE: tall, white to gray color, lyre-shaped horns.

MEAT: lean and flavorful, excellent for high-end cuts (prime rib, tenderloin, etc.).

SARDA

ORIGIN: Sardinia.

APPEARANCE: small size, wheat color of different shades.

MEAT: a highly prized veal.

MILK: breed bred above all for its milk (spun cheese from domestic production).

SARDO-MODICANA

Slow Food

ORIGIN: Sardinia since the nineteenth century.

APPEARANCE: medium height, dark red color, lyre-shaped horns.

MEAT: bright red, very flavorful.

MILK: for cheese making (*casizolu, fresa*).

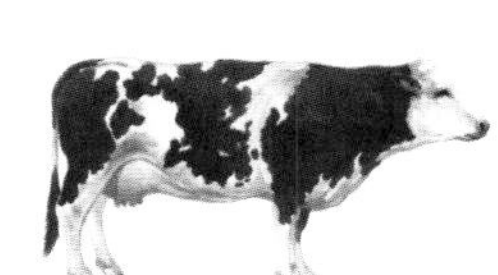

VALDOSTANA

Slow Food

ORIGIN: Aosta Valley since the fifth century.

APPEARANCE: medium height, red or black pied coat, short horns.

MEAT: very delicate.

MILK: rich, used for the fontina cheese.

VARZESE

Slow Food

ORIGIN: Varzi, Lombardy, since the sixth century.

APPEARANCE: medium height, wheat fawn color.

MEAT: excellent fresh.

MILK: used to make *pannerone*.

BEEF CUTS

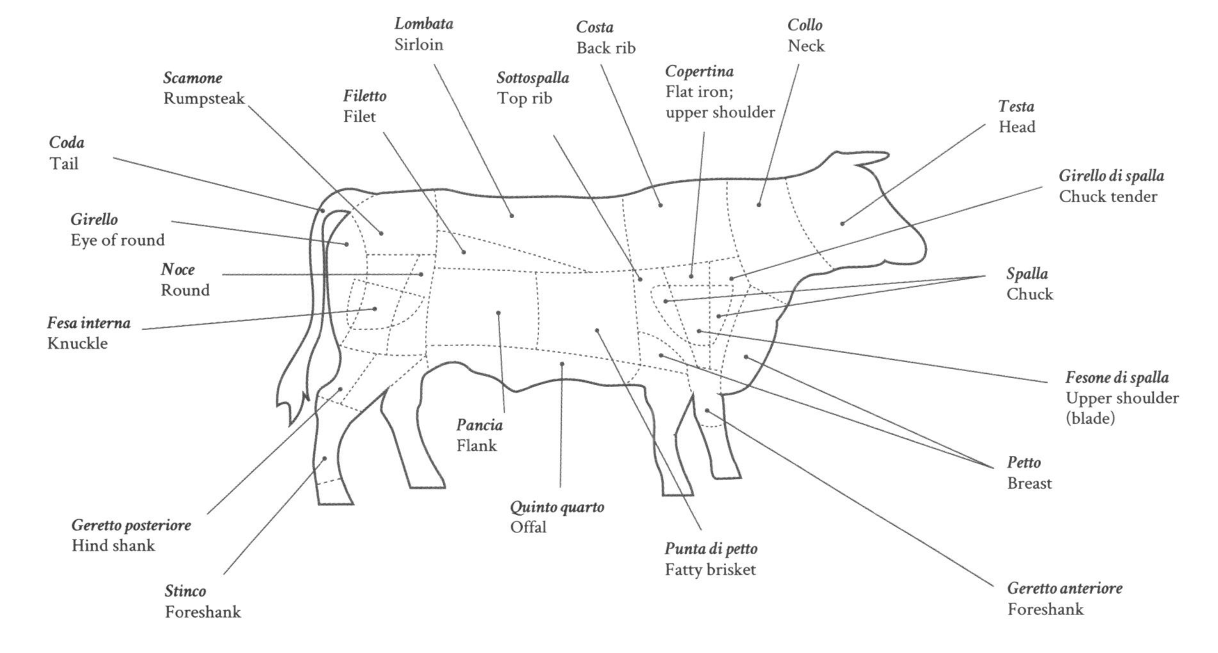

Italian bovine types

Vitello: milk-fed calf slaughtered before eight months. Its meat is tender and lean and is considered "white," and its flavor is less pronounced than that of *vitellone*. Ideal for pan cooking.

Vitellone: a calf slaughtered between eight and twelve months. Tender, lean red meat, richer in protein. The most popular of beef meats. Ideal braised or grilled.

Scottona: female generally slaughtered between fifteen and twenty-two months, in heat (hence the name, which means "burning") and who has never calved. Tender meat, with a strong flavor, bright red. Ideal for quick cooking or grilling.

Manzo: castrated cattle, around three to four years old. Fatty meat, intense red, rich in iron, with a pronounced flavor, marbled. Ideal for grilling but also for slow cooking.

Bovino: adult bovine (steer, bull, and heifer).

Bue: adult cattle slaughtered starting from four years old. A rather lean meat, with a very pronounced flavor, dark red. Ideal for slow simmering, in ragout.

Vacca: female over six years old who has calved; included in the category of adult bovine (*bovino*). Variable slaughter age, as well as meat quality. Industrial use.

GOATS

Among the forty-three Italian breeds, there are eight indigenous breeds registered in the genealogical book of the Associazione Nazionale della Pastorizia. Their sparse presence among Italy's regions explains their low representation in Italian cheeses.

GARGANICA *Slow Food*

ORIGIN: Gargano, Apulia.

APPEARANCE: medium height, black color with reddish tinges, large horns.

GIRGENTANA *Slow Food*

ORIGIN: province of Agrigento, Sicily.

APPEARANCE: medium height, long white coat, spiraling horns.

JONICA

ORIGIN: Taranto, Apulia.

APPEARANCE: large size, white color, long floppy ears.

MALTAISE

ORIGIN: Sicily.

APPEARANCE: medium height, yellowish white coat with long hair.

OROBICA *Slow Food*

ORIGIN: Valtellina, Lombardy.

APPEARANCE: medium height, color ranging from ash gray to purplish beige.

ROSSA MEDITERRANEA

ORIGIN: Sicily.

APPEARANCE: medium height, brown-red coat.

SARDA

ORIGIN: Sardinia.

APPEARANCE: medium height, white and brown coat with long hair.

GOAT CUTS

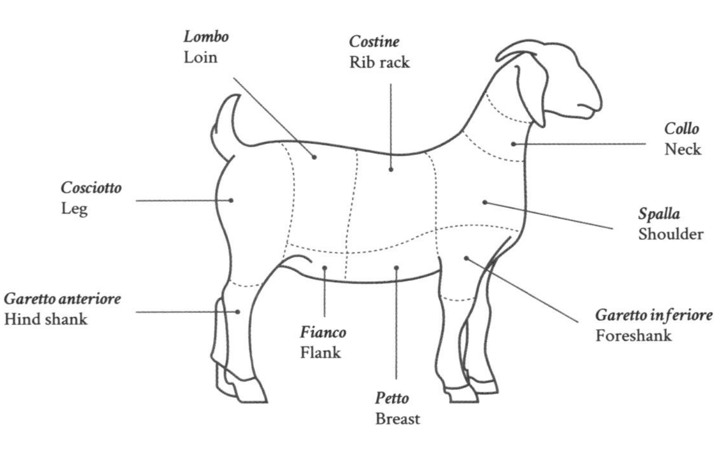

SHEEP

The Associazione Nazionale della Pastorizia lists seventeen principal breeds in a book of genealogy, but there are sixty-three indigenous breeds. Sheep are seldom cooked, but the milk is very prominent in the production of cheeses from central to southern Italy.

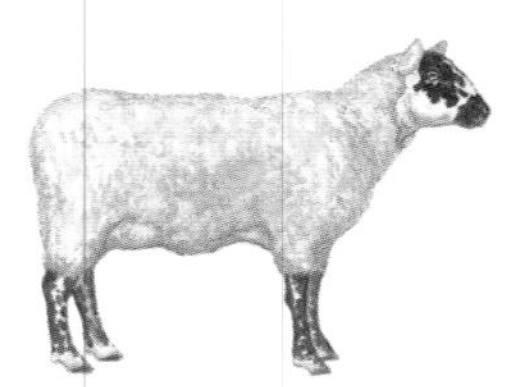

ALPAGOTA PRESIDI

Slow Food

ORIGIN: province of Belluno, Veneto.

APPEARANCE: white coat, black spots on the legs and head.

ALTAMURANA

ORIGIN: Altamurana, Apulia.

APPEARANCE: medium height, long-haired white coat with black spots.

APENNINCA

ORIGIN: the Apennines.

APPEARANCE: medium height, white coat.

BARBARESCA

ORIGIN: province of Caltanissetta, Sicily.

APPEARANCE: medium height, white coat, black spotted head, floppy ears.

BERGAMASCA

ORIGIN: Bergamo, Lombardy.

APPEARANCE: medium height, large floppy ears.

BRIANZOLA

Slow Food

ORIGIN: province of Brianza, Lombardy.

APPEARANCE: medium height, droopy ears.

COMISANA

ORIGIN: Sicily.

APPEARANCE: large size, white coat, floppy ears.

CORNIGLIESE

Slow Food

ORIGIN: upper Apennines, Emilia-Romagna.

APPEARANCE: tall, white coat, floppy ears.

FABRIANESE

ORIGIN: Fabriano, Marches.

APPEARANCE: large size, light coat with dark spots.

GENTILE DI PUGLIA

ORIGIN: Foggia, Apulia.

APPEARANCE: medium height, bushy white coat.

LANGAROLA

ORIGIN: Langhe, Piedmont.

APPEARANCE: large size, long forward ears.

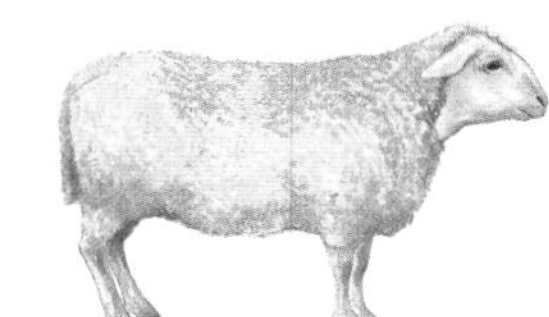

LATICODA

Slow Food

ORIGIN: Campania.

APPEARANCE: large size, white coat, long ears.

MASSESE

ORIGIN: province of Massa-Carrara, Tuscany.

APPEARANCE: medium size, brown coat and black skin.

MERINIZZATA ITALIANA

ORIGIN: Calabria, Basilicata, Apulia.

APPEARANCE: large size, white coat, short ears.

PINZIRITA

ORIGIN: Sicily.

APPEARANCE: small size, white coat, black spots on the legs and head.

POMARANCINA

Slow Food

ORIGIN: Pomarance and Montecatini Val di Cecina, Tuscany.

APPEARANCE: medium size, white coat, slightly drooping ears.

SAMBUCANA

Slow Food

ORIGIN: province of Cuneo, Piedmont.

APPEARANCE: medium size, yellowish coat, small horizontal ears.

SARDA

ORIGIN: Sardinia.

APPEARANCE: medium size, white, bushy coat.

SOPRAVISSANA

ORIGIN: province of Macerata, Marche.

APPEARANCE: medium size, thick white coat.

VALLE DEL BELICE

ORIGIN: province of Trapani, Sicily.

APPEARANCE: medium size, white coat.

VILLNÖSSER BRILLENSCHAF

Slow Food

ORIGIN: Trentino-Alto Adige.

APPEARANCE: medium size, white coat, dark spots on the head, long floppy ears.

ZERASCA

Slow Food

ORIGIN: province of Massa-Carrara, Tuscany.

APPEARANCE: medium size, white coat, slightly drooping ears.

SHEEP CUTS

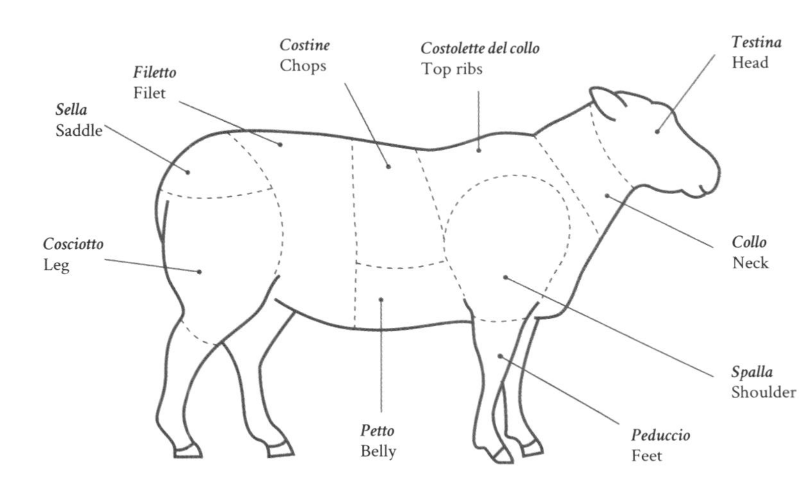

PIGS

In 1927, Italy had thirty breeds of pig. Here are the six listed today by ANAS (Associazione Nazionale di Allevatori di Suini).

APULA-CALABRESE

ORIGIN: Calabria and Puglia.

APPEARANCE: robust and of medium height, black hair, long muzzle and pointed ears.

MEAT: ideal in charcuterie (*n'duja, soppressata di calabrese, capocollo . . .*).

CINTA SENESE
(PDO since 2012)

ORIGIN: Montagnola Senese, in the province of Siena, Tuscany, in the fourteenth century.

APPEARANCE: medium height, dark color with a white band between the neck and abdomen, erect ears.

MEAT: perfect for curing; the source of Tuscan prosciutto.

MORA ROMAGNOLA
Slow Food Sentinel

ORIGIN: Emilia-Romagna since the nineteenth century.

APPEARANCE: stocky, dark hair, elongated muzzle and straight ears.

MEAT: melting fat and rich in fatty acids; makes *cacciatorini romagnoli*, small sausages for snacks.

NERO CASERTANA

ORIGIN: province of Caserta, Campania, since Roman times.

APPEARANCE: short, dark coat, long muzzle and floppy ears. Nicknamed *pelatella* for the bristles on its head.

MEAT: good for charcuterie or eaten fresh.

NERO SICILIANO

ORIGIN: Nebrodi Mountains, Sicily, since Carthaginian times (500 BCE).

APPEARANCE: medium height, dark hairy coat, elongated muzzle and straight ears.

MEAT: perfect in cured meats (*fellata, nebrodi* sausage, pancetta), excellent fresh.

SARDA

ORIGIN: Sardinia, since the fourteenth century.

APPEARANCE: short size, dark coat, erect ears, thick hair forming a mane on the back.

MEAT: when roasted young, it's used for *porceddu*, a succulent suckling pig on a spit.

PORK CUTS

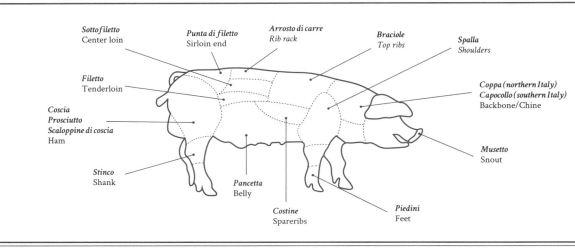

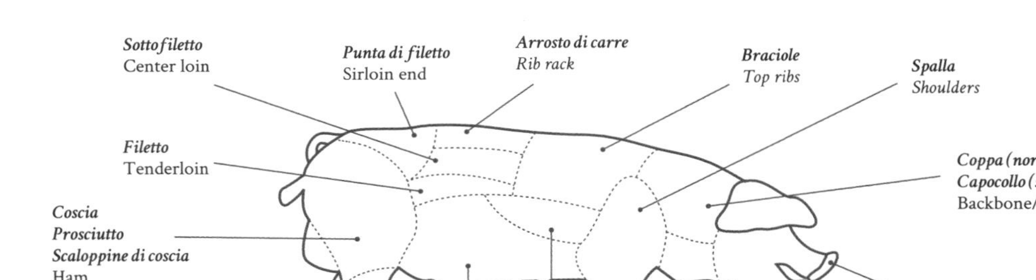

GEESE

Sacred squawking geese saved the Romans from an invasion by the Gauls who were attempting to sneak up Capitoline Hill. Here are five appreciated Italian breeds.

OCA CAMPANA

ORIGIN: Campania.

APPEARANCE: medium size, white plumage dotted with graying rings, orange beak.

OCA GRIGIA PADOVANA

ORIGIN: Padua, Veneto.

APPEARANCE: large, brownish-gray plumage, yellow-orange beak.

OCA DI LOMELLINA

ORIGIN: Valle Lomellina, Lombardy.

APPEARANCE: medium size, white plumage speckled with bluish-gray feathers, orange beak.

OCA PEZZATA VENETA

ORIGIN: Veneto.

APPEARANCE: very large, white-gray plumage that forms a heart shape on the back, pinkish orange beak.

OCA ROMAGNOLA

ORIGIN: Ravenna, Emilia-Romagna.

APPEARANCE: medium size, white plumage, imposing orange beak.

TAGLI DELL'OCA (GOOSE)

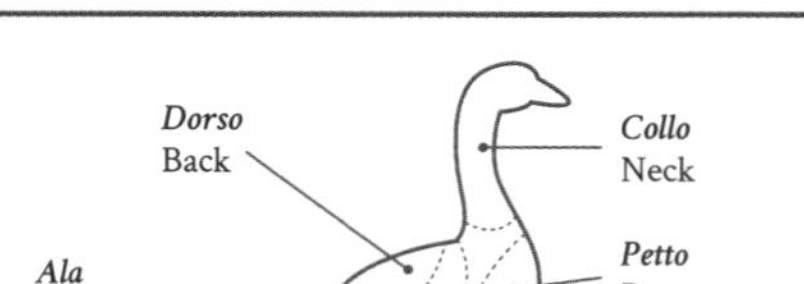

POULTRY

These ancient breeds make Italy one of the most beautiful lands for poultry in Europe. Here is a small tour of the best of the barnyard.

ANCONA
ORIGIN: Ancona, Marche.
APPEARANCE: red comb, bluish-gray plumage.

BIANCA DI SALUZZO
ORIGIN: Saluzzo, Piedmont.
APPEARANCE: large red comb, white plumage.

BIONDA PIEMONTESE
ORIGIN: Piedmont.
APPEARANCE: large comb, brown plumage.

COLLO NUDO ITALIANO
ORIGIN: Padua, Veneto.
APPEARANCE: bare red comb and neck, black and brown plumage.

CUCULA
ORIGIN: Veneto.
APPEARANCE: imposing comb, hawklike plumage.

EMELLINATA ROVIGO
ORIGIN: Rovigo, Veneto.
APPEARANCE: broad comb, white plumage, black tail.

FULVA DEL SANNIO
ORIGIN: Molise.
APPEARANCE: long comb, tawny plumage with golden tinges, black tail.

LIVORNO
ORIGIN: Livorno, Tuscany.
APPEARANCE: long comb, shiny plumage varying from white to black.

MERICANEL DELLA BRIANZA
ORIGIN: Brianza, Lombardy.
APPEARANCE: long red comb, white plumage.

MILANINO
ORIGIN: Province of Milan, Lombardy.
APPEARANCE: red comb, white plumage.

MILLEFORI DI LONIGO
ORIGIN: Padua, Veneto.
APPEARANCE: large comb, yellow and brown plumage.

MODENESE
ORIGIN: province of Modena, Emilia-Romagna.
APPEARANCE: long red comb, fawn to buff plumage.

MUGELLESE
ORIGIN: province of Mugello, Tuscany.
APPEARANCE: short comb, gold plumage.

NAPOLETANA O MONNEZZARA
ORIGIN: Naples, Campania.
APPEARANCE: long comb, gold plumage.

NERA DEL VAL FORTORE
ORIGIN: province of Benevento, Campania.
APPEARANCE: long red comb, black plumage with copper highlights.

NOSTRANA DI MOROZZO
ORIGIN: Cuneo, Piedmont.
APPEARANCE: large red comb, red-brown plumage.

PADOVANA RICCIA
ORIGIN: Padua, Veneto.
APPEARANCE: crest on the head, curly white plumage.

PEPOI
ORIGIN: Veneto and Friuli.
APPEARANCE: dwarf breed, small comb, golden plumage.

ROBUSTA LIONATA
ORIGIN: Rovigo, Veneto.
APPEARANCE: medium red comb, tawny plumage, dark tail.

ROBUSTA MACULATA
ORIGIN: Rovigo, Veneto.
APPEARANCE: red comb, dark white plumage with dark spots.

ROMAGNOLA
ORIGIN: Emilia-Romagna.
APPEARANCE: large red comb, black and white plumage.

SCODATA
ORIGIN: province of Caserta, Campania.
APPEARANCE: dark red comb, gold colored plumage, no tail.

SICILIANA
ORIGIN: Sicily.
APPEARANCE: large red comb, plumage ranging from gold to white through brown and black.

STORZA
ORIGIN: Campania.
APPEARANCE: thick red comb, white plumage.

VALDARNESE
ORIGIN: Valdarno, Tuscany.
APPEARANCE: folded red comb, white plumage.

VALDARNO
ORIGIN: Valdarno, Tuscany.
APPEARANCE: contoured comb, deep black plumage.

HEN CUTS

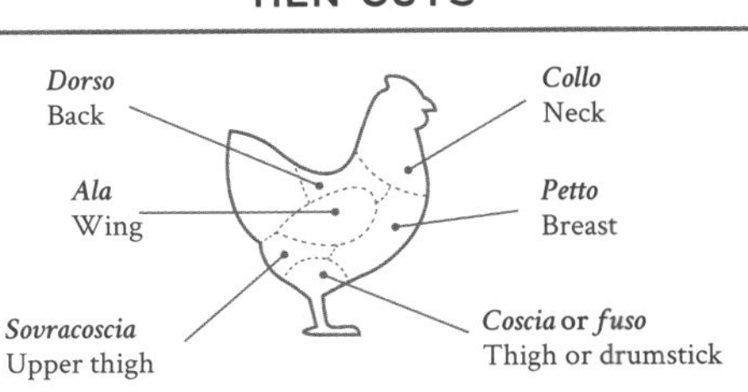

SEASON

TUTTO L'ANNO (YEAR-ROUND)

•

CATEGORY

ANTIPASTI, SECONDO PIATTO (APPETIZER/ MAIN COURSE)

•

LEVEL

FACILE (EASY)

ARROSTICINI

LAMB SKEWERS

Arrosticini, also called *rustelle* in the Abruzzian dialect, may be unassuming in appearance, but behind these simple meat skewers is the story of the entire pastoral history of Abruzzo.

CÉLINE MAGUET

A SHEPHERD'S SNACK

→ Arrosticini were born in the heart of the Gran Sasso e Monti della Laga national park in the north of Abruzzo during the 1930s. To tenderize the meat of older sheep, shepherds had the idea to cook the meat in small pieces combined with pieces of fat. For the sake of convenience, a skewer made from the twigs of nearby shrubs became an easy tool for handling the meat pieces.

→ At the time, street food was not yet a concept. Shepherds had simply found a convenient way to eat with their fingers. Starting in the 1950s, the tradition was gradually adopted by street vendors who came down from the mountains to the Adriatic coast.

What tradition dictates . . .

→ The skewers are served with grilled bread and olive oil, in this way turning your *arrosticino* into a bruschetta. They are the stars of local festivals, or they can be purchased from street vendors to take back to the beach.

→ Synonymous with popular food and the idea of sharing, cooking arrosticini represents reunions with family or friends or provides an excuse to get together, similar to the idea of a casual backyard barbecue.

A RUSTIC MEAT BREED

In Abruzzo, two breeds of sheep coexist: the Gentile di Apulia, the most common, and the Pagliorala, the most rustic—so rustic, in fact, that in winter, shepherds coming down from the mountains during transhumance can leave them in high-elevation pastures with just a little straw and simple shelter for survival. The Pagliorala takes its name from its winter feed: wheat stalks. This very thrifty sheep is content with the little food available to it, which compensates for its low production of milk. Bred mainly for its coarse wool, then secondarily for its meat and milk, it is the result of crossbreeding of various breeds, including Île-de-France, originating in the Paris Basin. The Pagliorala is threatened by extinction and has consequently become the focus of a plan for reintroduction and preservation.

THE RECIPE

Abruzzians rarely prepare their arrosticini themselves. Instead, they order them already prepared by the butcher. However, these skewers are easy to make so you don't need special skills or an arrosticini machine (yes, they do exist).

MAKES 40 *ARROSTICINI* (TO SERVE 4)

Mutton shoulder

Mutton breast

Salt

Material

40 small wooden skewers, 6 to 8 inches (15 to 20 cm) in length

Cut the meat into ¾-inch (2 cm) cubes.

Thread 6 pieces of meat onto each skewer, alternating lean pieces (shoulder) with fattier pieces (breast). To avoid drying out the meat, do not season with salt yet.

Cook over hot coals, 4 to 5 minutes per side (10 minutes in total).

Season the skewers with salt and serve immediately.

VARIATION

People hold firm to their traditional method of preparation, so variations aren't common, but some have ventured into replacing the sheep's breast and shoulder with pieces of liver or even lamb.

HOW DO YOU PASS FOR A TRUE ABRUZZIAN?

1. Choose arrosticini meat that has been knife cut, not machine cut. It can be spotted with the naked eye, so you can't go wrong.

2. Baking them in the oven is a real no-no! Cook your arrosticini over hot coals, on a *canaletta*—a long and narrow grill perfect for skewers—if possible.

3. Don't salt the skewers too soon. The perfect moment is just after they are cooked, to avoid drying out the meat and therefore wasting your efforts . . . and the meat with it!

4. Eat them by the dozen . . . and without fuss, straight off the skewer.

5. Drizzle them with a little Montepulciano d'Abruzzo, a red wine of the region.

And now you're authentically Abruzzian!

ARROSTILAND

THE *FESTA DEGLI ARROSTICINI*

Each year, one of the villages perched in the hills not far from Pescara is selected to organize a large festival in honor of arrosticini called Arrostiland.

•

On Easter Monday, dozens of *greggi* (flocks) selected for the occasion are rounded up and arrosticini are cooked for nearly 15,000 people, faithful to the motto of Arrostiland: "*Rostelle, montepulciano d'Abruzzo e amicizia*" ("Arrosticini, Montepulciano d'Abruzzo, and friendship").

SKIP TO
SAGRA, A SACRED FESTIVAL, P. 118.

HISTORIC CAFÉS

The famous *caffè* of Italy's grand cities stand out as guardians of tradition and of a way of life that has spanned the centuries.

ALESSANDRA PIERINI AND ILARIA BRUNETTI

A long history

When the first Piazza San Marco café opened in Venice in 1683, it marked the beginning of the active propagation of establishments characteristic of Italy's cities. Some of these cafés are now famous as veritable houses of culture. They serve as meeting places for ordinary folk as well as for artists, writers, and politicians to engage in literary, poetic, and patriotic expression and discussions.

CAFFÈ GILLI · *Florence, Tuscany*

The oldest café in Florence, founded in 1733 under the name Bottega dei Pani Dolci. Since the beginning of the twentieth century, it has been located next to Piazza della Repubblica and has preserved its Liberty-style decor, Murano chandeliers, and ceiling frescoes.

FAMOUS REGULARS: fashion designer Pucci.

TO TRY: the pastries, which are both traditional and creative.

CAFFÈ DEGLI SPECCHI
Trieste, Friuli-Venezia Giulia

Trieste is renowned for its historic cafés, which accommodated so many intellectual circles. The sophisticated Caffè degli Specchi, inaugurated in 1839, was the most sociable.

FAMOUS REGULARS: Joyce and Svevo.

TO TRY: the *nero in b*, an espresso served in a small glass (*bicchierino*), as it's called by the Triestinos.

PASTICCERIA LIQUORERIA MARESCOTTI DI CAVO · *Genoa, Liguria*

This café–pastry shop opened in 1780 in a thirteenth-century palace in the heart of Genoa's old town. Closed in 1979, it reopened in 2008 thanks to Alessandro Cavo, who preserved its Charles X–period decor and its fourteen crystal display cases.

FAMOUS REGULARS: the noble families of Genoa.

TO TRY: *amaretti di Voltaggio* (soft almond cookies) and *quaresimali* (monastic pastries).

COVA · *Milan, Lombardy*

Opened in 1817 as Caffè del Giardino next to La Scala theater, this elegant café–pastry shop moved to Via Montenapoleone in 1950. It is now part of the LVMH group and has locations around the world.

FAMOUS REGULARS: Verdi and Puccini.

TO TRY: the panettone.

FLORIAN · *Venice, Veneto*

The oldest and most famous café in Piazza San Marco, founded in 1720 by Floriano Francesconi. It has always welcomed great celebrities into its six luxuriously decorated lounges.

FAMOUS REGULARS: Casanova, Goldoni, and Mastroianni.

TO TRY: a Bellini cocktail and the *tramezzini* (small snack sandwiches).

ANTICO CAFFÈ SPINNATO · *Palermo, Sicily*

Since opening in 1860, this café has been owned by the Spinnato family, who preserve its neoclassical atmosphere and serve delicious Sicilian pastries.

FAMOUS REGULARS: artists from nearby Teatro Massimo.

TO TRY: *cassate*, cannoli, and frozen desserts.

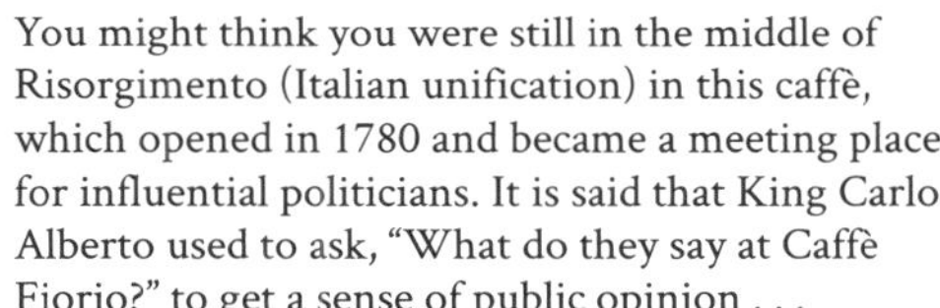

CAFFÈ FIORIO · *Turin, Piedmont*

You might think you were still in the middle of Risorgimento (Italian unification) in this caffè, which opened in 1780 and became a meeting place for influential politicians. It is said that King Carlo Alberto used to ask, "What do they say at Caffè Fiorio?" to get a sense of public opinion . . .

FAMOUS REGULARS: Camillo Benso, Count of Cavour.

TO TRY: hot chocolate, artisanal sabayons, and vermouths.

Caffè Greco
A.D. 1760

CAFFÈ GRECO · *Rome, Lazio*

This café has always served as a meeting place for the city's intellectuals, and today it hosts the Liberissima Università del Caffè Greco, a cultural group. In its rooms are exhibited more than 300 works of art.

FAMOUS REGULARS: Casanova, Goethe, and Byron.

TO TRY: *caffè e cornetto.*

CAFFÈ PEDROCCHI
Padua, Veneto

In 1831, Antonio Pedrocchi, along with architect Jappelli, transformed his father's small shop (opened in 1772 as Bottega del Caffè) into a building housing a public café and salons for the elite, where neoclassical and Gothic styles mingle. It has Venetian and exotic touches.

FAMOUS REGULARS: Balzac and Stendhal.

TO TRY: *caffè Pedrocchi*, an espresso with mint cream and cocoa, or the P31, a house-made herbal liqueur.

GRAND CAFFÈ GAMBRINUS
Naples, Campania

Opened as Grand Caffè in 1860 and renowned for its pastries savored by the House of Savoy, it expanded in 1890 and adopted its current name.

FAMOUS REGULARS: Empress Sissi, D'Annunzio, and Wilde.

TO TRY: *sfogliatelle* and their caffè.

But also: Al Bicerin (Turin, 1763) for its *bicerin* (an espresso-based drink); Mulassano (Turin, 1907), where the *tramezzino* was created; Caffè Tommaseo (Trieste, 1830), the oldest in the city; Caffè San Marco (Trieste, 1914), a café for intellectuals; Gran Caffè Quadri (Venice, 1775); Gran Caffè Renzelli (Cosenza, 1803); Tettamanzi (Nuoro, 1875); Giubbe Rosse (Florence, 1896).

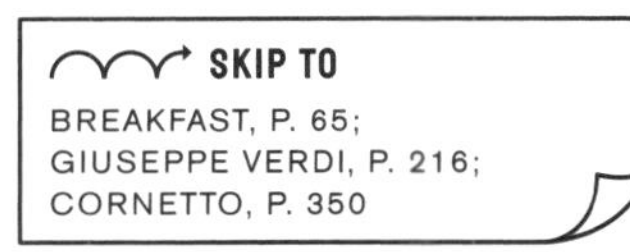
SKIP TO
BREAKFAST, P. 65;
GIUSEPPE VERDI, P. 216;
CORNETTO, P. 350

EGGPLANT

Whether served as parmigiana, caponata, or *alla Norma* . . . the *melanzana* is a triumph of *cucina Italiana.*

ALESSANDRA PIERINI

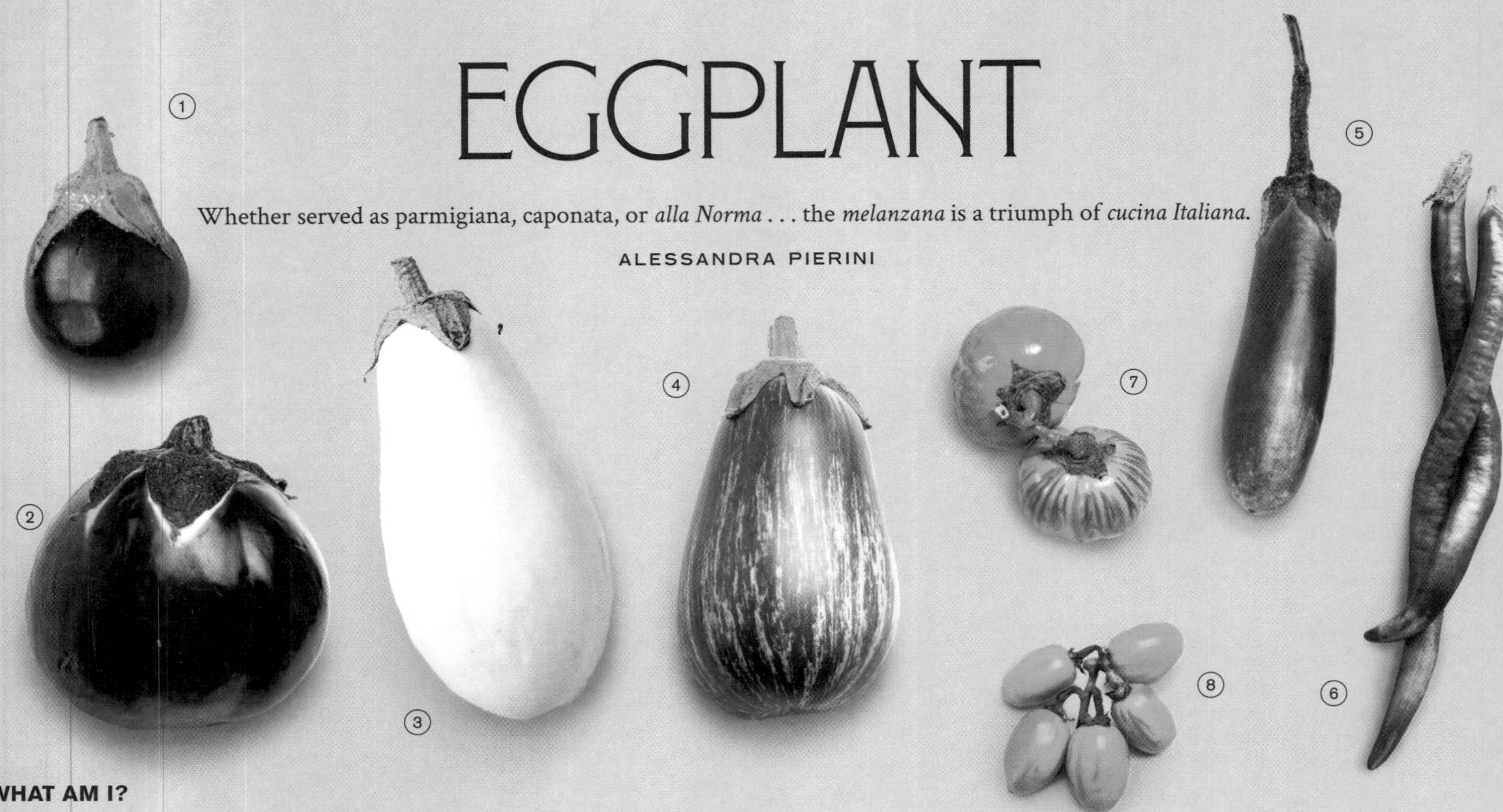

WHAT AM I?

NAME: *Solanum melongena.*

FAMILY: Solonaceae.

COMMON NAMES: *marignano* (Lazio), *molignana* (Campania), *mulinciano* (Sicily), *milangiane* (Calabria), *maranzana* or *malansana* (Piedmont), *meresgian* (Lombardy), *melongiana* (Veneto), *bulignama* (Abruzzo), *marangiana* (Apulia), *petonciano* (Tuscany).

ORIGIN: Asia. It was introduced to Sicily in the thirteenth century by Arab merchants.

FRUIT OR VEGETABLE? Since it is the product of a flower, eggplant—like tomato and zucchini—is actually a fruit.

Etymologies

There are different theories about the origins of its name:

→ From the Arabic *badingian*, preceded by the Italian word *mela* (apple), which medieval Italian used as a prefix to many foreign names of fruits and vegetables.

→ From the Low Latin *belangolus* and *merangolus* by way of the Spanish *berenjena.*

→ From *melainsana* ("unhealthy apple"). This third theory is the nickname of this vegetable-fruit that, for a long time, had a bad reputation: it was believed that its consumption could make people insane thanks to the small amounts of toxic alkaloids and solanine that plants of this family (including tomatoes, bell peppers, and potatoes) contain. Eggplant was mainly eaten by the poor classes in southern Italy, where the warm climate is more favorable for it. It only arrived in the 1970s innorthern Italy, with the exception of Liguria because of its ancient maritime connections with the southern portion of the country.

VARIETALS

They are generally grouped into three categories.

Round

Softer and fleshier, compact, with a tender texture. Fried, grilled, baked, stuffed; used in lasagna, *timballi*, parmigiana, *pasta alla Norma*; canned in oil.

VIOLETTA DI FIRENZE

Violette of Florence—Tuscany

Light purple, streaked with white, chubby, and ribbed.

① TONDA GENOVESE

Genoese round—Liguria

Shiny dark purple, small.

VIOLETTA CASALESE

Purple Casalaise—Piedmont

Bright violet-purple, sometimes streaked with white, a potbelly with a more elongated top.

② TONDA SICILIANA

Sicilian round—Sicily

From light to very intense purple, very bulbous.

Oval

The most common, medium size, uniform and shiny. It lends itself to all recipes, and especially to preparations made for its firm flesh and ability to hold together well during cooking.

DURONA A CALICE NERO OR A PEDUNCOLO NERO

With black calyx or black stem—Sicily

Dark purple, rather small.

③ BIANCA

White—southern Italy

Ivory white, very thin skin, medium to bulbous. There is also a miniature egg-shaped one (*bianca a uovo*).

VIOLETTA MESSINESE OR SETA

Purple Messina or "silk"—Sicily

Intense purple, medium size, tender, very soft.

④ ZEBRINA VIOLA

Purple zebra—southern Italy

Purple streaked with white, semilong, slightly curved.

Oblong

Thin and long, more pronounced taste, sometimes slightly bitter and pungent. In sauces with fish, panfried, batter fried, as confit, steamed, canned.

⑤ LUNGA VIOLETTA DI NAPOLI OR CIMA DI VIOLA

Long purple from Naples or purple tip—Campania

Intense purple, almost black, one of the most bulbous in the category from top to bottom. Perfect for parmigiana.

⑥ PERLINA

Small pearl—southern Italy

Violine, very thin (⅓ to 1⅛ inches/1 to 3 cm) and long (4¾ to 8 inches/12 to 20 cm), the sweetest.

In cooking

Eggplant is to be eaten cooked. To limit the absorption of cooking fats and oils and to reduce its bitterness, leave the skin on and, before cooking it, cut slices, sprinkle them with salt, and let them drain for an hour. You can steam the eggplant or bake it to prepare a purée or an eggplant dip after scraping out the flesh using a spoon. Because of its soft and delicate texture, it can also be incorporated as an ingredient in cakes. Italian cuisine has done justice to the eggplant: harvested between May and August, it becomes the featured ingredient of many cult summer recipes.

In Campanie

A FUNGITIELLI
Diced eggplant panfried in oil, garlic, parsley, capers, and tomato sauce, served cold.

A MANNELLA
Thin slices of fried eggplant, arranged in a dish with olive oil, vinegar, garlic, and oregano then baked, served cold or hot.

ALLA PULLASTIELLO
Eggplant sliced and stuffed with *caciocavallo* cheese, sausage, or ham, covered with a second slice, all dredged in flour, then in egg, and fried.

In Calabria

ALLA FINITESE
Boiled eggplant slices filled like a sandwich with caciocavallo cheese and basil, all dredged in flour, then in egg, then coated in dried bread crumbs and fried.

CHINE ("BOWED")
Eggplant halved lengthwise and fried, stuffed with dried bread crumbs, garlic, pecorino, parsley, egg, and tomato, baked in tomato sauce, and sprinkled with grated pecorino.

SOTTO SALE ("IN SALT")
Preserved eggplant cut into thick slices, boiled, and drained well, then layered in a clay pot with garlic, pepper, fennel seeds, and salt, covered, with a weight applied on top to press out excess liquid. Served with a drizzle of oil.

In Apulia

DI SANT'ORONZO OR PARMIGIANA DI SALENTO
Floured eggplant slices, dredged in egg, fried, and placed in a baking dish in layers alternating with tomatoes, onion, capers, pecorino, basil or oregano, and sometimes mozzarella slices, and baked.

SOTT'OLIO ("IN OIL")
Sun-dried eggplant slices layered in a pot with chile, oregano, and vinegar, covered with olive oil.

In Sicily

CAPONATA
Diced eggplant cooked with onion, capers, green olives, tomatoes, pine nuts, basil, vinegar, and olive oil.

PASTA ALLA NORMA
Fried eggplant slices or dice with tomato sauce and grated ricotta salata to dress pasta, preferably spaghetti.

A BECCAFICO
Fried eggplant slices, rolled with a stuffing made from dried bread crumbs, grated pecorino, raisins, basil, parsley, and baked in olive oil with bay leaves.

And also . . .

Parmigiana di melanzane (Emilia-Romagna, Campania, Apulia, Sicily), *a scarpone* (Campania), *ripiene alla ligure* (Liguria), *in saor* (Veneto), *a schibecci* (Sicily), *ammuttunate* (Sicily), *a picchipacchio* (Campania, Sicily), *a quaglia* (Sicily), *pasta 'ncasciata* (Sicily).

SHADES OF RED

The *rossa di Rotonda* (Rotonda red) DOP eggplant, a Slow Food sentinel (Basilicata) ⑦, in the local language *a pummadora* because it resembles a tomato, is small with a thin skin in intense orange color with green and red stripes. It is very fragrant, and mainly preserved. A new varietal is emerging in Campania and Sicily growing as a cluster, the Toga ⑧ eggplant, with the size and shape of an elongated yellow-orange cherry tomato with green striations. It is baked, fried, or stewed.

RECIPE

MELANZANE AL CIOCCOLATO (CHOCOLATE EGGPLANT)

Also called *parmigiana dolce*, this chocolate eggplant dish from Campania was prepared in convents located along the Amalfi Coast. Filomena Ventre Farano, from the town of Cava de' Tirreni (Salerno), shares her version of this traditional recipe served for the Assumption.

SERVES 4

2 medium eggplants
Coarse salt
Frying oil
⅓ cup plus 1 tablespoon (50 g) flour
2 large (100 g) eggs
1 cup (200 g) sugar
Zest of ½ unwaxed lemon
2 tablespoons (13 g) ground cinnamon
5½ tablespoons (30 g) crushed blanched almonds
1¾ ounces (50 g) candied oranges, cut into small cubes
1¾ ounces (50 g) hard amaretti cookies
½ cup (50 g) unsweetened cocoa powder
Just over ¾ cup (200 mL) milk
1¾ ounces (50 g) 70% cacao dark chocolate

- Wash and cut the eggplants lengthwise to make twelve ⅓-inch-thick (1 cm) slices. Sprinkle with coarse salt and let drain for 1 hour. Rinse and pat dry. Fry the slices in hot oil, completely submerging them, until they are softened but haven't developed too much color. Transfer them to paper towels to drain.
- Place the flour on a plate. Beat the eggs in a shallow bowl with a little salt.
- On a separate plate, combine ½ cup (100 g) of the sugar with the lemon zest and cinnamon.
- Dredge the eggplant slices on both sides in the flour, then dip them in the beaten egg and fry them again. Transfer them to paper towels to drain.
- Dredge the fried slices, still hot, in the sugar mixture to coat them well, then set aside. Place the almonds and oranges in a bowl. Using your hands, crumble the amaretti into the bowl. Add ¼ cup (20 g) of the cocoa powder and stir to combine. This makes the filling and topping.
- Heat the milk in a saucepan with the remaining ½ cup (100 g) sugar, remaining ¼ cup (20 g) cocoa powder, and the chocolate. Bring to a boil, stirring, until somewhat thickened.
- Pour a thin layer of the chocolate sauce on a serving platter and arrange 4 slices of eggplant on top. Sprinkle one-third of the amaretti mixture on top, then drizzle with more chocolate sauce. Repeat these steps to make two more layers, reserving a bit of the amaretti mixture.
- Finish by drizzling on chocolate sauce to completely cover the top, then sprinkle with the remaining amaretti mixture. Refrigerate, tightly covered, for 1 day before serving.

SKIP TO
PARMIGIANA DI MELANZANE (EGGPLANT PARMIGIANA), P. 274; CAPONATA (SICILIAN EGGPLANT SALAD), P. 220; PASTA ALLA NORMA (SICILIAN PASTA AND EGGPLANT), P. 238.

SEASON
TUTTO L'ANNO (YEAR-ROUND)

CATEGORY
SECONDO PIATTO (MAIN COURSE)

LEVEL
FACILE (EASY)

PIZZAIOLA

BRAISED MEAT WITH TOMATOES

No, *pizzaiola* is not the wife of a *pizzaiolo*! Instead, this is a simple, family-style, very tomatoey meat dish that can be made even using fish.

FRANÇOIS-RÉGIS GAUDRY

THE ORIGINS

Pizzaiola makes reference to pizza, and in particular the marinara sauce, whose ingredients it includes: tomato, garlic, oregano, and olive oil. This suggests the dish has Neapolitan origins, but little is known about its roots. Although it receives little mention, if any, in "official" recipe collections of Italian cuisine, this recipe is a very popular family classic in the south.

PIZZAIOLA WITHOUT MEAT BUT WITH . . .

PASTA: to use a Neapolitan saying, "*'a carne 'a sotto e i maccarùne 'a coppa*" ("the meat must be covered with *maccheroni*"). Although pizzaiola's sauce is used often as a sauce on maccheroni, it is preferable to serve the pasta with the pizzaiola sauce for the *primo piatto* (first course), then the meat and any remaining sauce for the *secondo piatto* (main course).

SALT COD: the salt cod is desalted for several days in water, sometimes fried, then cooked like the meat. This dish was once served for Christmas meals in Campania.

ITS INGREDIENTS

MEAT

Tender slices of veal or young beef, preferably cut from the rump. The *scannello* (rump steak) of beef and the *scamone* (rump) of veal are perfect options.

THE TOMATO

Nothing beats fresh, seasonal tomatoes, ripened hanging on the vine in the summer sun. But a good-quality canned tomato, peeled naturally, does well, too. For the canned version, the preference is the Neapolitan varietal San Marzano.

OREGANO

When used fresh, this aromatic herb develops an inimitable fragrance. But it works very well in its dried form also. No problem substituting it with basil, as is often seen in Italy.

GARLIC

Garlic, nothing but garlic, and use fresh and juicy garlic (for those who may be tempted to replace it with onion . . .)!

OLIVE OIL

This is the only fat allowed to make this Neapolitan creation . . .

THE RECIPE

SERVES 4

- 14 ounces (400 g) ripe cherry tomatoes or good-quality canned peeled tomatoes
- 2 cloves garlic
- Olive oil
- 4 slices (about 4¼ ounces/120 g) veal or beef rump
- Fresh or dried oregano
- Salt and freshly ground black pepper

Wash and dry the tomatoes. Remove any stems, and cut the tomatoes in half. Peel the garlic cloves.

Heat 4 tablespoons (60 mL) of olive oil over high heat in a large high-sided skillet.

Brown the meat slices on each side. Remove them from the skillet and set aside.

Brown the whole garlic cloves on each side.

Reduce the heat slightly and add the tomatoes. If using canned tomatoes, coarsely crush them with a wooden spoon to release their juices.

Add the oregano, using only the leaves if it is fresh or crumbling it if it is dried. Let the sauce simmer for about 10 minutes.

Add the browned meat, a pinch of salt, and a few turns of the pepper mill. Cover the pan and cook for another 10 minutes, turning the meat halfway through the cooking time to allow even cooking. The tomato sauce should be thickened but not too dry.

Set aside several minutes to cool slightly, then add a drizzle of olive oil and serve.

A CHEESY VARIATION!

To further justify its name, pizzaiola can accommodate mozzarella! Slice some *fior di latte* mozzarella and place the slices on the meat just before the end of the cooking time. Cover the pan and let the cheese melt slightly. This dish becomes truly irresistible!

SKIP TO
THE STATES OF THE TOMATO, P. 30;
OREGANO, P. 340.

LEONARDO DA VINCI
AND THE TABLE

Painter, engineer, philosopher, writer . . . this great Florentine made an indelible mark in history thanks to his vast body of internationally renowned work. However, his lesser-known interest happened to be a sincere love for the art of the table.

LOÏC BIENASSIS

1452	1503–1506 OR 1513–1516	1515	1519
BORN IN VINCI	PAINTS *LA GIOCONDA*	INVITED BY KING FRANÇOIS I	DIES IN AMBOISE
(Tuscany)	(*Mona Lisa*)	to move to France	(Touraine)

SHOPPING LISTS

Starting from the 1480s, Leonardo penned dozens of notebooks written in mirror image (reversed and from right to left). Only a few of these works are known. They included not only his ideas, reflections, sketches, and diagrams, but also his shopping lists: eggs, melons, blackberries, grapes, mushrooms, flour, spices, sugar, vinegar, wine . . . purchases that were just everyday items needed for him and his household.

Was Leonardo a Vegetarian?

SOME EVIDENCE SUPPORTS THIS CLAIM:

→ In his writings, he mentions, on various occasions, the cruelty of men toward animals and the suffering they endured.

→ Biographer Giorgio Vasari reports that Leonardo bought caged birds at the markets in order to free them.

→ One of his contemporaries, explorer Andrea Corsali, who did not know Leonardo personally, wrote in a letter: "Some infidels called *guzzarati* [Hindus] do not consume anything that contains blood, nor do they allow anyone to hurt a living thing, such as our Leonardo da Vinci."

However, no direct evidence confirms that the great artist refused to consume meat, and we have no writing from his hand advocating a meatless diet.

FORGERIES

In 1987, two English authors, Jonathan and Shelagh Routh, published *Leonardo da Vinci's Notes on Cookery*, a book allegedly based on the *Codex Romanoff*, a manuscript of the great man, found in Russia. Leonardo is said to have recorded his recipes there, a treatise on table manners, and proposed the design of various kitchen utensils, and inventions. It was too good of a find to be true—and alas, it was a hoax.

Principles of Healthy Living, According to Leonardo

If you want to stay healthy, follow this diet:

Do not eat if you are not hungry,
and have a light supper; chew well, and
that which you welcome in yourself,
be well prepared and simple.

Whomever takes of medicine does harm to himself. Avoid anger and distress; stand up straight when you leave the table; do not give in to sleep at noon.

Be sober about wine. Take it frequently in small quantities, but not without meals or on an empty stomach, nor delay visits to the toilet; if you exercise, it should be moderate.

Do not lie facedown or with your head down. Cover yourself well at night; rest your head and keep your mind joyous; flee from lust and observe the diet.

From Sandro Masci, in *Leonardo da Vinci e la cucina rinascimentale* (*Leonardo da Vinci and Renaissance Cuisine*), Rome, Gremese, 2006, p. 120.

1495 · THE LAST SUPPER · 1498

On this famous fresco (made for the refectory of the church of Santa Maria delle Grazie in Milan), where it is difficult to distinguish certain details, Leonardo chose not to put lamb (Easter) on the menu but instead included a lot of bread, fish, and pomegranates. Most notably, grilled eels with orange wedges are depicted, which was a pairing in vogue at the time in Italy.

GREAT ORGANIZER OF BANQUETS

Leonardo da Vinci designed the backdrops for many festivals, such as in Milan, in the service of the Sforza family (1482–1499). He is said to have even selected a single cheese in the shape of a wedding cake, the *Montèbore*, at the wedding of Isabella of Aragon and Gian Galeazzo Sforza.

A Few Tips from Leonardo

His notebooks included designs for several machines related to food.

A WEIGHTED ROASTER

A weight drives a drum fitted with a large flywheel that rotates a cogged wheel placed perpendicularly, which in turn rotates two other cogged wheels on which the pins are attached. An aerodynamic brake above the device controls the rotation of the drums.

A SMOKE ROASTER

Leonardo has sometimes been credited with inventing this system, although probably erroneously. It involves a horizontal wheel placed in the chimney flue and activated by hot air from the fireplace.

"This is the real method used to cook roasts: depending on the low or high temperature of the hearth, the piece to be roasted will turn slowly or quickly."

BUT ALSO . . .

Drawings of an olive-pressing machine, another for grinding grains, and even a recipe for "thirst-quenching and fresh rose water with sugar and lemon, strained through a cloth."

(*Codex Atlanticus*, fol. 482 r.)

SKIP TO
SACROSANCT CUISINE, P. 346; ITALY'S BEAUTIFUL CHEESES, P. 222; IMAGINARY MUSEUM, P. 72.

THE HISTORY OF PIZZA

How did the Neapolitan tradition of pizza and the art of the *pizzaiolo* get from the streets to the halls of UNESCO?

ANTONIO PUZZI

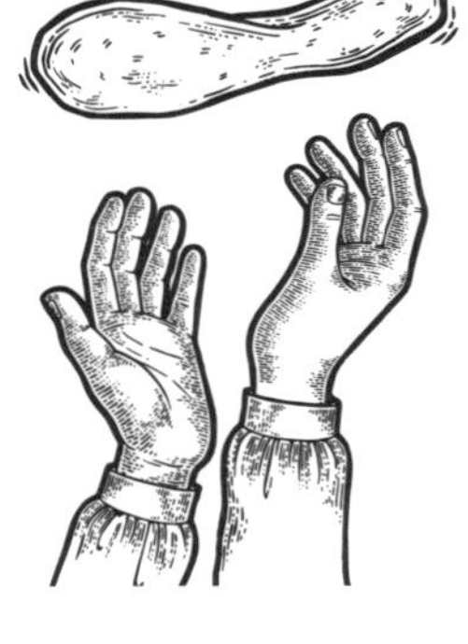

ETYMOLOGY

The word *pizza* is first mentioned in a Latin text dating from 997 CE, preserved in the archives of the Gaeta cathedral (Lazio). Its origins are debated, but could be either . . .

GREEK: the term *pizza* derives from the Greek *pitta* (flatbread or flaky cake), which would have spread, between the seventh and ninth centuries, to become part of the language of the people of southern Italy, controlled at the time by the Byzantine Empire.

OR GERMANIC: the Gothic word *bizzo* or *pizzo* (bite or piece of bread) is said to have been introduced in Italy in the sixth century during the Lombard invasion. This is the most likely theory.

Pizzaioli

UNESCO recognizes three categories of pizzaioli:

The *maestro pizzaiolo*, the person who prepares pizza. He is the guardian of tradition and the one who passes down the technique for making the dough.

•

The apprentice pizzaiolo (or *guaglione*, or the second pizzaiolo), who learns the secrets from the master.

•

The baker (*fornaio*), who shapes and bakes the dough into disks made from the *panetti*.

WHY IN NAPLES?

According to historians Antonio and Donatella Mattozzi, several factors contributed to Naples being the natural birthplace of pizza and encouraging its spread:

THE NATURAL ENVIRONMENT
Since the sixteenth century, flour-based doughs had been made in this region.

THE SOCIAL CONTEXT
Between the seventeenth and eighteenth centuries, Naples recorded enormous demographic growth, particularly from peasants escaping the misery of the countryside and local lords whose political power grew ever stronger. The city was heavily populated with often unemployed and homeless people who needed a nutritious and inexpensive meal.

DEMOGRAPHIC SPRAWL
in the sixteenth century, Naples was the most populous city in Europe.

· CHRONOLOGY ·

IT WAS AENEAS, the ancestor of the "Italian peoples," who ate the first "pizza" on the banks of the Tiber. In Virgil's *Aeneid* (VII, 107–34), the Trojans, gripped by hunger, eat their *mensa*, a word that, in this text, refers to a wheaten (*Cereale solum*) flat bread, usually used as a base on which vegetables (*pomis agrestibus*) were placed.

IN 1195, a document of the Roman Curia mentions *pizis* (pizzas) prepared with cheese and cooked over a wood fire in the town of Penne (Abruzzo). Then, several literary references appear: poet Benedetto Di Falco (1535) writes that *focaccia* is called *pizza* in Neapolitan; Bartolomeo Scappi cites the Neapolitan pizza in his *Opera* in 1570 and gives the recipe.

THE FIRST PIZZERIA is said to have been created in Naples in 1738 when, to diversify its offerings, a restaurant equipped with an oven decided to open what was to become Antica Pizzeria Port'Alba.

BETWEEN 1738 AND THE END OF THE NINETEENTH CENTURY, a new pizzeria opens every year in Naples.

IN 1834, tables appear in *pizzeries*. It is said that it was Antica Pizzeria Port'Alba that introduced this new idea.

ALEXANDRE DUMAS evokes *pizze* for delivery in *Le Corricolo* (1843), just like Matilde Serao, founder of the newspaper *Il Mattino*, in her book *Il ventre di Napoli* (*The Belly of Naples*, 1884). However, she considered these pizze were good only for the Neapolitans.

IN 1889, the visit of Queen Margherita of Savoy, first queen of the Kingdom of Italy, took pizza outside the walls of Naples to the lands of the Bourbons.

EMIGRATION from southern Italy to northern Italy and throughout the world did the rest. It was the beginning of a story that reached its climax on December 7, 2017, when UNESCO included the art of Neapolitan *pizzaiuolo* on the list of the Intangible Cultural Heritage of Humanity.

PIZZA-MAKING TOOLS	
THE HANDS	**THE PROOFING ROOM**
To make the dough and spread it out according to the artistic methods (as the pizzaiolo Franco Pepe does), to crush the San Marzano tomatoes, and to slice the mozzarella.	Traditionally, proofing and aging were done at room temperature, but today temperature-controlled rooms (*cella*) are used.
THE KNEADING MACHINE	**THE PEEL**
Today, the dough is barely kneaded by hand to prevent it from getting too hot and becoming too difficult to work with once it has risen. The use of an *impastatrice* (kneading machine) makes it possible to obtain a dough that is richer in water and closer to modern tastes.	The first *pala* (pizza peel) is the one on which the pizza maker places the pizza to transfer it into the oven. Using a second pala, smaller and more round, the baker turns the pizza during cooking. When the pizza is ready, the baker removes it from the oven using the first pala.
THE BOX	**THE MARBLE**
Formerly made of wood, *cassette* are now almost exclusively plastic. The *panetti* (small dough disks) wait there until cooked, once *staglio* (hand shaping) has been done.	Just before baking, the panetti are placed on a *banco in marmo* (marble work surface). Using a little semolina or rice flour, the dough disks are shaped by punching them (*ammaccatura*), then topped with ingredients taken from small bowls.

How to recognize Neapolitan pizza?

THE SIZE

According to the production specifications for Verace Pizza Napoletana (VPN, "True Neapolitan Pizza"):

→ Its diameter must not exceed 14 inches (35 cm); its *cornicione* (the edge) must be golden, 1/3 to 3/4 inch (1 to 2 cm) thick; and its center must have a thickness of about 4 mm, +/− 10 percent. The crust should be golden but not burnt.

→ It must be tender to the touch and to the taste, elastic, and easy to fold into a "wallet" (in fourths).

→ Its flavor must be a perfect balance between the tangy flavor of tomato, the sweetness of mozzarella, the fruity and spicy notes of garlic and oil, and herbaceous notes of basil and oregano. The cornicione should have the aroma and taste of freshly baked bread.

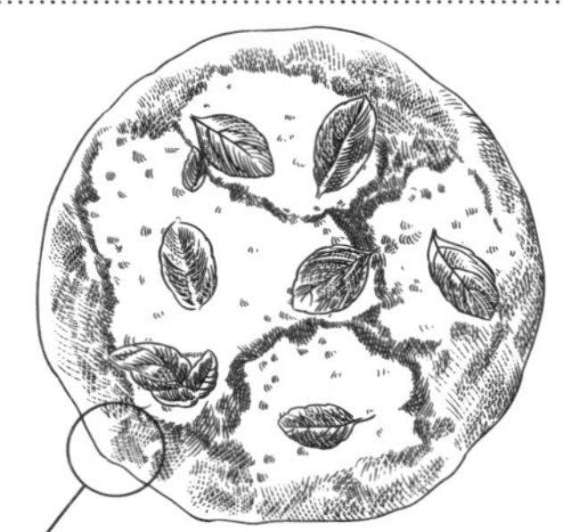

THE PREPARATION

Until 2019, the Disciplinare della Vera Pizza Napoletana (Specifications for True Neapolitan Pizza) required the use of baker's yeast. Today, the use of natural starter (sourdough) is also accepted thanks to the commitment of master pizzaiolo Salvatore De Rinaldi. You should dilute the yeast, incorporate *tipo* (type) 0 or 00 flour (or all-purpose or pastry flour), then the salt, and let the dough rise for several hours. After the first thirty minutes, the dough should be "folded," and two hours later, shaped into *panetti* (small dough disks) of approximately 10 ounces (280 g).

THE COOKING

Neapolitan pizza is baked in a Neapolitan dome-shaped oven, the inside of which is made of terra-cotta from Sorrento. This oven, built by specialized craftspeople, is fueled by wood (although there are modern gas or electric versions). Its temperature must reach between 800° and 900°F (430° and 480°C). Cooking is done by induction, convection, or thermal radiation.

Code Name

Neapolitan *pizzaioli* do not refer to the dough by a name but by number

50

When the "50" reaches the *punto di pasta* (point ready to be cooked), it is said to be *kalò*, which means "good" in Greek.

The number *50* is used because it represents the bread in the *Smorfia*, a book of interpretations of dreams derived from the Kabbalah and much appreciated by the Neapolitans.

HER MAJESTY MARGHERITA

"Majesty, allow this pizza to bear your name." This is what chef Raffaele Esposito said when, in 1889, the steward of Real Casa asked him to reveal to Queen Margherita of Savoy the name of his pizza topped with slices of mozzarella and San Marzano tomatoes and seasoned with basil and oil.

He may not be the inventor, but he was the one who prepared it for the queen in the bread oven in the Torre Garden of the Reggia di Capodimonte in the hills of Naples.

SKIP TO
PIZZE NAPOLETANE, P. 54; PIZZA FRITTA (FRIED PIZZA), P. 218.

GRAPES

Although primarily associated with the production of wine and condiments, the *uva* (grape), found in markets from July to December, can also be enjoyed raw, salty, sweet, or distilled into spirits.

ALESSANDRA PIERINI

FROM THE VINE TO THE TABLE

Italy is the largest producer of grapes in Europe, with the majority of the vines growing in Sicily and Apulia. The table varietals (*Vitis vinifera*, as for all grapes), as compared to the varietals used for winemaking, are less tart and less acidic and have a plumper pulp and thinner skin. These grapes were present on the tables of ancient Rome, but they became more prominent in Italy during the postwar years when imported varietals, which have now become part of everyday consumption, were added along with native varietals.

Uva Italia

Named the "ideal grape," the Italia cultivar has large and tempting clusters, sweet pulp, smooth skin, golden and spherical seeds, and good conservation. This grape, harvested starting in October, has all the best attributes and is one of the most produced and exported varietals, even if it is more desired for its name than for its attributes.

RECIPE

SUGOLI, OR CREMA D'UVA, SUGO D'UVA, BUDINO D'UVA, PAPPA D'UVA

Emilia-Romagna, Veneto, Lombardy

This is a thickened puddinglike mixture made from grape juice collected during harvest. It can be eaten on its own, with *sbrisolona* (a Lombard shortbread tart), or with a wine vinified from the same grape used to make it, such as a Lambrusco or Malvasia.

MAKES 4 RAMEKINS

2¼ pounds (1 kg) grapes
½ cup (100 g) sugar
⅔ cup (60 g) cornstarch

- Place the grapes in a saucepan with ¼ cup (50 g) of the sugar and 2 tablespoons (30 mL) of water. Bring to a boil, stirring to dissolve the sugar, then reduce the heat and cook for 15 minutes.
- Let cool, then strain the juice into a saucepan and add the remaining ¼ cup (50 g) sugar. Bring to a boil, then reduce the heat. Combine the cornstarch with a scant ¼ cup (50 mL) water and add it to the pan. Stir to combine. Cook, stirring frequently, until the mixture thickens, then immediately remove it from the heat and divide it among four ramekins.
- Let cool, then refrigerate until chilled before serving.

IN COOKING

RAW—to nibble as a treat or to add to fruit salad; with bread rubbed with garlic and tomatoes (*soma d'aj*, Piedmont); in a salad with Treviso radicchio and pears or with walnuts and a pungent Gorgonzola. Distilled into fruit-based alcohols or in grappa (*sotto spirito*); for granitas and sorbets.

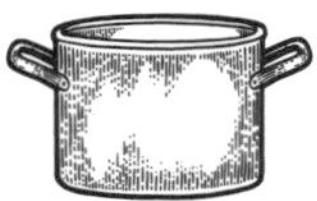

COOKED—with liver, game, quail, or pork; in *agrodolce* (sweet-and-sour sauce) for roasts, meat and vegetable stews, or with cheeses; *la cugnà*, a sauce for cheeses, or *bollito misto* (Piedmont). In pastries: on *schiacciata con'uva, pane pazzo* (Tuscany), crostata (a free-form rustic pie with fruit or preserves); gelled preparations.

DRIED—(*uva passa, uvetta*, or *sultanina*) in the sun or under hot air using very sweet varietals (Zibibbo, a grape varietal from the island of Pantelleria, is the most famous). Often used with pine nuts (*caponata, pasta con le sarde, sarde in beccafico*), pork, or fish. In pastry with orange, cinnamon, vanilla, and chocolate (panettone, *pandolce, zaleti*, Venetian cookies).

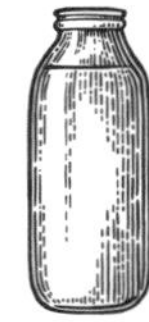

JUS—inspired by the Romans, the recipe consists of reducing the juice of ripe, sweet grapes by three-fourths to obtain a thickened, caramelized syrup. The syrup, known as *mosto cotto, vincotto* (Abruzzo and Molise), *saba* (Emilia-Romagna), *sapa* (Sardinia), or *savor reggiano* (Emilia-Romagna), is used as a sweetener or condiment.

① UVA VITTORIA

Southern Italy

HARVEST—July to August; round fruits, plump, greenish color, thick skin, and sweet and juicy flesh.

② UVA PIZZUTELLA OR UVA CORNA OR DITO DI DONNA (LADY'S FINGER)

Apulia

HARVEST—end of September; elongated and pointed golden-yellow fruits, crunchy and pleasant pulp, thin but firm skin. It can also be black and more acidic. Its name comes from the word *pizzuta*, meaning "pointed like a horn."

③ SUPERNOVA

South-central Italy

HARVEST—August to September; medium-size fruits, elongated, pinkish red, thin skin, juicy pulp, seedless, very aromatic and sweet taste. Ideal for drying.

④ UVA FRAGOLA (STRAWBERRY GRAPE) OR UVA AMERICANA OR UVA ISABELLA

Northern Italy

HARVEST—end of September; medium size, black-purple fruits, thick skin, syrupy pulp; pronounced flavor of red fruits, especially wild strawberries. Those of American origin are resistant to disease and proliferated after the phylloxera crisis. Widely trellised.

⑤ RED GLOBE

Apulia

HARVEST—from September to December; very large, red-violet, firm, crunchy, and very sweet.

⑥ NERA MICHELE PALIERI

Throughout Italy

HARVEST—August to September; round, medium, black-purple fruits, tough but thin skin, firm pulp, sweet, juicy, and fleshy. It is named after its creator.

⑦ MOSCATO NERO

Throughout Italy

HARVEST—August to September; medium-size purplish-black fruits, uniform and intense, thick and consistent skin, fleshy, sweet, and juicy pulp with a pleasant taste of muscat.

SKIP TO
GATHERING GRAPES, P. 158; COOKIES, P. 154; BALSAMIC VINEGAR, P. 280; PANETTONE, P. 96.

①
②
③
④
⑤
⑥
⑦

SEASON
ESTATE (SUMMER)

CATEGORY
PIATTO UNICO, SECONDO PIATTO (SINGLE COURSE/ MAIN COURSE)

LEVEL
FACILE (EASY)

PARMIGIANA DI MELANZANE

EGGPLANT PARMIGIANA

RICETTA *Iconica* RICETTA

Its beginnings are a geographic enigma, but the dish itself serves as an emblem of Italy's summertime cuisine. Here is a spotlight on this gratin of eggplant and Parmesan.

FRANÇOIS-RÉGIS GAUDRY

"MELANZANE ALLA PARMIGIANA" OR *"PARMIGIANA DI MELANZANE"*?

→ "*Alla parmigiana*" (Parmesan-style) has a relation with the city of Parma, according to the *Devoto-Oli* dictionary (1971), which states: "'in the style of the Parmesans,' that is to say the inhabitants of the city of Parma, means to cook the vegetables in layers."

→ To refer to the general recipe as discussed here, only the expression *parmigiana di melanzane* is valid, according to historian Massimo Montanari. The term *parmigiana*, as it was called in cookbooks from the fourteenth and fifteenth centuries, comes from the Latin *parma*, meaning "shield," due to the rounded appearance of the dish.

FROM PARMA, NAPLES, OR SICILY?

PARMA claims the use of Parmesan cheese in this recipe, although older recipes include only pecorino, Scamorza, or *caciocavallo*. In many cooking treatises, the phrase *alla parmigiana* attests to the presence of Parmigiano. In his famous work *Il cuoco galante*, culinary author Vincenzo Corrado (eighteenth to nineteenth centuries) describes *zucche lunghe alla parmigiana*, zucchini coated with flour, fried, and layered au gratin with a Parmesan and butter sauce. Could this be the ancestor of eggplant parmigiana?

NAPLES supports the writings of a local named Ippolito Cavalcanti, the first cook to codify a modern recipe for parmigiana. In the appendices, written in the Neapolitan language, added in 1839 to his work *Cucina teorico-pratica* (*Theoretical and Practical Cuisine*), he refers to *melanzane alla parmigiana*: "And you will fry them; then you will arrange them in a saucepan layer by layer with cheese, basil, and a ragout bouillon, or with tomato sauce; and, covered, you will stew them." The Neapolitans assure us that the cheese suggested was mozzarella.

SICILY, where this dish is called *parmigiana di melanzana*. The word *parmigiana* comes from the Sicilian *parmiciana* (itself derived from the Latin *parma*), which means wooden shutter slats, evoking the arrangement of the eggplant slices in the dish. Another theory: the name comes from the Arabic *al-badingian* (aubergine, another name for eggplant), the letters *p* and *b* having a similar pronunciation. Was Sicily, by way of the Arabs, the gateway to this vegetable-fruit in the fifteenth century? The word *petronciana*, the Sicilian term for the type of eggplant used in this dish, could confirm this theory . . .

History might agree with everyone: Naples and Sicily were part of the Kingdom of the Two Sicilies, and family ties with the Duchy of Parma may explain the strong culinary influences between the three regions.

THE RECIPE

Denise Solier-Gaudry has always made this recipe. She got it from her mother, a native of Bastia, who herself got it from an Italian aunt in the family, Lucile Montefusco.

SERVES 8

6 eggplant

¼ cup plus 2 tablespoons (100 g) coarse salt

3 balls *fior di latte* mozzarella

1 cup (250 mL) olive oil, plus more for drizzling

1 onion, finely chopped

1 clove garlic, finely chopped

1½ pounds (700 g) diced tomatoes

1 teaspoon (4 g) sugar

Salt

1½ cups (150 g) grated Parmesan cheese

8 basil leaves, coarsely chopped

Freshly ground black pepper

Wash and dry the eggplant, then trim them and cut into ⅓-inch-thick (1 cm) slices using a mandoline. Layer the slices in a colander, sprinkling coarse salt between each layer. Set a plate on top of the eggplant and a weight on top of the plate, and let drain for 1 hour.

Cut the fior di latte into cubes and drain in a separate colander.

In a saucepan, heat a drizzle of olive oil over medium heat. Add the onion and garlic, then the tomatoes, sugar, and a pinch of salt. Simmer for 30 minutes, until the sauce is fairly reduced and thickened.

Rinse the eggplants under cold water to remove the salt. Dry them thoroughly. Heat the 1 cup (250 mL) olive oil in a skillet over medium heat, then fry the eggplant slices on both sides. Transfer them to a paper towel–lined plate.

Preheat the oven to 400°F (200°C).

In a shallow baking dish, spread a little of the tomato sauce. Arrange the eggplant slices on top, overlapping them slightly. Cover with a little tomato sauce, sprinkle with some of the Parmesan, some cubes of fior di latte, and some basil. Season with pepper. Continue layering in this way until all the eggplant and fior di latte have been used. Finish with a layer of tomato sauce, then Parmesan. Bake for 1 hour 30 minutes.

THE VARIATIONS

NEAPOLITAN

Eggplant slices are lightly floured, dredged in beaten egg (or *pastella*, a kind of crêpe batter), and fried. This results in richer, but fattier, fried eggplant.

SICILIAN

Provola dei Nebrodi and pecorino cheeses are preferred here, with chopped hard-boiled eggs added between the layers. Sometimes you can find prosciutto or anchovy fillets added.

And the Salento version?

In Lecce (Apulia), they celebrate the patron saint of the city, Sant'Oronzo (August 26), by enjoying the traditional parmigiana di melanzane the evening before. This is a "poor man's" dish filled with all possible ingredients: mozzarella or Scamorza, eggs, sometimes even meatballs, mortadella, and ham.

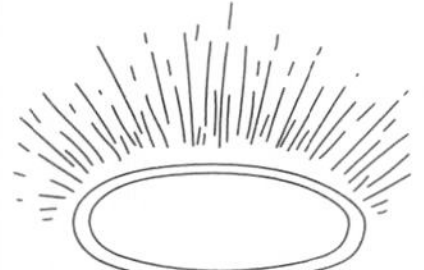

SKIP TO
EGGPLANT, P. 266;
PARMIGIANO-REGGIANO, P. 86.

THE FORK: AN ITALIAN INVENTION?

It is common to hear the claim that Renaissance Italy gave the fork to the rest of Europe. Is this legend or truth?

LOÏC BIENASSIS

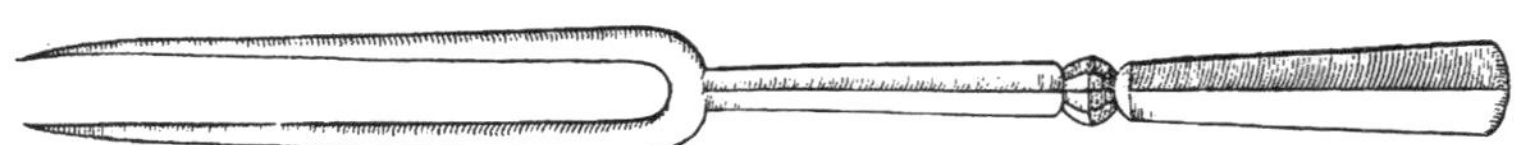

Is it Byzantium?

A Byzantine princess who arrived to marry a doge of Venice—probably Maria Argyre, who married the son of the doge Pietro II Orseolo in 1004—would have come upon the fork in Italy. This widely held historical theory is based on the account of the clergyman Pierre Damien (circa 1007 to 1072):

The Doge of Venice had a wife from Constantinople. . . . She did not touch the food with her hands, her food was cut by her eunuchs into tiny pieces, which she then held with sort of little golden two-pronged pitchforks, licking them with her tongue.

(Translated from *S. Petri Damiani . . . Opera Omnia*, II, Paris, Jacques-Paul Migne, 1853, col. 744.)

The use of the fork is not confirmed thereafter by any source. It therefore seems that in Italy, as elsewhere in Europe, it was the knife from which everyone would eat from their plate before eating with their hands.

However, several iconographic records suggest that two-pronged forks (*lingula*) may have been used as individual cutlery in certain regions of Italy during the eleventh century.

Conquering Europe

From Italy, the fork spread throughout the continent. In France, it began to attract the upper aristocracy in the sixteenth century, counter to legends that credit Catherine de' Medici with the fork's popularization. In 1713, Princess Palatine, sister-in-law of Louis XIV, reported in a letter that the Sun King had prohibited his grandsons to use forks. However, its use spread slowly, and it was firmly adopted only during the eighteenth century. It then increasingly became a luxury object, until eventually four-pronged forks became commonplace.

KEEPING OUR HANDS OUT OF OUR PASTA

It wasn't until the turn of the thirteenth and fourteenth centuries and the appearance of *Liber de coquina* that any mention of a fork can be found. This culinary manuscript, written anonymously in Latin in southern Italy, details the preparation of lasagna and recommends consuming the dish with a pointed wooden tool (*uno punctorio ligneo*).

In *Il trecentonovelle*, a book composed from 1380 to 1390 by the Tuscan Franco Sacchetti, the *forchetta* is indeed used to eat pasta. The adoption—or the return?—of the fork could be linked to this early taste for pasta among the Italians . . .

The small utensil became commonplace on the table of the elite classes in the following century, as a fresco by the painter Botticelli attests, and it finally conquered all social circles in the seventeenth century and later.

AND THE FOUR-PRONGED FORK?

The present iteration of the fork appeared, according to a Neapolitan legend, from the inventive spirit of Gennaro Spadaccini, the chamberlain of King Ferdinand IV of the Two Sicilies (1759–1816). The sovereign, not wanting to give up his favorite dish of spaghetti with tomato sauce, which was hardly suited to the decorum of the court, instructed his chamberlain to find a solution. By adding two additional prongs and making all four shorter and blunter, he allowed His Majesty—and his subjects!—to twirl their spaghetti and safely bring the utensil closer to their mouths. What a royal idea!

SKIP TO
EQUIPMENT, P. 6.

PASTA AND BEANS

The marriage between *pasta e legumi* is celebrated from north to south in Italy. Here is an inventory of these "poor" foods that are rich in flavor.

ILARIA BRUNETTI

 FAGIOLI 
COMMON BEANS

PASTA ALL'UOVO
EGG PASTA

PASTA E FASOI [SOUP]—*Veneto* (SEE OPPOSITE)
Borlotti or lamon IGP beans, partly puréed, cooked with pork rind or bacon. Tagliatelle or *maltagliati* is cooked in the soup. In Padua, add *soffritto* (cooked mixture of diced onion, celery, carrot), pancetta, and fresh bean broth and serve with garlic and parsley.

PASTA E FAGIOLI [SOUP]—*Piedmont*
Borlotti beans cooked with soffritto, potatoes, pancetta, and bacon; with maltagliati.

PASTA E FAGIOLI [SOUP]—*Emilia-Romagna*
Borlotti beans with tomato sauce and maltagliati cooked in the soup; very thick.

PASTINA
SMALL PASTA FOR SOUPS

PASTA E FAGIOLI [SOUP]—*Tuscany*
Cannellini beans, seasoned with garlic, sage, and rosemary, blended, to cook with *tubettini, ditalini rigati,* or *cannolicchi.*

PATARNOSCI CULLE COZZE E PASULI—*Apulia*
White beans (*pasuli*) with cherry tomatoes, mussels, and tubettini (*patarnosci* in local dialect) or cavatelli.

PASTA E FAGIOLI ALLA FRIULANA [SOUP]—*Friuli*
Soffritto, borlotti beans (from Carnia), potatoes blended with ditalini or broken spaghetti. You can season this dish with *pestât* (a mixture of bacon, vegetables, and herbs, a Slow Food sentinel). In Pordenone, pig's feet are added.

PASTA CORTA
SHORT PASTAS

PASTA E FAGIOLI ALLA NAPOLETANA [SOUP]—*Campania*
Cannellini beans, *tondini* (white beans) with garlic and cherry tomatoes, all seasoned with black pepper. Some of the beans are puréed. With *pasta mista* (a mixture of short pasta formats) cooked in the soup, very thick. Mussels can be added.

CAVATELLI, FAGIOLI E COZZE—*Apulia*
Typical of Taranto, with white beans from Zollino, mussels, garlic, and cherry tomatoes.

TACCOZZE E FAGIOLI—*Molise*
Beans, such as Acquaviva d'Isemia's white (Slow Food), are cooked just with a celery leaf and served with diamond-shaped pasta (*taccozze*) on the side; the entire preparation is seasoned with basil and chile.

CICERCHIE 
LEGUMES OR PEAS

PASTA CORTA
SHORT PASTA

SAGNE E CICERCHIE [SOUP]—*Molise* and *Abruzzo* (SEE OPPOSITE)
Legumes (vetch), onions, tomatoes, chile, and *adacciata* (the fat of ham cooked with basil, parsley, and garlic). Fresh pasta without eggs (*sagne*) is cooked separately.

PASTA LUNGA
LONG PASTA

LAGANE E CICERCHIE [SOUP]—*Campania*
Legumes (vetch) are cooked with garlic and tomatoes. Fresh pasta without eggs is cooked separately.

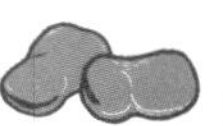 FAVE 
FAVA (BROAD) BEANS

PASTA CORTA
SHORT PASTA

FAVE CON I LOLLI [SOUP]—*Sicily*
A dish from Modica, with dried fava eans, boiled, then cooked with onions, carrots, and celery, then with *lolli* (a fresh pasta similar to cavatelli).

PASTA LUNGA
LONG PASTA

FAVE E LASAGNETTE—*Apulia*
Fresh pasta without eggs, served with a purée of dried fava beans.

 LENTICCHIE 
LENTILS

PASTA ALL'UOVO
EGG PASTA

LASAGNE ALLE LENTICCHIE—*Lazio*
Boiled lentils cooked with garlic, thyme, and bacon and blended into a purée. Alternating layers of lasagna noodles, lentil purée, whole lentils, and Parmesan cheese are then prepared.

PASTINA
SMALL PASTA FOR SOUPS

PASTA E LENTICCHIE [SOUP]—*Southern Italy* (SEE OPPOSITE)
Lentils cooked with garlic, sometimes tomatoes and/or celery or carrots. With broken tubettini, spaghetti, or linguine, cooked in lentils.

PASTA CORTA
SHORT PASTA

MACCO DI FAVE E FINOCCHIETTO [SOUP]—*Sicily*
Broken spaghettini cooked in a mash of dried beans. In season, squash purée can be added.

PASTA LUNGA
LONG PASTA

LAGANE E LENTICCHIE—*Basilicata*
Lentils, flavored with garlic and chile, added to *lagane* (fresh pasta made from durum wheat semolina flour and water, wider and shorter than tagliatelle), cooked separately. They are used in the same way as beans.

 CECI 
CHICKPEAS

PASTA ALL'UOVO
EGG PASTA

PAPPARDELLE O TAGLIOLINI E CECI [SOUP]—*Tuscany*
Pasta and chickpeas cooked with some tomatoes and rosemary. It is also found with ditalini.

PASTINA
SMALL PASTA FOR SOUPS

PASTA E CECI ALLA ROMANA [SOUP]
Latzio
Soffritto with anchovies, seasoned with rosemary. Made with ditalini.

MINESTRA DI CECI E ZARCHE [SOUP]—*Sicily*
Wild chard (*zarche*) and onions. With cavatelli or ditalini.

PASTA CORTA
SHORT PASTA

SAGNETTE E CECI [SOUP]—*Abruzzo*
Sagnette (small rectangular pasta without eggs) cooked with chickpeas (preferably from Navelli, a Slow Food sentinel), flavored with garlic and chile. Sometimes tomatoes or pancetta are added.

PASTA LUNGA
LONG PASTA

CICERI E TRIA—*Apulia*
Chickpeas cooked with garlic, cherry tomatoes, bay leaf, celery, onions, and parsley. The pasta (*tria*) is cooked separately, one part fried until crispy, the other cooked in the classic way. They are added at serving time.

LAGANE E CECI OU CICIARI [SOUP]—*Calabria, Campania, Basilicata*
Lagane pasta cooked with chickpeas.
Calabria: with garlic and chile.
Campania: with garlic, chile, and parsley, and finished with olive oil when serving.
Basilicata: a good amount of tomato sauce.

LAGANE, CECI, BACCALÀ—*Apulia*
Pasta and chickpeas served with tomato sauce and salt cod.

VIRTÙ TERAMANE (ABRUZZO), THE EVERYTHING SOUP

Commonly served on May 1, this bountiful soup is the coming together of the first vegetables of spring, the last ones of winter, and the leftovers from the pantry emptied to make room for the new season. Included are dried and fresh legumes; many vegetables and aromatic herbs; pork rind, bacon, or pancetta; meatballs; fresh pasta in different sizes; and stuffed pasta—all cooked separately before being stirred together at the end.

RECIPES

PASTA E LENTICCHIE (PASTA AND LENTILS)

This is a family recipe of Nadia Postiglione, a gourmet and food historian from Campania.

SERVES 4

1⅔ cups (320 g) dried lentils

2 cloves garlic, peeled

1 stalk celery, chopped

1 bay leaf

2 cherry tomatoes or Piennolo tomatoes, halved

Salt

8½ ounces (240 g) broken spaghetti or linguine, or ditalini

Freshly ground black pepper

Extra-virgin olive oil

- Rinse the lentils and place them in a large saucepan. Cover them with cold unsalted water (about three times their volume in water), add the garlic, celery, bay leaf, and tomatoes, and cook for 20 to 30 minutes.
- Season with salt, remove the celery and bay leaf, then add the pasta and simmer until the pasta is cooked, adding boiling water if necessary. The consistency of the soup should be quite thick. Season with pepper.
- Serve with 1 tablespoon (15 mL) of olive oil drizzled over the top of each bowl.

PASTA E FASOI (FASIOI IN BELLUNO DIALECT) (PASTA AND BEANS)

This recipe comes from Rosina Bridda (aka "Nonna Rosi" to contributor Max Bustreo) from Paiane, in the province of Belluno.

SERVES 4

3½ ounces (100 g) pork rind

Olive oil

1 onion, studded with several cloves

1 carrot, chopped

1 stalk celery, peeled and chopped

1 sprig rosemary

2¾ cups (500 g) dried lamon beans, soaked for 12 hours and drained

Salt and freshly ground black pepper

5¼ ounces (150 g) thick tagliatelle or ditalini

Wine vinegar

- Clean the pork rind, then blanch it in salted boiling water. Drain.
- Cut the pork rind into strips and brown it in a large saucepan with a drizzle of olive oil. Add about 6 cups (1.5 L) water, the clove-studded onion, the carrot, celery, rosemary, and beans. Season with salt and pepper. Bring to a boil, then cook over low heat for 2 hours, or until the beans are tender, adding water if necessary.
- Remove the onion. In a blender, combine the vegetables and three-fourths of the beans (without the broth) and purée. Return everything to the pan with the whole beans and pork rind. Stir to obtain a fairly thick consistency.
- Bring to a boil, add the pasta, and cook for 10 to 15 minutes. Turn off the heat, cover, and let sit for 15 minutes. Add a drizzle of vinegar and season with salt and pepper. Serve with a drizzle of olive oil. This soup is also excellent served cold the next day.

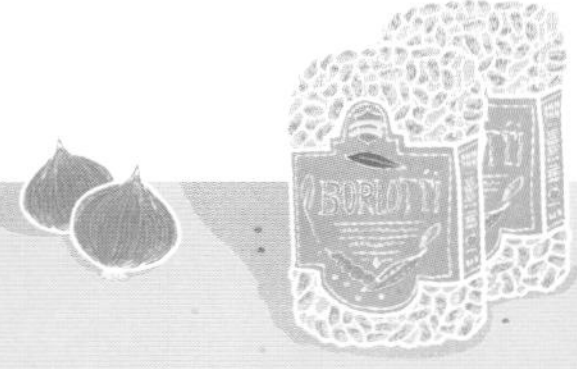

SAGNE E CICERCHIE SAGNE (RECTANGULAR PASTA) AND LEGUMES

This traditional recipe, which requires making pasta by hand, is the most widespread!

SERVES 4

4 cups (600 g) dried legumes (favas, peas), soaked overnight in water

1 clove garlic, peeled

Salt

For the *sagne* (pasta)

2 cups (250 g) all-purpose flour

1⅓ cups (250 g) durum wheat semolina flour

1 pinch salt

For the soup

1 clove garlic, peeled

1 onion

3 ounces (80 g) ham fat trimmings

Scant ⅔ cup (150 mL) olive oil

12 ounces (350 g) peeled tomatoes, diced

1 chile, seeded

1 small bunch basil, coarsely chopped

1 small bunch parsley, coarsely chopped

Salt and freshly ground black pepper

- Drain the legumes and transfer to a saucepan with 1 garlic clove and water to cover. Cook until the legumes become tender, about 1 hour. Season with salt, then drain, reserving the cooking water.

MAKE THE *SAGNE*

- Combine the all-purpose and semolina flours and the salt on a work surface. Add just enough water to obtain a soft but firm dough. Work the dough by hand until smooth and homogeneous. Cover and let stand for 30 minutes.
- Roll out the dough with a rolling pin or a pasta rolling machine to a thickness of 2 mm, then cut the dough into irregular diamond shapes about 1½ inches (4 cm) long.

MAKE THE SOUP

- Finely chop the garlic and onion. Chop the fat trimmings. Heat a drizzle of oil in a saucepan. Add the garlic, onion, and fat and cook until the onion is translucent.
- Add the tomatoes, chile, basil, and parsley and cook for 15 minutes.
- Add the beans along with a ladleful of the reserved cooking water.
- Cook the pasta in a pot of salted boiling water for several minutes, then drain and add it to the saucepan. Let cook for another 5 minutes over low heat. Season with salt and pepper and a drizzle of olive oil. Serve.

SKIP TO
THE SOUPS OF ITALY, P. 146.

THE OTHER PROMISED LAND

With a presence in Europe that extends far back into history, Italian Jewish communities have left innumerable imprints on the peninsula's culinary landscape.

FRÉDÉRIC LALY-BARAGLIOLI

CULTURAL CROSSROADS

→ Italy is a place where not only an original community of Jews settled—the Italkim—starting from the second century BCE, but also where Sephardic, Ashkenazi, and Asian diasporic communities settled.

→ After having surpassed a population of 50,000 at the beginning of World War II, Italian Jews have decreased to approximately 35,000 today.

→ Nearly a hundred *giudecche* (open Jewish districts) and around fifty Jewish ghettos from the past still thrive today with a rich culinary heritage.

The chicken or the egg?

Jewish and regional Italian culinary cultures are so intertwined that it is often difficult to determine which grew out from the other. This gives rise to the origin stories of many iconic recipes . . .

→ Dishes *alla giudia* or *alla mosaica* ("of Moses"), referring to dishes fried, marinated, or using pine nuts and raisins or simply tomato, are considered Jewish.

→ Certain dishes based on squash, artichoke, onion, fennel, and especially eggplant are attributed to Jewish origins because the community contributed to the dissemination of these vegetables. Pellegrino Artusi underlined this as early as 1891 in *La scienza in cucina e l'arte di mangiar bene* (*Science in the Kitchen and the Art of Eating Well*): "Eggplants were considered *cibo da ebrei* [Jewish food], which showed they always had a better sense for such things than did the Christians."

→ At the same time, Italian Jews claim culinary authorship of iconic Italian recipes because they are considered compatible with kosher regulations: *sarde in saor* and Venetian *bigoli in salsa, carciofi alla romana, cacciucco livournais, risotto alla milanese, tortelli di zucca ferrarais, pan di Spagna, bocca di dama*, or *torta al mascarpone* (an ancestor of tiramisu) . . .

From communities come cuisines

Despite their diversity, some factors of Italian Jewish foods are considered unchanging . . .

•

RELIGIOUS (KOSHER)

The ban on pork and certain other animals and no mixing of meat and dairy products have involved a necessary adaptation of Italian *ricettario* and the development of a cuisine rich in vegetables. Respecting Shabbat encourages specific cooking and preserving approaches.

•

SOCIOLOGICAL

The establishment of ghettos imposed from the sixteenth century onward led to the disappearance of an aristocratic Jewish cuisine, supplanted by *cucina povera*: offal and less noble meats, disregarded vegetables, fried foods, and street food . . .

•

GEOGRAPHICAL

As many Jewish dishes as there are Jewish communities—Roman, Venetian, Livorn, Ferraraise—were born out of the adaptation of local products and recipes to Kashrut (the food code of the Hebrew Bible.

•

EXOTIC

Asian traces of southern and Sephardic influences (spices, sweet-and-sour sauces, pine nut and raisin, eggplants . . .), Central European traces of Ashkenazi influences (goose fat, cured beef, fish in gelatin, cinnamon and nutmeg pastries . . .), and, more recently, borrowings from nearby Libyan, Egyptian, and Lebanese communities (meatballs, pastries with honey, etc.) are part of the makeup.

RECIPE

TAGLIOLINI COLLA BAGNA BRUSCA O SALSETTA GARBA (TAGLIOLINI WITH EGG AND LEMON SAUCE) *(Marche)*

Out of a need to reconcile a taste for pasta and a ban on cooking on Shabbat, Italian Jews very early on resorted to creating delicious recipes for cold pasta in sauce . . . perhaps inventing the pasta salad?

SERVES 6

2 cups (500 mL) chicken stock
2 large (100 g) eggs
2 large (38 g) egg yolks
Juice of 1 or 2 lemons
1 tablespoon (8 g) cornstarch
1⅛ pounds (500 g) tagliolini or tagliatelle
Olive oil
Salt and freshly ground black pepper

- Bring the stock to a boil in a saucepan, then reduce the heat to low. In a bowl, lightly beat the eggs, egg yolks, and lemon juice. While whisking, add a little of the hot stock and beat to combine. Pour the mixture into the pot with the stock and cook, stirring, until thickened. Stir a little water into the cornstarch, then add it to stock-egg mixture; do not let the mixture boil. Let cool.
- Cook the pasta al dente, lightly coat with olive oil, and season with salt and pepper. Let cool before adding the pasta to the sauce.

Celebrate the Italian Jewish year

1

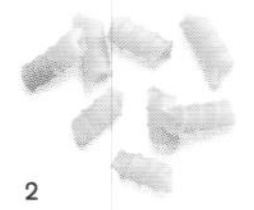
2

3

4

PASTA, ALWAYS PART OF CELEBRATIONS

For Yom Kippur, *tagliolini* (1), *ricciolini* (2), or *quadrucci* (3) are cooked in chicken stock; for Purim, it's spinach ravioli (4).

EDIBLE SYMBOLISM

For Passover, for example, bitterness—consumed as a reminder of the harshness of slavery endured in ancient Egypt—is found in bitter vegetables: *torzelli* (fried escarole) or Roman *carciofi* (artichokes) *alla giudia*. As well, *caponata ebraica* (sweet-and-sour vegetable ragout) or *melanzane* (eggplant) *alla giudia*, which highlight oil and frying, celebrate Hanukkah, the festival of lights.

SWEETS TAKE THE FOREFRONT

To add a little joie de vivre, sweetness takes center stage on festive menus: *cicerchiata* (a crown made from small pieces of fried dough coated with honey, with citrus and nuts) for Rosh Hashanah; *dolce di tagliatelle* (with almonds, cinnamon, and candied fruits) for Sukkot; *pizzarelle con miele* (matzoh-based cookies with honey) for Passover, or the theatrical *torta del monte Sinai* for Shavuot.

AN EMBLEMATIC AND SPECTACULAR DISH

The *ruota di Faraone* (Pharaoh's wheel), a long-cooking pasta dish combining sweet and savory, is eaten on Shabbat as remembrance of the parting of the Red Sea. Raisins and meatballs evoke the Pharaoh's soldiers, the round shape of the plates echoes the wheels of their chariots, and the tagliatelle represent the waves in which they drowned.

A JEWISH COUSCOUS

Cuscussù, emblem of Jewish cuisine in Livorno (Tuscany), has uncertain origins:

Of North African origin, couscous is said to have been adopted during the sixteenth century by the Jews of southern Italy, who then imported it to Tuscany during their exile.

•

The Granas, Jews of Portuguese culture who settled in Tunisia from the seventeenth century, disseminated it through Tuscany during their exchanges.

A concentration of Italian history!

SKIP TO
CLASH OF THE ARTICHOKES, P. 102;
CAPONATA (SICILIAN EGGPLANT SALAD), P. 220.

Geographical history of Jewish cuisine in Italy

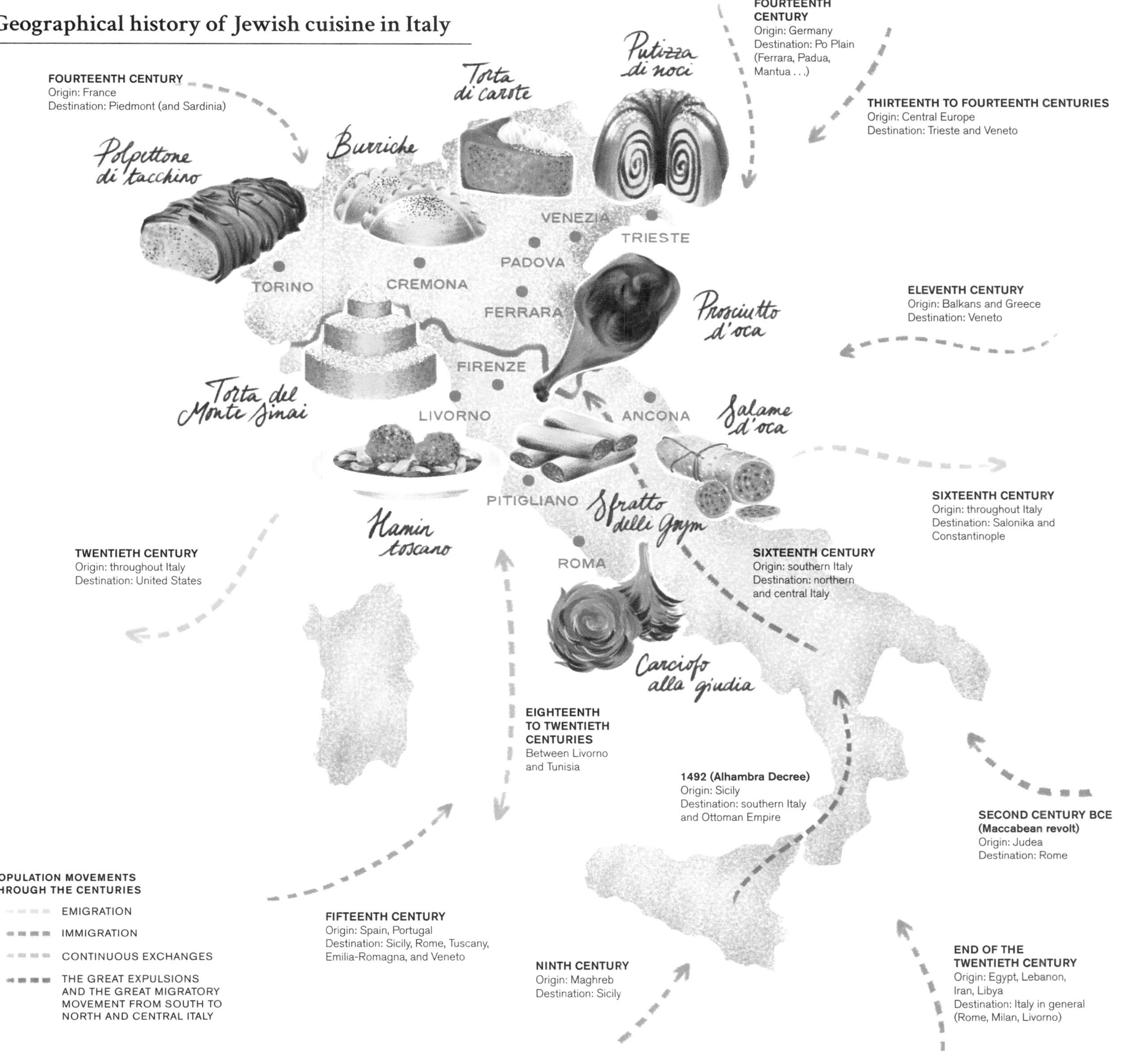

From the sixteenth century, Jewish communities concentrated in the northern and central areas of the country. By looking at strategies for replacing lard for cooking, historian Ariel Toaff distinguishes two traditional gastronomic zones: a Padan (northern) Italy, of Ashkenazi influence, where goose fat replaced lard; and a Tyrrhenian Italy, of Sephardic influence, where olive oil was used.

FAT FRONTIER

"PADAN ITALY" (GOOSE FAT)

"TYRRHENIAN ITALY" (OLIVE OIL)

Regional specialties

TURIN—Piedmont
Minestra dayenu (chicken stock with unleavened bread), *polpettone di tacchino* (turkey meatloaf)

TRIESTE—Friuli-Venezia Giulia
Paracinche (omelet tagliatelle in tomato sauce), goulash (meat ragout with spices), *putizza di noci* (rolled cake with nuts and spices)

VENICE—Veneto
Prosciutto d'oca (of goose), *tagliolini freddi alla salsa di pomodoro* (cold pasta in tomato sauce), *bigoli in salsa* (pasta with onions and anchovies), *sarde in saor* (sardines in sweet-and-sour sauce) . . .

PADUA—Veneto
Torta di pere di Succot (Sukkot pear tart), *torta di carote* (carrot cake) . . .

MANTUA AND CREMONA—Lombardy
Buricche (*böreks*, turnovers stuffed with meat or vegetables), *tortelli di zucca* (zucchini ravioli)

FERRARE—Emilia-Romagna
Buricche di fegatini (turnovers stuffed with chicken livers), *tortelli di zucca, zucca disfatta* (zucchini purée with cinnamon and onions)

FLORENCE—Tuscany
Hamin toscano (meat and bean ragout), *torta di mandorle e spinaci* (spinach and almond savory pie)

LIVORNO—Tuscany
Cuscussù (couscous), *triglie alla livornese* (red mullet in tomato sauce) or *alla mosaica* (with raisins and pine nuts), *torta del monte Sinai* (layered almond flour cake with citrus) . . .

PITIGLIANO AND SORANA—Tuscany
Sfratto delli Goym (log dough stuffed with nuts and spices, Slow Food), *bollo* (sweet rolls with anise, Slow Food)

ANCONA—Marche
Tagliolini colla bagna brusca, salami d'oca (goose sausages), *precipizi* (nougat made from fried dough balls) . . .

ROME—Lazio
Carciofi alla giudia (fried artichokes), *concia di zucchine* (sweet-and-sour zucchini), *torta di erbe* or *ebraica pizza* (savory herb pie), *milza ripiena* (stuffed spleen), *pizza dolce romana* (a sweet of dried and candied fruits), *torta di ricotta e visciole* (ricotta and morello cherry tart) . . .

BALSAMIC VINEGAR

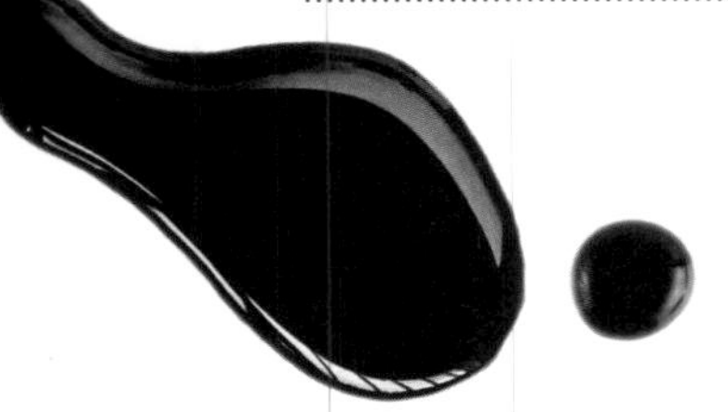

Formerly reserved for noble palates, this sweet-and-sour elixir is now a regular in everyone's pantry. But beware of counterfeits!

ALESSANDRA PIERINI

DEFINITION

Aceto balsamico tradizionale (traditional balsamic vinegar) is a condiment produced from fresh, cooked grape must. It is the result of alcoholic and acetic fermentations and is aged in barrels. Its nickname is "the black gold of Emilia-Romagna."

A FAMILY MATTER

Until 1796, balsamic vinegar was produced only in small quantities by the House of Este and a few noble families. But after the first Italian campaign led by Napoleon, French troops appropriated the property of the Ducal Palace, including barrels of this famous vinegar, and sold them at auction to the Modena aristocracy. These families became the custodians of a thousand-year-old heritage, still passed down today from generation to generation.

A little history

The cooking of grape must dates back to Roman times, when it was used to season meats, sweeten cakes, and preserve fruits.

In the Middle Ages, its production grew, and it became an indispensable ingredient in many recipes. Dating from 1046 is the first written testimony on the occasion of the donation of an *aceto perfettissimo* ("more than perfect vinegar") by Boniface III, Marquis of Tuscany, to Henry III, Holy Roman Emperor, during his passage through the present-day provinces of Modena and Reggio Emilia.

In 1747, the term *balsamico* appeared in Rubiera (in Reggio Emilia), in the registers of the cellars of the House of Este, which mention the therapeutic uses of this vinegar for its soothing and calming properties.

WHAT IS A BALSAMIC CONDIMENT?

These are the condiments made outside of the PDO or PGI labeling, which are . . .

AT BEST:

PDO balsamic vinegars sold before the twelve-year aging period required for certification, and PDO balsamic vinegars sold in different packaging from those required by the certifying consortium.

AT WORST:

Vinegars with a grape must percentage lower than 20 percent, or with other ingredients not admitted by the PGI certification requirements.

PGI vinegars that have not requested certification to be marketed in all sizes, even under 1 cup (250 mL).

Flavored vinegars (with truffle, raspberry, mango . . .) with additions of concentrated grape juice, modified starch, flavorings . . .

THE CASKS FOR AGING

The vinegar-aging casks provide flavor and infuse the vinegar with their essence over decades while contributing to the aging process. Each producer is free to make their casks according to their taste and to the results they want to achieve.

Softer and less compact woods (chestnut, mulberry, oak) are used for the first casks to facilitate an exchange with oxygen, which helps with evaporation and acetification.

Fruit-tree woods (pear, cherry, juniper, apple) are used halfway through the aging process to flavor and mellow the liquid.

The hardest and most compact woods (ash, locust) are recommended for the smallest casks, to slow down the concentration and avoid evaporation.

THE MANUFACTURING PROCESS OF TRADITIONAL BALSAMIC VINEGAR

→ The grapes, picked when very ripe, are pressed to obtain must.

→ The must is cooked at 200° to 205°F (90° to 95°C), uncovered, in a *paiolo* (kettle) made of stainless steel placed directly over a fire for twelve to sixteen hours to reduce by half and to caramelize.

→ The cooked must, after cooling and decanting, is placed in a large cask, the *badessa*. This is the first of a series of five to eight *vaselli* (casks) of successively smaller sizes and of different woods, called the *batteria*, in which the oxidation and double fermentation, both alcoholic and acetic, of the must will take place over one year.

→ The batteria is placed in the attic of the house where it is produced, if the vinegar is for domestic use, or in an *acetaia* (balsamic vinegar producer), if it is destined to be sold commercially. During this time, it is subject to seasonal temperature variations. As the vinegar ages, the contents of the cask are is transferred into smaller and smaller casks through a yearly operation that involves drawing off and filling of about 10 percent of the total cask content and sampling a certain quantity of the mature vinegar from the smallest barrel.

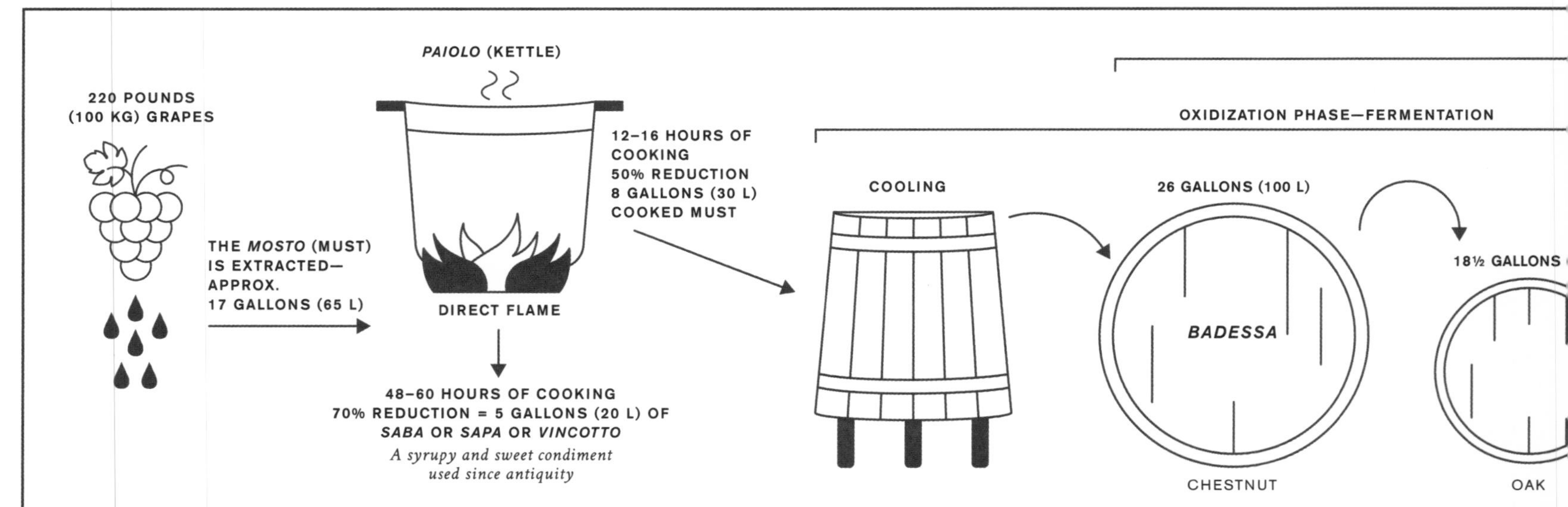

THE BALSAMIC UNIVERSE

A product of long and skilled tradition, balsamic vinegar has unfortunately suffered a fate similar to other great masterpieces in history: counterfeiting. This has necessitated the establishment of European certifications to guarantee its quality.

	 ACETO BALSAMICO TRADIZIONALE DI REGGIO EMILIA DOP	 ACETO BALSAMICO TRADIZIONALE DI MODENA DOP	  ACETO BALSAMICO DI MODENA IGP
INGREDIENTS	Fresh and cooked grape must.*		Concentrated grape must** (minimum 20%), wine vinegar. Added caramel permitted (E150b).
ORIGIN OF RAW INGREDIENTS	Grapes from Reggio Emilia.	Grapes from the province of Modena.	Worldwide
PRODUCTION PROCESS	Cooking, fermentation, acetification, aging, and bottling in the region of origin.		A combination of ingredients created in the region of Modena or Reggio Emilia.
AGING	Minimum 12 years (orange label). Minimum 18 years (silver label). Minimum 25 years (gold label).	Minimum 12 years (*affinato*, aged). Minimum 25 years (*extra vecchio*, extra old).	Classic: minimum 60 days. *Invecchiato* (aged): minimum 3 years in barrels.
BOTTLING AND SELLING	Bottled only by the control organization after organoleptic testing and chemical analysis, in official bottles of 100 mL, with a tied cork, stamped, and wax sealed.		Bottled by the producer or the reseller in bottles of a minimum of 250 mL.
CERTIFICATION	PDO since 2000.		PGI since 2009.
YIELD	220 pounds (100 kg) grapes = 2 pints (1 L) 25-year balsamic vinegar.	220 pounds (100 kg) grapes = 2 pints (1 L) 25-year balsamic vinegar.	220 pounds (100 kg) raw ingredients = 26 gallons (100 L) balsamic vinegar IGP.
FLAVOR PROFILE	**12 years:** amber, shiny, fluid, subtle flavor, lively and delicate, more acidity. **18 years:** brown, shiny, thick but fluid, concentrated, balanced acidity, complex and intense flavor. **25 years:** brown, shiny, syrupy but fluid, full-bodied, round, persistently aromatic.	**12 years:** amber, shiny, fluid, subtle flavor, lively and delicate, more acidity. **25 years:** deep brown, shiny, syrupy but fluid, full-bodied, round, less acidity, persistently aromatic.	Limpid and shiny, intense brown, balanced sweet-and-sour taste, vinegar flavor, woodsy if aged.
PRICE	Between €50 and €300 for 100 mL.		Between €2 and €100 for 250 mL.

**cooked must: grape juice partially caramelized by cooking in an open vat.*
***concentrated must: noncaramelized glucose and fructose syrup produced from the partial dehydration of grape juice from authorized varietals.*

PRECIOUS *SABA*

Fresh grape must, when cooked over direct heat for forty-eight to sixty hours and reduced by evaporation from 25 to 30 percent of its initial volume, provides a thick and honeyed syrup called *saba*, *sapa*, or *vincotto*, which has a long shelf life due to its sugar content. Already known at the time of the Romans, it is still used today as an accompaniment to cheeses and in sweet and savory cooking.

Attenzione!

White balsamic vinegar does not officially exist. The product *condimento balsamico bianco* (white balsamic condiment), which has a sweet and fruity taste and is made from wine vinegar, grape must, and sometimes other ingredients, is erroneously associated with certified balsamic vinegars.

BATTERIA (CASKS)

MATURATION

AGING

SAMPLING + SENSORY ANALYSIS

16 GAL (60 L) CHESTNUT

13 GAL (50 L) CHERRY

10½ GAL (40 L) BLACKBERRY

8 GAL (30 L) CEDAR

5 GAL (20 L) JUNIPER

2⅔ GAL (10 L) ASH

ACETO BALSAMICO TRADIZIONALE

IN COOKING

THE PDO—JUST A DROP

On strong and mature cheeses; a tiny drop on a slice of *zampone*, foie gras, or just before serving in a risotto; with a rotisserie beef filet, a duck breast; on octopus or oysters; as a topping with strawberries, pears, figs; as a final touch on a vanilla ice cream, panna cotta, or chocolate dessert, or in a cocktail.

Purists prefer to taste it with a porcelain spoon or, better yet, by placing a few drops on the top of the hand.

THE PGI—FOR EVERYDAY COOKING

In a vinaigrette; for deglazing white meat; in fish marinades; for cooking small onions; over grilled vegetables; reduced as a substitution for caramel; cooked in sweet preserves to enhance their flavor.

SKIP TO
PARMIGIANO-REGGIANO, P. 86.

CRUSTACEANS

Surrounded by four seas, Italians are spoiled by choice for seafood. From the Ligurian to the Adriatic, prawns and other crustaceans have made their home along the coasts—and in Italian cooking pots.

CÉLINE MAGUET

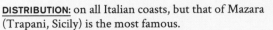

ARAGOSTA

Spiny lobster (*Palinurus elephas*)

DISTRIBUTION: mainly on the Sardinian coasts.

TASTE: very sweet flesh; when poorly cooked, it becomes elastic.

DISTINCTIVE ATTRIBUTE: unlike the European lobster, the spiny lobster has no claws and, while alive, its shell can turn violet.

CULT RECIPES: *fregula all'aragosta* (Sardinia), a shell and saffron broth, with *fregula* (small balls of pasta similar to pearl couscous) and spiny lobster meat; *zuppa di aragosta* (Sardinia), in a soup with tomatoes, herbs, olive oil, and a lot of white wine.

GAMBERO ROSSO

Giant red shrimp or prawn (*Aristaeomorpha foliacea*)

DISTRIBUTION: on all Italian coasts, but that of Mazara (Trapani, Sicily) is the most famous.

TASTE: briny flesh, juicy and delicate.

DISTINCTIVE ATTRIBUTE: medium in size, with an intensely red shell. Not to be confused with the *gambero viola* (*Aristeus antennatus*), blue-and-red shrimp, a rarer species, including that of Gallipoli (Apulia) and very sought after.

CULT RECIPE: raw, to enjoy in its simplest form.

CANOCCHIA (OR CICALA DI MARE)

Spottail mantis shrimp (*Squilla mantis*)

DISTRIBUTION: on all the Italian coasts.

TASTE: sweet and salty flesh.

DISTINCTIVE ATTRIBUTE: the spottail mantis shrimp has two small purple spots on the tail, which are used to fool its predators. Not to be confused with another species, *Scyllarus arctus*, larger and brown, highly sought after but protected.

CULT RECIPE: *canocchie al limone*, in which the shrimp are blanched or steamed and served with olive oil and lemon.

IN COOKING! *cicala e cicoria* (Abruzzo), a recipe combining the sweetness of the spottail mantis shrimp with the bitterness of chicory. Crack open the raw shrimp and use the shells to make a stock. Sauté the chicory in olive oil with a garlic clove. Add the stock, and serve with the raw shrimp meat.

GRANSEOLA (OR GRANCEVOLA)

Spinous spider crab (*Maja squinado*)

DISTRIBUTION: on the Sardinian coasts and in the Adriatic Sea.

TASTE: flesh with a pronounced nutty taste.

DISTINCTIVE ATTRIBUTE: to defend itself from its predators, its shell resembles rock, so that it disappears from sight.

CULT RECIPE: just boiled, to be eaten in its shell.

IN COOKING! spaghetti or gnocchi *alla granseola.* Immerse the crab in boiling water for 20 minutes, then remove the flesh. Reserve the juice from the shell. In a saucepan, brown garlic, deglaze the pan with the reserved juice, and add peeled tomatoes; let reduce. Mix boiled pasta with the sauce and serve topped with the crabmeat.

SCAMPO

Langoustine (*Nephrops norvegicus*)

DISTRIBUTION: on all the Italian coasts.

TASTE: saline and floral flesh.

DISTINCTIVE ATTRIBUTE: langoustine is closer to the European lobster than the spiny lobster.

CULT RECIPES: scampi, *aglio e olio* (Abruzzo), sautéed in olive oil with garlic and paprika; *scampi alla busara* (Friuli), a ragout of tomatoes, garlic, parsley, white wine, and dried bread crumbs, in which the unshelled langoustines are simmered.

GRANCHIO

Mediterranean shore (green) crab (*Carcinus aestuarii*)

DISTRIBUTION: Veneto.

TASTE: the flesh has an earthy taste, close to that of crayfish.

DISTINCTIVE ATTRIBUTE: the Venetians are fond of this crab when it's molting in spring and autumn. Its name then changes to *moeche.*

CULT RECIPE: *moeche fritte*, fried molted crabs (Venice).

MAZZANCOLLA

Striped (or caramote) prawn (*Penaeus* or *Melicertus kerathurus*)

DISTRIBUTION: Tyrrhenian, Ionian, and Adriatic seas.

TASTE: slightly sweet and bitter flesh.

DISTINCTIVE ATTRIBUTE: native Mediterranean species, varying in color from pale pink to orange-pink.

CULT RECIPES: *brodetto* (Adriatic coast), fish soup; *spaghetti allo scoglio* (throughout Italy), with shrimp, cockles, and mussels.

ASTICE

European (common) lobster (*Homarus gammarus*)

DISTRIBUTION: on the Ligurian and Tyrrhenian coasts and on the outskirts of Venice.

TASTE: soft and delicate flesh.

DISTINCTIVE ATTRIBUTE: a blue color streaked with yellow when alive; once cooked, it turns red like many crustaceans.

CULT RECIPE: linguine or *tagliolini all'astice* (throughout Italy).

IN COOKING! *astice alla catalana*, a recipe dating from the Catalan occupation in Sardinia and distributed today throughout Italy. Immerse a lobster in boiling water, then halve it lengthwise. Remove the flesh from the head and claws, as well as the juice, and make a sauce with olive oil and lemon. Serve it with chopped red onions and heirloom tomatoes, drizzled with its juice.

SKIP TO
THE LAGOON IS A TERROIR, P. 134.

SEASON

INVERNO (WINTER)

CATEGORY

PRIMO PIATTO (FIRST COURSE)

LEVEL

FACILE (EASY)

SPAGHETTI AI RICCI DI MARE

SEA URCHIN PASTA

This powerfully briny pasta, in which sea urchin is the star, is an explosion of Mediterranean flavors.

ELISABETH SCOTTO

WHAT INGREDIENTS?

The recipe is always the same: basic regional products—sea urchins, olive oil—to which garlic and chile are added and, if desired, chopped parsley and/or a little grated lemon zest at the time of serving.

WHICH PASTA?

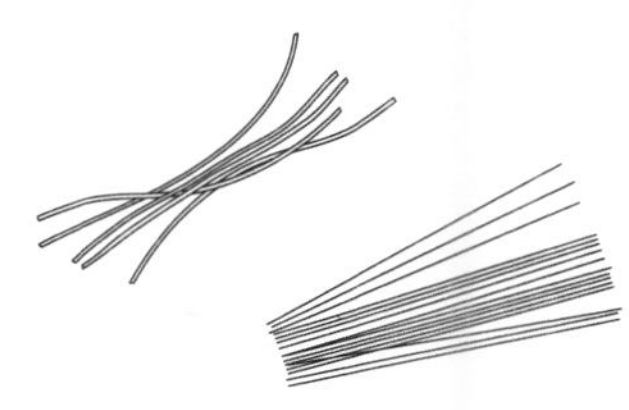

You can prepare this recipe with any format of spaghetti, from *spaghettino* to *spaghettone*, but also *spaghetti alla chitarra* or linguine.

Sea urchins in pasta

You might think that the sea urchin (*riccio di mare*) has always been part of the human diet since the day someone decided to break past the spines of this strange animal!

Savoring sea urchin roe with a small spoon when just plucked from the waters is probably the best way to enjoy it, but it should be noted that the urchin's powerful taste works wonders incorporated into cooked dishes.

Horace's *Satires* mentions that sea urchins and their briny water were used to season sauces. Pairing them with pasta therefore seems obvious . . .

THE RECIPE

SERVES 4

20 to 25 sea urchins

1 clove garlic

1 dried red chile (such as tabasco or cayenne)

Scant ½ cup (100 mL) extra-virgin olive oil

14 ounces (400 g) spaghetti

Butter (optional)

Pry open the sea urchins and remove and reserve the roe; strain and reserve the water contained inside. Peel the garlic and cut it into quarters, removing the center germ, if necessary. Remove the seeds from the chile and crumble the flesh.

Heat the olive oil in a skillet over low heat, add the garlic and chile, and cook for 5 minutes, or until the garlic is golden. Add half of the sea urchin roe and make an emulsion by crushing it with a fork. Remove from the heat and let steep in the oil.

Cook the pasta al dente in a pot of salted boiling water. Remove the garlic and chile from the oil in the pan. Reserve a few ladles of the cooking water, then drain the pasta and stir it into the pan. Add a little pasta cooking water and the sea urchin water while stirring. Off the heat, add the remaining sea urchin roe, stir well, and serve.

At the same time the sea urchin roe is added, you can stir in a pat of butter to act as a binder and for additional creaminess.

Where to try them?

Sicily, Sardinia, and Naples contend for the paternity of this recipe. Regardless of its origin, all of coastal Italy, from north to south, shares in this delight through the seasons, from autumn to early spring!

SKIP TO
CHILE PEPPERS, P. 359.

OSTERIE

Serving as ambassadors of local cuisine, these modest eating establishments offer a generous welcome, good wine, and affordable prices. Here is a tour through Italy via some favorite locations.

EUGENIO SIGNORONI

Zolin—Sandrigo (Veneto)

Ai Cascinari—Palermo (Sicily)

Kamastra—Civita (Calabria)

Entrà—Finale Emilia (Emilia-Romagna)

Lo Stuzzichino—Massa Lubrense (Campania)

Boccondivino—Bra (Piedmont)

Gallo Rosso—Filottrano (Marche)

THE TRADITIONAL

TRENTINO-ALTO ADIGE

***LOCANDA ALPINA*—BREZ**

→ *Piazza del Municipio, 23*

This osteria, run by the Segna family, offers dishes rich in flavors and aromas typical of this wonderous mountain region.

♥ ***Tortel di patate*** (flat potato cake), ***sella di cervo*** (venison saddle), ***strudel.***

***LOCANDA DELLE TRE CHIAVI*—ISERA**

→ *Via Vannetti, 8*

Over twenty years ago, Sergio and Annarita Valentini created this beautiful and warm osteria. They choose their suppliers carefully.

♥ ***Fanzelto con salumi*** (buckwheat crêpe with charcuterie), ***tortel di patate*** (flat potato cake), ***canederli*** (bread gnocchi).

***PITZOCK*—FUNES**

→ *Via Pizack, 30*

In this modern osteria, Oskar Messner excels with his traditional flavors using excellent ingredients from small producers.

♥ ***Frittelle di patate e crauti*** (flat cakes of potato and sauerkraut), ***plum canederli*** (bread dumplings).

LOMBARDY

***OSTERIA DELLA VILLETTA*—PALAZZOLO SULL'OGLIO**

→ *Via Marconi, 104*

This is one of the most beautiful *osterie* in northern Italy, with its Liberty-style rooms and contemporary works of art. Friendly operators Maurizio and Grazia Rossi offer simple home cooking.

♥ ***Polpette*** (meatballs), ***trippa in brodo*** (tripe in broth), ***baccalà in umido*** (salt cod in tomato sauce).

***ROVELLO 18*—MILAN**

→ *Via Tivoli, 2*

This old Milanese address, which still serves classics of Lombard cuisine, was one of the first restaurants in Italy to be awarded a Michelin star.

♥ ***Tagliatelle al ragù, costoletta alla milanese.***

PIEDMONT

***ANTICHE SERE*—TURIN**

→ *Via Cenischia, 9*

It is the *piola* (Piedmontese osteria) par excellence, with its family atmosphere and old-fashioned decor. Daniele Rota prepares Piedmontese classics according to artistic traditions.

♥ ***Vitello tonnato, insalata russa, panna cotta.***

***BOCCONDIVINO*—BRA**

→ *Via della Mendicità Istruita, 14*

This osteria, which is one of the oldest in Piedmont, is located in the building that houses the headquarters of Slow Food. It serves local dishes and wines.

♥ ***Tajarin*** (long, very thin egg pasta), ***agnolotti del plin*** (small meat ravioli), ***vitello tonnato.***

BASILICATA

***GAGLIARDI*—AVIGLIANO**

→ *Via Martiri Ungheresi, 18*

This temple to salt cod serves tasty and rustic dishes.

♥ ***Salt cod,*** from antipasto to *secondo* (main courses).

APULIA

***ANTICHI SAPORI*—ANDRIA**

→ *Frazione Montegrosso, Piazza Sant'Isidoro, 10*

This was one of the first restaurants to realize the importance of having its own vegetable garden.

♥ ***Tiella di agnello*** (baked lamb), ***cipollotti arraganati*** (stuffed onions), ***ricotta con sedano dolce*** (ricotta with celery confit).

ABRUZZO

***VECCHIA MARINA*—ROSETO DEGLI ABRUZZI**

→ *Lungomare Trento, 37*

This is the best place to savor fish from the Adriatic. Here Gennaro D'Ignazio cooks incomparable dishes.

♥ ***Crudi di pesce*** (fish crudo), ***scampi all'arrabbiata*** (spicy shrimp), ***frittura di paranza*** (fried fish).

CALABRIA

KAMASTRA—CIVITA
→ *Piazza Municipio, 4*
Enzo Filardi offers a gastronomic journey through the region's foods and the Arbëreshë culinary traditions (of Albanian origin), which have been interwoven for centuries with Calabrian culture.

♥ ***Dromësat*** (dough dumplings cooked in tomato sauce with oregano), ***capretto alla civitese*** (ragout of goat).

FRIULI-VENEZIA GIULIA

DEVETAK—SAVOGNA D'ISONZO
→ *Via Brezici, 2*
For over 150 years, the Devetak family has been located at this address bordering Slovenia, where the cuisine is a mix of influences; the wine list is excellent.

♥ ***Selinka*** (celery soup), **meats, gnocchi.**

MARCHE

GALLO ROSSO—FILOTTRANO
→ *Piazza XI febbraio, 4 bis*
Located in a medieval house, serving dishes typical of the hills of the Marche region, and with the best local products.

♥ ***Oca al verdicchio*** (goose with Verdicchio wine), **tagliatelle, cheeses.**

VENETO

ZOLIN—SANDRIGO
→ *Via Roma, 14*
Luigi Zolin and his sister Giuseppina offer authentic Veneto cuisine in a former hardware store.

♥ ***Gnocchi al pestat*** (with bacon and herbs), ***bigoli con ragù di anatra*** (long pasta with duck), **tiramisu.**

LIGURIA

LA BRINCA—NE
→ *Via Campo di Ne, 58*
The Circella family works with the best products from the land to offer rare and incomparable Ligurian dishes. Its wine cellar itself make the detour worthwhile.

♥ ***Lattughe ripiene*** (stuffed lettuce leaves), **mortar-made pesto, *punta di vitello*** (veal breast).

SARDINIA

SANTA RUGHE—GAVOI (NUORO)
→ *Via Carlo Felice, 2*
This welcoming osteria offers dishes that best represent the Sardinian countryside.

♥ ***S'erbuzu*** (wild herb soup), ***mahrrones curzos*** (pasta with tomato sauce), ***porceddu*** (suckling pig).

CAMPANIA

LO STUZZICHINO—MASSA LUBRENSE
→ *Via Deserto 1A*
The De Gregorio family serves local fish and vegetables with flavor and delicacy.

♥ ***Paccheri allo scorfano*** (scorpion fish pasta), ***involtini di pesce bandiera*** (silver scabbardfish paupiettes), ***delizia al limone.***

MIMÌ ALLA FERROVIA—NAPLES
→ *Via Alfonso d'Aragona, 19*
Since 1943, this address has been a place to enjoy traditional Parthenopean dishes.

♥ ***Insalata di polpo*** (octopus salad), ***ziti alla genovese*** (pasta with meat ragout), ***pesce all'acqua pazza*** (poached fish).

EMILIA-ROMAGNA

LA CAMPANARA—GALEATA
→ *Frazione Pianetto, Via Pianetto Borgo, 24 A*
Alessandra Bazzocchi and Roberto Casamenti offer rare traditional dishes from the Romagna region.

♥ ***Polpette di mora romagnola*** (pork meatballs), ***passatelli*** (pasta made with dried bread crumbs and Parmesan cheese), **tripe.**

ENTRÀ—FINALE EMILIA
→ *Frazione Massa Finalese, Via Salde Entrà, 60*
In their countryside osteria, Antonio and his sister Elvira Previdi prepare the best Emilian dishes, accompanied by an excellent choice of wines.

♥ **Tagliatelle, *tortelli di zucca*** (with pumpkin), ***faraona arrosto*** (roasted guinea fowl).

TUSCANY

DA BURDE—FLORENCE
→ *Via Pistoiese, 6R*
The Gori brothers offer an extraordinary choice of products and wines to accompany their authentic Tuscan dishes.

♥ ***Crostino con i fegatini*** (toasts with poultry liver pâté), ***peposo*** (slow-simmered meat), ***castagnaccio*** (chestnut flour cake).

LAZIO

DA CESARE—ROME
→ *Via del Casaletto, 45–49*
After touring the best restaurants in Europe, Leonardo Vignoli opened an osteria that has become a reliable location for fried foods, *primi piatti*, and natural wines.

♥ ***Trippa alla romana*** (Roman tripe), ***pasta carbonara, rigatoni con la pajata*** (with calf's intestines).

SORA MARIA E ARCANGELO—OLEVANO ROMANO
→ *Via Roma, 42*
Offering a festive atmosphere and cuisine amid the hills of the Roman countryside, using excellent and simply prepared products.

♥ ***Pappardelle al ragù bianco*** (pasta with meat ragout without tomatoes), ***abbacchio*** (suckling lamb), ***porcini arrosto*** (roasted porcini mushrooms).

SICILY

AI CASCINARI—PALERMO
→ *Via D'Ossuna, 43–45*
For over sixty years, the Riccobono family has been offering simple and traditional cuisine, including Sicilian seafood dishes.

♥ ***Spaghetti con brodo di pesce*** (with fish stock), ***bucatini con le sarde, falso magro*** (meat roulade stuffed with vegetables).

Trippa—Milan (Lombardy)

Trippa—Milan

La Madia—Brione (Lombardy)

Consorzio—Turin (Piedmont)

THE MODERN

For the past ten or so years, young *osti* (osterie operators) have renewed the concept of the osteria, highlighting small producers and great wines (often natural) and updating, though not betraying, traditional dishes.

CONSORZIO—TURIN (PIEDMONT)
→ *Via Monte di Pietà, 23*
Andrea Gherra and Pietro Vergano were the first to bring the osteria back to life in the twenty-first century; one of the best Italian wine lists.

♥ ***Quinto quarto*** (offal), ***animelle*** (sweetbreads), ***agnolotti*** (stuffed pasta).

TRIPPA—MILAN (LOMBARDY)
→ *Via Vasari, 1*
A cuisine of character, brilliantly crafted by Diego Rossi.

♥ ***Vitello tonnato, quinto quarto*** (offal).

LA MADIA—BRIONE (LOMBARDY)
→ *Via Aquilini, 5*
Excellent products combined with traditional and modern dishes from chef Michele Vallotti.

♥ **Sheep meats.**

OSTERIA FRATELLI PAVESI—PODENZANO (EMILIA-ROMAGNA)
→ *Frazione Gariga SS45, 8*
Giacomo Pavesi is among the best osti on the Italian peninsula.

♥ ***Bomba di riso*** (seasoned rice gratin), ***game.***

LOCANDA MAMMÌ—AGNONE (MOLISE)
→ *Contrada Castelnuovo, 86*
Stefania Di Pasquo offers cuisine that is faithful to the terroir, traditional but off the beaten track.

♥ ***Chitarrina al ragù di quaglia*** (long pasta with quail), ***baccalà in due consistenze*** (salt cod two ways).

SKIP TO
LET'S GO OUT TO EAT, P. 92.

CANDIES

Round, square, wacky, multi- or single-colored, these candies have been delighting for generations. Let's peruse a panorama of some highly addictive sweets!

ALESSANDRA PIERINI

THE ARTISANAL

Although becoming increasingly more rare, several artisanal confectioners continue to produce candies that Italians know from childhood.

1. *Zirele*—Lorandi (Trentino-Alto Adige): irregular square shape and pastel colors, made with sugar and natural flavors, often dropped into a glass of grappa to melt. Mint, cinnamon, cloves, strawberry, blackberry, lemon, rhubarb.

2. *Petalo di rosa*—Pietro Romanengo fu Stefano (Liguria): candied fresh rose petals. Used to dissolve into an herbal tea.

3. *Violetta*—Stratta (Piedmont): fresh violet petal soaked in warm sugar syrup to candy it. Traditionally served with candied chestnuts.

4. *Gocce di rosolio*—Pasticceria Giuliani (Lazio): also called *lacrime d'amore* (tears of love). Alcohol-based small drops of floral or spice infusions coated in a candy shell.

5. *Filo di cannella*—Pietro Romanengo fu Stefano (Liguria): elongated bead of cinnamon coated with sugar, similar to a dragée with an irregular surface.

6. *Balsamica*—Dolcezze Albino (Piedmont): chewy candy with essential oil of peppermint from Piedmont.

7. *Arancia confettata*—Pietro Romanengo fu Stefano (Liguria): orange peel covered with sugar, similar to a dragée with an irregular surface.

8. *Confettini*—Pietro Romanengo fu Stefano (Liguria): pistachios, pine nuts, coffee beans, fennel seeds, or orange blossoms in a colored-sugar shell.

9. *Ginevrine*—Pasticceria Mezzaro (Piedmont): sugared fruit lozenges. Lemon, anise, orange, mint, tangerine, blueberry.

THE CLASSICS

Produced on a larger scale, these traditional *caramelle* are loved by all Italians!

10. *Fruttini*—Eurodolciaria (Lombardy): small balls of sugar with fruit from Sicily, where they were created. Grape, orange, apple, lemon, strawberry.

11. *Mou polacche*—Vicentini (Veneto): soft, golden, rectangular caramels made from butter, sugar, and milk (traditional), all black (cream and licorice) and two-tone black and white (mint and licorice).

12. *Perla di sole*—Papillon (Campania): small sugar pearls with the flavor of limoncello.

13. *Orzo*—Valtonline (Lombardy): small square traditional honey-colored bar from Valtellina with sugar and barley, cooked in a kettle.

14. *Golia*—Perfetti (Lombardy): small round chewy licorice, a must!

15. *Mou Elah*—Elah Dufour (Piedmont): cubes of soft caramel rich with milk (classic), cream and licorice (*kremliquirizia*), peppermint, and two-tone licorice (900).

16. *Spicchi*—Cedrinca (Lombardy): hard candies in the shape of fruit wedges, with natural citrus juice centers. Orange, lemon, tangerine.

17. *Rossana*—Fida (Piedmont): pavé of sugar with a melting center made of hazelnut and almond; also called *la rossa* ("the redhead"), in reference to Roxane, Cyrano de Bergerac's beloved.

18. *Al miele*—Ambrosoli (Lombardy): hard, oval, and yellow candy with 23 percent honey.

19. *Selz*—Elah Dufour (Piedmont): oval and plump, hard and effervescent, with essential oils of lemon and orange.

20. *Galatina*—Sperlari (Lombardy): round bar of sweetened condensed milk.

Candies of Yesteryear

THE ETYMOLOGY OF THE WORD *caramellus* (candy) confirms its ancient roots: from the Latin *calamellus* (small reed), in reference to sugarcane. The ancestor of modern candy dates back to the eleventh century, when the Crusaders returned from the Middle East with pieces of sugarcane.

A cult candy in a collector's box of timeless beauty—this is the story of an Italian company that can boast of bringing Piedmont confections to the world.

In 1857, Luigi Leone, a Neapolitan pastry chef, began to produce his now legendary flavored hard candies in a confectioner in Alba (Piedmont). He then moved to Turin, where he became a supplier to the royal house. The company was sold in 1934 to the Monero family, which, after eighty years in operation, passed the reins to another private Italian company in July 2018. Its flagship product are soft and crunchy candies packaged in beautiful vintage cardboard or tin boxes and produced from essential oils and plant extracts, presented in different pastel hues obtained using natural products. Two families and more than forty flavors: those with flavors for "digestive" and more ancient virtues (mint, chamomile, gentian, rhubarb . . .) and those that are "thirst quenching": (blueberries, lemon, orange, tangerine, violet, strawberry . . .).

SKIP TO
THE DELIGHTS OF LICORICE, P. 138;
MINT, P. 202.

ITALY, THE HOMELAND OF PASTA?

The emblem of Italian cuisine, this simple and supple ingredient has conquered the world in all its forms and in all sauces. But is pasta really Italian after all?

SILVANO SERVENTI AND FRANÇOISE SABBAN*

Traveling wheat

→ Through the Middle East and Europe, the first pasta dates from the time of the ancient Romans. Evidence of vermicelli during the third century is found in Palestine and in the Arab world beginning in the ninth century. Starting from the twelfth century, Arab-Andalusian Sicily prepared pasta extensively.

→ In China, the first recipes for pasta steamed or cooked in broth date from the third century. Traditionally, these are pasta made of wheat flour.

THE BIRTH OF PASTA IN ITALY

SICILY, THE CRADLE OF DRY PASTA

The island of Sicily, located at the crossroads of the Christian and Muslim worlds, has cultivated durum wheat, imported by nomadic Arabs, since the Middle Ages. The inhabitants also passed on the technique of drying and molding pasta, an art mastered in a territory with a climate suitable for the task. Sicily's strategic commercial position enabled it to disseminate this practice across other regions. Sardinia in particular has become a second important location for durum wheat production.

GENOA AND THE FRESH PASTA TRADE

Both a maritime and financial power, Genoa was the trade center for Sicilian and Sardinian dry pasta in the Mediterranean basin from the Middle Ages to the fifteenth century. Gradually, *lasagnari* and *vermicellari*, makers and street vendors of fresh pasta, became important players in the city. Thanks to technical advances, eventually Genoa spread the vermicelli industry throughout the country, contributing to the reputation of "Italian pasta."

NAPLES, THE HEART OF ITALIAN PASTA

In Naples, maccheroni production is documented as far back as the thirteenth century, but this capital of Italy's largest kingdom did not establish itself as a producer of dry pasta until the eighteenth century, once technical advances and its *terroir* made it possible.

The figures of the *maccaronaro* in his stall and that of the maccheroni eater eating pasta with his bare hands in the street have fueled regional folklore. The Neapolitans thus universalized an Italian way of life.

FROM A SIMPLE SHEET

How does "dough" become "pasta"?

STRETCHING—Roll out the dough until you get a thin sheet, called *lasagna.* These wide strips or rectangles of fresh pasta are eaten soon after they are made. In the West, this quadrangular sheet is cooked in water before layering it with cheese (the first known condiment with pasta, dating from the Middle Ages) and baking it in the form of a casserole.

FILAMENTS—From this main sheet of pasta dough, small strips are cut, known as *tria* (vermicelli). These strips of unleavened dough can be dried and stored.

OTHER SHAPES—As early as the fifteenth century, distinct shapes other than large flat lasagna sheets began to appear. Wide noodles, thin threads sometimes rolled up, ravioli for encasing filling . . . the combinations are endless, and each region has its own technique: *maccheroni* in Naples, long pasta twisted into nests in Genoa, short dry pasta in Apulia, egg pasta in Bologna . . .

The long cooking of pasta, once recommended by medical and nutrition authorities, remained the norm in Italy until the twentieth century, after which the short cooking time of dry pasta made from durum wheat semolina flour infiltrated bourgeois circles in reaction to popular practices, in particular the idea of the maccaronaro who served passersby hot maccheroni dishes prepared to order and at low cost. This is the birth of the cooking technique referred to as al dente.

The Neapolitans were also the first to pair pasta with tomato, an exotic fruit introduced into the country via the commercial port of Campania, eventually adapting to the region's climate.

Polyglot pasta

In Italian, any type and shape of dough is referred to by the generic term *pasta*, from the late Latin *pasta* (third to sixth centuries) that meant "dough" in the broad sense, that is to say, a mixture of flour and water for kneading or cooking. But words like *pasta* have come a long way . . .

→ From the first century BCE to the sixth century CE: *itriumor* or *itriyya* (Arabic) in the East and *lagana* (from *laganon* in Greek and *laganum* in Latin) in the West designate a kneaded dough cooked in water, differentiated from leavened doughs that are part of religious preparations.

→ From the sixth to seventh centuries: the term *lagana*, of Greco-Latin heritage, comes to the forefront in Mediterranean countries. Its definition is close to the current word *lasagna.* In the south of Italy, *lagane* is still used to indicate types of tagliatelle without eggs.

→ In the thirteenth century: *pastasciutta* (drained pasta) as opposed to *pasta in brodo* (pasta in broth) appear as distinctions. The first pasta recipes appear in Italian cookbooks of the Middle Ages.

→ In the fourteenth century: there are two techniques, *lasagna* (fresh pasta) and *tri* or *tria* (dry pasta), result from the mixing of Greco-Roman and Arabic cultures in Italy.

→ In the fifteenth century: the terms *tortelli* (*torta*, or pastry-lidded pies), *ravioli* (stuffed pasta turnovers), *vermicelli* (sheets cut into threads), and *maccheroni* (sheets cut into strips or threads and rolled) appear.

→ In the sixteenth century *maccheroni* is the generic word for pasta of different formats, before the return of the word *pasta* in Italian treatises.

Marco Polo, the father of pasta?

Literature and cinema have popularized the myth of the spaghetti brought back from China by Marco Polo, the famous Venetian adventurer. But this isn't true! This idea is simply the result, and admittedly effective, of an advertising campaign launched in the *Macaroni Journal* by American industrialists. The legend began in the 1930s during the height of American marketing movements. In fact, pasta was consumed in Italy long before the explorer's return in 1295.

**Authors of* Les Pâtes, Histoire d'une culture universelle, *Actes Sud, 2000.*

SKIP TO
COOKING PASTA, P. 12; THE TASTE OF SHAPE, P. 317; SPAGHETTI VIP, P. 372; TOMATOES, P. 28.

SEASON

TUTTO L'ANNO (YEAR-ROUND)

CATEGORY

PRIMO PIATTO (FIRST COURSE)

LEVEL

FACILE (EASY)

SPAGHETTI AL POMODORO

SPAGHETTI WITH TOMATO

The marriage of pasta and tomato has become more than a national dish—it is a global symbol of Italianism.

FRANÇOIS-RÉGIS GAUDRY

A MARRIAGE OF LOVE

→ Roman cook Vincenzo Agnoletti recorded the first pairing of pasta with tomato in 1803, in *Nuova cucina economica.* The author describes a soup in which the small pasta are first "blanched," then cooked in a broth made from tomato sauce.

→ In the second edition of *Apicio moderno* (*Modern Apicius,* 1807) by Roman chef Francesco Leonardi, the recipe for *maccheroni alla napoletana* offers a variation in tomato sauce.

→ The marriage of spaghetti and tomato is formalized in 1839. In his collection *Cucina teorica-pratica* (*Theoretical and Practical Cuisine*), Neapolitan Ippolito Cavalcanti suggests combining pasta with fresh cooked and processed tomatoes, simply seasoned with a fat (olive oil or lard, depending on the season) in which garlic is to be fried. This recipe soon becomes a huge success throughout Italy and—thanks to innovations in the canning industry—around the world.

HAVING A HAND IN PASTA

Spaghetti al pomodoro is at the heart of one of the most famous scenes in Italian cinema. In *Miseria e nobiltà* (*Poverty and Nobility*) by Mario Mattòli (1954), Felice Sciosciammocca (the actor Totò) devours pasta with tomatoes with both hands, standing on a table, just before filling his pockets.

Sophia Loren, who plays a small role in the film, comments on this scene:

"It talks about the hunger of the common people. A hunger that can only be fought using a smile as a weapon, and only with the lightness of spirit which we, the Neapolitans, have plenty of."

THE RECIPE

Here is an authentically Neapolitan version.

SERVES 4

2 cloves garlic

2 tablespoons (30 mL) extra-virgin olive oil

2¼ pounds (1 kg) ripe fresh San Marzano tomatoes, or 1¾ pounds (800 g) canned peeled tomatoes

Salt and freshly ground black pepper

14 ounces (400 g) spaghetti

Leaves from 1 sprig basil

Peel the garlic and remove the center germ. Thickly slice the garlic. In a high-sided saucepan, heat the olive oil and cook the garlic until browned. Cut the tomatoes into quarters lengthwise and add them to the pan. Season with salt and pepper. Cook over high heat for about 10 minutes. If there is still too much liquid, continue cooking, and if the tomato pieces are too large, crush them with a wooden spoon.

Meanwhile, cook the pasta al dente in a large pot of salted boiling water. Drain the pasta, then add it to the sauce along with the basil leaves. Cook over medium heat for several minutes, stirring well to combine. Serve.

THE DILEMMAS

FRESH OR CANNED TOMATOES?

This dish is based on the quality of *pomodori da sugo* (tomatoes for sauce). They are ideally fresh, of the varietals San Marzano, Roma, beef heart, on the vine . . . The tomatoes must be in season, grown in the ground, and very ripe. However, instead of using mediocre fresh tomatoes, it is always better to select good-quality canned tomatoes, *pelati* (peeled) or *filetti* (in quarters). For a sweeter and quicker tomato sauce, choose small sizes: Pomodorini or Datterini.

SHORT OR LONG COOKING?

Some versions of *pasta al pomodoro* (typically northern Italy) suggest a gentle and very slow cooking of the tomato sauce to thicken it. In contrast, the Neapolitan school advocates rapid cooking over rather high heat to remove the water from the tomatoes but retain their fresh flavor.

OTHER PASTA?

Spaghetti is the universal format par excellence, but many other formats, long or short, lend themselves to tomato sauce: penne, rigatoni, orecchiette, *bucatini* . . .

ANOTHER HERB?

Basil is the best friend of spaghetti al pomodoro! For basil to deliver its fullest flavor, it must be used in the sauce as whole leaves and added only at the very end of the cooking time. In winter, it can be replaced with parsley.

CHEESE?

In Campania, they abstain. In Sardinia, they like pecorino. In Sicily, *caciovallo* or ricotta salata are not uncommon . . . In the north, you'll find a sprinkle of Parmesan and Grana Padano.

SKIP TO
HIS MAJESTY THE BASIL, P. 121; TOMATOES, P. 28; THE SPAGHETTI FAMILY, P. 201.

SEASON

TUTTO L'ANNO (YEAR-ROUND)

CATEGORY

PRIMO PIATTO (FIRST COURSE)

LEVEL

DIFFICOLTÀ MEDIA (MEDIUM DIFFICULTY)

RISOTTO ALLA MILANESE

MILANESE-STYLE RISOTTO

Butter and onion sizzle with rice; saffron ties it all together—Milan on a plate.

ANNA PRANDONI

THE LEGEND

It was in Milan where, for the first time, saffron was added to rice cooked with cheese and butter. It is said that a pupil of Flemish painter **Valerio De Perfundvalle** was responsible for adding a touch of saffron to make the yellow color of the dish more intense, earning him the nickname **Zafferano**. In 1574, the young man married the painter's daughter, and his friends jokingly added this spice to the risotto served at their wedding feast. The recipe immediately became famous.

The history

The first known mention of saffron in risotto can be found in the book of recipes by Cristoforo di Messisbugo, published in Ferrara (Emilia-Romagna) in 1549.

At the end of the last century, Milanese risotto was offered only in the city's trattorias and restaurants, but this historic dish was revived thanks to Gualtiero Marchesi, considered to be the founder of Italian nouvelle cuisine.

GUALTIERO MARCHESI'S RISOTTO

A native of Pavia who eventually settled in Milan, Marchesi revived the traditional recipe in the early 1980s.

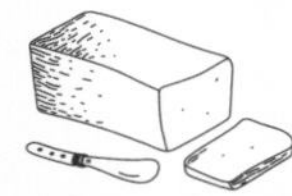

***IL BURRO ACIDO*—ACIDIC BUTTER**

After returning from France, the chef was inspired to use beurre blanc to create his light version of risotto: onions are simmered with white wine and vinegar and, off the heat, combined with butter to form a cream before being strained and added only at the creaming (*mantecatura*) stage of the risotto. This approach avoids burning the onions, the alcohol from the wine is cooked off, and, most important, the acidity of the risotto is controlled and can be adjusted at the end of the cooking time.

***LA FOGLIA D'ORO*—GOLD LEAF**

His final addition of a square of edible gold leaf and his serving the risotto on a black-rimmed plate enhanced with gold trim lent a luxurious allure to a dish otherwise often ignored.

THE RECIPE

This is *risotto Milanese all'antica* by chef Cesare Battisti, who, together with his wife and sommelier, Federica, owns the famous restaurant Ratanà (Milan). They use slices of bone marrow as tradition dictates, although today it is frequently omitted. Either way, be sure not to cook onions or white wine with the rice.

SERVES 4

- ½ onion
- 2 tablespoons (30 mL) extra-virgin olive oil
- 1⅓ cups (250 g) carnaroli rice (Riserva San Massimo)
- 8 slices bone marrow
- 3¼ cups (800 g) meat stock
- 1 pinch ground saffron
- 4 tablespoons (60 g) high-quality butter, preferably an alpine butter
- 3⅛ ounces (90 g) Lodigiano Típico or Grana Padano cheese
- 20 saffron threads

In a saucepan, cook the onion in the olive oil until soft and translucent. Remove the onion from the pan, then add the rice and 4 slices of the marrow. Sauté until the rice is translucent. Add the stock a little at a time, pouring in the next addition only once the previous addition has been absorbed by the rice. Stir in the saffron. Cook for 14 minutes. Turn off the heat, then add the butter and cheese, stirring vigorously to combine. Decorate with the remaining 4 marrow slices and the saffron threads. For a lighter version, serve it without the marrow.

THE TRADITIONAL VERSION

This version calls for broth made of beef, veal, and chicken with onion, celery, and carrots. Sautéing the rice in butter before adding the broth seems to be an addition of the Brianzoli—the inhabitants of Brianza, a historic Lombard region—who worked for wealthy Milanese families. Originally a red wine, the cooking wine used now is a white wine, to avoid coloring the rice.

SAUTÉED RICE, OR THE ART OF USING LEFTOVERS

Leftover Milanese risotto can turn into an equally famous *riso al salto* (sautéed rice), which is prepared by melting butter in a saucepan and adding the risotto to it. A beautiful golden crust forms on the side in contact with the pan, and the finished dish is served crust side up.

SKIP TO

GUALTIERO MARCHESI, P. 163; THE CULTIVATION OF RICE, P. 60.

SAFFRON

Neither a rhizome, seed, nor leaf, *lo zafferano* is the precious pistil of a flower. It colors, flavors, and ennobles many specialty dishes.

GIANNA MAZZEI

WHAT AM I?

SCIENTIFIC NAME: *Crocus sativus.*

FAMILY: Iridaceae.

APPEARANCE: mauve flowers composed of six tepals, three red stigmas, and three yellow stamens.

TASTE: sweet, slightly bitter; aromas of hay; warm notes of mild spice, sometimes saline.

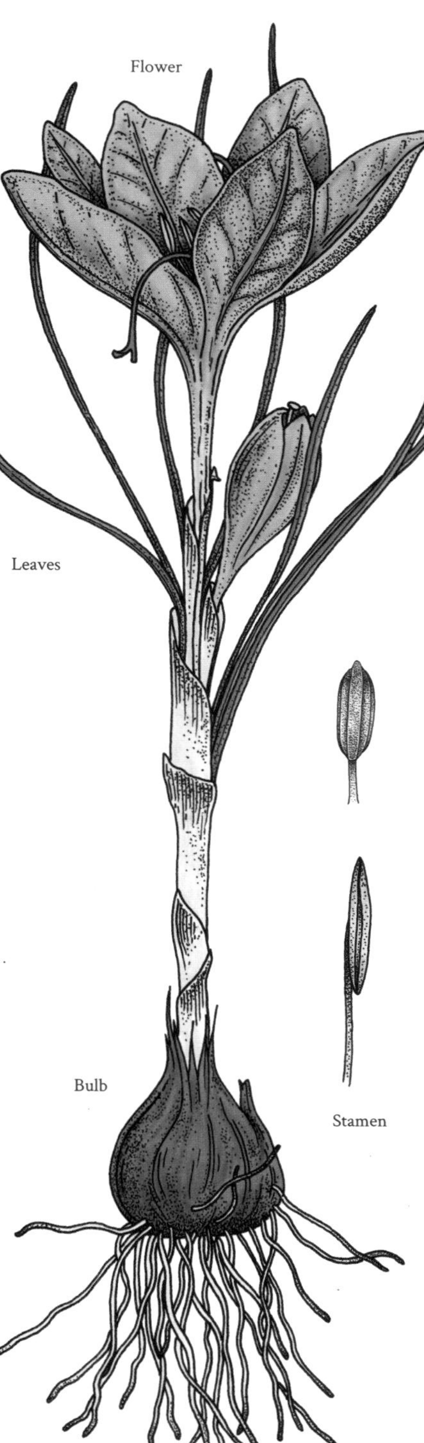

Saffron from L'Aquila PDO

In 1971, Giovannina and Silvio Sarra founded the Cooperativa Altopiano di Navelli in Civitaretenga to maintain the production of this spice, also involving chef Gualtiero Marchesi in their approach. Thanks to their efforts, this saffron from Abruzzo obtained a PDO.

Its cost varies from $45 to $75 (€35 to €60) per gram, depending on the method of cultivation and harvest. Between mid-October and November 1, the saffron must be harvested by hand, at dawn, before the flowers open. The stigmas are separated from the flower, placed in a sieve, and dried over wood embers.

Saffron from Sardinia PDO

It was the Phoenicians who brought the bulbs of this plant to Sardinia between the ninth and eighth centuries BCE. The Romans continued the production at the time. Today, it is cultivated according to ancestral techniques concentrated in the province of Medio Campidano (southwest).

Sardinian saffron has a higher-than-normal crocin, picrocrocin, and safranal content, which are responsible for its color, flavor, and aroma. It is used in the preparation of *malloreddus* (small Sardinian gnocchi) and *fregula* (pasta similar to Israeli couscous) and in broths, desserts, and fritters served during Carnival.

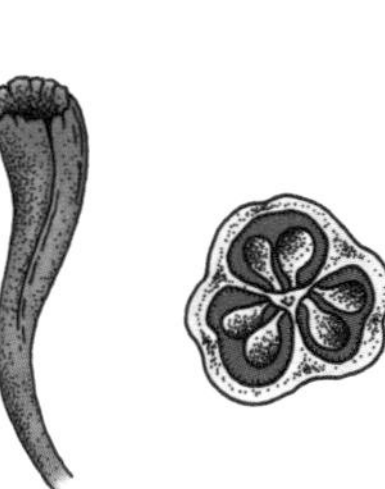

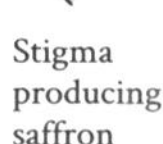

Stigma producing saffron

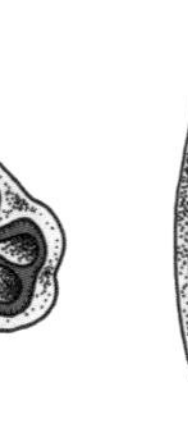

Ovary cross section

SKIP TO

RISOTTO ALLA MILANESE, P. 290;
SUPPLÌ VS. ARANCINI, P. 362;
EATING FROM THE SEA, P. 244.

ORIGIN AND LEGENDS

In Italy, saffron cultivation dates back to Roman times, but its reintroduction is thanks to the Arabs and dates from the ninth century (the period of occupied Sicily). The arrival of saffron in Abruzzo is linked to a monk from Navelli, who brought bulbs from Spain in the 1250s. The plant found an ideal habitat within the region. Saffron provided, among other things, a quality pigment to a penniless painter who painted a portrait of the Virgin, thus giving rise to the worship of the Madonna of Saffron in Civitaretenga.

Inventory of saffron dishes

SAVORY

ARANCINI (rice croquette), *Sicily.*

TORTA DI RISO, *Liguria*: very thin crust with a filling made from saffron rice, garnished with Parmesan.

CANNAROZZETTI ALLO ZAFFERANO, *Abruzzo*: short tube pasta, striped with saffron, and with ricotta.

SU SUCCU, *Sardinia*: *tagliolini* with a meat ragù with saffron and pecorino.

BRODETTO DI PORTO RECANATI, *Marche*: fish ragout with saffron.

SCAPECE ALLA VASTESE, *Abruzzo*: fish (dogfish) marinated in saffron vinegar, then fried.

COZZE E ZAFFERANO, *Abruzzo*: mussels with saffron.

RISOTTO ALLA MILANESE, *Lombardy*: saffron risotto.

PIACENTINU ENNESE, *Sicily*: sheep's-milk cheese flavored with saffron and black peppercorns.

BAGÒSS DI BAGOLINO, *Lombardy*: traditional cheese ripened with saffron.

DESSERTS

FIADONI DES ABRUZZES (see recipe below)

PANGIAL LO, *Lazio*: Christmas cakes.

PARDULAS, *Sardinia*: ricotta tartlets for Easter.

SAFFRON LIQUOR, *Abruzzo.*

RECIPE

FIADONI (RICOTTA AND SAFFRON CHEESECAKE)

This traditional recipe from Pescara has been perfected over the years, *fiadone* after *fiadone*.

MAKES APPROXIMATEY 12 *FIADONI*

FOR THE PASTRY

2¼ cups (280 to 300 g) high-protein all-purpose flour or type 65 flour
3 tablespoons (40 g) granulated sugar
2 large (100 g) eggs
3 tablespoons plus 1 teaspoon (50 mL) extra-virgin olive oil

FOR THE FILLING

4 large (200 g) eggs
Salt
14 ounces (400 g) cow's-milk ricotta
½ cup (100 g) granulated sugar
Zest of 1 lemon
½ ounce (15 g) saffron
Confectioners' sugar, for serving

- For the pastry, combine the flour, granulated sugar, eggs, and olive oil until you get a smooth mixture. Wrap in plastic wrap and let rest for 30 minutes at room temperature.
- For the filling, separate the egg yolks from the whites. Beat the egg whites to stiff peaks with a pinch of salt. Whisk the ricotta, granulated sugar, lemon zest, and saffron with the yolks until a foamy mixture forms. Gently fold in the egg whites.
- Preheat the oven to 350°F (180°C). Roll out the pastry dough to 2 mm thick and cut it into 4-inch (10 cm) squares. Place the squares in a greased muffin pan, leaving the excess dough at the corners sticking up. Fill each cavity with the filling, then fold down the corners without sealing the tops. Bake for 30 to 40 minutes, or until golden. Dust with confectioners' sugar.

ONIONS

From *agrodolce* to *soffritto*, the distinctive taste of *cipolle* is inseparable from the great classics of Italian cuisine.

ALESSANDRA PIERINI

WHAT AM I?

The onion, *cipolla* in Italian (*Allium cepa*), is a bulbous plant of the Liliaceae family, sometimes included among Amaryllidaceae. It has superficial roots, leaves, and a bulb as its edible parts.

It has been consumed since antiquity and is cultivated throughout Italy.

It is an essential ingredient in *soffritto*, the famous minced mixture containing equal amounts of carrot and celery, cooked over low heat in a fat (olive oil or butter, sometimes bacon fat, lard, or vegetable oil). It is the starting point for many dressings, sauces, and recipes: risotto, *Bolognese*, *spezzatino*, *sugo al pomodoro* . . .

LO SCALOGNO

Shallot

(Allium cepa var. aggregatum)

A bulb very close to the onion, but smaller in size and with a more delicate, sweet, and aromatic flavor with less pronounced sulfuric notes and a garlicky aftertaste. Formerly consumed as a snack on bread by peasants in Emilia-Romagna, today it is used in soffritto to replace onion, in *zuppa*, in bouillon, in agrodolce, with baked vegetables and fish.

IL LAMPASCIONE OR CIPOLLA CANINA

Tassel hyacinth

(Leopoldia comosa)

A small wild onion typical of Apulia and Basilicata, firm, very fragrant, and bitter. It is eaten fresh or jarred in vinegar or in sweet-and-sour dishes with *mentuccia* (lesser calamint) to accompany cheeses and charcuterie; fried; braised; in frittatas; with roast meat and fish.

OUR FAVORITE VARIETALS

CIPOLLA BIANCA

White onion

Cipollotto (spring onion—Liguria ⑨), *di Chioggia* (Veneto ③), *selvatica* (*Muscari comosum*, wild; central and south Italy ④)

TASTE—quite pronounced and crunchy, it becomes sweeter when cooked, releasing its aromas.

IN COOKING—raw, in a salad; in vinegar in *giardiniera*; marinade, *saor*; risotto; soffritto; braising; savory pies, focaccia; with peas, asparagus, zucchini; *fegato alla veneziana* (Venetian-style liver); baked with fish; with *luganega* (sausage) and *baccalà* (salt cod).

CIPOLLA DORATA OR RAMATA

Yellow or copper onion

Di Parma (Emilia-Romagna ⑦), *di Giarratana* (Slow Food, Sicily ②), *borettana* (Emilia-Romagna ⑤)

TASTE—powerful, fleshy; once caramelized, it becomes much more mild.

IN COOKING—the most versatile, too strong to eat raw. Slow-simmered stews, bouillons, roasts; with lentils; soffritto; ragù; *peperonata* (simmered peppers); pizza; *frittata rognosa* (omelet with sausage); *caponata*; for *scaccia* and *tirot* (two kinds of focaccia); the larger and flat ones stuffed and baked; *cipuddata* (a condiment of cooked onions); the smaller and softer as a topping, grilled, or in agrodolce.

CIPOLLA ROSSA

Red onion

Di Tropea IGP (Calabria ①), *di Acquaviva delle Fonti* SlowFood (Apulia ⑧), *Genovese* or *di Zerli* (Liguria ⑥)

TASTE—very mild, sweet, and delicate.

IN COOKING—less suitable for long cooking. Raw, in salad with potatoes, tuna, beans, or chickpeas; *panzanella* (Tuscan bread salad); *insalata bremese* (Lombard salad); compote; baked; savory tart; soup; *farinata* (socca); *frittelle* (fritters); *focaccia Genovese*; *baruat* (with frog legs and polenta); the larger ones stuffed.

SKIP TO

FEGATO ALLA VENEZIANA (CALF'S LIVER AND ONIONS), P. 243; CICCHETTI VENEZIANI (VENETIAN SNACKS), P. 228; RISOTTO, P. 78; PANZANELLA (BREAD SALAD), P. 168.

CHICKPEA, THE KING OF THE POOR

In the large family of *legumi* (legumes), chickpeas are an important ingredient. From *cibo di strada* (street food) to *cucina povera*, here is a tour of Italy via the *cece*.

STÉPHANE SOLIER

WHAT AM I?

The chickpea or garbanzo bean (*Cicer arietinum*) made its way across the borders of its native Anatolia to migrate, starting in antiquity, to the Indies and both shores of the Mediterranean, before finally landing on the Italian peninsula. Here are examples of its conquests, from northern to southern Italy, from appetizer to dessert . . .

STREET FOOD

WHEN CHICKPEAS HIT THE STREETS

BAKED CHICKPEA FLATBREADS

FARINATA
Liguria

CECINA/TORTA DI CECI
Tuscany

CECIATA
Emilia-Romagna

FAINÈ
Sardinia

SANDWICHES

FOCACCETTA, FUGASSETA
Stuffed with fried *panisse*, *Savona*

CINQUE E CINQUE
Filled with *torta di ceci, Livorno*

PANI E PANELLE
Topped with chickpea fritters, *Palermo*

SAVORY FRITTERS

CUCULLI
Liguria

PANELLE DI CECI
Sicily

RECIPES

PANISSE (FRIED CHICKPEA STICKS)

Savona, Liguria

SERVES 4 TO 6

4 cups (1 L) lukewarm water
3⅓ cups (300 g) chickpea flour
Salt
Olive oil
Freshly ground black pepper

- In a saucepan, gradually add the water to the chickpea flour and whisk to prevent lumps.
- Season with salt, set over very low heat, and stir continuously as you would when making polenta.
- After about 30 minutes, you should have a slightly dense consistency similar to yogurt.
- When the mixture begins to detach from the side of the pan, pour it into a cake pan measuring 9 by 4 inches (23 by 10 cm). Let cool for at least 2 hours or preferably overnight in the refrigerator.
- Unmold the panisse, cut into ¾- to 1⅛-inch-wide (2 to 3 cm) slices, then cut the slices into thick sticks, cubes, or diamond shapes.
- Fry the pieces in hot olive oil.
- Drain on paper towels and season with salt and pepper. Serve very hot.

☞ ***Il Tocco Della Nonna (Grandmother's Tip)***
Brown the pieces of panisse in a pan with chopped fresh onions, then season with salt and pepper (a specialty of La Spezia).

PASTA E CECI ALLA ROMANA (PASTA AND CHICKPEA SOUP)

Rome, Latium

SERVES 4

1⅓ cups (250 g) dried chickpeas
1 pinch baking soda
Olive oil
3 cloves garlic, peeled
3 small red chiles (such as tabasco or cayenne)
3 ounces (80 g) pancetta or bacon, thinly sliced into lardons
2 sprigs rosemary
Salt and freshly ground black pepper
6⅓ ounces (180 g) short tube dried pasta (*cannolicchietti, ditalini rigati . . .*) or *pasta mista* (a mixture of short pasta)
Pecorino Romano or Parmesan cheese

- The day before, soak the chickpeas in a bowl of cold water with the baking soda.
- The same day, heat 3 tablespoons (45 mL) olive oil in a large saucepan and brown the garlic, chiles, and pancetta.
- Drain the chickpeas and add them and the rosemary to the pan; cover with cold water (about 8 cups/2 L). Simmer, uncovered, for at least 2 hours 30 minutes, or until the chickpeas become tender. If necessary, add more hot water (up to 4 cups/1 L).
- Season with salt and pepper. Remove one-third of the chickpeas and mash them with a potato masher or a fork; set aside.
- Just before serving, bring the soup to a boil (add another 2 cups/500 mL water if necessary) and cook the pasta.
- Just before the end of the pasta cooking time, add the mashed chickpeas and stir well to combine. Serve hot, with grated pecorino and a drizzle of olive oil on top.

Quick version

- Use a pressure cooker and allow 45 minutes of cooking time.

☞ ***Il Tocco Della Nonna (Grandmother's Tip)***
Roman grandmothers cook two salted anchovy fillets, rinsed and sliced into thin strips, in olive oil, garlic, chile, and pancetta at the beginning of the recipe. This steps up the flavor without having a fishy taste. Magical!

You can also add 1 tablespoon of tomato paste to the olive oil at the beginning.

Sulla Punta Della Lingua (On the Tip of the Tongue)

Avere/parlare con il cece in bocca.
"Have a chickpea in your mouth."
To stammer, to stumble over your words.

È come cercare un cece in mare.
"It's like looking for a chickpea in the ocean."
Looking for a needle in a haystack.

A volte si perde la fava per cercare il cece.
"Sometimes we give up a bean to look for a chickpea."
We do not gain anything in exchange.

FRESH PASTA

From orecchiette of Apulia to *ravioli del Plin* from Piedmont, let's get our hands moving to make several of Italy's emblematic fresh pastas.

LAURA ZAVAN

1. MAKING *PASTA ALL'UOVO* (EGG PASTA)

SERVES 4

2¼ cups (280 g) type 1 flour or high-protein all-purpose (T65) flour

⅔ cup (120 g) fine durum wheat semolina flour

4 medium (175 g) eggs

PREPARATION

Combine the type 1 and semolina flours and pour them onto a work surface (preferably one made of untreated wood). Make a well in the center and add the eggs. Using a fork, gently beat the eggs (as you would when making an omelet) and gradually incorporate the flour. When the eggs are almost absorbed by the flour, start working the dough by hand. Knead for about 10 minutes. Add a little flour if the dough tends to stick to your fingers, or wet your hands if the dough is too firm. When the dough is smooth, form a ball, wrap it in a damp cloth or plastic wrap to prevent it from drying out, and let rest for 30 minutes to 1 hour at room temperature.

To roll out the dough

BY HAND

Flour the work surface. Roll out the dough using a rolling pin, always starting from the center and moving out. The thickness will not be perfectly even, but the pasta will hold the sauce better.

USING A PASTA ROLLING MACHINE

Work about 2 ounces (60 g) of dough at a time, keeping the remaining dough under a kitchen towel to prevent it from drying out. Flatten the dough into a disk using the palm of your hand. Lightly flour the top, then feed it through the pasta roller, opening the rollers as wide as possible. Fold the dough into thirds, then feed it again through the machine. Repeat this step until you get a rectangle fairly regular in size. Fold the dough in half and feed it through the pasta roller several more times, gradually tightening the rollers until the desired thickness is obtained: very thin for ravioli (second to last notch), about 1 mm thicker for long pasta. Cut it according to use.

2. CLASSIC PASTA FORMATS

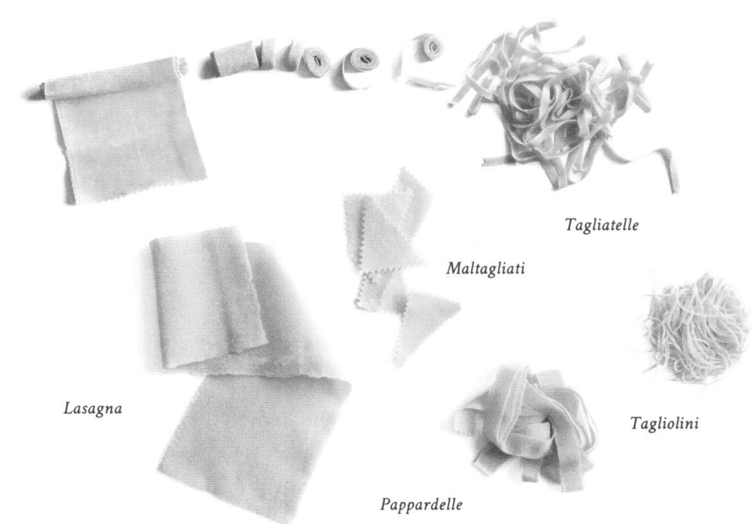

TAGLIOLINI, TAGLIATELLE, PAPPARDELLE, MALTAGLIATI . . .

Set the pasta sheets out for 10 minutes to dry on a cloth sprinkled with flour (or semolina) to prevent them from sticking when rolling them out.

CUTTING BY HAND: Roll up the dough and, using a sharp knife, cut sections that are:

→ Slightly less than ¼ inch (0.5 cm) wide for *tagliolini*.
→ ⅓ inch (1 cm) wide for tagliatelle.
→ ⅔ to ¾ inch (1.5 to 2 cm) wide for pappardelle.

Roll out the pasta and place them on a tea towel, forming small piles. Store them away from moisture and cook within 2 days.

Maltagliati (literally "badly cut") are irregular-shaped noodles cut with a knife or pasta cutter (these are often leftover pieces of rolled pasta dough that you use to avoid throwing anything away!).

LASAGNA NOODLES

With 2⅛ ounces (60 g) freshly rolled pasta dough you can form lasagna sheets measuring 4 to 4¾ inches (10 to 12 cm) wide and 15¾ inches (40 cm) long, to be cut according to the size of the dish. Precook the noodles for 2 to 3 minutes in salted boiling water, boiling no more than three or four noodles at a time. To stop the cooking, transfer them to a bowl of cold water, drain, then spread them out on a clean kitchen towel.

Tradition

Homemade pasta made with egg and soft-wheat flour is typical in northern Italy. The humid climate is not favorable to the cultivation of durum (hard) wheat. But soft wheat is lower in protein (gluten), thus the addition of egg.

LAURA'S ADVICE

To obtain a homogeneous dough, have your ingredients at room temperature.

The amount of flour needed may vary depending on its quality and the humidity in the room.

When using large eggs, plan on incorporating 5 to 10 percent more flour.

ORECCHIETTE

Orecchiette are traditional noodles from Apulia. This pasta is made from durum wheat semolina flour and water (like most pastas from southern Italy). The typical dressing is tomato sauce and *cacioricotta* cheese, or *cime di rapa* (broccoli rabe).

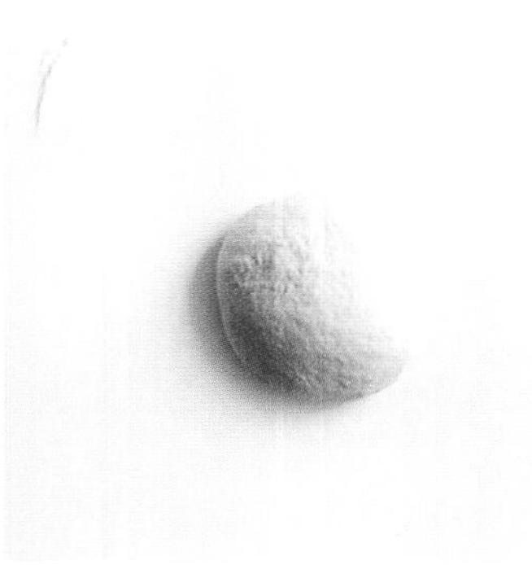

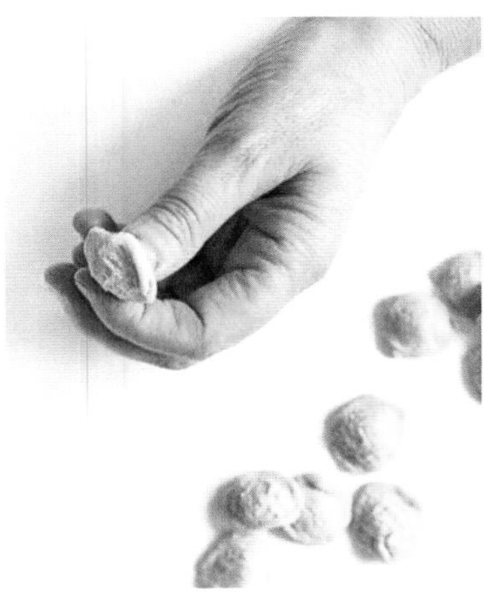

SERVES 4

1⅔ cups (300 g) fine durum wheat semolina flour (preferably whole grain)

About ¾ cup (200 mL) lukewarm water

- Place the flour in a bowl and make a well in the center. Gradually incorporate the water, mixing with your hands.
- Shape it into a ball. Knead the dough by hand on the work surface for 10 minutes, or until a smooth and homogeneous dough is achieved. If the dough sticks to your hands, add a little flour; if it is a little firm, wet your hands with water. Let the dough rest for 15 minutes, wrapped in a damp cloth or in plastic wrap.
- Cut a small piece of dough one piece at a time and make small sausages ⅓ inch (1 cm) wide with each piece. Cut each piece into ⅓-inch (1 cm) pieces, press them with the rounded end of a knife, and turn the dough over on your thumb: the concave shape obtained resembles a small ear (*orecchietta*). Place the pasta on a clean kitchen towel to air-dry, uncovered, for a few hours or overnight.

MACCHERONI AL FERRO

Maccheroni al ferro is a pasta, typical of southern Italy made from fine durum wheat semolina flour and water. The term *maccheroni* used to refer to all kinds of pasta. *Al ferro* ("with a rod") refers to the tool that is traditionally used in Calabria to roll the pasta, but a skewer will do!

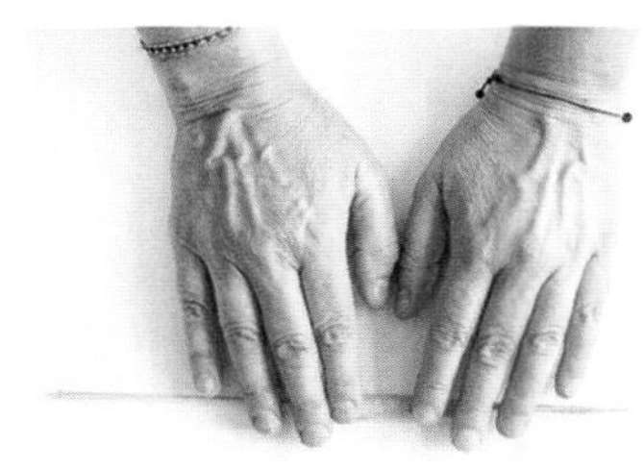
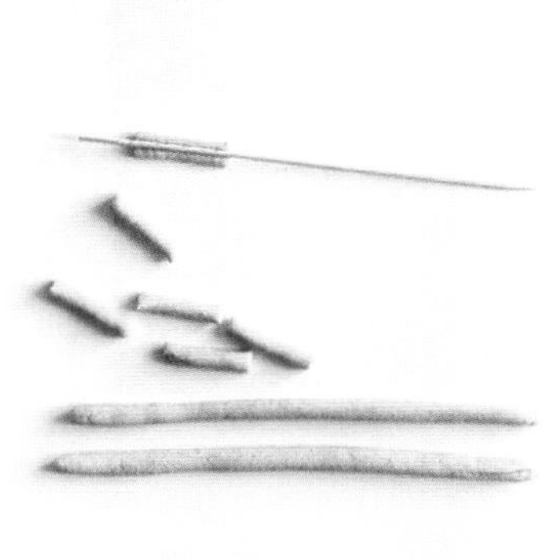

SERVES 4

2¼ cups (400 g) fine durum wheat semolina flour

About ¾ cup (200 mL) lukewarm water

Equipment

1 wooden skewer or 1 thin knitting needle

- Sprinkle the semolina onto a work surface to help aerate it, make a well in the center, and gradually incorporate the water by hand.
- Work the dough with your hands for 10 minutes, kneading until the dough becomes smooth and supple. If it is too sticky, add a little flour; if it is too dense, add a little water.
- Shape it into a ball and let rest, covered with a towel or plastic wrap, for 15 minutes at room temperature.
- Cut one small piece of dough at a time and roll it into a long sausage the diameter of a cigarette. Cut them into sticks of 1½ to 2 inches (4 to 5 cm).
- Roll the skewer on the dough log, pressing with a back-and-forth motion: the dough will wrap around the skewer, taking on its shape. Place the pasta on a clean kitchen towel and repeat with the remaining dough. Allow to air-dry, uncovered, for a few hours or overnight.

SKIP TO

ORECCHIETTE CON CIME DI RAPA, P. 374; LASAGNA VERDI ALLA BOLOGNESE (SPINACH PASTA LASAGNA BOLOGNESE), P. 47; THE BOAR, KING OF TUSCANY, P. 331.

RAVIOLI RICOTTA E SPINACI (RICOTTA AND SPINACH RAVIOLI)

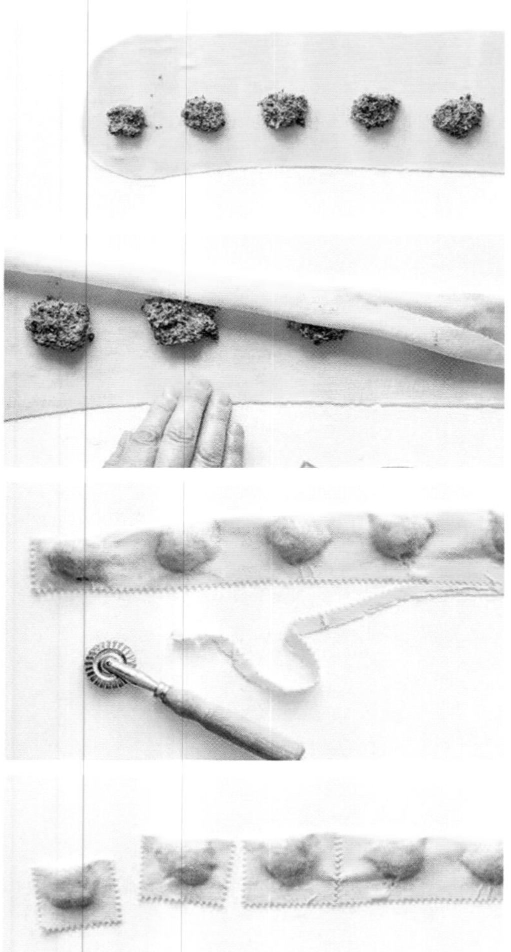

These ravioli, widely found throughout Italy, are stuffed with spinach (or, depending on the local variations, chard, nettles, borage . . .). Add fresh artisanal ricotta and a good grating of nutmeg. *Burro e salvia* (butter and sage) is the typical dressing, but this dish can also be made with a tomato sauce.

These ravioli are also called *ravioli di magro,* for "lean" days without meat following the principles of the Catholic Church that, since the Middle Ages, exclude meat on Fridays and during Lent.

SERVES 4

For the dough

1⅔ cups (200 g) all-purpose flour

½ cup (100 g) fine durum wheat semolina flour

3 medium (132 g) eggs

For the filling

14 ounces (400 g) fresh spinach (or a mixture of herbs), or 7 ounces (200 g) frozen spinach

1 clove garlic, peeled

2 tablespoons (30 mL) olive oil

Salt and freshly ground black pepper

3 pinches freshly grated nutmeg

3½ ounces (100 g) ricotta cheese

½ cup (50 g) freshly grated Parmesan cheese

For the sauce

3 tablespoons (40 g) unsalted butter

12 sage leaves

⅓ cup (40 g) freshly grated Parmesan cheese

· For the dough, follow the instructions on page 294.

· For the filling, remove the stems from the spinach and wash the leaves. Cut the garlic in half. Heat the olive oil in a pan and add the garlic. Add the spinach and cook until they release all of their water. Season with salt and pepper and the nutmeg. Remove the cooked spinach from the pan (discard the garlic) and chop it. Transfer it to a bowl. Add the ricotta and Parmesan, and toss to combine. Season again with salt and pepper or nutmeg, if needed.

· Roll out the dough until thin using a rolling pin or a pasta roller, setting the roller width to the second to last notch (see page 294). Place a spoonful of the filling every 2 inches (5 cm) along the length of the dough. Lightly moisten one edge of the dough with water using a brush or your fingertips to ensure the dough adheres together well. Fold the dough over, then press gently around the filling with your fingers to remove any air and seal the edges. Cut the ravioli with a fluted pasta cutter, trimming off excess dough horizontally around the edges, then cut vertically between each ravioli. Arrange them on a tray and cover them with a kitchen towel dusted with semolina flour.

· Bring a large pot of salted water to boil. Cook the ravioli for about 5 minutes, depending on the thickness of the dough.

· For the sauce, melt the butter in a skillet over low heat, then add the sage leaves to infuse the butter, adding a few tablespoons of the ravioli cooking water to create an emulsion.

· When the ravioli are done, remove them with a skimmer or slotted spoon and add them to the butter-sage sauce in the pan, or transfer them to a mixing bowl and toss them gently with the butter-sage sauce. Sprinkle with the Parmesan and serve.

Storing

All ravioli formats can be stored for twenty-four hours in the refrigerator: place them between two kitchen towels on a tray dusted with fine semolina flour (to absorb any moisture). You can also freeze them flat and, once frozen, store them in a freezer bag. Cook them frozen, without thawing them.

RAVIOLI DEL PLIN
(BEEF AND CURLY ENDIVE RAVIOLI)

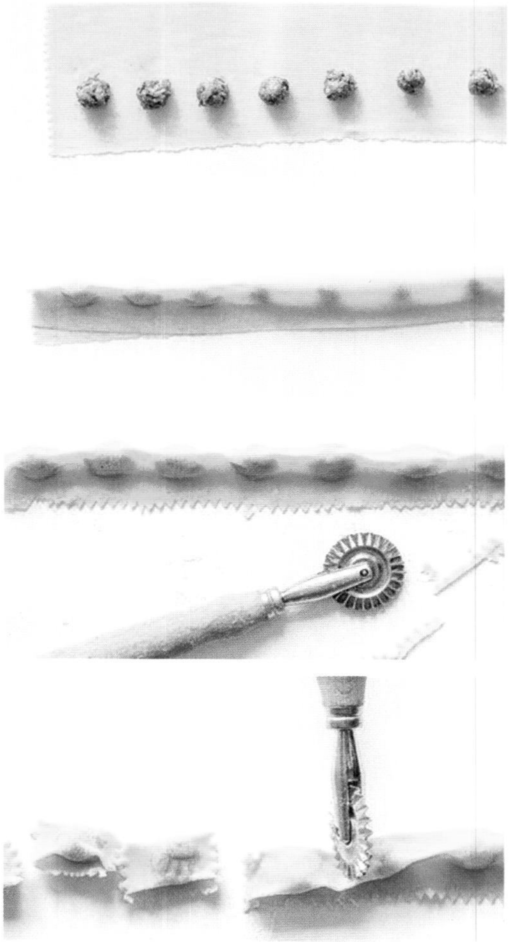

This recipe is typical in the hills of the Langhe, in Roero and Monferrato near Turin in the Piedmont region. The name *plin* refers to the pinch used to make these small ravioli. The filling consists of leftover *bollito* (meat and vegetable stew) or roast beef. This is the origin of all ravioli: the art of using leftovers!

SERVES 4

For the dough

(traditional recipe)

2½ cups (300 g) all-purpose flour

6 to 8 (114 to 152 g) egg yolks

OR

1⅔ cups (200 g) all-purpose flour

½ cup (100 g) fine durum wheat semolina flour

3 medium (132 g) eggs

For the filling

12 ounces (350 g) curly endive or spinach

2 tablespoons (30 mL) olive oil

1 clove garlic, peeled and halved

Salt and freshly ground black pepper

2 to 3 pinches freshly grated nutmeg

7 ounces (200 g) cooked beef (from a stew or roast)

1 large (50 g) egg

¾ cup (80 g) freshly grated 24-month Parmesan cheese

For the sauce

3 tablespoons (40 g) unsalted butter

12 sage leaves

⅓ cup (40 g) freshly grated Parmesan cheese

(Alternatively, replace the butter and sage with a scant ⅔ cup/150 mL juices obtained from roasted meat)

· For the dough, follow the instructions on page 294.

· For the filling, wash the endive, cut the leaves into quarters, and, without wringing them out, panfry them in the olive oil with the garlic until tender; add a little water if necessary. Season with salt and pepper and thenutmeg.

· Remove the cooked endive from the pan (discard the garlic) and finely chop it, then chop the meat. Combine everything in a bowl, then add the egg and Parmesan. Adjust the seasoning, if needed. Form the mixture into small balls, about the size of a hazelnut.

· Roll out the dough until thin using a rolling pin or pasta roller, setting the roller width to the second to last notch (see page 294).

· On a sheet of the dough, spoon a small amount of the filling spaced every 2 inches (5 cm), placing them 2 inches (5 cm) from the edge. Lightly moisten one edge of the dough with water using a brush or your fingertips to ensure the dough adheres together well. Fold the dough over, then press gently around the filling with your fingers to remove any air and seal the edges. Cut the ravioli with a fluted pasta cutter, trimming off excess dough horizontally around the edges, then cut vertically between each ravioli. Arrange them on a tray and cover with a kitchen towel dusted with semolina flour.

· Bring a large pot of salted water to a boil. Cook the ravioli for about 5 minutes, depending on the thickness of the dough.

· For the sauce, melt the butter in a skillet over low heat, then add the sage leaves to infuse the butter, adding a few tablespoons of the ravioli cooking water to create an emulsion.

· When the ravioli are done, remove them with a skimmer or slotted spoon and add them to the butter-sage sauce in the pan, or transfer them to a mixing bowl and toss them gently with the butter-sage sauce. Sprinkle with the Parmesan and serve.

· STUFFED PASTA ·

TORTELLONI AI CARCIOFI
(TORTELLONI WITH ARTICHOKES)

Italy is crazy about artichokes! They are enjoyed in all forms and preparations: raw, fried, sautéed, canned . . .

SERVES 4

For the dough

1⅔ cups (200 g) all-purpose flour

½ cup (100 g) fine durum wheat semolina flour

3 medium (132 g) eggs

For the filling

6 Poivrade artichokes or 9 ounces (250 g) artichoke hearts

Juice of ½ lemon

2 tablespoons (30 mL) olive oil

1 clove garlic, peeled and halved

⅓ cup (80 mL) dry white wine

Salt

½ bunch parsley, chopped

3½ ounces (100 g) cooked potatoes (cooled) or ricotta cheese

½ cup (50 g) freshly grated Parmesan cheese

Freshly ground black pepper

For finishing

2 tablespoons (30 mL) olive oil

2 ounces (60 g) Parmesan cheese shavings

· For the dough, follow the instructions on page 294.

· For the filling, clean the artichokes, cutting off the tips and removing several of the outer dark green leaves; place the artichokes in water with the lemon juice to help preserve their color. Cut the artichokes into quarters. In a skillet, heat the olive oil with the garlic clove halves over medium heat, add the artichokes, and cook for 10 minutes. Add the white wine in small quantities and cook until the liquid has evaporated. Season with salt, adding a little water if necessary. Finish cooking, covered. Sprinkle with the parsley.

· Remove and discard the garlic. Chop three-fourths of the artichokes. Set aside the remaining quartered artichokes for serving. Place the chopped artichokes in a bowl. Add the cooked potatoes, crushing them into the mixture, then stir in the Parmesan. Season with salt and pepper.

· Roll out the dough until thin using a rolling pin or a pasta roller, setting the roller width to the second to last notch (see page 294). Cut out 3-inch (8 cm) squares using a fluted pasta cutter. Using two small spoons, arrange a small pile of filling (⅓ to ½ ounce/10 to 12 g) in the center of each square. Lightly moisten two edges of each dough square with water, using a brush or your fingertips to ensure the dough adheres together well. Make a triangle by folding over two corners to meet and pressing the ends together to adhere, then wrap the other corners around the bottom and pinch them closed, forming a hat.

· Bring a large pot of salted water to boil and cook the ravioli for about 5 minutes, depending on the thickness of the dough. When the ravioli are done, remove them with a skimmer or slotted spoon and transfer to a bowl. Season with olive oil and 2 tablespoons of the ravioli cooking water. Serve with the remaining seared artichokes and the Parmesan shavings.

· STUFFED PASTA ·

CANNELLONI ALLA SORRENTINA
(CANNELLONI AS IN SORRENTINA)

A traditional recipe from Campania, typical on celebration days, delighting both young and old!

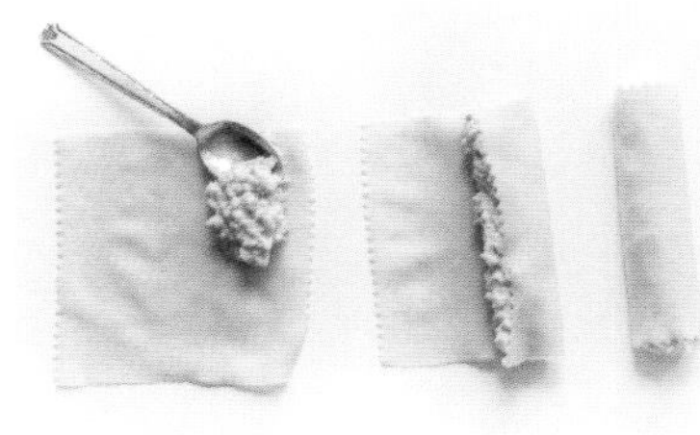

SERVES 4

For the dough

1⅔ cups (200 g) all-purpose flour

½ cup (100 g) fine durum wheat semolina flour

3 medium (132 g) eggs

For the meat sauce

1 medium onion

2 tablespoons (30 mL) olive oil

10½ ounces (300 g) ground beef (lower rib or other marbled meat)

Salt

¼ cup (60 mL) red wine

Freshly ground black pepper

14 ounces (400 g) peeled or diced tomatoes

For the filling

9 ounces (250 g) *fior di latte* mozzarella

10½ ounces (300 g) ricotta cheese

2 large (100 g) eggs

Several parsley leaves

1 cup (100 g) grated provolone cheese or Parmesan cheese

Salt and freshly ground black pepper

3½ ounces (100 g) cooked ham (lightly salted)

· For the dough, follow the instructions on page 294.

· For the meat sauce, finely chop the onion. Heat the olive oil in a cooking pot. Add the onion and cook until lightly browned. Increase the heat to high, add the meat, and cook it until it sticks to the bottom of the pan. Season with salt. Add the wine and cook until it has evaporated. Season with salt and pepper, then add the tomatoes. Cook over low heat for 1 hour.

· For the filling, cut the mozzarella into small cubes and let drain. In a mixing bowl, mash the ricotta with a spatula until creamy and smooth. Add the eggs, parsley, and most of the grated cheese (set aside a good handful for serving). Season with salt and pepper. Chop the ham using a knife, then fold it into the mixture along with the drained mozzarella.

· Roll out the dough until thin using a rolling pin or a pasta roller, setting the roller width to the second to last notch (see page 294). Cut out twelve squares of 4 to 4¾ inches (10 to 12 cm) each. Place four pasta squares at a time in salted boiling water with 1 tablespoon (15 mL) of olive oil for 2 minutes. Drain and transfer to a bowl of cold water to stop the cooking, then transfer immediately to a clean kitchen towel.

· On top of each square of dough, generously arrange the filling using two small spoons or a piping bag. Roll up the squares to create cannelloni.

· Preheat the oven to 350°F (180°C). In a baking dish, generously pour a layer of meat sauce over the bottom. Arrange the cannelloni on top. Cover the cannelloni with the remaining sauce and sprinkle with the reserved cheese. Bake for 15 to 20 minutes, or until the sauce is bubbling and the cheese is browned. Let the cannelloni rest for 10 minutes before serving.

MEZZELUNE AL BACCALÀ
(HALF-MOONS WITH SALT COD)

Salted *baccalà* is present in all Italian cuisine. It replaces fresh fish at any time (you just have to plan to desalt it forty-eight hours in advance). It can be replaced with shredded cod (a few hours is enough to desalt it) or with frozen cod already desalted, adding a few anchovies to make the dish even more flavorful.

SERVES 4

For the filling

10½ ounces (300 g) salt cod

1 bay leaf

½ bunch parsley with stems

1 clove garlic, peeled, halved, and germ removed

3½ ounces (100 g) cooked potatoes, cooled

3 tablespoons (20 g) capers in salt or good black olives

3 tablespoons (45 mL) olive oil

For the dough

1⅔ cups (200 g) all-purpose flour

½ cup (100 g) fine durum wheat semolina flour

3 medium (132 g) eggs

For the sauce

1 tablespoon (9 g) salted capers or more olives

2 tablespoons black olives

2 tablespoons (30 mL) olive oil

1 clove garlic, peeled and halved

9 ounces (250 g) cherry tomatoes, halved

A few small basil leaves, for garnish (optional)

· For the filling, desalt the cod 2 days prior to using it, changing the water regularly. In a saucepan set over very low heat, place the cod, bay leaf, parsley stems (reserve the leaves), and garlic. Cover with water and cook for about 10 minutes. Do not season the mixture with salt. Drain the cod and reserve the garlic. Remove the skin and bones from the cod.

· For the dough, see page 294.

· Rinse the capers under cold water and chop them (they will add salt). Chop the parsley leaves (reserving 1 teaspoon for serving, if you'd like). Mash the cooked garlic. Crumble the cod flesh and combine it with the cooked potatoes (mashed), capers, garlic, parsley, and olive oil. Adjust the seasoning, if needed.

· Roll out the dough until thin using a rolling pin or a pasta roller, setting the roller width to the second to last notch (see page 294). Cut out circles of dough using a cookie cutter. Place a spoonful of the filling in the center of each circle. Lightly moisten the edges of each dough circle with water, using a brush or your fingertips, and close the disk into a half-moon shape. Press around the stuffing with your fingers to remove air and seal the edges together well. Arrange the half-moons on a tray and cover with a kitchen towel dusted with semolina flour.

· For the sauce, rinse the capers under cold water and chop them. Remove the pits from the olives (if necessary) and halve the olives. In a pan, heat the olive oil and brown the garlic. Add the olives, capers, and tomatoes. Cook over high heat for 2 minutes. Remove and discard the garlic and adjust the seasoning, if necessary.

· Bring a large pot of salted water to boil and cook the pasta for about 5 minutes, depending on the thickness of the dough. When the pasta is done, remove it with a skimmer or slotted spoon, and transfer it directly to the pan with the tomatoes. Arrange a few basil leaves on top.

FISH

With its 4,660 miles (7,500 km) of coastline, Italy's boot is completely in the water!
Here is a catch of the twenty-one most common species found in the surrounding Italian seas—and how to cook them.

SERENA LANZA

1. Ombrina (Shi drum) / 2. Dentice (Common dentex) / 3. Scorfano (Red scorpion fish) / 4. Branzino (European sea bass) / 5. Triglia di scoglio and Triglia di fango (Surmullet and red mullet) / 6. Rombo (Brill or turbot) / 7. Lampuga (Common dolphinfish) / 8. Razza (Challenger skate) / 9. Acciuga (European anchovies) / 10. Cefalo or Muggine (Flathead grey mullet) / 11. San pietro (John Dory) / 12. Sarago (Sar) / 13. Sarda (Sardine) / 14. Palamita (Atlantic bonito) / 15. Ricciola or Seriola (Greater amberjack) / 16. Gallinella (Piper gurnard) / 17. Anguilla (Eel) / 18. Aguglia (Garfish) / 19. Spratto (European sprat) / 20. Orata (Gilthead sea bream) / 21. Rana pescatrice (Angler or monkfish)

① OMBRINA · Shi drum

LATIN NAME: *Umbrina cirrosa* (Sciaenidae).

COMMON NAMES: *corbello, corvo, corbo* (Adriatic regions).

SEASON: mainly fished in spring and summer; for commercial purposes, often farmed.

FLAVOR: white flesh, lean, with a delicate taste; rich in protein and mineral salts.

IN COOKING: baked, grilled, or simply boiled.

REGIONAL SPECIALTIES: *ombrina all'acqua di mare,* "with seawater" with lemon juice and white wine (Sicily).

② DENTICE · Common dentex

LATIN NAME: *Dentex dentex* (Sparidae).

COMMON NAMES: *dentat, tantatu, tentatu* (Apulia); *dental* (Veneto, Friuli).

SEASON: fished year-round, especially in spring and summer when it approaches the coast.

FLAVOR: firm flesh, intense taste; very lean, easy to digest.

IN COOKING: baked, in a flaky pastry with potatoes, grilled, in a sauce for pasta of different formats.

REGIONAL SPECIALTIES: *in umido,* in ragout (Sardinia); couscous from Favignana (Sicily)

③ SCORFANO · Red scorpion fish

LATIN NAME: *Scorpaena scrofa* (Scorpaenidae).

COMMON NAMES: *pesce scorfano rosso, scarpena, scorpena rossa* (Veneto); *scuorfano* (Campania); *ronola roscia* (Apulia); *capidazza* (Sicily); *cabbuni di mari* (Sardinia).

SEASON: fished year-round.

FLAVOR: white flesh, firm, subtle taste and delicately musky; rich in protein, low in fat.

IN COOKING: very sought-after flesh. Simmered, baked, in pasta sauces. Excellent grilled when of large size.

REGIONAL SPECIALTIES: linguine or *paccheri allo scorfano,* with garlic and cherry tomatoes (throughout Italy).

④ BRANZINO · European sea bass

LATIN NAME: *Dicentrarchus labrax* (Moronidae).

COMMON NAMES: *branzino* in the north, *spigola* in the rest of the peninsula and the islands. *Luassu* (Liguria); *spinola, spaine, spina* (Campania, Apulia, Sicily).

SEASON: fished year-round, but mostly present in markets in its farmed version.

FLAVOR: white flesh, light, firm; leaner when wild. Delicate taste.

IN COOKING: raw, baked, or grilled.

REGIONAL SPECIALTIES: in a salt crust (Friuli): a whole fish baked in the oven covered with coarse salt; *alla pitallara,* steaks cooked in a pan with tomatoes and bell peppers (Molise).

⑤ TRIGLIA DI SCOGLIO AND TRIGLIA DI FANGO
Surmullet and red mullet

LATIN NAME: *Mullus surmuletus* (surmullet), *Mullus barbatus* (red mullet) (Mullidae).

COMMON NAMES: *rusciole, triie* (Abruzzo); *trigghia, tregghia, treggh, treja* (Calabria and Apulia); *treggia* (Liguria); *triglia birdi, trigghjia birdu* (Sardinia); *trigghia, sparaganaci, sparacalaci, trigli pichi* (Sicily); *barbòn, tria, triola* (Veneto and Friuli-Venezia Giulia).

SEASON: fished year-round, especially in fall.

FLAVOR: delicate flesh, very tasty and fragrant; high in protein. Red mullet has a fattier flesh than surmullet, which is more refined and flavorful.

IN COOKING: the little ones are excellent fried, the larger ones are suitable for short cooking in the oven, grilled, or in a *guazzetto* (panfried cherry tomatoes with garlic, wine, or stock). Excellent in sauces for pasta or risottos.

REGIONAL SPECIALTIES: red mullet *alla livornese,* panfried with cherry tomatoes, garlic, and parsley (Tuscany); *cacciucco,* fish ragout (Tuscany); mullet risotto (throughout Italy).

⑥ ROMBO · Brill or turbot

LATIN NAME: *Scophthalmus rhombus* (*rombo liscio, rombo soaso,* brill); *Psetta maxima* (*rombo chiodato,* turbot) (Scophthalmidae).

COMMON NAMES: *rummulu, passira pitrusa, linguata, grumcu* (Sicily).

SEASON: fished year-round, especially in winter and spring.

FLAVOR: white flesh, firm, dense, with a delicate taste; lean, rich in proteins and mineral salts; very easy to digest.

IN COOKING: baked, broiled, or steamed. Excellent aroma with the head and bones.

REGIONAL SPECIALTIES: risotto with turbot; *boreto alla gradese,* sautéed turbot with garlic, vinegar, and a lot of black pepper (Friuli).

⑦ LAMPUGA
Common dolphinfish

LATIN NAME: *Coriphaena hippurus* (Coryphaenidae).

COMMON NAMES: *pappagallo* (Liguria); *lambuga* (Sardinia); *lambucha, capone* (Apulia); *pisci capunii* (Sicily).

SEASON: fished mainly in spring and fall as it approaches the coast.

FLAVOR: dense flesh, intense taste, lean and rich in mineral salts.

IN COOKING: excellent baked or grilled.

REGIONAL SPECIALTIES: *alla matalotta,* simmered with cherry tomatoes, onion, olives, and capers (Sicily).

⑧ RAZZA · Challenger skate

LATIN NAME: *Raja* spp. (Rajidae).

COMMON NAMES: *arzilla* (Lazio); *rascia* (Apulia); *pichira* or *picara* (Sicily).

SEASON: fished year-round, especially in winter.

FLAVOR: rosy flesh, very firm with a delicate taste; high protein and mineral content, low fat content. Excellent for broth with the head and bones, sought-after liver, with an intense taste.

IN COOKING: prepared in soup, in court-bouillon, or a breaded and fried fillet.

REGIONAL SPECIALTIES: *brodo di arzilla,* pasta and broccoli soup with skate broth (Lazio); *agliata di razza,* skate in sauce with garlic, sun-dried tomatoes, peeled tomatoes, vinegar (Sardinia).

⑨ ACCIUGA · European anchovies

LATIN NAME: *Engraulis encrasicolus* (Engraulidae).

COMMON NAMES: *anciua* (Liguria); *alice* (Campania and Apulia); *anciovitta, anciova* (Sardinia); *masculinu, anciova, aliccia, ancidda, corinedda, ancioja, anciojarina* (Sicily); *sardon, sardone* (Marche, Romagna, Veneto, Friuli-Venezia Giulia).

SEASON: fall and spring. The larger ones are fished between June and July.

FLAVOR: firm, semifatty flesh rich in omega-3s; distinct flavor.

IN COOKING: floured then breaded and fried; raw, marinated in vinegar or lemon; canned (in oil or salt). The fry are known by the name *bianchetti* or *neonata.*

REGIONAL SPECIALTIES: stuffed *alla ligure,* with bread crumbs soaked in milk, garlic, parsley, and Parmesan, breaded and fried (Liguria); *m'buttunate cilentane* (Campania); anchovy *tortino,* cut in half, placed on top of each other, and sprinkled with dried bread crumbs, herbs, and cherry tomatoes, then baked (Liguria and Sicily); *farinata with bianchetti* (Liguria); *bagnet verd* or *bagnet ross* sauces (Piedmont); *colatura di alici de Cetara* (Campania).

⑩ CEFALO OR MUGGINE
Flathead grey mullet

LATIN NAME: *Mugil cephalus* (Mugilidae).

COMMON NAMES: *muzao, musai* (Liguria); *cefolo, mattarello* (Rome); *capuozzo, capozze, capocefalo, ciefl* (Campania and Apulia); *mujelle, mugella* (Abruzzo, Marche); *volpina, sieul* (Friuli); *muza, muzzulu, muzzeru* (Sardinia); *mulettu, muletta* (Sicily).

SEASON: fished year-round, especially in spring and summer.

FLAVOR: flesh with an intense taste depending on the species, firm and easy to digest. Flavor strongly influenced by its environment in which it developed and fed.

IN COOKING: in a pan, baked, grilled, marinated, barbecued, or in a salt crust.

REGIONAL SPECIALTIES: *alla comacchiese,* marinated in oil, salt, rosemary, and lemon then grilled (Emilia-Romagna); bottarga from the eggs of females (Sardinia and Tuscany).

⑪ SAN PIETRO · John Dory

LATIN NAME: *Zeus faber* (Zeidae).

COMMON NAMES: *pesce gallo, san pietro* (Campania); *cetra, iotra, cetola, san piet* (Apulia); *ngitola, pisciu gaddru* (Calabria); *jaddu, gaddi, gaddu, pisci san petru* (Sicily).

SEASON: fished year-round, especially in spring and summer.

FLAVOR: white flesh, firm, lean, with a delicate and distinct taste; low in calories but high in protein, omega-3s, and potassium.

IN COOKING: in a flaky pastry with potatoes, *all'acqua pazza* (oil, garlic, cherry tomatoes, and parsley), or en papillote. Excellent steamed or grilled.

REGIONAL SPECIALTIES: couscous *alla trapanese* (Sicily).

NEXT PAGE

⑫ SARAGO · Sar

LATIN NAME: *Diplodus* spp. (Sparidae).

COMMON NAMES: variants depending on the species. For *sarago fasciato* (two-banded sea bream): *zacaro* (Lazio); *sparlo* (Liguria and Marche); *sacristanu, zacaro varaturu* (Sicily). For *sarago maggiore* (white sea bream), the most popular: *esperli, saagu* (Liguria); *sparagliuni 'mperiali* (Sicily); *sbaro, sbavo* (Marche).

SEASON: fished year-round, especially in fall and spring.

FLAVOR: white flesh, delicate and tasty, very easy to digest; low in fat and rich in minerals.

IN COOKING: grilled, baked, but also panfried.

REGIONAL SPECIALTIES: *alla ligure*, panfried with garlic, thyme, rosemary, white wine, or with pine nuts and Taggiasca olives (Liguria); on skewers with prosciutto, rosemary, bread, sage leaves (Tuscany); excellent in soups when the fish are small.

⑬ SARDA · Sardine

LATIN NAME: *Sardina pilchardus* (Clupeidae).

COMMON NAMES: *sarda* for fresh fish, *sardina* for fish preserved in oil. *Sardella, sardona, saracla, pesantone, cicinellijanculilli* (Campania); *sardela, palassiola* (Friuli); *sardella, melella* (Lazio); *sardenna, parasina, paasetta* . . . (Liguria); *sardèdde, falloppe, sard, sarachidd* (Apulia); *sardella, sarda fimminedda, sarduzza, saraca, sadda, varvaiolu, maiatica, muccu* . . . (Sicily); *sardella, parazzi* (Tuscany); *sardella, renga, rengheta, palassiola* (Veneto).

SEASON: fished year-round, especially in fall and spring.

FLAVOR: oily flesh, strong taste; rich in omega-3s and vitamin D.

IN COOKING: grilled, au gratin, baked, or canned (in oil or salt). The fry, known as *bianchetti* or *neonata*, are steamed or in fritters. When preserved in oil with chile and salt, the sardines are called *sardella* or *rosa marina* in Calabria.

REGIONAL SPECIALTIES: *a beccafico* (Sicily), *saor* (Veneto), *spaghetti con le sarde* (Sicily); *alla cetrarese*, baked with oil and oregano (Calabria); *incinte in agrodolce*, marinated in vinegar, stuffed with bread crumbs, raisins, garlic, pine nuts, and parsley, then baked in oil and lemon (Veneto).

⑭ PALAMITA · Atlantic bonito

LATIN NAME: *Sarda sarda* (Scombridae).

COMMON NAMES: *palamide* (Veneto); *bonnico* (Liguria); *cuvarita* (Campania); *pisantuni* (Sicily).

SEASON: fished mainly in spring and autumn.

FLAVOR: flesh with an intense taste; fatty, rich in omega-3s, vitamin A, and mineral salts.

IN COOKING: grilled, stewed, baked, boiled, or raw as carpaccio or tartare. Can be stored in oil.

REGIONAL SPECIALTIES: *spaghetti allo stufatu di palamita* (bonito stew), with cherry tomatoes, pine nuts, raisins, and wild fennel (Sicily); *bonito parmigiana*, eggplant and bonito with Parmesan (Sicily and Campania); Atlantic bonito from the Tuscan sea (Slow Food presidio), preserved in oil with bay leaf, black pepper, and chile.

⑮ RICCIOLA OR SERIOLA
Greater amberjack

LATIN NAME: *Seriola dumerili* (Carangidae).

COMMON NAMES: *eccia* (Liguria); *lissa* (Veneto and Friuli-Venezia Giulia); *saltaleone* (Tuscany); *alice grande* (Marche); *jarrupe* or *lecc* (Apulia); *aricciola, licciolu* (Sicily); *Servola* (Sardinia).

SEASON: fished year-round, especially from spring to fall, when it nears the coast.

FLAVOR: white flesh, firm, with an intense taste, slight spice; rich in omega-3s, vitamins A and B, and phosphorus.

IN COOKING: depending on the size, can be cooked whole or in slices, baked, grilled; excellent raw.

REGIONAL SPECIALTIES: *alla siciliana*, panfried with potatoes, olives, capers, and cherry tomatoes.

⑯ GALLINELLA · Piper gurnard

LATIN NAME: *Trigla lucerna* (Triglidae).

COMMON NAMES: *choeussano, organetto* (Liguria); *cappone, capone* (Lazio, Abruzzo); *cuoccio reale, faggiano* (Campania); *mazzola, mazzolina, mazziola* (Marche, Veneto); *luserna* (Veneto, Friuli); *angiloiedda, angiulu, teste* (Apulia); *cocciu* (Calabria); *cocciu, facianu* (Sicily).

SEASON: fished year-round, especially October to February.

FLAVOR: flesh with a delicate but pronounced taste; rich in mineral salts (potassium, magnesium, calcium) and vitamins A and D. High in protein, but very little fat.

IN COOKING: its flesh lends itself to different cooking methods, from soup to simply steaming.

REGIONAL SPECIALTIES: *in guazzetto*, cooked in a pan of tomatoes, garlic, wine, or stock; *in umido*, simmered with carrots, celery, onions, and tomatoes (Adriatic and Tyrrhenian coasts); Gurnard tomato sauce (with cherry tomatoes) with *paccheri* or spaghetti (Adriatic and Tyrrhenian coasts).

⑰ ANGUILLA · Eel

LATIN NAME: *Anguilla anguilla* (Anguillidae).

COMMON NAMES: *cieche* after the first metamorphosis. Galle eels (yellow eels) when they migrate into fresh water where they change color. After a few years, they still change color and become silvery. *Buratella* means silvery male eel, while *capitone* is a large female still young.

SEASON: fished year-round, mainly October to January.

FLAVOR: flesh with a marked flavor; very fatty, rich in protein, phosphorus, potassium, and vitamins.

IN COOKING: fried, in sauce, grilled, but also smoked and marinated.

REGIONAL SPECIALTIES: *alla maniera di Cascia*, marinated, then panfried and baked in the oven (Umbria); *su scabecciu*, floured with durum wheat semolina flour and fried (Sardinia); *bisato in speo*, on the spit (Friuli and Veneto).

⑱ AGUGLIA · Garfish

LATIN NAME: *Belone belone* (Belonidae).

COMMON NAMES: *becassin* (Liguria); *bisigola* (Veneto); *agora* (Marche); *guse* (Abruzzo); *ache* (Apulia); *agugghia* (Calabria); *augghia* (Sicily); *becculongu* (Sardinia).

SEASON: fished year-round, especially in summer.

FLAVOR: firm flesh, delicate taste. Green color along the back ridge due to biliverdin (pigment in the bile).

IN COOKING: fried, baked, or pan cooked.

REGIONAL SPECIALTIES: *in gratin* (Calabria); *alla ghiotta*, in a pan of tomatoes with garlic, wine, black olives, and capers (Sicily).

⑲ SPRATTO · European sprat

LATIN NAME: *Sprattus sprattus, Clupea papalina* (Clupeidae).

COMMON NAMES: *saraghina, saraghèna, saraghèina* (Emilia-Romagna); *papalina* (Romagna, papal states).

SEASON: fished from fall to spring.

FLAVOR: flesh is less firm than that of sardines but with a more pronounced taste; quite fatty, rich in omega-3s and mineral salts.

IN COOKING: grilled, au gratin, or canned (in oil or salt). In Emilia-Romagna, *colatura di saraghina* (rarer and less known than anchovy).

REGIONAL SPECIALTIES: *saraghina alla scotadeti* ("burned fingers"), grilled with garlic, parsley, and dried bread crumbs (Emilia-Romagna); *piada* (thin pancake) stuffed with *saraghina*, onion, and radicchio (Emilia-Romagna).

⑳ ORATA · Gilthead sea bream

LATIN NAME: *Sparus aurata* (Sparidae).

COMMON NAMES: *aurata* (Tuscany, Campania, and Liguria); *dorata* (Lazio); *cagnina* or *canina* (Sardinia).

SEASON: farmed sea bream are available all year round; wild caught in summer and autumn.

FLAVOR: white flesh, lean, moist, subtly briny; rich in important proteins, B vitamins (B1, B2, and B3), phosphorus, iodine, iron, calcium.

IN COOKING: consumed raw, baked, or grilled.

REGIONAL SPECIALTIES: *orata all'acqua pazza*, with oil, garlic, cherry tomatoes, and parsley (Campania); *alla San Nicola*, marinated with herbs, oil, lemon, and grilled (Apulia).

㉑ RANA PESCATRICE
Angler or monkfish

LATIN NAME: *Lophius piscatorius* (Lophiidae).

COMMON NAMES: *rana pescatrice* (monkfish) sold whole, *coda di rospo* (monkfish tail) sold whole but without the head or in steaks.

SEASON: fished year-round, in smaller quantities in summer.

FLAVOR: rosy flesh, very firm, light, and tasty; high protein and mineral content, low fat content. Excellent as broth with the head and bones, refined liver, with an intense taste.

IN COOKING: prepared in soup, baked, or pan cooked. Perfect in pasta or risotto sauces.

REGIONAL SPECIALTIES: *all'otrantina*, floured pieces, panfried with onion, garlic, tomatoes, and parsley, served on toasted bread (Apulia); monkfish liver pâté (Marche).

SKIP TO
THE AMAZING ANCHOVY, P. 236;
STOCKFISH AND SALT COD, P. 104;
BOTTARGA, P. 46.

FISHING HUTS

Along the Adriatic coast and in the lagoons, picturesque fishing huts stand as symbols of an authentic cuisine. Their charm has fascinated visitors as well as great writers.

ILARIA BRUNETTI

TRABOCCHI AND *CAPANNI*, FISHING ON STILTS

Trabocchi (Abruzzo and Molise, *trabucchi* in Apulia) and *capanni* (or *padelloni* in Emilia-Romagna) are huts built out over the water with large fishing nets, and these are sometimes strikingly beautiful.

HISTORY

Appearing on the coast of Ravenna starting from the fourteenth century, the huts were used in times of war as refuges. Today very few trabocchi are in operation, and several have been turned into restaurants. In some cases, the capanni are used by fishing enthusiasts, purchased by several co-owners and managed by one person. There is no signed contract, just a handshake.

ARCHITECTURE

The basic structure varies, but the fishing technique is the same: long antennas on stilts support a huge fishing net called a *bilancia* (Abruzzo, Molise, and Apulia) or *padellone* (Emilia-Romagna). These are located not far from the space where you can clean and cook the fish.

→ **Along the coast of Abruzzo and Molise** are where the most spectacular and imposing structures are observed, built with maritime pine wood, which is resistant to the salty air and water as well as to strong wind gusts from the mistral. They overlook the sea, anchored to the coast by long pontoons.

→ **In Apulia**, the *trabucco* stretches its arms above the sea but is attached to the shore, and its net is often twice as large.

→ **In Emilia-Romagna**, along rivers or the coastline, there are several kinds made of either wood or stone, or prefabricated. These are used for amateur and sport fishing but also for family or friendly gatherings.

Where do you find them?

→ On the Trabocchi coast, the coastline from Ortona to Vasto (Abruzzo).

→ In Gargano National Park (Apulia).

→ In the Po Delta Park (Emilia-Romagna).

→ At the end of the port of Cesenatico, only in Rimini, Marina di Ravenna, or Cervia (Emilia-Romagna).

The famous host

In his novel *The Triumph of Death* (1894), Gabriele D'Annunzio describes the trabocchi as "machines that seemed to live their own lives . . . , like the colossal skeleton of an antediluvian amphibious being."

The dishes

Brodetto alla vastese—Abruzzo: a succulent soup of fish, bell peppers, and tomatoes.

Fish ***escabeche***—Molise: fried fish marinated in vinegar and saffron.

Fried ***"fragagghjame"***—Apulia: fry that are floured and fried.

Fried ***"acquadelle"***—Emilia-Romagna: small whole fish fried without bread crumbs.

THE *CASONI*, REFUGES IN THE LAGOON

These reed huts are scattered along the lagoons of Friuli and Veneto, along the canals, or on small islands.

HISTORY

The first *casoni* date back to the Neolithic period! Originally, they were used as homes for fishermen. As fishing techniques evolved, they were gradually abandoned and are now rented by tourists who organize large festive meals there . . . on the condition that they catch the fish!

ARCHITECTURE

The supporting structure, in elm or alder wood, is covered with reeds that form high, sloping roofs. Inside is a single windowless room, clay or dirt floors, and a central fireplace; the smoke escapes naturally through the small cracks between the beams, themselves arranged lengthwise in a northeast–southwest direction so that they better withstand the strong local wind called the bora.

→ **In Marano** (Friuli) are found the best preserved casoni. Rectangular in shape, their shorter sides are rounded, and they are 5 feet (1.5 m) high.

→ **In Grado** (Friuli), only the rear of the building is rounded, but renovations using bricks or stones, or implementing windows, have often changed the original structure.

→ **In Caorle** (Veneto), these are oval-shaped and have no vertical walls, as the roof slopes to the ground.

SKIP TO
FROM THE SEA, P. 244.

Where do you find them?

→ In the regional nature reserve of the mouth of the Stella River (Friuli).

→ In Grado lagoon (Friuli).

→ On Fisherman's Island in Caorle (Veneto).

The famous host

The Grado lagoon and its casoni served as backdrop to the legendary land of Colchis in the film *Medea* by Pier Paolo Pasolini (1969), while Ernest Hemingway was attracted by the one in Caorle, where he stayed to write *Across the River and into the Trees* (1950).

The dishes

Bisato in speo—Marano, Friuli: eels on a spit.

Boreto graesano—Grado, Friuli: the local fish, often turbot or flathead grey mullet, cooked with garlic scorched in oil, vinegar, and a lot of black pepper.

Spaghetti coi canestrei—Caorle, Veneto: spaghetti with white sea scallops and parsley.

PECORINO

In Italy, they use the plural *pecorini* because there are so many different pecorino cheeses. Here is a spotlight on the five varieties of this salty sheep's-milk cheese, crowned with a PDO.

CÉLINE MAGUET

① PECORINO ROMANO, THE CELEBRITY

Don't be fooled by its name! Although Pecorino Romano was born 2,000 years ago near Rome in the mountains of Lazio, it has migrated over time to Sardinia, which today produces 90 percent of all Pecorino Romano.

ORIGIN—Sardinia, Lazio, and Tuscany (Grosseto).

TYPE OF CHEESE—aged.

PASTE (INTERIOR)—cooked.

MILK—raw or thermized sheep's milk.

SHEEP BREED—Commune.

FEED—pasture and hay.

RENNET—lamb or kid.

PRODUCTION—from October to July.

AFFINAGE—5 to 8 months.

WEIGHT—44 to 77 pounds (20 to 35 kg).

TASTE—aromatic, pungent, and salty.

PERFECT PAIRING—with fresh fava (broad) beans and a drizzle of olive oil.

IN COOKING—what do *amatriciana*, *cacio e pepe*, carbonara, and *gricia* all have in common? Pecorino Romano, of course, which binds, enhances, and makes creamier these four emblematic pastas of Rome.

② PECORINO SICILIANO, THE ARTISANAL

In Sicilian dialect, pecorino becomes *tumazzu* or *canistrattu*. Made from sheep from an island breed with a varied diet, it is one of the several pecorini that are most representative of a *terroir*.

ORIGIN—Sicily.

TYPE OF CHEESE—fresh, semiaged, or aged.

PASTE (INTERIOR)—semicooked.

MILK—raw, from indigenous sheep.

SHEEP BREED—Pinzirita, Comisana, and Valle Belice.

FEED—natural or cultivated pastures and fresh fodder.

RENNET—lamb.

PRODUCTION—year-round.

AFFINAGE—fresh, semiaged, and aged; addition of peppercorns allowed.

WEIGHT—31 pounds (14 kg).

TASTE—pungent, grassy, and spiced.

PERFECT PAIRING—with thinly sliced citron slices.

IN COOKING—Sicilian *pasta al forno*, baked pasta often accompanied by a meat sauce or a simple tomato sauce and baked au gratin with a Sicilian pecorino.

③ PECORINO TOSCANO, THE EVERYDAY

Formerly known as *cacio marzolino* because its production began during the month of March, it is now produced year-round. This cheese, dating back to the Etruscans, has fewer and fewer strict specifications.

ORIGIN—Tuscany, Umbria, and Lazio.

TYPE OF CHEESE—fresh or aged.

PASTE (INTERIOR)—cooked.

MILK—raw, thermized, or pasteurized sheep's milk.

SHEEP BREED—Commune.

FEED—natural pasture and fodder.

RENNET—veal or vegetable.

PRODUCTION—year-round.

AFFINAGE—4 months for the ripened.

WEIGHT—7¾ pounds (3.5 kg).

TASTE—sweet and buttery flavor.

PERFECT PAIRING—with artichokes in oil.

IN COOKING—ravioli stuffed with fresh ricotta, spinach or chard, and nutmeg, served with a meat ragout and grated Pecorino Tuscano, creating *tortelli maremmani*, a classic of Tuscan cuisine.

④ PECORINO SARDO, THE GENERIC

Once an island of dense forests, Sardinia has become, over the centuries and through empires, an island of food originating from plains and meadows, with a strong and deeply pastoral tradition.

ORIGIN—Sardinia.

TYPE OF CHEESE—fresh or aged.

PASTE (INTERIOR)—semicooked.

MILK—raw, thermized, or pasteurized sheep's milk.

SHEEP BREED—Commune.

FEED—pasture and hay.

RENNET—veal.

PRODUCTION—year-round.

AFFINAGE—2 months for the aged; it can even be smoked.

WEIGHT—3¾ to 8¾ pounds (1.7 to 4 kg).

TASTE—powerful and tangy.

PERFECT PAIRING—with pine nuts on *carasau* bread.

IN COOKING—what's a good use for stale bread? Dip it in a meat broth, of course! Add to it grated Pecorino Sardo, Casizolu (another famous cheese from Sardinia), add spices, and you have a *zuppa gallurese*, typical of the northeast of the island, served at weddings and large family gatherings.

⑤ PECORINO DI FILIANO, THE UNCOMPROMISING

There is a lesser-known PDO pecorino produced in Basilicata. Uncompromising in its specifications (native sheep breeds, farm rennet, long affinage, and a rind rubbed with olive oil from the region), this cheese, with its delicate and buttery taste, is becoming rare.

AND LAST BUT NOT LEAST

While only five pecorini hold the precious PDO, others, equally representative of their regions, are Slow Food sentinels:

Pecorino del Monte Poro
- Calabria -

Pecorino dei Monti Sibillini
- Marche -

Pecorino della Maremma
- Tuscany -

Pecorino di Farindola
- Abruzzo -

Pecorino bagnolese
- Campania -

SKIP TO
THE GENEALOGY OF ROMAN PASTA, P. 174; SHEEP, P. 260; ITALY'S BEAUTIFUL CHEESES, P. 222.

SEASON

TUTTO L'ANNO (YEAR-ROUND)

CATEGORY

ANTIPASTO (APPETIZER)

LEVEL

FACILE (EASY)

VITELLO TONNATO

SLICED VEAL WITH TUNA SAUCE

This classic pairing of land and sea hails from Piedmont.

CHARLES PATIN O'COOHOON

Genealogy

Its first traces date back to the eighteenth century in the region of Cuneo in Piedmont.

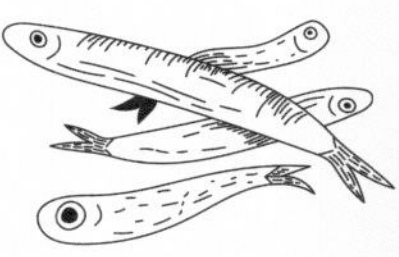

FROM VEAL TO ANCHOVIES

Originally, this dish contained no tuna. To season the dish, anchovies were used, which were less expensive than salt and abundant along the Ligurian coast. In the reference text *Il cuoco piemontese perfezionato a Parigi* (*The Piedmontese Cook Perfected in Paris*, 1766), written by an anonymous Piedmontese chef, anchovies and veal are paired in certain recipes such as *il petto di vitello all'alemanna*, veal breast served with a sauce of capers, anchovies, and chicken livers.

And the mayo?

When prepared homemade, the sauce takes on the appearance of a mayonnaise, and it made its appearance in 1950 in the collective reference work *Il cucchiaio d'Argento* (*The Silver Spoon*) and in the *Ricette regionali italiane* (*Regional Italian Recipes*) in 1967, in which Anna Gosetti della Salda recommends preparing a rich mayonnaise for the dish.

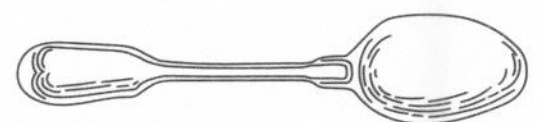

THREE WAYS TO ELEVATE THE TUNA

→ In Pergola, his three-star restaurant at the Cavalieri Waldorf Astoria Hotel in Rome, chef Heinz Beck serves "upside-down" *vitello tonnato*, or strips of red tuna grilled and placed on a veal gelée.

→ Marco Stabile, the Michelin-starred chef at Aria's Ora in Florence, offers *vitello palamitè*, slices of veal topped with a cream of bonito, served in an eggshell.

→ Carlo Cracco, chef of Cracco in Milan, serves the original version of vitello tonnato. No mayonnaise, but a creamy tuna sauce.

THE RECIPE

SERVES 6

- 1 carrot
- 1 stalk celery
- 1 yellow onion
- 1¾ pounds (800 g) veal
- 1⅔ cups (400 mL) dry white wine
- 2 cloves garlic, peeled and halved, germ removed
- 2 bay leaves
- 4 cloves
- A few peppercorns
- Extra-virgin olive oil
- Salt
- Capers, for serving

Very small dice the carrot, celery, and onion together. Place the veal, wine, diced vegetables, garlic, bay leaves, cloves, and peppercorns in a Dutch oven. Cover and refrigerate for 24 hours to marinate the veal. The next day, lightly score the veal on each side. Lightly oil a pan and warm over medium heat, add the veal to the pan and lightly sear both sides of the meat, 2 to 4 minutes on each side. Remove the meat from the pan and place it back in the pot containing the marinade. Add water to cover the meat. Season with salt, and cook over very low heat, covered. After 45 minutes, turn off the heat and let the veal cool in its juices. It should remain pink in the center.

To make the tuna sauce: Beat 2 large (38 g) egg yolks until thickened, then gradually add just over ¾ cup (200 mL) olive oil. Whisk in the juice of 1 lemon; this makes the mayonnaise. In a separate bowl, combine 10½ ounces (300 g) of tuna in olive oil (drained), 3 anchovy fillets, 10 capers in brine, and half a ladle of the cooled cooking broth from the veal. Gently fold this into the sauce; the sauce should be very creamy. Season with black pepper.

Very thinly slice the veal. On a plate, arrange six slices in a rosette pattern. Spoon the sauce into the center and sprinkle a few capers over the top. Serve.

THE ARRIVAL OF TUNA

In Piedmontese, it is called *vitel tonnè*. The term comes from the Old French *tanné*, meaning softened. This describes how to prepare the pieces of boiled veal. *Tanné* then evolved to *tonné* before finally becoming *tonno*. The introduction of tuna into the recipe can be attributed to the Milanese dermatologist Angelo Dubini in 1861. In his book *La cucina degli stomachi deboli* (*Cooking for Delicate Stomachs*), he describes a sauce composed of chopped tuna and anchovies, moistened in the veal cooking broth. The recipe was codified in 1891 by Pellegrino Artusi in his essential *La scienza in cucina e l'arte di mangiar bene* (*Science in the Kitchen and the Art of Eating Well*).

A NATIONAL DISH . . . IN ARGENTINA!

As the first foreign community settling in Argentina, Italians brought their cuisine with them. The vitello tonnato thus became a classic of Argentinian Christmas. Traditionally, the veal is replaced by *peceto*, beef shank.

SKIP TO

THE AMAZING ANCHOVY, P. 236; SPOTLIGHT ON CAPERS, P. 110.

SEASON
PRIMAVERA (SPRING)

CATEGORY
PRIMO PIATTO (FIRST COURSE)

LEVEL
FACILE (EASY)

PASTA CON LE SARDE

SICILIAN PASTA WITH SARDINES

Briny, anise-flavored, sweet and savory—this pasta dish with sardines brings together all the delicious flavors of Sicily.

ILARIA BRUNETTI

A dish of conquest

Legend credits the invention of this recipe to the cook of the Sicilian commander Euphemius of Messina. Driven from Sicily by the Byzantines, Euphemius allied with the Saracens to reclaim the island. Once landed in Mazara del Vallo, his cook, whose name has been lost to history, prepared pasta by mixing local ingredients (sardines and wild fennel) with an Arab touch (saffron).

ASSAULT ON ITALY

The recipe for *maccheroni con sarde alla siciliana* was included in the second edition of *La scienza in cucina e l'arte di mangiar bene* (*Science in the Kitchen and the Art of Eating Well*) by Pellegrino Artusi. This was its first appearance in a national cookbook, and it has contributed to its success beyond the island. This version includes only sardines, anchovies, and wild fennel.

VARIATIONS

WITHOUT SAFFRON
→ In Messina, they exclude this precious spice.

***MILANISA*-STYLE**
→ Paradoxically without saffron; the tomato makes an appearance, with a touch of paste or sauce added. Sardines can be fresh or in salt. The name (meaning "Milanese" in local dialect) comes from Sicilians who, after immigrating to Milan, modified the original recipe.

'NCASCIATA CON SARDINIA
→ The pasta is sautéed in a pan, then baked au gratin.

CON LE SARDE A MARE
→ The sardines have . . . stayed "in the sea" and do not appear in this dish! So even if the fishmonger is closed, the combination of other ingredients will provide a very tasty pasta.

THE BASE

· THE PASTA ·

Bucatini or *spaghettoni* (large spaghetti), preferably.

· INGREDIENTS ·

Fresh sardines, *finocchietto* (wild fennel), onions, canned anchovies, raisins, and pine nuts; the original Palermo version also uses saffron. The delicious addition of crunchy bread crumbs is common.

SKIP TO
THE AMAZING ANCHOVY, P. 236; FENNEL, P. 233; SARDE A BECCAFICO (SICILIAN STUFFED SARDINES), P. 186.

THE RECIPE

By Fabrizio Ferrara, chef of Osteria Ferrara (Paris, 11th).

SERVES 4

- 14 ounces (400 g) fresh sardines
- ¾ cup (180 mL) olive oil
- 1¼ cups (120 g) dried bread crumbs
- 2 cloves garlic, peeled
- 1 pinch cayenne pepper
- 7 to 9 ounces (200 to 250 g) fresh wild fennel (or store-bought)
- 3½ ounces (100 g) white onion
- ⅓ cup (80 g) tomato sauce
- ½ cup (80 g) raisins
- ⅔ cup (80 g) pine nuts
- 14 ounces (400 g) spaghettoni
- Salt

Rinse and gently scale the sardines. Cut off the heads and tails and remove the entrails. Cut off the dorsal fin, rinse the bodies, and place them in the refrigerator. Bring a large pot of water to a boil for the pasta. Heat 3 to 4 tablespoons (45 to 60 mL) of the olive oil in a skillet. Add the bread crumbs and 1 garlic clove. Toast the bread crumbs until crisp; be careful not to burn them. Set aside.

In a separate large skillet, heat the remaining garlic clove and the cayenne in ½ cup (125 mL) of the oil. Add the fennel, onion, tomato sauce, raisins, pine nuts, and sardines and cook over medium heat for about 5 minutes, adding a little water if necessary.

Once the water for the pasta reaches a boil, salt the water. Add the pasta and cook al dente. Drain (reserving a ladleful of the cooking water), then add the pasta to the skillet over high heat with the reserved cooking water. Serve, sprinkled with the toasted bread crumbs.

Il Tocco Dello Chef (Chef's Tip)

→ The chef adds garlic and cayenne because their scent goes perfectly with that of sardines and wild fennel.

→ He does not include the anchovy fillets traditionally added to the sauce because it is already sufficiently rich; he suggests, as an option, mixing them with the bread crumbs to make them even tastier.

PALERMO-STYLE

For the saffron version, infuse 4 saffron threads in 2 tablespoons (30 mL) of the pasta cooking water and add this when sautéing the pasta; add 2 anchovy fillets, desalted or in oil, to the onions. Tomato sauce is not included in this version.

BAKED

If you have leftover pasta, try the baked version: Sprinkle the bottom of a baking dish with bread crumbs, arrange the pasta on top, finish with more bread crumbs over the top, and add a drizzle of olive oil. Bake until browned on top.

INDIGENOUS GRAPE VARIETALS

Italy cultivates endemic grape varietals that contribute to the richness and distinctiveness of its wines. Here are five rare gems that were recently rediscovered and are being developed.

BERNARDO CONTICELLI

FRAPPATO

REGION OF ORIGIN
Grown exclusively in Sicily, and today mainly in its zone of origin around the town of Vittoria, in the southeastern part of the island.

GRAPE
Clusters of purplish-blue fruit with thick skin covered with abundant bloom (a substance produced by the skin of fruits and leaves), waxy and slightly powdery, which gives it a frosty or dusty appearance. It can withstand a fairly balanced and regular production, which serves as a guarantee of quality and quantity through the years.

GOOD TO KNOW
Traditionally used in a blend with Nero d'Avola, the second varietal authorized in Cerasuolo di Vittoria wine, the only DOCG from Sicily. For about the past ten years, some producers have vinified it on its own, to enhance its freshness and its floral aspect.

IN THE GLASS
Rather pale ruby-red color, with aromas of red fruits and flowers, sometimes full-bodied. The structure is graceful with a nice freshness, a flavor and silky tannins of great elegance. A wine that is easy to approach, but with aging potential.

A CUVÉE
Arianna Occhipinti, Il Frappato—IGT Terre Sicilian.

TIMORASSO

REGION OF ORIGIN
Historically present in Piedmont and Liguria, it is now cultivated on a few acres of the Colli Tortonesi area in the province of Alexandria, in southeastern Piedmont.

GRAPE
A medium-size cluster, not too compact, with yellowish-green fruits.

GOOD TO KNOW
Before the phylloxera crisis at the end of the nineteenth century, Timorasso was the most widely cultivated white grape in Piedmont, both for wine and as a table grape. Due to its production instability in the 1900s, it was replaced by Cortese and is now cultivated on only a few hundred acres.

IN THE GLASS
Straw yellow in color, it has floral, almond, and spice notes, with a presence of hydrocarbons with aging. The taste shows a vibrant acidity enhanced by minerality and palatability, which make it a white wine with great aging potential.

A CUVÉE
Walter Massa, Derthona—DOC Colli Tortonesi.

CESANESE

REGION OF ORIGIN
In Lazio, particularly east of the Castelli Romani (Roman Castles), around the towns of Piglio, Affile, and Olevano Romano, on the outskirts of Rome.

GRAPE
A medium-size cluster, made up of purplish-black fruits with very thick skin. The production is regular and abundant.

GOOD TO KNOW
The name comes from the town of Cesano near Rome. The grapes are traditionally used to give life to dry red wines, sweet wines, or even sometimes sparkling wines.

IN THE GLASS
With their intense ruby-red color with purple tinges, the wines from this grape offer notes of red cherry, black cherry, sour cherry, and dark fruits such as blackberry and plum, combined with some spicy and earthy undertones. Tannins are present, but not rough, supported by good structure, which allows this wine to be enjoyed young or aged for several years.

A CUVÉE
Damiano Ciolli, Silene—DOC Cesanese di Olevano Romano.

CILIEGIOLO

REGION OF ORIGIN
Historically present in central Italy, it is on the hills of Maremma (southern Tuscany) that it is best expressed, thanks to their clay soils and hot, dry climate.

GRAPE
A wide and long cluster, with two lateral wings. Very compact fruits of an intense blue-violet color.

GOOD TO KNOW
The name comes from *ciliegia* (cherry), in reference to the color and aromas that characterize the wines made from this grape varietal. Historically used in blends with Sangiovese to give flexibility, Ciliegiolo is increasingly vinified alone to enhance it.

IN THE GLASS
Fairly dark red color, very fruity aromas of cherry and morello cherry, spiced nuances. Thanks to its acidity, it already shows balance and structure when young. A crisp, easy-to-drink wine.

A CUVÉE
Antonio Camillo, Ciliegiolo Vallerana Alta—DOC Maremma Toscana.

PELAVERGA

REGION OF ORIGIN
Native to Piedmont, it is found exclusively around Verduno, the northernmost village in the Barolo area, in the Langhe.

GRAPE
Medium-size to large cluster, composed of late-ripening blue-black fruits covered with a thick bloom.

GOOD TO KNOW
A legend from the court of King Charles Albert of Sardinia attributed aphrodisiac virtues to this wine, probably linked to a low alcohol content that makes it possible to drink in large quantities, or perhaps for the grape's mischievously evocative name.

IN THE GLASS
The color is pale red with fragrant aromas of rose, raspberry, and spicy white pepper. Its moderate alcohol content and freshness mean it can be drunk young, and even at a slightly cool temperature.

A CUVÉE
Fratelli Alessandria, Speziale—DOC Verduno Pelaverga.

SKIP TO
GATHERING GRAPES, P. 158;
GRAPES, P. 272;
NATURAL WINE, P. 320.

— SALUMI —

Italy is, for many, synonymous with charcuterie. From the famous prosciutto di Parma to the precious *lardo di Colonnata*, here is an inventory of the most delicious cured meats from the peninsula.

ALESSANDRO DE CONTO

THROUGHOUT ITALY

Lonza di Maiale
BASE: pork loin.
CATEGORY: loin.
AGING: 1 month.
TASTE: pleasant and delicate.

CENTRAL-NORTH

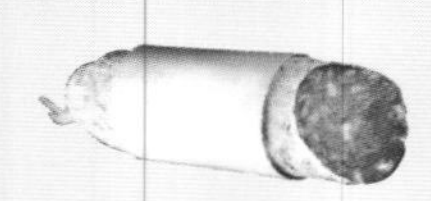

Salami italiani alla Cacciatora DOP
BASE: mixture of pork pieces.
CATEGORY: sausage.
AGING: 10 days minimum.
TASTE: pleasant, spice notes.

ABRUZZO

Mortadella di Campotosto Slow Food
BASE: mixture of pork pieces.
CATEGORY: sausage.
AGING: 15 days minimum.
TASTE: pleasant, intense, with a slight smoky aroma.

Salsiccia di Fegato Aquilana Slow Food
BASE: pork offal.
CATEGORY: charcuterie made from offal.
AGING: 1 month minimum.
TASTE: intense, powerful, ferrous.

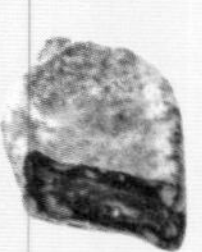

Salsicciotto Frentano Slow Food
BASE: mixture of pork pieces.
CATEGORY: sausage.
AGING: about 2 months.
TASTE: pleasant, fragrant, fruity.

Ventricina del Vastese Slow Food
BASE: mixture of pork pieces.
CATEGORY: sausage.
AGING: 6 months minimum.
TASTE: pleasant, slightly spicy, melting.

CALABRIA

Gammune di Belmonte Slow Food
BASE: pork thigh.
CATEGORY: raw, cured ham.
AGING: 16 months minimum.
TASTE: soft and melting, with notes of acorns and hazelnuts.

Pancetta di Calabria DOP
BASE: pork belly.
CATEGORY: pancetta.
AGING: 1 month minimum.
TASTE: aromatic and slightly spicy.

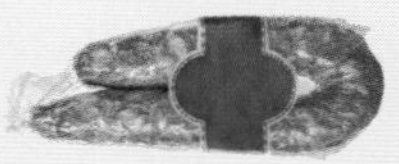

Salsiccia di Calabria DOP
BASE: mixture of pork pieces.
CATEGORY: sausage.
AGING: 1 month minimum.
TASTE: spicy and slightly spiced.

Capocollo di Calabria DOP
BASE: pork loin.
CATEGORY: *capocollo*.
AGING: 100 days minimum.
TASTE: melting, flavorful, with hints of black pepper.

Capicollo Azze Anca Grecanico Slow Food
BASE: boneless pork thigh.
CATEGORY: ham.
AGING: 6 months minimum.
TASTE: intense, with a scent of wild fennel and chile.

Soppressata di Calabria DOP
BASE: mixture of pork pieces.
CATEGORY: sausage.
AGING: 45 days minimum.
TASTE: intense, moderately spicy.

CAMPANIA

Salsiccia di Castelpoto Slow Food
BASE: mixture of pork pieces.
CATEGORY: sausage.
AGING: a few days.
TASTE: pleasant, with notes of bell pepper and garlic.

Soppressata di Gioi Slow Food
BASE: pork thigh.
CATEGORY: sausage.
AGING: 40 days minimum.
TASTE: pleasant, refined, and slightly spiced.

Salsiccia e Soppressata del Vallo di Diano Slow Food
BASE: mixture of pork pieces.
CATEGORY: sausage.
AGING: around 40 days.
TASTE: pleasant and aromatic.

EMILIA-ROMAGNA

Culatello di Zibello DOP
BASE: pork thigh.
CATEGORY: *culatello*.
AGING: 10 months minimum, but it's best from at least 18 months.
TASTE: intense, with notes of cellar and grilled fruits.

Spalla Cruda Slow Food
BASE: pork shoulder.
CATEGORY: shoulder butt.
AGING: 15 months minimum.
TASTE: intense, structured, with notes of cellar.

Spalla Cotta di San Secondo PAT
BASE: pork shoulder.
CATEGORY: shoulder butt.
AGING: not aged.
TASTE: tender, roasted meat.

Coppa Piacentina DOP
BASE: pork loin.
CATEGORY: capocollo.
AGING: 6 months minimum.
TASTE: complex, with cellar notes and a slight aroma of cloves.

Coppa di Parma IGP
BASE: pork loin.
CATEGORY: capocollo.
AGING: 2 months minimum.
TASTE: pleasant and delicate.

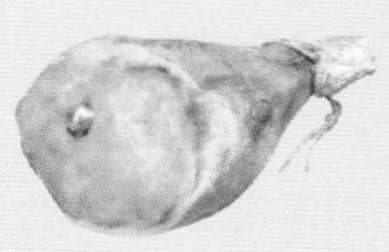

Prosciutto di Modena DOP
BASE: pork thigh.
CATEGORY: raw, cured ham.
AGING: 14 months minimum.
TASTE: pleasant and slightly spiced.

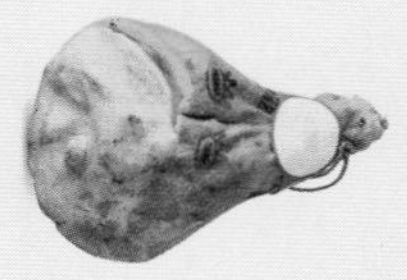

Prosciutto di Parma DOP
BASE: pork thigh.
CATEGORY: raw, cured ham.
AGING: 12 months minimum, but best from at least 16 months.
TASTE: pleasant, delicate, elegant.

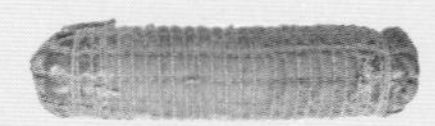

Pancetta Piacentina DOP
BASE: pork belly.
CATEGORY: pancetta.
AGING: 4 months minimum.
TASTE: pleasant, delicate, tender.

Salumi Rosa Bolognesi
BASE: mixture of pork pieces.
CATEGORY: cooked charcuterie.
AGING: not aged.
TASTE: pleasant, rustic, with an umami note.

Zampone di Modena IGP
REGION: Emilia-Romagna.
BASE: less noble pork pieces (fibrous tissue, parts of the head, fat, rind).
CATEGORY: cooked charcuterie.
AGING: not aged.
TASTE: pleasant, fatty, spiced.

Salame Piacentino DOP
BASE: mixture of pork pieces.
CATEGORY: sausage.
AGING: 45 days minimum.
TASTE: pleasant, persistent; the longer the aging, the more refined it is.

Mariola Slow Food
BASE: mixture of pork pieces.
CATEGORY: sausage.
AGING: around 12 months.
TASTE: pleasant, pronounced, slightly garlicky.

Cotechino di Modena IGP
BASE: less noble pork pieces (fibrous tissue, parts of the head, fat, rind).
CATEGORY: cooked charcuterie.
AGING: not aged.
TASTE: pleasant and spiced, with an umami note.

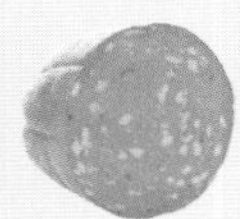

Mortadella Bologna IGP
BASE: mixture of pork pieces.
CATEGORY: cooked charcuterie.
AGING: not aged.
TASTE: pleasant, with notes of cooked meat, umami flavor, spices.

Salama da Sugo IGP
BASE: mixture of pork pieces.
CATEGORY: charcuterie for cooking.
AGING: 6 months minimum.
TASTE: intense, rich, aromatic.

Salame Felino IGP
BASE: mixture of pork pieces.
CATEGORY: sausage.
AGING: 1 month minimum.
TASTE: pleasant, very mild, with light notes of pepper.

PIEDMONT

Testa in Cassetta di Gavi Slow Food
BASE: pig's head.
CATEGORY: charcuterie made from offal.
AGING: a few days.
TASTE: intense, with hints of cinnamon and other spices.

Crudo di Cuneo DOP
BASE: pork thigh.
CATEGORY: raw, cured ham.
AGING: 10 months minimum, but best from at least 14 months.
TASTE: pleasant, slightly salty.

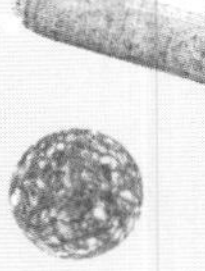

Salame Piemonte IGP
BASE: mixture of pork pieces.
CATEGORY: sausage.
AGING: 10 days minimum.
TASTE: pleasant, with a scent of red wine.

Salame delle Valli Tortonesi Slow Food
BASE: mixture of pork pieces.
CATEGORY: sausage.
AGING: 3 months minimum.
TASTE: pleasant, juicy, elegant.

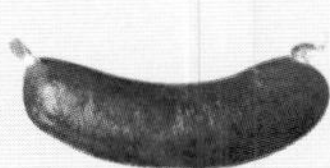

Mustardela della Valli Valdesi Slow Food
BASE: charcuterie made from offal.
CATEGORY: offal.
AGING: not aged.
TASTE: pronounced, ferrous, sort of sweet.

TRENTINO-ALTO ADIGE

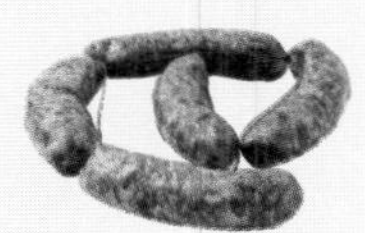

Ciuighe del Banale Slow Food
BASE: mixture of pork pieces and turnips.
CATEGORY: charcuterie made from trimmings.
AGING: a few days.
TASTE: intense and tender, also due to boiled turnips of between 30 and 40 percent of the mixture.

Speck Alto Adige IGP
BASE: pork thigh.
CATEGORY: raw, cured ham.
AGING: 20 weeks minimum.
TASTE: pleasant, with smoky and spiced notes.

AOSTA VALLEY

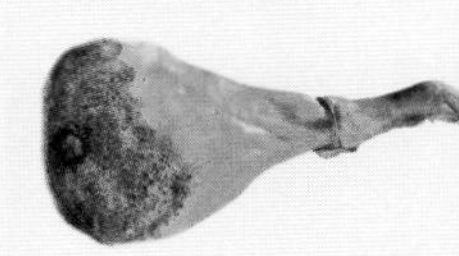

Jambon de Bosses DOP
BASE: pork thigh.
CATEGORY: raw, cured ham.
AGING: 12 months minimum, but better after 15 months.
TASTE: moderately intense, with notes of aromatic herbs.

Valle d'Aosta Lardo d'Arnad IGP
BASE: bacon.
CATEGORY: bacon.
AGING: 3 months minimum.
TASTE: delicate, with a note of sage and rosemary.

FRIUI-VENEZIA-GIULIA

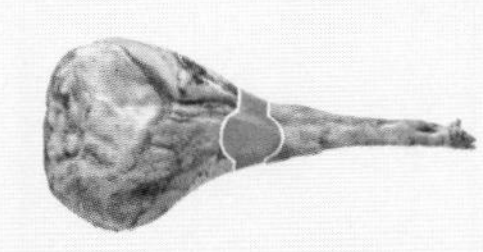

Prosciutto di San Daniele DOP
BASE: pork thigh.
CATEGORY: raw, cured ham.
AGING: 13 months minimum, but better after 16 months.
TASTE: pleasant, slightly salty, fragrant.

Prosciutto di Sauris IGP
BASE: pork thigh
CATEGORY: raw, cured ham
AGING: 10 months minimum, but more complex after 16 months
TASTE: fragrant, smoky note.

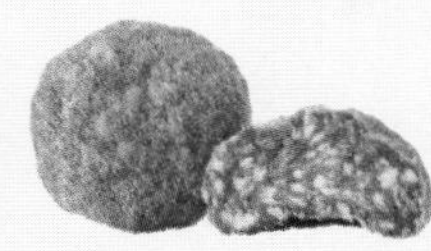

Pitina Slow Food
BASE: goat, sheep, or game meat.
CATEGORY: sausage.
AGING: 1 month minimum.
TASTE: pleasant, with varying intensity depending on the meat used.

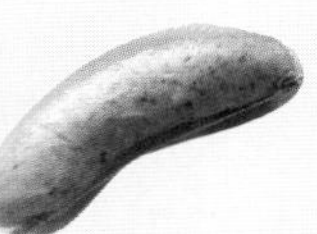

Pestat di Fagagna Slow Food
BASE: bacon, vegetables, and aromatic herbs.
CATEGORY: bacon.
AGING: not aged.
TASTE: pleasant, rich in vegetal notes, slightly spiced.

Varhackara Slow Food
BASE: bacon, different pieces of pork and aromatic herbs.
CATEGORY: bacon.
AGING: not aged.
TASTE: aromatic, with hints of nutmeg.

TUSCANY

Prosciutto Bazzone di Garfagnana Slow Food
BASE: pork thigh.
CATEGORY: raw, cured ham.
AGING: 24 months minimum.
TASTE: intense, slightly salty, very aromatic.

Prosciutto del Casentino Slow Food
BASE: pork thigh.
CATEGORY: raw, cured ham.
AGING: 24 months minimum.
TASTE: pleasant, tender, with aromas of grilled fruits.

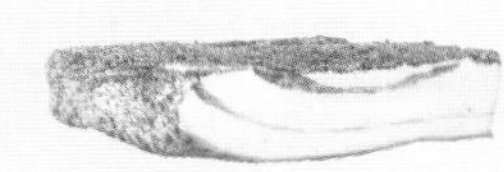

Lardo di Colonnata IGP
BASE: bacon.
CATEGORY: bacon.
AGING: 6 months minimum.
TASTE: pleasant, aromatic, slightly salty.

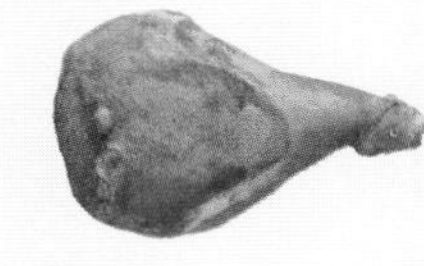

Prosciutto Toscano DOP
BASE: pork thigh.
CATEGORY: raw, cured ham.
AGING: 12 months minimum.
TASTE: pronounced, flavorful, slightly spiced.

Tarese Valdarno Slow Food
BASE: pork belly.
CATEGORY: pancetta.
AGING: 2 months minimum.
TASTE: pleasant, slightly salty, spiced.

Biroldo della Garfagnana Slow Food
BASE: pork offal.
CATEGORY: charcuterie made from offal.
AGING: a few days.
TASTE: ferrous, intense, with notes of wild fennel and spices.

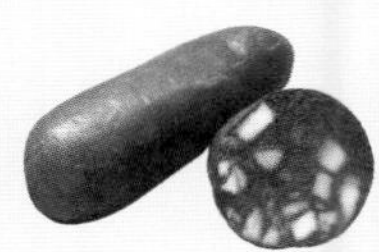

Mallegato Slow Food
BASE: pork offal.
CATEGORY: offal.
AGING: not aged.
TASTE: intense, ferrous, with a note of raisin, cinnamon, and other spices.

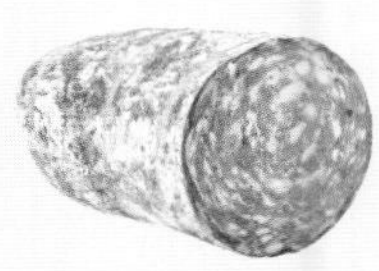

Finocchiona IGP
BASE: mixture of pork pieces.
CATEGORY: sausage.
AGING: 15 days minimum, but ideally more than 45 days.
TASTE: aromatic, with pronounced notes of fennel.

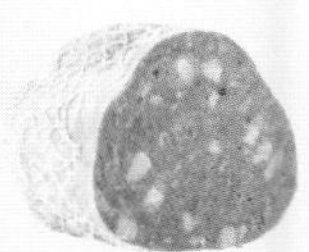

Mortadella di Prato IGP
BASE: mixture of pork pieces.
CATEGORY: cooked charcuterie.
AGING: not aged.
TASTE: pleasant and aromatic, with notes of Alkermes (a spiced Italian liqueur) and spices.

UMBRIA

Prosciutto di Norcia IGP
BASE: pork thigh.
CATEGORY: raw, cured ham.
AGING: 12 months minimum, but better after 15 months.
TASTE: pleasant, with light garlicky notes.

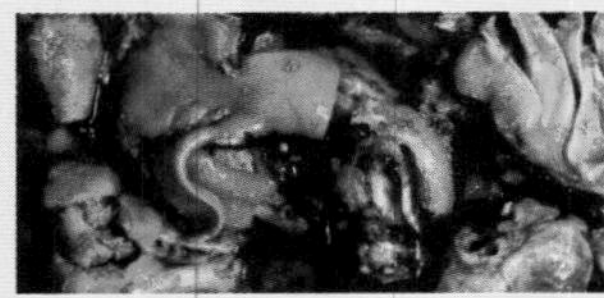

Cicotto di Grutti Slow Food
BASE: pork offal.
CATEGORY: offal.
AGING: not aged.
TASTE: rosemary, garlic and fennel, tender, intense, roasted meat flavor.

Mazzafegato PAT
BASE: charcuterie made from offal.
CATEGORY: sausage with offal.
AGING: a few days.
TASTE: pronounced, with iron notes and wild fennel.

LOMBARDY

Salame di Varzi DOP
BASE: mixture of pork pieces.
CATEGORY: sausage.
AGING: 45 days minimum.
TASTE: pleasant, with notes of cellar and noble molds.

Salame Brianza DOP
BASE: mixture of pork pieces.
CATEGORY: sausage.
AGING: 21 days minimum.
TASTE: pleasant, delicate, melting.

Bresaola di Valtellina IGP
BASE: beef (sirloin) pieces.
CATEGORY: charcuterie without pork.
AGING: 5 weeks minimum.
TASTE: delicate, light, iron notes.

Salame d'oca di Mortara IGP
BASE: goose meat.
CATEGORY: sausage.
AGING: about 1 month.
TASTE: very delicate and tender.

Violino di Capra della Valchiavenna Slow Food
BASE: goat thigh.
CATEGORY: charcuterie without pork.
AGING: 3 months minimum.
TASTE: intense, aromatic, ferrous.

Slinzega
BASE: chicken or beef thigh.
CATEGORY: charcuterie without pork.
AGING: 5 weeks minimum.
TASTE: intense, round, slightly spiced.

Salame Cremona IGP
BASE: mixture of pork pieces.
CATEGORY: sausage.
AGING: 5 weeks minimum.
TASTE: pronounced, with assertive notes of garlic and spices.

VENETO

Oca in Onto Slow Food
BASE: goose meat with its fat.
CATEGORY: cooked charcuterie without pork.
AGING: not aged.
TASTE: intense, of cooked meat and spices.

Sopressa Vicentina DOP
BASE: mixture of pork pieces.
CATEGORY: sausage.
AGING: 2 months minimum.
TASTE: melting, pleasant, with aromas of wine and garlic.

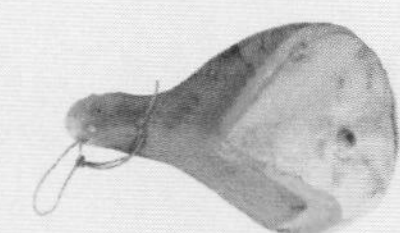

Prosciutto Veneto Berico-Euganeo DOP
BASE: pork thigh.
CATEGORY: raw, cured ham.
AGING: 12 months minimum.
TASTE: pleasant and delicate.

Stortina Veronese Slow Food
BASE: mixture of pork pieces.
CATEGORY: sausage.
AGING: about 1 month, then kept in lard.
TASTE: pleasant but intense.

APULIA

Capocollo di Martinafranca Slow Food
BASE: pork loin.
CATEGORY: capocollo.
AGING: 3 months minimum.
TASTE: delicate, very aromatic, slightly smoky.

LAZIO

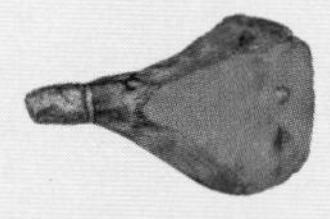

Prosciutto amatriciano IGP
BASE: pork thigh.
CATEGORY: raw, cured ham.
AGING: 12 months minimum.
TASTE: intense and aromatic.

Susianella di Viterbo Slow Food
BASE: pork offal.
CATEGORY: charcuterie made from offal.
AGING: 20 days minimum.
TASTE: intense, notes of red meat and wild fennel.

Porchetta di Ariccia IGP
BASE: whole pork, but without feet and innards.
CATEGORY: roasted charcuterie.
AGING: not aged.
TASTE: succulent, notes of roasted meat and rosemary.

Porchetta di Ariccia al pepe
BASE: pork cheek.
CATEGORY: guanciale.
AGING: 45 days minimum.
TASTE: pleasant, with peppery notes.

MARCHE

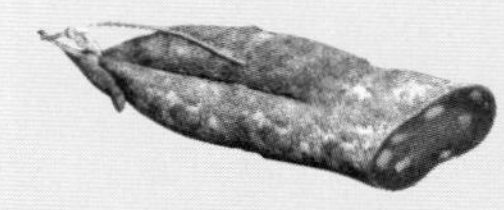

Salame di Fabriano Slow Food
BASE: pork thigh.
CATEGORY: sausage.
AGING: approximately 50 days
TASTE: pleasant, well rounded, complex.

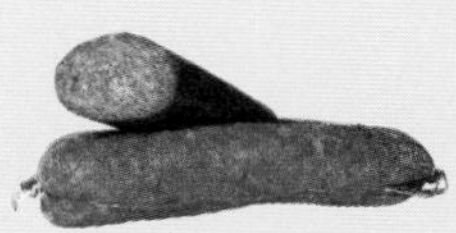

Ciauscolo IGP
BASE: mixture of pork pieces.
CATEGORY: sausage.
AGING: 15 days minimum.
TASTE: seasoned and melting.

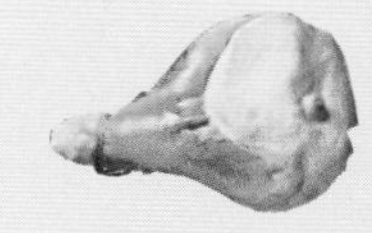

Prosciutto di Carpegna DOP
BASE: pork thigh.
CATEGORY: raw, cured ham.
AGING: 13 months minimum.
TASTE: pleasant and delicate.

BASILICATA

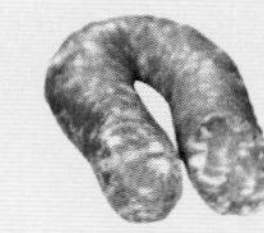

Lucanica di Picerno IGP
BASE: mixture of pork pieces.
CATEGORY: sausage.
AGING: 20 days minimum.
TASTE: pleasant, with notes of bell pepper and wild fennel.

Pezzente della Montagna Materana Slow Food
BASE: mixture of pork pieces.
CATEGORY: sausage.
AGING: 20 days minimum.
TASTE: pleasant, smooth, with light notes of pepper and spices.

MOLISE

Signora di Conca Casale Slow Food
BASE: mixture of pork pieces.
CATEGORY: sausage.
AGING: 6 months minimum.
TASTE: intense, slightly smoky.

SICILY

Salsiccia di Palazzolo Acreide Slow Food
BASE: mixture of pork pieces.
CATEGORY: sausage.
AGING: about 20 days, but can be eaten fresh grilled.
TASTE: pleasant and very mild, with notes of chile and wild fennel.

Salame Sant'Angelo IGP
BASE: mixture of pork pieces.
CATEGORY: sausage.
AGING: 1 month minimum.
TASTE: pleasant, fatty, slightly spiced.

THE WAR OF THE HAMS

These *prosciutti* are Italy's most iconic cured meats. Let's size up Parma and San Daniele hams in this head-to-head comparison.

CHARLES PATIN O'COOHOON

· PROSCIUTTO DI SAN DANIELE · VS. · PROSCIUTTO DI PARMA ·

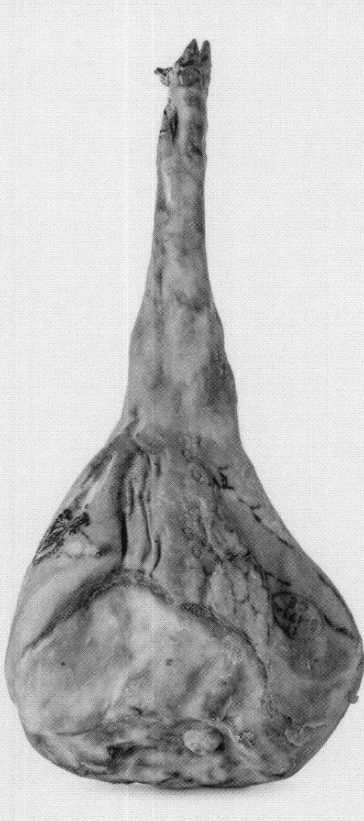

ORIGINS
In the manuscript *De conservanda sanitate* (1453), doctor Geremia Simeoni declares that "the lean parts of domestic pigs preserved in salt can be eaten as an aperitif."

PRODUCTION ZONE
Located along the Tagliamento River, its zone of production corresponds to the 13 square miles (34 sq km) around the municipality of San Daniele del Friuli (Friuli-Venezia Giulia).

APPELLATION
DOP since 1996.

CHARACTER
A guitar shape between 17½ and 22 pounds (8 and 10 kg), with the entire leg, which differentiates it from Parma, from which *il piedino* (the foot) is cut off. The fat layer is white and compact. The flesh is pinkish red, with white and pinkish-white marbling.

COMPOSITION
Only the whole leg of the pig and sea salt.

BREEDS
The Landrace, Large White, and Duroc breeds of pigs fed on noble grains and raised for at least nine months in Friuli-Venezia Giulia, Veneto, Lombardy, Piedmont, Emilia-Romagna, Umbria, Tuscany, Marche, Abruzzo, and Lazio.

AGING
Between fourteen and twenty-four months. In the thirteenth month, the part of the ham that is not covered by fat is protected by a mixture of pork fat and rice flour known as the *puntatura*. The ham dries in contact with the cold breezes from the Alps and the warm breezes off the Adriatic.

TASTE
The thin pink slices develop a very smooth flavor with delicate notes of chestnuts and undergrowth. Thanks to a faster drying time due to the climate, it is a little drier and more pronounced than Parma ham.

PAIRING
Finely cut with a knife, it fits wonderfully on a Montasio, a local pressed cow's-milk cheese.

STAMP
Branded with a hot iron with a ham-shaped symbol encircling the letters *S* and *D*.

PRODUCTION
Two and a half million hams are produced each year by thirty-one producers.

EVENT
Since 1985, the city of San Daniele has hosted the Aria di Festa in June, a major festival held in honor of its treasured charcuterie.

AMBASSADOR
Gabriele D'Annunzio, author of *The Flame* (1900), was a fan. He always asked a friend to bring him some.

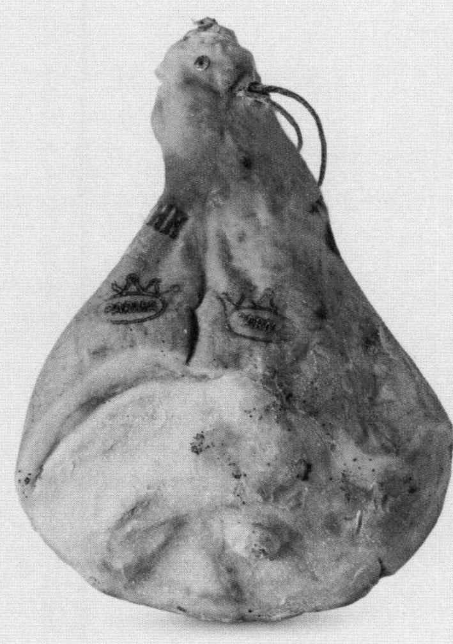

ORIGINS
The art of prosciutto has its roots in Cisalpine Gaul (the part of ancient Gaul south and east of the Alps) of which Parma was a part during Roman times. It was then codified by the corporation of Lardaroli, the Parma people (*parmensi*), during the Middle Ages.

PRODUCTION AREA
Most of the cured meats are concentrated around the village of Langhirano. The rest of the area is bordered by the rivers Enza to the east and Stirone to the west, in Emilia-Romagna.

APPELLATION
DOP since 1996.

CHARACTER
The rounded, thick ham weighs between 15 and 22 pounds (7 and 10 kg). The outer fat layer is orange-yellow and the flesh pinkish red.

COMPOSITION
Only the thigh of the pig and sea salt.

BREEDS
The Large White and Duroc breeds, fed on cereals and milk and raised for at least nine months in Piedmont, Lombardy, Veneto, Emilia-Romagna, Tuscany, Umbria, Marche, Lazio, and Abruzzo.

AGING
Between twelve and thirty-six months. The hams are caressed by the sea spray off the Emilian hills. In the seventh month, a mixture of fat, salt, black pepper, and rice flour is applied to the section not protected by fat.

TASTE
The thin rosy-red strips of flesh melt on the tongue and release woodsy and fragrant notes, typical of hazelnut. Evenly streaked with fat, this is one of the most pleasant-tasting hams.

PAIRING
Cut into thin slices, prosciutto is traditionally eaten with *grissini* (thin bread sticks), fresh figs, or melon.

STAMP
The ham is branded with a five-pointed golden ducal crown containing the name "Parma."

PRODUCTION
Nine million hams made by 160 producers.

EVENT
Festival del Prosciutto di Parma, in Langhirano, a large rally held every September.

AMBASSADOR
Italian opera composer Giuseppe Verdi, of course! The maestro from Parma was a big fan of this ham hailing from his home region.

SKIP TO
SALUMI, P. 308; THE FIG, P. 40; GIUSEPPE VERDI, P. 216.

SEASON

TUTTO L'ANNO (YEAR-ROUND)

CATEGORY

SECONDO PIATTO (MAIN COURSE)

LEVEL

DIFFICOLTÀ MEDIA (MEDIUM DIFFICULTY)

OSSO BUCO

ROASTED VEAL SHANK

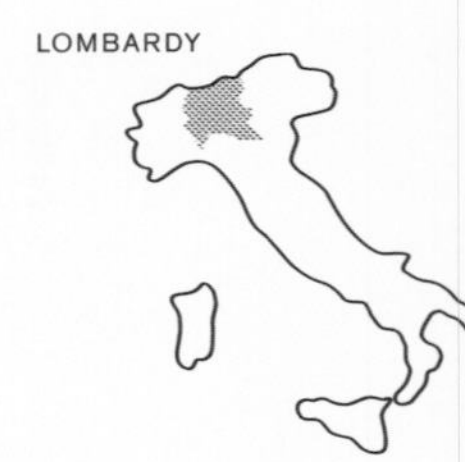

This recipe enjoys an international following, but outside the borders of its native region of Lombardy, the recipe can be misinterpreted. Here is the authentic Milanese version.

FRANÇOIS-RÉGIS GAUDRY

LOMBARD ORIGINS

→ The old Milanese spellings *òssbüs* and *òsbüüs* gave rise to *osso bucato* (bone with a hole), then eventually *osso buco.* In 2007, the city of Milan granted the dish the label *denominazione comunale* (De.Co.), an official municipal recognition.

→ Some historians trace its origins to the fourteenth century, when veal or beef marrow was widely used in culinary preparations. It became a classic in the nineteenth century; Giuseppe Sorbiatti, a prestigious cook for bourgeois families in Milan, highlights it in his collection *Memoriale della cuoca* (1879).

→ We owe its national influence to Pellegrino Artusi, who details the recipe in *La scienza in cucina e l'arte di mangiar bene* (*Science in the Kitchen and the Art of Eating Well*, 1891).

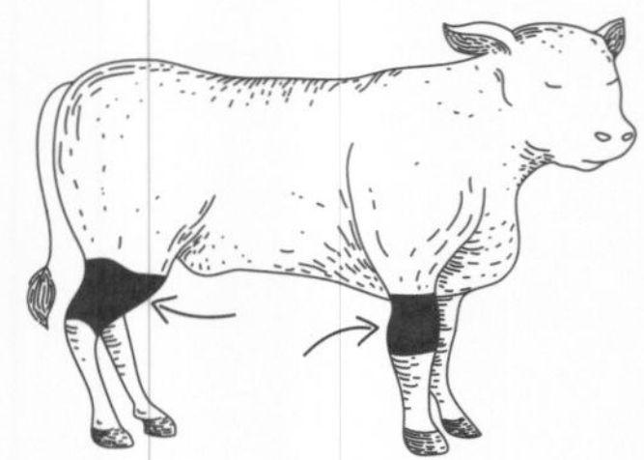

Which pieces?

OSSO BUCO

refers to the part of the bovine anatomy located in the shank (*garretto*), between the thigh and the calf. This 1- to 1½-inch-thick (2.5 to 4 cm) piece contains a central bone (the tibia), filled with marrow and surrounded by muscle. That of the hind legs has fewer tendons and is richer in meat. The foreleg is smaller and less meaty.

MARROW BONE

lends taste and texture. In some Milanese trattoria, this dish is still served with long, thin spoons specially designed to extract the marrow (amusingly called *esattori*, meaning "debt collectors," because they dig into every nook and cranny).

SKIP TO

PELLEGRINO ARTUSI, P. 32; POLENTA, P. 114; RISOTTO ALLA MILANESE, P. 290.

THE RECIPE

Here is a perfect Milanese version, the recipe for which is defended by the Confraternita dell'Ossobuco—an indication of how serious this subject is in Lombardy.

SERVES 4

1 carrot
1 large yellow onion
1 clove garlic
4 ossibuchi (veal shanks), 1⅛ to 1½ inches (3 to 4 cm) thick
Flour
4 tablespoons (60 g) unsalted butter
Scant ½ cup (100 mL) white wine
Beef, veal, or vegetable stock
1 bay leaf
1 sprig thyme
Salt and freshly ground black pepper

For the gremolata

1 clove garlic, peeled
Leaves from 3 sprigs parsley
Zest of ½ lemon

- Cut the carrot and onion into small cubes. Cut the nerve tissue that surrounds the ossibuchi, then flour each side.
- In a Dutch oven set over high heat, melt the butter. When the butter is no longer foaming, place the ossibuchi flat side down in the pot and cook for several minutes on each side to brown; remove and set aside.
- In the same pot, brown the vegetables and the garlic over medium heat in the fat that remains on the bottom, adding a little water if they begin stick. When the onion is translucent, place the ossibuchi back in the pot, pour the wine over the meat, and cook until the wine has reduced.
- Add just enough stock to cover the meat, then add the bay leaf and thyme. Season with salt and pepper.
- Cook, uncovered, over low heat for at least 2 hours. The secret to success: the meat must come off the bone. Do not hesitate to add a little more stock if the liquid reduces too quickly.
- Meanwhile, for the gremolata, finely chop the garlic and parsley together with the lemon zest.
- Near the end of the cooking time, sprinkle half the gremolata into the pot and cook for several minutes more.
- When serving the osso buco, sprinkle the remaining gremolata over the top. Serve with *risotto alla milanese* or a very creamy polenta.

GREMOLATA

→ From Milanese *gremolà*, "reduced to grains," gremolata (or *gremolada*) is osso buco's essential condiment! Composed of chopped parsley, garlic, and lemon zest, it flavors and perfumes the dish at the end of the cooking time and/or when it's served. An anchovy fillet can be added.

→ The use of lemon, a southern fruit, dates back to the Middle Ages when lemons were used as a spice because they came from varietals grafted poorly (or not at all) and therefore lacked sweetness.

A FLORENTINE-STYLE OSSO BUCO?

This is a very popular recipe in the United States (probably invented by Italian migrants), but some restaurants in Tuscany also serve it. This is the *rossa* version—made with an abundance of tomato—of the Milanese specialty, in which can be added just a bit of tomato sauce or tomato paste. For the Florentine version, add one can of peeled tomatoes per four *ossibuchi* at the moment when covering the meat with the stock.

WHEN RED WINE SPARKLES

Bubbles in red wine? It's perfectly acceptable in Italy, where effervescence and red grapes form a distinct cultural duo.

SAMUEL COGLIATI

ROOTS IN THE NORTH

In 1887, in the Marne region of France, Maison Giesler offered a red Champagne; it was a failure. For the French palate, marrying effervescence and tannins is a challenge not easily overcome.

This is not the case in Italy, where for centuries bubbles have been so popular that close to one hundred red wines with specific designations of origin, as well as table wines, highlight them.

This is especially a tradition in northern Italy: in 1825, the naturalist and botanist Giuseppe Acerbi praised the wines of Oltrepò Pavese (Lombardy) for their "finesse" and "rich foam."*

*Giuseppe Acerbi, *Delle viti italiane o sia materiali per servire alla classificazione*, Milan, 1825.

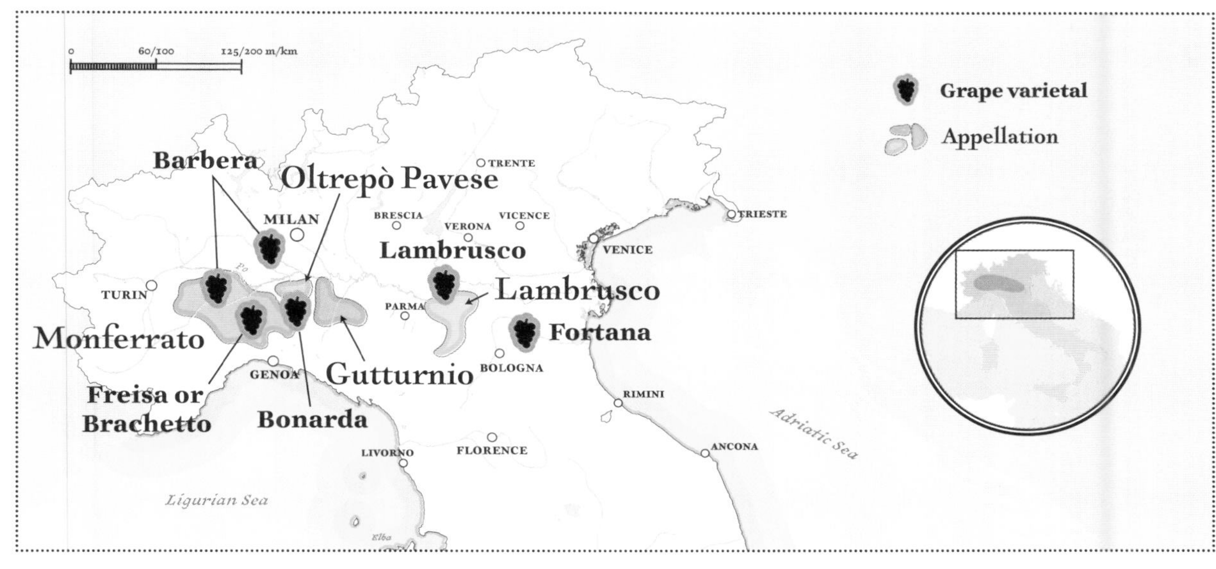

Where do the bubbles come from?

It's no accident that this unique form of wine production took root in northern Italy. Southern Piedmont and Lombardy, like Emilia-Romagna, are hot regions in summer but cool, if not cold, in autumn. This results in rich grapes and generous musts whose fermentation is slowed during harsh winter temperatures. As temperatures rise in spring, fermentation resumes in those wines left in barrels or bottles to develop their gases naturally. This so-called ancestral method develops the fine and elegant bubbles of natural sparkling wines. On a commercial scale, however, this process is replaced with the use of closed tanks, which makes the process faster but creates less elegant results . . .

A GOOD HABIT

Enhance the freshness of wines by serving them at 54° to 55°F (12° to 13°C), or even directly from the refrigerator in summer.

Ideal varietals

Not all red grape varietals are suitable for making sparkling wines. Varietals that yield wines that are a little harsh, or conversely a little weak, do not perform well for this type of wine, which fares best with rich varietals featuring developed tannins and a tolerance for sun. Among the most famous:

BONARDA (or Croatina between Pavia, Piacenza, and Parma).

BARBERA, especially Piedmontese and Lombard, with more intensity.

LAMBRUSCO (with multiple ecotypes in Emilia-Romagna and near Mantua), which has every attribute necessary to create sparkling wines and lively, easy-to-drink effervescent wines.

FREISA* OR *BRACHETTO (Piedmont).

FORTANA (Emilia-Romagna)

· DESIGNATIONS OF ORIGIN AND TYPES OF WINE ·

The most famous PDO wines are linked to these grape varietals, whose names they often bear:

→ **La Bonarda**, sparkling or still, is associated with the Oltrepò Pavese (Lombardy) appellation and one of Colli Piacentini (Emilia-Romagna).

→ **La Barbera** has the same, but its favorite sparkling *terroir* remains in southern Piedmont: the Monferrato.

→ **The Lambruschi family** is one of the most popular transalpine wines (over 17 million bottles sold in supermarkets in 2018, at an average price of €2.75/$3.25!). Its PDOs: Sorbara, Grasparossa di Castelvetro, Reggiano, Modena, Oltrepò Mantovano, Salamino di Santacroce . . . Some can be *spumante* (sparkling), made in closed vats or by the traditional method.

→ In Piacenza, **Gutturnio** is made from a blend of Bonarda and Barbera.

→ More specifically, **Malvasia di Casorzo d'Asti** and **Brachetto d'Acqui** from Piedmont, as well as **Sangue di Giuda dell'Oltrepò**, are red, effervescent, and sweet at the same time!

FOOD PAIRINGS

Tannins, acidity, gas, alcohol . . . Italian sparkling wines offer a wide array, from wines for serving at the beginning of a meal as an aperitif to those ideal for main courses to dessert. Their lively profile favors rich and fatty dishes: pork (sausages from Varzi or Felino, pancetta from Piacenza, mortadella and bacon), accompanied by *torta o gnocco fritto* (fritters made from bread dough), but also classic northern dishes: ravioli, *anolini*, and *cappelletti* stuffed with meat; *lesso* (meat and vegetable stew); tripe; *cotechino*; *zampone* . . .

Some beautiful locales

The bulk of production occurs from cooperative cellars and commercial heavyweights, mainly targeting quantity at low prices. An artisanal dimension remains preserved, however, and produces beautiful bottles.

A TOP 5

THE LAMBRUSCO OR THE BONARDA OF CAMILLO DONATI IN PARMA *(Emilia-Romagna).*

THE SOTTOBOSCO OF CA' DE NOCI IN REGGIO EMILIA *(Emilia-Romagna).*

THE BARBACARLO AND THE MONTEBUONO OF LINO MAGA IN BRONI *(Lombardy).*

THE BARBERA VIVACE OF BRICCO MONDALINO OF THE MONFERRATO VINEYARD *(Piedmont).*

THE BARBERA VIVACE DEL MONFERRATO OF BERA VITTORIO E FIGLI IN ASTI *(Piedmont).*

SKIP TO
TORTA FRITTA (FRIED DOUGH), P. 133;
NATURAL WINE, P. 320.

SWEET TREATS OF CHRISTMAS

Which of these many sweet Italian treats might Babbo Natale (Father Christmas) find waiting for him when he visits the homes of Italian children at Christmas? Here are fifteen delectable desserts to serve up for end-of-year celebrations.

STÉPHANE SOLIER

①

PANETTONE

Lombardy

A soft dome-shaped bread with raisins and candied fruits, sometimes filled. Descendant of medieval spiced breads.

PANDORO

Veneto

A soft vanilla-scented bread, shaped like a truncated cone of an eight-pointed star, dusted with confectioners' sugar. It was created at the end of the nineteenth century from Veronese *nadalin* or Venetian *pan de oro* in a comet-shaped mold designed by Impressionist painter Dall'Oca Bianca.

BOSTRENGO

Marche, Emilia-Romagna

A dense and flat pastry, round or rectangular, containing twenty standard ingredients and twelve possible varying ingredients, depending on what's on hand. Its base is often made up of stale bread or flour soaked in a broth of dried figs, cooked must, and nuts . . .

BUCCELLATO

Sicily

A wreath of crimped flaky pastry decorated with candied fruits and stuffed with figs, raisins, almonds, candied squash, orange zest, chocolate . . . This "little bite" eaten by Roman soldiers was ennobled in the sixteenth century with its *fichi incannati* filling (dried figs strung on reeds).

PARROZZO

Abruzzo

A half-dome cake made of semolina, ground almonds, eggs, citrus zest, and dark chocolate, invented in 1920 in homage to *pane rozzo* (peasant bread), from which it took its name, shape, and colors. It was named by poet D'Annunzio, who dedicated a song to it.

ZELTEN

Trentino-Alto Adige

A bread from medieval times, with honey, nuts, and candied fruits. The oldest recipe was found in an eighteenth-century manuscript in Rovereto. Its name comes from the German *selten*, meaning "sometimes," a reference to its seasonal character.

PANGIALLO

Lazio

A round or domed "yellow bread" with honey, nuts, candied citron, spices, and sometimes chocolate, coated with a saffron glaze. The recipe is mentioned in an eighteenth-century manuscript from Viterbo, but it's the descendant of golden cakes offered by the Romans during the winter solstice.

CERTOSINO DE BOLOGNE

Emilia-Romagna

A round medieval bread, slightly risen, brown, and in the shape of a Gothic rose window. It is flavored with honey, *mostarda Bolognese* (a plum and quince jam), dark chocolate, cinnamon, and red wine syrup with spices or with Marsala, decorated with candied fruit and almonds. It was made by the *speziali* (apothecaries) then by the *certosini* (Carthusian monks).

PANI 'E SABA

Sardinia

A dark bread with *sapa* (cooked grape must syrup obtained from grapes or prickly pears) or *abbattu* (a honey and pollen syrup) enriched with nuts, raisins, citrus zest, and aromatics. It was eaten during harvesttime.

PANDOLCE

Liguria

A "high" or "low" bread that is flavored (anise, fennel, bergamot, possibly Marsala) with nuts and candied fruits. It came about as a request by the Genoese doge Andrea Doria, who ordered a nutritious cake for his long voyages at sea.

PANPEPATO (OR PAMPEPATO, PAMPATATO)

Tuscany, Umbria, Emilia-Romagna

A bread made with nuts, candied fruits, and spices bound with flour and honey (and grape must in Umbria). Created in the thirteenth century by the Sienese Niccolò dei Salimbeni with new spices from the East, it is said to be the ancestor of various regional variations (*panforte, spongata* from Emilia-Romagna, Sardinian *pani 'e saba* . . .).

PANFORTE

Tuscany

A round, flat bread containing seventeen ingredients (for the seventeen Siena districts): honey, spices, nuts, and candied fruits. There are three versions: black (derived from *panpepato*, which dates back to 1280), chocolate (1820), and white (a glaze of vanilla sugar, 1879).

CARTELLATE (OR CRUSTELE, NEVOLE, CRISPELLE, ROSE...)

Apulia, Basilicata, Calabria

Crisp arabesque pastries flavored with white wine and citrus peel, fried, and coated with honey, spices, nuts . . . to soak in *vino cotto* (cooked grape must). Their shape symbolizes the halo or crown of thorns worn by Christ.

TURDILLI

Calabria

Flour-based gnocchi, grooved and rolled into a spiral, in reference to the sun's rays that connects them to the ancient pagan solar cult. Flavored with muscat, orange zest, and cinnamon, then fried and coated with amber-colored honey. They are served chilled, with a fortified wine.

STRUFFOLI

Campania

A spectacular composition made of balls of dough with eggs, butter, sugar, and lemon zest, fried in olive oil and coated with honey, orange zest, candied orange, and sugar. From Greek tradition, they were distributed by the Neapolitan convents in the seventeenth century.

~

And also . . .

GUBANA FROM FRIULI, MECOULIN FROM AOSTA VALLEY . . .

SKIP TO
PANETTONE, P. 96; MOSTARDA, P. 377; "MIELICROMIA," P. 338; ALMONDS, P. 173.

FELLINI, THE GOURMAND

Italian filmmaker and screenwriter Federico Fellini's films are chock-full of meal-centric scenes. Let's reveal more about this maestro's decadent genius through four starring ingredients.

LAURENT DELMAS

ABOUT ANCHOVIES . . .

Maddalena, Fellini's sister, reveals in her work *A tavola con Fellini* (2003) that one of his favorite dishes was anchovies with citrus, a preparation common in Italy's coastal regions.

RECIPE

ALICETTE AGLI AGRUMI
SMALL ANCHOVIES WITH CITRUS

SERVES 4

14 ounces (400 g) fresh anchovy fillets

White vinegar

Juice of 4 lemons, plus a little of the zest for finishing

¾ cup (185 mL) olive oil

1 small chile, chopped

Juice of 4 oranges, plus a little of the zest for finishing

Salt

Slices of rustic sourdough bread, toasted

· Place the anchovy fillets in a bowl and cover them with vinegar. Let marinate for 2 hours, then drain.

· Combine the lemon juice with ¼ cup (60 mL) of the olive oil and the chile. Cover the anchovies with this mixture and let marinate.

· Combine the orange juice with the remaining ½ cup (125 mL) olive oil, and season with salt. Remove the anchovies from the marinade and let drain. In a bowl, pour the orange juice mixture over the anchovies and sprinkle with the orange and lemon zest. Let stand 2 to 3 minutes. Serve with toasted bread.

ABOUT RAVIOLI . . .

In *La dolce vita* (1960), ravioli with ricotta and spinach plays a role. Marcello Rubini's (Marcello Mastroianni) companion believes she can hold on to him with this traditional recipe:

"Marcello, come home! I'm making dinner for you tonight, something light. Ah! I know what I'm going to make for you! Ravioli! I already have everything I need: pasta, cheese, and I'll go out to buy a salad . . ."

Unfortunately, it would take more than this to soften up this writer for gossip magazines, who was always eager to rendezvous with his favorite actresses, including Sylvia Rank, played by the voluptuous Anita Ekberg!

"La vita è una combinazione di pasta e di magia."

"Life is a combination of magic and pasta."

—

Federico Fellini
1920–1993

Palme d'Or 1960
for *La dolce vita*

ABOUT VEAL . . .

In *Fellini's Roma* (1972), he is clearly inspired by the time when, at age nineteen, he moved into a boarding house on Via Albalonga in Rome. He would dine in a small nearby trattoria. The film depicts large groups of outdoor tables where diners congregate, reaching for enormous plates of spaghetti and other specialties, such as calf's liver in all its forms, as evidenced by this dialogue among diners in the film:

—"Order what you like! Our specialty: liver with peppers!"

—"*Fettuccine alle vongole, maccheroni alla romana*, and the chef's specialty: liver with onions!"

—"Snails to start."

—"Just a small portion, my stomach was upset all night long."

—"Mamma is in the kitchen; she makes a fantastic *pajata*."

—"What is that?"

—"Calf's intestines! Fantastic!"

ABOUT SNAILS . . .

The Roman snails in *Fellini's Roma*, after being cooked in a flavored broth, are browned with garlic and onions in a mixture of oil and butter. Crushed tomatoes, chopped parsley, and a little rosemary are added, then everything cooks gently. The the owner of the restaurant where provincial young Fellini is seated sings their praises: *"Try our specialty. I'll show you the art of eating them! Take a needle and dig. We learn things when we eat snails. Your girlfriends will show you one day."*

As is often the case with Fellini, cooking and salacious suggestions go hand in hand . . .

And also . . .

• Sausage and a loaf of rustic bread at the beginning of *La Strada* (1954).

• Langoustine and caviar for Alberto Lazzari, chicken for poor Cabiria in *Le notti di Cabiria* (*Nights of Cabiria*, 1957) or for Carla (Sandra Milo) in *Otto e mezzo* (*8½*, 1963).

• Pork stuffed with sausages and birds from the Trimalcion banquet in *Satyricon* (1969).

• Tagliatelle from large family and Romagna tables in *Amarcord* (1973).

• Aphrodisiac oysters in *Il Casanova di Federico Fellini* (*Fellini's Casanova*, 1976).

SKIP TO
THE AMAZING ANCHOVY, P. 236;
GOURMET CINEMA, P. 68; POP PASTA, P. 221.

COOKING WITH SEAWATER

Although in recent years it has become a trendy technique used by top chefs, cooking *all'acqua di mare* was originally a trick of *cucina povera.*

ILARIA BRUNETTI

From Sea to Michelin Stars

In antiquity, the use of seawater in cooking was widespread around the Mediterranean, especially on ships. The great Spanish chef Ferran Adrià revived its use in haute cuisine, and it can be found as an ingredient being used in Italy today.

A LONG MEDITERRANEAN HISTORY . . .

→ The ancient Greeks used seawater to soften the tannins of olives from the Gallura region (Sardinia).

→ In ancient Rome, wild boar "Theban-style" was cooked with seawater and bay leaf.

→ Sailors and fishermen in Italy and Spain used seawater to clean and cook fish on board, as well as to soak their dry breads, such as *freselle* or *galette del marinaio.*

. . . WITH AN ITALIAN TOUCH

Some uses of seawater have spread on land, especially in southern Italy:

→ For fish soups, such as *quadaru* in Calabria or *gallipolina* soup in Apulia.

→ For cooking *all'acqua pazza* (crazy water), a method created in Campania.

→ To make breads (Apulia, Campania, and Calabria).

→ To cook poultry, such as *gadduzzu all'acqua di mare,* a chicken stuffed with meats and herbs cooked in seawater, typical of Calabria.

→ Until the 1970s, the *acquaiolo,* a traveling merchant, would sell water for drinking and seawater for cooking.

BETWEEN TRADITION AND EXPERIMENTATION

For environmental and hygienic reasons, it is illegal to directly sample and use seawater in cooking. Microfiltered seawater must therefore be purchased. Rich in trace elements and minerals (including potassium), it is also less concentrated in sodium chloride than table salt and therefore better for the body.

Some uses in cooking:

→ To clean fish and mollusks, because it keeps their flesh firm.

→ To cook vegetables, rice, or pasta: a simple *aglio e olio* with spaghetti cooked in seawater will make you feel like you hear the sound of ocean waves!

→ The innovative Birranova brewery (Apulia) created Margosa beer using water from Italian seas.

→ Some bartenders use it in their concoctions. In 2013, for instance, Donato Marzolla (at Palazzo Avino, Campania) created his Nettuno cocktail with rum, lime, kiwifruit, and rosemary—although the water used was not native to Ravello's neighboring sea (which you could admire while sipping it) but instead came from Spain!

→ Bakers and *pizzaioli* have (re)learned to integrate seawater into their recipes.

→ Many Italian chefs use it in unlimited and imaginative ways.

SKIP TO
PACCHERI ALLO SCORFANO, P. 206;
BREADS FOR SURVIVAL, P. 38;
SPAGHETTI AGLIO, OLIO E PEPERONCINO (SPAGHETTI WITH GARLIC, OLIVE OIL, AND CHILE), P. 193.

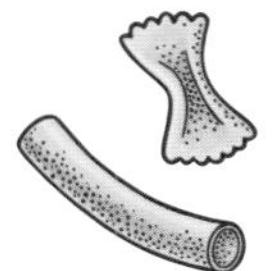

THE TASTE OF SHAPE

Sometimes the shape of pasta is not just a matter of looks.

ELEONORA COZZELLA

THE HISTORY

The vast number of pasta formats reflects a thousand years of history and culture. Over the centuries, 1,238 shapes have been identified, and 250 are still available for purchase today. What are the sources of inspiration for their names?

THE PLANT KINGDOM: *spighe* (wheat stalk), *semi di melone* (melon seeds), *sedani* (celery) . . .

THE ANIMAL KINGDOM: *lumache* (snails), *farfalle* (butterflies), *creste di gallo* (cock's comb) . . .

THE SKY: *stelline* (little stars), *tempestine* (in reference to hail during storms) . . .

HISTORY: *mafaldine* or *reginette* (dedicated to Queen Mafalda of Savoy), *tripoline* (created after the Italo-Turkish War from 1911 to 1912, where Tripoli was the focus).

RELIGION: *ave marie* and *pater noster* (because cooking times were measured in prayers) or *strozzapreti* (priest choker).

FEELINGS: *grattini* (the result of scratching . . .), *pizzicotti* (pinches), *cuoricini* (little hearts), *cieca-marito* ("blind husband," to be seasoned, of course, with the very spicy sauce known as *ammazza-suocera,* "mother-in-law killer").

FABRICS: *maniche* (sleeves), *cappellacci* (hats), *nastrini* (ribbons).

(Almost) Monogamous Marriages

Among pasta shapes and accompanying sauces, there are established and now famous pairings, such as:

Bucatini all'amatriciana
Trofie al pesto
Tagliatelle al ragù
Orecchiette alle cime di rapa
Paccheri con sugo di pesce (fish sauce)
Malloreddus e ragù di salsiccia (sauce with sausage)
Cavatelli con pomodoro e ricotta salata
Spaghetti ai ricci di mare (with sea urchins)
Ziti alla genovese
Pici all'aglione (garlics)
Pappardelle al cinghiale (wild boar)

FOR A PERFECT PAIRING

When it comes to pasta shapes and seasonings, there is an unspoken system of pairing rules based on the pasta's shape, and Italians are extremely sensitive to this.

THE BASICS

Harmony between structure and seasoning: for the most structured forms (such as rigatoni or *bucatini*), select rich sauces, such as those with meat. For smaller and/or thinner formats, select vegetable-based sauces.

Matching the pasta surface: if the surface is rough, it combines well with strong flavors; if it is smooth, simpler flavors are preferred.

LONG FORMATS

Small diameter (spaghetti, *spaghettini,* linguine . . .): vegetables, fish, mollusks, crustaceans; for tube pasta, cheeses and eggs work well.

Larger diameter (*spaghettoni, bucatini*): richly seasoned vegetables and meat-based sauces.

SHORT FORMATS

Penne, *maniche mezze,* rigatoni: select very thick sauces with chunks of meat, sausages, or vegetables.

Tubetti, ditali, lumache, and *conchiglie*: these are perfect with vegetables.

GIANT FORMATS

Lumaconi and *conchiglioni*: perfect baked au gratin because they withstand cooking well and support stuffing or toppings well.

Curiosity

Ziti and *candele* (candles), which are impossible to bend, are broken up prior to being cooked. It would seem easier to simply manufacture them in shorter formats, but the tiny pieces that result from breaking them by hand cook faster and therefore release more starch into the cooking water, creating a perfect creaminess. In this way, they are their own perfect accompaniment, but they also lend themselves to baking au gratin!

SKIP TO
PASTA INVENTORY, P. 124;
THE SPAGHETTI FAMILY, P. 201.

GORGONZOLA

This is without a doubt the most famous blue-veined cheese of Italy. And it divides its fans into two camps: *dolce* (sweet) or *piccante* (sharp).

ANGELA BARUSI

ITS ORIGINS

It was born in the city of Gorgonzola, near Milan, in 879. The city remained its largest center of production and trade for several centuries. The spread of Gorgonzola was slow but persistent, but it was with the development of a new manufacturing technique in the twentieth century's postwar period that its production attained the scale and fame that distinguish it today.

ITS CHARACTERISTICS

Gorgonzola is a soft cheese made from cow's milk from the PDO production area, which includes most of Piedmont and Lombardy.

•

Pasteurized whole milk is processed with the addition of natural lactic ferments and selected molds of the species *Penicillium roqueforti.*

•

Gorgonzola is produced in two types, sweet and sharp, which differ according to the type of penicillium and the length of affinage (aging and ripening). During ripening, the cheese is pierced with needles to allow the development of its characteristic green-blue veining.

SWEET OR SHARP?

THE DOLCE (SWEET) VERSION

is creamy and supple with a distinctive and slightly pungent flavor and biting aroma; it is often so fatty and soft that it is sold by the spoon. The minimum maturation period is 50 days, with a maximum of 150 days.

THE PICCANTE (SHARP) VERSION

has a more veined, firmer, and crumbly interior, with a more assertive and stronger flavor. The production requirements specify at least 80 days of affinage, and a maximum of 270 days.

In cooking

Gorgonzola is a great table cheese, but its natural creaminess also makes it an excellent culinary ingredient:

It is perfect spread on bread or polenta.

It makes a tasty base for sauces and creams and is an extraordinary ally of gnocchi and risottos, but also an ideal accompaniment to meats, fish, and vegetables.

It's a surprising ingredient in desserts, especially those containing dark chocolate, with which it pairs very well.

STORAGE TIPS

Gorgonzola is a living food that continues to evolve even after being cut into portions. It is therefore advisable to buy only the amount you need and to consume it soon after purchase.

PICCANTE (SHARP)

Store at the bottom of the refrigerator, wrapped in aluminum foil, for several days.

DOLCE (SWEET)

Store refrigerated, wrapped in plastic wrap and set in an airtight container to prevent oxidation. The rind can be the source of its pungent smell; therefore, removing it before enjoying the cheese is recommended.

RICH INSIDE AND OUTSIDE

Thanks to the proteolytic action of its penicillium, Gorgonzola is a very digestible cheese. Rich in vitamins, including B_2, B_6, and B_{12}, it is a valuable source of calcium and phosphorus.

It is almost lactose-free, since the milk sugar is naturally consumed by lactic acid bacteria during the natural fermentation that occurs during the cheesemaking process (when the milk curdles).

RELIABLE PAIRINGS WITH FOODS . . .

It works wonderfully with **mascarpone**, which enhances it due to its softness.

It is perfect with **raw vegetables** (celery, cherry tomatoes, peppers, radishes) and **cooked vegetables** (potatoes, squash, broccoli, zucchini). It is pleasant with fresh or dried fruits.

It goes well with citrus or fig **jams**, fruit or chestnut ***mostarde*** (sweet-and-sour garnishes), and **vegetable-based sauces** (tomatoes and red onions).

Another classic: Gorgonzola and **acacia or wildflower honey**.

. . . AND LIQUIDS

GORGONZOLA DOLCE (SWEET) goes well with red or white wines, particularly sweet and savory. Pairing is excellent with Riesling, Pinot Blanc, Orvieto Classico, Malvasia Secca, and Gavi. For reds, turn to Valtellina Superiore, Sassella, slightly sparkling Barbera, Chianti Classico, Sangiovese di Romagna.

GORGONZOLA PICCANTE (SHARP) prefers structured red wines aged in barrels such as Barolo, Barbaresco, Chianti Classico Riserva, Recioto, Amarone, Brunello di Montalcino, and straw wines such as Moscato Passito Liquoroso, Marsala Vergine, or Passito di Pantelleria.

SKIP TO
ITALY'S BEAUTIFUL CHEESES, P. 222;
MASCARPONE, P. 239;
BITTER LETTUCES, P. 170.

SEASON

TUTTO L'ANNO (YEAR-ROUND)

CATEGORY

STREET FOOD, ANTIPASTO (APPETIZER)

LEVEL

FACILE (EASY)

TRAMEZZINO

TRIANGLE SANDWICHES

These little finger sandwiches, very popular in bars and as aperitifs, have become a symbol of Italian gastronomy on the go.

MINA SOUNDIRAM

THE ITALIAN SNACK

Tramezzino—in the plural, *tramezzini*—is the diminutive of *tramezzo* (divide). Literally meaning "small divider," the word can be translated as "small snack." Tramezzini are frequently eaten between meals as a snack. Composed of two slices of crustless sandwich bread filled with mayonnaise, meat, cheese, vegetables, or fish or other seafoods, they are served in triangular portions (a sandwich cut on the diagonal) or as a square, and most often cold, although they can be offered toasted.

ITS ORIGINS

In 1925, Angela and Onorino Nebiolo, a couple who had lived in the United States, bought Caffè Mulassano, a Turin establishment. They had the idea of offering a "sandwich" inspired by American snacking habits and British teatime, which combine food and drink. Nineteenth-century dandy poet Gabriele D'Annunzio is said to have proposed the name *tramezzino*. It was a fitting idea, as the Fascist regime of the 1920s had banned the use of foreign words . . .

Today, Caffè Mulassano offers more than forty à la carte versions! Tramezzino *burro e acciughe* (butter and anchovies), *vitello tonnato* (veal with tuna sauce), and *acciughe, tonno, manzo* (anchovies, tuna, beef) are some favorites.

Venice vs. Turin

Although popularized in Venice where the humid climate is suitable for preserving the softness of the bread, this snack is considered just as much Turinese. In Turin, tramezzino filled with truffles or lobster had been consumed for a long time by the gastronomic aristocracy. In Venice, *tramesin* (in the local dialect) is more popular and is made with less-noble ingredients such as tuna, ham, egg, etc.

SKIP TO
APERITIVO, P. 59.

THE GOLDEN RULES

THE BREAD

Pancarrè, a sandwich bread without the crust, is the go-to.

THE TEXTURE

It is best to consume it immediately once made, when it is still soft but not too moist.

THE FILLING

There is no limit to the creativity of the filling, which can range from the simplest combinations to those with exceptional ingredients. The filled sandwich is recognizable by the "smiling mouth" shape: rounded in the center but with narrow edges. Be careful not to overfill it, or it will be difficult to eat. A recurring component? Mayonnaise!

THE MOST FAMOUS

PROSCIUTTO: with ham (pressed or cured), with mayonnaise, hard-boiled egg, and lettuce (romaine or arugula). You can add cheese.

POMODORO E MOZZARELLA: with tomato and mozzarella.

AL TONNO: to go with the tuna, capers and olives can be added, as well as tomatoes or artichokes.

AL SALMONE: smoked salmon is generally paired with fish roe.

VEGETARIANI: zucchini, eggplant, pickles, tomatoes . . .

TORTA DI TRAMEZZINI: tramezzini served up with assorted fillings, convenient for buffets or aperitifs for large groups.

THE RECIPE

***Tonno e carciofi* (tuna and artichokes): a marriage of love often found in tramezzini.**

SERVES 6

- 4¼ ounces (120 g) tuna in oil
- Zest and juice of ½ lemon
- 4 tablespoons (56 g) mayonnaise
- Salt and freshly ground black pepper
- 4¼ ounces (120 g) artichokes in oil
- 10 flat-leaf parsley leaves
- 6 square slices white sandwich bread, crusts removed
- 1 bunch cherry tomatoes (in season), sliced (optional)

In a bowl, crumble the tuna and add the lemon zest and lemon juice; stir to combine. Add 2 to 3 tablespoons of the mayonnaise and combine to a smooth consistency. Season with salt and pepper.

Drain the artichokes. In a separate bowl, combine the artichokes with the parsley leaves and the remaining 1 tablespoon mayonnaise to make a thick cream.

Arrange two rows of 3 slices of the bread. Spread the artichoke cream over the slices in the first row and the tuna mixture over the slices on the second row. Add a few slices of tomato, if using, on top of each slice with artichoke cream. Close the sandwiches by placing the slices with the tuna mixture on top, tuna side down. Wrap each sandwich in plastic wrap and refrigerate for 30 minutes.

Unwrap the tramezzini and, using a lightly dampened knife, cut each in half diagonally. You can cut them in half again on the diagonal into smaller servings, if you like. Serve chilled.

Good addresses to know

IN TURIN

Caffè Mulassano *(Piazza Castello, 15)*

IN VENICE

Bar Tiziano *(Fondamenta Trapolin, 5747)*

Do Mori *(San Polo, 429)*

Birreria Forst *(Calle delle Rasse, 4540)*

IN MILAN

Tramè *(Piazza San Simpliciano, Brera and Via Vittor Pisani 14, Centrale)*

NATURAL WINE

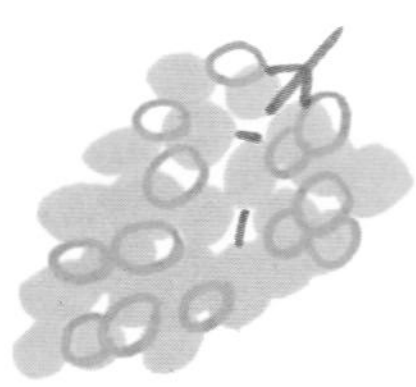

As a result of symbiosis between the vineyard and climate, and skillful handling in the cellar, Italian natural wines are making the grade.

FRANCESCA TRADARDI

DO YOU SPEAK THE LANGUAGE OF NATURAL WINE?

Vini veri (real wines), *artigianali* (artisanal), *contadini* (rustic), *trasparenti* (transparent): there are so many names for natural wines, but no European legislation or definition that standardizes the various terms.

Vini naturali (natural wines) are created with respect for the environment, without the application of synthetic substances or chemical fertilizers in the vineyard and without oenological additives in the cellar (except for modest amounts of sulfites, an approach that creates disagreements), in favor of indigenous yeasts naturally present during harvest and in cellars.

BORN IN ITALY

Unlike France, which saw the birth of this phenomenon in the 1950s led by Jules Chauvet in Beaujolais (in reaction to the growth of industrial agriculture), Italy saw its natural wine pioneers emerge only twenty years ago. Among them, Josko Gravner, Stefano Bellotti, Angiolino Maule, and Paolo Bea highlighted the desire for harmony between people and the planet. Initially a niche practice, the making of natural wine has developed in recent years. The first groups of producers to push the message of both traditional and innovation were ViniVeri, followed by VinNatur, both concerned with finding solutions compatible with climate change.

ORGANIC WINE

Organic wine is governed by European regulation published in 2012 after years of controversy. It is defined as "produced from grapes cultivated using organic farming methods," and all phases of wine production are rigorously controlled. No synthetic chemicals or GMOs are used in vineyards, and only authorized products can be used in cellars. The amount of sulfites is lower than in conventional wines:

RED WINES

UP TO 100 MG/L (150 mg/L for conventional wines).

WHITE AND ROSÉ WINES

UP TO 150 MG/L (200 mg/L for conventional wines).

The production process is only eligible for certification three years after its conversion to organic methods, following strict controls by bodies authorized by the Italian Ministry of Agricultural, Food, and Forestry Policies, themselves inspected by the same ministry as well as the regions.

Some winegrowers to know

Natural wine has created many skilled jobs, and women are particularly well represented in the field, in both the vineyards and the cellars.

ARIANNA OCCHIPINTI

DOMAIN: Azienda Occhipinti, Vittoria (*Sicily*).

CUVÉE: Fossa di Lupo 2016, red.

A new single-plot territorial approach that enhances a territory in which the charmed grape varietal Frappato, vibrant and deep red, is interpreted. Sand and limestone form the foundation of a deep and sun-drenched wine, with aromas of blackberry as well as balsamic notes and a very long tactile sensation.

ELENA PANTALEONI

DOMAIN: Azienda La Stoppa, Rivergaro (*Emilia-Romagna*).

CUVÉE: Ageno 2011, orange.

Produced by the historic company of Val Trebbiola, this wine of character is almost an archetype of macerated wines, a tribute to Cavaliere Ageno, founder of the estate. Ageno is the product of a blend of three white grape varietals: Malvasia di Candia Aromatica, Ortrugo, and Trebbiano. In the glass, it's a trip through flavors of the East, with enveloping notes of tea, spices, and citrus peel; to be shared with friends who appreciate its appeal.

ELISABETTA FORADORI

DOMAIN: Azienda Foradori, Mezzolombardo (*Trentino-Alto Adige*).

CUVÉE: Fontanasanta 2016, orange.

For more than thirty years, Elisabetta has been promoting the two indigenous grape varietals (Nosiola and Teroldego) from the Rotaliana plain surrounded by the Dolomites. Resulting from old-fashioned vinification with a long maceration on the skins in Spanish amphorae, this is a delicate wine but very long on the palate, to be enjoyed slowly.

BIODYNAMIC WINE

The biodynamic method was defined in the 1920s by the Austrian Rudolf Steiner (founder of anthroposophy). The only certification recognized in the world is issued by the Demeter Association and requires winemakers to operate with full respect for the course of nature and its resources, with particular attention to the phases of the moon. Chemical synthesis and GMO products are banned in favor of natural preparations obtained from fermentation, decoction processes, or even minerals.

ORANGE WINE: NEW FLAVORS

This method of winemaking, in which white grape varietals are vinified like red wines, finds a wide range of expressions among natural wines. The method spread to Italy in the 2000s thanks to Josko Gravner and Stanko Radikon.

WINES IN AMPHORAE

For the past twenty or so years, some Italian winegrowers have been reviving an ancient tradition dating back to the sixth century BCE by using vessels made from terra-cotta rather than wood for the vinification and aging of wine.

Amphorae are very popular because of their optimal thermal regulation and their porous nature, which provides good ventilation for the wine. In addition, unlike wood, their neutral material improves the expression of the grape varietal itself and of the territory.

Wines of great expression

ARIENTO 2016—ORANGE, Azienda Massa Vecchia (*Tuscany*).

Fabrizio Niccolaini was one of the first producers to promote environmentally friendly agriculture, converting to biodynamics. This wine made from the Vermentino varietal expresses a lively and juicy energy with a strong and flavorful tension. Maceration on the skins is perfectly managed. Extraordinary!

BARBACARLO 2003—RED, Azienda Barbacarlo (*Lombardy*).

Lino Maga himself is an extraordinary character, and his wine is legendary. In 2003, Barbacarlo was excluded from the Oltrepò Pavese Rosso DOC due to a sugar content higher than allowed by law. But this cuvée is a masterpiece, with a tannic impact accompanied by an intense force that combines acidity with sweetness. Nicely long on the palate, and with flavors reminiscent of Christmas pastries.

MARSALA SUPERIORE 1987—FORTIFIED, Azienda Marco De Bartoli (*Sicily*).

Marco De Bartoli is the guardian of the *soleras* method, an ancient technique for Marsala winemaking, and offers tasty gems with oxidative tones and briny flavors. A visit to his cellar is a journey back in time to discover a forgotten Sicily. A unique wine for a dense, almost three-dimensional sensation.

TREBBIANO D'ABRUZZO 2005—WHITE, Azienda Valentini (*Abruzzo*).

This estate, one of the oldest in the country (seventeenth century), has remained faithful to artisanal know-how. This wine is of great purity, endowed with a beautiful personality and a dense and luminous texture signed by Francesco Valentini. It's the perfect synthesis of authenticity and sensory excellence. The terroir and its personal interpretation are expressed in it.

NADIA VERRUA

DOMAIN: Azienda Cascina Tavijn, Scurzolengo (*Piedmont*).

CUVÉE: Ottavio 2018, red.

This family business is run by Nadia and her parents. Grignolino is one of the most interesting and least known indigenous Piedmontese grape varietals on the Italian wine scene. Its ideal land is in the Asti and Casalese regions. This is an easy-to-drink wine, but with a touch of austerity thanks to light tannins.

FRANCESCA AND MARGHERITA PADOVANI

DOMAIN: Azienda Fonterenza, Sant'Angelo in Colle (*Tuscany*).

CUVÉE: Alberello Rosso di Montalcino 2016, red.

Twin sisters have been harvesting and vinifying in the Montalcino commune since the early 2000s. Alberello takes its name from the way the vine is cultivated; that is, by giving it a shrub shape (*alberello* in Italian). The estate covers an area of 1¼ acres (0.5 ha) and offers around 5,000 bottles and a particularly careful selection of Rosso di Montalcino, a fragrant, floral Sangiovese with an excellent rhythmic flavor.

Events Not to Miss

Vini di Vignaioli (winegrowers' wines), Fornovo di Taro (Emilia-Romagna): one weekend between late October and early December.

Fiera di ViniVeri (Veneto): one weekend between late March and early April.

Fiera VinNatur, itinerant: variable dates.

La terra trema (trembling earth), Milan (Lombardy): one weekend between late November and early December.

Vi.vi. t., Verona (Veneto): four days in April.

SKIP TO
FRANCESCO "JOSKO" GRAVNER, P. 199; GATHERING GRAPES, P. 158; ORANGE WINE, P. 113.

MARINADES

Classic staples of Italian pantries, *scapece* and *carpione* are valuable methods of preserving food at home and attest to the Italian passion for sour flavors.

NADIA POSTIGLIONE

A FUNCTIONAL CONDIMENT

In Roman times, sweet-and-sour flavors were particularly popular, as found in the book *De re coquinaria d'Apicius*, with its instructions for cooking fish in vinegar and honey.

Undoubtedly inherited from this affinity, scapece and carpione are marinades prepared from wine vinegar, an ingredient that allows perishable foods to be consumed days after they are made. They are used mainly for fish but also for vegetables and meats, which give them a typical acidic note.

SCAPECE OR CARPIONE?

Scapece (escabeche in English) is a cold marinade for already-cooked food, usually one that is fried. Derived from the Spanish *escabeche*, a term for a vinegar marinade and itself borrowed from the Arabic *iskebeq* ("in vinegar"), the use of scapece has spread throughout the Mediterranean. The idea of cooking fried fish in a vinegar sauce was born in the Iberian Peninsula in the fourteenth century, and capece then spread through southern Italy and along the Tuscan and Ligurian coastlines.

Carpione involves marinating food in a vinegar-based sauce brought to a boil, often with the addition of wine, carrots, celery, and various aromatics. The preparation in carpione, widespread in northern Italy between Piedmont, Lombardy, and part of Veneto, takes its name from a typical fish from Lake Garda, the carpione, protected by the Slow Food Ark of Taste.

The mosaic of fish scapece

Muggine di scabecciu (Sardinia): fried mullet in a sweet-and-sour sauce of vinegar, sugar, and tomato.

Anguilla a scaveccio (Tuscany): once fried, eel is covered with a reduction of vinegar, bay leaf, chile, and rosemary.

Scabeccio (Liguria): floured and fried bogue marinated in vinegar with onions, sage, and mint.

Aggiadda (Liguria): small red mullet or bogue, floured and fried, then marinated in vinegar, white wine, and herbs, with a lot of garlic.

Scapece di vasto (Abruzzo): fried skate and dogfish, marinated in vinegar made from Trebbiano (a local white wine), with onions and saffron.

Scapece molisana (Molise): fried skate marinated in vinegar and saffron.

Alici di cetara alla scapece (Campania): anchovies, floured and fried, then seasoned with vinegar and mint.

Scapece gallipolina (Apulia): small fatty fish (sardines, sardinella, anchovies, garfish, etc.), floured and fried, then placed in wooden vats and covered with crumbled bread, soaked in vinegar and saffron.

Scapece di Lesina (Apulia): fried or grilled eel, marinated in vinegar, garlic, and mint.

Sarde in saor (Veneto): fried sardines marinated in vinegar, with onions, raisins, and pine nuts.

RECIPES

PESCI DI LAGO IN CARPIONE (MARINATED FRESHWATER FISH)

Characteristic of *cucina lariana* in the Como region, this preparation includes two freshwater fish, *alborella* (*Alburnus arborella*—a type of bleak fish) and *agone* (*Alosa agone*—a type of shad), which is fished in Lake Como, but the recipe is adapted to accommodate all small- and medium-size freshwater fish.

Wash and clean 1⅛ pounds (500 g) freshwater fish of your choice, lightly flour them, and fry them in olive oil or any frying oil. Chop 1 carrot, ½ celery stalk, ½ onion, and 1 garlic clove. Brown them in a drizzle of olive oil with 3 cloves, black pepper, and thyme. Add 2 cups (500 mL) dry white wine and 2 cups (500 mL) white wine vinegar and bring to a boil. Place the fish in an earthenware pot, then pour the marinade over them. Sprinkle with chopped parsley.

ZUCCHINE A SCAPECE (ZUCCHINI ESCABECHE)

A flagship of Neapolitan cuisine, this dish is perhaps the most popular version of this marinade.

Cut 6 zucchini into thick slices and fry them in olive oil. Season with ¼ cup (60 mL) white wine vinegar, a drizzle of olive oil, 3 cloves fresh garlic, salt, and a lot of fresh mint. Combine well. Set aside to marinate for 2 hours before serving. You can prepare this with eggplant instead.

TRIADE DEL CARPIONE PIEMONTESE (PIEDMONTESE-STYLE MIXED MARINADE)

Carpione Piemontese, a typical summer dish from the historic Langhe region, deserves special mention. It is made with poached eggs, veal scallops (sometimes chicken), and fried zucchini, all marinated together in a reduction of vinegar, onions, garlic, and sage.

Sulla Punta Della Lingua (On the Tip of the Tongue)

Scabeccio, in the Ligurian dialect, refers to an average person with limited abilities and few good qualities.

SKIP TO
FISH, P. 300; CICCHETTI VENEZIANI (VENETIAN SNACKS), P. 228.

Fulvio Pierangelini

PROFILE

He's considered a giant of gastronomy and a darling of Italian and global critics. Here is a portrait of a cook as larger-than-life as he is brilliant!

FRANÇOIS-RÉGIS GAUDRY

THE GAMBERO ROSSO PHENOMENON

From 1980 to 2008, Fulvio Pierangelini oversaw a gastronomic phenomenon: a modest structure by the sea, in a Tuscan village an hour from Livorno, with rattan armchairs, faded hangings, and old furniture . . . Nothing luxurious, but yet! In the early 2000s, it was Italy's most booked table. Traveling from locations such as Brazil, Iceland, and New Zealand, eager clientele made reservations up to five months in advance to taste his miracles. He could have increased the number of tables to accommodate more people, yet instead he did the opposite: he reduced the covers from thirty-six to eighteen. It was his way to get clear of the cumbersome restaurant codes endured through the years, to escape having to duplicate the same dish for multiple tables, and to be able to create on the spot, instinctively, all without sophisticated cooking equipment.

HIS BIOGRAPHY IN 5 DATES

MAY 11, 1953
Born in Rome.

1978
Internship with Roger Vergé at the Moulin de Mougins (Alpes-Maritimes).

1980
Opening of his restaurant Gambero Rosso in San Vincenzo (Tuscany).

1998
Two Michelin stars.

2008
Shuttering of Gambero Rosso.

MEMORABLE QUOTES

Regarding the Michelin Guide, which would never award him three stars: *"Last week, I pissed next to Jean-Luc Naret [ex-director of the Michelin Guides] in the toilets at the Plaza Athénée. Maybe my situation will get better . . ."*
RAI UNO, 2004.

"If I see a chef cutting broccoli tops with a knife, I know he's a blockhead! For many vegetables, I use the most sophisticated tool ever: my hands . . ."
L'EXPRESS, 2012.

RECIPE

INSALATA DI ARANCE, FINOCCHI E GAMBERI ROSSI (ORANGE, FENNEL, AND PRAWN SALAD)

The magic touch of this salad is delivered by a tangy orange sauce, which can also be used to season raw vegetables or fish.

4 juicing oranges
Salt and freshly ground black pepper
½ cup (125 mL) olive oil
2 fennel bulbs
2 tablespoons (30 mL) honey
1 pinch wild fennel, or 1 star anise pod
12 raw red shrimp

- Peel (removing the white pith) and quarter 2 of the oranges. Juice the remaining 2 oranges. In a saucepan, cook the juice over medium heat until reduced and syrupy. Using a small whisk, whisk the juice while adding 3 pinches of salt and a bit of pepper. Drizzle in the olive oil until a thick emulsified sauce is obtained.
- Finely chop the fennel bulbs. Combine half the chopped bulbs in a saucepan with the honey, a scant ½ cup water, and the wild fennel, and cook gently until only slightly softened; the fennel should remain crisp. Place the remaining raw fennel in ice water to keep the pieces crisp. Set aside a few of the fronds for presentation.
- Shell the shrimp, then immerse them in boiling water for 10 to 15 seconds.
- Compose each plate by alternating raw fennel and cooked fennel; arrange a few orange sections around, add fennel fronds, and 3 shrimp. Season with the orange–olive oil emulsion.

FLYING CHEF

Today he's chief consultant of the Hotel de Russie in Rome, the Hotel Savoia in Florence, the Verdura Golf and Spa Resort in Sicily, and the Hotel Amigo in Brussels, and a private chef traveling from Saint-Moritz to Venice via Miami . . . Since 2008, Fulvio Pierangelini has been an itinerant chef often experiencing jet lag. His motto: *"I want to experience cooking all over the world and no longer just do it twice a day in the same place."* The chef thus conquered his phobia of flying. For thirty-two years, he had refused to travel by air!

THE VIEWPOINT OF CRITIC ANDREA PETRINI

"The strength of his cuisine is based on its universality: It touches the heart of any Italian, and the most aesthetic gourmets always detect an innuendo, an allusion, a wink that makes it complex . . . Fulvio once served us his *ravioli al pomodoro.* On each plate there was a large ravioli stuffed with a sauce of semi-confit tomato. While I was discussing about my plate the relationship between the pasta and the tomato sauce, the outside and the inside, my son attacked his, and it was gone in two mouthfuls, and my wife was crying with emotion . . ."

HIS SIGNATURE DISHES

San Pietro ai carciofi, purè di patate all'olio extravergine d'oliva (1982): potato purée with olive oil, a world first! It was served accompanying John Dory with artichokes.

Passatina di cette con gamberi (1985): a chickpea purée topped with large shrimp, which has become a cult dish and a classic of Italian cuisine.

Ravioli di pomodoro, piccola insalata di mare (1995): a large ravioli with semi-confit tomato, served with a seafood salad.

Aragosta al lardo di Colonnata (1997): spiny lobster wrapped in the famous Tuscan bacon.

Capasanta, mortadella, mela e finocchio (2004): scallops studded with mortadella for a land-and-sea accord mediated by apple and fennel.

SKIP TO
CRUSTACEANS, P. 282.

LEGENDARY LABELS

A powerful player on the global wine scene, Italy has some prestigious cuvées (blends of different varietals or vintages) that every wine lover should taste at least once—as long as the price can be paid. Here are fourteen legendary bottles, uncorked.

GWILHERM DE CERVAL

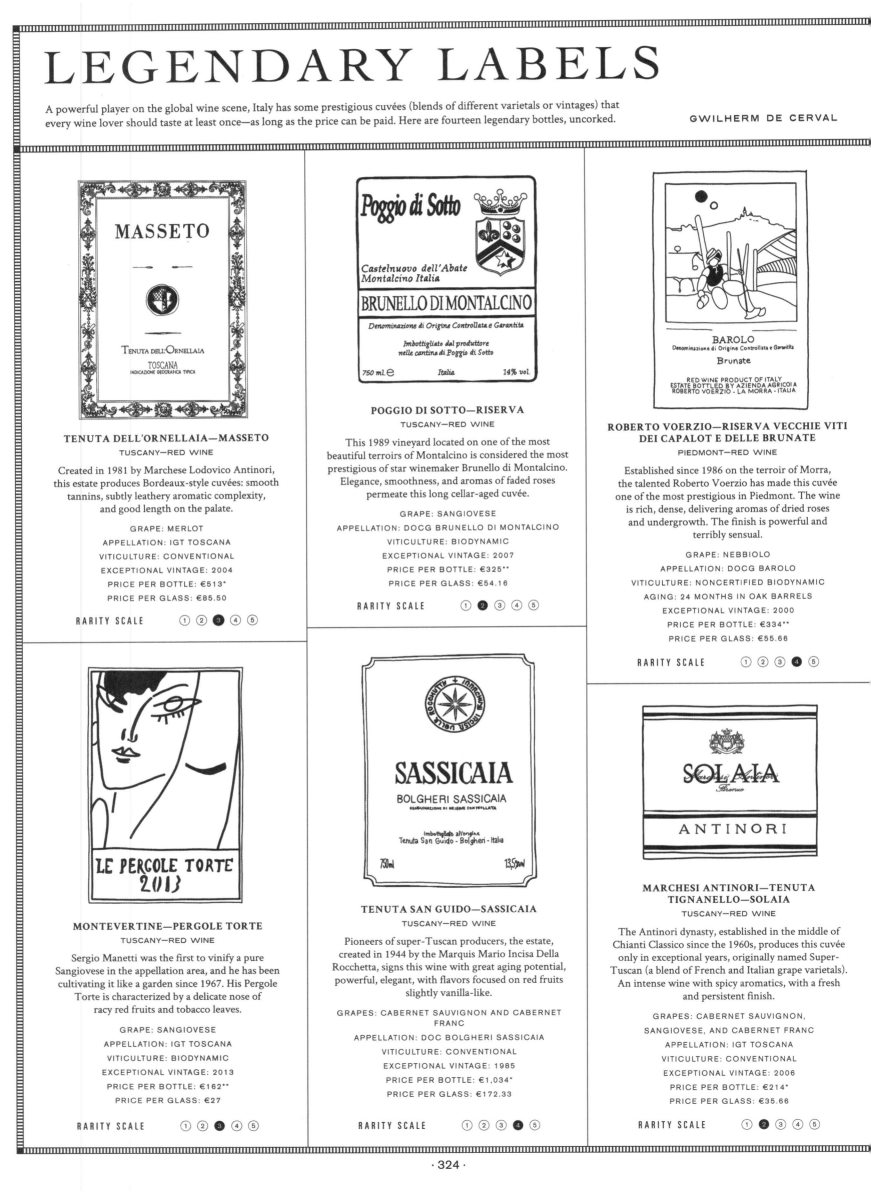

TENUTA DELL'ORNELLAIA—MASSETO

TUSCANY—RED WINE

Created in 1981 by Marchese Lodovico Antinori, this estate produces Bordeaux-style cuvées: smooth tannins, subtly leathery aromatic complexity, and good length on the palate.

GRAPE: MERLOT
APPELLATION: IGT TOSCANA
VITICULTURE: CONVENTIONAL
EXCEPTIONAL VINTAGE: 2004
PRICE PER BOTTLE: €513*
PRICE PER GLASS: €85.50

RARITY SCALE   

MONTEVERTINE—PERGOLE TORTE

TUSCANY—RED WINE

Sergio Manetti was the first to vinify a pure Sangiovese in the appellation area, and he has been cultivating it like a garden since 1967. His Pergole Torte is characterized by a delicate nose of racy red fruits and tobacco leaves.

GRAPE: SANGIOVESE
APPELLATION: IGT TOSCANA
VITICULTURE: BIODYNAMIC
EXCEPTIONAL VINTAGE: 2013
PRICE PER BOTTLE: €162**
PRICE PER GLASS: €27

RARITY SCALE   

POGGIO DI SOTTO—RISERVA

TUSCANY—RED WINE

This 1989 vineyard located on one of the most beautiful terroirs of Montalcino is considered the most prestigious of star winemaker Brunello di Montalcino. Elegance, smoothness, and aromas of faded roses permeate this long cellar-aged cuvée.

GRAPE: SANGIOVESE
APPELLATION: DOCG BRUNELLO DI MONTALCINO
VITICULTURE: BIODYNAMIC
EXCEPTIONAL VINTAGE: 2007
PRICE PER BOTTLE: €325**
PRICE PER GLASS: €54.16

RARITY SCALE   

TENUTA SAN GUIDO—SASSICAIA

TUSCANY—RED WINE

Pioneers of super-Tuscan producers, the estate, created in 1944 by the Marquis Mario Incisa Della Rocchetta, signs this wine with great aging potential, powerful, elegant, with flavors focused on red fruits slightly vanilla-like.

GRAPES: CABERNET SAUVIGNON AND CABERNET FRANC
APPELLATION: DOC BOLGHERI SASSICAIA
VITICULTURE: CONVENTIONAL
EXCEPTIONAL VINTAGE: 1985
PRICE PER BOTTLE: €1,034*
PRICE PER GLASS: €172.33

RARITY SCALE 

ROBERTO VOERZIO—RISERVA VECCHIE VITI DEI CAPALOT E DELLE BRUNATE

PIEDMONT—RED WINE

Established since 1986 on the terroir of Morra, the talented Roberto Voerzio has made this cuvée one of the most prestigious in Piedmont. The wine is rich, dense, delivering aromas of dried roses and undergrowth. The finish is powerful and terribly sensual.

GRAPE: NEBBIOLO
APPELLATION: DOCG BAROLO
VITICULTURE: NONCERTIFIED BIODYNAMIC
AGING: 24 MONTHS IN OAK BARRELS
EXCEPTIONAL VINTAGE: 2000
PRICE PER BOTTLE: €334**
PRICE PER GLASS: €55.66

RARITY SCALE   

MARCHESI ANTINORI—TENUTA TIGNANELLO—SOLAIA

TUSCANY—RED WINE

The Antinori dynasty, established in the middle of Chianti Classico since the 1960s, produces this cuvée only in exceptional years, originally named Super-Tuscan (a blend of French and Italian grape varietals). An intense wine with spicy aromatics, with a fresh and persistent finish.

GRAPES: CABERNET SAUVIGNON, SANGIOVESE, AND CABERNET FRANC
APPELLATION: IGT TOSCANA
VITICULTURE: CONVENTIONAL
EXCEPTIONAL VINTAGE: 2006
PRICE PER BOTTLE: €214*
PRICE PER GLASS: €35.66

RARITY SCALE   

EMIDIO PEPE—MONTEPULCIANO

ABRUZZO—RED WINE

The vines of this 1964 estate have never seen the slightest molecule of chemicals and have undergone biodynamic treatment since 2008. The wine has a deep color, is smooth and persistent on the palate, and has a finish that evokes spices and fresh black fruits.

GRAPE: MONTEPULCIANO
APPELLATION: DOC MONTEPULCIANO D'ABRUZZO
VITICULTURE: BIODYNAMIC
EXCEPTIONAL VINTAGE: 1983
PRICE PER BOTTLE: €322**
PRICE PER GLASS: €53.66

RARITY SCALE ① ② ❸ ④ ⑤

GAJA—COSTA RUSSI

PIEDMONT—RED WINE

Winemaker Angelo Gaja was the first to import French grape varietals and oak barrels into Piedmont for his estate established in 1859. This fruity cuvée is full-bodied, with a beautiful tannic structure that requires a few years in the cellar to refine further.

GRAPE: NEBBIOLO
APPELLATION: DOCG BARBARESCO
VITICULTURE: CONVENTIONAL
EXCEPTIONAL VINTAGE: 2001
PRICE PER BOTTLE: €226*
PRICE PER GLASS: €37.66

RARITY SCALE ① ❷ ③ ④ ⑤

CA' DEL BOSCO—ANNAMARIA CLEMENTI

LOMBARDY—EFFERVESCENT WHITE WINE

Recognized around the world as *the* benchmark for effervescent Italian wines, this 1960s *maison* vinifies using the Champagne method. This cuvée with fine bubbles reveals a pastrylike and gourmand nose and a full and complex palate.

GRAPES: CHARDONNAY, PINOT BLANC, AND PINOT NOIR
APPELLATION: DOCG FRANCIACORTA
VITICULTURE: NONCERTIFIED ORGANIC
EXCEPTIONAL VINTAGE: 2008
PRICE PER BOTTLE: €121**
PRICE PER GLASS: €16.66

RARITY SCALE ❶ ② ③ ④ ⑤

GIACOMO CONTERNO—RISERVA MONFORTINO

PIEDMONT—RED WINE

At the head of this 1920s estate, Roberto Conterno carries on the family tradition in an authentic and timeless Barolo style. His wine is ample, with smooth tannins. The aroma is complex and characterized by a slightly spiced finish.

GRAPE: NEBBIOLO
NAME: DOCG BAROLO
VITICULTURE: ORGANIC
EXCEPTIONAL VINTAGE: 2010
PRICE PER BOTTLE: €1,785**
PRICE PER GLASS: €297.50

RARITY SCALE ① ② ③ ❹ ⑤

GIUSEPPE QUINTARELLI—AMARONE DELLA VALPOLICELLA CLASSICO SUPERIORE

VENETO—RED WINE

Giuseppe Quintarelli (son of the founder of the estate, which dates from 1924; died in 2012) was considered to be the father of the Amarone, and he passed all his knowledge on to his daughter Fiorenza. The grapes are left to dry for at least five months before being pressed. The result is a concentrated wine with chocolate and licorice aromas.

GRAPES: CORVINA, MOLINARA, AND RONDINELLA
APPELLATION: DOCG AMARONE DELLA VALPOLICELLA
VITICULTURE: NONCERTIFIED ORGANIC
EXCEPTIONAL VINTAGE: 1997
PRICE PER BOTTLE: €364**
PRICE PER GLASS: €60.66

RARITY SCALE ① ② ❸ ④ ⑤

MASCARELLO GIUSEPPE E FIGLIO—RISERVA MONPRIVATO CÀ D'MORISSIO

PIEDMONT—RED WINE

This is one of the oldest Piedmontese estates (1881). Mauro, Giuseppe's son, isolated the Monprivato plot in the 1970s to stand out with this very fruity cuvée with silky tannins. The finish is enveloping, with floral and spicy aromas.

GRAPE: NEBBIOLO
APPELLATION: DOCG BAROLO
VITICULTURE: CONVENTIONAL
EXCEPTIONAL VINTAGE: 2010
PRICE PER BOTTLE: €849**
PRICE PER GLASS: €141.50

RARITY SCALE ① ❷ ③ ④ ⑤

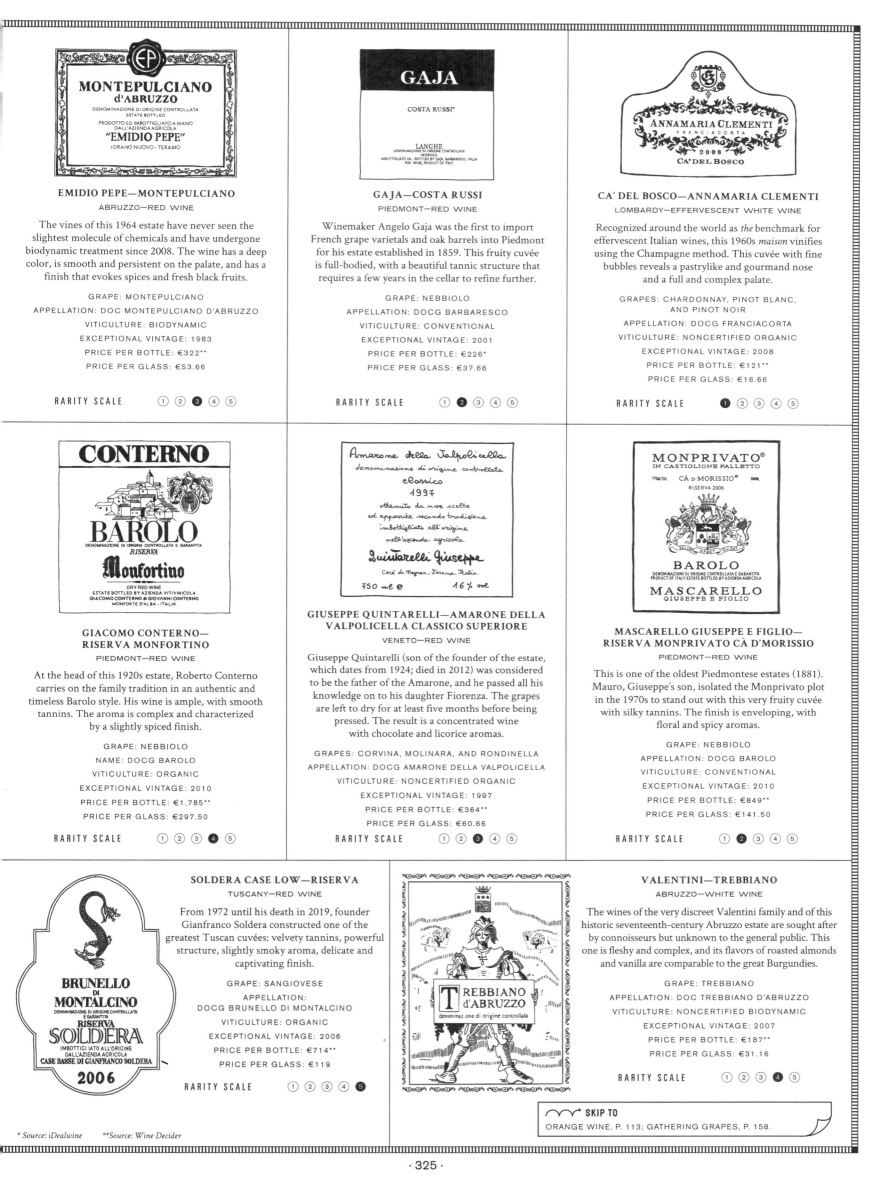

SOLDERA CASE LOW—RISERVA

TUSCANY—RED WINE

From 1972 until his death in 2019, founder Gianfranco Soldera constructed one of the greatest Tuscan cuvées: velvety tannins, powerful structure, slightly smoky aroma, delicate and captivating finish.

GRAPE: SANGIOVESE
APPELLATION: DOCG BRUNELLO DI MONTALCINO
VITICULTURE: ORGANIC
EXCEPTIONAL VINTAGE: 2006
PRICE PER BOTTLE: €714**
PRICE PER GLASS: €119

RARITY SCALE ① ② ③ ④ ❺

VALENTINI—TREBBIANO

ABRUZZO—WHITE WINE

The wines of the very discreet Valentini family and of this historic seventeenth-century Abruzzo estate are sought after by connoisseurs but unknown to the general public. This one is fleshy and complex, and its flavors of roasted almonds and vanilla are comparable to the great Burgundies.

GRAPE: TREBBIANO
APPELLATION: DOC TREBBIANO D'ABRUZZO
VITICULTURE: NONCERTIFIED BIODYNAMIC
EXCEPTIONAL VINTAGE: 2007
PRICE PER BOTTLE: €187**
PRICE PER GLASS: €31.16

RARITY SCALE ① ② ③ ❹ ⑤

SKIP TO
ORANGE WINE, P. 113; GATHERING GRAPES, P. 158.

* *Source: iDealwine* ***Source: Wine Decider*

NOUGATS

Though originally associated with Christmas holidays, the *torrone* can now be found all year round. Its origins are not in Italy, but its greatest versions were born there.

STÉPHANE SOLIER

TORRONE DE CREMONA (Lombardy)
Hard with almonds from Cremona (Fieschi) (1)

TORRONE DE BENEVENTO (Campania)
Hard with hazelnuts (Avellino—Torrone Del Casale) (2)

TORRONE OF PIEDMONT
Hard with hazelnuts, soft with hazelnuts (3), hard with almonds (4), hard with pistachios (5), soft with pistachios, small soft nougats with hazelnuts (6), hard, covered with dark chocolate (7) (Barbero)

TORRONE OF CALABRIA
Hard (called here torrone) with cinnamon (8), hard crunchy with honey (9), hard vanilla nougat (10), small delicacies (*chicche*) with almonds, pistachios, and vanilla (11) (Le Chicche di Francesco Taverna)

TORRONE OF BAGNARA IGP
with almonds, honey, pistachios (12)

SICILIAN TORRONE
With Bronte pistachios (13), *blu noto* (with Jamaican Blue Mountain coffee beans) (14), with Noto almonds (15) (Caffe Sicilia)

Bronte pistachios DOP, Sicilian black bee thistle honey, late mandarin of Ciaculli peel (16), Noto almonds, cocoa beans, Sicilian black bee dill honey (17), Noto almonds, Sicilian black bee orange blossom honey and Interdonato IGP lemon peel (18), grilled (*abbrustolito*) with Noto almonds, sainfoin honey (French honeysuckle) from Sicilian black bees, blood orange peel (19) (Sabadi)

Soft with almonds and pistachios, covered with white chocolate with lemon (20) and coated with white chocolate with orange (21) (Fiasconaro)

Soft with almonds, coated with vanilla (22), coated with lemon (23), coated with dark chocolate (24), coated with milk chocolate (25), coated with gianduja (red packaging) (26) (Condorelli)

TORRONE OF SARDINIA
Nougat with Sardinian honey and almonds (27), nougat with chestnut honey in wafers (28) (Pruneddu)

ALMOND TORRONE OF ALES (29)
(Maison Fiorenzo Atzori)

MANDORLATO DI COLOGNA VENETA
Mandorlato Bertolini Colonia, Veneta 6⅔ ounces (190 g) (30), 10½ ounces (300 g), 14 ounces (400 g) (31), 1⅓ pounds (600 g)

TORRONE MANDORLATO OF CREMONA
(Fieschi) (32)

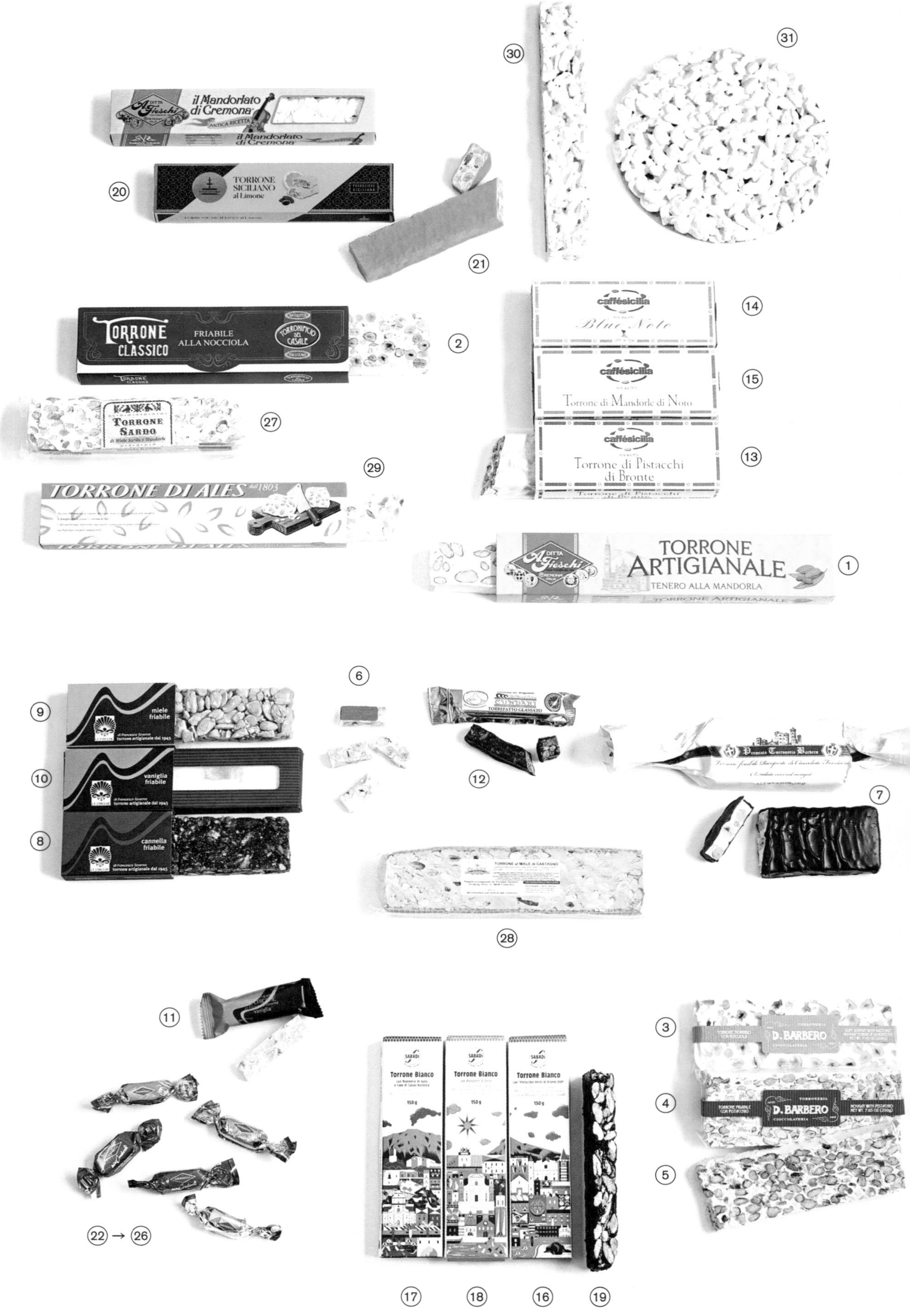

(30) (31) (20) (21) (2) (14) (15) (13) (27) (29) (1) (6) (9) (10) (8) (12) (7) (28) (11) (3) (4) (5)

(22) → (26)

(17) (18) (16) (19)

A WORLD OF SWEETNESS

Italian nougat comes in many regional variations.

THE TORRONE VERSION

Made from nuts, honey, sugar, and whipped egg whites, it can be hard (*friabile*) or soft (*morbido*).

TORRONE DI CREMONA, IGP

Lombardy

The first mentions of the most famous Italian nougat can be found in the fifteenth century. Vanilla, citron, or cinnamon can be added to the base of almonds (minimum 36 percent), sugar, honey, and egg white; and, since the seventeenth century, a coating of chocolate.

TORRONE DEL PIEMONTE

Grinzane Cavour, Asti

A connection recognized with the torrone of Cremona. Made with acacia honey or Piedmont wild flowers and IGP Langhe hazelnuts (minimum 50 percent) rather than almonds. Pastry chef Giuseppe Sebaste decided in 1885 to replace almonds with hazelnuts (of Piedmont, of course!), and despite this, this version is everything known as a "torrone."

TORRONE SARDO

At the crossroads of Catalan (seventeenth century) and Piedmontese (eighteenth century) traditions, it is produced throughout Sardinia but sees its best versions in the province of Nuoro. Specifics: no sugar, only Sardinian honey, soft and ivory color. Possible addition of citrus peel, vanilla.

TORRONE DI BENEVENTO, IGP

Campania

Referenced since the seventeenth century in this papal enclave of the kingdom of Naples, it claims an ancient heritage and is made with honey, egg white, almonds, or hazelnuts (variable quantity); varied flavorings, sometimes covered with chocolate.

TORRONE CALABRESE

Extremely varied nougats, some with southern Italian flavors (bergamot, licorice . . .). Torrone gelato is not an ice cream but instead a soft nougat with candied fruits. Particularly notable, the torrone di Bagnara IGP (Reggio Calabria) is flavored with cinnamon and ground cloves. Other versions: Martiniana (covered with superfine sugar) or *torrefatto glassato* (a bittersweet chocolate coating).

TORRONE SICILIANO

Many cities of Sicily dispute the Arab heritage of nougat and vary their recipes according to the almonds (varietal *tuono* for torrone *nisseno* PAT from Caltanissetta; the *romana de Noto* varietal, with an intense and aromatic taste, for others), flavorings, and the use of Bronte DOP pistachios . . .

THE MANDORLATO VERSION

It made its arrival into Venice thanks to the spice trade with the East and is mentioned as early as the sixteenth century. The mandorlato from Cologna Veneta (Veneto) is a confection with the consistency of a very hard and crumbly nougat, exclusively made from almonds, obtained by cooking honey, sugar, egg white, roasted almonds, and sometimes cinnamon in a copper kettle.

THE CROCCANTE VERSION

Made of nuts, whether whole or crushed, held together by caramelized sugar and/or honey, but without egg white. The Arab tradition has produced, from south to north: *cubbaita* or *giuggiulena*, meaning "pastry" and "sesame" in Arabic (Sicily, Calabria), and other *cumpittu* (Calabria), *cupeta, copata, copeta, cupett* (Apulia, Tuscany, Piedmont, Lombardy), *cubaite/cubaita* (Liguria), *gattò sardo* (Sardinia) . . .

And also . . .

TORRONE DI CREMA

Lombardy

LE TORRONE TENERO AL CIOCCOLATO AQUILANO *(Soft nougat with chocolate from L'Aquila)*

TORRONE NURZIA

Abruzzo

And if the Italians had invented the torrone?

Dissatisfied that their torrone owes a debt to the Catalan *torró/turrón*, derived from *torrar*, meaning "to toast" (from the Latin *torrere*), the citizens of Cremona tell of another origin to their sweet treasure: a pastry chef in the city was inspired by the shape of a tower (*torre*) of the *torrazzo* (belfry) of Cremona to make a nougat during the nuptial banquet of Francesco Sforza and Bianca Maria Visconti in 1441.

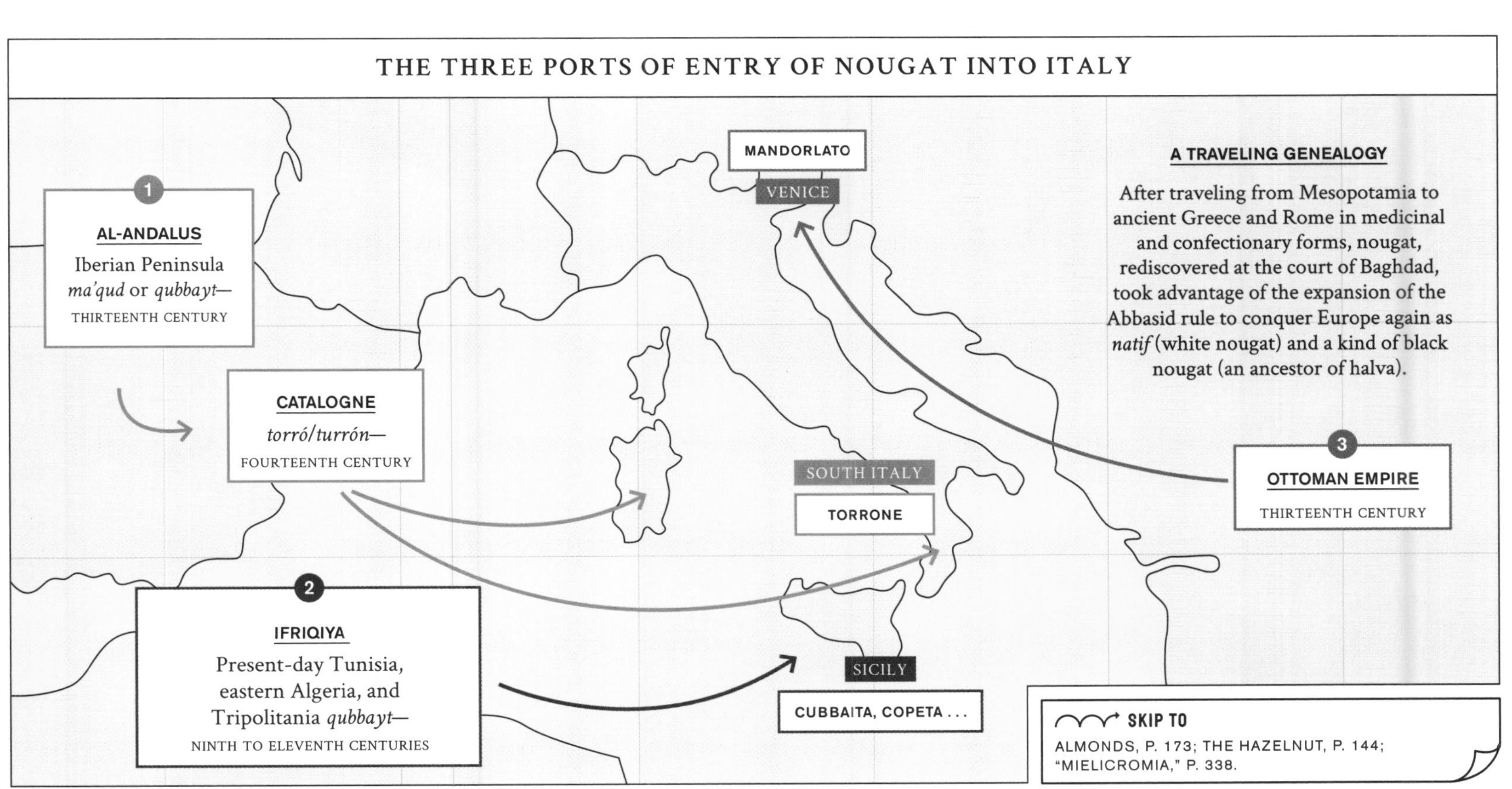

SKIP TO
ALMONDS, P. 173; THE HAZELNUT, P. 144; "MIELICROMIA," P. 338.

TORTELLINI IN BRODO

TORTELLINI IN BROTH

These little navel-shaped stuffed pastas, served in a delicious steaming broth, appear on all Emilian tables at Christmastime.

ILARIA BRUNETTI

THE TECHNIQUE

❶ ❷ Start by rolling out the dough very thinly. (You can use a pasta rolling machine.)

❸ Cut the dough into ¾-inch (2 cm) squares.

❹ Take a chunk of filling and roll it into a log. Pinch or cut off a hazelnut-size piece of the filling and place one in the center of each square.

❺ ❻ Fold each square diagonally into a triangle.

❼ Join the two opposite corners together around your index finger, making sure the tip of the tortellino is pointed up. Pinch gently to close.

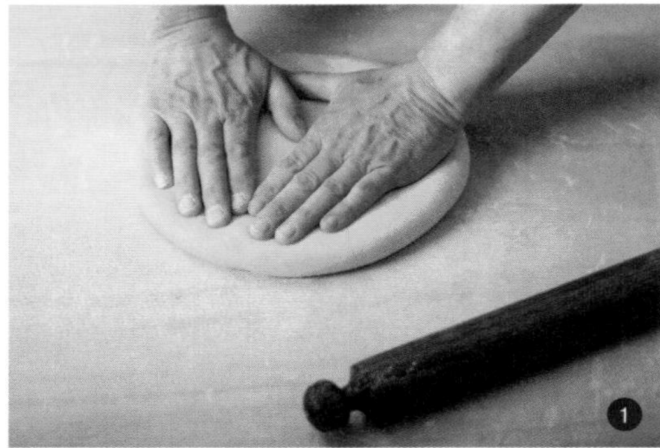

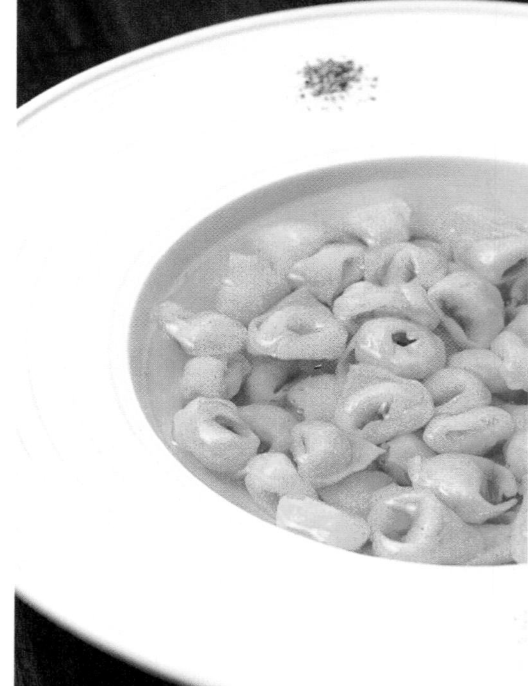

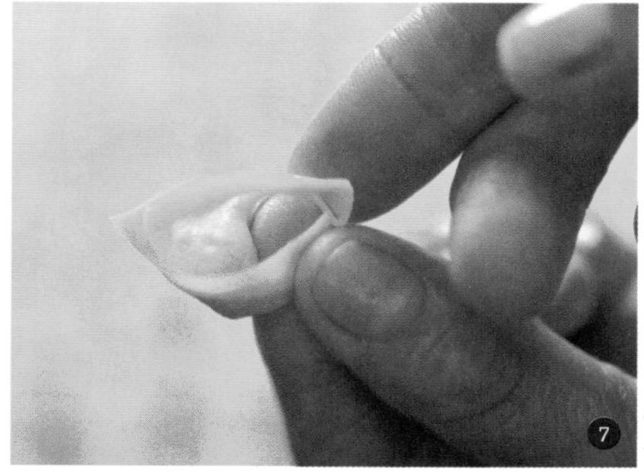

Muses and legends

Several navels boast of having inspired the shape of a *tortellino*:

HELEN OF TROY: in 1822, the Bolognese actor Vittorio Leonesi expressed in rhyme that Helen's navel ressembled a small *tortello*.

VENUS: at the end of the nineteenth century, the Tuscan engineer and intellectual Giuseppe Ceri wrote a parody of the poem *La secchia rapita* (*The Stolen Bucket*) by Tassoni, in which a guest from Castelfranco Emilia surprises Venus when she's quite naked; the beauty of her divine navel strikes him so much that he tries to imitate it with the pasta, thus creating a tortellino. The choice of the setting is a rather diplomatic one: Castelfranco Emilia is located halfway between Bologna and Modena, which fight over the claim to the origins of the tortellino.

MADAME LAVREINA: in Ostilio Lucarini's comedy *Quèll ch l'ha inventà i turtlein* (*He Who Invented Tortellini, 1925*), Pirulein del Burgatt, the cook for a family from Bologna, sees his boss Lavreina naked. Surprised by the husband, he risks being fired, but inspired by the beauty of the navel he witnessed, he invents the tortellino . . . and his creation saves his job!

THE GREAT COOKS AND THE EVOLUTION OF THE TORTELLINO

MIDDLE AGES—birth of tortello, stuffed fresh pasta.

1518—Maestro Martino describes round *tortelli*, with a stuffing of pork loin, Parmesan cheese, egg, and nutmeg, served in a capon broth.

Rosselli suggests that ravioli filled with pork, veal, and spices "no bigger than half a chestnut" be cooked for the time it takes to repeat the Lord's Prayer three times, then served with cheese.

1548—Cristoforo da Messisbugo gives the recipe for *tortelletti* as small as a hazelnut, made with saffron pasta, stuffed with beef, eggs, raisins, and cinnamon, and served in a fatty broth.

1602—in Giovanni del Turco's recipe for *agnoletti da minestra*, the shape of tortellino is described for the first time.

EIGHTEENTH CENTURY—tortellini appear on many menus in monasteries.

LATE EIGHTEENTH CENTURY—Alberto Alvisi adds marrow to the filling of tortellini, an ingredient that remained a trend for a long time (it is even found in the recipe by Pellegrino Artusi).

FOR AUTHENTIC TORTELLINI . . .

THE FILLING

Raw or cooked? There are two schools of thought: some cook the pork loin because cooking adds flavor, but many are opposed to this approach, claiming the raw filling remains tastier, more homogeneous, and digestible.

THE PASTA

→ ***Sfoglia:*** in Bologna, they claim the *sfoglia* (rolled-out dough) should be so thin that you can see the San Luca Sanctuary through it (located at the top of a hill overlooking the city).

→ **Making a square out of the circle:** although Artusi provides the circumference of the ideal tortellino, the Dotta Confraternità del Tortellino recommends cutting the dough into squares, a practice much more common today.

THE SAUCE

→ **The broth:** from beef and poultry, or only capon; a matter of quality and a rule of tradition.

→ **The cream:** in 1940, Cesarina Masi di Bologna, cook of the Bolognese restaurant that still bears her name, served tortellini for the first time with cream from fresh milk.

Massimo Bottura, the Michelin three-star chef, serves his legendary tortellini with Parmesan cream, but only when cheesemakers have the best quality cream from decanting milk available.

"They say that Bologna is famous for the university . . . Not true! It's thanks to tortellini and their consumption that it has become popular."

Alfredo Testoni, poet, 1881, Bologna

THE RIVALS

TORTELLINI DI MODENA

Although a war exists between these two gourmet rivalries, the tortellini are very similar. It's difficult to tell the difference between them, but in this version, the filling is most often cooked.

CAPPELLETTI ROMAGNOLI

The eternal rivalry between Emilia and Romagna (the northeast and southwest of the region) is also played out over stuffed pasta. Cappelletti are larger and folded slightly differently; they can be *di magro* (without meat) with a ricotta and Parmesan filling, or filled with capon meat and served in stock.

THE RECIPE

Lucia Antonelli, the undisputed queen of tortellino and chef of La Taverna del Cacciatore in Castiglione dei Pepoli, has twice won the chefs' challenge organized by the Tour'tlen association to honor the best "navel."

SERVES 8

For the pasta

- 3¼ cups (400 g) flour
- 4 large (200 g) eggs

For the filling

- 9 ounces (250 g) pork loin
- 1 tablespoon (14 g) butter
- 4½ ounces (125 g) mortadella
- ⅔ cup (80 g) grated Parmigiano-Reggiano, aged 24 months
- 1 teaspoon (7 g) salt
- Freshly ground black pepper
- Freshly ground nutmeg

For the stock

- 1 yellow onion, unpeeled, halved
- 1⅛ pounds (500 g) free-range poultry
- 9 ounces (250 g) top rib
- ½ beef kneecap
- 1 carrot, coarsely chopped
- 1 stalk celery, trimmed and coarsely chopped
- 1 small bunch flat-leaf parsley
- 1 tablespoon (15 g) coarse salt

For the homemade pasta, follow the instructions on page 294.

For the filling, cut the pork into large slices. Heat the butter in a skillet set over high heat and brown the pork on all sides. Finely process the cooked pork with the mortadella using a meat grinder, passing it twice through the grinder. (Alternatively, ask the butcher to do this for you.) Add the Parmesan, salt, and some pepper and nutmeg to the ground meat mixture and thoroughly combine. Chill the mixture for several hours, ideally overnight.

For the stock, roast the onion halves in a pan until softened. Place the onion, poultry, top rib, kneecap, carrot, celery, parsley, and coarse salt in a large saucepan. Add 1 to 1⅓ gallons (4 to 5 L) cold water. Bring to a boil and cook over low heat for at least 4 hours, partially covered. Regularly skim off any impurities from the top. Strain the stock and discard the solids.

Fill and shape the pasta (see opposite).

To cook the tortellini, bring the stock to a gentle boil, add the tortellini, and remove them as soon as they float to the surface; serve them in the stock.

THE COUSINS

TORTELLONI

From the outside, this pasta of Bolognese origin looks like giant tortellini made by the same folding technique, but the stuffing contains ricotta and vegetables (spinach, mushrooms . . .).

TORTELLINI DI VALEGGIO SUL MINCIO—VENETO

Lesser known, these wavy-edged tortellini are stuffed with roasted beef, chicken, and pork. They are served *asciutti* (dry), simply with butter and Parmesan.

SKIP TO
PELLEGRINO ARTUSI, P. 32;
FRESH PASTA, P. 294.

SEASON

TUTTO L'ANNO (YEAR-ROUND)

CATEGORY

PRIMO PIATTO (FIRST COURSE)

LEVEL

DIFFICOLTÀ MEDIA (MEDIUM DIFFICULTY)

RAGÙ BOLOGNESE

It's the queen of sauces, the one Mamma always makes better than anyone else. It's often served over spaghetti, but in the town from which it gets its name, tagliatelle is the choice.

GIORGIA CANNARELLA

THE STORY OF A MYTH

By ragù, we mean a hearty sauce for pasta consisting of tomato and meat that is ground (or cut into pieces) and cooked for several hours over low heat. Of all the Italian versions, the most famous is *ragù Bolognese*, a symbol of the city of Bologna and its culinary tradition. First traces of it date back to the sixteenth century, when it was served at the table of nobles as a single dish. It was a "white" ragù (without tomato) until the nineteenth century, when, with the addition of puréed tomato (an ingredient previously considered "toxic"), it took on the appearance we know today.

THE WORD *RAGÙ*

One of Italy's most famous preparations owes its name to . . . France. *Ragù* comes from the word *ragout,* itself probably derived from *ragoûter* or *ragoûtant,* meaning "flavorful" or "that which stimulates the appetite." During fascism, Mussolini tried to Italianize the term and ordered (but without success) that the preparation be called *ragutto.*

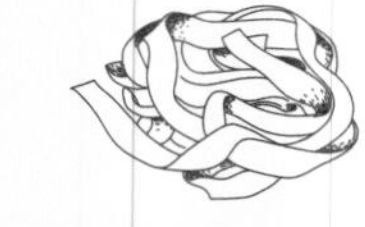

HOW DO YOU USE IT?

THE PERFECT COMBINATION of fresh tagliatelle onto which the sauce is added directly . . . and plenty of it!

WITH BÉCHAMEL in the legendary lasagna Bolognese or in baked pasta.

WITH POLENTA, prepared simply, or *pasticciata* (seasoned and placed briefly in the oven).

TO TOP potato gnocchi.

WITH DRY PASTA (penne *rigate,* rigatoni, *maniche mezze, conchiglie* . . .).

WITH BREAD, to mop up directly off the plate (*fare la scarpetta,* as the Italians say), the simplest and most delicious way possible!

THE RECIPE

Each family has its own recipe. The following recipe was filed at the Bologna Chamber of Commerce in 1982 by the Bologna delegation of the Academy of Italian Cuisine.

SERVES 4

5¼ ounces (150 g) pancetta, finely chopped

3 tablespoons (45 mL) olive oil, or 3½ tablespoons (50 g) butter

⅓ cup (50 g) finely chopped carrot

½ cup (50 g) chopped celery

⅓ cup (30 g) finely chopped onion

10½ ounces (300 g) ground beef (top sirloin, flank steak, top rib, foreribs, or center breast)

¼ cup (60 mL) dry white or red wine

5 tablespoons (75 mL) tomato sauce, or 2 peeled tomatoes

A little stock

¼ cup (60 mL) whole milk

Salt and freshly ground black pepper

Brown the pancetta in a pan (preferably terra-cotta or heavy aluminum, about 8 inches/20 cm in diameter). Add the olive oil, carrot, celery, and onion. Let cook.

Add the meat, stir well to combine, and press down on the meat using the bottom of a ladle or the back of a spatula. Cook until it is browned and no longer sizzles.

Pour in the wine, stirring gently until the liquid is completely evaporated. Add the tomato sauce, cover, and simmer for at least 2 hours over low heat, stirring in a little stock if necessary. Near the end of the cooking time, add the milk (this will counter the acidity of the tomato). Season with salt and pepper.

PELLEGRINO ARTUSI'S RAGÙ

Among the many recipes penned by nineteenth-century writer Pellegrino Artusi is *maccheroni alla Bolognese,* made of lean veal, butter, onion, celery, carrot, *carnesecca* (pork belly, rolled and dried), broth, flour, Parmesan, dried mushrooms, *fegatini* (small pieces of liver), and, optionally, half a glass of cream. In short, it's the ancestor of ragù Bolognese.

A tour of Italy's ragùs

CAMPANIA

→ For the Neapolitan *'o rraù,* beef, pork chops, sausage, and tomato sauce are cooked by *pippiare* (simmering) for several hours over very low heat. It is served with rigatoni, *paccheri* (large short tubular pasta), or *ziti tagliati* (thin tubular pasta).

→ Contrary to what it seems, *ragù genovese* originates from Campania. It is a "white" sauce made with onions and meat.

TUSCANY

→ *Ragù di cinghiale* (wild boar) with pappardelle or *pici* (large, thick spaghetti rolled by hand).

→ *Ragù bianco* with sausage, beef, and white wine, served with pici.

VENETO

→ Here can be found *oca* (goose) ragù with *lunghi bigoli* (long, thick tubular pasta, made from whole wheat flour and duck eggs, usually cooked fresh).

SARDINIA

→ *Ragù di agnello* (lamb) is accompanied by small gnocchi, *malloreddus.*

LAZIO, ABRUZZO

→ Mutton ragùs are very popular.

NORTH

→ Ragù made of game meat, such as various types of venison, is enjoyed.

SKIP TO
GENOESE PESTO, P. 20;
LASAGNA VERDI ALLA BOLOGNESE (SPINACH PASTA LASAGNA BOLOGNESE), P. 47.

THE BOAR, KING OF TUSCANY

Long appreciated as noble game and a formidable adversary, the boar reigns supreme on the tables of central Italy.

SACHA LOMNITZ

WHAT AM I?

A mammal native to Eurasia and North Africa, the wild boar (*Sus scrofa*) lives in groups (herds). Omnivorous and very resilient, it is now found throughout mainland Europe, most of Asia, and north Africa.

In Tuscany, it lives mainly in forests of oak trees, close to water sources, but also in the Mediterranean scrub.

The Tuscan wild boar (*Sus scrofa majori*) is generally smaller than other boars but has a larger and wider skull. It can reach 6 feet (1.8 m) long, 3 feet (1 m) at the withers, and 330 pounds (150 kg).

THE BOAR . . . SLICED

Wild boar meat is popular because it marries the taste of pork with that of wild game. Delicate and difficult to store when fresh, it's readily made into charcuterie in central Italy: *salame, salsiccia di cinghiale* (dried or uncooked sausage) . . .

FROM NEAR EXTINCTION . . .

From the Middle Ages, the natural habitat of the wild boar diminished with the expansion of agriculture and urbanization.

The hunt continued: because of its fighting spirit and its strength, the animal was hunted by nobility as a demonstration of valor. Even the Medici family maintained a strong passion for the art of boar hunting.

. . . TO PROLIFERATION

Of the indigenous breeds, only those of Maremma (*Sus scrofa majori*) and Sardinia (*S. scrofa meridionalis*) survive.

From 1950 to 1960, with the movement away from an agrarian society, along with the reintroduction of hybrid breeds raised for hunting purposes, the wild boar population in Italy resumed an upward curve, doubling within this decade. It numbers 2 million today, including nearly 500,000 in Tuscany.

RECIPE

RAGÙ DI CINGHIALE (WILD BOAR RAGÙ)

Carlotta Cioni, mother and grandmother of the butchers of the famous butcher shop Macelleria Cioni at the Cascine del Riccio (near Florence), offers this boar stew. It's ideal for serving with the famous pappardelle, a sort of large tagliatelle pasta that is an essential throughout Chianti and Maremma.

SERVES 4 TO 5

2¼ pounds (1 kg) boneless wild boar (shoulder, hind knuckle, and ribs, in equal quantity)
3 tablespoons (45 mL) extra-virgin olive oil
Salt
Black peppercorns
2 stalks celery
3 onions
5 sage leaves
1 sprig rosemary
5 cloves garlic, peeled
2 bay leaves
1¼ cups (300 mL) IGT Tuscan red wine, at room temperature
2 tablespoons (32 g) tomato paste
1⅛ pounds (500 g) diced tomatoes
10½ ounces (300 g) pappardelle

- Wash and roughly cut up the meat. In a skillet set over high heat, brown the meat in 2 tablespoons (30 mL) of the olive oil. Add a pinch of salt and a few peppercorns and stir frequently.
- Prepare a *battuto di odori*: finely chop the celery and onions together, then add and chop the sage, rosemary leaves, and garlic. Add the whole bay leaves.
- Remove the meat from the pan, add the remaining 1 tablespoon (15 mL) olive oil to the skillet, and cook the mixture over low heat just until softened.
- Return the meat to the pan. Add the wine. Cover and simmer over low heat until the wine is absorbed.
- Slightly dilute the tomato paste with water and add it to the pan. Add the diced tomatoes. Season with salt or with a mixture of salt, pepper, rosemary, and minced garlic. Add just over ¾ cup (200 mL) lukewarm water.
- Simmer over low heat, covered, for 2 hours 30 minutes.
- Remove the bay leaves. Cook the pappardelle al dente. Shred the meat in the sauce, then dress the pappardelle with the sauce. You can also serve the ragù on its own or with polenta.

Tip: Some Tuscans marinate the meat overnight in red wine and herbs, which are eventually added to the dish.

Wild boar in Renaissance sauce

It was one of the favorite animals of the Tuscan nobles. In Siena and Florence, it was cooked *in dolceforte*, a sauce made from *panforte* and crumbled *cavallucci* (cake and spiced cookies), chocolate melted in butter, raisins, pine nuts, walnuts, and vinegar. This offered strong contrasts between sweet and savory, which was particularly popular at the time.

THE *PORCELLINO* OF FLORENCE . . .

→ Isn't a "small pig" but instead a fountain in the shape of a boar in the Loggia del Mercato Nuovo.

→ Is a bronze statue of Pietro Tacca, a copy of an antique that Pius IV donated to Cosimo de' Medici in 1560.

→ Brings luck: put a coin in its mouth and rub its snout, and you will be *baciati dalla fortuna* (kissed by fortune) and return to Florence.

→ Inspired a fable by Hans Christian Andersen ("The Bronze Boar") and appears in several movies, including Ridley Scott's *Hannibal* and two Harry Potter films . . .

— SAUSAGE —

Tasty, meaty, and appetizing . . . sausages are the most ancient form of charcuterie in Italy.

ALESSANDRA PIERINI

DEFINITION

From Latin *salsum* (preserved with salt) and *insicium* (finely sliced), *salsiccia* is a preparation made from fresh pork (mostly), minced, seasoned, and encased in a natural casing. It is eaten fresh or cured, raw or cooked.

Cervellata or cervellatina

ORIGIN: Apulia, Calabria, Campania

INGREDIENTS: very finely minced pork; fennel and white wine (Calabria); red wine (Campania). Veal, mutton, and goat meat with garlic, basil, pecorino, salt, pepper (Apulia). In Taranto (Apulia), pork and/or veal with fennel seeds, red wine, salt, and pepper.

IN COOKING: grilled; with mashed beans and potatoes (Apulia); with the *friarielli* (Campania); in Calabria, a rare sausage made without chile but with broccoli.

Hirschwurst

ORIGIN: Trentino-Alto Adige

INGREDIENTS: venison, spices, nutmeg, white or red wine, black pepper. Smoked, aged for twelve days.

IN COOKING: with polenta or mushrooms.

Lucanica di Picerno IGP

ORIGIN: Basilicata

INGREDIENTS: premium pork, fennel seeds, chile, salt, black pepper. Lightly smoked.

IN COOKING: sliced; in sauces or slow simmered with vegetables.

Luganega trentina Slow Food

ORIGIN: Trentino-Alto Adige

INGREDIENTS: pork (and/or game, mutton, goat, or veal), garlic, salt, black pepper, sometimes cinnamon and cloves.

IN COOKING: typical in *smacafam* (a savory pie with various charcuterie).

Pasqualora

ORIGIN: Sicily

INGREDIENTS:pork, wild fennel, chile, white wine, salt, black pepper. Prepared with the meat trimmings from animals slaughtered at Easter (*Pasqua*).

IN COOKING: grilled and served with lemon juice.

Pezzente della montagna materana Slow Food

ORIGIN: Basilicata

INGREDIENTS: less noble pieces of pork, sweet peppers from Senise, chile, wild fennel, garlic, salt.

IN COOKING: in *sugo rosso* for pasta; in a casserole with chard, chicory, escarole.

Salsiccia del Vastese

ORIGIN: Abruzzo

INGREDIENTS: pork, sweet bell peppers, salt, fennel flower, chile. Dried for twenty days.

IN COOKING: raw, in slices; in savory pies.

Salsiccia di Calabria or zazicchiu DOP

ORIGIN: Calabria

INGREDIENTS: pork shoulder, ribs, and bacon; fennel, spices, wine, salt, black pepper. Sweet version with cream of sweet bell peppers; spicy version with chile. Keeps well for one year.

IN COOKING: raw sliced with a knife.

Salsiccia di Cinghiale

ORIGIN: Tuscany

INGREDIENTS: wild boar and very fine minced pork fat, salt, black pepper, garlic, wine. Aged for one month minimum.

IN COOKING: marinated in Chianti to soften it before being eaten with a knife.

Salsiccia di fegato aquilana or Cicolana Slow Food

ORIGIN: Abruzzo

INGREDIENTS: liver, heart, pork tongue and fat, garlic, chile, salt, black pepper. In the sweet version, with honey.

IN COOKING: Eaten on Easter morning with hard-boiled eggs and *pizza pasquale* (a lightly sweetened bread).

Salsiccia rossa di Castelpoto Slow Food

ORIGIN: Campania

INGREDIENTS: lean meat, bacon and pork belly, wild fennel, salt, black pepper, and infusion of garlic heads, ground sweet and spicy peppers (*papauli*) toasted in a wood-fired oven. Dried for twenty to fifty days.

IN COOKING: eaten sliced with a knife or added fresh in pasta.

Salsiccia sarda or Salstitza

ORIGIN: Sardinia

INGREDIENTS: lean pork, wild fennel, salt, black pepper, sometimes chile or myrtle.

IN COOKING: fresh, grilled, in *maloreddus alla campidanese*, rice or polenta; eaten dried, using a knife.

Salsiccia stagionata affumicata di suino nero

ORIGIN: Sicily

INGREDIENTS: lightly smoked black pork, black pepper, wild fennel. Dried for at least twenty days.

IN COOKING: eaten sliced with a knife.

Salsicciotto di Guilmi or Lumellu

ORIGIN: Abruzzo

INGREDIENTS: pork, salt, black pepper. Dried for twenty days then aged in fat or in oil for five months.

IN COOKING: with bread or in local recipes.

Salsicciotto frentano Slow Food

ORIGIN: Abruzzo

INGREDIENTS: ham, shoulder, loin, and part of the pork fat; salt, peppercorns and ground black pepper. Aged for three months maximum.

IN COOKING: raw, sliced with a knife.

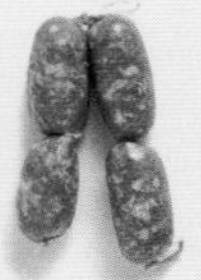

Verzini or Salamit de verz

ORIGIN: Lombardy

INGREDIENTS: pork, salt, black pepper, spices.

IN COOKING: in *cassoeûla* (a thick soup with pork and savoy cabbage); simmered dishes.

Julia Sammut's advice

A grocer in Marseille who loves transalpine products, Julia cooks salsiccia in all its forms!

Raw, slices on bread toasted *alla griglia* (over a flame); tossed with a fork with stracchino cheese, spread on bread to brown in the oven.

SERVES 4

Brown 2 peeled garlic cloves and 1 small chopped onion in a pan with a little oil. Add 14 ounces (400 g) crumbled sausage. Blanch 4 artichokes in water for 3 minutes then trim them, keeping the best leaves and the heart. Quarter them, then brown in the pan. Add 14 ounces (400 g) penne cooked al dente. Enjoy the treat!

SKIP TO
FENNEL, P. 233;
CHILE PEPPERS, P. 359.

SAVORY TARTS & PIES

A crust, a filling, and two approaches to preparation provide deliciously savory satisfaction.

ELISABETH SCOTTO

GLOSSARY— *torta, torta salata, torta rustica, tortino*... there are so many words to tell the same story: the successful marriage of a pastry crust and a filling. The Italian language typically uses the same word to describe either an open-faced filling on top of a single crust (a tart) or one baked between two layers of crust (a pie).

RECIPE

ERBAZZONE

Here is a very successful version of the famous Emilian *torta*. You can put all kinds of green vegetables and herbs in it. Zucchini is used for a touch of summer flavor.

SERVES 6

For the crust

2¾ cups (350 g) all-purpose flour
1 teaspoon (6 g) fine sea salt
1 teaspoon (4 g) superfine sugar
Scant ½ cup (100 mL) extra-virgin olive oil

For the filling

7 ounces (200 g) small zucchini
4 spring onions
1 clove garlic, peeled
2¼ pounds (1 kg) spinach leaves
3½ ounces (100 g) arugula
1 bunch chives
1 large bunch flat-leaf parsley
6 sprigs mint
6 tablespoons (90 mL) olive oil, plus more for brushing
1 dried small red chile
1½ cups (150 g) grated Parmesan cheese
Salt and freshly ground black pepper
8 pinches freshly grated nutmeg

- For the crust, combine the flour, salt, and sugar on a work surface. Make a well in the center and add the olive oil. Combine everything by hand, incorporating just over ¾ cup (200 mL) cold water; the dough should be smooth and homogeneous. Refrigerate for 1 hour.
- For the filling, finely grate the zucchini. Chop the onions and garlic. Rinse the spinach leaves and arugula, pat dry, and cut into thin strips. Chop the chives, parsley, and mint.
- Heat the olive oil in a skillet, and brown the garlic, onion, and chile (crumbled). Add the zucchini and cook for about 15 minutes, then add the spinach and arugula. Stir over high heat for 5 minutes, until all of the liquid is evaporated. Remove from the heat and add the chopped herbs and the Parmesan. Season with salt, pepper, and the nutmeg.
- Preheat the oven to 350°F (180°C). Divide the dough in half. Thinly roll out each piece into two disks measuring 9¾ inches (25 cm) in diameter.
- Lightly grease a baking sheet, line it with parchment paper, and place a dough disk in the center. Top with the filling. Place the second dough disk centered on top. Gently press the edges to adhere them together well. Brush the top all over with oil, then make a few slashes in the top crust to help steam escape. Bake for 30 minutes, or until the torta is golden. Serve warm or at room temperature.

DOUBLE CRUST (PIES)

ERBAZZONE, *Emilia-Romagna*: literally "large grass," an olive oil–based pastry, filled with a mixture of chard (or other leafy greens) lightly browned in olive oil, eggs, and Parmesan cheese (see recipe at left).

TORTA ALL'AGLIO, *Abruzzo*: a preparation from the Middle Ages. Between two pie crusts, spread a purée of blanched Sulmone pink garlic, then add bacon, egg, raisins, and saffron.

TORTA PASQUALINA, *Liguria*: a filling of chard (sometimes artichokes), ricotta, eggs, and Parmesan cheese, wrapped in an olive oil–based crust (*pasta matta*), served at Easter.

PIZZA RUSTICA NAPOLETANA, *Campania*: a filling of ricotta, Parmesan cheese, spicy provolone, cooked ham, spicy sausage, egg, and milk, baked in a short crust.

TORTA DI SCAROLA, *Campania*: olives, capers, pine nuts, and garlic lightly browned in olive oil, then with finely chopped escarole added, all baked in a yeast-raised dough.

CIPOLLINE CATANESI, *Sicily*: individual rectangles of puff pastry stuffed with simmered onions with tomato sauce, mozzarella, and cooked ham.

PANADAS DI OSCHIRI, *Sardinia*: individual pies with a lard-based crust made from semolina flour, stuffed with pork or lamb, bacon, garlic, and parsley. Rarer are the *panadas di Assemini*, made using eel.

PIZZA RUSTICA, *Basilicata*: an Easter pie with a lard-based crust, filled with a mixture of cheeses, dried sausage, and eggs.

CALZONE DI CIPOLLA, *Apulia*: an oil-based pastry stuffed with an onion confit with anchovies, olives, raisins, and Parmesan cheese. Prepared with *sponsali*, long white onions with a distinct flavor.

SINGLE CRUST (TARTS)

TORTA DI POTATO DELLA VAL NURE, *Emilia-Romagna*: blanched potatoes sautéed in butter, combined with leeks, Grana Padano cheese, and nutmeg in short-crust pastry. Formerly served in September after harvesting the potatoes, to use up the less desirable ones.

TORTA DI ALICI, *Liguria*: an aromatic base of dried bread crumbs, pecorino, egg, marjoram, parsley, garlic, and oregano, topped with fresh anchovies, topped with a little olive oil and bread crumbs browned on top.

TORTA DI RISO, *Liguria*: an olive oil–based crust filled with cooked arborio rice, crisped pancetta, regional cheese curd (*prescinseua*) or ricotta, Parmesan cheese, and eggs. Called *torta delle quattro palanche* (four cents), because making it is so inexpensive. Its little cousin, *torta verde*, contains also rice, zucchini, chard, and Parmesan.

TORTA DI ZUCCHINE, *Liguria*: an olive oil–based crust filled with zucchini sautéed with onions, regional cheese curd (*prescinseua*) or ricotta, Parmesan cheese, and eggs. Its little cousin, *torta di carciofi*, contains sautéed artichokes.

TORTA DI PEPE DI CAMAIORE, *Tuscany*: an olive oil–based crust filled with rice, chard, ricotta, Parmesan and pecorino cheeses, milk, eggs, and lots of black pepper. A recipe originally made for Easter, it is nicknamed *torta coi pizzi* (lace pie) because of its nicely crimped edges.

TORTA DELLA VIGILIA, *Apulia*: served on Christmas Eve (*vigilia*), filled with salt cod, escarole, onions, green and black olives, and raisins.

SKIP TO
ZUCCHINI, P. 234; RICOTTA, P. 219; THE HISTORY OF PIZZA P. 270; ONIONS, P. 292.

CABBAGE & COMPANY

Present in Italy for several centuries, these rustic vegetables from the Brassicaceae family seduce with their pronounced bitter and earthy taste.

ALESSANDRA PIERINI

① CAVOLFIORE BIANCO E VERDE

White and green cauliflower (*Brassica oleracea* var. *botrytis*)

ORIGIN—throughout Italy (*tardivo di Fano*, Marche; *di Moncalieri*, Piedmont; *gigante di Napoli*, Campania; *di Torbole* Slow Food presidio, Trentino-Alto Adige).

TASTE—musky and earthy notes, a perfect pairing with strong and spiced flavors such as cheese, chile, garlic. The green is milder and sweeter.

IN COOKING—cooked in water then sautéed, fried, cooked in omelet, or puréed; raw, marinated in vinegar for pickles (*giardiniera*); with pastas.

② CAVOLO ROMANESCO

Romanesco broccoli (*Brassica oleracea* var. *italica*)

ORIGIN—Lazio.

TASTE—halfway between broccoli and cauliflower, it has an intense aroma, a combination of power and sweetness, reminiscent of walnut and pine nut.

IN COOKING—cooked in water or steamed, then sautéed, as a purée, in puréed or chunky soups, baked au gratin.

③ CAVOLO CAPPUCCIO ROSSO E BIANCO

White or red cabbage (*Brassica oleracea* var. *capitata* f. *alba* or f. *rubra*)

ORIGIN—northern Italy (*gaggetta* and *lavagnino*, Liguria; *della val di Gresta*, Trentino-Alto Adige; *dell'Adige*, Veneto).

TASTE—the white is vegetal, slightly spicy, and sour; the red is sweeter, more subtle.

IN COOKING—ideal for sweet-and-sour preparations such as *crauti* (sauerkraut); in soup, salad, julienned with cumin and strips of speck; stuffed, steamed; in a stew with mutton or pork.

④ CAVOLO VERZA GRANDE E PICCOLO

Large and small savoy cabbage (*Brassica oleracea* subsp. *bullata* or subsp. *sabauda*)

ORIGIN—northern Italy (*di Montalto Dora, di Settimo Torinese* and *precocissimo di Asti*, Piedmont; *tardivo di Milano*, Lombardy).

TASTE—bitter, peppery, and earthy; the pale, tender leaves are sweeter.

IN COOKING—braised, stuffed, in a pork stew with chestnuts; with pork, goose, tripe, sausage; in risotto, soup; in *pizzoccheri* (buckwheat pasta).

⑤ CAVOLO NERO

Tuscan kale (*Brassica oleracea* 'Lacinato')

ORIGIN—central Italy and Tuscany (*nero riccio* or *braschetta, riccio nero di Lucca*).

TASTE—slightly grassy, subtle bitterness, sour aroma.

IN COOKING—in *ribollita*; in purées and stews, polenta, crostini; steamed, sautéed; the leaves can be stuffed.

⑥ CAVOLO RAPA

Kohlrabi (*Brassica oleracea* var. *gongylodes*)

ORIGIN—throughout Italy (*di Acireale "trunzu di Aci"* in Sicily).

TASTE—between turnip and wild cabbage; firm, juicy, and slightly fibrous flesh, intense flavor, sweet and aromatic.

IN COOKING—braised, in soup, with pasta, baked.

⑦ RAPA E RAPA BIANCA

Red and round white wild turnips (*Brassica rapa* subsp. *campestris*)

ORIGIN—northern Italy (*bianca piatta di Milano a colletto*, Lombardy; *di Nasino*, Liguria; *di Caprauna*, Piedmont).

TASTE—slightly sweet and earthy, sometimes a little pungent; juicy and crunchy flesh. Be careful not to confuse it with *cime di rapa*, from the same family but which are the leaves and not the roots.

IN COOKING—fermented in grape marc (*brovada*); in sweet-and-sour dishes; with bacon and sausage, in a selection of charcuterie; in purées and stews.

⑧ BROCCOLETTO OR GERMOGLI DI BROCCOLO RAMOSO

Broccolini (*Brassica oleracea* var. *italica* hybrid)

ORIGIN—throughout Italy (*vecchio di Rosolini* and *sparacello palermitano*, Sicily; *verde calabrese*, Calabria; *nero di Napoli*, Campania; *ramoso di Ruvo*, Apulia; *chiacchietegli di Priverno*, Lazio). Very similar to *cime di rapa*, but with larger, fleshy, and less tender stems, leaves, and tops.

TASTE—strong, vegetal, moderately bitter.

IN COOKING—steamed or sautéed; with pasta, in a savory pie.

⑨ BROCCOLO

Broccoli (*Brassica oleracea* var. *italica*)

ORIGIN—throughout Italy (*bronzino di Albenga*, Liguria; *precoce di Verona, di Bassano, fiolaro di Creazzo*, Veneto). Note that in Sicily, *broccolo* means cauliflower.

TASTE—between sweetness and bitterness, sometimes discreetly spicy and bitter.

IN COOKING—a perfect marriage with savory ingredients, goes well with *colatura*, anchovy, and Parmesan. Sautéed, au gratin, with pasta.

⑩ FRIARIELLI (Campanie), CIME DI RAPA (Apulia)

Broccoli rabe (*Brassica rapa* subsp. *sylvestris* var. *esculenta*)

ORIGIN—southern Italy (*aprilatico di Paternopoli*, Campania).

TASTE—assertive, vegetal, bitter if the shoots are late.

IN COOKING—with orecchiette; panfried, on pizza, in salad.

⑪ BROCCOLETTO DI CUSTOZA

Custoza broccoletto (*Brassica oleracea* var. *botrytis*)

ORIGIN—Veneto.

TASTE—tender heart, mild and delicate; more intense outer leaves.

IN COOKING—cooked in water, then sautéed; with pasta; in risotto, pesto, ragout, meatballs, savory pie, preserves.

⑫ RAPANELLI, RAFANELLI, RAVANELLI

Radish (*Raphanus sativus*)

ORIGIN—throughout Italy (*mezzo lungo rosso di Napoli*, Campania; *tabasso di Moncalieri* and *ramolass*, Piedmont; *ciliegia, candela di fuoco, candela di Ghiaccio*, throughout Italy).

TASTE—crunchy, fresh, spiced, moderately spicy, reminiscent of mustard.

IN COOKING—mainly eaten raw in salads, in sandwiches, in *pinzimonio*.

⑬ RUCOLA OR RUGHETTA

Arugula (cultivated: *Eruca vesicaria*; wild: *Diplotaxis tenuifolia*)

ORIGIN—throughout Italy.

TASTE—intense, bitter with a sharp finish (especially the wild), more moderate if the leaves are young.

IN COOKING—mainly used raw. Pesto, pizza, pasta salad, meat, and shellfish.

ATTENTION!

Be careful, although this plant below has rapa included in its Italian name, it does not belong to the same family!

⑭ RAPA ROSSA

Beet (*Beta vulgaris*, Chenopodiacee)

ORIGIN—throughout Italy.

TASTE—very pleasant, accentuated by cooking; very strong and earthy vegetal note, slightly acidic.

IN COOKING—leaves boiled and sautéed. The root (bulb), thinly sliced in sweet-and-sour dishes; baked, steamed; in stuffings, risotto, juiced.

SKIP TO

COLATURA DI ALICI, P. 237; ORECCHIETTE CON CIME DI RAPA (ORECCHIETTE WITH BROCCOLI RABE), P. 374; THE ART OF RIBOLLITA, P. 368.

SOPHIA LOREN, A GOURMAND MUSE

The undisputed face of Italian cinema since the 1950s, the "divine" Sophia has wonderfully embodied, in both her films and her life, the assertive Neapolitan spirit and its generous counterpart, Neapolitan cuisine.

STÉPHANE SOLIER

A PORTRAIT GOOD ENOUGH TO EAT

"Her lips are plump and red like the Pozzuoli tomatoes from her childhood, and her sinuous curves are like fresh homemade pasta. Sophia Loren is made of the stuff of the most raw and voracious dreams."
***MARIE-CLAIRE*, JANUARY 28, 2018**

"Everything you see I owe to spaghetti."
(*IN THE KITCHEN WITH LOVE*, SOPHIA LOREN, 1971)

Tributes to the Gourmand Muse

IN MOVIES

In *Totò, Fabrizi and the Young People Today* by Mario Mattoli (1960), the owner of the pastry shop compares the most beautiful of the *colombe* (Easter buns) to the diva: "It's the Sophia Loren of colombe!"

IN SONG

In *Sophia* (1955), Neapolitan singer Roberto Murolo openly declares his love to the beautiful *pizzaiola* from the movie *The Gold of Naples*: "Ah, Sophia, Sophia, I go crazy when I think of your *pizze*, I can't rest!"

IN COMICS

In the book *Asterix and the Chariot Race* (2017), the authors honor the cooking talents of the actress by depicting her bringing a pot of spaghetti to a competition (p. 39).

HER COOKBOOKS

1971

In the Kitchen with Love (In cucina con amore)

1999

Recipes and Memories

1954
L'Oro di Napoli
(The Gold of Naples)
VITTORIO DE SICA

In Naples, no one remains untouched by the charms of Sophia the *pizzaiola*, much to the chagrin of her jealous husband. Behind the counter of her single-story shop, she entices her customers . . . This is the actress's first personal success.

1955
La Donna del fiume
(The River Girl)
MARIO SOLDATI

A worker in an eel cannery in Comacchio, Nives turns all heads. Gino, a inveterate seducer, crosses swords with her against a background of skewered eels. Will it last long?

1960
La Ciociara
(Two Women)
VITTORIO DE SICA

1943: Cesira and her daughter flee the bombings of Rome to take refuge in her native Ciociaria. A comforting soup welcomes them when they arrive at Sant'Eufemia, before they are caught up in the turmoil of war . . . She wins an Oscar for best actress.

1964
Matrimonio all'italiana
(Marriage Italian Style)
VITTORIO DE SICA

After more than twenty years with Dummì (Marcello Mastroianni), Filumena feigns illness to get him to marry her. Now with her chance, she declares herself *signora Soriano* and rushes at a bowl of liberating leftover *pasta e fagioli* (pasta and beans) under the cries of the husband she has duped.

1967
Questi fantasmi
(Ghosts—Italian Style)
RENATO CASTELLANI

On the roof of his building, Maria gives her neighbor Pasquale (Vittorio Gassman) a lesson in making Neapolitan coffee . . . A marriage proposal is guaranteed!

1990
Sabato, domenica e lunedì
(Saturday, Sunday and Monday)
LINA WERTMÜLLER

Against a background of marital discord after a "gastronomic" betrayal by her husband, who overly praised a dish made by her stepdaughter, a quaint tiff takes place in a butcher's shop where a scathing Donna Rosa teaches a lesson in making *ragù napoletano* to customers!

1970
I Girasoli (Sunflower)
VITTORIO DE SICA

Giovanna marries Antonio (Marcello Mastroianni) to delay his leaving for war. On the menu of their extended days of happiness: an omelet with twenty-four eggs where everyone adds their two cents.

1971
La Mortadella (Lady Liberty)
MARIO MONICELLI

Maddalena, a worker in a meat factory, must join her fiancé in the United States. She is stopped at customs because of the mortadella she is carrying . . .

But also

The baked suckling lamb in *The Sign of Venus*, by Dino Risi (1955); the *ziti napoletani* in *Yesterday, Today and Tomorrow*, by Vittorio De Sica (1963); the gnocchi in *More Than a Miracle*, by Francesco Rosi (1967); the making of pasta and parmigiana in *Francesca and Nunziata*, by Lina Wertmüller (2001); stuffed peppers, Parmesan, *alici in soffitta* ("anchovies in the attic") in *Too Much Romance . . . It's Time for Stuffed Peppers*, by Lina Wertmüller (2004).

SKIP TO
PIZZA FRITTA (FRIED PIZZA), P. 218;
MORTADELLA, P. 160.

SEASON

TUTTO L'ANNO (YEAR-ROUND)

CATEGORY

PRIMO PIATTO (FIRST COURSE)

LEVEL

DIFFICOLTÀ MEDIA (MEDIUM DIFFICULTY)

GNOCCHI ALLA ROMANA

ROMAN GNOCCHI

This rustic recipe from Lazio with mysteries surrounding its origins brings back childhood memories for many Romans.

FRANÇOIS-RÉGIS GAUDRY

UNSETTLING DIFFERENCES . . .

→ They are referred to as "gnocchi," but this is misleading: they do not contain potatoes but instead durum wheat semolina flour, butter, and cheese. They have a pucklike shape, which is far from the oval shape of gnocchi. They are not cooked in boiling water but instead baked au gratin.

→ The fat used is butter, which is rather unusual in Lazio, where olive oil dominates.

→ Parmesan, the most popular cheese to use, would almost suggest this dish is from the north. But many recipes also use Pecorino Romano.

. . . BUT A PROVEN ROMAN ORIGIN

→ *Gnocchi alla romana* are one of the "seven dishes of Rome," according to Pellegrino Artusi in his 1891 book *La scienza in cucina e l'arte di mangiar bene* (*Science in the Kitchen and the Art of Eating Well*). Its recipe has the uniqueness of being made from flour and containing a good bit of Gruyère in addition to Parmesan. The recipe preceding this one is called gnocchi *di semolino* (semolina) and *looks* like today's gnocchi alla romana (milk, butter, and Parmesan).

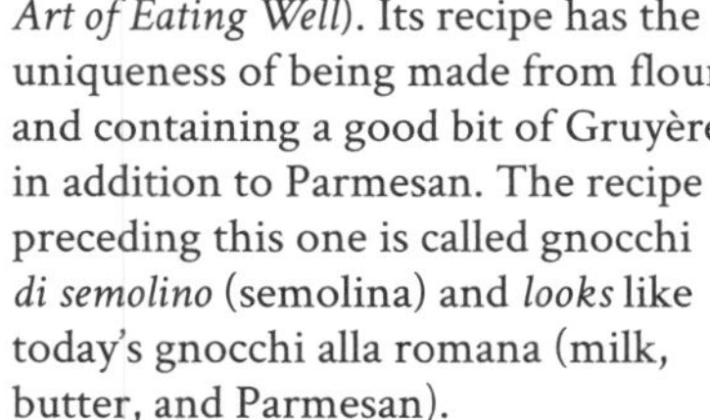

→ The cook and poet Adolfo Giaquinto also mentions them in 1899 in a work that contributed to the codification of Roman cuisine: *La cucina di famiglia. Raccolta di ricette prathe e consigli per ben cucinare Roma* (*Home Cooking: A Collection of Recipes and Practical Tips for Cooking Well Roman-Style*).

→ The use of durum wheat semolina flour, an ingredient common to *cucina povera*, indicates the peasant origins of this dish. In *La cucina romana* (1929), author Ada Boni explains: "Gnocchi alla romana was a festive dish prepared during baptisms and dinners for Carnival."

THE RECIPE

This is the Proustian madeleine for Giovanni Passerini. The Roman chef (Passerini restaurant, Paris 12th) revived the recipe his mother would prepare for him. Sometimes she added a little tomato and mozzarella. "I remember that bubbling magmalike temperature when she would place the glass baking dish down on the table; it looked like a living, singing being," says Giovanni.

SERVES 4

- 4 cups (1 L) milk
- 8½ tablespoons (120 g) butter
- Nutmeg, preferably freshly grated
- 1⅓ cups (250 g) finely ground semolina flour
- 1 teaspoon (7 g) salt
- 2 large (38 g) egg yolks
- 1 cup (100 g) grated Parmesan cheese
- ⅔ cup (60 g) grated Pecorino Romano cheese

In a saucepan, bring the milk, 3½ tablespoons (50 g) of the butter, and a little nutmeg to a boil. Add the semolina, stirring until the mixture thickens (as if making polenta). Season with the salt and cook for 5 minutes, stirring frequently. Let cool for several minutes, then add the egg yolks and Parmesan, stirring to thoroughly combine.

Divide the mixture in half. Scrape each half onto its own large sheet of parchment paper. Shape each half into a log measuring 2¾ to 3 inches (7 to 8 cm) in diameter, then roll it in its parchment. Place the rolls in the refrigerator for 1 hour. Alternatively, spread the mixture to a thickness of 1⅛ inches (3 cm) on parchment paper, then cut out circles using a cookie cutter.

Preheat the oven to 400°F (200°C). Cut the rolls into 1⅛-inch-thick (3 cm) slices. Place them in a well-greased baking dish. Melt the remaining 5 tablespoons (70 g) butter and pour it evenly over the gnocchi. Sprinkle with the pecorino. Bake until browned, about 20 minutes. Serve.

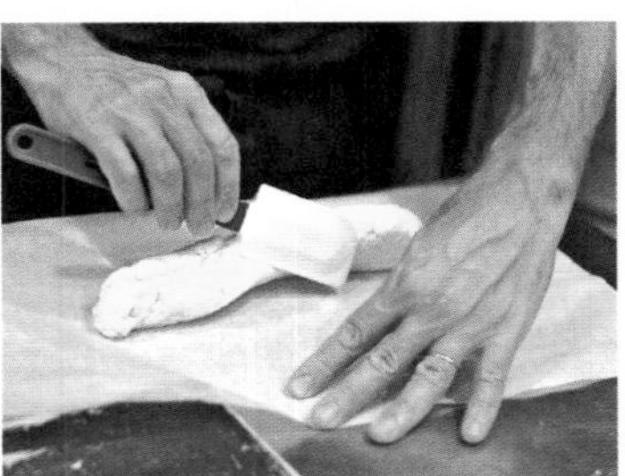

Thursday is gnocchi day!

Giovedì gnocchi, venerdì pesce e sabato trippa! ("Thursday is gnocchi, Friday is fish, and Saturday is tripe!")

In Rome, tradition dictates that on Thursdays, gnocchi is eaten as a *primo piatto* (first course), a rather substantial dish before lean Fridays. This rule applies to potato gnocchi as well as gnocchi alla romana.

SKIP TO

GNOCCHI DI PATATE CRUDE (RAW POTATO GNOCCHI), P. 164;
PELLEGRINO ARTUSI, P. 32;
TRIPPA ALLA ROMANA (ROMAN-STYLE TRIPE), P. 380.

"MIELICROMIA": A PALETTE OF HONEYS

Renowned beekeeper Andrea Paternoster depicts all the various shades of honeys as a scale he refers to as *mielicromia*. Here he reveals his collection of signature honeys that reflect the incredible botanical and climatic diversity of Italy, from north to south.

FRANÇOIS-RÉGIS GAUDRY

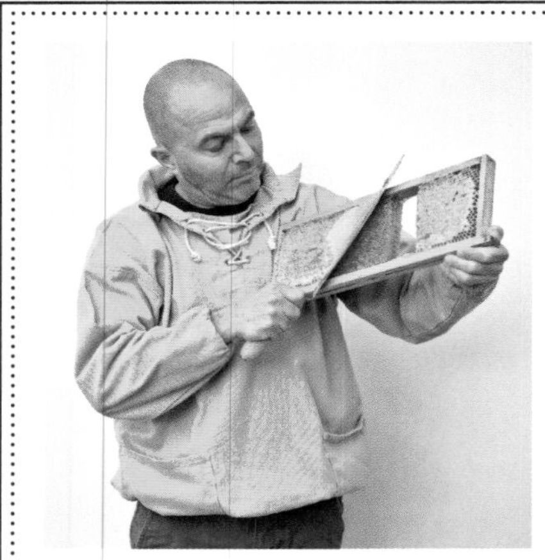

Andrea Paternoster founded Mieli Thun in Vigo di Ton in Trentino. He defines himself as a nomadic beekeeper, as he travels all over Italy with his beehives in search of exceptional biotopes.

www.mielithun.it

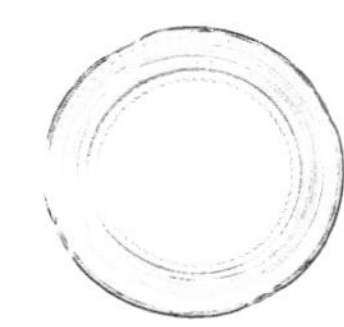

ACACIA · *Acacia*

ORIGIN—Lombardy, Veneto, Trentino-Alto Adige.

TASTING NOTES—scents of white spring flowers and Bourbon vanilla, very smooth on the palate, a touch of sweet almond.

A GOURMAND IDEA—1 teaspoon added to a slightly acidic tomato sauce.

ERBA MEDICA · *Alfalfa*

ORIGIN—northern Italy

TASTING NOTES—scent of cut grass, delicate palate with notes of cooked milk and grape must, with a slight acidity.

A GOURMAND IDEA—replace sugar with honey when preparing mulled wine.

ARANCIO · *Orange tree*

ORIGIN—southern Italy, Sicily, Sardinia.

TASTING NOTES—scent of orange blossom, honeysuckle, hawthorn, and yellow melon on the palate.

A GOURMAND IDEA—mix with lemon juice and olive oil to season raw vegetables.

CASTAGNO · *Chestnut tree*

ORIGIN—almost all of Italy.

TASTING NOTES—scent of dried chamomile, with hints of quinine. Bitter taste, slightly astringent, with notes of wood, tobacco, carob, and cocoa bean.

A GOURMAND IDEA—a drizzle on a whipped ricotta with crushed hazelnuts.

CORIANDOLO · *Coriander*

ORIGIN—Emilia-Romagna, Tuscany, Marche, Abruzzo.

TASTING NOTES—strong scent of spices, light smoky note and hint of cedar bark, refreshing and lingering citrus on the palate.

A GOURMAND IDEA—mix it with spices, chopped thyme, and vinegar to season grilled meats.

SULLA · *Sainfoin*

ORIGIN—central and southern Italy, Sardinia, and Sicily.

TASTING NOTES—delicate and floral scents, with notes of dried herbs, subtle and not very persistent on the palate, with a finish of cereals, legumes, and fresh nuts.

A GOURMAND IDEA—ideal for flavoring bread dough.

FIORE DELLE ALPI · *Alpine flowers*

ORIGIN—above 4,900 feet (1,500 m) in Aosta Valley, Piedmont, and Trentino-Alto Adige.

TASTING NOTES—the multitude of floral species represented in this honey gives it a complex bouquet of thistle, cooked artichoke, and rhubarb; fresh, minty, and persistent on the palate.

A GOURMAND IDEA—use to sweeten herbal tea or a toddy.

TIGLIO · *Lime (Linden) blossoms*

ORIGIN—northern Italy

TASTING NOTES—almost medicinal bouquet reminiscent of lime blossom, prolonged by incense and resin; refreshing and finely bitter on the palate, minty, with notes of sage and lime.

A GOURMAND IDEA—1 teaspoon diluted in the cooking water of spelt pasta.

BOSCO · *Honeydew from forest species*

ORIGIN—northern Italy

TASTING NOTES—penetrating scents of sweet wine and ripe fig, with a licorice finish. On the palate are rhubarb and green tomato preserves.

A GOURMAND IDEA—use it to coat lamb shoulder with mild spices for long roasting times.

MILLEFIORI · *All flowers*

ORIGIN—throughout Italy.

TASTING NOTES—this is snapshot of the area's surrounding vegetation. Depending on the biotopes, these honeys can be fruity, floral, mentholated, tannic, balsamic . . .

A GOURMAND IDEA—seasonings, marinades . . . any purpose!

RODODENDRO · *Rhododendron*

ORIGIN—northern Italy

TASTING NOTES—an ethereal nose, with notes of white flowers, round and intense palate, with a finishing flavor of wax.

A GOURMAND IDEA—use 1 teaspoon to glaze vegetables.

MARRUCA · *Christ thorn*

ORIGIN—Friuli, Tuscany, Umbria.

TASTING NOTES—scents of leather, hay, and licorice; on the palate, notes of deep caramel and coffee.

A GOURMAND IDEA—a small touch in tagliatelle pasta made with chestnut or spelt flour.

CILIEGIO · *Cherry tree*

ORIGIN—Piedmont, Veneto, Apulia.

TASTING NOTES—scents of toasted nuts and apricot jam, flavor of caramel, almond, and stone fruit. Slightly spicy finish.

A GOURMAND IDEA—slather on chicken with almonds.

EUCALIPTO · *Eucalyptus*

ORIGIN—southern Italy, Sardinia, and Sicily.

TASTING NOTES—an almost animallike scent, with hints of licorice that leans toward umami and dried porcini. Rich palate of dulce de leche, between sweet and savory.

A GOURMAND IDEA—a drizzle on warm grilled toast spread with goat's-milk cheese just out of the oven.

TOSCANO · *Tuscany region*

ORIGIN—Tuscany.

TASTING NOTES—a honey of immense complexity, like the botanical diversity that is expressed throughout the region—Mediterranean plants, stone-fruit orchards, sunflowers, eucalyptus . . .

A GOURMAND IDEA—a few spoonfuls to flavor a wild boar marinade with garlic and spices.

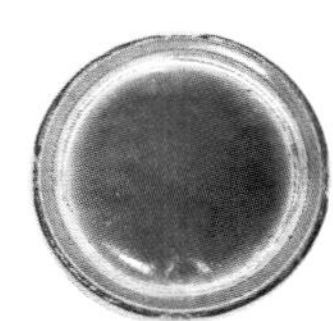

CORBEZZOLO · *Arbutus*

ORIGIN—Tuscany, Lazio, Campania, Sardinia.

TASTING NOTES—complex scents of roasted coffee, cocoa bean, and gentian; bitter taste of tobacco and chicory.

A GOURMAND IDEA—use it to sweeten a whipped cream with mascarpone and Bourbon vanilla.

TARASSACO · *Dandelion*

ORIGIN—northern Italy

TASTING NOTES—spicy scents, slightly sulfuric and vinegary, with notes of wet hay and root; moderately sweet on the palate, vanilla, with a flavor of chamomile tea.

A GOURMAND IDEA—combine with soy sauce, apple cider vinegar, olive oil, and black pepper to coat grilled meats.

MELO · *Apple tree*

ORIGIN—Dolomites and northern Italy.

TASTING NOTES—scents of cider, musk, and baked apple. Flowery and plant flavors on the palate, nearing that of cooked artichoke.

A GOURMAND IDEA—for a vinaigrette: 1 tablespoon (15 mL) honey, 1 tablespoon (15 mL) mustard, 2 tablespoons (30 mL) cider vinegar, 6 tablespoons (90 mL) vegetable oil, salt, and freshly ground black pepper.

ERICA · *Heather*

ORIGIN—west coast of Italy, from Liguria to Campania.

TASTING NOTES—rich bouquet of coffee, saffron, and apricot jam; generous and complex palate with flavors of caramel and tamarind, between acidity and bitterness.

A GOURMAND IDEA—ideal for alcoholic fermentations (beers, mead, etc.).

GIRASOLE · *Sunflower*

ORIGIN—central and southern Italy.

TASTING NOTES—scent of fresh-cut hay, pineapple, and passion fruit. Ripe apricot flavor, with sour notes and a star anise aftertaste.

A GOURMAND IDEA—1 teaspoon with olive oil, salt, and freshly ground black pepper to season steamed vegetables.

ABETE · *Fir tree honeydew*

ORIGIN—Dolomites, Tuscany, Piedmont.

TASTING NOTES—assertive smell of resin and candied citrus, with smoky notes. Malty palate, finely bitter, and slightly animallike, with a caramel finish.

A GOURMAND IDEA—use it to lacquer duck breast.

ALBERO DEL PARADISO · *Tree of heaven*

ORIGIN—Verona region.

TASTING NOTES—delicate nose, taste of muscat grapes, peach, and lychee syrup; umami, and fresh mushroom finish.

A GOURMAND IDEA—1 teaspoon added to fruit salad.

MIELE DELLA LUNIGIANA DOP

Acacia honey and chestnut honey, produced in the province of Massa Carrara, a historic region of Lunigiana (Tuscany).

MIELE VARESINO DOP

Very pure acacia honey produced at the foot of the Alps in the province of Varese (Lombardy).

MIELI DELL'APPENNINO AQUILANO SLOW FOOD

Honeys of *santoreggia* (*Satureja montana*, mountain savory) and *stregonia* (*Sideritis syriaca*, Greek mountain tea), produced in the region of Gran Sasso, Laga, and the Sirente Velino massif in the province of L'Aquila (Abruzzo).

MIELE DI ALTA MONTAGNA SLOW FOOD

Rhododendron honey, wild flower honey, and fir tree honeydew produced above 4,900 feet (1,500 m) in the regions of Lombardy, Piedmont, and Aosta Valley.

MIELE D'APE NERA SICULA

Honey of various monofloral profiles (eucalyptus, orange tree . . .) produced by the endemic black bee of Sicily (*Apis mellifera siciliana*, protected by Slow Food).

MIELE DELLE DOLOMITI BELLUNESI

Six types (mille fleurs, acacia, lime, chestnut, rhododendron, dandelion) produced in the region of Belluno (Veneto), giving a varied aromatic palate, marked by a mountainous and sweet profile.

SKIP TO
EASTER CAKES, P. 90; CARNIVAL & DELICACIES, P. 58; SWEET TREATS OF CHRISTMAS, P. 314; NOUGATS, P. 326.

OREGANO

A favorite companion with tomato sauce, this wild mountain herb is an essential flavoring in southern Italian cuisine.

GIANNA MAZZEI

WHAT AM I?

From the Greek *oros*, "the mountain," and *ganos*, "brightness/joy," *origano* belongs to the Lamiaceae family. Growing in hilly and mountainous areas, it prefers dry, limestone, and stony soils. It is harvested year-round. To best store it, pick between June and August, before flowering. Its herbaceous, Mediterranean aroma is tenacious: it does not weaken with drying. Plants with white flowers seem more aromatic than those with pink or purplish flowers.

Origano secco (dried) · *Origano fresco* (fresh) · *Maggiorana* (marjoram)

RECIPE

REGINETTE CO-E EUVE (WITH EGGS)

This thick soup is common in Liguria.

SERVES 4

2 to 3 large (100 to 150 g) eggs
1 clove garlic, peeled
1 tablespoon (2 g) fresh marjoram
1 cup (100 g) grated Parmesan cheese
¼ cup (60 mL) olive oil
Salt
6 cups (1.5 L) water or broth
7 ounces (200 g) *reginette* or *mafaldine* (pasta in the shape of a serrated ribbon about ⅓ inch/1 cm wide)

- Lightly beat the eggs in a bowl. Chop the garlic and marjoram, then add them with the Parmesan and the olive oil to the bowl. Season with salt and set aside.
- In a saucepan, lightly salt the water and bring it to a boil. Add the pasta. Halfway through the pasta cooking time, dilute the beaten egg mixture with two ladles of the pasta cooking water, adding it slowly to avoid lumps.
- One minute before the pasta is finished cooking, pour the egg mixture into the pan and continue stirring the pasta. The soup is now ready.

DRIED OREGANO

It's more delicate. It's excellent on caprese salad, pizza, and bruschetta; in *trito* (a chopped mixture) for roasting; and in compound butter.

ESSENTIAL FOR:

→ **Canned *sott'olio*** (in oil): artichokes, spring onions . . . (throughout Italy)

→ **Oregano liqueur** (throughout Italy).

→ ***Carne alla pizzaiola*** (Campania): meat cooked with tomato, olive oil, garlic, and white wine, of Neapolitan origin.

→ ***Sardenaira*** (Liguria): focaccia with tomato, onions, and anchovies.

USING

The leaves and flowers are eaten fresh or dried.

Dried oregano is easier to find than fresh oregano, which tastes more intense; however, they are interchangeable.

FRESH OREGANO

Perfect with meat, fish, and vegetables.

Excellent on veal scallops, mushrooms, tomatoes, grilled vegetables, *baccalà con patate o in umido* (salt cod with potatoes or simmered), and tuna en papillote or grilled.

ESSENTIAL FOR:

→ ***Pasta origanata*** (Calabria), with anchovies.

→ ***Rianata*** (*origanata* in the local dialect) ***trapanese*** (Sicily): pizza with sardines, garlic, parsley, tomatoes, and pecorino.

→ ***Salmoriglio*** (Sicily): a sauce prepared with two-thirds olive oil, one-third lemon juice, oregano, parsley, salt, and pepper, used to season meat and grilled fish.

MARJORAM

A more spiced and milder flavor than classic oregano, it is often used fresh.

In Liguria—where it's called *persa*—it is treated like royalty.

ESSENTIAL FOR:

→ **Stuffing for *pansòti***, ravioli with herbs.

→ ***Frittate*** (omelets).

→ **Added to dried bread crumbs.**

→ ***Cima alla genovese***, veal stomach or intestines stuffed with vegetables, offal, and eggs, then boiled.

→ ***Torta de anciöe*** (anchovies), also with oregano from southern Italy.

→ ***Torta pasqualina***, rustic savory Easter pie, with spinach and ricotta.

→ ***Polpettone di fagiolini***, potato bread and string beans.

→ ***Zucchine e fiori di zucca ripieni*** (zucchini and zucchini blossoms, stuffed).

→ ***Minestra di bianchetti***, soup of fish fry (anchovies, sardines).

→ ***Salsa de pegneu*** (pine nut sauce).

→ **Artichokes fricassee.**

→ **Lettuce soup.**

Throughout the remainder of Italy:

→ ***Coniglio all'ischitana*** (Campania), rabbit with garlic and tomato.

→ ***Spaghetti col rancetto*** (Umbria), with tomato, onion, and guanciale (cured pork cheek).

→ ***Cjalsons*** or ***agnolotti*** (Friuli-Venezia Giulia), ravioli with a sweet-and-savory filling.

→ **Potato croquettes with eggplant custard** (Sicily).

→ ***Persata*** (Tuscany), typical bread soup from Elba Island.

Varieties present in Italy

Common oregano, *Origanum vulgare*: found throughout the territory, its aroma is acrid. It is mainly used in herbal teas.

"Southern oregano" (green), *Origanum heracleoticum*: found in southern Italy, this is the most popular and the one traditionally used in Italian cuisine.

Sweet marjoram, *Origanum majorana*: more commonly known as marjoram. Cultivated throughout Italy.

Pot marjoram, *Origanum onites*: found in eastern Sicily, between Catania and Syracuse, making it more rare.

SKIP TO
PIZZE NAPOLETANE, P. 54;
HIS MAJESTY THE BASIL, P. 121.

SEASON
PRIMAVERA (SPRING)

CATEGORY
SECONDO PIATTO (MAIN COURSE)

LEVEL
DIFFICOLTÀ MEDIA (MEDIUM DIFFICULTY)

CORATELLA DI ABBACCHIO CON I CARCIOFI

LAMB'S OFFAL WITH ARTICHOKES

This stew of lamb's organs and artichokes is a cult dish in Rome, especially at Easter, when the sacrifice of lamb has religious associations. The Romanesco artichoke also takes center stage in this springtime dish.

MARIE-AMAL BIZALION

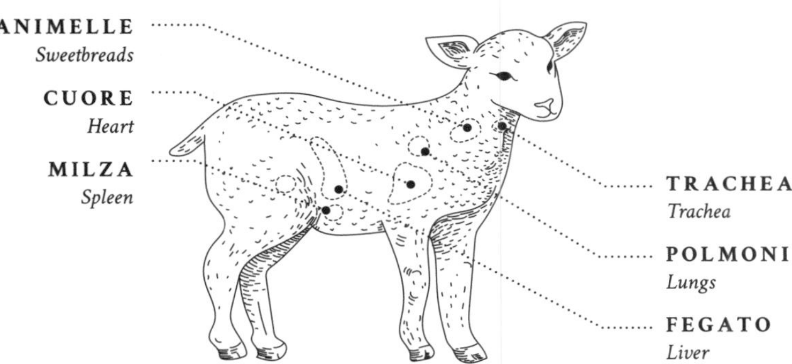

ANATOMY LESSON

The term *coratella* refers to both lamb's and kid's offal, or all of the attached central organs. Sold as a whole piece, this includes the lungs, heart, liver, spleen, sweetbreads (thymus glands), and part of the trachea.

How to purchase offal

SELECT CAREFULLY

It must come from an *abbacchio* (a milk-fed lamb, a term used in central Italy and especially Lazio), preferably organic, and of the utmost freshness. The liver should be dark red, and the lungs should be smooth, shiny, and soft pink.

They should be prepared shortly after purchase. Freezing is not recommended.

BE SENSITIVE TO TIMING!

Take care when cooking by respecting the cooking times noted for each part: if coratella cooks too long, the parts can become tough and will therefore need a much longer, slower simmering to tenderize them.

SKIP TO
ARTICHOKES, P. 100;
TRIPPA ALLA ROMANA (ROMAN-STYLE TRIPE), P. 380.

THE RECIPE

SERVES 4

- 4 Romanesco artichokes or similar purple artichoke
- 1 lemon
- Coratella of 1 fresh whole milk-fed (suckling) lamb (if possible, the liver, lungs, heart, trachea, and sweetbreads)
- 4 tablespoons (60 mL) olive oil
- 2 cloves garlic, peeled and lightly crushed
- Salt and freshly ground black pepper
- 1 onion, finely chopped
- ¼ cup (60 mL) white wine
- 10 sprigs parsley, chopped

Clean the artichokes and slice off the top third. Remove any other outer leaves flush with the cut end to reveal the heart. Cut the heart in half, then remove the choke. Cut the artichokes into quarters and place the pieces in a bowl of water with the juice of half a lemon.

If not already prepared by a butcher, remove the fatty tissue, nerve endings, and any bile from the coratella pieces. Rinse all the pieces with water, being sure to rinse the inside of the trachea and the heart. Gently pat the pieces dry with a paper towel.

Cut the lung and trachea into very thin slices (⅛ inch/3 mm) and set aside on a plate. Thinly slice the liver and set it aside on a separate plate. Chop the heart and dice the sweetbreads; set them aside on a third plate.

In a skillet set over low heat, heat 2 tablespoons (30 mL) of the olive oil with the garlic cloves. When the garlic begins to brown, remove them, then add the artichokes. Increase the heat to high. Cook the artichokes for 5 to 6 minutes, or until browned. Season with salt and pepper, add a little water, cover, and simmer for 15 minutes over low heat. Transfer the contents of the pan to a bowl or plate and set aside.

In the same pan, brown the onion in the remaining 2 tablespoons (30 mL) olive oil until browned. Add the lungs and trachea. Sauté over high heat, stirring for 5 minutes.

When the lungs are well browned, add the wine. When the juice begins to steam, add the heart and sweetbreads. Season generously with salt and pepper while stirring. After 3 minutes, add the liver. Stir over high heat for 2 minutes. Add the artichokes and garlic and stir for another 2 minutes.

Adjust the seasoning, if needed. Finish with a dash of lemon juice and the parsley. Serve piping hot.

FRITTO MISTO
MIXED FRIED FISH

Fritto misto all'italiana is a complete meal, where you'll find everything from savory to sweet.

ILARIA BRUNETTI

LIKE A FISH IN . . . OIL

Fritto misto di pesce (an assortment of fried fish) is a popular dish in Italian restaurants outside of Italy as well as in Italy's coastal towns. Its variations are determined by the day's catch more than by regional differences. You can find whole small fried fish (anchovies, sardines, red mullet, small sole, various other small fish . . .), larger fish fillets, squid, shrimp . . . all simply battered and fried in hot oil (either olive oil or other frying oils).

Two specialties not to miss

Frittura di novellame (fish fry, or larvae) (all coasts):

The *uomini nudi* (naked men) from Emilia-Romagna, or *fragagghjame* in Apulia, are an exquisitely prepared fried dish, although now rare; in Liguria, *bianchetti* or *gianchetti* mainly contain fry from the sardine family.

Fritto di paranza (south-central coasts):

This "poor man's dish" brings together small fish that are of little value in the market but that reign in the skillet! *Paranza* originally meant a trawler fishing boat, then referred to the trawl (the net) as well as the small fish it snares.

THE STREET FOOD VERSION

In Naples, fritto misto is served up by street vendors. You can walk down the street holding a *cuoppo* (paper cone) of either *di mare* (from the sea) with *zeppoline* (fritters made from yeast-raised batter) of salt cod or seaweed and fried fish, or select *di terra* (from the earth), with plain or vegetable zeppoline made with potato, vegetables, *mozzarelline*, etc.

Likewise, in Genoa, you can try cones of *frisceu* (or *cocculi*), similar to zeppoline.

Every spring since 2004, the town of Ascoli Piceno (Marche) has celebrated the countless variations of Italian-style fried assortments with a weeklong *sagra* (large festival).

Sulla Punta Della Lingua (On the Tip of the Tongue)

"Siamo fritti!"
"We are done for!"

Paranza, in the jargon of the Camorra (the Naples Mafia), refers to a group of Mafia.

RECIPE

FRITTO MISTO PIEMONTESE (PIEDMONT-STYLE FRITTO MISTO)

Though it's a rich dish served in finer restaurants, it stays close to its peasant roots. It was prepared to celebrate a slaughter. The *quinto quarto* (fifth quarter, or offal) was fried with fresh sausages. In 2003, the Accademia della Fricia association was founded to preserve and promote *fricia*, the version of fritto misto from Montferrato (Piedmont), which includes nine savory items, five sweet items, and two accompaniments. Here is a simplified version, but don't hesitate to add more items!

SERVES 6

7 ounces (200 g) pork sausage
7 ounces (200 g) veal and/or pork liver
3½ ounces (100 g) veal brains
3½ ounces (100 g) veal marrow
3½ ounces (100 g) veal sweetbreads
4 large (200 g) eggs
7 tablespoons (55 g) all-purpose or T55 flour
2 cups (200 g) dried bread crumbs
Olive oil
Butter
2 apples
Sparkling water
12 soft amaretti (almond cookies)
Salt

- Cut all the meat into cubes or strips of the same size.
- In a shallow bowl, lightly beat the eggs.
- Place 3 tablespoons (25 g) of the flour on a separate plate. Place the bread crumbs on a second plate. Dredge the meat pieces in the flour to lightly coat them, then dunk them in the egg (allow any excess to drain), then gently press them into the bread crumbs on all sides to evenly coat them.
- In a skillet (preferably cast iron) set over medium-high heat, combine an equal quantity of olive oil and butter until this frying fat is 2 to 3 inches (5 to 8 cm) deep. When the fat is hot, fry the pieces until golden.
- Peel and thinly slice the apples.
- Combine the remaining 4 tablespoons flour with just enough sparkling water to make a batter thick enough to coat the pieces but not too thick. Coat the apples and the amaretti in the batter, then fry them in butter or oil in a separate skillet.
- Season with salt. Serve with carrots cooked in butter and with *salsa verde* (a parsley-based sauce) for dipping.

SKIP TO
FISH, P. 300; CALAMARI, P. 242; ARTICHOKES, P. 100.

TOUR OF ITALY

It's called *all'italiana* (Italian-style), but fritto misto varies in ingredients and frying techniques depending on the region. What do they have in common? A wide variety of foods, ranging from meats and vegetables to cheeses and even small cakes, fried separately but served together as a single dish.

FRITTO MISTO . . .	MEATS	VEGETABLES	CHEESES AND OTHER PREPARATIONS	FRUITS AND CAKES	COATING	COOKING FAT
ASCOLANO (from Ascoli, Marche): more than just its famous fried olives	Lamb chops	Artichokes, zucchini and their blossoms	*All'ascolana* olives (pitted and stuffed with ground meat and Parmesan)	*Cremini* (cubes of pastry cream)	Flour + egg + dried bread crumbs	Frying oil
PIEMONTESE (←see recipe opposite): a feast of *quinto quarto* (offal)	Brain, liver, kidneys, sweetbreads, veal scallops; pork sausage, scallops; sometimes poultry liver, cock's comb; now rare: calf lungs and testes; modern additions: lamb chops, frogs, snails . . .	Tradition calls simply for buttered carrots on the side; modern additions (fried): mushrooms, cauliflower, fennel, zucchini, eggplant, artichokes		Apples, amaretti (almond cookies), *friciulin* (semolina-based cream squares)	Meats: flour + egg + dried bread crumbs Vegetables: flour + beer or sparkling water, with or without eggs	A mixture of butter and olive oil
LIGURE vegetables are the real heroes	Brain, liver, sweetbreads, and veal scallops; now rare: *stecchi* (skewers of meat and offal); *fritti nell'ostia* (fried veal offal and artichoke meatballs)	Sage and borage leaves, zucchini and their blossoms, artichokes, onions, cauliflower	*Latte brusco* (thick cream made from flour, milk, eggs, salt, parsley, lemon, and milk, cut into thick strips); sometimes *frisceu* (yeast-raised fritters with onion and lettuce)	Apples, *latte dolce* (thick cream flavored with lemon and cinnamon)	Flour + eggs + wine or sparkling water; sometimes for meats: just egg + flour	Olive oil (preferably local)
BOLOGNESE Emilian richness	Lamb chops; chicken croquettes; mortadella; sweetbreads	Zucchini and their blossoms, artichokes, potato croquettes, cauliflower, eggplant, mushrooms, fennel, green tomatoes, acacia flowers	Diced Emmental, *mozzarelline*, ricotta croquettes	Pastry cream, apple, semolina and rice fritters	Meats and cheeses: egg + dried bread crumbs Vegetables and cakes: flour + eggs + beer	Formerly lard; today frying oil
TOSCANO white meats delicacies	Chicken and rabbit; sometimes lamb and offal	Zucchini and their blossoms, onions, artichokes, sage			Meats: egg Vegetables: flour or flour + egg	Olive oil
ROMANO milk-fed lamb and artichokes are king	*Abbacchio* (milk-fed lamb) offal; on Christmas Eve, salt cod replaces offal	Artichokes; modern additions: zucchini, sometimes stuffed zucchini blossoms, cauliflower . . .	Sometimes: Roman ricotta, mozzarella, *pandorato* (slices of sandwich bread stuffed with prosciutto and mozzarella); modern additions: *supplì* (rice ball snacks)		Flour + egg	Traditionally lard; today vegetable oil
MILANESE veal offal, in all its simplicity	Veal offal (brain, sweetbreads, spinal cord, and liver); now rare: lungs	Mushrooms, zucchini, eggplant			Flour + egg + dried bread crumbs	Butter

PASTA AND POTATO

Can a marriage between two starchy foods lead to happiness?
Here are the best Italian love stories between *pasta e patate*.

ILARIA BRUNETTI

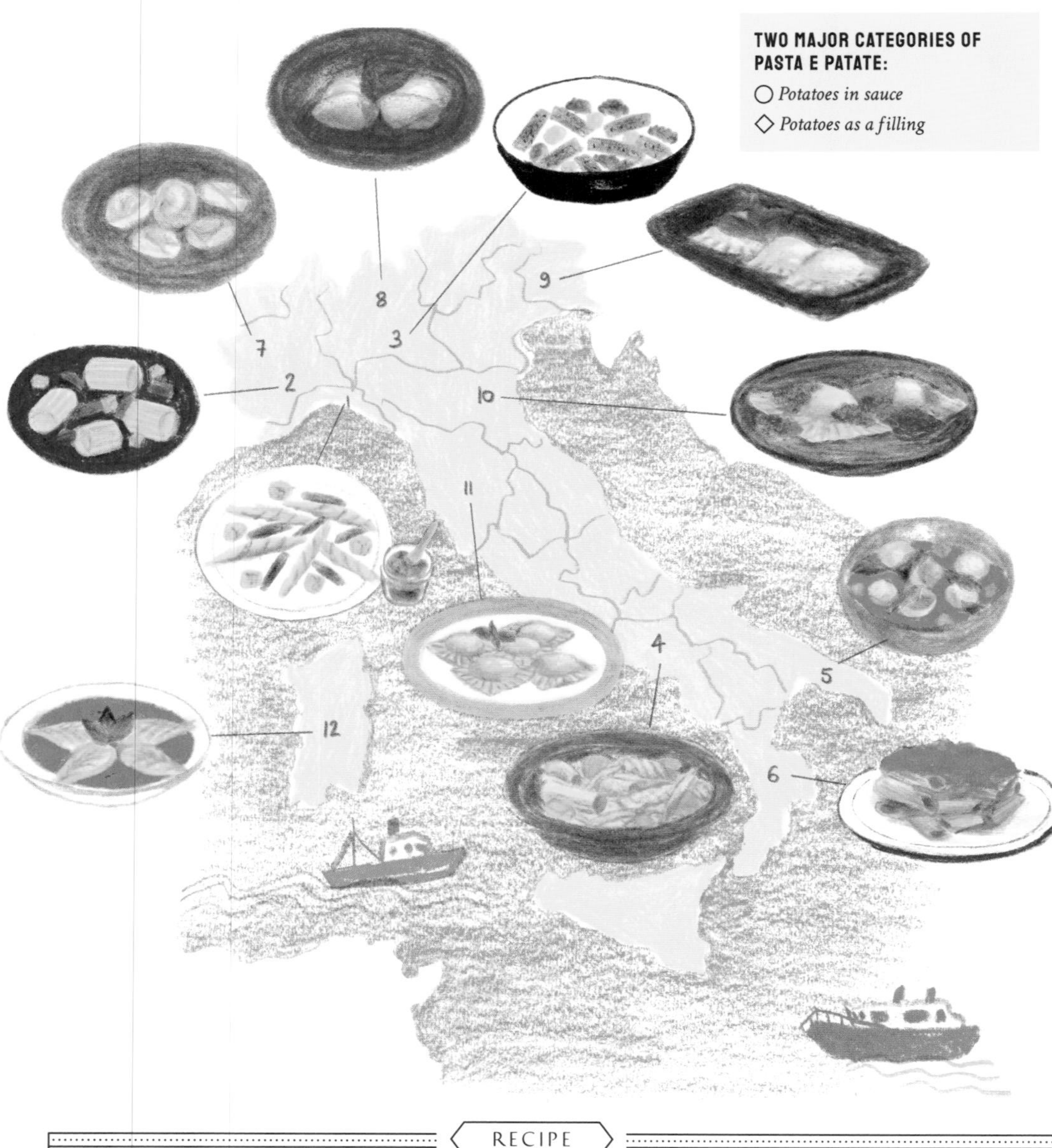

TWO MAJOR CATEGORIES OF PASTA E PATATE:

○ *Potatoes in sauce*

◇ *Potatoes as a filling*

1. PASTA AL PESTO
○ *Liguria*
Trofie (or *trenette*) are cooked with string beans and diced potatoes before adding pesto.

2. PASTA RUSTIDA
○ *Piedmont*
Ditalini tomatoes and potatoes are boiled, then pan-sautéed in butter, onion, pancetta, with an alpine-style cheese added.

3. PIZZOCCHERI VALTELLINESI
○ *Lombardy*
Short buckwheat tagliatelle pasta, cooked with kale and diced potatoes, then served with butter and Casera cheese.

4. PASTA E PATATE ALLA NAPOLETANA
○ *Campania*
A happy, creamy marriage of *pasta mista* and potatoes (and provola cheese). It is also often made au gratin.

5. ORECCHIETTE CON PATATE E ERBA RUTA
○ *Apulia*
Orecchiette cooked in water with diced potatoes and common rue (a bitter aromatic plant), then served with tomato sauce (and sometimes arugula).

6. PASTA E PATATE "ARA TIJEDDRA"
○ *Calabria*
In this ancient recipe, pasta is baked in the oven (originally wood-fired) without first cooking in water. Layers of penne or rigatoni alternate with sliced potatoes, tomato sauce, Parmesan, and oregano, all in an earthenware pan.

7. RAVIOLI ALLA VERNANTINA
◇ *Piedmont*
Large tortellini stuffed with potatoes and leeks, served with butter and Parmesan.

8. CASÔNSÈI DELLA VAL CAMONICA
◇ *Lombardy*
Egg ravioli stuffed with potatoes, chard or spinach, sausage, mortadella, Parmesan, dried bread crumbs, and parsley, served with melted butter and Parmesan.

9. CJALSONS DI TIMAU
◇ *Friuli*
These half-moon, egg-free pasta are filled with potatoes, cinnamon, onions, butter, and raisins. They are served with butter and smoked ricotta.

10. TORTELLI CON PATATE EMILIANI
◇ *Emilia-Romagna*
Egg pasta filled with potatoes, ricotta, pancetta, and Parmesan, served with butter and cheese or a meat sauce.

11. TORTELLI DI PATATE DEL MUGELLO
◇ *Tuscany*
Egg pasta filled with potatoes, garlic, Parmesan, sage, and rosemary, served with oil and Parmesan, a meat sauce, or mushrooms.

12. CULURGIONES
◇ *Sardinia*
Egg-free durum wheat semolina flour ravioli braided and filled with potatoes, mint, and sheep's-milk cheese, served with a tomato sauce and pecorino.

RECIPE

LA PASTA E PATATE (NEAPOLITAN PASTA AND POTATO*)

SERVES 4

- 1 yellow onion, thinly sliced
- 1 stalk celery, diced
- 4 tablespoons (60 mL) extra-virgin olive oil
- 3 firm-fleshed potatoes, such as Red Bliss, fingerling, or new potatoes, peeled and diced
- 2 to 3 tomatoes, preferably Piennolo, halved and seeded
- Salt
- 9 ounces (250 g) *pasta mista* (prepared by combining *tubettoni*, *tubettini*, *mafalde*, linguine, and broken spaghetti)
- 5¼ ounces (150 g) provola di Sorrento cheese or smoked mozzarella, diced (optional)
- ⅓ cup (40 g) grated Parmesan cheese
- Freshly ground black pepper

· Heat a pan of water until hot; set aside and keep hot.

· In a saucepan set over high heat, brown the onion and celery in the olive oil. Add the potatoes. Stir well to combine. Cook for several minutes, then add just over ¾ cup (200 mL) hot water. Add the tomatoes. Reduce the heat, cover, and cook for 15 minutes, stirring from time to time to ensure nothing sticks to the pan.

· Add 1¼ cups (300 mL) of the hot water and bring to a boil. Season with salt and add the pasta. Cook, adding additional hot water a little at a time while stirring constantly to create a thickened consistency. At the end of the cooking time, turn off the heat, add the diced cheese, if using, then sprinkle with the Parmesan and season with pepper. Stir to combine. Let stand for 5 minutes before serving.

Il Tocco Della Nonna* *(Grandmother's Tip)

Sauté the onion and celery in 1¾ ounces (50 g) bacon or pancetta to add flavor.

**Recipe by Nadia Postiglione, food historian and talented cook from Campania.*

PASTA MISTA

Pasta mista is now a type of pasta available for purchase, although originally it was a way to avoid waste by using scraps and broken pieces of dried pasta or leftovers that neighborhoods would donate in order to make nourishing meals. In the Neapolitan dialect, they are still called *munnezzaglia* (garbage). Potatoes were added to the munnezzaglia among the poor classes starting in the seventeenth century. When possible, a potato and pasta dish was enriched with the rinds of Parmesan wedges, still used today, or replaced by grated Parmesan cheese or provola. Whatever version you choose, there is one requirement: be sure to make the pasta *azzeccate*: creamy and melting.

SKIP TO
GENOESE PESTO, P. 20.

SEASON

TUTTO L'ANNO (YEAR-ROUND)

CATEGORY

PRIMO PIATTO (FIRST COURSE)

LEVEL

FACILE (EASY)

BIGOLI IN SALSA

ANCHOVY AND ONION PASTA

In this dish, one of the most popular of Venice, a typical Venetian long pasta meets anchovy and onions.

FRANÇOIS-RÉGIS GAUDRY

BIGOLI

THEIR NAME: from *bigat*, meaning "caterpillar" in Venetian, because of the spaghetti's plump, rough, and porous form, known for allowing the sauce to cling to it well. The *bigolo* is also the rod that rested on the shoulders of water carriers (a profession as important as that of gondolier in former times).

THEIR ORIGIN: made from whole wheat flour, a flour considered poorer than the white flour, which was reserved for nobility. They were created in the fifteenth century during the war between the Venetian Republic and the Turks. When ships carrying precious durum wheat sank, the pasta makers, finding themselves without the necessary raw ingredients, were forced to use leftover unrefined flour . . .

THEIR SPREAD: in 1604, Bartolomio Veronese, a master pasta maker from Padua, created the *torchio bigolaro*, a manual press in the form of a vertical wooden cylinder that made it possible to press the dough with a lever or a crank on a bronze die with two holes.

THEIR TYPE: today bigoli are often made with eggs. They can be bought in a fresh (with eggs) version at the market or *pastificio* (pasta shop), and in a dried version anywhere from Veneto to eastern Lombardy.

In the heart of Venice

Bigoi coea salsa in the Venetian dialect are bigoli simmered with a sauce made with anchovies (or sardines), salt, and onions (a pasta version of the *pissaladière*!). They were created, like many dishes made with onions, in the Jewish ghetto established in the Cannaregio district during the eleventh century. Over time, this recipe has become a classic for lean days: Christmas Eve, Good Friday, and Ash Wednesday.

ADAPTED VERSIONS

Bigoli con le sardelle—bigoli with sardines: a version from Mantua, made with sardines slowly cooked and sprinkled with cheese or dried bread crumbs sautéed in butter, thyme, and rosemary.

Bigoli con ragù d'anatra—bigoli with a duck ragout: this very popular sauce from Veneto can be made with or without tomato.

Bigoli mori—Moorish bigoli: elements of Bassano del Grappa (Veneto), the version made with buckwheat flour and eggs. It works well with a variety of sauces.

Pici—the Tuscan cousins, these thick spaghetti are traditionally cooked as fresh rather than dry pasta.

THE RECIPE

Simple and delicious, this dish reacquaints anyone with anchovies, whose flavor here is tempered by the sweetness of onions. Venetian cook Enrica Rocca* makes a wonderful version of this specialty.

SERVES 4

- 2 large onions
- 2 tablespoons (30 mL) olive oil
- 1 cup (250 mL) white wine
- 8 whole anchovies in salt, or 4 to 6 sardines in salt
- A few sprigs parsley, chopped
- Salt and freshly ground black pepper
- 14 ounces (400 g) bigoli, spaghetti, or *spaghettoni*

Finely chop the onions. In a skillet, heat the olive oil, then brown the onions over low heat, covering them for several minutes while they cook. They should be translucent but not browned. If there is water left in the pan, continue cooking until it has evaporated. Deglaze the pan with the wine and continue cooking for about 40 minutes, until the onions are almost caramelized (there should be some moisture left; add a little water if necessary).

Rinse the anchovies to remove the salt. Remove the bones, then mash the flesh with a fork. Cook the flesh in the pan with half the parsley. Season with salt and pepper.

In a separate saucepan, cook the bigoli al dente. Set aside a ladleful of the cooking water. Drain the pasta and transfer it to the pan with the onions, anchovies, and parsley. Stir to combine, adding a little of the pasta cooking water, if necessary, to loosen the sauce. Sprinkle with the remaining parsley and serve.

**Recipe taken from* Venise Gourmande et créative, *Éditions des Falaises, 2016.*

THE VARIATIONS

The recipes vary from family to family, with or without white wine, sometimes flavored with bay leaf, a hint of cinnamon and ground ginger, or sprinkled with toasted pine nuts . . .

SKIP TO
THE OTHER PROMISED LAND, P. 278; THE AMAZING ANCHOVY, P. 236; ONIONS, P. 292.

SACROSANCT CUISINE

Italian cuisine is much influenced by the worship of saints, which inspires fanciful feasts. Here is a collection of recipes according to the Catholic liturgical calendar.

SÉBASTIEN PIEVE

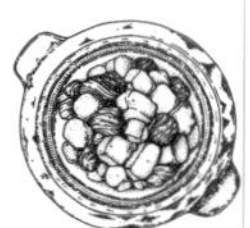

JANUARY 17

Milan-Varese, Lombardy

THE CELEBRATION: Sant'Antonio Abate (Saint Anthony the Abbot), a saint associated with the pig and very popular throughout Lombardy.

THE DISH: *cassoeula*, a winter peasant's dish from the region, similar to a pork stew. Cooked slowly and served hot, it uses the snout, ears, and feet with added green cabbage. It can be served with polenta.

FEBRUARY 5

Catania, Sicily

THE CELEBRATION: the breasts of Sant'Agata (Saint Agatha)! A Sicilian martyr from Catania, her breasts were cut off with pincers.

THE DISH: *minne*, breast-shaped desserts usually served in pairs. These pastries are filled with cream, candied fruit, and pistachios, glazed with a white glaze and topped with a candied cherry.

FEBRUARY 7

Manfredonia, Apulia

THE CELEBRATION: San Lorenzo Maiorano (Saint Lawrence of Siponto), patron saint of the city.

THE DISH: *farrata*, a traditional dish from Apulia, made with a layer of wheat pasta filled with spelt (*farro* in Italian), sheep's-milk cheese, marjoram, mint, and cinnamon. The ingredients are shaped into a ball before being baked.

MARCH 19

Naples, Campania

THE CELEBRATION: San Giuseppe (Saint Joseph), husband of the Virgin Mary.

THE DISH: *zeppola*, a cabbage in the shape of a crown fried and filled with citrus-flavored pastry cream . . . A nice break from fasting in the middle of Lent!

APRIL 23

Milan, Lodi, Monza . . . , Lombardy

THE CELEBRATION: San Giorgio (Saint George) is often represented as slaying a dragon, but, in a more peaceful role he is also the protector of dairymen.

THE DISH: *pan meino* or *pan de mej*, a small sweet focaccia bread flavored with elderflower and usually served with cream.

MAY 9

Nocera Inferiore, Campania

THE CELEBRATION: San Prisco (Saint Priscus), patron saint of this town located in the province of Salerno.

THE DISH: *zuppa* or *bubbetella*, a vegetable soup with peas, beans, and potatoes—and sometimes pancetta.

JUNE 24

Rome, Lazio

THE CELEBRATION: San Giovanni Battista (Saint John the Baptist), who was reportedly beheaded at the request of the Jewish princess Herodias and her daughter.

THE DISH: *lumache di San Giovanni*, snails cooked with peeled tomatoes, onions, garlic, and so-called San Giovanni herbs that include sage, thyme, rosemary, marjoram, and bay leaf. This preparation is supposed to drive out witches and demons called by Herodias and her daughter.

JULY 22

Atrani, Campania

THE CELEBRATION: Santa Maria Maddalena (Saint Mary Magdalene), the converted sinner.

THE DISH: *sarchiapone di Atrani*, along the Amalfi Coast. Local long green squash are seeded and filled (ground meat, mozzarella, diced hard-boiled egg, ricotta, and parsley), then breaded and deep-fried before being topped with tomato sauce and baked.

AUGUST 26

Lecce, Apulia

THE CELEBRATION: Sant'Oronzo di Lecce (Saint Orontius of Lecce), who offered a rooster to the city of which he became bishop.

THE DISH: *galletto di Sant'Oronzo* (Saint Orontius's rooster), cooked over low heat with fresh tomatoes and tomato sauce.

SEPTEMBER 19

Naples, Campania

THE CELEBRATION: San Gennaro (Saint Januarius), principal patron saint of Naples whose relics were carried in procession to stop the eruptions of Vesuvius.

THE DISH: *biscotti di San Gennaro*, cookies with a light texture often filled with cherry jam symbolizing both the blood of the saint and the lava from the volcano.

OCTOBER 4

Assisi, Umbria

THE CELEBRATION: San Francesco d'Assisi (Saint Francis of Assisi). The *poverello* (poor little boy) loved the cookies made by one of his faithful, Jacoba of Settesoli.

THE DISH: *mostaccioli*, famous hard cookies made with a dough of grape must, almonds, and cinnamon.

NOVEMBER 1

Siena-Grosseto, Tuscany

THE CELEBRATION: All Saints' Day, the feast of all saints.

THE DISH: *pan co' santi* or *pane dei santi*, a boule of bread filled with nuts and raisins and spiced with black pepper. It is best enjoyed with Tuscan *vin santo* (a dessert wine).

DECEMBER 13

Syracuse, Sicily

THE CELEBRATION: Santa Lucia di Siracusa (Saint Lucia of Syracuse). During a famine on the Sicilian lands, Lucia is said to have saved the population by growing wheat on the island.

THE DISH: *cucìa*, a porridge made from wheat. It comes in a savory version, with chickpeas and boiled broad (fava) beans, or in a sweet version made with ricotta, berries, orange zest, and cinnamon.

SKIP TO
COOKIES, P. 154; DISHES FROM THE VATICAN, P. 382; SWEETS FROM THE CONVENT, P. 204.

SPREADABLE SAUSAGES

For those who love savory bites, here are soft charcuteries, ideal for piling on toast or as an addition to pasta . . . but that's not all!

ALESSANDRA PIERINI

① 'NDUJA · *Calabria*

COMPOSITION—tripe, liver, lungs, and ground pork meat with fennel and a lot of chile, aged for at least three months. You can also find it jarred without the casing. Typical in the town of Spilinga, where the local chile pepper is used to prepare it.

APPEARANCE—appears in a fairly large casing, about 14 ounces (400 g), bright red.

TASTE—very spicy, intense, and fragrant.

ORIGIN—from French *andouille*, this traditional charcuterie made from pork stomach arrived in Italy in the Napoleonic period thanks to Joachim Murat, King of Naples, who had it distributed throughout the countryside to gain the approval of the common people. According to other sources, the recipe dates back to the sixteenth century and is an adaptation of the Spanish *soubressade*, following the introduction into Europe of chile pepper after the discovery of the Americas. Although it is very popular outside of Italy, it's less so in Italy itself.

HOW TO SERVE IT—first cut open the casing and discard it. Remove the bright, spreadable flesh. Warning: even a small bite is enough to ignite the taste buds! Add it to a pizza, bruschetta; in *fileja* (typical handmade pasta); or with beans.

② VENTRICINA TERAMANA · *Abruzzo*

Slow Food Sentinel

COMPOSITION—very finely chopped meat and fat (60 to 70 percent) from local pork, sweet salt of Cervia (Ravenna), bell pepper, chile, garlic, spices, and aromatic herbs, aged for at least three months. The filling can also be purchased in a jar. Typical of the town of Teramo.

APPEARANCE—contained in the bladder or stomach of the wild pig. It weighs about 4½ pounds (2 kg), with an orange-red flesh.

TASTE—slightly spicy and very fragrant.

ORIGIN—the name comes from the word *ventre* (belly), referring to the pig's stomach where the filling is placed. Ventricina is recorded for the first time in 1800 in the *Vocabolario dell'Uso Abruzzese*, by Italian physician Gennaro Finamore, but it was already being produced prior to that date as a "white" version. With the cultivation of red bell peppers and chiles in Italy during the nineteenth century, the red version began to appear.

HOW TO SERVE IT—for *bruschette* and *crostini*; to accompany roast pork and *arrosticini* (skewers of mutton).

③ CIAUSCOLO OR LU CIAUSCULU IGP *Marche*

COMPOSITION—pork meat and fat (30 to 50 percent), garlic, fennel seeds and flowers, white wine, salt, black pepper, orange peel. Best consumed fresh or after sixty days of aging, sometimes very lightly smoked (*sfumatura*).

APPEARANCE—very fine pork flesh, quite long, about 1⅛ pounds (500 g), a uniform pink.

TASTE—soft and delicate with aromatic and spicy notes.

ORIGIN—also called *ciauvuscolo* or *ciabbusculu*, from the Latin *cibusculum* (small food) or the derivation of three Latin words: *clausum* (closed), *ius* (sauce), and *colum* (colon). Best when enjoyed at Easter and for special occasions. There are some records of it as early as the late seventeenth century, but, as the etymology of its name suggests, the origins date from Roman times, and it was made only in winter.

HOW TO SERVE IT—for crostini as an aperitif; to top focaccia, *bruschette*, and pizzas; in soups. It can also be baked and served with mashed potatoes or lentils.

④ CREMOSO DI NORCIA · *Umbria*

COMPOSITION—pork meat and fat, garlic, salt, black pepper, and white wine, but each butcher has their own version; aged for about twenty days. Its popularity has been overshadowed a bit by a similar version from Marche with a quality certification, but locally it's a favorite.

APPEARANCE—finely chopped in a pork casing, weighing about 14 ounces (400 g), pinkish red with white specks.

TASTE—smooth and well spiced.

ORIGIN—the term *cremoso* (creamy, smooth) associated with this charcuterie attests to the high fat content that guarantees its spreadability. Traditionally, it was produced in January, when low temperatures allowed pigs to be slaughtered and their meat to be processed safely. It was a farmer's snack to provide nourishment for hard work in the fields.

HOW TO SERVE IT—on crostini and bruschette; in hot winter soups.

SKIP TO

SALUMI, P. 308; PIGS, P. 262; ARROSTICINI (LAMB SKEWERS), P. 264.

PASTA PASTRY

Simple and readily available, pasta is often a medium for art, even a little kitsch . . .
But these pasta cakes make spectacular displays!

ILARIA BRUNETTI

Its origins

→ While *frittata di pasta* (a pasta omelet) is a popular dish among poor people, the more complex preparations inspired by it are a legacy of noble Renaissance tables and influences from Arab cuisine.

→ The term *timballo* derives from the French *timbale*, from the Arabic *thabal*. It first meant a drum, then a cylindrical mold in which extravagant, spiced fillings were baked encased in a short-crust dough.

→ Very trendy in Sicily and Campania between the eighteenth and nineteenth centuries among French cooks—the Monsu or Monzu—in aristocratic houses, these preparations were eventually simplified: the quantities of spices and the variety of meats were reduced, and rather than encasing it in shortcrust dough, the preference moved to lining the mold with eggplant or simply coating it with bread crumbs.

①②③④⑤ **Frittata di maccheroni,** *Campania*
Created to use up leftover spaghetti, this large frittata is now an essential part of picnics and other excursions. Combine 1⅛ pounds (500 g) cooked spaghetti with 4 beaten (200 g) eggs and plenty of grated Parmesan and/or provola cheese, and season with salt and pepper. Cook in a heated pan with oil, as when cooking a traditional frittata. You can enrich it with charcuterie or vegetables . . .

①②③④⑤ **Frittatine di pasta,** *Campania*
Spaghetti is served in béchamel sauce with ham, peas, and provola or mozzarella. Large nests of pasta are created, then breaded and fried. It's eaten in Naples as a popular street food.

①②③④⑤ **Timballo di anelletti,** *Sicily*
Little rings of pasta are seasoned with a tomato sauce made from meat and *caciocavallo* cheese to which peas and/or eggplant are sometimes added. It is packed in a mold—cylindrical or ring-shaped—breaded or lined with thin slices of fried eggplant. It is then baked and unmolded. The result is spectacular! (See recipe below.)

①②③④⑤ **Torta di tagliatelle,** *Bologna, Emilia-Romagna*
A kind of frangipane made from almonds, sugar, and liqueur is set on a short-crust base, with fresh raw tagliatelle that, once baked, turns into a crispy filling.

①②③④⑤ **Cupola di ziti,** *Campania*
A monumental dome of ziti (a smooth pasta shaped like long tubes), served with Neapolitan ragù and cheeses (mozzarella, provola . . .). This is the only preparation where the ziti are not broken up before being cooked.

①②③④⑤ **Timballo di Bonifacio VIII,** *Lazio*
In this dish, a mold is lined with slices of prosciutto. The filling is tagliatelle seasoned with a sauce made of chicken liver, small veal meatballs, mushrooms, and tomato sauce. This dish is a tribute from the inhabitants of Anagni, where the Pope's summer residence was located, to their beloved Boniface VIII captured in 1303 by emissaries of King Philip IV of France during papal conflicts.

①②③④⑤ **Timballo di maccheroni in crosta,** *Sicily, Emilia-Romagna,* **timpano** *in Campania*
The crust and seasoning vary depending on the region, but the basic method is the same: richly seasoned pasta (meat sauce, chicken livers, cheese, meatballs, pigeon meat, truffle . . .) is enclosed in a crust of sweet short-crust pastry or flaky pastry. It's as eccentric as it gets in both form and content.

It's Not Just Pasta

→ The famous Neapolitan *sartù* is an opulent timballo made of rice seasoned with Neapolitan ragù and layers of chicken livers, peas, meatballs, and hard-boiled eggs . . .

→ The *bomba di riso* (rice bomb) from Reggio Emilia is a ring of rice with ragù, Parmesan, and porcini mushrooms (originally pigeon, chicken livers, and truffle were also added), wrapped in slices of ham.

→ In Abruzzo, *timballo di scrippelle* can be found, with layers of savory crêpes, meatballs, peas, tomato sauce, and cheese . . .

RECIPE

TIMBALLO DI ANELLETTI (BAKED PASTA)

The Sicilian chef Lorenzo Sciabica (chef of Pastore, Paris 9th) reinterprets a recipe of his father's, who would cook his timballi in large molds in a wood-fired oven, and without unmolding them. For smaller servings, these little timballi are the perfect size.

SERVES 6

- 9 ounces (250 g) veal breast
- 9 ounces (250 g) pork shoulder
- 1 carrot
- 2 stalks celery
- 1 onion
- 1 clove garlic, peeled
- Olive oil
- 1 small bouquet garni
- ½ teaspoon (6 g) tomato paste
- 1¼ cups (300 mL) red wine
- 4 cups (1 L) tomato sauce
- 3 purple eggplant
- 1⅛ pounds (500 g) *anelletti*
- 3½ ounces (100 g) pork sausage, preferably from the Nebrodi black pig, thinly sliced
- 1½ cups (150 g) grated caciocavallo cheese
- 9 ounces (250 g) *vastedda* cheese or any fresh and mild sheep's-milk cheese, diced
- 3 hard-boiled eggs, sliced
- 7 tablespoons (100 g) butter
- 1 cup (100 g) dried bread crumbs

Equipment

- 1 springform pan, 8 inches (20 cm) in diameter and 2⅓ inches (6 cm) high

· **The day before:** Brown the meat pieces in a skillet. Remove from the pan and set aside. Cut the carrot, celery, onion, and garlic into very small dice. In the same pan used to brown the meat, heat 3 tablespoons (45 mL) of olive oil and add the diced vegetables. Once the vegetables are tender, return the meat to the pan and add the bouquet garni and tomato paste. Cook until slightly browned. Deglaze the pan with the wine, and cook until the liquid has evaporated. Add 3 cups (750 mL) of the tomato sauce and a scant ½ cup (100 mL) water. Simmer for 4 hours. Remove the meat (it should be very tender), chop it, and place it back in the sauce. The result will be a very thick, dark red ragù. Allow the sauce to cool, transfer to an airtight container, and refrigerate overnight.

· **The day of:** Thinly slice the eggplant and fry them in a pan in 2 or 3 tablespoons (30 or 45 mL) olive oil. Cook the anelletti in salted boiling water until very al dente, then drain. Heat the remaining 1 cup (250 mL) tomato sauce and add the cooked pasta to it; stir to coat.

· Preheat the oven to 325°F (160°C). Line the sides of the springform pan with the fried eggplant slices. Arrange a layer of the pasta on the bottom, then sprinkle them with some of the caciocavallo. Generously distribute the ragù over the top, followed by the sausage, vastedda, and sliced eggs. Add another layer of ragù, sprinkle again with caciocavallo, and cover with a layer of the pasta. Top with the remaining slices of eggplant, then bake for 20 to 25 minutes. When done, let rest for several minutes. Using a kitchen towel, turn the pan over on top of a baking dish, and gently remove the sides of the pan. Sprinkle with bread crumbs and additional caciocavallo. Place a few pieces of butter on top, then place under the broiler for about 10 minutes, or until golden on top.

Variation: If you prefer a timballo completely covered with eggplant, line the bottom of the pan also with eggplant slices. Prepared in this way, it is not necessary to place it under the broiler at the end.

TIMBALLO MY LOVE . . .

•

The seductive Casanova regards a *"macaroni pâté (as it's called in France) made by a good Neapolitan cook"* as one of his greatest pleasures.

•

The most aristocratic timballo in Italian literature is undoubtedly the one with truffles that Fabrizio Corbera, prince of Salina, served at the family's first meal in his summer residence in Donnafugata, described in the novel *The Leopard* (1958) by Giuseppe Tomasi di Lampedusa.

•

In Stanley Tucci's film *Big Night* (1996), Primo and Secondo, two Italian brothers who immigrated to New York, conquer their guests with a majestic timballo during a dinner intended to save their restaurant from bankruptcy . . .

SKIP TO
RAGÙ BOLOGNESE, P. 330.

THE CHEESE IS CRAWLING!

This worm-filled cheese is illegal because it's considered a health risk, but for the most adventurous gourmets, it's a delight that is well worth the danger.

ILARIA BRUNETTI

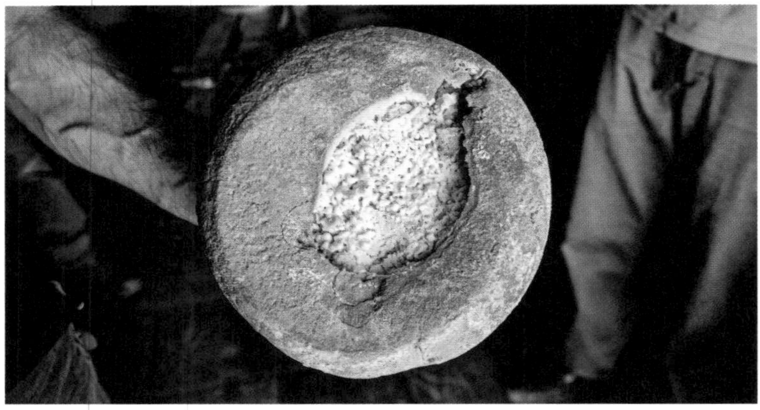

Casu marzu

The most famous cheese representing this cheese family is *casu marzu* or *casu frazigu* from Sardinia, meaning literally "rotten cheese." It is a sheep's-milk cheese filled with . . . live larvae of the cheese fly (*Piophila casei*), whose infestation causes the casu to reach its ultimate state of fermentation: the paste turns into a pungent creaminess with a very strong odor. It is also referred to as "the cheese that moves on its own" . . . It's a cousin of the Corsican *casgiu merzu* cheese.

A BRIEF HISTORY

While casu marzu was originally the result of an accident, today the cheese rind is pierced with holes, milk or oil is poured in, and flies are intentionally introduced for the purposes of infesting the cheese. In 2005, the European Union banned it, and in 2009, the Guinness Book of Records declared it the most dangerous cheese in the world. Despite this, it has been registered in the list of PAT (Traditional Italian Regional Food Products) of Sardinia, permitting it an exemption from typical health standards. It can therefore be produced—but not marketed. The Agricultural Entomology Institute of Sassari has created a fly-breeding system that meets EU standards. Sardinian producers have even requested it be protected by a PDO label.

ITS FLAVOR

It is terribly strong and pungent thanks to the extreme fermentation and the lamb rennet used in its production. In 2000, a *Wall Street Journal* reporter described it as "a viscous, pungent goo that burns the tongue and can affect other parts of the body."

How to taste it

The upper crust is sliced off (*su tappu*) and the cheese is eaten with a spoon, with *carasau* bread (a thin and crunchy Sardinian bread)—and an enormous amount of courage.

AND ELSEWHERE?

Other versions are even rarer, but there are many other such cheeses in Italy:

SALTARELLO (Friuli): a "cheese that jumps" made from a latteria-type cow's-milk cheese. The flies lay their eggs in it in spring, it is aged for three months in a room called a *celar*, and it is cut to enjoy in fall.

FURMAI CUI SALTAREI (Emilia-Romagna): near Piacenza, flies infest large wheels of sheep's-milk or cow's-milk cheese. Robiola, a fresh cheese made from cow's milk, is also macerated in a jar with grappa and honey. When the larvae appear, the *robiola nissa* is ready to enjoy.

MARCETTO OR CACE FRACECHE (Abruzzo): a spreadable cream obtained from the "rot" of a raw-sheep's-milk cheese wheel. In neighboring Molise, it is called *casu punto*, "stung" (by the fly).

CASU DU QUAGGHIU (Calabria): obtained from a young cheese of sheep's and goat's milk, produced to be infested.

And also . . .

Bross ch'a marcia (Piedmont), *Gorgonzola coi grilli* (Liguria), *Cas cu i vierm* (Basilicata) . . .

SKIP TO
GORGONZOLA, P. 318; ITALY'S BEAUTIFUL CHEESES, P. 222.

CORNETTO

It is not the Italian copy of the croissant, but rather a small brioche shaped like it.

ANNA MARÉCHAL

LET'S MAKE THINGS CLEAR!

The French croissant is a flaky roll made from puff pastry (a dough of flour, water, yeast, and a little sugar, alternated with layers of cold butter) rolled into a crescent-moon shape and baked.

The Italian brioche, inspired by the French version of brioche, starts with a leavened dough made from flour, butter, egg, sugar, yeast, and water. It is often round and in Sicily is topped with a ball of dough (*col tuppo*).

The *cornetto* is made with the same base as the Italian brioche but includes layers of butter. The pastry is laminated and rolled into a crescent-moon shape with two small "horns" (hence its name). It is therefore much sweeter and more tender than the French croissant.

WHEN AND HOW DO YOU TASTE IT?

In northern Italy, it is called *brioche* and is eaten almost exclusively for *colazione* (breakfast) with its faithful sidekick, the cappuccino. In central Italy, the term *brioche* is used to refer to any pastry.

In the south-central part of the country, the cornetto is enjoyed any time of the day! It's even a go-to midnight snack (bars and pastry shops are open all night to offer filled *cornetti*).

Origins in Vienna

The cornetto is a descendant of the Austrian *kipferl*, a sweet or savory crescent-shaped specialty. It arrived in Veneto at the end of the seventeenth century, a period of active trade between Vienna and the Republic of Venice. Venetian bakers reworked the recipe before disseminating it to other regions.

Attention!

Italians also have what's called the *croissant*. Invented in the second half of the nineteenth century and based on the French version, it is usually prepared without eggs (you can detect the buttery flavor more). Less sweet than its contemporary ,the cornetto, it can thus be eaten alone for breakfast (sweet) or filled as a sandwich with deli meats or cheese for a snack or a savory breakfast (a more northern practice).

CORNETTO AND CO.

It can be plain or filled (with apricot jam, cream, chocolate, honey . . .). It is often brushed with egg yolk to brown it, or is glazed.

The **cornetto** is also offered in an enjoyable version made *ai cereali* (with grains).

The ***cornetto vuoto*** (empty croissant) of Venice always has a bit of apricot jam! In the south central, it is called ***cornetto semplice*** (simple) and is enjoyed completely plain!

Polacca anconitana (*polonaise* of Ancona, Marche) is a cornetto in a straight shape, filled with marzipan, and glazed. It takes its name from Polish soldiers who, after liberating the city of Ancona, feasted on this version.

The ***polacca aversana*** (polonaise of Aversa, Campania). A Polish nun is said to have provided a recipe typical of her country to a pastry chef from Aversa, who created a cake and a cornetto by the same name.

SKIP TO
BREAKFAST, P. 65;
CAFFÈ AL BAR, P. 64.

PEPPERS

From antipasto to *peperonata*, sweet peppers are a staple in summertime Italian meals.

VALENTINE OUDARD

WHAT AM I?

Originally from Central America, the pepper (*Capsicum annuum*) arrived in Italy in the sixteenth century where it was cultivated from north to south.

The sweet pepper is part of the great Solanaceae family, as are the tomato, potato, eggplant . . . It is not to be confused with the chile pepper (*peperoncino* in Italian), whose shape can be similar, but whose taste is not!

There are three varietals: green (more bitter) or yellow or red (sweeter).

The most commonly available types are *grosso* (large), *quadrato* (square or bell), and *lungo* (long), with an elongated shape similar to a chile pepper.

TOUR D'ITALIE

① CORNO DI TORO ROSSO OR CORNELIO · *Sicily*

APPEARANCE: an elongated and conical shape, fleshy, orange-yellow and red.

TASTE: juicy flesh, somewhat mild; crunchy and fragrant.

IN COOKING: fresh, preserved; stuffed; sautéed; in sauce for pasta.

② CORNETTO LECCESE VERDE OR PIPI · *Apulia*

APPEARANCE: green, medium size, curvy appearance.

TASTE: mild with a hint of bitterness.

IN COOKING: raw in salad; in sweet-and-sour dishes; fried; preserved in oil.

③ LUNGO DI CARMAGNOLA OR CORNO DI BUE · *Piedmont*—Slow Food

APPEARANCE: horn-shaped, very long, green then yellow or red when ripe.

TASTE: mild and slightly sweet.

IN COOKING: stuffed; in sauté; in salad.

④ FRIGGITELLI OR PUPARUOLI FRIARIELLI *Campania* · OR FRIGGI FRIGGI ("FRY FRY") · *central and southern Italy*

APPEARANCE: green, small, curved.

TASTE: fruity with a slightly bitter aftertaste.

IN COOKING: fried; in vegetable stews.

⑤ PEPERONE NAPOLETANO CLASSICO · *Campania*

APPEARANCE: fleshy, elongated.

TASTE: mild, firm flesh; juicy and sweet. The yellow variety is more delicate.

IN COOKING: raw in salad; in vinegar; peperonata; baked.

⑥ PEPERONE DI CARMAGNOLA IGP *Piedmont*

APPEARANCE: bright red or dark yellow, squared or more elongated, depending on the varietal.

TASTE: mild; delicate and tender.

IN COOKING: with *bagna cauda*; in vinegar *giardiniera*; *pinzimonio*; peperonata.

⑦ QUADRATO ROSSO E GIALLO · *Apulia*

APPEARANCE: large, squared, thick, and crunchy flesh.

TASTE: fruity, sweet, juicy.

IN COOKING: fried; roasted; stuffed; stewed.

⑧ PEPERONE DI SENISE IGP *Basilicata - Calabria*

APPEARANCE: green to red, elongated, thin, and containing little water.

TASTE: mild or spicy depending on the varietal.

IN COOKING: harvested from August to September, they are tied together to dry in the sun in long necklaces. Fried as an aperitif (*peperone crusco*); ground to season dishes or charcuterie.

RECIPE

PEPERONATA (STEWED PEPPERS)

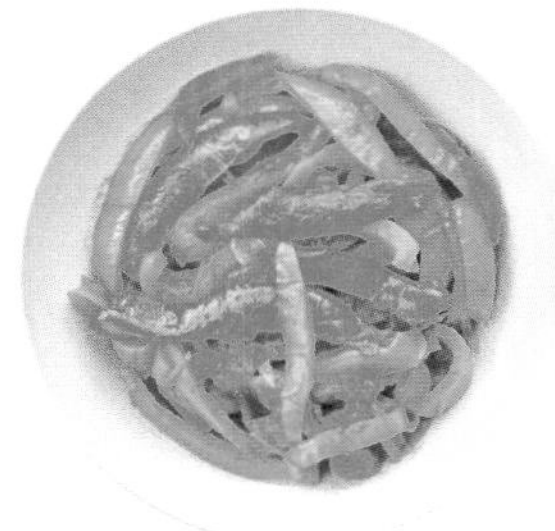

This family-style recipe is made with several variations throughout almost all regions of Italy. For lovers of sweet-and-sour dishes, add 2 tablespoons (30 mL) white wine vinegar and 1 teaspoon (5 g) sugar at the end of the cooking time.

SERVES 4

3 large red and/or yellow sweet peppers

¼ cup (60 mL) olive oil

1 onion

3 ripe red tomatoes, quartered, or 10½ ounces (300 g) diced tomatoes

A few basil leaves

Salt and freshly ground black pepper

- Cut the peppers into strips. Remove the seeds.
- Heat the olive oil in a saucepan. Thinly slice the onion and add the slices to the pan. Once they begin to brown, add the peppers and cook for 10 minutes. Add the tomatoes and basil. Season with salt and black pepper. Cover and cook over very low heat for 30 minutes, stirring occasionally. If necessary, add a ladle of hot water.
- Serve as an antipasto or *contorno* (side dish).

SKIP TO

CHILE PEPPERS, P. 359; BAGNA CAUDA (GARLIC AND ANCHOVY DIP), P. 119.

LAND OF LEMONS

From Sicily to Liguria to Campania, Italy loves lemons. Going from the orchard to the plate, here's everything about the king of citrus.

ALESSANDRA PIERINI

THE VOYAGE OF THE LEMON

The earliest traces of the lemon date to around 3000 BCE and are thought to occur around Kashmir. From its native Asia, the golden fruit traveled the Silk Road to the Middle East, where it was discovered and cultivated by the Hebrews.

Acclimatized to Mediterranean lands, it then moved to sunny southern Europe. Its presence has been evident in Italy since Roman times. Certain representations of these citrus fruits found in Herculaneum and Pompeii are evidence of this.

Its cultivation disappeared with the fall of the Roman Empire, and it was thanks to the Crusades in the Middle Ages that the lemon arrived in Liguria. In the thirteenth century, the Arabs started growing it in Sicily and the Kingdom of Naples.

- *Citrus limon* -

Lemon (*Citrus limon*) is a citrus fruit.
It is the fruit of the lemon tree belonging to the genus *Citrus* and the family Rutaceae. According to some genetic studies, it is an ancient hybrid, probably of the citron (*Citrus medica*) and bitter orange (*C. aurantium*). But for centuries, the lemon has been an autonomous species that proliferates through seedlings, cutting, or grafting.

EVERY PART OF THE LEMON IS GOOD

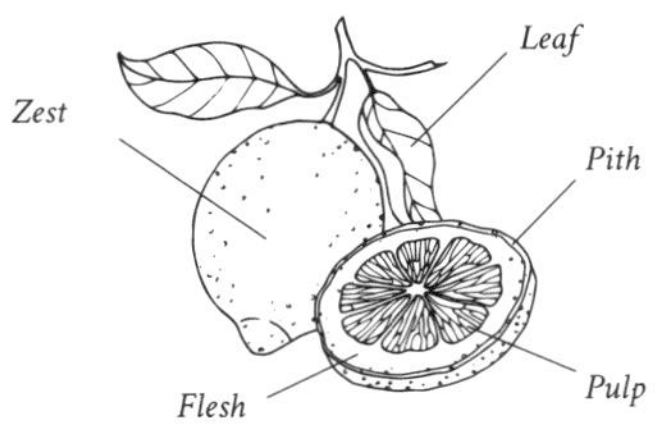

The zest (also called epicarp, flavedo, or *buccia* in Italian) is found on the rind of the lemon. It is the zest that deliciously flavors sweet and savory recipes. It can be dried and crushed to a powder to then use as a spice.

However, you should avoid grating the white membrane called the pith (*albedo* in Italian) just under the zest because of its bitter taste. Nevertheless, the pith can be used to help set jams and preserves. The pulp (*polpa* in Italian) is surrounded by a thin skin called the endocarp, and the juice, *succo*, boosts the flavor of salads, vinaigrette dressings, fish, white meats, cakes, creams, preserves, and dessert gels. The leaves, *foglie*, can be used as an infusion in a broth or as a wrapping for cooking en papillote in the oven.

RECIPES

SPAGHETTI AL LIMONE
(SPAGHETTI WITH LEMON)

If the lemons are good, this is a pure treat in just a few simple steps!

SERVES 2

7 ounces (200 g) spaghetti
2 tablespoons (30 g) unsalted butter
1 unwaxed lemon
2⅛ ounces (60 g) Parmesan cheese
Salt and freshly ground black pepper
A few sprigs flat-leaf parsley or basil, chopped

- In a large pot of salted boiling water, cook the spaghetti al dente.
- Meanwhile, in a large skillet, gently melt the butter. Add 2 tablespoons (30 mL) water and stir gently to combine.
- Zest and juice the lemon (to get about 2 tablespoons/30 mL juice). Reserve the zest.
- Add the lemon juice and the Parmesan to the pan, and stir vigorously to create an emulsion. Season with salt and pepper. Add the zest.
- As soon as the pasta is cooked, drain it and add it to the pan. Stir over medium heat to ensure the pasta is well coated.
- Serve immediately, sprinkled with the chopped fresh herbs.

CREMA AL LIMONE
(LEMON CREAM)

This lemon cream can be used to fill the famous *delizia al limone* of Amalfi or a crostata.

SERVES 2

3 large (150 g) eggs
½ cup plus 1 tablespoon (120 g) superfine sugar
Zest of 3 unwaxed lemons
Juice of 1 lemon
7 tablespoons (100 g) unsalted butter, at room temperature

- In a bowl, beat the eggs and sugar until frothy.
- Add the lemon zest to the egg mixture, then add the lemon juice.
- Scrape the mixture into a saucepan and add the butter.
- While stirring with a whisk, heat over medium heat to melt the butter; the mixture will slowly thicken.
- Bring the mixture just to a boil, then immediately remove the pan from the heat.
- Let cool; it will continue to thicken.

LIMONCELLO
(LEMON LIQUEUR)

The version of this fairly sweet liqueur offered here guarantees an intensely fruity experience!

MAKES 8 CUPS (2 L)

6 plump unwaxed lemons
4 cups (1 L) alcohol (95% ABV)
4 cups (1 L) water
3½ cups (700 g) sugar
. . . a bit of patience

- Wash and dry the lemons. Using a knife, remove the zest (avoiding the white pith) in large strips. Place the zest in a 2-quart glass jar.
- Add the alcohol. Close the lid tightly.
- Shake the jar vigorously, then place it on a shelf in the pantry or cupboard; shake it vigorously once each day.
- After 1 week, place the water and sugar in a saucepan. Bring the mixture to a boil, stirring to dissolve the sugar, then boil for 3 minutes, until syrupy. Remove from the heat and let cool.
- Remove the lemon zest from the jar with the alcohol, then pour the syrup into the jar.
- Using a funnel lined with cheesecloth (to filter out small debris), pour the alcohol-syrup mixture into bottles.
- Tightly close the bottles and set aside for at least 3 weeks.
- Enjoy the limoncello chilled or, even better, over ice.

CANARINO
(LEMON AND BAY TEA)

This excellent herbal tea owes its name to its special canary-yellow color.

SERVES 1

1 cup (250 mL) water
Zest of 1 unwaxed lemon
1 bay leaf

- Combine the water with the lemon zest and bay leaf in a small saucepan. Bring to a rolling boil, and let boil for 5 minutes.
- Enjoy very hot. You can sweeten it with honey, if desired.

SKIP TO
THE SPAGHETTI FAMILY, P. 201; LIQUORI, P. 366; CITRUS, P. 106.

THE BARILLA SAGA

How a small fresh-pasta company goes multinational by mastering the art of advertising.

ILARIA BRUNETTI

FROM 1910 TO THE 1930S
THE CREATION OF THE BRAND

↑ *A boy who breaks a gigantic egg inside a wooden trough*, by sculptor Emilio Trombara, becomes the brand image of the company from its official founding in 1910 until 1936.

↑ The Winged Cook, created in 1926, represents Barilla during the 1930s.

THE 1930S
FAMILY IMAGES WITH FUTURISTIC INFLUENCES

↑ Postcard from 1927: children and their mothers are the targeted consumers of Barilla's products and represent the Barilla image. Images move from photography to graphic art.

↑ "Flying high since 1877": an advertisement created by Carlo Mattioli, with graphics by Giuseppe Venturini. This becomes an important campaign that focuses on the company, not the product. After World War II, supply of the product is difficult and the quality is not the same, but Barilla endures beyond 1947.

1950S
MARKETING

Pietro Barilla, a marketing pioneer in Italy, moves to the United States. Understanding the importance of investing in communication, he entrusts the image of Barilla to Erberto Carboni, a well-respected pioneer of Italian advertising campaigns.

↑ "Pasta for everyone—the 100 best-spent lira of the day," advertisement by Erberto Carboni, 1959.

↑ "Barilla, real egg pasta," by Erberto Carboni in 1953.

1960S
A CHANGING SOCIETY

↑ Pietro Barilla himself hires the singer Mina for the *Carosello* in 1965. This collaboration would last until the 1970s.

↑ "There's a great cook inside you . . . and Barilla reveals it," 1965. A new marketing strategy: the woman, now emancipated from the home, cooks freely and for pleasure.

1970S

THE AMERICAN DECADE

Between 1971 and 1979, the large American multinational company W. R. Grace becomes the majority shareholder of Barilla.

← The first example of comparative advertising (1974–1978): after the Arab-Israeli war of October 1973 and the resulting inflation, the Italian government set a ceiling on the price of pasta; many producers adapted by lowering their pasta quality. Barilla reacts with a forceful campaign: "Barilla defends quality. Here's the proof."

FROM THE 1980S TO 2000

PIETRO BARILLA TAKES OVER THE COMPANY AGAIN

The company invests in acquiring new establishments and significantly increases the budget for advertising. Barilla begins to grow rapidly.

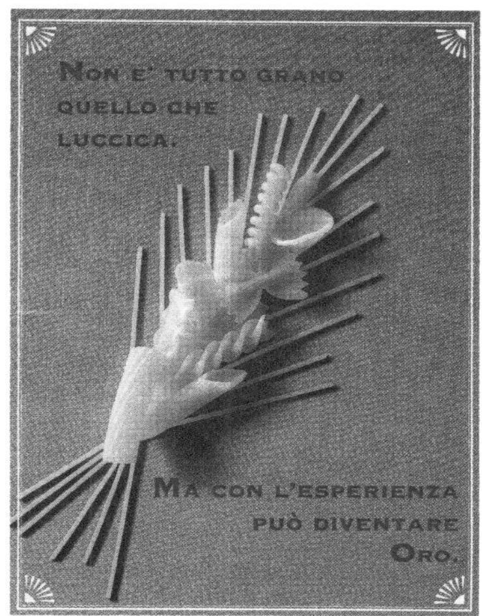

↑ Launch of the Selezione Oro product line in 1996: twenty-five pasta formats produced with the best blends of durum wheat, sold in packages designed by Gio' Rossi.

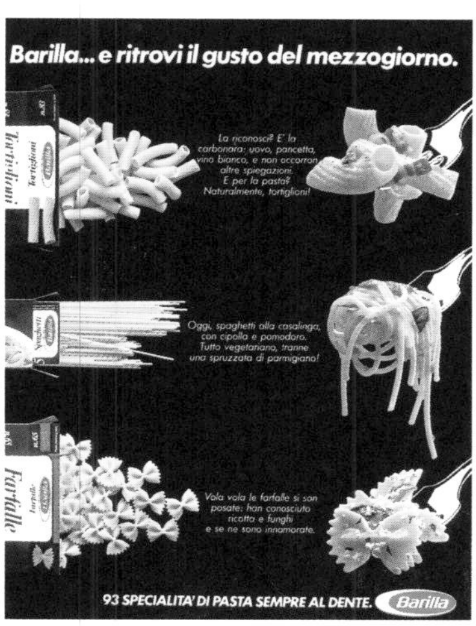

↑ "Rediscover the taste of the south" campaign from 1982, which launched special pasta formats.

↑ Pietro Barilla commissions the famous director Federico Fellini for a television commercial. This gives birth in 1984 to the campaign "High society," nicknamed "Rigatoni," where an elegant woman sitting in a high-end restaurant orders rigatoni after the waiter describes a long list of very refined French dishes.

↑ "*Dove c'è Barilla c'è casa*" ("Where you find Barilla, you find home") is created by ad agency Young & Rubicam in 1985. It launches now famous television spots and many posters. Shown here are images by Chris Broadbent, inspired by Caravaggio's *Basket of Fruit.*

A FAMILY HISTORY

1877

Pietro Barilla opens a small bakery selling fresh egg pasta in Parma's town center.

1910

His sons Riccardo and Gualtiero buy an establishment outside the city and ramp up production. They register the name of the Barilla brand.

1947

Pietro and Gianni, sons of Riccardo, invest in production technology.

1952

They stop producing bread in order to devote themselves to egg and durum wheat pasta; for the first time, pasta is sold packaged in cardboard boxes rather than in bulk.

1969

Barilla is the largest pasta producer in the world.

1971

The company passes into the hands of the US-based giant W. R. Grace.

1975

Barilla creates the Mulino Bianco brand, which produces breads and cakes.

1979

Pietro Barilla buys back the company from W. R. Grace.

2000

Barilla is a multinational company with many brands (Wasa, Harry's . . .) and the leader in pasta production in the US. Pietro's sons, Guido, Paolo, and Luca, are the fifth generation to run the company.

THE EVOLUTION OF THE LOGO

1908	BARILLA 1910	BARILLA 1916	BARILLA 1922
Barilla 1927	Barilla 1929	Barilla 1930	Barilla 1931
Barilla 1934	Barilla 1937	Barilla 1939	Barilla 1948
Barilla 1948	Barilla 1952	Barilla 1956	Barilla 1969
Barilla 1996	Barilla 2000	Barilla 2020	

SKIP TO
THE SPAGHETTI FAMILY, P. 201;
THE TASTE OF SHAPE, P. 317.

SEASON

TUTTO L'ANNO (YEAR-ROUND)

CATEGORY

ANTIPASTO, SECONDO PIATTO (APPETIZER/MAIN COURSE)

LEVEL

FACILE (EASY)

FRITTATA

This cousin of the omelet can be enjoyed seasoned simply with salt and pepper or enriched with added vegetables, meats, or cheeses. Over the centuries, it has served as an indispensable source of protein in everyday Italian cuisine.

NADIA POSTIGLIONE

A LONG HISTORY

From the Latin *frictus/frixus* (fried), the frittata is popular throughout the Mediterranean region. Eggs beaten and fried in oil, seasoned in various ways, already existed in Roman times, although some claim it originated with the Arabs. In *De re coquinaria*, the Roman cook Apicius offers as an appetizer a frittata prepared with garum (a condiment made from fermented fish) and wine, and he includes other recipes with elderflower, lettuce, or honey.

AS A SANDWICH

The omelet sandwich is a true Italian gastronomic totem. Although once considered a meal of Italian laborers who carried them in their bags, it's now a snack for picnics in the countryside or on the go.

A gesture that causes debate

Flipping the frittata over in the pan is a distinctive and "natural" approach for the Italians. This sets the frittata apart from the omelet, which is folded when cooked. In the past, however, the directions for frittata recipes differed. Culinary writers Maestro Martino and Pellegrino Artusi, for example, recommended cooking it on one side only.

UNIQUE OMELETS

→ *Filoscio*, from French *filoche* (a large-mesh fabric), is a classic of Neapolitan cuisine. A testament to French influence, it is not flipped in the pan like the classic frittata but instead folded over. What makes it unique? Its *fior di latte* (a cow's-milk mozzarella) filling from Agerola.

→ The *frittata di scàmmaro*, common during Neapolitan Lent, is an egg-free omelet made with vermicelli, anchovies, and olives.

→ In Abruzzo, the eve of Easter is celebrated with *zuppa imperiale abruzzese* (Abruzzo imperial soup) made of cubed pieces of omelet flavored with cinnamon and served in a capon broth.

FRITTATA ALLE ZUCCHINE

This zucchini omelet is an ideal *secondo piatto* (main course) for the summer, and even more delicious accompanied by a salad of tomatoes and mozzarella.

SERVES 4

3 medium zucchini
1 clove garlic, peeled
Scant ½ cup (100 mL) olive oil
6 medium (264 g) eggs
10 basil leaves, chopped
Salt and freshly ground black pepper

· Wash and dry the zucchini. Cut them into ⅓- to ¾-inch (1 to 2 cm) cubes. In a skillet, heat the garlic with a scant ¼ cup (50 mL) of the olive oil. Add the zucchini cubes and brown them. Set aside, leaving the oil in the pan; remove the garlic.

· Beat the eggs in a bowl. Stir in the cooked zucchini and basil. Season with salt and pepper. Add the remaining scant ¼ cup (50 mL) oil to the pan and heat until warm. Spread the zucchini mixture evenly in the pan. Cook for 5 minutes, cover, and cook over low heat for another 5 minutes, stirring occasionally. When the bottom is golden brown, place a flat plate on top of the pan and quickly flip the omelet upside down. Return the pan to the heat, add more oil if necessary, and slide the omelet back into the pan. Cook over low heat for 8 to 10 minutes, until golden brown.

A THOUSAND AND ONE *FRITTATE*

WITH VEGETABLES

Con le cipolle—with onions (throughout Italy)

Con carciofi di Albenga, o le bietole—with artichokes from Albenga, or with chard (Liguria)

Affogata, con i pomodorini—"drowned," with tomatoes (Tuscany)

Con le favette—with beans (Sardinia)

Con il silene o i bruscandoli—with campion or hop shoots (Friuli and Veneto)

Con gli asparagi—with asparagus (throughout Italy)

Con i fiori di zucca—with zucchini blossoms (Veneto)

Con la menta o i lampascioni—with mint or tassel hyacinth (Apulia)

WITH MEAT

Rognosa—with salami or sausage (northern Italy)

Con gli zoccoli—"with hooves," with pancetta (Tuscany)

Di Pasqua—Easter, with lamb's liver and pecorino (Molise)

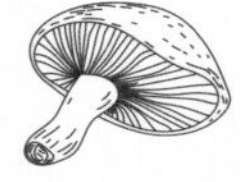

WITH MUSHROOMS AND TRUFFLES

Con i tartufi neri—with black truffle (Umbria)

Con i funghi prugnoli—with St. George's mushroom (Emilia-Romagna)

WITH FISH

Di gianchetti—with anchovy fry (Liguria)

Di uomini nudi—with sardine fry (Emilia-Romagna)

Di moeche—with molting green crabs (Veneto)

WITH CHEESE

Con mozzarella o ricotta—with mozzarella or ricotta (southern Italy)

SKIP TO

ZUCCHINI, P. 234; CICCHETTI VENEZIANI (VENETIAN SNACKS), P. 228; ASPARAGUS, P. 208.

PEARS

Italy claims an impressive 17 percent of the world's production and 30 percent of European production of *pere*, and they aren't just for dessert!

ALESSANDRA PIERINI

WHAT AM I?

SCIENTIFIC NAME

Pyrus communis.

FAMILY

Rosaceae.

GEOGRAPHIC ORIGIN

Originating from Asia Minor and Central Europe, the *pera* (pear) is a typical Mediterranean fruit enjoyed as far back as ancient Rome, where it was eaten raw or cooked in wine.

PRODUCTION

Half of the country's pear production is concentrated in northern Italy and Emilia-Romagna. The Pera dell'Emilia-Romagna and the Pera Mantovana (Lombardy) are among the common varietals, Conferenza, Decana, Kaiser, Max Red Bartlett, William, and—uniquely in Emilia-Romagna—Cascade, Passa Crassana, Santa Maria, and Carmen all benefit from PGI designation.

SLOW FOOD SENTINELS

→ Signora della Valle del Sinni (Basilicata) is a small yellow pear with delicate and fragrant white flesh. It's a great option for syrup, made into preserves, or dehydrated. It's harvested in July.

→ Cocomerina dell'alta Valle del Savio (Emilia-Romagna) is a very small pear with thick greenish-brown skin. It's also called Pera Cocomera (watermelon pear) for its intense pinkish-red flesh. It's sweet and fragrant, perfect for preserving in syrup or made into preserves. The early one is harvested at the end of August, the late one at the end of October in the Apennines of Cesena.

① ABATE

ORIGIN—Emilia-Romagna, Veneto.

APPEARANCE—white flesh, firm, grainy, sweet, juicy, and very aromatic.

HARVESTING—September–October.

IN COOKING—*crostate* (tarts); risottos with Gorgonzola or speck and Taleggio; fruit salads; enjoyed raw.

② DECANA DEL COMIZIO

ORIGIN—Emilia-Romagna, Lombardy.

APPEARANCE—soft, delicate, tasty, juicy, and compact flesh.

HARVESTING—September–October.

IN COOKING—it holds together perfectly when cooked; pressed for juice; preserves; tarts and pies; in syrup; baked; grilled; risottos; enjoyed raw.

③ CONFERENZA

ORIGIN—Emilia-Romagna, Lombardy.

APPEARANCE—juicy, melting, intense, fragrant, and slightly tart flesh.

HARVESTING—September–November.

IN COOKING—in filling for ravioli with pecorino cheese, with a carpaccio of bresaola and Parmesan cheese; chocolate cakes, tarts and pies; wine; in a compote.

④ MARTIN SEC OR MARTINA

ORIGIN—Piedmont Ark of Taste Slow Food.

APPEARANCE—yellowish, sweet, slightly astringent, not very juicy, and grainy flesh.

HARVESTING—mid-October–November.

IN COOKING—considered the best pear for cooking; *timballo* (similar to strudel); *cugnà* (grape-based condiment); preserves; tarts and pies; in spiced red wine, grappa; grilled; poached.

⑤ KAISER

ORIGIN—Emilia-Romagna, Lombardy.

APPEARANCE—white, slightly grainy, compact, crunchy, very aromatic, and sweet flesh.

HARVESTING—mid-September.

IN COOKING—it holds up well to cooking, baked with goat cheese, Taleggio or robiola, pies with Fontina and sage; in salad with shrimp, octopus, and walnuts; preserved; enjoyed raw.

⑥ BUTIRRA PRECOCE MORETTINI

ORIGIN—Emilia-Romagna, Marche.

APPEARANCE—juicy, fruity, sweet, and tender flesh.

HARVESTING—July.

IN COOKING—with charcuterie or cheeses; preserves; for juicing; enjoyed raw.

⑦ SUPERTINO

ORIGIN—Piedmont.

APPEARANCE—whitish flesh, quite delicate, slightly grainy, moderately firm, tasty, slightly aromatic.

HARVESTING—November–February.

IN COOKING—in a salad with fennel, walnuts, and pomegranate; in syrup with thyme; cooked in Alkermes liqueur, poached.

⑧ COSCIA OR COSCIA DI MONACA ("nun's thigh")

ORIGIN—Tuscany, Sicily.

APPEARANCE—white, melting, soft, juicy, and grainy flesh.

HARVESTING—July–September.

IN COOKING—with red wine; tarts and pies; in salads with spelt and barley, with ripened cheeses.

⑨ ANGELICA

ORIGIN—Emilia-Romagna, Marche.

APPEARANCE—medium to small in size, in the shape of an upside-down heart; green-yellow skin turning to red; juicy, sweet-sour, and firm flesh.

HARVESTING—September.

IN COOKING—with charcuterie; in grain-based salads; preserves, syrup, grappa.

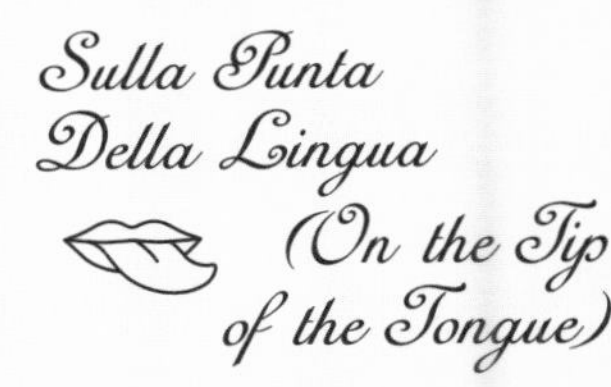

"Al contadino non far sapere quanto è buono il cacio con le pere" (literally, "Don't tell the farmer how good cheese is with pears"): Don't spread the secret.

SKIP TO

ITALY'S BEAUTIFUL CHEESES, P. 222; CROSTATA ALLA CONFETTURA, P. 66.

SEASON
TUTTO L'ANNO (YEAR-ROUND)

CATEGORY
SECONDO PIATTO (MAIN COURSE)

LEVEL
DIFFICILE (DIFFICULT)

BOLLITO MISTO

MIXED MEAT STEW

PIEDMONT, LOMBARDY, VENETO, EMILIA-ROMAGNA

This hearty meat stew of complex origins has spanned the history of Italian cuisine to become a popular dish among large families.

GIORGIA CANNARELLA

ITS ORIGINS

The regions of Piedmont, Lombardy, Veneto, and Emilia-Romagna each has its own recipe for stews made of slow-boiled, less noble cuts of meats. This dish is often associated with the centuries-old tradition of Piedmontese cattle markets, and the *gran bollito misto piemontese* is considered the most complex in terms of meat varieties and preparation.

At the beginning of the twentieth century, the dish had conquered all of Italy. It is said to be the favorite dish of Count di Cavour (the father of Italian unity) and Victor Emmanuel II (the first king of a united Italy).

THE *BOLLITI* CART

In restaurants, guests choose their desired pieces and sauces brought to the table by cart. At the end of the meal, it is customary to drink a cup of the cooking broth diluted with red wine.

THE RECIPE

For a simplified version of this Piedmontese recipe, opt for five meats and three sauces. This recipe is approximated for a large table of guests. Cooking times will need to be adjusted according to the meats and quantities selected.

SERVES 8 TO 10

- 1 bunch parsley
- 3 or 4 sprigs rosemary
- 3 onions
- 3 stalks celery
- 3 cloves garlic, peeled
- 1⅛ pounds (500 g) beef flank
- 1⅛ pounds (500 g) beef plate
- 1⅛ pounds (500 g) beef tail
- 1⅛ pounds (500 g) beef tongue
- 1⅛ pounds (500 g) veal's head
- ½ capon or hen, ready to cook
- 1 small (about 1½ pounds/700 g) *cotechino* (an Italian pork sausage)
- Coarse salt and freshly ground black pepper

Place one-third of each of the herbs and vegetables in a large pot of cold water, bring to a boil, and cook for 15 minutes.

Add the beef flank, plate, and tail to the pot. Bring to a boil and cook over high heat for 15 minutes. Reduce the heat to low and cook for 3 hours. Skim off any impurities from the surface from time to time.

If some pieces are done earlier than this, remove them and set them aside in a double boiler to keep warm. In a separate large pot, repeat these same steps with another one-third of the herbs and vegetables, adding the beef tongue and veal head, and cook for 1 hour 30 minutes. In a third pot, cook the poultry with the remaining herbs and vegetables for 1 hour 30 minutes. In a fourth pot, boil the cotechino, wrapped in a tied kitchen towel, for 2 hours. Reserve all the cooked meats in their pots until ready to serve.

Serve the meat with a ladle of hot broth, the sauces, the vegetables used for cooking, as well as other accompaniments such as spinach cooked in butter, boiled potatoes, sautéed mushrooms, and sweet-and-sour onions.

GRAN BOLLITO MISTO PIEMONTESE

The preparation for this version follows "the rule of seven" to guarantee a balance of flavors and a diversity of ingredients. Some go so far as to serve it with seven sides.

<u>Seven pieces of beef</u>

Rib, belly, neck, top blade or upper shoulder, bottom sirloin/flank, plate, coulotte (top sirloin cuts).

<u>Seven accompaniments and cheaper cuts</u>

Chicken, outer part of the beef head, veal shank, beef tongue, beef loin, tail, cotechino (a slow-cooking Italian pork sausage).

<u>Seven sauces</u>

A rich green sauce, rustic green sauce, red sauce, horseradish sauce, *mostarda* (sweet-and-sour condiment made from fruit), honey sauce, *cugnà* sauce (a sweet preparation made from grape must, with pears and apples and possibly other fruits).

SKIP TO
MOSTARDA, P. 377.

RED SAUCE

Peel and roughly chop 2¼ pounds (1 kg) tomatoes. Chop 1 onion, 1 carrot, ½ red bell pepper, 1 celery stalk, 1 sprig rosemary, and 2 cloves garlic. In a pan, combine all the ingredients and cook for 2 to 3 hours over very low heat. Season with salt and pepper. Add a little sugar for some sweetness. Process all the ingredients through a food mill. Add about a scant ½ cup (100 mL) olive oil and a pinch of chile powder or chile flakes, if desired. Stir to combine, then boil again for several minutes. Let the sauce rest before serving.

HORSERADISH SAUCE

Wash and peel 7 ounces (200 g) fresh horseradish. Grate it and combine it in a bowl with 1 tablespoon (15 mL) olive oil and ½ cup (118 mL) vinegar. Serve cold.

RUSTIC GREEN SAUCE

Using a blender (or a mortar), blend or grind 1 bunch parsley, 2 salted anchovies, 1 cup (100 g) dried bread crumbs soaked in a scant ½ cup (100 mL) wine vinegar, 2 cloves garlic, and some salt. While blending, add about a scant ½ cup (100 mL) olive oil and blend to obtain a smooth consistency. Finish by incorporating the juice of ½ lemon.

CHILE PEPPERS

The chile pepper arrived in Italy from America and at the time was considered the pepper of the poor. Today the *peperoncino* ignites the palate and provides an unexpected element to any dish.

JULIA SAMMUT*

**Gourmand grocer, explorer, seeker of products with a strong culinary identity, and managing chef of L'Idéal, a food market–restaurant located at 11, rue d'Aubagne in Marseille.*

Discovery

Originally from Central America and well known to pre-Columbian civilizations as *axi'*, the chile (*Capsicum*) arrived in Europe in 1493, brought back by Christopher Columbus. This was a very different path to Europe than that taken by other aristocratic and expensive spices from the East. The botanist Diego Alvarez Chanca started cultivating the chile in Spain in 1494, and it was introduced into Calabria during the sixteenth century.

IN COOKING

→ The chile can be eaten fresh (July to September) ① or dried ②; when dried, it is much stronger, and it can also be crushed ③ and ground to a powder ④. It is eaten raw, *sott'olio* (in oil), or incorporated into spicy creams or charcuteries (*'nduja, salsiccia,* soppressata, or Calabrian *spianata*).

→ It flavors pasta sauces such as *arrabbiata* or *aglio, olio e peperoncino.*

→ Infused in olive oil, it is called *olio santo* (holy oil) in Sicily, a devilishly spicy infusion that enlivens pizzas or is drizzled in dishes before serving ⑤.

→ When sun-dried then crushed and mixed with olive oil ⑥, it makes a *piccantissima* (terribly spicy) sauce to spread on a sandwich or to spice up *bruschette*, stews, or meats. It's for the brave!

→ When chopped with onions, sun-dried tomatoes, olives, or mushrooms in a *calabrese bomba* (Calabrian bomb), it used as a spread on toast.

→ It can be used on cheeses, with tomatoes, eggplant, potatoes, seafood, anchovies, and . . . dark chocolate.

One pepper, several names

Originally called *pepe* or *pepe d'India* (Indian pepper), it took the name of *peperone* (sweet pepper) starting in the eighteenth century. Since the middle of the nineteenth century, only the mild and large variety goes by this name.

The smallest and spicier pepper became the *peperoncino.*

A TRICKY NAME: in Tuscany, the chile is called *zenzero* (ginger).

LUCKY CHARM

In Naples, it is called *cornicello* or *curniciello* ("horn of luck"), worn as a pendant in the shape of a red pepper believed to ward off the evil eye.

SPICE OF THE POOR

1635

The first mention of this beneficial ingredient is in Tommaso Campanella's *Medicinalium iuxta propria principia.*

NINETEENTH CENTURY

The distribution of the chile in the kitchens of the working classes of the south goes by the name *lardo della povera gente* ("bacon of the poor," according to the Calabrian writer Vincenzo Padula) for its use as a spice, preservative of perishable foods, and a form of bartering.

TWENTIETH CENTURY

It gains gastronomic recognition after being used in a Futurism dinner held in 1931.

THE SOUTH: INSTANT *AMORE*

Capsicum annuum is the only species cultivated in Italy and more particularly in Basilicata and Calabria where, in 1994, the Accademia Italiana del Peperoncino was born. Its taste is aromatic and fruity, with a low to medium intensity of spiciness, depending on the cultivar.

The most popular varietals are:

Abbreviatum (or *diavolicchio*, "little devil," small, cone-shaped), the spiciest.

Acuminatum (or "Calabrian horn," in the shape of an elongated and curved cone), used especially when fresh.

Fasciculatum (narrow and straight, called a "cigarette"), dried or preserved.

Cerasiferum (small and round like a cherry), used in fillings.

SKIP TO
PENNE ALL'ARRABBIATA, P. 252; PEPPERS, P. 351; SPREADABLE SAUSAGES, P. 347; SPAGHETTI AGLIO, OLIO E PEPERONCINO (SPAGHETTI WITH GARLIC, OLIVE OIL, AND CHILE), P. 193.

Despite the Turkish or Persian origin of its name, *caviale* (caviar) has ancient roots in Europe. Italy has even made a specialty of these salt-cured sturgeon's eggs.

JACQUES BRUNEL

A SALTY STORY

At the banquets of the ancient Egyptians and Phoenicians, salted fish roe (especially those of sturgeon and mullet) were served to distinguished guests as early as 2400 BCE.

In the fifteenth century, the eggs of sturgeons taken from the Po River were prized by doges and popes, for whom the writer Bartolomeo Sacchi recorded the first known recipe for caviar in 1475. Leonardo da Vinci is said to have given this "ultimate sophistication" to Beatrice d'Este in a coffer encrusted with precious stones as a wedding gift. Caviar itself is a real gem!

The three species of sturgeon present in almost all the rivers of Italy (cobice [Adriatic], common, and beluga) gradually became scarcer due to overfishing, development, and pollution. At the end of 1970, a reduction in the supply of caviar from the East, which was impacted by poaching, prompted Lombard fish farmers to revive Italy's output.

A REVIVED RECIPE

Starting from the time of the Renaissance, *caviaro* from the Po was a specialty of the city of Ferrara. Cristoforo da Messisbugo, the Italian Renaissance chef, indicated how to salt and cook it. In the 1930s, the recipe was brilliantly interpreted by Nuta Ascoli, a grocer from the Jewish ghetto. She was killed in 1941 before passing on her recipe. The caviar of Messisbugo is now being produced again by a few artisans. This cooked caviar is lightly salted and preserved in a very delicate oil.

THE MARRIAGE OF CAVIAR, BY MASSIMO MORI

Manager of the Armani Caffè in Paris and the Mori Venice Bar, this Veneto-born gastronome enjoys caviar served as a canapé (*tramezzino*) with a mayonnaise made from mild lemon from Lake Garda and a glass of the noble Franciacorta sparkling wine.

OR PAIRED WITH:

→ Polenta, fried or grilled, risotto, or gnocchi.

→ Sole, as served in luxury hotels, cod, or a sturgeon tartare with white asparagus and citrus.

→ White beans or celery, reduced or not, in cream, salsify, wild asparagus, *agretti* (monk's beard).

→ Sweetbreads or veal kidneys, chicken gizzards.

RECIPE

SPAGHETTI AL CAVIALE DE GUALTIERO MARCHESI (GUALTIERO MARCHESI'S SPAGHETTI WITH CAVIAR)

This is one of the signature dishes of the great Italian chef from Milan. The spaghetti is served as a salad (that is to say, cold), because the delicacy of the caviar would not tolerate heat.

SERVES 4

3½ ounces (100 g) very thin spaghetti
Salt and freshly ground black pepper
Scant ¼ cup (50 mL) extra-virgin olive oil
Juice of ½ lemon
¼ cup (10 g) chopped chives
¾ ounce (20 g) caviar
⅛ ounce (5 g) shallot, finely chopped

· Cook the spaghetti in salted boiling water. Drain and let cool. Divide the spaghetti among serving bowls. Season with salt and pepper. Top with a drizzle of olive oil and a few drops of lemon juice.

· Sprinkle each serving with some chives, place a spoonful of caviar in the center, and finish with a pinch of shallot on the caviar.

TOP ASSETS

→ Italy has become the second largest producer of caviar in the world, with 53 tons in 2019 (25 million euros in turnover), ahead of Iran and Russia, but behind China (which produces three times more).

→ Eighty percent of Italian caviar is exported (to Europe, America, Arab countries, and even to the Kremlin in Russia). Its quality and almost fruity finesse make it the chosen caviar of airlines.

→ Resulting from state-of-the-art fish farming, Italian caviar is produced exclusively in the north (Piedmont, Veneto, Trentino-Alto Adige, etc.) from noble species (beluga, sevruga, osetra, etc.), and mainly in Lombardy under the brand Calvisius. A pioneer in the Italian revival of caviar, Calvisius remains the absolute leader and accounts for 20 percent of world production.

SKIP TO
FISH, P. 300;
GUALTIERO MARCHESI, P. 163;
TRAMEZZINO, P. 319.

SEASON
TUTTO L'ANNO (YEAR-ROUND)

CATEGORY
PRIMO PIATTO (FIRST COURSE)

LEVEL
DIFFICOLTÀ MEDIA (MEDIUM DIFFICULTY)

LINGUINE AL NERO DI SEPPIA

CUTTLEFISH INK LINGUINE

Although the cuttlefish may use its ink as a way to escape its enemies, the Italians love it as a unique ingredient combined with pasta. It's a simple yet memorable dish!

ILARIA BRUNETTI

THE INK

Nero di seppia (cuttlefish ink) is the liquid contained in a sac located between the gills of the cuttlefish. The animal ejects the ink to repel its predators. Used in food since the time of the ancient Greeks and Romans (Apicius provides three recipes for cuttlefish cooked in its ink in his fourth-century recipe collection *De re coquinaria*), the ink was also used for dyeing fabrics and for writing. Today it is especially popular in Spain and Italy, where it colors fresh pasta, especially linguine, and is used in a sauce in which the cuttlefish are cooked.

ONE DISH, TWO ORIGINS

Present throughout Italy's coastal regions, cuttlefish ink pasta is an especially important part of the cuisine of Venice and Sicily: in spaghetti or linguine in the south, or for linguine or *bigoli* around Venice.

Black and white

The ingredient also goes well with rice. In Venice, you can feast on *risotto al nero*. In Sicily, *ripiddu nivicatu* ("snowy volcano" in the local dialect) is a popular dish created about fifty years ago in Catania in homage to Mount Etna: a cone (the "volcano") of black rice is topped with a dollop of ricotta (the "snow") and filled with a tomato sauce (the "lava").

VARIATIONS

→ In Venice, it is also found without tomato sauce.

→ In Sicily, fresh tomatoes may be added.

INNOVATION

→ *Treppia*: this now classic contemporary interpretation has left its mark on the Parisian dining scene. Cuttlefish ink tripe (*trippe + seppia = treppia*) was created in 2014 by Roman chef Giovanni Passerini in his former gourmet bistro Rino.

THE RECIPE

Here is the Venetian version, enlivened with a hint of chile pepper, by chef Eleonora Zuliani of restaurant Il Bacaro (Paris 11th).

SERVES 4

- 2¼ pounds (1 kg) cuttlefish (preferably large) with ink
- ½ bunch flat-leaf parsley
- 2 white onions (approximately 9 ounces/250 g)
- 2 cloves garlic, peeled
- ¼ cup (60 mL) olive oil, plus more for drizzling
- Scant ½ cup (100 mL) dry white wine
- ⅔ cup (150 mL) tomato sauce
- 1 pinch ground chile
- Salt
- 14 ounces (400 g) linguine
- Freshly ground black pepper

Using a knife or kitchen shears, slice open the belly of the cuttlefish to extract the central cuttlebone. Open the membrane to release the ink sac: take it by the end attached to the body, pull it out gently to prevent tearing it, and rinse it. Place it in the refrigerator.

Separate the body from the head, remove the beak located between the tentacles, and remove the eyes and entrails. Place the cuttlefish on a board and, using a paper towel for gripping, pull the skin from the body and the side wings. Rinse the body, then cut it into ⅔-inch (1.5 cm) cubes. Place it in the refrigerator.

Wash and dry the parsley. Finely chop the onions and garlic.

Heat the olive oil in a large pot. Add the onions and garlic and cook until lightly browned. Add the cuttlefish pieces and sear for 5 minutes while stirring. Add the white wine, then half the parsley (with its stems), the tomato sauce, chile, and a scant ½ cup (100 mL) water. Season with salt and stir well to combine. Cook for 45 minutes over low heat, adding more water if necessary. Add the contents of the ink sac, then cook for another 5 minutes. Taste and season again with salt, if necessary. Remove the parsley stems and set the mixture aside to keep warm.

Cook the linguine in a pot of salted boiling water until al dente, then drain well. Add the linguine to the pot with the sauce; stir to combine. Add a drizzle of olive oil. Stir again.

Chop the remaining parsley leaves. Arrange the linguine on serving plates, sprinkle with the chopped parsley, and season with pepper.

Il Tocco Della Chef (Chef's Tip)

For a twist on this traditional recipe, Eleonora likes to add 1 teaspoon (2 g) fennel seeds to the sauce, as she learned from a Sardinian chef.

IN CASE OF ACCIDENT

If you accidentally puncture the ink sac while detaching it from the cuttlefish, you can use the contents of four single-dose packets of store-bought cuttlefish ink in its place, but they will not have as much flavor.

A DRESS CODE

Wearing a black dress or a large black bib is strongly recommended; a white shirt is not a good idea. It is difficult, if not impossible, to remove ink stains . . .

SKIP TO
CALAMARI, P. 242;
TRIPPA ALLA ROMANA (ROMAN-STYLE TRIPE), P. 380.

SUPPLÌ VS. ARANCINI

It's Rome versus Sicily! When rice gets rolled into balls, it's a "food fight" of delicious proportions.

FRANÇOIS-RÉGIS GAUDRY

SUPPLÌ—ROME

RECIPE

SUPPLÌ

Manning the ovens at Supplizio (Via dei Banchi Vecchi 143, Rome), Arcangelo Dandini is the Roman emperor of *supplì*. Here is his classic (and stringy!) recipe.

SERVES 6 (ABOUT 15 SUPPLÌ)

2 quarts (2 L) tomato purée (*passata*)
Salt
Olive oil
½ stalk celery, finely chopped
¼ white onion, finely chopped
2 pinches fennel seeds
3½ ounces (100 g) chicken livers, finely chopped
10½ ounces (300 g) sausage meat
1⅓ cups (250 g) carnaroli rice
¾ cup plus 2 tablespoons (80 g) grated Parmesan cheese
2 sprigs basil, coarsely chopped
1 *fior di latte* mozzarella (4½ ounces/125 g), well drained
High-heat oil, for frying
Flour
2 large (100 g) eggs
2 cups (200 g) dried bread crumbs

- In a large saucepan or skillet, cook the tomato purée for about 30 minutes over medium heat. Add 3 pinches of salt.
- In a separate large saucepan, heat 2 tablespoons (30 mL) olive oil over medium heat. Add the celery and onion and cook until softened. Add 2 pinches of salt, the fennel seeds, and the chicken livers and cook for 15 minutes. Stir in the sausage meat until thoroughly combined and cook for an additional 15 minutes. Add the tomato sauce, then the rice, and cook for 16 minutes.
- Turn off the heat, stir in ¾ cup (70 g) of the Parmesan and the basil, and season with salt.
- Keep the saucepan covered for 2 minutes, then stir to combine. Let cool.
- Cut the mozzarella into cubes. As soon as the rice mixture has cooled, scoop up a few tablespoons of it (about the size of a chicken egg), insert a piece of mozzarella in the center, then, using your hands, mold the rice into an egg shape to enclose the mozzarella.
- Place some flour on a plate. In a shallow bowl, lightly beat the eggs. Season the eggs with salt, add the remaining 2 tablespoons (10 g) Parmesan, and stir to combine. On a second plate, place the bread crumbs.
- In a heavy pan, heat 1 to 2 inches (3 to 5 cm) of oil to 338°F (170°C). Meanwhile, roll the rice balls in the flour to coat them, quickly dunk them in the egg mixture to coat evenly, then dredge them in the bread crumbs to fully coat them. Fry them in the hot oil for 4 minutes, or until golden. Serve hot.

ORIGIN OF THE NAME: derived from the French *surprise* (surprise) and probably dating from the Napoleonic era, the name is a reference to the stringy center of mozzarella hidden in the center . . .

HISTORY: supplì have been a rustic street food in Rome since the beginning of the nineteenth century during fairs and popular events. The first written testimony of them dates back to 1847, when the reference appeared on the menu of the Trattoria della Lepre in Rome, under the name *soplis di riso*.

SIZE: a cylinder 2 to 2⅓ inches (5 to 6 cm) in length, slightly flattened into an egg shape.

STATUS: served as an *aperitivo* (aperitif) or a *cibo di strada* (street food). Sold in the windows of *rosticcerie* (casual establishments focusing on roasted meats) and *tavole calde* (selling cooked foods).

ORIGINAL RECIPE

***Supplì al telefono*:** a cooked-rice croquette (traditionally using rice made the day before) cooked with a minced meat ragout (originally made with chicken offal), Pecorino Romano cheese, egg, and stuffed with a piece of mozzarella. It is breaded with egg and bread crumbs, then fried, and eaten very hot to reveal the stringy and stretchy mozzarella inside, which is thought to resemble the long stretchy cord of old telephones.

RICE TYPE: carnaroli, Arborio, Vialone Nano, originario . . .

FRYING FAT: peanut oil or other vegetable oil.

VARIATION: vegetarian, with tomato; *cacio e pepe*; carbonara . . .

POPULARITY: a recipe representing Roman pride, supplì play a role in the film *La Forza del passato* by Piergiorgio Gay (2002): the stressed Bogliasco lashes out, indecently swallowing up a bunch of supplì, in praise of rosticcerie.

Sulla Punta Della Lingua (On the Tip of the Tongue)

In the Catania region, people make fun of a plump and stout person by calling him *arancinu che 'peri* (*arancino con i piedi*), an "arancino with feet."

ARANCINO/ARANCINA—SICILY

ORIGIN OF THE NAME: in Palermo, Ragusa, Syracuse, and on the west of the island, it is a term whose spelling is represented in the grammatically feminine form *arancina* because the name derives from the word for orange (also grammatically feminine) in Italian, or *arancia*. In Catania and the eastern part of the island, the word *orange* in Sicilian (*arànciu*) is masculine and results in *arancinu*, the masculine form of the word, becoming therefore the masculine form of the word in Italian, or *arancino*.

ITS HISTORY: there are two theories:

→ The arancino dates back to Muslim rule in Sicily (ninth and eleventh centuries). The Arabs used the palm of the hand to shape saffron rice with lamb meat. Because of the saffron, the arancino appeared orange in color.

→ The arancino was a sweet dish prepared for the feast of Santa Lucia to commemorate the landing in Syracuse of a ship loaded with wheat on December 13, 1646, ending a long period of famine. In order to immediately consume the wheat (not ground but instead boiled), a dessert called *cuccì* was created, made of whole wheat grains, honey, and ricotta. The arancino therefore became a transportable version of this dessert, and one in which the wheat was eventually replaced with rice.

SIZE: a ball 3 to 4 inches (8 to 10 cm) in diameter, rounded in shape in Palermo and western Sicily. In Catania, it takes on a conical shape, with reference to Mount Etna.

STATUS: served as main course or cibo di strada today, although it is assumed that, like many breaded dishes, it was a meal to take on the go by field workers or hunters. Today it is sold on every street corner and in rosticcerie.

ORIGINAL RECIPE

Arancino al ragù: a saffron rice ball filled with a meat and tomato sauce, peas, sometimes diced hams, *caciocavallo* cheese, and/or mozzarella. There is no egg in the breading. Over time, the arancino has become a way for households to recycle leftover risotto.

RICE TYPE: Roma, originario, carnaroli, Arborio . . .

FRYING FAT: originally olive oil, but frequently replaced with peanut oil or vegetable oil.

VARIATION: *al burro* (in butter, with ham, mozzarella, and often béchamel sauce); *spinaci* (with spinach); *sarde e finocchietto* (sardines and wild fennel, in Palermo); *alla norma* or *alla catanese* (with fried eggplant, ricotta, tomato, basil); *pistacchio di Bronte* (Bronte pistachios, in the Etna region). More recently with seafood, pesto, cuttlefish ink, and a sweet version.

POPULARITY: spread throughout Europe and the Americas by Sicilian migrants, *arancini* have a famous ambassador: Inspector Salvo Montalbano, Sicilian author Andrea Camilleri's detective hero, who is addicted to his cook Adelina's arancini. He even gives the recipe for it in *Gli arancini di Montalbano* (1999).

SKIP TO

THE CULTIVATION OF RICE, P. 60; RISOTTO, P. 78; RAGÙ BOLOGNESE, P. 330.

RECIPE

ARANCINE AL RAGÙ

Here is the classic recipe by Sandro Pace (Via Giuseppe di Vita, 17, Comiso, Sicily), one of the best cooks of arancina. Between the preparation of the ragù and that of the rice, it is a long process, but the result is so worth it!

SERVES 6

(Makes 1 dozen arancine. The ideal weight of an arancina is 6⅓ ounces/180 g, with 2⅛ ounces/60 g ragù inside, making up one-third of its weight.)

For the rice

½ stalk celery
1 carrot
1 onion
3 tablespoons (45 mL) olive oil
1 cube vegetable bouillon
4 saffron threads
2⅔ cups (500 g) rice (a mixture of Arborio and carnaroli)
3½ tablespoons (50 g) butter, cubed
¼ cup (20 g) grated Caciocavallo or Parmesan cheese

For the breading

2 cups (250 g) flour
1⅔ cups (400 mL) water
2 cups (200 g) dried bread crumbs
High-heat oil for frying

1 recipe ragù bolognese (see page 330)

· For the rice, thinly slice the celery, carrot, and onion.

· Heat the olive oil in a large pot over medium heat. Cook the celery, carrot, and onion just until lightly browned. Add 4 cups (1 L) water, the stock cube, and the saffron threads. When the mixture begins to boil, add the rice, and stir once. Lower the heat slightly and cook for 18 to 20 minutes.

· As soon as the water has dropped below the surface of the rice, add the butter and grated cheese; do not stir. Once the butter has melted, turn off the heat. Stir the rice, turning slowly for several minutes. Let cool.

· Take a large pinch of the rice mixture and form a compact ball. Do not compress it too much. Holding the rice ball in one hand, push the index finger with the other hand into the center, rotating the ball and spreading it with your finger to create a slightly widened cavity; this will create the *camicia* (shirt) that will envelope the ragù filling. Fill the cavity with 1 spoonful of ragù, fold in the edges of the camicia around the filling, and shape the arancina with your hands and fingers, forming a cone shape. Repeat these steps to make the remaining ones.

· For the breading, combine the flour with a scant ½ cup (100 mL) water and whisk together to make a smooth batter. Dunk the arancina into the batter, making sure to have an even but thin coating. Gently roll the coated arancina in the bread crumbs.

· In a heavy saucepan, heat at least 1 to 2 inches (3 to 5 cm) of frying oil to 350°F (180°C); you need enough oil to fully submerge the arancina. Once the oil has reached the correct temperature, fry the rice balls in several batches; they should not be too close together in the oil. Fry them until they are evenly golden brown on all sides. Remove and place them on a paper towel–lined plate to drain. Serve.

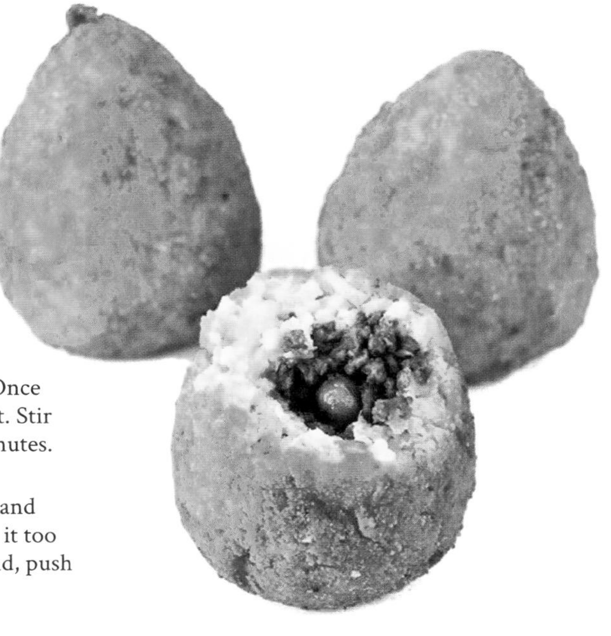

OTHER "RISI DI STRADA" (STREET RICE)

CRESPELLE DI RISO: also called *crispeddi* in Sicilian or *zeppole* in the local dialect, this specialty from Catania (Sicily) consists of a cylinder-shaped rice-based fritter cooked in milk with cinnamon and citrus zest, fried, then dusted with confectioners' sugar. It is then drizzled with honey. The *palline di risi di San Giuseppe* (rice balls) are their cousins from Palermo, eaten without honey.

PALL' E RIS': this is the name by which the *palle di riso* (rice balls) are known in Campania, the Neapolitan versions of the Sicilian arancini, thought to have been introduced during the reign of the Bourbons in the eighteenth century. They are round, smaller, usually filled with a ragù, peas, and mozzarella.

CHESTNUTS

Its spiney shell may act as a deterrent, but underneath, the *castagna* conceals a nutritious treasure.

SACHA LOMNITZ

THE BASICS

The edible chestnut is the fruit of the sweet, or European, chestnut tree (*Castanea sativa*), a deciduous tree of the Fagaceae family (including beech and oak) that can reach up to 100 feet (30 m) in height and live for several hundred years.

It is rich in vitamin C and minerals, and its high carbohydrate content (75 percent) has made it a "poor man's food" par excellence for centuries. The sugar level of the fruit changes over time and is usually highest just a few weeks after harvest.

Celebrating the "bread tree"

The sweet chestnut tree (*castagno* in Italian) is nicknamed the *albero del pane* (bread tree) in Italian and other cultures because of its high starch content. For centuries, chestnut flour has been used to make black bread, a good source for filling empty stomachs.

Late-nineteenth-century poet Giovanni Pascoli sings the praises of these "wintertime friends" in his Latin poem *Castanea* (1896) and glorifies "our bread tree" in a 1908 article:

"You should place a cross there, as you do with other sacred trees, so that no one touches them. This blessed tree is the true benefactor of the people."

Echoing this, a proverb from Garfagnana (Tuscany), where Pascoli spent the end of his life in the midst of beautiful mountains blanketed with groves of chestnut trees, states:

"Garfagnin della Garfagna,
se tu non avessi la castagna,
moriresti dalla famma!"

("Garfagnin of Garfagnana,
if you didn't have chestnuts,
you would starve!")

ITS PRESENCE IN ITALY

Probably native to the Caucasus and Anatolia, the chestnut tree has proliferated among the rain-soaked mountainous areas of the northern Mediterranean. Italy has the largest area of chestnut tree groves in Europe (around 1,900,000 acres/800,000 ha). A varietal typical of hilly and low-mountain regions, the chestnut tree is particularly populous from Calabria to Liguria and in the western area of the Alpine arc of Piedmont. Its name differs depending on the region: *tasatagne* (Aosta Valley), *crudèla, feruda,* or *gückiaröl* (Lombardy), *cjastine* (Friuli), *panella* (Liguria), and *pastiddha* (Calabria).

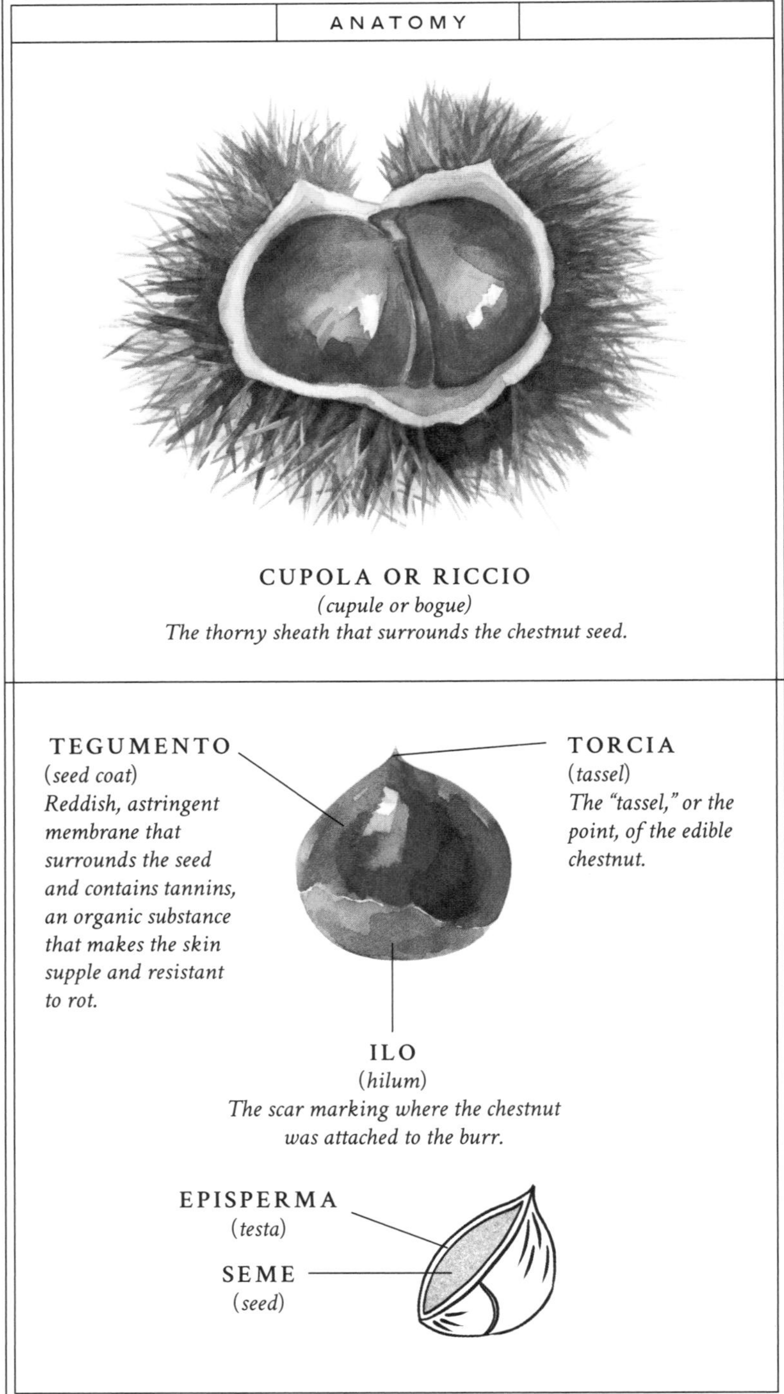

THE CASTAGNA THROUGHOUT ITALY

There are many Italian pastries and desserts made with chestnuts, and several of them are worth mentioning:

→ ***CASTAGNACCIO* AND *NECCI*** (Tuscany): a cake and crêpe, respectively, made from chestnut flour. These are must-haves in fall, from Arezzo to the Tyrrhenian coast, and along the Arno River.

→ ***CALZONCELLI*** (Campania, Apulia, Basilicata) (see recipe opposite): small fritters filled with chestnut cream and cocoa with many variations (hazelnuts, dried pears, lemon zest, chickpeas, . . .).

→ ***BUSECCHINA*** (Lombardy): a cake made from dried chestnuts and milk, the name of which refers to *busecca*, Milanese tripe (another example of chestnuts being used as a substitute for a richer food).

→ ***BUDINO DI CASTAGNE*** (Trentino-Alto Adige, Piedmont): custard made from chestnuts, milk, and rice flour.

→ ***MONTE BIANCO*** (Aosta Valley, Piedmont): probably of French origin, it can be found in restaurants and pastry shops throughout Italy; it is celebrated by Nanni Moretti in his film *Bianca* (1988), depicting a character being blown away by it as he tastes it.

But the chestnut can also be part of savory preparations:

→ ***GNOCCHI OSSOLANI*** (Piedmont): with boiled chestnuts and squash.

→ ***PASTA BASTARDA*** (Tuscany): fresh pasta prepared with part chestnut flour, typical of Lunigiana.

→ ***MAROCCA DI CASOLA*** (Tuscany): bread prepared with chestnut flour, typical of Lunigiana.

→ **CHESTNUT POLENTA** (central Italy).

There is also a great tradition of dried chestnuts widely used in Italy as a legume, especially in soups eaten year-round. They were also used as small snacks for peasants, who often carried them in their pockets.

THE CASTAGNA IN TWO RECIPES

CALDARROSTE (ROASTED CHESTNUTS)

Literally "hot roasted," chestnuts are scored and cooked in a perforated pan over low heat on a gas stove (in the absence of a fireplace) for about twenty minutes.

LES CALZONCELLI (CHESTNUT TURNOVERS)

These little stuffed pastries are prepared for Christmas in Basilicata.

SERVES 5 OR 6

- Boil 1⅛ pounds (500 g) fresh chestnuts with an orange peel for 30 minutes.
- Boil ⅔ cup (125 g) dried chickpeas, soaked overnight, for about 1 hour 30 minutes.
- Prepare a flaky pastry dough with 4 cups (500 g) flour, ½ teaspoon (2 g) sugar, ½ cup (100 g) olive oil, sweet white wine (or Marsala) as needed, and a pinch of salt. Let rest for 20 minutes.
- Roll the dough out to about 2 mm thick. Process the boiled chestnuts through a food mill.
- Remove the skins of the chickpeas; crush the chickpeas with a fork.
- Combine the mashed chestnuts and chickpeas together with 2½ cups (200 g) unsweetened cocoa powder and about ¾ cup (150 g) sugar (you can also add 5¼ ounces/150 g of *vincotto*, a cooked grape must).
- Taste and adjust the seasoning. Cut out circles of the dough measuring about 2¾ inches (7 cm) in diameter, place a small mound of the filling in the center, and fold them over into half-moons, pressing gently to seal the edges. They can be fried in very hot olive oil or baked on a greased baking sheet.
- Once cooked, dust these "Christmastime ravioli" with confectioners' sugar and cinnamon.

Sulla Punta Della Lingua (*On the Tip of the Tongue*)

Between sweet chestnuts and horse chestnuts, beware of the wrong choice . . . and how two terms in Italian referencing chestnut are used in certain expressions (and their meanings).

→ The seed of the horse chestnut tree (*Aesculus hippocastanum*) is contained in a wartlike husk with soft-tipped points (the seeds also have no tassel), while the sweet chestnut (*Castanea sativa*) is enclosed in a spine-covered burr with four chambers.

→ Horse chestnuts should not be eaten (they are considered toxic). In Italy, the term *marrone* is used to designate the best, more fleshy and tastier varietals of sweet chestnuts, but *castagne* is usually refers to the sweet chestnuts we like to "roast over an open fire."

→ "*Far girar i marroni/maroni*" is literally to "turn the chestnuts," but means to annoy someone.

→ "*Prisere in castagna*" means "to be caught red-handed."

So be aware of the two terms, *castagna* and *marrone*.

VARIETALS

It's impossible to list all the varietals of chestnuts grown throughout Italy, alternately called castagne or marroni, but here are those protected by an appellation:

CASTAGNA DI CUNEO IGP, Piedmont

MARRONE DELLA VALLE DI SUSA IGP, Piedmont

MARRONE DI COMBAI IGP, Veneto

MARRONE DI SAN ZENO DOP, Veneto

MARRONE DEL MONFENERA IGP, Veneto

MARRONE DI CASTEL DEL RIO IGP, Emilia-Romagna

CASTAGNA DEL MONTE AMIATA IGP, Tuscany

MARRONE DEL MUGELLO IGP, Tuscany

MARRONE DI CAPRESE MICHELANGELO DOP, Tuscany

CASTAGNA DI VALLERANO DOP, Lazio

MARRONE DI ROCCADASPIDE IGP, Campania

CASTAGNA DI MONTELLA IGP, Campania

Some delicious products:

FARINA DI CASTAGNE DELLA LUNIGIANA DOP (flour), Liguria and Tuscany (1)

FARINA DI CASTAGNE (NECCIO) DELLA LUNIGIANA DOP (flour), Tuscany

MIEL DELLA LUNIGIANA DOP (honey), Liguria and Tuscany

MIEL DELLE DOLOMITI DI BELLUNO DOP (honey), Veneto

CREMA DI CASTAGNE (chestnut cream), Lombardy (2)

CASTAGNA SECCA (chestnuts dried in dryers called *tecci*) from Calizzano and Murialdo, (Liguria) (3)

(1)

(2)

(3)

SKIP TO
CASTAGNACCIO (CHESTNUT FLOUR CAKE), P. 145;
THE GNOCCHI UNIVERSE, P. 76.

Liquori

From *aperitivo* to liqueurs, Italy is full of *liquori*: sweet alcohols infused with herbs, spices, or fruits. Here is an overview, from the artisanal to the most common.

CÉLINE MAGUET

Liquirigia (licorice)

ABV: 20 to 25%

ORIGIN: Calabria, Sicily, Basilicata, and Emilia-Romagna

BRIEF HISTORY: the cultivation of licorice didn't begin in Italy until the eighteenth century, but Franciscan monks quickly took up the practice, first for the plant's medicinal properties, then . . . to transform it into a liqueur.

INFUSION: licorice root

AROMA: refreshing and intense in licorice

IF YOU MUST HAVE ONLY ONE: Liquirizia Quaglia

Maraschino (marasca cherries)

ABV: 30%

ORIGIN: Veneto and Friuli

BRIEF HISTORY: it is a medieval tradition shared with neighboring countries along the Dalmatian coast: from Croatia to Albania through Montenegro and Bosnia and Herzegovina.

INFUSION: using fruits and pits of the sour marasca cherry varietal, then distilled.

AROMA: morello cherry

IF YOU MUST HAVE ONLY ONE: Maraschino by Morelli

Genziana (gentian)

ABV: 20%

ORIGIN: Abruzzo

BRIEF HISTORY: the star ingredient of a quintessential mountain liqueur, gentian grows at an elevation of 3,200 feet (1,000 m) or higher.

INFUSION: gentian root in white wine

AROMA: herbaceous, like a medicinal remedy, which at the end of a meal would put your taste buds back in line!

IF YOU MUST HAVE ONLY ONE: Liquore di genziana by L.AB, Liquoreria ABruzzese

Ratafià (cherry)

ABV: 14 to 26%

ORIGIN: Piedmont, Aosta Valley, Abruzzo, and Molise

BRIEF HISTORY: in Abruzzo and Molise, the cherries are infused in Montepulciano wine; in Piedmont, the cherry juice is mixed with alcohol and sugar.

INFUSION: black cherry or morello cherry

AROMA: ripe cherry

IF YOU MUST HAVE ONLY ONE: Ratafià Vini Praesidium

Sambuca (star anise)

ABV: 38 to 42%

ORIGIN: Lazio; and throughout Italy

BRIEF HISTORY: created under its current name in Civitavecchia (Lazio) in 1851 by Luigi Manzi, it became famous starting in 1945 thanks to perfumer Angelo Molinari. The old recipe included the addition of an elderberry distillate (sambuco), but the link with its name is not really attested. It's perhaps derived from the Arabic *zammut*, meaning "strong smell."

INFUSION: star anise and/or green anise

AROMA: anise

IF YOU MUST HAVE ONLY ONE: Sambuca Molinari

Nocino (walnut)

ABV: 30%

ORIGIN: Emilia-Romagna and throughout Italy

BRIEF HISTORY: spreading from France into Italy was an easy trip for this walnut liqueur, where it was quickly adopted beginning several centuries ago.

INFUSION: walnut shell or fresh green walnut

AROMA: undergrowth

IF YOU MUST HAVE ONLY ONE: Nocino di San Costanzo Nastro d'Oro

Mirto (red myrtle)

ABV: 30%

ORIGIN: Sardinia

BRIEF HISTORY: Corsica and Sardinia share the tradition of myrtle liqueur. You won't go wrong if you look for *mirto di Sardegna*.

INFUSION: fresh myrtle berry

AROMA: spices

IF YOU MUST HAVE ONLY ONE: Mirto Fratelli Rau

Some Big Names

APEROL
ABV: 11%

Created in Padua (Veneto) at the start of the nineteenth century, this tinted infusion made from bitter orange and gentian is perfect for cocktails, such as a spritz, which made it famous.

CAMPARI
ABV: 25%

In 1862, distiller Gaspare Campari opened a shop in Milan in what would become the Galleria Vittorio Emanuele, where he prepared a red liqueur made from *chinotto* (small citrus), aromatic herbs, and cochineal, a natural red dye. Gin + Campari + vermouth = Negroni!

FRANGELICO
ABV: 24%

This bottle, designed in the shape of a belted monk's robe, pays homage to Fra Angelico, a hermit monk from Piedmont (not to be confused with the Italian Renaissance painter of the same name), who created this liqueur based on cocoa and vanilla in hazelnut alcohol (using the hazelnut varietal *tonda e gentile*) in the eighteenth century.

STREGA (witch)
ABV: 40%

Concocted with seventy aromatic herbs and saffron, native to Campania, it takes its name from a legend that 2,000 witches gave birth to this potion to eternally unite all those who drink it together.

VOV
ABV: 18%

A pastry chef from Padua (Veneto), not knowing what to do with all the egg yolks he had left after making nougats, created this liqueur in 1845, made from egg yolk (*vovi* in the local language) and white Marsala wine.

SKIP TO
AMARO, P. 210; COCKTAILS, P. 190;
LAND OF LEMONS, P. 352; SPRITZ, P. 94.

SEASON

TUTTO L'ANNO (YEAR-ROUND)

CATEGORY

ANTIPASTO, PRIMO PIATTO (APPETIZER/ FIRST COURSE)

LEVEL

FACILE (EASY)

PAPPA AL POMODORO

TUSCAN BREAD SOUP

Tomatoes, bread, garlic, basil, and olive oil make for a Tuscan summer "porridge" whose origins are contended between Florence and Siena. This thick bread-and-tomato soup can be enjoyed warm or chilled.

SACHA LOMNITZ

MORE *PAPPA* THAN *POMODORO*

Pappa (pronounce the double *p*!) means a mush or porridge served to children. It is also a term adults use to refer to baby food. It is part of the tradition of ancestral *zuppe* (soups made from bread and vegetables). Tuscans substituted tomatoes for vegetables in the late eighteenth century when tomato cultivation spread across Europe. This soup making use of stale bread was originally a light pink color as it was prepared with very few tomatoes—just enough to fool both the eye and the stomach into believing the simple broth was richer than its humble ingredients.

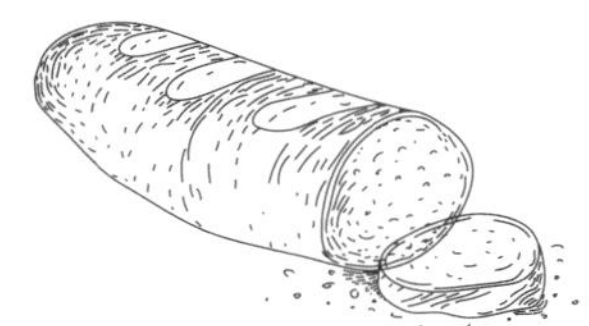

From a classic in children's literature...

Pappa al pomodoro is featured in the children's novel *Il giornalino di Gian Burrasca* (1907) by Vamba (Luigi Bertelli). In the story, the mischievous Jean la Bourrasque denounces the hypocrisy of adults and society. The name of this character was adopted into everyday language to designate a mischievous child.

... to a classic song!

In the story, the young hero manages to feed all his buddies with the much-adored pappa. In the 1965 television version, this episode inspired the very famous song "*Viva la pappa col pomodoro,*" sung by Rita Pavone (aka Gian Burrasca) to the music of Nino Rota, Federico Fellini's favorite composer.

TUSCAN INGREDIENTS . . . *MAGARI!*

"*Magari!*" ("maybe") is an expression with a very fluid meaning, used to express all nuances of hope. The exact meaning is all in the tone of how it's used.

For the recipe below, maybe—magari!—you will find **PANE SCIOCCO** (Tuscan bread without salt), some **BOMBOLINO** or **COSTOLUTO FIORENTINO** tomatoes, **GIGANTE TOSCANO** basil leaves and **TUSCANO IGP** extra-virgin olive oil from the hills of Florence. Ah, if only maybe—magari!—you could find **BOMBOLINO** tomatoes and dry them hanging in the fireplace or in your kitchen. Their more concentrated flavor will enrich your pappa.

THE RECIPE

Legend attributes powers to the pappa: heat it until a veil forms on its surface, stir it gently, then repeat this step seven times. The pappa is then ready, and the magic can happen . . .

SERVES 4

- 1⅓ to 1¾ pounds (600 to 800 g) ripe red tomatoes (Tuscan or San Marzano varietals, canned or as a sauce)
- 3 cloves garlic, peeled
- 5 tablespoons (75 mL) extra-virgin olive oil (preferably Tuscan)
- About 10 leaves basil (gigantic Tuscan or Neapolitan varietals)
- 7 to 9 ounces (200 to 250 g) stale Tuscan bread or another hearty unsalted bread, thinly sliced or diced
- 1 cup (250 mL) vegetable stock, warmed
- Salt and freshly ground black pepper

Wash, peel, seed, and chop the tomatoes (if purchased whole). Brown the garlic cloves in a large saucepan with 3 tablespoons (45 mL) of the olive oil. Add 5 or 6 basil leaves and the tomatoes. Stir in the bread and stock. Cook over low heat for about 10 minutes, until you get a dense mush, but one that still maintains some body and is not completely broken down.

Season with salt and pepper. Add the remaining 2 tablespoons (30 mL) olive oil, then set the pan aside off the heat for at least 30 minutes. Serve warm or chilled, garnished with 1 basil leaf per bowl.

The pappa can be prepared the day before; it will be even better the next day.

SKIP TO
TOMATOES, P. 28;
THE SOUPS OF ITALY, P. 146.

THE ART OF RIBOLLITA

This Tuscan winter vegetable stew with bread is a masterpiece of peasant cuisine!

CLAUDIO CAMBON

CLAUDIO'S RECIPE

***Ribollita* is not difficult to make, it just needs to be prepared ahead of time and rewarmed—after all, the name means "boil again" in Italian! Here is a great family recipe, with a few variations from tradition.**

SERVES 10 TO 12

3 DAYS IN ADVANCE

Purchase a loaf of rustic bread weighing about 1¾ pounds (800 g). Instead of the Tuscan *pane sciocco* (bread without salt), you can choose a whole wheat natural sourdough bread. Cut the bread into slices of about ⅓ inch (1 cm) thick, and set them out for a day to dry out. Once dried, store them wrapped in a kitchen towel.

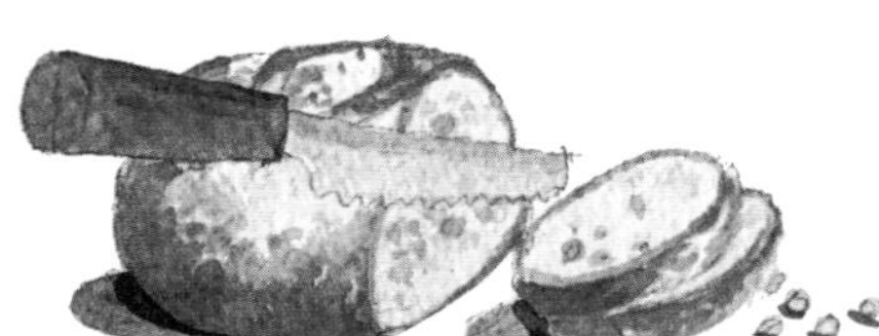

2 DAYS IN ADVANCE

Soak 2¼ cups (400 g) cannellini, borlotti, or Toscanelli beans (or great northern, Tarbais, or flageolet) overnight.

1 DAY IN ADVANCE

① Preheat the oven to 425°F (220°C). Drain and rinse the beans, then cook them with a little water, salt, and 1 garlic clove. Drain the beans, setting aside a little of the liquid. Purée about half the beans and stir the purée into the remaining whole beans. Quarter 2 onions and roughly chop 2 leeks and 3 carrots. Place them on a baking sheet lined with parchment paper, brush them with a little olive oil and salt, and roast them in the oven for 15 to 20 minutes, or until the vegetables start to brown and crisp.

② Add the cooked vegetables to a saucepan filled with 1½ to 1¾ gallons (6 to 7 L) boiling water, 3 canned peeled tomatoes, 2 celery stalks (with their leaves), 1 bunch parsley (stems and leaves), some fresh thyme, 1 bay leaf, and salt. Cook for about 1 hour 30 minutes (you'll need about 1⅓ to 1½ gallons/5 to 6 L of broth in the end). Season with salt and pepper near the end of the cooking time, and turn off the heat. Once the broth has cooled slightly, strain it and set it aside.

③ In a large pot, prepare a *soffritto*: finely chop then sauté 1 onion, 2 leeks (white part only), 2 large carrots, and 2 chopped celery stalks for several minutes in olive oil. Add 4 to 6 sage leaves, fresh thyme, 1 sprig rosemary, and half a not-too-spicy fresh pepper. Add 1 tablespoon (15 mL) tomato paste diluted in ½ cup (125 mL) of the reserved broth. Cut 6 to 8 leaves of kale into strips and add them to the soffritto. Remove and discard the tough outer leaves from a head of green cabbage, cut the cabbage head in half, and remove the core. Cut the leaves into strips about ¾ inch (2 cm) wide, then finely chop the core. Cut a bunch of chard into strips 1⅛ to 1½ inches (3 to 4 cm) wide.

④ Add the cabbage and chard to the soffritto, along with 1 cup of the reserved broth to prevent the vegetables from sticking. Cook for about 10 minutes over medium heat, until the cabbage leaves soften slightly. Add the beans and cook for several more minutes to combine the flavors. Season with salt. Preheat the oven to 325°F (160°C). Place a layer of bread in the bottom of a separate large ovenproof lidded pot, cover with a nice layer of the vegetables (1½ to 2 inches/4 to 5 cm deep), and drizzle the top with the broth without covering the bread and vegetables completely. Repeat this step until the pot is full. Place the lid on the pot and set it in the oven. Add hot broth after about 45 minutes, then cook for another 45 minutes. Remove the pot from the oven and let cool.

D-DAY!

Add more broth to the pot and gently heat the ribollita in the oven for about 45 minutes. It should have the consistency of a fairly thick soup. It gets better each time you reheat it. Serve with a Sangiovese wine, such as a Chianti!

A RUSTIC VEGETARIAN RECIPE

Ribollita is a stew of winter vegetables and a classic example of peasant cuisine, in which the simplest ingredients—bread, cabbage, and beans, cooked in a vegetable broth—meld into a rich and tasty soup.

It is thought to have originally been a vegetarian dish. First indications of the recipe were in the cookbook by the gastronome Giovanni del Turco (printed between 1602 and 1636). Pellegrino Artusi calls it in *La scienza in cucina e l'arte di mangiar bene* (*Science in the Kitchen and the Art of Eating Well*, 1891) the *zuppa di magro alla contadina*, a lean peasant soup made for days abstaining from meat. However, the recipe lists smoked ham or dried beef among the ingredients! But according to tradition, the poorest families would use *aringa essiccata* (dried herring) to rub on the bread.

THE FIRST INGREDIENT: *PANE SCIOCCO*

Ribollita without *pane sciocco*, a Tuscan salt-free bread, is no ribollita! But some may say the bread doesn't have much flavor and that no one really wants to eat it because it dries out quickly. And they'll point out to you that *sciocco* doesn't just mean "salt-free" but also "foolish."

CHANGE IT UP

No two recipes are the same. Although each person can add something new, ribollita should always maintain a spirit of simplicity in ingredients.

→ If you have a ham bone, go for it! Corsican smoked bacon is a adds great flavor. So is a piece of Parmesan rind.

→ String beans are a tasty addition in spring, with possibly some chopped fresh green onions on the side. Several recipes call for potatoes, but others find this makes the soup too starchy.

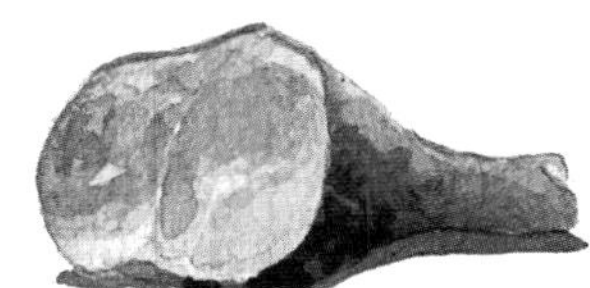

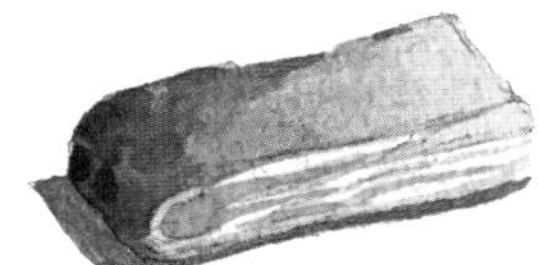

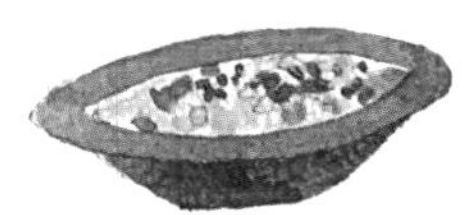

A question of cabbage

An equal amount of collard greens, *cavolo nero* (a Tuscan black kale), and chard is a great option. You can replace the cavolo nero with easier-to-find green kale, but be aware the Tuscan kale will have a stronger flavor and firmer texture. Traditionally, Tuscans waited until after the first frosts to use kale, when the leaves would soften, but it should be sufficient to simply remove the stems and any tough veins.

SKIP TO
LEGUMES, P. 150; ARTE BIANCA, P. 136; THE SOUPS OF ITALY, P. 146.

COOKING BY TELEVISION

Here we're not talking about turning on an Antonella Clerici cooking show or sitting in front of Italy's top chef . . . but instead following the tempo of Italian TV to successfully execute your recipe!

STÉPHANE SOLIER

Here is the procedure to follow according to Bianca, a native Italian through and through, in *La Commedia des ratés* (1991), by police-thriller author Tonino Benacquista:

"Will you turn on the TV, please, Antonio? . . . At this hour, there is nothing good on, but it helps me to cook. . . . Watch, I'm going to teach you how to make an *all'arrabbiata* sauce. It's 7:45. Turn it to RAI [Radiotelevisione italiana]." *A series of commercials begins . . .*

7:45

TV commercials on RAI
Bring the water to a boil and sauté the garlic in the oil.

"Bring your water to a boil. Meanwhile, cook a whole peeled garlic clove in a hot skillet, just until the commercials are finished. The smell of garlic will waft through the air."

The commercials end. She asks Antonio to turn it to channel 5 where a guy in front of a map of Italy is predicting a very hot day for tomorrow.

8:05

Weather on channel 5
Remove the garlic clove and dump the peeled tomatoes into the pan.

"As soon as the weather starts, you can remove the garlic clove from the pan. We don't need it anymore, the oil has absorbed as much of its flavor as it can. Dump your peeled tomatoes into the pan. When the weather report is over and the water is boiling, throw in the penne. Turn it to channel 4."

8:10

Game show on channel 4
A game-show host, audience, models, giant dice, numbers lighting up, excited contestants . . .

8:22

The big game-show finale on channel 4
Adjust the tomato sauce by adding a little tomato paste and peppers, and the pasta is done: drain the penne.

"When the winner is announced, you can stir the sauce a little and add a small can of tomato paste, just to give it a little color, then add two small chile peppers, no more, turn up the heat, without covering the pan; it will spit everywhere, but they say that an all'arrabbiata sauce is successful only when the kitchen is splotched in red. Turn to Channel 2."

8:25

Brazilian soap opera on channel 2
Cook the penne in the pan with the spicy tomato sauce.

On a Brazilian soap opera shot in video, two heated lovers fight with each other in the living room.

8:30

TV News (TG) on channel 2
Serve the pasta.

"At the end of the soap opera, the news will come on, and we can finally sit down to dinner. The sauce and the pasta will be ready at exactly the same time. Fifteen minutes. Did you get all that? . . ."

"Your recipe isn't bad, but I don't have TV."

"Fine, then eat chickpeas."

"The hot pasta was spooned out onto my plate. It's a delight that ignites the palate. I have always been wary of girls who know how to cook."

SKIP TO
PENNE ALL'ARRABBIATA, P. 252; POP PASTA, P. 221.

ROSÉ WINES

As with its other wine styles, Italy offers a wide selection of beautifully produced *vini rosati.*

SAMUEL COGLIATI

PRODUCTION TECHNIQUES

Grape skins contain the aromas, pigments, and tannins that become part of a wine. In general, for a rosé wine, winemakers attempt to capture the aromas and pigments, not the tannins. How is this achieved?

Combining white wine with red wine is not allowed in the production of a true rosé wine, therefore there are three possible approaches to achieving the desired result:

DIRECT PRESSING: when the grape skins are a sufficiently dark color, the grapes are pressed just enough to color the juice to the depth desired.

MACERATION: this approach results in more elements from the grapes being extracted, enabling the skins to infuse in the grape must for a few hours or a few days.

BLEEDING: this process is also maceration, with the distinction that juice is drawn from a vat intended for red wine production, therefore tinting the juice to a rosé color.

Revenge of the bubbles

The traditional, closed vat, or "natural sparkling" method: effervescence is a perfect match for rosé wines. Sparkling rosé wines have been increasing in popularity for some time. Is this a fad, or is it a legitimate trend toward a wine style with a solid future? As evidence of a well-established future, the most famous appellations (Franciacorta, Trento, Alto Adige, Oltrepò Pavese) are producing wines of this style. Lambrusco lends itself to this style (look for Casalpriore or Paltrinieri estates), and even Prosecco recently decided to risk producing a rosé as part of its offerings!

PAIRING WITH FOOD

Rosé is probably the most versatile wine to serve, and even more so paired with the flavors of Mediterranean cuisine.

THREE SUGGESTIONS

→ It's hard to beat a rosé paired with a simple pizza, such as a Margherita (tomatoes and mozzarella), a marinara (tomatoes, garlic, oregano), or one with added anchovies—the wine envelopes these flavors and prolongs their pleasure.

→ The vigor of an Abruzzo Cerasuolo will pair wonderfully with *guazzetto di pesce*, a "red" fish soup (one with added tomato and chile).

→ How about pork loin skewers with bacon and bell peppers? Turn to an opulent and tasty pink Cirò!

SKIP TO
ORANGE WINE, P. 113; PROSECCO & CO., P. 250; GRAPES, P. 272.

• NORTHERN ROSÉS •

In northern Italy, rosé is synonymous with delicacy. Containing little or no tannins, these wines benefit from the cooler climate and are often supple and flavorful.

PIEDMONT The few rosés of the Coste della Sesia DOC take advantage of the choice of Nebbiolo and Vespolina grape varietals. To taste: Antoniolo or Proprietà Sperino estates.

TRENTINO-ALTO ADIGE Lagrein is the origin of Kretzer-style wines, with an appreciable spirit. To taste: Weingut Nusserhof estate.

LAKE GARDA The Valténesi Chiaretto appellation offers smooth wines (a blend of Groppello, Marzemino, Sangiovese, and Barbera; Costaripa estate).

BETWEEN LOMBARDY AND VENETO The Riviera del Garda (shores of Lake Garda) also offers gentle wines from the same varietals. To taste: Cà dei Frati estate.

NORTH

SOUTH

N W E S

ABRUZZO The Montepulciano grape produces wines of character under the appellation Cerasuolo d'Abruzzo. To taste: Emidio Pepe, Valentini, or Praesidium estates.

SOUTH OF APULIA Alezio, Salice Salentino DOPs, Leverano, or the Salento IGP are from vines like Negroamaro or Primitivo. To taste: Michele Calò or Leone de Castris estates.

CALABRIA Thanks to the Gaglioppo grape varietal, Cirò rosés can offer sensual bottles with aging potential. To taste: 'A Vita or Tenuta del Conte estates.

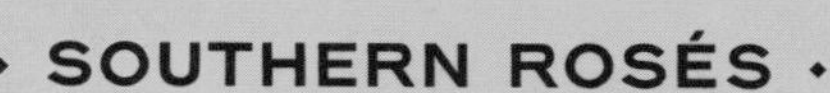

• SOUTHERN ROSÉS •

The central and southern portions of Italy are probably even better located to produce this style of wine—as long as you like your rosés racy, powerful, fleshy, tasty, and sometimes bordering on the color red.

ROSÉ PRODUCTION IN ITALY	WORLDWIDE CONSUMPTION 2002–2017	ITALY'S WORLD RANKING	MAIN IMPORTING COUNTRIES FOR ITALIAN ROSÉ
10% of world production	+23%	Production: 4th place Consumption: 5th place	Germany, United Kingdom, United States

SEASON

AUTUNNO, INVERNO (AUTUMN/WINTER)

CATEGORY

PRIMO PIATTO (FIRST COURSE)

LEVEL

DIFFICOLTÀ MEDIA (MEDIUM DIFFICULTY)

TORTELLI DI ZUCCA

PUMPKIN RAVIOLI

This is one of the most famous ravioli dishes, combining winter squash, almonds, and cheese. Born in Mantua, it has become a symbol of Italian cuisine.

GIORGIA CANNARELLA

A SURPRISING ASSOCIATION

The recipe for *tortelli* dough is classic, using eggs and flour . . . Square and rectangular shapes are common, but the shape can also be a half-moon or a kind of "bonbon." The most important thing is what's inside!

The filling consists of winter squash (pumpkin), Grana Padano or Parmesan cheese, nutmeg, amaretti (almond cookies), and *mostarda* from Mantua (a condiment of candied fruit and mustard; the one from Mantua is made with quince).

THROUGHOUT HISTORY

Their beginnings lie somewhere between Mantua and Ferrara, during the Renaissance.

→ In the treatise *Dello scalco,* written in 1584 by Giovan Battista Rossetti, the butler at the House of Este court, *tortelli di zucca con butirro* (with pumpkin in butter) are mentioned for the first time.

→ Tortelli di zucca became common at court banquets during the Renaissance.

→ Over time, the dish became more widespread, including among the working classes. It is generally eaten as a lean dish, especially during Lent in Mantua.

Mantua vs. Ferrara

Mantua is not the only city to boast a tradition of tortelli di zucca, and its main rival is Ferrara.

	Mantoue	Ferrare
NAME	*Tortelli* or *tortei ad süca* (in local dialect).	*Cappellacci* or *capelaz* (in local dialect) IGP.
SHAPE	Square (most popular), rectangular, half-moon, or strips.	Round hat.
FILLING	Pumpkin, amaretti, mustard, mostarda from Mantua, Grana Padano.	Winter squash (pumpkin), Parmesan, nutmeg. In Cremona, they are sweeter due to the use of mostarda.

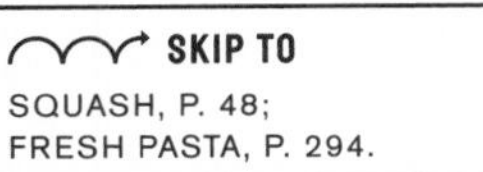

SAUCE

You never fix what isn't broken, so tortelli di zucca are invariably served in melted butter, sage, and grated cheese (preferably Grana Padano or Parmesan). In Ferrara, it is not uncommon for them to be served in a ragù made with various meats.

SKIP TO
SQUASH, P. 48;
FRESH PASTA, P. 294.

THE RECIPE

Here is the traditional version from Mantua.

SERVES 4

- 1⅓ pounds (600 g) Mantua winter squash or pumpkin
- 5¼ ounces (150 g) mostarda from Mantua
- 3½ ounces (100 g) amaretti (almond cookies)
- 1½ cups (160 g) grated Grana Padano or Parmesan cheese
- Zest of ½ lemon
- ½ teaspoon (2 g) freshly grated nutmeg
- Salt and freshly ground black pepper
- ¼ to ⅓ cup (20 to 30 g) dried bread crumbs (optional)
- Pasta dough consisting of 3 large (150 g) eggs and 2½ cups (300 g) flour (see p. 294)
- 5 to 7 tablespoons (80 to 100 g) butter
- 6 to 8 sage leaves

Preheat the oven to 425°F (220°C). Wash the squash, then peel and seed it. Quarter the flesh. Place the quarters on a baking sheet lined with parchment paper. Bake until cooked through (the squash should be soft enough to mash with a fork). Let cool.

Chop the mostarda and mash the amaretti. Process the squash through a food mill, then combine it with the mostarda, amaretti, 1 cup (100 g) of the cheese, and the lemon zest. Add the nutmeg. Season with salt and pepper. If the filling lacks a thick enough consistency, add a few bread crumbs.

Roll out the dough, cut it into 2-inch (5 cm) squares, place a small mound of filling in the center, cover with another square of dough, and seal the edges with a little water. Cook the tortelli in a pot of salted boiling water until they float to the surface (a few minutes will suffice).

When ready to serve, melt the butter over low heat with the sage, pour over the pasta, and top each serving with a sprinkling of the remaining ½ cup (60 g) cheese.

SPAGHETTI VIP

When stars slurp pasta . . . they are sometimes caught red-handed!

ANNA MARÉCHAL

The French actor from Piedmont **FERNANDEL** (Fernand Contandin, 1903–1971), decked out in Don Camillo's cap, bends head-down into a plate of spaghetti and a glass of Chianti. A perfect model for the Don Patillo of Panzani (Albert Augier).

↑ License to kill . . . and to feast! Well-escorted British actor **SEAN CONNERY** (1930–2020) doesn't know which way to turn!

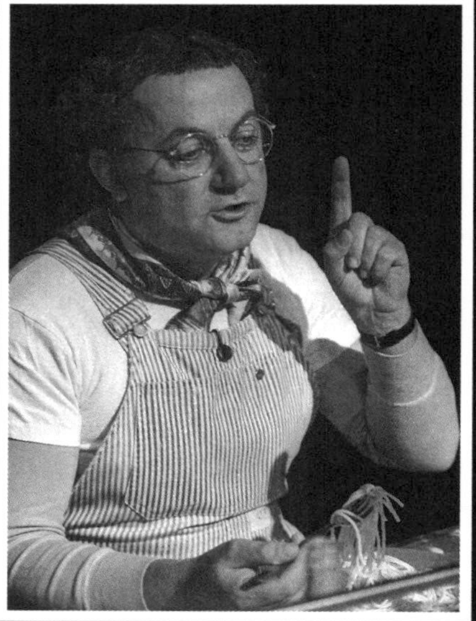

↑ It's the story of a guy . . . who ate pasta. Michel Colucci, alias **COLUCHE** (1944–1986), French actor, clown, and founder of Restos du Coeur, took off his red nose just long enough to eat.

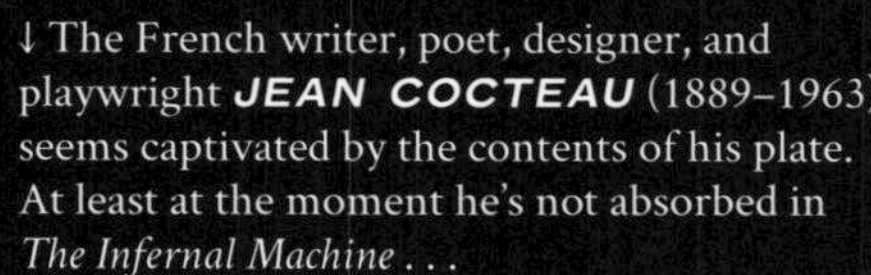

↓ The French writer, poet, designer, and playwright **JEAN COCTEAU** (1889–1963) seems captivated by the contents of his plate. At least at the moment he's not absorbed in *The Infernal Machine* . . .

Son of Italian immigrants, American baseball player **JOE DIMAGGIO** (1914–1999) gazes fondly at his mamma. You can feel all the sharing, the love, and the recognition of such good food in the eyes of this future husband of Marilyn Monroe.

← Face-to-face partners in cri actors and frie **ROCK HUD** (1925–1985) and **CLAUDI CARDINAL** 1938). It's a bit a spaghetti wes played out at t table between American and Italian

← Actor **KIRK DOUGLAS** (1916–2020) entertains the gallery (and not to be missed: **SOPHIA LOREN**, who laughs heartily!) as he manages his plate of spaghetti at the dinner for the premiere of *The Vikings* in 1958.

↑ American actress and dancer **RITA HAYWORTH** (1918–1987) seems as comfortable as a femme fatale (*Gilda* and *The Lady from Shanghai*) as she does a spaghetti-and-meatballs housewife.

Great Roman actor of the postwar period and notorious gourmand **ALDO FABRIZI** (1905–990) remains speechless in front of his neighbor at the table . . . No doubt because he's being nterrupted as he enjoys his favorite dish, *aglio, olio e peperoncino* (garlic, olive oil, chile) . . .

← It's pasta on the go for the Italian pin-up **GINA LOLLOBRIGIDA** (b. 1927), probably between shoots in France or the United States.

← When **CHARLTON HESTON** (1923–2008) trades his chariot and breastplate for a fork and a suit!

Quiet on the set, I'm eating! The multi Oscar–winning Italian director **FEDERICO FELLINI** (1920–1993)—never seen without his white scarf—eats from his lap in the middle of filmi

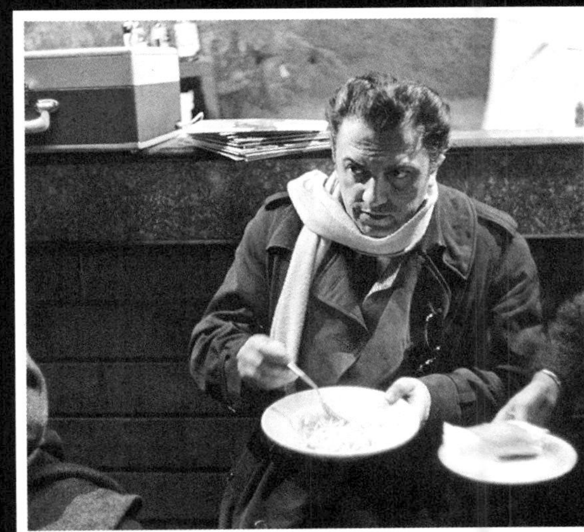

SEASON

INVERNO (WINTER)

CATEGORY

PRIMO PIATTO (FIRST COURSE)

LEVEL

FACILE (EASY)

ORECCHIETTE CON CIME DI RAPA

ORECCHIETTE WITH BROCCOLI RABE

It's the meeting between a common pasta format and a common vegetable: one of the most famous combinations in Apulia.

FRANÇOIS-RÉGIS GAUDRY

ORECCHIETTE . . .

Orecchiette (little ears) first appeared in the region of Sannicandro di Bari, a municipality of Apulia, between the twelfth and the thirteenth centuries.

→ Are they Jewish?
The claim is they are related to *orecchie di Haman*, a kneaded, concave-shaped sweet dough popular in the local Jewish community.

→ Are they French?
Some say in southern Provence a type of thick pasta was made in the shape of a disk bulging in the center created by pressing with the thumb. This dry pasta may have reached Apulia and Basilicata during the control of Charles of Anjou, owner of the county of Provence starting in 1246.

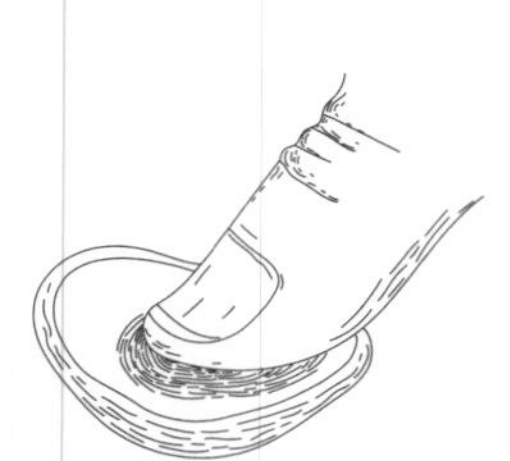

. . . CON CIME DI RAPA

Grown in family gardens and vegetable farms, broccoli rabe is popular throughout southern Italy. It was formerly used to feed pigs and horses, as well as the poor peasants during times of famine.

LATIN NAME
Brassica rapa ssp. *sylvestris* var. *esculenta*.

OTHER NAMES
Friarielli (Campania), *broccoletti* (Lazio), *rapini* (Umbria, Tuscany), *broccoli di rapa* (Apulia, Campania) . . . The varietal *broccolo aprilatico di Paternopoli* (Campania) is a Slow Food sentinel.

ATTRIBUTES
Long stems, large crumpled leaves, tousled flower clusters. It literally means "turnip tops," but it has a close resemblance to broccoli.

DISTRIBUTION
Apulia (those of the region of Fasano are famous), Lazio, Molise, Campania, Basilicata, Calabria . . .

FLAVOR
Vegetal, smooth, and bitter. Notes of cabbage.

THE RECIPE

This is the traditional Apulian version, which involves cooking orecchiette and broccoli rabe in the same pot. The pasta is therefore saturated with the aroma of the vegetables . . . and you use less water.

SERVES 4

- 3⅓ pounds (1.5 kg) broccoli rabe or broccoli
- Olive oil
- ½ cup (50 g) dried bread crumbs
- 1 clove garlic, peeled and crushed
- 4 anchovy fillets in oil
- 1 pinch dried chile pepper or ground cayenne
- 1⅛ pounds (500 g) fresh orecchiette (see recipe on page 295) or 14 ounces (400 g) dry orecchiette
- Salt

Remove the most fibrous outer leaves from the broccoli rabe and cut up the more tender leaves from the heart, the younger stems, and the flower clusters, to obtain at least 2¼ pounds (1 kg) of greens. Wash and set aside.

In a large Dutch oven, heat a drizzle of olive oil over medium heat. Add the bread crumbs and lightly toast them. Remove them and set aside.

Cook the broccoli rabe for 5 minutes in a separate large pan of salted boiling water.

Meanwhile, heat a scant ½ cup (100 mL) olive oil in the Dutch oven set over medium heat, and brown the garlic clove. Add the anchovies and cook them while crushing them with a wooden spoon. Add the chile. Remove the garlic clove.

After the broccoli rabe cooks for 5 minutes, add the orecchiette to the pan and cook for another 5 minutes, stirring with a wooden spoon. If using dry pasta, adjust the cooking time according to the package instructions.

Drain the pasta and the broccoli rabe through a colander, then sauté them in the pot with the anchovy and chile, making sure the pasta is neither too dry nor too wet. Season with salt, if necessary, and divide the pasta among four serving plates. Drizzle with olive oil, sprinkle with the toasted bread crumbs, and serve.

The variations

POMODORINI?
In some recipes, fresh or canned cherry tomatoes add a *rossa* touch to this dish.

RICOTTA SALATA?
This dry, salty cheese can replace the toasted bread crumbs.

SALSICCIA?
In a more modern version, anchovies are replaced with crumbled sausage (plain or with fennel).

SKIP TO
CABBAGE & CO., P. 334;
RICOTTA, P. 219.

PEACHES

Fragrant, juicy, delicate, irresistible: peaches are popular throughout the peninsula.

ILARIA BRUNETTI

Peaches in Italy—*Prunus persica*

Native to China, the peach tree was discovered in Persia in the fourth century BCE by Alexander the Great, who introduced it to Greece before conquering the Mediterranean. There are different families and, for each, many local varietals. The season runs starting from May for a few early varietals or from mid-June, lasting through September.

In cooking, the peach is eaten raw, alone, or in fruit salads; in preserves; in ice cream, sorbets, *crostata*, and cakes. For cocktails, it is used in the famous Venetian cocktail, the Bellini.

A delicious idea

Inhabitants of Friuli like to end their summer meals with *piersolada*: slice peaches, sprinkle them with a little sugar and lemon juice, and drizzle them with a very light white or red wine. Chill for at least three hours, then enjoy. Also good with mint leaves or elderflower syrup.

False peach

Pesche dolci (sweet peaches) are small cakes common in Emilia-Romagna and Tuscany, where the peach is just . . . part of the shape! These are made by joining two hemispheres of sponge cake that have been soaked in Alkermes red liqueur and joined with a layer of chocolate cream. They are then coated in sugar, and a small mint leaf is placed on top—all to resemble a peach.

RECIPE

PESCHE AL FORNO CON GLI AMARETTI (BAKED PEACHES WITH AMARETTI)

Chef Giovanna Guidetti (Osteria La Fefa, Finale Emilia) explains one of the easiest and most delicious ways to enjoy the harmony between peaches and amaretti, the bitter almond cookies.

SERVES 8

8 ripe yellow peaches

1¾ ounces (50 g) hard amaretti cookies, crumbled

3½ tablespoons (50 g) butter, melted, plus 1 tablespoon (20 g) for greasing the baking sheet

¼ cup (50 g) superfine sugar

1¼ cups (100 g) unsweetened cocoa powder, sifted

1 large (19 g) egg yolk

· Preheat the oven to 325°F (170°C). Grease a baking sheet with 1 tablespoon (20 g) butter. Clean the peaches, peel them, halve them, remove the pit, and, using a spoon, scoop out a little of the flesh from the center. In a bowl, crush the peach flesh with a fork. Add the amaretti, 3½ tablespoons (50 g) butter, the sugar, cocoa, and egg yolk. Stir to thoroughly combine.

· Stuff the peach halves with this mixture. Place them on the prepared baking sheet and bake for about 1 hour. Serve warm or cold, lightly dusted with cocoa.

THE MAIN FAMILIES

① PESCA BIANCA

ORIGIN—throughout Italy.
→ White flesh; delicate and fragrant.

② TABACCHIERA OR SATURNINA

ORIGIN—Sicily, Emilia-Romagna, Marche.
→ Meaning "snuffbox" in Italian due to its shape, it has an intensely fragrant and sweet white flesh.

③ PESCA GIALLA

ORIGIN—throughout Italy.
→ Velvet skin and yellow flesh.

④ NETTARINA GIALLA OR PESCA NOCE

ORIGIN—throughout Italy.
→ Smooth skin and firm flesh. It is also found with white flesh.

⑤ PERCOCA

ORIGIN—Campania, Calabria, Basilicata, Apulia and Emilia-Romagna.
→ Very firm and compact flesh, most often used in juices, syrup, and preserves.

⑥ PESCA ROSSA OR SANGUIGNA

ORIGIN—throughout Italy.
→ Late varietal, recognizable by its red or white flesh streaked with red.

SOME RARE GEMS

About ten endangered varietals are Slow Food sentinels or Ark of Taste, such as:

IRIS ROSSO

ORIGIN—Friuli.
→ White flesh and red skin.

BUCO INCAVATO

ORIGIN—Emilia-Romagna.
→ Very light yellow flesh.

BIANCA DI VENEZIA

ORIGIN—Veneto.
→ White flesh.

TABACCHIERA DELL'ETNA

ORIGIN—Sicily.
→ The most delicate, but also the one with the most intense fragrance.

PESCA NEL SACCHETTO

ORIGIN—Sicily.
→ Very intense yellow, it is ripened until October or November, each fruit in its own protective parchment bag.

SKIP TO
COCKTAILS, P. 190;
CROSTATA ALLA CONFETTURA, P. 66;
COOKIES, P. 154.

SEASON

TUTTO L'ANNO (YEAR-ROUND)

CATEGORY

SECONDO PIATTO (MAIN COURSE)

LEVEL

FACILE (EASY)

CODA ALLA VACCINARA

OXTAIL BRAISED WITH TOMATO AND CELERY

Whether made with veal or beef tail, this slow-simmered stew with tomato is a Roman favorite!

FRANÇOIS-RÉGIS GAUDRY

WHO INVENTED IT?

A gladiator? Around 98 CE, gladiators who succeeded in defeating a bull in the Flavian amphitheater—aka the Colosseum—were offered the animal's ears and tail. From there, it's easy to conclude this trophy may have been simmered by the victorious gladiator armed with a spatula . . .

The *vaccinari*? These are the cattle butchers who lived in the Regola district from the thirteenth century. Among the trimmings not sold to the rich was the tail, which the butchers learned to cook. This recipe gained in popularity with the slaughterhouse located in the Testaccio district (1888–1975). Slaughterhouse workers used the remains of the carcasses as a way to supplement their pay by either using the tail as food or by selling it to nearby taverns.

Ferminia? The daughter of Lorenzo and Clorinda Mariani, the founders of Checchino dal (1887), an osteria in Testaccio, was the first to codify *coda alla vaccinara*. This restaurant always offers a delicious version, with pine nuts and raisins added.

THE CODES OF THE *CODA*

Coda alla vaccinara is a ragout of beef (or veal) tail simmered in a tomato sauce with white wine, onion, carrot, and a lot of celery.

GAFFI?

An old tradition is to add *gaffi* (beef cheeks) along with the tail to make the dish even more succulent.

LARD?

This was the original fat used but was gradually replaced, either totally or partially, by olive oil or guanciale (cured pork cheek).

SPICES?

The poet, chef, and songwriter Adolfo Giaquinto added a touch of cinnamon. Nutmeg and cloves are also frequently used.

RAISINS, PINE NUTS, AND COCOA POWDER?

These are more recent additions and evidence of this dish being adopted by the upper classes. The cocoa makes the sauce smooth and shiny and rounds out the flavor.

THE RECIPE

Roman chef Sergio Risdonne, from Chez Marie en Corse, the restaurant he heads with his partner Pascal Orsini in Linguizzetta (Haute-Corse, France), offers a wonderful family recipe.

SERVES 6

- 4 carrots
- 2 yellow onions
- 8 stalks celery
- Extra-virgin olive oil
- Ground cayenne
- 12 pieces veal (or beef) tail
- ¼ cup (60 mL) white wine
- Salt and freshly ground black pepper
- 14 ounces (400 g) peeled tomatoes

For finishing the sauce

- ⅔ cup (80 g) pine nuts
- ½ cup (80 g) raisins
- 1 teaspoon (2 g) unsweetened cocoa powder

Very small dice the carrots, onions, and 4 of the celery stalks. Divide the mixture in half.

In a casserole dish, such as a Dutch oven, set over medium heat, brown half the diced vegetables in olive oil with a pinch of cayenne. Add the tail pieces, cook until browned, then deglaze the pot with the wine. Reduce the heat and add just enough water to cover the meat. When the mixture begins to boil, add the remaining diced vegetables, season with salt and pepper, and simmer for 1 hour.

Add the tomatoes and cook for another 4 hours (if using beef tail, plan for 5 to 6 hours), or until the meat is tender.

For finishing the sauce, cut the 4 remaining celery stalks into 4-inch (10 cm) sticks and blanch them in salted water. Add them to the pot 1 hour before the end of the cooking time along with the pine nuts and raisins.

In a small bowl, combine the cocoa with a little of the sauce to dilute it, then stir it into the pot.

RIGATONI ALLA VACCINARA

The sauce can also be served with rigatoni, traditionally sprinkled with pecorino and topped with a piece of veal tail.

JULIEN DELLI FIORI'S VARIATION

The former manager of FIP radio network in France, this Roman jazz specialist composes an excellent version of the dish, somewhat inspired by osso buco. There is no trio of raisins, pine nuts, or cocoa in his recipe, but 2 cloves and 2 bay leaves are added during cooking, as well as a small can of tomato paste in addition to the *passata* (tomato purée), because "the sauce must be good and red." When ready to serve, he grates in the zest of an organic lemon and an orange, chops up some parsley, and sprinkles it over the top gremolata-style (without garlic).

SKIP TO

CORATELLA DI ABBACHIO CON I CARCIOFI, P. 341; OSSO BUCO, P. 312; ONIONS, P. 292.

MOSTARDA

It's neither mustard nor jam. This very Italian specialty made from syrup-flavored fruit is a multifaceted condiment.

JACQUES BRUNEL

LES INCONTOURNABLES

① *Mostarda di Cremona*
(Cremona, Lombardy)
As the homeland of *mostarda*, this city dedicates two days of celebration to it every year. It is most often whole candied fruits (orange, apricot, cherry, pear, fig, clementine) in a mustard oil syrup. It has a crunchy texture and a pronounced fruity and spicy flavor with earthy accents.

② *Mostarda di mele cotogne senapata* (quince with mustard, Lombardy)
Typical of Cremona and Brescia, it comes in a round, compact, and gelatinous form. Rich in pectin, it is enlivened with orange zest and a just a tad of spiciness. It is served cut into thin wedges to accompany cheeses (Asiago, stracchino, mozzarella, Parmesan . . .).

③ *Mostarda mantovana*
(Mantua, Lombardy)
An ingredient in *ravioli di zucca* (with pumpkin), it consists of either quince or small sour apples (called *contadine*) in slices in a rather spicy syrup. It is translucent with a long finish in flavor. Melon, watermelon, and other *mostarde* also come from this region . . .

④ *Mostarda veneta*
(Veneto)
Made of quince, apples, and pears crushed or in small pieces, preserved in a syrup made of white wine delicately flavored with mustard. It has a grainy texture and very fruity flavor.

BUT ALSO . . .

Viadananese (Lombardy): close to the one from Mantua, but with pears.

Milanese (Lombardy): sweeter, made mostly of apples.

Vicentina (Veneto): close to the Veneta one, but with a more pronounced spiciness and lemon juice.

Veronese (Veneto): made from vegetables.

Bolognese (Emilia-Romagna): with pears, quince, and oranges.

Toscana (Tuscany): grape must with apples, pears, and vin santo (a dessert wine).

Tutti frutti

Always fruity and sweet, mostarda is as varied as Italy itself. Whether represented as candied fruit, jams and preserves, or pâte de fruits, it often has a little spiciness. It is enjoyed at Christmastime with *bollito misto* (a meat and vegetable stew), chicken in bladder, or *zampone* (stuffed pig's feet), but also with cheese (sheep's milk or blue-veined), charcuterie, fish (such as swordfish), and desserts (ice cream, panettone, or panna cotta).

⑤ *Mustadda*

This is an ancient Sicilian mostarda recipe using grape must, cinnamon, and cloves, prepared at harvesttime. It is a kind of cake gelled with cornstarch (ashes from grapevine, olive wood, or almond wood were used in former times) before being molded into different shapes, often of religious meaning. Red-brown in color with a slightly stretchy texture, it can be stored for a very long time, and often accompanies ripened cheeses.

SKIP TO
TORTELLI DI ZUCCA, P. 371;
BOLLITO MISTO, P. 358.

A TRULY UNIQUE CONDIMENT

Mostarda, seemingly untranslatable, is little known outside of Italy. It is very different from French mustard or English or American mustards. This fruity chutney sometimes incorporates (for an addition of spiciness) mustard seeds or oil.

THE HEAT OF WILD MUSTARD

The mustard plant is a cousin of wasabi, horseradish, watercress, turnip . . . and belongs to the large Brassicaceae family with spicy flavors. It was cultivated to replenish the soil or to use in medicines (as tonics or on bandages, etc.). It also provided mankind, starting about 3,000 years ago, its oldest and most widely used condiment: mustard.

The Renaissance of mostarda

During the Middle Ages, monasteries in northern Italy carried on the tradition of creating spicy must and fruits, ideal for preserving these small delicacies. Sweet-and-savory flavors came into fashion during the fifteenth century, so *mostarda di frutta* was found on the tables of the doges and that of the Gonzaga family in Venice, Catherine de' Medici having preferred the one from Cremona. This rustic luxury product is made from perfectly ripe fruits whose juices are cooked for a long time before the fruits are added, followed by the mustard in the form of oil or seeds.

During Antiquity

Succeeding the Greeks, the Romans used mustard seed to preserve fruits, vegetables, and juices, especially wine—where its addition to mixtures produces a "fiery must," hence the term *mustard*, a derivation of the French words *moût* (grape must) and *ardent* (fierce, or fiery). From the first century, agronomist Columelle provides a recipe, followed in the fifteenth century by the cook Maestro Martino.

FAGIOLI AL FIASCO

· TUSCANY IN A BOTTLE ·

This bean recipe evokes an old way of preserving food using Chianti bottles. A descendant of Tuscan *cucina povera*, it represents a method of cooking in a closed container to concentrate flavors.

SONIA EZGULIAN

Beautiful bottle

The Chianti bottle is heir to the tradition of Greek and Roman amphorae, wrapped in straw or wicker to withstand long trips by carts or boats. In past times, the demijohn (a bottle enclosed in wicker) with a capacity of 5½ to 13 gallons (20 to 50 L) was transported across roads and seas to deliver wine and olive oil. The *fiasco*, a smaller bottle of about 2 pints (1 L) and very rounded at the base, appeared in the Middle Ages in Italy. The Florentine fiasco as early as the sixteenth century stood out because it had no wickerwork on the neck of the bottle and proudly wears on its neck a wax seal with the coat of arms of the Grand Duchy of Tuscany.

AT WORK

Until the early twentieth century, production of the *fiasco di Chianti* employed legions of women working with *sala*, a marsh weed bleached with sulfur and dried in the sun to become straw (*gita*), while a large group of glassblowers gave shape to the bulbous bottle with a flat bottom, and in which battalions of basket weavers enclosed in strips of the straw.

IN COOKING

In the Tuscan countryside, the Chianti bottle has been used as a preserving jar to store such things as *passata di pomodoro*, a tomato purée. To achieve this, the bottle is first stripped bare of its straw then submerged into a saucepan of water to cook.

In peasant families, beans with herbs were cooked slowly inside these bottles, placed above the embers of the oven before the embers extinguished so as not to waste heat generated from a previously prepared meal. It was a gentle, economical, and flavorful way of cooking.

This tradition is still honored in some *trattorie*, which offer beans cooked in rounded bottles placed over embers. Today the Italian food calendar even has a designated day to honor it: November 23!

SKIP TO
LEGUMES, P. 150.

RECIPE

To honor the Florentine spirit, opt for cannellini (white) or borlotti (striped deep pink) beans. Otherwise, choose fresh coco white beans, preferably from Paimpol if available, or great northern beans, or even dried beans, in which case they should be soaked overnight in a bowl of fresh water. Depending on the variety and size of the beans, the cooking time may need to be extended for 15 to 20 minutes, adding a little water or broth along the way if necessary.

SERVES 3 TO 4

10½ ounces (300 g) fresh borlotti beans, shelled

1 clove garlic, unpeeled

4 sage leaves

Salt and freshly ground black pepper

2 cups (500 mL) chicken stock

Scant ½ cup (100 mL) white wine

3 tablespoons (45 mL) olive oil

6 sprigs flat-leaf parsley, chopped

⅓ cup (40 g) shaved Parmesan cheese

<u>Equipment</u>

A 2-pint (1 L) Chianti bottle, with the wicker covering removed. Otherwise, use a different bottle or jar; the important thing is that the glass must be thick, with a wide neck to easily empty out the beans once cooked.

- Arrange the beans in the bottle (up to two-thirds of the bottle maximum). Add the garlic clove and the sage leaves. Season with salt and pepper, then add the stock, wine, and a drizzle of the olive oil. Close the bottle with a cork stopper wrapped in cheesecloth, leaving some fabric hanging out (this will make it easier to remove the cap during or at the end of the cooking time).
- Place the bottle in a saucepan filled with water, tilting it at a 45-degree angle, then simmer for 1 hour. If necessary, add a little water to the bottle during cooking (the beans should always be covered in liquid).
- Remove the bottle from the water, pour the contents into a large shallow dish (almost all the liquid will be gone), and serve the beans with a drizzle of olive oil, a sprinkling of the parsley, and the Parmesan shavings.

SEASON

TUTTO L'ANNO (YEAR-ROUND)

CATEGORY

DOLCI (DESSERT)

LEVEL

DIFFICOLTÀ MEDIA (MEDIUM DIFFICULTY)

STRUDEL

The inhabitants of northern Italy are fond of this German apple-filled pastry.

FRANÇOIS-RÉGIS GAUDRY

THE RECIPE

Giulia Segna, chef of Locanda Alpina in Brez (Trentino-Alto Adige), takes this recipe from her grandmother Anna. Its secret? A thin and flaky dough, plus an apple filling—without pine nuts or raisins—flavored with brandy!

MAKES 1 STRUDEL

For the pastry

- 1 large (50 g) egg
- 2 tablespoons (25 g) sugar
- 1 pinch salt
- Zest of 1 lemon
- 1 tablespoon (20 g) grappa or other brandy
- 4 tablespoons (60 g) unsalted butter, at room temperature
- ⅓ cup plus 1 tablespoon (100 g) milk, at room temperature
- 3¼ cups (400 g) flour

For the filling

- 10 assorted apples (Rennet, McIntosh, Golden Delicious . . .)
- 1 teaspoon (2 g) ground cinnamon
- ¼ cup (50 g) sugar
- Juice of 1 lemon
- Splash of rum, brandy, or other liquor
- ½ cup (50 g) dried bread crumbs

For finishing

- 1 cup brewed coffee
- 1 tablespoon (25 g) superfine, granulated, or confectioners' sugar

For the pastry, whisk together the egg, sugar, and salt in a bowl. Add the lemon zest and grappa, then incorporate the butter and milk. Whisk well to combine.

Stir in the flour, and, using your hands, combine the mixture until you achieve a smooth, consistency that can easily be rolled out. Shape the dough into a ball and let stand 10 to 15 minutes wrapped a kitchen towel.

For the filling, peel the apples and cut them into thin wedges, then cut the wedges into squares. Transfer the pieces to a mixing bowl. Add the cinnamon, sugar, lemon juice, and rum. Toss everything together using your hands. Stir in the bread crumbs to absorb the moisture from the filling, then toss again.

Using a rolling pin, roll out the dough until very thin (¼ inch/5 mm) in the form of a large rectangle measuring approximately 27½ by 12 inches (70 by 30 cm). Flour the dough while rolling it. Cut the dough in half lengthwise and transfer the two rectangular pieces to a parchment-lined baking sheet.

Arrange the apples in a mound down the center of each dough rectangle, equally dividing the apples between the two pastries.

Fold the long edges of the dough over to envelope the apples. Tightly close the ends and trim off any excess dough from the ends. Repeat for the second pastry. Transfer both strudels to a parchment-lined baking sheet.

For finishing, preheat the oven to 320°F (160°C). In a bowl, combine the coffee and sugar to make a syrup. Brush the syrup equally over the top of the two doughs, covering them entirely. Bake for 1 hour.

ITS GENEALOGY

Strudel means "swirl" in German, referring to its rolled-up shape, filled with apples, spices, and sometimes nuts. It has an eventful history as a popular pastry throughout central Europe, with distant origins, but just as much Italian.

ASSYRIA—EIGHTH CENTURY BCE

A cake with thin layers of dough filled with honey and nuts exists.

ANCIENT GREECE AND CENTRAL ASIA—THIRD CENTURY BCE

The ancestor of baklava (a flaky pastry topped with honey, pistachios, walnuts and other nuts) appears.

OTTOMAN EMPIRE—FOURTEENTH CENTURY

Baklava spreads during the conquests of Suleiman the Magnificent (1494–1566).

AUSTRO-HUNGARIAN EMPIRE—FROM 1699

The pastry evolves closer to the strudel (a pastry filled with apples) thanks to the progress of flour milling and the adoption of white flour.

TRENTINO-ALTO ADIGE—1867

Strudel spreads throughout northern Italy (part of the Austro-Hungarian empire).

INGREDIENTS

THE FRUITS

The apple has found a perfect spot among the Dolomites through many local varietals (Golden Delicious, Renetta, McIntosh, and Red Delicious from the appellation Mela Val di Non DOP). Some strudel recipes include pears, apricots, red berries, or rhubarb, and even potatoes in a savory version.

THE NUTS AND DRIED FRUITS

Traditionally: raisins and pine nuts, sometimes walnuts or hazelnuts.

THE PASTRY

Pasta frolla (similar to flaky pie dough); *pasta sfoglia* (puff pastry); or *pasta matta* ("crazy" dough), which hardens during cooking and provides a good wrapping for the steaming filling.

THE ALCOHOL

Rum is used in most recipes, but some people prefer brandy.

SKIP TO

"MIELICROMIA," P. 338; PEARS, P. 357; GRAPPA, P. 189.

SEASON

TUTTO L'ANNO (YEAR-ROUND)

CATEGORY

SECONDO PIATTO (MAIN COURSE)

LEVEL

FACILE (EASY)

TRIPPA ALLA ROMANA

ROMAN-STYLE TRIPE

In the family of Italian tripe dishes, those from Rome are some of the best! They are slow simmered, covered with tomatoes, fragrant, and deliciously tender.

FRANÇOIS-RÉGIS GAUDRY

A Roman delight

→ Made from the intestines of bovines, tripe is typically at the bottom of the scale in terms of options among animal trimmings, but they were an inexpensive source of protein for the common people of Rome and in particular for the workers of the Testaccio district slaughterhouses.

→ *Trippa alla romana's* particular appeal comes from two ingredients typical of the region of Lazio: Pecorino Romano (sheep's-milk cheese) and *mentuccia* (lesser calamint).

→ *Sabato trippa*: Roman-style tripe traditionally eaten on Saturdays for lunch.

	IN ITALIAN	IN LOCAL DIALECTS	IN ENGLISH
	Rumine	*Croce, ciapa, larga, panzone*	*Rumen*
	Omaso	*Foiolo, centupezzi, centopelli, libretto, millefogli*	*Omasum*
	Reticolo	*Cuffia, beretta, nido d'ape*	*Reticulum*
	Abomaso	*Lampredotto, quaglio, caglio, frezza, ricciolotta, francese*	*Abomasum*

A famous fan

Elena Fabrizi (1915–1993), aka Sora Lella, sister of actor and gastronome Aldo Fabrizi, was a famous actress (*We All Loved Each Other So Much* by Ettore Scola; *Bianco, rosso e Verdone* by Carlo Verdone . . .) and renowned restaurateur in Rome. Her trattoria, Sora Lella, opened on Tiber Island in 1940. Operated today by her grandchildren, it still serves up a true trippa alla romana.

THE RECIPE

Giovanni Passerini (Passerini, Paris 12th) has made trippa alla romana one of his restaurant's cult dishes. He slips in a bit of guanciale and uses peppermint instead of menturcia.

SERVES 6

- 2 stalks celery, trimmed
- 2 carrots
- 3 onions
- 2½ tablespoons (50 g) salt, plus more for seasoning
- 1 cup (250 mL) white vinegar
- 2 large strips orange peel
- 3 cloves
- 2¼ pounds (1 kg) beef tripe, cleaned, rinsed, and cut into large chunks
- 4¼ ounces (120 g) guanciale (cured pork cheek)
- Scant ¼ cup (50 mL) olive oil
- ½ cup (125 mL) white wine
- 1½ pounds (700 g) peeled tomatoes
- 1 pinch peperoncino (chile)
- 20 peppermint leaves, chopped
- 3½ ounces (100 g) grated pecorino cheese
- Freshly ground black pepper

Wash the celery, carrots, and onions. In a large pot, bring 1⅓ gallons (5 L) water to a boil with the salt, vinegar, orange peels, cloves, 1 celery stalk, 1 carrot, and 1 onion.

Add the tripe pieces, ensuring they fit down into the pot. Cook for 45 minutes, then remove with a skimmer; reserve the broth. Let the tripe cool, then cut it into strips about 2¾ inches (7 cm) long and ⅔ inch (1.5 cm) thick. Set aside about 2 cups (500 mL) of the cooking broth.

Cut the guanciale into pieces. Cut the remaining celery stalk, carrot, and 2 onions into very small dice. Heat the olive oil in a saucepan and add the guanciale, onions, celery, and carrot. Cook for several minutes, until the vegetables are softened. Add the tripe and cook until browned. Deglaze the pan with the white wine, then add the tomatoes, mashing them with a wooden spoon. Add the reserved broth and simmer over medium heat for 2 hours 30 minutes.

At the end of the cooking time, season with the pinch of chile. Divide the tripe among six plates. Top with the mint leaves and pecorino, and season with pepper.

Sulla Punta Della Lingua (On the Tip of the Tongue)

"No c'è trippa per gatti," or ***"Nun c'è trippa pe' gatti"*** in Roman dialect: "There is no tripe for cats."

This expression is used when a goal cannot be achieved. Its origin dates from 1907 when Ernesto Nathan became mayor of Rome and was eager to save money. He decided to strike from the city budgets the tripe that the city would purchase to feed the cats who hunted mice in the city's center. He publicly announced that there would be no more tripe for cats.

SKIP TO

CODA ALLA VACCINARA, P. 376; CORATELLA DI ABBACHIO CON I CARCIOFI, P. 341; MINT, P. 202.

HIGH-ELEVATION WINES

They are often referred to as "extreme wines," produced from vines located above 1,600 feet (500 m) in altitude and on 30-degree or more slopes . . . Let's take a hike to discover them!

ANTOINE GERBELLE

Flavors from Above

Produced in the foothills of the Alps, these terrace wines with invigorating flavors have in common an original aromatic power due to the direct and concentrated sunlight that the grapes are exposed to during ripening.

AOSTA VALLEY

With Mont Blanc in the spotlight, some vines peak at over 3,900 feet (1,200 m) in elevation! The climate of the valley is distinguished by dry summers, which explains why the young vines must be irrigated and why 75 percent of the wines are red.

THE VINES: one-third of the 1,400 acres (600 ha) is on land with a gradient of more than 30 percent, especially in the Valdigne or the upper valley, the favorite growing place for Prié Blanc, an indigenous white grape variety grown on short pergolas.

THE WINES: the small white appellation of Morgex and La Salle makes the Prié Blanc shine over some 70 acres (30 ha). The production of the greatest red wines from rare grape varietals is concentrated in the central valley: Fumin, Mayolet, Cornalin, Petit Rouge, Vien de Nus, and Premetta.

NOT TO BE MISSED: the trilogy of Prié Blanc (still, effervescent, and late harvest) by Ermes Pavese (Morgex); Didier Gerbelle (Aymavilles).

LIGURIA

The Cinque Terre is surely among the most breathtaking stretches of wine villages in the world.

THE VINES: 370 acres (150 ha) of vines suspended between sky and sea, clinging to plunging cliffs. The terraces are held back by hundreds of miles of drystone walls.

THE WINES: in the province of Imperia, the local gem is an original red grape, Rossese. It delivers a delicate red wine of red fruits, thyme, rosemary, and pine. From three main grape varietals—Bosco, Albarolla, and Vermentino—the Cinque Terre appellation produces in small collections two white wines, one dry and one sweet, obtained by drying grapes on the vine, with delicate sugars and a finely sea-air stony taste.

NOT TO BE MISSED: Cantina Sociale delle Cinque Terre (Riomaggiore); Rondelli (Camporosso); Maccario Dringenberg (San Biagio della Cima); Testalonga (Dolceacqua).

TRENTINO-ALTO ADIGE

Located in far northeastern Italy bordered by Switzerland and Austria, the province of Bolzano, with a long wine-growing tradition, is at the heart of a huge amphitheater formed by the neighboring mountains.

THE VINES: perched between 2,600 and 3,200 feet (800 and 1,000 m) above sea level, they are renowned for Pinot Grigio, an easy-drinking dry white, and for their light and precise reds, made from Schiava (or Vernatsch).

THE WINES: many are of particular appellations: Alto Adige (or Südtirol), Caldaro (or Kalterer), Santa Maddalena.

NOT TO BE MISSED: Franz Haas (Montagna); Cantina Terlano (Terlano); Alois Lageder (Magrè sulla Strada del Vino); Hofstätter (Tramin); San Michele Appiano (Appiano).

PIEDMONT

Along the banks of the Dora Baltea in the direction of Turin lies the village of Carema and its amphitheater of vineyards, which runs up Mount Maletto up to an altitude of 2,200 feet (700 m).

THE VINES: on less than 49 acres (20 ha), the vines grow on terraces built in the fifteenth century, covered with high pergolas supported by massive, truncated pillars carved from a block of stone.

THE WINES: Nebbiolo red with vertical, aromatic, and floral acidity, to be found in the Carema appellation.

NOT TO BE MISSED: DOC Carema de Ferrando (Ivrea).

LOMBARDY

Close to the Swiss border along the Adda River around the main village of Sondrio are found the beautiful wine-growing hillsides of Valtellina.

THE VINES: up to 2,700 feet (850 m), they are nestled on terraces that are sometimes so steep and narrow that they only accommodate one row of vines. Extraordinary reds from dried grapes (dried before pressing) are produced.

THE WINES: the Chiavennasca grape makes up the majority of the wines. The elevation, the orientation of the valley, and the granite soils give it more delicacy and freshness than the Piedmontese vintages made from this same grape varietal. The production of great dry reds for cellaring in Valtellina Superiore—fresh, pure, expressive, and mineral-y—is concentrated between 1,400 and 1,900 feet (450 and 600 m).

NOT TO BE MISSED: Sandro Fay (San Giacomo); Dirupi (Ponte in Valtellina); Arpepe (Sondrio).

TO GO EVEN FURTHER . . .

→ The selection of "extreme" wines from the Proposta Vini association.

→ The Extreme Wines Fair in the Aosta Valley.

SKIP TO
GATHERING GRAPES, P. 158; WINE FROM FIRE, P. 165; MIGRANT CUISINE, P. 194.

DISHES FROM THE VATICAN

Gluttony may be one of the seven deadly sins, but many pontiffs have succumbed to delicious temptation. Here is a list of the most gourmet popes, whose inspired dishes may appear on the Vatican's dinner table.

CHARLES PATIN O'COOHOON

FIFTH CENTURY • Gelasius I

492–496

The tradition of crêpes at Candlemas is attributed to this pope from Africa. He offered pilgrims passing through Rome flat cakes made from flour, salt, and water.

THIRTEENTH CENTURY • Martin IV

1281–1285

This French pope was fascinated by eels. He brought them still alive from Lake Bolsena to the aquariums of the papal palace and enjoyed them with a Vernaccia wine. His epitaph testifies to his passion.

FOURTEENTH CENTURY • Boniface IX

1389–1404

Born Pietro Tomacelli, this Neapolitan pope contributed his name to *tomaselle,* small dumplings made of liver that he consumed often.

FIFTEENTH CENTURY • Paul II

1464–1471

A great consumer of *maccheroni*, the Venetian Paul II organized on March 13, 1466, before Lent, a sumptuous feast for the faithful. In a book of order forms of his famous cook, Maestro Martino, a shopping list reads: 8,571 eggs, 3,112 wheels of Parmesan cheese, and 5,141 sheep's-milk cheeses.

SIXTEENTH CENTURY • Leo X

1513–1521

Leon X loved Florentine gastronomy. A great hunter and organizer of sumptuous dinners, this Medici-family pope was also a prankster. One evening, he allegedly served guests ropes of hemp, passing them off as eels.

SIXTEENTH CENTURY • Julius III

1550–1551

The table was the main side occupation of the Roman pope Julius III. His Holiness loved stuffed peacocks, in which he frequently indulged. He is said to have said, "Since God became angry over an apple, I, his vicar, can I not make a fuss at my leisure over a peacock which has even greater value?"

SIXTEENTH CENTURY • Pius V

1566–1572

A lover of caviar and fish from Lake Garda, Milanese pope Pius V indulged in the services of the most famous cook of the time, Bartolomeo Scappi, author of the cookbook *L'opera dell'arte del cucinare.*

SEVENTEENTH CENTURY • Alexander VIII

1689–1691

Aware of the pleasures of the flesh and good food, Venetian pope Alexander VIII spent his nights drinking and singing erotic verses.

EIGHTEENTH CENTURY • Clement XIV

1769–1774

A connoisseur of figs, Clement XIV was said to have been poisoned by the Jesuits using a fig picked from the most beautiful garden in Rome into which *aquetta*, a powerful poison, had been injected.

NINETEENTH CENTURY • Leo XIII

1878–1903

Originally from Lazio, he sent emissaries to his hometown of Carpineto Romano to collect *ciambelle*, crown-shaped cakes flavored with anise, to adorn his breakfasts.

TWENTIETH CENTURY • John XXIII

1958–1963

The Sisters of the Poor of Bergamo were hired to cook him traditional peasant dishes from Lombardy, his home region. On the papal table: polenta, Taleggio, and *stracchino.*

TWENTIETH CENTURY • John-Paul II

1978–2005

Karol Wojtyła had his passion: the *kremowka*, a custard tart from Poland. The Holy Father also brought in Polish nuns to prepare him pierogi, dumplings filled with potatoes or chicken.

TWENTY-FIRST CENTURY • Benedict XVI

2005–2013

This Bavarian pope was a fan of Tyrolean cuisine. His favorite dishes? A salad of cold sausage and a stuffed suckling pig, cooked in beer and served with *passatelli* (a small pasta with bread crumbs, Parmesan, and eggs).

TWENTY-FIRST CENTURY • Francis

Since 2013

When he was small, he dreamed of becoming a butcher. A son of Italian immigrants, the Argentine pope was fed *cappelletti* in tomato sauce, Milanese risotto, and stuffed squid family-style. At the Vatican, he's an aficionado of beef empanadas and *colita de cuadril,* beef simmered in Madeira.

SKIP TO

SACROSANCT CUISINE, P. 346; POLENTA, P. 114.

THE *BELLA SQUADRA*

EDITORIAL DIRECTOR
François-Régis Gaudry
with
Alessandra Pierini
Stéphane Solier
Ilaria Brunetti

COORDINATION
Anna Maréchal

EDITIONS MARABOUT
Élisabeth Darets
Christine Martin
Audrey Genin assisted
by Emmanuel Le Vallois

EDITIONS RADIO FRANCE
Anne-Julie Bémont

PROOFREADING
Cécile Beaucourt
Emmanuelle Pavan
Aurélie Dombes-Beaucourt
Irène Colas

IMAGE ARCHIVES
Candice Renaud

GRAPHIC DESIGN
ARTISTIC DIRECTION
Sidonie Bernard, Line Monthiers
(Hic et Nunc studio)
Pierre Boisson

LAYOUT
Sidonie Bernard, Line Monthiers
(Hic et Nunc studio)
Pierre Boisson
Francine Thierry

FOOD STYLIST
(ICONIC RECIPES)
Sabrina Fauda-Rôle

PHOTOGRAPHERS
Richard Boutin
Marielle Gaudry
Rebecca Genet
Pierre Javelle
David Japy
Yannick Labrousse
Charlotte Lascève
Sandra Mahut

ILLUSTRATORS
Lucie Barthe-Dejean
Angela Barusi
Gianluca Biscalchin
Aurore Carric
Giulio Castagnaro
Chroniques de bouche
Charlotte Colin
Camille de Cussac
Francesco Del Re
Sophie Della Corte
Marie Doazan
Jyothi Godin
Adrien Grant Smith
Flora Gressard
Jean Grosson
Stefano Marra
Junko Nakamura
Mathieu Persan
Alice Piaggio
Sophie Rivière
Victoria Roussel
Gaia Stella
Coline Tinevez
Yannis Varoutsikos

CONTRIBUTORS
Angela Barusi
Loïc Bienassis
Marie-Amal Bizalion
Christophe Brouard
Jacques Brunel
Ilaria Brunetti
Claudio Cambon
Giorgia Cannarella
Alberto Capatti
Gwilherm de Cerval
Serena Ciranna
Samuel Cogliati
Bernardo Conticelli
Samanta Cornaviera
Hippolyte Courty
Jill Cousin
Eleonora Cozzella
Alessandro De Conto
Laurent Delmas
Julien Delli Fiori
Déborah Dupont
Sonia Ezgulian
Adriano Farano
Marie-Laure Fréchet
Jérôme Gagnez
Francesca Gamberini
François-Régis Gaudry
Marielle Gaudry
Antoine Gerbelle
Frédérick Ernestine Grasser-Hermé
Gabrielle Kerleroux
Frédéric Laly-Baraglioli
Serena Lanza
Pierre-Brice Lebrun
Martina Liverani
Sacha Lomnitz
Laura Lupo
Céline Maguet
Paolo Marchi
Anna Maréchal
Elvira Masson
Xavier Mathias
Gianna Mazzei
Patrizio Menchi
Morgane Mizzon
Jordan Moilim
Massimo Montanari
Massimo Mori
Valentine Oudard
Carlo de Pascale
Charles Patin O'Coohoon
Alba Pezone
Alessandra Pierini
Sébastien Pieve
Laura Portelli
Nadia Postiglione
Anna Prandoni
Antonio Puzzi
Emmanuel Rubin
Françoise Sabban
Julia Sammut
Elisabeth Scotto
Silvano Serventi
Eugenio Signoroni
Stéphane Solier
Mina Soundiram
Zazie Tavitian
Paolo Tegoni
Francesca Tradardi
Martina Tuscano
Sylvie Wolff
Laura Zavan

CHEFS AND COOKS
Lucia Antonelli
Corrado Assenza
Cesare Battisti
Luana Belmondo
Rosina Bridda
Massimo Bottura
Paolo Burde
Alessandro Candido
Mattia Carfagna
Luigi Chezzi
Carlotta Cioni
Alain Cirelli
Ilaria Conti
Enrico Crippa
Arcangelo Dandini
Francesco Di Natale
Paolo Dolzan
Michele Farnesi
Riccardo Ferrante
Fabrizio Ferrara
Guillaume Grasso
Maria-Luisa Grementieri-Menchi
Giovanna Guidetti
Nabil Hadj Hassen
Andrea Maggi
Alfonso Mattozzi
Virgilio Mazzei
Christian Menchi
Mirjam Montefusco
Maria Oliveri
Sandro Pace
Giovanni Passerini
Norma Pielli
Fulvio Pierangelini
Maurizio Pinto
Alfredo Proto
Oscar Quagliarini
Sergio Risdonne
Enrica Rocca
Niko Romito
Nadia Santini
Lorenzo Sciabica
Giulia Segna
Silvana Segna
Denise Solier-Gaudry
Irene Stefanelli
Giacomo Timpanaro
Marisa Tondo
Simone Tondo
Annamaria Troiano
Rosetta Pierini
Daniele Rota
Anna-Rita Valentini
Filomena Ventre Farano
Daniela Vettori
Eleonora Zuliani

ACKNOWLEDGMENTS

Giovanni Assante
Francesca Ballestrieri
Brigitte Barbier
Anne-Julie Bémont
Stefania Benvenuti
Enrico Bernardo
Mario Di Bernardo
Andrea Bezzecchi
Michèle Billoud
Laurence Bloch
Gaia Bottone
Irene and Carlo Brunetti
Max Bustreo
Jeannot Carnasciali
Alessandro Casi
Alessandro Cavo
Isabella Cereda
Nadia Chougui
Yann Chouquet
Gianfranco et Silvio Di Cocco
Claudio Corallo
Giovanni Fancello
Marco Ferrari
Monica Fiumara Jancarossa
Luca Funedda
Jean-Pierre Gabriel
Pierre Gaudry
Filippo Giarolo
Fabrice Gour
Coraline Hery
Mathieu Joselzon
Vincent Josse
Gianluca and Antonio Di Lello
Nathalie and Frank Maréchal
Maria Antonietta Mazzone
Masseria Mirogallo
Marc Montarello
Domenico Morabito
Christian Nicola
Jean-Antoine Ottavi
Roberto Panizza
Clément Parant
Manuela Passerino
Rosetta, Alfredo and Carlo Pierini
Simone Sabaini
Matteo De Santi
Alberto Santini
Pierre-Olivier Savreux
Yves Solier
Akié Takizawa
Lauranne Thomas
Giampiero Ventura
Masseria Perugini
Tiphaine Vierne
-
Antica Macelleria Cioni
Azienda Agricola Maida de Vastola Francesco
Harry's Bar
-
Alessi
Bialetti
Lavazza
Luigi Guffanti Formaggi
Fondazione Marchesi
Accademia Barilla
Accademia della cucina italiana
Agricola Quei Mille
Confraternita del Bollito Misto
Casa Madre Italiana
Consorzio del Prosciutto di Parma
Consorzio Prosciutto San Daniele
Fratelli Corrà salumi
Identità Golose
Il Parodi Nocciola Ligure
Missoni
Museo Internazionale della Ceramica di Faenza
Olivieri 1882
Pasta Garofalo
Pino Cossu Bontà Sarde
Qualitalia
Re Fiascone Effetto Costiera
Valsana
-
Brandon Nickerson (typographical design)

CONTENTS

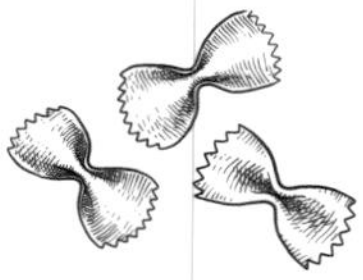

ITALIAN CUISINE: A USER'S GUIDE

PASTA

GNOCCHI

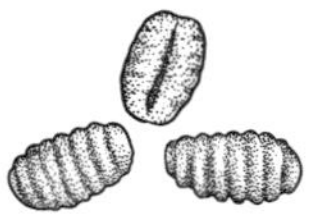

RICE

PIZZA

BREAD AND CEREALS

MEAT AND EGGS

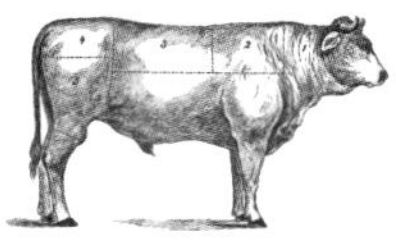

FISH AND SEAFOOD

VEGETABLES

BEANS AND LEGUMES

FRUITS AND NUTS

CHARCUTERIE

CHEESE

DESSERTS AND PASTRIES

CONFECTIONERY

CONDIMENTS AND SEASONINGS

WINE

LIQUOR AND COCKTAILS

COFFEE

TRADITIONS AND CUSTOMS

HISTORY AND HERITAGE

ARTS AND CULTURE

PEOPLE

Recipes are in a separate recipe index, beginning on page 396.

A

B

C

D

E

F

G

H

I

J

K

L

M

N

O

P

Q

R

S

T

U

V

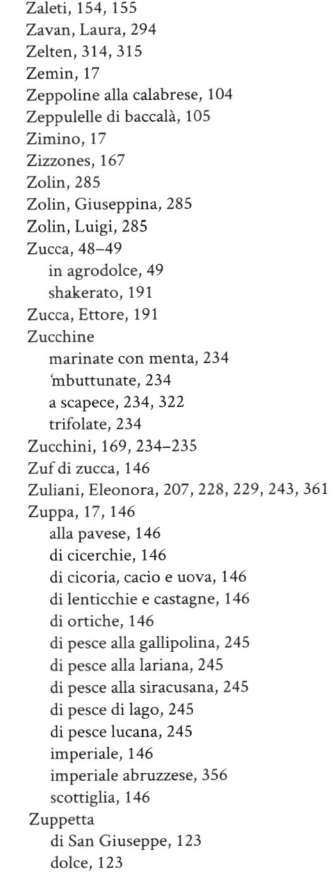

RECIPE INDEX

Iconic recipes and techniques have bold page numbers

FRENCH AND ITALIAN BIBLIOGRAPHY

→ Agostini, Pino, and Alvise Zorzi. *A tavola con i dogi*. Arsenale editrice, 2004.

→ André, Jacques. *L'Alimentation et la cuisine à Rome*. Les Belles Lettres, 1981.

→ Anselmi, Gian Mario, and Gino Ruozzi, eds. *Banchetti letterari*. Carocci editore, 2017.

→ Aragona, Raffaele. *Pizza, Petit Précis de gastronomie italienne*. Editions du Pétrin, 2017.

→ Arnaldi, Valeria. *L'asparago*. Iacobelli editore, 2017.

——. *Il carciofo*. Iacobelli editore, 2017.

——. *Il radicchio*. Iacobelli editore, 2017.

→ Artusi, Pellegrino. *La Science en cuisine et l'art de bien manger*. Actes Sud Editions, 2016.

→ Ascoli Vitali-Norsa, Giuliana. *La cucina nella tradizione ebraica*. Giuntina, 1993.

→ Aucante, Pierre. *Le Safran*. Actes Sud, 2000.

→ Baur, Eva Gesine, and Isolde Ohlbaum. À la table de Verdi. Éditions du Chêne, 2001.

→ Barbagli, Annalisa. *La cucina di casa del Gambero Rosso. Le 1000 ricette di Annalisa Barbagli*. Gambero Rosso Editore, 2012.

→ Beaugé, Bénédict. *Michel Troisgros et l'Italie*. Glénat, 2009.

→ Beauvert, Thierry, and Nathalie Le Foll. *Rossini. Les Péchés de gourmandise*. Éditions Plume, 1998.

→ Bernardi, Ulderico. *Il profumo delle tavole. Tradizione e cucina nelle Venezie*. Santi Quaranta, 2006.

→ Bistolfi, Robert, and Farouk Mardam-Bey. *Traité du pois chiche*. Sindbad, Actes Sud, 1998.

→ Bloch-Dano, Evelyne. *La Fabuleuse Histoire des légumes*. Le Livre de poche, 2011.

→ Bottura, Massimo. *Ne jamais faire confiance à un chef italien trop mince*. Phaidon, 2015.

→ Boudier, Valérie. *La Cuisine du peintre. Scène de genre et nourriture au Cinquecento*. PUFR/PUR, 2010.

→ Bresson, Aïté. *L'Artichaut et le cardon*. Actes Sud, 1999.

→ Brioist, Pascal, and Florent Quellier, eds. *La Table de la Renaissance. Le mythe italien*. PUR, 2018.

→ Brouard, Christophe, and Sophie Laroche. eds. *La Grande Bouffe. Peintures comiques dans l'Italie de la Renaissance*. Éditions Lienart, 2017.

→ Brunet, Jacqueline, and Odile Redon, eds. *Tables florentines. Écrire et manger avec Franco Sacchetti*. Stock, 1984.

→ Buisine, Alain. *Cènes et banquets de Venise*. Zulma, 2000.

→ Campo, Stefania. *I segreti della tavola di Montalbano. Le ricette di Andrea Camilleri*. Il leone verde Edizioni, 2018.

→ Capasso, Lydia, and Giovanna Esposito. *Santa Pietanza. Tradizioni e ricette dei santi e delle loro feste*. Guido Tommasi editore, 2017.

→ Capatti, Alberto. *Le Goût du nouveau. Origines de la modernité alimentaire*. Albin Michel, 2014.

——. *L'osteria nuova. Una storia italiana del XX secolo*. Slow Food editore, 2000.

——. *Pellegrino Artusi. Il fantasma della cucina italiana*. Mondadori Electa, 2019.

——. *Storia della cucina italiana*. Guido Tommasi Editore, 2014.

→ Capatti, Alberto, and Massimo Montanari. *La Cuisine italienne. Histoire d'une culture*. Seuil, 2002.

→ Cilli, Fiorenza. *La lenticchia*. Iacobelli editore, 2018.

→ Clausel, Jean. *Venise exquise*. Payot, 1990.

→ Clerici, Luca, ed. *Mangiarsi le parole. 101 ricette d'autore*. Skira, 2018.

→ Colella, Amedeo. *Mille paraustielli di cucina napoletana*. Cultura Nova, 2018.

→ Cozzella, Eleonora. *La carbonara perfetta*. Cinquesensi editore, 2019.

→ Danneyrolles, Jean-Luc. *L'Ail et l'oignon*. Actes Sud. 1998.

——. *Le Piment et le poivron*. Actes Sud. 2000.

——. *La Tomate*. Actes Sud, 1999.

→ Davidson, Alan. *Le Monde merveilleux des poissons de la Méditerranée. Comment reconnaître et préparer les 250 principaux poissons et fruits de mer*. Solar, 1973.

→ De Bernardi, Alberto. *Il paese dei maccheroni. Storia sociale della pasta*. Donzelli editore, 2019.

→ Delli Colli, Laura. *Il gusto del cinema italiano in 100 ricette*. Elleu Multimedia, 2002.

——. *Pane, film e fantasia. Il gusto del cinema italiano*. Rai Com, 2015.

→ De Rosamel, Chantal. *L'Asperge*. Actes Sud, 2000.

→ Dickie, John. *Delizia! Une histoire culinaire de l'Italie*. Buchet/Chastel, 2009.

→ Dubois, Philippe. "Tables italiennes.' Tradition et savoir contemporain." *Revue Critique*, no. 685–686: La gastronomie. Editions de Minuit, 2004.

→ Dumas, Alexandre. *Grand Dictionnaire de cuisine*. Phébus, 2000.

——. *Lettres sur la cuisine napolitaine à un prétendu gourmand napolitain*. Mercure de France, 1996.

→ Faccioli, Emilio, ed. *L'arte della cucina in Italia. Libri di ricette e trattati sulla civiltà della tavola dal XIV al XIX secolo*. Einaudi Editore, 1987.

→ Farina, Salvatore. *Dolcezze di Sicilia. Storia e tradizioni della pasticceria siciliana*. Edizioni Lussografica, 2009.

→ Gho, Paola, ed. *Dizionario delle cucine regionali italiane*. Slow Food Editore, 2010.

→ Goust, Jérôme. *Basilic, marjolaine et origan*. Actes Sud, 1999.

→ Hordé, Tristan. *Mots et Fourneaux. La Cuisine de A à Z*. Éditions Sud Ouest, 2013.

→ Kermoal, Jacques, and Martine Bartolomei. *La Mafia se met à table*. Actes Sud, 1986.

→ Leon, Donna, and Roberta Pianaro, À table avec le commissaire Brunetti. Un *avant-goût de Venise*. Calmann-Lévy, 2011.

→ Luciani, Luciano. *Il guerriero dal tenero cuore. Storia e ricette del carciofo*. Maria Pacini Fazzi editore, 2010.

→ Mangolini, Mia. *L'Encyclopédie de la gastronomie italienne*. Flammarion, 2013.

→ Marchesi, Gualtiero. *La Cuisine italienne réinventée*. Éditions Robert Laffont, 1984.

→ Marinetti, Filippo Tommaso, Jr. *La Cuisine futuriste*. Éditions A.M. Métailié, 1982.

→ Massaro, Costantino. *La poetica della pancia. Viaggio gastronomico nell'anatomia letteraria degli scrittori italiani dell'Otto-Novecento*. Edizioni ETS, 2018.

→ Metz, Vittorio. *La cucina del Belli*. SugarCo edizioni, 1984.

→ Michel, Dominique, and Thierry Thorens. *Le Goût des fruits. Encyclopédie culinaire*. Actes Sud, 2004.

→ Monaco, Franco. *Guide des fêtes folkloriques italiennes*. Automobile Club d'Italia, 1967.

→ Montanari, Massimo. *La Faim et l'abondance. Histoire de l'alimentation en Europe*. Seuil, 1995.

——. *Le Manger comme culture*. Université de Bruxelles, 2010.

——. *Il mito delle origini. Breve storia degli spaghetti al pomodoro*. Editori Laterza, 2019.

——. *Nuovo Convivio. Storia e cultura dei piaceri della tavola nell'età moderna*. Laterza, 1990.

——. *Il sugo della storia*. Editori Laterza, 2016.

→ Montanari, Massimo, ed. *Alla bolognese. Dalla città grassa a fico*. Il Mulino, 2018.

→ Novelli, Silverio, ed. *Mario Soldati. Da leccarsi i baffi*. DeriveApprodi, 2013.

→ Oliveri, Maria. *I Segreti del chiostro. Storie e ricette dei monasteri di Palermo*. Il Genio Editore, 2017.

→ Ottaviani, Giancarlo. *La cucina dell'era fascista*. Todariana editrice, 2005.

→ Parasecoli, Fabio. *Al dente. Storia del cibo in Italia*. Leg edizioni, 2015.

→ Pierini, Alessandra. *Le Citron. Dix façons de le préparer*. Éditions de l'Épure, 2016.

——. *La Fleur d'oranger. Dix façons de la préparer*. Éditions de l'Épure, 2020.

——. *La Friture. Dix façons de la préparer*. Éditions de l'Épure, 2019.

——. *La Mozzarella. Dix façons de la préparer*. Éditions de l'Épure, 2018.

——. *Le Panettone. Dix façons de le préparer*. Éditions de l'Épure, 2019.

——. *Parmigiano*. Petit Précis de gastronomie italienne, Éditions du Pétrin, 2014.

——. *Le Pesto. Dix façons de le préparer*. Éditions de l'Épure, 2018.

——. *La Polenta. Dix façons de la préparer*. Éditions de l'Épure, 2014.

——. *Le Vinaigre balsamique. Dix façons de le préparer*. Éditions de l'Épure, 2019.

→ Pierini, Alessandra, and Sonia Ezgulian. *La Pasta allegra*. Éditions de l'Épure, 2019.

→ Pignataro, Luciano. *La cucina napoletana*. Editore Ulrico Hoepli, 2016.

→ Piras, Claudia, ed. *Italie. Encyclopédie gourmande*. H. F. Ullmann, 2008.

→ Porzio, Stanislao. *Natali d'Italia*. Guido Tommasi editore, 2005.

→ Rabaa, Claudine. *L'aubergine*. Actes Sud, 2001.

→ Rabaa, Claudine, and Thierry Thorens. *Le riz dans tous ses états. Encyclopédie culinaire*. Actes Sud, 2002.

→ Ragagnin, Luca. *Canzoni da mangiare. Piccolo dizionario gastropop*. Il Leone verde edizioni, 2003.

→ Puzzi, Antonio, ed. *Pasta. Le forme del grano*. Slow Food editore, 2017.

→ Rebora, Giovanni. *La civiltà della forchetta. Storie di cibi e di cucina*. Edizioni Laterza, 1998.

→ Redon, Odile, Silvano Serventi, and Françoise Sabban. *La Gastronomie au Moyen Age: 150 recipes de France et d'Italie*. Stock, 1991.

→ Roden, Claudia. *Le Livre de la cuisine juive*. Flammarion, 2012.

→ Romain, Hippolyte, and Daniel de Nève. *Casanova. Les Menus plaisirs*. Éditions Plume, 1998.

→ Saint-Bris, Gonzague. *La Grande Vie d'Alexandre Dumas*. Minerva, 2001.

→ Salaris, Claudia. *Cibo futurista. Della cucina nell'arte all'arte in cucina*. Stampa Alternativa, 2000.

→ Sandri, Amedeo. *La Polenta nella cucina veneta*. Franco Muzzio Editore, 1985.

→ Serventi, Silvano, and Françoise Sabban. *La Gastronomie à la Renaissance—100 recettes de France et d'Italie*. Stock, 1997.

——. *Les Pâtes*. Histoire d'une culture universelle. Actes Sud, 2000.

→ Servi Machlin, Edda. *La Cuisine juive italienne*. Editions MJR, 1981.

→ Soldati, Mario. *Vino al vino. Alla ricerca dei vini genuini*. Bompiani, 2017.

→ Solitro, Antonio, and Pasquale Troia. *A tavola con i santi. Un anno per l'Italia tra la buona cucina delle feste patronali*. Edizioni Essegi, 1991.

→ Spector, Sally. *Venezia e i suoi sapori*. Arsenale Editrice, 1998.

→ Stefani, Bartolomeo. *La cucina ai tempi dei Gonzaga* (expanded edition from the original *L'arte di ben cucinare* of 1662). Rizzoli/Skira, 2002.

→ Thorens, Thierry. Étonnants légumes. Encyclopédie culinaire. Actes Sud, 2001.

→ Thorez, Jean-Paul. *La Pomme de terre*. Actes Sud, 2000.

——. *Les Salades*. Actes Sud, 1999.

→ Toaff, Ariel. *Mangiare alla giudia. La cucina ebraica in Italia dal Rinascimento all'età moderna*. Il Mulino, 2000.

→ Toesca, Catherine, and Jean-Bernard Naudin. *Casanova. Un Vénitien gourmand*. Editions du Chêne, 1998.

→ Vianello, Toni. *Risotto*. Flammarion, 2001.

IMAGE CREDITS

Italian Cuisine in 20 Dates pp. 4–17: Lucie Barthe-Dejean / **Gourmand Geographies** p. 18: Lucie Barthe-Dejean / **The Wine Map of Italy** p. 19: La Carte des vins s'il vous plaît / **Genoese Pesto** p. 20: Rebecca Genet (recipe), Coline Tinevez (drawings) / **Naples: The Top 10 Pizzerias** p. 22: Marie Doazan / **Minestrone** p. 23: Rebecca Genet (recipe), Coline Tinevez (drawings) / **Polpette (Meatballs)** p. 25: Marielle Gaudry / **A Love for Tomatoes** p. 26: AdobeStock / **Homemade Tomato Sauce** p. 27: Marielle Gaudry (recipes), AdobeStock (drawings) / **Tomatoes** p. 28: Pierre Javelle / **The States of the Tomato** p. 30: Richard Boutin / **Pellegrino Artusi** p. 32: Charlotte Colin (portrait), Ilaria Brunetti (recipe) / **Panna Cotta** p. 34: Rebecca Genet (recipe), Coline Tinevez (drawing) / **The Bronte Pistachio** p. 35: François-Régis Gaudry / **Grissini & Co.** p. 36: David Japy / **Breads for Survival** p. 38: David Japy / **The Fig** p. 40: AdobeStock / **Co(s)toletta alla Milanese** p. 41: Rebecca Genet (recipe), Coline Tinevez (drawing) / **La Commedia dell'Arte** p. 42: AdobeStock, Coline Tinevez (masks) / **Focaccia** p. 43: Rebecca Genet (recipe), Coline Tinevez (drawing) / **Lasagne Verdi alla Bolognese** p. 47: Rebecca Genet (recipe), Coline Tinevez (drawing) / **Squash** p. 48: Pierre Javelle / **In the Land of Gelati** p. 50: Stefino, Marielle Gaudry (granita), AdobeStock (map) / **Homemade Pizza** p. 52: Marielle Gaudry / **Pizze Napoletane** p. 54: David Japy, AdobeStock (marble) / **Aperitivo** p. 59: Stefano Marra / **Carnival & Delicacies** p. 58: Pierre Javelle / **Bottarga** p. 46: Sandra Mahut, Marielle Gaudry (recipe) / **Alimentari** p. 84: Giuseppe Ippolito / **Coniglio alla Ligure** p. 57: Rebecca Genet (recipe), Coline Tinevez (drawing) / **The Cultivation of Rice** p. 60: AdobeStock (drawings), David Japy, lecinqueerbe.it (recipe) / **Carlo Petrini** p. 62: Charlotte Colin (portrait), Marcello Marengo Archives Slow Food, ShutterStock (drawings) / **Slow Food** p. 63: AdobeStock, ShutterStock / **Caffè al Bar** p. 64: Yannis Varoutsikos / **Breakfast** p. 65: Chroniques de bouche / **Crostata alla Confettura** p. 66: Rebecca Genet (recipe), Coline Tinevez (drawing) / **Octopus** p. 67: Sophie Rivière / **Gourmet Cinema** p. 68: *We All Loved Each Other So Much* (*C'eravamo tanto amati*), director: Ettore Scola - producer: Pio Angeletti, Adriano De Micheli - release: 1974; *Viva Italia* (*I nuovi mostri*), sketch "Hostaria!", director: Ettore Scola, producer: Pio Angeletti, Adriano De Micheli, release: 1977; *Poverty and Nobility* (*Miseria e nobiltà*), director: Mario Mattoli, producer: Dino De Laurentiis, Carlo Ponti, release: 1954; *Big Deal on Madonna Street* (*I soliti ignoti*), director: Mario Monicelli, producer: Franco Cristaldi, release: 1958; *La Grande Bouffe* or *Blow-Out* (*La grande abbuffata*), director: Marco Ferreri, producer: Vincent Malle, Jean-Pierre Rassam, release: 1973, Sunset Boulevard/Corbis via Getty Images / **La Genovese** p. 69: Rebecca Genet / **The Art of Pork Fat** p. 70: David Japy / **Imaginary Museum** pp. 72–73: Annibale Carracci, *The Beaneater*, Electa/Leemage; Umberto Boccioni, *The Drinker*, Electa/Leemage; *Still Life with Peaches and a Water Jar*, National Archeological Museum of Naples Luisa Ricciarini/Leemage; Maître Hartford, *Still Life with Birds*, Electa/Leemage; Caravage, *Basket of Fruit*, Photo12/Alamy/Art Library; Jacopo da Ponte, *The Last Supper*. Painting by Jacopo da Ponte known as Bassano (1515–1592), 1546–1548. Oil on canvas. Roma, Galleria Borghese (Rome, Borghese Gallery) © Electa/Leemage pse162171; Renato Guttuso, *Vucciria*, "La Vucciria." Scene of fruit and vegetable market in Sicily. Painting by Renato Guttuso (1912–1987), Palermo, University of Palermo © Aisa/Leemage © ADAGP; *The Ricotta Eaters*, Painting by Vincenzo Campi (1536–1591). Photograph, KIM Youngtae, Lyon, Musée des Beaux Arts de Lyon. © Youngtae/Leemage;Bartolomeo Passarotti, *The Butcher's Shop*, De Agostini Picture Library / Bridgeman Images; Giuseppe Arcimboldo, *The Cook*, Tarker / Bridgeman Images; Giovanni Paolo Castelli known as Lo Spadino, *Autumn*, Photo12/Alamy/Zip Lexing / **Gnocchi di Patate** p. 74: Marielle Gaudry / **The Other Home of Couscous** p. 81: AdobeStock / **Modica Chocolate** p. 81: AdobeStock, Simone Sabaini / **The Gnocchi Universe** p. 76: Yannis Varoutsikos / **Risotto** p. 78: David Japy (grains), AdobeStock (drawings), Akiko Ida, Marie-Pierre Morel, Pierre Javelle, Alessandra Pierini, ShutterStock, Marielle Gaudry (step by step) / **Mozzarella in Carrozza** p. 82: Rebecca Genet (recipe), Coline Tinevez (drawing) / **Nadia Santini** p. 83: Charlotte Colin (portrait), ShutterStock (drawings) / **High-Elevation Wines** p. 381: AdobeStock / **Parmigiano-Reggiano** p. 86: Pierre Javelle / **The Religion of Coffee** p. 88: AdobeStock, ShutterStock / **Easter Cakes** p. 90: Flora Gressard / **Let's Go Out to Eat** p. 92: Coline Tinevez / **Insalata Caprese** p. 95:Rebecca Genet (recipe), Coline Tinevez (drawings) / **Panettone** p. 96: Pierre Javelle / **Behind the Scenes of the Panettone** p. 98: Flora Gressard, AdobeStock, Olivieri (photoreport) / **Spritz** p. 94: Marie Doazan / **Bagna Cauda** p. 119: Rebecca Genet (recipe), Coline Tinevez (drawings) / **Artichokes** p. 100: Pierre Javelle, Marielle Gaudry (recipe) / **Clash of the Artichokes** p. 102: Rebecca Genet (recipes), Coline Tinevez (drawings) / **Stockfish and Salt Cod** p. 104: Marie Doazan / **Citrus** p. 106: Pierre Javelle / **Massimo Bottura** p. 108: Charlotte Colin (portrait), Francescana DR (recipes) / **Zabaione** p. 203: Rebecca Genet (recipe), Coline Tinevez (drawings) / **Spotlight on Capers** p. 110: Sophie Rivière (illustration), David Japy (photos) / **Spaghetti alle Vongole** p. 112: Marielle Gaudry (recipe), Coline Tinevez (drawings) / **Orange Wine** p. 113: Charlotte Lascève / **Polenta** p. 114: David Japy, Marielle Gaudry (recipes), *Paìsa* director: Roberto Rossellini, producer: Mario Conti, Rod E. Geiger, Roberto Rossellini, release: 1946; *Novecento (1900)* director: Bernardo Bertolucci, producer: Alberto Grimaldi, release: 1976; *Preparing the Polenta* (oil on canvas) Longhi, Pietro (c.1701–85) Credit: Ca' Rezzonico, Museo del Settecento, Venice, Italy/Bridgeman Images / **Cannolo** p. 116: AdobeStock, *The Godfather*, director: Francis Ford Coppola, producer: Albert S. Ruddy, release: 1972 (film), Coline Tinevez (drawings), Marielle Gaudry (recipe) / **Sagra, A Sacred Festival** p. 118: Coline Tinevez / **Dante and** The Divine Comedy p. 120: Luisa Ricciarini/leemage / **His Majesty the Basil** p. 121: David Japy, Pierre Javelle, Sidonie Bernard (illustration), AdobeStock (drawing) / **Piadina Romagnola** p. 122: Rebecca Genet (recipe), Coline Tinevez (drawing) / **Neapolitan Pastries** p. 123: Sophie Rivière / **Pasta Inventory** p. 124: Pierre Javelle / **Torta Fritta** p. 133: Rebecca Genet (recipe), Coline Tinevez (drawings) / **The Lagoon Is a Terroir** p. 134: Sidonie Bernard (map), AdobeStock / **Puntarelle alla Romana** p. 135: Marielle Gaudry (recipe), Coline Tinevez (drawing) / **Arte Bianca** p. 136: Flora Gressard (map), AdobeStock, Museo Archeologico Nazionale, Naples, Campania, Italy/Bridgeman Images (fresco) / **The Delights of Licorice** p. 138: Pierre Javelle / **Mafia Dishes** p. 139: *Goodfellas*, 1990, Martin Scorsese, producer Irwin Winkler (executive producer: Barbara De Fina, associate producer: Bruce S. Pustin); *The Godfather*, 1972, Francis Ford Coppola, producer Albert S. Ruddy; *Once Upon a Time in America*, 1984, Sergio Leone, producer Arnon Milchan (executive producer: Claudio Mancini) / **Spezzatino** p. 85: Rebecca Genet (recipe), Coline Tinevez (drawings) / **Olive Oil** p. 140: AdobeStock / **Bottles of Green Gold** p. 142: David Japy / **The Hazelnut** p. 144: David Japy, Marielle Gaudry (recipe) / **Castagnaccio** p. 145: Rebecca Genet (recipe) / **Gualtiero Marchesi** p. 163: Charlotte Colin (portrait), ShutterStock (drawings), M. Borchi (recipe 2) / **Cacio e Pepe** p. 175: Coline Tinevez, AdobeStock / **Bistecca alla Fiorentina** p. 132: Marielle Gaudry, Coline Tinevez (drawing) / **The Soups of Italy** p. 146: Marie Doazan / **Macco di Fave** p. 148: Rebecca Genet (recipe), Coline Tinevez (drawing) / **Cooking with Bread** p. 149: ShutterStock / **Legumes** p. 150: David Japy / **Fregula con le Arselle** p. 152: Rebecca Genet (recipe), Sophie Della Corte (drawings) / **Persimmon** p. 153: ShutterStock / **Cookies** p. 154: Pierre Javelle, Valéry Guédes (cantuccini, amaretti), AdobeStock / **Gathering Grapes** p. 158: Yannis Varoutsikos / **Mortadella** p. 160: David Japy, AdobeStock (drawings), ShutterStock (pistachios) / **Seadas** p. 157: Rebecca Genet (recipe), Coline Tinevez (drawings) / **Saltimbocca alla Romana** p. 33: Rebecca Genet (recipe), Coline Tinevez (drawing) / **Pasta Pazza** p. 162: Alice Piaggio / **Gnocchi di Patate Crude** p. 164: Marielle Gaudry / **Wine from Fire** p. 165: Jyothi Godin / **Panino** p. 166: AdobeStock / **Panzanella** p. 168: Rebecca Genet (recipe), Coline Tinevez (drawings) / **The (Re)naissance of Vegetables** p. 169: British Library Board. All Rights Reserved/Bridgeman Images, AdobeStock / **Bitter Lettuces** p. 170: Pierre Javelle / **Salame di l'Italia Cioccolato** p. 172: Rebecca Genet (recipe), Coline Tinevez (drawing) / **The Genealogy of Roman Pasta** p. 174: Lucie Barthe-Dejean / **Cacio e pepe** p. 175: Rebecca Genet (recipe), Coline Tinevez (drawing) / **Gricia** p. 176: Rebecca Genet (recipe), Coline Tinevez (drawings) / **Amatriciana** p. 177: Rebecca Genet (recipe), Coline Tinevez (drawings), AdobeStock / **Carbonara** p. 178: Marielle Gaudry (recipe), Coline Tinevez (drawing) / **Gianduja** p. 180: David Japy, AdobeStock (drawings) / **Malloreddus alla Campidanese** p. 167: Rebecca Genet (recipe), Coline Tinevez (drawing) / **The Mozzarella Family** p. 182: Charlotte Lascève, AdobeStock, ShutterStock / **Sarde a Beccafico** p. 186: Rebecca Genet (recipe), Coline Tinevez (drawing) / **Gnocchi Dolci** p. 187: Chroniques de bouche / **Tiramisu** p. 188:Marielle Gaudry / **Grappa** p. 189: Sidonie Bernard, AdobeStock (grapes) / **Risotto alla Milanese** p. 290: Rebecca Genet (recipe), Coline Tinevez (drawing) / **Cocktails** p. 190: Pierre Javelle / **Garlic** p. 192: Pierre Javelle / **Spaghetti Aglio, Olio e Peperoncino** p. 193: Marielle Gaudry (recipe), Coline Tinevez (drawings) / **Migrant Cuisine** p. 194: Aurore Carric / **Pizza Journeys** p. 196: Aurore Carric / **Carpaccio** p. 198: Rebecca Genet (recipe), Coline Tinevez (drawings) / **Francesco « Josko » Gravner** p. 199: Charlotte Colin (portrait), AdobeStock (drawing) / **The Spaghetti Family** p. 201: Pierre Javelle / **Mint** p. 202: Sophie Rivière, AdobeStock / **Risi e Bisi** p. 207: Rebecca Genet (recipe), Coline Tinevez (drawings) / **Sweets from the Convent** p. 204: Marielle Gaudry, I Segreti del chiostro / **Paccheri allo Scorfano** p. 206: Rebecca Genet (recipe), Coline Tinevez (drawing) / **Asparagus** p. 208: Charlotte Lascève / **Amaro** p. 210: Lucie Barthe-Dejean / **Pollo alla Diavola** p. 212: Rebecca Genet (recipe), Coline Tinevez (drawings) / **Farro, Ancient Grains** p. 213: ShutterStock, François-Régis Gaudry (recipe) / **Olives** p. 214: Sophie Rivière / **Giuseppe Verdi** p. 216: Charlotte Colin (portrait), ShutterStock / **Spaghetti alla Puttanesca** p. 217: Rebecca Genet (recipe), Coline Tinevez (drawings) / **Pizza Fritta** p. 218: Alba Pezone / **Ricotta** p. 219: Richard Boutin / **Pop Pasta** p. 221: *Lady and the Tramp*, 1955 (Walt Disney) Everett / Bridgeman images; Gossini, Attanasio © Le Lombard (dargaud-lombard s.a.), 2020;*The adventures of Marco Polo*, 1938, Real Archie Mayo., COLLECTION CHRISTOPHEL © The Samuel Goldwyn company; Spaghetti-Harvest in Ticino BBC 1957 / **Caponata** p. 220: Rebecca Genet (recipe), Coline Tinevez (drawing) / **Italy's Beautiful Cheeses** p. 222: Sandra Mahut, Valsana, Luigi Guffanti / **Cicchetti Veneziani** p. 228: Rebecca Genet (recipe) / **Gourmand Adornments** p. 230: ALBERTO PIZZOLI / AFP, Antonio de Moraes Barros Filho/WireImage/Getty, Ernesto Ruscio/ Getty Images, TIZIANA FABI / AFP, Philadelphia Museum of Art, Pennsylvania, PA, USA Gift of Mrs. Elsa Schiaparelli, 1969/Bridgeman Images, AdobeStock, Claudio Tajoli (recipe) / **Zucchini** p. 234: Charlotte Lascève, Marielle Gaudry (recipe) / **The Amazing Anchovy** p. 236: Angela Barusi / **Pasta alla Norma** p. 238: Rebecca Genet (recipe), Coline Tinevez (drawings) / **Mushrooms** p. 240: Gianfranco et Silvio Di Cocco (Gruppo Micologico Fiorentino - P.A. Micheli) / **Calamari** p. 242: Marielle Gaudry (recipes), AdobeStock / **Fegato alla Veneziana** p. 243: Rebecca Genet (recipe), Coline Tinevez (drawings) / **Cooking with Seawater** p. 317: Junko Nakamura, ShutterStock (drawing) / **Pizza as Pop Icon** p. 246: *The Pizza Triangle/Drama of Jealousy, Dramma della gelosia*, 1970, Real Ettore Scola, Monica Vitti., COLLECTION CHRISTOPHEL © Dean Film / Jupiter Generale Cinematografica; *Eat, Pray, Love,* 2010, Real Ryan Murphy, Julia Roberts., COLLECTION CHRISTOPHEL © Plan B Entertainment / Red Om Films;*Small Time Crooks*, 2000, Real Woody Allen, Woody Allen, Carolyn Saxon, Tracey Ullman, Collection Christophel © DreamWorks SKG / Sweetland Films; *Friends*, Marta Kauffman and David Crane, 1994–2004, Producers: Ted Cohen, Andrew Reich, Michael Curtis, Ira Ungerleider; *Breaking Bad*, Vince Gilligan, 2008–2013, producer: Karen Moore / **Baba** p. 247: Rebecca Genet (recipe), Coline Tinevez (drawing) / **Spreadable Sausages** p. 347: Pierre Javelle, Coline Tinevez (drawing) / **Prosecco & Co.** p. 250: Mathieu Persan / **Penne all'Arrabbiata** p. 252: Rebecca Genet (recipe), Coline Tinevez (drawings) / **Amarena** p. 253: Pierre Javelle / **Enrico Crippa** p. 254: Charlotte Colin (portrait) / **Farinata** p. 255: Marielle Gaudry (recipe), Coline Tinevez (drawings) / **Fennel** p. 233: Pierre Javelle / **Porchetta** p. 256: Marielle Gaudry, Coline Tinevez (drawings) / **Sage** p. 257: Pierre Javelle / **A Chart of Rustic Breeds** p. 258: Jean Grosson, Pierre Boisson (diagrams / **Historic Cafés** p. 265: Sidonie Bernard / **Eggplant** p. 266: David Japy, Pierre Javelle, Marielle Gaudry (recipe), AdobeStock (drawing) / **Pizzaiola** p. 268: Marielle Gaudry (recipe), Coline Tinevez (drawings) / **The History of Pizza** p. 270: Bibliothèque des Arts Décoratifs, Paris, France Archives Charmet/ Bridgeman Images; L. Romano/De Agostini Picture Library /Bridgeman Images; akg-images / Picture Alliance / Peter Endig; AdobeStock (drawings) / **Arrosticini** p. 264: Rebecca Genet (recipe), Coline Tinevez (drawings) / **Liquori** p. 366: AdobeStock, ShutterStock / **Grapes** p. 272: Pierre Javelle, AdobeStock / **Parmigiana di Melanzane** p. 274: Marielle Gaudry (recipe), Coline Tinevez (drawings) / **Pasta and Beans** p. 276: Coline Tinevez / **The Other Promised Land** p. 278: Lucie Barthe-Dejean (map), AdobeStock, Stéphane Solier (recipe) / **Crustaceans** p. 282: AdobeStock, ShutterStock / **Spaghetti ai Ricci di Mare** p. 283: Marielle Gaudry (recipe), Coline Tinevez (drawings) / **Balsamic**

Vinegar p. 280: Sophie Della Corte (diagram), David Japy (bottles), AdobeStock, ShutterStock / **Osterie** p. 284: Marielle Gaudry (Ai Cascinari, Kamastra, Boccondivino, Trippa) / **Candies** p. 286: David Japy / **Spaghetti al Pomodoro** p. 289: Marielle Gaudry (recipe), Coline Tinevez (drawings) / **Pastiera** p. 91: Marielle Gaudry (recipe) / **Saffron** p. 291: Sophie Rivière / **Onions** p. 292: Sandra Mahut / **Fresh Pasta** p. 294: Rebecca Genet / **Fish** p. 300: Francesco Del Re / **Fishing Huts** p. 303: AdobeStock, ShutterStock / **Pecorino** p. 304: Pierre Javelle / **Vitello Tonnato** p. 305: Rebecca Genet (recipe), Coline Tinevez (drawings) / **Pasta con le Sarde** p. 306: Marielle Gaudry (recipe), Coline Tinevez (drawing) / **Chickpea, the King of the Poor** p. 293: Marielle Gaudry (recipe), Stéphane Solier (recipe), AdobeStock, ShutterStock / **Osso Buco** p. 312: Rebecca Genet (recipe), Coline Tinevez (drawing) / **When Red Wine Sparkles** p. 313: Adrien Grant Smith (map), AdobeStock / **Sweet Treats of Christmas** p. 204: David Japy / **Fellini, The Gourmand** p. 316: Louis Goldman / Gamma-Rapho via Getty Images, AdobeStock / **Cooking with Seawater** p. 317: AdobeStock / **The Taste of Shape** p. 317: AdobeStock / **Gorgonzola** p. 318: Chroniques de bouche, AdobeStock (cow) / **Tramezzino** p. 319: Rebecca Genet (recipe) / **Natural Wine** p. 320: Camille de Cussac / **Marinades** p. 322: Chroniques de bouche / **Fulvio Pierangelini** p. 323: Charlotte Colin (portrait), AdobeStock, ShutterStock / **Legendary Labels** p. 324: Pierre Boisson / **Nougats** p. 326: David Japy, Pierre Boisson (map) / **Trippa alla Romana** p. 380: Rebecca Genet / **Tortellini in Brodo** p. 328: Nicolas Boi (recipe), Coline Tinevez (drawings) / **Ragù Bolognese** p. 330: Rebecca Genet (recipe), Coline Tinevez (drawing) / **The Boar, King of Tuscany** p. 331: Marielle Gaudry (recipes), AdobeStock / **Sausage** p. 332: Richard Boutin, Sandra Mahut / **Savory Tarts & Pies** p. 333: Marielle Gaudry (recipe), AdobeStock / **Cabbage & Company** p. 334: Pierre Javelle / **Sophia Loren, a Gourmand Muse** p. 336: *L'Oro di Napoli* (*The Gold of Naples*), director: Vittorio de Sica, producer: Carlo Ponti, Dino De Laurentiis, Marcello Girosi, release: 1954; *La Donna del fiume* (*The River Girl*), director: Mario Soldati, producer: Carlo Ponti, Dino De Laurentiis, Basilio Franchina, release: 1955; *La Ciociara* (*Two Women*), director: Vittorio de Sica, producer: Carlo Ponti, Joseph E. Levine, release: 1960; *Matrimonio all'italiana* (*Marriage Italian Style*), director: Vittorio de Sica, producer: Carlo Ponti, Joseph E. Levine, release: 1964; *Questi fantasmi* (*Ghosts—Italian Style*), director: Renato Castellani, producer: Carlo Ponti, release: 1967; *Sabato, domenica e lunedì* (*Saturday, Sunday and Monday*), director: Lina Wertmüller, producer: Thierry Caillon, Renato Camarda, Alex Ponti, Carlo Ponti, release: 1990; *I Girasoli* (*Sunflower*), director: Vittorio de Sica, producer: Carlo Ponti, Arthur Cohn, Joseph E. Levine, release: 1970; *La Mortadella* (*Mortadella*), director: Mario Monicelli, producer: Carlo Ponti, Fred Wallach, Danilo Sabatini, release: 1971 / **Gnocchi alla Romana** p. 337: Marielle Gaudry / **Almonds** p. 173: Pierre Javelle, Marielle Gaudry (recipe) / **"Mielicromia": A Palette of Honey** p. 338: Pierre Javelle, Marielle Gaudry (producer) / **Oregano** p. 340: Pierre Javelle, AdobeStock (drawing) / **Coratella di Abbacchio con i Carciofi** p. 341: Rebecca Genet (recipe), Coline Tinevez (drawing) / **Fritto Misto** p. 342: Rebecca Genet (recipe), AdobeStock / **White Truffle, the Gem of Piedmont** p. 109: François-Régis Gaudry, AdobeStock (drawings) / **Pasta and Potato** p. 344: Junko Nakamura / **Bigoli in Salsa** p. 345: Rebecca Genet (recipe), Coline Tinevez (drawing) / **Sacrosanct Cuisine** p. 346: AdobeStock / **Spreadable Sausages** p. 347: Sandra Mahut / **The Cheese Is Crawling!** p. 350: François-Régis Gaudry / **Cornetto** p. 350: AdobeStcok / **Peppers** p. 351: Pierre Javelle, Marielle Gaudry (recipe) / **Land of Lemons p. 352:** Coline Tinevez (recipes), ShutterStock, Adobe Stock (lemon) / **The Barilla Saga** p. 354: Barilla Historical Archives- Parma - Italy / **Rosé Wines** p. 370: AdobeStock / **Frittata** p. 356: Rebecca Genet (recipe), Coline Tinevez (drawings) / **Pears** p. 357: Pierre Javelle / **Bollito Misto** p. 358: Rebecca Genet (recipe) / **Chile Peppers** p. 359: Pierre Javelle / **A Leading Country for Caviar** p. 360: © FONDATION MARCHESI (recipe), Adobe Stock, Shutterstock / **Linguine al Nero di Seppia** p. 361: Rebecca Genet (recipe), Coline Tinevez (drawings) / **Supplì vs Arancini** p. 362: Marielle Gaudry / **Chestnuts** p. 364: David Japy (products), AdobeStock (drawings) / **Pappa al Pomodoro** p. 367: Rebecca Genet (recipe), Coline Tinevez (drawing) / **The Art of la Ribollita** p. 368: Chroniques de bouche / **Cooking by Television** p. 369: AdobeStock / **Tortelli di Zucca** p. 371: Rebecca Genet (recipe), Coline Tinevez (drawings) / **Spaghetti VIP** p. 372: *Le petit monde de Don Camillo*, 1952, director: Julien Duvivier, Fernandel, Collection Christophel © FIlmsonor; Gamma-Rapho; Bettmann/Getty Images; Agip/ Bridgeman Images; Archivio Cameraphoto/leemage; © MP/Portfolio/Leemage; Peter Stackpole/The LIFE Picture Collection via Getty Images; Everett /Bridgeman images; © MP/ Portfolio/Leemage; Everett / Bridgeman images; © MP/ Portfolio/Leemage; Reporters Associati/MP/Leemage / **Orecchiette con Cime di Rapa** p. 374: Rebecca Genet (recipe), Coline Tinevez (drawings) / **Peaches** p. 375: Pierre Javelle / **Coda alla Vaccinara** p. 376: Rebecca Genet (recipe), Coline Tinevez (drawing) / **Mostarda** p. 377: Richard Boutin / **Fagioli al Fiasco** p. 378: Mauro Santella / **Strudel** p. 379: Rebecca Genet (recipe) / **Dishes from the Vatican** p. 382: Gianluca Biscalchin.

Originally published in French as *On Va Déguster L'Italie*

Translated from the French by Zachary R. Townsend

Library of Congress Cataloging-in-Publication Data

Names: Gaudry, François-Régis, author.
Title: Let's eat Italy! : everything you want to know about your favorite cuisine / François-Régis Gaudry with Alessandra Pierini & Stephane Solie, presents.
Description: New York : Artisan, a division of Workman Publishing Co., Inc., 2021. | Includes index.
Identifiers: LCCN 2021015464 | ISBN 9781648290596 (hardcover)
Subjects: LCSH: Cooking, Italian. | LCGFT: Cookbooks.
Classification: LCC TX723 .G288 2021 | DDC 641.5945--dc23
LC record available at https://lccn.loc.gov/2021015464

Book design by Marabout
Cover illustration by Aurore Carric

Artisan books are available at special discounts when purchased in bulk for premiums and sales promotions as well as for fund-raising or educational use. Special editions or book excerpts also can be created to specification. For details, contact the Special Sales Director at the address below, or send an e-mail to specialmarkets@workman.com.

For speaking engagements, contact speakersbureau@workman.com.

Published by Artisan
A division of Workman Publishing Co., Inc.
225 Varick Street
New York, NY 10014-4381
artisanbooks.com

Artisan is a registered trademark of Workman Publishing Co., Inc.

Published simultaneously in Canada by Thomas Allen & Son, Limited

Printed in China

First printing, October 2021

10 9 8 7 6 5 4 3 2 1